797,885 Books
are available to read at

Forgotten Books

www.ForgottenBooks.com

Forgotten Books' App
Available for mobile, tablet & eReader

ISBN 978-1-333-92075-3
PIBN 10703426

This book is a reproduction of an important historical work. Forgotten Books uses state-of-the-art technology to digitally reconstruct the work, preserving the original format whilst repairing imperfections present in the aged copy. In rare cases, an imperfection in the original, such as a blemish or missing page, may be replicated in our edition. We do, however, repair the vast majority of imperfections successfully; any imperfections that remain are intentionally left to preserve the state of such historical works.

Forgotten Books is a registered trademark of FB &c Ltd.
Copyright © 2017 FB &c Ltd.
FB &c Ltd, Dalton House, 60 Windsor Avenue, London, SW19 2RR.
Company number 08720141. Registered in England and Wales.

For support please visit www.forgottenbooks.com

1 MONTH OF
FREE
READING

at

www.ForgottenBooks.com

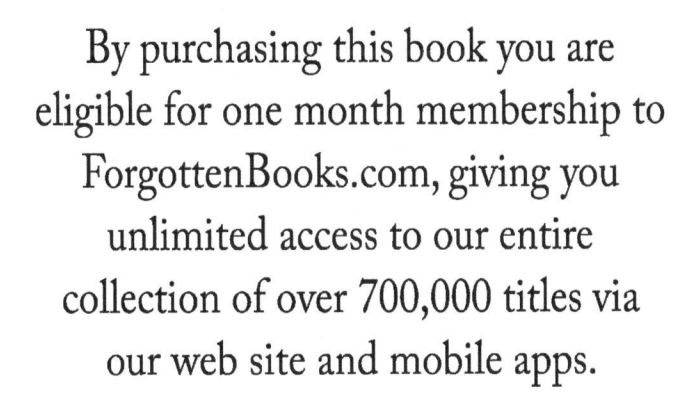

By purchasing this book you are eligible for one month membership to ForgottenBooks.com, giving you unlimited access to our entire collection of over 700,000 titles via our web site and mobile apps.

To claim your free month visit:
www.forgottenbooks.com/free703426

* Offer is valid for 45 days from date of purchase. Terms and conditions apply.

English
Français
Deutsche
Italiano
Español
Português

www.forgottenbooks.com

Mythology Photography **Fiction**
Fishing Christianity **Art** Cooking
Essays Buddhism Freemasonry
Medicine **Biology** Music **Ancient Egypt** Evolution Carpentry Physics
Dance Geology **Mathematics** Fitness
Shakespeare **Folklore** Yoga Marketing
Confidence Immortality Biographies
Poetry **Psychology** Witchcraft
Electronics Chemistry History **Law**
Accounting **Philosophy** Anthropology
Alchemy Drama Quantum Mechanics
Atheism Sexual Health **Ancient History**
Entrepreneurship Languages Sport
Paleontology Needlework Islam
Metaphysics Investment Archaeology
Parenting Statistics Criminology
Motivational

A COLLECTION

OF

STATE PAPERS

RELATIVE TO THE

WAR against FRANCE

Now carrying on by GREAT BRITAIN and the several other EUROPEAN POWERS:

Containing AUTHENTIC COPIES of

ARMISTICES,	MEMORIALS,
TREATIES,	REMONSTRANCES,
CONVENTIONS,	OFFICIAL LETTERS,
PROCLAMATIONS,	PARLIAMENTARY PAPERS,
MANIFESTOES,	LONDON GAZETTE ACCOUNTS
DECLARATIONS,	OF THE WAR, &c. &c. &c.

Many of which have never before been published.

VOL. VIII.

LONDON:

Printed by S GOSNELL, Little Queen Street, Holborn,

For J. DEBRETT, opposite Burlington House, Piccadilly.

MDCCC.

PREFACE.

WE have now completed the Eighth Volume of this Collection; and important and eventful as the former ones have been, the present, we will venture to affert, in the magnitude and multiplicity of the events it embraces, is certainly not inferior to any that have preceded it.

The war againſt France has been carried on with additional vigour: other powers have acceded to the conteſt; and nations, whoſe names rarely occur in the preceding volumes, will be found in this, amongſt the warmeſt ſupporters of the war. Ruſſia has been one of the principal pillars of the coalition, and, uniting her forces with thoſe of Auſtria and the Porte, has been one of the chief inſtruments in expelling the French from their conqueſts in Italy.

In the Eaſt, Tippoo Sultaun, whoſe hoſtile and perfidious conduct towards this country was little more than ſuſpected when our laſt volume made its appearance, has ſince that period furniſhed the moſt unequivocal proofs, and, in the proſecution of that hoſtility, has been juſtly deprived both of his ſovereignty and his life. The important documents relative to that war, which has eſtabliſhed on a baſis of the moſt permanent ſecurity the whole of the Britiſh poſſeſſions in India, and forming a ſeparate government under the Mihiſſoor Maharaj Kiſhenraj Wudiar, a deſcendant of the ancient Ranas of Myſore, of a part of the territories poſſeſſed by Tippoo, will be found in this volume.

Of

PREFACE.

Of the papers relative to the progress and termination of the Congress at Rastadt, and the catastrophe that followed, some have never before been published in this country—others have only appeared in an imperfect and mutilated state.

The remainder of the documents relative to the negotiation between the United States of America and the French republic, and the detailed Report, hitherto unpublished in this country, of the American Secretary of State on that procedure, are extremely important.

The brilliant success of the campaign in Italy, Switzerland, and Germany, has rendered the London Gazette account a very principal feature in this volume: to prevent distortion in the work, it has been thought advisable to bring down the military and civil operations to nearly the same point of time.

December 20*th*, 1799.

CONTENTS

ties, Armistices, &c. — — — — — Page 1

rious, Manifestoes, &c. — — — — — — ...

relative to the War in India — — — — 346

rts of the Committees of Secrecy of the Houses of
ards and Commons — — — — — 371

iamentary Papers — — — — — — 414

APPENDIX.

ory of the War — — — — — — 1

Books printed for J. DEBRETT.

I.

MEMOIR of the OPERATIONS Of the ARMY of the DANUBE, under the Command GENERAL JOURDAN, 1799:
Taken from the MANUSCRIPTS of that Officer. Translated from the French.—Price 4s.

Of whom may be had,

II.

CAMPAGNE DE JOURDAN,
1799.—Price 4s.

⁂ This Memoir must interest the Public, as it unfolds the system the French Directorial Government; and will instruct or amuse Soldier, by a minute History and Comment on the last Battle wh JOURDAN fought with the Archduke CHARLES; written by the Gen himself.

III.

Dedicated, by Permission, to Earl SPENCER, K. G. First Lord of Admiralty, &c. &c.

Elegantly printed in Two Pocket Volumes, Price 8s. bound,

A VOCABULARY of SEA PHRASES and TERMS of AR'
USED IN
SEAMANSHIP and NAVAL ARCHITECTURE.

In Two Parts.

1. English and French. 2. French and English. Carefully collec' from the best Authorities, written and oral, aided by a long and intim Acquaintance with the Nautical Language of both Countries; and conta ing all the Orders necessary for working a Ship, and carrying on the D on board, as well at Sea as in Port.

By a CAPTAIN of the BRITISH NAVY.

"This is evidently the work of an experienced professional man, w in his preface acquaints his readers, that it has been his endeavour to o no term or phrase that could be useful, either to the Sea Officer, the Na Architect, the Reader of Voyages, or the Translator. The Author not neglected to consult the best printed authorities; and he acknowled himself to have been favoured with important communications fr French Officers of distinguished talents. His Work is executed with gr ability, and in a small compass, the terms in each language being b concisely and well explained; and we strongly recommend it to all (aval Officers." Monthly Review, Sept. 1799

STATE PAPERS.

TREATIES, ARMISTICES, &c.

Negotiation at Seltz.
The following, which came in Manuscript from Hamburgh, is given as the Substance of the Secret Negotiation at Seltz.

IN the first conference between Count Cobenzel and Neufchateau, the former declared, that although his Imperial Majesty was ready to grant ample satisfaction for what had happened in regard to Bernadotte, yet from a due regard to the sentiments of the people of Vienna, it was necessary to conduct this business without precipitation and *eclat*. The interest of both powers seemed to require that the conferences at Seltz should be chiefly devoted to settle some material points which called for a definite arrangement. Neufchateau having acquiesced in this proposition, the Count went a step farther, and proposed, that as the congress at Rastadt was a mere farce, acted on the part of the Empire, under the vote and absolute guidance of the Imperial cabinet and ecclesiastical courts, the negotiation for peace should be entirely carried on and brought to an issue at Seltz, at the close of which it would be easy to force Prussia and the Empire to submit to what had been agreed upon between Austria and France. By command of the Directory, Neufchateau rejected the latter proposition, but entered into the discussion of the subjects alluded to by the Count, who proposed, first, "That, as the cession of Bavaria, stipulated in the secret articles of the treaty of Campio Formio, seemed to meet with great obstacles, even in regard to the guarantee promised by the Directory, Austria would for the present desist from demanding this cession, on condition that such parts of the borders of Bavaria and of the Upper Palatinate as were necessary for the greater convenience and safety of the Austrian frontiers, be ceded to Austria, together with

Saltzburgh, Paſſau, Bechtoldſgaden, and all the former poſſeſſions of the *ci-devant* republic of Venice."

This propoſal not having been accepted by the Directory, the Count offered his ſecond propoſition, wherein he once more demanded the ceſſion of the remainder of the ancient Venetian dominions, together with the three Roman legations, and the dutchy and fortreſs of Mantua, &c. and inſiſted on the treaty of Baſle being reſcinded, and that neither Pruſſia nor the Houſe of Orange would receive any indemnification in Germany. Upon this condition Auſtria relinquiſhed her claim of being indemnified by a part of the German territory.

Neufchateau declared this propoſition to be altogether inadmiſſible; in conſequence of which, Count Cobenzel made a third propoſition, which was in ſubſtance as follows: " Auſtria, as well as Pruſſia, is to relinquiſh all pretenſions of being indemnified by any part of the German territory. Such German ſtates as have loſt their all, are to be indemnified; and for this purpoſe the ſecularization of eccleſiaſtical poſſeſſions is to be reſorted to, but only as far as it is indiſpenſably neceſſary for that object. Auſtria demands in return the country of the Griſons, the Valteline, the reſt of the ancient Venetian poſſeſſions, the dutchy and fortreſs of Mantua, and as much of the Ciſalpine territory, as is neceſſary for the ſafety of the frontiers, &c. As to Pruſſia, ſhe is to receive no indemnification for the territory ceded on the left bank of the Rhine, at leaſt not in Franconia, &c."

Neufchateau paid great attention to this project, inſiſting however on the preſervation of the treaty of Baſle; but at length he received diſpatches from the Directory, ſeverely cenſuring his conduct, in giving Cobenzel ſo much hopes, and directing him to declare, " That the French government could neither diſpoſe of the country of the Griſons, nor of the Ciſalpine territory, &c.; that the ſubſiſting treaties with Baaden, Wirtemberg, Caſſel, and Deux Ponts, obliged the French republic to favour their indemnification, &c.; that for this purpoſe eccleſiaſtical poſſeſſions muſt be ſecularized, and France would not prevent the King of Pruſſia from ſeeking his indemnification in Weſtphalia, &c."

In conſequence of this declaration, the negotiations were ſuſpended for a conſiderable time; and upon Neufchateau's urging the termination of the buſineſs, Count Cobenzel offered as an excuſe the exiſtence of an important correſpondence between Berlin, Vienna, and Peterſburgh, throwing out at the ſame time looſe hints of a cloſe connexion being formed between Auſtria and Pruſſia, ſo that not only Neufchateau, but alſo the Directory, grew uneaſy and diſtruſtful. Count Lehrbach, whom Cobenzel had already introduced to Neufchateau, on offering the third propoſition, appeared at Seltz, and made the following fourth

and

and laft propofition, viz. "France may poffefs herfelf of Piedmont. Auftria agrees to cede all her poffeffions in Upper Suabia, by which the Elector of Cologne and the Elector Palatine are to be indemnified; Deux Ponts being the prefumptive heir of the latter, is not to receive any indemnification, &c. Wirtemberg is to be indemnified by a part of the Auftrian poffeffions in Upper Suabia, &c. The King of Pruffia fhall be permitted to fecularize the bifhopric of Hildefheim for his indemnification (which has already been offered him on the part of the Imperial court); nor will Auftria object to France endeavouring to obtain for the Swifs republic the Thurgaw, or fome part of Upper Suabia. Auftria demands in return that the reft of the ancient Venetian dominions be ceded to her, together with the Valteline, the dutchy of Mantua, and a part of the Tufcan and Cifalpine territory, &c.

" The King of Sardinia fhall be indemnified by the Roman territory, and a part of Cifalpinia; but Naples is alfo to receive as much of the ancient ecclefiaftical ftate as is neceffary to render her frontiers more fafe and convenient.

" The three Roman Legations and Lucca are to be allotted to the Grand Duke of Tufcany by way of indemnification, &c.

" The point relative to the Batavian dominions is to be adjufted by Pruffia, &c.

" No fort of exchange fhall be fuffered to take place between Pruffia and Batavia, in regard to the dutchy of Bergues, &c."

Immediately after this propofition had been offered by Counts Cobenzel and Lehrbach, Neufchateau was directed by the Directory to confine his negotiation to the fole point of fatisfaction, and to declare, that as all the propofitions made on the part of the Imperial court merely tended to aggrandize Auftria at the expenfe of other powers, unlefs Count Cobenzel could and would agree to the promifed fatisfaction, the conferences at Seltz fhould be broken off, which they accordingly were.

Treaty of Campo Formio.

Secret Articles, and additional Convention of the Treaty of Campo Formio, of the 20th Vendemiaire, 6th Year (October 17, 1798).

Article I.

HIS Majefty the Emperor, King of Hungary and Bohemia, confents that the boundaries of the French republic fhall extend to the under-mentioned line, and engages to ufe his influence, that the French republic fhall, by the peace to be concluded with the German Empire, retain the fame line as its boundary: namely, the left bank of the Rhine from the confines of Switzerland, below Bafle to the branching off of the Nette above Andrenach; including the head of the bridge at Manheim, the town and fortress of Mentz, and both banks of the Nette from where it falls into the Rhine, to its source near Bruch. From thence the line passes by Kenscherade and Borley to Kerpen, and thence to Luderfdorf, Blantenheim, Marmagen, Coll, and Gemund, with all the circles and territory of these places, along both banks of the Olff to where it falls into the Roer, and along both banks of the Roer; including Heimbach, Nideggen, Durin, and Juliers, with their circles and territory; as also the places on the banks to Linnig included. Hence the line extends by Hoffern and Kylenfdalen, Papelernod, Lutersforst, Rodenberg, Haverstoo, Anderscheid, Keldekuchen, Vampach, Herrigen, and Grosberg, including the town of Venloo and its territory. And if, notwithstanding the mediation of his Imperial Majesty, the German Empire shall refuse to consent to the above-mentioned boundary line of the republic, his Imperial Majesty hereby formally engages to furnish to the Empire no more than his contingent, which shall not be employed in any fortified place, or it shall be considered as a rupture of the peace and friendship which are restored between his Majesty and the republic.

II. His Imperial Majesty will employ his good offices in the negotiation of the peace of the Empire to obtain, 1. That the navigation of the Rhine from Hunningen to the territory of Holland shall be free both to the French republic and the states of the Empire on the right bank: 2. That the possessors of territory near the mouth of the Moselle shall never, and on no pretence, attempt to interrupt the free navigation and passage of ships and other vessels from the Moselle into the Rhine: 3. The French republic shall have the free navigation of the Meuse; and the tolls and other imposts from Venloo to Holland shall be abolished.

III. His Imperial Majesty renounces, for himself and his successors, the sovereignty and possession of the county of Falkenstein and its dependencies.

IV. The countries which his Imperial Majesty takes possession of, in consequence of the 6th article of the public definitive treaty, this day signed, shall be considered as an indemnification for the territory given up by the 7th article of the public treaty, and the foregoing article. This renunciation shall only be in force when the troops of his Imperial Majesty shall have taken possession of the countries ceded by the said articles.

V. The French republic will employ its influence that his Majesty the Emperor shall receive the archbishopric of Saltzburg, and that part of the circle of Bavaria which lies between the archbishopric of Saltzburg, the river Inn, Salza, and Tyrol;
including

including the town of Wasserburg on the right bank of the Inn, with an arrondissement of 3000 toises.

VI. His Imperial Majesty, at the conclusion of the peace with the Empire, will give up to the French republic the sovereignty and possession of the Frickthal, and all the territory belonging to the House of Austria on the left bank of the Rhine between Zurzach and Basle, provided his Majesty, at the conclusion of the said peace, receives a proportionate indemnification. The French republic, in consequence of particular arrangements to be made, shall unite the above-mentioned territory with the Helvetic republic, without farther interference on the part of his Imperial Majesty or the Empire.

VII. The two contracting powers agree, that when, in the ensuing peace with the German Empire, the French republic shall make an acquisition in Germany, his Imperial Majesty shall receive an equivalent; and, if his Imperial Majesty shall make such an acquisition, the French republic shall in like manner receive an equivalent.

VIII. The Prince of Nassau Dietz, late Stadtholder of Holland, shall receive a territorial indemnification; but neither in the vicinity of the Austrian possessions nor in the vicinity of the Batavian republic.

IX. The French republic makes no difficulty to restore to the King of Prussia his possessions on the left bank of the Rhine. No new acquisition shall, however, be proposed for the King of Prussia. This the two contracting powers mutually guarantee.

X. Should the King of Prussia be willing to cede to the French and Batavian republics some small parts of his territory on the left bank of the Meuse, as Sevenger and other possessions towards the Yssel, his Imperial Majesty will use his influence that such cessions shall be accepted and made valid by the Empire.

XI. His Imperial Majesty will not object to the manner in which the Imperial fiefs have been disposed of by the French republic in favour of the Ligurian republic. His Imperial Majesty will use his influence, together with the French republic, that the German Empire will renounce all feudal sovereignty over the countries which make a part of the Cisalpine and Ligurian republics; as also the Imperial fiefs, such as Laniguiana, and those which lie between Tuscany and the states of Parma, the Ligurian and Lucchese republics, and the late territory of Modena, which fiefs make a part of the Cisalpine republic.

XII. His Imperial Majesty and the French republic will, in concert, employ their influence, in the course of concluding the peace of the Empire, that the princes and states of the Empire, who, in consequence of the stipulations of the present

sent treaty of peace, or in consequence of the treaty to be concluded with the Empire, shall suffer any loss in territory or rights (particularly the Electors of Mentz, Treves, and Cologne, the Elector Palatine of Bavaria, the Duke of Wirtemberg and Teck, the Margrave of Baden, the Duke of Deux Ponts, the Landgraves of Hesse Cassel and Darmstadt, the Princes of Nassau Saarbruck, Salm, Korburg, Lowenstein, Westheim, and Wied Runckel, and the Count De Leyn), shall receive proportionable indemnifications in Germany, which shall be settled by mutual agreement with the French republic.

XIII. The troops of his Imperial Majesty, twenty days after the ratifications of the present treaties, shall evacuate the towns and fortresses of Mentz, Ehrenbreiastein, Philipsburg, Manheim, Kunigstein, Ulm, and Ingolstadt, as also the whole territory appertaining to the German Empire, to the boundaries of the hereditary states.

XIV. The present secret articles shall have the same force as if they were inserted word for word in the public treaty of peace this day signed, and shall, in like manner be ratified at the same time by the two contracting powers; which ratifications shall be exchanged in due form at Rastadt.

Done and signed at Campo Formio, the 17th of October 1797, 16th of Vendèmaire, in the 6th year of the French republic, one and indivisible.

(Signed) BUONAPARTE.
Marquis de GALLO.
LOUIS Count COBENZEL.
Count MEERFELDT, Major Gen.
Count DEGELMANN.

Provisional Treaty between his Majesty the King of Great Britain and his Majesty the Emperor of all the Russias. Done at St. Petersburgh the 29th (18th) of December 1798.

In the name of the most holy and indivisible Trinity.

HIS Majesty the King of Great Britain, and his Majesty the Emperor of all the Russias, in consequence of the alliance and friendship subsisting between them, being desirous to enter into a concert of measures, such as may contribute in the most efficacious manner to oppose the successes of the French arms and the extension of the principles of anarchy, and to bring about a solid peace, together with the re-establishment of the balance of Europe, have judged it worthy their most serious consideration and earnest solicitude to endeavour, if possible, to reduce France within its former limits, as they subsisted before the revolution. They have, in consequence, agreed to conclude a provisional treaty

treaty; and for this purpose they have named as their plenipotentiaries, namely, his Majesty the King of Great Britain, Sir Charles Whitworth, K. B. his envoy extraordinary and minister plenipotentiary at the Imperial court of Russia; and his Majesty the Emperor of all the Russias, the Chancellor Prince Besborodko, a privy counsellor, director general of the posts, senator, and knight of the orders of St. Andrew, of St. Alexander Newsky, of St. Anne, and Grand Cross of those of St. John of Jerusalem and of St. Vladamir, of the first class; the Sieur Korschouby, vice-chancellor, privy counsellor, and chamberlain, knight of the order of St. Alexander Newsky, and Grand Cross of that of St. Vladamir, of the second class; the Sieur Rostopschin, a privy counsellor, member of the college for foreign affairs, knight of the order of St. Alexander Newsky, and of that of St. Anne, of the first class; who, after having reciprocal'y communicated their full powers, have concluded and agreed upon the following articles:

Art. I. The two contracting powers, in the intention of inducing the King of Prussia to take an active part in the war against the common enemy, propose to employ all their endeavours to obtain that end. Immediately on his Prussian Majesty's consenting to this measure, his Imperial Majesty of all the Russias is ready to afford him a succour of land forces, and he destines for that purpose 45,000 men, infantry and cavalry, with the necessary artillery, upon the following conditions:

II. This body of troops shall be put in motion as soon as the high contracting parties shall be assured of the determination of his Prussian Majesty being conformable to what has been before stated.

With regard to the further movements of this corps, and its combined operations with the Prussian troops, his Majesty the Emperor of all the Russias will arrange them with his Majesty the King of Prussia, and communication shall also be made of them to his Britannic Majesty, in order that by such a concert between the high allies, the military operations against the enemy may be made with the greater success, and that the object which is proposed may the more easily be ascertained.

III. In order to facilitate to his Majesty the Emperor of all the Russias the means to take such an active part in the present war against the French, his Britannic Majesty engages to furnish the pecuniary succours herein-after specified; his Imperial Majesty of all the Russias nevertheless reserving to himself the right to recall the aforesaid body of troops into his own territories, if, by any unforeseen event, the whole of this pecuniary succour should not be furnished him.

IV. The amount and the nature of these pecuniary succours have been fixed and regulated upon the following footing:—1st.

In order to enable his Imperial Majesty of all the Russias to expedite, as soon as possible, and in the most convenient manner, the troops destined to be employed in favour of the good cause, his Majesty the King of Great Britain engages, as soon as he shall receive advice that the Russian troops, in consequence of the determination of his Majesty the King of Prussia, are to march, in order to co-operate with those of his said Majesty, to pay for the first and the most urgent expenses, 225,000*l.* sterling, dividing the payments in such manner, as that 75,000*l.* sterling should be paid as soon as those troops shall have passed the Russian frontiers; that the second payment, amounting to the same sum, should be made on the expiration of the first three months and on the commencement of the fourth; and that the third payment, completing the sum total, should be made in like manner, after three months and on the beginning of the seventh. 2d. His Majesty the King of Great Britain engages also to furnish to his Majesty the Emperor of all the Russias a subsidy of 75,000*l.* sterling per month, to be computed from the day on which the corps of troops above mentioned shall pass the Russian frontiers. This subsidy shall be paid at the commencement of each month, and being destined for the appointments and maintenance of the troops, it shall be continued during the space of twelve months, unless peace should be made sooner. 3d. The two high contracting parties, besides, shall come to an understanding before the expiration of the term of a year above specified, whether, in case the war should not be terminated, the subsidy above mentioned shall be continued.

V. The two high contracting parties engage not to make either peace or armistice without including each other, and without concerting with each other; but if, through any unforeseen events, his Britannic Majesty should be under the necessity of terminating the war, and thereby of discontinuing the payment of the subsidy, before the expiration of the twelve months above stipulated, he engages, in that case, to pay three months advance of the subsidy agreed upon of 75,000*l.* sterling, reckoning from the day on which the information shall be received by the general commanding the Russian troops.

VI. In like manner, if any aggression on Russia should take place, by which his Majesty the Emperor should be obliged to recall his army into his own dominions, the above-mentioned subsidy shall, in such case only, be paid up to the day on which the army shall re-enter the Russian frontiers.

VII. His Majesty the Emperor of all the Russias shall come to an understanding with his ally his Majesty the King of Prussia, respecting all the other expenses which this corps of troops and its operations may require. His Britannic Majesty shall take no further share in those expenses than the sum of 37,500*l.* sterling per month, during all the time that the above-mentioned troops shall be employed, by virtue of this treaty, for the common cause. That sum shall be advanced by his Majesty the Emperor of all the Russias; but his Britannic Majesty acknowledges it as a debt due by Great Britain to Russia, which he will discharge after the conclusion of a peace made by mutual agreement.

The mode and dates of the payment shall then be settled by mutual concert, according to the reciprocal convenience of the two allied powers.

VIII. The above-mentioned subsidies shall in this manner be considered as a sufficient succour for all expenses, including those which may be necessary for the return of the Russian army.

IX. This treaty shall be considered as provisional; and its execution, as it has been stated above, shall not take place until his Majesty the King of Prussia shall be determined to turn his forces against the common enemy; but, in case he should not do so, the two high contracting parties reserve to themselves the right and the power to take, for the good of their affairs, and the success of the salutary end they may have in view, other measures analogous to the times and circumstances, and to agree then upon those which, in such a case, they shall judge to be most necessary, adopting always as a basis (in as much as it shall be compatible) the stipulations of the present treaty. His Imperial Majesty of all the Russias, in order nevertheless to give a still more striking proof of his sincere dispositions, and of his desire to be as much as possible useful to his allies, promises to put, during the course of the negotiation with his Prussian Majesty, and even previous to its termination, the above-mentioned corps of 45,000 men upon such a footing that they may immediately be employed wherever, according to a previous concert amongst the allies, the utility of the common cause shall require.

X. The present provisional treaty shall be ratified by his Britannic Majesty and his Imperial Majesty of all the Russias; and the ratifications shall be exchanged here in the space of two months, to be computed from the day of the signature, or sooner, if it can be done.

In witness whereof, we the undersigned, furnished with the full powers of his Majesty the King of Great Britain and the Emperor of all the Russias, have, in their names, signed the present treaty, and have affixed the seals of our arms thereto.

Done at St. Petersburgh, the 29th (18th) of December 1798.

        (L. S.)   A. P DE B...BERODKO.
        (L. S.)   KOTSCHOUBEY.
        (L. S.)   ROSTOPSCHIN.

(L. S.)   CHARLES WHITWORTH.

Declaration.

BY the provisional treaty concluded between his Majesty the King of Great Britain and his Majesty the Emperor of all the Russias, the 29th (18th) of Dec. 1798, it is stipulated, that the body of 45,000 men, furnished by his said Imperial Majesty for the support of the common cause, should be employed in co-operating with the troops of his Prussian Majesty, if that sovereign should be induced to join his forces to those of their Majesties; but the endeavours which their Royal and Imperial Majesties have employed for this purpose having been unsuccessful, and that prince persisting in his adherence to his system of neutrality; the two high contracting parties, in order to neglect nothing on their part which may contribute to the success of the good cause, have resolved that the said body of 45,000 men, originally destined to second the hostile demonstrations of Prussia against France, shall be equally employed against the common enemy in whatever other quarter their Majesties may judge to be most advantageous to their common operations.

For this purpose the plenipotentiaries of their said Royal and Imperial Majesties have signed the present declaration, which is to be considered as forming a part of the provisional treaty above mentioned, concluded between the two courts the 29th (18th) of December 1798.

Done at St. Petersburgh, this 29th (18th) of June 1799.

(L. S.)   Le Comte de KOSCHOUBEY.
(L. S.)   Le Comte de ROSTOPSCHIN.
(L.S.) CHARLES WHITWORTH.

The Convention between his Britannic Majesty and his Majesty the Emperor of all the Russias, signed at St. Petersburgh the 22d (11th) of June 1799.

In the name of the most holy and indivisible Trinity.

HIS Majesty the King of Great Britain and his Majesty the Emperor of all the Russias, in consequence of the friendship and the ties of intimate alliance which exist between them, and of their common and sincere co-operation in the present war against the French, having constantly in their view to use every means in their power most effectually to distress the enemy, have judged that the expulsion of the French from the Seven United Provinces, and the deliverance of the latter from the yoke under which they have so long groaned, were objects worthy of their particular consideration, and wishing at the same time to give effect, as far as possible, to a design of that importance, their said Majesties have resolved to conclude with each other a

convention

…ation relative … … to the most proper means of …ng it into th… … …ition. For this purpose they …amed as their plenipotent…ies, to wit, his Majesty the King …reat Britain, Sir Charles Whitworth, his envoy extraordi…and minister plenipotentiary to the Imperial court of Russia, …t of the order of the Bath; and his Majesty the Emperor of …e Russias, the Count of Kotschoubey, his vice-chancellor, … privy counsellor, actual chamberlain, knight of the order … Alexander Newsky, commander of that of St. John of Jeru…, and great cross of the order of St. Vladamir of the second … and the Count of Rostopschin, his actual privy counsellor, …er of the college of foreign affairs, director-general of the … knight of the order of St. Alexander Newsky, and of St. … of the first class, great chancellor and great cross of that … John of Jerusalem; who, after having reciprocally commu…d to each other their full powers, have agreed upon the fol…g articles:

. I. His Majesty the King of Great Britain, thinking that …ject above announced cannot be better attained than by the …, a body of Russian troops, his Imperial Majesty, notwith…ing the efforts which he has already made, and the difficulties …employing an additional body of forces to act at a distance …his dominions, has, nevertheless, in consequence of his con…solicitude in favour of the good cause, consented to furnish se…n battalions of infantry, two companies of artillery, one …ny of pioneers, and one squadron of hussars, making in all …3 men, to be destined for the said expedition to Holland. … that number of troops, according to the plan proposed by …itannic Majesty, is not sufficient, and as it has been judged …,000 men would be necessary for that purpose, his said Ma…rill, on his side, furnish 13,000 men of English troops, or at …,000 men, if that smaller number should be deemed sufficient, …nongst whom there shall be a proportion of cavalry sufficient …e services of such an army.

This corps of troops of 17,593 men, together with the …ry artillery, shall assemble at Revel, in order that they may …n thence conveyed to their destination, either in English …er vessels freighted by his Britannic Majesty.

. In order to enable his Majesty the Emperor of all the Rus…afford to the common cause this additional and efficacious …r, his Majesty the King of Great Britain engages to furnish …dermentioned subsidies, upon the condition that his Imperial …ty of all the Russias shall have a right to recall into his domi…the above-mentioned corps of troops, if, through any unfore…vent, such subsidies should not be regularly furnished to him.
…. The amount and the nature of those pecuniary succours …een settled and regulated in the following manner: 1st. In

order to enable his Imperial Majesty to assemble and expedite this corps as soon and as well equipped as possible, his Majesty the King of Great Britain engages, as soon as he shall receive advice that the above-mentioned troops have reached the place of their rendezvous, that is to say, at Revel, and that it shall be declared that they are ready to embark (whether the transports be arrived or not), to pay for the first and most urgent expenses, the sum of 88,000*l.* sterling, dividing the payments into two parts, to wit, that 44,000*l.* sterling be paid immediately after it shall have been declared, either by the commander in chief of that corps to the English commissary, or by the ministry of his Imperial Majesty to the minister of his Britannic Majesty resident at St. Petersburgh, that the said corps is ready; and that the second payment, completing the sum total of 88,000*l.* sterling, shall take place three months afterwards and at the commencement of the fourth. 2dly. His Majesty the King of Great Britain engages in like manner to furnish to his Majesty the Emperor of all the Russias, a subsidy of 44,000*l.* sterling per month, to be computed from the day on which the above-mentioned corps of troops shall be ready. This subsidy shall be paid at the commencement of each month, and destined for the appointments and the entertainment of the troops. It shall be continued until they shall return into Russian ports, in English or other vessels, freighted by his Britannic Majesty.

V. If this corps of Russian troops should meet with difficulties, in procuring, during the expedition to which it is destined, or in case of its wintering, as shall be hereafter mentioned, in England, or during the voyages it shall have to make, its necessary subsistence, by means of the measures which the Russian commanders or commissaries may take for that purpose, his Britannic Majesty, upon the requisition of the minister of his Majesty the Emperor of all the Russias, residing at his court, shall furnish whatever may be necessary to the Russian troops; and an exact account shall be kept of all the provisions and other articles so delivered, in order that their value may be afterwards deducted from the subsidy, such provisions and other articles being valued at the price paid for them by his Majesty for his own troops.

VI. As the transport of the horses necessary for the officers, the artillery, and the baggage, would require a great many vessels, and as that arrangement would lead to many other inconveniencies, and more particularly to that of a delay, prejudicial to the above-mentioned expedition, his Britannic Majesty engages to furnish, at his own expense, the necessary number of horses, according to the statement which shall be delivered, and to have them conveyed to the place where the Russian troops are to act: his said Majesty will, in like manner, maintain them at his own expense during the whole time these troops shall be employed, and until they shall be re-embarked, in order to return to the ports of Russia.

His

(xiii)

His Britannic Majesty will then dispose of them in such a manner as he shall judge proper.

VII. In case that the Russian troops, after having terminated in Holland the projected expedition, or in consequence of its being deferred through any unforeseen circumstances, should not be able to return into the ports of his Imperial Majesty during the favourable season, his Majesty the King of Great Britain engages to receive them into his own dominions, to provide them there with good quarters, and all other advantages, until the troops shall be able to return on the opening of the navigation, or shall be employed upon some other destination, which shall be previously settled between their Royal and Imperial Majesties.

VIII. As the principal object of the employment of this corps of troops is a sudden attack to be made on Holland, by means of which his Britannic Majesty hopes to produce there a favourable change; as, besides, no fixed term for the continuance of the subsidies is stipulated, whilst on the other hand the said troops, after their return to Russia, must be reconducted to their ordinary quarters, mostly at a great distance; and as the marches which they will have to make will require considerable expenses, his Majesty the King of Great Britain hereby engages to make good this charge by a payment of subsidies for two months, to be computed from the day of the arrival of those troops in Russian ports. In like manner his Majesty the Emperor of all the Russias, without fixing any term, reserves to himself the right of causing the said corps of troops to return into his dominions, in the spring of the next year 1800; or if any hostile aggression upon Russia, or any other important event, should render it necessary: in these two cases, the above-mentioned engagement of his Britannic Majesty, concerning the payment of two months subsidy, shall equally take place.

IX. As it is understood that the expedition to Holland, which has given rise to the present convention, is to be effected in common by Russian and English troops, each party shall follow, relative to the employment and to the command of the troops, literally the treaty of defensive alliance concluded between the two high contracting parties the 7th (18th) of February, in the year 1795. In like manner, if any difficulties should arise either between the commanders of the respective forces or otherwise, which may regard the above-mentioned troops of his Majesty the Emperor of all the Russias, the solution of such difficulties shall be looked for in the stipulations of the said treaty of the year 1795, or likewise in that concluded with the court of Vienna the 3d (14th) of July 1792.

X. The present convention shall be ratified by his Majesty the King of Great Britain, and by his Majesty the Emperor of all the Russias; and the ratifications shall be exchanged here in the space

of

of two months, to be computed from the day of its signature, or sooner, if it can be done.

In witness whereof, we the undersigned, furnished with full powers by his Majesty the King of Great Britain, and by his Majesty the Emperor of all the Russias, have in their names signed the present convention, and have affixed thereto the seal of our arms.

Done at St. Petersburgh, the 22d (11th) of June 1799.

     (L. S.) Le Comte de KOTSCHOUBEY.
     (L. S.) Le Comte de ROSTOPSCHIN.
(L. S.) CHARLES WHITWORTH.

SEPARATE ARTICLE.

I. Although it be stated in Article II. of the convention concluded this day, that the corps of Russian troops, forming 17,593 men, destined for the expedition to Holland, shall be conveyed to its destination in English, or other vessels freighted by his Majesty the King of Great Britain; nevertheless, in order so much the more to facilitate this important enterprise, his Majesty the Emperor of all the Russias consents to furnish six ships, five frigates, and two transport vessels, which being armed *en fluttes*, will receive on board as many troops as they shall be able to contain, whilst the remainder of the said corps shall be embarked on board of English or other transport vessels, freighted by his Britannic Majesty.

II. His Majesty the Emperor of all the Russias will lend these ships and frigates upon the following conditions: 1st. There shall be paid by England, upon their quitting the port of Cronstadt, in order to go to the place of rendezvous, which is Revel, the sum of 58,927*l*. 10*s*. sterling, as a subsidy for the expenses of equipment, &c. for three months, to be computed from the day, as it is above stated, of their departure from Cronstadt. 2dly. After the expiration of these three months, his Britannic Majesty shall continue the same subsidies, that is to say, of 19,642*l*. 10*s*. sterling a month, which shall be paid at the commencement of each month. 3dly. Independently of this pecuniary succour, his Britannic Majesty shall provide for the subsistence of the crews; and the officers and sailors shall be treated on the same footing as are the English officers and sailors in time of war, and as are the Russian officers and sailors, who are at present in the squadron of his Imperial Majesty, which is united to the English squadron. 4thly. All these stipulations shall have full and entire effect until the return of the above-mentioned ships and frigates into Russian ports.

III. If it should happen, contrary to all expectation, that those six ships, five frigates, and two transport vessels, should not be able, through some unforeseen event, to return to Russia before the close of the present campaign, his Britannic Majesty engages to admit them into the ports of England, where they shall receive every possible

(xv)

IV. As the six [...] frigates, and two transports, above mentioned, having been originally intended for another destination, were furnished with provi[sions] for three months, his Britannic Majesty, instead of furnish[ing] them in kind, as it is stated in the second article, engages to p[ay], according to an estimate which shall be made, the value of these p[rovisions]. With regard to the officers, his Majesty the King of Great Britain will adopt the same principle as has been followed t[ill] the present time, respecting the officers of the Russian squad[ron] which is joined to the naval forces of England. That shall serve as a rule for indemnifying them for the preparations which they may have made for the campaign, such as it had been originally intended to take place.

This separate article shall be considered as forming part of the convention above mentioned, as being inserted therein word for word; and it shall be ratified, and the ratification exchanged in the same manner.

In witness whereof, we the undersigned, furnished with the full powers of his Majesty the King of Great Britain, and of his Majesty the Emperor of all the Russias, have, in their name, signed the present separate article, and have affixed thereto the seal of our arms.

Done at St. Petersburgh, this 22nd (11th) of June 1799.

(L. S.) Le Comte de KOTSCHOUBEY.
(L. S.) Le Comte de ROSTOPSCHIN.
(L. S.) CHARLES WHITWORTH.

Treaty of Alliance defensive between his Majesty the Emperor of the Ottomans, and his Majesty the Emperor of Russia.

In the name of God Omnipotent.

HIS Majesty the Emperor of the Ottomans, and his Majesty the Emperor of all the Russias, equally animated with a sincere desire, not only to maintain for the good of their respective states and subjects the peace, friendship, and good understanding which happily subsist between them, but further to make them contribute to the re-establishment and security of the general tranquillity so salutary for humanity, and at present so much disturbed, have resolved to draw still more close the bonds which unite them by the conclusion of a treaty of defensive alliance. Accordingly their Majesties have chosen and nominated for their plenipotentiaries, that is to say, his Majesty the Emperor of the Ottomans, Essaid Ibrahim-Ihmed Bey, with the title of Cadileskier of Romelie *ci-devant* Istamboul-Effendi, and Achmed Alif, Reis-Effendi; and his Majesty the Emperor of Russia, the noble Vassili Tamara his privy

counsellor

(xvi)

counsellor and ambassador extraordinary at the Ottoman Porte; who, after having exchanged their full powers in due and proper form, have agreed upon the following articles:

I. There shall be always peace, friendship, and good understanding between his Majesty the Emperor of the Ottomans, and the Emperor of all the Russias, their empires and subjects as well by land as by sea, in such manner as that by this defensive alliance there shall be established between them an union so intimate that they shall in future have the same friends and the same enemies; in consequence, their Majesties promise to open their minds without reserve, the one to the other, upon all subjects which concern their respective tranquillity and safety, and to take all necessary measures to oppose themselves to every hostile enterprise that might prove injurious to them, and for the re-establishment of general tranquillity.

II. The treaty of peace concluded at Jassy, the 29th December 1791, of the Egira 1206, the 15th of the moon of Gemaziel Coxel, as well as all other treaties comprised in it, are hereby confirmed in their full tenour and extent, as if they had been inserted word for word in the present treaty of defensive alliance.

III. To give to this alliance full and complete effect, the high contracting powers reciprocally guarantee their possessions. His Majesty the Emperor of all the Russias guarantees to the Sublime Porte all its possessions without exception, such as they existed before the invasion of Egypt: and his Majesty the Emperor of the Ottomans guarantees all the possessions of the Court of Russia as they at present exist, without exception.

IV. Although the two parties reserve to themselves the right of entering into negotiations with other powers, and of concluding with them all treaties that their interests may require, they bind themselves, however, one to the other, in the most formal manner, to insert nothing in such treaties that may be able to cause the least prejudice, injury, or loss to either of the two, or affect the integrity of their states. On the contrary, they bind themselves reciprocally to do every thing which may be able to preserve and maintain the honour, security, and advantage of both the one and the other.

V. If there should be formed any plan or enterprise hurtful to the two powers, or one of them, and that the forces which may be employed to baffle such hostile enterprises shall not be found sufficient, then the one party shall be bound to assist the other by land or by sea, either to act in concert or to make a diversion, or it shall assist with money according as the common interest of the allies and their security shall require. In such case they shall previously communicate to each other with frankness, they shall make all necessary dispositions with the greatest possible promptitude, and shall immediately fulfil their obligation with fidelity.

VI. The

VI. The choice of such assistance, whether it consists in auxiliary troops or money, shall depend on the party attacked; and in case that it requires the former, they shall be furnished within three months after demand made. If it prefers subsidies in money, they shall be paid, year by year, at fixed periods, from the day of the declaration of war by the aggressor on the commencement of hostilities.

VII. The two high contracting parties thus making common cause, whether with all their forces or only with stipulated succours, neither of the two shall conclude a treaty of peace or armistice without comprizing in it the other, and providing for its security; and in case there should be formed any enterprise or attack against the party called upon, in contempt of the alliance concluded, on the succours lent, the other party shall be obliged to fulfil with fidelity and punctuality the same obligations for the defence of the former.

VIII. In case where the two high allied powers are called upon to act in concert with all their forces or a stipulated aid, they promise to communicate reciprocally to each other, with frankness and without reserve, the plan of their military operations, to facilitate as much as possible their execution, to communicate their intentions relative to the duration of war and the conditions of peace, and to understand themselves on this subject as guided by pacific and moderate principles.

IX. The auxiliary troops shall be provided by their sovereign, in proportion to their number, with artillery, ammunition, and other necessaries. They shall be also paid and kept by him. The party requiring them shall furnish them with provisions and forage in kind or money, according to certain prices to be fixed and agreed upon, from the date of the day on which they shall quit their frontiers. The party requiring them shall procure them quarters and other accommodations, such as his own troops enjoy, or such as those of the country called upon have been used to in time of peace.

X. The party requiring shall furnish the auxiliary squadron with all provisions that it shall want, on certain terms which shall have been agreed upon, to commence from the day of its arrival, and during all the time it shall be employed against the common enemy. The party requiring shall furnish without hesitation from its arsenals and magazines, at the ordinary prices, every thing necessary for the squadron, should it stand in need of repairs. The ships of war and transports of the two allied courts shall have, during the whole time of the continuance of the common war, free entrance into their ports, either to winter there or repair.

XI. All trophies taken from the enemy, and all the prizes, shall belong to the troops which shall acquire them.

XII. Their Majesties, the Emperor of the Ottomans and the

Emperor of all the Russias, having no views of conquest by the present treaty of defensive alliance, but only to maintain the integrity of their respective possessions, for the security of their subjects, and also to support the other powers in the respectable situation in which they are at present placed; and according to which they may form a political counterpoise, if necessary, for the maintenance of the general tranquillity, their Majesties will not fail to invite his Majesty the Emperor, King of Bohemia and Hungary, the Kings of Great Britain and Prussia, and also all other potentates, to accede to this treaty, the object of which is so just and so salutary.

XIII. However sincerely the two high contracting powers may intend to maintain this engagement to the most remote period of time, yet as it may happen that circumstances should hereafter require some changes to be made in it, it is agreed to limit its duration to eight years from the date of the day of the exchange of the Imperial ratifications. The two parties, before the expiration of that term, shall concert, according to the state of affairs at that period, on the renewal of the said treaty.

XIV. The present treaty of defensive alliance shall be ratified by his Majesty the Emperor of the Ottomans, and by his Majesty the Emperor of all the Russias, and the ratifications shall be exchanged at Constantinople within the term of two months, and even sooner if possible.

In faith of which, we the undersigned, by virtue of our full powers, have signed the present treaty of defensive alliance, and have hereunto put our seal.

Constantinople, 23d *December* 1798.

(Signed) ESSEID-IBRAHIM-ISMET, with the title of Kadileskier of Romelia—ACHMED-ATIF, Reïss - Effendi — VASSILI - TAMARA, Privy-Counsellor.

Copy of the Treaty between Champicnnet and Prince Pignatelli

Armistice concluded between General Championnet, Commander in Chief of the Army of Rome, on one Part, and M. Prince de Miliano, and the Duke of Gesso, Plenipotentiaries of the Captain-general Pignatelli, Viceroy of the Kingdom of Naples, on the other Part.

Article I.

THE city of Capua, in its present state, with the magazines of all sorts, shall be given up to-morrow morning at ten o'clock, to the French army. It is to be understood, that the artillery and ammunition, which may have been taken out for the entrenched camp, shall be returned. A

French

French officer and commissary at war shall enter the town this evening, to verify the state of the magazines, and to receive them.

II. The French army, having its right upon the Mediterranean, shall occupy the right bank of the mouth of the Neapolitan lakes, Acerra, and the road from Naples which passes through Acerra, Azienzo, and Benevente; and shall keep garrisons in all the towns and villages of this country.

III. The line of demarcation shall extend from Benevente to the mouths of the Ofanto (beyond the Gulf of Manfredonia, in the Adriatic sea), taking the left bank of that river, and the right bank of the Lombardo.

IV. The Neapolitan troops which may be upon the Roman territory shall immediately evacuate it.

V. The ports of the Two Sicilies shall be declared neutral; those of the kingdom of Naples immediately after the signing of the present act, and those of Sicily as soon as the King of Naples shall have sent from Palermo an ambassador to Paris, to treat for peace. Consequently, no ship of war shall sail from any of the ports of the two kingdoms, nor shall any of the ships belonging to the powers at war with the French republic be received therein; and all the ships belonging to those powers who may be there at that moment shall be immediately sent away.

VI. During the continuance of the armistice, no change shall be made in the administrative authorities of the countries occupied by the French.

VII. No individual shall be troubled upon account of his political principles.

VIII. The King of the Two Sicilies shall pay to the French republic ten millions of livres tournois; five millions to be paid on the 26th Nivôse, corresponding with the 15th of January 1799, and the other five millions on the 6th Pluviôse, which corresponds with the 25th of January of the same year. These payments shall be made at Capua, and the ducat shall be received as equal to four livres of France.

IX. The usual commercial relations between Naples and the territory occupied by the French army, shall continue as heretofore, with the reserve, that the provisioning of the French army shall not suffer at all thereby. It is also agreed upon, that the reciprocity of the commerce of the French army, with the territory occupied by the Neapolitans, shall take place, with exemption from all duties.

X. The present treaty of armistice shall be submitted to the approbation of the governments of the two powers. If either refuse to ratify it, the generals commanding shall give notice three days before the recommencement of hostilities.

(Signed)   CHAMPIONNET.
Done at the Camp before Capua,   The PRINCE de MILIANO.
*** *** **** * Jan. 10., 7th   The DUKE de GESSO.
Year of the French Republic.

Conditions of the Treaty of Union between the Country of the Grisons and the Helvetic Republic.

Article I.

THE people of Rhetia acknowledge and accept, without reserve, the Helvetic constitution.

II. They submit themselves to all the laws of the Helvetic republic, as well those now in being as those which shall be hereafter enacted.

III. All the debts of the ci-devant Grison state, contracted legally and according to the ancient constitution of the country, are acknowledged debts of the Helvetic republic.

IV. On the contrary, they declare as national goods all the goods belonging to the ci-devant state of the Grisons, and generally all the funds, which, according to the law of the 3d April 1799, on the difference between goods of the state and goods of the communes, are in the class of national goods.

V. Rhetia shall constitute a canton of the Helvetic republic, under the denomination of the canton of Rhetia.

VI. From the day that the present treaty of union shall have received the sanction of the Executive Directory and Legislative Councils of the Helvetic republic, the people of Rhetia shall enter into the enjoyment of all the rights and privileges which the Helvetic constitution secures to every Helvetic citizen; and they, on their part, bind themselves, from the same day, to the same imposts, and generally to the faithful observance of the same duties of citizen, without the least exception, in like manner as all Helvetic citizens.

So concluded under the reserve of the sanction of the Executive Directory and Legislative Councils of the Helvetic republic, one and indivisible.

At Coire, 21st April 1799.

In the name of the Executive Directory of the Helvetic republic. Commissioners of Government,

SCHWALLER,
HERZOG.
President of the Provisional Government, SPZEGHER.
Secretary-general, OTTO.

Treaty of Commerce between the French Republic and the Helvetic Republic.

THE French republic and the Helvetic republic, in execution of the article XV. of the treaty of alliance concluded at Paris the 2d Fructidor in the 6th year of the French republic (19th August 1798), and being desirous to secure in a manner the

the most invariable and reciprocally advantageous, the commercial relations of the two countries, have nominated, for the purpose of carrying a treaty of commerce into completion and effect, to wit, the Executive Directory of the French republic, on the one part, Citizen Charles Maurice Talleyrand, minister of foreign affairs, and the Executive Directory of the Helvetic republic, on the other part, Citizens Pierre Joseph Zeltner, and A... le Jenner, ministers plenipotentiary; who, after having exchanged their full powers, have agreed to the following articles:—

Art. I. Neither of the two republics shall ever be at liberty to prohibit the importation, consumption, or carriage of any merchandise of the growth or manufacture of the other republic its ally, on condition that such merchandises shall be accompanied with certificates of their origin.

II. Neither of the two republics shall ever prohibit the exportation of any produce of its territory or manufactures destined for the republic its ally, except corn or flour, and that only when the same prohibition shall have taken place by a general regulation extending to all nations: and as a prohibition at present exists in France, against the exportation of grain, the French republic, considering the indispensable want of this article under which the Helvetic republic labours, and desirous to give it a particular proof of its affection, consents that it shall be authorized to export annually, on its own account, from the French territory a million of myriagrammes of corn or flour, on condition that it shall be carried by the following places, viz. Verfoix, Jougnes, Verrieres-de-Joux, and Bourg Libre, on Swiss carriages, conducted by Swiss carriers; and in certain cases when this importation of corn or flour should not be sufficient for the manifest wants of Helvetia, the French republic further consents that in such case, by particular treaties to be yearly renewed, it should be at liberty to import to the amount of four million of myriagrammes, but in no event whatever to exceed that quantity.

III. The duties on the import and export of merchandises of the growth or manufacture of the two allied republics, in their passage from one to the other, and which are fixed by the weight according to existing tariffs, shall continue to be collected in the same way, taking, however, for a basis the value of the merchandise, so far that in no case the duty paid shall exceed six per cent. of the value: and for this purpose, invoices of each kind of merchandise shall be made out by the respective governments, who shall transmit a table of the various articles of their growth and manufacture, and regulate the form of the certificates which are to authenticate their origin. And in the mean time, and until said regulations shall be carried into complete

plete effect, it is agreed that the perception of duties shall take place on the basis of the declared value of the merchandises, saving to the comptrollers the privilege of detaining them, paying at their said avowed value, with ten per cent. over, and upon condition that the articles exported from Helvetia shall not enter France except through the offices designated in the preceding article, to which shall be added one of the offices of the department of Mont-Terrible.

IV. The duties paid in Helvetia on retailed wines shall be the same on the wines of France as on those of the growth of Helvetia.

V. Whereas the reciprocal liberty of transfer of goods and manufactures is stipulated by the first article, the duty on the transfer shall not exceed one half per cent. of the value of the articles so transferred. The taxes for the maintenance of routes, as well by land as by water, shall not exceed those payable by the citizens of the republic which levies them. Waggoners, carriers, and watermen, on entering the territory of the one republic or the other, shall conform themselves to the laws and regulations respectively established in each of them.

VI. The two republics agree that their respective monies shall be struck after the same model, and that then they shall have a legal circulation in the two countries, reciprocally.

VII. If a merchant or any other French citizen shall die in Switzerland, the Helvetic republic undertakes to treat his heirs, or other persons having a right to his property, as if they were natives, and so reciprocally in France, in case of the demise of a Swiss citizen.

VIII. French citizens domiciliated in Helvetia, and Helvetic citizens domiciliated in France, shall have their passports verified by the consul of their respective nation.

IX. French citizens and Helvetic citizens, who shall travel for an unlimited term in the states of either allied republic, shall be at liberty to leave them with passports of their nation, on having them verified by the respective legation or consuls, and conforming to the police laws in force in the countries in which they shall so travel.

X. It is agreed that the treaties or conventions which the French and Helvetic republics shall make with other states shall never injure in any respect the execution of the present, but, on the contrary, that each of them, on such occasions, shall use its efforts to secure the commercial advantages hereby stipulated to its allied republic.

XI. Nothing herein contained shall change or affect the commercial and political articles of the treaty of alliance.

The ratifications of the present treaty shall take place in the space of three decades, reckoning from the day of its being signed, and

and its full execution within four decades after the exchange of the ratifications.

Concluded and signed at Paris, the 11th Prairial, 7th year (30th May 1799).

   (Signed) C. M. TALLEYRAND.
          P. J. ZELTNER.
          A. JENNER.

Alleged Treaty between Tippoo Saib and the French Republic, in the latter End of 1797.

THIS is said to have consisted of thirty-two articles, of which the following are the principal:

Article II. The French engaged to furnish him with a force of ten thousand men, including cavalry, artillery, and infantry.

III. For this force he was to pay 20,000 rupees per day, or seventy-two lacks of rupees per annum.

IV. The men were to be landed in French ships at Mangalore, or other places in that neighbourhood.

V. The negotiation was conducted by emissaries, with instructions from Pondicherry, and to be completed by the government of the Mauritius.

VI. It was stipulated, that whatever of the former French possessions should be conquered, should be restored to them entirely; and that such of the territories ceded by Tippoo to Lord Cornwallis, should in like manner be restored to the Sultan entirely.

VII. Such foreign conquests as should be made by the joint forces, were to be equally divided between Tippoo and the French.

VIII. It was stipulated that the first object to be attempted was the siege of Madras, and nothing was to be attended to until this should have been achieved.

IX. After this the French engaged to carry their arms to Hyderabad, Poonah, and ultimately to Delhi.

X. All naval expenses to have been borne by the French exclusively, and they, in consequence, to enjoy exclusively the advantages of all victories or conquests which might be obtained at sea.

XI. If the French should be attacked, Tippoo was to march to their assistance. If Tippoo should be attacked, they, in like manner, to move to his assistance.

XII. It was stipulated, that the French troops should move out of Tippoo Sultaun's dominions whenever they should be required.

XIII. It was stipulated, that barracks should be built for the French soldiers at Malapoor, and that place entirely appropriated to them.

Substance

Substance of a Treaty of Peace, Commerce, Fishery, and Navigation, alleged to have been concluded between his Catholic Majesty and the Emperor of Morocco at Mequinez.

[The difference of religious opinions is no longer made an obstacle with the Mahometans; and the latter, who offered to Christians no other alternative than slavery or the sword, speak in this treaty of their wishes to live in friendship, good understanding, and harmony with all Christian powers. In the XIIIth article the Emperor of Morocco declares that he desires the odious name of slavery may be effaced from the memory of man.]

THIS treaty regulates four different objects.
    I. The conditions upon which peace shall continue to exist between the two nations.
    II. The regulations relative to the reciprocal commerce between them.
    III. The navigation.
    IV. The fishery.
    The Spaniards and the inhabitants of the Canaries are permitted to fish in the seas to the north of St. Croix in Barbary.
    The XIXth article is a step towards the abolition of privateering. The Morocco sailors and effects taken on board ships at war with Spain are to be restored, without ransom, by the Spaniards. The same is to be done by the subjects of Morocco. Morocco ships and effects captured by a power at war with the Emperor are not to be sold in the ports of Spain. This condition is also reciprocal.
    Christian slaves, of any nation whatever, who, having escaped from captivity, shall seek an asylum on board Spanish ships, or in the forts which his Catholic Majesty has on the coast of Africa, shall not be reclaimed by their masters.
    The articles XXVI. to XXXV. regulate the custom duties, &c. The XXXth article declares that the company of the Cinco Gremios of Madrid shall continue to enjoy the exclusive privilege of drawing corn from Morocco, by the port of Darbeyda.
    An article states, that in case of a rupture between the two powers, the prisoners shall not be treated or considered as slaves; but they shall be exchanged as those of European nations are.

Proclamations, Manifestoes, Correspondence, &c.

Speech of the President of the United States of America to both Houses of Congress, on Saturday, Dec. 8, 1798.

Gentlemen of the Senate, and Gentlemen of the
House of Representatives,

WHILE with reverence and resignation we contemplate the dispensations of Divine Providence, in the alarming and destructive pestilence with which several of our cities and towns have been visited, there is cause for gratitude and mutual congratulations, that the malady has disappeared, and that we are again permitted to assemble in safety at the seat of government for the discharge of our important duties. But when we reflect that this fatal disorder has, within a few years, made repeated ravages in some of our principal sea-port towns, and with increased malignancy; and when we consider the magnitude of the evils arising from the interruption of public and private business, whereby the national interests are deeply affected; I think it my duty to invite the Legislature of the Union to examine the expediency of establishing suitable regulations in aid of the health-laws of the respective states; for these being formed on the idea, that contagious sickness may be communicated through the channels of commerce, there seems to be a necessity that Congress, who alone can regulate trade, should frame a system which, while it may tend to preserve the general health, may be compatible with the interests of commerce and the safety of the revenue.

While we think on this calamity, and sympathize with the immediate sufferers, we have abundant reason to present to the Supreme Being our annual oblations of gratitude for a liberal participation in the ordinary blessings of his providence. To the usual subjects of gratitude, I cannot omit to add one of the first importance to our well-being and safety—I mean that spirit, which has arisen in our country, against the menaces and aggression of a foreign nation. A manly sense of national honour, dignity, and independence, has appeared, which, if encouraged and invigorated by every branch of the government, will enable us to view undismayed the enterprises of any foreign power, and become the sure foundation of national prosperity and glory.

The course of the transactions in relation to the United States and France, which have come to my knowledge during your recess, will be made the subject of a future communication. That communication will confirm the ultimate failure of the measures which have been taken by the government of the United States towards an amicable adjustment of differences with that power. You will at the same time perceive, that the French government appears solicitous to impress the opinion, that it is averse to a rupture with this country, and that it has, in a qualified manner, declared itself willing to receive a minister from the United States for the purpose of restoring a good understanding. It is unfortunate for professions of this kind, that they should be expressed in terms which may countenance the inadmissible pretention of a right to prescribe the qualifications which a minister from the United States should possess; and that, while France is asserting the existence of a disposition on her part to conciliate with sincerity the differences which have arisen, the sincerity of a like disposition on the part of the United States, of which too many demonstrative proofs have been given, should even be indirectly questioned. It is also worthy of observation, that the decree of the Directory, alleged to be intended to restrain the depredations of French cruisers on our commerce, has not given, and cannot give, any relief; it enjoins them to conform to all the laws of France relative to carrying and prizes, while these laws are themselves the sources of the depredations, of which we have so long, so justly, and so fruitlessly complained.

The law of France enacted in January last, which subjects to capture and condemnation neutral vessels and their cargoes, if any portion of the latter are of British fabric or produce, although the entire property belong to neutrals, instead of being rescinded, has lately received a confirmation, by the failure of a proposition for its repeal. While this law, which is an unequivocal act of war on the commerce of the nations it attacks, continues in force, those nations can see in the French government only a power regardless of their essential rights, of their independence and sovereignty; and if they possess the means, they can reconcile nothing with their interest and honour but a firm resistance.

Hitherto, therefore, nothing is discoverable in the conduct of France which ought to change or relax our measures of defence; on the contrary, to extend and invigorate them is our true policy. We have no reason to regret that these measures have been thus far adopted and pursued; and in proportion as we we enlarge our view of the portentous and incalculable situation of Europe, we shall discover new and cogent motives for the full developement of our energies and resources.

But in demonstrating by our conduct that we do not fear war, in the necessary protection of our rights and honour, we shall give no room to infer that we abandon the desire of peace. An efficient preparation for war can alone ensure peace. It is peace that we have uniformly and perseveringly cultivated, and harmony between us and France may be restored at her option. But to send another minister, without more determinate assurances that he would be received, would be an act of humiliation to which the United States ought not to submit; it must therefore be left with France, if she is indeed desirous of accommodation, to take the requisite steps. The United States will steadily observe the maxims by which they have hitherto been governed. They will respect the sacred rights of embassy; and, with a sincere disposition on the part of France to desist from hostility, to make reparation for the injuries heretofore committed on our commerce, and to do justice in future, there will be no obstacle to the restoration of a friendly intercourse. In making to you this declaration, we give a pledge to France and the world, that the executive authority of this country will attend to the humane and pacific policy which has invariably governed its proceedings, in conformity with the wishes of the different branches of the government and of the people of the United States. But considering the late manifestations of her policy towards foreign nations, I deem it a duty deliberately and solemnly to declare my opinion, that, whether we negotiate with her or not, vigorous preparations for war will be alike indispensable. These alone will give to us an equal treaty, and ensure its observance.

Among the measures of preparation which appear expedient, I take the liberty to recall your attention to the naval establishment. The beneficial effects of the small naval armament provided under the acts of the last session are known and acknowledged. Perhaps no country ever experienced more sudden and remarkable advantages from any measure of policy, than we have derived from the arming for our marine protection and defence. We ought, without loss of time, to lay the foundation for an increase of our navy, to a size sufficient to guard our coast and protect our trade. Such a naval force, as it is doubtless in the power of the United States to create and maintain, would also afford to them the best means of general defence, by facilitating the safe transportation of troops and stores to every part of our extensive coast.

To accomplish this important object, a prudent forefight requires that fyftematical meafures be adopted for procuring at all times the requifite timber and other fupplies. In what manner this fhall be done, I leave to your confideration.

I will now advert, Gentlemen, to fome matters of lefs moment, but proper to be communicated to the national legiflature.

After the Spanifh garrifons had evacuated the pofts they occupied at the Natchez and Walnut Hills, the commiffioner of the United States commenced his obfervations to afcertain the point near the Miffifippi, which terminated the northernmoft point of the thirty-firft degree of north latitude. From thence he proceeded to run the boundary line between the United States and Spain. He was afterwards joined by the Spanifh commiffioner, where the work of the former was confined; and they proceeded together to the demarkation of the line. Recent information renders it probable that the Southern Indians, either inftigated to oppofe the demarkation, or jealous of the confequences of fuffering white people to run a line over lands to which the Indian title had not been extinguifhed, have, ere this time, ftopped the progrefs of the commiffioners. And confidering the mifchiefs which may refult from continuing the demarkation, in oppofition to the will of the Indian tribes, the great expenfe attending it, and that the boundaries which the commiffioners have actually eftablifhed, probably extend at leaft as far as the Indian title has been extinguifhed, it will perhaps become expedient and neceffary to fufpend further proceedings, by recalling our commiffioner.

The commiffioners appointed in purfuance of the fifth article of the treaty of amity, commerce, and navigation, between the United States and his Britannic Majefty, to determine what river was truly intended under the name of the river St. Croix, mentioned in the treaty of peace, and forming a part of the boundary therein defcribed, have finally decided that queftion. On the twenty-fifth of October, they made their declaration, that a river called Schoodiac, which falls into Paffamaquoddy Bay, at its north-weftern quarter, was the true St. Croix intended in the treaty of peace, as far as its great fork, where one of its ftreams comes from the weftward, and the other from the northward; and that the latter ftream is the continuation of the St. Croix to its fource. This decifion, it is underftood, will preclude all contention among individual claimants, as it feems that the Schoodiac and its northern branch bound the grants of lands which have been made by the refpective adjoining governments. A fubordinate queftion, however, it has been fuggefted, ftill remains to be determined. Between the mouth of the

St.

St. Croix, as now settled, and what is usually called the Bay of Fundy, lie a number of valuable islands. The commissioners have not continued the boundary lines through any channel of these islands, and unless the Bay of Passamaquoddy be a part of the Bay of Fundy, this further adjustment of boundary will be necessary. But it is apprehended that this will not be a matter of any difficulty.

Such progress has been made in the examination and decision of cases of captures and condemnations of American vessels, which were the subject of the seventh article of the treaty of amity, commerce, and navigation, between the United States and Great Britain, that it is supposed the commissioners will be able to bring their business to a conclusion in August of the ensuing year.

The commissioners acting under the twenty-fifth article of the treaty between the United States and Spain, have adjusted most of the claims of our citizens, for losses sustained in consequence of their vessels and cargoes having been taken by the subjects of his Catholic Majesty, during the late war between France and Spain.

Various circumstances have concurred to delay the execution of the law for augmenting the military establishment; among these, the desire of obtaining the fullest information to direct the best selection of officers. As this object will now be speedily accomplished, it is expected that the raising and organizing of the troops will proceed without obstacle, and with effect.

Gentlemen of the House of Representatives,

I have directed an estimate of the appropriation which will be necessary for the service of the ensuing year to be laid before you, accompanied with a view of the public receipts and expenditures to a recent period. It will afford you satisfaction to infer the great extent and solidity of the public resources from the prosperous state of the finances, notwithstanding the unexampled embarrassments which have attended commerce. When you reflect on the conspicuous examples of patriotism and liberality which have been exhibited by our mercantile fellow-citizens, and how great a proportion of the public resources depends on their enterprise, you will naturally consider whether their convenience cannot be promoted and reconciled with the security of the revenue, by a revision of the system by which the collection is at present regulated.

During your recess, measures have been steadily pursued for effecting the valuations and returns directed by the act of the last session, preliminary to the assessment and collection of a direct tax. No other delays or obstacles have been experienced, except such as were expected to arise from the great extent of our country,

try, and the magnitude and novelty of the operation ; and enough has been accomplished to assure the fulfilment of the views of the Legislature.

Gentlemen of the Senate, and Gentlemen of the
House of Representatives,

I cannot close this address without once more adverting to our political situation, and inculcating the essential importance of uniting in the maintenance of our dearest interests ; and I trust that, by the temper and wisdom of your proceedings, and by a harmony of measures, we shall secure to our country that weight and respect to which it is so justly entitled.

JOHN ADAMS.

December 12, 1798.

THIS day the Senate of the United States, in a body, waited on the President, and presented him the following Answer to his Speech :

To the President of the United States.

Sir,

THE Senate of the United States join you in thanks to Almighty God for the removal of the late afflicting dispensations of his providence, and for the patriotic spirit and general prosperity of our country. Sympathy for the sufferings of our fellow-citizens from disease, and the important interests of the Union, demand of the national legislature a ready co-operation with the state governments, in the use of such means as seem best calculated to prevent the return of this fatal calamity.

Although we have sincerely wished, that an adjustment of our differences with the republic of France might be effected on safe and honourable terms, yet the information you have given us of the ultimate failure of the negotiation has not surprised us. In the general conduct of that republic we have seen a design of universal influence, incompatible with the self-government, and destructive of the independence, of other states. In its conduct towards these United States, we have seen a plan of hostility pursued with unremitted constancy, equally disregarding the obligations of treaties and the rights of individuals. We have seen two embassies formed for the purpose of mutual explanations, and clothed with the most extensive and liberal powers, dismissed without recognition, and even without a hearing.

The government of France has not only refused to repeal, but has recently enjoined the observance of its former edict, respecting merchandise of British fabric or produce, the property of neutrals, by which the interruption of our lawful commerce, and the spoliation of the property of our citizens, have again received a public sanction. These facts indicate no change of system or
dispo-

difposition; they speak a more intelligible language than professions of solicitude to avoid a rupture, however ardently made. But if, after the repeated proofs we have given of a sincere desire for peace, these professions should be accompanied by infinuations, implicating the integrity with which it has been pursued; if, neglecting and passing by the constitutional and authorized agents of the government, they are made through the medium of individuals, without public character or authority; and, above all, if they carry with them a claim to prescribe the political qualifications of the minister of the United States to be employed in the negotiation, they are not entitled to attention or confideration, but ought to be regarded as designed to separate the people from their government, and to bring about by intrigue that which open force could not effect.

We are of opinion with you, Sir, that there has nothing yet been discovered in the conduct of France, which can justify a relaxation of the means of defence adopted during the last session of Congress, the happy result of which is so strongly and generally marked. If the force by sea and land which the existing laws authorize should be judged inadequate to the public defence, we will perform the indispensable duty of bringing forward such other acts as will effectually call forth the resources and force of our country.

A steady adherence to this wife and manly policy, a proper direction of the noble spirit of patriotism which has arisen in our country, and which ought to be cherished and invigorated by every branch of the government, will secure our liberty and independence against all open and secret attacks.

We enter on the business of the present session with an anxious solicitude for the public good, and shall bestow that consideration on the several objects pointed out in your communication which they respectively merit.

Your long and important services, your talents and firmness, so often displayed in the most trying times and most critical situations, afford a sure pledge of a zealous co-operation in every measure necessary to secure us justice and respect.

Reply of the President.

Gentlemen,

I THANK you for this address, so conformable to the spirit of our constitution, and the established character of the Senate of the United States, for wisdom, honour, and virtue.

I have seen no real evidence of any change of system or disposition in the French republic towards the United States. Although the officious interference of individuals without public character or authority, is not entitled to any credit, yet it deserves to be considered, whether that temerity and impertinence of individuals, affecting to interfere in public affairs between France and the United States, whether by their secret correspondence or otherwise, and intended to impose upon the people, and separate them from their government, ought not to be inquired into and corrected.

I thank you, Gentlemen, for your assurances that you will bestow that consideration on the several objects pointed out in my communication which they respectively merit.

If I have participated in that understanding, sincerity, and constancy, which have been displayed by my fellow-citizens and countrymen, in the most trying times and critical situations, and fulfilled my duties to them, I am happy. The testimony of the Senate of the United States in my favour is an high and honourable reward, which receives, as it merits, my grateful acknowledgments. My zealous co-operation in measures necessary to secure us justice and consideration may be always depended on.

Philadelphia, Dec. 12, 1798.   JOHN ADAMS.

Answer of the House of Representatives to the Speech of the President.

Sir,

THE House of Representatives unite with you in deploring the effects of the desolating malady by which the seat of government, and other parts of our country, have been visited. In calling our attention to the fatality of its repeated ravages, and inviting us to consider the expediency of exercising our constitutional powers in aid of the health-laws of the respective States, your recommendation is sanctioned by the dictates of humanity and liberal policy. On this interesting subject we feel the necessity of adopting every wise expedient for preventing a calamity so distressing to individual sufferers, and so prejudicial to our national commerce.

That our finances are in a prosperous state, notwithstanding the commercial derangements resulting from this calamity, and from external embarrassments, is a satisfactory manifestation of the great extent and solidity of the public resources. Connected with this situation of our fiscal concerns, the assurance that the legal provisions for obtaining revenue by direct taxation will fulfil the views of the Legislature, is peculiarly acceptable.

Desirous as we are that all causes of hostility may be removed, by the amicable adjustment of national differences, we learn with satisfaction that, in pursuance of our treaties with Spain and Great Britain, advances have been made for definitively settling the controversies relative to the southern and north-eastern limits of the United States. With similar sentiments have we received your information, that the proceedings under commissions authorized

thorized by the same treaties, afford to a respectable portion of our citizens the prospect of a final decision on their claims for maritime injuries committed by subjects of those powers.

It would be the theme of mutual felicitation, were we assured of experiencing similar moderation and justice from the French republic, between which and the United States differences have unhappily arisen. But this is denied us by the ultimate failure of the measures which have been taken by this government towards an amicable adjustment of those differences, and by the various inadmissible pretensions on the part of that nation.

The continuing in force the decree of January last, to which you have more particularly pointed our attention, ought, of itself, to be considered as demonstrative of the real intentions of the French government—that decree proclaims a predatory warfare against the unquestionable rights of neutral commerce, which, with our means of defence, our interest and our honour command us to repel. It therefore now becomes the United States to be as determined in resisting as they have been patient in suffering, and condescending in negotiation.

While those who direct the affairs of France persist in the enforcement of decrees so hostile to our essential rights, their conduct forbids us to confide in any of their professions of amity.

As therefore the conduct of France hitherto exhibits nothing which ought to change or relax our measures of defence, the policy of extending and invigorating those measures demands our sedulous attention. The sudden and remarkable advantages which this country has experienced from a small naval armament sufficiently prove the utility of its establishment. As it respects the guarding of our coasts, the protection of our trade, and the facility of safely transporting the means of territorial defence to every part of our maritime frontier, an adequate naval force must be considered as an important object of national policy. Nor do we hesitate to adopt the opinion that, whether negotiations with France are resumed or not, vigorous preparations for war will be alike indispensable.

In this conjuncture of affairs, while with you we recognise our abundant cause of gratitude to the Supreme Disposer of events for the ordinary blessings of providence, we regard as of high national importance the manifestation in our country of a magnanimous spirit of resistance to foreign domination. This spirit merits to be cherished and invigorated, by every branch of government, as the inestimable pledge of national prosperity and glory.

Disdaining a reliance on foreign protection; wanting no foreign guarantee of our liberties; resolving to maintain our national independence against every attempt to despoil us of this inestimable treasure; we confide, under Providence, in the patriotism triotifm and energies of thefe United States, for defeating the hoftile enterprifes of any foreign power.

To adopt with prudent forefight fuch fyftematical meafures as may be expedient for calling forth thofe energies wherever the national exigencies may require, whether on the ocean or on our own territory; and to reconcile with the proper fecurity of revenue the convenience of mercantile enterprife, on which fo great a proportion of the public refources depends, are objects of moment, which fhall be duly regarded in the courfe of our deliberations.

Fully as we accord with you in opinion, that the United States ought not to fubmit to the humiliation of fending another minifter to France, without previous affurances fufficiently determinate that he will be duly accredited, we have heard, with cordial approbation, the declaration of your purpofe, fteadily to obferve thofe maxims of humane and pacific policy by which the United States have hitherto been governed. While it is left with France to take the requifite fteps for accommodation, it is worthy the chief magiftrate of a free people to make known to the world, that juftice on the part of France will annihilate every obftacle to the reftoration of a friendly intercourfe, and that the executive authority of this country will refpect the facred rights of embaffy. At the fame time, the wifdom and decifion which have characterized your paft adminiftration, affure us no illufory profeffions will feduce you into any abandonment of the rights which belong to the United States, as a free and independent nation.

Reply of the Prefident.

Gentlemen,

MY fincere acknowledgments are due to the Houfe of Reprefentatives of the United States for this excellent addrefs, fo confonant to the character of reprefentatives of a great and free people. The judgment and feelings of a nation, I believe, were never more truly expreffed by their reprefentatives, than thofe of our conftituents, by your decided declaration, that with our means of defence, our intereft and honour command us to repel a predatory warfare againft the unqueftionable rights of neutral commerce; that it becomes the United States to be as determined in refiftance as they have been patient in fuffering, and condefcending in negotiation; that while thofe who direct the affairs of France perfift in the enforcement of decrees fo hoftile to our effential rights, their conduct forbids us to confide in any of their profeffions of amity; that an adequate naval force muft be confidered as an important object of national policy and that,

that, whether negotiations with France are refumed or not, vigorous preparations for war will be alike indifpenfable.

The generous difdain you fo coolly and deliberately exprefs, of a reliance on foreign protection, wanting no foreign guarantee of our liberties, refolving to maintain our national independence againft every attempt to defpoil us of this ineftimable treafure, will meet the full approbation of every found underftanding, and exulting applaufes from the heart of every faithful American.

I thank you, Gentlemen, for your candid approbation of my fentiments on the fubject of the negotiation, and on the declaration of your opinion, that the policy of extending and invigorating our meafures of defence, and the adoption, with prudent forefight, of fuch fyftematical meafures as may be expedient for calling forth the energies of the country wherever the national exigencies may require, whether on the ocean, or on our territory, will demand your moft fedulous attention.

At the fame time I take the liberty to affure you, it fhall be my vigilant endeavour, that no illufory profeffions fhall feduce me into an abandonment of the rights which belong to the United States, as a free and independent nation.

United States, Dec. 14, 1798. JOHN ADAMS.

The following Papers accompanied the Letter from Mr. Gerry to the Secretary of State immediately on his Arrival from France, dated Nantafket Road, October 1, 1798.

No. I.

Sir, *Paris, 12th May* 1798.

BEING informed that Meff. Prince and Brownfield, who expected to fail in the fame fhip with General Marfhall, are yet at Bourdeaux, I embrace the only favourable opportunity which has occurred fince his departure, to enclofe you a copy of a note which I received from Mr. Talleyrand, minifter of foreign relations, dated the 14th Germinal (April 3d), of my anfwer the 4th of April, and of my letter of the 20th of the fame month, being the day after General Pinckney left Paris. I had intended to have fent Dr. Tazewell, who is now in my family as fecretary, with my difpatches to our government, that no time might be loft in obtaining from it fuch arrangements for fupplying my place, as might have enabled me, immediately on his return, to leave France; but the meafure is become unneceffary, by the profpect that I have of being able foon to embark for the United States with the acquiefcence of this government.

The decifion of the Executive Directory, with refpect to my colleagues, after we had obtained, what we had been informed, in our first conference with Mr. Bellamy, was impracticable, a joint interview with the minister of foreign relations; and after the latter had seemed disposed to suspend matters, until we could obtain from our government an answer to our letters, was not less perplexing than surprising; and their proposition to treat with me separately was inadmissible. It was a proposition to which I had given my negative above a month before, when made to me under an injunction of secrecy by the minister of foreign relations. I was then informed, that an immediate rupture would be the result of my departure from France; and the same communication being again made, with information, that if I was determined not to negotiate separately, this government would be satisfied with my residence here, until the government of the United States could take their measures, I consented to this from public considerations solely; for every private one was opposed to it. In my embarrassed situation, not losing sight of the great object of our mission, a reconciliation with this powerful republic, I have taken a position, by which I mean to ascertain, if possible, without compromising the government of the United States, or myself, the ultimate views of France with respect to them. It would have been impossible for me, under existing circumstances, to have consented to a separate negotiation, had the provision been made in our powers and instructions; for two of my colleagues, one from the southern, and the other from the middle States, having been sent back, I could have had no prospect of forming a treaty, which could have given general satisfaction to my country; and I could never have undertaken any negotiation without that prospect. It is therefore incumbent on me to declare, that should the result of my present endeavours present to our government more pleasing prospects, it is nevertheless my firm determination to proceed no further with this negotiation. The want of time and health preventing further communications at present, I have the honour to remain, Sir, with great esteem and respect,

Your most obedient and very humble servant,
(Signed). E. GERRY.

*To the Secretary of State of the
United States of America.*

No. II.

Dear Sir, *Paris, 13th May 1798.*

I HAVE the honour to inform you, that the brigantine Sophia arrived at Havre the 11th instant; and last evening, at the moment of enclosing my dispatches to you of yesterday, Mr. Humphreys delivered me your letter of instructions of the 23d of March,

March, which shall be duly observed. The arrival of this vessel is a fortunate circumstance for me, and I shall embark in her for the United States, in lieu of taking my passage, as I had proposed, in one of the American merchantmen now in the ports of France. The ultimate views of this government, which their minister has promised in writing in a few days, shall be obtained if possible. I remain, Sir, with much esteem and respect,

Your very humble servant,

(Signed) E. GERRY.

To the Secretary of State of the United States of America.

No. III.

(TRANSLATION.)

Exterior Relations Office.—Liberty and Equality.

Paris, 14th Germinal, 6th Year of the French Republic, one and indivisible (April 3, 1798).

The Minister of Exterior Relations, to Mr. Gerry, Envoy Extraordinary of the United States of America to the French Republic.

I SUPPOSE, Sir, that Mr. Pinckney and Marshall have thought it useful and proper, in consequence of the intimations which the end of my note of the 28th of Ventose (18th March 1798) presents, and the obstacle which their known opinions have induced to the desired reconciliation, to quit the territory of the republic. In this supposition I have the honour to point out to you the 5th or the 7th of this decade, to resume our reciprocal communications upon the interests of the French republic and the United States of America.

Receive, I pray you, the assurances of my perfect consideration.

(Signed) CH. MAU. TALLEYRAND.

No. IV.

Paris, 4th April 1798 (Germinal 15th, An 6).

I HAD the honour, Citizen Minister, of receiving your letter of the 14th Germinal (the 3d inst.); and Mr. Deutrement, who delivered it, informed me, that it was intended to be shown to General Pinckney and General Marshall.

Whilst my colleagues and myself, to whom the government of the United States have entrusted the affairs of the embassy, had a joint agency therein, I have carefully imparted to them all the propositions which you have requested, and the relative conferences, as to yourself our decisions thereon; regretting, at the

the same time, the unfortunate and embarrassing circumstances which imposed on me this disagreeable task. But as, by the tenour of your letter, it is now expected that they will quit the territory of the French republic, it will be impossible for me to be the medium of, or to take any measures which will be painful to my colleagues, or not to afford them all the assistance in my power; and it would be moreover inconsistent with the line of conduct which, you well know, Citizen Minister, I have uniformly observed, for removing the unfavourable impressions which existed on the part of this government against them. Indeed, in our last letter, there is a conditional application for passports, which, as it appears to me, supersedes the necessity of a hint to them on this subject; and General Marshall is waiting impatiently for an answer to that part of it which respects a letter of safe conduct for the vessel in which he and his suite may take passage for the United States, to determine whether he shall embark from France or from Great Britain; but the unfortunate situation of General Pinckney, with respect to the critical state of his daughter's health, renders it utterly impossible for him to depart under existing circumstances.

You have proposed, Citizen Minister, the 5th or 7th of this decade for me to resume *(reprendre)* our reciprocal communications upon the interests of the French republic and of the United States. The reciprocal communications which we have had, were such only as I have alluded to in the beginning of this letter; unless your proposition, accompanied with an injunction of secrecy for me to treat separately, is considered in that light. To resume this subject will be unavailing, because the measure, for the reasons which I then urged, is utterly impracticable. I can only then confer informally and unaccredited on any subject respecting our mission, and communicate to the government of the United States the result of such conferences, being in my individual capacity unauthorized to give them an official stamp. Nevertheless, every measure in my power, and in conformity with the duty I owe to my country, shall be zealously pursued to restore harmony and cordial friendship between the two republics. I had the honour of calling on you last evening for the purpose of making this communication verbally; but as you were absent, to prevent misconceptions, I have thought it best to reduce it to writing.

Accept, I pray you, Citizen Minister, the assurances of my perfect esteem and respect.

     (Signed)   E. GERRY.

To the Minister of Foreign Affairs
 of the French Republic.

No.

No. V.

Paris, April 20, 1798 (1 Floreal, An 6).

Citizen Minister,

MY colleagues having been under the necessity of departing from Paris, have left me in the most painful situation, as it respects themselves, the government and nation which I had the honour with them to represent, and my personal circumstances. The alternatives presented to my choice, were, the continuance of my residence here, or an immediate rupture on my departure: I have chosen the former, prompted by every consideration of the duty I owed my country.

The object of this government in my remaining here, as announced in your official note of the 14th Germinal (3d April), was, " to resume our reciprocal communication on the interests of the French republic and of the United States." My answer informed you, that " I could only confer informally and uncredited on any subject respecting our mission, and communicate to the government of the United States the result of such conferences; being, in my individual capacity, unauthorised to give them an official stamp." This then I consider as the line of conduct well understood to be observed on my part; and in the present state of affairs, Citizen Minister, I flatter myself, that propositions for terminating all differences, for the restoration of harmony and friendship, and for the reestablishment of commerce between the United States and France, will be promptly made on the part of the latter; that they will be such as, corresponding with the justice and magnanimity of this great nation, and with sound policy, will ensure success; that I shall have an opportunity of soon embarking for the United States, and presenting them to my government for their consideration; and that all further depredations on our commerce, by French cruisers, will in the interim be prohibited. If in forming this arrangement I can render any services, you may be always sure of my immediate and cheerful co-operation.

Measures like these will at once extinguish those coals of discord, which, kindled into a flame, must be destructive of the respective interests of the two republics; will not only restore, but increase, if possible, their former confidence; and terminate in a competition for excelling each other in mutual acts of generosity and kindness.

In any event, Citizen Minister, I flatter myself it will not be thought necessary for me to remain long in France, as the state of my family and affairs requires my immediate return to the United States; and as their consul-general will continue his residence here, which, pending negotiation, will answer every political

litical purpose. I pray you, Citizen Minister, to accept the assurances of my most perfect esteem and regard.
  (Signed)   E. GERRY.
*To the Minister of Foreign Affairs
of the French Republic.*

No. VI.

(TRANSLATION.)

Paris, 11th Prairial, 6th Year of the French Republic, one and indivisible (May 30, 1798).

The Minister of Exterior Relations, to Mr. Gerry, Envoy of the United States.

I COMMUNICATE to you, Sir, a London Gazette of the 26th of last Floreal (May 15, 1798). You will therein find a very strange publication. I cannot observe without surprise, that intriguers have profited of the insulated condition in which the envoys of the United States have kept themselves, to make proposals and hold conversations, the object of which was evidently to deceive you.

I pray you to make known to me immediately the names denoted by the initials W, X, Y, and Z; and that of the woman who is described as having had conversation with Mr. Pinckney upon the interests of America: if you are averse to sending them to me in writing, be pleased to communicate them confidentially to the bearer.

I must rely upon your eagerness to enable the government to fathom those practices, of which I felicitate you on not having been the dupe, and which you must wish to see cleared up.

Accept the assurance of my perfect consideration.
  (Signed)   CH. MAU. TALLEYRAND.

[For Nos. VII. and VIII. vide our last volume, pp. 432, 433.]

No. IX.

Citizen Minister,   *Paris, June 1st, 1798.*

BEING officially informed that sundry letters for General Marshall, Mr. Murray, our minister at the Hague, Mr. Bourne, our consul at Amsterdam, the house of Lange and Bourne, and myself, captured in the American ship Farmer, some time since, and sent to Rotterdam, were, by order of Mr. Delacroix, transmitted to Paris, in pursuance of the instructions he received from this government, and having made several unsuccessful efforts to
  recover

recover thefe difpatches, permit mè to requeft your affiftance for obtaining them without further delay.

Accept, Citizen Minifter, the affurance of my perfect efteem and refpect.

(Signed) E. GERRY.

To the Minifter of Foreign Affairs of the French Republic.

[For Numbers X. and XI. vide laft vol. pp. 433, 434.]

No. XII.

Paris, June 1798, *Prairial* 6 *An.*

THE names of the perfons defignated in the communications of the envoys extraordinary of the United States to their government, publifhed in the Commercial Advertifer of the 12th of April laft, at New-York, are as follow:

X, is Mr. ———*.
Y, is Mr. Bellamy.
Z, is Mr. Hautval.

(Signed) E. GERRY.

To the Minifter of Foreign Affairs of the French Republic.

No. XIII.

Citizen Minifter, *Paris,* 10*th June* 1798.

HAVING been informed by my fecretary on the 7th, that you propofed to write to me the beginning of decade, I have impatiently expected, but have not yet received your communications.

The arrival of the newfpapers, containing the difpatches of the envoys to the government of the United States, after embarraffing and detaining me a fortnight, has produced a publication, wherein it is declared, that this republic " will never ceafe to manifeft her difpofitions to live in peace with America."

If this declaration really is, as it appears to be, official, and expreffive of the fenfe of government, and is followed by a fyftem of policy fuperior to unimportant confiderations, permanent friendfhip may be foon eftablifhed between the two republics.

When it is confidered that nine months have elapfed fince

---

* Mr. Gerry has inferted the proper name of X, in this document, as given to Mr. Talleyrand: but the perfon defignated by X, not having (like Y) avowed himfelf, the promife made by the envoys to him and Y, "that their names fhould in no event be made public," is ftill obligatory on the executive in refpect to X; and therefore his name is here omitted.

T. PICKERING.

Vol. VIII. D the

the arrival in Paris of the minifters who were charged with this important negotiation, and fix weeks fince the departure of two of them; when this delay, and a feries of the moft unfortunate events have inevitably produced alarming apprehenfions on the part of the government and citizens of the United States, that France is hoftile towards them, and waits only for a favourable opportunity to evince it; when France herfelf, in the publication mentioned, has declared that her enemies flatter themfelves with the hope of exciting in the United States a war againft her; when in this belief fhe muft be convinced, that in fuch a critical ftate of affairs, events are too rapid to admit of delay; when fuch is the decifion and ability of this government, in fome of its moft important negotiations, as to require but a few days to complete them: I flatter myfelf that fuch an arrangement on the part of this government will fpeedily be made, as will manifeft its amicable difpofition towards the United States, quiet the apprehenfion of their government, open on a liberal fyftem the channels of their commerce with this country, and afford them a well-grounded affurance of a fpeedy and happy iffue to their efforts for peace.

The brigantine Sophia, Henry Geddes mafter, in which I mean immediately to embark, is national property; but neverthelefs fubject, as is reprefented, to detention at Havre. I muft requeft, therefore, an order for exempting her from this prohibition.

My paffport, and the letter of fafe conduct for the veffel, are not yet received.

Accept, I pray you, Citizen Minifter, the affurances of my perfect confideration.

(Signed)   E. GERRY.

To the Minifter of Foreign Affairs
  of the French Republic.

No. XIV.

The Minifter of Exterior Relations of the French Republic, to Mr. Gerry, Envoy Extraordinary of the United States of America.

Paris, 22d Prairial, 6th Year (10th June 1798).

YOU could hitherto have remarked, Sir, in my letters of the 11th, 13th, and 16th of this month, nothing but my eagernefs to fathom the dark intrigue therein referred to, and difcover its ramifications. All further explanation in this refpect would be beneath the dignity of the French government.

But I will not preferve the fame filence on the intention manifefted by the meffage of the Prefident of the United States to the legiflature, of the 14th Germinal (April 3d, 1798), by the nature of
                                                                               the

the document [...]ed as pertaining to the basis of a negotiation, by the rapid publicity given to this strange collection, by the concealments made of the official communications. That intention is too well perceived in France and in America to require a developement. It is sufficient to repel the rumour so injuriously spread of the hostile dispositions of France. I will therefore refer myself to the note I addressed to the envoys on the 20th of last Ventose (March 18, 1798).—I doubt not that they will have promptly forwarded it to the President of the United States, and I must believe, that as soon as it shall be made public, it will efface from the minds of the American people the ill-founded uneasinesses which they have been made to entertain. As to the French government, superior to all the personalities, to all the manœuvres of its enemies, it perseveres in the intention of conciliating with sincerity all the differences which have happened between the two countries: I confirm it to you anew. The French republic desires to be restored to the rights which its treaties with your government confer upon it, and through those means it desires to assure yours. You claim indemnities; it equally demands them; and this disposition being as sincere on the part of the government of the United States, as it is on its part, will speedily remove all the difficulties.

It remains for me to ask you, Sir, whether you are at length in a situation to proceed towards this important subject.

Receive, Sir, the assurance of my perfect consideration.

(Signed) CH. MAU. TALLEYRAND.

No. XV.

Mr. Gerry, to the Minister of Foreign Relations of the French Republic.

Paris, 13th June 1798.

I HAVE received, Citizen Minister, your letter of the 22d Prarial (10th June), wherein, after informing me that all further explanation respecting the dark intrigue in question, will be below the dignity of the French government, you say, that you will not keep the same silence upon the intention manifested in the message of the President of the United States to the legislature, the 3d of April, in the nature of the pieces produced, as forming part of a negotiation; in a rapid publicity given to this strange collection, and in the concealment of official communications, by which, in the subsequent part of you letter, you allude to your note to the envoy, of the 28th Ventose (18th March last).

If the wishes and interests of the two republics call loudly for an accommodation of their differences (and of this the government of France, as well as that of the United States, appears to be convinced), is not a restoration of friendship between them, one of the most direct means for accomplishing that most desirable object?

D 2 —And

—And is it not altogether neglected? The unfounded prejudices against the President of the United States, in regard to his message, will be manifest, by comparing it with his official duty, designated by the constitution, and also by referring to the dates of your note, and of his message; whereby it will appear that the latter was but sixteen days later than the former, and that it was impossible that the President could have received your note, or concealed it from the public. The government of the United States, pure in its principles, just in its objects, and wise in its councils, is also superior to all personalities—and I wish they may for ever cease; for sure I am, that from such a source, no good, but infinite injuries, may result to the two republics. You conceive that your note, which was duly transmitted by the envoys to the government, when published, will efface from the minds of the American people their unfounded inquietude. Of this I can form no judgment; but before you addressed that note to the envoys, the proposition therein contained had been made to me to treat separately, and I had stated that the measure was in itself impolitic, and, as it respected myself, impossible.

I have, nevertheless, contrary to my wishes and interests, complied with your subsequent proposition for remaining here to prevent a rupture. I have been happy since, by your repeated assurances, that this government was sincerely disposed to reconcile all differences between the two countries, and probably would soon make an arrangement adequate to the object.—Indeed, I had great reason to hope, that I should have been furnished with a copy of it before my leaving Paris, and I earnestly wished it, lest the disappointment which might result from my return to the United States without it, should produce unhappy effects. But the vessel in which I am to embark being ready for sea, waits only my arrival at Havre, with the requisite documents for the voyage.

The sincerity of the disposition of the government of the United States to meet this government, on the ground of the existing treaties between the two countries, and to do justice to France, as well as to receive it from her, is too evident to admit for a moment of the least doubt; but I again repeat that I have no powers to enter on the negotiation. Nevertheless, the proposed arrangement might be made by this government, and a minister be sent to America to complete it; as it is of little consequence to either, in which nation the negotiation is concluded; but of great importance to both, that it should terminate in an immediate accommodation, and in the restoration of their friendship. I presume that in this, our wishes are alike sincere and ardent, and that the magnanimous policy of this government, to persevere in the intention, to reconcile, with sincerity, all the differences between the two countries, will have a speedy and happy effect.

Accept, Citizen Minister, the assurances of my perfect respect.
(Signed)   E. GERRY.

No. XVI.

Paris, 30th Prairial, 6th Year (18th June 1798).

The Minister of Exterior Relations, to Mr. Gerry, Envoy of the United States.

I HAVE received, Sir, your anfwer of the 27th of this month to my letter of the 22d. You take the trouble to obferve to me, that my note of the 28th Ventofe (18th March 1798) could not have made a part of the documents communicated by the Prefident of the United States, on the 14th Germinal (April 3, 1798). Do me the juftice to believe, that I have not committed this miftake.

You perfift in thinking that your powers and your inftructions do not permit you to proceed to the conciliating the differences between our two republics. You even announce to me pofitively, your departure for the United States, in the veffel which your government has difpatched to Havre. I fhould have prefumed, that, after having received and tranfmitted to Philadelphia my note of the 28th Ventofe, one of the envoys, whofe impartial difpofitions appeared to promife a reconciliation, would wait at Paris for further inftructions and powers, if he had need of them. It even appears to me, that thefe documents cannot now be long in reaching you, provided your government is as averfe to a rupture as you affure me. The part you take tends to give room to conjecture, that the veffel arrived at Havre, has only brought your orders, fimilar to the acts of which I complained on the 22d of this month.

Neverthelefs, Sir, fuch is the fincerity of the affurances which I have given you in the name of the Executive Directory on the 28th Ventofe, and which I have fince repeated to you, notwithftanding the moft irritating provocations, that I do not hefitate to explain myfelf to you, as if you were in a fituation to receive my overtures.

All negotiation between France and the United States muft effentially reft upon three principal points.

1. Frank and amicable declarations concerning certain circumftances, which malevolence has, and may yet mifreprefent.

It is utterly falfe, notwithftanding the public and private infinuations which have been made, in private writings, and in folemn acts, that the French government has ever fought to detach the people of the United States from the conftitution they have given to themfelves. It has complained of the American government, but to the government itfelf. Juftice demanded it fhould render homage to the fympathy of a free people for the caufe of liberty; and it did not go farther.

The

The secretary of state, Mr. Pickering, has inserted in his public letter to Mr. Pinckney (of the 16th of January 1797), assertions against the good faith of France in the negotiations of 1782, which have no other foundations than the interested communications of the English negotiator. It is a long time that this insidious weapon, forged by the enemies of France, has been used in the dark.

It is of importance to the two countries, to understand each other equally concerning the true value of several documents published as emanating from the French government, and of the private acts of certain agents, whom it has disavowed. In effect, it is only by destroying all the germs of distrust, that a good understanding can reappear, and continue hereafter without being obscured.

2. Fixing the meaning of several articles of the treaties between the two countries, and the absolute enjoyment of the rights which flow from them.

Long before the war, the 9th and 12th articles of the convention of the 14th of November 1788, the first relative to deserters, and the second relative to the jurisdiction of the consuls, were a continual source of altercations. They have become completely null by interpretations foreign to their manifest intent. It is necessary to perfect them.

By the 6th article of the treaty of alliance, France has renounced the Bermudas, New Brunswick, Nova Scotia, Cape Breton, Canada; in other words, it has renounced the procuring for itself one of the ports which would have been so necessary for it to possess for the protection of its sugar-islands. It devoted, in preference, the effort of its arms to the defence of the United States. It was understood that it should find proportionate advantages in their ports. One of these advantages is found implicitly in the 17th article of the treaty of commerce of the same day. The French ships, public and private, may freely enter into the American ports with the prizes which they may take. The ships, public and private, of the enemies of France, who may have taken prizes from it, shall not, on the contrary, have any asylum in those ports. Such is the literal sense, such is the intended sense. Does good faith permit a distinction between the vessels of the enemies of France who leave their prizes without the port, and those who come in with them? Can it be decided that the latter only should be excluded, without evidently violating the clause of the treaty which is the most important to France? Can it be invalidated by subsequent engagements? Doubtless not.

In virtue of the same 17th article, no authority whatever of the United States is permitted to interfere with the prizes taken by the French ships public and private. The captains are bound only to show their commissions, because it is necessary to be able

to

to distinguish the pirate from authorized vessels. It is also lawful to demand the release of a prize taken within the extent of the jurisdiction, that is to say, within the reach of cannon shot. But what abuse, what vexations, what odious chicanery, have flowed from the deviation from the meaning of the article? The government of the United States has rejected the precautions suggested to remedy the evil. Experience has shown that without those precautions the article is illusory.

The United States permitted the sale of French prizes until Prairial, 4th year (May, or June, 1796). At this period the supreme court decreed the revocation of this advantage, in virtue of the 24th article of the treaty with Great Britain. The 27th article nevertheless adds, that that treaty shall in no respect alter these which the United States may have previously contracted. But the liberty enjoyed by the French vessels of war of selling their prizes, is derived from the 17th and 22d articles of the treaty of commerce of the 6th February 1788. The 17th article would be of little value, if it were confined to the right of asylum. The 22d article would be mere surplusage, if it did not declare a right for the French, and an interdiction for their enemies. Great Britain obtained a similar right only on condition that it should be without force in all cases wherein France should be interested. When the United States concluded their treaty with Holland in October 1782, the memory of the treaty of 1778 was not yet weakened; and the exclusive privilege of the 22d article of the latter is formally acknowledged in the 22d article of the former.

The same 22d article of the treaty of 1778, must be appealed to against the refusal given to French vessels of war to make any change of their armament in the United States. If the desire to prevent the disorders, of which the American government complained, induced the committee of public safety, in the beginning of the 2d year, to cause all original armament in the name of the republic, in the United States, to be stopped, it did not intend that the abandonment of a doubtful pretension should carry with it that of an explicit right.

In the 23d and 24th articles, France and the United States have agreed, that the neutrality of the flag should determine that of the cargo, and have contracted the too-extended catalogue of contraband merchandise. It would have been pleasing to the republic to see in general prevalence, a system conformable with found justice, and which it flatters itself one day to extend. But how could the obligation remain reciprocal between it and the United States, when there no longer remained a parity of situation?

The English government has abused the liberality of France to her injury, since the commencement of 1793, and has not even
spared

spared American cargoes bound to French ports. Principles, contrary to thofe which influence the republic, have been confecrated fince, in the 17th and 18th articles of the treaty of London. It is doubtlefs a forced conceffion on the part of the United States, who, until then, made it their glory, in all their treaties, to aim at the liberty of the feas; but finally, it is a conceffion made by them in favour of England. France ought to enjoy it, in virtue of the fecond article of the treaty of Paris; its regrets cannot render it infenfible to its rights.

It ought, in virtue of this fecond article, which renders immediately common to it every favour accorded by the United States to any nation whatever, to claim fome other parts of the treaty of London.

3. The impartial examination of the damages which have refulted from the deviation from the treaties of 1778.

The treaties which bind the two nations have been infenfibly rendered infignificant by fophiftical interpretations. The cleareft claufes have been finally denied. The American government has never paid regard to the fucceffive complaints of the minifters plenipotentiary of the republic. It has never admitted them to enter into conference on this fubject. It has always taken upon itfelf to decide; although in every reciprocal contract, neither party poffeffes the exclufive right of interpretation. After having exhaufted itfelf in reprefentations, the French government was obliged to caufe its complaints to be unfolded for the laft time, on 25th Brumaire, 5th year (Nov. 15, 1796). Stripped of the advantages which the moft facred, the moft liberal treaty affured to it, it has been forced, in order to bring the United States back to their obligations to France, to imitate the conduct which England purfued previoufly to the treaty of London.

The court moderated its meafures, after its object was accomplifhed: the prefent complaints of the United States might have been prevented, if thofe of the French government had been attended to. The complaints which the United States now make are, in fine, only the confequence of a ftate of things which had coft the French republic and its citizens the moft confiderable damages. The French government neverthelefs has not ceafed to offer the exact juftice which it demands. It has never refufed, and never will refufe, to enter into difcuffion upon every proper fubject.

I have given, Sir, to thefe three points a large developement. We are very near an agreement, when we really defire it on both fides, and when we candidly admit the ftate of the queftion. You fee the negotiators require very general inftructions, in order to obviate the inconveniencies which are prolonged even until now. I believe, to fix the meaning of our treaties, it will be proper to draw up a declaration concerning it, to be hereafter obligatory

upon

upon the two parties, and confidered as making a part of the original acts; a declaration which, that it may have the force of law, should be eftablifhed by the ratifications which the conftitutional forms refpectively require.

The United States are placed in that happy unconnected ftate, which makes them, doubtlefs, fet a peculiar value upon the claufes of their treaties relative to their commerce and navigation. It is the effect of the long neutrality which they have the hope of maintaining. But France, although firmly determined, fince it has become a republic, to live in peace with all nations, cannot flatter itfelf with efcaping the fcourge which periodically torments Europe; and prudence requires that it preferve the rights which treaties fecure to it, in neutral ports, in time of war. With this double view, the American negotiators digefted the treaty of commerce of 1778. Although it be reciprocal upon the whole, fome provifions are more efpecially applicable to the fixed pofition of the United States; and others have allufion only to the eventual pofition of France. The latter has made great facrifices for the independence of the former. France has ftipulated few advantages; advantages which do not in any refpect injure the United States, and the lawfulnefs of which no foreign nation can conteft. The French republic will never renounce them.

It is now in the power of the United States to realize the difpofitions which you manifeft in their name. The prudence of your connexions in France has preferved you from the prejudices which it is difficult not to contract, when one is lefs on his guard againft foreign and even domeftic intrigues. I perfuade myfelf that you will tranfmit to your government only accurate documents. It will belong to it to purfue the beft meafures to effectuate a prompt reconciliation; and I ardently defire that they may correfpond with the wifh of the Executive Directory.

I continue however to think, that, inftead of returning to the United States, it would be preferable that you fhould afk for the inftruments neceffary to the negotiation. Nothing could more accelerate the drawing together of thofe ties, which the French republic and the true Americans have regretted to fee relaxed. Your prefence at Paris, if the powers, which muft be fuppofed to be on the road, fhould foon arrive, may momently accomplifh the object, which we both ambitioufly purfue.

Your departure, on the contrary, will give a new activity to the plots laid for precipitating the two countries into meafures which are as repugnant to their inclination as to their interefts.

The French government being, befides, penetrated with the fame fentiments which you teftify, will hereafter wait for what may be addreffed to it, and with pleafure will behold you as the organ.

Accept, Sir, the affurances of my perfect confideration.

   (Signed) Ch. Mau. Talleyrand.

No. XVII.

Paris, 22d June 1798.

I RECEIVED, Citizen Minister, on the evening of the 20th instant, your letter of the 30th Prairial (18th of June), in answer to mine of the 13th. You say you have not made the mistake respecting your letter of the 28th Ventose. I am not disposed to impute to you a mistake if you have not made it; although I think that your letter will warrant the construction I gave it: be this as it may, justice requires that the President of the United States should be free from the imputation of having concealed official communications, when he had published all, which it was possible for him to have received.

You should have presumed, as you state, that after having received and transmitted to Philadelphia your note of the 28th Ventose (the 18th of March), I would wait at Paris for instructions, and further powers, if necessary. But I had a right to expect, from what had passed between us before the arrival of the brigantine Sophia, and indeed after it, that I should have received, for the consideration of the government of the United States, propositions on the part of this government, for reconciling the differences, and restoring friendship between the two republics; that I should, ere this, have been on my passage to the United States; and that a French minister would have been sent to Philadelphia to complete the negotiation.

I accordingly informed you, before the arrival of the brigantine, that I should embark for America in June; and after her arrival, that I should take my passage in her, as soon as she could be fitted for sea.

You have stated and developed three points on which you conceive the negotiation between France and the United States ought essentially to rest. Your letter on this subject I will carefully communicate to my government: and if, after the voluminous official discussions, on the part of each of the republics, of the subjects in dispute between them, you conceive that a reconciliation will best be promoted by this mode only, I sincerely wish it success.

You say that France, in her treaty with the United States, has stipulated few advantages, which in no wise injure them, and the legality of which cannot be contested by any foreign nation. You then add, that the French government will never renounce them.

The government of the United States never desired of France a renunciation of any right to which she is entitled by their existing treaties: in construing some parts of these, the two governments have different opinions; but this is not unusual between nations;

nations; and when they are amicably difpofed, and governed by the principles you have juftly laid down, that neither party has the right of exclufive interpretation, they are generally fuccefsful, if direct meafures fail, in adjufting their difputes by arbitration: this mode has been fuccefsfully adopted by the United States with other nations.

My connexions in France, Citizen Minifter, have neither preferved me from, or fubjected me to prejudices. I am governed by my own principles: thofe, you may be affured, will always prompt me, in the difcharge of my duty, to prefent to my government exact documents and ftatements of facts.

It is impoffible for me to apply to the government for the neceffary inftruments to conduct the negotiation. On the other hand, fhould fuch a propofition be made to me, I fhould certainly, under exifting circumftances, decline it. Neverthelefs, I again affure you, that it will give me the greateft pleafure, if, by any other means, I can contribute to a juft and honourable accommodation of the differences between the two republics.

My return to the United States, which is indifpenfable, cannot, as I conceive, be attended with the effect you mention; more efpecially as the connexion between the two countries will be ftill kept up by their refpective confuls.

Accept, Citizen Minifter, the affurances of my perfect refpect.

     (Signed)   E. GERRY.

To the Minifter of Foreign Affairs
 of the French Republic.

No. XVIII.

Mr. Gerry, to the Minifter of Foreign Relations of the French Republic.

Citizen Minifter,   Paris, 25th June 1798.

I AM again under the neceffity of applying for neceffary documents to enable me to return to the United States; and as you cannot be infenfible of the manifeft difadvantages on my part refulting from the delay of them, I prefume that they are now in readinefs.

Accept my affurances of efteem and refpect.
     (Signed)   E. GERRY.

No. XIX.

Exterior Relations.
Paris, 9th Meffidor, 6th Year (27th June 1798).
The Minister of Exterior Relations, to Mr. Gerry, Envoy of the United States.

IN anfwering, Sir, your letter of the 4th of this month (22d June 1798), I regret that I am obliged to recur to the firft paragraph. I complained that the publications made at Philadelphia on the 19th Germinal (8th April 1798) did not contain all that your government then knew. You fuppofed that I alluded to my note of the 28th Ventofe (18th March), which could not however have reached the Prefident. I begged you not to attribute that miftake to me. You appear to adhere to your interpretation. From refpect to your fincerity, of which I cannot doubt, I will furmount my repugnance to minute digreffions, and will point out to you that one of the concealments which is the moft ftriking.

I have been furnifhed from the United States with the cleareft proofs, fupported even by articles extracted from the American papers, of the knowledge which fubfifted there before Germinal (before the 21ft of March), of the objection of the Executive Directory to any negotiation with two of the envoys, and of its *exprefs defire of treating with you.* In effect, I early teftified to you thefe difpofitions; and the declaration on this fubject inferted in my note of the 28th Ventofe (18th of March) was only the official expreffion of a thing already comprehended as well at Philadelphia as at Paris.

For the reft, Sir, let us hereafter pafs over thefe ufelefs epifodes, and let not our communications further bear the tint of recriminations. Thofe who are truly impartial will, perhaps, difcover a degree of generofity in this propofition coming from my fide.

Let us ferioufly refume our explanations. It is for facts to prove the reality of the intentions proteffed on both fides. My laft letter attefted to you very forcibly thofe of the Executive Directory. You do not allow thofe of the Prefident of the United States to be doubted. How then happens it, that, after having received propofitions, wherein every thing is combined for a frank and prompt conciliation, you in fome fort fhut the door againft all future advance?

You feem to infinuate that thefe propofitions have long been delayed. They could not have been made until after the departure of your colleagues: the firft open negotiations upon the differences

ferences which subsist between the two countries take their date only since that recent period: nothing was entered upon as long as the three envoys were present: one alone manifested a temper of reconciliation. Afterwards, some time was necessary to unite the views you suggested with the determination the Executive Directory has made, to place the respective interests in front. I did not, above all, partake in your opinion concerning the utility of your carrying the overtures of the French government personally to Philadelphia; and I never thought it advantageous to send thither a minister plenipotentiary from the republic, before the happy issue of the negotiations commenced. I was, nevertheless, about to transmit the result of my reflections in the beginning of Prairial (between the 20th and the last of May), when the incident happened which for a moment suspended the principal object. I do not see what delay I could have prevented. I am mortified that circumstances have not rendered our progress more rapid; and it is in order to accelerate it, as well as to obviate every new casualty, that I have pressed you, in my last letter, to remain at Paris.

Did you not come here, Sir, to establish friendship between the two republics, and determined to spare nothing to attain this end, as desirable to the United States as to France? Do not the full powers given to the envoys authorize them to negotiate separately? Is it after what has passed at Philadelphia that you can withdraw yourself? Ought you to do so when the French government, superior to all resentments, and never listening to any thing but justice, manifests itself anxious to conclude a solid and mutually satisfactory agreement? I have invited you to request promptly new powers, if you thought you stood in need of them, and they were not on their passage. You answer, that this step *is for you impossible*, and *that you would, besides, under existing circumstances, decline taking upon yourself the conducting of the negotiation*, if it was confided to you. I cannot reconcile this language with the avowed object of your voyage to France, with your full powers, with your attachment to your country, with the assurances you do not cease to give of the sincerity of your government.

I commend these observations to you, Sir. Reflect on the possible consequences of your departure, and judge for yourself, whether he who truly wishes for peace ought to consent to it.

Let us continue more and more to advance the work we have entered upon. I may almost venture to say that it is your duty. The propositions which I have made to you embrace three points.

The first will take but little time, and may be postponed.

The third will doubtless experience no difficulty on either side, after the second shall be amicably settled.

It

It is to the second, therefore, that we should first attend; and it is so much the more important, as it embraces the source of all our differences. A calm and candid discussion will successively clear up every article of them. I do not see that the voluminous discussions which have been entered into at Philadelphia have shed any light upon it. They have rather contributed to set up the passions in the seat of reason. Ours shall always be followed by a conclusion either in the cessation or admission of the right reclaimed. It is necessary in order to effect the act declaratory of the meaning of our treaties. As to the eventual arbitrament of a third power, I do not know whether the United States have sometimes had recourse to it. The French republic has never experienced the want of it; and I am persuaded that on this particular occasion, it will readily come to an understanding with the United States, if they are determined to be just towards it, as it desires to be towards them.

Let us begin with the ninth article of the consular convention of the 14th November 1788. I annex a note upon the difficulties its execution meets with in the ports of the United States. It shall be followed by similar notes, upon each of which we will endeavour to come to an agreement.

Accept, Sir, the assurances of my perfect consideration.

   (Signed)   Ch. Mau. Talleyrand.

Note upon the ninth Article of the Convention between France and the United States, of the 14th November 1788.

THE beginning of this article declares, " That the consuls and vice-consuls may cause to be arrested captains, officers, mariners, sailors, and all other persons, being part of the crews of the vessels of the respective nations, who shall have deserted from the said vessels, in order to send them back and transport them out of the country. For which purpose the said consuls and vice-consuls shall address themselves to the courts, judges, and officers competent." Before 1792, it frequently happened that the judges acting under the authority of the individual states, have pretended that they were incompetent. On the 14th April 1792, an act of Congress declared, that the district judges, acting under the authority of the United States, should be competent. All the judges of the individual states have since thought themselves justified in declining to render their aid; but as there are many more ports in the United States than district judges, and as they do not even always reside at a port, the French consuls and vice-consuls have often been unable to hinder desertion, to the great detriment of the vessels of their nation. The consuls of the

the United States do not experience those difficulties in the ports of the republic. Reciprocity, as well as the meaning of the article, require that it should be declared, " that all the officers of justice having power to order the arrest of mariners, shall be considered competent, and as such bound to comply with the request of the consuls, in the manner and in the cases stipulated.

The article proceeds, " and shall demand the said deserters in writing, proving, by an exhibition of the registers of the vessel's or ship's roll, that those men were part of the said crews."

The mariners have often waited till the departure of their vessel to desert, and have afterwards not only braved the authority of the consul, but served to debauch other crews. It has often been sufficient for them to go from one port to the nearest neighbouring port, to be secure from all pursuit. The consul being no longer able to produce the roll with ease, or not having it in his power to detach it from the vessel where it should remain, is no longer admitted to make a claim. He in vain produces a copy of the roll made in chancery, and duly authenticated—no faith is ascribed to it, notwithstanding the tenour of the first paragraph of the 5th article of the convention; it is maintained that the original roll is necessary; and thus the spirit of an important stipulation is destroyed, by the ambiguity attributed to the letter. It would be requisite to declare, " that by the register or ship's roll, not only the original is understood, but every authentic copy or extract, certified to be conformable to the original, by a judge of the country, before the departure of the vessel, and that this extract or copy shall have, in all the ports of the respective powers, the same force with the original, for three months."

Paris, 9th Messidor, 6th Year.
 The Minister of Exterior Relations,
  (Signed) CH. MAU. TALLEYRAND.

No. XX.

Mr. Gerry, to the Minister of Foreign Affairs of the French Republic.
         Paris, 1st July 1798.

I HAVE received, Citizen Minister, on the 11th, your letter of the 9th Messidor (27th of June); but without an answer to mine of the 25th of June, or the documents therein demanded for my voyage to America. You say, " they have furnished you from the United States, with the most clear proofs, supported even by articles extracted from the American papers, of the
               knowledge

knowledge which they had there, before Germinal (20th of March), of the objections of the Executive Directory to any negotiation with two of the envoys, and of its formal defire to treat with me." Admitting this, it does not prove to my mind, that the President of the United States had received official communications, and concealed them; but it is a convincing proof, that the information of thefe facts muft have been fent from hence to the United States, when fecrecy refpecting them, impofed on me previoufly to their communication, was ftrenuoufly infifted on.

You have made what you confider a generous propofition, that our communications fhould not be tinged with any more recriminations: is the fubfequent part of your letter altogether free from them? My filence on the abufe offered to the government of the United States, its envoys in general, and myfelf in particular, in an anonymous, but apparently official publication of the 7th of June, muft afford you unequivocal evidence that I had already adopted the meafure you have propofed.

It is inconceivable to me, that, being without powers to negotiate, my return to the United States, after fuch long notice, can be fuppofed in any degree to clofe the door to fubfequent fteps for a reconciliation. The door has always been, and ftill is open, on the part of the government of the United States. It is impoffible for any government to exceed it, in the moderation and juftice of its meafures towards France, or in its perfeverance and patience to execute them; but it having failed in two attempts, will not France make one effort to obtain a reconciliation between the two republics? Confider the difagreeable predicament in which the government of the United States has been involuntarily placed, and it is conceived you cannot fail to fee the propriety and policy of this meafure.

I have, in my laft letter, ftated to you truly what I conceived was well underftood between us, refpecting my return to the United States with the overtures of France, and her fending a minifter there to complete the negotiation. How we could mifunderftand each other on thefe points, is to me incomprehenfible. Be this as it may, it is not very material who is to be the bearer of the propofitions, if they are fuch as to be accepted by the United States.

You inquire whether I am not come to eftablifh friendfhip between the two republics, and determined to fpare no pains to attain this defirable object? Judge yourfelf, Citizen Minifter, whether I have not faithfully difcharged my duty in this refpect.

You afk, whether I am not authorized to treat feparately? Had my colleagues relinquifhed their office, been recalled, or by phyfical means been difqualified to act, my powers would have

been

been adequate to a separate negotiation, and I would have entered on it without delay. As matters are circumstanced, I have no such powers. You differ from me in opinion on this subject, but I must abide by my own judgment.

You declare that France, superior to all resentment, and only listening to justice, manifests a zeal to conclude a treaty solid and mutually satisfactory. Be assured, Citizen Minister, that the United States will with ardour meet such a disposition on the part of France; and that it cannot fail of success, if accompanied with a suspension of the long and ruinous depredations on our commerce, and with proper arrangements for a negotiation.

In my last letter you will perceive, that, having particularly referred to the mode adopted by the United States with other nations, I could only allude to that of deciding by commissioners, disputes which could not be adjusted by direct means. You have misconceived my intention, if you supposed it extended to the eventual arbitration of a third power.

My frequent applications for a passport, letter of safe conduct for the vessel, and her exemption from the embargo at Havre, have been altogether unnoticed. I hope you will not, by the continuance of this unusual mode of conduct, render an explanation of it immediately necessary.

Accept, Citizen Minister, the assurances of my perfect respect.

To the Minister of Foreign Affairs
of the French Republic.   (Signed)   E. GERRY.

No. XXI.

Ministry of Exterior Relations.

Paris, 18th Messidor, 6th Year of the French Republic
(July 6, 1798).

The Minister of Exterior Relations, to Mr. Gerry, Envoy of the United States.

I HAVE received, Sir, your answer of the 13th of this month, to my letter of the 9th. I will not conceal from you, that this kind of correspondence gives me the more pain as it injures the progress of our business.

It is clear that *before Germinal* (before 21st March) the intentions of the Executive Directory could not be known at Philadelphia, but by communication from Paris; but I attest, that they did not proceed either from the French government, or its agents, or from any one whatever, to my knowledge.

In the mean time, let us admit the gratuitous suppoſition that you make upon this ſubject. Is it therefore leſs true, that my overtures to treat with you were known in the United States, when it was there declared, that France refuſed all negotiation ?

You tell me, that the United States having been twice baffled in their attempts, it belongs to France to make an effort in order to effect a reconciliation between the two republics. What name therefore do you give to the indefatigable zeal which I maniſeſt to ſmooth all the difficulties, and bring about an honourable accommodation ? It is a genuine effort, Sir, the merit of which might be better appreciated. What, on the other hand, are the two attempts of the United States ? I know of no other miſſion on their part, in conſequence ot the declaration made at Philadelphia on the 25th of Brumaire, 5th year (Nov. 15, 1796), than that confided jointly and ſeparately to Meſſ. Pinckney, Marſhall, and yourſelf. I will not retrace the cauſes which have prevented the envoys collectively from attaining the moſt complete ſucceſs; but I will affirm that they are foreign to the French government, and that in any ſtate of the cauſe, it depends upon you to fulfil the expectation of the two countries.

You deny, Sir, that there was ſome generoſity on my part in propoſing to you to baniſh hereafter from our communications, all uſeleſs epiſodes, and eſpecially no longer to give a place in them to recriminations. This is another epiſode; but ſince you force me to it, it is neceſſary that I ſhould explain myſelf more fully. If now and then ſome anonymous publications, of a nature diſagreeable to the American government, have crept into the French papers, it would not become me to complain. For a long time, certain papers of the United States, the editor of one of which is the printer of the Senate, daily ſpread abroad the moſt atrocious calumnies, the moſt injurious inſinuations, the moſt baſe reflections upon the French people, their inſtitutions, their government, their legiſlators, the heads of their executive, their miniſters, their agents, their glorious defenders. Yes, thoſe ſame warriors, who reſpect their enemies, receive the moſt ignominious appellations among a friendly people, for whom many have combated. Nay, more; within the walls of the national repreſentation of the United States, how many deeply inſulting ſpeeches have been and yet are delivered ? Nothing is ſpared in order to endeavour to degrade the French republic in the opinion of the American people ; and the ſilence ot your government leaves an open field to this torrent of invectives, whilſt ſcarcely now and then a word of reply eſcapes, notwithſtanding our vigilance, from the indignation of ſome French citizen. Is it not repeated in the United States, that the Executive Directory repels negotiations, in order to wait an opportunity of carrying the war there ? This odious aſſertion has been credited; and

your

your government, which ought to know that such a thought was never conceived, opposes no corrective to the impression which it is calculated to make. Whatever may be your opinion of it, Sir, it is generous to stifle all the sentiments which arise in abundance on reading your public papers, and even the debates of your legislature upon the subject of France. And yet until the two governments shall be so far reconciled as to concert the means of remedying these abuses, it is expedient that those who are to treat upon the interest of the two nations adopt a conciliatory language, and hereafter avoid what may give rise to painful recollections. I repeat to you, that it is my desire; that I will set the example; that I am impatient to abjure reproaches; and that I insist that this point may be well understood.

This is the last time I shall yield to these digressions, which ought to be as disagreeable to you as they are to me.

You have not transmitted to me any opinion, Sir, upon the note annexed to my letter of the 9th of this month. I have delayed until now sending you the following ones. I flatter myself that the long conference which I have had with you, will have produced some modification of the resolution in which you might appear to persevere. I therefore recommend to your attention two fresh notes, one upon the twelfth article, and the other upon the sixteenth article of the convention of the 14th of November 1798. They contain every thing which it is important to explain at present, in relation to this act. We will immediately after proceed to the treaties of February 1778. You desired that I might send you some propositions. I did so on the 30th Prairial (18th June), and you should have had them sooner, had it not been for the incident which has happened. I have therein traced the plan of the negotiation. I have therein pointed out generally the intentions of France; I have therein entered into an engagement to discuss every proper subject; I have assured you, that the Executive Directory would render to the United States that justice which it expects itself; I have excluded nothing which we can suggest on either side, to strengthen still more the good understanding between our two republics.

But it is not enough to transmit these propositions to your government; they are only the foundation of the necessary discussions upon every question of detail of which we ought to find the solution. The reconciling of the different points upon which we shall have fixed our ideas, will form the act to be drawn up. I do not think that we could come to conclusions in any other manner. It even appears to me, that there will be an evident loss of time, if, in the state of things, this discussion is adjourned. I have already given you to understand, that it would be inconvenient to give it in charge to a minister plenipotentiary at Philadelphia. Circumstances have rendered this inconvenience more

important,

important, and I will not conceal from you that I should fear fresh incidents.

I therefore urge you more preffingly than ever, Sir, whilst I refer to what I have already written to you on this subject, to postpone your departure, and to attend quickly to the discussions which I urge. I know that you are not of the same opinion with me, with respect to the validity of your full powers; but reflect, that, in any case, you can in nothing bind your government, which has reserved the right of ratifying.

I will add, that, in the situation in which you stand, it is contrary to all usage to depart, without notifying that you have received an order therefor; that the usage, on the contrary, is, when a doubt is raised upon the full powers, the envoy waits the decision of his government, without breaking off the negotiation.

Receive, Sir, the assurance of my perfect consideration.

CH. MAU. TALLEYRAND.

Foreign Affairs.

Note upon the twelfth Article of the Convention between France and the United States, of the 14th November 1788.

THIS article has been executed in France in its literal meaning, and in its implicit meaning: that is to say, that all the differences between the citizens of the United States in France, have been left to the decision of their consuls, and that the sentences of the latter have been executed, when coercion was necessary, in the same manner and by the same officers of justice as the sentences of the French tribunals.

Nothing has been changed in this respect, since the establishment of the republican form of government, notwithstanding the jealousy which is peculiar to it, and which the judiciary authorities of every country possess in general.

It has been judged, as to the literal meaning, that the jurisdiction given to the consuls of the United States over their countrymen, was not in any respect optional. The 12th article does not declare in effect that all the differences *may be* determined, &c. which would imply only a power in persons of the nation to sue before their consuls, and a power in the latter to admit or decline. It declares formally that all differences *shall be* determined, &c. which implies a reciprocal obligation upon the persons of the nation and their consuls. This obligation is confirmed by the last paragraph, which pronounces an absolute interdiction upon the territorial officers, civil or military, to interfere in any manner whatever; and consequently obliges the persons of the nation to apply to their consuls, and the consul to decide their differences.

It has been judged, as to the implied meaning, that the stipulation

tion being exprefs, mutual, and guaranteed by the public faith, included within it the engagement to give it effect. It would have been ridiculous to put the citizens of the United States in France under the neceffity of referring exclufively their differences to their confuls, and the neceffity of taking them up, as the only competent judges, without intending the execution of the fentences. But this execution can proceed only from the territorial power which difpofes of the force.

It has finally been judged, that this kind of jurifdiction was not in any refpect repugnant to the local fovereignty, becaufe its admiffion was mutually agreed upon; that it did not ftand in competition with the French tribunals, becaufe it did not embrace objects common to them; that it did not abridge the territorial rights, becaufe it extended only to foreigners.

There has been no reciprocity on the part of the United States, wherein this queftion has been viewed under a different afpect; and the French government has conftantly received complaints upon this fubject. In 1792, attention feemed to be paid to the reprefentations which it caufed to be made. An act of Congrefs of the 14th April of that year declares, "that in all cafes wherein, by any article of the convention, the confuls of France are entitled to aid in the execution of any order, the marfhals of the diftrict courts of the United States, or their deputies, fhould be the officers competent, and fhould give their aid according to the tenour of the ftipulations." The fame act having provided, in the preceding paragraphs, for the execution of the 7th and 9th articles of the convention, that which has been juft cited is applicable only to the 12th article, the laft of the three which were forefeen, and the only one wherein an order might be iffued. But, foon after, the officers defigned eluded this provifion.

Since that time fome courts in the United States have declared that they would not take cognifance of actions at law between Frenchmen. Thefe actions have been fuftained in other courts, notwithftanding the remonftrances of the defendants. On the other hand, the confuls of the republic decided in vain upon the differences fubmitted to their judgment. One while the juftice of the country was refufed by arguing from the tenour of the 12th article; at another time the confular jurifdiction was palfied by arguing from its pretended filence, and fometimes it was entirely forgotten.

It is of preffing importance to put an end to thefe uncertainties, which are difcouraging to the French merchants, and embarraffing to their government, whofe protection they claim.

The 12th article of the convention between France and the United States, gives to the confuls a judiciary authority over their countrymen, to the exclufion of the refpective tribunals.

This

This authority is not optional; it does not derogate from the rights of sovereignty of either republic; it is founded on a reciprocal agreement; it is conformable with the principles asserted by the most enlightened writers upon public law; it meets with no opposition in France, and it ought to be faithfully facilitated in the United States.

The French government will not insist upon a particular mode of executing the sentences of the consuls in the United States. It asks only the express recognition of the implied meaning of the 12th article, and a promise to provide for it fully at the next session of Congress, in the manner most consonant with the forms used in the country.

Paris, 18th Messidor, 6th year (6th July 1798).
The Minister of Foreign Affairs,
(Signed) CH. MAU. TALLEYRAND.

Note upon the sixteenth Article of the Convention between France and the United States, of the 14th November 1788; and general Observations.

THIS article declares that the convention shall be fully and completely executed during the space of twelve years, to be reckoned from the day of the exchange of the ratifications.

The exchange took place in January 1790, and the term appointed will expire in January 1802.

It will be proper, before that period, to set about the revision of the convention. Many articles require it. The French republic will show itself less jealous of the privileges of the consuls, than of the stipulations useful to its merchants and navigators. The United States will doubtless be guided by the same laudable views. The two republics will the more readily agree on this subject, as they are founded upon the same principles.

But it is possible that on the one side or the other the parties may not be prepared at the time fixed for the intended negotiation; that more experience may be desired; or that they may not even agree as to the best system to be adopted. The French government proposes, that it be declared, " that, on account of the events which have prevented a judgment upon the effect of the present convention, it shall be prolonged for six years after the expiration of the twelve first years, if it be not renewed in the interval."

The French government also proposes, " that in all quotations of any article of the convention, the denomination of *French citizen* be substituted for that of *subject;* and that the words *French Republic*

Republic be placed in the stead of *Most Christian King, Most Christian Majesty.*

Paris, 18th *Messidor*, 6th year *(July 6, 1798).*
The Minister of Exterior Relations,
(Signed) Ch. Mau. Talleyrand.

No. XXII.

Mr. Gerry, to the Minister of Foreign Affairs of the French Republic.

Citizen Minister, Paris, 10th July 1798.

I RECEIVED on the 9th instant your letter of the 6th, being the 18th Messidor, and shall briefly reply to it.

You inform me that the communication of the intentions of the Executive Directory, sent to Philadelphia before Germinal, the 20th of March, did not proceed from the French government, its agents, or any person whatever, to your knowledge: and I affirm that it did not, directly or indirectly, proceed from me.

The rumour then must have been vague, and could not have merited the attention of the President of the United States; much less could it have authorized his formal communication thereof to Congress.

The two attempts of the United States to obtain a reconciliation between the republics, to which I referred in my last, were those of the mission of a minister to efface unfavourable impressions, sooth suspicions and restore cordiality between them, and afterwards of the three envoys, whose powers were more extensive. I made no allusion to your conduct, and with respect to my own, have done every thing incumbent on me.

You complain that certain newspapers of the United States, one of which has for its editor the printer of the Senate, calumniate daily the French people, their institutions, government, legislators, and others. The envoys, in their letter to yourself of the 3d of April, have discussed this subject so fully as to leave nothing further necessary to be said thereon.

You also complain of some speeches of the national representation of the United States, degrading the French republic in the opinion of the American people, and of the silence of our government thereon. The constitution of the United States expressly provides, that the senators and representatives, for any speech or debate in either House, shall not be questioned in any other place. So essential is the freedom of debate in each House, as to be sacredly preserved by the constitution, and to be above the control of every other department of the government. The government of the United States, on their part, pay no regard to offensive speeches in foreign legislatures, well knowing that, however amicably disposed

posed governments may be towards each other, such a mode of conduct must be productive of perpetual sources of discord between them.

And now having replied, Citizen Minister, to your observations on these subjects, I assure you, that nothing can be more disagreeable to me than such discussions. I did not give rise to them, and here I shall terminate them.

On the 27th of June, about six weeks after I had demanded my passport, and when my baggage was on board the Sophia, you sent me a note containing some remarks on the consular convention, and expected a formal discussion of them; to this, without powers, I could not have consented at any time; I have repeatedly refused it, and must adhere to my determination.

You conclude by observing, that in my situation, which is that of an unaccredited minister, it is contrary to all usages to depart without notifying that I have received orders therefor: and that, on the contrary, it is customary when a doubt arises upon full powers, to wait the decision of the government of which one is the envoy, without breaking the negotiation. On my part there has been no doubt of a want of powers, and there has not been any negotiation; there cannot then be a rupture of it by my departure. I am to judge of the necessity of demanding my passport. I now renew my demand of it, and the other documents necessary for the voyage, and request a definite answer.

Accept, Citizen Minister, the assurances of my perfect consideration.

(Signed)   E. GERRY.

To the Minister of Foreign Affairs of the French Republic.

No. XXIII.

Ministry of Exterior Relations.
      Paris, 24 *Messidor*, 6th *Year of the French Republic*
                (July 12, 1798*).*

The Minister of Exterior Relations, to Mr. Gerry, Envoy of the United States.

AS long as I could flatter myself, Sir, with fulfilling the wish of the Executive Directory, by endeavouring with you to re-establish the good understanding between the French republic and the United States, I used my efforts, both in our conferences and in my correspondence with you, to smooth the paths, to establish the basis, to enter on the business, and to convince you of the utility of your presence at Paris. It is in your character of envoy of the American government that I received you and wrote to you: it depended upon yourself to be publicly received by the Executive Directory. Without partaking in your opinion with respect to the

the change which the departure of Messrs. Pinckney and Marshall might produce in the full powers, wherein I have read that you have been authorized to treat *separately;* it appeared to me that in the hypothesis even in which you placed yourself, you ought to refer the question to your government, and in the interval fix with me, by a calm and friendly discussion, all the questionable points of our differences.

This proceeding was the more natural, as, setting aside the premature knowledge which your government had of the offer to treat with you, after the departure of your colleagues, my note of the 28 Ventose (18th March), which must have reached Philadelphia about the end of Floreal (May 19th), left no more doubt upon this subject. It comprehends three objects perfectly distinct. It begins by rectifying, with the dignity which becomes the French government, the statement of grievances of the United States, drawn up by their envoys in the inverted order of facts, on the 28 Nivose preceding (17th January). It next points out the reasons which prevented the negotiation from being carried on with the envoys collectively. It finally declares solemnly the conciliatory dispositions of the Executive Directory, its express desire of restoring between the two countries the ties of their former friendship, and the intention to treat with you. A declaration so explicit was made only to furnish the President of the United States with a infallible mean of accommodation. It was a pledge of peace that might be taken up. I presumed you could not be long in receiving analogous instructions, and even other powers, if they were necessary; or that, at least, if you had announced to the President a wish to return to America, another envoy would come to consummate the happy work which we should have had the satisfaction to prepare.

With such well-grounded hopes were mingled considerations upon the inconveniences of your departure. I have given you to understand, that notwithstanding the assurances you have given me, many would believe that it was owing solely to your inclination, to a thorough conviction of the invalidity of your powers, or to a wish to see the care of the negotiation confided to other hands. I have conversed with you respecting the conjectures which it would give rise to; on the means it would furnish the British cabinet, which spares nothing to draw France and the United States to extremities, from which it calculates to derive the sole profit; and on the suspicions even which the French government would be made to conceive. I endeavoured to make you see into its possible consequences. The occurrence of several circumstances has already retarded the reconciliation of the two republics. It may be permitted to him, who sincerely wishes for peace, to fear new ones. These views, for which I shall ever honour myself, induced me to resist, as much as I could, the desire you manifested of

Vol. VIII.   G   quitting

quitting France. You decisively infist upon it in your letter of the 22d of this month (10th July). The Executive Directory has consequently authorized me to send you the passports which you request, for yourself and the vessel which awaits you at Havre. You will find them enclosed.

May your return to the United States, and the communication of what has passed between us, since you have solely represented your government, remove there the injurious opinion of hostile intentions on the part of France. You have often repeated to me, since you pressed your departure, that if you could not treat here as an envoy, your good offices in the United States should not be spared as a citizen. You have it not in your power to render the two countries a more signal service, than by contributing to make their political and commercial relations accord with their inclination and interest. Assure your government that the Executive Directory perseveres in the intention of conciliating with sincerity the differences which have arisen between the French republic and the United States, as soon as an opportunity for that purpose shall be sincerely presented. If it be really true, that the dispositions of your government correspond therewith, let it give a proof of it, and you may answer beforehand for the success.

You cannot dissemble, Sir, that, if nothing prevented you from pursuing with me the examining and reconciling of the grievances which divide the two countries, we should not long stand in need of any thing but the respective ratifications.

Who will doubt of the sincerity of the French government, when it shall be known, that for nearly three months every pressing solicitation came from me, and that, faithful to the engagements I made in my note of the 28th Ventose (18th March), I have been the first seriously to press the negotiation after the departure of Messrs. Pinckney and Marshall? It will not be said, I hope, that the refusal to treat with them, is a refusal of conciliation, because this refusal was accompanied with a promise to treat with you, and your full powers presented you as separately authorized.

I shall incessantly appeal to that document, because it is the foundation of the opinion which the government must have formed; and even admitting that you were tied down by secret restrictions, I could not in my mind oppose what I did not know, on account of the credence due to the ostensible power.

Yes, Sir, when scarcely informed of the departure of Messrs. Pinckney and Marshall, I endeavoured in every conference I afterwards had with you, to demonstrate to you the urgency, the propriety, and the possibility of an active negotiation. I collected your ideas; they differed from my own; I endeavoured to reconcile them, and I was about to transmit some propositions to you, when a packet from your government arrived at Havre. You then

then appeared to be preparing to depart. Until then I never supposed you entertained the design of embarking before we had come to an agreement upon the definitive articles to be ratified by your government. A few days afterwards I received some dispatches from Philadelphia, the contents of which for a moment gave a new course to my correspondence with you On the 22d Prairial (10th June, I notified you that the dispositions of the Executive Directory were the same, and I prayed you to inform me, whether you were finally in a situation to negotiate On the 30th Prairial (18th June) I transmitted to you a complete plan of the negotiations. On the 9th Messidor (27th June I sent you my first note for discussion upon one of the points of our treaties, which are unexecuted in the United States. You declined answering it. It is necessary however to be agreed upon the details, in order to arrive at the conclusions. On the 18th Messidor (6th July) I sent you two others. In vain I accompanied these documents with the most cordial invitation rapidly to run over with me this series of indispensable discussions upon all our grievances. You have not even given me an opportunity of proving what liberality the Executive Directory would use on the occasion. You never wrote, in fact, but for your departure. And it is the French republic, which is accused in the United States of not wishing for peace! Perfidious instigators will insinuate that it never wished it. I will therefore ascend to the period when the first symptoms of discontent manifested themselves, that is to say, to the arrival of the Minister Genet at Philadelphia in Prairial of the 1st year. An universal joy burst forth in the United States at the declarations he was charged to make. He then expressed the friendly and generous intentions of the French government, which, powerful in the national energy, forbore to claim aid from its allies. Some of his measures soon afterwards gave umbrage They were the effect of a zeal badly adapted to local circumstances, and unfortunately still worse interpreted. The President caused his complaints concerning them to be made in France at the close of the same year. The committee of public safety immediately rendered satisfaction; and other agents arrived at Philadelphia in the beginning of Ventose, 2d year: their instructions will bear the utmost publicity: not to interfere in any party matter, to respect the government, to prompt it to maintain its neutrality with vigour, to repress all armaments which might endanger it, to maintain the rights secured to France by its treaties—such is the substance of them: such also were the instructions given to the Minister Adet, who succeeded them in the 3d year. Surely nothing can be more pacific. Nevertheless the rights of France were insensibly forgotten, the most important clauses of its treaties were rendered insignificant; its vessels experience the most discouraging vexations; England sports with impunity with the neutrality of the United States, which to France, who is too confident in it, becomes a source of loss. A transaction clandestinely negotiated, ends by consecrating, to the detriment of a friendly nation, the pretensions of its implacable enemy. After that time nothing has passed between the American government which the representations thwart, and the ministers plenipotentiary of the republic, who could not avoid making them, but a correspondence gradually increasing in asperity. The French government never interferes in them: it reposes upon the hope, that their own interest would lead the United States to perceive that England was drawing them within its vortex. Far from taking an hostile attitude, it affects indifference, in order to show itself patient with dignity. The crowd of complaints which it receives obliges it finally to change this line of conduct. It causes its grievances to be declared on the 25th Brumaire, 5th year (Nov. 15, 1796), and in order to produce a negotiation, too long delayed, it draws from the treaties of Paris and of London the most suitable means of hastening it. It is animated by no view of aggression, by no hostile intention. In order to obtain from the United States some degree of justice, it places them in a situation to be obliged to demand an arrangement themselves. Let us now see whether it has rejected any honourable propositions.

Mr. Pinckney had departed before the declaration of the 25th Brumaire (Nov. 15, 1796), which suspended the customary relations. He came to succeed Mr. Monroe, and, like him, to explain and palliate the conduct of the United States, without any special power for the negotiation demanded by France. He could not be received, because he was not in a situation to fulfil the conditions required, upon the resumption of political connexions. The President of the United States thought it his duty to call an extraordinary meeting of the legislature. I shall not review the opening speech, nor the turn which the debates took in that session. But I will say, that the impression which resulted therefrom, at Paris, was unfavourable previous to the arrival of the envoys; that this circumstance alone raised an obstacle, which ought to have been foreseen at Philadelphia; that the envoys themselves, unwilling to comprehend the natural effect of this kind of provocation, have contributed to render the impression more durable. It has finally, however, yielded to the primitive desire of a sincere reconciliation. You find a proof of it in the very expedient suggested, of treating with you separately; for a government hostilely disposed would not have taken the delicate course, which guards its honour and fulfils its pacific intentions.

You have given me to understand, Sir, that it would have been well, had the Executive Directory supported the declarations which I have made to you in its name, by a change in the measures which affect the commerce of the United States.

I might

I might answer you, that your government might have also secured its object by restoring at first the French republic to the rights which flow from its treaties. But let us exact less rigidly, and be more equitable towards each other. Although the measures of France are no more than the consequence of those of the United States, you must have remarked, that in my propositions of the 12th Prairial (18th June), the intention of the Executive Directory is, that the respective pretensions may be collaterally examined and adjusted. It intends to place, in a single act, a durable monument of the future friendship of the two republics, and the justice which they owe to each other; and no idea of false glory enters its mind. On taking leave of you, Sir, I have supposed that I owed you a testimony of my esteem: it consists altogether in the unreservedness with which I have just spoken to you, and in the expression of the regret which your departure, under the present circumstances, gives me.

Receive the assurance of my perfect consideration.

(Signed)   CH. MAU. TALLEYRAND.

P. S. of the 27 Messidor (July 15, 1798).

A circumstance, Sir, of infinite importance has delayed the dispatching of this letter. I do not know how it happens that at every step towards a reconciliation, a cause of irritation intervenes, and that the United States always give rise to it. Some days since different advices were successively received by the Executive Directory. It seems that your government, hurried beyond every account, no longer preserves appearances. A law of the 7th of the last month authorizes it to cause every French vessel of war to be attacked, which may have stopped, or intended to stop American vessels. A resolution of the House of Representatives suspends, from the 13th of this month, all commercial relations with the French republic and its possessions. Several plans of a law have been proposed for banishing the French, and sequestrating French property.

The long suffering of the Executive Directory is about to manifest itself in the most unquestionable manner. Perfidy will no longer be able to throw a veil over the pacific dispositions which it has never ceased to manifest.

It is at the very moment of this fresh provocation, which would appear to leave no honourable choice but war, that it confirms the assurances which I have given you on its behalf. In the present crisis, it confines itself to a measure of security and self-preservation, by laying a temporary embargo on American vessels, with a reserve of indemnities, if there be occasion for them. It is yet ready, it is as much disposed as ever, to terminate by a candid negotiation the differences which subsist between the two countries.

Such is its repugnance to consider the United States as enemies,

that,

that, notwithstanding their hostile demonstrations, it means to wait until it be irresistibly forced to it by real hostilities.

Since you will depart, Sir, hasten at least to transmit to your government this solemn declaration.

(Signed)   CH. MAU. TALLEYRAND.

PROCEEDINGS *of the* CONGRESS *at* RASTADT.

Conclusum of the Deputation of the Empire, of the 16th Brumaire, 6th of November; transmitted the 7th.

THE deputation of the Empire cannot explain how, upon the very detailed note of the 17th October (26th Vendemiaire), the ministers of the French republic could confine themselves, in their note of the 7th Brumaire (28th October), to an absolutely negative reply, and to simple reference to their note of the 12th Vendemiaire (3d October), without entering into any ulterior details upon still contested articles; and rendering that reply still more bitter by expressions and declamations as unexpected, in the very moment of a reconciliation so near at hand, as contrary to usage in public and diplomatic negotiations between two pacificators esteeming themselves reciprocally. If the deputation of the Empire cannot remove difficulties which arise from the nature of affairs, they certainly do not seek to prolong labour, but to give it, on the contrary, a fixed direction: and as they endeavour, above all, to conceive all objects clearly, and thereby to avoid all double meaning, they could have wished to have been informed of the passages in the note, in which the French ministers think, nevertheless, double meanings are to be found.

The deputation employ themselves, and insist only upon propositions just and equitable in themselves: and if their declarations have not always been as close and brief as those of the French plenipotentiaries, the principal reason is, that he who thinks only of waving demands, and of diminishing as much as possible the sum of his loss, is obliged to enter into more ample details upon modifications, than he whom the fate of arms has placed in the situation of making only general demands, to be able to content himself with more or less gain; but if the French ministers reproach the deputation of the Empire with not wishing seriously for peace, and with doing nothing but *speak of it*, they have only to cast an eye upon the negotiation to the present period, and to take an exact account of all that the deputation have *effectually done* to obtain peace, to prevent any one whatever from considering this accusation as a serious one.

They have not only acceded to the principal bases of peace, and abandoned to France all the finest countries of the left bank of the Rhine, in extent, situation, population, wealth, and consequently is important to the aggrandifement of the French republic; but they have, befides, acceded to demands of the higheft importance. They have renounced the rights of the Empire upon the Auftrian Low Countries and Savoy, as well as upon the fiefs of the Empire fituated in the Cifalpine. They have confented to the abolition of the tolls of the Rhine. For the fecurity of Mentz, they have abandoned the Ifle St. Pierre, fituated on the Thalweg. They have even given an affurance of the demolition of the fortrefs of Ehrenbreiftein, fituated upon the right bank of the Rhine. They have come to an underftanding, with fome modifications reciprocally convenient, upon the Thalweg and the courfe of the Rhine, which is to form the limits of the two ftates, upon the free navigation of that river, and the keeping up a towing road. They have confented to the re-eftablifhment of the commercial bridges of the Rhine which have exifted hitherto, and they have not oppofed the building of other bridges: they have folely placed as a condition of it, the ufe, neceffity, and at each time the confent of the Emperor and the Empire. With refpect to the dependences of the ecclefiaftical eftablifhments, the deputation have entirely acceded to the convention refpecting the principal object propofed by France. They have confined themfelves fimply to the making of propofals upon the application with regard to the perfonals and capitals comprifed in it. They have confented to the demand, not to conftruct new forts or fortreffes on the right bank of the Rhine, for three thoufand toifes from Kehl and Caffel. Finally, they have even determined to charge themfelves with the private debts as well as thofe of the countries contracted for the war of the Empire, together with the debts of the ftates of the left bank, which fhall be indemnified upon the right bank.

No nation that is and will remain free and independent could make greater facrifices. No ftate will confent to fimilar ceffions and conditions, unlefs it very fincerely defires peace as the termination of the fufferings of humanity.

On what then can the reproach, that the deputation do not wifh for peace, be founded? Is it, perhaps, becaufe they refufe to charge the right bank with the communal debts of the war contracted on the left bank? (which are not even charged upon the French republic as national debts, and of which the republic will rather be, in the event, the moft confiderable creditor.) Is it becaufe they demand that individuals, who have hitherto been citizens of the German ftates, fhould not be treated as French emigrants, that thofe whom the war has rendered miferable, fhould not become more fo by peace? The German Empire will religioufly fulfil the future articles of the peace: but conditions which in their foundation are contrary to the firft bafes of peace agreed upon, becaufe they would, in reality, extend the pretenfions of France to all the right bank of the Rhine; conditions

which

which are incompatible with the German national honour; which would be prejudicial to the glory of the citizens of the German states—would endanger the political existence of Germany; conditions which would oblige almost all the German people to a permanent tribute, that would every where paralyse all the means of existence, and enervate all the forces of the states: such conditions it is impossible for the deputation to fulfil, and they cannot adhere to them. The well-being of Germany is entrusted to them; their duties, consequently, prescribe to them, notwithstanding their love for peace, which cannot be made a matter of doubt. It is those same duties, justice and equity, which dictated to the deputation the observations contained in their last note.

To so great a number of individuals become miserable, these observations and demands no longer concern cessions of countries, fixing of limits, commercial advantages, but the rights, property, tranquillity, and even the lives of German subjects. The national dignity has imposed upon the deputation the law of speaking with warmth in favour of those Germans; they demand only that which has been granted at every peace, and every cession of territory, according to the general right of nations.

The deputation think they may submit, with full confidence, to the judgment of their contemporaries, and of posterity, the whole of their conduct to the present moment, as well as the observations contained in the present note: they rely, nevertheless, always upon the justice and equity of the French government: they hope that these considerations, so true, will be deeply weighed by them; and they flatter themselves that the French plenipotentiaries, fully convinced that the deputation have made every effort to arrive at an entire reconciliation, will no longer hesitate to explain themselves in a favourable and tranquillizing manner upon all the observations and demands made in the communication of the 17th October (26th Vendemiaire).

Second Conclusum of the Deputation of the Empire, of the 16th Brumaire, 6th November; transmitted the 7th.

THERE shall be made with the consent of the Imperial plenipotentiaries, the following reply to the second note of the French legation concerning the supplying of Ehrenbreitstein with provisions.

The deputation of the Empire have seen by the second note of the French plenipotentiaries of the 7th Brumaire (28th Oct.) relative to the supplying of Ehrenbreistein with provisions, that the said ministers regard that measure as belonging to the military part, and as out of their competence, and that, for that reason, they

they solely reiterate the assurance that the French government is disposed to extend to all the objects susceptible of them, suitable ameliorations and alleviations; but that they observe, at the same time, that it is peace alone that can arrange all these affairs; and that nothing shows more that peace is not wished for, than these instances continually renewed. Yet in the nature of the thing it is impossible that military objects, if even their execution should depend upon military authorities, should be excluded from a negotiation for peace, if it is to be complete, and should not be in the competence of those who, in affairs of that kind, are the sole organs of their respective government. The demolition of the fortress of Ehrenbreitstein belongs also, with respect to its foundation, to the military part, and yet it is the deputation of the Empire that have consented to it, on condition that the actual blockade of the fortress, as well as the prohibition of furnishing the inhabitants of the Thal and of Ehrenbreitstein with provisions and other articles necessary for subsistence, should be removed, conformably to existing conventions. These conventions explain themselves clearly. When on the 18th of April 1797, the suspension of arms was stipulated at Leoben for Germany, and consented to by the two parties, the generals in chief of the two armies, Werneck and Hoche, agreed on the 18th April 1797, "In case hostilities should recommence, Mentz and Ehrenbreitstein shall be victualled for as many days as the armistice shall have lasted. The Austrian generals shall inform the French generals of that victualling, in order that it may be ascertained; it shall be done from week to week during the time the armistice shall last only."

On the 12th of May, *the charge* of the generals in chief of the Austrian and Imperial armies on one part, and of the French general on the other, assembled at Heidelberg, to fix the mutual positions. It was declared by *the charge* of the general in chief of the Austrian and Imperial armies: Article V. Every thing fixed by the convention of Generals Werneck and Hoche, with respect to the victualling of fortresses, as well as the free navigation of the Mein, Rhine, and Moselle, shall continue to be maintained upon the same footing.

Adjutant-general Antoine, who assisted in the name of General Hoche, replied, " The fifth article is recognised, &c

The commander of the fortress of Ehrenbreitstein, and the French General Gouthon, afterwards entered into particular conventions.

The first, on the 25th of April 1797, states:—

" The inhabitants of the Thal provisionally may, with the express authority of the commandant of the fort, go to Coblentz upon affairs of commerce: the same permission shall extend to those of Coblentz, who shall obtain leave from the French general."

And the 10th of June 1797:—

"The importation and exportation of all commercial merchandise shall be permitted upon each bank of the Rhine:

"Are nevertheless excepted from this article all that relates to military matters, such as lead, powder, iron, wood for building, other warlike ammunition, &c. the entrance of which into the Thal is absolutely prohibited, &c. &c."

The very words of those conventions already shew, that they were not to take place but during the interval from the armistice to the peace, or to a new war. The hindrance then to the victualling of Ehrenbreitstein for several months cannot be the consequence of a peace yet to be concluded ; and by insisting continually upon the fulfilling of these conventions, the deputation can still less draw upon them the suspicion that they have not a serious desire to accelerate peace.

The conclusion of it, however speedy it may be, cannot keep pace with the urgent wants of the fortress and the Thal.

The victualling from week to week during the whole time of the armistice, is, by the solemn and repeated assurances given of it, an object so much the more decided, as the ministers of the French republic have themselves acknowledged diplomatically, and again recently in their note of the 28th Fructidor (Sept. 14), the armistice concluded, and the lines fixed for the two armies: and in what moment can the deputation expect with more confidence the fulfilling of existing conventions, than in that in which negotiators are assembled to conclude fresh ones of the highest importance? They therefore still hope that the plenipotentiaries of the French republic will hesitate no longer in giving a speedy declaration, conformably to the demand of the 23d of October (2d Brumaire).

Substance of the Memorial of the Prussian Ministers communicated on the same Day as the above.

THE ministers plenipotentiary of his Prussian Majesty can by no means approve the statements in the French note of the 7th Brumaire (October 28), in answer to the note of the deputation of the Empire, that the revictualling of Ehrenbreitstein did not belong to them, but to the military department. This point is no more of a nature purely military than the demolition of that fortress, which, however, was treated of at Rastadt. The French ministers, as negotiators for peace, could treat of every thing which concerns the state of possession, and the relations between the two contracting powers. The blockade of Ehrenbreitstein is directly repugnant to the armistice which was agreed upon. It might be

almost

considered as an act of hostility, and even special conventions it still more expressly. This blockade too is quite super-
since the deputation of the Empire have agreed to the
tion of that fortress from a love of peace. The French ple-
atiaries too must recollect the friendly, the amicable repre-
ons which they presented to his Prussian Majesty on the
, stating that the French government had totally renounced
ws upon this place. Were it to fall into other hands, the
of Germany would be more exposed, and an important dif-
: would arise on its means of defence, and consequently the
ts of his Majesty would be directly affected. The army of
lity would then be no longer adequate to its object: it
be necessary to increase it, and to take other measures. In
l, the ministers of his Prussian Majesty expressly state their
t that the matter should be represented to the French govern-
and that the blockade of the fortress be given up, and its
talling permitted.

s from the French Ministers to the Deputation of the Empire.

FIRST NOTE.

IE undersigned ministers plenipotentiary of the French re-
: for the negotiation with the German Empire, have received
ne of the deputation of the Empire, communicated to them,
rth Brumaire (November 7), by the ministers plenipotentiary
Emperor.

at spirit of conciliation which the undersigned have ever
d, with a degree of firmness conformable to circumstances,
ustifies them in making those observations, for which many
es of that note furnish sufficient grounds. Without regard-
e language of opinions dictated by partiality, it is now only
ed by this answer to bring back the negotiation to its real
. It is wholly contained, with respect to its basis and gene-
inciples, in the note of the undersigned of the 12th last
maire, which is supported by all precedents, the dispo-
of which it has not annulled. It is to that point the depu-
ought to concentrate its attention; it is there it will find
, notwithstanding so many obstacles which seem to unite to
the progress of affairs.

note of the 12th Vendemiaire is, in fact, if it is properly
ered, the most complete proof the French government
have given the Empire of its pacific resolutions, and of the
it places to its force and advantages. It would be super-
to enumerate the 3d, 4th, 5th, 7th, 8th, and 10th arti-
me of then have been either expressly or impliedly agreed
the deputati of the Empire; and the unimportance of

the

the difficulties thrown in the way of the others, affords a presumption that the obstacles will soon yield to better reflection. For instance, is it possible that the 7th article can leave wise negotiators any thing to desire on the subject, or that it should be necessary to declare that the French laws against emigration are not applicable to the German nation?

The first article, relative to the limits of the Rhine and the isles, is of the number of those to which the deputation of the Empire has acceded. But it has proposed a doubt, and made a demand, which is explained according to the meaning of these words:—The French government will never consent that the Empire, or any of its members, should in any manner enjoy any rights or property on the side situate to the left of the Thalweg; and so it has determined. It never could have been thought that so clear and definite a text as this passage, fortified also by the body of the article, should have required interpretation. The exemptions can in no case be extended, and far less supplied. Therefore, the undersigned explicitly declare, in order to satisfy the desire of the deputation of the Empire, that the said article extends generally to all the isles situated to the left of the Thalweg, established in the middle of the course of the Rhine, properly so called; and consequently, that those pointed out in the note of the deputation of the 26th of last Vendemiaire, should belong to the French republic, notwithstanding all former arrangements, which are incompatible with the present conventions. With respect to the observation respecting *les ouvrages riverains*, it is not refused on the part of France to provide materials, in case those of Germany fail, subject to the conditions of the said article, and the exigency of circumstances.

The second article is not susceptible of any modification, or any difficulty: the deputation, if it attends to it, must be satisfied of its propriety. With regard to what concerns the toll-gate of Elsfleth, it is precisely because the undersigned are ignorant of the origin and nature of that right, that they have demanded of the deputation of the Empire its abolition in favour of the French republic. Surely nothing is more common than to see things established by a treaty, annulled or modified by a subsequent treaty; and when the contracting parties are essentially the same as in the preceding case, what doubt can there be about making such agreements as are convenient? The Empire has conceded the right in question. It is the business of the Empire to be acquainted with the propriety of a demand relative to the object of its concession. If it did not depend on the Empire (which the undersigned cannot suppose the contrary of) to decree the suppression required, it at least belongs to it to authorize and render it valid, by its formal consent. At the moment of the re-establishment of peace, and of the ancient relations between the two powers,

the

the Empire ought not to refuse French commerce a franchise which many other states enjoy.

The second article includes a second demand, namely, that by a special clause to be inserted in the future treaty, the free and imperial cities of Hamburgh, Bremen, and Frankfort, should be confirmed and maintained in the plenitude of their rights and constitutional independence. It is a reasonable demand, and it ought to be agreeable to the Empire in general, that the French republic should seize so solemn an occasion, in order to give those deserving cities, with which it is intimately connected, a public testimony of that friendship which they know how to appreciate. The republic will not renounce that satisfaction; and the deputation of the Empire cannot oppose it, without a failure in that respect, which it is impossible to attribute to it.

The sixth article relates to debts. The arrangement made on this subject leaves no question, except with regard to the communial debts. The undersigned will explain themselves in a few words upon that subject, lest misrepresentation should one day bring it before the public in a point of view unfavourable to the government, by insinuating, that it would throw the burden of the debts in general upon the Empire. No one is ignorant that the undersigned have consented that the communial debts contracted for the public benefit should remain chargeable to that part to become subject to France. Except with regard to the debts of princes, and debts for carrying on the war, is there an impartial man who can say any one will be injured? Every well-disposed person, notwithstanding the endeavours to mislead his judgment, will acknowledge that the quarrel which they have brought against France should be equally borne by the Empire in mass, and not by a portion of the Empire which has ceased to be German; and will they, therefore, less desire the conclusion of a peace, which they may reasonably regard as a perpetual one? It is further to be observed, that the deputation of the Empire, by consenting to charge itself with the debts of princes, and debts contracted on account of the war, has acknowledged the principal it owes to France. Why, therefore, would they now introduce an arbitrary difference between debts which have the same cause, and the same destination? It does not deny that the Empire, both before and pending hostilities, has drawn from the communes and bailiwicks, in every possible way, part of its military expenditure; from whence it follows, that it is, on the part of the French government, a mark of great self-denial, that it consents to leave to the ceded bank of the Rhine those communial debts which have been contracted since its occupation by the French troops. The republic is ever disposed, as is evident, to open the doors of accommodation; but it will never act so as to lose sight of its interests, or compromise its dignity.

After

After thefe explanations, the underfigned hope to fee a ftruggle put an end to, which has been already too much prolonged, and a speedy adoption of that principle which is the bafis of the negotiation, and which it is their duty to fee adhered to. They do not doubt but the fecret or declared enemies of peace will endeavour to miflead the policy of the deputation of the Empire; but at the fame time they are perfuaded that it will be able to efcape every fnare by its own aid; and by its ideas of its own intereft well underftood, that it will ferioufly confider the inequality of the war in which pernicious councils have involved it; that it is a war in which France, befides that it already poffeffes more than it demands for peace, may in all probability gain ftill more, whilft the Empire cannot even hope to regain its loffes, and would be expofed, whatever events took place, to confequences very different to thofe which peace and amity with the republic now offer.

The minifters plenipotentiary of the French republic confirm to the minifter plenipotentiary of his Majefty the Emperor, fentiments of their moft diftinguifhed regard.

BONNIER.
Raftadt, 21ft Brumaire (Nov. 11),   JEAN DEBRY.
7th Year of the French Republic.   ROBERJOT.

The following is the Tenour of the fecond Note.

THE underfigned minifters plenipotentiary of the French republic for the negotiation with the Germanic Empire, have received the fecond note of the deputation of the Empire, tranfmitted to them the 17th Brumaire, by the minifter plenipotentiary of the Emperor.

The document, of which this note contains a few extracts, was not known to the underfigned. It confirms them in their opinion, that the object it treats of belongs to the military diftrict, and confequently is unconnected with the negotiations for peace. They cannot, therefore, referring to what they have already faid on the fubject, but exprefs to the deputation of the Empire, the conftant defire of the French government to conclude peace, until that happy period, which wholly depends on the Empire, to ameliorate the prefent ftate of things as much as the national fafety will permit.

The underfigned affure the minifter plenipotentiary of his Majefty the Emperor of their moft diftinguifhed regard.

Raftadt, 21ft Brumaire (11th November),
   7th Year of the French Republic.

Substance of the Note of the Imperial Minister to the French Ministers.

Rastadt, 2d Frimaire (Nov. 22).

THE Imperial minister expresses his satisfaction at seeing that the confidence of the deputation of the Empire in the justice of the French government has not been deceived, and that their declarations on some points promise a favourable issue to the negotiations. He says that they admit, with the French ministers, the articles 3d, 4th, 5th, 8th, 9th, and 10th, of the French note of the 12th Vendemiaire, which may soon be regulated by means of some ulterior explanations.

With respect to those contained in the note of the 21st Brumaire, they consent, first, that the isles situated on the left bank of the Thalweg, which before the war were under the sovereignty of the Empire in the upper part of the Rhine, and formed the ancient limit between the Empire and France, shall pass under the sovereignty of France, with the express reserve of the rights of property, and the free enjoyment in favour of their ancient properties, states, communes, or private persons of the Empire, and in the hope that on their side the French government will cede the isle of Buderich, to the preservation of which the King of Prussia attaches an extreme importance, as a necessary post to defend the fortress of Wesel. Secondly, reference is made to what has been previously said on the subject of the toll of Elsfleth, on the Weser; so much the more because the envoys of Denmark, Oldenburg, and Sweden, claim that toll as a property of the house of Holstein, absolutely independent, and forming part of the domains of that house, and because their means are supported by the Prussian legation.

3. It is far from being wished to refuse the demand made by the French ministers in favour of Frankfort, Hamburgh, and Bremen. The observations which have been made were solely intended as a stipulation for the preservation of the rights of the states, the actual nobility, and of all the members of the Empire, and, above all, for the maintenance of the German constitution.

4. The deputation suggests fresh modes of appreciating the refusal of transferring to the Empire part of the debts of the left bank, which the French ministers pretend to give up to the Empire to the discharge of the ceded countries.

5. The Imperial minister accepts the declaration made by the French ministers, *that the French laws, with regard to emigration, are not applicable to the German nation*, as an act of justice on the part of the French government, which removes the most important difficulty in the negotiation. All the Germans, he says, designated in the note of the 26th Vendemiaire, without exception, are assured that the laws of emigration are applicable to their

their perfons, not their property, whether in thofe countries which are ceded by the peace, or in France. By this declaration, the diftinction, fo little conformable to the law of nations, which was made between the united countries and thofe which were not, is done away; and the fubjects of Germany will not feel themfelves releafed from their relation with their ancient governments, except through a folemn treaty of peace, which will fix the limits of the two ftates.

The Imperial minifter fent fame day a note to the French minifters, in which he ftrongly infifts on the victualling of Ehrenbreitftein.

Reply of the French Minifters to the laft Notes of the Deputation of the Empire.

FIRST NOTE.

Raftadt, 5th Frimaire. (Nov. 25).

THE underfigned, wifhing to fhorten the difcuffions, which are profitable only to the common enemy, and wifhing to put the finifhing ftroke to the proofs of moderation and love of peace which the government have never ceafed to give, declare, that the French republic will confent that the *communal* debts on the left banks of the Rhine fhall remain at the charge of the French; but at the fame time they declare, that a conceffion fo liberal is propofed only under the condition *fine qua non et refolutiva*, that the députation of the Empire on their fide fhall accede completely, without any referve, and without any delay, to their note of the 12th Vendemiaire laft, explained by their pofterior notes of the 21ft and 25th Brumaire, and by the following difpofitions:

1. Relative to the firft article of the faid note of the 12th Vendemiaire, concerning the *delimitation* of the courfe of the Rhine and its ifles, the underfigned are agreed that the property of the ifles poffeffed on the left bank of the Thalweg by private perfons, fhall be preferved to them by their conforming to the laws; but with refpect to thofe on the faid fide which belong to princes and ftates of the Empire, and to immediate nobles having voices in the diet, it is underftood that the fovereignty and the property of all the ifles, without diftinction, are ceded and transferred to the French republic; all arrangements, conventions, and obfervances contrary to this point being to ceafe, as incompatible with the limit folemnly and irrevocably fixed and recognifed in the prefent negotiation by the two contracting powers.

2. In what concerns the toll of Elsfleth, the abolition of which

to the French republic is claimed by the second article of the said note of the 12th Vendemiaire, the undersigned do not conceive that the deputation of the Empire can think themselves incompetent to pronounce the partial suppression of that toll, when they have pronounced the suppression of all the tolls of the Rhine, belonging the greater part to members of the Empire. At the furthest, the German Empire is only asked for what is dependent upon it; that is to say, the abandonment of its rights, or the formal declaration that it has none; and with respect to individual interests, no doubt the loss resulting from a cession effected, would be indemnified in the same manner as all the others which the actual pacification shall have occasioned.

3. What has been said by the undersigned in their note of the 21st Brumaire, touching the seventh article of that of the 12th Vendemiaire, relative to emigrants, cannot be, and is in fact but an explanation in confirmation of the said article, the substance of which cannot by that be at all changed. The countries become French by their effective union, form no longer a part of the German nation; consequently they are under all the French laws. The undersigned declare anew, that the republican constitution opposes the extension which the deputation of the Empire would give to the said seventh article; that they formally reject the forced sense which is given by a false analogy to the terms made use of in their note of the 21st Brumaire. With respect to the rest, as the laws relative to emigration admit just exceptions, and in great number, the deputation may be very little disquieted upon their application.

In concluding this note, the undersigned may justly submit to the eyes of the deputation the importance of the new sacrifice which they have just offered to peace, compared with that which they demand at this moment; but full of confidence in it, they rely upon the wisdom of the deputation, and are persuaded that they will not, by a resistance, which hereafter would be founded only upon interests purely individual, compromise the general well-being and safety of Germany.

SECOND NOTE.

WHATEVER desire the undersigned have to give a proof of their deference for the deputation of the Empire, they cannot partake of their opinion upon the object of this new note; but they invite them, by all the considerations of an interest well understood, and of true humanity, to direct all their attention to their principal note of this day, in which they will find the assured pledge of a speedy peace, and the possible melioration of affairs.

(Signed)   BONNIER.
                        JEAN DEBRY.
                        ROBERJOT.

Address of the Deputation for the Pacification of the Empire to the Imperial Plenipotentiary, on the 10th December.

THE deputation extraordinary for the pacification of the Empire submit to the legation appointed by his Imperial Majesty, our gracious Emperor and Sovereign—

That the deputation for the pacification of the Empire consider it proper that the following answer should be given to the two notes of the plenipotentiaries of the French republic of the 6th inst. that is to say, to the first note as follows:

"The deputation for the pacification of the Empire have found, with the most unaffected grief, from the principal note of the ministers of the French republic, of the 6th December, that these ministers continue to assert that the deputation seeks to render the negotiations for peace more difficult, and to lengthen them without cause, while it is uninterruptedly employed in making the most sincere efforts to attain a prompt and sure peace. This it has sufficiently proved, and has only been diligently engaged in seeking to lessen the losses of the Empire.

"Full of confidence, it therefore submits all its conduct to the judgment of its cotemporaries, and of posterity. The work of peace is already so far advanced, that, in all the series of objects which have formed the subject of negotiation, there are none on which it has been thought proper to break off the negotiation. On the contrary, all the articles which formed the basis of the peace, excepting only those which related to emigration, and some points, modifications, and questions, have been accepted.

"In this situation of peace, the French ministers have declared that their notes of the 12th Vendemiaire, 21st, 23d Brumaire, and 3d and 16th Frimaire, are to be considered as the ultimatum of their government; and they require on that head a categorical and satisfactory answer.

"As to what relates to the subject of emigration, which has been mentioned, and which is yet in contest, the deputation is convinced, from all that has been said on this subject by the French ministers, that the French laws on emigration, and their application of them, are irreconcilable in principle. But, as the French ministers have given an assurance in their preceding notes, that there are ways and means of procuring to the dependants of the Germanic Empire, in whose behalf the deputation has been warmly

warmly interested, that tranquillity, which is so desirable, both with respect to their persons and fortune, it accepts this assurance, and relies on the justice of the French government, for efficacious protection for these unhappy persons, and that they shall be sheltered from all the arbitrary passions of the lower ranks. As to the remaining articles in the notes of the 12th Vendemiaire, 21st and 23d Brumaire, and 3d and 16th Frimaire, it appeared to the deputation more desirable to come to some conclusions as to those articles which required some further explanation; but, as the French ministers require still further a categorical answer on all these points, they think proper to assent to them, and to declare that they accede to all the articles of the ultimatum, and think it right that such of those articles as require more precise determinations and discussions, shall be settled when the treaty of peace shall be definitively arranged.

"The deputation of the Empire having, by the categorical declaration, entirely done away the principal obstacles to the approaching conclusion of peace, they entertain confident hopes, that, in conformity to former promises, the fate of the countries occupied on the right bank of the Rhine will, from this moment, be ameliorated as much as possible, and that the new demands for contributions and requisitions will be speedily revoked."

In answer to the second note of the French ministers, relative to the victualling of Ehrenbreitstein, the deputation propose to return the following answer:

"The French ministers refer, on the subject of victualling Ehrenbreitstein, to their last note of the 6th December, and to their preceding ones on this subject, and they assign as a reason, the present situation of the negotiation. But, as this situation is changed by the chief note of this day, the demands made by the deputation in their preceding notes acquire new weight; and they are persuaded that the French ministers will return without delay a satisfactory answer on the subject.

"At a moment when it was doubtful whether a rupture would take place, or the negotiation for peace would continue, the deputation of the Empire have been obliged to take into consideration every thing relative to these negotiations, to balance the hopes and the dangers, and to weigh the actual state of defence of the Empire. On this conscientious examination they found the reasons of their conclusion, very firmly convinced, that, in so doing, they act for the benefit of the Empire; and they trust, that for this reason they need not doubt that the Imperial legation will join them in this conclusion.

"The plenipotentiaries of the deputation for the pacification of the Empire, and of the electors, princes, and states, present their respects to the Imperial legation."

Rastadt, Dec. 10.

Answer of the French Plenipotentiaries, containing their Acceptance of the last Ultimatum of the Deputation of the Empire.

THE underfigned ministers plenipotentiary of the French republic for negotiating with the Germanic Empire, have received the note of the deputation of the Empire, communicated on the 21st Frimaire (December 11), by the minister plenipotentiary of the Empire. They will not defer the agreeable sensations they have experienced, by seeing that their confidence in the prudence and enlightened humanity of the deputation of the Empire has not been deceived. They accept with pleasure the declaration made by them; they accede to the just and last proposals of their government announced in the ultimatum delivered on the 6th inst. and in the preceding relating to it. And the deputation of the Empire is assured, that they will concur with all their efforts in every thing that may make the present appearance of affairs serve to promote the reciprocal advantage of the two contracting parties. As by means of this act of full and formal adhesion to the said ultimatum, every essential of the first basis of the negotiation is definitively settled and agreed on, nothing more is necessary than to attend to the application of the acknowledged principle of indemnity by the way of secularization, which forms an integral and indivisible part of the future treaty, which the respective negotiators must complete. This object, which will be directed with the same views of general interest which have conducted the negotiation to a point of maturity so satisfactory, deserves still to be considered before it is submitted to discussion; but the underfigned mean to present, without delay, their propositions in this respect to the deputation of the Empire, who, as well as themselves, must find a favourable augury in the decisive character of acceleration and unity which affairs have now assumed.

(Signed)   BONNIER.
                         JEAN DEBRY.
Rastadt, Dec. 12.   ROBERJOT.

Decree of the Imperial Commission with the Deputation of the Empire for negotiating a Peace.

THE commission appointed by his Imperial Majesty, our most gracious Emperor and Lord, with the deputation of the Empire, has taken into serious consideration the conclusum formed on the 10th of this month (20th Frimaire) by the deputation of the Empire, in answer to the two notes of the French legation of the 6th instant (16th Frimaire). After the numberless proofs which the Empire has given of its great love for peace, it would not be proper either in the ministers plenipotentiary of the French republic, or their constituents, to make, in opposition to the
                                             unanimous

unanimous opinion of Europe, and to their own conviction, those reproaches so unfavourable which are expressed in their last principal note. If the deputation of the Empire for negotiating peace have thought it their duty to yield still in this point, the Imperial commission does not wish to fetter the laborious steps which must at length ensure peace; but the real reasons of its resolution would be mistaken, were they not seen solely in the desire repeatedly manifested by it, of avoiding, considering the diversity of sentiments, a rupture with the deputation of the Empire for effecting a peace. The Imperial commission consequently now communicates to the ministers plenipotentiary of the French republic, the conclusum of the deputation of the Empire by the two notes, copies of which are here subjoined. The undersigned presents to the gentlemen of the deputation assurances of friendly respect.

(Signed) FRANCIS GEORGE CHARLES, COUNT DE METTERNICH WINNEBURGH BEILSTEIN.

Substance of a Note transmitted by the French Ministers to Chateauneuf Randon.

WE invite the General Chateauneuf Randon to forward the enclosed to the minister for foreign affairs by the military telegraph.

" The ultimatum remitted on the 6th of December by the French legation, was accepted on the 9th by the deputation of the Empire. The conclusum to which the Imperial commissary adhered, has been officially transmitted to the French ministers."

Rastadt, Dec. 21.

Note from the French Ministers to the Deputation of the Empire.

THE undersigned ministers plenipotentiary of the French republic do make this formal declaration to the deputation of the Empire, that if the Diet of Ratisbon should consent to the entry of the Russian troops on the territory of the Empire, or if even it does not effectually oppose it, the march of the Russian army through the German territory will be regarded as a violation of neutrality on the part of the Empire; that the negotiation at Rastadt will be broken off; and that the republic and the Empire will then be in the same relative situation in which these two powers were, previously to the signing of the preliminaries at Leoben, and the conclusion of the armistice.

To this declaration, dictated by the importance of the circumstances, the undersigned add with pleasure the express assurance of their government, for the tranquillity and satisfaction of the

Empire,

Empire, both of the sincere desire it has that an incident so unforeseen as that which is the object of this note, and which might become so destructive of the tranquillity of the interior of Germany, may not take place to destroy the hopes, almost realized, of a perfect reconciliation, and of a perpetual peace between the two nations.

No one can be deceived as to the motives and the aim of the cabinet of Petersburgh: the deputation of the Empire particularly is too well acquainted with the affairs of Europe, not to perceive clearly that Russia, after having promoted the war six years, without taking a part in it, now takes such open measures of aggression against France, for the purpose of interrupting the pacification of the continent, and with a view, not less evident, of covering the grand usurpation she has so long meditated.

The undersigned, therefore, do not doubt that the deputation will see, in this proceeding, on the part of the French government, a further proof of its pacific sentiments, and an opportunity for the Empire, in avoiding a personal danger, to acquire additional claims to the friendship of the republic.

(Signed) BONNIER.
Rastadt, 12th Nivose (2d January) JEAN DEBRY.
of the French Republic. ROBERJOT.

Note of Count Metternich to the Ministers Plenipotentiary of the French Republic.

THE undersigned, together with the deputation for the peace of the Empire, has received the note of the French ministers, dated the 2d January, relative to the supposed march of a body of Russian troops upon the territory of the German Empire. At the earnest entreaty of the deputation of the Empire, he immediately transmitted an account of it to his Imperial Majesty. The deputation of the Empire also did not fail to communicate the note without delay to the Diet at Ratisbon, of which it has the honour to inform the ministers plenipotentiary of the French republic, renewing at the same time the assurances of its distinguished consideration.

Rastadt, January 4.

Substance of the French Note delivered to the Minister of his Imperial Majesty, as King of Hungary and Bohemia, by the French Plenipotentiaries, on the 13th January.

IT states, " that in leaving a free passage to an army of a power which has declared war against France, and in permitting
it

it to traverse his states for the purpose of reaching the French troops, the Emperor reduces the republic to the necessity of regarding this act as a rupture of the ties which unite the two states, and that, in consequence, the Emperor is required to give on this a precise and satisfactory explanation."

Resolutions adopted at the Diet of Ratisbon, on the 8th of January, in Answer to the French Note of the 2d, communicated to the French Legation the 15th.

1. THAT the constituted legations shall demand, as soon as possible, instructions from their constituents with regard to this important point.

2. That the principal commissioner of the Emperor shall be requested to report the subject to his Imperial Majesty.

3. That this article shall be communicated to the deputation of the Empire at Rastadt, with the express remark, that no requisition has yet been made to the Empire concerning the entry of the Russian troops into the territories of the German Empire.

Substance of a Note from Count Metternich, the Imperial Minister to the Deputation of the Empire; transmitted the 17th January.

IT states, that he had observed to the French ministers that at the time they sent their ultimatum, and when it was accepted by the deputation, they had promised to engage their government to relieve the people of the right bank of the Rhine from the burdens of contributions, impositions, and the quartering of troops; that notwithstanding this, far from seeing their promises carried into effect, these countries were more burdened then ever, and the blockade of Ehrenbreitstein still more severely pressed. He added, that it would be to the interest of the French government to inspire confidence in its engagements, by its exactness in fulfilling existing treaties and promises. That the French ministers replied, that they had informed the Directory, sending to them the note of the deputation of the Empire, both of their promises and their observations, and had entreated that they might have the wished-for success: that in doing so they had fulfilled their engagements, and could do no more. The Imperial minister concludes by engaging the deputation of the Empire to take into consideration the measures that it shall deem proper to attain the object of its solicitude.

Memorial

Memorial transmitted to the Deputation of the Empire, relative to the Contributions imposed by French Agents in the Circle of Westphalia.

THE annexed letter of the French commissioners Haynier and Gauthier, of the 16th Frimaire (6th December), by which the part of the Dutchy of Westphalia which is occupied has been subjected anew to a contribution of 150,000 francs, ready money, per month, and of 130 quintals of hay, 75 quintals of straw, and 59 quintals of oats, to be delivered daily into the French magazines of Lennep and Remschaid, had already been transmitted to the undersigned, in order that he might claim the intervention of the deputation for the pacification, to obtain the removal of this new oppression of war: but he then thought that he ought not to make it known to the deputation, because he expected that the tranquillizing assurances given by the French ministers relative to the charges of this unhappy war would be realized, and would themselves put an end to the new contributions and requisitions, under which the Dutchy of Westphalia, and the other occupied countries, groaned.

But the subsequent letter of the French commissaries of war to the deputy of the Dutchy of Westphalia of the 24th Nivose, contains unhappily the fatal certainty that these new contributions and requisitions are to be collected by military executions: that at this very moment they have commenced, and with the grievous assurance, that it is the will of the Executive Directory of Paris. All sincere friends of peace see with grief that, at the very time in which the French government manifest, by their ministers plenipotentiary, their pacific sentiments towards the Empire upon all occasions, their agents drain, to the last drop of blood, the countries of the Empire occupied by the French troops. None but eye-witnesses can form to themselves an idea of the oppression and exhausted state of the innocent inhabitants of the Dutchy of Westphalia, so poor since the cessation of hostilities agreed upon by the suspension of arms at Leoben.

It is time at length that this uncertainty between peace and war, ten times more oppressive than open war, should cease; and that the inhabitants of the right bank of the Rhine should participate, at least provisionally, in the benefits of that peace: the evils resulting from the delay of which cannot fall upon these innocent persons, without the most crying injustice.

The undersigned, therefore, acquits himself of the commission with which he is charged, by entreating the deputation for the pacification of the Empire instantly to take the most energetic measures, to obtain without delay the cessation of the new contributions and requisitions imposed upon the right bank of the Rhine.

(Signed)   COUNT D'ERBACH.

Rastadt, 30 Nivose (19th January).

Substance of the Emperor's Answer, relative to the March of the Russian Troops.

1. HIS Imperial Majesty is surprised that the French ministers should have addressed themselves to the deputation for the pacification of the Empire upon a subject with which it has no concern.

2. His Imperial Majesty testifies his satisfaction that the deputation has unanimously referred this affair, upon which it was not competent to decide, to those whom it concerns, and who ought to be acquainted with it.

30. His Imperial Majesty will, however, wait for the report which shall be made to him on this subject by the diet of Ratisbon.

[This answer was communicated *verbally* by Count Metternich to the directory of the deputation of the Empire, on the 21st January.]

Text of the Resolution of the Deputation of the Empire, addressed to the Imperial Minister, the 7th Pluviose (January 26th).

THE minister plenipotentiary is informed of the resolution which the three colleges of the general diet of the Empire came to, on the 21st Nivose (10th January), upon the report made to them by the deputation on the 5th of January, upon the subject of the supposed march of a Russian army upon the territory of the Empire, and the reply which the general diet has just transmitted to them. The deputation, on their side, have received, through the medium of the directorial minister, the contents of the resolution of his Imperial Majesty, of the 21st of January (2 Pluviose), sent to his Imperial minister. They think it conformable to the present state of things, and the progress of affairs, to communicate it to the ministers plenipotentiary of the French republic. The deputation, in consequence, think, that a note couched in these terms should be sent to them:

"The minister plenipotentiary of his Imperial Majesty has received the resolution taken by his Majesty, in conformity with the demand of the deputation of the Empire upon the subject of the eventual march of the Russian army upon the territory of the Empire, and containing the declaration that the deputation is not competent to take cognisance of the object of the French note, which relates to that army; and that it regards only the Empire assembled under the authority of its chief, from which they must wait for ulterior resolutions.

"The general diet of the Empire has demanded upon this subject instructions from its constituents, and makes known to the deputation, that it has not yet received either official advice, of the Rhine than open war. We may, then, flatter ourselves, with confidence, with the confolatory hope, that his Imperial Majefty, and the general diet of the Empire, will take this into deep confideration; his Electoral Highnefs of Mentz being determined to fulfil faithfully to the diet of the Empire all that his duty as arch-chancellor of the Empire impofes upon him in fo critical a fituation.

Conclufum.

That the notes of the 4th and 27th ult. as well as the new French note of the 12th Pluviofe, be fent to the general diet of the Empire; that they be made known to the Imperial plenipotentiary; and that this laft note be communicated according to cuftom to the particular deputies.

Note and Proclamations delivered by the French Minifters to the Deputation of the Empire.

Note of the French Legation to the Deputation of the Empire.

THE underfigned minifters plenipotentiary of the French republic for the negotiation with the Germanic Empire, have received orders from the Executive Directory to tranfmit to the deputation of the Empire the proclamation fubjoined. They acquit themfelves of this commiffion, by annexing to the prefent note a copy, certified by them, of this proclamation; as alfo a copy of the addrefs of General Jourdan to the army he commands.

The underfigned are charged at the fame time to declare, that the march of the army is only to be confidered as a meafure of precaution impofed by circumftances; that the defire for peace on the part of the French government is ftill ardent and fincere; and that it will proceed to conclude it with the Empire, provided the Empire fhall declare againft the march of the Ruffians.

Raftadt, 11 *Ventofe (March* 1), 7*th Year of the French Republic.*

BONNIER.
JEAN DEBRY.
ROBERJOT.

LIBERTY—EQUALITY.

THE troops of his Majefty the Emperor, King of Bohemia and Hungary, in contempt of a convention concluded at Raftadt, on the 11th of Frimaire of the 6th year (December 1, 1797), have paffed the Inn, and advanced beyond the boundaries of the hereditary countries. This movement is connected with the march of the Ruffian troops now in the ftates of the Emperor, who openly declare that they come to attack and combat but the French republic. Ever faithful to the obligations it has imposed on itself; ever animated with the desire of maintaining a state of peace; and ever disposed to ascribe to his Majesty the Emperor the same sentiments, the French government has demanded a satisfactory declaration relative to this march of the Russian troops, and the passage which has been granted them. The Emperor has been silent. The Executive Directory, therefore, sees itself compelled by the necessity of self defence, and the obligation which every state is under to provide for its security, to order the French armies to take such positions as circumstances require; but it declares, at the same time, that its desire for peace is unchanged; and that the moment his Majesty the Emperor shall make known, by an amicable declaration, that the Russians have evacuated his states, and that his troops have resumed the positions determined on in the convention concluded at Rastadt, the French armies shall return to the positions they have hitherto occupied.

Approved by the Executive Directory,
2d *of Ventose,* 7th *year.*
(Signed) L. M. REVELLIERE LEPAUX, President.
LAGARDE, Secretary-general.

LIBERTY—EQUALITY.

Head-quarters of the Army of Mayennce, the — Ventose, 7th *Year of the French Republic, one and indivisible.*

The Commander in Chief to the Army.

SOLDIERS! In contempt of a solemn convention, the troops of Austria have passed the first, the stipulated line of demarcation, the Emperor, deceiving the pacific dispositions of the French government, has called into the bosom of Germany armed strangers, less known by their military success than their ravages in former wars; and while, scrupulous observers of the faith of treaties, you remained behind your lines, in a firm but peaceable attitude, this prince dared to concert hostile movements with his new allies, and avail himself, under favour of a perfidious silence, of the advantages which your security gave him. This manifest infraction, this outrage on public faith, respected by all civilized nations, has at length compelled the Executive Directory to make reprisals. It has done every thing for peace; but if war is wished, it will make it. Soldiers, let us come out of our lines, and recommence that career we have hitherto pursued with so much glory. We will fight, if we meet with opposition to our assuming the military positions towards which the army advances; we will fight, if the Emperor

peror does not promptly and strictly execute the existing conrention; but, faithful to the principles of moderation which have hitherto characterized the French nation, we will retreat and enter our former lines as soon as the republic shall have received the satisfaction which it has a right to expect. Soldiers, in resuming your arms, recollect that the scourge of war ought only to fall on the enemies of the republic. Your glory will be effaced, your laurels withered, the wishes of your enemies fulfilled, if you are guilty of blameable excesses. You know that your enemies have employed all their arts to arm the nations of Europe against the French people. Let your conduct give the lie to all their perfidious accusations. Remember constantly, that the army must respect general and individual property, and that every disorder will be restrained by force, and punished with severity. It is you especially, superior officers, chiefs of corps, commanders, whom I shall render personally responsible for the strict execution of my intentions, and those of the government. Maintain the most exact discipline, provide for the wants of the troops under your command, watch over them incessantly; tell them that every mean action is unworthy of the French name; remind them that it would stain the glory of the armies of the republic; and no doubt they will return to good order. Animated with the principles of justice and equity, the Executive Directory has ordered me to inform you, that its firm intention is to reimburse the people and governments friendly to the republic for whatever they may furnish to supply the unforeseen necessities of the army. It is requisite, therefore, that there shall be delivered with the most scrupulous punctuality, *bons* (or certificates) of whatever shall be required or furnished for the army; and to prevent impositions, I hereby give notice, that the commissary general, authorized by me, shall alone be empowered to levy requisitions of every kind, though the generals and commanders of detached troops may levy requisitions on occasions of urgence; but in every case a copy shall be transmitted to me, and every imposition punished with the utmost severity; though I trust, soldiers, you will spare this pain to your general. In consequence of these just regulations, worthy of the French nation, the inhabitants of Germany, encouraged to disregard the reports propagated by the malevolence of our enemies, will, I hope, remain calm in the midst of the storm, and be convinced, that the best means they can take to preserve their property will be to remain peaceably in their habitations. But if, on the contrary, notwithstanding what I have engaged, the French army shall find the towns deserted, and villages abandoned; if their inhabitants shall oppose its march, or refuse to procure it the succours in their power, then I declare with the same frankness, that I will take

other

other measures to punish them, and make them repent their temerity.

(Signed)   JOURDAN, General in Chief.
(A true copy.)
(Signed)   ERNOUF, General of Division,
Chief of the Staff.

12th Ventose (March 2).

THIS day the deputation of the Empire having met for the purpose of deliberating on the note delivered on the preceding day by the French ministers, agreed to the following conclusion:

"That the note of the French plenipotentiaries should be immediately sent to the general diet of the Empire, with the documents annexed to it; that it would at the same time be remarked by the diet, that the majority of the deputation was convinced, in consequence of that note, that the general diet must be persuaded how urgent it was to put it in the power of the deputation to give an answer to the note of the French legation of the 2d of January, for the purpose of resuming the negotiations already too long suspended; that the present deliberation should be transmitted, according to custom, to his Imperial Majesty's commissioners; that he should be requested to communicate to the French ministers the decision of the deputation, and to express to them the lively sentiments with which it is animated to concur with all its powers in procuring a speedy and lasting peace; and that finally the French note, and the documents annexed to it, should be communicated to all the respective deputies who are at Rastadt."

Note, with Proclamation annexed, presented by the French Ministers this Day, to the Deputation of the Empire.

Rastadt, March 9.

THE undersigned plenipotentiaries of the French republic have received orders from the Directory to communicate to the deputation of the Empire the annexed proclamation of General Massena, commander in chief in Helvetia: they have likewise received orders to repeat the explanation given in their note of the 1st, that the movements of the French army are to be considered as a measure which circumstances have dictated, and which will form no interruption of the earnest and sincere desire of peace, by which the French government is animated: they are formally empowered to repeat the assurance,

ance, that the Directory persevere in their desire to conclude a peace with the Empire, still under the condition, however that the Empire shall declare against the march of the Austrian troops.

(Signed)   BONNIER.
JEAN DEBRY.
ROBERJOT.

Massena, Commander in Chief of the French Army in Helvetia to the Grisons.

People of the Grisons,

THE enemies of your independence have called in a foreign power to support their tyranny; the friends of your liberty claim, in their turn, the assistance of the French republic. The army which I have the honour to command, is coming to second your wishes: their sole design is to restore you again to yourselves: the moment the court of Vienna shall respect your independence, and declare that it will send no more troops into your country, the French army shall evacuate your territory. During their stay, individual liberty, property, political and religious opinions, shall be inviolably respected. And you French soldiers, who are summoned to restore liberty to the people of the Grisons, you know the intentions of your government and those of your general: respect a people that will be freed by you, and let your conduct teach and convince them that a rigid discipline, and the respect of the rights and property of nations, are the peculiar characteristics of the French armies.

(Signed)   MASSENA.

Note of the French Minister to the Deputation of the Empire, relative to Citizen Bacher.

Rastadt, March 14.

THE undersigned ministers plenipotentiary of the French republic have received information of the following fact:

M. Von Hugel, the Austrian commissary at the diet of Ratisbon, on the 20th of Ventose (10th of March) repaired to Citizen Bacher, chargé d'affaires from the French republic to the diet, and communicated to him an order from the Archduke Charles, general in chief of the army of the King of Hungary and Bohemia, importing that an Austrian officer was ready to escort the said chargé d'affaires to the French advanced posts; to which Citizen Bacher answered, that his stay at Ratisbon

(73)

████ of
██ received ██   █ █ █
████ unless compelled. Notwi   ██
███, only twenty-four hours were a   d hi to
his journey. The undersign   e to the depu
the Empire this violation of every p: of right,
they must immediately send notice to their   ernment.
   The ministers plenipotentiary of ██   h republic assure
the minister plenipotentiary of his Ma██y the Emperor of their
high consideration.
                    (Signed)   BONNIER,
████, 24 Ventose (March 14), 7th Year   JEAN DEBRY.
    of the French Republic.   ROBERJOT.

██blished by Austria, in the College of Princes, 17th March, and transmitted to the Legation.

THE legation has received orders to make the following de████tion in the name of his Majesty the Emperor, relative to ██ject in deliberation.

██ is with reason we express our surprise that a foreign power, ██ which the Empire has not yet concluded peace, and at a ██ too, when the issue of the negotiations remains uncertain, ██ war seems on the point of being renewed, should, in a tone ██ very unbecoming, make demands relative to the measures of ██cy which may be necessary in the Empire; demands which, ██ must be evident, circumstances will not admit of answering, ██ which are far from being consistent with the dignity of an independent state.

Without referring to the considerations which present themselves under this point of view, we will only remark, that during fifteen months that the negotiations have lasted, the deputation of the Empire, for the attainment of a just, solid, and general peace, has in every instance made the greatest condescensions, and has consented to the greatest sacrifices; that notwithstanding these sacrifices in territory as well as in subjects, France has not till now given any satisfactory assurances relative to the important and justly-founded conditions by which the fairest provinces of the Empire are to be ceded to her; but, far from it, without any regard to the suspension of hostilities solemnly agreed ██, the provinces of the Empire, as well on the right as on ██ bank of the Rhine, are treated in an hostile manner, by ██butions and vexations of all kinds; and finally, the fortress ██renbreitstein, although its provisioning was stipulated by ██ most formal agreements, has been so closely invested and

VOL. VIII.   L   blocked

blocked up, that it has been forced by famine to surrender, and has been arbitrarily taken possession of by the French. Such conduct, which so little flatters the hopes of a peace consistent with the safety of the Empire, necessarily inspires well-founded apprehensions for the maintenance of the tranquillity of the Empire; and the more so, as, on the other hand, France, during the course of the negotiations, has overturned the government of Rome, of Switzerland, and Piedmont, and is proceeding, by arbitrary acts, to destroy the integrity of the members of the Empire, and the rights of supremacy and sovereignty of the Emperor and the Empire: that furthermore, by a levy of two hundred thousand men in its own country, by alliances offensive and defensive, obtained by force in the new *soi-disant* free states it has created, and by the forced levy of troops in Switzerland, and the other provinces occupied by its armies, it has so augmented its forces, that the measures of the French government cannot but be obviously hostile to the pacific intentions and general wishes of the states of the Empire. In this situation of affairs it is left to the world to judge whether circumstances, and the present prospects of peace, afford the least hope of such a one as is compatible with the true interests of the Germanic body; and whether it is prudent to defer measures of precaution, or to refuse the assistance of a powerful court, which manifests a real regard for the interest of the Germanic Empire, and of which, in circumstances less dangerous, five circles of the Empire and other states have demanded aid? Finally, whether it is prudent to renounce the hope of a powerful protection for the defence of the frontiers of Germany, and the preservation of the Empire?

Further, in case his Imperial Majesty shall deem it necessary to add any thing upon the subject in deliberation, he formally reserves the right of an ulterior declaration.

The majority in the College des Villes leaves every thing to the wisdom of his Imperial Majesty.

Verbal Declaration of the Motives which induced the Imperial Committee to refuse its Sanction to the Conclusum of the Deputation of the Empire of the 2d of March, made to the Directory by the Deputation, in consequence of its repeated Request.

WHEN the majority of the deputation of the Empire conceived it had grounds for earnestly recommending to the general diet of the Empire the object of the note of the French ministers plenipotentiary of the 1st of March (11th Ventose), and of expressing the sentiments of the Empire relative to an affair of the utmost importance; when it required of the general diet an answer

⁂ the former note of the French plenipotentiaries of the January (13th Nivose), to the effect that the negotiations ⁂ce, so long suspended, might take their course, and that ⁂ it would know whether the wish of the French government expressed in this note, would be acceded to; the deputa⁂y so doing, exceeded the limits of that relation in which ⁂enipotentiary stood with respect to him who invested ⁂ith his power. Thus the deputies of the state at congress desirous of exercising a right which can alone emanate ⁂ participation in the deliberations and decisions of the su⁂ power, and which can only be exercised in the assembly ⁂ general diet, where the views, the reasons, the situation, ⁂ judgment of each state concur and influence every mea⁂oper to be adopted, in the same proportion as the other ⁂rs who vote with it.

⁂vever, as this is only a question of the internal relation of ⁂utation with respect to the Empire, the Imperial com- ⁂ would have willingly passed it over in silence; but the ⁂ty of the deputation have further resolved to inform the ⁂ plenipotentiaries of this pressing recommendation, and at ⁂ne time to declare, that it has ever been desirous of con⁂g a speedy and lasting peace. The French government, ⁂above-mentioned declaration of the 2d of January (13th ⁂), as well as in its later ones of the 1st and 9th of March ⁂and 19th Ventose), have attached the conclusion of peace, ⁂ speak with more propriety, the continuation of the nego⁂s of peace, to a condition of the highest importance, upon ⁂ the Emperor and the Empire have as yet come to no de⁂; and on which it is possible their opinion may be different ⁂hat of the majority of the deputation. The moment such ⁂ility exists, it is contrary to that subordinate relation in ⁂ a plenipotentiary stands with respect to him from whom ⁂ives his power: it is also contrary to that degree of pru⁂ which ought to be observed in every negotiation; it can ⁂ case be productive of any real advantages; and it may be ⁂icial to offer recommendations and premature overtures to ⁂ a foreign power, particularly one which has proved by a ⁂ most unexpected towards its own plenipotentiaries at ⁂t, in what light it considers such recommendations and ⁂ces, which have not the sanction of the supreme authority. ⁂en it is also considered that the declarations which the ⁂ity of the deputation of the Empire have made to the French ⁂otentiaries, at a period when, by the marching of the ⁂ troops through the territory of the Empire on the banks ⁂ Rhine, by the capture and occupation of the fortresses and ⁂ on the right bank, by exactions and oppressions of all ⁂, and, finally, by the violent subversion of all those rela-

tions

tions eftablifhed by the armiftice, and which fhould have formed the bafis for the negotiations for peace, the Emperor and the Empire find themfelves reduced to the neceffity of holding a different language, and taking more ferious meafures, which we cannot here anticipate, even in the moft diftant manner.

All thefe confiderations fo evidently point out why a prudent circumfpection fhould be obferved in the anfwer to be made to the French plenipotentiaries, that it is unneceffary to enlarge further upon them. Thefe motives are at the fame time of fuch a nature, that the Imperial committee expects to be informed of the reafons which actuated the majority of the deputation in the firft inftance. It was therefore out of regard to the majority, and in the confidence that it would be convinced of the propriety of the refufal of the Imperial committee to give its fanction, that the latter avoided the painful tafk of publifhing its motives in the decree of the committee of the 14th of this month.

Vienna, March 27.

Raftadt, 22d Germinal (April 11).

Note of the French Plenipotentiaries to Count Metternich, returned fame Day by him to them.

THE underfigned have received the note addreffed to them on the 19th of the prefent month, by the minifter plenipotentiary of his Majefty the Emperor. If the object of that note was fuch as to excite their furprife, they have been ftill more aftonifhed at the motives which are expreffed in it, and which are all fupported by affertions deftitute of any foundation. Multiplied acts atteft the ardour and fincerity of the wifhes, the efforts, and the facrifices made by the Directory for a prompt and folid peace. The armiftice and negotiation ftill fubfifting between the Germanic Empire and the French republic belies every contrary affertion; and as to what is hinted at in the faid note refpecting the fecurity of correfpondence, and of the place where the congrefs is held, the underfigned are perfuaded that an infinuation of that kind cannot be directed againft their government. Such violations of the law of nations are unexampled upon its part; nor is it capable of committing them.

The underfigned affure the minifter plenipotentiary of his Majefty the Emperor of their moft diftinguifhed confideration.

(Signed)   BONNIER.
                               JEAN DEBRY.
Raftadt, 20th Germinal   ROBERJOT.
    (9th April).

Note of the French Ministers, declaring their Determination to leave Rastadt.

THE undersigned ministers plenipotentiary of the French republic, for negotiating a peace with the German Empire, having been officially informed by the Baron d'Albini, the directorial minister, of the result of the sitting held the day before yesterday by the deputation of the Empire, of which a certified copy has been transmitted to them, cannot but see with great regret, that arbitrary acts, equally contrary to the right of nations, and the express declaration of the letter of his Majesty the Emperor, of the date of the 13th of Brumaire, 6th year, together with the mournful prospect of the continuance of these vexatious proceedings, have compelled the deputation to suspend for the present the negotiations for peace.

The undersigned could the less expect such a conduct, as a totally different example had been given by the general of the French army, who, passing the Rhine on the 11th of Ventose, to resume his former position, in conformity to the orders of the French government, paid the most inviolable respect to the place where the congress was held, the freedom of its deliberation, the safety and inviolability of its members, and deprived calumny of every pretext.

The undersigned have seen with the greatest astonishment the deputation reduced to less than two thirds of its members, by several of the states having recalled their envoys, so that it was impossible it should come to any resolutions agreeable to the terms of its instructions. They had supposed, that though the states of the Empire had the undoubted right of changing their sub-delegates at the congress, it only appertained to the Diet, considered as a body, to withdraw the powers of the states themselves.

In this situation of things and persons, the undersigned, to whom the Executive Directory, ever disposed to peace, has recommended not to leave the place of congress till the last extremity, eager to seize the hope offered them by the deputation of resuming the course of the negotiations, since they are only momentarily suspended; persuaded that the excesses which have impeded them, will serve to convince the states of the Empire of the lively interest they have taken to remove the scourge of war, and in general, all the obstacles which violence or ill faith may oppose to the peace; considering besides,

1. That the deputation has formally declared in its conclusum, and made it the principal motive of its resolution to quit Rastadt, that there was no longer either tranquillity or safety for the congress, whence it results that it was in an actual state of oppression:

2. That the existence of a congress between two free states
ought

ought to depend upon the will of the contracting parties, and can never be subordinate to the intervention of any foreign force:

They therefore remit to the deputation of the Empire the following protestation and declaration:

The undersigned protest, 1st, Against the violation of the rights of nations committed, with respect to them, by the Austrian troops, and of which the object is positively announced in their note of the 30th Germinal.

2dly, Against the answer which the commander of the Austrian troops stationed at Gernsbach has returned to the directorial letter of the 1st of Floreal; an answer which the deputation, by making it the ground of its deliberation the day before yesterday, has considered as the expression of the general orders of the Austrian army, and which is conceived in these terms:

" To his Excellency the Baron d'Albini, intimate Counsellor of his Imperial Majesty, and Electoral Minister of Mentz, Rastadt.

" I regret much to be under the necessity, in conformity to my duty, of stating, in answer to your letter remitted to me by Counsellor Baron Munich, that in the present circumstances of the war, in which the safety as well of the military as of the country requires that patroles should be placed at Rastadt and in the environs, it is impossible to make any satisfactory declaration relative to the maintenance of the diplomatic body now there: since the recall of his Excellency the Imperial plenipotentiary, we can no longer, on our part, consider Rastadt as a place which the presence of a congress protects against hostile events; and that city, after this, must feel the necessity of conforming to the laws of war like any other place.

" I entreat your Excellency, however, to be assured, that except in the case of necessity imposed by the events of war, our military will consider personal inviolability as sacred; and that, on my part, I will continually, to my utmost, testify to you the profound respect with which I am your Excellency's most humble servant, (Signed) BARBACSY, Colonel."

They call, in the name of the French republic, insulted in its rights, the serious attention of the Diet to an act, equally contrary to its own independence, and subversive of all the principles hitherto practised among civilized nations. They expect a just and full redress.

In fine, in consequence of what has been stated, the undersigned inform the deputation of the Empire that in three days they will quit Rastadt; but, wishing to give to Germany a last and signal proof of the forbearance of the French government, and its wish for peace, they declare that they will repair to Strasburgh, where they will wait the recommencement of the negotiations,

tiations, and attend to such propositions of peace as shall be made.

         (Signed) BONNIER.
Rastadt, 6th of Floreal (April 25),   JEAN DEBRY.
7th Year of the French Republic.   ROBERJOT.

Letter from Colonel Barbaefy to the Ministers of the French Republic.

 Ministers,

YOU see it cannot square with military plans, that citizens of the French nation should be tolerated in countries where the Imperial and Royal army may be. You will not therefore take it ill, if the circumstances of war oblige me to signify to you, ministers, to quit the territory of the army in the space of twenty-four hours.

Dated head quarters of the etat-major, at Gernsbach, 28th of April 1799, seven at night (two hours before the massacre).

Letter from Colonel Barbacfy to the Deputies at Rastadt, in Reply to their Note relative to the assassinated French Ministers.

              April 29.

I FEEL myself deeply oppressed with anxiety, caused by the account of an horrible act which was perpetrated on the persons of the ministers of the French nation by some common plunderers, who had availed themselves of the protection of the night for that purpose. Your Excellencies must be persuaded, that in a breast hardened by battle there still beats a heart which shudders at such cruelties, and is afflicted at such an unnatural revenge as that which has been perpetrated. I gave orders on the spur of the occasion, that an officer with a command should afford a safe escort as far as the Rhine, to that part of the embassy which had the good fortune to escape. It has ever been the practice of my life, to place under confinement every man under my command, who has been guilty of wanton trespasses. With respect to the safe escort of the embassy in question, the situation of the country did not permit me to restrain my troops from over-running this neighbourhood; and I am convinced that no danger would have arisen, nor would this cruel act have been committed, by any criminals blinded by a thirst for plunder, if the French embassy, who had twenty-four hours to arrange their affairs, had set out on their journey in the day-time. I beg your Excellencies

lencies will vouchsafe to believe I remain with the profoundest respect,

Your obedient servant,
VON BARBACSY, Colonel.

Letter from Jean Debry's Secretary to Citizen Noblet, relative to the Assassination of the Deputies.

Citizen Representative,   *Strasburgh, April* 30.

ON the 28th of April the law of nations was horribly violated; the French ministers were assassinated by 400 Austrian hussars, who were charged with escorting them as far as the French advanced posts. Roberjot and Bonnier are no more; the former was assassinated in the arms of his wife. The life of Jean Debry is preserved for the republic: he received forty *coups de sabre*, and is wounded in thirteen places, but not one of his wounds is mortal. We arrived almost dead at one o'clock after midnight. He made his escape while the banditti were engaged in pursuing the persons in the other carriages: it was at thirty paces from Rastadt that this horrible action was committed; those who were to have escorted them became their assassins.

Jean Debry is not in a feverish state; his little children are about to write to you. Unhappy ones! they were on the point of witnessing the assassination of their father.

(Signed)   BELIN.

YOU will not believe all we have to relate to you; we have beheld the murders; we have heard the Austrian cries of fury.— The monsters!

(Certified as a true copy.)   NOBLET.

Assassination of the French Ministers.

Report of the Ministers Plenipotentiary at Rastadt, on the Events of the 28th and 29th of April.

THE Imperial plenipotentiaries being recalled from Rastadt, and having quitted that town on the 13th of last month, the deputation of the Empire declared in its sitting of the 23d that its functions were suspended, and notified to the French legation the motives of that declaration. On the 25th, the ministers of France also declared that they would depart within three days.

In the evening of the same day, the courier of the French legation, furnished with a passport and his badge, and charged with
                                                                dispatches

dispatches to Strasburg, was arrested on the road to Seltz, between the village of Isteldorf and Rastadt by some Austrian hussars, and conducted to the head-quarters of the Imperial colonel Barbatzy, at Gernsbach, after having had his papers taken from him. On the requisition of the French legation, the directorial envoy of Mentz, in the name of all the members of the deputation, interposed his good offices, in the same manner as the Prussian legation, in order that, "according to the universal principles of the rights of nations, the courier who had been arrested should be set at liberty, along with his dispatches—and that the security of the correspondence of the French ministers should not be interrupted during the short delay of three days fixed for their departure."

The letter of the minister of Mentz was sent on the same night to Gernsbach, by a courier, who returned with a short reply from Col. Barbatzy, stating, that "he had rendered an account to his superiors of the arrestation of the French courier—and that he could not yield to the views of the French deputation; until he received farther orders." The letter of the Prussian legation was sent on the 25th, at five in the morning, by the Count Bernstorff, counsellor of the legation, with an injunction to support the contents of it verbally. The French legation having also addressed themselves to Baron d'Edelsheim, minister of state to the Margrave of Baden, to claim the protection of the Margrave, that minister judged it proper to accompany Count Bernstorff, and to make every representation suitable to the circumstances of the case to Col. Barbatzy. The verbal answer of the Colonel was, that " he would transmit these representations to his superiors, along with the letter of the Prussian legation, and that he would communicate the result as soon as possible; but that until then he could not, in any manner, farther explain himself." The account of the mission, written by the Count de Bernstorff, proves that this refusal to explain himself was positive.

Meanwhile the French ministers resolved to depart for Seltz, on the third day, the 28th, at eight in the morning. Every preparation was made, and the carriages, loaded with their baggage, were already in the court of the castle. But looking at circumstances—considering that patroles of hussars were constantly passing on the road from Rastadt to Seltz; that they had already, on the 19th, arrested several German ministers, and among others the minister of Wurzburg, from whom they had taken and detained his papers—considering, besides, that the declarations of Col. Barbatzy, both on this affair, and on the arrest of the French courier, were no way encouraging for the journey of the French legation, it was impossible to be without some uneasiness on that subject—for it appeared at least possible that the ministers might be arrested out of contempt; a transaction from which great inconvenience

VOL. VIII. M venience

venience might result. For these reasons, all the diplomatic persons, who still communicated with the French ministers, advised them to defer their journey for some hours, or to the next day; the reply of Col. Barbatzy to the representations of the ministers of Prussia, Mentz, and Baden, being expected every moment.

The French ministers yielded to this advice, particularly on the observation, that it was proper to wait the result of the steps taken by the other ministers, for whom the French legation testified much gratitude. As at eleven in the morning no answer had arrived, the minister of Mentz, Baron d'Albini, wrote again to Col. Barbatzy, and required from him a categorical reply to this question, " Whether the French ministers, who were ready to depart, and who were furnished with passports from Baron d'Albini, were likely to meet with any interruption?" It was hoped that the officer of the Margrave of Baden, who was dispatched with this letter, would return about three or four o'clock in the afternoon with a reply: but these expectations were disappointed.

In the evening, between seven and eight o'clock, an officer of hussars arrived with some soldiers. The officer proceeded immediately to the ministers of France and Mentz in the castle, and according to the testimony of the undersigned ministers, the Counts de Goertz, de Dohm, and de Solms, who were present, he begged them to excuse Col. Barbatzy, who was too busy to reply in writing, but he declared in his name, that the French ministers might travel in perfect safety, and that for that effect the term of twenty-four hours was fixed for them. As to the Prussian legation, they received no letter from Col. Barbatzy, either written or verbal.

The Imperial officer delivered a letter to the French ministers. —M. de Dohm is the only other minister who saw it, and that was by accident*.—He guarantees its contents to be as follows:

" Ministers—You will easily conceive that no French citizen can be tolerated within the chain of posts occupied by the Imperial troops; you will therefore excuse me if I find myself obliged to signify to you, that you must quit Rastadt in the space of twenty-four hours.

" *Gernsbach, April* 28. BARBATZY."

---

* It happened that M. de Dohm, who, with the other diplomatic persons, was eager to know the object of the Imperial officer's mission, and the arrival of the troops, passed before the chamber of the secretary of legation, Rosenueil, as he came out of that of Jean Debry, where the three French ministers had assembled. Citizen Rosensteil had then the letter alluded to in his hand, which, of his own accord, he gave to M. de Dohm to read; and while the secretary wrote a receipt, which was required by the Imperial officer, he (M. de Dohm) had time to read the letter twice over with attention.

The French ministers resolved to depart immediately, and would not be dissuaded by the observation, that they could not arrive at the Rhine before night, and that the passage of that river might then be dangerous. They set out on the 28th, within half an hour after they received the above letter, in four carriages, chiefly drawn by horses belonging to the Margrave. With the officer who brought the letter, there arrived fifty of the hussars of Szeklers, who were posted at the gate of Etlingen, and had caused the other gates to be occupied in the same manner. It was soon known that an order was given to allow no person belonging to the congress to enter or to leave the town, and that the captain of the hussars had signified to Major Harrant, commander of the troops of Baden, that he required that his soldiers should remain at the gates to point out to the Austrians the persons belonging to the congress, whose passage in or out of the town was prohibited. Notwithstanding this restriction of the prohibition to the members of the congress, no person whatever was permitted to pass even the bridge of communication between the town and the suburbs. The commandant of the town himself could not obtain leave to go without the gates, though he demanded it very pressingly when he was informed of subsequent events. The Danish minister had fixed his departure for the same day, and only waited the result of the steps taken by the deputation relative to the French ministers. After having learnt the reply of Colonel Barbatzy, he went home to make preparations for his journey; but on being informed, as he passed near the gate, that no person was permitted to go out of the town, he crossed the garden of the castle towards the causeway, where the captain of the hussars was posted with his troop, and asked if he might depart that evening.

The officer replied, that he was ordered to allow no person to pass: but when he was informed that the French ministers were summoned to depart, and that they were at that moment leaving the town by the gate of Rheinau, the captain replied that he had no orders to prevent the departure of the French legation. The minister of his Danish Majesty afterwards asked if he would give them an escort. He said he had no orders to do that; and when it was strongly represented to him how much the honour of the German nation required that every means should be taken to prevent any disorder from happening on the departure of the ministers, the captain replied, that he had nothing to do but to provide for his own security; adding also this remark, that the Imperial plenipotentiaries had gone away a sufficient time ago to have allowed all the other German envoys to have departed also.

When the members of the French legation presented themselves at the gate of the town, they were informed that they could

could not be allowed to pafs.—The three minifters immediately alighted, and leaving their carriages, with their families and fuite, proceeded to the minifter of Mentz in the caftle. No one could reconcile this contradiction: the order to leave the town within twenty-four hours, and the obftacle oppofed to the departure of the minifters at the gates of the town. The envoy of his Danifh Majefty, who had, after this new incident, repaired, with feveral others, to the minifter of Mentz, gave an explanation, founded on his converfation with the captain of huffars, and this explanation was foon after officially confirmed by M. de Munich, fecretary of legation, who had been fent to that officer by M. d'Albini. He ftated, that when the Imperial officer took poffeffion of the gates of the town, and ordered that no perfon fhould be permitted to pafs, he had forgotten to except the French minifters from that order. But M. de Munich added, that this neglect was now repaired, and that the minifters might depart without interruption. The French legation thought that it would be neceffary to demand a military efcort, in order that they might not be ftopped by the patroles which they would probably meet on their road as far as Plittefdorf. The fecretary of the legation of Mentz charged himfelf with requefting this efcort from the captain, and the French envoys proceeded in a carriage of the Margrave's to join the others at the gate. They were obliged to wait there a long time for the anfwer, which was at laft brought by M. de Harrant, a major in the fervice of the Margrave of Baden, and ftated, that " the captain could not give an efcort, becaufe he had no orders to that effect; but that the French minifters would find no interruption in their route." On Major Harrant's afking if it was to be underftood by this anfwer that the French minifters might pafs to the other fide of the Rhine in fafety, and if he might give them that affurance; the captain anfwered, Yes. After fome deliberation, the French envoys then preferred departing immediately, without an efcort, to returning to the caftle and waiting there until next morning—a ftep to which feveral perfons advifed them, and which the women were anxious they fhould take. At laft, between nine and ten o'clock, the French minifters left the town. The night was very dark, and torches were carried before the carriages.

A quarter of an hour had fcarcely paffed when the news arrived from different quarters that the French legation had been arrefted by the violence of fome Auftrian huffars, who had ftruck the coachmen and the bearers of the flambeaus with their fabres. The greater part of the members of the diplomatic corps were at this time affembled in Caffino. The Ligurian envoy, Boccardi, and his brother, who had efcaped, brought the firft intelligence of the affair. It was inftantly determined that the different minifters fhould repair to the

the captain to demand an explanation, and, above all, the moſt ſpeedy ſuccours. In a few minutes after the report arrived that *one*, that *two*, that all the *three* French miniſters were aſſaſſinated by the Emperor's ſoldiers. To reaſon, ſuch a crime appeared improbable, and the heart could not believe it poſſible. It was the univerſal opinion that it was falſe. The deſire, however, of terminating as ſoon as poſſible an unfortunate miſunderſtanding, cauſed the deputies to haſten towards the commanding officer, whoſe quarters were about twenty paces diſtant from the gate of Etiingen, at the inn called The Lantern.—The guards at the gate would not allow them to paſs, although they declared themſelves to be the envoys of the regal and princely courts. It was not without the greateſt trouble that an inferior officer was prevailed upon to announce their arrival. They were again aſked what envoys they were? and it was declared to them with a troubleſome exactneſs, that only *three*, *four*, or *ſix* miniſters could be permitted to go to the captain. At laſt that officer appeared. Count de Goertz, the underſigned envoy of his Pruſſian Majeſty, in the name of all the other deputies, made a ſhort ſtatement to the captain, requeſting to know what meaſures he had taken in conſequence of the melancholy intelligence which had doubtleſs reached him. He replied, that in conſequence of the application of the miniſter of Mentz, who had already called upon him, he had diſpatched an officer with two huſſars. We thought that this was not ſufficient; and we entreated him, in the name of all the ſentiments of humanity—in the name of the welfare of Europe, and of the German nation, about to be ſtained by a crime unparalleled in the annals of civilized countries—in the name of his auguſt ſovereign—in the name of his Imperial Majeſty's ſervice—in the name of his own individual honour and of his life, to take as quickly as poſſible every meaſure in his power to ſave whoever could be ſaved. The captain replied, that the affair was an unfortunate miſtake; that doubtleſs the patroles roamed about the environs during the night; that ſuch a misfortune might eaſily happen, and that the French miniſters ſhould not have departed at night. He was reminded that he had refuſed an eſcort, and that he had ſaid to Major Harrant, that there was nothing to fear for the French legation. He replied, that he had no orders to give an eſcort, and that it ſhould have been aſked of the commandant. Count Bernſtorff, counſellor of the Pruſſian legation, ſaid, that he himſelf aſked the colonel, when he was ſent to him for an eſcort. " Did he grant it to you?" was the captain's reply. The underſigned envoy of Denmark having afterwards reminded him of the converſation which he had with him, as ſtated above, " Would you (ſaid he) eſtabliſh an inquiſition upon me?" Finally, paſſing from all conſiderations which we ought to have felt, after the treatment we were obliged to endure, we preſſed,

prayed,

prayed, supplicated him not to lose a moment in endeavouring yet to save the lives of some men, and to rescue the honour of his service. He asked us where the carriages of the ministers were, and required other explanations from us, whom his orders retained prisoners in the town—from us, who came to him to obtain information, and to learn what measures he had taken to prevent, if possible, a crime which so nearly concerned his own honour and that of his sovereign. At last we procured from him the promise of detaching an officer and six hussars to accompany Major Harrant, and two hussars of Baden, on the great road of Plittesdorf.—Meanwhile there arrived several fugitives from the field of carnage, who confirmed the report that the French ministers had been assassinated by the hussars of Szeklers.—The murder of Bonnier was reported by an eye-witness, viz. the flambeau-bearer. Major Harrant, of Baden, with whom there was dispatched only a marechal-des-logis, instead of an officer, as had been promised, found the carriages on the spot where the scene of horror had passed. They were surrounded by about fifty hussars of Szeklers holding flambeaus (among whom, however, he could not discover any officers), and employed in conducting around the town the carriages, and the unfortunate persons with them, who were still in a state of profound stupor. When M. de Harrant declared to the hussars that the carriages must be brought into the town, the hussars would not at first listen to him, maintaining, that they were their booty. It was not without the strongest menaces, and after M de Harrant had declared to them that, in his quality as commandant, the disposition of the carriages belonged exclusively to him, that he succeeded in making them desist from their project. M. de Harrant found the dead bodies of Roberjot and Bonnier on the ground, horribly mangled. Not finding the body of Jean Debry, he took every imaginable pains to search for it. He even proposed to search for it in the forest, and for that purpose demanded an escort of some Austrian hussars who had joined him, and the two hussars who had accompanied him; but this escort was refused him, under the pretext that other Austrian patroles might easily be met with, and that in the obscurity of the night they might run the risk of being attacked. M. de Harrant was therefore obliged to delay the execution of his design until daylight, but in the mean time he brought the carriages into the city. The wives of Jean Debry and Roberjot, the daughters of the former and the domestic, came with him: none of them were wounded, though several of them had been robbed of their money, their watches, &c. The three ministers only were attacked by the murderers. The carriages stopped before the castle. Every one hastened to approach the unfortunate persons who were in them, in order to give them assistance, but all were kept back without distinction, even the most consider-

able

able of the foreign ministers; because, no officer being present, it was found necessary to wait for orders.

At last permission was obtained to carry to the apartments of M. de Jacobi, minister of the King of Prussia, Madame Roberjot, who was extended half dead in her carriage, which stopped before the door of that minister. Madame Debry and her two daughters were obliged to descend from their carriage into the street, on the pretext that carriages were never permitted to enter the court of the castle. They were conducted to the gate of Erlangen. The horses of the court were demanded to conduct them the next day to Gernsbach; this was countermanded, however, the same day. The women were conducted on foot to their former lodgings in the castle by several members of the diplomatic corps; but they were soon after removed to the house of the undersigned minister of Brandenburg, in order that they might be more within the reach of succour. The details of the assassination of Roberjot were learnt from his valet-de-chambre, who was in the same carriage. He deposed, that " Some hussars presented themselves at the door of the coach, broke the glasses, and asked the minister if he was Roberjot? Upon which the minister answered, Yes, in French, producing at the same time the passport of the directorial envoy of Mentz; that the hussars tore this passport; that they forced the minister out of his carriage, and struck him several very violent blows; that Roberjot still giving some signs of life, and his wife having cried, Save him! save him! the hussars redoubled their blows; that Madame Roberjot then threw herself on the body of her husband; but that he (the valet-de-chambre) seized her fast in his arms, and covered her ears, to prevent her from hearing the groans of her dying husband; that he (the valet-de-chambre) had been dragged out of the carriage by a hussar, who asked him if he was a servant; and having answered in the affirmative, the hussar gave him to understand, by signs, that he had nothing to fear for himself; that, notwithstanding, his watch and his purse were taken from him; and that Madame Roberjot experienced the same usage." It was remarked, however, by several of us, that the carriage was not entirely pillaged, but that money and other valuable effects were left in it. When Madame Roberjot came out of her carriage, she fell repeatedly into fits, calling out frequently, " They have torn him away from me, before my eyes!"

The secretary of legation, Rosenstiel, who was in the last of the carriages, and consequently nearest the town, escaped through the gardens about the commencement of the affair. He was found at the house of the minister of Baden in a state of delirium. All the other persons attached to the French legation arrived in succession, either as fugitives on foot, or with the carriages. The minister Jean Debry was still missing; no proof of his death was established by eye-witnesses. It was then considered to be ab-

folutely

solutely essential that every thing should be attempted to save him. Some of us applied to the captain of the Austrian hussars, and solicited him to grant an escort to Major de Harrant; who, accompanied by some hussars of Baden, wished to go in search of Jean Debry. The undersigned, Count de Solms de Laubach, offered to accompany him, in order to call the French minister by his name, as his voice was known to Jean Debry. The captain granted him the escort, and at daybreak, about four in the morning, Count Solms, Major Harrant, and two hussars of Baden, under the escort of a corporal and four Imperial hussars, mounted on horseback to search the environs, and particularly the forests of Steinmaner and Plittesdorf. They had not the satisfaction of finding Jean Debry, but they learnt some circumstances connected with the transactions. Major Harrant having addressed himself to the baillie of Rheinau, to obtain information of the absent minister, the baillie informed him, that some Imperial hussars had already made very strict inquiries relative to a wounded Frenchman, whose discovery, they said, was of great importance to them; that they had recommended strongly, in case a Frenchman should be found resembling the person they described, to take care not to conduct him to Rastadt, but to make him pass without the town, and bring him to them at Muckenstrum by a road which they pointed out, or simply to take care of him, and give them notice of his being found.

Every thing had been hitherto done to ameliorate, as much as possible, this horrible state of things. The present business was to provide for the safety of the members of the diplomatic body and their families. The undersigned, therefore, addressed themselves to Colonel Barbatzy, by a letter (No. 5.) with which M. Jordan, secretary of the Prussian legation, was charged, and who set out at four in the morning on the 29th, accompanied by an Imperial ordonnance. At seven in the morning, Jean Debry came to the house of the Prussian minister, M. de Goertz. His appearance caused as much pleasure to those who were present as the state in which he was inspired them with interest. They were the witnesses of the first transports of his joy, and his gratitude towards Providence, when he learned that his wife and children were still alive. His clothes were torn; he was wounded in the left arm, the shoulder, and the nose. His wig and his hat had saved him from the cut of a sabre in such a manner that he only received a contusion from the blow. Every necessary succour was immediately administered to him, and we heard the affecting relation of the miraculous manner in which he had escaped. " A hussar asked him, in French, if he was Jean Debry? to which he answered in the affirmative, and produced his passport, which was instantly torn. He, his wife, and his daughters, were then dragged out of the carriage. The hussars struck him, and

threw

threw him into a ditch by the side of the highway. He had the presence of mind to counterfeit death, and to allow himself to be stript. This saved him. When the hussars went off, he rose, and ran into the forest. Not wishing to lay himself down on the ground, which was wet with rain—notwithstanding the severe wound in his left arm, he climbed a tree, where he slumbered from time to time, in consequence of lassitude and fatigue. He remained there till morning, when he proceeded towards Rastadt. On approaching the town he mingled with the multitude who had come out to see the dead bodies, and, without being observed, either by the Austrian paroles or the guards posted at the gate, he arrived safely in the town. The most distressing spectacle for him was the dead bodies of his two colleagues, by which he was obliged to pass."

The answer of the colonel had not yet arrived, but in the mean time we were extremely desirous that those of the French legation who were saved should have an opportunity of passing the Rhine. M. de Rosenkranz and Gemmingen, therefore, waited on the captain, about nine o'clock, and stated to him, that as soon as the situation of Jean Debry and the widow of Roberjot would permit them to be removed, they should proceed to the Rhine, with their effects, under the escort of the military of Baden, if the captain would answer for their safety on his honour, and give them the escort of an officer and a few hussars. After having started some difficulties, the captain granted this request, but required that it should be presented to him in writing, which was done. During this conversation, several expressions dropped from the captain, which deserve notice—" It was a misfortune, but who was to blame?—It was ordered!" M. M. Rosenkranz and Gemmingen expressed to him the horror which they thought the mere mention of such a supposition ought to excite in the mind of every man of honour. He then endeavoured to extenuate the crime, by saying—" Our generals have been killed also." The sensations which such discourse could not fail of exciting in us, since it was held by a man to whom our safety was confided, was only capable of being calmed by the answer of Colonel Barbatzy, which M. de Jordan at last brought about eleven o'clock. He had not seen the colonel himself; he sent notice to him that he came not only in the name of the Prussian legation, but of all the deputation of the Empire assembled at Rastadt: the reply he received was, " that the colonel could not speak to him, even though he were come in the name of God the Father and God the Son." M. Jordan had indeed much trouble in engaging the captain, whom he met at Rotenfels, to transmit his letter, because, said he, " the colonel has already received couriers and estafettes enough during the night." The reason why M. Jordan was detained so long, was a false report circulated at Gernsbach, of an attack being made by the French on the side of Rastadt. The letter of the colonel, however, announced a man of honour and humanity: he promised an escort for the French legation; as for us, he declared that it was useless and inconvenient that we should accompany them.

Every measure was instantly adopted for a speedy departure. The physician and the surgeon were of opinion, that the journey would be less dangerous for Jean Debry than the continuation of the alarming crisis in which he was placed. He and Madame Roberjot were equally desirous of setting out; our sentiments coincided with theirs. The captain had received orders to accompany them, but he declared that he was expressly prohibited from allowing us to accompany them; and that the German legations might retire to their own states, but not towards the Rhine. However disgusting this treatment was, our representations might have created farther delays, and we were therefore silent. Baron de Gemmingen began to stipulate for the conditions of the journey. The escort was to consist of Major de Harrant, with six hussars of Baden, and an Imperial officer with eight hussars of Szeckler. M. de Jordan, the Prussian secretary, who had become acquainted with these troops, in consequence of his mission to Gernsbach, was the only person who obtained permission to accompany the carriages; and his presence afforded much satisfaction to the persons attached to the French legation. They commenced their departure for the third time at one o'clock. Was it surprising to see these unfortunate victims covered with the paleness of death, on exposing themselves anew to the greatest dangers, or to find that it was impossible for us to convince them that they had nothing to fear? They seemed to place confidence in our assurances; but among themselves, and to those who were near them, they whispered—" We are going to death—we shall be assassinated!" Jean Debry took leave of his wife, who was big with child, and his daughters, in the most affecting manner. M. Rosenstcil recommended his family, who have long been at Strasburgh, to his brother-in-law, M. Wieland, counsellor of the legation of Weimar. Our reason blamed them; but could it be expected that they should have already forgotten what had happened? They were shocked to see among their escort the uniform of their murderers. God be praised! their terrible apprehensions were vain. The journey was made without any disagreeable accident.

The escort of Imperial hussars increased on the road to about the number of thirty men, and it was not yet known whether the French or the Austrians occupied Plittesdorf; the latter were, however, found at that place. After having travelled five

hours,

hours, the ferry-boat was hailed with a trumpet, and every person belonging to the French legation was soon embarked. It is impossible to describe the expression which appeared on all their countenances. It was the transition from the fear of a terrible death to the hope of being saved. No words can express the gratitude they testified towards Major de Harrant and M. de Jordan. Jean Debry also thanked the Imperial officer of the escort, in a few words, which M. de Harrant translated to him. He assured him, that though it was impossible for him to forget the past, he should always remember the escort that he had at last obtained, and that if ever the fortune of war should occasion any of his regiment to fall into the hands of the French, he should do his utmost to make this last action be recollected, and to repress every sentiment of vengeance. He made a present to the escort; and, on leaving Rastadt, his wife gave one hundred louis to Baron de Edelsheim, for the poor of the town. In half an hour they reached the French side of the Rhine. The horrible crime was not yet known there, and according to the report of the coachmen of the Margrave, who are returned, Jean Debry himself endeavoured to prevent it from being immediately known. M.M. Harrant and Jordan returned to Rastadt, which the German legations had left at five o'clock. Not having heard any accounts of the travellers, they had every reason to believe that they had accomplished their journey in safety.

The undersigned attest upon their honour and their duty, that all the facts above stated are most correctly true. We have been eye-witnesses of the greater part of these events, and we have verified the others with the most scrupulous attention upon the evidence of persons who were present and concerned in the transactions. We have had only in view the proving the facts in all their purity, and the placing them beyond the reach of any future misrepresentation. We have avoided, as much as possible, giving any opinion of our own, making any observations, or yielding to the impulse of sensibility.

Carlsbrue, May 1, 1799.

    The Count de Goertz.
    The Baron de Jacobi, de Dohm,
     de Rosenkranz, de Rechberg,
     de Reeden.
    The Baron de Gatzert.
    The Count de Solms Laubach.
    The Baron Otto de Gemmingen.
    The Baron de Kreuen.
    The Count de Taube.

The Minister Plenipotentiary of the French Republic to the Congress, to Citizen Talleyrand, Minister for Foreign Affairs.

Citizen Minister,   Strasburgh, 12th Floreal *(May* 1*).*

I ENDEAVOUR to recollect myself, in order to dictate the details of the dreadful events of which the French legation were the victims, on the 9th Floreal (April 28), and from which, wounded and mutilated, I have escaped by a miracle, of which I cannot give an account.

Long before the 30th Germinal (19th April), the French legation perceived that means of all kinds were employed by the enemies of peace, to produce the dissolution of the congress; and we reckoned upon seeing it expire insensibly, by the successive retreat of those who composed it; but on that day (30th Germinal) the carrying off of the ferry-men who served to transmit our correspondence by way of Seltz, informed us that our enemies would not, undoubtedly, have the patience which the French government showed: we exclaimed against this violation of the rights of nations; the deputation exclaimed on their side; and the result of these steps was a military letter, which announced to us that no tranquillizing declaration for the safety of the members of the congress could be made. The deputation, assembled anew, declared that they were no longer free; that, besides, the recall of several members rendered them, according to the terms of their instructions, unable to adopt any deliberation whatever. It was upon this conclusum, officially transmitted to us by the directorial minister, himself recalled, that we founded our note of the 6th Floreal (25th April), protesting against the violence exercised, and declaring that we should repair within three days to the commune of Strasburgh, to continue the negotiations there. The next day, the 7th (I give you all these details from memory, because our papers were carried off, as you shall hear; but I do not think I am mistaken respecting dates), Citizen Lemaire, courier of the legation, was seized at Plittesdorff by an Austrian parole, and sent to Gernsbach, the colonel's quarters. Informed by us of this outrage, unheard of till then, but which was soon to be surpassed, all the members of the diplomatic body, especially the minister of Baden, the Prussian legation, and the directorial minister, applied to the Austrian colonel for reparation: they demanded from him particularly the assurance that we should be respected in returning to France. No answer was given. On the 9th (27th April) preparations were made for our departure; we might have gone without doubt with safety, had we stolen away on the 8th (26th April), when there were no Austrian patroles on the Rhine: but having once introduced the question of the right we had to return in safety, we should

have

have thought ourselves wanting to the dignity of our character, had we not required some solution; and perhaps this sentiment facilitated the execution of the crime upon which I am about to enter.

I resume my recital, Citizen Minister:—On the 9th Floreal (April 28), at half past seven in the evening, a captain of hussars of Szekler, stationed at Gegenbach, came, on the part of his colonel, to declare verbally to Baron d'Albini, that we might quit Rastadt in safety; and afterwards came to signify to us an order to leave that city in twenty-four hours. Already had the hussars of Szekler taken possession of it, and occupied all the avenues: at eight o'clock we got into our carriages: when we arrived at the gate of Rastadt, we found a general prohibition against letting any one enter or go out. An hour was spent in parleys. It appears that they stood in need of this delay, in order to organize the execrable execution that followed, and of which, I say it with conviction, all the details had been commanded and combined beforehand. At length the Austrian commandant gave an order for the departure of the French legation only. We demanded an escort: it was refused, and the commandant declared, that we should be as safe as in our own rooms. In consequence of this, we began our journey. We were not fifty paces from Rastadt, ourselves and the Ligurian legation, who did not quit us, and who participated our dangers with unequalled devotion, when a detachment of nearly sixty hussars of Szekler, in ambush upon the canal of La Murg, fell upon our carriages, and made them stop. Mine was the first of them. Six men, armed with drawn sabres, tear me out with violence—I am searched, and robbed of all that I had. Another, who appeared to command this expedition, arrives, on horseback, and asks for the minister Jean Debry: I thought he came to save me. It is I, I said, who am Jean Debry, minister of France. Scarcely had I said so, when two cuts from a sabre stretched me upon the ground. I was immediately assailed on all sides with fresh blows. Tumbled into a ditch, I feigned to be dead: the banditti then quitted me to go to the other carriages I availed myself of this instant, and escaped—wounded in different places, losing blood on all sides, and indebted for my life, perhaps, only to the thickness of my clothes. Bonnier was killed in the same manner I was to have been, and Roberjot massacred almost in the arms of his wife.

The same question was put to my ill-fated colleagues as to me: Are you Bonnier? are you Roberjot? Our carriages were pillaged, every thing became the prey of the brigands; the papers of the legation were carried off, conveyed to the Austrian commandant, and claimed in vain. The secretary of the legation threw himself into a ditch, and by favour of the night escaped the blows of the assassins. I crawled to an adjoining wood, hearing the
yells

yells of the cannibals, the screams of the victims, and particularly of their companions, of the wife of Roberjot, of my wife seven months gone with child, and of my two daughters calling out for their father: my private secretary, Citizen Belin, was held by six men, to be witness to all these scenes of horror. My valet-de-chambre was thrown into the river.

I know that all the members of the diplomatic corps made the greatest efforts to break through the line of the assassins, and to come to the assistance of those to whom assistance might yet be administered. But it was not till one in the morning that the wife of Roberjot could get to M. de Jacobi's, the Prussian minister; and my wife and daughters, to M. de Redon, minister from Bremen and Hanover. I wandered about the wood during the whole of that dreadful night, fearful of the day, which might expose me to the Austrian patroles. About six in the morning, hearing them go about, and seeing that I could not avoid them, penetrated besides by the rain and the cold, and growing more and more enfeebled by the blood I lost, I took the desperate resolution of returning to Rastadt. I saw on the road the naked bodies of my two colleagues. The dreadful weather, and perhaps the weariness of the assassins, after the commission of such crimes, facilitated my journey; and I arrived at length, out of breath, and covered with blood, at the Count de Gortz's, the King of Prussia's minister.

It is out of my power to depict to you the torment, and to relate to you the recitals of all the persons attached to the legation, who were the witnesses or the objects of these execrable scenes; I will collect them when I have strength. Notwithstanding her virtuous courage, the wife of Roberjot is like a mad person with grief. I implore for her all the interest of the government. Fatigued with the recital which I have just made at two different times, I confine myself now to express to you how much gratitude each of the persons saved owes to the generous devotion of the members of the diplomatic corps. I name none of them, because it would be necessary to name them all. Besides generous attentions and sweet consolations, we are indebted to them for our return here; a formal act, signed by all of them, was conveyed to the Austrian colonel, declaring to him that their constituents made him responsible both for the crime and all its consequences. The minister of the Margrave gave us an escort of his troops for our return. It was necessary to suffer it to be joined by the hussars of Szekler, who appeared to see that I had escaped with regret. The Prussian legation, prevented by them from accompanying us, charged their secretary, M. de Jordan, not to quit us till we had embarked. My God! why was it that so much care could not prevent the fatal catastrophe of my two ill-fated colleagues?

I should

(95)

I should also [say], that almost the whole of the inhabitants of Rastadt, shed tears at the outrage, loaded it with merited execration, and could not dissemble the opinion which attributes the atrocious conception, and all the direction of it, to Austria ; to Austria, whose minister, Lherbach, now commissary with the army of the Archduke, obtained, without the smallest difficulty, at his departure from Rastadt, all the passports he demanded from the French legation; to Austria, who dared to signify to us, by the Count de Metternich, that that Imperial commissioner could no longer remain at Rastadt, in consequence of the want of safety for his correspondence ; to Austria, in short, who, according to every probability, gave the order for massacring three ministers, carrying off their papers, and promised the plunder as the reward.

There are many other approximations that might be made; but they will be felt. Pardon the disorder of my ideas; the horrible images which I have incessantly before my eyes do not leave me free reflection, and oppress me more than the pain I feel. My wounds are in a good state, and hitherto announce nothing dangerous.

Health and respect. (Signed) JEAN DEBRY.

[The above letter was communicated by a message from the Directory to the Councils of Five Hundred and Ancients, on the 5th of May, and referred to a committee of seven members.]

Letter from the Archduke Charles to General Massena, relative to the Assassination of the French Deputies.

General,

THE reports, which have reached me this day, inform me of an event which has happened in the line of my advanced posts. The officer in command acquaints me that the French ministers, Bonnier and Roberjot, having crossed, during the night, the chain of his posts, were attacked by hussars, and unfortunately perished. The circumstances of this event are still unknown to me; I have, in the mean time, caused the commander of the advanced posts to be arrested, and have also appointed a commission to make the most exact and rigorous inquiries respecting the causes of that accident. I hasten to assure you beforehand, that, should my advanced posts be found in the slightest degree culpable in that affair, I shall exact signal satisfaction from them, as my orders relative to the personal safety of the French ministers were precise and reiterated. I cannot sufficiently express my regret that such a disaster should have happened in the line of my advanced posts. I reserve to myself, General, the opportunity of communicating to you, without delay, the result of the inquiries which I ordered to be made, the moment the intelligence reached me. Receive, General, an assurance of my high consideration.

Head-quarters, Stockach, May 2. CHARLES.

Procla-

Proclamation of the Executive Directory on the Assassination of the French Plenipotentiaries at the Congress of Rastadt.

Frenchmen! 17 *Floreal (May* 6).

YOUR plenipotentiaries have been recently massacred in cold blood, by the orders and satellites of Austria; and those illustrious victims, whose character was sacred, have been sacrificed only because they were the image of the active representation of a nation, which your ferocious enemy would have been happy to have butchered without a single exception; similar to that other Emperor, who in his brutal ferocity wished the Roman people had but one head, that he might strike it off with a single blow. You have read the horrible details of this assassination, which was meditated in the silence of the cabinet, preconcerted by treachery, and executed in the sight of the members of the congress, as if designed to defy in their persons all the powers whose representatives they also were, and to give the dreadful signal of a war of extermination.

Frenchmen! you have, on the recital of such horrors, demanded vengeance. Be assured that it will prove terrible. It is not the cause of liberty alone which we must defend, but even that of humanity; and in this struggle of civilization against barbarity, should the indignation of Europe promise to supply you with auxiliaries, it will be your duty to hold out the glorious example that is calculated to rally them in support of your cause. There has never yet occurred any instance in which an outrage of the law of nations has stained your successes or accompanied your misfortunes. Your enemy, on the contrary, has only attempted to repair his defeats by treachery, and has celebrated an ephemeral success only by assassinations: a perseverance in your generous conduct will render the contrast more dishonourable to him. If the battalions of Austria have not shared in its crime, they will refuse to associate themselves with assassins, and will break their arms. If they continue to fight against us, they must be considered as accomplices in the guilt. A memorable punishment is necessary to preserve the world from the new outrages and crimes which are reserved for it by the impious league of the monarchs of Russia and Austria, formed by ambition, cemented by crimes, and which, in the madness of their projects, threatens the destruction of Europe.

The Executive Directory decrees, that the preceding proclamation shall be inserted in the bulletin of the laws, and that it shall be reprinted and affixed in all the communes of the republic in the usual places.

The minister of justice is charged with the execution of the present decree.

(Signed)   P. BARRAS, President.
                LA GARDE, Sec. Gen.

The Executive Directory of the French Republic to all People and all Governments.

THE news of an excessive outrage has already resounded in Europe; and the circumstances of a crime the most unheard-of, with which the pages of the history of civilized nations have been stained, are now collecting with horror from all parts. It was at the gates of Rastadt, on the territory of an independent and neutral prince, and in the sight of all the members of the congress violently detained in that town, and forced to be no less impotent than indignant spectators of a crime which affected them in the deepest manner, and threatened them all, that in contempt of a sacred character, in contempt of assurances given, in contempt of every thing which constitutes humanity, justice, and honour, the plenipotentiaries of the republic, victims ever to be regretted of the mission of peace with which they were entrusted, and of the unlimited devotion with which they fulfilled the instructions of government, and maintained the national dignity, were massacred in cold blood by a detachment of Austrian troops. But how much more detestable do all the circumstances of this assassination render it!

Already, in the first days of the month Floreal, the communication of the French legation with the republic had been intercepted; one of its couriers had been carried off, and the spirited remonstrances of the congress had only produced an insolent declaration, which made its separation necessary.

On the 9th Floreal (28th of April), at seven o'clock in the evening, the colonel of the regiment of Szeklers caused a declaration to be made by a captain to Baron Albini, the directorial minister, that the French legation might leave Rastadt in security. The same captain proceeded afterwards to the French ministers, and signified to them an order to depart from Rastadt in twenty-four hours. At eight o'clock they got into their carriages, and were stopped at the gates of the town. So sudden a departure no doubt had not been expected, and the assassination was not completely organized. Another hour was still wanting. At nine o'clock the prohibition against passing the gates was taken off with respect to the French legation only. The French ministers demanded an escort, but the Austrian commander refused to grant it, and answered in the following terms:—"You will be as secure on your journey, as in your apartments." But the legation had scarcely advanced fifty paces, when it was surrounded by a numerous detachment of the same corps, whose commander had just before promised every kind of security. The carriages are stopped; Citizen Jean Debry, who was in the first, is forced to alight, and he is asked, "Are you not Jean Debry?"— "Yes," he answers, "I am Jean Debry, minister of France."

He inflantly falls to the ground pierced with wounds. The Citizens Bonnier and Roberjot are ftopped in the fame manner, and interrogated. They tell their names, and are killed. Roberjot is maffacred in the arms of his wife. The crime being perpetrated, the papers of the legation are carried off, and conveyed to the Auftrian commander. In confidering thefe faithful details, who is there that cannot perceive the premeditation of this affaffination, and its firft author?

Such a facrilege will doubtlefs only tend to the accumulation of infamy and execration, and fhould any other punifhment be wanting, hiftory referves one for thofe who have been guilty of the crime. It would be in vain for the court of Vienna to attempt to fhake off the dreadful refponfibility that attaches to this accufation. All its previous conduct now comes forward in evidence againft it. It will be recollected that it commenced hoftilities by an outrage of a fimilar nature, in caufing two French ambaffadors to be arrefted on the territory of the confederacy, who were afterwards thrown into the dungeons of Mantua. It will be remembered that the prifons of Olmutz alfo received, and confined for three years, reprefentatives of the people, and a minifter who was delivered up by treachery. It will be remembered, that Auftria was not unacquainted with the affaffinations committed at Rome on the French, and that it received and protected the authors of them. It will, finally, be recollected, that the firft ambaffador of the republic at Vienna experienced only outrages and affronts there. Thefe ftatements are fufficient to imprefs conviction that the affaffination recently perpetrated at Raftadt is but the confequence and the horrid completion of the feries of atrocities with which Auftria has aftonifhed Europe, fince Charles the Fifth firft furnifhed the example of ftepping beyond all focial laws, by caufing the ambaffadors whom Francis the Firft fent to Venice and to Conftantinople to be maffacred.

The proofs exifting in hiftory of the indignation which was manifefted at that period by all the European powers, convince us that a crime ftill more execrable will alfo excite more horror and deteftation.

And when the conftant moderation and boundlefs generofity of the French republic fhall be compared with the crimes of Auftria; when it fhall be confidered, that even in the midft of the moft violent ftorms of the revolution, the law of nations has not received the flighteft injury in France; that the envoy of the Britannic government entered twice into the territory of France, and departed from it free and refpected, although juftly fufpected to have come rather to excite troubles than to negotiate peace; that the minifter of Naples obtained permiffion to return to his mafter, and to continue his journey in a fecure and uninterrupted manner, at the very moment when the French general had re-

pulfed

pulsed the Neapolitan troops, and when he was informed that the ambassador of the republic had been refused passports to retire by land, and had been compelled to embark at Naples, with a certainty that such a measure was but to deliver him into the hands of the African states; that the cruel treatment to which the French have fallen victims in the dominions of the Grand Signior, however great and just the national resentment on that account may have been, has not given rise to any reprisals; when the congress at Rastadt, peaceable and respected as long as the French armies were near it, shall be compared with the congress thrown into confusion, and dissolved on the approach of the Austrians; when the voluntary departure of M. M. de Lehrbach and de Metternich, protected by French passports, shall be compared with the premeditated massacre of the ministers of the republic: these different contrasts, already so odious, will become still more dishonourable for Austria by the comparison which must be made between its satellites, whose cowardly ferocity is a subject of astonishment even to the people of the North, who have been called upon to co-operate with them, and the agents of the government of England, who, though it is the most essential enemy of the French government, and the most determined to injure it, have recently given proofs at Constantinople that they understood the law of nations, and set a value on preventing the violation of it. Is it possible then, that any people, that any government who may not have abjured every principle of civilization and of honour, can hesitate for a moment to declare itself in favour of good faith against perfidy; in favour of continued moderation against unmasked ambition; in favour of abused confidence against atrocious and premeditated crimes?

It is therefore with the just hope of being attended to with effect, and of obtaining for the illustrious victims who have been immolated at Rastadt, a deep regret; for the French republic an honourable approbation, and an union of execration against Austria; that the Executive Directory now addresses this solemn appeal to the conscience and honour of every people and of every government, accepting thus early as a pledge of the generous determination which will be formed by them, the particular indignation which has been expressed with so much energy at Rastadt by all the members of the congress, and at Paris by the ambassadors and ministers of friendly or neutral powers.

The Executive Directory decrees, that the preceding manifesto shall be transmitted to all governments by the minister of the foreign department; that it shall be printed in the bulletin of the laws, and solemnly read, published, and affixed in all the communes of the republic, and be inserted in the orders of all the armies.

(Signed)   BARRAS, President.
LA GARDE, Sec. Gen.

May 7.

Substance

Substance of a Note from Citizen Zeltner, Minister Plenipotentiary from the Helvetic Republic at Paris, transmitted 5th August 1798, to the Minister for Foreign Affairs, with a Request to communicate it to the Executive Directory.

AFTER recapitulating the vexation which certain French commissaries have exercised in Switzerland, it adds:

" The consequences of a conduct so irritating ought to be seriously apprehended from a people, who are neither distracted by pleasure, nor to be intimidated by force, and with whom gentleness alone will succeed. It is exceedingly impolitic not to study their character better, and to act towards them as if they possessed that happy thoughtlessness with which the French adopt novelties, the apathy of the Batavians, or the docile pliability of the Italians. This irritable and courageous people adhere firmly to their religion, to their democracy, and to their ancient manners. Every thing which bears the stamp of infidelity and oppression, fills them with indignation and resentment. When they have nothing more to lose, when they are driven to despair, they are capable of every excess; and Helvetia may become the theatre of scenes still more horrible than those of La Vendée. The undersigned trembles to use this language, but it is his duty to employ it: not to unveil to the French Directory the whole truth were a crime.

" The Grisons have already discovered a disposition to decline all connexion with us, on hearing of the deplorable state into which Switzerland is plunged. They prefer a yoke which formerly inspired them with horror; the chains of the Tyrol are rivetted; Suabia, on the point of embracing the system of liberty, rejects it with disdain. Those who formerly had sworn to propagate it, now swear to oppose it with all their might; and the neighbours of Helvetia refuse with horror fruit which seems poisoned.

" The true republicans of Helvetia will be the first victims of so great disorders. The towns, the only support, the only asylums of the new order of things, will be exposed to the fury of the inhabitants of the country, who accuse them of having caused their misery and ruin, by giving the first impulse to the revolution: upon them will fall the first ebullition of their frantic rage. The English consider themselves as protected from the resentment of the great nation, because the latter allows useful neighbours to tear their own vitals, and allows her enemies to avail themselves of the most valuable advantages. Situation, history, experience, every thing proves the importance of this neighbourhood to France; every thing excites the enemies of France to unite themselves with a brave and estimable people, whose fate at present inspires such general interest."

The

The minister plenipotentiary concludes with the following demands on the part of the Helvetic republic :

1. That the funds of every denomination, which have been sequestrated, or which have been taken from the Helvetic nation, should be restored to its new government, to enable it to meet the expenses of its revolution ; to organize an armed force which may render the Helvetic republic worthy of an alliance with the French republic ; to pay for articles of the first necessity which France may furnish to Switzerland, such as grain, salt, &c.

2. That the different parts of Helvetia, on which contributions have been laid, should be exempted from them.

3. That the artillery, arms, magazines, and, in general, every thing taken from the Helvetic nation, should be restored to the constitutional government.

4. That the number of French troops in Switzerland, especially cavalry, be reduced to what shall be absolutely necessary ; and that these troops evacuate the country as soon as possible.

5. That the constitutional government of the Helvetic republic be favoured, in every possible way, in the exercise of its authority ; and for this purpose it is necessary,

That orders be given to the agents of the French government in Helvetia to take measures, in concert with the Directory of the latter power, upon every point in which it is concerned, to act only in its name, with its consent ; observing, at the same time, all the respect which is due to it.

That the French troops which remain in Switzerland be auxiliaries ; that, instead of traversing the operation of the government, they shall support it ; that they shall assist it as often as required.

That the advantages given to the canton of Berne, respecting the maintenance of troops, be extended to all Helvetia.

(Signed)   ZELTNER.

The Executive Directory of the Helvetic Republic to the General in Chief of the French Army in Helvetia.

Citizen General,   Lucerne, September 12, 1798.

THE Executive Directory of Helvetia present to you, and, under your auspices, to the brave army which you command, the decree of the legislative body, which proclaims their gratitude, and invokes that of the whole nation for your common labours for the establishment of the republic. The legislature is informed only of your cares by their happy consequences ; but we, Citizen General, who were the depositaries of your confidence and your wise measures ; we, whom you acquainted beforehand with those skilful and rapid combinations which prepared your successes, we cannot

cannot doubt that the folicitude and intereft of friendfhip have been united to the talents and duties of the general; and our gratitude is fo much the greater, becaufe it has motives more profound.

To-day our firft fitting at Lucerne has been devoted to your correfpondence, and to the deliberations which it gave rife to. Your military difpofitions, fo well calculated for our fafety; your counfels full of wifdom; your deference for our opinion; the magic of a ftyle which gives to affairs the life and animation of fentiment; that politenefs which one loves fo much to find in the firft ftations, and which is natural to you; all thefe circumftances have won our hearts, and fo rule over them, that, leaving for ordinary compliments the common forms, each of us has declared the determination to place his individual fignature to the authentic declaration of our attachment to your power, and of our tender gratitude.

Health and confideration.

The prefident and members of the executive power:

PIERRE OCHS,   OBERLINE,
LEGRAND,   LAHARPE.
GLAYRE,

The Minifter of War to the Executive Directory.

Paris, 6th Vendemiaire, 7th Year
Citizens Directors,   (September 28).

I HAD the honour, on the 29th Fructidor, and the third complementary day laft, to tranfmit you an account of the victory which the French army in Helvetia had gained over the rebels of the canton of Waldftallen *(ci-devant* Schwitz), Ury, Zug, and Underwald.

General Schawembourg has juft fent me a detailed report of the events which preceded, accompanied, and followed the defeat of the rebels of Underwald and their auxiliaries, of which I fubjoin a copy.

You will perceive, that every meafure of mildnefs and conciliation had been exhaufted to gain the fubmiffion of thofe mifguided men, and induce them to take the oath of fidelity to the Helvetic conftitution; but the priefts, thofe irreconcilable enemies of all order, and foreign emiffaries, took advantage of circumftances to prevent the eftablifhment of the conftitution, to pervert the minds of thofe mountaineers, and even to raife them to fuch a pitch, that they returned a letter unopened, which the Helvetic Directory had addreffed to them in the form of a declaration, granting them a few days to return to order, and deliver up their principal chiefs.

General

General Schawembourg, perceiving there were no further hopes of bringing them to their duty by reason, took his dispositions accordingly, and appointed the 22d Fructidor for the attack; but the different columns not having been able to effect their junction, and a heavy rain having fallen, which considerably augmented the difficulties of the march of the troops, who had to climb steep rocks and exceedingly high mountains, he postponed the attack until the next day, the 23d.

The rebels, emboldened by the failure of the attack the preceding day, as well as by the arrival of a portion of the inhabitants of the district of Schwitz, who, yielding to the solicitations of Father Paul, a Capuchin, had joined the insurgents, defended themselves with the greatest obstinacy; but the valour of our troops again triumphed over every obstacle, and restored order among these fanatic spirits.

We found among the slain many Capuchins and priests.

General Schawembourg is at present engaged in repairing, as well as he is able, the miseries of war, and particularly in indemnifying the patriots of this country for the losses they have sustained; and you will see, Citizens Directors, by the copy of the letter addressed by the Helvetic Directory to General Schawembourg, which I have also subjoined, that it has approved of his proposal of making the weight of the indemnities due to the patriots of Stanz fall upon the district of Schwitz, and particularly on the communes which have marched to the assistance of the rebels.

I have to observe, that the inhabitants of Underwald, who fled at the approach of our troops, have returned to their homes in great numbers, and have delivered up their arms. They have also surrendered some of their subaltern chiefs; but those who possessed the greatest influence, and among them Father Paul, have either found the means of escaping, or remain on the field of battle.

Health and respect.
(Signed) SCHERER.

Manifesto of the Roman Consuls against the King of the Two Sicilies.

Rome, 8th Brumaire (October 29).

The Roman Consuls to the Citizens Commissioners of the French Republic.

Citizens Commissioners,

THE consuls, proud of the august functions with which they have been clothed by you, owe to France, to Rome, to all the republicans of Italy, a solemn declaration of their sentiments. A longer silence would be criminal; it would excite impatience, and

and entirely paralyze the energy of that crowd of friends to liberty, who await from you the signal of triumph.

An enemy, made powerful by our weakness, has placed his hopes in our subjection. He has placed the certainty of his successes, not in the valour of his slaves, but in the lethargy of freemen, whose destruction he meditates; not in his mercenary phalanxes, but in the hostile dispositions of counter-revolutionists, who surround us on every side. Shall the native soil of Brutus be disgraced by the presence of the partisans of tyranny? Shall the insolence of a monarch trample upon the descendants of the masters of the world? Ah! since the moment when, thanks to French intrepidity, and our patriotic sentiments, we recovered our rights from despotism, a neighbouring despot menaces us, insults us, plans our destruction! He seeks to smother the republic in her cradle; he incites against her her own children, whose affections he alienates. He arms against her, internal enemies, whom he keeps in pay. His hatred has fomented a sedition in the department on her frontiers; he pays the rebels; he applauds their crime; he gives them for chiefs officers of his own; he opens in his state an asylum for the assassins of the French army, for those who burn and destroy republican property; he lavishes upon them provisions and stores of every kind.

This is not all: he inundates our countries with incendiary plans, with seditious letters, with counter-revolutionary promises, with destructive menaces; his agents circulate them in cities, in the country, in public places, and private societies. His spirit infests a part of the authorities; it insinuates itself into the tribunals. They who expect his approach with impatience no longer dissemble their joy; they who execrate royalty, ask if they have been sold to tyranny?

Public credit, which only exists by security, is every day diminishing under the terrors that besiege us in all the parts of the republic. How shall we keep up the value of domains which may be to-morrow invaded, and which perhaps, to-morrow, will no longer exist in a land inhabited by liberty?

How can we conceive hopes of a substantial credit, when we every where behold a scandalous pillage; dilapidations which would make even common brigands shudder; and management of money and provisions in the hands of a crowd of plunderers, who only know the republic by the treasures of which they strip her?

How shall we flatter ourselves with an amelioration of public spirit, while the sword of royal and theocratic despotism shall remain brandished over the heads of republicans; while patriotism shall not be held in esteem; while it shall have no means of developing its character; while the enemies of liberty shall live menacing and audacious; while they shall not be driven from

a soil

hich they   with their deadly aristocracy; and while
udent hav   sacerdotal and monarchical manifestoes
    punished? Do you wish for arms? we shall have them.
 sul call to witness the taking of the Bastile. Do you
r money, subsistence, stores of all kinds? we shall had
 The consuls know the sublime determinations of the Na-
 Convention of France. Do you wish that the Roman
   should be disembarrassed of all the enemies that over-
 it? Speak the word! Do you wish we should avenge the
    republic and her daughter, by punishing the dissoluteness
  g? At your voice, at ours, at that of the French, the
    friends of our prosperity, phalanxes will appear, whose
 e is not even suspected by those who only superficially
 e men who live under our constitution. We know their
  their means, their love for that liberty which they have
  from the French, which they inherit from their ancestors;
  tural hatred to Naples, which braves us; their conviction
  impossibility of being tranquil and happy, without re-
  g their neighbours from an abhorred sway, even to the
    om of Naples itself. The diplomacy of republics is not
  t of courts. Republics, when attacked, can acknowledge
  otiators but cannon and bayonets. Monarchical powers,
  unfortunate in war, retrieve their affairs by treaties. Re-
  s know no alternative but death or victory. We will not
  the victims of the perfidy of our neighbours; we will not
  them to pollute this sacred ground; we will not pay the
  rs furnished by them to an enemy who conspires against the
  h republic, and the republics her allies. Naples finds
  s; we shall have heroes. Naples has dismissed a minister
  did not watch over the magazines of despotism. We will
  e Naples to the advantage of liberty. Naples supports
  y, aristocracy, and the hypocrisy of fanaticism. We shall
  r our country from royalists, from aristocrats, and fanatical
  rites. Naples holds the patriots in subjection and debased.
  patriots shall raise their heads and resume their dignity.
  s insults the government of Rome, of Milan, of Paris:
  will avenge Paris, Milan, and Rome.
  tizens Commissioners, one cause invites all; it is the cause
  l the defenders of the republican system: we shall conquer
    wish to conquer. Should the committee unite with the
  late; should they sanction the measures which we shall pro-
  ; should they communicate to us those which their zeal for
    public has suggested, and come to a resolution fatal to
    y; Rome will learn its regeneration, and Naples its
    ement.

President of the Consulate, PIERELLI.
By the Consulate, Secretary, BASSAL.

OL. VIII.   P   *Executive*.

Executive Directory.

Decree of the 15th Brumaire (5th November), 7th Year.

THE Executive Directory, upon the report of the minister of marine and the colonies, and considering the law of the 29th Nivose, 6th year, and the decree of the 25th Priarial, relative to ships laden with English merchandise subject to re-exportation, decrees—

Article I. The regulations of the decree of the 25th Prairial, 6th year, are applicable to ships laden with English merchandises, produced immediately by the sale of prizes carried into foreign countries and the colonies, by French corsairs or the ships of the republic.

II. To identify these merchandises to neutral vessels, it will be sufficient, in the first instance, to produce,

1. A copy of the judgment of confiscation.
2. A detailed inventory of the merchandise.

In the colonies this inventory shall be certified by an officer of the customs at the port from whence the ship shall sail, and by the comptroller of the marine.

In foreign ports it shall be by the consul or vice-consul; or for want of them, by some other of the republic's agents of the ports from whence the ship shall have set sail.

III. There shall be mentioned at the foot of the said inventory, the day when the ship carrying it shall have put to sea, with its place of destination, according to the declaration of the captain, who shall in no case conceal fraudulent expeditions.

IV. This present decree shall be inserted in the bulletin des lois. The ministers of justice, finance, and marine, are charged with its execution, each in their respective departments.

(Signed)   TREILHARD, President.
LAGARDE, Secretary-General.

MANIFESTO.

BEFORE the commencement of hostilities, the King of Naples published the following manifesto:

San Germano, Nov. 22, 1798.

Dear, faithful, and beloved Subjects,

AFTER having, for almost forty years, exerted every effort to render you happy, and to succour you in all the calamities which it has pleased God to send you, I am now about to leave my beloved country, for the sole purpose of defending our holy religion,

religion, almost overthrown; to reanimate the divine worship; and to secure to you and to your children the enjoyment of the blessings which the Lord has given you. If I had been sure of attaining that object by any other sacrifice, believe me, I should not have hesitated a moment to prefer that alternative; but what hopes could be entertained of success after the many fatal examples with which you are well acquainted? I set out, therefore, at the head of the brave defenders of their country, full of confidence in the Lord of Hosts, who will guide our steps and protect our operations. I go to brave all danger with the greatest cheerfulness, because I do it for my fellow-citizens, for my brothers, for my children, for such I have ever considered you. Be always faithful to God, and to her whom I leave in my stead to conduct the government of these states, my dear and well-beloved consort. I recommend to you, then, your tender mother. I recommend to you my children, who are not more mine than they are yours. At all events, remember that you are Neapolitans; that those are brave who are willing to exert their courage, and that it is better to die gloriously for God and our country, than to live shamefully oppressed! Meanwhile, may God bestow upon you all the blessings and the happiness which is the wish of him, who is, and while he lives shall be, your most affectionate father and sovereign,

FERDINAND.

Copy of a Letter from General Championet to General Mack, November 23.

General,

I AM informed by the commanders of the advanced corps of the French army stationed in the Roman republic, that you have caused them to be summoned to evacuate their posts; threatening, in case of refusal, to march your army against them; and that some of them, giving way to superior force, have retreated. This conduct, on your part, requires a frank and candid explanation, and I demand it of you; entrusted by my government with the command of the army destined to protect the independence of the Roman republic, I am responsible to it for every breach of that independence. On your side, General, you are not less responsible for the blood which is about to flow, and the flames which you shall kindle. Consider that peace exists between the French republic and the court of Naples; that the two ambassadors of the two governments, and all their diplomatic agents, still reside at Paris and Naples; and finally, that nothing has broken the ties established by the last treaty of peace

between

between the French republic and the King of the Two Sicilies. In this state of things, to summon the French troops to evacuate the Roman territory, the defence of which is entrusted to them, is to violate the right of nations, which allows not solemn aggressions of government against government until after a declaration of war. It is to assume the part of an aggressor, and to be answerable for the events of war, which can only tend to the detriment of humanity; these, General, are the observations to which I expect your answer.

Answer of General Mack to General Championet.

General, November 24.

I DECLARE to you that the army of his Sicilian Majesty, which I have the honour to command, under the king in person, passed yesterday the frontiers, in order to take possession of the Roman state, which has been revolutionized, and usurped since the peace of Campo Formio, and has never been recognised or acknowledged by his Sicilian Majesty, or by his august ally the Emperor and King. I demand that you will cause, without the smallest delay, all the French troops stationed in the said Roman state to retire into the Cisalpine republic, and to evacuate the places occupied by them.

The generals commanding the different columns of his Sicilian Majesty's troops, have received the most positive orders not to commence hostilities, if the French troops withdraw in consequence of the notice which shall be given to them; but they are also ordered to have recourse to force in case of opposition.

I further declare, I shall consider it as an act of hostility, should the French troops enter the territories of the Grand Duke of Tuscany.

General, I expect your answer without the smallest delay; and request you will dispatch Major Reinhart with it, whom I send to you, within four hours at farthest after the receipt of my letter.

The answer must be positive and categorical, both with respect to the demand of evacuating the Roman state, and of not setting foot on that of Tuscany.

A negative answer will be considered as a declaration of war, and his Sicilian Majesty will be enabled to carry into effect his just demands, which I state to you in his name. I have the honour to be, &c.

Letter of Citizen Alquier to the Bavarian Minister.
Munich, November 27.

THE undersigned resident, chargé des affaires of the French republic to his Serene Electoral Highness of the Palatinate of Bavaria can no longer defer claiming, in the name of his government, the execution of the treaty of armistice concluded at Pfaffenhofen, the 21st Fructidor, 4th year of the republic (Sept. 7, 1796), between General Moreau, commander in chief of the French army, and the commissioners of his Serene Electoral Highness. The whole of the conditions agreed to by the commander of the French troops have been rigorously fulfilled; property has been respected, and even protected, by the troops of the republic. Neither the religion, the laws, nor the constitution of the state, have experienced the least detriment; on the contrary, all parts of the states of his Serene Electoral Highness have been restored to the most perfect tranquillity. None of the obligatory clauses on the part of the Bavarian government have been carried into execution, though it is more than two years since his Highness has enjoyed the happy effects of a suspension of arms. It has preserved the most absolute silence with respect to the engagements contracted by the commissioners in its name. By the eagerness with which the general of the French army subscribed to the pacific intentions of his Highness, the republic has manifested, in a manner the most unequivocal, the desire it had to renew the connexion which anciently subsisted between the two powers.

Its resident has been charged to offer the most ample reparation for the losses occasioned by the war. He has even declared, that the Executive Directory will consent, not to insist upon the complete execution of the treaty of armistice, but that, from its attachment to the Bavarian government, it shall obtain a diminution of the stipulated sums, provided the minister of his Serene Highness, at congress, shall receive orders to second the views of France, to procure for Europe a speedy peace, for Bavaria an increase of power, and for the Germanic Empire a real independence. The undersigned will not recall all those facts, which demonstrate that the councils of his Serene Highness, far from manifesting that satisfaction, which propositions so advantageous for Bavaria ought to have inspired, and of answering the unreserved advances, of which the republic has given the example, has, on the contrary, submitted its principles to the will of the enemies of France; and that daily preparations, concerted with those powers, announce the resolution of seconding their projects, and of embracing their cause.

The undersigned desires that the Bavarian government, deceived by the result of events, may return to a system more conformable

formable to its real interests. He confines himself, for the present, in claiming rights that are incontestable, acquired by force of arms, and sanctioned by a formal convention. Existing circumstances prescribe to him as a duty, to require the most prompt execution of the treaty of armistice. His Highness has just obtained a bull from the Pope, permitting him to raise fifteen millions of florins upon the property of the clergy; a favour the more valuable, as it does not exhaust the source from whence it is derived; and that the rich possessions of the order of Malta, and the chapters formerly excepted by the bull from the number of taxable properties, may hereafter become the object of a new demand, and the relief of new wants. The tenths exacted in the name of his Highness have been sold, as well as the *fonds des bailliages*. So considerable an amelioration of the finances places the government in the happy possibility of fulfilling its engagements; and there can be no one more powerful or just than that which it has entered into with the French republic.

The undersigned therefore requests the Count de Vicregg to order the payment as soon as possible of the sums stipulated to be paid to the French government or its agents, according to the tenour of the treaty of Pfaffenhofen.

The undersigned has the honour of offering the Count de Vicregg assurances of his high consideration.

(Signed) ALQUIER.

Summons of the Neapolitan General to the Commander of the French Troops in the Castle of St. Angelo in Rome.

THE commandant in chief of the Neapolitan army has desired me to inform you, he has learned with the most lively indignation that you have dared to fire on his troops; and still more so, because General Championet had notified to him that he would evacuate Rome without making the smallest exception. He desires me to declare to you, that all the French who are sick in the hospitals at Rome, as well as the guards whom your general has left there, and who have been detained as prisoners, will be considered as hostages, and that every shot which you may fire upon the Neapolitan troops shall be followed by the death of a French soldier, who shall be given up to the just indignation of the inhabitants. You will yourself be answerable for the fate of these unhappy victims.

Rome, Nov. 28. Gen. BOUCHARD.

Copy of the Letter written to General Mack, Commander of the Neapolitan Army, by General Macdonald, from his Head-quarters at Monterisi, on the 29th November 1798.

THE commander in chief, Sir, has sufficient confidence in me, to recognise as his own the reply which I make to your letter of the 28th of November. I well know that he has not given any answer to your letter respecting the evacuation of the forts and strong places, and we consider the castle of St. Angelo as one of these. The silence of contempt was certainly what was due to your insolent menaces on this subject, and this was the only answer that could be expected consistently with the dignity of the French name. You speak of a regard for justice, and yet you invade the territory of a republic in alliance with France, without provocation, and without its having given you the least reason for such conduct. You have attacked the French troops, who trusted in the most sacred defence, the law of nations, and the security of treaties. You have shot at our flags of truce which were proceeding from Trivoli to Vicavero, and you have made the French garrison at Rieti prisoners of war. You have attacked our troops on the heights of Terni, and yet you do not call that a declaration of war! Force alone, Sir, constrained us to evacuate Rome; but believe me (and you, Sir, know better than any one what I say), the conquerors of Europe will avenge such proceedings.

At present I confine myself merely to stating our injuries: the French army will do the rest. I declare to you, Sir, that I place our sick, the commissary of war, Valville, and the other Frenchmen who have remained at Rome to take care of them, under the protection of all the soldiers whom you command. If a hair of their head be hurt, it shall be the signal for the death of all the Neapolitan army. The French republicans are not assassins; but the Neapolitan generals, the officers and the soldiers, who were taken prisoners of war the day before yesterday, on the heights of Terni, shall answer with their heads for their safety. Your summons to the commander of the fort of St. Angelo is of such a nature that I have made it public, in order to add to the indignation and to the horror which your threats inspire, and which we despise as much as we think that there is little to be dreaded from them.

(Signed)   MACDONALD.

Answer

Answer of the Count de Vicregg to the Minister Alquier.

Munich, November 30.

IN presenting Citizen Alquier, at Munich, with those respects due to an individual honoured with the confidence of his government, and possessing all that confidence which his personal qualities, joined to the favourable declarations which he had constantly reiterated with respect to the amicable intentions of his powerful nation towards the Palatine, have inspired, I have to inform him that his Serene Electoral Highness had constantly flattered himself, that, far from indirectly augmenting the embarrassments which certain disaffected of his subjects endeavour to oppose to all the operations of the finances, aided by the unhappy effects of war, the loss of one half of his states, and the anticipation of the resources of the revenue, added to the daily and urgent exigencies of the state, he would, on the contrary, have referred to the wisdom of the government of the Elector all those details which relate to the internal administration of Bavaria; and that, faithful to the principles with which he commenced, he would have shut his eyes to the insidious insinuations of a few ill-advised intriguers, who seek to interpret according to their own manner, all the proceedings of the Elector, and even his future intentions. It is therefore with much pleasure that the undersigned, as well as all the members of the Bavarian government, render every justice to that wise and perfect good conduct, by which Citizen Alquier has hitherto preserved the esteem of the public, and of the ministers of the Elector, and are persuaded that he would never enter into any of the views of the disaffected above mentioned. On this subject the undersigned can only repeat what he has often declared, " That his Serene Electoral Highness, in fulfilling all the duties imposed on him as Prince of the Empire, and defender of his people, has not ceased to manifest at all times, and on all occasions, his sincere desire to see a period to those calamities at which humanity shudders, by the conclusion of a just, solid, and durable peace, for the advancement of which he has made at Rastadt sacrifices greater and more important than any other sovereign; and that, faithful to these principles, it shall certainly not be his fault if peace, so much desired, shall delay the establishment of those ancient connexions which have so long subsisted between the French nation and the palatine Bavarian government." With respect to the treaty of Pfaffenhofen, upon the form of the execution of which there are so many things to be said, the undersigned contents himself with observing to Citizen Alquier, " That the contributions, requisitions, and other military regulations demanded since that period in the different states of the Elector occupied by the French troops, surpass exceedingly the pretensions resulting from that treaty." Besides, as this discussion relates so intimately to the negotiations of Rastadt, where all the interests of the Empire with the French republic seem to be concentrated, it cannot at present be allowed that those difficulties which have retarded peace with the Empire should be brought forward at Munich by Citizen Alquier, who is requested to accept these confidential observations, together with assurances of the most distinguished consideration of the undersigned.

(Signed)   VICREGO.

Arreté of the 14th Frimaire, 7th Year (December 4).

THE Executive Directory having considered its arreté of the 21st Fructidor, 6th year, decrees as follows:

Article 1. Every Frenchman not usefully employed with, or in the train of the army of Italy, or that of Rome—every Frenchman employed only by a commission posterior to the 21st Fructidor last—every Frenchman employed even by a commission anterior to that date, but whose presence in Italy may be injurious to the interests of the republic, whether from his correspondence or connexions, or from the vexations, impositions, or extortions in which he may have taken part, shall likewise be expelled from the territories occupied by the arms of the republic, upon a very short notice, which shall be determined by the civil commissaries with the armies.

2. Every Frenchman who has remained in Italy in contravention of the above-cited arreté of the 21st Fructidor, 6th year, and every one who shall continue there in contravention of the first article of the present arreté; in short, all those who, on having been expelled from the states occupied by the armies of Italy, shall have retired into those occupied by the army of Rome, or reciprocally, shall be apprehended, and conducted as spies before the council of war.

Head-quarters of the Army at Milan, December 5.

Joubert, Commander in Chief.

General Orders.

AT length the court of Turin has filled the measure of its guilt. It has thrown off the mask; it has required delays to furnish its contingent, and in the mean time it is directing its force against Loano and Oneglia, there to welcome the enemy of the French nation, which is its ally: it appoints to the chief military employments those men who are most hostile to the French name: it is making open preparations to bear part in

VOL. VIII.   Q   the

the coalition, its tools no longer conceal themselves, and they have even openly violated the territory of the Cisalpine republic. For a long time crimes have been committed; the blood of French and Piedmontese republicans has flowed, in consequence of the orders of this atrocious court. The French government, delighting in peace, was in hopes to be able to bring them back to peaceable measures; it was desirous of healing the wounds which had been inflicted in a long war, of restoring tranquillity to Piedmont, and of every day more closely cementing the alliance between them. But this hope has been deceitful, and it has given orders to its general to avenge the honour of the great nation, no longer giving credit to a court which is faithless in its treaties; and to secure peace and happiness to Piedmont. Such are the motives which have led the French army to enter Piedmont. All the friends to liberty are placed under the safeguard of the French army, and are invited to join it.

Property, personal safety, and religious worship, shall be respected. The Piedmontese army forms part of the French army in Italy: promotions shall in future be given only to patriotism and talents.

Those who shall oppose by force of arms the entry of the French, shall meet with the most violent persecution.

(Signed)   JOUBERT.

Message from the Directory to the Council of Five Hundred, December 5.

Citizens Representatives,

THE court of Naples has crowned its perfidies: you see by the letters of Generals Joubert and Championet, and by the copy of a letter from the Neapolitan General Mack to General Championet, that the French troops in the Roman republic have been attacked by the Neapolitan troops. Thus the moderation of the French republic only serves to increase the audacity of its enemies. The details which will be sent you, will convince you that both the one and the other have been carried to their height.

Now the first care of the government will be to take measures to repel the insolent attack of a perjured court.

The Executive Directory has likewise to declare to you, that the court of Turin, equally perfidious, makes common cause with our enemies; and this crowns a long train of crimes against the French republic.

Citizens Representatives, the Executive Directory does not dissemble that the danger is imminent; but republican energy is still great; and if all differences of opinion now disappear, and all

wishes

wishes unite, and the legislative body will second, by every means in its power, the efforts of government, the projects of the enemies of the republic will again be confounded, and the triumph of liberty will be for ever secured.

The Executive Directory proposes to you, formally to declare war against the King of Naples and the King of Sardinia.

[After reading the letters (for which see pages 107 and 108), the Council of Five Hundred passed a resolution, declaring war against the Kings of Naples and Sardinia. This resolution was immediately sent to the Council of Elders, approved of, and passed into a law.]

The Executive Directory to the Armies of the Republic.

Citizen Soldiers,

THE will of the nation again calls you forth to battle. The French nation had hitherto spared the courts of Naples and of Turin; but insult, treachery, and assassination were the first fruits of their gratitude. The Executive Directory sacrificed for perhaps too long a time their sense of injury to their profound desire for peace: but what has been the fruit of their uniform moderation? The Neapolitan troops have attacked the soldiers of liberty! You shudder, Frenchmen—you will shudder still more when you shall hear what was the insolent menace which accompanied the unjust aggression of your enemy. The moment of vengeance is come.——The Directory have done all in their power for peace. You, citizen soldiers, on your part, will do all that is in your power for the honour and for the glory of your country. France has all her eyes upon you. Recollect all that she is entitled to expect from your courage. Recollect that the temples of the republic should every ten days resound with the fame of your exploits. Recollect that thirty millions of your brethren follow you with their eyes and with their hearts in your glorious career. March: you will find among every people defenders and friends. Your cause is that of the whole human race, while perjured courts seek to plunge mankind in darkness and superstition, and in the horrors of slavery.

Given at the Directorial Palace, Dec. 7, 1798.

(Signed)   La Reveilliere, President.
LAGARD, Secretary.

Head-quarters, Turin, December 9.

Act of Renunciation of the King of Sardinia.

THE commander in chief gives orders that the present act shall be printed in both languages, French and Italian, and made public.

Article 1. His Majesty declares, that he renounces the exercise of all power, and he especially orders all his subjects whatever to obey the provisional government which is about to be established by the French general.

2. His Majesty orders the Piedmontese army to consider itself as an integral part of the French army in Italy, and to obey the French commander in chief as their own.

3. His Majesty disavows the publication of the proclamation circulated by his ministers, and he gives orders to M. le Chevalier Danigen to surrender the citadel of Turin, as a pledge that no resistance whatever shall be attempted against the present act, which has emanated purely from his own will.

4. His Majesty issues orders to the governor of the city of Turin to receive and execute precisely all orders which the French general commanding the citadel shall think proper to order for the maintenance of public tranquillity.

5. No change shall be made that can affect the Catholic religion, or the safety or property of individuals.

The Piedmontese who are anxious to change their abodes, shall have liberty to take with them their moveable effects, to sell and liquidate their property, in order to export the value. The Piedmontese who are absent are at liberty to return to Piedmont, and to enjoy the same rights there as other citizens, nor shall they, on any account, be questioned as to any actions or writings previous to this present act.

6. The King shall be at liberty to repair to . . . . . . [Sardinia was afterwards determined upon as the place]. In the mean time no arrangement shall be made that can affect the security of his person. Until the moment of his departure his palaces and country-houses shall not be taken possession of by the French troops, nor shall any property be carried off, and the guard shall be kept by those who have hitherto been employed in that service.

7. The passports and necessary orders shall be given; that his Majesty and all his family may arrive in safety at the place of their retreat. They shall be accompanied by an equal force of French and Piedmontese.

8. In case the Prince de Carignan shall remain at Piedmont, he shall enjoy his property there, and shall be at liberty to leave it, as provided for the other subjects of Piedmont.

9. The

9. The f............ ic archives, chests, &c. shall be immediately given ....eal shall be placed on the chests.

10. The ships or powe.. at war with the French republic shall not be received in the ports of the island of Sardinia.

Done at Turin, this 9th of December 1798.

    (Signed) CLAUVEL, Adj. General.

Consented to and approved by me, C. EMMANUEL.

    RAIMOND DE ST. GERMAIN, Chamberlain.

I undertake that I will throw no impediment in the way of the execution of this treaty. VICTOR EMMANUEL.

Approved and accepted, JOUBERT, Commander in Chief.

Army of Rome.

Championet, General in Chief, to the Army.

Soldiers,

IF you had been vanquis.d ... Nepi, you would have been put to the sword. Such ... the horrible orders which the Neapolitan general gave previ..ly to the battle. Tremble with horror at the execrable c...ct of your enemies, who are as cowardly as they are barb.ro.. At Arcoli three French soldiers were taken prisoners, ..a tied to a tree and shot. At Otricoli thirty sick, the g..er part of whom had their arms cut off the day before, were ...not; and some others, who were lying upon straw, were burnt. Undoubtedly this conduct will call for dreadful reprisals on our part, and we have the means of vengeance; but no—let us prove that republicans are as generous and humane after the action, as they are dreadful in it. Let us march against the enemy with republican courage; let us revenge our brethren in arms by destroying the army of this perfidious and barbarous king; but let their soldiers who have submitted and are disarmed, be treated with all that mildness which we have ever shown to the conquered. This sentiment exists in the hearts of all the children of the great nation.

The commander in chief, considering that justice and courage have always been the characteristics of the French nation, that cowards are always cruel, and that brave republicans, dreadful in action, are humane and gentle in victory, and never imitate the conduct of assassins, notwithstanding the cruelties practised by the Neapolitans to our wounded, decrees,

1st. All the Neapolitan prisoners shall be treated with the humanity due to a conquered and disarmed enemy.

2d. The officers shall take care to see that this order shall be carried into execution.

3d. Every French soldier, who is guilty of any violence to a disarmed prisoner, shall be severely punished.

              4th.

4th. The present order and the proclamation which precedes it shall be printed in both languages, inserted in the general orders, read at the head of every corps in the army, and copies of it sent to the generals of the Neapolitan armies.

(Signed) CHAMPIONET.

Head-quarters at Terni, 11th Dec. 1798.

Proclamation of the General in Chief of the Army of Rome, to the Neapolitans.

THE inhabitants of Civita Ducale fled at the approach of the French: they abandoned their asylums and their property. What an error! Inhabitants of these beautiful countries, reassure yourselves. The French entering the Neapolitan territory, do not wish to injure the people. The people ought not to suffer for the absurdities of a delirious government, which alone is guilty, and which shall alone be punished. Recall your children from these standards, under which they are kept by force. Let the impotent militia of a king who imposes upon you, march; they will be beaten wherever we find them. Be calm; return to your houses; let the rich inhabit their palaces, and the poor return to their cottages; rely confidently upon French justice, upon my word, and upon my protection. Your perfidious king will fall from his throne; but your religion, your altars, your opinions, and your property, shall be respected. I repeat it, reassure yourselves; but tremble if one single Frenchman is insulted.

(Signed) CHAMPIONET.

Army of Rome.

GENERAL Championet has addressed the following letter to the Roman consuls:

Monte Rotondo, 24th Frimaire (Dec. 14).

Rome is free, but it is not yet worthy to receive the French within its walls. I have demanded that the guilty should be given up to me. Rome, distracted by the spirit of fury and of revenge, ought not to present a spectacle of sorrow to its lawful representatives. I order you, therefore, citizens consuls, not to return to that capital, till tranquillity shall be re-established, and Rome shall be worthy to receive you.

(Signed) CHAMPIONET.

Message of ... ve Directory of the French Republic to the Council ... red, 24th Frimaire (December 14).

Citizens Representatives,

THE Executive Directory, in their message of the 6th inst. announced to you, that they should shortly transmit to you the details which make manifest the long train of perfidy of which the court of Naples have been guilty, brought to its height by an audacious attack on the French republic. It this day lays before you details which will prove not less clearly the hostile connivance of the court of Turin, which, joined to the machinations of the Sicilian King, have rendered that proposition necessary which they made to you, to declare war against the Kings of Naples and Sardinia. For a long time has Europe resounded with accounts of the perfidy of the Neapolitans; and for a long time must it have been astonished at the magnanimous moderation of the Executive Directory; while, on the other hand, the sincere desire of the French government to live at peace with the King of Naples was not less manifest. Superior to the just indignation which this court had provoked in so many ways, a court that, during the whole course of the war of the coalesced monarchs, distinguished itself by the most infensate fury against the republic, the French government received, with the most pure benevolence, the first propositions which were made to them for a good understanding between the two states; they made no other use of the superiority which our victories gave them, than for the purposes of moderation; in a word, all the advantages of the treaty were as reciprocal as if the successes of the war had been equal.

Such magnanimity should have for ever put an end to the malevolent dispositions of this court, and should have attached them to the republic by the ties of gratitude as well as of interest; but its blindness prevented it from laying aside its hostile prejudices; it gave way, without reserve, to all the hopes to which the idea of the destruction of the republic gave rise, while we alone were capable of defending them; and it took advantage of peace only for the purpose of carrying on secret hostility, while we, on our part, were the most rigid observers of the treaty. This contrast will be made to appear from incontestable facts. It would be needless here to recall to the recollection of our readers the odious and revolting conduct which distinguished the cabinet of Naples during the continuation of the war. Let us begin from the period when the republic, putting a stop to the progress of their victories, consented to grant it peace. From that period, from October 1795, by what inexplicable conduct has that perfidious court been distinguished!

When

When the French government showed itself resolute to overthrow that impious government which caused our warriors to be assassinated, the court of Naples, whose agents, it is obvious, were not strangers to these crimes, after having in vain attempted to aggrandize themselves with the ruins of that of Rome, which they feigned to respect, opposed all the resistance in their power to prevent the establishment of a republic on that soil, which was become the conquered land of liberty; this court increased her armaments, and marched towards the frontiers troops prepared to enter the Roman territory. All these extraordinary preparations she justified on futile pretences. She received the discontented at Rome with open arms; fomented the troubles which she had excited there; furnished the rebels with provisions and an asylum; and never ceased to assume towards this new republic the most threatening attitude. While she dared not openly to declare war against France, she sought to destroy in Italy all the free states which were under her protection.

The French government might, without doubt, have inflicted signal vengeance for this public protection, which was granted to the frequent insurrections formed at Rome against the French army, as well as for the increased number of spies with which our agent at Naples was surrounded; but, far from giving way to this just sentiment, the Directory did not think proper to oppose the taking possession of the dutchy of Benevento; they even offered their mediation to deliver the King of Naples from the feudal pretensions which Rome had on his estates. But this was not all; they sent to Naples a new ambassador, furnished with the most amicable and conciliatory powers. At the moment in which the army commanded by Buonaparte sailed, the Executive Directory were anxious to satisfy the King of Naples as to the object of this expedition. In short, they addressed to him the most repeated protestations of their unalterable desire to maintain tranquillity in Italy; adding, it is true, a not less energetic wish, that the Roman republic, which had been placed by the current of events under the special protection of the French republic, might be able to consolidate its political existence.

But neither friendly intercourse, nor the voice of reason, nor the necessity of peace, could inspire these sentiments in the breast of that court. Every pretence was made use of to justify her complaints, her threats, and, at length, her numerous infractions of treaty.

The French republic replied to the manifesto of Malta by the conquest of that island; at that moment the court of Naples, with the most ridiculous hauteur, dared to revive its pretensions on a country which it had neither governed by its laws nor by its arms; and the French government did not disdain to reply

at

at length to this nonsensical pretension, as if it could have been supported by the least appearance of reason.

From the moment of signing a peace, all the acts, as well public as private, of this court have been distinguished for perfidy and hatred towards the French. The treaty was signed, and the court delayed to publish it from motives of respect for the courts of London and Vienna. The seventh article promised liberty to all the French who were detained for political opinions, and all the Neapolitans suspected of having any connexion with them, who were imprisoned. At the solicitations of our agents, some of the peaceful friends to the French republic were restored to liberty; but upon the most vain pretences they were loaded with fresh chains. At length the French, whom commercial affairs alone detained in the states of the King of Naples, were every day, merely because they were French, publicly insulted, attacked, and even assassinated; and these attempts remained unpunished.

The third article of the treaty stipulated, that " his Majesty, the King of the Two Sicilies, shall observe the most strict neutrality towards all the belligerent powers; and he, therefore, engages to forbid, without distinction, the entry into his ports of all armed vessels belonging to the hostile powers, exceeding the number of four at least, according to the known laws of neutrality. All ammunition or merchandise known as contraband shall be refused to them."

How has this article, the sense of which is by no means ambiguous, been executed?

Forty days after the conclusion of the treaty, the English had seven frigates in the port of Naples; on the 9th Thermidor, the fourteen vessels of Admiral Nelson entered at full sail the ports of Augusta and Syracuse; and in whatever manner this article be interpreted, it is obvious that this was an infraction of it. The government of Naples thought themselves obliged to justify this proceeding, by representing that it was not in their power to resist force, a contemptible subterfuge, because it did not even attempt resistance, and because the senate of Syracuse received the English admiral with honours. About this period, too, the 17th Thermidor, five Portuguese ships of war, and three English ships, were received with equal eagerness in the port of Naples.

With respect to the furnishing of articles forbidden by this treaty, is it not notorious, that, immediately after the conclusion of peace, the French, attempting to prevent the English from getting provisions, the Neapolitan government gave orders to the governor of Orbitello to hinder them from passing, while he suffered a considerable corps of emigrants, who were in the service of England, to be disembarked? Is it not notorious, that the fleet of Admiral Nelson was first victualled in the ports of Sicily;

Vol. VIII.   R   that,

that, on its return afterwards to Naples, it received from the arfenal of the King the ftores of which it ftood in need? Is it not notorious, that, long before this epoch, on the 29th Prairial, the whole of the Englifh fleet having appeared before Naples, a brig was detached, which anchored in the port, and two officers, who came from on board it, had a converfation with General Acton and the Queen, in order to fecure whatever might be neceffary to the fuccefs of the attack upon the French fleet; that in addition to the affiftance and the affurance that they received from them, pilots were alfo furnifhed to clear the Straits of Meffina; a paffage which no fquadron, without fuch affiftance, would have dared to attempt; and in confequence of which they hoped to be able to cut off the French fleet, which were fuppofed to be yet at Malta? In a word, is it not clear that nothing that could be injurious to France has been refufed, by the court of Naples, to our implacable enemies?

If, in addition to this, the conduct which Naples has directly manifefted towards us be confidered; if it be recollected that, in fpite of the fourth article of the treaty, which ftipulates, " that the King of Naples fhall be bound to grant, in all his roads and ports, furety and protection to all French merchant-fhips, however numerous, and to all fhips of war which fhall not exceed four;" feveral of the convoy of the French fleet having been obliged to anchor in the roads of Sicily, commotions, evidently excited by the government of Naples, broke out at Trapani, at Gergonti, and at Meffina, in which feveral of the French foldiers who went on fhore were affaffinated: if it be recollected that, fince Malta has been in the hands of the French, the Maltefe boats, which came as ufual to take in provifions in Sicily, were prevented, the gates fhut againft them, and they were repulfed with fire-arms; that the plan of furprifing Malta, while it remained in the hands of the French, was not even diffembled by the Neapolitan government; and that a Maltefe bark, which was carrying French commiffaries fent to the Viceroy of Sicily, having been forced by an Englifh fhallop to take refuge at Alciata, the crew, having landed, were immediately purfued with mufketry by the Sicilians, and forced to re-embark, when the veffel was immediately taken by the Englifh, without the Neapolitan government making the fmalleft reprefentation to caufe the neutrality to be refpected: if too it be added, that on another occafion one of our corfairs having been carried off by force in the port of Baratto, the governor of that place did not condefcend to take any meafures to prevent fuch an attack upon the fovereignty of the King of the Two Sicilies; and, in fhort, that fuch are the hoftile delirium and hatred of the King of Naples towards the French and their allies, that in contempt of all the ties which fhould bind him to the King of Spain, he

had

had had the impudence to receive in his ports a Spanish prize taken by the English: if, too, we recollect the inconceivable joy which was manifested at Naples on the fight of the English fleet, the public honours which the court itself lavished on Admiral Nelson, in going out to welcome him; his triumphal entry; the large reward granted to the messenger who brought the first account of his victory; and the illuminations and rejoicings which took place on the occasion: if it be remembered that, from the time of this victory, the audacity of the Neapolitan government has known no bounds; that lately an unrestrained populace broke the windows of our consul at Naples, without the Neapolitan government having taken any measures to repress such an insult; that the late sedition at Malta was openly protected in the Neapolitan states; that the markets and all the public places resounded with the most terrible invectives against us; that all who were inclined to encourage peace with France were persecuted with the most acrimonious rage; that at length a barbarous order was issued by the King of Naples, menacing with death whoever should carry provisions to the French at Malta: if all these circumstances are considered, it must be allowed that more hostile sentiments were never manifested than on one side, nor more patience shown than on the other.

The Executive Directory, however, put off as long as possible the moment in which it was to wreak the vengeance of the nation. It was made clear by demonstration to them, that the court of Naples did not confine its hostility against the republic to complaints, menaces, or fury; that after having for a long time after the conclusion of the peace, shown the most hostile disposition, it had for a long time been at open hostility, and had furnished succours of all kinds on our most cruel enemy; that, in short, she was become the ally of Great Britain, and as useful to that power as she was prejudicial to us; and yet the French government, faithful to its desire of preserving peace even with Naples, was willing to hope that there was yet a possibility of repentance. This honourable illusion has been, however, dissipated by the Neapolitan government, which has brought its long train of perjuries to the height; it has dared to attack suddenly the French army, and to accompany this aggression with the most insolent menaces. The republican energy, long confined, will now break forth with the strength of thunder; and this court, too long spared, which, imitating the illegal conduct of the British government, has dared to be guilty of breaking the laws of peace, without having the courage to declare war, will at length receive the reward of its demerits.

But it is necessary, too, that those who have shown themselves its accomplices should also share the same fate. The Sardinian government has been the associate of its perfidies, and a similar fate awaits it; its guilt, as an accomplice with Naples, is manifest from a thousand circumstances; its sentiments, its language, and even its actions, in proportion to its means, have been the same; and its artifice and hypocrisy exactly resemble that of Naples. It would be difficult to account for its recent conduct towards France, if history did not, in all ages, make manifest the cunning and versatile politics of this court, constantly occupied in fomenting war among its neighbours; in taking a part in all the wars of Italy, and in shamelessly deserting its allies; in constantly joining that side which appeared most strong, in order to oppress the weak; in gratifying its revenge and its ambition; and in offering its support for sale to whoever was inclined to purchase it.

Independently of every other cause of complaint, who would believe that the treaty which we designed to conclude with the court of Turin, and which they ought to have considered as a signal favour, has not yet been published in all the states of the King of Sardinia? The agents of the republic have in vain requested that this might be done; their resistance has been invincible, and the most futile reasons have been assigned as a pretence for this delay, or rather for this refusal. In fact, they have never ceased to make war in every way which their imbecility and their cowardice suffered them to put in execution. Our most cruel enemies, the emigrants and refractory priests, have constantly met with a welcome reception in his dominions; there they have been suffered to give free vent to their hatred, and to the expressions of their barbarous wishes against the republic. They have even been able to excite the people against the French by the most atrocious calumnies. This is not all; from the moment in which peace was signed, the French, almost under the eyes of their ambassadors, have been assassinated in cold blood, and that chiefly by the regular troops. The assassinations have been committed almost daily, and the number of them is dreadful when the total amount shall be known. Some of them have fallen by the stiletto; some have been mutilated in the most dreadful manner. A volunteer of the 68th demi-brigade was buried alive, after having been barbarously wounded; he was seen coming alive out of the grave in which he had been buried; he was destined to escape, in order to offer a proof of this dreadful cruelty.

The agents of the French republic have expressed, in the name of the republic, the most energetic indignation; but they have been unable to prevent these crimes from going unnoticed or unpunished. Some banditti, enrolled under the name of barbets,

whose

whose business it is to rob and pillage, but whose amusement is to kill republicans, far from being dissipated by public authority, appear to be encouraged by it. Their thefts on the Piedmontese were forgiven, in consideration of their murder of the French. On this subject a long negotiation was entered into, which was considered by the Sardinian government as a public calamity, the object of which was not to obtain the suppression of, but the mere promise to repress, these banditti. On this condition the support of our arms was promised to them. But the Sardinian government was unwilling to obtain tranquillity at this price, and, after all, would not consent to issue a law against stilettoes and concealed arms; so fearful were they that the French should, by any means, be secure in their states! and during the course of the negotiation, and in spite of the formal promise to suspend a proceeding in which the most serious passions were manifested, several Frenchmen, who were implicated in an unhappy affair, were shot without pity.

Besides this enrolled banditti, besides judiciary banditti, the Duc d'Aost, a monster, the brother of the king, and the heir to the throne, like another Old Man of the Mountain, never ceased to keep under his orders, and in his pay, a band of cut-throats, to whom he issued orders to assassinate such and such a Frenchman; and these orders were but too faithfully executed.

It is in vain to suppose, that all these crimes were not imputable to the Sardinian government, since the whole of its conduct has proved that it was privy to every one of them. The principal places in Piedmont were occupied by French troops; for those no provisions were to be obtained. The friends of the republic were constantly thrown into prison, the Frenchmen insulted, and even their dress turned into derision; the emigrants were encouraged in their audacity; those public officers, who were most distinguished for their hatred towards the French, chiefly promoted, the barbets protected, even openly, by their civil magistrates; poniards forged, and distributed to a vast number; in short, the most dreadful plots against the French planned, and ready to be carried into execution. From an interrogatory ex...ed to one of the chiefs of the barbets, it appears that a person who was employed in the custom-house at Turin, and who was commissioned to pay this banditti, had received from the Sardinian government orders to distribute among the chiefs of them boxes of poison, to be thrown into the wells which lay near to the French camp.

It is evident that there exists the most intimate connexion between the conduct of such a government as this and that of the court of Naples, in their hostility to the French republic; this connexion, maintained and supported by so many crimes, would alone be sufficient to implicate the court of Turin in the guilt of

the

the other: but a stronger proof is added in the circumstances of the preparations for war being increased at Turin, in proportion as those at Naples were multiplied; the militia in the former place were called forth, and 30,000 stand of arms were delivered to them.

The Piedmontese troops marched towards Loana and Oneglia at the same moment in which the Neapolitan army attacked the French troops in the territory of the Roman republic, in which 6000 Neapolitans disembarked at Leghorn, and in which a new disembarkation was threatened on the coast of Liguria. It was in the same moment that the order to march on the first signal was given; that Turin was filled with troops; that 1500 poniards were distributed; that the citadel was nearly besieged; that the heights which command it were furnished with an extraordinary number of cannon; and that the Sardinian government dared to require the evacuation of the citadel, and the diminution of our troops in Piedmont.

In this situation of affairs it was impossible for the French government to separate two courts obviously so hostilely united against the French republic. But the Directory declares solemnly to Europe, that whatever may be the result of this war, no ambitious views shall intermeddle in the purity of the motives which have induced them to take up arms; and they declare to all governments, guiltless of the perfidy of the Neapolitans, that the treaties which bind them shall never have been more faithfully observed in times past than they shall be in times to come.

(Signed)   LA REVEILLIERE LEPAUX.

Army of Rome.

Head-quarters at Rome, December 17th.

Order of the Day.

Championet, General in Chief, to the Army.

Comrades,

WHILE you were beating the Neapolitans, the army of Italy was dethroning the King of Sardinia. That of Naples must also tumble from his throne. To-morrow we march. In all your contests with the enemy, you have been uniformly victorious. But six days march, and Naples shall be conquered. The general in chief orders, that every person employed in the army, subject to requisition or conscription, shall immediately cease his functions, and be incorporated in a demi-brigade, or regiment of cavalry. The generals, chief commissioner, and chiefs of the corps, are charged with the execution of the present order.

Turin,

Turin, December 18*th.*

Details respecting the Piedmontese Revolution, addressed to the Editor of the Feuille du Jour, *by A. Blondeau, Captain, acting immediately under the Order of the Adjutant General.*

ON the 30th November it was reported at Milan, that a great insurrection had taken place at Turin, and that the revolutionists had, with the protection of the French, dethroned and imprisoned the King. The general of division, Victor, was entrusted by the commander in chief, Joubert, with the superintendance of the expedition destined to give liberty to Piedmont. On the 3d of December his division, which was at Modena, set out on its march. On the 6th, Novare, the first place of strength, was taken by stratagem. It was our duty to prevent the effusion of blood. Fifteen brave grenadiers, with an officer of the staff at their head, being placed in carriages, which had the appearance of a convoy, demanded entrance, and the gate was opened to them. When they arrived at the guard-house, they threw themselves out of the carriages, seized the arms, and made the guard prisoners. The porter who had the care of the keys, attempted to lock the gate upon them; but having received a slight blow of a sword from one of the grenadiers, he ran off, and according to a preconcerted signal, the 15th regiment of light horse entered at full gallop into the town, and took possession of the head-quarters and the adjacent streets. It was soon after followed by a considerable column of infantry, which surrounded the barracks, and received the arms of the garrison, consisting of about 1200 men, both horse and foot. The column, after leaving two battalions in the place, continued its march, and halted at a small distance. On the 7th some Piedmontese troops at Vercelli, a small town on the way to Turin, retreated towards the metropolis. The French troops entered it the same night. The republicans were received there with the acclamations of the people, a general illumination took place, and the effigy of the King of Sardinia was carried throughout the town, and burnt, with his arms, in the principal square. On the 8th, the town of Chivasso, with a garrison of about 800 men, opened its gates to us without any resistance. The Piedmontese troops being thus disarmed in every place, the republican columns proceeded from all directions against Turin. The commander in chief entered the citadel the same day, and sent a notification to the King of the intentions of his government. This prince certainly was not ignorant that his troops had been disarmed, with the exception of those in garrison at Turin, and accordingly did not hesitate to consent to every proposition which was made to him, even to that of evacuating the city in person, which he

did

did about ten o'clock at night, with all his family, a part of his retinue, and some of his friends. I have never seen any thing which bore a greater resemblance to a funeral than this departure. There were about 30 carriages, each with two servants behind, carrying flambeaux in their hands, escorted by a numerous guard of dragoons, who observed the most profound silence in an obscure night, and during the most inclement weather. The French troops entered Turin on the 10th, and were received with universal acclamations. Every countenance manifested the most lively joy. A proclamation had been previously issued by the commander in chief, which announced to the Piedmontese troops, that they were to constitute part of the armies of the French republic, and they were in every respect to be considered as such. The proclamation produced every desired effect, and on the same night all the posts were given up to the French. At present the service is carried on in concert, and the French, the Piedmontese, the Swifs who were in the service of the *ci-devant* King, and the civic guard, are seen on the parade together. They all rival each other in zeal and patriotism. The tree of liberty was planted on the 12th, and although the weather was foggy and cold, the concourse of people was prodigious. All the troops of both nations, the civic guard, and even the body guards of the *ci-devant* King, were under arms. The air resounded with the shouts of " Long live the republic! Long live the French, the assertors of the liberty of oppressed countries!" The city was illuminated during the whole of the night; and the next day the fifteen members of the provisional government were installed with every solemnity. They were appointed by Citizen Eymar, commissioner of the French government.

Letter which the King of Naples addressed to his Subjects, after his Return to his Capital.

19*th December.*

NO sooner had I seen that the enemy were directing their force to attack my states, than I came in the midst of you, dear, faithful, and beloved subjects, in order to provide energetically for your defence, and to employ the most efficacious means to preserve to you religion, honour, prosperity, and life. I went myself to meet the danger, in order to ward off from you that loss, which the enemies of religion and of thrones had for a long time determined upon. The common safety depends upon you, my dearest subjects. The enemy are small in number. If you will it, you will be saved. Let all those who have courage, who love God, our sacred religion, and what they possess, take up arms to defend them. Recollect that the provincial

vincial militia, not numerous, but brave, levied in haste, and taken from the plough, maintained upon the head of my august father the crown of these kingdoms, which a skilful and experienced enemy wished to wrest from him. The Neapolitan never was a coward; and now, that it is the cause of God, your King, and yourselves, will you now suffer yourselves to be conquered? No, my dearest friends and brethren! Do not be deceived; if you do not hasten to defend yourselves, you will lose every thing, religion, life, property; and you will see your wives, your daughters, and your sisters dishonoured. Rise then, my faithful subjects; arm; defend yourselves; march bravely against the enemy, prevent them from entering the kingdom, or make them find in it their death and graves. March: call to your aid our great protector, St. Januarius: have confidence in God, who always protects his cause, for which each of you ought to fight, unless he means to deny his faith.

(Signed)   FERDINAND.

Joubert, Commander in Chief, to the Executive Directory.

Head-quarters at Turin, 23 Frimaire (December 20th).

Citizens Directors,

I INFORM you that the provisional government was installed on the 21st Frimaire (December 11th). Turin that day was what Paris was during the first days of the revolution. The shouts of *Vive la Liberté! Vive la Nation régénératrice!* were continued the whole day. The citizens were busily employed in congratulating each other. The enthusiasm was general. It was remarked, above all, in the Piedmontese troops, who, proud of being associated in the glorious labours of the French army, swore to render themselves worthy of it. I shall leave to your ambassador, who was present at this imposing ceremony, to transmit to you the interesting details. All the letters which I receive from the interior of Piedmont, assure me of perfect tranquillity and general satisfaction. The municipalities are installed in all the principal cities, and the Piedmontese troops cantoned there are eager to receive my orders. Health and respect.

(Signed)   JOUBERT.

VOL. VIII.   S   *Proclamation*

Proclamation of General of Division Serrurier, commanding a Corps of French Troops, on their entering the Territories of the Grand Duke of Tuscany, and the Republic of Lucca.

THE commander in chief of the French army orders me to enter the territories of the Grand Duke of Tuscany, not to inflict upon them the scourges of war, but to drive from them the English and Neapolitans, who have there established themselves, contrary to the faith of treaties. I will defend the person and property of the inhabitants; the existing form of government shall be preserved, and religion respected. Let the Grand Duke avoid all hostile influence, and he may remain tranquil in his possessions. Inhabitants of Lucca, I repeat, I come not to destroy your government; your persons and properties shall be religiously respected, but in other respects the conduct of your government must regulate mine.

(Signed) SERRURIER.

Head-quarters, Modena, 8th Nivose (December 28).

Proclamation of Buonaparte to the Inhabitants of Cairo, dated Nivose (December 28th).

PERVERSE men had succeeded in misleading a party amongst you: they have perished. God has ordered me to be merciful towards the people, and I have been clement and merciful towards you: I have been incensed against you on account of the revolt; I have deprived you for two months of your Divan: but this day I restore it to you; your good conduct has effaced the stain of your rebellion. Sherifs, vimas, orators of the mosque, cause the people well to understand, that those who, through any levity, shall become my enemies, shall find no refuge in this world or in the next. Shall there be a man so blind, as not to see that all my operations are conducted by destiny? Can there be a man so incredulous as to doubt that every thing in this vast universe is subjected to the empire of destiny? Instruct the people, that since the world has existed it was written, that, after having destroyed the enemies of Islamism (Mahometanism), and destroyed the cross, I should come from the farthest part of of the west to fulfil the task which was imposed upon me. Make the people see that, in the second book of the Koran, in more than twenty passages, that which has happened was foreseen, and that which shall take place, has also been explained: let those then whom the fear of our arms alone prevents from pronouncing imprecations on us, now change their dispositions; for in offering prayers to Heaven against us, they solicit their own condemnation: let the true believers then offer their vows to Heaven

for

for the success of our arms. I could call to account each individual amongst you for the most secret sentiment of his heart; for I know every thing, even that which you never communicated to any person: but the day will come when all the world shall see it proved, that I am commanded by orders from above, and that all human efforts are of no avail against me. Happy those who in good faith shall be the first to attach themselves to me.

(Signed)   BUONAPARTE.

Proclamation of General Hedouville to the Inhabitants of St. Domingo, dated 22d October.

AFTER having done all the good in my power to this colony, I have only, before I quit it, to warn you against an evil which I am unable to avert. A long while have the emigrants cast their eyes on Saint Domingo, which they hoped would become their prey. Beaten every where by our victorious armies, they have been received in all the different places of this colony, occupied by the English; civil and military employments have been given to them; and when they were thought sufficiently strong to put in execution their plans of independence, connected with the cabinet of St. James's, and the federal government, the English commanders made a show of retiring, but without taking with them the troops in the pay of England, not even the officers who commanded them. It was in vain that, in order to destroy the sources of the evil, I had excepted from the amnesty every individual who had filled civil and military employments in the service of the King of England; for a crowd of emigrants, from without, came and joined them. Firm, notwithstanding, in the resolution of driving from the colony these dangerous enemies, I ordered the strict execution of the law against emigrants; but the *arrêté* relative to this measure either never came to the hands of the proper authorities, or remained without execution on the part of those who have sold themselves to England.

Then the enemies of the republic dropped the mask, and spoke openly of independence. It was against the national authority that they began their attack. The most atrocious calumnies were invented; and whilst all my acts tended only to the execution of the laws, they dared to attack their motives, and to ascribe to them consequences injurious to the public welfare; as if the public functionary and the simple citizen could have any other proper guide and safeguard than the laws.

Whilst general liberty is the object of their profound hatred, they go so far as to insinuate that I wish to destroy it. But know, citizens, that at the same instant, aware of the vexations that the citizens of colour underwent in the United States, when their misfortunes had induced them to seek an asylum, I invited the consuls of the republic to send them back again in preference to all other refugees.—Know that I agreed with the governor of the isle of Cuba for the transport of 300 black citizens and Caraibs of the island of St. Vincent's, who had been banished by the English, and sent to the island of Rattan.—Know that those who, at this moment, offer you their protection, are the most cruel enemies of your liberty.—Know, in short, that those who oppose the establishment of the constitutional order, are only fearful of seeing an end put to their domination and their tyranny.

Will you be free, citizens? Recognise no other empire than that of the law; and let the voice of the magistrates, which speaks in its name, always find you ready to obey it. Rally then round the constitutional act, before which all prejudices ought to disappear, and let France reckon you among the number of her children.

Done at the Cape, 1st Brumaire, 7th year of the French republic, one and indivisible.

T. HEDOUVILLE.
GAUTIER, Secretary.

To the Merchants of France.

Address of Citizen Cafe, Aide-de-Camp of the General in Chief of St. Domingo, 31st December.

CHARGED with the last dispatches of General Toussaint Louverture, commander in chief of the army of the republic in St. Domingo, I have brought to the Executive Directory incontestable proofs of the attachment of that chief to the mother-country, of his love for the republic, his zeal for its interests, and his earnest desire to establish in that colony that order and tranquillity, union and confidence, which ambitious intriguers, the enemies of France and of her prosperity, seemed to have for ever removed.

After having accomplished my mission with the government, it is my next duty to destroy the disagreeable impressions which have been made on the public opinion by the calumnious reports, designedly circulated in the English journals, and repeated by the French papers, of a plan of independence, or criminal connivance, between General Toussaint and the English.

It would doubtless be sufficient to remind you of the frank and honourable conduct of this general since he was invested with the command of St. Domingo, and of the unequivocal testimony of all those who have had an opportunity of estimating his morality and his intentions, in order to show the absurdity

absurdity of the frantic project that is ascribed to him, were it not obvious, that a plan of this kind (had the commander in chief conceived it) would never obtain the consent of the people who inhabit this colony, nor of the army and its officers who defend it. Were such a plan in existence, it will at least be allowed that it must be carried on in concert with all the parties interested.

It never entered into the imagination of any of the present defenders of St. Domingo to detach themselves from the mother-country, to whom they owe their liberty and their existence, and to throw themselves into the arms of a rival, who has done every thing to reduce them again to slavery, or to annihilate them.

The late events which have taken place in St. Domingo, are not of a nature to give credit to the ill-founded suspicions which have been circulated as to the fidelity of General Toussaint Louverture. They were not preceded, and have not been followed, by any symptom which ought to be considered alarming for the republic, whose sacred interests will always be the object of the most earnest solicitude of that disinterested chief, who is zealous to show himself worthy of the reputation his virtues have acquired him, and of the confidence placed in him by a government which is the declared protector of liberty, the friend of order and of national prosperity.

It is particularly the merchants of France whom the British agents at London and Paris have endeavoured to inspire with distrust as to the disposition of the chiefs of St. Domingo; this is done in order to suspend the relations of the mercantile interest of France with St. Domingo, which would produce the double object of depriving France of the immense resources which this rich country affords, and to compel St Domingo to give its produce to the English traders, in exchange for their manufactures: but let not the French merchants be led into this snare; let them, on the contrary, redouble their activity, and they will soon be convinced of the perfidy of our enemies.

The planters of St. Domingo, duped by the bad faith of the neutral islands, have long since been desirous of renewing their commercial connexions with their brethren in Europe. The abundance of the productions of the country, and the scarcity or bad quality of foreign merchandise and stores, promise to the French speculators the most profitable return. The national interest and the private advantage of individuals ought not to induce the French merchants to re-establish, as soon as possible, the commercial relations which formerly subsisted between the mother-country and her colonies. This is the most intimate bond with which France can be united. It is time to rescue the colonies from the English monopoly, to which the apathy of
commerce

commerce has reduced them, and to re-open those channels which will give facility to the industry of the inhabitants of both the French hemispheres.

(Signed) CASE, junior.

Head quarters at Capua, December 31.
Copy of a Letter from General Mack to the General in Chief Championet.

Monsieur General,

I HAVE received an order from my government, to propose to you an armistice, to afford some repose to the troops of both armies in this inclement season, and after so much fatigue, occasioned by the frequent marches which they have made, and continual snows and rains.

If this proposition be agreeable, Monsieur General, the bearer of the present, my Adjutant General, Pignatelli, is authorized to treat with the person whom you shall be pleased to nominate for that purpose, and to conclude a limited or unlimited armistice, upon the basis of the line of the outposts of the two armies.

I am, Monsieur General, with consideration,

Captain General MACK.

St. Germano, 12th Nivose, 7th Year of the French Republic, one and indivisible, January 1.

Letter from the General in Chief Championet to Captain General Mack.

I HAVE received, Monsieur General, your proposals for an armistice. Humanity alone is the burden of your letter; bad roads, rain, snow—these are your motives.

But the army, with its ordinary patience, has surmounted every thing. Nothing more remains for it but the invasion of Naples. I march to accomplish its wishes, and to execute the orders of my government, which, in consequence of your declaration of war at the mouth of the cannon, has charged me with punishing that insult.

I am sorry, for my part, that my instructions lead me to reject your proposals.

(Signed) CHAMPIONET.

Message from the Executive Directory to the Council of Five Hundred,
January 14.

Citizens Representatives,

THE Executive Directory was upon the point of laying before you new observations upon maritime legislation, as it respects prizes, when it received your message of the 16th Frimaire. By now addressing to you general views relative to privateering and its consequences, it is persuaded it perfectly fulfils those intentions by which it has been actuated.

The practice of privateering is the natural consequence of a state of war; but it is not a private act, by which a citizen of a country, of his own accord, and at his own expense, associates in enterprises against the general enemy. The government, being alone invested with the right of carrying on hostilities, has the sole direction and guidance of whatever forms a part of the means of war; and it is in virtue of that right it gives the private adventurer its express authority to seek, fight, and capture enemies' ships; an authority without which he cannot act.

Thus the direct object of privateering is to intercept and destroy the commerce of the nation with which we are at war; therefore all ships which sail under an enemy's flag are evidently liable to seizure. But if it may happen, on the one hand, that an enemy's ship may contain the property of a government, or an individual, neutral or friendly; so on the other, it ought to be remembered that belligerent nations, who cannot navigate with safety under their own flags, borrow those of neutral powers, in order to protect their property, and thus secure the continual and easy exportation of the produce of their soil and industry. The repeated and partial practice of this deceit diminishes that respect which is due to a neutral flag, and renders it necessary to adopt the means of discovering and seizing enemies' property wherever it may be met with on the sea, and by whatever flag it may be protected.

It is therefore a duty to form a legislation, with respect to privateering, applicable to that object alone, not only to determine and regulate its action, but to judge and decide upon its consequences.

In this legislation two objects are distinguishable; the law by which the practice of privateering is exercised, and the mode by which its action is judged.

The first act of French jurisprudence relative to privateering was towards the close of the fourteenth century, and until the middle of the seventeenth this part of maritime legislation remained among all the nations of Europe in a chaos of contradiction and obscurity, which first began to dissipate by the stipulations included in the 19th and 20th articles of the treaty of the Pyrennees, importing, " that merchandises seized in an enemy's ship are liable to confiscation,

fication, whomsoever they may belong to; nevertheless, merchandise the property of an enemy, if on board a neutral ship, shall not be confiscated, except it is contraband."

This double principle, that an enemy's flag should cause the condemnation of whatever it protected, whilst a neutral flag should guarantee its safety, was again recognised by the 8th article of the treaty of Aix-la-Chapelle, and prevailed in France until the publication of the ordinance of 1681, which still remains the basis of our maritime legislation; the 7th article of which, under the head Prizes, restrains those of the treaty of the Pyrennees, by declaring, " that every ship laden with effects belonging to enemies, and merchandise of every kind found in an enemy's vessel, shall be equally considered as good prize."

The regulation of 1704 went still farther, and declared " seizable all merchandise coming from, supposed to belong to, or of the manufacture of, an enemy."

But we must remark, that as the government which made the law proceeded at the same time to its application, its severity was advantageous, because it could be relaxed as suited the occasion. Thus it may be seen that in all wars which have taken place anterior to the present one, as often as the rigorous application of the regulations could compromise the political interests of the state, the government did not fail, by a declaration or by a ministerial letter, to determine what decision was to take place, and sometimes to modify that which had taken place: and it is precisely, because, in a free constitution, no executive or judicial authority can have the right of interpreting or modifying the law, that it is indispensable in the legislative body itself to reform that which may be demonstrated vicious.

Further, the ancient government took care at the beginning of every war, wherein it was necessary to arm privateers, to revise the former laws on that subject, to confirm or modify their application by reference to treaties which it had entered into, or upon principles which it judged important should prevail.

Thus the regulation of 1744 is founded upon the changes which had occurred since 1704, with respect to the connexion between France and certain states; and the 14th and 15th articles establish formal exceptions in favour of Denmark, Sweden, Holland, and the Hanse Towns.

That of 1778 had for its basis more liberal principles, because the American war, having for its object the revenging the injuries and losses of an age, by the freedom of the English colonies, and of protecting, at the same time, the liberty of the sea, the French government was induced the more to appreciate the rights of neutral nations, and to feel that whatever it did in favour of them was a blow struck against England.

Immediately after the powers of the North had formed a treaty for an armed neutrality, the French government was eager, in most earnestly manifesting its regard for neutral navigation, by acceding to the principle announced in the treaty, by inviting Spain to admit it, by ordering privateers to respect neutral flags, and by prescribing to the council of prizes, to conform its judgments to the new declaration.

Such was the French legislation on the subject of prizes in the American war; such it was in preceding wars. At the same time that government granted permission to arm privateers, it definitively judged all the consequences of privateering; and as it judged them by laws it had made, and which it could modify at its pleasure, the perfection of those laws was necessarily of little importance, because the government could, according to its views, conciliate the interests of the privateerer with those of the country and of commerce in general.

The evil then was not in the judgments of the government being unjust, but because the law was of its own making, and depended on its will alone.

The evil has since been, that in giving up to the government, according to the most sacred principle of a free constitution, the right of making or modifying laws, instead of entirely reforming those which existed relative to privateering, and which were inconsistent with a republican regime, it has been thought proper to refer the application of them to the executive authority.

What happened in fact at the beginning, and in the course of the war?

It was the National Convention which, finding itself invested with full powers, permitted privateering, determined upon the delivery and form of letters of marque; and by its decree of the 14th February, in attributing to the tribunals of commerce the decision upon prizes, directed "that the ancient laws should continue to be executed until otherwise ordered."

By the ancient laws, if thereby we may understand the regulation of 1778, and the unrepealed dispositions of those of 1681, 1701, and 1744, it was difficult not to admit equally the modifications that resulted from particular decisions, which the importance of circumstances had made the ancient government adopt; so that, in remitting to the ordinary tribunals the right of pronouncing upon the validity of prizes, they abandoned them to an incomplete and superannuated jurisprudence, often contradictory, and of which no authority in the republic could correct or direct the application.

During the first years of the present war, the inconveniences of this legislation were less felt:—1. Because privateering was almost exclusively directed against the ships of direct enemies, and because the capture of a ship under an enemy's colours seldom gives room for contest. 2. Because the National Convention,

Vol. VIII.　　　　　T　　　　　having

having speedily perceived the danger of the powers granted to the commercial tribunals in matters of commerce, had, by their decree of the 18th Brumaire (second year), restored to the executive provisional council the right of pronouncing through the medium of administration upon the validity of prizes: a right which, after the suppression of the executive council, continued to be exercised by the committee of public safety, to the epoch in which the law of the 3d Brumaire, 4th year, completed by that of the 8th Floreal of the same year, committed again to the ordinary tribunals the decision upon contests in matters of prizes.

It was then privateering commenced against neutral flags, and that the questions upon prizes were seen to multiply, and to be rendered complicated daily. To the ancient regulations were annexed some recent laws, which served to strengthen the opinion that privateering could not be too much encouraged, to obtain full success: and to judge with certainty of the utility of the system followed in this respect, it is necessary to examine the results of privateering under the double relation of the internal prosperity of the republic, and of her consideration, or of her external credit: for it might happen that the means taken, with the view of a real advantage, might not have fulfilled the object of their institution.

In the most flourishing times of the French commerce and marine, the population of the maritime inscription amounted to 80,000 men. At present there are not half left. The corsairs alone have, in three years, placed more than 20,000 individuals in the balance of exchange in favour of England. The fate of almost all the ships armed as privateers, is, to fall either sooner or later into the hands of the enemy.

But, without being taken, a corsair often loses the greater part of his crew, because he is obliged to send his best men on board the prizes taken; and thus, when they are intercepted, either at sea or on the coast, which frequently happens, the men and ships are lost at once.

The law of the 31st of January 1793 directs, " that vessels armed for privateering shall not have more than a sixth of their crew in sailors." Whatever efforts the Directory may make, this law is too frequently evaded. The person fitting out the privateer, contends with money in his hand against the service of the republic, obtains the preference, excites desertion, embarks the best sailors: and privateering, instead of forming sailors, according to the spirit of its institution---instead of recalling to the sea-service those who retired from it, employs only sailors already formed, and among them the best, who, too often captured, are lost to the republic.

If the privateers have introduced into France some provisions; if they have given activity to some commercial places; if they
have

have appeared to be the sole acting portion of the naval force of the republic; on the other hand, the yards and docks of the republic are deserted; her armaments cannot be completed for want of sailors; and it is for this reason that privateering has been too numerous, and too much encouraged, and that the armaments of the republic have been struck with a kind of palsy.

It is for the same reason, that neutral ships, driven from our ports, afford no market for our territorial productions: and when we speak of the benefits of privateering, we must examine if it is not concentred in five or six places, whilst the whole republic, deprived of the more extensive advantages which the peaceful and respected commerce of neutral ships would procure, pays double the natural value for colonial produce, sees her own articles disparaged, and her resources destroyed, by the absolute failure of exportation; for, in short, if privateers import into France some articles, they export more; and, what is unhappily too true, there is not a single merchantman trading under French colours! What other means of exportation have we but the employment of neutral ships? And is it proper to drive them from our ports, when they are so indispensable to us, under two capital relations, for the supplying our colonies and our marine?

We cannot have forgotten, that northern cargoes, the most rare, rich, and most impatiently expected, shipped on board neutral ships on account of government, have been taken by French privateers---some condemned, and others escaping condemnation with difficulty.

It is, then, impossible to be concealed, first, that the number and sort of sailors that remain, forming no proportion to the wants of our navy, every arming of a privateer is, in some sort, an attack at present upon the naval force of the republic. Second, that the supplies of our navy, of our colonies, and the exportation of our own articles, not being able to be effected without the aid of neutral ships, they are paralysed by our own measures.

And if we examine next the effect of privateering with relation to our external credit, we shall see that it is not less adverse.

Let it be recollected what was the moderation of the French government to neutral powers during the first years of the war. The piracies of England increased the merit of that moderation in the eyes of all Europe. It was against them that neutral ships armed at our solicitation; at the same time our negotiations announced to the maritime powers, " that the plan of our government was not to give peace to England, but upon condition of subscribing to a fundamental charter of the rights of neutrality, which should constitute in future the safeguard of peaceful nations."

These

These words, confirmed by all our proceedings, and which should, without doubt, have rallied round us all neutral powers to labour in common for the destruction of the usurpation of the English, produced, however, on the part of the states of the North, only cold looks towards the republic, interested services, and inefficacious resistance to the continual violation of their neutrality by the English.

Affected at once in her dearest interests by the conduct of the British government, and the slothful resignation of neutral powers, France was then obliged to renounce, for a time, the liberal principles which she had attempted to establish; and, not to be the victim of a false generosity, she announced at last to neutral powers, "that we should behave to them as they suffered the English to behave."

This measure produced a very good effect: the English ceased to capture, indiscriminately, all neutral ships which they supposed destined for France. Neutral powers even assert, that they accelerated the payment of sums due for preceding captures; and if, at the same time that the arret of the 14th Messidor was become to privateers an encouragement which they laid hold of, the government has not been deprived of the right of pronouncing definitively upon the effect of their expeditions; it must have had the power of regulating and preventing them from being carried beyond the just reprisals, which the unrepressed audacity of the English had rendered necessary: perhaps even it might obtain from neutral nations more energetic conduct and useful efforts for the maintenance of their rights; whereas the privateers having gone beyond what the well-understood interest of their country claimed, the effect of their unlimited action has been to drive entirely from our ports the neutral flags, which it was of importance to encourage, for the purpose of keeping, by competition, at a higher price, our productions and merchandise, and at a lower rate the price of freight and insurance.

It is, therefore, wrong to regard as a real source of riches, as a means of prosperity, the too great latitude given to the practice of privateering. Its utility is essentially relative, subordinate to circumstances, to the position and the wants of countries; and certainly a state, whose prosperity depends on its agriculture, on its own productions and industry, which consumes much, and has much left to export, should be always the most interested that commercial relations should be maintained in their fullest integrity, and in complete security.

It is time then, that we should adopt, upon the subject of privateering, juster ideas, and a system more conformable to the interest of the country, and more truly organized for the destruction of the monopoly and rapacity of the English.

If the practice of privateering has failed in attaining that object,

(141)

ject), it is because its legislation is defective, particularly with respect to the mode by which its consequences are determined.

Citizens representatives, place again before your eyes the message which the Directory sent you the 2nd Floreal, of the 6th year. It is there demonstrated, that the disputes relative to prizes are not to be decided by the ordinary forms of justice; and that, as privateers are but auxiliaries to the armed force, and privateering but a mean of war in the hands of government, the consequences which result from it can only be judged by those who have authorized and directed it.

Every other consists in this: "that constantly assimilating the disputes relative to prizes with those between citizens of the same state, a regulation relative to privateering, to a law purely civil or criminal, it is feared that the *arbitrament* given to government may partake of a judicial power."

But if it is true that the ancient regulations have blended those things which ought now to be distinguished, and which cannot be referred to the same mode of determination, this is of itself a sufficient reason for the necessity of reforming them.

That which the law should grant to the government is the right of pronouncing definitively upon prizes, and upon the validity or non-validity of them, conformably to treaties; because this attribute is truly inherent in the functions delegated to government, and is indispensable for enabling it to employ privateers to the advantage of the state.

This decision should emanate from government alone; for when all governments have consented that prizes should be judged of in the countries of the captors, they have supposed that the decision always emanating from the executive power, they could on all occasions be parties through the medium of their ambassadors, in a cause which relates to their immediate interest, and that of their subjects. It is therefore manifest that there can be no question relative to prizes, which does not more or less concern the interests of the country, especially when it is considered that, in the present state of our maritime legislation, every tribunal pronouncing in the last resort relative to a prize under a neutral flag, is really invested with the terrible right of placing the republic in a state of war, against the wish, and without the knowledge, of its government.

War is rekindled on the continent; and this scourge renewed, attests the intrigues and influence of England. It is her we must pursue, it is her we must destroy. But let us avoid deceiving ourselves as to the means, the object of which is to revenge all nations; and let us not imprudently prepare for the Britannic cabinet, by means which seem directed against it, a new source of success for its intrigues, and an increase but too certain to that monopoly which it already exercises on all the seas, and in all the markets.

Penetrated

Penetrated with the force of these considerations, the Directory has less hesitation in informing you, citizens representatives, that it answers your demand made in your message of the 16th Frimaire, by sufficiently proving that instead of giving at this time greater latitude to the practice of privateering, it is essentially necessary to modify and regulate its action.

The Executive Directory considers, therefore, that it is its duty specially to invite you to revise the legislation relative to prizes, and previously to decide as an essential basis, that from this time contests relative to prizes shall be in the last resort determined administratively.

(Signed)   REVEILLIERE LEPAUX, President.
LAGARDE, Secretary General.

Proclamation of the Governor to the Inhabitants of the several Provinces of Naples.

HIS Majesty's paternal care for his subjects increases in proportion to the dreadful events of the present war. His enemies being aware of the weakness of their forces against a faithful people, have employed the arms of corruption to weaken and divide them, and by such base means have obtained possession of a part of his kingdom. Cowardice and treachery only have rendered this invasion dreadful. The bravery and the attachment of the people to their religion, their sovereign, and to their country, must speedily have the effect of rendering their enemies contemptible. A pretended armistice, illegally negotiated, and more illegally concluded with the enemy on the 11th instant, far from producing any benefit to his Majesty's subjects, cannot fail to increase the evils and dangers to which they are already subject: enormous contributions, cessions of fortresses, strong holds, extent of territory very important to the enemy, a free intercourse and communication with our traitors and seducers, in order to delude and subjugate the inoffensive and unwary people, under the appearance of a short and deceitful reconciliation, are part only of the evils with which this armistice is pregnant. The French have employed the same means in Piedmont and Rome: what has been the consequence? Those devoted people have been stripped of all their property, and now groan under the most oppressive tyranny.

His Majesty, who never gave powers to his servants to treat for such an armistice, declares it null and void: the happiness and safety of his beloved subjects, his honour, his fidelity towards his allies, who assist, and will assist him, required from him this declaration. In these circumstances, his Majesty relies on the readiness and fidelity of his provinces, whose government he

has

has been pleased to confer on me, directing me to supersede the ordinary forms, too slow and unequal to the present emergency; the objects of my administration are the speedy embodying of all those who are willing to preserve whatever is dear to man, the active administration of justice, and the prompt and equal distribution of rewards and punishments. By such means, inhabitants of these countries, if you are willing to preserve your religion, your country, your property, and your families, you will succeed; but not an instant must be lost: his Majesty, from the neighbouring kingdom, will support your exertions with all the vigour with which he is inspired: he has taken, and he is still taking, the most effectual measures in your behalf, in concurrence with his allies; and you, people of these countries, besides the preservation of all that is dear to you, and the reward I am directed to bestow on those whose exertions shall deserve it, you will have the glory of having preserved the throne of your excellent King, who for these forty years has been wholly intent on your happiness and prosperity.

Letter from the King of Naples to General Pignatelli, Commander in Chief at Naples during the Absence of his Majesty; dated Palermo, January 15th, 1799.

AT the time when, from the urgency of circumstances, and the good dispositions manifested by my people, to which in your former letters you have done justice, I expected a general rising in defence of the capital of my kingdom, I receive yours of the 12th instant, which informs me of the disgraceful treaty which has been concluded, in consequence of the most absurd instructions given by you to persons directed to negotiate with the enemy, and by which I see the greatest part of my realm, though unconquered, given up with a view of sparing the capital, when it is obvious that these concessions must lead to the irretrievable loss of my whole kingdom. I have been more surprised that you have acted in this unwarrantable manner, as you had no powers from me for such negotiations. The instructions I left with you were of a tendency very different. In concluding such a treaty, you may either have forgotten you have a master, or remember it only for the purpose of imposing the most scandalous and disgraceful terms on him.

You may suppose how much I am incensed at finding the trust I had reposed in you betrayed in such a manner, and how indignant I feel against your unworthy advisers.

F. R.

French

French Palace at Pera, near Constantinople, Jan. 15, 1799.

Letter to his Excellency Mr. Spencer Smith, Minister Plenipotentiary of his Britannic Majesty at the Sublime Porte, from the Officers and other French Soldiers, Prisoners to the English, who have this Day come from Prison.

WE owe to your Excellency our gratitude for the first steps which, in conjunction with the efforts of your brother, have been crowned with success for our liberation; and we embrace the first moments of freedom to discharge the debt of thanks. Europe need not be told all that your Excellency and your brother have done here in favour of the unfortunate French, in order to judge of the generosity of the nation whom you represent with so much credit to yourself; but forty-six families, who are indebted to you for the restoration of children, of husbands, and of fathers, will feel the necessity of making this public; and we are anxious to be the medium of it. Unable to pay our respects in person to your Excellency, we request the favour of you to accept our grateful acknowledgments, and our profound respect.

The Chief of the Battalion of Engineers,

PASCAL VOLLONGE,

For himself and Comrades.

Note transmitted by the Sublime Porte to the Ambassador from the Republic of Holland.

THE present government of France, entirely disregarding every law of nations, having adopted as a principle to attack all powers without distinction, whether friends or enemies, and every where to disseminate disturbance and confusion, in consequence of this principle secretly prepared the means to subjugate Egypt, the most valuable province of this sublime empire, and which is the gate of the two sacred and revered cities, Mecca and Medina. In vain was it officially declared, that if such a project were engaged in, it must inevitably produce a sanguinary war between every Mussulman nation and France; the republic still persisted in its base design, suddenly attacked, and Egypt was plunged into confusion and anarchy. The Sublime Porte has, in consequence, found itself under the absolute necessity of repelling force by force, as it had previously and solemnly declared to the Directory all these facts; and the measures taken by the Sublime Porte to resist these unjust and shameful proceedings are of public notoriety. The republic of Holland is the ancient friend of the Sublime Porte; no cloud until the present day had ever overcast this friendship on either side; and it is certain, that the

the Dutch, who maintain a very lucrative commerce with the Ottoman empire, have always endeavoured, during the time of their independence, to render themselves agreeable to the Sublime Porte. But, since the entrance of the French into Holland, two parties have arisen, who have submitted to the French—the one voluntarily, and the other by force. The former of these, under the phantom of a perfidious alliance, have seized on the maritime force, and all the revenues of the country, which they employ to ruin, and plunge it into the most disastrous condition. Holland is, therefore, now deprived of its independence, and reduced beneath the yoke of the five French Directors like the provinces of France; its inhabitants are, in fact, become their subjects.

The Sublime Porte is, without doubt, animated with the desire of maintaining its ancient friendship with this republic; but it is evident, that the reasons above alleged render it improper that the ambassador of Holland should continue to reside near it. He is, therefore, hereby enjoined to quit this residence within a week, and informed, that the ancient amity and most perfect good understanding will be re-established between the Sublime Porte and the republic of Holland, as soon as the latter shall be separated from the French, a separation which will promote its true interests, and restore it to its former dignity.

January 16, 1799.

Proclamation of General Grouchy, Commander in Chief of the Army of Piedmont.

Head-quarters, Turin, January 18.

EMANUEL Grouchy, general of division commanding in Piedmont, being informed that the balls which have been held at the theatre of Carignan have been attended with disorders of different kinds; that citizens have been insulted and threatened there; that the measures taken to repress these disorders by the armed force have been calumniated; and that proposals contumacious to the French government have been advanced: being also informed, that in the streets of Turin, as well as in the different coffee houses, anarchists, no doubt excited and paid by royalism and aristocracy, have persecuted citizens, either on account of their dress, or in compelling them to acts contrary to personal respect and individual liberty; orders the commandant of the place to cause the ball held at the theatre of Carignan to be suppressed, enjoins him to get all those arrested who may in public insult the authorities established by the commander in chief, form meetings, wear marks of their parties, and who may finally, by their acts or proposals, endeavour to

Vol. VIII. U substitute

substitute licentiousness for liberty, in order that they may be tried conformably to the French laws. The commandant of the place, the commander of the national guard, and the chief officers of police, shall adopt measures in concert to carry into execution the present order.

(Signed)   EMANUEL GROUCHY.

Proclamation of General Championet to the Neapolitans on the 23d January, the Day on which the French obtained Possession of Naples.

Citizens,

I HAVE for a moment suspended the military vengeance, provoked by the horrible licentiousness and frenzy of some individuals hired by your assassins. I am well convinced that the Neapolitans are a good people, and I am heartily sorry for the evils they have suffered. Profit, then, Citizens, of this opportunity; return to order, surrender your arms at Chateau Neuf, and your religion, your persons, and your property shall be protected. The houses from which a musket shall be fired shall be burnt, and the inhabitants shot; but if tranquillity be re-established, I shall forget the past, and happiness shall spring up in these smiling countries."

Championet, Commander in Chief of the Army of Naples, to all the Inhabitants of the ci-devant Kingdom of Naples.

YOU are at length free; your love is the only price which France desires to obtain from you for your liberty, and the only clause of the treaty of peace, which the army of the republic comes to ratify by a solemn oath with you within the walls of the capital, and on the subverted throne of your last king. Misery be to the wretch who shall refuse to sign with us this honourable compact, in which the fruit of victory is given to the vanquished, and which only leaves to the conqueror the glory of having consolidated your happiness; he shall be treated as a public enemy, against whom we remain in arms. If there are still among you hearts so ungrateful as to reject that liberty which we have gained for you at the expense of our blood, or men so insane as to regret a king deprived of the right of commanding them, in consequence of his violating the oath which he had sworn to defend them; let them fly for protection to standards which are disgraced by perjury! War shall be prosecuted against them to extermination. Republicans, the cause under which you have so generously suffered is ultimately victorious. What the brilliant victories of the army of Italy had not been able to accomplish, has been happily ply effected by the blindness of your last king. Let him then blame his own mad pride, and his audacious aggressions, for the happiness of your fate, and the disgrace which he has experienced; but let him be justly punished for having attacked, against the faith of oaths, a nation in alliance with him; and for having attempted to deprive a neighbouring nation of their liberty: let him be punished by the loss of a crown which he has dishonoured, and by the chagrin of having been the principal instrument in making you free: let no apprehension embitter the sentiment of an happiness so unexpected. The army which I command remains in the midst of you for your defence; it will lose its best men, it will shed its last drop of blood, before it will allow your last tyrant to entertain even the hope of renewing the proscriptions of your families, and of opening again the dungeons in which he has caused them so long to pine. Neapolitans, if the French army assume now the title of the army of Naples, it is in consequence of the solemn engagement into which it has entered to die for your cause, and to make no other use of its arms than to maintain your independence, and to preserve your rights, which it has vindicated. Let the people, therefore, be assured of the full enjoyment of their religion, and cease to be alarmed with respect to the rights of property. The force of interest has maintained the tyrants in the great exertions they have made to calumniate, in the eyes of the world, the integrity, generosity, and good faith of the French nation; but, to a nation so generous, a few days are sufficient to divest credulous men of the odious prejudices to which tyranny has recourse, to incite them to deplorable excesses. The organization of plunder and assassination projected by your last king, and excited by his corrupt agents, as a mean of defence, has produced the most dreadful and horrible consequences; but, in removing the cause of the evil, it will be easy to check its effects, and to repair even the fatal mischief which it has produced. Let the republican authorities, which are about to be established, restore order and tranquillity on the basis of a paternal administration; let them dissipate the idle alarms of ignorance, and oppose the fury of fanaticism, with a zeal equal to that which has been employed by perfidy to increase them; and, in a short time, the severity of discipline, which re-establishes with so much facility order among the troops of a free people, will not delay to put a period to the disorders produced by hatred, and which have been with difficulty repressed. (Signed) CHAMPIONET, Commander in Chief of the Army of Naples.

Naples, January 24.

Proclamation of General Championet to the Inhabitants of Naples, dated Head-quarters at Naples, February 5, 1799.

I HAVE ordered a difarming—it is not yet effected; this difobedience is a crime—it covers perfidious projects. I give the difaffected twenty-four hours to lay down their arms; I declare that I fhall then take terrible meafures againft them—evil to the rebel who fhall not have obeyed! A reward of twenty-four francs fhall be given to every one who fhall difcover a concealed mufket; I promife a ftill greater recompence for the difcovery of a depôt of arms. CHAMPIONET.

Extract of a Letter from General Touffaint Louverture to Citizen Guybre, his Secretary and Bearer of his Difpatches to Paris, dated Port Republicain, 11th February.

I WRITE to you, by triplicate, to fend you my memorial to the Executive Directory. The duplicate is ftill at the Cape, which place I was obliged to leave to come to Port Republicain, to meet the agent of the Directory, Roume, who is arrived there from St. Domingo: but it will not be long before it reaches you; for as foon as I arrive at the Cape with the agent, a veffel will be difpatched to France, which will carry it to you. At length, after the ftorms which had obfcured our political horizon at the latter end of Vendemiaire and beginning of Brumaire, the dawn of happinefs again appears for the people of St. Domingo. Their exertions, aided by the wife meafures of the Directory, have given to the colony an agent, who, by wifdom and prudence, will eftablifh the public tranquillity. You know me well enough to be convinced that, affured of the agent of government, I wifh to fecond him by all the means in my power; and which I will never exert, but to contribute to the happinefs of my country, and to preferve it to France; for, in fpite of calumniators, I will prove to the world, that, faithful to my oaths, I have never merited the opprobrium which they have endeavoured to heap upon me I ferved Spain when royalifm in France held liberty in chains, and perfecuted thofe who declared themfelves its defenders; but when France offered its affiftance, and admitted me to rank as one of its children, I immediately placed myfelf under the ftandard of the republic, and have never ceafed to fight in its defence. And how can it be faid, that I have entered into a compact with England, when I have never ceafed to make a war of extermination againft its hirelings in St. Domingo? In battles deception is allowed, and becaufe I have fucceffively employed it againft a commander of George the Third, is it thence to be concluded that I am the partifan of England?

On

On the contrary, it ought to furnish another proof of my attachment to liberty, and of my desire to augment its conquests; at present there are no more to make in St. Domingo.

The army of St. Domingo has no more laurels to gather; and when it devoted itself to the triumph of liberty, and the defence of the republic, it desired no other recompence than that of enjoying its rights and the fruit of its labours. I have employed my power for the happiness of the colony, and if its welfare be established my wishes will be fulfilled. Satisfied with the happiness of all the inhabitants of the colony, and of the triumph of France, I shall die content; and my last sigh will be an expression of gratitude to the republic. See my dear children as often as you can; give me an account of them; you know how dear they are to me, how much I am attached to them: give them the counsels which they ought to expect from a friend of their father. Let them be industrious, and endeavour, by their application, to render themselves worthy the attention and benevolence of the mother-country. My attachment to them, as well as that of their tender mother, for whom you will embrace them, will then be redoubled.

(Signed)   TOUSSAINT LOUVERTURE.

Letter from the French Minister Alquier to Baron Hompesch, dated Munich, 24th Pluviose, 7th Year (February 12, 1799).

M. Baron,

I AM informed that on the 22d instant (10th February) Mr. Paget, the King of England's minister, said to the circle at the court of his Electoral Highness, that he had it for certain, that Citizen Trouve was employed by order of the Directory of France in revolutionizing the states of the Duke of Wirtemburg; that I corresponded on the subject with the minister; and that, in concert with him, I was labouring to excite troubles in Bavaria; to this absurdity I oppose the dignity of the Executive Directory, and the wisdom and loyalty of the minister at Stutgard. With respect to what is personal to myself, I shall not descend so far as to justify myself: I appeal from this scandalous reflection upon my conduct to the esteem which his Electoral Highness and his ministers have for me, and to the public, whose good opinion, I think, I have deserved; yet as I owe to a declaration made by a foreign minister, before the whole court, a clear and precise reply, it is as follows: I give the most formal contradiction to the author of this lying assertion. I entreat you, M. Baron, to accept my assurances of high consideration.

(Signed)   ALQUIER.

P. S. What I have just written to you, M. Baron, I should have

have had the honour to say to his Electoral Highness, if circumstances had allowed me to be presented to him. I hope you will communicate my letter to the Prince.

Message of the Directory to the Councils, relative to the War with Turkey, February 16.

THE Ottoman Porte, informed that the expedition to Egypt was only directed against its real enemies, had begun to look upon it with a favourable eye; but it was soon led astray by the perfidious insinuations of England and the coalesced powers. The war which it has declared against its ancient and faithful allies has been the fruit of this error, and will lead to its total ruin. It has drawn the Barbary powers into a war with France. The French government has adopted measures of reprisal, and it gives you notice of having done so.

PROCLAMATION.

The Ministry of the Sublime Porte to the Generals, Officers, and Soldiers of the French Army in Egypt.

THE French Directory, forgetful of the rights of nations, has deceived you, surprised your good faith, and in contempt of the laws of war, sent you to Egypt, a country subject to the dominion of the Sublime Porte, by persuading you that the Sublime Porte itself had consented to the invasion of its own territory.

Can you entertain any doubts but that the only object of the Directory in sending you to a remote country was to banish you from France, and to plunge you into an abyss of dangers? If, completely ignorant of the truth, you have invaded the territory of Egypt, and are made the instruments to violate treaties of the most solemn kind, must you not attribute this to the perfidy of your Directors? Egypt must however be freed from so iniquitous an invasion, and vast armies are now in march, and the sea is covered with formidable squadrons, for the attainment of that object.

Those among you, of whatever rank they may be, who wish to extricate themselves from the imminent peril to which they are exposed, are called upon to signify their intentions without delay to the commanders of the land and sea forces of the allied powers. They may be confident of a safe conduct to whatever place they may be desirous to proceed, and they shall receive passports to protect them on their voyage from the squadrons and cruisers of the allied powers. Let them then hasten to take advantage of the benignant disposition of the Sublime Porte, and let them consider

sider it as a propitious occasion for extricating themselves from the horrible gulf into which they have been precipitated!

Done at Constantinople the 11th of the Moon Ranarzan, in the year of the Hegira 1213, the 5th (16th) February 1799. From the royal printing-office at Hasſkeng, in the environs of Constantinople.

Circular Letter issued from the Adjutant General's Office, to the Generals, &c. commanding the several Districts in Ireland, dated Dublin, 21st February 1799.

IT being now certain, that the enemy is using every exertion to fit out another and a more formidable armament destined to act against this country; I am directed by his Excellency Marquis Cornwallis, to refer you to the standing orders of the 12th of April 1797, and to desire you will take the necessary measures for ascertaining whether the several regiments under your command be complete in every article requisite to march against an enemy; and for procuring a supply of their respective deficiencies, should, at this late period, any such exist; and the Lord Lieutenant desires you will point out to the commanding officers of regiments the indispensable necessity of the utmost precision on this subject, and their own responsibility for the complete equipment of their men for the field. I am further directed by his Excellency to desire that you will order all officers now absent, not recruiting, or under very strong circumstances, to be immediately called to their regiments; and that you will not forward any further memorials for leave of absence, except such very extraordinary cases as you may judge necessary to attend to.

I have the honour to be, &c. G. HEWITT, Ad. Gen.

Extract of a Letter from the Governor in Council at Fort St George to the Directors of the East India Company, dated 25th February 1799.

IN the month of June last we were informed by the commanding officer at Masulipatam, that two Frenchmen, named Du Chiens and Bligny, had arrived at that place, and claimed protection and support, having been shipwrecked on the coast of Coromandel, on their way to the Isle of France, whither they were proceeding with the permission of the Governor General of Bengal. We gave orders, in consequence, that they should be paid the usual subsistence, and treated like other prisoners of war on their parole; but upon communicating these circumstances to the supreme government, we were told in reply, that as Du Chiens and Bligny had broken their paroles, it would be proper to place

their

their persons under restraint, their conduct having been such as to deprive them of all indulgence or favour from the British government. Instructions were accordingly given to the commanding officer of Masulipatam for confining their persons: but from this confinement they found an opportunity of escaping, in the month of December, with several other Frenchmen. Having passed the gates disguised as natives, they stole a boat, and put to sea. As soon as we were apprised of this transaction, our president wrote to Governor Anker, the governor of Tranquebar, requesting, in case a boat should touch at that port, he would give directions for her detention, and for delivering up to the British government the people who had arrived in her. The demand was founded upon the circumstance of their having broke their parole in Bengal, and been clearly convicted in a piratical act, in the mode by which they effected their escape from Masulipatam. We learned by Governor Anker's reply, that the boat had arrived at Tranquebar, and that in consequence of our president's letter, accusing the men of an act of piracy, orders had been given for confining their persons; but that he could not deliver them up to the British government without the sanction of his council, to whom he was bound by his instructions to submit the case. He added, that Du Chiens had reported that he had been detained a prisoner at Masulipatam, notwithstanding the permission of the Governor General of Bengal for his proceeding to the Mauritius. Lord Hobart answered this letter very fully, stating the conduct of Du Chiens in Bengal, to show that he had broken his parole; and, to confirm the charge of piracy, his Lordship acquainted Governor Anker, from information received from Cuddalore, that an English vessel in the roads of Porto Novo had been boarded and plundered by Du Chiens and his party in their passage to Tranquebar: it was therefore urged that this man ought not to be protected by a neutral state, and the demand was renewed for his being delivered up with the other persons concerned with him. Lord Hobart further acquainted Governor Anker that the whole of the conduct of the government of Tranquebar with respect to the British nation, appeared indeed so inconsistent with that cordiality and good will which had been professed, that it would become a very serious consideration with his Majesty's ministers in Europe.

We have gone at large into this subject, with a view of drawing the attention of our government at home to the very improper conduct of the government of Tranquebar. But it is not only in this instance that we have to complain: the case of Captain Walker, commander of the Danish ship the Dorothea Elisabeth, is before you; and if it were necessary to add other instances of a manifest breach of neutrality, we might refer to the notorious practice at Tranquebar of granting passes to privateers, fitted out

out at the Mauritius, which have enabled the vessels to elude the vigilance of our cruisers (when it suited their safety) by announcing themselves to be under the protection of Denmark; and whenever opportunities offered for making prizes, the national colours of France were hoisted, and the vessels declared to be privateers.

Orders of the General in Chief, 8th September.

Article 1.

ALL the inhabitants of Egypt shall wear the tricoloured cockade.

2. All vessels which navigate the Nile shall carry the tricoloured flag.

3. The generals, the commanders of provinces, the officers, shall not admit any person to speak to them, unless they have the national cockade. The commanders of Borta, of Rosetta, and Damietta, shall cause the same to be observed, and inform the masters of all vessels, that after the 16th Vendemiaire no vessel will be suffered to navigate without the tricoloured flag.

4. The members of the Divan only may carry a tricoloured shawl upon the shoulder.

5. On the 1st Vendemiaire, the tricoloured flag shall be erected on the highest spire in Cairo, and by all other provinces.

(Signed)   BUONAPARTE.

A Letter written November 5, by Toussaint Louverture, to Citizens Penckinat, Br thier, Raigner, and other Representatives of the People.

WOULD you expect to hear that when the nomination of General Hedouville to the government of St. Domingo announced that happiness which his great reputation promised to this unfortunate country, we should expose them to the most imminent dangers, from which I have just had the good fortune to preserve them?

The copy which I send you of my address to the Directory, will show you how much this agent, having the best means of doing good if he wished it, has disappointed the true friends of liberty, in disgusting a whole people by his impolitic measures, and the arbitrary acts he exercised in the name of the laws, which were themselves the palladium of which he took advantage to light up the torch of discord, and bring on a civil war, which was on the point of breaking out.

Notwithstanding this, in order to excuse his having shamefully abandoned his post, he writes to you, citizens representa-

Vol. VIII.   X   tives,

tives, as he has had the impudence to proclaim here, that I had separated the colony from France; and that with the troops in the pay of England I had erected the project of independence which I had long had in view.

But I trust in the impartiality of the two Councils, and in the justice of the Directory. The storm which thunders over my head does not affright me.

Invariable in my principles, sincerely attached to France and to liberty, I will continue to sacrifice every moment of my life to assure the prosperity of St. Domingo.

Salut à la république Françoise.

(Signed)   TOUSSAINT LOUVERTURE.

Leghorn, Nov. 30.

Extract from a Notification drawn up by the Commander of the Garrison of Leghorn, in consequence of a Summons sent on Shore by the Commander of the English and Portuguese Fleets.

THE illustrious Jacob Lavillette, major general of the troops of Ferdinand III. Grand Duke of Tuscany, notifies and makes known that there appeared in the road of Leghorn a squadron composed of English and Portuguese ships of war, having on board a considerable number of troops for landing, belonging to his Sicilian Majesty, the commander of which required of the governor of Leghorn to permit their landing, menacing, at the same time, in case of refusal, to effect it by force.

The general, major commandant of the place, the civil authorities, and a deputation of the houses of commerce, assembled to deliberate on the summons of the commander of the said squadron, and being sensible of the superiority of their forces, the smallness of the garrison, and the impossibility of defending the port, resolved immediately to allow the said troops to disembark, under the express condition of respecting the neutrality of the port of Tuscany.

Message of the Executive Directory to the Council of Five Hundred, 7th of February.

THE army of Rome, now the army of Naples, was attacked the 2d Pluviose, by an innumerrble multitude, composed of the remains of the Neapolitan army, the Lazzaroni, and peasants well armed, well conducted, and inflamed by the torch of the most delirious fanaticism. The soldiers of liberty, surrounded on all sides, routed the assailants in every point; and after three days, signalized by prodigies of valour, which the preceding vic-

tories

tories of the republicans can alone render credible, all the obstacles were surmounted, and the army established itself in Naples.

The energy of the Neapolitan patriots, so long restrained, was reanimated with vigour; their voice was heard, and, united with the clemency of the conqueror, it converted into a holy enthusiasm for liberty the fanaticism with which the hearts of a deluded multitude had been inflamed. The Neapolitan republic was proclaimed, and a provisional government organized.

Summons of General Bernadotte, Commander of the French Army of Observation, to the Rhinegrave Salm, Commander of the Fortress of Philipsburg; dated 2d March.

General,

THE Austrian government, contrary to the treaty of Campo Formio, has taken possession of the fortress of Ulm, which aggression renders it necessary for us to have a garrison in the fortress which you command. It will be in vain, General, that you will attempt to make opposition, for your garrison is not strong enough to sustain an assault; and the peace which is on the point of being signed between the German Empire and the French republic renders it your duty to prevent the effusion of blood by delivering up a depot which you cannot protect from the attacks of the Austrian army. I will not suppose, General, that you would deliver it up voluntarily to that army; but were your inclination such, it is at present too distant to afford you the smallest support. The army of General Jourdan is at this moment marching through the Schwartzwald (Black Forest) to seek the Austrian army in the interior of Bavaria. I must tell you still more, General: I know that your garrison is discontented, that the officers of it are too wise and enlightened to lavish their blood to gratify the selfishness and caprice of a few arrogant men, and the soldiers only wait the signal of attack to declare their dissatisfaction. When the inhabitants shall see that their houses are soon about to become the prey of the flames, they will presently determine which side to take. The artillery of Landau, which is advancing, will quickly furnish them with what they have long waited for—a sufficient motive to compel their commandant to deliver up the keys. The terrible example of General Mack, to all those who lead soldiers to battle against their will, must have furnished you with matter for alarming reflections. But, without all these advantages, the army under my command has sufficient means to compel the fortress to surrender. I hope I shall not be compelled by your obstinacy to shed human blood, and make the inhabitants of

Philipsburg

Philipsburg the innocent victims of the destructive contest. I cannot repeat sufficiently often, General, that I will not place a garrison in your fortress as an enemy. Far from it: I only mean to hold the place for the German Empire; and I call the whole world to witness, that I declare that I will restore Philipsburg to the Empire as soon as the French government shall be certified that the Empire can defend it against the ambition of the House of Austria. On you alone, General, depend the lives of many men, and the safety of the inhabitants of Philipsburg; and you will render yourself accountable for the manner in which you shall act, not only to your cotemporaries, but to posterity. Should you oblige me to make the assault, I doubtless cannot but succeed, as the number of troops I have with me renders it impossible I should fail. But the punishment will be terrible of those who have been the cause of resistance to the French republic; nor will I restrain the rage of the soldiers, which will be furious against you.

I have the honour, &c.
(Signed) BERNADOTTE.

Answer of the Commandant of Philipsburg to General Bernadotte, dated Auttenhein near Philipsburg, March 2.

General,

YOUR letter of the 2d of March, which was brought me by Adjutant General Gardin, is of such a nature as I could not have expected to receive at this moment when peace is on the point of being signed between the German Empire and the French republic. You yourself must perceive, General, that I should be culpable were I to deliver up a fortress, the command of which has been entrusted to me by the general in chief of the army of the Empire. His residence is not far distant; and still nearer to the place of meeting of the deputies to the congress for the peace of the Empire. The orders and instructions which I may receive from these two quarters will regulate my conduct. While in expectation of these orders, which when I receive I shall immediately communicate to you, I can only act as every man of honour must act in my place. The situation of the fortress under my command is not such as you appear to believe; nor do I know of any discontent among the garrison. I must therefore declare to you that I will not receive a French garrison into the place, nor commence hostilities, though I will resist every attack. The assailants will be answerable to our contemporaries and posterity for all the calamities which may follow in consequence of an attack.

(Signed) The RHINEGRAVE SALM, Lieut. Gen.

On the 3d of March General Ernouf published a Proclamation at Gengenbach, it which he orders that

THE horses, &c. belonging to the post-offices shall not be liable to requisition, as it is of the utmost consequence that the post in the countries occupied by the French armies should suffer no interruption. The houses in which the post-offices are shall not have any troops quartered in them, and the postmasters shall not have any services imposed upon them.

A PROCLAMATION of the Duke of Wirtemberg, dated March the 3d, orders persons of every description, civil and military, to remain at their post, and to take care that the inhabitants of the communes through which the French pass keep quiet, and behave towards those troops in the manner agreed upon by the treaty of peace between his Highness and the republic; since, according to that treaty, his Highness is assured that the French will not exercise any hostility against his states.

The Protest of the King of Sardinia against the Conduct of the French in driving him from his Dominions, has been published in all the foreign Journals: it is dated from the Road of Cagliari, 3d of March.

HIS Majesty declares that the honour of his person, the interest of his family and of his successors, his connexions with friendly powers, impose it on him as a duty to protest loudly, and in the face of Europe, against the proceedings by which he has been compelled to quit his territories on the continent, and to abandon for a time the exercise of his power. He declares upon the faith and word of a king, that not only he never infringed, even in the slightest degree, the treaties made with the French republic, but, on the contrary, that he observed them with such scrupulous exactness, with such demonstrations of amity and condescension, that he far exceeded the obligations contracted with the republic. It is notorious that all the care and solicitude of his Majesty were continually directed to secure respect to every French citizen, particularly the troops stationed in his territory and passing through it, to repress and punish those who insulted them, to obviate even the well-grounded resentment of those who, outraged by military licentiousness, might have been led to violence. He protests likewise upon the faith and word of a king against any writing wherever published, insinuating that his Majesty carried on any secret intelligence with the powers hostile to France. In proof of this he refers not only to the accounts transmitted to the French government, and to what has been advanced by its generals, but

the

the impartial evidence which the ministers and public representatives who were at Turin have given to their respective courts. It is easy for any one to decide, from the facts before the public, that the adherence of his Majesty to whatever was imposed upon him by the superior forces of the French republic was only temporary, and could have no object but to save his subjects in Piedmont the evils which a just resistance would have occasioned, his Majesty being surprised by an unexpected attack, which he could never have suspected from a power, his ally, and at a moment when, in consequence of an application from the agents of the republic, his forces were put upon the footing of the most profound peace. Impelled by all these motives, his Majesty resolved, whenever it was in his power, to make known to all the powers of Europe the injustice of the proceedings of the French generals and agents, and the nullity of the reasons urged in their manifestoes, and at the same time to reclaim his reinstatement in the dominions of his ancestors.

Head-quarters at Friedberg, March 3.
Address of the Archduke Charles to all the Generals of the Imperial Armies, and of the Armies of the Empire.

THE movement made by the French army on the 1st instant, to march forward from the positions which it had occupied until that time, induced me to offer to the generals of the armies of the Emperor and of the Empire a short review of the events which have happened for about a year past, with respect to ourselves, and which have at length brought us to the point in which we are now placed. Scarcely were the most solemn treaties concluded between the Emperor and the Empire on the one part, and France on the other, when the French government began to show its intention to take advantage, with the most manifest injustice, of the retreat of the armies into the military positions which they had taken, relying on the security of public faith. The peaceable people of Switzerland were subjugated, and the most violent means were adopted by the French to change that country into a slavish ally, and to establish themselves on the flank of Germany. They refused to let provisions into the fortress of Ehrenbreitstein, in opposition to the most precise agreements. They blocked up that fortress, and without any respect for the rights of nations and the indignation of Europe, they devoted the quiet and inoffensive inhabitants of the Thal, and the brave garrison of Ehrenbreitstein, to the miseries of famine. What remained of the garrison thus starved into a surrender were compelled to evacuate the place at a moment when such acts of atrocity were committing, unheard of in the history of the world;

at

at the moment when they continued to levy contributions and impose requisitions on the right bank, when the tone of the French ministers at Rastadt became every day more imperious, and they accumulated new pretensions in a manner injurious to the German nation; they did not hesitate to demand of us, on the part of France, if we were disposed to prepare any resistance to future operations of that kind? To our answer, if hostilities were put an end to by the French, if Ehrenbreitstein was evacuated, if the French army was retreating from the right bank, if the French troops in Switzerland which threatened Germany were withdrawn, and if a reasonable peace was concluded at Rastadt, founded on the rights, not on the slavery of the Empire, no other reply was made on the part of France, than that it was hoped the diet would agree to such a resolution as France might wish; a conduct which implied, in other terms, that the French should be suffered to continue at their pleasure acts of hostility which the Germans, as well as other people, were to consider as amicable and pacific acts. To that ministerial answer of the French has been this moment added the declaration of the general of the French army, stating that it is at present thought proper they should prepare themselves by taking advantageous military positions, probably to enable them, when they are sufficiently prepared, to fall with their combined force on the Germans; to push on at the first instant the Helvetic republic as far as the Danube, to make that river and the Leck its limits, and to penetrate still more forward. The first military measure dictated by prudence against the French army, which has advanced from its positions, should be the adoption of every step which the security and tranquillity of Germany renders indispensable. I am impressed with the fullest conviction, that the army under my orders will execute the arrangements which I have made in passing the Leck, for that grand, national, and sacred object, with the confidence and unlimited attachment, of which I have received such multiplied proofs in so many epochs decisive of the fate of Germany, and in a manner which will immortalize in the annals of war its inviolable loyalty and its unshaken bravery. I have taken every precaution that my brave troops shall not be in want of necessary provisions, I remain therefore in the most positive confidence that all and every one of them will conduct themselves towards the inhabitants of the towns and countries, who are our friends, with the attention and scrupulous care required by equity and justice, as well as by the first principles of morality. But should any individuals be so far forgetful of their duties as to stain by excesses the honour and glory of the army to which they belong, I solemnly declare that they shall be punished with all the rigour of military law. As I am not less certain that it is in the power of every commanding officer to prevent excesses of all kinds,

by

by the maintenance of order and difcipline, I hereby make the different commandants of regiments and corps perfonally refponfible for every inftance of that nature which may happen.

Letter from the Minifter for Foreign Affairs to Bernadotte, Commander in Chief of the Army of Obfervation.

THE Executive Directory having received the moft favourable proofs with refpect to the difpofition and fentiments of the Elector Palatine, and inclined to find him in a fhort time the friend of the republic, haftens to give you information of it, that you may take off the fequeftration laid upon the public treafury and revenue of the palatinate government at Manheim, and that you may treat every part of the territories of the Elector through which your army may pafs with all the refpect and care which the Directory wifhes fhould be obferved towards a prince whom it diftinguifhes from his predeceffors, and from whom it expects a conduct directly oppofite. It alfo defires, fhould any horfes or effects of the Elector have been feized in purfuance of your firft orders, that they fhould, if poffible, be reftored to him.

(Signed) TALLEYRAND.

Proclamation iffued by Order of his Imperial Majefty, dated March 4.

THE troops of the French republic have not only extended their encroachments on the right bank of the Rhine, and the other boundaries of Auftrian ftates, but, notwithftanding the military conventions, the fortrefs of Ehrenbreitftein, which ferved as a barrier to the whole Empire, has, during a ceffation of hoftilities, been required to furrender by means of an hoftile blockade, in order that it might fall into their poffeffion. The hoftile attempts of the French, combined with the confcription of 200,000 men in France, as well as the powerful levies which they made in Switzerland, have afforded a fufficient reafon to apprehend their views, and have rendered it neceffary for his Imperial Majefty, on his own part, to adopt meafures of fafety.

His Majefty, always accuftomed to fulfil the treaties entered into by him, has been defirous of maintaining peace, with a moderation, under all circumftances fo ftrikingly feafonable, that he could not have entertained the fmalleft ground for fuppofing a contrary difpofition, in this refpect, on the part of the French government. But now, fince the reftlefs and increafing attempts of the French republic have rendered it every day more neceffary to confult the prefervation of tranquillity, his Majefty is unavoidably placed in a fituation which obliges him to extend his

preparations

preparations for general safety in proportion to the strides of the French, and to order his troops also to advance beyond those places where they had hitherto remained in a state of tranquillity. His Imperial Majesty has been led to adopt these measures of precaution, not less from a consideration of the dangers with which the greater part of the Empire is threatened, than from a regard to the security of his own hereditary dominions; and he can entertain no doubt that prompt measures will be taken for the general safety and defence of all the boundaries of the Empire, by which means his Majesty's hereditary dominions may at the same time be preserved.

Army of the Danube.

Head-quarters, Villengen, March 8.

JOURDAN, commander in chief of the armies of the Danube, of Helvetia, and of observation, considering that the reigning Prince of Hoenzollern Heckingen is connected by the ties of blood with the house of the King of Prussia; that a good understanding subsists between his Prussian Majesty and the French republic; and also that the reigning Prince of Hoenzollern Heckingen has always observed the strictest neutrality towards the French republic, expressly orders that the military, and all those in the train of the army, shall respect the person of that prince, and all the persons who belong to his house, or are in his service, as well as their properties. The prince shall be enabled, in case of necessity, to demand assistance from the commanding officers, and the latter are enjoined to employ the armed force to carry into effect the present order.

(Signed)   JOURDAN.

Letter written by Buonaparte to Ghezzar Pacha, dated 19th Ventose (March 9).

SINCE my arrival in Egypt I several times informed you, that I had no design to make war against you, and that my only object was to expel the Mamelucks. You returned no answer to the overtures which I made to you. I announced that I desired you would drive Ibrahim Bey from the frontiers of Egypt; but, instead of that, you sent troops to Gaza, you formed there large magazines, and gave out that you intended to march against Egypt. You indeed began to put this plan in execution, and you threw 2000 of your troops into the fortress of Arifeh, which is only six miles from the frontiers of Egypt. I was obliged then to depart from Cairo, to direct in person the war which you seemed to invite. The districts of Gaza, Ramle, and Jaffa, are already

Vol. VIII.

already in my power. I have treated with generosity such of your troops as surrendered at discretion; but I have been severe towards those who violated the rights of war. In a few days I shall march against Acre; but why should I go to deprive an old man, with whom I am not acquainted, of the few remaining years of his life? What are a few miles more of territory, in comparison of those which I have already conquered? And, as God grants me victory, I will, like him, be clement and merciful, not only towards the people, but towards the great.

You have no solid reason for being my enemy, since you were that of the Mamelukes. Your government is separated from that of Egypt by the districts of Gaza, Ramle, and impassable marshes. Become my friend, be the enemy of the Mamelukes and the English, and I will do you as much good as I have already done you hurt, and I can still do you more. Send me a short answer by some person invested with full powers, that I may know your views. He needs only present himself to my advanced guard with a white flag, and I have given orders to my staff to send you a pass of safety, which you will find here annexed. On the 1st of Germinal (March 21) I shall march against Acre. I must therefore have an answer before that day.

BUONAPARTE.

Message from the Executive Directory to the Councils, proposing to declare war against the Emperor of Germany and the Grand Duke of Tuscany: delivered on the 13th March.

Citizens Representatives,

WHATEVER may have been the magnitude of the events that have taken place since the conclusion of the treaty of Campo Formio, we have still the remembrance of those that preceded it. We have not forgotten that it was after five years of triumphs, and at the moment in which the French armies were no more than thirty leagues from Vienna, that the republic consented to suspend the course of her victories, and preferred to the success of some last efforts, the immediate establishment of peace. It may be recollected, that when the treaty was concluded, the moderation of the conqueror appeared so great, that it wanted in some sort an apology.

Could we have foreseen that this compact, in which force showed itself so indulgent—in which the most liberal compensation ought to have silenced all regret, so far from obtaining the promised stability, would have been from the beginning but the deceiving pledge of an ephemeral reconciliation, and that the sudden attacks made against it should all come from a power which was indebted to it for an ample indemnification for the losses she had experienced by the war? What a strange contrast! Whilst the republic with constant care fulfils every stipulation of

a treaty,

a treaty, which is in proportion neither with her succeses, nor with what she might deduce as legitimate revenge for the plans of destruction formed and pursued against her; Austria, instead of showing herself satisfied with an approximation that has spared her the greatest misfortunes, appears to be occupied only with deteriorating and destroying the compact that has formed her safety.

Among the violations of the treaty which that power has been guilty of, some have been so manifest, that they have already excited the surprise of Europe, and the indignation of republicans:—others, less public, or less perceived, have yet not been less hostile; and the Directory can no longer defer marking out to the Legislature the circumstances of the conduct of the cabinet of Austria;—a conduct truly offensive, invasive of the state of peace, and which no effort nor example has been able to bring back to the observance of engagements contracted.

At the period of the concluding of the treaty of Campo Formio, it was reciprocally stipulated by an additional act to the treaty, that all that part of the German territory extending from the Tyrol and the frontier of the Austrian states to the left bank of the Mein, should be evacuated at once by the French and Imperial troops, except the post of Kehl, which was to remain with the republic. A convention still more particular, concluded and signed at Rastadt, the 11th Frimaire, 6th year, renewed that engagement, and marked a fixed term for its execution.—On the part of the republic that execution was prompt and entire. On the part of Austria it was deferred, eluded, and is not yet obtained. In Philipsburg the Emperor has kept a garrison and provisions which belong to him, in spite of the pretence that covers them. In Ulm and Ingoldstadt he has not ceased to keep troops, and an etat major to receive more. All the places of Bavaria have remained at his disposal; and so far from that dutchy having been evacuated, according to the terms of the treaty, we see that it contains 100,000 Austrians destined at once to resume hostilities against the republic, and to invade a country so long coveted by the court of Vienna. If that court had intended to have shown itself faithful to the treaty, the first effect of this disposition would without doubt have been to press the reciprocal establishment of the respective legations:—but so far from Austria having entertained a wish of making any beginning upon this head, what was the surprise of the Directory when they were informed it was considered at Vienna, that the plenipotentiaries sent on both sides to the congress of Rastadt were sufficient to keep up the communications between the two states, and that the treaty of Campo Formio was to receive by the treaty with the Empire ulterior developements, before the habitual relations of perfect understanding could be entirely established!

So cold an interpretation of the treaty, so formal a distance, did not presage that it would be long respected.

In the mean time, a government, whose existence attested also the moderation of the republic, dared to provoke anew her vengeance by the most horrible attacks. The Pope expiated his crime, and Rome acquired liberty; but the Directory, foreseeing that persons would not fail to alarm the Imperial court, and to give to the most just reprisals the aspect of ambitious aggression, thought proper to wave all considerations of etiquette, which might have prevented them, and to send to Vienna Citizen Bernadotte, as ambassador from the French republic, to make it understood that the destruction of the Pontifical government at Rome would make no change in the limitation of the states of Italy: that the existing and recognised republics would not be increased by any part of the Roman territory, which left the treaty of Campo Formio in all its integrity, since, by fixing the extent of the Cisalpine republic, it could not foresee nor prevent, with respect to their result, the events which might change the form of other states of Italy on account of their own aggressions. Yet the ambassador of the republic was received at Vienna with coldness. This mark of the most loyal eagerness, this sending of an agent invested with the most august character, was without reciprocity: and soon an event less injurious by the circumstances that accompanied it than by the impunity which it has obtained, manifested the secret sentiments of the court of Vienna. If, at the first news of this event, the Directory had not had some foundation for seeing in it only the work of two courts eager to revive the war upon the continent; if they could have believed that the Emperor knew the plot woven under his eyes; they would not have hesitated a moment in inciting the national vengeance against so outrageous a violation of the state of peace and the rights of nations, so religiously respected by the republic in the midst even of the most violent storms of the revolution. But it was possible that the cabinets of London and Petersburgh might have prepared and directed by their agents a tumult neither known nor approved by the Emperor. The expressions of regret conveyed in the first moment to the ambassador of the republic by M. de Colloredo, the announced appointment of M. Degelmann to Paris, were the motives for thinking that the Imperial court would hasten to pursue and punish an attack, whose existence it acknowledged, and of which it feared to appear the accomplice. When it was known besides, that the minister who was accused of having seconded the fury of England and Russia, had given up his place to the Count de Cobenzel, and that the latter was going to Seltz to make reparation, the Directory could not repent having incited these conferences, by showing herself less ready to follow the first

first impulse of a legitimate resentment, than eager to do away by common explanation every thing that might oppose the establishment of the most perfect harmony.

Such was their desire to produce conciliation, that the envoy extraordinary of the republic had for his definitive instruction to content himself, in reparation for the event at Vienna of the 21st Germinal, with a simple disavowal, and a declaration that the guilty should be sought after. But scarcely had the conferences been opened at Seltz, when the Imperial court altered its tone and its conduct—Baron Degelmann did not proceed to Paris —M. de Thugut returned to the ministry—the informations commenced remained unavailing and ineffectual. The Count de Cobenzel, instead of asking or giving the reparation which was the principal object of his mission, affected a wish to direct the discussion to other points, and concluded by declining all satisfaction, even that with which the republic would have contented herself, when he was convinced that the Directory would not listen to the insinuations by which the court of Vienna wished to render her, in the midst even of peace, an accomplice in the most strange spoliation.

The negotiators separated, and soon afterwards the negotiator who had been sent to Seltz, by his Imperial Majesty, to make profuse and vain protestations of peace, received a mission to Berlin and Petersburgh, to connect himself with all the incitements of the British government to revive the war. The Directory must have been animated with a profound love for peace, not to have yielded from that time to the evidence of the hostile dispositions of the House of Austria, and to have avoided answering the provocations received. They saw that at Rastadt, from the very opening of the congress, both the Imperial minister and the minister of Austria had incessantly shown themselves adverse to all the propositions of the republic, and to all those which might lead to a definitive and stable pacification. They knew the difficulties made at Vienna to the acknowledgment of the Cisalpine minister; a circumstance calculated to bring in question points decided by the treaty of Campo Formio. They were informed that the Austrian cabinet (whatever might be their personal opinion of the Emperor), yielding more than ever to the impulses of England, gave to the cabinet of Naples a confidence which led it into the most extravagant measures, directed, in a more secret manner, Piedmont, which, a short time before, it had devoted to dismemberment, and endeavoured to wrest from its neutrality the Prussian government, which it wished to arm against France, after having endeavoured to arm France against the Prussian government.

What motives for abjuring a treaty not acknowledged, violated by Austria, and which ceased to be binding upon the republic!

But

But the patience and the resolution of the Directory were to show themselves superior even to a provocation more direct. At the moment in which the factious, who had usurped the power in the Grison league, testified some uneasiness at a French army being near, and at the projects which they supposed to be formed against their independence and neutrality, affecting, at the same time, a perfect security with respect to Austria, from whom they said they had received the most encouraging protestations, the Directory thought proper to make known to the inhabitants, that their territories would be respected, as long as they were respected by Austria. Some months only had elapsed since that declaration was made, when a corps of Austrian troops invaded and established themselves in the country of the Grisons. Nothing that was hostile in that invasion, nothing of secret machination that was included in it, escaped the Executive Directory. It was evident that Austria was thus preparing the means of disturbing Helvetia, of making an irruption into the Cisalpine, and of giving at the decisive moment her aid to the King of Piedmont, in order to attempt, in concert with him, to cut off all retreat to the French, who were to be attacked by 100,000 Neapolitans, and whom they dared to suppose conquered.

The Directory were not blind to all these perfidious combinations, but they avoided seeing in them a formal aggression; and it was not till the moment in which the premature attack of the King of the Two Sicilies opened a new war, that the Directory, having the full proof of the King of Sardinia being an accomplice, and wishing to turn aside the effect of it, seized his strong places, thus getting the start by some days of the Austrians, who were to have occupied them themselves; the anterior invasion of the Grison territories being but the prelude to such a step.

But at the same time that the republican armies repelled the aggression in Italy, and prevented the perfidy, the Directory, though they had intelligence of the treaty between Vienna and Naples, though they saw an Austrian general at the head of the Neapolitan army, though they knew the movements of troops which had taken place in the Tyrol and the north of Italy, persisted still in professing a desire to remain at peace with the Emperor; and the sincerity of their wishes was sufficiently apparent by their conduct to Tuscany; for a long time had elapsed since they had found it impossible to make a distinction between the court of Florence and the court of Vienna.

The Directory had known that the journey of M. Manfredine to Vienna related to the same object that had brought the Prince of Montechiaro from Naples; and had usefully prepared the success of his mission, by contributing to give the Emperor the desire of increasing his influence in Italy, of seeking a new aggrandisement, under the pretence of indemnity, of checking

the

the establishment of the Cisalpine republic, and of opposing, above all, the existence of the Roman republic. The Directory knew also, that at the epoch in which the King of Naples was making dispositions to march his army to Rome, the Grand Duke was himself employed in preparations for war; accelerating and extending in a manner very unusual to the country, and ordering, in addition to the complete armament of the troops, voluntary enrolments in every town and village; establishing a forced loan, demanding from the churches, monks, and nobles, their plate; and taking, in short, all the measures that denoted a secret participation in the greatest enterprises: yet, notwithstanding the art with which these traces of hostility were sought to be concealed, the Directory obtained proofs that the Grand Duke relied so much on the defeat of the French, that he shut up all the passes by which they might have retreated through his states, and fortified them with a numerous artillery, which was to have completed the destruction of the remnant of the French army, whilst on another side a troop of Neapolitans, and some English ships, took possession of Leghorn; an event that would never have taken place, if that prince had only declared that he would not consent to it.

Thus the first movement of the French army ought to have been to march to Leghorn and Florence; and if the Directory (who only knew since with certainty to what an extent the Grand Duke, who is still arming secretly, had carried his culpability) suspended the effect of their resolution, it was because, looking upon the court of Tuscany as less immediately connected with the interests and enterprises of the court of Naples than with those of the court of Vienna, they still hesitated in believing that the latter wished to revive the war. Soon, however, a fact more decisive than all the former ones, left no doubt of the disposition of Austria, and consequently afforded a full insight into that of the Grand Duke. Twenty-five thousand Russians advanced towards Germany, they were to be followed by several corps equally numerous.

The Russian monarch had proclaimed throughout Europe his hostile designs against the republic; and whilst his fleets, obtaining leave to pass the straits, interest the Mediterranean to attack the possessions of France, his troops sought a passage on the continent to attack the troops of the republic: it was at the moment in which the Emperor was still in a state of peace, in which the Empire, neutralized by a special armistice, was near the period of pacification, that a prince committing an aggression, that an ally of London and Constantinople, wishing to unite his efforts to theirs, appeared upon the limits of the Austrian territory, his army was received without any obstacle: it is evident that it was expected.

The Emperor quits his capital, goes himself to meet the
Russians,

Ruffians, accepts their congratulations, and affociates himfelf to their projects, by heaping upon them prefents and attention. Struck with the fcandal of fuch a conduct, inftructed that the Ruffians were to pafs from the Auftrian territory to the territory of the Empire, the Directory, ftill reprefling the firft impulfe of the national pride, contented themfelves with demanding explanations from the Emperor and Empire. The Emperor was filent: his plenipotentiary wifhed to deny that he had received the note of the French minifters. The deputation of the Empire referred to the diet, and the diet to the Empire. The march of the Ruffians continued: they traverfed Moravia and Auftria: they approach Bavaria: and the amicable reprefentations of the republic have not been liftened to more than the intereft of Germany, which is againft this foreign invafion. The moment was then arrived, in which the Directory could no longer temporife, and hold a language which might compromife the national dignity and the fafety of the ftate. The republic had given peace as foon as it was afked: fhe had exhaufted herfelf in efforts to maintain what fhe had granted: but it was neceffary, at length, that fhe fhould know her enemies, and that thofe who wifhed for war fhould be forced to explain themfelves. Such were the fpirit and object of the two notes tranfmitted, on the 12th of laft Nivofe, to the Auftrian minifter at Raftadt, and to the deputation. A delay was fixed for his Imperial Majefty to give a categorical and fatisfactory reply, in failure of which, his filence or his refufal would be regarded as an hoftile act. That delay expired on the 27th Pluviofe, and no reply is yet arrived.

Such, citizens reprefentatives, has been the conduct of the court of Vienna. It is by fuch a fucceffion of facts, that the treaty of Campo Formio, not acknowledged from the commencement, unexecuted on the part of Auftria in feveral of its principal parts, compromifed and invalidated daily by hoftile preparations or actions, is at length facrificed to the rapacity of the Ruffian monarch, and the perfidious combinations of England. It is thus that the Emperor, carried perhaps beyond his own refolutions, compromifes at the fame time the fate of the Empire, deprives himfelf of the benefits of a peace begun, and gives up Germany anew to all the chances of a war, in which the Emperor and the Empire are no more than the auxiliaries of Ruffia. It is thus that, the determinations of the court of Vienna carrying with them thofe of the court of Tufcany, it is not permitted to the Directory to feparate one from the other. Forced then, in the terms of the declaration made at Raftadt, to confider the filence of the Emperor as a hoftile meafure; inftructed befides that the Auftrian troops have already made aggreffive movements in Bavaria towards Suabia, the Directory, renouncing with regret the hope of maintaining peace in Germany, but

ftill

still disposed to listen to suitable propositions for a new and complete reconciliation, inform you, citizens representatives, that they have already taken such measures as they have thought necessary for the defence of the state; and propose to you to declare war against the Emperor, King of Hungary and Bohemia, and against the Grand Duke of Tuscany.

(Signed)   BARRAS, President.
                  LAGARDE, Sec. General.

Copy of a Letter from the Executive Directory to General Jourdan, dated March 15.

THE emissaries of Austria, Citizen General, are busily employed in Suabia, in organizing with *éclat* a pretended insurrection against the present governments. The desire of forming republics is the mask under which they conceal their plans; their real object is to carry alarm into all the Germanic states, and drive them into a coalition against the republic, by representing it as the irreconcilable enemy of every state which is not democratic. These artful enemies have perhaps even found means to associate with themselves some patriots, more active than enlightened, and of making even their love of liberty contribute to the success of the plans of our enemies. The Executive Directory wishes you to fix your attention on these perfidious intrigues. It expects from your wisdom, that in all the governments where you shall find the dispositions of the people friendly and pacific, far from favouring agitators, you will, on the contrary, endeavour by every means in your power to blast their hopes and their efforts.

With respect to governments which shall declare themselves against the republic, they deserve, undoubtedly, no interference on the part of the Executive Directory; therefore, it is no consideration of their interest which induces it to prescribe to you not to favour insurrections in their bosom; but you must be sensible that the Germanic states in Suabia are so intersected, that it would be difficult to prevent the flame, if kindled in the one, from communicating to the others; and in such case you ought to confine yourself to apprising the government with precision of all the movements which shall come to your knowledge. You will afterwards receive orders according to circumstances.

P. S. You would do well to transmit the orders contained in this letter to Generals Bernadotte and Massena, who command under you, the one, the army of observation, the other that of Helvetia.

Proclamation of General Massena to the French Army, dated 16th March.

Brave Soldiers,

WHEN the Executive Directory of the French republic, yielding to the wishes of an oppressed people, instructed me to call upon the Austrian commander to evacuate the Grison territory with his troops, you did not expect that you should be called upon to fight; but you were compelled to it by the resistance with which you were opposed. The passages of the Rhine, forced marches, difficult roads, privations of every sort, extreme cold, entrenchments, redoubts, forts, all you have surmounted; and in five days you have made 10,000 prisoners, taken 40 pieces of cannon, a considerable quantity of ordnance stores, and five standards. I do not mention the other twenty standards from the Grison companies in the enemies pay. They were deluded peasants, and not formidable enemies. In a word, you have taken positions in the Voralberg, you occupy all the Grison country, and you have restored that people to themselves and to liberty. Such are your labours and their consequences. These labours do you honour, and their result must teach the enemy, that the brave troops of the armies of the Rhine and of Italy have not degenerated. Your glory is pure, brave soldiers! I do not now suspect that any excess which I have had to punish is to be ascribed to you. It is the work of a few cowardly, insidious individuals; but those men are always the scourge of the vanquished, and frequently they have tarnished the glory of the vanquishers;—soldiers, remove them from you, and let justice, when it strikes, ever find them out of your ranks. Then, while you are the example of courage and bravery, you will never cease to be the models of good conduct and discipline.

(Signed) MASSENA.

The General in Chief of the Armies of the French Republic in Germany to the Commander in Chief of the Austrian Troops in Suabia.

Monsieur General,

Head-quarters at Pfallendorf, 17th March.

THE French government has ordered me to penetrate into Suabia with the army under my command. In executing the movements necessary for carrying these orders into effect, I every where meet posts of Austrian troops; and not having had an intention of exercising the least hostility against them, I summoned these posts to retire; which they consented to do without hesitation. But, as they now threaten to make resistance, I have the

honour

honour to apprife you, M. General, that I am refolved to employ force of arms to make the troops under your command evacuate the pofitions which I muft take, in compliance with the orders of my government. Receive, M. General, my affurance of the moft perfect confideration, with which I am, &c.

JOURDAN.

Refolution publifhed by Citizen Reinhart in the Name of the French Republic.

Article 1.

ALL perfons attached to the perfonal fervice of the Grand Duke and his family fhall receive, exclufive of what is due to them for the paft, a month's falary, to begin from the 1ft of April.

2. Thofe who are infirm, and proved to be incapable of fervice elfewhere, fhall be entitled to penfions.

3. A particular ftatement fhall accordingly be made of all the individuals attached to the Grand Duke's fervice, with an account of their ages, the number of years they have ferved, and the falaries they have enjoyed.

4. Citizen Laguerre, treafurer to the Grand Duke's houfehold, is charged with drawing up that ftatement, and is empowered to add any obfervations which he may think neceffary.

5. He fhall, at the fame time, give an account of the current expenfes which have not been paid till the prefent moment.

(Signed) REINHART.

Extract of a Letter from General Maffena to the Helvetic Directory.

Citizens Directors,   Head-quarters at Azmoos, March 6th.

I HAVE the honour to inform you that I have received orders from my government to drive the Auftrians from the Grifon territory, in order to reftore to their rights the patriots who had fled into Helvetia. As the Auftrian general returned no anfwer to my fummons, I, to-day, attacked him in feveral points.

(Here follows a detail of the engagement.)

(Signed) MASSENA.

Proclamation of the King of Pruffia.

HIS Majefty the King of Pruffia, &c. has received information, that in his provinces of Cleves, Meurs, and Gueldres, on the other fide of the Rhine, the inhabitants are now actually proceeding

ing in the sale of farms, lands, and others effects, without the concurrence of the authorities appointed by his Majesty; and as those alienations can have no legal validity, in the present provisional state of the said provinces, and before their destiny has been decided by the conclusion of a definitive peace with the Empire, his Majesty, therefore, causes it to be herewith announced, by way of advertisement, that he shall not consider himself bound by any alienations of this kind, which may take place before the conclusion of the aforesaid peace; but that, on the other hand, he shall regard them all as void and of no effect.

Dated Berlin, March 12th.
        (Signed)   FINKENSTEIN, HEINITZ,
                         GOLBECK, ALVENSLEN,
                         HAUGWITZ, THULEMEYER,
                         MASSO, D'ARMIN.

Decree of the French Executive Directory explaining that of the 14th January, relative to neutral Vessels.

CONSIDERING that the article 4th of the decree, which concerns the roles d'equipage of neutral ships, has given rise to abusive interpretations relative to the roles d'equipage of the American vessels; and as it is important to put an end to the impediments which have resulted therefrom to the American commerce; after having heard the foreign minister and the minister of justice, they declare, that by article 4th of the above decree it was not intended that the navigation of American ships, relative to the form of their roles d'equipage, should be subject to other conditions than those imposed on all neutral bottoms, by the 12th article of the regulation of 1744, and by article 9th of that of the 26th July 1788. And this is ordered to be inserted in the bulletin of the laws.

Extract of a Message from the Helvetic Directory to the Grand Council, March 17th.

AMONG the monarchic governments, none have given the Helvetic republic more sincere marks of friendship than that of Spain. Several Princes of the Empire have also hastened, not only to acknowledge the republic, but to enter into negotiations on the subject of their common interest, and ours, and the relations of good neighbourhood, which have hitherto subsisted between their subjects and the citizens of Helvetia. The republic may in particular rely on the sister republic, whose interests are identified with hers. The Cisalpine envoy has arrived at
                                                      Lucerne,

Lucerne, and the appointment of a Ligurian envoy has been announced to us. The Roman republic has, since the moment of its birth, maintained with us intimate relations, which, though interrupted during the late crisis, have now resumed their usual course. The provisional government of Piedmont has, in the name of the people, renewed those relations which formerly subsisted between us and the King of Sardinia. The Batavian is the only republic that has not made a return to the advances of the Executive Directory. This, however, can be imputed to no other cause than the distance and the difficulty of communication. The King of Prussia, connected with Switzerland by his title of Prince of Neufchatel, has not yet answered the dispatch which announced to him the regeneration of our government; but the government of Neufchatel continues to maintain its ancient relations with us, and the Helvetic citizens are received as friends in all the Prussian states. The House of Austria has not treated us with the same respect; under the pretext of obtaining a pledge for the indemnities which the republic has promised to the German states, who possessed some feudal rights on our territory, the Helvetic funds invested in the bank of Vienna have been sequestrated, and the Austrian subjects have been prohibited paying their debts due to Switzerland. Our counter-revolutionists receive protection and support in the Austrian states, while numerous emissaries from all quarters announce that the Imperial armies are marching to re-establish the ancient government. Our intimate connexion with the great nation is sufficient to make us forget every act of injustice. The interests of the two republics are so identified, that, notwithstanding the disproportion of their power, the destruction of the less republic would be attended with very disagreeable consequences to the greater. While France preserved the hope of concluding a peace at Rastadt, the execution of the decree for levying 18,000 men remained suspended, but since the hope of peace has vanished, that law has been carried into effect.

Diplomatic Note distributed in Germany by Order of the Court of Vienna.

THE French Directory continues to advance the most exaggerated pretensions, and the Imperial court will not suffer itself to be degraded by republicans, whose object is to humble all princes. Twenty-five millions of faithful and devoted subjects, the best army in Europe, and immense resources of all kinds, are strong inducements to inspire the Emperor with a just sentiment of his dignity and power. With such means, the Emperor will not allow himself to be dictated to, and his example will be followed by every monarch whose throne is now threatened by innovation

innovation and anarchy. The caufe of kings, when united, can no longer be doubtful : but if they remain divided, their reigns muft foon be at an end, and Europe muft be expofed to the moft dreadful calamities.

Extract from a Proclamation in reply from Bernadotte to the People of Germany, iffued from his Head-quarters at Manheim.

TYRANTS and their iniquitous counfellors have miftaken our patience for fleep, and our prudence for death. But nations who have reconquered their liberty are no more liable to fleep than death.

Germans! the hoftilities which we now commence are entirely defenfive. You will no longer mifapprehend the odious machiavelifm of the Houfe of Auftria. Ever defirous of engaging you in its quarrels, it would again convert a war undertaken for its own purpofes into a war of the Empire, in order to increafe its own ftrength by exhaufting yours.

You will perceive how much it has directed againft your interefts its monftrous alliance with England, which fupports itfelf only by the troubles of the continent; and with Ruffia, which wifhes to impofe upon civilized Europe the chains of Afiatic barbarifm.

Germans! the maintenance of your religion, your fafety, your liberty, and the independence of your governments which are on terms of friendfhip with us, enjoin the neceffity of your uniting your efforts to ours to drive thefe confpiring hordes to their native dens.

Your property will be held facred. The laws of the republic punifh with death thofe who dare to violate the afylum of the peaceful inhabitant, and they fhall be rigoroufly executed.

Unite with us, Germans! in declaring war againft the Houfe of Auftria, and againft the barbarians of the North, who are again defirous of inundating your territory.

General Orders, given on the 20th of March, by his Royal Highnefs the Archduke Charles, to all the Generals of the Army under his Command.

THE hoftile intentions, of which the firft approach of the French troops left no room to doubt, are daily more apparent; and it is at length clearly feen what the French announced by the occupation of the military pofitions, until the general affembling of all their troops. On the 6th of March, Maffena commenced hoftilities on the fide of Switzerland, againft the Grifon country and the Voralberg: he even began by furprife, without

without any previous declaration of war. An enemy's corps advanced on the 15th towards Stockach, attacked our posts which were placed there, and repulsed them. The same proceeding took place against the posts of Klosterweld and Zolnegg. At the same time, that is to say on the 16th, General Thurreau planted cannon against our post Sallmansweiller, and made himself master of it with the detachments of cavalry and infantry; the post of Uberlingen was attacked on the same day. The posts of Major-general Piazeck were driven in as far as Ravensburg; one of his guard was even wounded in a perfidious manner. Major Loweck informed the French commander on the 20th of this event; but as the major was referred to General Thurreau on this subject, the latter by a trumpet demanded a conference. The major having approached him, the French general made him prisoner with his detachment; an action till now unheard of, and which the laws of war only allow of in the cause of the most violent wars.

By advices which I have received, the French army approached against my advanced guard, and having driven in some of the advanced detachments, penetrated to Kofkirchen, and the convent of Jieften.

A series of such offensive actions was followed by a letter from the French commander in chief: it is of that tenour which admits of no other answer than from the mouth of our cannon; and the hostile actions, cited only as examples, which have been connived at from the 6th current until the present time and progressively, against the troops which are under my orders, are such as leave no other alternative then taking revenge for the treason, and answering insults, such as the history of war offers nothing equal to, in such a manner as the offended honour of the troops under my command imperiously requires. All the incalculable consequences which insulted humanity must suffer from this new struggle are to be attributed to those who, almost at the same moment when they were reiterating their pacific assurances, attacked our troops in a hostile manner in their positions, and by surprise carried their depredations to the highest degree possible, founding their conduct upon reasons which can in no respect be justified, and are contrary to common sense, or pretences which are adverse to the practice of our times, and contrary to every admitted principle.

Edict of the Emperor of Russia respecting Hamburgh.

WHEREAS we have remarked for some time past in the government of Hamburgh a disposition for the principles of anarchy, and an attachment to the forms of the French government, which are destructive of all legitimate power: we order
that

that an embargo shall be laid upon all Hamburgh vessels in our ports, and which belong to Hamburgh subjects; and we also order that a return shall be made to us of the number of the said vessels which are in each of our ports.

Given at St. Petersburgh, March 21, 1799.   PAUL.

Downing Street, March 21, 1799.

THE King has been pleased to cause it to be signified by the Right Honourable Lord Grenville, his Majesty's principal secretary of state for foreign affairs, to the ministers of neutral powers residing at this court, that the necessary measures having been taken, by his Majesty's command, for the blockade of the ports of the United Provinces, the said ports are declared to be in a state of blockade; and that all vessels which may attempt to enter any of them after this notice, will be dealt with according to the principles of the law of nations, and to the stipulations of such treaties subsisting between his Majesty and foreign powers, as may contain provisions applicable to the cases of towns, places, or ports in a state of blockade.

Proclamation of the Duke of Tuscany, in consequence of the Determination of the French to occupy Florence.

WE shall regard it as a proof of fidelity, attachment, and affection on the part of our faithful subjects, if, at the time of the entry of the French troops into Florence, they respect the French corps, and all the individuals who compose it, and abstain from all acts that might give occasion to any kind of complaint: this prudent conduct will secure to them new claims to our good-will.

(Signed)   FERDINAND.
Done at Florence, March 24.   J. FRACISCO SEBAT.
                          GAETANO RENIOLDE.

Leghorn, 24th March.

THE consul of the French republic at Leghorn will put seals upon all the property belonging to England, or English merchants, the subjects of the Emperor, the Grand Signior, the Emperor of Russia, the Queen of Portugal, the States of Barbary, and, in fine, of all the potentates and subjects of the powers with whom the French republic is at war.

The necessary measures shall be taken to discover and procure the surrender of all the articles subject to the preceding order, which may

may be in the possession of merchants or private individuals of Leghorn.

Rewards will be given to such as assist in the necessary searches.

(Signed) MIOLLES.

Proclamation of the Governor of Inspruck, dated March 28.

MAJOR General Baron Laudon has retired with part of his troops near Bergeis in the vicinity of Glugens. But however agreeable this event may be, the danger is not therefore diminished; and it requires the most prompt and energetic measures to raise the country *en masse*, in order to oppose the further progress of the enemy, and by this means second, in the most efficacious manner, the royal Imperial troops. All the districts in which the summons of the 26th has been made, are called upon anew by the present, in the most pressing manner, to march as soon as possible; particularly as it is understood that a report was spread, without any foundation, that the call of a levy *en masse* had been revoked.

FERDINAND, COUNT BISSENGEN, Governor.
Inspruck, March 28.

Proclamation of the Archduke Charles, Commander in Chief of the Imperial Armies, and of the Empire, to the Swiss.

AFTER two victories gained over the French army, who, without any declaration of war, advanced beyond their positions; who, without any declaration of war, had on all sides exercised their power and made attacks; the troops under my command have entered the territory of the Swiss, not to make war against the Swiss, who are actuated by amicable dispositions, but to pursue the common enemy, against whom you have yourselves fought with so much bravery, in defence of your liberty and independence, and whose superiority of force alone has reduced you to the wretched situation of which you are so deeply sensible, and at which you have already so loudly expressed your discontent. Among the attempts and means employed to retain you in a state of dependance and subjection, they have endeavoured to make you believe, that the Imperial and royal court entertained plans to dismember your country, or had other designs against Switzerland. They have also endeavoured to alarm you, by filling you with apprehensions of oppression and pillage on the part of the Imperial army. It is my duty, therefore, solemnly to declare to the Swiss of all descriptions, that his Imperial Majesty, in conformity to those assurances which he has on every occasion given to the Helvetic league

league of his amity and good neighbourhood, is firmly resolved to preserve towards her, in the most active manner, the ancient friendly relations; and also that his Imperial Majesty has no other view than that of contributing to the utmost of his power, that Switzerland may enjoy, without interruption, its independence, its integrity, its privileges, its rights, and its possessions.

On my part, I confidently expect that the troops under my command, whose entry into the Swiss territory, occasioned by circumstances sufficiently evident, has no other object than that of the common safety, will be treated in a friendly manner, and assisted by all the members of the Helvetic league, satisfied they have the good of their country at heart, and that the people of Switzerland will carefully avoid whatever may augment the miseries of war.

Among the happy effects of such a conduct to Switzerland, may be ranked the suppression of those measures which hostilities and violence have occasioned, and the re-establishment of the relations of commerce and communication between Germany and Switzerland.

March 30th, 1799. The ARCHDUKE CHARLES.

Extract of a Letter from Lord Robert Fitzgerald to Lord Grenville, dated Copenhagen, 23*d January* 1798.

I HAVE received information, through a private, but, I believe, authentic channel, of a very scandalous practice, in which, your Lordship will hardly credit it, the gentlemen of the Royal College of Commerce in this city are principally concerned. This is nothing else than the mean traffic which is carried on through the channel of an individual of Tranquebar, who is their agent for the sale of sea-passes to all such vessels as are disposed to purchase them, for the purpose of skreening themselves from the vigilance of the British cruisers in the Indian seas. The name of the person at Tranquebar, whose agency is thus employed, and whose modern principles fit him for the office, is Lichtenstein. He is head man to the Danish factory at Tranquebar, and to him it is that the charge of filling up the blanks in the passes, and of distributing them, is committed, from hence, after they are regularly prepared and signed by the College of Commerce.

This hint may possibly be of some use, my Lord, to the officers commanding his Majesty's ships of war on the Indian station; and it is with that view only I mention the circumstance, as I have not sufficient proof to make it a matter of formal complaint to the Danish minister, though I have the fullest reliance on the veracity of the person from whom I have the information. It is

said

said that the communication between the Mauritius and Batavia is principally maintained by the aid of these false passes.

[The above extract was transmitted to Sir Hugh Christian, by the Lords Commissioners of the Admiralty, and was the primary cause of the detection of the ships suspected of illicit traffic.]

29th March.

THIS day the Helvetic Directory proposed to the two Councils to issue a formal declaration against the Emperor. The proposition was adopted.

Answer of the Diet of Ratisbon to the Note of the Deputation of the Empire at Rastadt, with respect to the Affairs of Citizen Bacher.

IT states in substance, that on the subject of the notification made to the diet on that transaction, the three colleges of the Empire have declared they have had no share in that event, and that if any resolution to such an effect is to be adopted on the part of the Empire, they ought, in conformity to their duty, previously to communicate it to their constituents.

N. B. The note alluded to, was written in consequence of a complaint made by the French ministers at the deputation of the Empire at Rastadt, 14th March, for which see page 72.

Ratisbon, April 2.

YESTERDAY the plan of the Electoral conclusum relative to the march of the Russians was presented in the college of Electors. It was approved and adopted by the majority, consisting of the ministers of Bavaria, Palatine, Saxony, Brandenburgh, Brunswick, and Mentz. In this sitting, the minister of the Elector of Cologne caused the following declaration to be inserted in the Protocole, as a supplement to his vote; viz. " That the French government has committed new acts of hostility against the Empire by marching its armies into the circles of Suabia and the Upper Rhine, by summoning Philipsburg, by contributions imposed upon the Palatinate and other parts of Germany, by the enormous requisitions recently made for the fortress of Ehrenbreitstein, and by the last proclamation of General Bernadotte.—That the deliberations on the march of the Russian troops have entirely lost their object, in consequence of the formal declaration of war which has been made against Austria, and still more so in consequence of the direction which, according to all accounts, the Ruffian troops have taken.—That a reprefentation, on the part of his Imperial Majefty, conceived in general terms, could not produce any effect.—That as the Houfe of Auftria has not only been attacked; but as the aggreffion againft its ftates has taken place on the territory of the Empire, in confequence of the French advancing into the circle of Suabia, Auftria will not fend back thofe troops, and will make ftill lefs difficulty in employing them, according to circumftances, on the fide on which the attack was made. Now that the war has broke out anew, a more hoftile treatment than that which the Empire expériences at this moment does not depend upon the diet, but on the fortune of arms. The Elector is, therefore, of opinion that he ought to confine himfelf to declaring, that as no requifition has been made on the fubject in queftion, no legal determination can be made."

In the fitting of the college of Princes on the fame day, Schwarzbourg, grand mafter of the Teutonic order, Hildefheim, Paderborn, Lubeck, and the Counts of Suabia, gave in their votes; only nine votes are wanting; viz. the four of Mecklenbourg, Brunfwick-Wolfenbutel, Holftein-Gluckftadt, Pomerania, Arenfberg, and Schwarzenberg. We are ftill ignorant as to when the conclufum will be prepared in this college.- In the college of the towns, the majority coincides with the vote of the Imperial city of Frankfort, but no conclufum has as yet been drawn up.

Proclamation of the General in Chief to the People of Helvetia, dated Head-quarters at St. Gall, April 3.

Helvetians,

THE French commanders inform me that perfidious or fanatical perfons commit acts of violence againft the French troops when they march fingle or in fcattered bodies. I learn, likewife, that fymptoms of infurrection have appeared in feveral quarters of Switzerland.—Helvetians, why this fudden change? Why do you deftroy that indifpenfable harmony which exifted between you and the French army? Why do you difturb that peace which reigned in your abodes? It would thus feem that you give ear to the infinuations and atrocious plots of the enemies of the French republic, who are alfo your enemies! It would thus appear that you conceive the French army is not longer in a ftate to refift the Auftrian forces. The army which I command has beat them at every point where it has been engaged; and will ftill beat them, fhould they dare to enter your territory. But can you imagine, that amidft the efforts of courage, and the facrifices which that brave army makes for your defence,

it

it will coolly see its heroes falling under the attacks of cowardly assassins? Do you think that I myself will hesitate to take terrible vengeance on these infamous enormities? Helvetians, who remain attached to France and your constitution! save your country from the evils which threaten it, by repressing the guilty; point them out to your government, that their crimes may be instantly overtaken with punishment. As to myself, I have shown that I know how to protect you, whilst I beheld in you a faithful ally; so will I show myself capable of punishing you if you become traitors and violators of the faith of treaties. The security of the French army, and your own security also, will be the rule of my conduct.—I therefore declare, that from this moment I shall hold the several communes responsible for all the events which shall happen within their territory, to the annoyance of Frenchmen. I farther declare, that columns of the French army will march with rapidity towards the cantons which shall show any disposition to insurrection, and that such canton shall be ravaged with fire and sword. This proclamation shall be printed in the two languages, published and posted up through the whole of Helvetia, and copied into the general orders of the army.

(Signed) / MASSENA.

Correspondence between Commodore Trowbridge and General Macdonald.

Sir, *Culloden, off Naples, April 3.*

HAVING learned that the French privateer the Championet, a prize belonging to one of his Majesty's vessels under my command, has been driven by bad weather into the port of Castellamare, and having, within a little more than a month, released nearly 4000 French prisoners, I hope that your Excellency will set at liberty the midshipman and seven English seamen, now in your power. It is necessary for me farther to inform your Excellency, that on the 30th ult. I sent a cartel from Palermo to Nice with 300 French prisoners. It is with real concern I hear that the effects of our minister, Sir W. Hamilton, are detained in his house at Naples. You, Sir, both as an officer and soldier, ought to know that the property of ambassadors has never been considered as falling within the right of conquest; and I am convinced that what has taken place, in that respect, has happened without your knowledge. An ambassador is obliged to follow the court to which he has been sent. I beg you to reflect on our conduct towards your consul and merchants at Leghorn, when we took possession of that port.

I am

I am also to acquaint you, that I captured at the heights of Alexandria, a Monsieur Beauchamp, dressed in the Turkish fashion, on his way to Constantinople as a spy, with secret instructions, and about 600*l*. concealed about him, which I restored to him, from conviction that it is the duty of all officers to alleviate the miseries of war, which should as little as possible affect individuals, and to treat prisoners with every proper attention. I wish I had it in my power to say, that our officers, soldiers, or sailors, have been treated in that way by the Directory. I trust, Sir, after this explanation, that you will make no difficulty of giving up the above-mentioned midshipman and seamen to my officer, who is charged with the delivery of this letter, and that you will also put into his hands all the English whom you may have in your power. I shall take care to have their names registered, and the officer will give you a receipt for the men whom you shall send back to me.

I have the honour to be, with great respect,
Your very humble and obedient servant,
T. TROWBRIDGE.

Sir,

THE crew of the small vessel which was forced into Castellamare by bad weather, are still performing quarantine; but as soon as the officer of health shall declare there is no danger in opening the communication with them, I shall give the necessary orders for sending them on board your squadron. Your officer, who brought your letter, has been enabled to satisfy himself that your minister has left nothing here but the walls of his house. At least it was found in that state on the conquest of Naples. You, Sir, who are so well versed in the rights of nations, should put the ex-King of Naples in mind of them, who now keeps in chains, without any reason or motive, the vice-consul of the French republic. I beg, Sir, you will be satisfied that your prisoners are treated with all the attention and care which misfortune and humanity prescribe. I wish I had it in my power to say as much in favour of the agents of your government, and of you in particular.

I am, Sir, with respect, &c. MACDONALD.

The Commander in Chief Macdonald, to M. Acton, Minister of his Neapolitan Ex Majesty.

Naples, April 13th.

I LEARN, Sir, with the greatest surprise and the most lively indignation, that the *ci-devant* King of Naples exercises his impotent vengeance against Citizen Ribaud, vice-consul of the
French

French republic at Messina, and that he has loaded him with chains, and thrown him into a dungeon. Such extraordinary conduct cannot fail to provoke reprisals, and it is on your brother that they have fallen. I am astonished, Sir, that humanity and the ties of blood have not spoken in favour of him. I propose, Sir, however, to exchange him for our estimable fellow-citizen Ribaud.

MACDONALD, Commander in Chief.

Letter of the Helvetic Directory to General Massena, Commander of the Armies of the Danube and Helvetia, upon the Union of the Grison League to the Helvetic Republic; dated 10th April.

Citizen General,

THE legislative body of the Helvetic republic has solemnly accepted the accession of Rhetia to the compact which has united into one family the members of the ancient confederation. Annexed is the decree of union and the message which gave rise to it.

On this day, which unites to us a people whose energy and simplicity of manners promise a real accession of strength to that of the simple but estimable Helvetia, our first regards are led towards the author of this blessing, who, in opposition to the efforts of Austria, its contemptible agents, and the ignorant people they had enslaved, succeeded in rendering them free, and, even in the moment of victory, proved himself their benefactor.—Citizen General, the Helvetians and the Grisons, through us, as their organ, acknowledge that it is to you they will be indebted for a continuance of that security and strength which their union assures to them.

Their gratitude accompanies you in the labours of a campaign which you will render glorious for the cause of liberty.—Massena, say they, is great, because he has long conquered, but he is still greater, because he loves and confers happiness on the people conquered. We trust, though farther removed from us, since double command has been confided to you, that Helvetia will still be dear to you, that she will not cease to be the object of your cares. We shall think her in safety, as long as you are to direct the efforts she makes for the protection of her soil and her liberty.

Receive the expression of our esteem and attachment.

BAY, the President of the Executive.

General Massena to the Executive Directory of the Helvetic Republic.

Citizens Directors,

WITH your letter of the 10th of April (old style) I have received the decree uniting the Grison league to the Helvetic republic. The interest and policy of the two countries demanded this measure, which would have been long ago adopted, if some dangerous leaders, sold to the House of Austria, had not drawn the Grison league into proceedings which might have led to their own destruction, and which threatened also to involve Helvetia in their fall. But we shoud not revive the remembrance of painful events. The domains of liberty are increased, and the Helvetians and Grisons now form but one people and one family. I apply to the French army the tribute of praise with which you present me, Citizens Directors, for the acts which have preceded and led to the accomplishment of this union. I have no personal wish but that which I have strongly expressed, of serving the cause of republics, and of being useful to Helvetia. Yes, Citizens Directors, Helvetia is dear to me (to use your expression), and my labours shall have no other object than that of defending her from internal enemies, of protecting her against the Austrian armies, as my constant wishes shall be that she may preserve her independence, and that, under your paternal and beneficent government, she may reach that degree of strength and prosperity, to which she is called by her destinies and her union with the French republic.

Health and respect.

(Signed) MASSENA.

Sir, *King's House, Jamaica, April* 18, 1799.

I AM commanded by his Honour the Lieutenant Governor, to send to you an order of his Majesty in council, dated the 9th of January 1799, which you will please to publish in the Royal Gazette.

I have the honour to be,
Your most obedient humble servant,
J. ALSTON.

Alex. Aikman, Esq. his Majesty's Printer.

AT the court at St. James's, the 9th day of January 1799; present, the King's most excellent Majesty in council:

It having been represented to his Majesty, that it would be expedient to allow certain articles, under certain restrictions, to be exported from Jamaica to certain ports in the island of St. Domingo,

Domingo, and to import the produce of the said island in return for such articles; his Majesty, by and with the advice of his Privy Council, is pleased to authorize, and doth hereby authorize the governor or lieutenant-governor of the island of Jamaica, or, in his absence, the commanding officer of his Majesty's land forces for the time being, and the officer commanding his Majesty's naval forces on that station, jointly or separately, to grant (L. S.) licences, under their hands and seals, but in his Majesty's name, to any person or persons (the name of every such person or persons to be inserted in such licence), to export from the said island of Jamaica, in any British ship or vessel navigated according to law (the name of every such ship or vessel, and of the master thereof, to be inserted in every such licence), any articles (naval and military stores excepted), the same being the produce or manufacture of his Majesty's dominions, or being the produce of the United States of America (such articles, and their respective quantities, in every such licence to be expressed), and to convey the same to such port or ports (in every such licence to be named) of the said island of St. Domingo, as may be approved of by the said governor or lieutenant-governor of the island of Jamaica, or the commanding officer of his Majesty's land forces for the time being, and the officer commanding his Majesty's naval forces on that station, and to bring back in the said vessels, and import into the said island of Jamaica, from the said port or ports of St. Domingo, any of the produce of the said island of St. Domingo, which may be received in return for articles carried thither under the authority of the said licences, and subject to such further regulations and restrictions, to be inserted in the said licences, as to the said governor, lieutenant-governor, and commanding officer as aforesaid, shall, from time to time, seem fit and expedient.

And his Majesty doth hereby order and command all and every the commanders and officers of his ships and vessels of war, and the commanders of all private ships of war, and all others whom it may concern, to suffer all and every such ships and vessels, having such licences as aforesaid, and conforming to the regulations and restrictions therein prescribed, to pass and repass to and from the said island of Jamaica, and to and from such port or ports in St. Domingo, as shall be described in such licence. And in case, through ignorance, or in breach of this his Majesty's order in Council, any ship or vessel, having such licence as aforesaid, should be brought in for adjudication, his Majesty doth hereby further order and command, that they shall forthwith be released by his Majesty's court of admiralty, upon proof that the parties have duly conformed to the regulations and restrictions prescribed in the said licences.

W. FAWKENER.

Extract from the Registry of the Deliberations of the Agency of the Executive Directory at St. Domingo, 25th April.

THE agent of the Executive Directory at St. Domingo, considering that the infractions committed upon the law of nations by French privateers, or vessels pretending to be such, have occasioned great discontents amongst the neutral nations, and particularly the United States of America, where a rupture appears on the point of breaking out between that government and ours:

That the agent Hedouville, impressed with the necessity of taking competent measures to prevent the cessation of commerce between St. Domingo and the United States, excepted, by his arreté of the 9th Floreal, year 6, from the dispositions of the law of the 29th Nivose of the same year, neutral vessels bound for ports of St. Domingo, of whatsoever nature their cargo; and stipulated by a second arreté of 30th Messidor following, new guarantees in favour of those vessels, and particularly for the Americans, even in case of hostilities between the republic and one of those said powers at present neutral:

That the Executive Directory has proclaimed its arreté of the 13th Thermidor, year 6*, which establishes precautions against the abuses of which our allies, the Americans, complain:

That, in spite of the wisdom and the publicity of those decrees, things have arrived at such a pitch of animosity, that the government of the United States has judged it necessary to persist in the hostile attitude it had before taken:

That, in the mean time, the general in chief Toussaint Louverture, finding himself solely charged with all the burden of the government during the vacation of the agency; and wishing, after having quieted the colony, to avert the horrible famine with which it was threatened, had the prudence and the patriotism to commission the Citizen Bunel to go and offer to the American government his views for the re-establishment of a commerce no less necessary to American than to St. Domingo:

That, in virtue of that authority, the president has appointed the Citizen Stevens to reside at the Cape in quality of consul general, to effect the renewal of commerce, provided that the privateers be prevented from continuing their excesses, and that all the abuses which may exist be suppressed:

That the object of the mission of Citizen Stevens having been

---

* A copy of which will be found in No. 29 of the series of papers transmitted by Mr. Gerry after his return to America, in a subsequent page.

discussed,

discussed, between him, the general in chief, the agent, the comptroller Dumain, and the ordonnateur Idlinger, it has been agreed, that the articles adopted on either part shall be firmly established by a decree of the agency:

Considering, that, besides the complaints adduced to the Executive Directory by the government of the United States, other griefs of the same nature have been laid before the agents of the Directory at St. Domingo, by the Batavian governor of Curaçoa, and by the Spanish chiefs of the captaincy general of the Caracas, who have positively assured that their colonies would fall into a total dearth of food and raiment, if they (the agents) suffered longer to subsist in those seas, those rigorous dispositions of laws and decrees, which the Legislative Body and the Directory have promulgated upon considerations solely concerning European relations, and by no means with the intention of ruining the colonies of France, or of its allies:

Considering, finally, that until, in the expectation of the French and American governments agreeing between them, on the reciprocal reparations which may be required, the agency cannot suppose that they will ever come to a declaration of war, by which our common enemies alone would profit in the annihilation of the commerce of America, as well as that of the produce of St. Domingo:

And that upon this principle it is the duty of the agency to take upon itself the responsibility of all measures necessary to the preservation of St. Domingo and the colonies of our allies; those measures being too urgent to be adjourned until the receipt of new orders from the national government, decrees:

Art. 1. The decree of the Executive Directory, of 13th Thermidor, year 6, relative to French privateers and to neutral vessels, shall be published immediately in the chief places of the departments of the north, the east, and the south of St. Domingo, to be executed according to its form and tenour, excepting with the explanation contained below in the second article. In consequence, there shall be no more letters of marque delivered, either for cruising, or for war and merchandise, but by the agent himself; and those which he left signed in blank at his departure from St. Domingo, are annulled.

All those heretofore issued shall be regarded as void after the expiration of thirty days from the date hereof: the privateers which bear them are required to return and deliver up their commissions within the same time, upon pain of incurring the risk of being considered as pirates.

The agency shall cause carefully to be respected the persons and effects of Americans and other neutrals or allies: the administrators of the marine shall not treat for their cargoes but by

mutual

mutual consent, and shall satisfy them punctually according to the conditions of their agreements.

2. The owners and captains of privateers, furnished with the commissions of the agency, shall conform themselves exactly to the laws of the 23d Thermidor, year 3, and 3d Brumaire, year 4, as well as to the ordinances and rules which have preceded them; and the first of those laws shall be maintained in operation.

The laws of the Legislative Body, and the decrees of the Executive Directory, posterior to the date of 3d Brumaire, year 4, shall have no operation relative to the American vessels of commerce, armed or unarmed, nor to those of other allied or neutral nations.

3. American vessels of state, singly, or convoying vessels of commerce to the French ports of St. Domingo, as well as all other American vessels, shall be free to harbour therein, and to purchase those objects of which they may stand in need; they shall be under the safeguard of the national honour, at their arrival, during their stay, and at their departure.

4. The former decrees of the agents of the Directory at St. Domingo are annulled, so far as they may be found contrary to the present dispositions.

5. The security prescribed by the law of 23d Thermidor, year 3, shall continue to be in the sum of fifty thousand francs, money of France: nevertheless, if, to defeat the execution of the present decree, the privateers send their prizes elsewhere than to St. Domingo, or to our allies, in those ports where reside French receivers, the owner and his security shall answer wholly for all the charges, expenses, and damages, which shall result from a definitive judgment, to the profit of the owners of the vessel captured.

6. No change is to take place relative to sentences yet to be passed upon the neutral vessels already captured.

Those which shall be captured through ignorance of the present decree, during the term of thirty days, dated from this day, shall be immediately released on their entry into port, and the captors shall be held to indemnify them.

After the same term, the captains of privateers who shall make prizes in violation of these presents, shall answer personally for all the damages which shall result therefrom, and shall be incapable of commanding during the rest of the war.

7. The Citizen Edward Stevens is provisionally authorized to exercise the functions of consul general of the United States at St. Domingo, per interim, until definitively authorized by the Executive Directory.

The Citizen Jacob Mayer shall exercise those of provisional consul at the city of the Cape and its dependencies.

The provisional consul general may discuss the solidity of the securities which shall be offered, before the controller, the ordonnateur,

nateur, and the commiffary of the executive power at the municipal adminiftration, who fhall pronounce upon the queftion.

8. The agency fhall alfo authorize American confuls provifionally, in other towns of the colony, as may be found convenient.

9. All thofe who fhall contravene any of the preceding difpofitions, fhall be punifhed conformably to the laws.

10. The prefent decree fhall be tranfmitted immediately to the Executive Directory, to be fubmitted for its approbation, and fhall be provifionally executed.

It fhall be moreover addreffed to the military and civil authorities of the colony, as alfo to the commiffion of St. Domingo and to the receivers of the republic in the neighbouring iflands, tranfcribed into the regifters of the tribunals civil and of commerce, enregiftered in the comptrolloire of the marine, printed, read, publifhed and pofted wherefoever need fhall be.

Done at Cape Français, the 6th Floreal, year 7 of the republic, one and indivifible.

(Signed) in the regiftry of the deliberations, the particular Agent of the Executive Directory, ROUME.

The Secretary-general of the Agency,
L. BLANCHARD.

The following is a Tranflation of the Law of 23d Thermidor, 3d Year, referred to in the Arrêté of the Agency of St. Domingo.

In National Convention, 23d Thermidor, 3d Year.

THE National Convention, on the report of the Committee of Public Safety, decrees as follows, viz.

Art. 1. It is lawful for all French citizens to arm veffels to cruife againft the enemy.

2. The commiffioners of the marine and colonies are authorized to iffue letters of marque, to be figned by five members of the Committee of Public Safety, and counterfigned by the commiffioner of the marine.

3. Every owner of a veffel who fhall intend to fit out a privateer, fhall apply to the commiffioners of the colonies, and fet forth to them the nature and advantages of the intended armament; the commiffioners fhall inform the committee thereof, and deliver the letters of marque if there be ground therefor.

4. The owners fhall enjoy the benefit of the law of 31ft January 1793 (O. S.), which allows of compofing one fixth of the crews of privateers of regiftered failors; but they fhall not employ any requifition-men, nor any of thofe whofe fervices are indifpenfably neceffary to the republic.

5. The

5. The owners shall purchase all necessary articles at their own expense, except produce with which they will be supplied by government.

6. Each owner shall find security in the sum of 5000 livres.

7. All former laws of police and discipline, respecting privateering, the distribution of ships, money, and indemnities in cases of illegal captures, shall continue to be executed in so much as they do not derogate from these presents.

8. Grants an amnesty to deserters, and settles the mode of claiming and recovering the benefit of it.

AMERICAN PAPERS.

(Continued from Page 46.)

No. XXIV.

Citizen Minister,   *Paris, July 20, 1798.*

I RECEIVED, on the 27th Messidor (15th July), your letter of the 24th (the 12th of July), on which permit me to make some observations.

You allege, that in the United States the French republic is accused of not wishing for peace, and to show that it was always desirous thereof, you recur to the arrival of Mr. Genet in America. Far from accusations of any kind, I wish to cultivate harmony between the two governments, as the solid basis of peace. From that epoch, to the departure from the United States of Mr. Adet, the correspondence of the secretaries of state of the United States, with the French ministers in America, and the American ministers in France, contains the history, to that time, of the unhappy differences between the two republics, and evinces the sincere desire of the government of the United States, amidst the inevitable embarrassments resulting from the convulsed state of Europe, to preserve harmony and friendship with the French republic, and to perform with scrupulous attention the duties of neutrality. If, by any unfortunate events, France had sustained injuries during that term, still the manifest disposition of the government of the United States to justice and moderation, was a sure pledge of redress.

When Mr. Monroe was recalled, a minister was sent to supply his place, and you say, "he could not be received, because he was not in a situation to fulfil the conditions necessary for the renewal of the political connexions." Had he been received, he could have applied for other powers if necessary: nothing is more usual. The application, which you have so strenuously urged on my part, must have been for the renewal of powers annulled

by

the act of sei   g away the other envoys: surely then your
arguments w   d have applied with much more force to the case
of a minister, whose powers were only supposed inadequate to the
objects of his mission. The act of rejecting his minister, accompanied with circumstances of high displeasure on the part of the government of the French republic, could not fail to wound deeply
the government of the United States, and to produce observations
on such an important event. Let the cause and effect be buried
in oblivion; the remembrance thereof cannot promote harmony.
This you will readily accede to, when you consider the amicable and attentive conduct immediately adopted by the American
government, in sending three envoys extraordinary with adequate
powers to effect a reconciliation and a renewal of a commercial
intercourse between the republics.

From the arrival of the envoys at Paris to the departure of two
of them, the objects of their mission were defeated, by insupe-
rable bars arising from demands of loans, which, violating the
neutrality of the United States, would have involved them in
immediate war, and of procuring reparations for the observations hinted at. Towards the end of that period, after imposing
on me secrecy, you stated the embarrassments and dissatisfaction
of the Executive Directory, on account of the opinions and conversations of my colleagues, its determination not to treat with
them, and its desire to negotiate with me; and you added, that
my departure would produce an immediate rupture. Astonished
as I was at this communication, I informed you that I had no
powers to treat separately; the measure was impossible; and
that, had my powers been adequate, a treaty made under such
circumstances could never be ratified by my government. You
differed from me, we reasoned on the subject, and each adhered
to his opinion. I urged in vain the unreasonableness of admitting prejudices against my colleagues, without informing them
of the causes thereof; the good effect in removing these, which
might result from such information, and the necessity of making
known to them all that had now passed between us. You held
me to the promise of secrecy, adding, that if I would negotiate,
we could soon finish a treaty; for the Executive Directory were
not in the habit of spending much time about such matters. You
desired another interview, in which, after a discussion of the
subject, I confirmed and adhered to my determination. In this
state affairs remained for some time, and I flattered myself with
the hope, that, failing in the proposition for negotiating with me
separately, your next would be to accredit the three envoys; in
such an event the secrecy mentioned would have been proper.
This expectation was strengthened by the two subsequent interviews which they had with you; and you may judge of my surprise on the receipt of your letter of the 28th Ventose (18th
March),

March), containing a refusal to treat with two of the envoys, and renewing the proposition to treat with me. Finding that I was the person alluded to, and that all hopes of our being jointly accredited were at an end, I again refused, in the most positive terms, to negotiate separately: another proposition was then made, that, to prevent a rupture, I should remain here till information could be sent to my government of the events. Embarrassing as such a state was, I submitted to it, rather than to bring on a war. You afterwards sent me your note of the 14th Germinal (3d April), proposing that I should resume our reciprocal communications upon the interests of the French republic and the United States. To this I replied, on the 4th of April, " that I could only confer informally and unaccredited, on any subject respecting our mission, and communicate to the government of the United States the result of such conferences; being, in my individual capacity, unauthorized to give them an official stamp." The day after the departure from Paris of the last of my colleagues, I again addressed you, and, quoting the above paragraph, informed you, that this I considered as the line of conduct well understood to be observed on my part: to this you made no objection, verbally or by writing, and thus acquiesced in it. Had you not, I should have immediately demanded my passport.

At one of our first interviews, after that letter, you stated a difficulty in adopting the plan proposed by my letter of the 20th of April, from your not being informed of the wishes of the government of the United States, in regard to a treaty: these were so reasonable, that I thought it best to communicate them to you; and according to your own opinion, since expressed, they would require little or no time for discussion: nothing can exceed them for moderation or justice. Believing that you was seriously disposed to bring forward the plan of a treaty, for the consideration of the government of the United States, and being also convinced, that the subject thereof had been so fully discussed, and was so well understood, as not to require much time to accomplish it, I informed you that I should embark for America in June; and although you objected to it in the first instance, you afterwards appeared to be fully convinced of the necessity of it, promised to digest the plan proposed without delay, and to send it to me for examination. I conferred with you at different times, on the expediency of sending a minister to Philadelphia to complete the negotiation; and you promised to consider of it. At length the Sophia arrived, and a few days afterwards you informed me, that I might make myself quite easy, that France did not wish a war with the United States, that she had no thoughts of it, that the American affairs were before the Executive Directory, and that every thing would be arranged to my wishes. I again stated the necessity of sending a minister to America to complete the negotiation, tation. You say you would propose one to the Executive Directory. This I could not suppose was for the purpose you have since stated of residing there after the ratification of the treaty.

Thus were matters circumstanced until the arrival of the gazettes, containing the dispatches of the envoys to their government, which gave more than a momentary turn to your correspondence with me. When I informed you that I should embark in the Sophia, as soon as she could be fitted for sea, there was still time to finish the plan of the treaty, and to send it by me, if expedient. You desired me to remain here; I told you my return was indispensable, and gave you no other reason. I thought that sufficient. You conceive it depended on me to be publicly received by the Executive Directory; but our opinions are different on this point. A government sends three envoys to treat with another government; this rejects two of them, and proposes to treat with the third. Candour must admit, I think, that the latter cannot accept the proposal, without transferring in this instance the executive authority of his government, who would only have *nominated* three envoys, to the foreign government, who would have *appointed* one of them. You say, that if my powers were altered by the departure of my colleagues, yet, on my own hypothesis, I ought to have referred the question to my government, and in the interim, to have fixed with you, by a calm and amicable discussion, all the contentious points of our differences. If my government, as you repeatedly have asserted, was apprized before the 20th of March of the proposition to treat with me separately, it is evident, that it was not disposed to send me new powers; for the Sophia sailed on the 28th of that month; and knowing this, you still urged me to make the application. I have been always ready, and, had you come forward with the project of a treaty, would have entered into a calm and amicable conference with you on every part of it, but not into a formal epistolary discussion, which was not proposed till some time after I was ready to embark, was only relative to the consular convention, which will soon expire, was contrary to my stipulation relative to conferences, in which you acquiesced, and would have required months to be completed.

You was the first, you affirm, to press seriously the negotiation: you will agree with me, that the merit would have been *greater*, had the measure itself been *feasible*.

You frequently remind me of your exertions, which I am disposed as much as possible to appreciate, regretting at the same time their circuitous direction. On my part, I think you will be convinced, that every thing has been done which circumstances, herein truly detailed, would admit.

It is with pleasure I learn, that the Executive Directory is still ready, and is as much disposed as ever to terminate by a

liberal

liberal negotiation the differences which subsist between the two countries.

This disposition has always existed on the part of the government of the United States. A negotiation then, if set on foot free from all propositions of loans and explanations of speeches, to be held, if necessary, in a city of some neutral nation, and providing for a decision, by three or five commissioners, of all points which may not be determined by direct negotiation, would still be accompanied, in my opinion, with success: but having no authority, I cannot make the proposition. A preliminary measure appears to be requisite, in which the dignity of this government is as deeply concerned, as the interest of the United States. The depredations, outrages, and cruelties committed on our commerce and citizens, in the West Indies and on our coasts, by French privateers, some of which it is said have no commissions, are perhaps seldom paralleled amongst civilized nations. It is said, that this government has not been already apprized of these events, which have been a great source of irritation in the United States, and a principal cause of the repressive measures adopted by them. A recall of the commissions of the privateers, and restraining them by severe penalties to the proper objects of capture, cannot fail to have a happy effect.

You claim a promise of my good offices, as a private citizen in America. These shall not be wanting, to represent truly every measure of this government, and to render successful all such as may be well adapted to effect a reconciliation. This is all that can be expected of me, and the duty which I owe to my country will require it.

And now, Citizen Minister, having given you a testimony of my esteem, such as results from a frank and candid conduct, I bid you adieu, wishing sincerely a speedy renewal of amity and commerce between the two republics.

Accept, Citizen Minister, the assurances of my perfect consideration. (Signed) E. GERRY.

To the Minister of Foreign Affairs
of the French Republic.

No. XXV.

Exterior Relations.---Liberty, Equality.

Paris, 4 Thermidor, 6th Year of the French Republic, one and indivisible (July 22, 1798).

The Minister of Exterior Relations, to Mr. Gerry, Envoy of the United States.

ALLOW me, Sir, to confine myself to the two last paragraphs of your answer of the 2d of this month to my letter of the 24th Messidor

Messidor (July 12). Easy as it may be to rectify those which go before, it were [...] to enter uselessly into the circle of digressions. It is my duty to feel what in the state of things you think due to your government; and this consideration would be alone sufficient to stop me, if I set a less value upon conciliation.

You repeat to me that the government of the United States has always been disposed to terminate amicably the differences which subsist between the two republics. This fresh assurance, at a time when hostile demonstrations have just been made, could not but temper their effect; but let then a frank, candid, and truly amicable act speedily realize those dispositions. Far from entering into the answers of the President to the addresses which have been presented to him from different parts of the United States, whatsoever they may be, I would fain behold in his expressions nothing but a political expedient. I do not thence judge less favourably of the true intentions, which you profess in his name; and I would not have engaged you to warrant the success of the first proof which he will render of them, if the Executive Directory, which was ready to receive you, had not made a fixed determination upon the subject. A negotiation may therefore be resumed even at Paris, where I flatter myself you have observed nothing but testimonies of esteem, and where every envoy who shall unite your advantages cannot fail to be well received. Moreover, I know not, Sir, why you tell me that it would be requisite to lop from this negotiation every preliminary respecting a loan, and explanations on the subject of the speeches delivered. Be pleased to read over again the propositions which I transmitted to you on the 30th Prairial (June 18); they contain all the ideas of the French government; and you will not find in them a word which justifies your recurring to those two questions. An odious intrigue had got possession of them: the dignity of the French government could not permit this mixture; and it did not with that views as pure as its own should be associated therewith hereafter. As to the preliminary measures, which you suggest, Sir, the government has already anticipated your desire. By information which it has just received, it indeed learns that violences have been committed upon the commerce and citizens of the United States in the West Indies, and on their coasts. Do it the justice to believe, that it needs only to know the facts, to disavow all acts contrary to the laws of the republic and its own decrees. A remedy is preparing for it, and orders will soon arrive in the West Indies calculated to cause every thing to return within its just limits, until an amicable arrangement between France and the United States shall re-establish them respectively in the enjoyment of their treaties.

This period, Sir, cannot be too near at hand. I do not cease to regret, that you should refuse yourself the accelerating of it, by yielding to circumstances, persuaded, as I ever am, that you were fully authorized.

Accept my wishes for your happy passage, and the assurance of my perfect consideration.

    (Signed) CH. MAU. TALLEYRAND.

No. XXVI.

Paris, July 25, 1798.

MR. Gerry having seen in the Redacteur of this morning, the publication of a letter to him from the minister of foreign affairs of the French republic, dated the 24th Messidor (12th of July), requests him to order a just translation of the answer dated the 20th of July, to be also published. Mr. G. being on the eve of his departure from Paris, presumes the minister will readily comply herewith, to prevent partial and undue impressions against him in his absence.

No. XXVII.

Exterior Relations.—Liberty, Equality.

Paris, 16th Thermidor, 6th Year of the French Republic, one and indivisible (August 3, 1798).

The Minister of Exterior Relations, to Mr. Gerry, Envoy of the United States.

PRESUMING, Sir, that you have not yet embarked, I address to you a decree of the Executive Directory, wherein you will find a part of the measures which I announced to you the fourth of this month. Its solicitude will not be confined to that. Neutrals, in general, will have reason soon to be convinced of its firm attachment to the principles to which it is desirous that all the maritime nations might agree. It depends upon the United States in particular, to cause every misunderstanding immediately to disappear between them and the French republic.

Accept, Sir, the assurance of my perfect consideration.

    (Signed) CH. MAU. TALLEYRAND.

No. XXVIII.

Havre, August 8, 1798.

AT the moment of my embarkation, Citizen Minister, I have the honour of receiving your letter of the 16th Thermidor (3d August), with the arrêté of the Executive Directory of the 13th,

13th, both of which shall be communicated to the supreme executive of the United States, immediately after my arrival there.

Accept, Citizen Minister, the assurance of my perfect respect.
(Signed)   E. GERRY.

To the Minister of Foreign Affairs
of the French Republic.

No. XXIX.

Extract from the Registers of the Deliberations of the Executive Directory.

Paris, the 13th Thermidor, 6th Year of the French Republic (July 31, 1798).

THE Executive Directory having heard the report of the minister of marine and the colonies:

Considering that information recently received from the French colonies and the continent of America leaves no room to doubt, that French cruisers, or such as call themselves French, have infringed the laws of the republic relative to cruising and prizes:

Considering that foreigners and pirates have abused the latitude allowed at Cayenne, and in the West Indian islands, to vessels fitted out for cruising, or for war and commerce, in order to cover with the French flag their extortions, and the violation of the respect due to the law of nations, and to the persons and property of allies and neutrals;

Decrees:—

Article 1. Hereafter no letters of marque, authorizations of permissions to fit out vessels either for cruising, or for war and commerce, shall be issued in the colonies of America, but by the special agents of the Directory themselves, who shall not delegate that power to any one: they shall exercise it only in favour of owners of vessels whose principles and responsibility are well known to them; and they shall be bound to conform themselves to all the laws relative to cruising and prizes, and especially to those of the 1st of October 1793 (O. S.).

Art. 2. All letters of marque, authorizations or permissions granted in the colonies of America by the particular agents of the Executive Directory, and all other agents civil and military, under their orders, to fit out vessels either for cruising, or for war and commerce, shall be considered as not having been done, after the thirtieth day from the publication of the present decree in the said colonies.

Art. 3. All agents and other deputies in the neutral possessions, appointed to decide there upon the validity of prizes taken by the French cruisers, and who shall be suspected of having a direct or
indirect

indirect interest in the vessels fitted out for cruising, or for war and commerce, shall be immediately recalled.

Art. 4. The special agents of the Executive Directory at Cayenne, St. Domingo, and Guadaloupe, shall studiously take care that the interests and property of vessels belonging to neutrals or allies be scrupulously respected, and they shall in no case bargain for their cargoes, but by mutual consent, and to the full and entire satisfaction of the contracting parties.

Art. 5. The said special agents of the Executive Directory, the commanders of all vessels of the republic, the consuls, vice-consuls, and all others invested with powers for that purpose, shall cause to be arrested and punished, conformably to the laws, all those who shall contravene the provisions of the present decree, which shall be printed in the bulletin of the laws, and with the execution of which the ministers of foreign relations, and of the marine and the colonies, are charged.

For a true copy, as the President of the Executive Directory,
(Signed) MERLIN.
By the Executive Directory, as the Secretary-general,
(Signed) TREILHARD.
For a true copy, the Minister of Exterior Relations,
CH. MAU. TALLEYRAND.
By the Minister, the Secretary-general,
(L. S.) PAGANES.

No. XXX.

Sir, *Paris, June 9, 1798.*

IN your letter to the minister of foreign affairs of the 13th Prairial, published in the Bien Informé of this day, you have deviated in some points, not very material, from the statement communicated by the envoys of the government of the United States respecting a conference which I had with the minister aforesaid on the 22d of October last, viz. that I requested the interview instead of the minister, and that I met him twice on this communication, whereas I saw him but once. I wish therefore you would revise the statement referred to, and inform me, whether it is not, to the best of your memory, literally true; it is precisely the same, without changing a word, which we communicated to my colleagues.

I am, Sir, with much esteem and respect,
Your very humble servant,
Mr. Hauteval. (Signed) E. GERRY.

No. XXXI.

Sir,

I HAVE received the letter which you did me the honour to write to me yesterday, relative to that which I deemed it my duty to write to the minister of exterior relations, on the 13th of this month, and which the government caused to be printed.

It is not at all astonishing that my memory may not have served me with precision upon a subject which passed more than six months ago, and of which I have not taken notes. I undertook merely to repeat with exactness the essential heads, which I believe I have done.

I indeed recollect, that having been together at the minister's, and not having met with him, I left our names with his porter; that having returned there the next day alone, he expressed to me his regret at not having been at home, when you called there the day before, and charged me to tell you that he would receive you with a great deal of pleasure on a day he assigned to me: the appointment therefore proceeded from the minister, and not from your request, as I have said in my letter; but the matter appears to me to be of little consequence.

The second error which you remind me of having committed, is that of having separated into two conferences what passed in one. On every occasion, when I have had the pleasure to see the minister, I have always conversed with him on matters relating to the negotiations with the United States of America, the success of which I have never ceased anxiously to desire. In my letter, I might be mistaken in some details; but you, Sir, could not, having immediately taken a written note of what had just passed between the minister, yourself, and me. I regret that I had not the pleasure to see you before I transmitted my letter to the minister: by communicating it to you, I should have rectified the two slight errors which crept into it; but I was constrained by the occasion, and was very far from thinking that it would be printed.

I shall ever be anxious to render homage to the truth, and to seize occasions of assuring you of my respectful attachment.

I have the honour to be, Sir,
Your very humble and very obedient servant,
Paris, the 22d Prairial,   (Signed)   L. HAUTEVAL.
6th Year (10th June 1798).
To Mr. Gerry, Envoy of the United States
of America, Rue de Vaugirard, Paris.

No. XXXII.

Dear Sir,   *Paris, July* 16, 1798.

SOME part of the last instructions of the secretary of state of the United States to the envoys, and to Mr. Humphreys, who brought the dispatches, induces me to think, that, in the precarious state of our affairs with France, you may have conditional instructions, which may require particular information of what respects the existing state of affairs here. I have therefore thought it best to enclose in the most perfect confidence, by my secretary, Mr. Tazewell, the documents necessary to attain this object, and contained in the schedule annexed, for your use only. If you have not received such instructions, your prudence will dictate the necessity of observing the most profound secrecy, pending any subsequent measures which may take place for restoring friendship between the two republics.

I shall leave Paris for Havre as soon as possible, and expect, on my arrival there, to embark immediately for the United States.

            Be assured that I remain, dear Sir,
                Your friend and very humble servant,

Mr. King, Minister Plenipotentiary   E. GERRY.
of the United States at London.

Schedule enclosed in a Letter to Mr. King.

Letters from Mr. Gerry to the Minister of Foreign Affairs.	*Letters from the Minister to Mr. Gerry.*
No. 1. April 4.	No. 1. Germinal 14, April 3.
2. —— 20.	2. Prairial 11, May 30.
3. May 31.	3. ——— 13, June 1.
4. June 3.	4. ——— 22, —— 10.
5. —— 10.	5. ——— 30, —— 18.
6. —— 13.	6. Messidor 9, —— 27.
7. —— 22.	7. ——— 18, July 6.
8. July 1.	8. ——— 24, —— 12.
9. —— 10.	9. Thermidor 4, —— 22.
10. —— 20.	
To Mr. Pickering.	
No. 1. May 12.	
2. —— 13.	

No. XXXIII.

Extract of Mr. Gerry's Letter to Doctor Tazewell, as far as it relates to Mr. King, Minister of the United States at London.

Dear Sir, Mignon, 27th of July 1798.

THE dispatches for Mr. King are to be delivered to him by yourself; in the interim, you will please not to let them be put out of your possession, or communicated to any one.

No. XXXIV.

Substance of a Conference with the Dutch Minister the 25th July 1798.

JUST before dinner, the Dutch minister called on me, and said, he had received from Mr. Talleyrand a printed copy of his letter to me, dated 24th Messidor (12th July), that the Dutch government took a friendly part in the disputes between France and the United States, and that he came to offer his services, and the mediation of his government, who had authorized and instructed him on this head.

I answered, that the conduct of Mr. Talleyrand, in publishing his letter to me, had an hostile appearance: that if a mediation could be supposed necessary, it must be offered to the government of the United States: I had no authority to accept it: that if the government of France was sincere in its declaration, made through Mr. Talleyrand its minister, all that was wanting was to open a negotiation, for he had expressed a desire to show by treaty how well disposed France was to put an end to these disputes; that the government of the United States was so reasonable and just in its demands, that it could not fail to evince a good disposition to a reconciliation; that the etiquette of setting on foot a negotiation appeared at present to be the only embarrassment; more especially as the principal obstruction to a negotiation had ceased, this government having relinquished all claims of loans and reparations on account of the President's speeches; that, as the United States had been twice defeated in sending ministers to Paris, the government might not be disposed to send them a third time; and that if the French government would propose some city, in a neutral nation, as a place for opening a new negotiation, or, which would be better, would send a minister to the United States, I did not doubt it would succeed: that this was a mere matter of opinion, for I had no instructions on the subject, neither was I informed whether my government had or had not formed an alliance with any other nation, as had been frequently reported. The Dutch minister answered, that the proposal of a mediation must go to the government, and inquired in that case if I would stay at Paris; I anfwered, No, it was not neceffary; neither did I conceive the propriety of offering at this period a mediation: the proper mode of fettling difputes was, in the firft inftance, by treaty; if in any points this fhould fail, ftill there were other means befides the mediation of a third power, which might be adopted; but that if his government wifhed to make the propofition, I would carefully tranfmit it to the government of the United States.

He faid that Mr. Talleyrand, who had ftyled his letter a pacific manifefto, and had fent a printed copy to each foreign minifter, had no hoftile intention in publifhing it; but confidered it as a friendly meafure. I anfwered, we then had different views of the fubject. I then fhowed the anfwer to that letter, which the Dutch minifter read. I thought it neceffary for the information of his government to make to him the communications mentioned.

No. XXXV.

Upon the Communications made by the Prefident of the United States to the American Congrefs, on the 14th Germinal, 6th Year (April 3d, 1798.)

THE American and Englifh papers have lately refounded with the publication of the moft ftrange communications which the envoys of the United States have thought it their duty to make to their government. It is with refpect to thofe envoys a deplorable monument of credulity and contradictions: and it is with refpect to that government a provocation ftill more deplorable.

It is requifite, by the evidence of facts and the very words of the envoys themfelves, to fhow their inconceivable error. It is requifite, by the force of reafon and the mere fentiment of the happinefs of the two republics, to anfwer to the provocation fo vifibly fuggefted by the Britifh government.

That government indeed, after fo many and fuch ridiculous efforts againft the French republic, endeavours to organize corruption around it. Grown defperate on account of fo many glorious treaties of peace, which the latter has concluded, it has flattered itfelf, by its peculiar perfidies, to rekindle the former wars in Europe, and to excite againft it a new war in America; but all this fyftem of Britifh corruption fhall be expofed and confounded; and the American people fhall know the height of the precipice to which they are urged by the fervile friends of their former oppreffors.

For a long time the French republic complained, and certainly it had a right to do fo, againft the inexecution of the moft important

ant parts of ⟨ ⟩ concluded between France and the United s. 1 t it hostilities were soon followed by the most aggravat⟨ed⟩ injuries. It was in vain that the republic made a sacrifice of arma⟨me⟩nts, which might compromit the American neutrality.

The most legitimate of its armaments was soon after contested. The French vessels experienced a thousand vexations. Their prizes were no longer under the protection of the treaties. The courts of justice arrogated a jurisdiction over them: lengthy and ruinous chicaneries discouraged the captors: the French ports in the two worlds were soon declared to be blockaded by British proclamations: the vessels which departed from them were stopped on a loose suspicion of being enemies' property: those which carried provisions thither were turned back. On the other hand, the British ships of war entered the ports of the United States, after seizing French property or property claimed to be such. By degrees they became stationary there, and made of them military stations, whence they attacked both the French and the Americans in connexion with France. The republic however confined itself to appealing to its treaties with the United States, and to pressing their government to cause their own neutrality to be respected. They answered it with a treaty clandestinely negotiated and concluded with Great Britain.

Does this treaty, however, secure the neutrality of the United States? No.—It renders the presence of the English forces in their ports lawful: it gives to England rights, which, in the midst of war, ameliorate its situation to the prejudice of France: it allows the facility of again starving France and its colonies: it sacrifices the generous principles established in favour of the liberty of the seas, in former treaties.

France makes complaints: the American government eludes, and wanders from them; it multiplies official notes without approaching the main point of the question. Reparations are demanded: they are not made. It speaks of nothing but wrongs experienced by the United States: it skips over those which it makes France suffer. The treaty of 1778 is rendered more and more insignificant; and the last blows are struck at the French cruisers in the American seas, by the prohibition to sell their prizes. The republic is under the necessity, in order to manifest its too long suspended resentment, and bring about a negotiation, to appropriate to itself the same clauses of the English treaty. At length the United States, sensible only to the disagreeable consequences which have resulted therefrom to themselves, appeared to wish a reconciliation.

Three commissioners have been sent for that end to the French republic: two of them, General Pinckney and Mr. Marshall, manifesting against France prejudices brought from America, or imbibed

imbibed from the nature of the connexions which they loft no time in forming here; and the third, Mr. Gerry, announcing more impartiality, and manifesting himself more difpofed to lend a' favourable ear to every thing which might reconcile the two republics

From this ill-fuited union, which difclofed difpofitions not very conciliatory, there muft needs refult, and there has in fact refulted, a crooked and embarraffed career on the part of thofe commiffioners; hence their conftant averfion to do what might reconcile, their eagernefs to write what might difguft.

At firft they manifefted a defire to be acknowledged; but explanations of fome expreffions evidently infulting to the republic, which were contained in the opening fpeech of the Prefident of the United States, were demanded from them as a previous condition. They did more than to refufe; they did not even comprehend this demand, and had recourfe to groundlefs recriminations. Soon afterwards a willingnefs appeared to fpare them the embarraffment of the difavowals; and in order to detach them from England, and to reftore in a fmall degree the balance fo ftrongly inclined in favour of that power by the laft treaty, it was wifhed that an unequivocal proof of attachment to our caufe, which fo recently was their own, might be obtained from them: it fuited the finances to exchange, at that period, for fpecie, fome Batavian infcriptions at gradual infta'ments: the Minifter of Foreign Relations gave them to underftand, that their offering to purchafe a certain quantity of them, would be confidered as a friendly act. They faid that they did not poffefs the power; and they fhowed that they had not the will.

To come at fome accommodation, fome friendly explanation, frequent communications with the Minifter of the Exterior were neceffary. The latter complained publicly that he did not fee them, and they avowed that he caufed them to be often informed of this reproach; but two of the commiffioners, fhielding themfelves under ceremony, refufed to comply with the defire. Mr. Gerry at length refolved to go, fpoke twice with the minifter; and whether from embarraffment in explaining himfelf, or fear of compromitting himfelf, he faid but little; and did not venture to decide on any thing.

In the mean time the envoys thought themfelves bound to tranfmit to the Prefident of the United States a very voluminous account of their negotiation.—Of what then could this account be compofed? It was neceffary to fill it with the defpicable manœuvres of all the intriguers, who, feeing the commiffioners charged with the moft important interefts, fecluding themfelves from the government with which they ought to treat, haftened to gather round them, and infatuated them with the idea of their credit and the opinion of their importance.

One

One of these intriguers appears to have grounded himself on some acquaintance, which, as a foreigner having a recommendation, he had succeeded in obtaining with the minister: another (and it is the one who is the most active) grounds himself solely upon the acquaintance which he had with the first intriguer; for he declares that he does not even know the minister. Such moreover is the situation of the man, whoever he may be, who is placed at the head of this department, that he is obliged to receive and listen to many persons, who are far from having any share in his confidence, and he has no means of preventing the abuse they may make, in his absence, of the most insignificant visits, of which they avail themselves, as suits their interest with men of no experience.

In the publication which the American government has made of the report of its envoys, these persons, without being avowed, are designated each by a letter. The minister, impatient to know their names, demanded them with importunity, and finally obtained the communication, which he immediately handed to the proper authority. It will be learned with pleasure that they are foreigners, and it will be readily believed, that they did justice to themselves by hastening to quit the territory of the republic. Only one of those letters, Z. designates a Frenchman, who hastened to declare himself *. The language he held is irreproachable: he is represented as having sometimes served as interpreter; but it is clearly seen that he interpreted none but honourable propositions.

As to the foreigners who are seen figuring in this negotiation, it appears that the object of their whole intrigue was to obtain from the Americans a sum of 1,200,000 livres, to be distributed for corrupt purposes. Hence begin and end all the bustle, all the conversations, all the proceedings, minutely detailed in the report of the envoys.

It will be for ever inconceivable, that men authorized to represent the United States near the French republic, could have been for an instant deceived by manœuvres so evidently counterfeit, and that there should exist a temptation to convert the error in this respect into bad faith.

What? Three men are sent envoys from America to France to negotiate there a reconciliation between the two republics: embarrassed in a preliminary matter, they cannot at once confer with the minister as commissioners; but they have a thousand ways of seeing him as individuals, either at his own house or elsewhere; and two of them constantly refuse all the facilities which are offered to them.

---

* See his letter printed at the end of these reflections.

This

This is not all: we see them present the details of their negotiations, as if persuaded that the disgusting propositions which they say were made to them, were addressed by a man clothed with the confidence of the government; and nevertheless, in the course of their recital, they suffer an avowal to escape, that they several times suspected these clandestine communications, and that they finally decided to reject them for the future. Mr. Gerry even declares positively, that these meddlers did not produce any authority or any documents of any kind whatever*. At the same time, they continued to decline the direct communications, which were offered to them continually by the minister. Is not all this a labyrinth of contradictions?

And when we examine by what a series of intermediate persons they thought to approach the minister, whom it was so easy to them to consult immediately, is it not rendered impossible for us to think that they have seriously adopted the consequences of their recital?

Here it is a lady, known to be connected with Mr. Pinckney, who holds with him the most innocent discourse, which has been repeated to him from one end of France to the other: Lend us (says she to him one day) money in our war; we lent it to you in yours: and a conversation thus simple is taken up by Mr. Pinckney, who finds it necessary to write every thing and to poison every thing; it is mysteriously sent by him to his government, as if it had any relation to the clandestine propositions made by the intriguers. Thus minute is distrust! thus is prejudice led astray in its reasonings! In this manner are the politics of some men a pest to social intercourse!

There it is one W. whom we have not succeeded in discovering, who introduces to General Pinckney one X. a very hasty fellow, who says he is charged with a message from the minister; who being soon afterwards pressed to answer whether he is personally known to him, is forced to say, No; but that he has the propositions which he made from Y. who, he says, has connexions with the minister; and nevertheless when they want to intrust Y. with the negative answer to his proposition for the 1,200,000 livres, he declines being charged with it, and is compelled to avow, through a kind of shame, and at the risk of discrediting the part he was playing, that the proposition did not come from the Directory, nor even from the minister; and that it came solely from him Y. who was desirous of saving the envoys the mortification of the disavowals. If these same men have afterwards held a different language, was it not natural for the envoys for ever to mistrust their reports, and above all to en-

---

* See, at the end, his first answer to the minister.

deavour to reach the fource? They have not done fo. How can this conduct be reconciled either with reafon or good faith?

In the fame report they manifeft themfelves defirous of informing their government, with the utmoft detail, of every thing which paffed in relation to their commiffion: and whilft with fuch a fcrupulous care they collect fo many abfurdities and miferable puerilities, they are filent upon the official communications, which the perfons employed in the office of exterior relations had with them on behalf of the minifter. It is without doubt, becaufe thofe communications, agreeing with the few which the minifter himfelf made, were pure, upright, and calculated to do honour to the French government. It was part of their plan to pafs them over in filence. The others, fo fufpicious in their origin, were defamatory in their object: they had the utmoft impatience to make them known*.

They had juft prefented a voluminous memorial fetting forth their pretended grievances: they well knew, that the minifter was about to addrefs a note to them in anfwer, which ought to have formed one of the authentic documents of the negotiation, and which in fact was fent to them in the month of Ventofe laft (March 19). They haftened to publifh every thing that evidently did not come from the minifter, and which they endeavour to impute to him, in order, doubtlefs, to weaken thereby the very different impreffion which muft have been produced by the note, wherein every thing breathes a fincere defire to conciliate.

This group of facts prefents fuch a tiffue of incongruities and contradictions, that the mind is loft in it. One is at a lofs to fpecify with precifion the reproaches to be made to the American envoys. But it is very evident that they have been moft ftrangely deceived, if they did believe, and that they are moft perfidious, if they did not believe what they relate. [In the expreffion of thefe reproaches which efcape from indignation, it is requifite to haften to except Mr. Gerry, who doubtlefs may have been deceived both by the foreign intriguers, and perhaps alfo by his very colleagues, but to whom no fufpicion of bad faith or infincerity can attach.]

Now, what could be the fecret motive which caufed fuch puerile communications to be circulated with fo much eclat? How then can they juftify the pompous affectation, by which the American people has been prepared to hear them? How can we

---

* See in the fecond letter of Mr. Gerry, dated 15th Prairial (June 3, 1798), which follows thefe reflections, the exprefs declaration of Mr. Gerry, that, in the courfe of the negotiations, he faw perfons employed by the office of exterior relations, and the juftice he does them of never having uttered a word, which had the leaft relation to propofitions, fuch as the intriguing foreigners X. and Y. appeared to have made.

conceive

conceive that it was hoped to render the farce more imposing by fasts and public prayers?

Doubtless a great object caused them to hazard the holding up as discoveries of the greatest importance, the incoherent prating of two intriguers, who were foreigners with respect to France. Perhaps it was supposed that the citizens of the United States would judge of the French government by these caricatures, and that the French government would be sensible to such a marked provocation. The effect of the outrage was calculated from the malignity of the intention, and not from the littleness of the means.

In one word, they flattered themselves with exciting indignation instead of pity. They wished for war; and they wished that insulted France might declare it against a people, whose cause she defended, and that it might be restored by her to the arms of England.

By that war, the British cabinet would gain an ally, who would labour for its interest, second its projects upon the French and Spanish colonies, and retard the moment of its humiliation: by that war too the British government would accelerate the execution of a favourite plan of which it has never lost sight.

It is known, that since it despaired of reuniting to the triple crown, the states whose independence it was obliged to acknowledge, it aspired at least to prejudice them in favour of limited monarchy; that it endeavoured to fortify, by the similarity of constitutional forms, the habits common to the English and American people; and that it took care to keep for a long time one of the sons of George III. in the vicinity of the United States. Can it then be true, that, to the disgrace of the human mind, many citizens of the United States should be found who are seriously reconciled to the English form of government? Can it then be true, that men, called by the public confidence to the head of the government of the United States, have written in favour of the British constitution, merely to prepare its adoption in their own country? Can it be true that a thirst for honours, greediness of wealth, and a desire of perpetuating power, have already ripened this conspiracy against liberty?

If this ought to be no longer considered as a suspicion, all is explained. War is necessary in order to raise troops and obtain supplies: an unnatural war against old friends, against brothers, against republicans, is more especially necessary: it is necessary that this war should excite civil commotions, shock every idea of morality, and rouse to resistance the true sons of America: and pretences will arise in abundance for stigmatizing with sedition the honourable defenders of principles, and for substituting a monarchical in the room of a representative government.

It would be hereafter unnecessary to dissemble. Such are the

criminal

criminal pri   cabinet. Such is the blind propensity of a   e ent   it influences: and it is the French republic which sacrificed the blood and fortune of its citizens in the cause of liberty; it is the French republic that is instigated to strike the fatal blow! But superior to the influence of her resentments, she will be actuated by nothing but the happiness of the two republics, and she will appeal to the whole universe to judge of the sincerity of the dispositions, which she has never ceased, and which she will never cease to manifest, for living in peace with America.

P. S. It is of extreme importance to lay before the public the letters written to Mr. Gerry, envoy of the United States, by the minister of exterior relations, as soon as this strange publication came to his knowledge; and it is of equal importance to know the answers given by Mr. Gerry. Both are as follow. [See the preceding numbers VI. VII. VIII. X. XI.]

Note, The names were in fact sent to the minister, who immediately deposited them in the proper place.

[*The following Letter of the Citizen designated by the Letter Z. it is not less essential to publish.*]

13th Prairial, 6th Year (June 1, 1798).

To the Minister of Exterior Relations.

MR. Gerry having communicated to me the letter which you yesterday wrote to him, by which you expressly desire, that he may make known to you the persons meant by the letters W. X. Y. Z. in the correspondence of the American envoys, printed in a public paper of the United States of America, dated 12th of April (O. S.);

My sensibility must be much affected on finding myself, under the letter Z. acting a part in company with certain intriguers, whose plan it doubtless was to take advantage of the good faith of the American envoys, and make them their dupes. Finding myself implicated in this affair, and wishing to remove my uneasiness respecting the disagreeable impressions, and the consequence which the publication of your letter to Mr Gerry might produce, I thought it my duty to hasten to you, and pray you, Citizen Minister, to be pleased to declare in writing, that, in the conferences I had with those gentlemen, I pursued the communications which you authorized me to make to them, in the manner I shall state below.

In the beginning of last Brumaire (October 22, 1797), having been to pay my respects to the citizen minister of exterior relations, and the conversation turning upon the United States of America, he expressed to me his surprise, that news of the Americans, and especially the new envoys, ever came to his house that this was not the way to open a negotiation, the success which they had more reason than we to wish; that he wou receive them individually with great pleasure, and particular Mr. Gerry, whom he had known at Boston. Knowing my friend connexions with Mr. Gerry, he charged me to impart to the what he had said. I accordingly waited on Mr. Gerry, wh having sent for his colleagues, I communicated to them the co versation I had had with the Citizen Minister.

Messrs. Pinckney and Marshall declined waiting on the minist upon the ground of ceremony; but, as the same reason did n apply to Mr. Gerry, it was agreed that he should go the next da and that I should accompany him, Mr. Gerry at that time n being able to express himself in French. The next day we wen but not finding the minister at home, Mr. Gerry requested him to a point a time for an interview, which was fixed for a few days afte We attended accordingly, and after the usual compliments, M Gerry having expressed to the minister his desire to see harmo and a good understanding re-established between the two repu lics, the minister answered him, that the Directory had made determination not to treat with them, unless they previously ma reparation for some parts of the President's speech at the openii of Congress, and gave an explanation of some others; that I could not delay, but for a few days, communicating this dete mination officially to them; that until then, if they had any pr positions to make, which could be agreeable to the Directory, would communicate them, with alacrity; that considering the ci cumstance, and the services of the same kind which France h formerly rendered to the United States, the best way would be f them to offer to make a loan to France, either by taking Batavi inscriptions for the sum of fifteen or sixteen millions of florins, in any other manner. Mr. Gerry, after having replied in a polit but evasive manner, to the first article, added on the subject the loan, that their powers did not extend so far, but that would confer with his colleagues upon the subject. It is to observed, that, as the minister spoke nothing but French, I r peated in English to Mr. Gerry what he had said to him, and th although certain that he very well understood the answers of M Gerry, I repeated them to him in French. We took our lea of the minister who just received a courier, and he charged n on parting to repeat to Mr. Gerry and his colleagues what he h said to us. Accordingly I repeated to Messrs. Pinckney a Marshall, in the presence of Mr. Gerry, the conversation whi we had had with the minister.

A few days afterwards Mr. Gerry requested me to accompar him again on a visit to the minister, and having repeated to hi the extreme desire he felt to see the most perfect union re-est
blish

blished between the two nations, he resorted to the insufficiency of their powers, and proposed, in the name of his colleagues and himself, that one of them should immediately depart for America with the propositions which the French government might make. The minister answered, that it would require six months to have an answer, and that it was of importance to have a speedy determination; that he was extremely desirous to have frequent communications with them individually and amicably; this course appearing to him to be the best adapted to come at the issue of a speedy negotiation: he therefore lamented that he had yet had no communication with them.

Such, Citizen Minister, as far as my memory serves me, are the particulars of the only two conferences at which I was present. I shall add that no person has had a greater desire than myself to see this negotiation succeed.

Health and respect.
(Signed) HAUTEVAL.

Mr. Skipwith's Communications.

To the Secretary of State of the United States of America.

Sir,

I HAVE the honour to send you enclosed, the official copy of an arrêté of the Executive Directory of the French republic, concerning the French privateers in the West Indies, which was transmitted to me by the French minister of foreign affairs.

I have the honour to be, Sir,
Your most obedient humble servant,
Paris, August 4, 1798. FULWAR SKIPWITH.
Hon. Col. Timothy Pickering, Secretary
of State of the United States.

Sir, Paris, August 8, 1798.

HAVING had the honour of transmitting to you three official copies of the arrêté of the Directory of the 13th Thermidor*, concerning their privateers in the West Indies, the present is merely to enclose you a copy of a letter which I yesterday received from the minister of foreign relations, on the subject of that arrêté.

I have the honour to be, Sir,
Your most humble servant,
The Secretary of State. FULWAR SKIPWITH.

---

* July 31, 1798. The arrêté here referred to.

*Paris, 19th Thermidor, 6th Year of the
French Republic (August 6, 1798).*

The Minister of Exterior Relations to Citizen Skipwith, Consul-general of the United States of America.

Citizen,

YOU will have seen in No. 961 of the Redacteur, a copy of a decree made by the Directory, in order to cause the privateers to return within the rules and limits whence they ought never to have departed.

By this measure foreign powers will be convinced that the Executive Directory, when informed of the abuses which may be directed against them, takes every pains to stop them, and to prevent their return.

You will doubtless see in the intention and the acts of the Directory, cause for feeling a security with respect to the commerce of your fellow-citizens, so long as it shall be confined within just bounds.

I wish, Citizen, that, for the good of the two countries, the conduct of the federal government may correspond with that of the Directory. In this supposition, the friendly relations of the two people would be soon re-established.

(Signed)   C. M. TALLEYRAND.

Consulate-general of the United States of America.

Fulwar Skipwith, Consul-general for the United States, near the French Republic, to Timothy Pickering, Esq. Secretary of State of the United States.

Sir,   *Paris, 22d August 1798.*

WITH a copy of a letter I have just received from the minister of foreign affairs, I have the honour, under cover hereof, to transmit to you copies of two letters, which have been officially communicated to me, from the minister of marine, to all principal civil and military officers, at the different ports of this republic, concerning the safety and protection of American citizens in general, and those seamen in particular, who were detained, or are in confinement at those ports. Agreeably to the intimations contained in the minister's letter to me, I have this day made application to the minister of police in favour of the American seamen, who, by means of one of the public authorities at L'Orient, had been arrested as Englishmen, and are at present confined at Orleans as prisoners of war. In a few days I expect to obtain their liberation, and shall procure their passages home.

I have

I have likewise the pleasure of forwarding to you an official copy of an arrêté of the Directory for raising the embargo, imposed by government on all vessels belonging to the United States, in the ports of this republic.

I deem it my duty to observe, that, from informal communications, which I have recently and repeatedly had with some of the best informed individuals of the government on the subject of American vessels and property, now under trial before the different tribunals of this republic, I have derived such information of the present disposition and intentions of the Directory, as to be satisfied myself, that they will ere long endeavour to provoke in the legislature a revision of their maritime laws, and that such a system will be organized as will secure the most important rights of neutrality upon the seas: this pleasing event is generally expected, and will, I am persuaded, arrive before this can reach you. Though many of the late arrêtés of the Directory have certainly encouraged the tribunals in the most pernicious applications of existing laws in regard to neutral property captured and brought in for adjudication, yet it may not be unimportant to remark to you, Sir, that the Directory, however well disposed, cannot change the conduct of the tribunals in regard to American and other neutral vessels now before them, without legislative interference, and that, owing to particular circumstances, it appears evidently that some time is necessary for them to prepare and dispose that body to alter some laws and make others, which shall cause the tribunals and privateers to respect neutrals in general, and the flag of the United States in particular: but from the present manifest dispositions and endeavours of the Directory to produce that end, I am happy to add, that the tribunal of cassation, before whom appeals have been made on most of the American property condemned in France, appear disposed to procrastinate pronouncing upon them until the sentiment of the legislature shall be declared upon the laws which are operating against their success.

I have the honour to be, Sir,
Your most humble servant,
FULWAR SKIPWITH.

Liberty.   *Equality.*

Paris, 3d Fructidor, 6th Year of the French Republic (August 20, 1798).

The Minister of Foreign Relations, to Mr. Fulwar Skipwith, Consul-general of the United States to the French Republic.

I SEND you, Sir, copies of two letters written by the minister of marine to all the principal officers civil and military of the ports

ports of the republic. Their contents will prove to you the attention of the government to remedy the abuses committed against its intentions.

With respect to the persons detained in the civil prisons of Orleans, because they are not possessed of papers to prove that they are not English, and who claim to be Americans, be pleased to call upon the minister of general police, to whose functions belong all the measures of safety. The minister of marine informs me, that he has transmitted their petition to him, and I am going to write to him myself, in order to request him to admit your declaration in their favour, in the absence of other proofs.

Receive, Sir, the assurance of my consideration.
  (Signed) CH. MAU. TALLEYRAND.

Copy of a circular Letter, written by the Minister of Marine and the Colonies, to all the principal Officers of the Ports, civil and military, on the 29th Thermidor, 6th Year (16th August 1798).

OUR political situation with regard to the United States, Citizen, not having as yet undergone any change which can affect the respect due to neutral nations, I do not think I have need to remind you, that no injury should be done to the safety and liberty of the officers and crews of any American vessel found to be in order, and that the same conduct ought to be observed towards all passengers and other citizens of the United States, furnished with the necessary passports or protections. You will be pleased to use a vigilant attention, that the intentions of the government in this respect may be pursued by all those under you, and when any of them has departed from them, you will do justice upon the complaints which may be addressed to you, after ascertaining their validity.

The Minister of Marine and of the Colonies,
  (Signed) E. BRUIX.
For a true copy, the Minister of Exterior Relations,
  (Signed) CH. MAU. TALLEYRAND.

Copy of the circular Letter written by the Minister of Marine and the Colonies, to the Agents of the Marine in the Ports of the Republic.

    Paris, the 24th Thermidor, 6th Year
     (11th August 1798).

I OBSERVE, Citizen, by the correspondence of the greater part of the administrators of the ports, that the embargo recently laid upon the American vessels has occasioned the detention of the crews. The intentions of the government were very badly understood, when a measure was adopted, which, in the first place,
hazards

hazards the safety of thefe veffels, and in the fecond place appears to place us in a hoftile attitude with refpect to the United States, whilft the acts of the government evince, on the contrary, that it defires a good underftanding between the two republics. I therefore charge you, Citizen, immediately upon the receipt of this, to order the difcharge of all the Americans who may have been confidered as prifoners of war, in confequence of the embargo of their veffels. You will be pleafed to render me a prompt account of the execution of this order.

The Minifter of Marine and of the Colonies,
(Signed) E. BRUIX.
For a true copy, the Minifter of Exterior Relations,
(Signed) CH. MAU. TALLEYRAND.
True and exact copies,
FULWAR SKIPWITH.

Department of Exterior Relations.—Liberty, Equality.

(Copy of a Decree.)

Extract from the Regifter of the Decrees of the Executive Directory, of the 29th Thermidor, 6th Year of the French Republic, one and indivifible 16th Auguft 1798).

THE Executive Directory confidering that, notwithftanding the hoftile manifeftations of the government of the United States, which have occafioned a momentary embargo upon their veffels, it muft be believed that, unlefs abandoned to the paffions of the Britifh cabinet, that government, faithful to the interefts of the American nation, will take meafures conformable to the pacific difpofitions of the French republic, after it fhall receive a confirmation of them,

And wifhing to purfue the friendly and fraternal habits of France towards a people whofe liberty it defended,

Decrees as follows:

Article 1. The embargo laid upon the American veffels fhall be immediately raifed.

Art. 2. The minifter of marine and of the colonies is charged with the execution of the prefent decree, which fhall not be printed.

For a true copy, as Prefident of the Executive Directory,
(Signed) MERLIN.
By the Executive Directory, as Secretary-general,
(Signed) J. M. REVEILLERE LEPEAUX.
For a true copy, the Minifter of Exterior Relations,
(Signed) CH. MAU. TALLEYRAND.

Letter from Mr. Gerry, on his Return from France, accompanying the previous Correspondence from No. I. inclusive; dated Nantasket Road, 1st October 1798.

Sir,

I HAVE the honour to inform you of my arrival here this morning, in the brigantine Sophia, Captain Geddes, from Havre, but last from Portsmouth in Great Britain; and to enclose copies of my letters to yourself of the 12th and 13th of May last, No. I. and II.; of the correspondence between Mr. Talleyrand, the French minister of foreign affairs and myself, numbered according to the respective dates from III. to XXVIII. inclusively; of an arrêté enclosed in his last letter, No. XXIX.; of my letter to Mr. Hauteval and his answer, No. XXX. and XXXI.; of my letter to Mr. King, our minister at London, and an extract to Dr. Tafwell, the bearer thereof, No. XXXII. and XXXIII.; also the substance of a conference with the Dutch minister, a day or two before I left Paris, No. XXXIV.; and an anonymous publication " on the President's communication" of our dispatches, said to have issued from the French office of foreign affairs, No. XXXV.

When I left the United States in August 1797, the citizens in general appeared to be earnestly desirous of a reconciliation with France, on terms consistent with the honour, interest, and welfare of the two republics; these, being free from claims and controversies in regard to territory, boundaries, and many matters which embroil states; and from competitions relative to their productions, manufactures, and commerce, had a mutual and manifest interest in the renewal of their commercial and friendly intercourse with each other. Nature seemed to have entitled the United States, in their remote situation, to the peaceable pursuit of their industry, by means whereof, in its various branches, their wealth and power were rapidly increasing: and to an exemption from the conflicts of Europe; which, involving them, would check their population, drain their resources, and ensure their poverty. On a candid investigation then of the causes of the unhappy differences between the two governments, on a disposition to correct errors, to which all governments are more or less liable, and on their mutual resolution to reciprocate justice, the success of the mission was conceived to depend; and as this temper marked the plan of pacification adopted by the government of the United States, there was a rational prospect of success.

Soon after our arrival at Paris, the scene was changed, and the hope of a reconciliation being diminished, the necessity of harmony in the United States was proportionably increased, as the only mean for preserving their welfare and independence at home, their rights and respectability abroad. In case of a war, there was every reason to believe that they would be able to defend

themselves

themselves against any nation, or coalition that could be formed against them; whilst their citizens should consider the government, chosen by themselves, as the pole-star of their salvation; should rally round its standard, when raised for their defence; should rise superior to foreign intrigues, always expert in fomenting divisions, and often aided by popular elections, legislative debates, and clashing opinions and interests; and should promote unanimity, by toleration amongst themselves. Nevertheless, the critical state of our affairs required that France should not be furnished with pretexts for charging the American government, or ministers, with neglecting of means for obtaining a reconciliation.

When the minister of foreign affairs, in October last, unauthorized by the Executive Directory, as Mr. Y. had informed the envoys, to have any communications with them, had expressed a desire to see them in their private capacities, I was opposed to a compliance, *individually;* not from considerations of etiquette, which had no weight in my mind, but because it would infer on me a separate agency in matters wherein I was but jointly authorized: to prevent, however, the imputation of the failure of the negotiation, then daily expected, to the United States, I submitted to the measure, was unsuccessful in my attempts to make it general, and was thereby subjected to a series of embarrassments.

The particular attentions of the minister to me, left they should be insidious, were in every instance but two declined, and in one of these I yielded to importunity: preferences I viewed as a source of division.

The second conference which I held with the minister, being on the 17th of December, and his propositions to the envoys, were published with their dispatches. Their answer, which was unanimously in the negative, was delivered by me to his secretary. Mr. Y. had expected it, and expressed a surprise that the secretary had applied for it.

On the 4th of February, the minister, by order of the Executive Directory, proposed that I should treat separately: the circumstances thereof, and of my refusal, are generally detailed in the correspondence enclosed.

The minister afterwards desired me, by his secretary, to communicate to the other envoys his proposition for a loan subsequent to the war; which he soon relinquished. On this subject, our first instructions were silent; the last were explicit, and necessary to determine my judgment.

In consequence of his letter to the envoys, of the 28th Ventose (18th of March), the minister renewed his proposition for me to treat separately; and again received a negative answer. He then proposed that I should remain at Paris, until the sense of the government should be obtained: declaring, as before, that an immediate rupture would be the consequence of my departure. To have left France under such circumstances, was a measure which I could not justify. The power of declaring war was not entrusted with the supreme executive of the United States, much less with a minister; and to have thus provoked it, would in my mind have been tantamount to a declaration thereof. Indeed, to have plunged the nation into a war suddenly, even if it was inevitable, appeared to me in other respects unwarrantable. Congress, who alone had the right to adopt this measure, might, by such a premature step, have been defeated in their previous arrangements, and subjected to other manifest inconveniencies, and the executive might have been placed on ground less advantageous for forming alliances, &c. Whereas, my detention at Paris gained time, if this was requisite; and could not procrastinate a declaration of war, if the United States were prepared for it. Other considerations had their weight. France at that time was making very formidable preparations, with a professed design to overthrow the British government; and such were the exertions and enthusiasm of her citizens, armies, and administration, as to spread a general alarm throughout Great Britain. It was evident then to common observation, that should France succeed, she would acquire, by the powerful navy and resources of Britain, such strength, as to be able to give law to Europe, and to regions more remote; and it was rational to suppose, that a coalition would be formed, of such European powers as were not in the interest or under the influence of France, to put an end to the war, by offering their mediation, and declaring their intention to oppose the power which should refuse it: the temporizing negotiations at Rastadt had this aspect. Moreover, the internal affairs of France were in an agitated state, and threatened civil commotions. If then, on the one hand, a new coalition against France, a change in her government, or even a successful resistance on the part of Great Britain, had happened, a favourable opportunity would have presented itself to the United States, for obtaining of her a just and advantageous treaty; and this would have been lost, by a previous rupture in consequence of my departure. If, on the other hand, Great Britain unaided had fallen, the United States would have been in a much better condition at peace, than in war with the most formidable power the world had exhibited. In such an event, they could have had but small hopes of resisting France; and it might have been deemed madness in them even to have attempted it. For these reasons, I thought it my indispensable duty to remain a short time at Paris.

The tenour of our instructions, the last as well as the first, shows that the government did not anticipate the proposition for
treating

treating separately, and made no provision for such an event. The French minister has uniformly insisted, that I had power to treat; because in the instrument he saw that the envoys had a separate and joint authority. If the position could be established, it would authorize a foreign government, at pleasure, to reduce the number of a commission consisting of two or more members, and thus to deprive the constituting government of the joint abilities of its ministers; or absurdly to insist on a separate negotiation with each minister, and to choose from their several treaties, that which should best answer its purpose: besides, in case of the misconduct of ministers, their government has a right to expect information thereof, and an opportunity of substituting others in their stead; but I trust that the arguments stated in the correspondence enclosed, are sufficient to show that the power to treat did not exist; or, if it did, that I was justified, under existing circumstances, in refusing to exercise it.

On the 3d of April I received the minister's note No. III. and apprehending that he proposed to draw me into a negotiation, notwithstanding my resolution to the contrary, I sent him an answer on the 4th of April (No. IV.), to which he made no reply.

On the 20th of April, considering the unpleasant situation in which I was placed, detached from the other envoys, destitute of power to negotiate, irreconcileable to an application for it, and even to an acceptance of it, if offered, I addressed to the minister the letter No. V. urged him to come forward with propositions for a reconciliation, and to release me from my confinement.

At our next interview, on the 28th of April, the minister informed me, that he could not comply with my proposals, not knowing the views of the United States in regard to a treaty. To remove this obstacle, I gave the information, and in it the fullest extent to the claims of the American citizens against France, but I was silent with respect to the guaranty of the eleventh article of the treaty of alliance, and to what relates to the Barbary powers; and left it with him, in the first instance, to provide for a liberal commerce to the French colonies in the East and West Indies, and to express the views of France in regard to the proposed treaty. We afterwards conferred on the necessity of sending a French minister to the United States; and he promised to deliver me, within three or four days, the project of a treaty. On the evening of the 12th of May, Mr. Humphreys arrived, and delivered me your letter of the 23d March, which, the next morning, was deciphered. Our government could not then have been apprized of the new state of affairs; but, as it had signified " that suspense was ruinous," I thought myself authorized to give immediate information to the minister of foreign affairs, that I should return to America in the Sophia, as soon as she could be fitted for the sea; and that it was necessary to expedite the measures we had contemplated, for effecting a treaty. The Executive Directory, as well as the minister, had, it was said, during the three preceding weeks, been indispensably occupied by the new elections; and these being finished, they could now proceed on American affairs: had the latter required more time than I had allotted for them, I was determined to have detained the Sophia a short period, rather than to have defeated the proposed arrangements. This I considered as my duty; for whilst the government manifested in their instructions a just indignation at the treatment which their envoys had received, it evinced a disposition to peace; and, as far as I could judge, the same temper now existed on the part of France.

On the 24th May, the minister sent the principal secretary of his bureau to inform me, that his government did not wish to break the British treaty, but expected, in the new treaty, such provisions as would indemnify France, and put her on a footing with that nation: to this I answered, that the information gave me pleasure; that it was impossible for the United States, by violating that treaty, to become perfidious; that the treaty itself was an evidence of their good faith, inasmuch as it contained a provision, " that it should not be construed or operate contrary to former and existing public treaties with other sovereigns or states;" that if, in its construction or operation, France had sustained injuries, still she was sure of redress by the provisions thereof, as well as by her own treaty with the United States; and that the latter ensured to her an extension of favours, in regard to commerce and navigation, if any such had been granted to Great Britain.

He said, there was a second point, which respected the claims of American citizens on the French republic; that, if the latter should not be able to pay them when adjusted, and the United States would assume and pay them, France would reimburse the amount thereof. To this I answered, that the measure was impossible; but that the claims might be adjusted, funded, and made transferable by France; and be redeemed, pursuant to such stipulations, as might be agreed on between the two governments.

He then stated a third point, which respected the consular convention. I answered, that perhaps it would be best, as its duration would be short, to let it expire. But if the present war should soon terminate, and commerce revive in France, it may be well to revise it in order to prevent further disputes, respecting the evidence for apprehending deserters, the judicial officers for issuing warrants, and the mode of executing consular decisions; stating, at the same time, that foreign tribunals could never be admitted within the jurisdiction of the United States. The secretary reported the conference, and informed me the next morning,

morning, that the minister would send me his answer, in writing, in a few days.

On the 26th May I had a conference with the minister, the substance of which is stated in my letter No. XXIV. Having pressed on this, as well as former occasions, the necessity of sending a minister to the United States, he now readily acceded to it: this would have enabled France to relax from any stipulations, which she might have urged there, but which might be found by her minister in the United States to endanger the treaty.

In this state were affairs on the 27th May, when I was called on by one of the city gazettes, which announced the publication of our dispatches, to deny their authenticity. Having reason to suppose that the result of this new embarrassment, if not pacific, would be very violent, I prepared for the event, being obliged to abide the consequences.

On the 30th May I received from the minister his letter, No. VI. and returned for answer No. VII. In this I repeated, what was published in our dispatches, that X. and Y. had not produced a document of any kind, for authorizing their conference with us. I was not disposed to accuse or exculpate the French government or minister: the latter had disavowed the intriguers, as they were styled, and they, in their conferences with us, had declared that they were not authorized by the government: the matter was therefore left with the republic, as it had been referred to their tribunal.

On the 1st of June the minister sent me his letter No. VIII. and I desired to know of the bearer, why application was again made to me for the names of the intriguers, when they could be otherwise ascertained? He answered, that he believed, by the exertions of the bureau and of the police of the city, the names were discovered; and he mentioned them to me. But he added, that matters had become very serious; that the Directory expected something from me in confirmation of this discovery; that this was the use which would be made of my letters; and that the minister did not wish for any declaration from me, but what should be perfectly consistent with truth. I assured him that no extremity should produce from me any other declaration, and sent the minister my letter No. X. In this I guarded against the publication, on my authority, of the names thus communicated; and did justice to certain individuals, who being suspected, were nevertheless innocent.

On the 7th June, the publication No. XXXV. appeared in the Redacteur. In this, contrary to assurances received, I was made to act a very conspicuous part; and was attacked under a thin veil of insidious compliments: the cause thereof was the detail, in the dispatches, of my particular conferences. The next day I prepared a letter to the minister, for detecting the artifices,

and

and correcting the abuses, of that curious performance. But having considered, that it might open a door to altercation and delay, if not defeat the great object in view; or produce a mere disavowal of the anonymous publication, which afterwards was made in No. XXI. I suppressed the letter, and on the 10th June addressed to him No. XIII. In this, availing myself of the pacific declaration contained in the strictures, I urged the expedition of pacific measures, as a requisite to their success.

On the 11th of June I received from the minister No. XIV. in which, as he had informed my secretary, he revived the disagreeable subject of the dispatches; and he concluded by formally demanding whether I was in a situation to treat? Every circumstance concurred now to prove, that the dispatches had excited the resentment of the minister against the government, as well as myself; and had changed his plan in regard to the United States.

On the 13th June I answered that letter by No. XV. and on the 20th received a reply, No. XVI. In this the minister, in lieu of the proposed plan of a treaty, presented a general plan of negotiation: notwithstanding, as he had stated it, "my persevering to think my powers were inadequate," and " the most irritating provocations:" by the first " point" of this plan, a door would have been open to endless altercations, respecting the supposed abuse of the French government, by private writings, public acts of the United States, official letters, and the dispatches of the envoys; by the second point, the sense of the treaties was to be fixed, and the rights flowing therefrom were to be established; and by the third point, the damages of deviations from the treaties were to be examined: he then stated, that " very general instructions" were necessary for the negotiations; and proposed that I should apply for them: very general indeed must the instructions have been, to have negotiated such a plan as this; and it was impossible to view it in any other light than that of an evasion of the arrangements proposed. It was easy to have pointed out the misinterpretations and misrepresentations, as well as the impolicy of the plan; but I was under the necessity of avoiding this, or of entering into a formal negotiation. To allure me into it, was probably the object of the minister; for, soon afterwards, he invited me to discuss in writing some articles of the second point. In my answer therefore of the 22d June (No. XVII.) I merely observed, that, " if he conceived a reconciliation would be best promoted by his mode only, I sincerely wished it success."

On the 29th June I received the minister's letter No. XIX.; in which, after relaxing from the first point of his general plan, and suggesting that the third would not meet with much difficulty, as soon as the second should be amicably adjusted, he for the first time

time propofed, that I fhould difcufs, in writing, fome articles of the treaty comprized under the fecond point. Nearly three months had then elapfed, fince I had declared I could only confer with him informally on the objects of the miffion; nearly two months fince he was informed of the views of the United States in regard to a treaty, and had promifed to come forward in a few days with the project thereof; and fix weeks fince I had apprized him of my intention to embark in the Sophia. As then a compliance with his wifhes would have given a fanction not only to his departure from the plan we had agreed on for forming an arrangement; but alfo to the meafure adopted by his government, of accrediting at pleafure the whole or a part only of a commiffion; and as I had frequently demanded my paffport, by letters, as well as by my fecretary, I paffed in filence his propofition for difcuffion, as a meafure he well knew was inadmiffible, and urged in my letter of the firft of July (No. XX.), in a more decided tone, the demand for the paffport, &c.

On the 5th July, not having received an anfwer to my laft, I called on the minifter, to know the caufe of his detaining my paffport, and to give him an opportunity, before my departure, of removing the obftacles to a plan of pacification. He began by obferving, that, in a note accompanying his laft letter, he had ftated two points refpecting the confular convention, expecting that I would difcufs them, as he had done, but I had not taken any notice of them; that I had faid I had no powers.—He had powers; and of confequence, I fhould not compromit my ftate, whilft he would compromit his: that I might take the difcuffion to the United States, and my government might judge of it; that when my colleagues were here, the government could not treat with them; that when they were fent off, it was ready to treat with me; that although I had no powers, I might fend for them; or, remaining there, might give my government an opportunity of fending other minifters, if I did not choofe to proceed in the bufinefs; that in this, there would be no refponfibility on my part; that there were but a few points for difcuffion, which might foon be finifhed; and that if a war was the confequence of my leaving the country, it would be chargeable to me. To which I replied, that the laft propofition of the Directory for me to treat, was one which I had before rejected; that in April laft, he knew I would only confer on the fubjects of the miffion, and made no objection to the meafure; that on the 29th June, after my baggage was on board, and I was ready to embark, he firft propofed a difcuffion in writing, of the articles of the treaty; that I confidered this, however qualified, as a formal mode of negotiation, which I had uniformly declined; that had he brought forward, as he had propofed, the plan of a treaty, and in it comprized the articles which I had ftated, we might have paffed on it expeditioufly, and might have made it acceptable

ceptable to both governments; that the moft important parts might have been firft confidered, and, if not adjufted, might have precluded the neceffity of paffing on the reft ; that in addition to the objection already ftated to his mode, it commenced with the confular convention, which would foon expire ; that fhould we agree on this, and on the leffer points of the commercial treaty, he may referve to the laft the weighty articles thereof; and failing in thefe, we might wafte feveral months, by a fruitlefs negotiation ; that fhould we unite in all the points which he has fuggefted, his mode of difcuffion would require feveral months ; that the lofs of time, by thefe or other means, might compromit the government of the United States, and myfelf likewife ; that if a war fhould be the confequence of his departing from the plan we had agreed on, for obtaining a treaty, he would be chargeable as the caufe of it. The minifter faid, the mode he had propofed was generally adopted by France. I replied, the other was not unufual, and in the prefent cafe was preferable, if not indifpenfable ; he obferved that the notes which I had lent him, refpecting the views of the United States, were informal. I anfwered, it was true, but that I would remove that difficulty. He then propofed the 7th July for another interview ; but afterwards put it off till the 9th. On the 6th I reduced the notes to form, for conftituting a part of the treaty.

On the 9th of July I called on the minifter ; and he inquired whether I had received his letter of that morning: I anfwered in the negative, and defired to know the contents ; he replied, " A difcuffion of two other points of the confular convention ; on which I want your opinion in writing." I informed him, that I had ftated the views of the United States without difcuffion, and expected the fame of him on the part of France ; that when this was done, I would proceed to a conference on each point, but not to an epiftolary difcuffion; that fuch a mode would require, of diligent negotiation, three months, and with his official engagements, double that time. He faid, No ; that it would not require as much time as I had conceived; that there were at moft but fix other points. On your fide, I replied, but many on ours. He anfwered, "*Pas d'avantage,*" none befides. I faid that I was glad to hear it ; but to fuch a difcuffion as he propofed, I fhould prefer treating effectually. Some of the converfation was repeated which we had on the 7th, and I renewed my demand for the paffport. He anfwered, that my refufal to difcufs muft firft be given in writing, and we parted. This is the fubftance of the two interviews.

On the fame day I received the letter mentioned at the interview (No. XXI.), dated the 18th Meffidor (6th July), in which, fpeaking of his general plan in No. XVI. he fays, "But it is not fufficient to fend thefe propofitions to your government; they are only the bafis of difcuffions, neceffary on each queftion of detail ; the folution of which we ought to find :" although, in the laft-mentioned

(225)

~~~~ number ~~~~ said in reference to them, "I am per~~~~ that you will transmit to your government exact documents ~~~~ be its province to take the best measures for accomplishing ~~~~ reconciliation." In the letter first mentioned, the mi~~~~ also observes, "I have apprized you, that it would be incon~~~~ to charge with this discussion a minister plenipotentiary at ~~~~elphia. Circumstances have rendered this inconvenience ~~~~ serious: and I do not conceal from you, that I fear new in~~~~." The fact was, as I ascertained to my satisfaction, that the arrival of the dispatches and other intelligence from the ~~~~ States, the Executive Directory apprehended if a minister ~~~~ there, that he would not be accredited; and that over~~~~ or any plan unaccompanied by a minister, would meet a ~~~~ fate.

~~~~ the 10th July, in my letter No. XXII. I refused an episto~~~~discussion; and demanded a definitive answer to my application ~~~~ passport and other documents.

~~~~ the 15th July I received the minister's letter of the 24th Mes~~~~ (the 12th July), No. XXIII. in which he appeals to me for ~~~~th of his assertion, "that if nothing had prevented me from ~~~~ing, with him, the examination of the grievances which se~~~~ the two countries, we should have needed nothing more ~~~~heir respective ratifications." Before the arrival of the dis~~~~es of the envoys, the minister appeared to me sincere, and ~~~~us to obtain a reconciliation. He had proposed by his secre~~~~ an assumption of the debts due to American citizens; which ~~~~ed: but he had made no other proposition of a loan what~~~~ and never renewed that. Indeed his views in general, as ~~~~ I could then ascertain them, were liberal in regard to a ~~~~: it is nevertheless impossible for me to determine whether ~~~~ould have united in opinion, on every point of dispute between ~~~~publics. I had a full expectation, that, by the middle of ~~~~ at farthest, we should have agreed on the plan of a treaty; ~~~~et a French minister would have been sent to America for ~~~~leting it. I was likewise informed of the candidate: but ~~~~the arrival of the dispatches, although the minister, in the ~~~~ of the Executive Directory, declared that they persevered in ~~~~pacific intentions, he probably, for the reasons stated in ex~~~~ng No. XXI. abandoned the plan we had at first agreed on, ~~~~ed a general plan of negotiation, discussed some articles ~~~~f in writing, and insisted, contrary to stipulations, on my ~~~~ing him in the same mode. At this period, a reconciliation ~~~~quite problematical, one of his objects evidently was, to ~~~~materials for a manifesto, in the event of a war, to show ~~~~ was a matter of necessity, and not of choice. He says, ~~~~after the arri of the Sophia, I was disposed to depart; ~~~~ time he t ver conceived that I had a design to em~~~~. VIII.   G g   bark,

bark, before we should have agreed on the definitive articles to be ratified by my government." Before and after the arrival of the Sophia, I had announced my intention to embark early in June; conceiving that the arrangements might be made by that period. I had no design, however, of departing before they were completed, provided there should have been no reason to doubt of the minister's disposition, or of the success of our endeavours, for obtaining a reconciliation. His general conduct would have been the criterion of the first, and our progress in this business, of the last point: but having abandoned our original plan, he has not given me an opportunity to judge effectually of either.

On the 20th July I sent the minister No. XXIV. and received on the 22d, his reply, No. XXV. In this he declines a contest in regard to the facts stated by me in No. XXIV. which I was ready to support: he complains of my proposition for lopping from any future negotiation, every preliminary of a loan, and of explanations upon speeches; and refers to his letter of the 30th of Prairial, No. XVI. to prove that this step was unnecessary. But although the first point of his plan in that letter is silent on these demands, they might, as I conceived, be hereafter revived, and were for this reason brought again into view: by these means they were effectually renounced.

The minister having, the day before I left Paris, published his letter No. XXII. rendered necessary the publication of my answer No. XXIV. and the note No XXVI. as a preliminary thereto.

On the 8th of August I received at Havre the minister's letter No XXVII. to which No. XXVIII. is an answer: the former contained the arrêté No. XXIX. and his desire to send it by the Sophia, probably produced the official impediments which for several days prevented her sailing. The minister is unwilling to admit that the arrêté was the effect of my representations: I believe there is no doubt of the fact; but it is a matter of little consequence.

No. XXX. and XXXI. will show that Mr. Hautval, in his letter to the minister, relative to our first interview, committed some errors, and candidly corrected them.

No. XXXII. and XXXIII. require no explanation.

No. XXXIV. will show the object of the Dutch minister in his conference with me, and requires no comment. I was before informed that this gentleman, if requested, would interpose his good offices; but did not think it proper to make the application.

No. XXXV. has already been the subject of some general remarks.

To No. IX. a verbal answer was sent by the minister, that the letters and dispatches therein mentioned " had never reached the government."

On the 26th of July I left Paris: and from the best information which I could obtain relative to the disposition of the Executive

tive Directory (for I never had any direct communication with them), they were very desirous of a reconciliation between the republics. Every impediment to my departure had been adopted by the French minister; and he would have prevented it, had he succeeded in his plan of an epistolary discussion: his object was, as I conceived, to gain time for ascertaining, whether the United States were then disposed to a treaty; of this he manifested doubts, being persuaded that their resentment was too great to admit of it. He seemed also to apprehend, that in consequence of the incredible exertions of Great Britain, and the unequivocal evidence she had given of her ability to defend herself, they were inclined to avenge their injuries by an alliance with her; and that should France come forward with overtures, or the plan of a treaty, she would fail therein, and compromit her honour. I was nevertheless of opinion, that should France be just and liberal in her measures, the government of the United States would still meet her on the ground of accommodation. My judgment was the result of their instructions; for I had never received any other official intelligence since my departure from America: I have therefore uniformly inculcated that sentiment.

Having been thus in a situation, wherein, amidst a series of events, each has been productive of fresh embarrassments, I have invariably pursued what to me appeared the honour, interest, and and welfare of my country, and been guided by the sense of the government, as far as I could ascertain it.

If the door is still open to peace, the establishment of it must be an happy event to the United States, as it will exempt them from calamities, which, notwithstanding delusive appearances, will, with short intervals, probably continue for half a century to exhaust and depopulate Europe.

But if the national pulse beats high for war, and the wise and constitutional councils of the United States shall consider it as the only safe and honourable alternative, may that Omnipotent Being who controls events, protect them; and may they commence the war with ardour, continue it with vigour, and terminate it with glory! That this will be the issue there can be no doubt, whilst the American republic shall choose Union for her motto; and profiting by the misfortunes of other nations, shall be convinced that discord will insure dependence, and concord independence in war and peace.

I shall probably, when at leisure, give you some other details of less consequence, and in the interim remain, Sir, with much esteem and respect,

         Your very humble servant,

Timothy Pickering, Esq. Secretary of   E. GERRY.
State of the United States.

Letter from the Secretary of State to Mr. Gerry, dated June 25th, 1798, transmitted to him at Paris in the Interval of the previous Correspondence.

Department of State.

Sir, Philadelphia, June 25, 1798.

BY the instructions dated the 23d of March, which, agreeably to the President's directions, I addressed to Generals Pinckney and Marshall and yourself, and of which six sets were transmitted, one by a dispatch-boat sent on purpose, and some of which doubtless reached you during the last month, you will have seen that it was expected that all of you would have left France long before those instructions could arrive, and which were transmitted rather from abundant caution than necessity, seeing no probability or hope existed that you would accomplish the object of your mission. The respect due to yourselves and to your country irresistibly required that you should turn your backs to a government that treated both with contempt; a contempt not diminished but aggravated by the flattering but insidious distinction in your favour, in disparagement of men of such respectable talents, untainted honour, and pure patriotism, as Generals Pinckney and Marshall, and in whom their government and their country reposed entire confidence; and especially when the real object of that distinction was to enable the French government, trampling on the authority and dignity of our own, to designate an envoy with whom they would condescend to negotiate. It is therefore to be regretted that you did not concur with your colleagues in demanding passports to quit the territories of the French republic, some time before they left Paris.

General Marshall has arrived, and delivered to the President your letter of April 16th, with its enclosures; all which were, on the 21st instant, laid before Congress, accompanied by a message in which the President declares the negotiation at an end, and that " he will never send another minister to France without assurances that he will be received, respected, and honoured, as the representative of a great, free, powerful, and independent nation."

It is presumed that you will consider the instructions of the 23d of March, before mentioned, as an effectual recall: left, however, by any possibility, those instructions should not have reached you, and you should still be in France, I am directed by the President to transmit to you this letter, and to inform you, that you are to consider it as a positive letter of recall.

I am respectfully, Sir,
Your obedient servant,
(Signed) TIMOTHY PICKERING.

Elbridge Gerry, Esq.

Address of the President on presenting the previous Correspondence of the French Minister with Mr. Gerry, after the other Plenipotentiaries had left Paris.

Gentlemen of the Senate, and Gentlemen of the House of Representatives,

THE communication relative to our affairs with France, alluded to in my address to both Houses, at the opening of the session, is contained in the sheets which accompany this. A report of the Secretary of State, containing some observations on them, will be sent to Congress on Monday.

January 18, 1799.   JOHN ADAMS.

Message from the President of the United States, accompanying the following Message and Report of the Secretary of State.

Gentlemen of the Senate, and Gentlemen of the House of Representatives,

ACCORDING to an intimation in my message on Friday last, I now lay before Congress a report of the Secretary of State, containing his observations on some of the documents which attended it.

January 21*st*, 1799.   JOHN ADAMS,

Message of the Secretary of State to the President of the United States.

THE Secretary of State respectfully submits the following report on the transactions relating to the United States and France, since the last communications to Congress on that subject.

Department of State,   TIMOTHY PICKERING.
Jan. 18*th*, 1799.

Report of the Secretary of State on the Transactions relating to the United States and France, since the last Communications to Congress on that Subject.

THE points chiefly meriting attention are the attempts of the French government,

1. To exculpate itself from the charge of corruption, as having demanded a douceur of fifty thousand pounds sterling (222,000 dollars) for the pockets of the directors and ministers, as represented in the dispatches of our envoys:

2. To detach Mr. Gerry from his colleagues, and to inveigle him into a separate negotiation; and,

3. Its

3. Its design, if the negotiation failed, and a war should take place between the United States and France, to throw the blame of the rupture on the United States.

1. The dispatches of the envoys published in the United States, and republished in England, reached Paris towards the last of May: and on the 30th of that month, the French minister, Mr. Talleyrand, affecting an entire ignorance of the persons designated by the letters W. X. Y. and Z. (calling them intriguers, whose object was to deceive the envoys,, writes to Mr Gerry, and "prays him immediately to make known to him their names."

Mr. Gerry, in his answer of the 31st, wishes to evade Mr. Talleyrand's request; and with reason, for he and his colleagues had "promised Messrs. X. Y. that their names should in no event be made public." Mr. Gerry, in his letter of October 1, in noting the repetition of Mr. Talleyrand's request for those names, states as an objection to giving them up, "that they could be otherwise ascertained;" and that Mr. Talleyrand's messenger, admitting the fact that they were already known, immediately mentioned their names. Mr. Gerry nevertheless certified in writing the names of X. Y. and Z.; with the reserve "that they should not be published on his authority: and besides formally certifying to Mr. Talleyrand the names of his own private agents, added, that "they did not produce, to his knowledge, credentials or documents of any kind"—"Credentials" in writing were certainly not to be expected to be produced by agents employed to make corrupt propositions: but Mr. Gerry had Mr. Talleyrand's own assurance that Mr. Y. was acting by his authority. It is recited in the envoys' dispatches, and upon Mr. Gerry's own report to his colleagues, that on the 17th of December 1797, Mr. Y. "stated to him that two measures which Mr. Talleyrand proposed, being adopted, a restoration of friendship between the republics would follow immediately; the one was a gratuity of fifty thousand pounds sterling; the other a purchase of thirty-two millions of Dutch rescriptions," and after conversing on these topics, Mr. Gerry and Mr. Y. rode to Mr. Talleyrand's office, where "Mr. Gerry observed to Mr. Talleyrand, that Mr. Y. had stated to him that morning, some propositions as coming from Mr. Talleyrand, respecting which, Mr. Gerry could give no opinion," and after making some other observations, Mr. Talleyrand answered, "that the information Mr. Y. had given him (Mr. Gerry) was just, and might always be relied on." This declaration stamps with the minister's authority, all the communications made by Mr. Y. to the envoys. And Mr. Y. himself, who is Mr. Bellamy, of Hamburg, in his public vindication, declares, that "he had done nothing, said nothing, and written nothing, without the orders of Citizen Talleyrand." The same may be asserted in regard to Mr. X.; for he first

introduced

introduced Mr. Y. to the envoys; and his separate communications were substantially the same with those of Y. and both together were present with the envoys when the communications were more than once repeated.

It also deserves notice, that in stating the preliminary demands of the French government, the private agents, X. and Y. and the minister, use a similar language. The agents declare, that the Directory are extremely irritated at the speech of the President, and require an explanation of some parts of it, and reparation for others; that this must give pain to the envoys, but the Directory would not dispense with it: and that as to the means of averting the demand concerning the President's speech, the envoys must search for them, and propose them themselves. Being asked to suggest the means, the answer is, "Money," the purchase of the Dutch rescriptions, and "the fifty thousand pounds sterling, as a douceur to the Directory."

The minister told the envoys, that the Directory were wounded by the President's speech; and, in his conversation with Mr. Gerry on the 28th of October, said, "the Directory had passed an arret, which he offered for perusal; in which they had demanded of the envoys an explanation of some parts, and a reparation for others, of the President's speech to Congress of the 16th of May 1797, that he was sensible that difficulties would exist on the part of the envoys relative to this demand; but that, by their offering money, he thought he could prevent the effect of the arret. Mr. Z. (the "interpreter"), at the request of Mr. Gerry, having stated that the envoys have no such powers, Mr. Talleyrand replied, they can in such case take a power on themselves, and proposed that they should make "a loan." But this "loan," as will presently appear, did not mean the "money," which would "prevent the effect of the arret." Mr. Gerry then making some observations on the powers of the envoys, that they "were adequate to the discussion and adjustment of all points of real difference between the two nations; that they could alter and amend the treaty; or, if necessary, form a new one;" added, "that as to a loan, they had no powers whatever to make one: but that they could send one of their number for instructions on this proposition, if deemed expedient."—"That as he (Mr. Talleyrand) had expressed a desire to confer with the envoys individually, it was the wish of Mr. Gerry, that such a conference should take place, and their opinions thus be ascertained."—"Mr. Talleyrand, in answer, said, he should be glad to confer with the other envoys individually; but that this matter about the money must be settled directly, without sending to America; that he would not communicate the arret for a week; and that if we could adjust the difficulty respecting the speech, an application would nevertheless go to the

United

United States for a loan." Now this matter of the money that must be settled directly, could only refer to the douceur ; for a loan in the purchase of millions of Dutch rescriptions, or in any other form, could only be the subject of a stipulation to be afterwards fulfilled by the United States; but the douceur of fifty thousand pounds sterling was a sum within the immediate reach of the envoys; for their credit would certainly command it: in fact, a mercantile house had offered to answer their drafts: and this Mr. Talleyrand unquestionably well knew; for it was a member of the same house who first introduced the minister's agent, Mr. X. to General Pinckney, in the manner stated in the envoys' dispatches. A collateral evidence, that in " this matter of the money that must be settled directly," Mr. Talleyrand referred only to the douceur, arises from this circumstance: The very next day (October 29th) Mr. X. called on the envoys, and said, " Mr. Talleyrand was extremely anxious to be of service to them, and had requested that one more effort should be made to induce us to enable him to be so." After a great deal of the same conversation which had passed at former interviews had been repeated, the envoys say, " the sum of his proposition was, that if we would pay, by way of fees (that was his expression), the sum of money demanded for private use, the Directory would not receive us, but would permit us to remain in Paris as we now were; and we should be received by Mr. Talleyrand, until one of us could go to America, and consult our government on the subject of a loan."

Although the envoys' dispatches, and the facts and circumstances hereinbefore stated, cannot leave a doubt that X. as well as Y. and Z. was well known to Mr. Talleyrand, it will not be amiss to add, that on the 2d of December X. Y. and Z. dined together at Mr. Talleyrand's, in company with Mr. Gerry; and that after rising from table, the money propositions, which had before been made, were repeated, in the room and in the presence, though perhaps not in the hearing, of Mr. Talleyrand. Mr. X. put the question to Mr. Gerry in direct terms, either, " whether the envoys would now give the douceur," or, " whether they had got the money ready." Mr. Gerry, very justly offended, answered positively in the negative, and the conversation dropped.

Mr. Z. who has avowed himself to be Mr. Hauteval, was the person who first made known to the envoys the minister's desire to confer with them individually on the objects of their mission : he it was, who first introduced Mr. Gerry to Mr. Talleyrand, and served as the interpreter of their conversations; and in his letter to Mr. Talleyrand, at the close of Mr. Gerry's document No. XXXV. he announces himself to be the agent of the minister to make communications to the envoys.

Mr. Hauteval declares, " his sensibility must be much affected on on finding   r the letter Z. acting a part in company with certai   s,   iofe pl..n," he fays, " it doubtlefs was to take advantage of the go   faith of the American envoys, and make them their dupes:" yet this perfon, the avowed agent of the French minifter, apparently fo anxious to fkreen himfelf from the fufpicion of an agency in foliciting the bribe required by Mr. Talleyrand, did himfelf urge a compliance with that corrupt propofition *.

The fenfation which thefe details irrefiftibly excite, is that of aftonifhment at the unparalleled effrontery of Mr. Talleyrand, in demanding of Mr. Gerry the names of X. Y. and Z. after Y. had accompanied him on a vifit to the minifter, with whom the converfation detailed in the printed difpatches then paffed, and who then affured Mr. Gerry, " that the information Mr. Y. had given him was juft, and might always be relied on ;" after Z. had, in the firft inftance, introduced Mr. Gerry to the minifter, and ferved as their mutual interpreter, and when the converfation between them had alfo been ftated in the difpatches ; and after X. Y. and Z. had all dined together with Gerry at Mr. Talleyrand's table ; on rifing from which X. and Y. renewed the propofition about the money. The very circumftance of Mr. Talleyrand's being continued in office, after the account of thefe intrigues had been publifhed to the world, is a decifive proof that they were commenced and carried on with the privity, and by the fecret orders of the Directory. It was to accomplifh the object of thefe intrigues that the American envoys were kept at Paris unreceived fix months after their credentials had been laid before the Directory ; and it was only becaufe they were fuperior to thofe intrigues, and that no hopes remained of wheedling or terrifying them into a compliance, that two of them were then fent away, and with marks of infult and contempt.

2. The fact that the French government attempted to inveigle Mr. Gerry into a feparate negotiation will not be queftioned : at firft it was made privately, and under an injunction of fecrecy towards his colleagues : it was afterwards plainly infinuated by the minifter, in his letter of the 18th of March 1798, in which he tells the envoys, that the Executive Directory was difpofed to treat with one of the three ; and that one he openly avowed, in his letter of the 3d of April, to be Mr. Gerry. The pretence

---

* Extract of a Letter, dated June 15th, 1798, from Mr. King, Minifter of the United States in London, to the Secretary of State.

" Col. Trumbull, who was at Paris foon after the arrival there of the commiffioners, has more than once informed me, that Hauteval told him, that both the *douceur* and the *loan* were indifpenfable, and urged him to employ his influence with the American commiffioners to offer the *bribe* as well as the *loan*."

Vol. VIII.   H h   for

for selecting him was, that his " opinions, presumed to be more impartial, promised, in the course of the explanations, more of that reciprocal confidence which was indispensable." But when before have their " opinions" been stated as a justifiable ground for rejecting the ambassadors of peace? Ambassadors too of established probity, whose characters were of the first distinction in their own country, and whose demeanour towards the government to which they were deputed was decent and respectful; who had, with a frankness which the candour of their instructions warranted, communicated the important points which they contained; and who unremittingly, and with the most anxious solicitude, entreated that the negotiations might be commenced: what more proper or more honourable qualities ought ministers deputed to negotiate with a foreign nation to possess? But why should a foreign government question the opinions of the ambassadors sent to negotiate with it on subjects of difference between the two nations? If wisely chosen, and faithful to the interests of their own country, they must of course possess different opinions from the government to which they are sent, the differing opinions maintained by the two nations on their respective rights and interests, being the cause and objects of the negotiation. A government really disposed to treat on fair principles would never object to the opinions of foreign ambassadors: it would receive them, and appoint its own ministers with proper powers to treat with them, propose its terms, and receive those offered; and discuss both: and if then they could not agree, put an end to the negotiation. The French government did not wish to negotiate; it desired to impose a treaty on the United States. To this practice it had been accustomed towards the minor powers in Europe, whom it had subjected to its will; and it expected equal submission from the United States. Hence Mr. Talleyrand's secret declaration to Mr. Gerry, " that if he would negotiate, they could soon finish a treaty; for the Executive Directory were not in the habit of spending much time about such matters." Hence the objections to Gen. Pinckney and Gen. Marshall; they manifested a discernment superior to the intrigues of the French government, and an invincible determination not to surrender the honour, the interest, or the independence of their country. It was necessary then to get rid of them; and seeing that neither despair of negotiating, nor studied indignities, could induce them to quit their posts, passports were sent to them to quit France: it was with difficulty that Gen. Pinckney could obtain permission to stay two or three months for the recovery of his sick daughter, to whom an immediate voyage would probably prove fatal. Unembarrassed by the presence of these envoys, the French government, if it really desired a treaty on any terms, hoped to prevail on Mr. Gerry to negotiate separately, although from the

first

first overture declined and continued to decline it. But after the expulsion of his colleagues, it hoped, by its seductive arts, to prevail over his scruples, and gain his consent to terms which, while they were present, would be rejected; or, at all events, to retain him, with the semblance of negotiating, regularly or informally, and thus keep the United States in the torpor of indecision, without preparation for offence or defence. Unfortunately, Mr. Gerry was induced, by the threats of immediate war against the United States, to separate from his colleagues and stay in Paris; threats which, viewed with their motives, merited only detestation and contempt. Four or five months before, the threats of immediate orders to quit France, and the terrors of war in its most dreadful forms, had been held up to all the envoys, to frighten them into a compliance with the groundless, unjust, and corrupt demands of the French government. Those threats had not been executed, and the unworthy purposes for which they had been uttered had been obvious. Happily for the United States, the character of the French government, as delineated in the official dispatches of all the envoys, and the knowledge of its conduct towards other countries whose governments it had overturned, and whose people, in the names of Liberty and Equality, it had enslaved, so operated as not to leave us exposed to all the evils which suspense was calculated to produce. Mr. Gerry, indeed, resisted all the arts of the French minister to entice him into a formal negotiation, after that government had driven his colleagues from Paris: a negotiation which, in its nature, would have been a surrender of our independence, by admitting a foreign government to choose for us the minister who should represent our country, to treat of our important rights and interests, which that government had itself violated and deeply injured.

The Directory, and their minister Mr. Talleyrand, hoped and expected that General Pinckney and General Marshall would voluntarily have quitted France, after the minister's letter of the 18th of March, in which he made the offensive distinction between them and their colleague Mr. Gerry, on the pretence that his " opinions" were more " impartial" than theirs. Accordingly Mr. Talleyrand, in his letter to Mr. Gerry of the 3d of April, says, " I suppose, Sir, that Mess. Pinckney and Marshall have thought it useful and proper, in consequence of the intimations which the end of my note of the 18th of March last presents, to quit the territory of the republic." Yet Mr. Talleyrand had given them neither passports nor letters of safe-conduct! The fact is, the French government wished to avoid the odium of sending them away, and the blame of a rupture, which Mr. Talleyrand predicted would be the consequence; while it was privately intimated to them that they must leave the country. The minifter's conduct on this occasion towards General Marshall (as detailed in his journal) was particularly marked with indignities. When it was observed to Mr. Talleyrand, that this was not the manner in which a foreign minister ought to be treated, Mr. Talleyrand replied, that General Marshall was not a foreign minister, but was to be considered as a private American citizen; and must obtain his passport, like others, through the consul. To this it was answered, that General Marshall was a foreign minister[*], and that the French government could not deprive him of that character, which was conferred upon him, not by Mr. Talleyrand, but by the United States; and though the Directory might refuse to receive or to treat with him, still his country had clothed him with the requisite powers, which he held independently of France; that if he was not acceptable to the French government, and in consequence thereof it was determined to send him away, still he ought to be sent away like a minister; that he ought to have his passports, with letters of safe-conduct which would protect him from the cruisers of France. Mr. Talleyrand replied, that if General Marshall wished for a passport, he must give in his name, stature, age, complexion, &c. to the American consul, who would obtain a passport for him: that with respect to a letter of safe-conduct, it was unnecessary, as no risk from the cruisers would be incurred. The result of these conversations was a plain demonstration of the intention of the minister, that in consequence of his intimation at the close of his letter of the 18th of March, that the "opinions" of two of the envoys were not agreeable to the government of France, Generals Pinckney and Marshall should appropriate to themselves the character which the minister had drawn generally. The envoys, aware of this snare, in their answer of the 3d of April to the intimation that "the Directory was disposed to treat with one of the envoys," declare to the minister, "that no one of the envoys was authorized to take upon himself a negotiation evidently intrusted to the whole," and "that no two of them could propose to withdraw themselves from the task committed to them by their government, while there remained a possibility of performing it;" but that if "it should be the will of the Directory to order passports for the whole or any number of them," it was desired that such passports might be accompanied with letters of safe-conduct, to protect them against the cruisers of France.

These endeavours of the French government, whether real or

---

[*] On the 9th of October 1797, the day after the envoys had delivered to the minister a copy of their letter of credence, "cards of hospitality were sent to them and their secretaries, in a style suitable to their official character." (See page 184, 7th volume of this work.) And in the minister's letter to them of the 18th of March 1798, he calls them "the Commissioners and Envoys Extraordinary of the United States of America." (See French minister's letter, p. 275, 7th volume of this work.)

affected,

affected, to draw Mr. Gerry into a separate negotiation, constitute the substance of the correspondence between him and Mr. Talleyrand. They appear to merit consideration in several points of view.

1. Because if real, it was only in the hope and expectation, that by intrigues and terrors the French government might influence Mr. Gerry to enter into a formal treaty, on the terms which he and his colleagues had repeatedly rejected as incompatible with the interest, honour, and independence of their country. For at this time Mr. Talleyrand had not renounced the demands of loans and a douceur as the indispensable preliminaries of a treaty. Accordingly we see Mr. Talleyrand, in his letter of the 3d of April to Mr. Gerry, proposed "to resume their reciprocal communications upon the interests of the French republic and the United States of America." And in his letter of July 12th, to Mr. Gerry, having mentioned the arrival at Havre of a packet, the Sophia, from the American government, he says, " until then I never supposed you entertained the design of embarking before we had come to an agreement upon the definitive articles to be ratified by your government." 2. Because if that government had so far succeeded, it would have insisted on its ratification by the President and Senate, on the ground constantly taken by Mr. Talleyrand, that the powers of the envoys being several as well as joint, Mr. Gerry, when alone, even after the French government had ordered his colleagues to leave France, were adequate to the formation of the treaty; and that therefore the public faith would be violated, if it were not ratified. 3. Because under such circumstances, the French government, doubtless, calculated at least on a division of the public opinion in the United States in favour of the ratification of such a treaty; by means of which it might enforce the ratification, or effect still greater mischiefs. 4. But these endeavours to draw Mr. Gerry into a formal negotiation are chiefly remarkable because they were persevered in during near five months, against his constant, direct, and positive refusals to treat separately; Mr. Talleyrand asserting, and Mr. Gerry denying, the competency of his powers.

We have seen the envoys, from the 6th of October 1797, the date of their first letter to the French minister, to the 3d of April 1798, when their last was delivered to him, expressing their earnest desire to enter upon and prosecute the great business of their mission: we have seen them during that long period patiently enduring neglect and indignities, to which an ardent zeal to re-establish harmony and peace could alone induce freemen to submit. We have seen them, while held in suspense—neither received nor rejected—yielding to the importunities of private agents of the French government, and hearing and discussing their propositions, insulting as they were, in the hope that when these should be

shown

shown to be utterly inadmissible, others, founded in reason and equity, and in the usual course of diplomatic negotiation, might be brought forward. Doubtless they also wished, when their astonishment at the first overtures had subsided, by listening still longer to such dishonourable propositions, to ascertain the true character of the French government. We have seen them, after waiting five weeks from the presentation of a copy of their letters of credence, entirely unnoticed, " solicit an attention to their mission," and soliciting in vain. Thus denied an official hearing, they hoped by an unusual step to excite the attention of that government: they determined to transmit to the minister a letter representing the views of their own government in relation to the subjects in dispute with France. This letter, dated the 17th, was delivered the 31st of January 1798. Waiting near a month without an answer, and " still being anxious to hear explicitly from Mr. Talleyrand himself, before they sent their final letter, whether there were no means, within their powers, of accommodating our differences with France, on just and reasonable grounds," on the 27th of February they desired " a personal interview on the subject of their mission ;" and afterwards a second interview. They remark on what passed at these meetings, " that the views of France, with regard to the United States, were not essentially changed since their communications with its unofficial agents in the preceding October."

At length they received Mr. Talleyrand's letter of the 18th March 1798, in answer to theirs of the 17th of January. The minister's letter represented the complaints of France; as usual, charging the American government with the inexecution of the treaties with France—with dissimulation—insinuating, that our tribunals were subject to a secret influence—holding up the British treaty as replete with evil and injury, and " the principal grievance of the republic"—accusing the American government of a wish to seize the first favourable occasion to consummate an intimate union with Great Britain, and suggesting that a devotion and partiality to that power have long been the principle of the conduct of the federal government.

To this letter of the French minister, the envoys sent their reply on the 3d of April. This reply and their former letter detect the sophisms and erroneous statements of the minister, expose his naked assertions, refute his arguments, repel his calumnies, and completely vindicate the fidelity, the justice, and, as a neutral power, the impartiality of the government of the United States; and, at the same time, exhibit the weighty and well-founded complaints of the United States against the French republic.

Hitherto, instead of a desire to obtain a reconciliation, we can discover in the French government only empty professions of a desire to conciliate; while it haughtily refused to receive our

envoys,

envoys, and during six months disregarded their respectful and ardent solicitations to negotiate: and after one of them, whom it induced to remain in France, had declared that "he had no powers to treat separately, that the measure was impossible," then the Directory expelled the other two!

If now we survey Mr. Gerry's individual correspondence, we shall find no solid evidence of any change in the disposition of the French government.

In his first letter to Mr. Gerry, Mr. Talleyrand's artifice is visible: he addresses him as "envoy extraordinary of the United States of America, to the French republic;" and proposes to him to "resume their reciprocal communications." Mr. Gerry, apprehending that the minister intended to draw him into a negotiation, repeats what he had often before declared, that for him to treat separately was impracticable; and that he can only confer with him informally.

On the 20th of April, Mr. Gerry addresses a letter to the minister, and presses him to come forward with propositions for terminating all differences, restoring harmony, and re-establishing commerce between the two nations. He receives no answer. On the 28th he confers with the minister, who says he cannot make propositions, because he does not know the views of the United States in regard to a treaty. Mr. Gerry gives him the information. He then promises in three or four days to deliver Mr. Gerry the project of a treaty: this promise was never performed. On the 12th of May, the new instructions of March 23d, sent by the Sophia packet, reached Mr. Gerry; and he gave immediate notice to the minister that he should return to America in the Sophia, as soon as she could be fitted for sea.

" On the 24th of May, the minister sent his principal secretary to inform Mr. Gerry, that his government did not wish to break the British treaty; but expected such provisions as would indemnify France, and put her on a footing with that nation." Yet that treaty had been made, by the French government, its chief pretence for those unjust and cruel depredations on American commerce which have brought distress on multitudes, and ruin on many of our citizens; and occasioned a total loss of property to the United States of probably more than twenty millions of dollars; besides subjecting our fellow-citizens to insults, stripes, wounds, torture, and imprisonment. And Mr. Talleyrand, in his letter of the 18th of March to the envoys, declared that treaty to be " the principal grievance of the republic." But now, instead of breaking that treaty, France desires to be put on the same footing. This the United States would at any time have done, and the envoys were now explicitly instructed to do; and seven months before, all the envoys, in their conversation with Mr. Bellamy (Y.), the confidential and authorized agent of the

French

French minister, told him "that he might be assured that their powers were such as authorized them to place France on equal ground with England, in any respects in which an inequality might be supposed to exist at present between them, to the disadvantage of France."

The secretary also mentioned the claims of the American citizens on the French republic: he said, if the latter should be unable to pay them, when adjusted, and the United States would assume and pay them, France would reimburse the amount thereof. This has the semblance of candour; but on the 4th of March, when the envoys were in conference with Mr. Talleyrand, and they disclosed their principal instructions, "General Pinckney and Mr. Gerry told him they were positively forbidden to assume the debts to our own citizens, even if we were to pay the money directly to them." And doubtless it was because the proposition was already known to be inadmissible that it was now renewed.

The secretary and Mr. Gerry had also some unimportant conversation about the consular convention. And it is plain that the whole object of the secretary's visit was to amuse, by keeping alive Mr. Gerry's hopes of some pacific arrangements.

On the 26th of May Mr. Gerry had a conference with the minister; pressing on this, as on former occasions, the necessity of sending a minister to the United States with powers to negotiate, to which, he says, the minister acceded; but afterwards explained himself to mean a minister to reside there after the ratification of the talked-of treaty.

Such are the proceedings of the French government, by its minister, Mr. Talleyrand, before the arrival of the printed dispatches of the envoys. We discover nothing but a proposition for treating with Mr. Gerry alone, which he had repeatedly declared to be impossible, and on terms which Mr. Gerry himself, as well as the other envoys, had long before pronounced to be utterly inadmissible, because directly repugnant to their instructions. We shall now see, by an examination of Mr. Gerry's subsequent communications, that the publication of the envoys' dispatches, far from causing a discontinuance of negotiations with him, or any change in the disposition of the French government more unfriendly to the United States, incomparably greater zeal for negotiating was exhibited afterwards than before.

On the 30th of May the minister announces to Mr. Gerry the publication of the envoys' dispatches. In his letter of the 27th of June, he says this incident only "for a moment suspended the principal object," the negotiation with Mr. Gerry; and in his letter of June 10th, he declares, that "the French government, superior to all the personalities, to all the manœuvres of its enemies, perseveres in the intention of conciliating with sincerity all the differences which have happened between the two countries."

tries." On the 18th of June the minister sends him a plan for conducting the negotiations; for the first time states the "three points" on which he says "all negociations between France and the United States must essentially rest," and "gives (what he calls) a large developement" of them; concluding by pressing him to remain at Paris, to accelerate the negociation, " the drawing together of those ties which the French republic and the true Americans have regretted to see relaxed."

On the 27th of June the minister again writes to Mr. Gerry; and in language the most importunate, such as had never before been used, urges him not to withdraw, " when the French government, superior to all resentments, and never listening to any thing but justice, manifests itself anxious to conclude a solid and mutually satisfactory agreement." The minister even observes that the first of the " three points" mentioned in his preceding letter (respecting amicable declarations about mutual recriminations) might be postponed, that the third (about the consular convention) would doubless experience no difficulty on either side, after the second should be amicably settled: that it was to the second therefore they should first attend; it being so much the more important, as it embraced the source of all the differences between the two nations. And on the 22d of July the minister renounces all demands of " loans and explanations on the subject of speeches;" and even affects to be hurt that Mr. Gerry should have mentioned them: although both he and his private agents had before so long and so obstinately persevered in demanding them of the envoys, as the indispensable preliminaries to a negotiation. And doubtless it is partly owing to the publication of their dispatches, thereby exposing to the world those shameless demands, with the scandalous proposition of the douceur, that they are now relinquished.

In adducing these circumstances to show the increased zeal of the French government, since the publication of the dispatches, to negotiate on its differences with the United States, it is not to be understood that they afford a shadow of evidence of its sincerity. But as professions, verbal or written, furnished the only ground on which Mr. Gerry could form his opinion, that " before the arrival of the dispatches of the envoys, the minister was sincere and anxious to obtain a reconciliation," much more, professions stronger and more importunate, afterwards made, afford proportionably higher evidence of sincerity. But the present details demonstrate that all those professions were merely ostensible. In the minister's last-mentioned letter, after saying that his " second point" (to fix the meaning of the treaties between the two countries) was most important, " as it embraced the source of all the differences," and that to this they should first attend; he purposely passes by the most interesting questions which it involves,

involves, and sends Mr. Gerry a note on the consular convention, of all possible subjects in difference the most insignificant, as it would have expired by its own limitation in two years and a half, within which time, the commerce of France, judging from its present state of annihilation, would probably not furnish a single ship to visit the ports of the United States. In his next letter, dated July 6th, he pursues his speculations on the consular convention, and sends Mr. Gerry two more notes upon it, complaining that he had not transmitted to him his opinion upon his first note, and recommending the two last to his attention: although Mr. Gerry had repeatedly and positively declined a formal discussion, such as the minister now urged in writing. Mr. Gerry states also that this first note of the minister on the consular convention, was sent to him six weeks after he had demanded his passport, and when his baggage was actually on board the Sophia!

In a word, the more clearly the impossibility of entering on a formal negotiation appeared, the more was it pressed by the French minister. Mr. Gerry, in his letter to Mr. Talleyrand of July 20th, as justly as pointedly exposes the boasted zeal of the minister: "You was the first, you affirm, to press seriously the negotiation: you will agree with me that the merit would have been greater, had the measure itself been feasible." Again he says to the minister, " You frequently remind me of your exertions (to negotiate), which I am disposed as much as possible to appreciate, regretting at the same time their circuitous direction."

From this detail of facts, the following are the necessary conclusions:

That by the exclusive attentions of the minister to Mr. Gerry, the French government intended to excite the jealousy of his colleagues, to promote dissensions between them, to separate him from them, and induce him to remain in France, expecting either to seduce him into a formal negotiation of a treaty, on terms exclusively advantageous to France, and injurious and dishonourable to the United States; or, failing in this, to hold the United States in suspense, and prevent any measures for our security, in the event of a war; while we, amused and deluded by warm but empty professions of the pacific views and wishes of France, and by "informal conferences," might wait in spiritless torpor, hoping for a peaceful result: and

That by this course of proceeding, this ostentatious display of zeal to adjust differences, and restore harmony and a friendly intercourse between the United States and France, the French government intended, in case of a rupture, to throw the blame on the former.

It

It is neceffary to make a few obfervations on the decree of the Executive Directory of the 31ft July 1798.

This decree was fent after Mr. Gerry to Havre; and he fuppofes that the official impediments, which for feveral days prevented his failing, are to be afcribed to the minifter's defire of fending the decree by him. The minifter introduces it as "a part of the meafures which he had announced to Mr. Gerry on the 22d of July." In his letter of that date to Mr. Gerry, the minifter fays, "By information which the government has juft received, it indeed learns that violences have been committed upon the commerce and citizens of the United States in the Weft Indies, and on their coafts. Do it the juftice to believe that it needs only to know the facts, to difavow all acts contrary to the laws of the republic and its own decrees. A remedy is preparing for it, and orders will foon arrive in the Weft Indies, calculated to caufe every thing to return within its juft limits." This "remedy" is the decree of the 31ft of July.

1. The firft article of this decree confines to the fpecial agents of the Directory, the right of iffuing commiffions to cruifers; and requires thefe to conform themfelves to all the laws relative to cruifing and prizes, and efpecially to thofe of the 1ft of October 1793. Although the injunction to conform to all the laws of the republic relative to cruifing was ominous, as the laws moft recently promulgated and beft known were themfelves the fources of the depredations and evils of which we complained; yet not imagining that a decree introduced with fo much folemnity, of which one copy was fent to Mr. Gerry, another to the American conful-general at Paris, and a third to Mr. Létombe, late conful-general of France, all to be communicated to the executive of the United States, and all of which have been received, could be a mere parade of words, I was difpofed to conclude that the law of the 1ft of October 1793, to which all cruifers were efpecially enjoined to conform, might contain regulations that would afford fome relief from French depredations. By the favour of Mr. Létombe I obtained a copy of that law; and to my aftonifhment found its object, conformably to its title, was "to determine the mode of dividing prizes made by French veffels on the enemies of the republic *." And the only reftriction, in this lengthy law of fix and forty articles, impofed on the individuals, officers, and all others, compofing the crews of their armed vef-

---

* " Decret de la Convention Nationale du 1. 8bre 1793, l'an 2d de la république française.

" Que détermine le mode de répartition des prifes faites par les vaiffeaux François fur les ennemis de la république."

fels, is, "that they shall not sell beforehand their eventual shares of prizes."

2. The second article declares that all commissions granted by the agents in the French colonies in America, to fit out vessels for cruisers, or for war and commerce, shall be void in thirty days after the publication of the decree in those colonies.

It has been supposed that by this regulation the agents may gather a fresh harvest of fees for new commissions; and that this would be its only effect. The agents however had before taken care of this; they had been accustomed to limit the duration of privateers' commissions; and if they continued to cruise after their expiration, such privateers should have been considered as destitute of commissions, and consequently, if they made any captures, as pirates. But the agents knew their interest better: they did not punish the piratical captors, they did not declare their captures void, and restore the property to the neutral owners, but, declaring such captors to have no title to the captured vessels and cargoes, took the whole to themselves. A remarkable instance occurred in the last year, in the case of the East India ship New Jersey, belonging to Philadelphia, to redeem which, the owners have paid to General Hedouville, special agent of the Executive Directory in St. Domingo, upwards of two hundred thousand dollars in cash. Whether any, and what portion of such prize-money goes into the chest of the republic, I am not informed.

3. The third article declares that all agents and other deputies in the neutral possessions, appointed to decide there on the validity of prizes taken by the French cruisers, and who shall be suspected of having a direct or indirect interest in the cruisers, shall be immediately recalled.

It is remarkable that this article, apparently designed to correct the monstrous abuse of public officers sitting in judgment in their own causes, should be limited to such of the French agents and their deputies as were appointed to reside in neutral places. I do not know that an instance of the kind exists. For although the French privateers and their prizes find asylums in the Swedish and Danish islands, yet the papers are carried thence to Guadaloupe, and there the captured vessels receive their doom under the superintendance of another special agent of the Executive Directory, Victor Hugues. And even the captured American vessels carried into the West India ports of Spain and Holland, do not there receive sentence: these cases are decided by the agent or his deputies, or other French tribunals, established in the island of St. Domingo, frequently, if not generally, in the absence of the masters and supercargoes. The French agents and judges find no difficulty in this mode of proceeding; justice being administered with more facility and dispatch, when only one of the parties is present at the trial, especially when the agents or other

judges

judges are interested in the privateers, and this the present decree impliedly allows; the penalty of "recall" being applicable, as above suggested, to such agents only as reside in neutral places, if any such there be.

It is also remarkable, that this decree, which was to give the United States a proof of the justice of the French government, (a government, Mr. Talleyrand says, "never listening to any thing but justice"), and of its desire of a reconciliation with the United States, should be limited to the West Indies, when as great, if not as numerous abuses, were practised by French agents and tribunals in Europe, and even France itself, as in her remote possessions. This too many of our citizens well know. For captures and condemnations are not the less abuses, because made under the colour of municipal laws and decrees, which directly violate treaties, the law of nations, and the plainest principles of justice. At present I shall only mention, that, in a report made by Major Mountflorence, chancellor of the American consulate at Paris, to General Pinckney, in December 1796, and which was laid before Congress in May 1797, he states, " that the tribunals of commerce in every port of France, take cognizance, in the first instance, of every matter relative to captures at sea;" and " these tribunals (he adds) are chiefly composed of merchants, and most of them are, directly or indirectly, more or less interested in the fitting out of privateers; and therefore are often concerned in the controversies they are to determine upon."

4. The fourth article requires the special agents of the Executive Directory at Cayenne, St. Domingo, and Gaudaloupe, studiously to take care, that the interests and property of vessels belonging to neutrals and allies, be scrupulously respected.

We have too long witnessed the studious and scrupulous care of these gentlemen respecting the property of neutrals and allies, and experienced its ruinous consequences; and as the same laws which authorized that " care" remain in force, and with a fresh injunction of a strict conformity to them, we can expect only a continuance of the same abuses.

5. The fifth article enjoins the special agents of the Executive Directory, consuls, and all others invested with powers for that purpose, to cause to be arrested and punished all who shall contravene the provisions of the present decree. Unfortunately, these special agents, consuls, and their deputies, are themselves the aggressors, and justify their proceedings under the laws of the republic and the decrees of the Executive Directory.

This analysis of the present decree manifests its futility; and, with some remarks on its preamble, will demonstrate it to be a bold imposture, intended to mislead the citizens of the United States into a belief, that the French government was going to put an end to the depredations of French cruisers on American commerce;

commerce; while the means propofed are fo grofs as to be an infult on our underftandings.

The preamble to the decree fets forth, " that information, recently received from the French colonies and the continent of America, leaves no room to doubt that French cruifers, or fuch as call themfelves French, have infringed the laws of the republic relative to cruifing and prizes;" and " that foreigners and pirates have abufed the latitude allowed at Cayenne and the Weft India iflands, to veffels fitted out for cruifing or for war and commerce, in order to cover with the French flag their extortions and the violation of the refpect due to the law of nations, and to the perfons and property of allies and neutrals." And Mr. Talleyrand, in one of his letters before noticed, dated the 22d of July laft, fpeaks of this information as having been " juft received."

But what has been more notorious than French depredations on neutral, and efpecially on American commerce, in violation of treaties, and the law of nations? Thefe have been coeval with the exifting war in Europe; but were multiplied under the loofe decree of the Executive Directory paffed the 2d of July 1796, declaring that " the flag of the French republic will treat neutral veffels, either as to confifcation, to fearches, or to capture, in the fame manner as they fhall fuffer the Englifh to treat them."

This decree committed the whole commerce of neutrals, in the firft inftance, to the rapacity of French privateers, and then to the difcretion of their agents, confuls, and tribunals. Thefe had only to fay, truly or falfely, that the Englifh treated neutrals in any given way, and then they were to treat them in the fame manner. Accordingly we have feen Santhonax and Raimond, commiffioners of the French government in St. Domingo, in their adjudication of an American veffel, on the 10th of January 1797, declare, " That the refolution (or decree) paffed by the Executive Directory, on the 2d of July 1796, prefcribes to all the armed veffels of the republic, and the armed veffels belonging to individuals, to treat neutral veffels in the fame manner as they fuffer the Englifh to treat them;" and " that it is in confequence of the above refolution of the Executive Directory, and in confequence of the manner in which the Englifh government in the Antilles treats neutral veffels, that the commiffion paffed their refolution of the 7th of January, by which they declare all neutral veffels bound to or from Englifh ports, to be legal prize." From thefe facts, and the tenour of the decree itfelf, we can form but one conclufion, That it was framed in fuch indefinite terms, on purpofe to give fcope for arbitrary conftructions, and confequently for unlimited oppreffion and vexation.

But without waiting for this decree, the commiffioners of the French government at St. Domingo began their piracies on the
commerce

commerce of the United States: and in February 1797, wrote to the minister of marine (and the extract of the letter appeared in the official journal of the Executive Directory of the 5th of June), " That having found no resource in finance, and knowing the unfriendly dispositions of the Americans, and to avoid perishing in distress, they had armed for cruising; and that already 87 cruisers were at sea; and that for three months preceding, the administration had subsisted, and individuals been enriched, with the product of those prizes."—" That the decree of the 2d of July was not known by them until five months afterwards. But (say they) the shocking conduct of the Americans, and the indirect knowledge of the intentions of our government, made it our duty to order reprisals, even before we had received the official notice of the decree."—" They felicitate themselves that American vessels were daily taken; and declare that they had learnt, by divers persons from the continent, that the Americans were perfidious, corrupt, the friends of England, and that therefore their vessels no longer entered the French ports, unless carried in by force."

After this recital, before the Council of Five Hundred, Pastoret makes the following remarkable reflections:

" On reading this letter, we should think that we had been dreaming; that we had been transported into a savage country, where men, still ignorant of the empire of morals and of laws, commit crimes without shame and without remorse, and applaud themselves for their robberies, as Paulus Æmilius or Cato would have praised themselves for an eminent service rendered to their country. Cruisers armed against a friendly nation! Reprisals, when it is we ourselves who attack! Reprisals against a nation that has not taken a single vessel of ours! Riches acquired by the confiscation of the ships of a people to whom we are united by treaties, and whom no declaration of war had separated from us!" The whole discourse of the agents may be reduced to these few words. " Having nothing wherewith to buy, I seize; I make myself amends for the property which I want, by the piracy which enriches me; and then I slander those whom I have pillaged."— " This is robbery justified by selfishness and calumny." Yet Santhonax, one of these robbers, and the chief of those Directorial agents, continued in office, and going a few months afterwards from Saint Domingo to France, was received as a member into one of the legislative councils.

Pastoret also adverts to a letter from Merlin, then minister of justice, and now a member of the Executive Directory, to Mr. Skipwith, consul general of the United States, which also appeared in the journal of the Directory; and quotes the following passage: " Let your government break the inconceivable treaty which it concluded on the 19th of November 1794, with our most implacable enemies; and immediately the French republic will cease to apply in its own favour the regulations in that treaty, which favour England to the injury of France; and I warrant you that we shall not see an appeal to those regulations, in any tribunal, to support unjust pretensions."—" Have I (says Pastoret) read this rightly? Unjust pretensions! Could it be possible that they should thus have been characterized by the minister, who is himself their agent and defender?"

After all, this " inconceivable British treaty" was itself but a pretext to countenance the " unjust pretensions," as Merlin himself calls them, used by the French government in its tribunals, for the purpose of condemning American vessels. The details I have already given prove it. I beg leave to adduce other evidence. It is the testimony of Mr. Barlow, an American by birth, but for several years past a citizen of France, a man of acknowledged discernment and talents, devoted to the French republic, and intimate with her leading men. Mr. Barlow has long resided at Paris, and cannot have mistaken the views of the French government, nor the motives of its conduct. Mr. Barlow's letter, dated at Paris the 1st of March 1798, to his brother-in-law Mr. Baldwin, has doomed the writer to infamy: yet when it describes the principles and conduct of the French republic, it merits attention. He says, " that act of submission to the British government, commonly called Jay's treaty, is usually considered, both by its friends and enemies, as the sole cause, or at least the great cause, of the present hostile disposition of the French republic towards the United States. This opinion (says he) is erroneous." He then proceeds to an enumeration of a variety of matters which he says have influenced the conduct of France. But the most provoking, and the most unpardonable of all the offences of the United States against France, was, fortunately, not an act of the government, but an act of the people. The freemen of the United States, " the true Americans," dared to exercise their independent rights, and, contrary to the wishes of the French government, and the endeavours and practices of its minister Adet, elected Mr. Adams to the office of president. Mr. Barlow's observations on this event further develope the character and the principles of that government. He says, " When the election of Adams was announced here, it produced the order of the 2d of March*, which was meant to be little short of a declaration of war:"—" the government here was determined to fleece you of your property, to a sufficient degree to bring you

---

* It will be recollected that this is the decree of the Executive Directory, ordering the capture and condemnation of American vessels, not having a *role d'equipage*— that truthful source of plunder to Frenchmen, and of ruin to American citizens; and which also declared all American seamen, making a part of the crew of enemies' ships, even when put on board them by force, to be pirates, and directed them to be treated as such.

to your feeling in the only nerve in which it was prefumed your fenfibility lay, which was your pecuniary intereft." And what was this "feeling" to produce? The anfwer is obvious—Submiffion to the will of the French government. The myftery of French politics is here unveiled. The United States did not fubmit: hence the non-reception of her envoys, and their haughty treatment: hence the infulting demands of tribute as a preliminary even to their reception; and hence the expulfion of two of them from France.

But to return to the decree of the Executive Directory of the 31ft of July laft.

I have already fhown that the mafs of depredations on the commerce of the United States, under the French flag, of which we fo juftly complain, are not thofe committed, as the Directory in their preamble infinuate, "by foreigners and pirates," but by French armed veffels commiffioned by the government or its agents; or whether commiffioned or not, whofe acts in capturing American veffels receive the fanction of French confuls, of French tribunals, and of the fpecial agents of the Directory. I have fhown that the laws of France and the Directorial decrees are themfelves the fources of thofe violations of treaties and the law of nations, which have caufed fuch immenfe loffes to the citizens of the United States. And to the proofs already offered, that the information of fuch aggreffions and abufes, particularly in the Weft Indies, and on the coaft of America, was not, as the preamble fuggefts, but "recently received," I may add, that their "fpecial agents" authorized thofe depredations and violations of the law of nations, by decrees affuming the laws of the republic, or the acts of the Executive Directory, for their bafes—by decrees printed and publifhed, and undoubtedly from time to time reported by thofe agents to the Directory itfelf. Further, thefe outrages on the American commerce have for years paft been the theme of every tongue, and filled columns in our newfpapers—thofe newfpapers which Mr. Barlow fays, "the office of Foreign Affairs (at Paris) regularly receives." I will conclude this point with the teftimony of Mr. Letombe, late conful general of the French republic, and ftill refiding in Philadelphia. He has long fince, and repeatedly, affured me, that he collected all thofe accounts of depredations and outrages committed by French privateers, and tranfmitted them to his government at Paris.

In relation to the depredations and outrages committed by the French on the commerce of the United States, I have faid that as great, if not as numerous abufes were practifed by the French in Europe, and even in France itfelf, as in her remote poffeffions: and that this fact was but too well known to our citizens, who had felt feverely their effects. Among thefe we have feen the cafe of the fhip Hare, Captain Hayley; but never in all its difgufting

Vol. VIII. K k

gusting features. With this I will close my observations on the preamble of the Directorial decree of the 31st July.

Extract of a Letter from Rufus King, Esq. Minister of the United States in London, dated September 3, 1798, to the Secretary of State of the United States.

"The pretence for this arreté (the decree of the Directory of July 31st) is of a piece with the vindication of Talleyrand respecting X, Y, and Z.; and the justice and sincerity of the Directory should be ascertained, not by their word, but by the following cotemporaneous fact.

"Hayley, an American citizen, master of the American ship Hare, lying in the port of London, laden with a rich cargo, the property of Americans, and bound to New York, went with my passport from London to Paris, where, in a personal interview, not with the agents of the minister of marine, but with the minister himself, he disclosed his plan of bringing the ship Hare and her cargo into France; and to enable him to receive the profits of the fraud, without risking the punishment of piracy, he demanded and received from the minister of marine a commission naming him the commander of a privateer that did not exist; with which in his pocket he returned to London; and soon after carried the ship Here and her cargo as a prize into France.

"The ship and cargo were both claimed by the American owners; and upon the unveiling of this infamous proceeding before the lower tribunals, the judges hesitated, and finally refused to sanction so unheard-of a fraud; though, instead of restoring the property to its lawful owners, they on some frivolous pretence adjudged both ship and cargo to be good prize to the nation. Lately the tribunal in the last resort, upon the appeal of Hayley, has reversed the judgment of the lower court, and 'decreed the ship and cargo to be condemned as good prize to this renegado.'

"If a transaction more grossly corrupt and infamous has occurred in the West Indies, I have not heard of it; and yet with this case of unequalled infamy and corruption before them, sanctioned by the highest tribunals of the nation, the Directory expect to amuse us with a disavowal of the conduct of a few subaltern agents, in a remote part of their dominions!!!"

Besides the communications from Mr. Gerry, I have received from Fulwar Skipwith, Esq. consul general of the United States at Paris, three letters, dated the 4th, 8th, and 22d of August, copies of which, and of the papers therein referred to, are herewith presented, excepting the decree of July 31st, which appears among the communications from Mr. Gerry. Mr. Skipwith's letter of August 22d, with its enclosures, was delivered to me by Doctor Logan; I had previously received the original, which had been brought over by Mr. Woodward of Boston.

Doctor Logan having been the bearer of the last-mentioned commu-

communications from the French government, and his embaſſy having not only engaged the attention of the public, but been made the ſubject of debate in Congreſs, I truſt it will not be deemed improper to introduce into this report ſome circumſtances reſpecting it.

On the 12th of November the Doctor came to me at Trenton—he advanced with eagerneſs, and handed me the packet from Mr. Skipwith. On examining its contents, I told the Doctor that I already poſſeſſed the ſame papers. I made ſome remarks on the decree of the Directory of the 31ſt of July, to ſhow that it was only oſtenſible and illuſory; and that it would not give any relief to the commerce of the United States. The Doctor, not conteſting my arguments or opinion, ſaid, that more was intended to be done; but that the Directory could not accompliſh it of themſelves; ſeeing it depended on the laws, which the legiſlative councils alone could change. I anſwered, that this was eaſy to be done; that as the Directory, on the 18th Fructidor (Sept. 4th, 1797), had garbled the two Councils, and baniſhed ſome and diſmiſſed others of the beſt members, all who were firmly oppoſed to their views; and as on the new elections to ſupply the vacancies and the new third of the Councils, the Directory ſent home every new member who was not agreeable to them, every body muſt ſee that the Directory had but to declare its will, and it would be obeyed. The Doctor ſaid, that the Directory was very well diſpoſed towards the United States, and deſired a reconciliation; that they would promote a reviſion of the laws in regard to privateering, ſo as to put the rights of neutral nations on a juſt footing; but that it would take ſome time to bring this about, " the people concerned in privateering having gained a very great influence in the two Councils!" ———! ———! Is it neceſſary to inquire how this " very great influence" has been obtained? Are the leading members owners of privateers? or do they receive their ſhares of prize-money from thoſe who are? Do the legiſlative Councils really act independently of the Directory? or does the ſame " influence" actuate both?—The printed diſpatches of our envoys, under the date of October 29, 1797, ſtate, on the information of Mr. Talleyrand's private agent X. that Merlin, one of the members, and now or late preſident of the Directory, was to receive no part of the douceur demanded of the envoys, becauſe he was paid by the owners of privateers; and in reſpect to the loan then demanded, on which ſubject it was ſuggeſted that one of the envoys ſhould go to America to conſult the government, the envoys " aſked Mr. X. if in the mean time the Directory would order the American property not yet paſſed into the hands of the privateerſmen, to be reſtored? He ſaid explicitly that they would not. The envoys aſked him whether they would ſuſpend further depredations on our commerce? He ſaid they would not:—but Mr. Talleyrand obſerved, that on this ſubject we could not ſuſtain

much

much additional injury, becaufe the winter feafon was approaching, when few additional captures could be made." Here we fee our envoys inquiring, not whether the two Councils would fufpend thofe depredations, but whether the Directory would do it; and Mr. Talleyrand's agent X. without intimating that the Directory wanted power, or that they could only " endeavour to provoke in the Legiflature a revifion of their maritime laws," anfwered peremptorily, that the Directory would not fufpend the depredations. The truth is, that it was an act of the Directory alone (their decree of the 2d of March 1797), which authorized and produced more extenfive depredations on the commerce of the United States than any other decree or law of the French republic. To effect a repeal of that decree, no application to the legiflative Councils could be neceffary. They could alfo have repealed another of their own decrees, that of the 2d of July 1796, which fubjected neutral property, and particularly that of American citizens, to the difcretion of their confuls and cruifers in the European feas, as well as of their privateers and agents in the Weft Indies, and on which thefe agents have founded other numerous decrees, which have occafioned thofe fhocking depredations and abufes there and on the coaft of the United States, which the Directory by their decree of the 31ft of July laft affect to reftrain.

When the Executive Directory wifhed to enlarge the field of depredations on neutral commerce, and on the 4th of January 1798 propofed to the two Councils the project of the iniquitous law, " to declare to be good prize every veffel and her cargo, to whomfoever belonging, if any part of the cargo came from England or her poffeffions," there was a ready obedience. " The Directory thinks it urgent and neceffary to pafs the law." The plan of a decree is reported to the Council of Five Hundred on the 11th; and, " urgency" being declared, is immediately and unanimoufly adopted. It goes to the Council of Ancients; that Council approves the act of " urgency ;" and on the 18th of January the project of the Directory becomes a law.

This law was neceffary for the French government. So many American veffels had been entrapped by the Directory's decree of March 2d, 1797, requiring the *rôle d'equipage*, that the refidue were now generally provided with that paper: fome new pretext was therefore requifite for " fleecing" the people of the United States of their property: and an ordinance of one of the kings of France, made near a century paft, having declared lawful prize the veffels and their cargoes in which was found Englifh merchandife belonging to enemies," the Directory declare that the provifions of this ordinance ought to be extended, to comprehend the veffels and cargoes of friends; that is, of allied and neutral nations. The Directory knew that the United States, whofe inhabitants were chiefly cultivators, required a greater fupply of Eng-

lifh

lish manufactures than any other neutral country of equal population; and those manufactures too were, from the course of American commerce, combined with almost all our mercantile operations, and pervaded entirely our great coasting trade. Hence it is evident that this law was chiefly aimed at them.

It will be remembered also, that this law was passed while our three envoys were at Paris, where they had passed three months unheeded by the French government, except by its indignities; and where they had in vain solicited to be heard on the just claims of our citizens, plundered and ruined under the former decrees of the republic. This time was preferred, in order to add insult to injury. The envoys had firmly resisted her demands of loans and douceurs; and when speaking of their country, dared to intimate, that it was independent: it was therefore requisite, on the French system, to "chastise," as well as to "fleece" it.

In closing this subject, it will be proper to notice an assertion of Mr. Talleyrand in a conversation with the envoys on the 2d March 1798. In reply to some observations of his respecting the proofs of friendship required by France from the United States, General Pinckney observed, "that the envoys being in France was a proof of the friendly disposition of our government; and that while they were there, the French government had passed a decree for seizing neutral vessels having on board any article coming out of England; which in its operation would subject to capture all our property on the ocean. Mr. Talleyrand replied, that this was not particular to us, but was common to all the neutral powers." This assertion of Mr. Talleyrand is not true. Although the decree in its terms is general, and applicable to all the neutral powers, yet, in its operation, it was not designed to be, and has not been so applied: it has not touched a vessel of Prussia. The motives to this exemption are obvious: France wished not, by irritating Prussia, to add so powerful a nation, and one so near at hand, to the number of her enemies, while her peace with Austria remained precarious. But this exemption of Prussian vessels from the operation of a general law, merits particular notice. It demonstrates that there exists in the French republic a dispensing power—a power above the laws—a power which can prevent their execution: and it is alike demonstrable, that this sovereign controlling power can exist, and in fact does exist, in the Executive Directory. It might then, if the Directory desired it, be exercised in the exemption of American as well as Prussian vessels: but the Directory do not desire it: we have not yet been sufficiently "fleeced" and "chastised."

Mr. Skipwith's letter of the 4th of August enclosed the decree of the Executive Directory already noticed, passed the 31st of July, respecting French depredations in the West Indies and on the coast of the United States. His letter of the 8th of August enclosed Mr.

Mr. Talleyrand's letter to him of the 6th, refpecting that decree, in which it is plain that the minifter fuppofes the world, and particularly the United States, will be amufed by that illufory device, and imagine that it was intended to ftop abufes, and give fecurity to neutral commerce.

Mr. Skipwith's letter of the 22d of Auguft covers another letter from Mr. Talleyrand, dated the 20th of Auguft, in which he enclofes copies of two letters from the minifter of marine refpecting American feamen who had been imprifoned. When in July laft an embargo was laid on the American merchant-veffels in the ports of France, the agents of the marine took out their crews, and threw them into prifon; thus hazarding the lofs of the veffels, and injuring the men by confinement and the bad provifions of their jails. Thefe feamen were ordered to be releafed. The other letter from the minifter of marine required that no injury fhould be done to the fafety and liberty of the officers and crews of American veffels found to be in order, nor to paffengers and other citizens of the United States having paffports and protections.

The fame letter from Mr. Skipwith enclofed the copy of a decree of the Directory paffed the 16th of Auguft, for taking off the embargo laid a month before on American veffels.

The decree itfelf occupies but two lines: but its preamble is extended, for the purpofe of infulting the government of the United States, when an act of common juftice was done to fome of their citizens; by infinuating that the government was "abandoned to the paffions of the Britifh cabinet." This, however, is but the repetition of a calumny familiar in French diplomacy, refpecting other nations as well as our own. Barras, prefident of the Directory, in his valedictory addrefs to Mr. Monroe, declared that "France would not abafe herfelf by calculating the confequences of the condefcenfion of the American government to the fuggeftions of her former tyrants:" profeffing at the fame time great "efteem for the American people." Mr. Adet had before charged the American government with a "perfidious condefcenfion to the Englifh;" and after making his laft communications to the government, he, by their immediate publication under his orders, appealed from the government to the people of the United States. Yet Mr. Talleyrand fays, that the French government has indeed "complained of the American government, but to the government itfelf;" meaning to have it underftood, though carefully avoiding the expreffion, that it had complained to the government alone. With the like fophiftry he attempts to evade our well-founded allegations, that the French government has made reproachful and injurious diftinctions between the government and people of the United States, endeavouring to feparate the latter from the former. He fays, "it is utterly falfe, notwithftanding the public and private infinuations which have been made, in private writings and in fo-

lemn

lemn acts, that the French government has ever sought to detach the people of the United States from the constitution they have given themselves." Such a charge against the French government has not, that I know, ever been made by the American government: but we have accused them, and truly, with endeavours to detach the people of the United States from the government chosen by themselves to administer that constitution: and this the minister does not attempt to deny. The Directory would perhaps be contented that the people should retain the forms of " the constitution they have given themselves," and to which they are attached, provided they would elect, to administer it, men devoted to France, and ready to obey the intimations of her will. And because the people have not been thus obsequious, but have dared to make a different election, the French government has expressed its " terrible" resentment. Mr. Barlow has assured us, in the passage already cited from his letter, that for this single act of the people of the United States, in exercising freely their right of election, the Directory passed a decree " which was meant to be little short of a declaration of war;" by which it " was determined to fleece the people of their property:" certainly in expectation that, by touching their feeling in that " nerve," they would be induced, in order to save their property, to submit implicitly to the government of France. Failing in this attempt, the French government made another, in the decree of the 18th of January 1798, which, though general in its terms, I have shown to have been levelled directly and chiefly at the commerce of the United States; and this at the time (as I have before remarked) when three envoys extraordinary were waiting, month after month, and most respectfully soliciting to be heard, and to enter on the discussion of all the subjects of difference between the two countries; and among these, on the French depredations on our commerce. Yet Mr. Talleyrand has the confidence to assert, and to Mr. Gerry too, one of those envoys, that the French government " never refused, and never will refuse, to enter into discussion upon every proper subject!" Does the minister mean that those depredations are not " a proper subject of discussion?" Yes, with respect to a vast proportion of them. Mr. Y. his private agent, explicitly told our envoys, that the condemnations of vessels for want of the rôle d'equipage were not to be questioned; " that being a point on which Merlin, while minister of justice, had written a treatise, and on which the Directory were decided."

It is fit here to recollect another and a peremptory refusal of the French government, " to enter into discussion" upon the subjects of difference between France and the United States.

General Pinckney, appointed the minister plenipotentiary of the United States to the French republic, went to Paris in the autumn

of

of 1796. There was at first (as in the case of the envoys extraordinary in 1797) a show of receiving him: but soon the scene was changed; and he was not only refused a hearing, and, after bearing a thousand indignities, ordered to leave France, but the predecessor of Mr. Talleyrand, Charles De La Croix, in a letter to Mr. Monroe, intended to be communicated to General Pinckney, declared (being specially charged to do so by the Directory, and Mr. De La Croix repeated the declaration to General Pinkney's secretary), " that it will not acknowledge nor receive another minister plenipotentiary from the United States, until after the redress of the grievances demanded of the American government, and which the French republic has a right to expect from it." To this resolution we have seen the Directory adhere; and we have also seen, in the demands it made to our envoys extraordinary, as the indispensable preliminaries to any negotiation, what it meant by a " redress of grievances," prior to the reception of a minister from America: it consisted in a douceur for the pockets of the Directors and ministers, in the purchase at par of thirty-two millions of Dutch securities, then worth but half that sum, and in loans as immense and indefinite as their depredations on our commerce.

The same letter from the French minister De La Croix to Mr. Monroe affords another proof of the aim and endeavours of the French government to separate the people from the government of the United States. In the sentence next following the above quoted passage, Mr. De La Croix says, " I pray you to be persuaded, Citizen Minister, that this determination having become necessary, allows to subsist between the French republic and the American people, the affection founded upon former benefits and reciprocal interests."

If I were to allow myself to make any further reflections on the conduct of France towards the United States, it would be to illustrate the truth of Mr. Barlow's assertion, that the French government determined to fleece us. If the French government " listened (as Mr. Talleyrand says it does) to nothing but justice," and really desired a reconciliation, it would have proposed to fix some measure of satisfaction for the injuries it said it had received. Or, if too proud to propose to us, at least it would have prescribed to itself some limit to reprisals; or, any rate, it would not have spurned us from its presence, when we respectfully presented ourselves, sought a reconciliation, and offered to make a just satisfaction for every injury we had committed. And if (as Mr. Talleyrand asserts) " the French government has not ceased to offer the exact justice it demands," it would also have permitted us to state our claims. But it would have been so easy to ascertain all the damages we had done; and their amount would have been so small, even if we agreed to pay for all English, Spanish,

and

and Dutch veſſels brought by French cruiſers into our ports, while all thoſe nations were at war with France, a few of which the juſtice of the federal courts, in vindication of the ſovereignty of the United States, reſcued from the hands of the French conſuls, agents, and privateerſmen; and if to that amount we alſo added ten times the value of the miſerable corvette Le Caſſius, a veſſel which had been unlawfully fitted out for war in the United States, but which had been the burden of every note from Adet's in 1795, to De La Croix's and Talleyrand's in 1796 and 1798, the amount of the whole, it was known, would be ſo ſmall, the French government did not chooſe to have it aſcertained: for then the injuries done by the French to the commerce of the United States muſt alſo have been examined and adjuſted; and when adjuſted, payment muſt have been made or ſtipulated: but in this, the French government doubtleſs thought " it would find only a real diſadvantage:" the amount of its own demands deducted from thoſe of America, would hardly ſeem to have diminiſhed the latter.

Such a mutual adjuſtment would alſo have been accompanied with a ſettlement of all queſtions and diſputes about the conſtruction of treaties, and all other ſubjects of difference: but in this alſo the French government, upon its own ſyſtem, " would have found real diſadvantage." For it would have vaſtly reduced the field for privateering in the European ſeas; and in the Weſt Indies it would have been nearly annihilated: for there, for every veſſel taken from the enemies of France, her cruiſers have probably captured twenty belonging to the United States. But the French government, by always abſtaining from making ſpecific demands of damages, by refuſing to receive our miniſters, by at length propoſing to negotiate in a mode which it knew to be impracticable, with the perſon who had no powers, and who therefore conſtantly refuſed to negotiate, and thus wholly avoiding a negotiation, it has kept open the field for complaints of wrongs and injuries, in order, by leaving them undefined, to furniſh pretences for unlimited depredations. In this way " it determined to fleece us:" in this way it gratified its avarice and revenge, and it hoped alſo to ſatiate its ambition. After a long ſeries of inſults unrelented, and a patient endurance of injuries aggravated in their nature, and unexampled in their extent, that government expected our final ſubmiſſion to its will. Our reſiſtance has excited its ſurpriſe, and has certainly increaſed its reſentment. With ſome ſoothing expreſſions, is heard the voice of wounded pride. Warmly profeſſing its deſire of reconciliation, it gives no evidence of its ſincerity, but proofs in abundance demonſtrate that it is not ſincere. From ſtanding erect, and in that commanding attitude requiring implicit obedience, cowering, it renounces ſome of its

Vol. VIII. L l unfounded

unfounded demands. But I hope we shall remember "tiger crouches before he leaps upon his prey."

Department of State,   TIMOTHY PICKER
January 18, 1799.

House of Representatives.

Message of the President of the United States to both Hou Congress, on Tuesday, January 8, 1799.

Gentlemen of the House of Representatives,

IN compliance with your desire, expressed in your re of the 2d of this month, I lay before you an extract of from George C. Morton, acting consul of the United S the Havannah, dated the 18th November 1798, to the f of state, with a copy of a letter from him to L. Trezev; William Timmons, Esqrs. with their answer. Althoug request extends no farther than such information as has b ceived, yet it may be a satisfaction to you to know, that, as this intelligence was communicated to me, circular notic given by my direction to all the commanders of our ve war, a copy of which is here transmitted. I also direct intelligence and those orders to be communicated to his B Majesty's envoy extraordinary and minister plenipotentiar United States, and our minister plenipotentiary to the C Great Britain, with instructions to him to make the proper sentations to that government upon this subject. It is but to say, that this is the first instance of misbehaviour of the British officers towards our vessels of war that has come knowledge. According to all the representations I hav the flag of the United States, and the officers and men, ha treated by the civil and military authority of the British in Nova Scotia, the West India islands, and on the ocean uniform civility, politeness, and friendship. I have no that this first instance of misconduct will be readily correct

January 8, 1799.   JOHN ADA

Extract of a Letter from G. C. Morton, Esq. acting Consu United States at the Havannah, dated there, November 18, to the Secretary of State.

"BY the delegation of Daniel Hawley, Esq. I am at acting as consul of the United States in this district, with he will most probably have acquainted you. It imposes u the mortifying task of informing you, Sir, of a partial of an American fleet under the convoy of the Baltimore f war, ——Phillips, Efq. commander, by a British fquadron off this harbour, accompanied with circumftances rather grating to the feelings of Americans, and by no means analogous to that good harmony which feems to fubfift between the two governments. The anfwer of Meffrs. Trezevant to my annexed note of the 17th inftant, requefting an exact relation of the occurrence, will, I prefume, be deemed as impartial a narration as can be given of the whole tranfaction, they having been paffengers on board one of the captured veffels, and removed to the Baltimore."

Mr. Morton adds, that Commodore Loring ordered the fifty-five men out of the Baltimore, " on board his fhip, previous to any propofal of exchanging the natives of one nation for thofe of the other; and retained five of the hands as being Britifh fubjects, without giving an equal number of Americans, whom he acknowledges to have on board."

To L. Trezevant and W. Timmons, Efqrs.

Gentlemen,

AS acting American conful for this city and diftrict, and of courfe obliged to forward the moft correct ftatement poffible to the government of the United States officially, I would beg the favour of you, Gentlemen, to furnifh me with an exact relation, under your fignature, of the unpleafant occurrence which took place off the Moro Caftle, on the 16th inftant, by which you will much oblige,

Havannah,
November 17, 1798.

Gentlemen,
Your moft obedient fervant,
(Signed) G. C. MORTON.

N. B. It would be proper to premife, that you were paffengers, and your diftance from the Moro Caftle at the time of capture.

Sir, *Havannah, Nov. 17, 1798.*

AGREEABLY to your requeft, we now commit to writing the beft account we are able to give you of the conduct of Captain Loring, commodore of the Britifh fquadron which was lately off the Moro, towards the United States fhip the Baltimore. We muft obferve, however, that all we can fay of it is from the information of Captain Phillips, as we were not on board of the Baltimore when fhe was vifited by Captain Loring's officers. In the morning of the 16th inftant we difcovered this fquadron when we were in fight of the Moro, and afterwards found

found it was composed of Captain Loring's ship the Carnatic, of 74 guns; Captain Cochet's ship the Thunderer, of the same force; Captain Dobson's ship the Queen, of 98 guns; Captain Donnelly's frigate the Maidstone, of 32 guns; and Captain Hardy's frigate the Greyhound, of the same force. We were passengers in the brig Norfolk, Captain Butler, which, together with the ship Eliza, Captain Baas, and the brig Friendship, Captain Fuller, were cut off from their entrance into port, and were all made prizes within gunshot of the Moro. We obtained leave to go on board the Baltimore without our baggage, and did so. When Captain Phillips discovered they were English ships, which was before we were taken, he stood towards them and spoke the commodore. After we got on board the Baltimore, the captain informed us that he had been on board the Carnatic, and the commodore had told him he should take out of the Baltimore all such men as had not American protections; that he had remonstrated with him against showing such an indignity to our flag; that to do so would leave him in a very defenceless state, and would deprive him of nearly all his men, as not even those who were really Americans, or at least very few of them, could show protections, because it was always thought our flag on board a government ship was a sufficient protection. All this, however, was urged in vain. Captain Phillips returned to his ship, and the commodore sent an officer on board the Baltimore, who carried away fifty-five of her men to the Carnatic. Captain Phillips remained in expectation that nearly all the rest would be taken from him; but whether the commander, on reflection, thought better of it, or whatever else might have been his motive, he sent back fifty, and kept five, among whom was the ship's boatswain. Captain Loring proposed to give up a number of American seamen, who, he said, were in his fleet, if Captain Phillips would give him English subjects for them. Captain P. refused this offer, and the American seamen were not delivered to him. Before any of the men were returned, he sent a message to Captain L. to let him know if he, or one of his officers, would go on board of him and point out who were Americans and who were not, he would return all the Americans; but this was declined also. After we got on board of the Baltimore, he sent a letter to Captain P. which he showed to us, in which the commodore "*demanded*" that he would give up all the British subjects on board the Baltimore. To this Captain P. replied, he could not know any of his men as British subjects, nor could he, as commander of a ship in the service of the United States, voluntarily give up any of his men; but if he thought fit to send an officer on board to take any number of his men, he should not oppose it. In this answer, Captain P. mentioned he should lay before the executive of the United States a full account of the occurrences of the day. Shortly after

sending

sending this squadron set sail and left the Baltimore. Commodore L. y polite to us, and was so to Captain P. when he went on board; but Captain P. complained of indecent behaviour from the inferior officers.

     LEWIS TREZEVANT.
     WILLIAM TIMMONS.
     G. S. MORTON, Esq. Vice-consul of the
      United States at the Havannah.

Circular Letter to the Commanders of armed Vessels in the Service of the United States, given at the Navy Department, December 29, 1798: alluded to in the above Message of the President of the 8th January.

Sir,

IT is the positive command of the President, that on no pretence whatever you permit the public vessel of war under your command to be detained or searched; nor any of the officers or men belonging to her to be taken from her by the ships or vessels of any foreign nation, so long as you are in a capacity to repel such outrage on the honour of the American flag. If force should be exerted to compel your submission, you are to resist that force to the utmost of your power, and when overpowered by superior force, you are to strike your flag, and thus yield your vessel as well as your men, but never your men without your vessel. You will remember, however, that your demeanour be respectful and friendly to the vessels and people of all nations in amity with the United States; and that you avoid as carefully the commission of, as the submission to insult or injury. I have the honour to be your obedient servant,

        BENJAMIN STODDERT.

New Negotiation between the United States of America and France.

Congress of the United States.

President's Message.

Gentlemen of the Senate,

I TRANSMIT you a document which seems to be intended to be a compliance with the condition mentioned at the conclusion of my message to Congress, of the 21st of June last.

"Always disposed and ready to embrace every plausible appearance of probability of preserving or restoring tranquillity, I nominate William Vans Murray, our minister resident at the Hague, to be minister plenipotentiary to the French republic.

If

If the Senate shall advise and consent to his appointment, effectual care shall be taken in his instructions, that he shall not go to France without direct and unequivocal assurances from the French government, signified by their minister of exterior relations, that he shall be received in character; shall enjoy the privileges attached to his character by the law of nations; and that a minister of equal rank, title, and powers, shall be appointed to treat with him, to discuss and conclude all controversies between the two republics by a new treaty.

United States, Feb. 18, 1799. JOHN ADAMS.

(Copy.)

Liberty. (L. S.) Equality.—*Exterior Relations, 3d Division.*

Paris, 7th Vendemiaire, 7th Year of the French Republic, one and indivisible.

The Minister of Exterior Relations to Citizen Pichon, Secretary of Legation of the French Republic to the Batavian Republic.

I HAVE received successively, Citizen, your letters of the 22d and 27th Fructidor; they afford me more and more reason to be pleased with the manner you have adopted, to detail to me your conversations with Mr. Murray. Those conversations, at first merely friendly, have acquired consistency by the sanction I have given to them by my letter of the 11th Fructidor. I do not regret that you have trusted to Mr. Murray's honour a copy of my letter. It was intended for you only, and contained nothing but what is conformable to the intentions of government. I am thoroughly convinced, that, should explanations take place with confidence, between the two administrations, irritations would cease, a cloud of misrepresentations would disappear, and the ties of friendship would be more strongly united, as each party would discover the hand that sought to dispute them.

But I will not conceal from you, that your letters of the 2d and 3d Vendemiaire, just received, surprise me much. What Mr. Murray is still dubious of, has been explicitly declared, even before the President's message to Congress of the 3d Messidor last was known in France. I had written it to Mr. Gerry, namely, on the 24th Messidor and 4th Thermidor. I did not repeat it to him before he set out. A whole paragraph of my letter to you of the 11th Fructidor, of which Mr. Murray has a copy, is devoted to develope still more the fixed determination of the French government, according to these bases. You were right to assert, that whatever plenipotentiary the government of the United States should send to France, to put an end to existing differences between the two countries, would be undoubtedly received with the

respect

respect due to the representative of a free, powerful, and independent nation.

I cannot, Citizen, conceive that the American government need any farther declaration from us to induce them, in order to renew the negotiations, to adopt such measures as would be suggested to them by their desire to bring the differences to a peaceable end.

If misunderstandings on both sides have prevented former explanations from reaching that end, it is presumable that those misunderstandings being done away, nothing henceforth will bring obstacles to the reciprocal dispositions. The President's instructions to his envoys at Paris, which I have only known by the copy given you by Mr. Murray, and received by me the 21st Meſſidor, announcing (if they contain the whole of the American government's instructions) dispositions which could only be added to those which the Directory has always entertained; and notwithstanding the irritating and hostile measures they have adopted, the Directory has manifested its perseverance in the sentiments which are set forth both in my correspondence with Mr. Gerry, and in my letter to you of the 11th Fructidor, and which I have herein before repeated in the most explicit manner. Carry, therefore, Citizen, to Mr. Murray those positive expressions, in order to convince him of our sincerity, and prevail on him to transmit them to his government.

I presume, Citizen, that this letter will find you at the Hague; if not, I ask that it may be sent back to you at Paris.

  Health and fraternity.
  (Signed) CH. MAU. TALLEYRAND.

 Gentlemen of the Senate,

THE proposition of a fresh negotiation with France, in consequence of advances made by the French government, having excited so general an attention, and so much conversation, as to have given occasion to many manifestations of the public opinion, by which it appears to me that a new modification of the embassy will give more general satisfaction to the nation, and perhaps better answer the purposes we have in view:

It is upon this supposition, and with this expectation, I now nominate Oliver Ellsworth, Esq. chief justice of the United States, Patrick Henry, Esq. late governor of Virginia, and William Vans Murray, our minister resident at the Hague, to be envoys extraordinary and ministers plenipotentiary to the French republic, with full powers to discuss and settle by a treaty all controversies between the United States and France.

It is not intended that the two former of these gentlemen shall

shall embark for Europe until they shall have received from the Executive Directory direct and unequivocal assurances, signified by their secretary of foreign relations, that they shall enjoy all the prerogatives attached to that character by the law of nations, and that a minister or ministers of equal power shall be appointed and commissioned to treat with them.

February 25, 1799. JOHN ADAMS.

Turco-Russian Proclamation to the People of Corfou, published after the Capitulation of that Place.

THE commanders of the combined squadrons of his Majesty the Emperor of all the Russias, Vice-admiral Uschakow, and of his Majesty the Grand Seignior, Capitan Bey, Cadir Bey, to all the inhabitants of the city and island of Corfou. Corfou has surrendered to the victorious arms of the two Empires, and obtained a generous capitulation. The French garrison is at liberty on its parole, and has been granted safety and protection until it shall embark for France. A full and complete amnesty to the inhabitants of all classes: their religion, properties, and persons are guaranteed, and an entire oblivion of the past has been required. People of all ranks, and of all nations, respect these dispositions dictated by humanity. Let animosities cease; let the spirit of revenge be silent; let peace, order, and concord, reign through the whole island. If any one shall dare to violate these principles, we declare he will incur our indignation, and shall be severely punished. It is strictly forbidden to the Russian, Turkish, and Albanian troops, to exercise the least usurpation of power. The Russian troops will enter to take possession of the ports of Corfou. The Ottoman troops, pursuing their destination, will march under the command of Patrona Bey. The other troops, and particularly the Albanians, shall not be at liberty to enter the forts and cities without leave from the commanders in chief of the two squadrons. Those who shall dare to transgress this order, and to enter them by force, shall be punished as rebels and violators of the supreme wills of the government and the Emperors, his Majesty of all the Russias, and his Majesty the Grand Seignior.

Given on board the admiral's ship, St. Paul, the 21st of February.

(Signed) CAPITAN BEY.
CADIR BEY.
VICE-ADMIRAL USCHAKOW.

Declaration

Declaration of War against the United States.

Arreté.

THE particular agent of the Executive Directory at Guadaloupe and its dependencies, has, ever since his arrival in the colony, confirmed the dispositions of the Executive Directory of the French republic, with respect to neutral and allied nations; his measures have been calculated to keep union and harmony, and to cause their colour and their property to be respected.

Those measures were scrupulously observed with regard to the Americans. The citizens of that nation, who were detained, on his arrival have been released. Those who were destitute of means have been supplied with succours which their situation required; and cartels were dispatched at the expense of the republic, to convey them to New York. The cargoes and ships seized and carried into the ports of Guadaloupe and its dependencies, were restored to the owners; and, to add to the proofs of our aversion from vexations and hostilities, the armed schooner of the United States, the Revenge, was sent back to the President.

The particular agent of the Directory could not, without astonishment and indignation, be informed, that in contempt of the free and open conduct observed in respect to that nation, Mr. Truxton, commanding the American ship Constellation, mounting 50 guns, insulted the colours of the French republic, and took, in an action wherein he was aggressor, the frigate Insurgent, whose captain had positive orders to respect the American flag.

Such a piece of hostility, exercised without a declaration of war, has induced measures, the event of which leaves no doubt that the American officer, in thus acting, followed the orders and instructions of his government.

From the above facts, and the hostilities which are daily committed by the Americans since the capture of the Insurgent,

The particular agent of the Executive Directory,

Considering, that it is his duty to cause the flag of the French republic to be respected, to protect commerce and the seamen from the risks they have to run from the Americans, who are cruising in force on these coasts;

To adopt measures which may be the least prejudicial to negotiations that may have begun between the two nations; and which may justify self-defence against aggression and insults, and even to prevent them;

Resolves as follows:

I. The captains and officers who command the vessels of the republic, and those armed from the ports of Guadaloupe and its dependencies, are authorized, from the date of the publication of the present resolve, to pursue all American vessels, whether belonging to the government or to individuals, to seize and capture them without distinction, and bring them into the ports of Guadaloupe and its dependencies.

II. The vessels belonging to the American government shall be kept to be used according to the order of the Executive Directory.

III. Such as are the property of individuals, and which may contravene the laws of the republic, and the resolves of the Executive Directory, respecting neutrals and allies, and liable to condemnation, agreeably to the purport of those same laws and resolves, shall be, as well as their cargoes, condemned by a judgment of the tribunal of commerce, and sold for the profit of the captors, according to custom.

IV. The merchant-vessels, the papers of which shall have been acknowledged by the tribunal to be regular, and not liable to condemnation, shall be sold, together with their cargoes, and the proceeds thereof deposited in the public coffers, that it may afterwards be delivered either to the captors or owners, agreeably to the orders of the Executive Directory.

V. In the foregoing dispositions are included all American vessels and their cargoes, detained in the ports of Guadaloupe and its dependencies ever since information was received of the capture of the Insurgent.

The present resolve shall be read, published, posted up, and registered in the tribunal of commerce and control of the navy.

All public functionaries, owners and commanders of the ships of the republic, and privateers, whom it concerns, are hereby ordered to conform to the same.

Done at Basseterre, in the national house of the agent, the 24th Ventose (14th March 1799), 7th year of the French republic, one and indivisible.

(Signed) DESCHAMPS,
Particular Secretary for the
General Secretary.

A true copy. (Signed) DESFOURNEAUX.

Proclamation of General Klenau to the Inhabitants of Outrè-Po, published 19th April 1799.

WE, Comte de Klenau, general of brigade and commandant of the province of Polesine for his Royal Imperial Apostolic Majesty, having been informed, that the inhabitants of Outrè-Po have taken up arms, cannot approve in anywise of such a measure, unless in the case of their being called upon for the defence of their properties, or to protect themselves against the incursions of the common enemy. In consequence, we invite and command them, in the name of his Majesty the Emperor, our august sovereign, not to take up arms but in the above cases, and to abstain from

making

making excursions, the consequence of which would be to introduce disorder into their country. A people good and faithful to their sovereign ought to remain tranquil in their habitations, and leave to the victorious army of his Majesty the care of conquering and punishing those who shall have proved traitors to their country and their sovereign. In such case where the military force may judge it proper to invite the people to unite themselves to it, then only should the inhabitants march, lend their assistance, and give proofs of their attachment to the good cause. But, in any other case, the commanders of my troops have orders not only to prevent all kinds of excess, but further to punish whoever shall have the audacity to plunder or mal-treat their fellow-citizens, whose sentiments his Majesty reserves to himself the right of examining, and judging their opinion.

Head-quarters at Sustinenti, 19*th April* 1799.

Address from the Emperor of Germany to his former Subjects.

People of Lombardy,

IT is not your sovereign but your sincere friend who now addresses you: it is a tender parent, who, pitying your extreme misery, would again receive you to his bosom with open arms; in one hand he shows you the thunder of his artillery; in the other, the olive-branch of peace. With the first, he would defend you from your oppressors, with the other, he wishes to restore peace, justice, and your holy religion. Dear children! receive your friends in your devastated plains, and you will soon perceive new life springing all around.—Cordially unite with your parent to re-open the way to happiness, a foreign power not less than his own has joined him, by which religion must once more triumph.

April. 22*th*, 1799.   FRANCIS.

Proclamation of J. M. Musset, Commissary of the French Government in Piedmont.

Piedmontese,   *Turin, April* 26.

THE enemies of liberty, the men who will never forgive you for breaking your chains, are employed anew, and threaten to disturb your tranquillity. I will point them out to you by certain marks. One time they will tell you, that your religion and your worship are menaced; another time, that the public fortune is to be invaded, or else they will complain, with the perfidious zeal of hypocrisy, that the benefits of the new organization do not extend to communes rendered interesting by their patriotism and population; that certain men, invested with public functions, do
not

not deserve your confidence. Such, Piedmontese, are the discourses of those vile persons in the pay of Austria and England, who assume and throw off by turns, and according to circumstances, the emblems of liberty and the colours of royalism. By these speeches, equally perfidious and absurd, you may recognise your real enemies, those who would excite between you and the French people oaths of hatred and discord, and deprive you of a faithful and generous friend; repel them with horror and indignation; and recollect, that free men are strong only by unanimity.

Need I repeat, that your religion and your form of worship shall be maintained and protected; and that such is the express will of the French government? After this authentic declaration, let malevolence and hypocrisy be silent.

Every commune not being able to bear the establishment necessarily too expensive, the distribution of the advantages which they present, shall be made with strict impartiality.

If in the choice of citizens invested with public functions some do not deserve the general confidence, they shall be removed as soon as the voice of the people shall have made them known. Piedmontese, who have entered upon the career of liberty with so much energy and courage, will you draw back at the voice, at the perfidious suggestion of those men who would again bend you ignominiously under the yoke of despotism? Shall your brave brethren who fight with glory at the side of republican phalanxes, hear that you know not how to preserve in your homes that liberty which they are cementing with their blood in the field of honour?

No: Piedmontese! you will be calm and tranquil. You will resist the hypocritical insinuations of your cowardly oppressors; you will watch over them, you will unmask those men, slaves by choice and habit; the constituted authorities shall second your efforts; and you shall not have sworn to be free in vain.

Vive la liberté!   J. M. MUSSET.

Proclamation of Massena, General in Chief, to the Inhabitants of Helvetia, published about the 28th April.

Citizens,

THE enemy, who is advancing towards your territories, and who knows the resolution which you have taken to defend, even to death, your homes, your independence, and your constitution, less confident than he affects to appear, is endeavouring to deceive and disunite you. He talks of his victories, as though he had already forgot his defeats, or as if he flattered himself, by terrifying you, to avoid the necessity of fighting you. He represents himself as having been attacked, while his aggression is manifest in every quarter: in Italy, by the audacity excited at Naples, by the plots concerted at Turin, by the acknowledged conspiracy at Florence; in Germany, by the shackles put on the negotiations at Rastadt, by a constantly active participation in the intrigues of England, by the calling in and march of the Russians, as also by the invasion of the territory of the Leagues, which would still groan under a foreign tyranny, if the French republic had not given the orders which I executed, to expel from the country of the Grisons, after a previous summons, the troops which had entered there, in contempt of an acknowledged neutrality, for the purpose of restraining the wishes of a people who solicited a prompt and complete union with Helvetia. Citizens of Helvetia! let not Austria impose on you. To-day she flatters you; to-morrow, if she was received, she would carry among you slavery or death. Since the commencement of 1798 she has formed a plan of invading you, since that æra she has formed a party among you, and caused it to present her with addresses, in one of which the Abbé of Notre-Dame-des-Hermites tells her, "that Helvetia wished to become a province of Austria." But your indignation has rejected her councils and her promises: you have associated your cause with that of the French; they are inseparable. Let us unite our efforts, our labours, and successes. Every thing shall be in common to us both. The army which I command is to be entirely employed in securing the integrity of your territory. Let your battalions be organized, and combat in the ranks with ours, and shortly the enemy, driven from your frontiers, shall have received from his aggression nothing but the chagrin of seeing Helvetia, increased, fortified, and ready to assume a more advantageous situation, the fruit of an organization of which Austria wishes to deprive her, because she foresees and dreads its effects.

      (Signed) MASSENA.

Examination of the Six Couriers belonging to the Margrave of Baden, who were taken by the French Plenipotentiaries to Seltz; taken in consequence with the Demand of the Sub-delegation of Baden.

1. ANDREW Caspar declares in his deposition, that he drove the carriage of the minister Jean Debry; that at his departure, he had been ordered by the minister Bonnier to answer, in case he should be stopped and asked whom he drove, that they were the French ministers; that he was in effect stopped by some of the Royal Imperial hussars at the entrance of the valley of Rheinau, that the aforesaid question was put to him, to which he gave the answer as directed; that being asked where Bonnier was, and the name of the person whom he drove, he answered, Bonnier was in the second carriage, and Jean Debry was in his; that on
                this

this information, a greater number of huffars rode up to the carriage, and dragged out of it the minifter Debry, and the ladies with him, and immediately attacked the former with their fabres, pulled the women after them, and fearched them; that he himfelf received a blow with the flat of a fabre, on which he dropped down between his horfes; that he was then afked who he was, and having anfwered he was coachman to the Margrave, he was affured no injury fhould be done to him.

2. James Ohnweiler depofes, that he faw Jean Debry receive feveral blows with fabres; but at the fame time fome huffars rode up to his carriage, which was the third, and afked him who was in it; that having anfwered he drove Bonnier, feveral huffars rode up to the door on both fides of the carriage, and cried, " Alight, Bonnier!" They inftantly broke the windows, dragged the minifter out, and maffacred him before his eyes at the fide of his faddle-horfe; that they afterwards plundered the minifter, and the contents in the carriage; that he alfo thought he heard Bonnier make lamentations in French, and pronounce the word " Pardon."

3. James Weifs depofes, that he drove the fourth carriage, in which was the fecretary of legation Rofentiel; that he faw Debry and Bonnier dragged out of the carriages which were before: the treatment experienced by the former happened at too great a diftance for him to make obfervations, but he diftinctly heard the huffars cry, " Where is Bonnier?" that he faw them drag Bonnier out of the carriage, and ftrike him at the fame time with their fabres on the legs, and cut him to pieces, when he fell on the ground. With refpect to Roberjot, the huffars, after the maffacre of Bonnier, galloped to his carriage, and cut him to pieces. Roberjot, bathed as he was in his blood, giving ftill fome figns of life, a huffar on foot ftruck him fix times with his fabre.

4. The 4th coachman depofes, that his carriage was at the fame time attacked by the huffars; he was afked the name of the minifter whom he drove, but as he did not know, they applied to the fervant on the coach-box, and having learned that it was Roberjot, they faid, " Ah! 'tis he:" they opened the door, dragged out the minifter, and by the order of one of the under-officers, who fpoke Hungarian, they maffacred him in a horrible manner, ftripped him of his clothes, and renewed their attacks while there appeared the leaft fign of life. Madame Roberjot was alfo torn out of the carriage, and entreated them repeatedly, in bad German, to put her to death with her hufband.

(Signed)   J. H. W. MULLER.

Done at Raftadt 10th Floreal (29th April), in the prefence of M. Poffelt.

Proclamation

Proclamation of General Suwarrow to the Inhabitants of Lucerne and St. Martin, in the West of Piedmont.

PEOPLE, what part have you taken? Seduced peasants, you support the French, the disturbers and enemies of the public tranquillity, while tranquillity can alone secure our existence and happiness. The French have declared themselves the enemies of Jesus Christ; and the ancient attachment of your fathers to the precepts of Christianity has procured you the protection of England. The French are now the enemies of that power, your benefactress, our ally at this very moment. Supported by our forces, and animated by our victories, as well as by the assistance which the God of the Christians deigns to grant his warriors, we are arrived at the foot of your mountains, and on the point of entering them, if you continue to persist in your blindness. Inhabitants of the vallies of St. Lucerne and St. Martin, the time of repentance is not yet past; hasten to join our banners; for they are blest by Heaven, and victorious on earth. The fruits of the plain are at your disposal, if you become our friends; and the mighty protection of England shall be continued to you; the more so, as your conscience will never permit you to expose yourselves to the galling reproach of having been the satellites of your tyrants and seducers, in uniting with us you will become the defenders of true liberty and tranquility.

(Signed)   SUWARROW RIMNISKOY.

The following is the Declaration published by M. Von Steiger, late Schultheiss, or Mayor of Berne, and entitled, " The Declaration of the United Swiss, who have returned for the Restoration of their Country."

SWISS, brethren, confederates! who yet wish well to your country, collect your last strength, and exert it to obtain vengeance; for now is the time : come, unite with those worthy Swiss who have assembled to deliver their country, and extirpate the common enemy, who has subjugated you. Confide in God, who will protect the just cause ; confide in German integrity and fidelity, which never has broken its word. Receive as friends the Austrian armies, who come for your deliverance, and solemnly assure you that they will again restore your ancient independence, your laws, rights, and government. They have the same views and wishes with yourselves; unite with them, follow their directions, and assist them with your advice and exertions as much as may be in your power. At their head is a prince of the House of Austria, who, by his splendid yet modest virtues, has acquired the greatest glory throughout Europe, and the love of millions of men who honour

nour him as their father and deliverer. Under his orders is a distinguished general (Hotze), who himself is a native and a brave Swifs; who seeks the crown of his military glory in the deliverance of his country, and the freedom of his fellow-citizens.

He will lead you on, and share all labours and all dangers with you. Fear not, therefore, but prove yourselves worthy of your noble ancestors, who shall look down upon you from heaven with complacence. They would have expired with shame, could they have known that their descendants would ever have submitted to so disgraceful a yoke. Fall then upon the enemy, who infolently calls you to his affiitance, and extirpate him, that your country may be freed and fecured from fimilar violence for ever. Then may we expect from our endeavours, with the powerful support and blessing of God, that the reign of crime shall have an end, guilt receive its punishment, religion and justice again return among us, agriculture, manufactures, and trade flourish, oppression of every kind cease, and public tranquillity and domestic happiness be once more restored. Then shall we be again a free and virtuous people, respected abroad, and happy at home, as we formerly were.

With these views, we return to you, to fight for you, or die with you.

Dated Ravensbourg, FREDERICK VON STEIGER,
1st May. Late Mayor of Berne, in the name
 of all the United Swifs.

Proclamation of Suwarrow to the Italians.

Nations of Italy,

THE victorious army of the Roman and Apostolic Emperor is now here; it is only fighting for the re-establishment of your holy religion, of the clergy, nobility, and the ancient government of Italy. People, unite with us for your God and faith: we are at Milan and at Placenza to support you.

 (Signed) SUWARROW,
Castel Pasterlengo, Commander in Chief of the Austro-
May 2d, 1799. Russian Army.

Proclamation to the Inhabitants of the Bas-Vallais.

WE the undersigned generals, commanding in chief the two invincible and combined armies of Austria and Russia, moved with pity, invite the people of the Bas-Vallais, by these presents, to lay down their arms without delay, in consideration that it is not our intention to bring upon them the pestilence of war,

war, and make conquests, but that our arms are directed by the sacred and immutable principles of justice, and are wielded only for the re-establishment and preservation of our holy religion, and of good order, which has received an universal shock. If, in contempt of our proclamation; if, notwithstanding the ties which unite you to the *ci-devant* Haut-Vallais; if, in disregard of the desire of his Royal Imperial Majesty, announced in the proclamation of Prince Charles, dated the 30th of March last, to see re-established in Helvetia the former and legal order of things, any of you shall be found in arms, we now declare to you, that he shall be put without mercy to the sword; that his goods shall be confiscated, and that not even the wives and children of such shall be spared, as an example to all mutineers. Christian brethren, become, therefore, yourselves: turn your arms against your real enemies, who impose on you under the name of friends; think that it is your last hour, and that you have only an instant to choose your part.

Done at Brigue, the 11th of May 1799.
(Signed)   MILLORADOWITZ.
                WUKASSOVICH.

Proclamation of Field-marshal Suwarrow, May 12th.

Nations of Italy!

TAKE up arms; unite under banners which are fighting for God and the faith; and you shall triumph over perfidious enemies. The army of his Majesty our most exalted Emperor and King are fighting, provoked by the French, and shedding their blood in defence of our most holy religion, for the recovery of your property, and the re-establishment of your former government. Do not the French demand every day immense sums of you? do not they demand uncommon requisitions? and all this under the chimerical name of liberty and equality, which are even so painful to the heads of families, deprive them of their dear children, and force them to take up arms and fight against your lawful sovereign, your loving father, and most zealous defender? Nations, be of comfort! there is a God who protects, and armies that defend you. See the number of troops! See a new complete army sent by the allied Emperor of Russia; behold those prudent nations, every where full of enthusiasm, to terminate this bloody war in the most speedy manner. That faithful numerous army, consisting of brave warriors, comes to deliver Italy. Fear nothing: wheresoever the armies combating against the French republic shall come, you shall see the laws restored, religion exalted, and private and public tranquillity revived, which has been for these three years past under a heavy yoke. The faithful ministers of religion,

ligion, too, shall be re-installed in their offices and property. But hear! should there ever be found among you one so perfidious, that shall either take arms against our sovereign, or favour in any manner the enterprises of the French republic, such a perfidious man shall immediately be shot, without regard to quality, birth rank, office, or condition; and his family, houses, and property shall be persecuted and destroyed. Your prudence, nations of Italy! gives hopes, that being now convinced of the justice of the cause, you will furnish no occasion of inflicting those rigorous measures and irremissible punishments, but that you will rather manifest proofs of your fidelity and attachment towards so beneficent and loving a sovereign.

(Signed)   L. Suwarrow.

Extract from the Register of Deliberation of the Agency of the Executive Directory at St. Domingo.

Decree relative to the Re-establishment of commercial Connexions between the Colony of St. Domingo and the United States of America.

THE agent of the Executive Directory at St. Domingo, considering that the infractions done against the rights of nations by the French privateers, or those calling themselves so, have occasioned great discontents amongst several neutral nations, particularly the United States of America, where differences appear to be on the point of breaking out between that government and ours:

That the agent Hedouville, penetrated by the necessity of taking measures capable of preventing the cessation of commerce between St. Domingo and the United States, excepted by his decree on the 9th Floreal, 6th year, from the dispositions of the law of the 29th Nivose of the same year, neutral vessels bound for St. Domingo whatever might be the nature of their lading; and stipulated by a second decree of the 30th Messidor following, new assurances in favour of these vessels, particularly for the Americans, even in case of hostilities between the republic and one of the powers actually neuter:

That at the same epoch, the Executive Directory published it decree of the 13th Thermidor, 6th year, which establishes the securities, against the abuse of which our allies the American complain:

That notwithstanding the wisdom and publicity of these three decrees, things have arrived to such a degree of animosity, that the government of the United States has judged it proper to persist in the hostile attitude which it has taken:

That nevertheless, the general in chief, Toussaint L'Ouverture, finding himself alone charged with the whole burden of the government during the vacancy of the agency, and desirous, after

having

having pacified the colony, to turn away the horrible famine with which it was threatened, had the prudence and patriotism to commission the Citizen Bunel to go to offer to the American government, views for the re-establishment of a commerce not less necessary to America than to St. Domingo:

That in consequence of propositions of the General in Chief, the Congress has given power to the President to renew the transactions of commerce with the French, if it should appear to be of utility to his country:

That in virtue of this authority, the President has charged the Citizen Stevens to pass to the Cape, in quality of consul general, for the purpose of renewing commerce, on the ground that the privateers shall be prevented from continuing their excesses, and that all the abuses which may appear to exist shall be suppressed:

That the objects of the mission of Citizen Stevens having been discussed between him and the General in Chief, the Agent, the Comptroller Dumaine, and the Ordonnateur Idlinge, it has been agreed that the articles adopted on the one part and the other, shall be formally established by a decree of the agency:

Considering that besides the complaints made to the Executive Directory by the government of the United States, other complaints of the same nature have been made of the agents of the Directory at St. Domingo, by the Batavian governor of Curaçoa, and by the Spaniards, chiefs of the captaincy-general of Curaçoa, who have positively assured them, that their colonies would become totally bare of provisions and clothing, if, for a longer time, there are permitted to subsist, in these seas, the rigorous dispositions of the laws and decrees which the Legislative Body and the Directory did not promulgate, but from a single consideration applicable to Europe, and not with an intention to ruin the colonies of France and her allies:

Considering, in short, that while the French and American governments are agreeing on the reciprocal reparation which may be required, the agency ought not to suppose that they will ever come to a declaration, of which our common enemies would alone profit, by the annihilation of the commerce of America, and the destruction of the produce of St. Domingo:

And that from this principle, it is the duty of the agency to take upon its responsibility all the measures necessary for the preservation of St. Domingo, and the colonies of our allies; as these measures are too urgent to postpone until the reception of new orders from the national government: decrees,

Art. I. The decree *(arrêté)* of the Executive Directory, of the 13th of Thermidor, 6th year, relative to French privateers, and to neutral vessels, shall be published immediately in the principal places of the departments of the north, of the west, and of the south of St. Domingo, in order that it shall be executed according to its form and tenour, except so much of it as is altered by the second article of this decree. In consequence, therefore, there shall not in future be any commissions granted to cruising vessels or merchantmen, but by the agent himself; and those which he left signed, blank, on his departure from the city of St. Domingo, shall be annulled. All those heretofore granted, are to be regarded as not of force after the 30th day from the date of this decree; and the privateers shall return to port and deliver up their commissions within the same period of thirty days, under pain of encountering the risk of being considered as pirates.

The agent will carefully cause to be respected the persons and property of the Americans, and other neutrals and allies. The administrator of the marine shall not be permitted to treat for, or take their cargoes, contrary to their own will, and they shall punctually comply with the conditions of their agreements.

II. The owners *(armateurs)* and captains of the privateers furnished with commissions by the agency, shall conform themselves exactly to the laws of the 23d of Thermidor, and the 3d of Brumaire, 4th year, as well as to the ordinances and regulations which preceded them, and which the first of these laws maintains in activity. The laws of the Legislative Body, and the decrees of the Executive Directory, posterior to the law of the 3d Brumaire, 4th year, shall not be carried into execution against American vessels of commerce, whether armed or not, nor against those of other nations, neutral and allies.

III. The state vessels of America alone, or convoying vessels of commerce to the French ports of St. Domingo, as well as all other American vessels, may remain in them, and purchase such articles as they may have occasion for; they shall be under the safeguard of the national honour on their arrival, during their stay and at their departure.

IV. All preceding decrees of the agents of the Executive Directory shall be considered as null, whenever they counteract the dispositions of the present decree.

V. The security prescribed and required by the law of the 23d Thermidor, shall continue to be 50,000 livres of France; and if to evade the present decree, the privateers should send their prize otherwise than to St. Domingo, to our allies, or to those ports where there are French receivers, the owner *(armateur)* and his security shall be held effectually to answer, for the benefit of the proprietor of the captured vessel, all costs, expenses, and damages which may result from a definitive judgment.

VI. Nothing is changed relative to the sentences on neutral vessels already captured. Those which shall be captured through ignorance of the present decree, during the thirty days from the date hereof, shall be immediately released without indemnity o
th

the part of the captors; after the expiration of that term, the captains of the privateers who shall make prizes in violation of this decree, shall answer personally for all damages, and shall be incapable of commanding during the war.

VII. The Citizen Edward Stephens is provisionally authorized to fulfil the powers of consul-general of the United States, but subject to the definitive authorization of the Executive Directory.

The Citizen Jacob Mayer is provisionally authorized to perform the functions of consul at the Cape. The provisional consul-general may discuss and object to the solidity of the securities (to be given by privateers) before the comptroller and ordonnateur; and the commissary of the executive power shall decide on the question.

VIII. The agency will also authorize, provisionally, American consuls in the other towns of the colony, where such establishments may be necessary.

IX. Whoever shall contravene any of the foregoing dispositions, shall be punished conformably to law.

X. The present decree shall be immediately transmitted to the Executive Directory for its approbation; and, in the mean time, shall be provisionally executed. It shall also be addressed to the civil and military authorities of the colony, to the commission of St. Domingo, to the receivers of the republic in the neighbouring islands, and shall be inscribed on the registers of the civil and commercial tribunals.

Done at Cape François, the 6th Floreal (May 12), 7th year of the French republic, one and indivisible.

Signed on the register of deliberation, the particular Agent of the Executive Directory,

ROUME.
BLANCHARD, Secretary
of the Agency.

Note of Citizen Bertolio, Ambassador from the French Republic, to the Roman Consulate.

Citizens Consuls, Rome, May 13th.

I HAVE this moment received a letter written from Ancona, in which I find an evident proof of the falsity of the news which is circulated here. The report is false, Citizens Consuls, that the cantons of Pezaro, Rimini, and Sinegaglia, are in a state of insurrection. It is false that the French have evacuated that part of the country. It is also false that Bologna and Ferrara are in the possession of the enemy. The French couriers have arrived at Ancona without experiencing any obstacle in their ordinary course. All the rumours that circulate in Rome are so many phantoms,

phantoms, created by fear and malevolence. They should be ranged in the clafs of thofe impoftures which are often the offfpring of ill-regulated imaginations. For example, it was this morning ftated in Rome that I had departed for Florence. How contemptible are the authors of this abfurdity! I declare that I have never for a moment formed the defign of abandoning Rome; I declare that it is not the intention of my government that I fhould; I declare that I will not abandon my poft, even though there fhould be as much danger as there is now fafety in remaining in Rome; I declare that I am perfectly confident of being able, within a few days, ftill better to confound the impoftors and the evil-minded; and I hope to have to announce to all the Roman patriots, new victories of the French, and triumphs for liberty.

(Signed)   BERTOLIO.

Notice publifhed by the Senate of Hamburgh againft libellous Remarks on political Relations, &c.

THE Senate has with the greateft difpleafure underftood, and it has been affirmed in feveral public prints, that certain focieties and meetings exift in this city, whofe criminal object is, by the diffemination of feditious principles, to difturb the public tranquillity and good order of fociety in general; to excite commotions and infurrections againft the exifting governments and magiftracies, and by every means in their power to be aiding and affifting to the confpirators againft them in their wicked defigns.

In confequence, indeed, of the care and caution exerted by this Honourable Council to prevent and crufh all fuch flagitious attempts, it cannot give entire credit to all the reports circulated on the fubject: yet, as fuch reports, whether well or ill founded, may deprive the city of the valuable confidence of foreign powers, it is a duty incumbent on its magiftracy to make the ftricteft inquiries to detect, and adopt the moft vigorous meafures to punifh, fuch dangerous practices.

All perfons, therefore, who think they have any knowledge of fuch focieties, or their connexions, are hereby required and reminded, that it is their duty to their neighbours and fellow-citizens, to give all the information in their power to the magiftrates, of any fecret meetings or practices tending to difturb the tranquillity of this city, or of foreign ftates. The names of thofe giving fuch information fhall be concealed, and they fhall receive a fuitable reward.

And forafmuch as a variety of highly offenfive pamphlets, on political fubjects, and daily prints, are now more than ever publifhed, by which party differences and a factious fpirit are nourifhed and promoted, and various evil confequences produced,

the

the Senate finds itself under the necessity of repeating the warning on the same subject published in 1793; and reminding all printers, publishers, and bookfellers, and all who are in any manner accessary to the sale and circulation of such writings, especially those in which the opinions, views, and actions of governments and magistrates shall be harshly canvassed and criticised, or ludicrously libelled and held up to contempt; or such as inculcate seditious principles, and tend to undermine and overthrow the existing constitutions and governments, that they shall not only suffer the confiscation of such books, but shall be further punished with the utmost severity of the law.

On this occasion also, the inhabitants of this city are hereby admonished to refrain, in all public places and social meetings, from any violent or intemperate expressions, or such as may be capable of double meanings, on the present state of political affairs; which prudent conduct may prevent disagreeable consequences both to themselves and others.

Foreigners resident here are likewise required, agreeably to the tenour of the notice published here in the year 1798, to abstain from taking any violent part on either side, fully to avoid giving any offence in the way of ridicule, as the maintenance of the peace of the city, and its respect among foreign powers, will render it necessary that those who offend against these restrictions shall be punished with the utmost rigour, as disturbers of the public tranquillity.

Given in the Assembly of the Senate, Hamburgh, May 15, 1799.

Ratisbon, May 20.

Declaration made to the Diet of the Empire, in the Name of the King of Sweden, as Duke of Pomerania.

HIS Majesty having already declared that he considered the congress of peace at Rastadt no longer constitutional, after the renewal of the war, and in consequence thereof having recalled his minister, this congress ought to be considered as dissolved.

No legation of the states of the Empire can remain at Rastadt, without evident breach of that respect which each state owes to the supreme chief of the Germanic body. The present war, in his opinion, ought to be regarded as a war of the Empire; indeed, it was declared as such at first; and as the congress was convened for the sole purpose of negotiating the peace during the armistice, he conceives that things should remain on the same footing as before.

It is the duty, then, of each member of the Empire to take an active interest in this war, by furnishing his contingent; no state, in his Majesty's opinion, can be difpenfed from this obligation except thofe whofe local pofition, and want of means, render impoffible. A contrary opinion feems to him inadmiffible an unconftitutional. Our principal obligation is obedience to th chief fupreme of the Empire, and attachment to the conftitution to enfure the enjoyment of our rights and prerogatives.

It may perhaps be alleged, that the interefts and well-being of fome of the ftates of the Empire prefcribe to them what is terme a neutrality; but, as his Majefty has already excepted thofe fove reigns and countries, which, from imperious circumftances, a prevented from fupporting the burdens of the war, he does not fe any reafon for fuch conduct in thofe whofe fituation excludes th like excufe; and even fhould the part they would take in the w be attended with difficulties and expenfe, they have no folid mo tives which juftify a breach of their engagements.

No; and it is much to be wifhed that private intereft fhou never lead to the like proceedings; and that promifes fo facre fhould be revered among us, as they were by our anceftors.

It is by thefe means alone, not by infulating one's felf, a difregarding that fubmiffion which is due to the chief fuprem that the integrity of the Empire will be maintained.

Do we not already owe thanks to the Emperor, who, thou left to himfelf, foon after the commencement of the firft war the Empire, fuftained alone with his faithful people a war of fi years duration? And if the peace which he afterwards ma with the republic was not entirely to the general advantage Germany, it was perhaps merely becaufe fuch an expectati could not be juftified, after the fupreme chief had been abandon to himfelf. We fovereigns, who exact from our people fideli and obedience, fhould deem it our duty to fhow them the exai ple by fulfilling our own obligations. And what advantages ha been obtained by the neutrality? Has it been refpected? A have not a fufficient number of events occurred fince, which oug to convince us of the contrary?

As the fulfilling of his Majefty's obligations is to him m fatisfactory, he could not behold any longer with indifference t general filence; he alfo has confidered that a longer filence on l part might be prejudicial, and judges his breaking it here to be great utility. He that reads in the hearts of men is his judge; a he will affuredly fee that no motive of ambition has induced him take this ftep; and that his only incitement is the defire of 1 eftablifhing union, confidence, and integrity, in the Germanic bo

He declares then here to his co-eftates, that he is ready at t moment to make his contingent march, as Duke of Pomerani and wifhes that all the well-difpofed members of the Empire, p ticularly thofe who have the power to do it effectually, may ir tate his example.

Sx

Second Proclamation of the Archduke Charles to the Swiss.

IN the state of dependance and conftraint in which you are held by the oppreffion of the enemy, you are not only ignorant of all that paffes abroad, but they conceal from you what might encourage you in your misfortunes. I take it for granted, that meafures have been taken to conceal from a part of the Swifs the declaration by which I ftated to you the pacific and amicable intentions of his Majefty the Emperor, by the entry of the troops under my command in the canton of Schaffhoufe. It is that which has determined me to renew the undermentioned proclamation, in order to diffeminate the fentiments of his Imperial Majefty throughout the cantons.

Helvetians! for three ages have you enjoyed uninterrupted peace, and have never beheld foreign troops upon your territories; it is the ambition of conqueft in the French government that has deftroyed your happy tranquillity; it is by a violence and perfidy unexampled in hiftory, that it has feized upon your country. Injuries of every kind have been the refult. The enemy pretends to your affiftance; your population is to be facrificed to its intereft alone, and to fubject yourfelves to its dominion.

It is thus through Switzerland that the people of Germany are to be attacked and fubjugated to the yoke. Such was the object of the plans of the enemy, which their defeat has prevented his carrying into execution. The purfuit of our triumphs is not lefs neceffary to our deliverance than your fafety. If you fear the evils neceffarily attached to war, confider that within a year you have had all its fcourges in the midft of you; and that to drive them from you, and obtain repofe, peace, fecurity, and your ancient fecurity, you have no other means left than to oppofe the enemy which has brought on you this fecond war.

Befides, equity and juftice towards the Swifs always accompany our armies. The troops under my orders obferve a rigorous difcipline, and only require lodging of you. What their immediate wants may render indifpenfable, care fhall be taken to arrange an equitable indemnification for. I repeat to you, then, all the proteftations which I have made you in the name of his Majefty the Emperor, as well in my firft proclamation as in this; and I expect with confidence not only that the Swifs will undertake nothing hoftile to the Imperial armies, but that for their own advantage they will favour and fecond its pure and beneficent views. On the other hand, I fhould declare to you not lefs folemnly, that every town, community, or individual, who fhall afford affiftance to the enemy, or fhall fight againft the Imperial troops, fhall be excluded from thefe amicable affurances, and fhall be dealt with as enemies. I require, therefore, all thinking men, thofe to whom the fafety of their country is dear, to oppofe thofe meafures which only tend to its destruction, and to unite against the common enemy, for the deliverance of their country, which I am resolved to save.

 Given at my head-quarters at Paradies (in Switzerland), the 23d May 1799.
(Signed)   CHARLES.

Third Proclamation of the Archduke Charles to the Swiss.

IN some parts of Switzerland certain ill-disposed persons have shot from the houses upon our troops, who were in pursuit of the enemy.

I found this the more contrary to my expectation, as, by my proclamation of the 30th March and 23d May, I had given the most positive assurances to all the inhabitants of Switzerland of the sincere and friendly designs of his Imperial Majesty.

Highly convinced as I am, that none but individuals can commit such hostile acts, the safety of the army entrusted to my command requires me to take all possible measures of military precaution against it; and to make hereby responsible, in the most rigorous manner, the magistrates of the towns and the chiefs of the villages, for every occurrence of this kind.

Done at the head-quarters in Paradies, May 27, 1799.
(Signed)   CHARLES.

Official Correspondence.

Sir,   *Philadelphia, May* 6, 1799.

THE government of the United States appears to be nearly in the same situation with regard to the Shawenese Indians, that that of Canada is with respect to the Mohawks. The Shawenese wish the United States to make some alteration of their limits as fixed by the treaty of Grenville; and at the same time to confirm the sales of lands they have already made, and authorize future alterations. The American ministers, on the other hand, are determined not to grant this favour, and are embarrassed by the persevering importunity of the Indians. Advices lately arrived from Fort Wayne inform the administration, that the Shawenese intended this spring to call a general council of the nation (composed of representatives from the several tribes), with a view to take such measures as may be thought best calculated to obtain some modifications of the Grenville treaty. And the information adds, that this idea was first suggested by the late Colonel M'Kee, deputy superintendant of Indian affairs.

The government consider this interference as unfriendly, and
injurious

injurious to their interests; and a complaint has been made to me on the subject by the secretary of state, with a request that I would make such representation of the matter to you as might produce a defeat of the project at present, and prevent all intervention of a similar nature in future.

I informed the secretary of state that I could scarcely bring myself to credit the report respecting Colonel M'Kee; that, at all events, I could not conceive that any thing unfavourable to the United States could have been contemplated by a public officer in the service of Great Britain, but that I would of course make the representation requested; that I made no doubt of its having the desired effect, because I was confident that you were sincerely disposed to ward off every incident that could give just cause of misunderstanding between the two nations.

The situation of public affairs in this country continues the same as at the date of my last letters, unless it be that government has given a new subject of provocation to France, by encouraging (in conjunction with us) the negro chief, Toussaint, in measures which appear ultimately to tend to a separation of the island of St. Domingo from the mother-country. Whether this affront will be pocketed by the Directory, I do not pretend to decide; but I cannot persuade myself that it is probable.

I have the honour to be, &c.

The Hon. President Russel. ROBERT LISTON.

Sir, Philadelphia, *May* 23, 1799.

MY last having been entrusted to a person who was not going directly to Upper Canada, I am uncertain whether it may yet have reached your hands, and therefore take an opportunity of transmitting a duplicate.

On public affairs I have scarcely any thing to add. One step further on the road to a formal war, between France and the United States, has been taken by the governor of Guadaloupe, who, in consequence of the capture of the Insurgente frigate, has authorized French ships of war to capture all American vessels, whether belonging to the government or to individuals; but the resolution of the Directory on the great question of peace or war is not yet known. Perhaps the new explosion on the continent of Europe may give them a degree of employment that may retard their decision.

In the interior of this country the declamations of the democratic faction, on the constitutionality and nullity of certain acts of the legislature, have misled a number of poor ignorant wretches into a resistance to the laws, and a formal insurrection. This frivolous rebellion has been quelled by a spirited effort of certain volunteer

volunteer corps lately embodied, who deserve every degree [of] praise.

But the conduct of these gentlemen having been shamefu[lly] calumniated by some of the popular newspapers, they have v[en]tured to take the law in their own hands, and to punish one [or] two of the printers (by a smart flogging), a circumstance wh[ich] has given rise to much animosity, to threats, and to a commen[ce]ment of armed associations on the side of the democrats (parti[cu]larly the United Irishmen); and some apprehend that the af[fair] may lead to a partial civil war! The portion, however, of the Ja[co]binic party, who would carry matters to this extremity, is small; the government is on its guard, and determined to act w[ith] vigour; and I do not on the whole apprehend any serious dan[ger].

I have the honour to be, &c.
ROBERT LISTON.

Proclamation of General Gauthier; published at Florence 5th of J[uly].

A PEOPLE which has been treated by the French army w[ith] a mildness unexampled in the history of war; a people w[ho] has never been loaded with new imposts, or disturbed in its p[oli]tical or religious opinions, has dared to take arms against [the] troops of the Great Nation; already the tri-coloured cockade [has] been insulted, and French blood been shed, without any prev[ious] provocation. The shouts of "Long live the Emperor! Dea[th to] republicans!" have resounded on all sides. I can no lo[nger] tolerate such audacity, and in consequence order the follow[ing] regulations:

1st. Every commune which shall permit any tumultuous seditious assemblings of the people, shall be considered as re[bel]lious, and treated as such. All the inhabitants found with a[rms] in their hands shall be immediately shot, if they do not surre[nder] them at their first summons.

2d. The communes which shall have rung the alarm=b[ell] and offered any resistance to the troops, shall be given up to pill[age] and burned. The inhabitants who shall not give up their a[rms] or who shall wear the enemy's cockade, shall be shot. The [citi]zens who shall not take part in these assemblings, shall be [pro]tected, and their property respected.

3d. The nobles and priests shall answer with their heads t[o the] French army for the safety of the republicans in Tuscany; they are in consequence placed under the permanent inspec[tion] of the military commanders.

4th. When a commune shall be in a state of insurrection, curates and priests shall use their influence with the insurgen[ts] induce them to return to their duty; and all those who shall refuse to perform this act of civism and attachment to their country, shall be considered as ringleaders in the plot, and punished as such.

Count Cocastelli, the Emperor's Commissioner at Milan, published there the following Proclamation early in June.

HIS Majesty the Emperor and King, the sovereign and father of his faithful subjects of Lombardy, whom the bravery of his troops has just restored to his dominion, and to his heart, has directed his first attention to whatever may increase their welfare and their felicity. The integrity and lustre of the holy Catholic religion, the pure administration of justice, the known morality and probity of all the persons employed in the public service, the destruction of those nefarious maxims which were broached in order to seduce and corrupt that good people, the punishment of those who have made the scandalous profession of them; such are the principles which his Majesty, in the plenitude of his justice, and of his love for his subjects of Lombardy, has prescribed to the undersigned commissary, in his letter of the 17th May, and in that of Baron Thugut, minister of foreign affairs, and supreme director in that department of his Majesty's provinces in Italy. In order not to retard the execution of those views of the sovereign, it is just that this illustrious city should begin to experience their happy effects by a wise and enlightened administration, wholly devoted to the good and advantage of the public. In consequence, instead of the present provisional administration, which is dissolved and abolished from the moment of the publication of the present proclamation, there shall be created an administrative body, under the denomination of a delegated congregation for the city and province of Milan, to be divided into six departments, corresponding to the six branches of administration, which shall be entrusted (until new dispositions shall have been made) to the direction of that body, under the immediate inspection of the government of its representatives.

Ratisbon, June 13.

ON the 11th instant, the diet of the Empire, assembled here, received the following

Imperial Aulic Decree to the German Diet respecting the late Catastrophe near Rastadt.

HIS Imperial Majesty received on the 3d ult. the melancholy intelligence, in a report signed by the Margrave of Baden himself,

himself, that the French ministers plenipotentiary sent to the congress of peace with the Empire, were stopped late in the evening of the 28th of April, on their departure in the night from Rastadt (against which they had been advised by several different persons), at a small distance from the said city, by a troop of people dressed in the Imperial military uniform ; and that the ministers Bonnier and Roberjot were murdered by many cuts of sabres, but that the minister Jean Debry, who escaped from death only by a happy accident, had been much wounded, and all of them were robbed of a great part of their effects.

His Majesty is scarcely able to express, by word, the great shock his sentiments of justice and morality have received, and the whole force of impression of abhorrence which has been excited in him on the first account of this act of barbarity committed on the territory of the German Empire, upon persons whose inviolability was under the special guarantee of the right of nations; nor can his Majesty express the indelible impression which this disastrous catastrophe has left in his revolted mind, which always entertains the most inviolable respect for the dignity of man, for morality, and the sacred principles of the law of nations.

It is not by illiberal suspicions and rash conjectures, not by calumnious imputations and partial reports of audacious fictions, nor by the passionate sallies of a depraved heart, and the licentious fabrications of foreign and domestic editors of public journals—it is not by inimical representations, calculated for an increase of power, for exactions of money, or for other secret designs, nor by furious speeches in conventions, and vindictive proclamations to the French nation and all other states—but only by a conscientious, fair, and impartial inquiry, instituted according to the prescription of the laws, and conducted with every juridical rigour, that the horrid act may be traced in all its circumstances, its authors and accomplices be truly discovered, and the imputation of the offence be properly fixed both in a subjective and objective view.

To this end the most eligible directions and orders have accordingly been given ; and his Imperial Majesty doth at the same time most solemnly declare before the general diet of the Empire, of the whole public of Germany and all Europe together, that nothing short of the most perfect satisfaction, regardless of all other considerations, shall gratify the just feelings of the chief of the Empire, respecting him whom the impartial sentence of avenging justice may pronounce guilty.

But it is also the will of his Majesty the Emperor, that the manner in which this melancholy event happened, an event which his Majesty considers in various respects as a national concern of Germany, be not only examined with the most conscien-

tious

tious impartiality, and that the moſt perfect ſatisfaction be given; but his Imperial Majeſty further cheriſhes the moſt lively wiſh, and feels himſelf partly and moſt urgently induced to it by the domeſtic and foreign opinions encroaching upon the legal inquiry whoſe deciſion is thereby prejudged; that even the poſſibility of a ſuſpicion of any connivance be removed, ſo that in this reſpect no ſort of blame owing to a want of the moſt deliberate attention ſhall be attributed either to the chief of the Empire himſelf, or to the Empire collectively taken.

In order to accompliſh this deſign moſt effectually, the general diet is hereby charged, upon mature deliberation, to appoint deputies of their own, who are to be preſent at the inquiry which has been opened, and to adviſe every thing with a patriotic and noble frankneſs as to the ſteps, which are to be taken as ſoon as poſſible, with regard to whatever the importance of ſo unheard-of and deteſtable an event may in its wiſdom and prudence ſeem to require: and thus farther to convince the whole impartial world by giving its conjoint advice, that both the Emperor and the Empire are animated with the ſame uniform ſentiments for the execution of the moſt rigorous juſtice, and the granting of the moſt perfect ſatisfaction, and by an equal and juſt abhorrence of ſo ruthleſs and infamous an act, as well as by an equal and dutiful reſpect to morality and the ſacred principles of the law of nations.

His Roman and Imperial Majeſty expects therefore the advice of the Empire with all poſſible ſpeed; and with all the fervency of his wiſhes as chief of the Empire, his Majeſty remains in other reſpects, &c.

(Signed) FRANCIS, Mor.

Done at Vienna, June 6, 1799.

YESTERDAY the members of the Germanic diet held a conference, in which the following reſolutions were agreed upon, reſpecting the new Imperial Aulic decree:

I. The deliberation upon the decree of his Imperial Majeſty ſhall commence on the 12th of July.

II. The Imperial commiſſioner ſhall be aſked, whether the decree implies in its meaning, a deputation of the ſtates or individuals of the Empire.

III. That, in the latter caſe, Ratiſbon ſhall be propoſed to the Emperor as the place of diſcuſſion; but in the former caſe, a ſafe place, which ſhall not be too diſtant from that where the deed was perpetrated, ſhall be propoſed to his Imperial Majeſty.

IV. Only a deputation of four ſtates of the Empire ſhall be deſired, which, excluding the Imperial cities, ſhall conſiſt of two electoral and two princely deputies.

V. The French government ſhall afterwards be invited to delegate

delegate some person to assist in the inquiry, and to communicate the legal dispositions of the injured parties.

VI. That the Emperor shall be entreated to give directions to the military commission, which is already subsisting, to communicate all its proceedings to the deputation, and to make the said commission conform itself to the propositions of the latter.

VII. The deputation shall be provided with unlimited power—

VIII. Both the deputation and the military commission shall be instructed, either to agree together upon a sentence, or to send the acts of their deliberations to impartial quarters.

These resolutions have been sent by the envoys of the different states with the diet of Ratisbon, to their respective courts, expecting such instructions as shall enable them to form a decision by the majority of the diet, as required by its chief.

Proclamation of General Moreau, Commander in Chief of the Army of Italy, to the Ligurian People.

Head-quarters at Genoa, 16th June, 7th Year of the French Republic.

THE General in Chief is unwilling to quit Genoa without testifying his satisfaction and gratitude to the Ligurian people. The army has received from them the most hospitable treatment.

The General in Chief saw them, in the midst of the insurrection that surrounded them, divide their subsistence with the French army, and join their battalions to repulse the common enemy. He recognised the descendants of those Genoese, who, more than once, proved themselves the friends of the French, and the dreadful enemies of the Austrians.

The General in Chief hastens to acquaint the French government of the loyal and courageous conduct of so faithful an ally, and assurés the Ligurian people, that the army will cover its territory with the same firmness as if it defended its own country; that the French republic regards it as a brother, and will divide with it, equally, its resources of every kind, in the same manner as it has partaken its dangers. Numerous convoys of grain have already left the French ports for the use of both the people and the army.

If disorders, inseparable from a dangerous and difficult march, have given birth to any private injuries, let the government be informed of it, who will immediately make it known to the General in Chief, and reparation will instantly be made. Of this an example has already been given.

The General in Chief recommends to the Ligurian people concord and harmony between all the citizens. Let all party spirit

spirit vanish before the dangers of the country; let them be animated by one common sentiment—that of repulsing the enemy, and saving the country.

(Signed)   MOREAU.

Proclamation of the provisionary Government of the City of Zurich, published the 18th of June.

HIS Royal Highness the Archduke Charles, commander in chief of the Imperial army, has formally declared to the Swifs, in his two proclamations of the 30th of March and the 23d of May, that his Majesty the Emperor had no other design, with regard to our country, than to contribute in an amicable manner to the maintenance of the independence of Switzerland, and to the inviolate preservation of its rights and possessions. The declaration made by his Majesty's generals, immediately upon entering this country, was a proof of his beneficent views; this declaration expresses, that immediately upon the army's entering Switzerland, dispositions be made, so that the course of business be not interrupted, and that justice continue to be rendered, and the public resources employed to the greatest advantage of the country, until the contribution of each part of the Helvetic confederation, and the union between all its members, can be re-established, or otherwise determined. This declaration farther said, that during the interval, a provisionary regency should be formed, to exercise the authority which was vested in the ancient magistrates of Zurich. In consequence, a provisionary government, consisting of fifteen members, chosen from among the inhabitants of this city and its environs, has been formed, &c. &c.

The following Proclamations were published by the French and Spanish Admirals, previous to their leaving Carthagena.

LIBERTY.   EQUALITY.

In the Name of the French Republic.

In the Road of Carthagena, on board the Admiral's Ship the Ocean, dated the 24th June, in the 7th Year of the French Republic. Eustache Bruix, commanding the French naval Forces.

Frenchmen and Republicans,

AT last, united with our faithful allies, we approach a period in which we shall punish England, and relieve all Europe from its tyranny. Although I have no doubt, my brave friends, of the sentiments which you have professed, I feel myself bound to call upon you to give proofs of their sincerity by every means in your power. Recollect that it is for the interest of your country, and for your own honour, to give to a nation whom we esteem the highest opinion of us. That word alone is sufficient for Frenchmen. Do not, above all, forget that you are come among a just and generous people, and our most faithful ally—respect their customs, their usages, their religion; in a word, let every thing be sacred to us. Think the least departure from that which I am now prescribing to you, will be a crime in the eyes of the republic, and it will be my duty to punish it. But, on the contrary, I am convinced that you will give me an opportunity of praising your conduct, and that will be the greatest recompence I can receive.

E. BRUIX.

Spanish Proclamation.

A GREAT interest commands the junction of the naval forces of the King my master, with those of the French republic. This natural, this happy alliance, is the only curb which can restrain the plan which England has always formed of tyrannizing over the seas. There is no reason to apprehend that our fleets will not show themselves in a manner worthy of the two great nations. The principle of a good alliance is fraternity and reciprocal esteem; and they are implanted in the hearts of Spaniards and Frenchmen, as has appeared on many occasions, particularly in the war from 1779 to 1783. It cannot therefore be necessary for me to recommend good order to you. Nevertheless, for the purpose of greater security, I exhort all the crews to preserve discipline. My confidence in the worthy admirals who command under me, in the captains and officers, and in the discipline and valour of the soldiers and sailors, promises me the most happy success to the two fleets.

MASSAREDO.

On board the Conception, in Carthagena Roads, June 24, 1799.

A Proclamation by the President of the United States of America.

WHEREAS by an act of the Congress of the United States passed the 9th day of February last, entitled, "An Act further to suspend the commercial Intercourse between the United States and France, and the Dependencies thereof," it is provided, that at any time after the passing of this act, it shall be lawful for the President of the United States, if he shall deem it expedient and consistent with the interests of the United States,

by

by his order to remit, and difcontinue for the time being the reſtraints and prohibitions by the faid act impofed, either with refpect to the French republic, or to any ifland, port, or place belonging to the faid republic; with which a commercial intercourfe may fafely be renewed; and alfo to revoke fuch order, whenever in his opinion the intereft of the United States fhall require; and he is authorized to make proclamation thereof accordingly: And whereas the arrangements which have been made at St. Domingo, for the fafety of the commerce of the United States, for the admiffion of American veffels into certain ports of that ifland, do, in my opinion, render it expedient and for the intereft of the United States, to renew a commercial intercourfe with fuch ports: Therefore, I John Adams, Prefident of the United States, by virtue of the powers vefted in me by the above recited act, do hereby remit and difcontinue the reſtraints and prohibitions therein contained, within the limits and under the regulations here following, to wit:

1. It fhall be lawful for veffels which have departed, or may depart, from the United States, to enter the ports of Cape François and Port Republicain, formerly called Port-au-Prince, in the faid ifland of St. Domingo, on and after the 1ft day of Auguſt next.

2. No veffel fhall be cleared for any other port in St. Domingo than Cape François and Port Republicain.

3. It fhall be lawful for veffels which fhall enter the ports of Cape François and Port Republicain, after the 31ft day of July next, to depart from thence to any other port in faid ifland, between Monte Chrifti on the north, and Petit Goave on the weft; provided it be done with the confent of the government of St. Domingo, and purfuant to certificates or paffports, expreffing fuch confent, figned by the conful general of the United States, or conful refiding at the port of departure.

4. All veffels failing in contravention of thefe regulations, will be out of the protection of the United States, and be moreover liable to capture, feizure, and confifcation.

 Given under my hand, and feal of the United States, at Philadelphia, the 26th day of June, in the year of our Lord 1799, and of the independence of the faid States the twenty-third.   JOHN ADAMS.
  By the Prefident,
  TIMOTHY PICKERING, Secretary of State.

Proclamation of Moreau to the Piedmontese, published before he quited Voltaggio.

Piedmontese,

THE French descend from the Alps and the Appennines to exterminate those men who call themselves the harbingers of peace and happiness: they are nothing but barbarous destroyers. If a Frenchman should injure you in your properties, persons, or opinions, make it known. A speedy justice shall avenge you. It shall be terrible, and calculated to terrify others from similar attempts. But I must warn you, that if the blood of a single Frenchman, shed by the sword of an assassin, should pollute your soil, I shall destroy, I shall burn the village or city which shall tolerate or commit that crime. Finally, I promise protection to the obedient, and extermination to rebels.

Manifesto addressed to the Roman Nation on the Approach of the combined Armies.

WORTHY descendants of Romulus, the dawn of peace at length opens upon your horizon. The happy days of Numa Pompilius, of Augustus, and of Trajan, are about to return. Impiety and fanaticism give place to true religion and honour. The mask of wantonness and libertinism is about to fall. The tree of discord is rooted out of your soil; the tri-coloured standard will no longer dishonour the Capitol. Remember that you are Romans, and your breasts will glow with indignation against a race which has constantly been your enemy, which persecuted Rome, both in its infancy and in its state of maturity, and which at all times was averse to its prosperity; which at this juncture has robbed it of its treasures, its monuments, its many rarities, and violated its religion; which has overthrown its good order, and deprived it of that dignity and consequence which all nations of the universe were wont to ascribe to it. Romans! where are the statues collected with so much labour and fatigue from the most distant regions? Where are your famous pictures, and those celebrated manuscripts which you have preserved with so much care from the ravages of time? Where are your vessels of gold and silver, your precious jewels, and rich ornaments? All is become the prey of that French nation which had promised and undertaken to guarantee your properties. Where are the decorations and magnificent attributes of your churches? Where is the Supreme Pontiff, the sacred pledge, whose honourable custody was committed to your charge for the general interest of the Catholic church? All has been barbarously torn from you by those French commissioners and generals,

who

(293)

who had folemnly contracted with you for the protection of your public worfhip.

Where is your liberty? that liberty which was deceitfully held out to you as the bafis of your revolution, and the deareft wifh of your hearts. The moft oppreffive tyranny, the moft humiliating defpotifm, has fettered you, and ftill afflicts you. Some vile Frenchmen, without honefty, without birth, without education, have annihilated the Roman name, and with their impure and deceitful breath have profaned the lafting fame of your noble anceftors, Curtius, Horatius, Fabius, Brutus, and Caffius; they have plundered you of your inheritance, your authority, and your tranquillity. But, people of Rome! you fhall be avenged; the Imperial eagle has again directed its flight towards the Italian fhores; it is guided by the valiant Suwarrow, the hero of Ruffia, the hero of Italy, the hero, whofe name refounds from the Euxine to the Viftula and the Volga, on the banks of the Po, the Adige, and the Trebbia, and who is immortalized by the victories he has gained. The united forces of the two empires and the greateft powers in Europe are conducted by the greateft commander, the terror of whofe name alarms the enemy. Victory accompanies his ftandard, and overthrows every bulwark; the humbled Frenchman flies at his approach, and feeks to fave himfelf in the Alps; but there is no retreat nor fafety for him; purfued, beaten, difcomfited, he abandons Italy, and is detefted and abhorred by all its inhabitants, who found the alarm to deftroy and annihilate him.

People of Rome! we likewife ought to follow this laudable example; you have your vengeance to claim, and fhould participate in the common glory. In the name of General Suwarrow, I invite you to do it; he is perfuaded that you will not hefitate to unite yourfelves with the victorious armies of the two empires, and doubts not but, with that force and energy which has always diftinguifhed your illuftrious nation, you will yourfelves expel from your city, and the Roman ftate, the fmall remainder of Frenchmen who ftill keep you under fubjection, and opprefs you; and that you will liberate your families from fuch unwelcome and dangerous guefts.

Let no apprehenfions detain you from this refolve. A total oblivion of what is paft, and an abfolute pardon for all who may return to their duty, are promifed you by the allied princes, and guaranteed by the General. He cannot fuppofe you blind enough to be attached to your enemies, and the enemies of Heaven—the foes of all the human race; or that you would wifh to retard the general peace of Italy, by abufing the bounty of fo many fovereigns. He loves you, and dreads the thought of being obliged, if you continue refractory, to confider you as the enemies of religion and the allied powers; in which cafe he would

be

be under the painful necessity of fighting and exterminating you with the common enemy. May God avert such a calamity from you, and inspire you for the public good, to act in such a way as to merit his grace, the praises of Suwarrow, and the commendation of Europe.

     GEORGE, COUNT OF ZOUCCATO,
    Lieutenant-colonel in his Imperial Russian Majesty's Service, Volunteer in the Army of Italy, Knight of the Orders of St. George, St. Volodomir, and the Prussian Order of Merit.

Manifesto addressed to the Belgians, distributed by the advanced Posts of General Sztarray's Corps.

Brave Belgians,

WE are now arrived on the frontiers of the Empire, whose chief is your lawful sovereign, his Majesty the Emperor and King. It now depends upon you, brave Belgians! to abandon the banners of your usurpers, and repair to the standard of your ancient and illustrious Sovereign, where you will be received with open arms. The victorious troops are advancing with great strides, and only wait your arrival to receive you in their bosom, and, supported by your courage, to lead you back to your country. Belgians! his Imperial Majesty promises, from this moment, to all those who have been guilty of desertion, the total oblivion of their offences, and a general amnesty.

 (Signed) COUNT SZTARRAY, General in Chief.
Head-quarters at Donaueschingen,
 July 1, 1799.

Embargo on Swedish Vessels in France.

Translation of a Letter from E. Signeul, his Majesty's Consul-general at Paris, to Claes Grill, Consul-general in London, dated the 5th of July.

I HASTEN to advise you, that the Directory have decreed an embargo to be laid on all Swedish ships, which at present are, or may hereafter arrive in the ports of France. I hope you will make use of this advice as you shall think the most proper for the interest of our commerce.

Impeachment of the Ex-Directors.

THE following is a full and correct statement of the charges brought against the four ex-Directors—Reubell, La Revelliere, Merlin, and Treilhard:

               Charge

Charge I.—*They have violated the right of nations,*

1. By attacking, without any previous manifesto or declaration, without the concurrence of the Legislative Body, the Ottoman Emperor, our ally, by the invasion of Egypt, a country under his domination, and that at a time when the Ottoman government, so far from being in a state of imminent or commenced hostilities, or of threats or preparations of war against the republic, had still, on the contrary, an ambassador amongst us.

2. By invading Switzerland without a previous manifesto or declaration, and without the concurrence of the Legislative Body, when the Helvetic government was neither in a state of imminent or commenced hostility, of threats or preparations of war against the republic; and while the wrongs or complaints which we had to impute to them might be redressed either by such changes as the operation of public opinion prepared in that state, or by such arrangements as our situation and the force of treaties had given us a right to propose and to expect.

Charge II.—*They have refused to acknowledge the sovereignty of the people,*

1. By modifying by the means of violence only the constitution which the Cisalpines and the Batavians had accepted and sworn to maintain immediately on the recovery of their liberty; by causing to be enforced by violence, and in the name of the French republic, the changes introduced into the constitution of a people declared free, acknowledged as independent, and as our ally.

2. By subjecting the general will of the Roman people, who had been declared free and independent, and who had an ambassador amongst us, to the will of a commander in chief, or of a commissary; and by forcing that people to accept of a constitution, the 360th article of which sanctioned their slavery.

Charge III.—*They have violated our constitution,*

1. By usurping the legislative authority by issuing decrees, ordaining that such and such a law shall be executed, as far as it is not modified by such decrees; by issuing decrees which crippled or rendered nugatory those laws, and thus reduced the administrators to the alternative, either of being deprived of their places, if they did not obey the law, or of being prosecuted for contumacy if they disobeyed the decree.

2. By neglecting to lay before the Councils such accounts and information as they called for, either respecting the finances, or the situation of the country, which constitutes a formal refusal to obey the will of the constitution.

Charge IV.—*They have endangered our external security,*

1. By raising an additional enemy against the republic, namely, the Ottoman Porte, and compelling it to unite with the coalition of the North.

2. By

2. By neglecting to take any measure during the peace with the Emperor and the armistice with the Empire, for keeping the armies on a respectable footing, for filling the vacancies, providing the cavalry and artillery with horses, or for furnishing the fortified towns with provisions, arms, and ammunition.

3. By permitting to be taken the cannon, muskets, stores, &c. both in the fortified towns and the magazines of the army.

4. By proposing to the Legislative Body to declare war against the King of Hungary and Bohemia, when the French armies were either disorganised or spread out on an immense extent of territory, or reduced to a number infinitely inferior to the forces which all the reports of the generals announced as marching against us; by deceiving the Legislative Body by fallacious statements of our military force, and by leaving upwards of an hundred thousand men in the interior of the republic.

Charge V.—*They have endangered the internal security,*

1. By arming the citizens against one another; by exposing the true republicans to proscription under the designation of anarchists, either in the directorial proclamations or the circular letters of their ministers, acknowledged by them, inasmuch as they did not censure them: and by provoking and encouraging, by means of these designations, the removing of republicans from all public functions, and instigating to their assassination.

2. By dismissing at the same time, and in the most summary manner, an immense number of public functionaries appointed by the people; thus introducing anarchy at a moment when the operative influence of the laws became of the utmost importance to facilitate the permanent improvement of the new taxes, the perfection of the old ones, the departure of the French for the defence of the country, and, above all, the repression and punishment of robberies and assassination.

Charge VI.—*They have refused to acknowledge the sovereignty of the French people,*

1. By sending into different departments of the republic agents to influence the elections, by forcing promises, by means of threats, and by employing every art and seduction to entrap the votes of the citizens in favour of those who were pointed out by those agents.

2. In neglecting or refusing to punish the agents who had caused to be arrested electors and presidents of primary assemblies, and those who were denounced to them for having by their intrigues endeavoured to annihilate the suffrages of the people.

Charge VII.—*They invaded the liberty and security of citizens,*

1. In arbitrarily imprisoning citizens, in detaining them illegally, and subjecting them to lettres-de-cachet. Among these citizens,

......, Ge Vernon, whom they drove from Italy; and exiled from France.

2. In perverting the 24th article of the law of 19th Fructidor, year 5, so far as to transport citizens who could not be comprehended under that law.

Charge VIII.—*They attempted to dissolve the national representation,*

In proposing to certain military commanders to arrest a number of members of the Legislative Body; in consulting its chiefs on the possibility or difficulty of this measure.

Charge IX.—*They have dissipated the public revenues, and permitted pillage and peculation,*

1. In taking no steps to prevent or punish dilapidation, robbery, excess, violence, despotism, and vexation of every kind, by which the people on whom we pretended to bestow liberty were overwhelmed; and in having done nothing more than issue decrees which proved their knowledge of these crimes, and the impotence of the measures adopted against them.

2. In prosecuting General Championet, because he opposed the arbitrary proceedings and depredations of one of their commissaries, by which that agent drove to insurrection against the army and the French republic, a nation disposed to receive with gratitude the liberty which we offered. Thus did they bring death and destruction upon an army of French heroes, against whom a people, driven to despair, let loose their vengeance, as reprisals for the tyranny, oppression, and violence of the agents of the Directory.

Imperial Aulic Decree to the Diet of Ratisbon, published at that Place on the 12th of July.

THE preliminaries of peace between the Austrian and French plenipotentiaries were signed at Leoben on the 13th of April 1797; and, at the earnest solicitation of his Imperial Majesty, it was resolved, on that remarkable day, that all hostilities should be suspended between the Emperor and the French republic, that a peace might be securely negotiated. But this desirable work accomplished so ineffectually the paternal views of his Majesty the Emperor, that, on the part of the French (notwithstanding the Empire's constant desire of peace), almost every day was marked with acts which removed to a greater distance the object so anxiously wished for. In contempt of the just remonstrances of the states of the Empire, and of the deputation, they not only made the severest military exactions, and seized the fortress of Ehrenbreitstein (contrary to a former convention), but incorpos. with the new Helvetic republic, which they created,

created, those territories and fiefs of the Empire situated in Switzerland, and, overturning it by the vilest machinations, they carried throughout Helvetia the destructive torch of their revolution to the frontiers of Germany. The French government, always true to the spirit of this revolution, was constantly occupied with plans to destroy the political relation of the Empire with Italy. Amidst the negotiations for peace, it strove to strengthen its formidable power by new abettors and alliances, and by a levy of 200,000 men. In short, the French government, in all its political relations with the Empire, without examining the evils it hath caused, and in defiance of the truce and negotiations for peace, only sought to render its condition the worst possible, by the numerous evils it committed.

Even this state, however quiet, could only be considered as a state of war; yet, from a humane disposition for peace, representations were the only arms opposed to the domineering arrogance of the French Directory, which had, however, no other effect (as their rash plans had hitherto succeeded) than the perpetration of fresh acts of injustice and violence. No other arguments are wanting to confirm these facts than the facts themselves, viz. the orders given to repair the fortifications of Ehrenbreitstein; the supplying that place with provisions, by extorting them from the neighbouring subjects of the Empire; and the avowed will of the French government, seriously declared, to keep possession of that fortress, against the law of nations, and in contempt of solemn conventions:—the occupation of Manheim, and the disarming of the garrison; the prevention of the exercise of their official functions, which was only provisorily granted to the magistrates of that city, by way of a revolutionary prelude to the bold menaces made by the French plenipotentiaries, in an official note of the 3d October, last year, to introduce the destructive principles of France into Germany:—the memorable, but not dissembling letter, of the French Executive Directory, addressed in the same revolutionary spirit to the French commander in chief, Jourdan, on the 15th of March 1799; the rapid advancing of the French troops, by several directions, into the very heart of Germany, even without giving due notice of the truce with the Empire being broken off, and with a visible violation of the laws of armistice:—the summons sent, in the most singular expressions, on the 1st of March, to the Imperial fortress of Philipsburgh to surrender, and with violent and shocking threats against its commandant, for him to give up the fortress from terror:—the immoral written invitation to treason against the Emperor and the Empire, addressed to the civil magistrates, on the 14th of March:—the batteries raised close to the fortress, and the unjust attempt made to seize the fortress by offers of subornation:—the exciting of all

Germans to rebellion againſt their lawful chief, contained in the horrid proclamations of Bernadotte, together with ſeveral other occurrences of the ſame pernicious tendency, remarked in the Imperial decree of commiſſion, of the 4th of April of the preſent year:—all theſe are deeds of ſuch a nature, as to combine all the attributes of an actual ſtate of warfare; and which can never be reconciled by ſmooth profeſſions of pacific intentions, and by an unnatural and contradictory diſcrimination of ideas.

The war therefore actually exiſts againſt Germany by facts —war! the ſole terrible work of the ambitious, revolutionary, and all-confounding politics of the French government. And the late political relations of the German Empire with Italy and Switzerland, would be irretrievably loſt; the ſtandard of revolution would already be hoiſted in a great part of the German Empire, as it has been in other ſubjugated ſtates and provinces, and the brighter proſperity of Germanic freedom be perſecuted by the ungrateful French ſyſtem of liberty and equality, had not the prudence and heroiſm of the Imperial generals, and the victorious armies, put a ſtop to the incurſions of the daring enemy. Thus, while hoſtilities have been renewed, and the proſpect of a ſucceſsful negotiation of peace, ſo much deſired by the Empire, is vaniſhed, the former ſtate of warfare between the Germanic Empire and France actually exiſts; and, according to the public declarations forced from the Empire by this ſtate of war, it muſt ſtill combat, at the higheſt price, for the inviolability of the deareſt treaties, for religion, property, the maintenance of ſocial order and conſtitution, the honour, dignity, liberty, exiſtence, and preſervation of the Germanic Empire; and muſt ſtill combat for an acceptable, juſt, becoming, and laſting peace, agreeable to the ſpirit of the former reſolutions of the Germanic diet.

His Imperial Majeſty, therefore, places his confidence, as chief, in the electors, princes, and ſtates, and deems himſelf entitled to expect from them, in the ſacred name of their common country and conſtitution, and by virtue of the manifold aſſurances given, that no ſtate of the Empire will recede from the moſt conſcientious execution of all the duties which are impoſed againſt the common enemy, by the very nature of the ancient Germanic confederation, the ancient poſitive ſtatutes, and the concluſions of the Empire, promulgated ſince the preſent war has been declared; eſpecially that concluſion of the Empire which relates to the augmentation of the armament to a quintuple; and in conformity to which, his Majeſty the King of Sweden has lately declared himſelf, in his quality as a ſtate of the Empire, to the diet, with as much cordiality as generoſity, to revive German patriotiſm in general. It is equally urgent
and

and proper, and the particular wish of his Imperial Majesty,
the diet do direct its deliberations towards granting a suffic
number of Roman months to defray the expense of the v
and that it do accelerate, as much as possible, its approbation
be transmitted to the chief of the Empire.

Decree of the Prince of Brazil, declaring himself Regent
Portugal.

TAKING into consideration that, in virtue of the laws
which is founded the Portuguese monarchy, all the rig
of sovereignty have devolved upon my person, on account of
sorrowful, verified, and very notorious infirmity of the Qu
my mother, and her incapability of continuing to exercise the
and finding myself convinced (by the prolonged experience
seven years, in which the care and assistance of the most
puted physicians have been entirely ineffectual) that the s
infirmity, humanly speaking, should be considered an insani
it has appeared to me, that in the actual circumstances of pu
affairs, as well as to what respects the foreign concerns, as
the internal administration of the kingdom, the good of
faithful Portuguese subjects, and my personal honour,
equally interested, in that (by my revoking my decree of the 1
of February 1792, which was solely dictated by the sentim
of respect and filial love, of which I have always desired,
do desire, to give to the Queen my sovereign and mother
most superabundant proofs) the government of these kingd
and their dominions should continue from this day forward
der my proper name and supreme authority; on which acco
without withdrawing myself from the said sentiments, but
knowledging that they from their nature ought to be subordi
to the good of the people, and to the honour of the sovereig
I have resolved that from the date of the present decree all l:
acts, decrees, resolutions, and orders (which ought to be n
out in the name of the Queen my sovereign and mother, if
was actually governing this monarchy), shall be formed
made out in my name, as Prince Regent, which I am du
her actual impediment; and that, in like manner, shall be
dressed to me all consultations, petitions, requests, and re
sentations, which in future may ascend to my presence.

Joseph Scarra de Sousa, counsellor of state for the affair
the kingdom, shall make it to be so understood, and cause
be executed, sending copies of this decree to those parts whe
they belong.

Done at the Palace of Quelenz, on the 15th of July 1
(Signed) J. S. DE SOUS.
(The Prince's seal, &c.)

Talleyrand's Vindication.

TWO articles of the journal which I have repeatedly cited, will give an astonishing specimen of contradiction. In No. xviii. p. 64, the journalist asserts—" That it was Talleyrand who was the cause of the return of Malmesbury, after he had been (says he) dismissed by Charles Lacroix. But (adds he) it was not to Paris, that was undoubtedly no longer necessary, but to Lisle, to the very centre of our military bulwarks. Is not this easy to be seen through? Never was there a clearer conviction of any fact; if we have been blind, let us be so no longer."

I shall not here examine with how much more advantage the journalist would have attacked me, if he had established that it was Charles Lacroix who fixed the negotiation at Lisle, and that I was at Paris. In fact, on the 13th Prairial of the 5th year (June 1, 1797), Lord Grenville proposed a negotiation. The 16th Prairial (June 4) the proposition was accepted. The 23d Prairial (June 12) Charles Lacroix sent passports to England, and appointed the commune at Lisle.

On the 29th Prairial (June 17) Lord Grenville accepted the appointment of that place, and announced the nomination of Lord Malmesbury by the King of England. On the 2d Messidor (June 20) the Directory consented to the opening of the negotiation. On the 18th Messidor (July 6) the conferences began at Lisle, and then I was not minister, not having been appointed till the 28th Messidor, (July 16). Next day the journalist, knowing these facts, mentions that an error had crept in respecting Lord Malmesbury; and how is this corrected? I copy his words (p. 85): " We did not mean to say that Lord Malmesbury was sent from England to Lisle after the appointment of the Bishop of Autun to the office of minister of foreign affairs. This was not exactly the case, but (adds he boldly) this makes the matter still more conclusive."

These people have imputed to me all the operations of every department of government during my ministry. They ask me why the Grand Duke of Tuscany was not kept as an hostage (as it it were my province to give instructions to generals); they dare to shut their eyes on all evidence; and affirm that I have alienated from us the United States, when they knew well that at the moment when they printed that strange accusation, the American negotiators had arrived in France, and they could not be ignorant of the part I took in this business, and of the language, full of deference, moderation, and I may add dignity, with which I addressed them in the name of the French government, while those who attack me to-day, allow me nothing but violent and irritating language. They pretend that I provoked

against

against Citizen Truguet a kind of rigour that to me ever appeared inexcusable.

And what have I done to deserve such a suspicion? Have ever appeared vindictive or persecuting? During all my administration can I be accused of one act of severity? Have the citizens associated with me in business, ever received any thing but testimonies of confidence and friendship? Have they ever seen any caprice on my part? Have they for one moment been disturbed by me? Last year, when the walls were covered with libels against me, dictated by fury, did I do the least injury to the young man who directed them against me? Whoever knows me must be satisfied that these are not my principles or character.

I have done. I am certain that I have satisfactorily answered my accusers. I despised them in the beginning of the revolution, and I despise them still.

Observations, by Charles Delacroix, upon the Reflections published by Talleyrand Perigord.

AS I have been named or referred to twice in the reflections which Citizen Talleyrand has published, I owe it to truth and to my own character to establish those facts with respect to which I have been alluded to in this work.

It is very true, as Citizen Talleyrand observes, that it was from me Lord Grenville demanded a passport for Lord Malmesbury, that the negotiations were commenced during my administration, and that it was I who pointed out Lisle to him, in consequence of the express orders of the Directory. I do not see how these facts can excite suspicion; but if it were necessary to justify them, I should state, that the facility of the telegraph communication, and the remembrance of the intrigues formed by Lord Malmesbury when at Paris, were the principal motives which determined the Directory to prefer the commune of Lisle.

"The expedition to Egypt," says Talleyrand, "was prepared before the period of my administration. It is a certain fact, that Citizen Magallen, consul general of the republic of Egypt, in consequence of a great number of memorials dispatched by him, and all relative to an expedition against Egypt received, previous to my entering into administration, leave to return to France. It was not, it could not be for any other purpose than to give information in support of these memorials."

It would seem from this passage, that it was I who prepared the expedition to Egypt. I owe it to truth to declare the fact without attempting here to judge of the merit of the enterprise.

It is very well known that different projects, particularly under the ancient government, were proposed relative to Egypt; but what is not known, yet is not less true, is, that these memorials remained wholly neglected during my administration; that neither myself on the part of the Directory, nor the chief of division, paid any attention to them; that I had not any idea of the contents of the memorials of Citizen Magallen; that his memorials in no respect influenced the permission given him to return; but, on the contrary, it was granted on the ground of his ill health and the danger he was in of dying if he remained longer in Egypt.

Let Citizen Talleyrand cast an eye over the account I gave the Directory of my conduct in administration, on the 12th Thermidor in the 5th year, under the article Ottoman Porte, and he will find that there is not a single word in it relative to that expedition, and that every expression breathes the desire and the hope of securing for ever the most perfect harmony between the two powers.

Citizen Talleyrand might even recollect that in my first conference with him, on my return from my mission to the Batavian republic, after having conversed with him a long time on the horrible counter-revolution which had destroyed there, in one day, the fruits of six months labours, and the outrages offered in my person to the French republic, I mentioned to him the report which began to get abroad, that Egypt was the immediate destination of Buonaparte's expedition. "I shall not attempt," I observed, "to penetrate into your secret; but I do not give credit to the report in circulation. It is not to Egypt, but the Black Sea, that Buonaparte is to proceed. It will be his object to destroy in that quarter the establishments of the Russians, who are absolutely determined to engage in a war with us; to restore the Poles to the number of nations; to keep the House of Austria in awe, and to prescribe a definitive peace. If you entertain any future designs with respect to Egypt, the Porte, grateful for the important service which you shall have performed for it, will readily co-operate in carrying them into effect." Citizen Talleyrand left me in a pleasing illusion, which events but too soon dissipated.

My regard for truth has dictated these short observations. It will plead my excuse to Citizen Talleyrand.

CH. DELACROIX.

Charenton, 27th Messidor (15th July),
7th Year of the French Republic, one
and indivisible.

The Minister Plenipotentiary of the Batavian Republic to the Citizen Minister for Foreign Affairs.

Paris, 21st July, 5th Year of Batavian Liberty (3d Thermidor).

Citizen Minister,

I HAVE received orders from my government to submit the following reflections to the French Directory. The new efforts of despotism against the representative government, the sentiment of duty, and even of necessity, which results from thence for the allied republics, to strengthen the bands which ought to unite them for the safety of the common cause, have dictated this frank and amicable communication, this explanation of the salutary and protecting principles which should actuate all republicans, inflamed with the love of their country, and only directed by that sentiment they owe a people who have entrusted their dearest interest to them. Since the formation of the Batavian constitution, the legislative body, the directory, the tribunals, the departmental administrations, in short, every authority generally composed of men most remarkable for their patriotism and understanding, have strove to assure the stability of that constitution, and to procure their fellow-citizens all the happiness that had been promised to them. The immense majority of the Batavians, attached by sentiment to the laws which have been given them, impressed with a generous esteem for the magistrates honoured by their choice, will second by every means in their power, with the whole strength of their ability, the painful labours of their delegates. This union between the nation and its magistrates presents to the philosopher and the friends of humanity the consoling hope of being soon able to prove, by an eloquent example, the excellence of a well-tempered democracy, and of establishing by facts, that the practical execution of this system is as easy and as simple, as the conception of its theory is grand and sublime. But this example of a happy republic, without patricians, without privileges, exercising the rights of its sovereignty with dignity, must be too flattering to the people, too alarming to kings. England, dreading its power, has hitherto directed its artificial and criminal policy, in endeavouring to weaken and destroy it. The cabinet of Saint James's has seen with affright the fall of the Stadtholder. Thus this cabinet has calculated the fatal consequences to its commerce, which must be produced by the alliance between the Batavians and the French republic. Its menaces, its arms, not having been able to prevent that alliance, it endeavours to defeat the benefits resulting from it. Force having become useless in the accomplishment of its plans, it has established itself as the banker of intrigue, and by dark manœuvres and machiavelian combi-

nations

nations has attempted to sow jealousies between the two nations, to destroy those sentiments of mutual benevolence which subsisted between them, to divide and to exasperate them against each other. It is thus, on the one hand, to alienate the Batavians, that the disguised emissaries of that cabinet report, with as much affectation as insolence, that the French government will have only tributary republics near it; slaves rather than allies; people vainly decorated with the title of sovereigns, geographically independent, but politically enchained; and that at a peace, Holland, parcelled out and abandoned to a foreign yoke, will leave to Europe only the remembrance of its name and its virtues. It is thus that in France the disguised apostles of tyranny essayed to surprise the confidence of the Directory; to inspire it with fears as to the fidelity of the Batavians; to raise doubts as to their patriotism; to call in question their known attachment to the republican system, by describing as suppliers of England, as engrossers on the account of England, as partisans of England, those who are the implacable enemies of the Britannic government, and the eternal rivals of that haughty ruler of the main. Alas! who are the organs of these horrible blasphemies? Men rendered infamous by the most culpable excesses; men who, having shaken off the restraint of the laws, and renounced all morality, all idea of social organization, set up as the only patriots and privileged defenders of liberty, and, under pompous titles, endeavour to submit all to their fury and despotism. They are men, who, establishing themselves as the disposers of character, describe as a Stadtholderian the citizen who obeys the laws; as a tyrant, the functionary faithful to his duties; and as an egotist and friend to England, the merchant, who by his indefatigable industry is able to pay the enormous contributions which circumstances have rendered necessary, and which have hitherto saved the republic. It is by fomenting hatred, and exasperating republicans, that these promoters of civil discord daily bring down new misfortunes on their country, and insensibly prepare the ruin and overthrow of the state. Indifferent as to the means, they indiscriminately embrace all those they think likely to favour their designs; sometimes humble, sometimes insolent, but always perfidious, they flatter or destroy; informers by profession, infamous in character, they calumniate those they cannot corrupt; and, after having mysteriously fabricated pretended plots, and feigned treasons, they loudly invoke the vigilance of the French agents, in order to avert evils which never had any existence, except in their disordered imagination, and their fantastic projects. By what fatality is it they have preserved the appearance of good faith, when they have been spreading their fears? How have they been able so easily to affright us with vain fears? How have they been able to circulate such unfounded

Vol. VIII. R r reports,

reports, such sinister predictions, such denunciations, as ridiculous as impudent, and render themselves the echoes of them to the French government? How is it we have not foreseen the disastrous effects which must necessarily be produced by the suspicions with which they have surrounded a rising administration? How is it that it has not been felt that the insinuations of a violent and unruly patriotism may destroy the confidence and esteem which the chief magistrates of two friendly and independent nations ought reciprocally to possess? How is it they have not felt, that to annihilate the credit of the Batavians, already so much impaired by the shocks inseparable from a great revolution, was serving the most ardent wishes of the British minister; and that, from the day on which its credit, the very principle of its existence, strengh, and power, should be destroyed, the republic would present nothing to its allies but foetid marshes, and to Europe the dreadful spectacle of a nation cruelly disappointed in its hopes, and writhing in the convulsions of an horrible agony? Yes, it is to the infernal system of informers—to the odious proscription of whatever is good, honest, and upright, to that perfidious art of altering and corrupting every thing, that crafty England owes its successes, republics their losses, republicans their misfortunes, and Batavians that want of regard and deference, that offensive treatment, which have so often occasioned their deep regret, and been the subject of their complaints. The Batavian government is so intimately persuaded of having pointed out the source of all its evils, that it is convinced of the necessity of a prompt and efficacious remedy. It is time to prove to England and to Europe that the French republic is too generous, too magnanimous, to adopt a system of making republics tributary; on the contrary, it acknowledges that it wishes, in its full extent, the equality of the people; and, rich in its own resources, it only desires friends, powerful and faithful friends. The Batavian government, confiding in the purity of its intentions, neither has nor can have any secrets which it wishes to conceal from the French Directory. It knows that by fate the two nations are inevitably united with each other; that they must triumph or perish together; destroy the same enemies, or be destroyed by them; that they must inspire respect for republics by a manly energy, and the example of their internal happiness; that they must suppress factions; and that in the bloody contest of republicanism against royalty, it is necessary that republicans should unite to prudence and prodigies of valour the courage to make every sacrifice. The Batavian nation will not be behind in this perilous struggle. During the storms which have preceded the establishment of its constitution, it has learnt to distinguish its real friends from its vile seducers. It will honour the one, and punish the disturbers of

its

its repose, whatever disguise they may assume. Fatigued with the long commotions which have shaken its credit and annihilated its commerce, it feels that it is only by internal peace that it can repair its losses; that new revolutionary tempests will wreck the vessel of the state; and that the general safety demands general order, calmness, and wisdom. For these considerations the Batavian Directory, jealous of dissipating the clouds by which the enemies of the two nations have endeavoured to obscure the first days of a sworn alliance, calculated for the prosperity of the two republics; jealous also of destroying every pretence for calumny, of obviating all suspicion of establishing those legitimate relations which ought to subsist between the two governments, is eager to make a profession of its faith, and to explain publicly the whole of its policy and system. This system, which will ever actuate the Batavian government, is the result of its inviolable attachment to the democratic constitution and republican principles; to the faithful accomplishment of the engagements of the Batavian republic towards the French republic; to the firm resolution of rigorously repressing Orangism and public disturbers; of restraining and chastising the factious; to its deep-rooted hatred against the government of England; to the direction of its resources, in order to second the measures which the French government may adopt against the enemy; to place upon the most respectable footing, and to the full extent of its means, the forces of the Batavian republic by sea and land; to offer its forces in aid of the common cause; to concert with the French republicans as to their destination and employment; and to leave to France, in the combination of its military plans, that ascendency which it naturally derives from its situation.

Doubtless, the Directory, convinced of the sincerity of the Batavian government by the rigorous execution of its solemn promises, will hasten to second its intentions. Doubtless it will show, that the independence of its ally is dear and sacred to it; that it will make it respected by respecting itself; that it will instruct its agents in Holland, that there can be no durable influence but that which is founded on esteem and public opinion; that it is upon these principles they should regulate their conduct in their relations with different authorities; and that it is the more necessary to conform to these principles, inasmuch as the Batavian nation, long characterised by its noble frankness, by its hatred of pride and haughtiness, by its extreme sensibility to the slightest marks of benevolence, only distinguishes and appreciates men according to their virtues, their talents, the amenity of their deportment, their modesty with regard to social relations, and their inflexible severity against the enemies of public order. It will, doubtless, instruct them, that Batavia is not a conquest;

R r 2   that

that its ancient history attests the undaunted firmness it has ever opposed to tyranny; that its inhabitants, long previous to the arrival of the French, combated against the Stadtholder; and that the reception they gave them has proved to the whole world they were received rather as brethren than conquerors, rather as friends than oppressors . . . . ; but what chiefly cannot escape the sagacity of the Directory is, the necessity of restoring and protecting the commerce of the Batavians in its ancient splendour. The Directory will then convince its agents, what they have not sufficiently been impressed with, that commerce is to Holland what agriculture is with respect to France; and that as without agriculture the colossal size of the republic would soon be a skeleton, without vigour and without life; so also the Batavian republic, without commerce, would disappear: that England alone desires to behold such a catastrophe; that its policy and its jealousy, its luxury and its taxes, its avarice and its prodigality, its ambition and its pride, its factitious existence and its vanity, its expenses and its paper credit; that all these circumstances impose upon it the execrable duty of aspiring to an exclusive commerce, an exclusive navigation, a monopoly of the universe; that it is this monopoly which includes the secret of the resources and the means of England; that to the dominion it exercises over the seas, the misfortunes which in the course of the present war have been heaped upon all neutral nations are to be attributed; that it is to the violation of this neutrality it is indebted for the gold with which it pays its taxes; and that, proud of such advantages, it will constantly oppose the efforts of an active and industrious republic, which, independent of its influence, too well understands its own interests, ever to become the instrument of its domination and caprice.

Such is the fertile system from which glory and happiness must result. Such is the system which becomes two generous nations, which alone is worthy their honour and their loyalty. England wishes to disunite, in order to subject them. England can only be conquered by their union. May the most perfect confidence succeed the efforts of malevolence; may they rival each other only in good offices, and in mutual sacrifices for their common good; may our energy redouble with our dangers; may th French and Batavians compose but one family under differen titles; and may they soon appreciate according to its just value th friendship of a nation, as jealous of its rights as its indepenc ence, and as respectable by its manners and its industry, distinguished by its courage!

Inviting you, Citizen Minister, immediately to lay this no before the Directory, permit me to applaud myself for being upon this occasion the solemn interpreter of a government which

manifes

manifests the purest intentions and most liberal ideas. You know with what constancy, I may say with what tenacity, since my arrival in this capital, I have discussed with you plans equally salutary to both nations, and calculated more closely to cement that union which ought to exist between them.

May the fraternal conduct which I have this day adopted in its name, unite every mind and every heart! May the destinies of our two republics dissipate every storm! May a glorious and speedy peace, hastened by a redoubled increase of our efforts and energy, procure to the French and to the Batavians all that prosperity which they have a right to hope for from an alliance founded upon sentiment and reason!

Receive, Citizen Minister, the homage of my high consideration.
(Signed) R. J. SCHIMMELPENNINCK.
As an attested copy,
(Signed) J. M. SMITS.
C. G. HULTMAN.

Answer of the Insurgents of Arezzo to the Proclamation addressed to Rivani, the President of the Government of Florence, by the French during their Stay in Italy.

THE French government, disciplined in the art of conquering provinces and kingdoms by means of perfidy, faction, and intrigue, are enraged and dismayed at beholding the extent, and consequently the formidable attitude, of the insurrection. They are far, however, from being willing to awake from the flattering dream which induces them to imagine that they can scatter and dissolve it by a mere sheet of paper. Fatigued neither by holding out threats at one time, and offers of pardon at another; confounded by the shame of drawing back, and shrinking with fear, after the boastful publication of their terrific proclamations, they endeavour to convert you into an instrument for enforcing the persuasion that they are sincerely disposed to adopt measures of mildness and moderation: but who is unacquainted and unprovoked by the insidious language, the fallacious policy of the French ministers and their satellites?

This gracious pardon they hold out does not flow from the goodness of their heart, but is extorted by the imperious necessity of the moment. When Rusca fell back on St. Quirico, he marched against Arezzo by order of that braggart Macdonald, who in his imagination already sacked and ravaged every town, and reared in their room some romantic pyramids. Were we then more guilty than at present in his imagination? The retreat of that general, and the pacific offers that are now addressed to us, are not so much dictated by emotions of sensibility,

as by the difasters and defeats which they have fustained in c
ferent parts of Italy, and particularly on the confines of Tufca
Thefe virtuous Frenchmen, whom you reprefent as fo concern
at our misfortunes, and fo anxious to fraternize with us as
have employed the intervention of the minifters of the gofpel
folicit our return from what they call our fatal error, are th
not the very fame who have fpread defolation all over Europ
who have every where perfecuted religion, and loaded it w
fcoffs and fcorns; who have reduced unfortunate Tufcany to t
loweft ebb of diftrefs by mifery and famine; are they not '
very men who applauded the docility of the good-natured T
can people, becaufe they imagined that by fuch hollow flatte
they might the more eafily undo them? Are they not the ve
men who, though they feemed to hold the name of impofitic
in execration, defpoiled, notwithftanding, all the wealth of
public treafuries; gathered up all the money of the ftate, a
enriched themfelves with the plunder of all the churches; w
ftole or put into requifition all the horfes, and carried off all
provifions, under the pretext of maintaining a body of troops
the protection of the ftate; and that from perfons who, fo
from wifhing any connexion with the French, would, on
contrary, have given all they poffeffed, that they might ne
fee them, except, perhaps, a few defperate wretches, who lool
forward to the French for protection and employment? Are th
not the very men, who, providing only for their own fafety, a
regardlefs of that of others, have difarmed, by one order,
whole of Tufcany; and after having poffeffed themfelves of
the arms, fold them afterwards at a low rate, under the e
of their very owners? Are they not the men, who, hav
nothing at heart, or in view, but plunder and robbery, exp
to fale all the furniture, the houfes, and the lands of the in
bitants, and who are ready even to fell their blood, did there e
a nation fo bafe and perfidious as their own, with whom th
might contract for it? The pardon therefore, which they of
proceeds merely from the defire to afflict with the fame mif
and defolation thofe whom they ftigmatize as the infurger
among whom, however, are to be found plenty and tranquilli
bleffings wholly unknown to the cities and provinces who h
admitted within their bofoms thofe defolating monfters.

Let the Tufcan people who have been thus lulled with
promifes of fovereignty, carefully confider the ftate of mifery i
which they are reduced; let them compare it with that of
Lombards, the Neapolitans, the Romans, who have allov
themfelves to be inveigled by fimilar promifes. For your p
Tufcans, you have always beheld with fcorn and indignat
thofe execrable innovators, who deprive nations of their fo
reigns, in order to bow their necks before the nod of a thouf

base and barbarous tyrants. Your rage would have burst out against them from the very moment of their arrival, had not the best of princes and of fathers repressed your resentment and arrested your avenging arm. You submitted, and withheld your tears and your lamentations at the moment the beloved Ferdinand was tearing himself from your embrace. But your silence was an inauspicious omen for those unhappy sufferers...... But the Imperial cohorts, so anxiously looked for, rapidly approach your frontiers, daily winning and crowning their brows with new laurels, which French perfidy would fain conceal from your knowledge. The miserable remains of the republican armies that have concentrated themselves in Tuscany, are straining their last efforts, but to no purpose. The Divine Justice, justly enraged, has at the close of ten years appointed the hour of punishment. The dejection of their leaders, the desertion of their soldiers, the motions of their troops—every thing bespeaks a defeat and ruin, which they themselves have accelerated by the very means which they exerted to avert or retard it. Even the talent of lying, that magic instrument, which opened to them the gates of so many towns and fortresses, is disarmed of all its power. In their proclamations they would fain hold out victories, and attempt to triumph over a few prisoners; to these they add false, imaginary details of the assassination of their ministers, whose funeral rites they perform with a ridiculous ostentation and pomp, in order to amuse and deceive the credulous; but henceforth the eyes of Italy are open to the means, and resolve upon the execution of vengeance. The time of its servitude is no more. Tuscans, be not apprehensive that our numbers shall decrease, or our spirit be relaxed. Forty thousand soldiers are willing and prepared to die on the field of battle, or to restore the beloved Ferdinand. Let that name be the signal for a general insurrection! The moment is not far distant—when it comes, display all your energies; and your very despair will furnish you with those arms which you have concealed from the vigilance of your executioners. Do you, president, advise the tender-hearted Reinhard to reserve his tears of condolence for that fatal day.

The following is the Answer which the President of the Batavian Directory made to Fouche de Nantes, Minister of the French Republic, on presenting his Credentials, at the End of July.

THE Executive Directory of the Batavian republic, rejoicing to receive a minister from their ally the French republic, testify to you, Citizen, the pleasure they feel in seeing that character vested in your person. Organ of the French government, placed in a manner as such between it and the Batavian government, you

will

will be enabled to contribute effectually, as well to the promoting the common prosperity of both, as to remove whatever might become a source of disagreeable misrepresentations, suspicions, and mistrust, so prejudicial to nations naturally connected by the same interests. I shall not enter, Citizen Minister, into the particulars of what would essentially prejudice that common interest; your own information will make them sufficiently obvious to you. All that their mutual relations induce us to observe is, that on our part, faithful allies, being neither infested with principles of Anglo-mania, nor with a leaven of aristocracy or an inclination for arbitrary power, we wish to direct all our efforts, all our measures, against the common enemy. Devoted to the grand principles of the revolution, which has happily brought about among us a new order of things; jealous of the liberty and independence which have taken root on the Batavian soil, we shall evince ourselves, on every occasion, ready to combat whatever might have a tendency to shackle them. And as nothing is more calculated to attain that end than the cementing of a good understanding and reciprocal confidence between the two allied republics, we shall, on our part, most eagerly seize at all times the opportunity of cultivating them. Considering France as the guarantee of that liberty, of that independence which are become the precious right of the people, whose care is entrusted to us, we shall co-operate with a sincere attachment and true zeal to the maintaining and nourishing the happy harmony which subsists between both. But, Citizen Minister, that zeal, that affection, that truth, give the Batavian nation a right to be seconded by the dispositions of its great ally; they require a concert and reciprocity of efforts and actions. Above all, it is necessary that the Batavian people should enjoy in reality the fruit of so many sacrifices, which they have made with the frankness that forms their character, in order that nothing may be able to alienate them from a government which has its basis on the true and sacred principles of equality, and on the rights of man and the citizen. We moreover more ardently wish that your stay among us, attended with satisfaction to yourself, may be salutary to the two republics, and tend to make them prosper for ever.

The Batavian Executive Directory, on sending to the first Chamber the Legislative Body the Speech of the Minister Fouche, and the Answer of the President Director, wrote to that Chamber the following Letter.

CITIZENS representatives, Citizen Fouche, minister of the French republic to this, who is come to replace Citizen Lombard delivered to us this day his credentials, and has commenced the exercise of his functions among us. We make known this event to you, by sending you his speech of introduction, with the answer of our President. We doubt not, citizens representatives, that you will
fir

find in the speech of that minister, sentiments which do honour to the nation which he represents; which contain the most unequivocal assurances, that the true grandeur of a republic consists neither in the extent of its territory, nor in the number of its trophies; and that the Batavian nation, which has made itself beloved and respected among all other people, by its prudence, activity, and integrity, may rely on the consolidation of that liberty and independence which have cost it so many sacrifices.

Declaration of War of the Emperor of all the Russias against Spain.

WE, by the grace of God, Paul I. &c. &c. do hereby make known to all our faithful subjects, that we, and our allies, have resolved to overthrow the lawless government now ruling France, and we have, therefore, risen against it with all our forces. The Almighty has blessed our arms to this very day, and crowned all our enterprises with victory and success. Among the small number of European powers, apparently attached to the French government, but, in fact, powers that are only afraid of the vengeance of this government, the outcast of God, struggling with the last agonies of dissolution, Spain has, more than all the rest, shown her fear of, or attachment to France, not by giving her actual succours, but by armaments. In vain have we made use of all our resources to open to that power the real path to honour and glory, by combining with us; she has persisted obdurately in the measures and wanderings destructive of herself; and thus have we at last found ourselves under the necessity of sending back her chargé d'affaires at our court, Odie. But having since that received information, that our own chargé d'affaires, too, Counsellor Butzow, has been compelled to quit the King of Spain's dominions within a term unto him limited, we deem this an insult committed upon our Imperial dignity, and do hereby declare war; giving orders at the same time to impose sequestration on all Spanish ships in our harbours, and to confiscate the same, as also to send orders to the commanders of all our land and sea forces, to act with hostility every where against all the subjects of the King of Spain.

Done at Peterhof, July 26, 1799.

(Signed) PAUL.

The Prince of Orange's Proclamation.

WE William, by the grace of God Prince of Orange and Nassau, Hereditary Stadtholder, &c. &c. To all those to whom these presents shall come, greeting.

Dear Countrymen,

THE long-wished for moment when you are at last to be delivered from so many calamities, under which you have suffered more than four years past, is, we hope, arrived, and we now enjoy the satisfaction again to address you under that pleasing prospect. It would be superfluous to enumerate the different hardships under which you have groaned, ever since the violence you have suffered in consequence of the French invasion, and the events which have followed it. If cruel experience has made you feel them but too severely, and if our ardent wishes could be sooner fulfilled, you would have been relieved long ago from that intolerable burden. We have been but too long obliged to confine ourselves to the deploring your fate in silence, without having it in our power to alter it. At last that time is come. His Majesty the King of Great Britain, moved by his affection and friendship towards the republic of the United Provinces, and pitying your misfortunes, has taken the generous resolution, as soon as the general circumstances of Europe have allowed it, to employ, in concert with his allies, vigorous measures for your deliverance. The military force which is now sent for that purpose is to be followed by still more numerous troops.

The object of this expedition is made known to you in the name of his Britannic Majesty, by the commander in chief of the first body of troops which is to open this glorious career. Those troops do not come to you as enemies, but as friends and deliverers, in order to rescue you from the odious oppression under which you are held by the French government, and by the French troops, and to restore you to the enjoyment of your religion and liberty, those invaluable blessings for which, with the Divine assistance, your and our own ancestors fought and conquered. Hesitate not, therefore, brave inhabitants of the United Provinces, to meet and to assist your deliverers. Receive them among you as friends and protectors of the happiness and welfare of your country. Let every difference of political sentiments and opinions vanish before this great object. Do not suffer the spirit of party, nor even the sense of the wrongs you have suffered, to induce you to commit any acts of revenge or persecution. Let your hands and your hearts be united in order to repel the common enemy, and to re-establish the liberty and independence of our common country. Let your deliverance be as much as possible your own work. You see already, and you will experience it still more in future, that you may depend upon being vigorously and powerfully assisted. As soon as the first efforts which are making towards your delivery shall have acquired some consistency, our dearly beloved son, the Hereditary Prince of Orange, who is in possession of our entire confidence, and is deserving of yours, and who is perfectly well acquainted with our intentions, will join you, put himself at your head, and, following the steps of our illustrious ancestors, spare neither his property nor his life, in order to assist with you, and for your sake, in bringing this great undertaking to a successful issue. We ourselves also will then, as soon as circumstances shall allow it, proceed to join you. And as
we

we have always confidered our own happinefs and welfare as infeperably connected with that of our dear country, we will then, after having feen your laws and privileges reftored, and yourfelves re eftablifhed in the poffeffion of thofe benefits which belong to a free people under a lawful government, make our greateft and moft heartfelt fatisfaction confift (under the Divine bleffing) in the advancement of the public good, and of that profperity and welfare which formerly made our once happy country an object of admiration to the furrounding nations.

Done in the palace of Hampton Court, the 28th of July 1799.
(Signed)   W. PRINCE OF ORANGE.

Manifefto publifhed at the Head-quarters of the Auftro-Ruffian grand Army, Auguft 1ft.

THE army is on the eve of entering the territory of the republic of Genoa; it does not come as an enemy, but to free that republic from the yoke of her oppreffors and their fatellites. It comes to reftore the old government, and holy religion, polluted with impiety. It grants a general oblivion of the paft to the malevolent, if they will return to virtue, good order, and their lawful government.

Secret Convention entered into on the 5th of Auguft 1796, between his Majefty the King of Pruffia and the French Republic.

ANIMATED with the fame defire of feeing the unfortunate war under which Europe groans, brought to a fpeedy termination, and entertaining the fond hopes that the time is not far diftant when this falutary wifh fhall be accomplifhed, his Majefty the King of Pruffia and the French republic have thought it neceffary to enter into an amicable treaty. His Pruffian Majefty, in purfuance of the declarations made by him at the peace of Balle, has not withheld the wifh which his own dignity as a ftate of the Empire, and his bounden duty, pointed out to him; namely, that the conftitution and boundaries of the Empire might be preferved in their full integrity. In like manner his Majefty, confiding in the French government, has difclofed the wifh of the Houfe of Orange, that this family might be reinftated in their former rank and dignity in Holland, under fuch juft modifications as might be agreed upon. His Majefty has alfo made ufe of every amicable means which he conceived neceffary for accomplifhing this object; but as the French republic perfifted in the opinion that circumftances did not permit them to participate in thofe wifhes, or to favour their completion, therefore both parties have entered into a further agreement

agreement with each other, through the medium of their mi*
M. Christian Henry Curt, Count de Haugwitz, Minister c
to his Prussian Majesty, on the one part, and M. Anton. B
Caillard, Plenipotentiary of the French republic, on the othe
These have agreed to the following eventual capitulation.

1. As the French government has expressed a wish th
republic of the United Netherlands, by way of compensat
the territory given up to France, might receive that part
bishopric of Munster which extends from the place wh
Ems enters East Frieseland, and up this river towards Wi
from thence in a direct line over Heyden and along the bou
of the dutchy of Cleves to the point where it meets the bo
Holland; his Prussian Majesty declares, that in order to g
French republic an assurance of his amicable sentiments,
not oppose such a measure whenever negotiations shall be
into concerning the cession of the left bank of the Rh
France; and because the principle of secularization is unav
necessary for indemnifying the temporal princes who mus
losses by such a disposition, his Majesty consents to the adop
that principle accordingly, as an indemnification for the
vinces which lie on the left bank of the Rhine, including th
tory of the bishopric of Munster, with the country of Rec
hausen. His Majesty, however, reserves to himself the
claim such further additions as may appear best calculated t
him a complete indemnification; an object concerning wh
two contracting powers will entertain an amicable underst

2. The second article of the treaty of Basle of April 5,
remains in full force; consequently the French republic
the mediation of the King of Prussia in favour of other pri
the Empire who might wish to enter into negotiation
France.

3. In the statements set forth in the article concerning t
sion of the left bank of the Rhine to France, and concern
adoption of the principle of secularization, his Prussian M
and the French republic pledge themselves to use their unit
deavours to effect, in favour of the princes of the House of
the secularization of the ecclesiastical states, which shall
the most convenient compensation to them, in lieu of the la
property which they may lose on the left bank of the Rhin
also to procure the Electoral dignity for the line of Hesse (

4. His Majesty the King of Prussia pledges himself to m
the cities of Hamburgh, Bremen, and Lubeck, in their i
and present independence.

5. If at the future pacification the restoration of the H
Orange to its rank and dignity in Holland should be deeme
missible, in that case his Prussian Majesty and the French r
pledge themselves that they will use every mediation in thei

to bring about a proper accommodation between the Batavian republic and the princes of Naſſau Orange; the chief conditions of which ſhall be, on the one part, a renunciation of all claims to the dignity of Stadtholder, as well as to all the immoveable property of thoſe princes on the left bank of the Rhine, and in the Belgic provinces; on the other ſide, the Batavian republic ſhall make a compenſation to the Princes of Orange equivalent to what they had poſſſeſſ in the United Provinces, and in the Dutch colonies, unleſs the Batavian republic would rather give up to the Houſe of Orange the immoveable property juſt mentioned, in order that they might themſelves agree upon a fair exchange of this property; or ſuffer it to be done by an arbitrator choſen by both parties. In order to effect this accommodation, the French republic pledges itſelf ſtill further, that it will do its utmoſt endeavour to promote the advantage of the ſaid Prince of Orange and his male heirs; to effect the ſecularization of the biſhoprics of Wurtzburgh and Bamberg; and make ſuch an arrangement, that the reverſions of the ſaid biſhoprics ſhall be ſettled on the Houſe of Brandenburg, in caſe the male branch of the Houſe of Orange ſhould become extinct.

6. The preſent ſecret convention ſhall be ratified by the contracting parties; and the ratification ſhall, within ſix weeks, or ſooner, if it can be done, be exchanged at Berlin. In teſtimony of the ſame, this convention has been ſigned and ſealed by the undernamed plenipotentiaries.

Done at Berlin, Auguſt 5, 1796.

CHRISTIAN HENRY CURT, COUNT DE HAUGWITZ,
ANTON. BERNARD CAILLARD.

Extract of an Order from St. Peterſburgh to Major-general and Port-captain Burmaneligen, dated Auguſt 1799.

WHEREAS in the city of Copenhagen, and throughout the whole kingdom of Denmark, clubs and ſocieties have been formed, upon principles ſimilar to thoſe which have brought about the revolution in France, and overturned the lawful monarchical power of that country; and whereas theſe have been permitted by the Daniſh government: it is ordered by us, that all Daniſh ſhips of war, as well as merchantmen, and alſo all ſubjects of that kingdom, ſhall be ſtrictly forbidden to enter into any of the ports of our dominions.

Circular

Circular Letter of his Royal Highness the Archduke Charles, in Capacity of Field-marshal-general of the Imperial Troops, and those of the Empire, to all the Princes who are Members of concerning the furnishing of their Contingents to the Army of Empire; dated August 19, 1799.

THE high decree of commission to the general assembly of Empire, respecting the renewed state of war of the Empi and the duties to which that state subjects its members, affords an opportunity to communicate to you my thoughts upon a su ject with which my mind has been occupied for some time, absolutely necessary for the honour and welfare of our comm country, namely, the furnishing of contingents for the Imper army and the army of the Empire.

The proceedings of France at the negotiations of Rasta when Germany sincerely wished for peace, are universally know It is also known, how, during an armistice, the German Empi has been offended, and exposed to fresh dangers of invasion a revolution, by the subjugation of Switzerland. Its proceedin against the fortress of Ehrenbreitstein, during the negotiatior and contrary to existing treaties, are circumstances unparallel in history. In short, its offences against the rights of nations general, of which it had been guilty ever since the opening the negotiations for peace, could leave no doubt that it had n only resolved on the renewal of war against Germany, but al the destruction and subjugation of this ancient confederation, formidable when undivided. Preparations were actually maki for this purpose. The enemy's plan of operations, in its mater points, was the same as that on which they proceeded in 1796 a 1797. Jourdan's army was to occupy Suabia, to penetrate in the heart of the Empire, in conjunction with the armies of Ita and Switzerland. The only difference was in the manner of e ecuting their plan, as the faithless policy of the French gover ment wished to deceive us, under the mask of peaceable sent ments, to weaken our means of defence, and to carry on th most dangerous war of extermination with less resistance. was pretended, artfully distorting the true sense of the word that they only took such military positions as the circumstanc required, but without stating their extent. The whole army France advanced from its positions; ambiguous proclamatio (the object of which was nevertheless evident), accompanied l threats of the Directory as well as of the generals, preceded thi The line marked out, at the conclusion of the armistice, w transgressed, without previous notice being given, as had bee agreed upon; Suabia was invaded, and treated worse than a hostile country, at least amongst civilized states. Already on th 6th of March, in the present year, was the Grison country, a

th

... of Vorarlberg, attacked by Massena, without giving any previous notice to General Auffenberg, who commanded in the Grison country; while, on the other hand, Jourdan's army advanced from different points in Germany, without the least declaration of war. The enemy made himself master of the town and fortress of Manheim, and disarmed the garrison in the most disgraceful manner. General Bernadotte summoned the commandant of Philipsburg, threatening him in a letter in which the most sacred principles of the rights of nations were trodden under foot; called upon the magistrates to become traitors against the Emperor and the Empire; and attempted to get possession of Philipsburg by bribery, intrigue, and secret plans; he published proclamations which laid open the atrocious views of the enemy, and filled the breast of every German with detestation.

In consequence of all these hostile proceedings of the French, I advanced across the Leck with the troops under my command, took such positions, and employed such measures of precaution, as circumstances absolutely demanded, for the honour and preservation of Germany. The enemy, having advanced as far as Ostrach, was beaten there and at Stockach. By pursuing the enemy to Switzerland, I endeavoured to secure the left flank of Germany; and several states of the Empire are already restored to their rights, possessions, and revenues. From the many acts which had taken place, and from the avowal of the French Directory, their generals and commissaries, it remained no longer a secret what would be the fate of the neighbouring circles of Suabia, Bavaria, and Franconia, should the enemy's plans succeed; and it must be confessed, that much has been done for the security of Germany by the victories gained over him. A convincing proof of this is, the tranquillity which some German states already enjoy, when compared with former times, in which they were exposed to French intrigues, arbitrary threats, and oppression: this confirms it, that the war into which we are again forced is the only and best means for effecting a speedy, true, and lasting peace. Another object, of similar importance, yet remains; namely, to consolidate the advantages we have gained, to drive the enemy entirely from the German territory; and to secure its frontiers. Still are German frontier-fortresses in his possession, still are countries kept under his oppressive yoke, which form a considerable part of the strength of the Germanic body, and who wish to be joined again to their common country. The negotiations at Rastadt clearly show how much it was the intention of the French to retain full power to invade Germany again whenever they pleased, with little danger to themselves. But the present moment, when so much has already been done for the safety of Germany, is particularly adapted to regain its ancient limits, and to acquire its former dignity, integrity, liberty, and independence;

pendence; to reinstate in their rights, possessions, and pr
princes and individuals, saved from the most humiliating
sion, and to conclude an honourable and lasting peace.
obtain this grand object, it is absolutely necessary that the C
states, who have hitherto been equally offended by the proc
of the French, whose future security and independence ha
exposed to the same danger, should no longer suffer the
to be treated with contempt, but, without delay, unite a
strength to attack the enemy in his position, from which th
danger threatens every member of this powerful confed
which, united, has given so many proofs of its bravery.
is the moment in which, with mutual sincerity, with ii
public spirit and harmony, all means must be employed to
our country against the rapacity, ambition, and plans of o
mies. It cannot be doubted that, when every state of t
pire fulfils its duties, particularly by furnishing its quintup
tingents, the enemy will soon be forced to accede to the cor
of peace, which have been laid down as a basis in the re
of the Empire of the 22d of December 1794, 10th of Fe
3d of July, and 19th of November 1795. We may be
persuaded, that then the enemy will not only be driven bac
ancient limits, but that he will also be obliged to desist f
farther plans against the security and independence of Ge
As I am fully convinced that the present is the proper i
when the Empire, and every individual member of it, may
future security and welfare, I think it my duty, as Field-m
general of the Empire, forcibly to enjoin the furnishing
tutional contingents, which I am particularly bound to de
the pressing circumstances, and according to the orders i
from his Majesty and the Empire.

His Imperial Majesty having carried on the measures of
for so many years, at an immense expense, and by every
in his power, and the preservation of Germany havir
effected almost alone by Imperial troops, I think I am en
expect, and have that confidence in the members of the E
that they will fulfil their duty, and take the necessary
furnish their contingents as soon as possible.

To the Officer commanding the Dutch Troops.

Sir,

ENCLOSED I send you a proclamation of his Serene H.
the Prince of Orange, and one of my own, by comr
his Majesty the King of Great Britain. I demand that y
render instantly, on the grounds contained in this proclar
should you refuse, it will be my duty to treat you as an

and you may ...ly conceive that my army, which is ready for the attack, will im... y defeat you. The officer who is the bearer of this has o...s to return to me immediately with your anſwer. I have the honour to be, &c.

RALPH ABERCROMBY.

On board the Waſhington Man of War, in the Roads of the Texel, Aug. 22.

Anſwer.

General,

I HAVE received your letter, to which I have the honour to anſwer, that my life belongs to my country: I therefore expect you quietly, General, with the brave troops whom I have the honour to command. This is my reply.—Greeting and reſpect.

GILQUIN, Colonel.

Proclamation of General Muller, Commander in Chief of the Army of the Rhine, dated Manheim, Aug. 24.

LIBERTY! EQUALITY!

Officers and Soldiers!

THE left wing of the army of the Danube, for a long time reduced to act on the defenſive, has offered merely a paſſive reſiſtance to the enemies of the republic; but now changed by the orders of the Directory into the army of the Rhine, it is called upon to maintain the former reputation attached to that diſtinguiſhed name by victory, and is about to enter upon the campaign. Soldiers! your country invokes you to undertake new achievements.—Carry terror into the dominions of the enemies of the republic and of liberty. Let every chain be broken, and every ſocial inequality be diſſolved at the appearance of your battalions! Let the unfortunate find in you deliverers and avengers; but let the weak and the oppreſſed reſume confidence at your approach! Suppreſs, by ſubordination and diſcipline, the fears of the peaceable inhabitants. The ſlighteſt error might excite againſt you a people ſimple and good, whoſe attachment it is your duty to conciliate by your conduct, and by your reſpect for unarmed perſons and private property; and finally evince yourſelves the true friends of the people by diſplaying yourſelves as Frenchmen armed for their country, for juſtice, and liberty.

(Signed)   LEONARD MULLER, Commander in Chief of the Army of the Rhine.

Proclamation of the Batavian Directory to the Batavian People, dated Hague, August 26.

BATAVIANS! the moment is arrived in which your enemy is endeavouring to realize her menaces, and to snatch from you the fruit of your numerous sacrifices. Intrigue, cunning, flattery, violence, every thing will be employed to immolate to her pride and ambition the prosperity of our country; but the Batavian, a jealous lover of the liberty and independence of his country, feels strongly at this crisis all the duties which the title of citizen impose upon him, and he will brave with intrepidity the most imminent dangers. This, then, is the moment in which the ancient heroism which rendered your forefathers illustrious, will be found entire in their descendants. Batavians! be worthy of your ancestors!

In these circumstances, the most efficacious measures, the most energetic efforts, will be paralysed by perfidious machinations, or by imbecility, if the authority, hitherto indulgent, did not rise now against those who should manifest the desire of another order of things. The safety of the state imperiously requires that all those should be treated as foes, who, by their conduct or their speech, shall appear to approve of the enterprises directed against the republic. The same state reason prescribes also equal severity against all those who shall check or delay the execution of the legitimate orders; against all who shall warn the enemy by signals, correspond with them, hoist any sign of sedition, utter cries of revolt, or form or foment any insurrection; against all who shall propagate sinistrous reports with guilty intentions, calumniate the constituted authorities, the civil or military officers, and insult their orders; against all, in short, who, by their actions, words, or writings, shall announce hostile intentions.

It is no longer an intermediate government, which, without any permanent or solid basis, may be easily overthrown or modified, that is now threatened—it is our constitution, which we have solemnly sworn to defend; it is not the fear of some, or the caprice of others—it is the voice of all which cries aloud that the country is in danger, and that we ought to save it.

Batavians! we respect your will; deaf to adulation or promises, supported only by the idea that the most terrible catastrophe cannot produce more evils to the country than those which result from cowardice and inactivity, we will remain unshaken in the midst of dangers; and we will prove to the public and private enemies of our political regeneration, that we only desire the constitution and the republic to perish with ourselves.

Ye too, who may be called to the defence of the common cause, may this declaration, this solemn promise, which is not

the

the result of an hasty decision on our part, but which is inspired by the sentiment of our duties, and fidelity to the oaths we have taken, animate you! May it become a pledge for your devotion to your chief magistrates, who, by calling you to arms, have finally resolved to sacrifice themselves to your liberty and your safety! May this declaration particularly carry conviction to those who may have contrived secret plots, in order to kindle the flames of revolt in the interior at the moment of the invasion of the enemy!

Batavians! the engagements we have bound ourselves to are vast; but Heaven favours us, and will enable us to fulfil them. We are borne up by the consciousness of wishing to do what is right. The leading principles of our constitution are too immutably true to have ruled the Batavian soil but for a moment, and then to disappear for ever. Events too weighty have taken place ever to induce us to abandon to a precarious destiny, that system of civil and political liberty which we have assisted in establishing.

All these considerations, added to the justice and holiness of our cause, ought to destroy that calumny which delights in reporting, sometimes, that we are betrayed by the French; at others, that we betray ourselves; and the more so, as at this moment the French government has, with the utmost frankness and good faith, promised the Batavians every assistance in its power.

Batavians! your national representation has, in its wisdom, weighed every circumstance; it has considered, that by the terms of the constitution it is bound to neglect no means of enabling the executive power to display a vigorous resistance to our enemies, and to ensure internal tranquillity.

If the respect which they bear to the constitution directs them not to deviate from what it prescribes, the same sentiment also imposes on them an obligation to defend it against every attack, and to take care that the literal observance of an article of the constitution shall not be made an instrument of overturning the constitution by the constitution itself:

That in case of an hostile invasion, their endeavours should not be confined merely to repel that invasion by the most efficacious methods; but that moreover they may, and they are bound in duty to recur to extraordinary means to repress the revolt in the interior, and to ensure the quiet and tranquillity of the citizens:

That it is the duty of the legislative body to prevent disaffection from embarrassing the measures taken for the public safety; and that, in a word, the occurrence of extraordinary circumstances renders it necessary also to resort to extraordinary means to rouse the courage of the patriots, to increase the energy of the brave defenders of their country, and to preserve each individual from the perfidious suggestions of the enemy.

The Executive Directory of the French Republic to the Executive Directory of the Batavian Republic.

Citizen Directors,·   Paris, 12th Fructidor (29th Aug.), 7th Year of the French Republic.

WE learn that the enemy which has appeared on your coasts has dared to proclaim, " that it comes to deliver the Batavian nation from the yoke which the French republic has pressed upon it." But we also know with what energetic indignation you have repelled the perfidious insinuations and the injurious charges addressed to you. You have sworn to defend, even to death, both your liberty and the constitution upon which that liberty is founded. The whole nation has participated in your oath ; and that glorious unanimity is a terrible answer to the calumnious assertions of the common enemy.

Nevertheless, however confident our two nations may be of their mutual dispositions in a circumstance so serious, we think it a duty and a pleasure to declare anew, " that the French republic, so far from ceasing to respect the independence of the Batavian people, its first ally, is resolved to defend it against every attack, and by every means in its power."

Receive, Citizen Directors, this solemn assurance ; transmit it to your fellow-citizens ; they know how to distinguish the sincere ally, the constant ally, whom policy as well as liberty attaches to the success of Batavia, from the jealous nation, from the inimical government, which, wishing to usurp the commerce of the universe, and fearing the efforts of the industrious Dutchman, endeavours to reduce Holland once more under its dependance, by destroying the association to which it is indebted for its prosperity by entailing on it opprobrium and slavery.

(Signed)   SIEYES, President.
            LAGARDE, Sec. Gen.

The following Letter from the French Ambassador to the Dutch Minister of Foreign Affairs was read in the Sitting of the Legislative Body on the 30th of August.

WHEN two united powers endeavour to conquer the territory of the Batavian republic, and to destroy her navigation and commerce ; when they take off the mask, and dare to call upon the Batavian people to return to the dominion of their lawful sovereign ; when traitors have the boldness to express a criminal joy at these proce ings; my government has chosen this critical moment to rene w, through me, its positive declarations, that it will strain every nerve to procure to the Batavian republic the victory over her enemies, and to strengthen her independence. I can also add, Citizen Minister, that my government, far from withing to leave the Batavian government to its own strength, and to recall the French troops, has this moment sent off fresh battalions to complete the army, as stipulated by treaty. My government is also forming an army of observation adjoining the Batavian frontiers, which shall immediately march where danger and glory calls. Malicious reports are spread, that the Batavian government had attempted secretly to treat with the enemy, and that it would sacrifice Batavian liberty to the false expectation of peace and prosperity; but my government requires no refutation of these calamities, invented by the cabinet at St. James's. As this, however, might diminish the patriotic confidence of the Batavian people, the Directory knows how to refute these calumnies. This may be effected by uniting more closely the friends of liberty and equality, by forming an assembly of them against internal and external enemies, by vigorous measures against traitors, by watching their secret machinations, and by ridding the Batavian territory of French emigrants and English agents. Receive, Citizen Minister, the assurances of my respect, &c.

The Ex-Director Merlin's Vindication, in an Address to the Council of Five Hundred.

LONG before the 30th Prairial (18th June), the idea of giving in my resignation occurred to my mind, and I still hesitated upon the subject, when Citizen Jean Debry arrived from Rastadt; I communicated to him my ideas, adding, that if I really did adopt this conduct, my intention was to demand the legiflative body, upon accepting my resignation, to send me before the supreme court of justice, that the purity of my conduct, so long calumniated, might be established in the face of day. I begged him at the same time to consider this idea, and to give me his advice, after having maturely weighed it in his mind. I saw him again in a few days, and he said to me that my project did not appear to be advantageous for myself, nor useful to the republic. Well, said I to him, let there be no more said about it. On the 29th Prairial many representatives of the people made others advise me, and even some of them advised me themselves, to give in my resignation, giving me to understand that it was the only means of withdrawing myself from that destruction which for some time had been impending over my head. I replied, that if my resignation could have been of advantage to the republic, I would have given it in long before,

before, and that I would still give it in upon this supp
should it even cost me the sacrifice of my honour; but tha
vinced of the contrary, I could not reconcile it with my
that a decree of accusation had nothing in it that could
me, and that I would much rather die with glory, than live
grace a few years longer.

In the evening, I learned from my colleague Reveilliere I
that the same proposals had been made to him as to me, and
had replied in a similar style. We separated, promising
yield, and to surrender ourselves peaceably to the high c
justice, should we be put in accusation. On the morrow n
new instances were made, which met with a new refusal.
two hours after mid-day, the Directory being assembled, a
keeper announced that a deputation from the Council c
Hundred wished to speak to Citizens Reveilliere Lepai
Merlin. We went, my colleague and I, into the minister's
where we found the representatives of the people, Lauffat,
Chapsal, Perrin, Faurela-Bremerie, Regnier, and Chaffet,
bers of the Council of Elders, accompanied by five or six m
of the Council of Five Hundred.

Citizen Perrin first informed us, that all the members
Council of Elders had been assembled in the Room of Lib
place adjoining to the usual place of their sittings; that,
with the dangers which menaced the country in the state o
rescence which existed in the precincts of the Council c
Hundred, they had unanimously agreed to send us a depu
the members of which the president himself had named, to
us to give in our resignation, assuring us upon the honour
Council, that nothing more should be done in the plan fo
and publicly announced, of putting us under accusation; t
deputation, before coming to us, had gone to the Council c
Hundred; that it had communicated to the assembled com
of that House, the object of the mission which they were ge
discharge, and that all the members of these committees h
tified their hearty concurrence in the sentiments and disposit
the Council of Elders.

We replied, as we had formerly done to the same propos.
we added, that, disposed as we were to wait calmly the dec
accusation with which we were threatened, and to confort
selves peaceably to it in surrendering ourselves to the high
of justice; we could not conceive how this decree could co
mise the public tranquillity, as we had not on our part eith
plan or the means of resistance. Citizen Perrin and his coll
successively spoke, and informed us, with tears in their eyes,
was not for our personal security that they demanded our re
tion, but solely to arrest the commotion which was disp
itself with the most alarming symptoms; that the conduct

this commotion, strangers to the two Councils, only infifted on our expulfion from the Directory, by means of a decree of accufation, as a pretext for the troubles and deftruction which they were meditating ; that it was then of the firft confequence to deprive them of this pretext ; that it was impoffible, if we perfifted in our generous determination, to calculate how far their fury might be carried, and that they once more conjured us to yield, not for our own fakes, but for the fafety of the republic. Thefe confiderations, repeated in an accent of fenfibility truly affecting, ftaggered our refolution ; the reprefentatives of the people perceived it. They preffed upon us with new energy. At laft we declared to them, that before having heard them we were determined to facrifice our exiftence to our honour, but that, overcome by their reafonings, we were ready to facrifice our honour to the country ; and that in confequence we fhould go and fign our refignation if things were ftill entire in the Council of Five Hundred; that is to fay, if at the time at which we fpoke that council had come to no refolution which tended to our accufation. They immediately departed, after having preffed us in their arms, and went to the Council of Five Hundred. Half an hour after, the reprefentatives of the people Regnier and Chaffet returned with the reprefentatives Jourdan and Boulay (de la Meurthe), members of the Council of Five Hundred. They declared to us that the two Councils had not yet taken any refolution with regard to us, and that they came to affure us that fince we had agreed to abdicate our office, nothing farther would be done in the bufinefs of putting us under accufation. Citizen Boulay even engaged to proclaim us from the tribune the faviours of the country. It was upon the fecurity of this confidence that our refignation was drawn up, figned, and fent to the two Councils. I have thought it proper to make thefe details, not to prevent the examination which they now wifh to make into my conduct, but to affure thofe who are ignorant that this refignation was not on our part the effect of an indolent and pufillanimous work, and that it could only be confidered as a facrifice generoufly offered to the tranquillity of our fellow-citizens, and to the fafety of the republicans.

Part of the Replies of Merlin to the Accufations brought againft the Ex-Directors.

FOR having fent our brave men, without arms, to be murdered on the Danube, &c.—Jourdan wrote, that he would have gained, on the 5th Germinal, a complete victory, if Hautpolt had executed his orders. He had then fufficient forces. Our reverfes muft be attributed to the infubordination of the generals to their chief. The Directory put upon trial thofe whom Jourdan pointed out. This general faid, at dinner with Merlin, that his reverfes in the 4th year were owing to the bad underftanding which an evil genius

had

had caused between him and his generals of division. The first thing which he said to the Directory upon his last return was, that he had been perpetually opposed by those who ought to have obeyed him. Scherer owed his reverses in Italy to the same cause. Each general wished to be commander in chief, &c.

For having transported 40,000 men into the deserts of Arabia.—It will not be supposed that I have wished to deprive myself of the only son that I have in the world; of a son, who, at the age of 14, took arms in the defence of the republic: it is this son whom I am accused of transporting with the immortal general, who wished much to take him for his aide-de-camp. Buonaparte, for two months, minuted himself all the orders, all the instructions. He did, in a certain degree, a violence to the Directory, by hastening a departure which we had twice delayed by couriers, who twice retained the impatient general; and the third time it was no longer possible to put off an expedition directed against England, for Egypt is the advanced post of India. The power that is master of the one will soon become master of the other. The affair of Aboukir has delayed the conquest of India, and made England and the enemies of the Directory to triumph.

For having dismissed General Championnet, and appointed General Scherer.—The constitution says that the armed force is necessarily subservient to the civil authority, and Championnet, by a general order, broke through a decree of the Directory. Scherer, in the 2d year, took from the Austrians, Landrecies, Quesnoy, and Nord Libre. He was nominated by the Convention general in chief of the army of the Eastern Pyrennees, and twice general of the army of Italy. He gained in the 4th year, on the 2d Frimaire, a brilliant victory over the Austrians. Joubert proposed him to take the command of the army of Mayence, and testified his regret that Jourdan had been preferred to him. Bernadotte, at the moment of his departure for the army of observation, said, "Scherer is a father to us all. He is the first general whom the republic has actually in Europe." It belongs to the tribunals to determine whether Scherer has not been more unfortunate than criminal, and whether, like Jourdan, he does not owe his reverses to the insubordination of the generals of division.

For not having caused to be punished the agents accused of plundering the republican allies.—The Directory demanded precise facts from the authorities of Helvetia. Their answer had not arrived on the 30th Prairial, and it was still expected. Brune was charged by an arret to prosecute them. Why did he not do it? Brune, by a simple military order, overturned the authority of the Directory and the Cisalpine Legislative Body, notwithstanding the contrary instructions which he had received from the French Directory. Why did he not accuse them? It was; our duty; to annul the arbitrary operations of Porune, and to restore things to their

their ancient footing. The Secretary of State obliged the Directory to hold a direct correspondence with foreign agents; no law forbid, this precaution; the 143d article of the constitution, on the other hand, authorizes it.

Finally, for having endangered the existence of the republic by the vices of the administration.—For three years, answers Merlin, I was insulted by the injuries and calumnies of the friends of the throne; I voted for the death of the King; I presided in the Committee of Five on the 13th Vendemiaire (Oct. 4); I, as minister, prosecuted Brotier, Preslé, Serisy, Besignan, Baruel-Beauvert; I displayed the greatest zeal against the emigrants and refractory priests; I do not sufficiently despise my existence to confide it to the re-establishment of a king. It is said, that it is on our account we attempted the usurpation of the national sovereignty. It is known, that after the 13th Fructidor there was formed in the legislative body, a very powerful party, in order to continue for seven years the powers of the then sitting members, and to ten years those of the men who formed the Directory. If my ex-colleagues and I had had the ambition which is now imputed to us, the opportunity was favourable, and there was no occasion for great efforts in order to satisfy it; it was only necessary for us not to refuse the offer. Meanwhile we each declared in private to every one that proposed the plan to us, that we never would make such an attack upon the sovereignty of the people. They insisted we were immoveable. At length the re-union at the Pavilion of Flora (such was the name of the numerous congress who abetted th project of the prolongation of power) adopted the resolution of sending a deputation to us of two of its members, who had most deeply investigated the merits of the plan, and most thoroughly ascertained its consequences: and the representative of the people, Regnier, of the Council of Elders, who had uniformly and pertinaciously abetted their views, was called upon to accompany them as a witness of the transaction. A long conference took place between this deputation and the Directory. The members of the deputation went very much at large into representations and arguments to convince the Directory that they were exceedingly in the wrong, for not binding themselves to an arrangement which, to themselves in particular, must prove so advantageous. The Directory continued obstinate; and concluded by a declaration, that if a law should be enacted for the adoption of such an arrangement, they would appeal to the people against it, and would never consent to sanction or to promulgate it. This declaration completely defeated the system of prolongation; and it is well known that since that time two members of the Directory have successively gone out by lot at the period appointed by the constitution.

Is it thus, I ask, if any person who has any regard to the dictates of good sense, is it thus that magistrates who aspire to tyranny would

would conduct themselves, magistrates who wish to sacrifice to their ambition the liberty of their fellow-citizens?

How then ought you to consider these addresses which accuse us of having meditated the overthrow of the national representation?

To overthrow the national representation! we, without whom there would have been no election, either in the sixth or seventh year! we, without whom the legislative body would have been nothing but a monstrous oligarchy! we, who never ceased in all our private conversations with the representatives of the people to protest against every idea of a new 18th Fructidor, which malevolence endeavoured to render creditable by the most audacious and extravagant suppositions! yes, I have often repeated it, and I am satisfied with the numerous witnesses who have heard my asseverations, that a new 18th Fructidor would ruin the republic, because, however legitimate in appearance the cause might be, entirely disregarded the legislative body, and that without a very respectable legislative body France could no longer have republic.

Proclamation of General Suwarrow to the Piedmontese.

SENSIBLE of the necessity of establishing public order in these provinces, happily conquered by the combined Austro-Russian forces, and considering it as a duty not only to watch over the distribution of justice, but also to maintain in activity all the branches of public economy and administration, on the footing and according to the system established by the late government of his Majesty the King of Sardinia, we order as follows:

1. The laws, and political and civil establishments, which existed before the order of things which has just ceased, are to remain in force.

2. Lieutenant-general Baron Latour is invested by us with the most extensive powers, to make all the dispositions necessary, as well in the military as in the civil and economical department, and appoint persons who shall be deemed fit on account of their probity and talents to fill the places.

3. The persons appointed by Lieutenant-general Baron Latour shall exercise the functions entrusted to them conformably to the aforementioned laws and establishments; and in unforeseen cases they shall act as most expedient for maintaining public order.

4. The dispositions relative to the financial department, and the extinction of the public debt at present existing, shall continue to be observed; however, until it shall be otherwise ordained, the circulation and issuing of royal notes bearing interest, shall be suspended.

ALEXANDER SUWARROW RIMNISKY.

Head-quarters at Voghera,
  8th May 1799.

Proclamation of the Hereditary Prince of Orange to the People of the United Netherlands.

WE, William Frederic, Hereditary Prince of Orange Nassau, &c. Providence having crowned with the happiest success the endeavours of the allied powers, who have taken up arms in defence of their religion and independence; the moment being at last arrived, when, with the powerful assistance of his Britannic Majesty, and of his allies, our country will at length be liberated from the yoke under which it has groaned for four years; and his Highness the Prince of Nassau Orange, Hereditary Stadtholder, Governor, Captain-general, and Admiral of the United Netherlands, as well as Hereditary Captain and Admiral-general of the Union, &c. our father, having in a proclamation, dated at Hampton Court, the 28th of July 1799, already declared his sentiments and the intentions with which he is animated towards the good inhabitants of the state; we invite you, empowered and ordered by our father, by a decree dated December 19, 1798, and agreeably to his intentions, to assist us in gaining the object by which we are animated, namely, the re-establishment of religion and liberty, according to the principles of our legal constitution. Instead of the long slavery which has hitherto oppressed you, that true liberty is again offered to you which alone is able to promote your happiness. You may rest assured that you have to expect the protection of the laws, and freedom of persons and property, if you offer no resistance to your deliverers, but assist them as much as lies in your power. Be therefore united, lay aside all discord and party spirit; abstain from revenge; endeavour to maintain tranquillity and order, and be persuaded, that on our part we are animated by the same sentiments, and that it is our most ardent desire to awake peace and harmony among the inhabitants, to establish which we shall do every thing in our power.

We promise to all those who shall return to their duty, and assist in liberating our dear country, that their sentiments and actions during the revolution shall be forgotten, and that they shall receive protection; those in particular, who have been in any official capacity have nothing to fear upon that head, excepting that they have neglected their duty, or been guilty of crimes which are considered as such in every country, and are punishable before every impartial judge. All inhabitants may therefore rely upon perfect security, and we expect that no opposition will be made to our endeavours. Should, unexpectedly, the contrary be the case, every one will have to ascribe the disagreeable consequence to his own conduct, as such persons will experience the rigour of the laws. We caution likewise all present rulers and public functionaries, not to offend any one belonging to the ancient legal government,

vernment, or who shall be known as a partisan of the House
Orange, as they will have to answer for their safety with their p
sons and property.

It being also neceſſary, to prevent anarchy, immediately to e
bliſh a government, we invite and requeſt all thoſe, who, bef
the invaſion of the Seven Provinces and of the country of Dren
by the French, have been employed in the departments of poli
finance, and juſtice, immediately to take upon themſelves the p
viſional adminiſtration of thoſe departments, till a government ſl
be properly re-eſtabliſhed; and alſo to put again into activity the
miniſtration of government of towns and villages, with except
of thoſe who have had a ſhare in the revolution, or who have m
any declaration for ſupporting that illegal form of government,
given evident proofs of their attachment to it.

We likewiſe order all public functionaries of the preſent ill
government to continue in the exerciſe of their duties, till the p
viſional government ſhall be eſtabliſhed; enjoining them, howe
not to embezzle any money, or ſecrete documents or papers.
particularly forbid all receivers to make any payments to th
whatever, and they ſhall be anſwerable with their property.

Concerning the United States in general, we have tho
proper, till the proper government ſhall be re-eſtabliſhed, to
point a proviſional government, conſiſting of able perſons f
the reſpective provinces, which we ſhall appoint by letters, t
preſent the States of the United Netherlands.

Laſtly, we order the army and navy to contribute to the r
tabliſhment of the legal government, to maintain order and t
quillity, and to obey the commands of the officers nominated b
Highneſs. The officers in the ſervice of the illegal governn
who ſhall aſſiſt in effecting this, ſhall be particularly rememb
     (Signed) WILLIAM FREDERI
        Hereditary Prince of Or

Hague, 23 Fructidor (9th Sept.
Meſſage of the Executive Directory of the Batavian Republic t
 firſt Chamber of the repreſentative Body of the Batavian Peop

Citizens Repreſentatives,

AFTER having laſt night informed your preſident, an
morning early your aſſembly, of the appearance of an Engliſh
off the Texel roads, we have deliberated more maturely on
reply which the commander in chief of the republican fleet
give to the letter and the ſummons of Admiral Duncan, to v
he has merely ſent a proviſional reply; in conſequence of v
we have commiſſioned the agent of the marine to reply t
ſaid letter and ſummons, in the manner which you will ſee b

extract of our resolutions, which we join to this message, not being willing to fail in giving you information.

    Health and respect,   E. EMERINS.
By order of the Directory,
 HULTMAN.

       On board his Britannic Majesty's Ship
Sir,   Kent, 20th August.

MORE than 20,000 men being at this moment disembarked at the Helder, who will be followed by many others, you have now a favourable opportunity of manifesting your zeal for your legitimate sovereign, the Prince of Orange, by declaring for him, together with all the ships which may choose to follow your example. All those who shall declare for him in like manner, hoisting the Orange flag, shall be considered as allies and friends. As soon as I shall have made Sir Ralph Abercromby, commander in chief of the British land forces, and Admiral Mitchell, who commands the naval part of the expedition under me, acquainted with this declaration, all the ships which are desirous of so doing, may come out and join me; they will be treated with the most sincere friendship as allies, and will be received in the bosom of the English fleet, with which they may remain until they shall receive the commands of the Prince of Orange, with respect to the conduct which they are to pursue.

    I have the honour to be, &c.
           DUNCAN.

 The bearer of this letter, Captain ———, is commissioned to assure the officers of the Batavian fleet of my esteem for them.
          DUNCAN.

The Commander in Chief of the Batavian Fleet, to Admiral Duncan, Commander of the English Fleet in the North Sea.

       On board the Washington, Texel Road,
Admiral,   August 22, 1799.

I SHOULD be unworthy of Lord Duncan, and should forfeit the esteem of every honest man, were I to accept the proposal you make me. I know the duty which I owe to the flag I obey, and to my country; were your force double, my sentiments would still remain the same. Your Lordship may therefore expect from me a defence worthy of my nation, and of my honour. I shall, however, immediately send your summons to my government, and if you please to await its determination, I will inform you of the result.

 Be assured, my Lord, that I am, with esteem,
      (Signed)   STOREY.
          Extract

Extract from the Register of the Deliberations of the Executive Directory of the Batavian Republic, 23d August, 5 o'clock in the Morning.

THE Executive Directory having read an address, written by the minister of the marine this morning at a quarter before 3 o'clock, in which he states the appearance of the English fleet before the Texel, and the summons of Admiral Duncan, decree, that the agent of the marine shall be commanded to make, in the name of the government, by means of the commander in chief of the fleet, the following answer to Admiral Duncan:

That the English admiral has formed an erroneous supposition in his letter of the 20th of this month which he addressed to him, in which he states that General Abercromby had disembarked with 20,000 men at the Helder; that dispositions had been made to make him repent of this enterprise; and that even if the disembarkation had succeeded, that would not induce the brave and faithful commanders of the Batavian ships to surrender to a hostile power, as they are disposed to put in force every means of defence to protect the Batavian flag, and from which they expect the happiest result. The answer already given by the commander of the Batavian fleet, and from which Lord Duncan might have anticipated the present, with which it agrees in substance, would have been deemed sufficient, if the conduct of one of the officers who brought the summons did not deserve to be reported to Lord Duncan, in the persuasion that it will not only be disavowed by him but severely punished; that that officer having taken advantage of the opportunity, to put into the hands of one of the Batavian officers who fell in his way, a pretended proclamation in Dutch and English, the object of which was to seduce and alienate, if possible, the minds of the inhabitants of the Batavian republic from the confidence which they repose in their constituted authorities; that this perfidious conduct having been discovered after the departure of the English officer, it was not possible to seize him as a seducer of the military; that it was expected no such proceedings in future should take place, as otherwise those who should behave in a manner so inconsistent with the laws of war, must be answerable for the fatal consequences; that henceforth no flags of truce could be received, the object of which was merely to bring summonses and messages, which patriotism requires should be rejected. In future, therefore, those who bring these proclamations, will be considered not as the bearers of flags of truce, but as prisoners of war.

———

Hague, Sept. 3.

Letter from the French Directory to the Batavian Directory.

Citizen Directors,

WE are informed that the enemy, who has made his appearance off your coasts, has dared to declare that he is come to liberate the

Batavian

(335)

...tion, from the yoke of the French republic, un...
...ks. We know also the energetic manner in which
rejected his offers. You have sworn to defend your liberty
constitution with your lives; the whole nation has joined
it oath, and this laudable harmony is a dreadful answer to
...es of the common enemy. But, much as our two na...
convinced of their reciprocal sentiments, yet we feel plea...
...ain solemnly declaring, that the republic of France, for
...ntinuing to respect the independence of the Batavian
...r first ally, has resolved to defend it to the utmost against
...ck. Receive, Citizen Directors, this solemn assurance,
...ate it to your fellow-citizens; they will know how to
... the sincere and steady ally (whom policy as well as
...ites with the Batavian republic) from that jealous nation
...cal government which is desirous of subduing the com...
the whole world, and which, fearful of the concurrence
zeal, strains all its powers to annihilate an alliance which
...ffect the happiness of Holland, in order to make it de...
...n itself, and to deliver it up to slavery.

(Signed)   SIEYES.

---

from General Brune to the Municipality of Amsterdam.

...istrates of the People of Amsterdam,

...finity of reports have been propagated in consequence of
...ng of the English. That event has added numbers and
...o the Orangists and French emigrants. Magistrates of
...ian people! behold the shades of Van Tromp, De Witt,
...er, and Barneveld, burst through their sacred tombs, that
...e animated by their spirit, and denounce death against those
...raitors to their country—Guard yourselves against French
...: oppose yourselves to the impious attempts of Orangists;
... the Batavian people, and stand your ground against the

BRUNE.

I wish that this letter may be published in the French and
...anguages.
Sept. 3.

---

*...the President of the Batavian Directory on the Surrender of
the Fleet.*

...re an honest man, citizens representatives, whatever party
...belong to, who does not feel the highest indignation
...ccasion of so infamous a treason? a treason which re...
...much to the disgrace of those by whom it was pro...
...of those by whom it was carried into effect. Good
Heaven!

" Heaven! has the Batavian people so long cherished those monsters in order that they should at last be betrayed in so base a manner by them? May the enemy always receive those vile wretches whom we do not acknowledge as Batavians, nor as fellow-citizens! May the punishment of the crime fall upon the heads of those who were the authors of it! Revenge will overtake them in due time. Meanwhile, my fellow-citizens, this misfortune, deeply as it must be felt by every patriotic heart, ought not to suffer our spirits to be dejected. We know the duties which we owe our country and the people. These we will fulfil; and sooner shall the land of our forefathers, and the soil on which we stand, be converted into a heap of ruins than the enemy shall triumph over our firmness. The Batavian army, which is united with our French brethren, and at this moment is fighting in defence of its country's liberty, will prove, to a certainty, that generous blood boils in their veins. On these our expectations rest, and may God assist them!

Proclamation of Sir Ralph Abercromby to the Dutch.

LIEUTENANT-general Abercromby, to whom his Majesty the King of Great Britain, the ancient ally of the United Provinces, has entrusted the command of a body of troops destined to recover the freedom of the said United Provinces, has by his Majesty's orders issued the following proclamation, containing the intentions both of his Britannic Majesty, and of the kings and sovereign princes his allies in this great undertaking.

IT is not as enemies, but as friends and deliverers, that the English troops enter the territory of the United Provinces. This undertaking has no other object in view, but to deliver the inhabitants of this country, heretofore free and happy, from the oppression under which they groan, to protect their religious worship against the persecuting intolerance of incredulity and atheism, to rescue their administration from the violence which they experience from anarchy and rapaciousness, and to re-establish them in the possession of their ancient liberty and independence, so closely connected with the privileges of that constitution, by means of which their ancestors fought and conquered under the standard of the Princes of Orange; privileges, whose influence has proved to the United Provinces a perennial source of prosperity, under the auspices of the amity and the alliance of Great Britain.

His Majesty entertains no doubt, but that, eager to re-assert those privileges, the inhabitants of the United Provinces will rekindle in their bosoms, and with equal success, the courage and the self-devotion of their ancestors. The hand of Providence has already appeared in the deliverance of a large portion of Europe from those measures, into which it hath permitted that they should for a time be involved by the arms and principles of the French republic.

The military forces which his Britannic Majesty has assembled under the command of Lieutenant-general Abercromby, joined to those which his high allies have destined for the same object, are sufficient fully to protect those who shall stand forward in the cause of their country.

The allied sovereigns are desirous that the deliverance of the Batavian republic should be principally brought about by its own citizens, in all the deliberations and in all the exertions that shall be connected with this interesting object. His Majesty recommends to them in the most pressing manner, to act together with concert and unanimity, to forget and to forgive the past, and to form an unshaken determination to protect and defend against all excesses of revenge, the lives and property of their fellow-citizens, even of those whose errors and whose faults have perhaps contributed to aggravate the sufferings of their country; but who now, reclaimed by the irresistible conviction of experience, are ready to make common cause with us in this arduous task.

" It is consistently with these principles, and agreeable to this spirit, that the British army shall conduct themselves in the midst of a people whom the English nation has been so long accustomed to regard as friends and allies. But if, hereafter, and from the present moment, there should be found Batavians, who at the approach of the deliverance of their country should still remain devoted to its oppressors, and show themselves unworthy of the invaluable enjoyment of the tranquillity and security of a legitimate government, as well as of religious and civil liberty, such only shall be looked upon, and treated by his Britannic Majesty, as the obstinate and irreconcilable enemies, not only of his said Britannic Majesty and his high allies, but also of the happiness of their country, as well as the general interests and security of Europe.

R. ABERCROMBY, Lieut. gen.
FREDK. MAITLAND, Sec. of the Commander in Chief.

Copy of the Summons which the French sent to Count Salm, Commandant of Philipsburg.

Sir,

THE fortress whose defence is entrusted to you, is attacked on from many sides, and its blockade is covered by a numerous army. Every thing is ready to cause you and the garrison un-

Vol. VIII.　　　　　X x　　　　　der

ts ruins. In the name of humanity I call on you to
render the fortrefs of Philipfburg to the French troops,
prevent the fhedding of human blood, and your inevitable
I grant you two hours to confider of it, after the expiration of which I fhall only be guided by the law of force. Greet-
ings and refpect.

  (Signed)   Laroche,
      General of Divifion, commanding the
20th Fructidor (6th Sept.). Blockade of Philipfburg.

The Commandant returned the following Anfwer.

General,

YOUR fummons, which I have juft received, I can only anfwer as becomes a man of honour and an old foldier, that is
I fhall do my duty, and employ all the means in my power to
defeat the attack which you inform me you intend to make.
affure you, General, of my perfect efteem.

  (Signed)   Count de Salm, Lieut.-gen.

---

*The Archduke Charles's Letter to Count Salm, Commandant of Philip-
burg, dated Head-quarters, Enzwelhingen, September 13.*

I HAVE received your letter of yefterday, in which you
informed me of the fiege of the fortrefs of Philipfburg be
raifed. I haften to exprefs to you my entire fatisfaction
applaufe of the brave and diftinguifhed defence which you
made, and beg you will thank the brave officers and garrif(
my name. This able and glorious defence proves that I
made the happieft choice in filling that poft, and fully
fies the high opinion which I had, during the whole w:
your great military fkill. A courier is juft fetting off to 1
mend you and your brave garrifon to his Imperial Majeft
I am convinced that he will be highly fatisfied with you
viour. I expect a full account of the whole of your pro
with anxiety, which, I am perfuaded, will be a laftin-
ment of the deeds of the brave garrifon in the annals of
fent war.

  (Signed)   Charles, Arc

Proclamation, addressed in the Name of his Sicilian Majesty to the Inhabitants of Rome, and the other Towns belonging to the Roman States, in the Beginning of September.

Romans,

THE army of Ferdinand IV. again enters within your walls. It is not composed of those warriors, who, after coming amongst you, suffered themselves disgracefully to be driven away. The troops which I have the honour to command, are the same which, faithful to their king, and advancing from the extremity of Calabria, have reconquered his Majesty's kingdom, by an uninterrupted course of victories. They now come to deliver you from the degrading yoke to which you have been subjected under the false denomination of liberty and equality. The king my sovereign has led his victorious army towards you, in order to restore to religion its former splendour, to put an end to oppression, disorder, and massacre, and to re-establish upon the ruins of anarchy the throne of truth and justice.

His Majesty, inspired by these sentiments, and guided by such pure motives, has ordered me, and I am also charged by his vice-general, the most eminent Cardinal Ruffo, to make known to all the Romans his fixed resolution to pardon those who might have been led astray, as well as those who, seduced, intimidated, or constrained by force, have embraced the republican party, provided they do not take arms against his Majesty's troops under my command, nor by opposing their entrance render themselves deserving of the severe punishment which will be otherwise reserved for them.

It is therefore ordered that all persons, as well soldiers as others, shall lay down their arms on the arrival of his Majesty's troops. All who have assembled for the preservation of the *soi-disant* Roman republic are also required to abandon the Roman territory on our approach, as on the contrary there shall be employed against them the same force and valour with which the army has already surmounted the obstacles that were opposed to it.

What satisfaction, Romans, must you not feel at the arrival of this auspicious moment? Those now coming amongst you are the adorers of the cross, of that sacred sign which victory attends, and at the appearance of which the enemies of God, of the throne, and of humanity, are terrified and dispersed—of that cross whose greatest triumphs were performed in the midst of you---which is the asylum of the just, and the scourge of the wicked.

On the appearance of the triumphant standard borne by my soldiers, all the males shall exhibit this sign, worn on the right side of their hats, and all the women on their breast: on the left fide they shall wear the Neapolitan cockade. Hasten, Romans, to tear up that infamous tree, which to your disgrace is suffered still to remain within your territories. In the room of that fatal sign of irreligion, diffolution, and all the most abominable vices, plant the sacred sign of the crofs, the purest source of all the virtues; receive amongst you those courageous soldiers: it is a duty which religion imposes upon you. They come to defend your honour, your families, your existence. Draw a veil over the past, and in the hope of a happy future, bury the recollection of all the evils you have suffered.

You know the abundance which prevails in the happy kingdom of Naples. Although the enemy, to whom bribery and treason had opened its gates, employed during their fatal stay of seven months in that fine country, all those means which were likely to impoverish it, its natural fertility can enable it, by means of an amicable union, to furnish your states with all those necessaries of which they were hitherto deprived. My conduct in regard to you shall be regulated by your own line of conduct, &c. &c.

Letter of the French Ambassador in Spain, enclosing to the Commander of the tenth military Division, Copies of the following Notes, addressed to him by the Secretary of State of his Catholic Majesty.

THE annexed notes will inform you of the happy refult of my application to the minister of his Catholic Majefty; I have no doubt but that his agents will hasten to conform to such positive orders, and that the delivering up of all the rebels who may have been arrested will be speedily and faithfully effected. My love for our country is a sure guarantee, Citizen General, of the zeal by which I shall second the means you may think conducive to the restoring of tranquillity in the division which you command, and to deprive those who may attempt to rekindle the flame of civil war in France, of all hopes of a retreat into this country.

(Signed)   GUILLEMARDEST.

Note addressed by the Secretary of State of his Catholic Majesty to the Ambassador of the French Republic in Spain.

Citizen,   *St. Ildephonfe, September 2.*

I RECEIVED the note you did me the honour to fend me yesterday, giving an account of the revolt which had broken out in feveral departments of the fouth of the French republic, and informing me of the defeat of the rebels by the republican

republican troops; you acquaint me that a great many insurgents have retreated on the Spanish territory, and you seem convinced that his Majesty will not delay a moment to order that they be immediately sought for and delivered up to the French authorities, to undergo the punishment they have incurred.

It is a particular satisfaction for me to assure you, in the name of his Majesty, that his direct interest in the tranquillity of the French republic, and in the perfect preservation of its government, is of such weight in his eyes, that your observations were not necessary to engage him to act conformably to what his sincere friendship for and close alliance with the French republic require. In fact, I was no sooner informed by the captain general of the kingdom of Arragon, and more particularly by the governor of the castle of the Venasco, of the troubles which had broken out on those frontiers, than I enjoined them in the most positive manner to observe a conduct entirely conformable with the intimate relations which unite us to the government and the constitution of France; and I ordered them particularly, as soon as I was informed that some of the rebels had passed into Spain, to take all the necessary steps to seize them and deliver them up, with proper precautions, to the tribunals of the republic.

I doubt not but that the officers will conform exactly to the orders of his Majesty, and that you will hasten to transmit to your government this new proof of his cordiality, and of the solid friendship which his Majesty testifies towards it on all occasions; and being animated with the same sentiments, I renew my sincere desire of convincing you of my high consideration.

(Signed)   M. L. D'URQUIJO.

Second Note addressed by the Secretary of State of his Catholic Majesty to the Ambassador of the French Republic in Spain.

Citizen,   *St. Ildephonse, Sept. 4.*

IN answering, on the 2d instant, your note of the day before, I had the honour to inform you of the vigorous steps ordered to be taken by his Majesty, as soon as he was informed that on the frontier of the kingdom of Arragon some of the revolted, who had disturbed the public tranquillity in the southern departments of the French republic, had entered on the Spanish territory, and that, by virtue of the dispositions already announced, they were all to be delivered up to the nearest French authorities, in order that they may suffer the punishment due to them. This day I have the satisfaction of informing you further that the king has ordered similar injunctions to be extended to the captains general of Catalonia and Guipofcoa, and to the viceroy of Navarre, charging them likewise to cause all the royalists who shall retire
into

into Spain to be disarmed, and, as soon as they shall be arrested, to deliver them up, as I have already announced. His Majesty has enjoined them also to examine with the greatest attention, in the present circumstances, the passports and papers of individuals who enter Spain and present themselves as republicans, in order to avoid, by this precaution, the artifices and frauds of the royalists, who might thus attempt to conceal their true character. I trust that you will see, in the employment of these means, an effectual desire and a continual attention, on the part of his Majesty, to contribute with all his power to the advantage of the French republic, and to the preservation of its government. I also flatter myself that you will second, as much as possible, these dispositions, by the orders you will address to the French agents on those points of the frontier which may most facilitate the escape of the guilty.

Convinced that you will not lose a moment in the execution of these measures, I avail myself with pleasure of this opportunity of repeating the assurance of my sincere desire of rendering service and doing what may be agreeable to you.

(Signed) M. C. D'URQUIJO.

Answer of the King of Spain to the Manifesto of the Emperor of Russia.

Madrid, Sept. 11.

THE religious exactness with which I have endeavoured, and shall endeavour, to maintain the alliance which I have entered into with the French republic, and the bonds of friendship and of good intelligence which subsist between the two countries, and which are cemented by the evident analogy of their common political interests, have excited the jealousy of some powers, particularly since the formation of the new coalition, of which the object, instead of the chimerical and ostensible desire of re-establishing order, is only to disturb it by despotizing over those nations who will not submit to their ambitious views. Among them, Russia has thought proper to appear very prominent with respect to me. The Emperor, not content with arrogating to himself titles which cannot in any sense belong to him, and with thus manifesting his views, has just published a decree declaratory of war against me, in consequence, as he says, of not having experienced from me the condescension which he expected. The publication of this decree may alone suffice to prove his want of justice. The translation of it is literally as follows.*(Here the Manifesto of the Emperor is recited.)*

I have seen, without surprise, this declaration of war, because the conduct observed towards my chargé d'affaires, and other proceedings

ceedings not less extraordinary on the part of this sovereign, some time since, informed me what I was to expect. In dismissing, therefore, from my court and dominions, the Russian chargé d'affaires, M. le Conseiller Butzow, I have not been so much governed by motives of resentment as by the imperious considerations of my dignity.

In consequence of these principles, I am far from intending to examine at length the inconsistent and offensive contents of the Russian manifesto—offensive not only to me, but to other European powers; and well knowing the nature of the influence of England upon the reigning Czar, I consider it below me to answer this manifesto, being accountable for my political connexions to none but the Almighty, by whose aid I shall be able to repel every unjust aggression, which the presumption of a system of false combinations may direct against me and my subjects, for the protection and security of whom I have taken and am taking the most efficacious precautions; and in making known to them this declaration of war, I authorize them to act hostilely against Russia, its possessions, and its inhabitants.

Substance of the Opinion of the Empire on the Renewal of the War of the Empire, and the Duties of its Members in furnishing Contingents, published in the Diet of Ratisbon, 18th Sept.

AFTER due consideration of the Imperial decree of commission of the 17th of July, it was resolved to return thanks to his Imperial Majesty for his paternal care and protection; that the Empire in general was fully convinced of the necessity of recommencing the war, in consequence of the hostilities of the French, carried on even during the negotiations at Rastadt; and that therefore a due observance of those regulations which were found necessary since the beginning of the war, ought again to take place, by which all members of the Empire were bound to give all assistance in their power to defend their country, to renounce all private views, and to make every necessary sacrifice, that they should furnish their quintuple contingents, in such a manner as to be able to repel and keep off every attack of the enemy. To obtain this great object, the Empire should grant one hundred Roman months to defray the expenses of the war, payable at three different periods, of six weeks each, commencing from the publication of the Imperial ratification.

Speech

Speech of the President of the French Directory to M. d'Azara, Ambassador from Spain, on his taking leave of the Directory, on the 23d September.

YOU have seen, during your residence among us, how solicitous the Directory has been to cultivate the friendship of his Majesty the King of Spain. It will never forget the zeal which you have shown in drawing closer the alliance between two amicable nations by the junction of their naval forces. The interests of both nations required that junction to oppose the common enemy. You carry with you, Sir, the satisfaction of having, by your honourable mission, usefully served your own country, and merited the esteem of ours.

Speech of M. Musquiz, the new Ambassador.

Citizens Directors,

THE King of Spain, in appointing me his ambassador to the Executive Directory of the French republic, has commanded me to present to you the sincere testimony of his unalterable desire to maintain and strengthen the alliance and friendship which subsist between the two powers, by every possible means accommodated to their reciprocal advantages and their common good. Never was a duty of so great importance prescribed with more sincerity and good faith.

It is by directing all my efforts to accomplish it, with the zeal and fidelity enjoined to me by the sincerest wishes of the King of Spain, according with the immutable interests of the nation which he governs, that I shall endeavour to merit the esteem and good opinion of the Executive Directory, and of all France; the most perfect prosperity of which I shall not cease to desire with all that sincerity and truth, of which the King of Spain has appointed me the interpreter, and of which, Citizens Directors, you will find the assurance in the credentials which I have the honour to present to you.

Reply of the President of the Directory.

THE Executive Directory of the French republic receives with pleasure the new assurances of attachment and friendship which the King of Spain has charged you to convey to it. There are nations between whom nature herself has drawn up a treaty of alliance. The bravery, generosity, and sacred respect for treaties, which characterize the two nations, which the Pyrenees ought to separate only in territory, has long since laid the foundation of the treaty by which they are united. This treaty, founded on the virtues

virtues, as w] interests of both countries, does honour to the wisdom of governments.

The reciprocal sentiments inspired by this alliance, acquired a still more affecting interest from their being expressed on the day when the French nation celebrates the foundation of the republic. This immortal epoch is a new pledge of the unalterable union of the two powers. The French nation will never forget that the King of Spain was her first ally. She will not, for a moment, forget that this generous ally has kindly united his naval forces to hers. The choice which the King of Spain has made of you to be his representative in the republic, is a further proof of his attachment to her. Your character, your personal qualities, assure her that the constancy of her friendship for the Spanish nation will be daily represented to the monarch who governs it, with that generous frankness which distinguishes the two countries.

Proclamation of the Batavian Directory.

THE people of Batavia are invited to rise in a mass, and arm.

I. All those who shall join the standing army, shall receive, besides the bounty of six ducats, a premium of twenty-one florins (2*l.*).

II. All those who shall serve with the army until the enemy shall have been driven from the national territory, shall receive a recompence of thirty florins (3*l.*).

III. All the authorities of the departments and municipalities are enjoined to favour and encourage this sort of recruiting; and if there are no recruiting parties near, to send the volunteers to the next garrison places, where the aforesaid bounties and premiums will be paid, as soon as they are approved of and enlisted in their respective corps.

Done at the Hague, by the Batavian Directory, Sept. 23, 1799, 5th year of Batavian liberty.

WAR IN INDIA.

Papers relating to the late War in the East Indies with Tippoo Sultaun.

Copy of a Letter from the Right Honourable the Earl of Mornington to the Court of Directors; dated 20th March 1799 (received per Sarah Christiana, 13th Sept. 1799); detailing the Causes of the War with Tippoo Sultaun.

To the Honourable the Court of Directors.

Honourable Sirs,

IN my separate dispatch of the 21st of November, by the Eurydice, I informed your Honourable Court, that although I had deemed it my duty to call your armies into the field in every part of your possessions, my views and expectations were all directed to the preservation of peace in India.

2. In the letter of the 13th of January, from the Governor General in council at Fort St. George, I apprized your Honourable Court of my arrival at this presidency, to which I thought it my duty to proceed from Bengal, in the hope of opening a negotiation with Tippoo Sultaun, for the amicable adjustment of the differences which had arisen between that prince and the Honourable Company's government.

3. In my dispatches to the Secret Committee of your Honourable Court, I have regularly transmitted advices of the state of political affairs in India, and I have fully explained the principles which have governed my conduct, not only towards Tippoo Sultaun, but towards all the native powers, since I have taken charge of the government general.

4. Having ultimately been compelled to commence hostilitie against Tippoo Sultaun, it is now become my duty to lay befor your Honourable Court an accurate detail of the causes of th war in which we are engaged.

5. For this purpose, it will be necessary to draw your attentio to a period of time as remote as the month of June 1798, and t trace from that date the progress of those events which hav finally produced the necessity of resorting to arms for the securit of your interests committed to my charge.

6. A proclamation issued by the Governor General of the I of France, in the month of February 1798, made its first aj pearance at Calcutta on the 8th June of the same year. (A. Er closure, No. 1 *.)

---

* In the course of this letter will be found references to several doc ments, which, as the substance of them is herein stated, we do not think necessary to lay at full length before the public.

7. Th

7. This proclamation states, that an embassy had arrived at the Isle of France with letters from Tippoo Sultaun, addressed not only to the government of that island, but to the Executive Directory of France, proposing to conclude an offensive and defensive alliance with the French, to subsidize and to supply whatever troops the French might furnish to the Sultaun, and to commence against the British power in India a war of aggression, for which the Sultaun is declared to be fully prepared, waiting with anxiety the moment when the succour of France shall enable him to satisfy his ardent desire of expelling the British nation from India. The proclamation concludes by offering encouragement to the subjects of France to enter into the service of Tippoo Sultaun, on terms to be fixed with his ambassadors then on the spot.

8. Although I was inclined, in the first instance, to doubt the authenticity of this extraordinary publication, I thought it advisable to transmit a copy of it, on the 9th of June, to Lieutenant-general Harris (then governor of Fort St. George, and commander in chief on the coast of Coromandel), informing him, that if the proclamation should prove authentic, it must lead to a serious discussion with Tippoo Sultaun; and directing Lieutenant-general Harris to consider without delay the means of assembling the army on the coast of Coromandel, if necessity should unfortunately require such a precaution.

9. On the 18th of June 1798, I received a regular authentication of the proclamation, in a letter from his Excellency the Earl of Macartney, dated the 28th of March; and at the same time several persons arrived at Calcutta who had been present in the Isle of France at the time of the publication of the proclamation.

10. By a strict examination of the most respectable of these persons, I was enabled to obtain an authentic and accurate statement of all the material circumstances attending the publication of the proclamation at the Isle of France; the substance of which statement I have already forwarded to your Secret Committee, and now have the honour to submit to your Honourable Court.

11. Tippoo Sultaun dispatched two ambassadors, who embarked at Mangalore for the Isle of France, and arrived at Port Nord-ouest in that island, towards the close of the month of January 1798. The ambassadors were received publicly and formally by the French government, with every circumstance of distinction and respect, and they were entertained at the public expense during their continuance on the island.

12. Previous to the arrival of ambassadors on the island, no idea or rumour existed there of any aid to be furnished to Tippoo Sultaun by the French, or of any prospect of a war between that prince and the Company; but within two days after the arrival of

of the ambaſſadors, the proclamation in queſtion was fixed up in the moſt public places, and circulated through the town of Port Nord-oueſt.

13. The ambaſſadors, far from proteſting againſt the matter or ſtyle of the proclamation, held without reſerve, in the moſt public manner, the ſame language which it contains with reſpect to a war of aggreſſion to be commenced by Tippoo Sultaun againſt the Britiſh poſſeſſions in India; and they even ſuffered the proclamation to be publicly diſtributed by their agents at the place of their reſidence.

13. The ambaſſadors were preſent when the French government proceeded to act under the proclamation in queſtion; and the ambaſſadors aided and aſſiſted the execution of the proclamation, by making promiſes, in the name of Tippoo Sultaun, for the purpoſe of inducing recruits to enliſt in his ſervice.

15. The ambaſſadors propoſed to levy men to any practicable extent, ſtating their powers to be unlimited with reſpect to the force to be raiſed in the name of Tippoo Sultaun. They entered into certain ſtipulations and engagements in the name of the Sultaun (according to the tenour of the laſt paragraph of the proclamation) with ſeveral Frenchmen, and others, particularly with Mr. Dubuc, whom the ambaſſadors engaged in the ſervice of their ſovereign, for the expreſs purpoſe of aſſiſting in the war to be immediately commenced againſt the Britiſh power in India.

16. The proclamation therefore originated in the arrival of Tippoo's ambaſſadors at the Iſle of France; it was diſtributed by their agents, it was avowed in every part by their own public declarations, and finally it was executed, according to its tenour, by their perſonal aſſiſtance and co-operation.

17. On the 7th of March 1798, the ambaſſadors embarked at Port Nord-oueſt, on board the French frigate La Preneuſe, together with the force thus raiſed in the name of Tippoo Sultaun, amounting to about two hundred men, incluſive of ſeveral officers, the chiefs of whom were M. M. Dubne and Chapny.

18. Such is the ſubſtance of the evidence obtained from the perſons who were preſent in the Iſle of France during the reſidence of Tippoo's ambaſſadors; from other authentic ſources I learnt the ſequel of the tranſaction.

19. The French frigate La Preneuſe, with the Sultaun's ambaſſadors and the French troops levied for his ſervice, arrived at Mangalore on the 26th April 1798.

20. An opportunity now occurred of aſcertaining, beyond the poſſibility of doubt, whether the acts of the Sultaun's ambaſſadors in the Iſle of France were conformable to the inſtructions of their ſovereign. For although the preſumption was already ſufficiently powerful, that the ambaſſadors would not have ventured to tranſgreſs the limit of their commiſſion in a matter of ſuch

momentous

momentous importance, as the conclusion of offensive engagements with the French against the English East India Company, it yet remained a question, whether Tippoo Sultaun would venture openly to avow proceedings, which could not fail to expose him to the just resentment of your government.

21. This question was immediately solved, for the Sultaun, without hesitation, permitted the French force to land publicly at Mangalore; and, far from manifesting the least symptom of disapprobation of the conduct of the embassy in any part of the negotiation, he formally received his ambassadors, and the French officers, and principal persons in their suite, with public and extraordinary marks of honour and distinction; and finally, he admitted the greater part of the French force raised for the purpose of making war upon the Honourable Company, into his service, in which it is still entertained.

22. By this public and unequivocal sanction, he must be considered not only to have personally ratified the engagements contained in the proclamation of the Governor General of the Isle of France, but to have taken the preliminary measures for accomplishing the design which the ambassadors had avowed in his name.

23. Tippoo Sultaun, therefore, having actually concluded offensive and defensive engagements with the French against the Honourable Company; having collected, by the aid of the French, a force openly destined to carry those engagements into effect; having applied to the Executive Directory of France for a more powerful force destined to the same end; having signified through his public ambassadors to the enemy, that his preparations for war (as far as they depended upon himself) were actually complete; having avowed the object of those preparations to be the subversion of the British empire in India; and finally, having declared the delay of the meditated blow to proceed from no other cause, than his expectation of receiving further aid from the enemy; I could not hesitate to pronounce, that he had flagrantly violated the treaties of peace subsisting between him and the Honourable Company; and that he had committed an act of direct hostility and aggression against the British government in India.

24. To confirm the conclusions necessarily resulting from the facts already stated, I received undoubted information, that Tippoo Sultaun had for some time past been employed in military preparations, conformably to the hostile spirit of his engagements with the enemy; that the greater part of his army was actually in a state of equipment for the field; and that a large portion of it was then encamped under his personal command.

25. To your Honourable Court it would be superfluous to observe, that no provocation had been offered by any of your governments in India, to justify or to palliate any act of hostility, or even

any

any emotion of jealoufy or fufpicion on the part of Tippoo Sultaun; but I think it neceffary to remark in this place, that at the very moment of receiving the authentic copy of the proclamation iffued in the Ifle of France, I had ordered the difputed diftrict of Wynaad to be delivered to the Sultaun, after a public acknowledgment of the juftice of his claim to that poffeffion, and I had propofed to open an amicable negotiation for the purpofe of adjufting his recent claims to a part of the diftrict of Cooya, on fimilar principles of equity, according to the tenour of the feventh article of the treaty of Seringapatam.

26. The Sultaun himfelf had not attempted to allege even the pretext of a grievance againft the Britifh government: in his letters to Sir John Shore (written a fhort time before the return of the Myforean ambaffadors from the Ifle of France, and received at Fort William on the 26th of April 1798, the day on which the French force landed at Mangalore) Tippoo declares, "that his friendly heart is difpofed to pay every regard to truth and juftice, and to ftrengthen the foundations of harmony and concord between the two nations;" and he fignifies his defire, that "Sir John Shore would imprefs Lord Mornington with a fenfe of the friendfhip and unanimity fo firmly fubfifting between the two ftates."

27. This is not the language of hoftility, nor even of difcontent; from what difpofition in the friendly heart of the Sultaun thefe amicable profeffions have proceeded, how they are connected with a regard to truth and juftice, or calculated to ftrengthen the foundations of harmony and concord, and to imprefs me with a fenfe of the firmnefs of the Sultaun's friendfhip, your Honourable Court can now determine without difficulty, fince it is now proved, that thefe letters were written at the very crifis when he was in anxious expectation of the hourly arrival of that military fuccour which he had earneftly folicited from the enemy, for the exprefs purpofe of commencing a war of aggreffion againft the Company's poffeffions.

28. That Tippoo Sultaun had not yet received the effectual fuccour which he had folicited from the French, might have been afcribed either to the diftracted ftate of the government of Mauritius, or to their want of zeal in his caufe, or to the rafhnefs and imbecility of his own councils; but neither the meafure of his hoftility, nor of our right to reftrain it, nor of our danger from it, were to be eftimated by the magnitude of the force which he had actually obtained, for I knew that his demands of military affiftance were unlimited; I knew that they were addreffed not merely to the government of the Mauritius, but to the Executive Directory of France, and I could not afcertain how foon, either by fome revolution in the government of the Mauritius, or by direct intercourfe with France, thofe demands might be fatisfied to the full extent of his acknowledged expectations.

29. Under

29. Under all these circumstances an immediate attack upon Tippoo Sultaun, for the purpose of frustrating the execution of his unprovoked and unwarrantable projects of ambition and revenge, appeared to me to be demanded by the soundest maxims both of justice and policy.

30. The act of Tippoo Sultaun's ambassadors, ratified by himself, and followed by the admission of a French force into his army, was equivalent to a public, unqualified, and unambiguous declaration of war. But while his hostile purpose had been clearly manifested, the immediate means of accomplishing it had happily disappointed the order of his hopes.

31. The inconsiderable amount of the aid which he had already received from the French, while it could not be construed as a limitation of my just right to vindicate the public safety, afforded strong argument of policy in favour of attacking this desperate, implacable, and treacherous enemy, before he could either complete the improvement of his own army, under the French officers whom he had already admitted into his service, or could receive a further accession of strength under the progressive operation of his alliance with France.

32. In the moment of his comparative weakness, of his disappointment and probable dejection, the principles of justifiable self-defence, and of prudential precaution, required that we should strike such an instantaneous blow against his power and resources, as should preclude the possibility of his deriving any substantial advantage from the aid of France, whenever it might reach his dominions.

33. Such was the tenour of my opinions as early as the 20th of June 1798. Although at that early period I could not ascertain from what quarter the French would attempt to assist the Sultaun, I recorded my conviction that some attempt to assist him would be among the earliest of their operations. The conclusion of peace upon the continent of Europe, the weak state of our allies in India (particularly of the Nizam, whose councils and army were at that period subjected to the overbearing influence of a powerful French faction), might appear both to Tippoo and to France to offer a favourable crisis for the attack of the British possessions in India. The disposition of the French government to attempt such an enterprise has never been disguised; and although I had not obtained positive proof that any formal and regular correspondence between Tippoo Sultaun and the Executive Directory of France, had existed previous to the embassy and letters which arrived at the Mauritius in January 1798, yet the nature of that transaction afforded a strong presumption that a previous intercourse of the same hostile character had taken place. This presumption was further corroborated by my certain knowledge, that for some time past various emissaries of France had reached the councils of Tippoo

Sultaun,

Sultaun, and that through their reprefentations he had been ta
to entertain a confident expectation of fpeedy and effectual fup[

34. Even admitting that this expectation was likely to be
trated, either by a failure of faith on the part of France, or by
vigilance and fuperior power of his Majefty's fleets, I was appr
that Tippoo had alfo difpatched an embaffy to Zemaun Shah,
object of which could be no other than to encourage that pr
in the profecution of his long-threatened invafion of Hindo
The whole tenour of my advices from the north-weftern coun
of Hindoftan, led me to believe that Zemaun Shah would crofs
Attack, and would endeavour to purfue his avowed project o
vafion in the courfe of the enfuing feafon; and it appeared
bable that his approach, which muft neceffarily engage the at
tion of the army in Bengal, might be the fignal to Tippoo Sult
for an irruption into the Carnatic.

35. In addition to thefe confiderations, it appeared by no m
improbable, that the impetuofity of Tippoo Sultaun's temper,
afperated by the affiduous and unremitting inftigations of the e
faries of France, might break forth into hoftilities without wai
for the actual movement of any Indian or European ally.
late embaffy to the Ifle of France fufficiently manifefted a di
fition capable of purfuing its favourite object of vengeance ag
the Britifh nation with more zeal than difcretion. It is my
further to remark, that in the month of June 1798, the diftribu
and condition of the army on the coaft of Coromandel, to w
I fhall advert more fully in a fubfequent part of this difp
offered but too ftrong a temptation to the enterprife of a faitl
and active enemy. Under fuch circumftances it would have
an unmanly and weak policy to have confided the fafety of
Carnatic to the precarious forbearance of Tippoo Sultaun,
have left him any longer in the undifturbed poffeffion of
powerful advantage of being able to choofe, according to his co
nience, the time and mode of the attack which he had op
menaced.

36. I therefore recorded my decided judgment, that it was
ceffary to affemble the armies on the coaft of Coromandel
Malabar without delay, and I iffued my final orders for this
pofe on the 20th June 1798.

37. To affemble the army on both coafts was an indifpenf
precaution, which I could not have been juftified in omitting,
the moment that I was apprized of Tippoo Sultaun's offenfive
gagements with the French, and of the landing of a French f
at Mangalore. But, being refolved on all occafions to fubmi
your Court a full and diftinct view of the whole fcope of my
tives and intentions, I have no hefitation in declaring, that
original refolution was (if circumftances w have admitted
have attacked the Sultaun inftantly, and on both fides of his d

sions, for the purpose of defeating his hostile preparations, and of anticipating their declared object; I was concerned however to learn, from persons most conversant in military details at Fort St. George (notwithstanding the distinguished discipline of your army on the coast of Coromandel, and the eminent valour, activity, and skill of its officers), its dispersed state, and certain radical defects in its establishments, would render the assembling a force equal to offensive movements against Tippoo, a much more tedious and difficult operation than I had apprehended.

38. Some officers of approved military talents, experience, and integrity, at Fort St. George, declared that your army in the Carnatic could not be assembled for offensive purposes before the commencement of the year 1800, and that a period of six months would be required for its equipment, even for the purpose of defending the Carnatic against any sudden attack. The difficulty of assembling and moving your army on the coast of Coromandel, furnished indeed an alarming proof of the defenceless and perilous state of the Carnatic in that arduous conjuncture. But in proportion to the pressure of that difficulty, the necessity of an instantaneous and active exertion became more urgent; for whether the army, when assembled, was to anticipate or wait the attack of Tippoo, it appeared an equally indispensable measure of precaution to resume, without delay, the power of meeting that vindictive and restless prince in the field. I was not therefore discouraged, either by the suggestions to which I have referred, or by subsequent representations of a similar character and tendency, from insisting on the immediate execution of my orders for assembling the army; and adverting to the fatal consequences which have formerly been experienced in the Carnatic, by neglecting to keep pace with the forwardness of hostile equipments in Mysore, I resolved to entrust the protection of your possessions on the coast of Coromandel to no other security than a complete and early state of preparation for war.

39. At Bombay, my orders for assembling the army were executed with great promptitude and alacrity, unaccompanied by any symptoms of indisposition to those united and zealous efforts, which the exigency of the crisis demanded from every branch of your civil and military service.

40. The unavoidable delay which obstructed the assembling your army in the Carnatic, having compelled me to relinquish my first intention of striking an immediate blow against the power and resources of Tippoo Sultaun, I applied myself to the formation of such a permanent system of preparation and defence, as, while it tended to restore to the government of Fort St. George, with all practicable dispatch, the power of repelling any act of aggression on the part of Tippoo Sultaun, might ultimately enable me to demand both a just indemnification for the expense which the Sultaun's

taun's violation of treaty had occasioned to your government, and a seasonable security against the consequences of his recent alliance with the enemy.

41. With this view, while the army was assembling on the coasts of Coromandel and Malabar, my early attention was directed to strengthen and improve the defensive alliance concluded between the Honourable Company, and their Highnesses the Nizam and Peshwah, under the treaties of Paangul, Poonah, and Seringapatam, for the purpose of establishing a barrier against the ambition and revenge of Tippoo Sultaun.

42. The state of this alliance afforded abundant matter of painful anxiety; I found both the Peshwah and the Nizam (whose respective power it was the object of the treaty of Seringapatam to maintain) in such a state of efficiency as might render them useful allies in the event of a war with Mysore, reduced to the lowest condition of depression and weakness, the former by the intrusion of Doulet Row Sindia, and the latter by the threatened hostility of the same chieftain, by the establishment of a numerous and active French faction in the centre of the Decan; and while the internal convulsions of each state had diminished the resources of both, their co-operation against Tippoo Sultaun had become impracticable by the progress of their mutual animosities and dissensions.

43. In this scene of general confusion, the power of Tippoo Sultaun alone (which it had been the policy of all our alliances and treaties to reduce) had remained undisturbed and unimpaired, if it had not been augmented and improved.

44. The final result to the British government appeared to me to be, first, the entire loss of the benefit of the treaty of triple alliance against Tippoo Sultaun, by the utter inability of our allies to fulfil their defensive engagements with the Company, and, secondly, the establishment of a French army of 14,000 men, in the dominions of one of our allies, in the vicinity of the territories of our irreconcilable enemy, and on the confines of the Carnatic and of the Northern Circars.

45. In this state of our political relations, the Company was exposed, without the aid of a single ally, to the hazard of a contest with the united force of Tippoo Sultaun and of the French.

46. My separate dispatch under date the 21st of November, forwarded by the Eurydice, will have apprized your Honourable Court of the measures which I took for the purpose of restoring to his Highness the Nizam, the power of fulfilling his defensive engagements with the Company.

47. At the same time my endeavours were employed, with equal assiduity, to give vigour and effect to the treaties subsisting with his Highness the Peshwah. The return of Nana Furnaveese to the administration, afforded, for some time, a just expectation that

alliance with the Mahrattahs would speedily be restored with [addi]tional vigour and advantage; but the increasing distractions [of th]e Mahrattah empire unfortunately frustrated the wise coun[sels] of that experienced and able statesman, and disappointed my [hope]s at the court of Poonah; I had, however, the satisfaction [of being] certain, that the disposition of that court, under the admini[stra]tion of Nana, continued perfectly favourable to the British [intere]sts; and that want of power would be the sole cause of its [inacti]on, in the event of a war with Tippoo Sultaun.

Towards the commencement of the month of August 1798, [I le]rnt the preparations making by the French in the Mediter[ranea]n. Various circumstances attending the equipment of that [armam]ent, inclined me to apprehend, that at least a part of it [would] be destined for an expedition to India, although I could [not b]elieve that the attempt would be made through Egypt. [Unde]r these impressions, I took the earliest opportunity of di[rectin]g the attention of Rear-admiral Rainier to the coast of Ma[labar;] and at the same time I proposed to strengthen his Majesty's [squad]ron in those seas, according to any arrangement which his [Excel]lency might suggest; and I issued orders to the governments [of For]t St. George and Bombay, to attend to his Excellency's [sugges]tions on this important subject. I am happy to inform [your] Honourable Court, that his Excellency, with the utmost [readin]ess, acceded to the proposition which I had suggested to [him,]with respect to the defence of the coast of Malabar, al[thoug]h his original intention had been to proceed, in the first in[stance], to the straits of Malacca.

On the 18th of September I ratified the new subsidiary [treaty] with the Nizam, of which I have stated the substance in [a se]parate dispatch of the 21st of November by the Eurydice. On the 18th of October I received the first authentic in[forma]tion of the invasion of Egypt by the French, and of the [succe]ss of their arms in that country.

It is unnecessary to call the attention of your Honourable [Court] to the evident connexion of the invasion of Egypt with [the]designs of the French and of Tippoo Sultaun, against the [Britis]h power in India; and I trust it is now equally superfluous [to ent]er into any detailed reasoning for the purpose of satisfying [you of] the security which, at that period of time, would have [accrue]d to your interests in India, if my original intention of [anticip]ating the hostile projects of Tippoo Sultaun could have [been c]arried into immediate effect, according to my anxious wish. [The n]ecessity, however, of either compelling Tippoo Sultaun to [detach] himself from the interests of France, or of depriving [him of] the power of co-operating with the French, if they [should] be enabled to reach India, now became too evident to [admit]of any doubt. My opinion had long been decided, that

Z z 2 no

no negotiation with Tippoo Sultaun could be fuccefsful, unlefs accompanied by fuch a difpofition of our force as fhould alarm him for the fafety of his capital, and that no military operation could effect an adequate or fpeedy reduction of his power, unlefs directed immediately to the fiege of that city.

52. On the 20th of October, therefore, I gave peremptory orders to the government of Fort St. George, for completing the equipment of their battering train, and for advancing it with all practicable difpatch to the moft eligible ftation on the frontier of the Carnatic, with a view of proceeding towards Seringapatam at the earlieft poffible period, if fuch a movement into Myfore fhould become neceffary. At the fame time I fignified to the government of Fort St. George, my intention of reinforcing their army with 3000 volunteers from the native infantry, on the eftablifhment of Bengal, who had offered their fervices with the utmoft alacrity and zeal.

53. To the government of Bombay I iffued further orders for the collection not only of their troops, but of the largeft poffible fupplies on the coaft of Malabar.

54. On the 22d of October (as I have already informed your Honourable Court) the difmiffion of the French faction in the Nizam's army was happily accomplifhed at Hydrabad.

55. On the 31ft of October I received the intelligence of the glorious victory obtained by his Majefty's fquadron under the command of Sir Horatio Nelfon; but being ftill uncertain of the fate of the French army in Egypt, and ignorant whether an additional force might not have been intended to co-operate with it in India, by the ordinary paffage round the Cape of Good Hope, I did not relax any part of the naval or military preparations which had been commenced under my orders. The opportunity now appeared favourable for opening a negotiation with Tippoo Sultaun. I had already communicated to the allies, the Nizam, and the Pefhwah, a circumftantial detail of the conduct of that prince, and had received from both the moft unequivocal affurances of their entire concurrence in my fentiments and views, as well as of their determination to fupport my juft claims of fatisfaction for the infraction of the treaty of Seringapatam.

56. On the 8th of November, therefore, I addreffed to Tippoo Sultaun a letter, of which a copy (No. 2, A. and B.) accompanies this difpatch.

57. Your Honourable Court will perceive, that in this letter I have carefully avoided every hoftile expreffion, merely apprizing the Sultaun of my knowledge of the nature of his intercourfe with the French nation, and propofing to him to receive Major Doveton on the part of the allies, for the purpofe of proceeding to an amicable arrangement of all fubfifting differences.

58. My expectation was, that the neceffary impreffion of the

fuccefs

success of his Majesty's fleet against the French in Egypt; the revival of our defensive alliance with the Nizam; the destruction of the French influence in the Decan; the declared disposition of the Peshwah to fulfil his defensive engagements to the utmost extent of his power; the presence of his Majesty's squadron on the coast of Malabar, reinforced by such of the Honourable Company's ships as had been equipped for the purpose; and, finally, the progress of our military preparations on both coasts, might have induced the Sultaun to accede to my proposals for opening the channels of pacific negotiation; and, under these circumstances, I trusted that the terror of the British arms might have rendered their actual employment unnecessary.

59. With such expectations I resolved to proceed to Fort St. George, for the purpose of conducting the expected negotiation with the Sultaun, which I flattered myself my presence on the coast of Coromandel might enable me to bring to an issue, before the season should be so far advanced as to relieve Tippoo Sultaun from those alarms for the safety of his capital, on which I founded my sole hope of obtaining any satisfactory adjustment with him.

60. On the 10th of December I addressed the letter marked No. 3. to the Sultaun, informing him of my intention to proceed to Fort St. George, and again urging him to receive Major Doveton. On the 25th of December I embarked on board his Majesty's ship the Sybille, Captain E. Cooke, and arrived at this presidency on the 31st of the same month.

61. A few days previous to my arrival, the corps of native volunteers from Bengal had landed in perfect safety, and in the highest spirits, and soon after a corps of artillery arrived from Fort William, under the command of Colonel Montague.

62. The letter marked No. 4. was delivered to me on my arrival at Fort St. George.

63. In this letter your Honourable Court will observe the prevarication and falsehood which mark the Sultaun's statement of his late intercourse with the French, and you will perceive the evasion by which he eludes the moderate and amicable proposition of the allies for opening a negotiation.

64. To this letter from the Sultaun I returned the answer dated 9th of January, and marked No. 5. in which I renewed the proposition of opening a negotiation, and urged the Sultaun not to delay his reply beyond the period of one day after my letter should reach him; intimating that dangerous consequences might result from a longer delay.

65. The advanced period of the season absolutely required that I should ascertain the Sultaun's views within a short time; my proposition contained nothing derogatory to the honour or dignity of the Sultaun. It was now urged for the third time without

variation,

variation, and it related simply and distinctly to the admission of an ambassador, for the purpose of opening a negotiation; to demand an immediate answer to a proposition of such a nature, could not, therefore, be deemed either offensive or unreasonable.

66. Subsequently to the dispatch of my letter No. 5. I received from the Sultaun the letter No. 6. in reply to my letter No. 3. dispatched from Fort William. The Sultaun's silence in his letter No. 6. with respect to the admission of Major Doveton, afforded an additional proof of his disposition to evade the pacific advance of the allies.

67. I now employed every effort to advance the military preparations in the Carnatic, which had already made a considerable progress during the months of November and December. From the moment of my arrival at Fort St. George, all the inhabitants of this settlement, and every officer, civil and military, appeared to be animated by an unanimous determination to discharge their respective duties with a degree of cheerfulness and ardour, correspondent to the exigency and importance of the occasion; and I was soon satisfied that the disposition, of which I lamented the appearance in the months of July and August, had either been subdued by the just exercise of authority, or corrected by reflection, and by the more full disclosure of the views of the enemy. The zeal, alacrity, and public spirit of the bankers and commercial agents at Madras, as well as of the most respectable of your civil servants at this presidency, enabled me, within a few weeks, to raise a large sum of money, by loan, for the public service. Previous to my departure from Bengal, I had remitted twenty lacks of rupees in specie for the use of this presidency; I now dispatched the Sybille to Calcutta for a further supply; and the extraordinary exertion of his Excellency the Vice-president in council, assisted by the diligence and ability of Mr. Thomas Myers, the accountant-general of Bengal, furnished me with an additional aid of twenty lacks, within so short a time, that the movement of the army was not delayed for an instant, on account of a deficiency of treasure; and Lieutenant-general Harris was provided with a sufficient supply of specie to maintain his army in the field until the month of May.

68. Tippoo Sultaun remaining silent for a considerable time after the receipt of my letter of the 9th of January, I concluded that his object must be to delay his answer until the season should be so far advanced, as to render the capture of Seringapatam impracticable during the present year.

69. In the mean while the advices from Bussorah, Bagdad, Constantinople, and Bombay, were of so uncertain a nature, as to leave me still in doubt with respect to the condition of the French army in Egypt; the only safe conclusion which could
be

drawn from those advices being, that the French still maintained the possession of that country with a large army.

70. No intelligence had been received from the Red Sea respecting the arrival of any of his Majesty's ships on that station; or had I been able to ascertain with any degree of accuracy, that means the French might either have provided, or might find on the spot, to enable them to reach the Sultaun's dominions.

71. In addition to these circumstances, I knew that while Tippoo Sultaun had declined to receive an ambassador from the Honourable Company, and had omitted to answer my late letters, he had dispatched native vakeels from Seringapatam, who, together with Mr. Dubuc (one of the leaders of the French force raised in the Isle of France, under Mr. Malartie's proclamation), were on the point of embarking at Tranquebar, with an avowed mission from the Sultaun to the Executive Directory of France.

72. On the 3d of February I had received no answer from the Sultaun to my letter of the 9th of January, although the communication between Seringapatam and Fort St. George does not require, at the most, a longer time than eight, and is sometimes effected in four days.

73. In order, therefore, to defeat the object of the Sultaun's silence, and to avail myself of the actual superiority of our force, and of the advantages of the present season, before the French could effect any junction with him, I determined to commence hostilities without delay, and to suspend all negotiation, until the united forces of the Company, and of their allies, should have made such an impression on the territories of Mysore, as might give full effect to our just representations.

74. With these views, on the 3d of February, I directed Lieutenant-general Harris to enter the territory of Mysore with the army assembled under his command; on the same day I issued orders to Lieutenant-general Stuart to be prepared to co-operate from Malabar; and I signified to Rear-admiral Rainier, and to the several allies of the Company, that I now considered the British government in India to be at war with Tippoo Sultaun.

75. At length, on the 13th of February, I received from Tippoo Sultaun the letter marked No. 7. informing me, that being frequently disposed " to make excursions and hunt," he was " accordingly proceeding upon a hunting excursion," and desiring " that I would" dispatch Major Doveton " slightly attended."

76. But the season for negotiation through the pacific channels, so often offered by me, was now elapsed. After mature deliberation on the grounds already stated, I had directed the advance of the army into the territory of the Sultaun; and I had signified to the allies my determination to proceed to hostilities. To have delayed the advance of the army, would at once have thrown

the

the advantages which I then poſſeſſed into the hands of Tippoo
Sultaun, and have rendered the ſiege of his capital impracticable
during the preſent ſeaſon. On the other hand, an embaſſy
combined with the hoſtile irruption of any army into Myſore
would have been liable to the imputation of inſincerity toward
Tippoo Sultaun ; and while it bore the appearance of indeciſion
in the eyes of the allies, would have promoted, and perhaps wa
ranted, a ſimilar degree of inſtability in their councils and op
rations.

77. The deſign of this tardy, reluctant, and inſidious aſſert
the admiſſion of an embaſſy from the Britiſh government, c
be conſidered in no other light than that of a new artifice
the purpoſe of gaining time, until a change of circumſta
and of ſeaſon might enable the Sultaun to avail himſelf of
aſſiſtance of France. This concluſion was now confirmed
my knowledge of the actual embarkation of Mr. Dubuc and t
native vakeels, on an embaſſy from Tippoo to the Executi
Directory of France ; an event which took place at Tranqueba
on the 7th of February.

78. I therefore replied to the letter of Tippoo Sultaun in th
terms of the encloſure No. 8. ; in which I have declared Lieu
tenant-general Harris to be the only perſon now authorized b
me to receive and to anſwer whatever communications the Sultau
may think fit to make, with a view to the reſtoration of peace
on ſuch conditions as appear to the allies to be indiſpenſably ne
ceſſary to their common ſecurity. This letter I directed Gener:
Harris to forward to the Sultaun on the day on which the arm
under his command ſhould paſs the frontier, and, at the ſam
time, I inſtructed him to iſſue, in the name of the allies, th
accompanying declaration, marked No. 9.

79. The Nizam's contingent conſiſts of above 6000 of th
Honourable Company's troops, ſubſidized by his Highneſs,
about the ſame number of his own infantry (including a portio
of Mr. Peron's Sepoys, now commanded by Britiſh officers), an
a large body of cavalry.

80. This force, under the general command of Mur Allum
formed a junction with the Britiſh army on the 19th
February ; and it is with the greateſt ſatisfaction that I re
mark to your Honourable Court, the beneficial effects whic
the Company have already derived from the recent improvemen
of our alliance with the court of Hydrabad. The Nizam's con
tingent actually arrived in the vicinity of Chittoor, in a ſtate c
preparation for the field, before General Harris was ready to pro
ceed on his march from Vellore.

81. I have annexed to this diſpatch, No. 10. the laſt return
of Lieutenant-general Harris's army previous to his paſſing th
frontier, an army more completely appointed, more amply an
liberall

supplied in every department, or more perfect in its
, and in the acknowledged experience, ability, and zeal
cers, never took the field in India. The army on the
Malabar (of which I also enclose a return, No. 11.) is
ally efficient and respectable condition; and the extra-
efforts which have been made by Lieutenant-general
d Major-general Hartley, seconded by the cordial at-
and unremitting assiduity of the Rajah of Coorga, have
, within a very short period of time, a supply so abun-
it I am induced to transmit the particulars of it to your
ble Court, as a testimony of the distinguished merits of
uable officers, and of the loyalty and active exertions of
ful tributary of the Honourable Company. (No. 12.)

considerable force, under the command of Lieutenant-
Read and Brown, will co-operate with Lieutenant-gene-
s in the southern districts of the Carnatic and Mysore.
nder these circumstances General Harris entered the
of Mysore on the 5th of March, with orders to proceed
o Seringapatam.

aving thus submitted to your Honourable Court, ac-
o the order of dates, a detailed relation of the events
ve led to the war in which we are actually engaged, and
eclared to you the motives and objects of my conduct
stage of this important transaction, I must request your
n to conclude this dispatch with such reflections as arise
nd from the review of my past measures, and from the
of their ultimate consequences and permanent effect.

rom the first disclosure of the nature and object of
Sultaun's embassy to the Isle of France, every principle
and policy demanded from your government in India,
nstantaneous effort should be made to reduce his power
rces, before he could avail himself of the advantages
iance which he had concluded. The defect of means is
consideration which can justify me, for not having made
t at the early period when its success would have placed
ty of your possessions on a foundation, which the inva-
ndia by a French force could not have impaired.

, without the aid of some native power, it is scarcely
hat the French should ever make any permanent im-
n your empire in India; and no native power (excepting
Sultaun) is so infatuated as to be disposed to assist or re-
ench army.

he progress of events since the date of my orders of the
une 1798, has not only confirmed the principles of
d policy, by which an attack upon the Sultaun was at
demanded, but has manifested that the designs of

VIII.   3 A   France,

France, as well as of the Sultaun, were of a much more e˙
five and formidable nature, than any which have ever bee
tempted againſt the Britiſh empire in India ſince the hour ⟨
firſt foundation.

88. While the magnitude and danger of theſe deſigns
gradually diſcloſed, I had the ſatisfaction to feel that the r
of averting them were augmenting in a proportion nearly e
by the ſucceſs of the negotiations at Hydrabad, and by the ad˙
of the military preparations which I had ordered throughout
poſſeſſions.

89. At the commencement of the month of February
criſis arrived in which I was called upon to form my ult
deciſion on the important queſtion at iſſue with Tippoo Sul
and to determine the final reſult of the whole ſyſtem o:
meaſures.

90. On the one hand, the apparent eſtabliſhment of the F
army in Egypt, and the uncertainty of the ſtate of our
power in the Red Sea, rendered the danger ſtill urgent from
quarter; while Tippoo Sultaun's repeated evaſions of my
poſals for negotiation, combined with his embaſſy to the E
tive Directory of France, under the conduct of Mr. D⟨
appeared to preclude all hope of detaching the Sultaun fro
recent alliance with the enemy. On the other hand, I now
ſeſſed ample means of fruſtrating the moſt dangerous effe
that alliance, by a ſeaſonable application of the powerful ⟨
which the treachery and aggreſſion of the Sultaun had comp
me to collect at a heavy expenſe to your finances.

91. Your Honourable Court will determine, whether, ir
ſtate of affairs, my orders of the 3d of February were prem⟨
and whether I ſhould have been juſtified, on the 13th of Febr
in recalling thoſe orders, for the purpoſe of admitting, a
late period, a negotiation which would have enabled T
Sultaun to defeat every object of the armament of the alli⟨
the preſent ſeaſon, and would have afforded him ample ti⟨
reap the full benefit of his connexion with France, befor
ſeaſon for beſieging his capital ſhould return.

92. In deciding theſe important queſtions, you will nece˙
conſider what degree of reliance was to be placed on the ſin⟨
of the Sultaun's diſpoſition to conclude an amicable adjuſt
with your government, at the very moment when he had ac
diſpatched, on an embaſſy to the Executive Directory of Fr
the commander of the French troops raiſed in the Mauritiu⟨
admitted into the Sultaun's ſervice, for the expreſs purpo⟨
carrying on a war of aggreſſion againſt your poſſeſſions in In

93. The admirable condition of your armies on both ⟨
and the unequalled perfection of their equipment in ever
part⟨

partment, added to the extraordinary spirit and animation with which the campaign has been opened, afford every reason to hope, that the issue of the war will be speedy and prosperous, and that it must terminate in a considerable reduction of Tippoo Sultaun's resources and power.

94. The wisdom of your Honourable Court will anticipate the extensive benefits which must result to your interests, from an event now become essential to the peace and security of your possessions in India.

95. The policy of the treaty of Seringapatam certainly was not to maintain Tippoo Sultaun's power in such a state as should leave him a constant object of alarm and apprehension to the Company: that he has been justly so considered for some years past, cannot be doubted by any person acquainted with the records of any of your governments in India. The present is the second crisis within the last three years, in which the Government-general has thought it necessary to assemble the army on the coast of Coromandel, for the sole purpose of checking his motions; and the apprehension of his intentions has obstructed our operations against our European enemies in India during the course of our present war.

96. The continuance of Tippoo's power on its actual scale, and under such circumstances, must have proved to the Company a perpetual source of solicitude, expense, and hazard. But the engagement which he has contracted with the French, the public proofs which he has given of his eagerness to receive in Mysore as large a force as they can furnish, combined with the prodigious magnitude of their preparations, and the incredible progress of their arms, evidently directed to the destruction of the British power in India, form new and prominent features in our political situation in this quarter of the world.

97. Admitting the wisdom of that policy which dictated the preservation of Tippoo Sultaun's power, at the close of the last war with Mysore, the spirit of our present councils must be accommodated to the variation of circumstances, and to the actual position, character, and views of our enemies.

98. In such a conjuncture of affairs, I am persuaded that your Honourable Court will be of opinion, that no object can be deemed so urgent, or so necessary to the safety of your possessions, as the effectual reduction of the only declared ally of France now existing among the native powers of India.

99. If Tippoo Sultaun had been disposed to content himself with the quiet possession of his present dominions; if he could have been brought to a sense of his own peril in forming a connexion with the French, the representations which I addressed

3 A 2

to

to him would have produced an early and falutary impreffion. Whatever fpeculative opinions might have been entertained with refpect to his interefts, views, and power, the juftice and moderation of the Britifh government would never have difturbed his tranquillity. But he refolved to attempt the recovery of his loft dominions, at the hazard of thofe which he ftill retains; and in the ardour of his paffionate purfuit, he overlooked not only the certain deftruction of his own independence, the inevitable confequence even of the moft profperous fuccefs of any alliance with France, but alfo the predominant influence of the Englifh Eaft India Company, which would detect his treachery, and turn againft his own empire the ruin which he had meditated againft theirs.

100. The fecrecy of his councils, the promptiude of his refources, his conftant and active ftate of equipment for war, added to the facility of his intercourfe with the French through his remaining territories on the coaft of Malabar, form the moft dangerous circumftances in the actual condition of his power and dominion, and conftitute his principal means of offence.

101. If fuccefs fhould attend your arms in this war, I entertain a firm confidence that thofe dangers will either be wholly averted, or fo confiderably diminifhed, as to afford to your government in India the profpect of durable fecurity and genuine peace.

102. I cannot clofe this letter without repeating to your Honourable Court the cordial expreffions of my entire fatisfaction in the zealous and honourable co-operation of Lord Clive, as well as of all the members of this government. The beneficial effect of their cheerful and ready concurrence in forwarding all my views, is manifeft in the rapid progrefs and perfect completion of the equipments of the army in the field, and furnifhes a ftriking and falutary example of the ineftimable advantages of unanimity and concord among your fervants in India. I have the honour to be, Honourable Sirs, with the greateft refpect,

Fort St. George,   Your moft obedient and faithful fervant,
20*th March,* 1799.   MORNINGTON.

Copy of a Letter from Tippoo Sultaun to the Executive Directory.

The Circar Condabad to the Executive Directory, reprefenting the French Republic, one and indivifible.

IN the name of the friendfhip which the Circar Condabad and his nation vow to obferve towards the French republic, a friendfhip and alliance which will endure as long as the fun and moon
                                       fhall

shall continue to shine in the heavens, and will be so solid that the most extraordinary circumstances shall never break or disunite either the one or the other.

The English, jealous of the connexion and friendship which for a long time reigned between my Circar and France, have united themselves to the Mahrattahs, to the Nizam Ali Khan, and to my other enemies, for the purpose of declaring war against me; a war as odious and unjust as that which had lasted for some years before, and which was attended with such fatal consequences to me, by taking from me my finest provinces, three crores and thirty lacks of rupees.

The republic is not ignorant of any of these unfortunate circumstances; and of my having endeavoured to dispute every inch of territory, which I was forced to give up to our common enemy. I should not have been compelled to make those cruel sacrifices had I been assisted by the French, my ancient allies; who, deceived by the perfidious projects of Governor-general Conway at Pondicherry, together with Governor Campbell at Madras, agreed to the evacuation of the place which they commanded. The French republic, by expelling the English from their rich possessions in India, will certainly repair the faults of their ancient government.

Animated for a long time by these sentiments, I have communicated them to the government of the Isle of France through the medium of two ambassadors, from whom I have just had the high satisfaction of receiving such answers as I wished for; as well as the republican colours from the Chief of Brigade Chappins, and Naval Captain Dubuc, who have brought to me such succours in soldiers and officers as circumstances have permitted General Malartic and Rear-admiral Sercey to send me.

I keep near me the former officer, and send you the second in quality of an ambassador, for the purpose, at the same time that he demands your alliance offensive and defensive, of obtaining forces sufficient to attack and annihilate our common enemies. I will transmit to you by his means my standard, which, united to that of the republic, will serve as a basis of the alliance which the two nations are about to contract. I have also charged him to communicate particular orders to you.

I join with him in the embassy Sheik Abdoubraim and Mahomet Bismilla, my subjects, who are equally directed to represent me in all affairs which they have to transact with you.

Whatever may be the circumstances in which the two nations may hereafter find themselves, whether together or separately in all their transactions, may the good, the glory, and the advantage of both be always the end of them! May their respective sentiments

ments be guaranteed by the appearances of fidelity, and the solemn pledges given by each of them! and may the heavens and earth draw near to each other and unite, sooner than our alliance shall experience the slightest alteration!

Given at my palace at Seringapatam, July 20, 1798.

(A true copy)   C. MACAULEY, Sec.
(A true copy)   N. B. EDMONSTONE, P. T.

Copy of Articles of Engagement proposed by Tippoo Sultaun to the Directory.

RECAPITULATION of the demands which my ambassadors are to make of the Executive Directory at Paris:

Article I. Ten or fifteen thousand troops, consisting of infantry, cavalry, and artillery.

II. A naval force to carry on hostilities on the coast where our armies may be, in order to favour their operations, or reinforce them, if necessary.

III. The Circar shall furnish all warlike stores and provisions to the armies of the republic, as well as horses, oxen, and every necessary article, with the exception of European liquors, which he has not in his country.

IV. The orders of the King shall be taken with respect to all the marches and military operations.

V. The expedition shall be directed against some point of the coast of Coromandel, and in preference against Porto Novo, where the disembarkation of the troops shall take place; and the King shall first repair thither with his army, his intention being to commence his operations in the heart of the enemy's country.

VI. The King demands, that notice shall be given to him by the republic, in dispatching two corvettes from Europe, at a distance of twenty days from each other, of the number of ships and troops to be sent to him, that he may immediately enter upon the campaign, and make himself master of the coast of Coromandel before the arrival of the republican forces.

VII. All the conquests made from the enemy shall, with the exception of the provinces which the King has been obliged to cede to the English, to the Mahrattahs, and to Nizam Ali Khan, be equally divided between the two nations, and according to the respective conventions; the same division shall take place of the enemy's vessels and the Portuguese colonies, for the purpose of indemnifying the King for the expenses of the war.

VIII. If any difficulty shall arise between the allied armies, each of them shall possess the right of referring to their modes of justice according their laws and customs, and every discretionary

tionary article shall be agreed upon in writing between both nations.

IX. That whatever may be the wish of the republic to make peace with England, or to continue the war, it shall always consider the King as its friend and faithful ally, and include him in all its treaties, and communicate to him all its intentions.

X. All French who now are in, or may come into the states of the King, shall be treated as friends and allies; and they shall be empowered to come and go, and carry on trade, without being liable to any trouble or molestation, but shall, on the contrary, receive every assistance of which they may stand in need.

XI. This article relates to bringing into the service of the Sultaun several French artists and mechanics, skilled in casting cannon, in paper and glass making, with some engineers and builders.

Given in my palace of Seringapatam, under my signature, that of my prime minister, and authenticated with the state seal, on the 20th of July 1798.

(A true copy)   C. MACAULEY, Sec.
(A true copy)   N. B. EDMONSTONE, P. T.

Copy of a Letter from Dubuc to the Rajah of Travencore's Minister at Aleppo.

My Lord,

I EXPECT, with impatience, the arrival of some vessels from India, to hear from you, and to learn from you that your health is perfectly re-established, if, as it has been reported here, it has been in a bad state.

As the means of sending intelligence to India are very fluctuating, I take the opportunity of a vessel which is sailing for the coast of Coromandel, to write to the Prince Tippoo Sultaun, with whom I have the honour to correspond. I request he will be pleased to communicate my letter to you, after having caused it to be translated into the Oriental language, that it may not be necessary for you to show it to any one.

I have often considered in my own mind, why your prince was not in alliance with the Sultaun; and in recollecting that the great Nabob Hyder Ali, his father, had been the friend and ally of Ram Rajah, I was astonished that that friendship, which had been deranged by some event, had not been renewed. It is very common in Europe for a power which has been at war with its neighbour to become its friend and ally. You have been at war with the Pacha. I feel the sincerest conviction that every resentment should be forgotten; that all former disputes should be
consigned

consigned to oblivion; and that it is the duty of the two princes to enter into a treaty of alliance and friendship, in a way solid and suitable to their reciprocal interests. Were I in India, I should give you, as well as the Sultaun, such substantial grounds for that proceeding, that I am confident my wishes would be fulfilled; but it will be peculiarly your glory to unite these two powers. You are the counsellor and the friend of your king; you direct his affairs so advantageously, that if you find this alliance profitable (and I do not doubt but you will), it will be sufficient for you to propose it to him, and the two princes will readily come to a good understanding Should my hopes be gratified in this respect, my joy will be complete, for you will be considered our ally in becoming that of a prince who has been for a long time united with France. I pray Heaven to grant you long and happy days; and that those of your king may be prosperous, is the sincere wish of your servant and friend,

Isle de France, March 5, 1798.   MAL. DESCOMBRE.
(A true copy)   C. MACAULEY, Sec.
(A true copy)   N. B. EDMONSTONE, P. T.

Copy of a Letter from Dubuc to Tippoo Sultaun; dated 10th December 1798, O. S.

Grand Pacha—Health and Respect!

THE men have fortunately arrived, but we are in want of the most essential thing—the letters which they left on their way. I however hope they will arrive in a few days. They have been four months on their journey, and you may judge of their dispatch and of their punctuality in their services to you. The Hircarrahs whom I dispatched to you the 11th of last month, returned yesterday with your Majesty's answer of the 29th of the same month, and I hasten to send them back, as they are very faithful persons, and I wish them to be liberally rewarded. The person who was to have furnished the money has not made his appearance, and I fear there will be considerable difficulty in getting them paid. I think it indispensably necessary for you to expedite an order for taking up immediately all the money which is at Mercieu's, and to annex it to a letter of credit, as I had requested of you, on the republic. The importance of my mission is such, and the result of it must prove so advantageous to your Majesty, that I cannot too often repeat, money must be considered as nothing when affairs of such immense moment are carrying on. It will be necessary for me to depart, and without money I cannot. In all countries money is the sinew of war; and if your Majesty does not wish to be ruined by the English, and lose the assistance

assistance of my friends the French, give me a sufficient demonstration of your confidence in giving me the proper means of proceeding. Socars with money will not be stopped, more particularly if it be in pagodas with stars. Use difpatch in fending it to me, and I shall inftantly set off. The cloths are not yet come, and I have difpatched people to forward them. I requeft your Majefty will authorize me to take a year's falary in advance, as you promifed me, in order to provide for the fubfiftence of my family in my abfence, fince the fix months for which I have been paid expire on the 8th of next month, and I have been compelled to expend every thing in my poffeffion. The Englifh having taken my fhip and my property, you will confider my demand juft in every point of view, when you reflect that my family are in a foreign country, deprived of every refource. I once more repeat my earneft defire, that your Majefty will give me full powers in that refpect, and order me immediately to be provided with the neceffary funds. The Hircarrahs have promifed to return within thirty days, and I fhall be able to depart in forty. It would be prudent to have fome other Hircarrahs here, that you may receive intelligence every eight days. I beg leave to recommend earneftly to you the Ouaquil, who is not fufficiently paid, and has received nothing for eight months paft. He alfo fhould have a palanquin; for the envoy of a great prince, fo truly noble and generous as you are, ought not to walk on foot like a cooly. Are you content with my conduct? Speak candidly. You know how much I am attached to you, and you fhall have certain proofs of my fidelity. I befeech your Majefty to countenance with your bounty and protection my good friend and colleague, General Chaprus. See him often, and the more you fhall fee him the more you fhall know that he is worthy of your efteem, as a man of honour and prudence.

I have learned, that your Majefty has written to the government of Madras and to Lord Mornington. What will be the iffue of their anfwer? Be on your guard againft them; be ready either to defend yourfelf, or to make an attack. The preparations for war are going on with great rapidity. The army of the Nizam is already on its march; it muft be ftopped. The Englifh were defirous of carrying away Ouaquil Sadas Chidevaram; but I difcovered the plot, and it has not fucceeded. It is neceffary that your Majefty fhould inftantly write to the government of Tranquebar, by a fwift courier, to demand its immediate protection for your general in chief Dubuc, his Major Fillietag, the interpreter De Bay, and your Ouaquil. Lord Mornington, Governor-general of Bengal, and General Clarke, are coming to the coaft about the end of this month, for the purpofe of entering into negotiations with your Majefty; which, if they are not advantageous to them, they will caufe you to declare war againſt them. The refult of that meafure will be the invafion of your country, and the dethroning of you, by fubftituting for you and your heirs a nabob of their own making. Your Majefty muft perceive, that nothing leſs is in agitation than the deftruction of your kingdom. You muft exert yourfelf, and negotiate every where to maintain your power, until the moment when I fhall be able to fecure it for ever for yourfelf and your auguſt children. It is very eafy for the Englifh, in confequence of their intrigues in every part of India, to caufe troubles of a ferious kind, and deprive you of all your allies. Should they fucceed in the war againſt your Majefty, they would afterwards effect the deftruction of the power of the Mahrattahs, and deprive them of every poffeffion which might be ceded to them by a new treaty of peace. It is therefore evidently their intereft to treat jointly with you for the purpofe of finding a certain and mutual guarantee, and that each member may defend the ftipulations and ceffions made by each at the peace which you figned in your capital with the contracting parties. The Englifh threaten you, the Mahrattahs are bound to fupport you, and not fuffer you to be overcome. The barrier which feparates you from the former fhould exift without any encroachment. You may rely on your allies as long as you poffefs interefts in common, and you would be abandoned by them were thefe common interefts to ceafe.

The time is fhort and precious. You muft give proofs of your good intentions, and gain over the Englifh; and, at the fame time, throw obftacles in the way of their negotiations a Poona. In fuch a conjuncture, the Mahrattahs ought to give to the law of treaties all poffible weight, and not to omit recalling to the minds of the Englifh the affiftance granted by them againſt your Majefty. Should their remonftrances be neglected, and the means of conciliation prove fruitlefs, let them inftantly take up arms, and threaten the nation guilty of a breach of the treaties Such a proceeding would, perhaps, ftop all military defigns and operations againft your Majefty. But if the event fhould prove different, the fword muft be drawn, and the fheath thrown fo fa as to render every fearch for it ufelefs. We have no intelligence of any peculiar intereft from Europe. The republic is uniformly victorious, and continues to refufe peace to England. Scindi has already taken Delhi; and I think he muft have alfo finifhed the conqueft of Agra. It would be prudent in your Majefty to difpatch couriers to him, to acquaint him with the fituation in which you are placed. I entreat your Majefty to read my letter attentively. It has been dictated by candour, truth, and fenfe of your intereft.

I pra

I pray God to grant fuccefs to the exertions of your Majefty, to whom I have the honour to be, with refpect,
(Signed)   Dubuc,
Commander in Chief, Naval Captain of the French Republic, one and indivifible.
(True copy)   C. Macaulry, Sec.

Major Filletat begs you to accept his homage and attachment to your Majefty.
(A true copy)   N. B. Edmonstone, P. T.

Report of the Committee of Secrecy of the Britifh Houfe of Commons, printed the 15th March 1799.

THE Committee of Secrecy, to whom the feveral papers which were prefented (fealed up) to the Houfe by Mr. Secretary Dundas upon the 23d day of January 1799, by his Majefty's command, were referred, and who were directed to examine the matters thereof, and report the fame, as they fhall appear to them, to the Houfe, have proceeded, in obedience to the orders of the Houfe, to the confideration of the matters referred to them. They have been prevented from fooner laying before the Houfe the refult of their examination, not only from the extent of the matters which came before them, but becaufe fome of the recent circumftances which they have to ftate, could not, with propriety, have been difclofed at an earlier period.

In the whole courfe of their inquiry, your Committee have found the cleareft proofs of a fyftematic defign, long fince adopted and acted upon by France, in conjunction with domeftic traitors, and purfued up to the prefent moment with unabated perfeverance, to overturn the laws, conftitution, and government, and every exifting eftablifhment, civil or ecclefiaftical, both in Great Britain and Ireland; as well as to diffolve the connexion between the two kingdoms, fo neceffary to the fecurity and profperity of both.

The chief hope of accomplifhing this defign has refted on the propagation of thofe deftructive principles which originally produced the French revolution, with all the miferies and calamities fince experienced in France, and now extended over a large part of Europe.

The moft effectual engine employed for this purpofe, has been the inftitution of political focieties, of a nature and defcription before unknown in any country, and inconfiftent with public tranquillity, and with the exiftence of regular government. The effects of this fatal caufe, operating in its fulleft extent, have been unhappily felt and exemplified in the diftractions and calamities of Ireland. The fame caufe is known to have prepared the way for

all the different revolutions by which France has fucceedec
verting fo many of the governments of Europe, and red
many independent ftates to vaffalage and fubjection.
country fimilar meafures have been attempted; and althou
have been hitherto defeated, by the precautions of the Leg
by the vigilance of his Majefty's government, and ftill mo
general good fenfe and loyalty of the nation, the objec
abandoned. The utmoft diligence is ftill employed in en
ing, not only to fuftain and revive thofe focieties, whofe
and treafonable purpofes long fince attracted the notice
liament, but to extend their correfpondence to every par
kingdom, to Ireland, to France, and to thofe places on
tinent where French emiffaries are eftablifhed; and to
new focieties, formed precifely on the fame plan, and dir
the fame object, as thofe whofe influence in Ireland has p
fuch pernicious and formidable effects; and of which, th
quences might have proved fatal to that kingdom, if they
been averted, in a feafon of the greateft difficulty, by the
firmnefs, and exertion of his Majefty's government, and
liament of Ireland. The extent and uniformity of this fy
confpiracy are equally ftriking. The formation and ftru
all thefe focieties, in this country, in Ireland, and on
tinent, are fimilar; their views and principles are the f
well as the means which they employ to extend their ir
A continued intercourfe and concert has been maintain
their firft origin to the prefent moment; fometimes betw
focieties themfelves, fometimes between their leading m
and a frequent communication has been kept up with the
ment of France; to which they appear to look as their p
and ally, and which has repeatedly furnifhed an afylum
who, on account of their principal fhare in thefe crimin
actions, have become fugitives or outlaws from the Br
minions.

In ftating the grounds of this opinion, although your Co
will have much and important new matter to lay before the
yet they will alfo be obliged to recall to the recollectior
Houfe, many particulars which have already been brougl
the confideration of Parliament, but on which new ligl
been thrown by the events which have fince occurred, an
fubfequent intelligence which has been received. The i
tion which has been produced to your Committee, on th
of this fubject, has been moft ample and extenfive. Th
penfable neceffity of fecrecy, with refpect to the fources c
parts of that intelligence, muft be felt by the Houfe, as
from confiderations of good faith as well as public fafety.
are convinced, that the early and uniform defeat of all
to difturb the public tranquillity of this kingdom, is,

great degree, be   ed to the meritorious and laudable diligence of the   fi   ing those departments of his Majesty's government to which this duty has peculiarly belonged. They appear, during a long period of time, to have obtained early and accurate information of the chief designs and measures of the conspirators; and the striking manner in which the most important particulars of the secret intelligence thus procured, have, in a great variety of instances, been completely confirmed, by events now notorious to the world, and by the confession of parties concerned, entitles, in the opinion of your Committee, the whole of the information derived from the same sources, to the fullest credit.

§ 1. *View of the Nature and System of the Society of United Irishmen, as fully established in Ireland.*

Your Committee are induced, in the first instance, to state the nature, extent, and influence, of the Society of United Irishmen; because this Society has proved the most powerful engine, in the hands of the conspirators, against the government of their country, which has ever yet been devised; and because its proceedings place in the clearest view, the real object of all societies of this description, either in Ireland or Great Britain; the peculiar means by which they act; and the extreme danger which such societies must produce, whenever they are fully established. It is this which has given exertion, consistency, solidity, and force to the Irish rebellion; which has enabled the conspirators to form themselves, under the eye and in defiance of Government, into one body, compacted by one bond of union, under an oath of fidelity and secrecy; engaging themselves, in the first instance, to misprision of treason, and, successively, to the perpetration of the most atrocious crimes. This Society, thus united and combined, extended itself, by its subdivisions, through every part of the kingdom; and was enabled to involve in one general confederacy, a very numerous description of individuals of almost every class, connected with each other by a pledge of secrecy, by consciousness of guilt, and by the sense of personal danger, either from the violated laws of their country, or from the resentment and power of their associates. These bonds of union were strengthened by the use of secret signs, frequently changed, and applied to different ranks in the conspiracy, for the purpose of preventing discovery.

The system, thus established, gradually acquired the means of disturbing the tranquillity of the country in all its parts; of impeding the execution of justice, by forcible resistance to the authority of the laws; by the protection of accused persons; by the rescue of prisoners, the seizure of arms, and, at length, by the assassination of informers, of witnesses, of magistrates, and

of

of jurymen; till, by the general terror which was diffuse loyal inhabitants in different counties were succeffively drive the towns, or compelled wholly to quit the kingdom. head of this extenfive confpiracy was placed a committee, te itfelf " An Executive Directory," extending its influenc power over the difaffected through every part of the ki by " Provincial and Baronial Committees;" through whor by the miffion of itinerant delegates over the country, ar verfal correfpondence was eftablifhed between this execut rectory and all the fubordinate powers and members of th tem. An intercourfe was maintained, in the name of the with individuals and focieties in this country, as well a the governments of his Majefty's enemies; and the confpi were thus enabled to conceal or difplay their numbers a and confequently to magnify their power, or to hide their nefs; to circulate, with rapidity and effect, the moft atr calumnies againft his Majefty's perfon and government againft all defcriptions and bodies of men whom they tho their intereft to vilify; to raife contributions, extortec quently even from thofe who had not become members o union; to procure, difperfe, and conceal arms, ammunitio artillery; to collect military information: and, finally, t an army formed of all thofe among them capable of bearing and placed under the command of officers, in military di correfponding with thofe eftablifhed for the general purp the confpiracy.

* It is material to ftate, in detail, the formation of the d branches of this fyftem, in order to compare it with the i tions of a fimilar nature, which have been fince formed in Britain, and which will be hereafter mentioned. Each inferior focieties confifted, according to their original inftu of thirty-fix members; which number was afterwards redu twelve. Thefe twelve chofe a fecretary and treafurer; a fecretaries of five of thefe focieties formed what was ca " Lower Baronial Committee;" which had the immediate dir and fuperintendance of thofe five focieties. From each lov ronial committee, thus conftituted, one member was delega an " Upper Baronial Committee;" which, in like mann fumed and exercifed the fuperintendance and direction lower baronial committees in the refpective counties. Th fuperior committees were, in populous towns, diftinguifl the name of " Diftrict Committees;" and in counties, name of " County Committees," and were compofed of

---

* Report of Secret Committee of Houfe of Lords of Ireland, Au 1798.

were delegated by the upper baronial committees, each upper baronial committee delegating one of its members to the district or county committee; and the district or county committees had the superintendance and direction of the upper baronial committees. Having thus " organized" (as it is termed) the several counties and populous towns, a committee, called a " Subordinate Directory," was erected in each of the four provinces of Ulster, Leinster, Munster, and Connaught, composed of two members or three, according to the extent and population of the districts which they represented; who were delegated to a provincial committee, which held the immediate direction and superintendance of the several county and district committees in each of the four provinces; and a " General Executive Directory," composed of five persons, was elected by the provincial directories; but the election of this directory was so managed, that none but the secretaries of the provincial directories knew on whom the election fell. It was made by ballot, but not reported to the electors; the appointment was notified only to those on whom the election devolved; and the executive directory, thus composed, assumed and exercised the supreme and uncontrolled command of the whole body of the Union, which, by these secret modes of election, was kept utterly ignorant who were the persons to whom this implicit obedience was paid.

§ 2. *Institution of United Irishmen in* 1791; *and Rise of different Societies in Great Britain.*

For the purpose of obtaining a comprehensive view of the attempts which have been repeatedly made, in the course of the last eight years, for establishing a similar system in this country, and of the means by which they have been hitherto defeated, as well as in order to enable the House to judge fully of the perseverance with which the system is pursued, and of the nature and tendency of the measures which are carrying on at the present moment, your Committee deem it necessary, before they advert to more recent transactions, to go back to that period, when societies of this tendency first appeared in both kingdoms, and to trace, as shortly as they can, their progress and intercourse to the present time.

The Society of United Irishmen was established in the year 1791; and other societies in Great Britain, particularly the Constitutional Society (which had long existed, but about this time assumed a new character), the Corresponding Society (which was instituted in the spring of 1792), and the societies of persons in Scotland terming themselves " *The Friends of the People*" (which originated at nearly the same period), appear to have adopted, in their fullest extent, all the extravagant and violent principles of the French revolution. The events which
followed,

followed, in the courfe of that year and the year 1792, raged among the leading members of thefe focieties, an perfons of fimilar principles, a fanguine hope of intr into both countries, under pretence of the "reform of a what they termed a "*new order of things,*" founded on the ples of that revolution. The degree of bigotry and enti with which they attached themfelves to thefe principle manifefted, as well by the fpeeches and writings of the m of the focieties, as by the zeal with which they laboured pagate among the lower claffes of the community, a f[hatred and contempt for the exifting laws and government country.

It can hardly be neceffary to recall to the recollection Houfe, the induftry with which they endeavoured to diffe thefe fentiments, by the circulation of their own proceedi refolutions; uniformly directed to vilify the forms and pri of the Britifh conftitution; to reprefent the people of thi try as groaning under intolerable oppreffion; to eradicate ligious principle; and to recommend a recurrence to exper of defperate innovation, fimilar to thofe which were at th: adopted in France. For the fame purpofe, the works of and other feditious and impious publications, were diftr throughout almoft every part of the kingdom, with an and profufion beyond all former example.

So confident were the focieties of the efficacy of thef fures, that they appear almoft univerfally to have looked f from the beginning, to the entire overthrow of every (eftablifhment in thefe kingdoms, and to the creation of fo mocratical form of government; either by uniting the w the Britifh empire into one republic, or by dividing it ir or more republics. The confpirators in Ireland, unquefti always meditated the complete feparation of that countr Great Britain: all, however, confidered themfelves as eng one common caufe, as far as related to the deftruction exifting conftitution; all looked to the fuccefs of the dif in each country as forwarding their common views; an was ready to fupport the other in any refiftance to the lav vernment: a frequent intercourfe among them was th confidered as important to their ends; and they all invi expected, the countenance and aid of France.

The attempts made in the beginning of this confpi difguife the real objects under falfe pretences, which o no time to have impofed even on fuperficial obfervers, ha fince been abandoned. Subfequent tranfactions have not fhown the extremes to which the nature and principles c focieties naturally led, but have completely unveiled the (and fettled defigns of the perfons chiefly concerned in

Your Committee beg leave, in this place, to refer the House to his Majesty's Proclamation* of the year 1792, and the several Addresses of both Houses of Parliament thereupon; to the Reports of the Committees of Parliament in this kingdom and in Ireland; and to the different trials for treason and sedition in both kingdoms: and they are confident, that an attentive examination of those documents can leave no doubt in the opinion of the House (even on the circumstances known at that early period) respecting the real nature and extent of the original conspiracy.

§ 3. *First open Attempt in Scotland.*

The groundwork having been thus laid in each kingdom, the first public attempt which was openly directed to the object of overthrowing the government, and effecting a revolution, was made in Scotland, under circumstances which even then evidently marked the connexion between the disaffected throughout his Majesty's dominions. An assembly, styling itself " A General Convention of Delegates from the Societies of the Friends of the People throughout Scotland," met at Edinburgh on the 11th of December 1792. Thomas Muir, a leading member of this assembly, endeavoured to prevail upon its members, at one of their meetings, to receive and answer a paper, intituled, " An Address from the Society of United Irishmen in Dublin to the Delegates for promoting a Reform in Scotland," dated the 23d of November 1792, and set forth in the Appendix (No. 1.); in which the United Irish address the Scotch delegates in what they term " the spirit of civic union in the fellowship of a just and common cause;" and rejoiced, " that the Scotch did not consider themselves as merged and melted down into another country;" but that in the great national question to which the address alluded, " they were still Scotland." They added, " that the cause of the United Irish was also the cause of the Scotch delegates;" that " Universal Emancipation, with *Representative Legislature*, was the polar principle which guided the Society of United Irish-

---

* Proclamation and Addresses - - - - - - 1792.
Lords Report - - - - - - - - - - 1794.
Commons Report - - - - - - - May 1794.
Do. do. - - - - - - - - - June 1794.
Irish Lords Reports - - - - - - - - - 1798.
  Commons do. - - - - - - - - - - 1798.
Trial of Muir, Skirving, Margarot, Gerald, Palmer, and others, for sedition in Scotland, in 1793 and 1794.
— of Watt and Downie, for treason in Scotland, in 1794.
— of Hardy and others, for treason, in 1794.
— of Redhead, *al.* Yorke, for sedition, in 1795.
— of Stone, for treason, in 1796.

men,"

men;" that their end was " a national legiflature, their mea[ns] an union of the whole people." And they recommended affe[m] bling the people in each county in (what they term) " peacea[ble] and conftitutional convention;" the object of which they [at] tempted to difguife by the pretence of reform and petition to P[ar] liament. Several members of the Scotch Convention appear[ed to] have been alarmed at the language of this addrefs, and, notwi[th] ftanding the efforts of Muir, no anfwer was fent; and the me[et] ing adjourned to April 1793. The conduct of Muir in this a[f] fembly formed part of the charge of fedition upon which he w[as] afterwards tried and found guilty. His zeal, however, reco[m] mended him to the confpirators in Ireland; and on the 11th [of] January 1793, he became a member of the Society of the Uni[ted] Irifhmen of Dublin.

He was abfent in France at the time of the fecond meeting [of] the Scotch Convention, which affembled in April 1793, a[nd] again adjourned itfelf to the 29th October following; when [it] met a third time at Edinburgh, after the trial of Muir, who w[as] convicted and fentenced to tranfportation in Auguft 1793. It [is] well known that he afterwards efcaped from the place of [his] tranfportation, and has recently refided in France, purfuing [a] conduct marked by the moft inveterate hoftility to his country.

This meeting * of the Scotch Convention in October 17[93] appears to have been held in concert with feveral focieties [in] England, and particularly the Conftitutional Society and [the] London Correfponding Society, already mentioned. Thefe [so] cieties afterwards fent delegates to the Scotch Convention; [the] terms of whofe inftructions demonftrate the dangerous views [of] thofe who fent them.

Hamilton Rowan, a member of the Society of United Irifhm[en] of Dublin (now a fugitive from Ireland, and attainted of h[igh] treafon), and the Honourable Simon Butler (likewife a mem[ber] of the Society of United Irifhmen), attended this meeting; a[nd] Hamilton Rowan had previoufly been folicited, by letter fr[om] Scotland, on the fubject of fending delegates from Ireland [to] the Convention. It does not appear, however, that thefe p[er] fons bore the diftinct character of delegates, but they were [re] ceived with marked attention; and the Convention refolv[ed] on the 5th November 1793, " That any of the members of [the] Society of United Irifhmen of Dublin fhould be admitted to fp[eak] and vote in the Convention." On the 22d of November 17[93] the Convention had changed its title to that of " The Britifh C[on] vention of Delegates of the People, affociated to obtain Unive[rfal] Suffrage and Annual Parliaments." They affumed, in alu[fion]

---

* Report of Secret Committee of the Houfe of Commons, June 1794.

every particular, the ſtyle and mode of proceeding adopted by the National Convention of France: they divided themſelves into " ſections, committees of organization, inſtruction, finance, and ſecrecy;" granted honours of ſitting; made honourable mention in their minutes of patriotic donations; entered their minutes " in the firſt year of the Britiſh Convention;" inſtituted " primary ſocieties, proviſional aſſemblies and departments;" received from their ſections a variety of motions and reports, ſome of which, in their ſtudied affectation of French phraſes, had the words " *Vive la Convention*" prefixed to them, and ended with " *Ça Ira;*" and ſome were dated " firſt year of the Britiſh Convention, one and indiviſible."

The views of this dangerous aſſembly appear from the minutes of their proceedings, and from the correſpondence of Skirving their ſecretary, Margarot and Gerald, the delegates of the London Correſponding Society, and Hardy, the ſecretary of that ſociety; which are ſtated in the Report of the Committee of this Houſe in 1794, and in the Appendix to that Report, and were given in evidence on the trials above referred to.

It is obſervable upon the face of theſe minutes, that the funds of this Convention were extremely low; ſo low, that perhaps at firſt ſight the aſſembly itſelf may appear to have been rather an object of contempt, from the apparent inadequacy of its pecuniary means, than an object of alarm from the dangerous extravagances of its revolutionary deſigns. It is happy for the peace of this country that the means of theſe ſocieties, in their different ſhapes and ſtages, have not been more equal to ſuch deſigns. But the recent proceedings in Ireland too plainly ſhow, that though the want of money may retard the progreſs, and cripple the exertions of ſuch conſpiracies, yet numbers thus leagued together for the total ſubverſion of the government and conſtitution of a country poſſeſs means which (if not ſeaſonably counteracted) may introduce ſcenes of the moſt horrid confuſion, rebellion, and blood.

This Convention continued to hold its meetings in the city of Edinburgh until the 4th of December 1793; when its objects evidently tending towards open rebellion, ſome of the leading members were arreſted, together with Skirving, their ſecretary; and Skirving, Margarot, and Gerald, were afterwards tried in Scotland for ſedition, and ſentenced to tranſportation. The members of this Convention, notwithſtanding the arreſt of ſome of their body, aſſembled again on the 5th of December, and refuſed to diſperſe till compelled by the magiſtrates; but they continued for ſome time to meet privately, in different ſocieties, and to carry on a ſecret correſpondence with various parts of England and Scotland.

The Society of United Irishmen of Dublin, who had already shown the interest they took in the meeting of this Convention appear (as was to be expected) to have considered its dispersion as hostile to their views, and declared their sentiments, by a resolution of the 20th December 1793; in which, after noticing what they called "the oppressive attempt in Edinburgh to stifle the voice of the people through the British Convention, and a truly patriotic resistance to that attempt," they resolved, "That all or any of the members of the British Convention, and the patriotic societies which delegated members to that Convention, should be received as brothers and members of their society."

§ 4. *Attempts to assemble a Convention of the People in England.*

The leading English societies, which have been already stated to have sent delegates to the Scotch Convention, had, during its sittings, and for a considerable time previous thereto, been actively employed in measures directed to similar objects. For the purpose of promoting their seditious projects, they had carried on a constant correspondence with all the numerous country societies which had been formed in many populous towns in different parts of the kingdom. They had, as early as in May 1792, presented an address, sufficiently expressive of their principles, to those whom they styled "the Friends of the Constitution at Paris known by the name of Jacobins." In the end of the same year, after receiving a letter of approbation from persons calling themselves "Friends of Liberty and Equality in France," they instituted a regular committee of foreign correspondence; and they had even proceeded to present addresses to the National Convention in France, which had then assumed the whole legislative and executive power, and was assembled for the purpose of framing a new constitution, and proceeding to the trial of the King. In one of these addresses (particularly noticed in the Report of 1794, but which your Committee think it material again to advert to) they styled the Convention "Servants of a sovereign People, and Benefactors of Mankind." They rejoice that the revolution had arrived at that point of perfection which enabled them to address them by such a title. They extol the proceedings of the 10th of August as a glorious victory, and add, "*The honour will in part be ours,* but the glory will be all your own; and is the reward of your perseverance, the prize of virtue." January following, at the eve of the murder of the French King and of the commencement of hostilities against this country, Barrere, Roland, and St. André, active members of the French Convention, had been elected honorary members of the Constitutional Society: and two speeches, made by Barrere and André, delivered for the express purpose of accelerating the catastrophe demnation and execution of the King, afferting the doctrines of the fovereignty of the people, and deducing, as its confequence, the unlimited rights of a National Convention, and the perfonal refponfibility of the monarch, were entered on the books of the Conftitutional Society; and the refolution for this purpofe was publifhed in the newfpapers. Actuated by thefe principles, the Englifh focieties perfevered in their defign; and notwithftanding the difperfion of the meeting at Edinburgh, which had affumed the appellation of " the Britifh Convention," proceeded on a plan which they had long had in contemplation, for affembling in England a fimilar but more extenfive meeting, under the appellation of " a Convention of the People."

At a general meeting of the Correfponding Society, held at the Globe Tavern on the 20th January 1794, a refolution and addrefs to the people of England were agreed to, and ordered to be publifhed, exprefsly directed to the object of affembling a general convention of the people.

At another general meeting of the fame Society, held at Chalk Farm on the 14th of April 1794, among a variety of inflammatory refolutions, they declared, that the whole proceedings of the late Britifh Convention at Edinburgh claimed their approbation and applaufe. They, at the fame time, returned thanks to Archibald Hamilton Rowan, prifoner in Newgate, in the city of Dublin (who had, in March 1794, been chofen an honorary member of the Conftitutional Society), as well as to the Society of United Irifhmen in Dublin, whom they exhorted to perfevere in their exertions to obtain juftice for the people of Ireland. The language held on different occafions evidently fhowed their intention of endeavouring to eftablifh, by force, the authority of fuch a Convention. They exhorted each other " to prepare courageoufly for the ftruggle which they meditated," and openly avowed that they meant to obtain the redrefs, which they profeffed to feek, " not from Parliament, not from the executive government, but from themfelves, and from their own ftrength and valour; from their own laws, and not from the laws of thofe whom they termed 'plunderers, enemies, and oppreffors'." For the purpofe of affembling fuch a Convention, and of preparing the people at large to look to its proceedings with refpect, and to adopt and countenance the doctrine and practices which it might recommend, itinerant members of the focieties above mentioned difperfed themfelves throughout different parts of the country, proceeding from town to town, and from village to village, endeavouring to inculcate into the minds of thofe with whom they converfed, the neceffity of fuch a meafure as that which they had in contemplation for the reform of the abufes of the government, and the redrefs of the grievances of the people; and defcribing, in language varied according to the paffions or prejudices of different

ferent claffes whom they addreffed, the nature and extent of t
different political purpofes which might be effected by a cc
vention once affembled. The difperfion of Paine's works, a
other works of a fimilar tendency, was at the fame time contin
with increafed induftry; and the focieties flattered themfelves tl
they had, by thefe means, really made a progrefs towards p
paring a large portion of the nation to favour their project.

The zeal, indeed, of many of the country focieties appears
have outrun the inftructions of the agents, and to have carr
them into difcuffions beyond thofe limits which the perfons v
planned and inftigated the meafure thought it prudent, in the f
inftance, to prefcribe. The agents were inftructed to confine
views of the feveral focieties to whom they were deputed, a
to point the wifhes of individuals purely to the attainment
univerfal fuffrage, from which, once eftablifhed, it was rep
fented that all the reforms which could be defired would na
rally flow; and it appeared to have been the defign of thofe v
directed the bufinefs to prevent the premature difcuffion of
of thofe points, which they reprefented as fubordinate, until a
the Convention fhould have been affembled, and this prim
object of univerfal fuffrage obtained. No caution or prohibiti
however, could prevent many of the country focieties from fho
ing how confidently they anticipated, as the refult to which
deliberations of that Convention muft neceffarily lead, the abc
tion of monarchy, of ariftocracy, and of other eftablifhmer
which they deemed equally oppreffive; and the fubftitution of
reprefentative government, founded on the new doctrine of t
rights of man; and uniting, in one body, all the legiflative
executive powers of the ftate.

This intended Convention was prevented from affembling
the arreft of the fecretaries, and of feveral members of the t
focieties, called " the London Correfponding Society," and " t
Conftitutional Society." The fecretaries and leading members
the focieties at Sheffield and Norwich (which, together wi
feveral other fubordinate focieties in different parts of the kin
dom, were in conftant correfpondence with them; were al
taken into cuftody. The attention of Parliament was at th
period directed to thefe proceedings; and in confequence of tl
evidence then laid before a Secret Committee of this Houfe, tl
power of detaining fufpected perfons was entrufted to his M
jefty.

The fubfequent proceedings are fufficiently known. Some
the perfons fo arrefted were profecuted for high treafon. A gra
jury for the county of Middlefex found a bill againft Thom
Hardy, the fecretary of the London Correfponding Society, ar
eleven others. Three of the perfons fo indicted, viz. Thom
Hardy, John Horne Tooke, and John Thelwall, were tried, ar

... trials ... charge in the indictment,
... the evidence ... hose trials established, in the clearest
... ner, the grounds on which the Committees of the two
... ses of Parliament had so ... Reports in 1794; and
... wed, beyond a possibility of ... by, the views of these
... sons and their confederates ... r nature, completely
... ile to the exiting govern... constitution of this king-
... m, and went directly to the subversion of every established and
... gitimate authority.

After these acquittals, Henry Redhead, alias Yorke, who had
... n committed at the same time on a charge of high treason, was
... ught to trial at York in July 1795, upon an indictment for a
... ditious conspiracy; in which Joseph Gale, the printer of a
... wspaper at Sheffield, and Richard Davison of Sheffield, both of
... om had fled from justice, were included. Upon the trial of
... rke on this indictment, he was found guilty, and sentenced to
... o years imprisonment.

§ 5. *Further Proceedings subsequent to the Arrests in 1794.*

The disclosures made upon these trials; the detentions already
... ioned; and the powers vested in Government by the Act
... empower his Majesty to secure and detain such Persons as his
... jesty shall suspect are conspiring against his Person and Govern-
... ent," which received the royal assent on the 23d of May 1794;
... oke for a time all the measures which had been concerted by
... e disaffected, and obliged them to proceed with more caution
... d reserve. But they never appear for a moment to have relin-
... ished their original design; and the nature and constitution of
... Corresponding Society (which still subsisted) peculiarly qua-
... ed it secretly to continue its machinations, and to extend and
... fuse its pernicious principles among the lower orders of the
... ple. The plan of this constitution, as originally proposed,
... having been stated in the Reports before referred to, is in-
... ted in the Appendix. It is evident, that the overthrow of
... ery part of the government and constitution of this kingdom
... in the immediate contemplation of those by whom this plan
... formed; and that it was contrived with the view of being
... plied to the most extensive purposes, if they had succeeded in
... object, and of enabling the conspirators, after the overthrow
... the existing government, to usurp and exercise an uncontrolled
... thority over the whole kingdom. It does not appear that this
... was ever formally adopted; but so much of it ... led to the
... ablishment of a secret system of direction, resembling that of
... United Irishmen, was agreed to, and reduced to practice.
... ot contented with employing these means gradually to ex-
... d their influence through different parts of the kingdom; the
... ing members of these societies, shortly before the opening of
the

the seffion of Parliament in October 1795, called togeth[er]
unlawful meeting in a field near the metr[op]olis, evidently [with]
a view of trying the temper of the popu[lac]e. Under the [pre]tence of "debates," language of the moſt ſeditious and in[flam]matory nature was held to a large multitude, whom curi[osity]
or other motives, had aſſembled there, and the moſt dari[ng li]bels were uttered againſt every part of the conſtitution of [these]
realms.

The public tranquillity appears to your Committee to [have]
been greatly endangered by this ſtep; ſo exactly reſembling [that]
which fifteen years before had nearly led to the deſtructi[on of]
the metropolis: and your Committee are decidedly of opi[nion]
that the ſhameful and highly criminal outrages which ſoon [after]
took place on the firſt day of the ſeſſion, are, in a great de[gree,]
to be aſcribed to the influence of theſe inflammatory pro[ceed]ings, and of this public and open violation of the laws. [It is]
not without regret that your Committee feel themſelves ob[liged]
to recall to the recollection of the Houſe, the horrid and [sacri]legious attempt againſt his Majeſty's perſon, with which [these]
outrages were accompanied.

This alarming proof of the dreadful and deſperate c[onſe]quences, which meetings and proceedings of ſuch a deſcri[ption]
naturally tend to produce, made a deep impreſſion on the m[inds]
of the public, and neceſſarily engaged the attention of P[arlia]ment. On a full conſideration of all the circumſtances, [the]
Legiſlature, by ſalutary laws, ſtrengthened the authority o[f the]
magiſtrate for the repreſſion of ſedition and tumult; pro[vided]
freſh checks againſt meetings of a dangerous tendency, and [a]
deſcription unknown in the hiſtory and conſtitution of this c[oun]try; increaſed the penalties of obſtinate and repeated guilt, [and]
added a freſh ſafeguard to the ſacred perſon of his Majeſty.

One of the immediate effects of theſe meaſures was to [put a]
ſtop to a practice which had too long been ſuffered in the [me]tropolis, to the diſgrace of all order and government—the [open]
and regular delivery of public lectures, inculcating the doct[rines]
of ſedition and treaſon; inciting the hearers to follow the exa[mple]
of France, and animating them to the commiſſion of the [most]
atrocious crimes. This practice has not ſince been reviv[ed in]
the ſame ſhape; but many of the debating ſocieties which ſ[ubſiſt]
at the preſent time appear to your Committee to be, in a [great]
meaſure, directed to the ſame pernicious objects, and to re[quire]
farther animadverſion and correction. Some check was [also]
given to the licentiouſneſs of the preſs, which had, till [then,]
been in a great meaſure unreſtrained. That licentiouſneſ[s had]
furniſhed, in every part of Europe, one of the moſt dang[erous]
inſtruments in the hands of conſpirators. The induſtry [with]
which every ſpecies of inflammatory and ſeditious libels had [been]

diſſemin[ated]

ated, applyi[illegible] passions and prejudices of [illegible] of society, [illegible] of that which is the least in- and therefore [illegible] to seduction, is an unanswer- [illegible] both of the extent and [illegible] zeal of the conspiracy in [illegible]

[illegible] the passing of these bills, the London Corresponding So- [illegible] their delegates into the country, to point out the method [illegible]ng them, and for the purpose of feeling the disposition of [illegible]le. Two persons, in this character, John Binns and John [illegible]nes, were sent by the London Corresponding Society to [illegible]ham, where they were arrested. They were found ad- [illegible] a meeting of persons in that town. Upon the person of [illegible] were found two papers; one a letter of credence from the [illegible] signed by John Ashley their secretary, introducing Binns [illegible]es as their accredited delegates; and the other, the instruc- [illegible] the Society for the conduct of these delegates; both which your Committee have inserted in the Appendix (Nos. [illegible] they wish particularly to notice, that after directions [illegible] the delegates, to persuade the people whom they were to [illegible] that the sole object of the Society was parliamentary re- [illegible]nd that the bills last referred to need not prevent their con- [illegible] to meet, the 7th article of the instructions is in these words: [illegible]e design of the above articles is to remove misapprehensions [illegible] to the safety of our association under the new laws. This your mission being effected, you are to strain every power [illegible] mind to awaken the sleeping spirit of liberty; you are to [illegible] our fellow-citizens to be ready with us, to pursue our [illegible] object, if it must be, to the scaffold, or rather (if our ene- [illegible] desperate enough to bar up every avenue to inquiry and [illegible]n) to the field, at the hazard of extermination; convinced [illegible] temper less decided than this will suffice to regain liberty [illegible] bold usurping faction. But, to the end that we may suc- [illegible] the irresistible voice of the people, you are to excite in every [illegible]he desire which animates our bosoms to embrace the [illegible] brethren, and the resolution to bear every repulse from [illegible] and prejudice which fails to deprive us of the sure grounds [illegible]ment." And in the 13th article are the following ex- [illegible]

[illegible] a word, you are always to reflect, that you are wrestling [illegible] enemies of the human race, not for yourselves merely, for [illegible] not see the full day of liberty, but for the child hanging [illegible], and that the question, whether the next generation [illegible] free or not, may greatly depend on the wisdom and inte- [illegible] your conduct in the generous missions which you and your [illegible] now take upon yourselves."

[illegible]standing this disposition to resist and evade the effect of [illegible], yet the seasonable and effectual check thus for a second time,

time given to the progress of sedition and treason, averted immediate danger; and if it did not extinguish the hopes of the conspirators, at least deterred them from the public avowal and pursuit of their projects. But the attempt to poison the minds of the lower orders of the people, and to prepare the means which might be resorted to on any favourable occasion, was pursued with unabated perseverance.

During the remainder of the year 1796, the system continued to operate silently and secretly; but in the beginning of the following year its contagious influence was found to have extended to a quarter where it was the least to be suspected, and produced effects which suddenly threatened the dearest interests and immediate safety of the country with the most imminent danger.

The mutiny which took place in the fleet, if considered in all its circumstances, will be traced to an intimate connexion with the principles and practices described by your Committee, and furnishes the most alarming proof of the efficacy of those plans of secrecy and concert, so often referred to, and of the facility with which they are applied for inflaming and heightening discontent (from whatever cause it proceeds), and for converting what might otherwise produce only a hasty and inconsiderate breach of subordination and discipline, into the most settled and systematic treason and rebellion. These principles and this concert could alone have produced the wide extent of the mutiny, and the uniformity of its operation in so many and such distant quarters. The persons principally engaged in it, even in its early stages, were many of them United Irishmen. The mutineers were bound by secret oaths to the perpetration of the greatest crimes. An attempt was made to give to the ships in mutiny the name of "The Floating Republic," and this attempt was countenanced both by papers published in France, and by a paper here, called, "The Courier," which has on many occasions appeared almost equally devoted to the French cause. In some instances a disposition was manifested to direct the efforts of the mutineers to the object of compelling the government of this country to conclude a peace with the foreign enemy; and they at length even meditated betraying the ships of his Majesty into the hands of that enemy. All these circumstances combine to impress your Committee with a firm persuasion that whatever were the pretences and misrepresentations employed to seduce from their duty a brave and loyal body of men; yet a spirit, in itself so repugnant to the habits and dispositions of British sailors, must have had its origin in those principles of foreign growth which the societies of the conspirators have industriously introduced into this country, and which they have incessantly laboured to disseminate among all descriptions of men; but especially among those whose fidelity and steadiness is most important to the public safety. A striking instance of the desperate extent to

which

which these principles were carried appears in the proceedings of a court martial held in the month of June 1797, an abstract of which your Committee have thought it right to insert in the Appendix (No. 17). The opinion stated by your Committee will be still more confirmed by the repeated and atrocious attempts (bearing still more evidently the character of those principles in which they originated, which have been made in a great number of instances since the general mutiny was suppressed; and of which it will be necessary for your Committee hereafter to take notice. At the period now referred to, these systematic attempts made to seduce both the sailors and soldiers from their duty and allegiance, to incite them to mutiny, and to engage them in plans for the subversion of government, had become so apparent and frequent as to attract the immediate notice of the Legislature. Among these attempts, that made by a person of the name of Fellows, convicted at Maidstone in July 1797, deserves particular attention. The seditious hand bill which he was proved to have distributed among the soldiers, is inserted in the Appendix (No. 5); and it appears from a letter (also there inserted) No. 6, written by him to Evans and Bone, two of the most active members of the London Corresponding Society, and who have successively filled the office of secretary to that society, shortly before his arrest, that he had gone to Maidstone for the purpose of circulating seditious papers, as well as of making reports of the Society at Maidstone.

In consequence of the prevalence of these dangerous practices, two acts of Parliament were passed in the year 1797 *; one inflicting severe penalties on any person guilty of inciting any of his Majesty's forces by sea or land to mutiny; the other for more effectually preventing the administering or taking of unlawful oaths. The propriety and necessity of both these acts was farther evinced shortly after. A person of the name of Fuller was detected two days after the passing the first act, in attempting to seduce a soldier belonging to the Coldstream regiment of guards, was found guilty at the following sessions of the Old Bailey, and sentenced to death; and one Charles Radcliffe, prosecuted under the second act, at the last court of session held for the county palatine of Chester, was found guilty of administering the oath or test of the Society of United Englishmen. The paper found upon Fuller, and which formed the chief ground of his conviction, is inserted in the Appendix No. 7, and deserves particular attention.

Your Committee have thus traced the chief transactions which took place in this country connected with the general design of the conspiracy, nearly to the period when its effects were manifested in their most dreadful and formidable shape in Ireland, by the atrocious and unexampled rebellion which broke out in the begin-

---
* 37 Geo. III. c. 70. 37 Geo. III. c. 123.

sing of the last summer. About this time, either with
that very rebellion, or in consequence of it, the societie
country entered into still closer connexion with the S
United Irishmen, and assumed a shape, more similar tha
to that extraordinary combination, the nature and effects
have been already fully described. It will therefore be
for your Committee, in this place, shortly to review the
of this Society, and of the steps by which it gradually pre
way for all the recent miseries and calamities which have
perienced in Ireland.

§. 6. *Progress of the Society of United Irishmen in Ireland
Period of the Rebellion; its Intercourse with France,
leading Members of Societies in this Country.*

The transactions of the conspirators in that country ar
detailed in the different Reports of the two Houses of the I
liament, that your Committee do not think it necessary
them at length; and will only call the attention of the
such parts of them as prove, from the subsequent condu
conspirators, the falsehood of the early pretences by which
tempted to disguise their real views, as well as the interco
up by them with the French Directory, chiefly through
and the communication between leading members of th
of United Irishmen, and those of similar societies in Great

As early as in the year 1793, hopes and expectations
out of French assistance; prayers were publicly offered
fast, from the pulpit, for the success of the French arms;
associations were entered into without any legal autho
repeated attempts were made to seduce the soldiery from t

In February 1794, Jackson, an Irish clergyman, pa
France through England, into Ireland, for the purpose of
on a treasonable correspondence with a view to an invasio
kingdoms. He was particularly recommended to son
leading members of the English societies; and he trans
the French government, both from London and from
papers on the subject of his mission, which had been
communicated to other persons in each kingdom *.

In April 1794 he had many confidential conversations
lin on this subject, with Hamilton Rowan, a leader of th
Irishmen, before mentioned, who was then in prison,
his escape has been attainted for high treason; wit
Tone, also a leading member of the same society, who v
taken on board the French ship the Hoche, in the actua
to invade Ireland; and with Lewins, now the resident en
the United Irish at Paris.

* Vide Jackson and Stone's Trial, and Report of Commons in

Although the trials of Jackson and Stone, and the arrest and flight of Hamilton Rowan and Tone, checked these projects for a time, the Society of United Irishmen pursued their measures with unabating activity. The Government of Ireland acquired information respecting the conduct of particular persons, whom they had even at that time sufficient ground to consider as chiefly engaged in this treasonable conspiracy; particularly Lewins, above referred to; Henry and John Sheares, since convicted of high treason, and executed; Oliver Bond, and Wolfe Tone, convicted of the same crime, and both since dead, the latter by his own hands, to escape the punishment due to his crimes; Lord Edward Fitzgerald, who died in prison in consequence of the wounds he received in resisting the officers of justice, and has been since attainted of high treason; and Arthur O'Connor, M'Nevin, and Emmet, whose individual guilt, as well as that of the whole conspiracy, is sufficiently proved by their own confessions.

It is stated, in the confessions of the three persons last named, that the first communication which came to their knowledge between the Irish and the French Directories, was an offer made by the latter, in the year 1796, to send a French army to Ireland to the assistance of the republicans. But the Committee of the House of Lords in Ireland have stated it as their opinion, that Lewins had been dispatched to France, in the summer of 1795, to request this assistance; and your Committee are convinced, from secret intelligence which has been laid before them, that this opinion was well founded.

The invasion of Ireland, which was attempted in December 1796, was arranged at an interview which took place on the frontier of France between Lord Edward Fitzgerald, Arthur O'Connor, and General Hoche, in the summer of that year. After the failure of this attempt, the solicitations of the Irish Directory were renewed; a proposal, which arrived from France early in 1797, was accepted, and an answer transmitted, through England, by the means of Arthur O'Connor; Lewins was dispatched to Paris in April, and M'Nevin in June. Both were employed in urging the invasion of Ireland, and in counteracting the negotiation for peace with the French republic, which his Majesty's minister was then carrying on at Lisle. A conference was held in the same summer, in London, between Lord Edward Fitzgerald and a French agent who came from Hamburgh, in which further arrangements were made for the intended invasion.

The arrest of several persons in Ireland, and the flight of others; and the memorable defeat, by Lord Duncan, of the fleet intended to protect the expedition fitted out from Holland, again disconcerted the projects of the conspirators. After this event the French government appears to have repeatedly urged the leaders of the Irish Union to immediate insurrection; but the more cautious among

among them were unwilling to act, until the French should actually have landed; and their opinion for a time prevailed.

The correspondence was in the mean time continued: the projects of rebellion and invasion were ripening; and at this period the hopes of the Irish conspirators derived fresh encouragement from reports of the progress of new societies in Great Britain, formed on the same plan with themselves. A regular communication was kept up between the Irish and English committees, through Arthur O'Connor, who had come from Ireland to England early in January 1798; and in the reports transmitted by the English societies to Ireland, the force of the United Englishmen (a society which had been recently formed on the model of the United Irish, and of which a more particular account will be given hereafter) was represented to be considerable, though your Committee have reason to believe that there was much exaggeration in these reports. Arthur O'Connor [*], in a letter to his brother, dated London, 13th February 1798, and seized in Lord Edward Fitzgerald's apartments at Leinster-house, states, " That Scotland is Irish all over—that the people here give no opinion, though it is easy to learn they look for a change."

At a provincial meeting in Ireland, held on the 1st of February 1798, it was stated to the meeting, by a person just arrived from Dublin, that " The French were going on with the expedition, and that it was in a greater state of forwardness than was expected; but what was more flattering, three delegates had been sent from the United Britons to the Irish national committee, and from that moment the Irish were to consider England, Scotland, and Ireland all as one people, acting for one common cause." An address was at the same time produced, which it was stated the delegates from Britain had brought with them to the Irish national committee. It was also stated, that the priest O'Coigly was one of the delegates mentioned to have been then lately returned from France; and was added, that he, and another priest who had fled from Ireland, were the principal persons who had opened the communication with the United Britons.

At another provincial meeting, held on the 27th February 1798, it appears to have been stated, " that a delegate had arrived from France; that the French were using every endeavour to have the expedition for Ireland completed; and that the Irish delegate came home to cause the United Irish to put themselves into a state of organization to join them, as the Directory positively assured the Irish delegates, that the expedition would set out for Ireland the end of April or the beginning of May." It was also stated, that there had been a meeting of all the delegates in England and Scotland held in London; but that their resolutions could not be obtained

---

[*] Vide Trial of O'Connor.

tained till the next provincial meeting, to be held on the 25th of March.

The addrefs which the delegates of United Britons were fo ftated, at the provincial meeting of the 1ft of February 1798, to have brought with them to the Irifh national committee, your Committee have inferted in the Appendix (No. 8). About the fame time a moft feditious paper, fent from the London Correfponding Society to the Society of United Irifhmen, figned J. T. Crosfield, Prefident—Thomas Evans, Secretary—dated 30th January 1798 (alfo inferted in the Appendix, No. 9), was publifhed in Ireland, in a paper called "The Prefs," and the original feized in March 1798, in confequence of the apprehenfion of Arthur O'Connor in England.

The prieft O'Coigly, referred to in thefe tranfactions, and who has fince been convicted and executed at Maidftone, was a native of Ireland, and went from that country to Cuxhaven in 1797, with another Irifhman, who was obliged to fly from Ireland, and paffed into Holland at the time when the Dutch fleet under Admiral de Winter was about to fail, with a large body of troops, on an expedition deftined againft Ireland. When that fleet had failed without the troops, O'Coigly and his companion went to Paris, where finding themfelves thwarted by the jealoufy of the refident envoy from the Irifh Union, O'Coigly returned to England about the middle of December 1797, and went to Ireland in January 1798.

Whilft in Ireland, he appears to have had interviews and correfpondence with Lord Edward Fitzgerald, and others of the Irifh confpirators; and he returned to England about the middle of February 1798.

Intelligence was conveyed to Government of this man's defigns, and particularly of his intention to pafs into France, for the purpofes which afterward appeared to be the object of his miffion; he was therefore narrowly watched; and on the 28th of February 1798, he was, together with Arthur O'Connor, John Binns, Allen, and Leary, taken into cuftody at Margate, in the attempt to obtain a paffage to France. The particular circumftances attending thefe attempts are detailed in the evidence on his trial. One of the papers feized by the officers who apprehended him, was an addrefs from "the Secret Committee of England to the Executive Directory of France," fet forth in the Appendix (No. 10); clearly demonftrating the traitorous views of thofe who formed the addrefs, and were inftrumental in the attempt to tranfmit it to France.

It appears alfo to your Committee, both from previous and fubfequent information, that Arthur O'Connor, who had been, to the moment of leaving Ireland, one of the members of the Irifh Directory, was not only going to France in the confidence that, when there, he fhould be confidered and received as an accredited

agent,

agent, but was confidentially employed by the remaining members of that Directory, who were at that time diffatisfied with the conduct of Lewins.

§ 7. *Further Intercourse between the United Irishmen, the French Government, and the British Societies; Formation of new Societies, and their Proceedings.*

At the meetings of the London Corresponding Society, for above two years before this time, it had been avowed, that the object of the Society was to form a republic, by the affiflance of France. Reform in Parliament, or even annual elections, or universal suffrage, were therefore no longer mentioned. Your Committee have abundant reason to believe, from the information laid before them, that a person of the name of Afhley (one of the persons arrested in 1794), and who had, for a long time, been secretary to this Society, was now acting as their agent at Paris, and had recently given them hopes of the succour of a French army. Meetings were held, to contrive the means of procuring arms, to enable them to co-operate with a French force, in case of an invasion. The leading members of the disaffected societies were also in the habit of frequenting an occasional meeting, which was held at a cellar in Furnival's Inn, and was first formed for the purpose of reading the libellous and treasonable publication called "The Press." This place gradually became the resort of all those who were engaged the most deeply in the conspiracy. It was particularly attended by Arthur O'Connor and O'Coigly, previous to their attempt to go over to France; and by the persons chiefly instrumental in carrying on correspondence with the Irish conspirators; and secret consultations were repeatedly held there, with a view to projects, which were thought too dangerous and desperate to be brought forward in any of the larger societies. Among these plans, was that of effecting a general insurrection, at the same moment, in the metropolis and throughout the country, and of directing it to the object of seizing or affaffinating the King, the Royal Family, and many of the Members of both Houses of Parliament. An officer, of some experience in his Majesty's service, was selected as their military leader; and sanguine hopes were entertained, that they could command a sufficient force to effect their desperate purpose, in the first instance, by surprise. But although the apprehension that they could not as yet collect sufficient numbers to maintain and secure their advantage, appears, for the time, to have deterred them from the attempt; yet the general language held among these persons, at this period, proved, that they had brought themselves to the opinion that matters were nearly ripe for measures of open violence.

Attempts were at the same time made to form in London, upon the plan of the United Irishmen, the Society of United Englishmen

men or United Britons, before referred to: and O'Coigly and John Binns appear to have been leading persons in that design. It was proposed to divide this Society into four districts, including a large part of the coasts of this kingdom the most exposed to invasion: and it was also in contemplation to combine the operations of this Society with those of a Society of United Irishmen; of which your Committee will find it necessary separately to take notice.

Most of the societies through England, which had used to correspond with the London Corresponding Society, had also about this time adopted the same plan of forming societies of United Englishmen; and finding their communications by writing to be hazardous, they avoided, as far as possible, the keeping any papers; used ciphers or mysterious words, in the few writings that passed between them, and principally carried on their intercourse by agents, who went from place to place, and were recognised by signs, which were frequently changed. Many ignorant or inconsiderate persons, throughout the country, were gradually involved in these criminal transactions; and the influence of the destructive principles from which they proceeded, was still farther extended by the establishment of clubs, among the lowest classes of the community, which were open to all persons paying one penny, and in which songs were sung, toasts given, and language held, of the most seditious nature.

Information having been received of a meeting of United Englishmen, to be held at a house in Clerkenwell, warrants of arrest were issued, and persons were apprehended on the 18th of April 1798. There was found upon the secretary of the London Corresponding Society (who appears to have officiated as president at that meeting) the oath proposed for the United Englishmen, set forth in the Appendix (No. 11), another oath, of the same nature, was found under the table; and also a printed constitution of the Society of United Englishmen, set forth in the Appendix (Nos. 12 and 13).

Information having also been received of an extraordinary meeting of the delegates and secretary of the London Corresponding Society, intended to be assembled at a large room in Wych-street, on the 19th of April 1798, the persons there assembled were likewise arrested, and from the discoveries made in consequence of these arrests, the connexion between the London Corresponding Society and the London Society of United Englishmen was clearly established.

It appeared, that about forty divisions of United Englishmen had been formed in London; about twenty of which had their regular places and days of meeting; and that many similar societies were forming in different parts of the country. With respect to these latter, it was intended that the different counties in Great Britain

Britain should respectively be divided into districts; in each of which a central society was to be established in the princip[al] town, and was to carry on a constant correspondence, both wi[th] the smaller societies in that district, and with the general society [in] London. And this system was so constructed, as to admit of sti[ll] further subdivision, if the increase of numbers had been such as t[he] leaders hoped.

It appears to your Committee, that the chief progress made i[n] the formation of societies of United Englishmen, was in Londo[n] and the parts adjacent; and in Lancashire, and some parts of th[e] west of England and of Wales, more immediately communicatin[g] with Ireland, and in which there were many United Irishmen either as residents or as fugitives from their country.

At Manchester, and in the adjacent country in particular, th[e] plan of these conspiracies was extending itself in the most alarming manner; and they were much promoted by the activity of th[e] United Irishmen, of whom there are very large numbers residen[t] in that neighbourhood. Great numbers of printed copies of th[e] "Constitution of United Englishmen" have been discovered i[n] Manchester and the neighbourhood; and it is evident that the So ciety was making great progress, when it was checked by the arre[st] of several of its leaders in 1798.

A Society of United Englishmen had been established in an[d] about Manchester before the year 1797. In the beginning of th[at] year it consisted of about fifty divisions, and in the year 1798 ha[d] extended to about eighty. Each of these divisions consisted of n[o] less than fifteen members, and was again subdivided when th[e] number of its members exceeded thirty-six. This Society has bee[n] particularly active in the most wicked attempts to seduce the sol[-] diers in different regiments; for which purpose they adopted system of more particular secrecy, and it has therefore been difficu[lt] to discover the extent of these crimes; but the general good co[n]duct of his Majesty's forces, of every description in this kingdo[m] affords the most satisfactory proof that these diabolical practic[es] have not been successful in any considerable degree. The te[st] used for the soldiers is set forth in the Appendix (No. 14). I[n] other respects the Society has followed the United Irish and t[he] United English formed in London, in their constitution, their tes[ts] and their signs of secrecy; and its operations have been conducte[d] with the same mystery, and under the same direction; the who[le] being governed by the persons who form the Committee of Unit[ed] Englishmen, styled "The National Committee of England[,]" who are, apparently, unknown to the rest of the members of th[e] Society, though their dictates are implicitly obeyed. They wer[e] the more induced to acquiesce in this system, and to obey impli[-] citly the directions of their leaders, from the persuasion with whic[h] they appear to have been universally impressed, that persons [of]

highe[r]

higher fituations in life afforded them countenance and pecuniary aid; though, from circumftances of caution, thofe perfons had not become actually members of the Society; or, if they were members, concealed the fact with confiderable care, and did not attend the meetings. In fome degree this perfuafion may have been well founded; but your Committee are induced to think, that fome art was ufed to ftrengthen this impreffion, for the purpofe of giving greater encouragement to the members in their hopes of final fuccefs.

The focieties in the country connected with Manchefter have been formed into twelve diftricts, each of which fent a delegate to the committee called The County Committee; which appears to have corresponded, not only with the National Committee of England, but alfo with the National Committee of Ireland.

The intercourfe between the United Englifhmen in thefe parts and the United Irifh, appears indeed to have been continual; many of the United Irifh frequently paffing and repaffing between Chefhire or Lancafhire, and Ireland, and frequently vifiting the Englifh focieties. Among the perfons who have been thus travelling from one country to the other, your Committee have remarked O'Coigly, who repeatedly vifited Manchefter, Stockport, and other places in the neighbourhood; and particularly in the year 1797, when he was received with marked attention. He came there again in 1798, on his return from Ireland after his journey into France before mentioned. He then wore a military drefs, and paffed by the name of Captain Jones, the fame appellation by which he was introduced, by Arthur O'Connor, to Mr. H. Bell, of Charterhoufe Square, from whofe houfe O'Connor took his departure, previous to his arreft at Deal. The accounts which have been obtained of his converfation and conduct at Manchefter, leave no room to doubt the objects of his different journies between Great Britain, Ireland, and France, and particularly of his intended journey to France, which was prevented by his arreft; and there appears alfo little reafon to doubt, that many, both of the United Englifhmen and United Irifh, at Manchefter and in its neighbourhood, were aware of the general purport, at leaft, of his miffion, and anxioufly expected that affiftance from France, of which they received, from him, very ftrong affurances.

The Society at Manchefter feems to have been the central fociety of an extenfive diftrict; and to have been managed by a very zealous and active committee. It frequently fent delegates to places in the neighbourhood, and to various parts of Yorkfhire, Derbyfhire, Nottinghamfhire, and Chefhire. Their correfpondence appears to have extended to the moft diftant parts of England, as well as to Edinburgh and Glafgow.

Liverpool alfo became the feat of another central fociety, prefiding over a furrounding diftrict, and correfponding with other parts

parts of England, and with Scotland and Ireland; and diffe[r] emiſſaries, ſome of whom were foreigners, about this time w[ere] ſent through various parts of the kingdom, for the purpoſe of certaining the numbers and diſpoſitions of the ſocieties of Un[ited] Engliſh and United Iriſh.

Whilſt the ſocieties in England were thus endeavouring to f[orm] a Society of United Engliſhmen, or of United Britons, on [the] model of the Iriſh Society, attempts were made in Scotland to f[orm] a diſtinct Society of "United Scotſmen" on the ſame plan. [As] your Committee cannot forbear to remark the induſtry w[ith] which it has been attempted in this inſtance, as well as in oth[ers] to ſeparate Scotland as well as Ireland from England, and to fou[nd] on the ruins of the eſtabliſhed government, three diſtinct repub[lics] of England, Scotland, and Ireland.

The attempts to form a Society of United Scotſmen had m[ade] little progreſs till the ſpring of 1797; but from the month of A[pril] 1797 until November following (when a diſcovery was mad[e in] the county of Fife, on which George Mealmaker was brough[t to] trial, and convicted of ſedition) theſe attempts appear to have b[een] attended with more ſucceſs, and particularly in the neighbourh[ood] of Glaſgow, and in the counties of Ayr, Renfrew, Lanerk, D[um]barton, Fife, and Perth. Glaſgow, and the county of Ayr, w[ere] the places in which this ſpirit firſt manifeſted itſelf, and from w[hich] emiſſaries were ſent into different parts of the country, for [the] purpoſe of increaſing the numbers of the Society, and diſſe[mi]nating what they termed "political knowledge."

The ſocieties thus formed in Scotland, appear to have been [re]duced to a ſyſtem almoſt as regular and complete as that which eſtabliſhed in Ireland; the outlines of the plan were the ſame, the ſtudied ſecrecy of the proceedings, and the gradations of [in]ternal arrangement, formed its great characteriſtic. By a [ge]neral rule of their aſſociation, no ſociety was to conſiſt of m[ore] than ſixteen members, and when any ſociety had obtained a n[um]ber of members exceeding ſixteen, it was to divide itſelf into [two] ſocieties. In ſome ſmall towns there were three or more [ſuch] ſocieties, all of which were ſometimes aſſembled, by their i[ndi]vidual members, or by a committee from each ſociety: and [theſe] aſſemblies were termed "Parochial Meetings." Each of t[heſe] Parochial Meetings had a ſecretary, who was alſo treaſurer; one or two delegates were choſen to repreſent the Parochial at [the] County Meeting, which was compoſed of delegates from all [the] Parochial Meetings within the county or diſtrict, and was [held] every ſix weeks. The delegates were elected by ballot; but [the] ballot was ſo conducted that no perſon knew on whom the ch[oice] fell, except the ſecretary and the perſon choſen. This elec[tion] was ſometimes made, by each member whiſpering in the ea[r of] the ſecretary the name of the perſon for whom he gave his v[ote] and as there could be no material check on the declaration of the secretary, it is evident that the election of delegates might be managed in any manner most agreeable to the leaders of the Society. The meetings called " County Meetings" were not restricted to the known divisions of the counties, but were composed of delegates from Parochial Meetings, within either larger or smaller districts, according to the number of United Scotsmen in each neighbourhood. At the County Meetings, delegates were elected, to represent the societies at a " National Meeting," in the same secret manner as was used for the election of the delegates to the County Meeting; and the place of that meeting was not generally disclosed. The secretary of the County Meeting gave the delegate, when chosen, a small slip of paper, containing the name of a person to whom he was to apply, and who was to take him to the place of the National Meeting. This person was called " The Intermediate." The counties were also distinguished by numbers, and not by their names; and the delegate received, on another slip of paper, the number of the county, and the time appointed for the National Meeting.

The meeting assuming this name was a committee formed of delegates from the County Meetings, and assembled every seven weeks; and there the most important business of the Society was transacted. This meeting received reports from a secret committee and nominally directed its conduct, but the secret committee really had the chief management. This committee was elected, from amongst the delegates at the National Meeting, in the same secret manner as those delegates had been chosen at the County Meeting, the persons elected being only known to the secretary; and the committee, thus secretly formed, did not disclose itself in the transaction of business; all of which was conducted through the intervention of a person (already noticed) called " The Intermediate;" who delivered their orders, and who was the same person to whom the delegates had been directed to apply for information respecting the place of assembly of the National Meeting. Except therefore to the intermediate, to the secretary, and to each other, the persons composing the secret committee remained wholly unknown.

Every proceeding was involved in the same mysterious secrecy; and though this system of blind obedience had the effect of disgusting and alarming some of the delegates, who perceived themselves to be instruments in the hands of an unknown authority, for purposes, of which the extent was never fully disclosed to them; yet the committee, thus formed, continued to preserve its general influence; disbursing at its pleasure the money collected, giving all orders for the places of the National Meetings; sending missionaries, disseminating papers, receiving information, and conducting every part of the business without control.

The

The National Meeting was generally, if not always, held in or near Glasgow; and from reports of what passed at those meetings it appears that they corresponded with the Society of United Britons, and sent delegates to England, and received delegates from thence. When the meeting broke up, each delegate received note of the time appointed for the next meeting; which he was to deliver to the secretary of his own County Meeting, when the new delegate was elected.

Their communications with different parts, and particularly with England, were seldom carried on in writing: some papers however, have been discovered, which clearly show that the Society had the most dangerous objects in view; and that some of its members were sanguine enough to profess an opinion, "that if the flattering accounts which they received from London were real, the emancipation of the country was at no great distance when they should rally round the standard of Liberty."

This system of Union, as well as that of the United Englishmen, was evidently borrowed from Ireland; and there is reason to believe that it was introduced by delegates from that country. Signs were adopted for the purpose of distinguishing the members as was practised in Ireland; but the knowledge of the signs seems to have been only imperfectly diffused; they never have been generally understood; or having been altered at different times in different places, without concert, were never uniform in all parts of the country.

In their sanguine expectation of success, these conspirators formed wild and extravagant plans of seizing, in the same night all the leading people over the whole island. If these persons should resist, they were to be put to death; if they submitted quietly, their lives and property were to be spared, but they were to be kept in custody till a new constitution should be formed, which was clearly meant to be conformable to French principles.

An oath or test was formally administered, and printed papers were circulated under the title of "Resolutions and Constitution of the Society of United Scotsmen," a copy of which is set forth in the Appendix (No. 15).

The measures of this conspiracy were disconcerted by the arrest of Mealmaker, of Dyer, and of Archibald Gray, the latter of whom, after his indictment, escaped to the continent, and has become a member of a Society at Hamburgh, which will hereafter be noticed, by the name of "The Philanthropic Society."

In addition to this view of the proceedings of the societies both in England and Scotland, at this period, it is material to remark that whilst the rebellion was at its height in Ireland, there were found individuals in this country who so strongly manifested their desire to support the cause of the rebels, that they became the objects of criminal prosecution. Among these a man of the name of

Martin

unknown was indicted, for distributing at Gosport the
     in the Appendix (No. 16), entitled, "An Irishman's
     his Countrymen in England;" the contents of which
     ight have warranted a prosecution for a higher crime;
     striking a specimen of the intentions of the disaffected,
     gh the particular instance relates only to the conduct of
     lual, your Committee have thought it highly deserving.
     This man was convicted at the last summer assizes at
     r, and sentenced to two years imprisonment.
     uance of the same plan, the United Irishmen, in this
     ave been incessantly labouring to disseminate their prin-
     h by means of secret combinations among such of them
     und their way into the naval service, and by extending
     ties both in the metropolis and in different parts of the
     The extent to which these practices have prevailed,
     ithstanding repeated instances of detection and punish-
     still carried on in the fleet, has been too fully demon-
     the evidence which has appeared in a variety of courts
     te proceedings of which have been laid before your Com-
     id which contain matter so serious and important, that
     mittee have thought it right to insert an abstract of them
     pendix (Nos. 17, 18, 19, 20, 21, 22). It appears, that
     : been tendered by the mutineers to the crew, "to be
     rishmen, equal to their brethren in Ireland, and to have
     5 do with the King or his Government:" that they
     l in the professed expectation of assistance from France,
     express view of co-operating, for the expulsion of the
     s from Ireland, and the erection of a Roman Catholic
     nt; and it has been part of their plan to murder their
) seize on the ship, and carry her to France or Ireland,
     ther occasion, the oath has been as follows: "I swear to be
     : Free and United Irish, who are now fighting our cause
     rants and oppressors, and to defend their rights to the last
     y blood, and to keep all secret: and I do agree to carry
     nto Brest the next time the ship looks out ahead at sea,
     ll every officer and man that shall hinder us, except the
     ind to hoist a green ensign with a harp in it, and after-
     kill and destroy the Protestants."
     utineers on board one of his Majesty's ships, appear to
     engaged in the plan of carrying the ship to France, in
     an that they would there be promoted in proportion to
     ies; that one of their ringleaders was to be appointed
     and that they were then to proceed with the French
     sland; and this deep laid villany was disguised and ag-
     by a degree of hypocrisy and imposture scarcely to be pa-
     the particulars are stated in the Appendix (No. 20).
     utineers in another ship were proved to be connected
                                                     with

with Corresponding Societies at Nottingham. The oath which they attempted to administer was, " to carry the ship into an " enemy's port, either French, Dutch, or Irish;" and they meant, in the event, of being brought into action with an enemy's ship, to shoot their own officers on the quarter-deck.

While these proceedings of the United Irishmen in the fleet exhibit so dreadful a picture of their sanguinary designs, and of the similarity of their views and principles to those which have produced so much calamity and bloodshed in Ireland, their conduct on shore has not been less deserving of the most serious attention. Your Committee have no hesitation in stating, on the clearest proof, strongly confirmed by recent circumstances, that among the various bodies enlisted, in any part of Great Britain, for the purposes of sedition and treason, the societies which have been formed by the United Irishmen in this country are in al respects the most formidable, particularly at the present moment whether considered with a view to their combination, their ac tual numbers, or the atrocious nature of the designs of whic they are preparing, in a very short time, to attempt the executio in direct co-operation with France.

The danger to be apprehended from these societies is muc increased, from the constant communication which they mai tain with the societies in Ireland; their mutual confidence each other; and the alarming circumstance of their being this moment subject to the same secret direction and the sa chiefs.

These societies have been instituted not only in London in different parts of the country, and have formed themsel into subdivisions. In the Appendix (Nos. 23 and 24) are ferred printed forms of certificates of election to the Socie which were seized among the papers of a person long engag in this conspiracy. One of these forms has been framed fo " London Society." The other appears to relate to a soci called an " *External Society.*" The impression of the seal on t former of them is the same with that of the seal found in t custody of Lord Edward Fitzgerald, when he was appr hended. The reference in these certificates to the constitutic and the test confirm the unquestionable information whic your Committee have received, that these societies form a pa of the dreadful system which was unhappily established Ireland. The constitution of the United Irishmen, such as was acted upon in Ireland, appears to regulate their proceed ings; and copies of this constitution have been found in th possession of persons principally concerned in promoting the meetings. The views which they entertain at this moment and the sanguine hopes with which they look to their accom plishment, are apparent in an inflammatory and treasonabl

pape

paper recently found at one of thofe meetings, of which Government had received intelligence, and the perfons prefent at which were confequently apprehended. This paper is inferted in the Appendix (No. 25). Other papers, feized at the fame meeting, ftrongly confirm the account which your Committee have received, that a mode has lately been adopted by thefe focieties (fimilar to that practifed both in Ireland and Scotland), of keeping the accounts of the Society, by fubftituting different numbers for the names of the members. Your Committee think it alfo not immaterial to infert in the Appendix (No. 26) copy of a printed card, which has been found in the poffeffion of different perfons, and particularly, among other feditious papers, in that of a perfon recently apprehended, who, there is reafon to believe, has been very lately chofen to act as general fecretary to the different focieties of United Irifhmen now in London. The perfon named in this card, and the tranfaction to which it relates, are fuch as to require no comment.

Your Committee have received different accounts of the numbers of this Society; but, though their force is probably exaggerated by themfelves, for evident reafons, there is fufficient ground for believing that their numbers have been long confiderable. Many Irifh, ordinarily refident here, chiefly among the loweft claffes of the community, have been gradually induced to become members of this Society. But the moft active part confifts of thofe Irifh rebels who have fled to this country, rendered defperate by their crimes, not daring to return to Ireland, and either unable to make their way to the countries fubject to France, or not receiving fufficient encouragement to attempt it, they remain here, waiting for the opportunity of executing thofe violent and defperate projects to which they have become familiar. And they appear to be under the direction of fome perfons of a higher clafs, who fometimes furnifh pecuniary aid and form the committee; by means of which a conftant correfpondence is carried on through Hamburgh, with France.

Among thefe plans, there is good reafon to believe, that early in 1798 it was ferioufly in agitation among the confpirators in Ireland to convey, in fmall veffels, from Ireland to England, a great number of United Irifhmen; and to land them on different parts of the coaft, with inftructions to divide themfelves into fmall bodies, and to endeavour to make their way to the capital in the manner leaft liable to fufpicion, under the difguife of thofe trades and occupations in which the Irifh, commonly reforting hither, are principally engaged. Their object is reprefented to have been that of co-operating with the Correfponding Society in effecting an infurrection in London at the time of the rebellion breaking out in Ireland, for the purpofe of diftracting the military force, and preventing reinforcements being fent to that country; and the plan is faid to have failed from the Corre-

Vol. VIII.   3 F   fponding

sponding Society shrinking from the execution of it. Abo[ut the] same period another project was secretly formed (of which [the] Committee have received more distinct information) for [se-] lecting, at one point, a chosen body of the most deter[mined] from among the United Irish employed on the river Tham[es,] whom a new oath of secrecy, obedience, and fidelity, was administered; large rewards were to be promised; they w[ere to] be kept wholly ignorant of the precise service they were int[ended] to perform till the moment of its execution, which was t[o take] place as soon as an attack on some part of the coast w[as an-] nounced on the part of the French: they were then to b[e pri-] vately armed with daggers, to be put under leaders of k[nown] tal[e]n's and courage, and formed into three divisions; and w[ere to] make an attack, by surprise, at the same moment, on [the] Houses of Parliament, on the Tower, and on the Bank.

The intelligence obtained from time to time by Govern[ment] respecting the proceedings and plans of the conspirator[s, the] seizure and detention of some of the intended leaders, an[d per-] haps the timidity or reluctance of some of the parties conc[erned,] prevented any open attempt to realize these extravagant d[esigns] when they were first in contemplation.

But, notwithstanding the continuance of every precautio[n, and] although these conspirators cannot be ignorant of the pr[epared] and formidable force, and the determined spirit and general [zeal] with which such an enterprise would be immediately r[esisted,] your Committee have received undoubted proof that plans [of this] nature are now, more than ever, in agitation. Attemp[ts are] actually making, by agents from Ireland, to concert wi[th the] French government the time for a fresh and general insurr[ection] in Ireland. Intelligence has been received, that in the p[orts of] France the utmost diligence is used in preparing another e[xpedi-] tion to co-operate with the rebels in that kingdom. Th[e time] for making this attempt seems to be in a great measure [fixed.] The expectation which appears to be generally entertained [by] the traitors in Ireland tallies, in this respect, with the intell[igence] which has been laid before your Committee; and this expe[ctation] has been particularly communicated from thence to their to command an expedition against Cornwall, which are in the Appendix to this Report (Nos. 27 and 28). For ... of co-operating with these attempts, and particularly ... same view as that to which the measures before enu... were directed in the beginning of 1798, that of preventing, ...ossible, reinforcements being sent from hence to Ireland; ...o part of the plan, that an effort should be made to ...n insurrection in the metropolis, and in some other ... the kingdom where these societies are most numerous. ...ommittee are fully confident, that while plans of this na...tinue to be traced and known, and while Government ...he means which it at present possesses, such wild and ... projects may be expected to lead only to consequences ...re to their authors; but your Committee are, at the ...ne, so forcibly struck with the view they have had of this ... the system, and with the peculiar danger continually ...rom the Society of United Irishmen, which they deem ... its nature incompatible with the secure maintenance of ...anquillity, that they have thought it necessary to bring ...tinctly under the immediate consideration of the House.

§ 8. *Societies at Hamburgh.*

...dition to this mass of treason in Great Britain and in ...your Committee find, that, for the purpose of more ...nt communication between France and Ireland, a com... ...f United Irishmen has been formed at Hamburgh. That ...s long been the receptacle of those disaffected persons ...e fled from Great Britain or Ireland, either from ap... ...n of the consequences of the treasonable practices in ...hey have been engaged, or for the purpose of assisting ...piracies carried on against their respective countries; ... the latter view it has been the centre of a correspond... ...ich has long subsisted among the British and Irish so... ...stablished at that place, as well as in London and Paris; ... correspondence with Great Britain and Ireland has fre... ...been covered by the pretence of commercial transactions, ...mmunicating intelligence for the public newspapers. ...urgh has also been the resort of the disaffected of every ...ntry, whose intrigues are constantly directed to the object ...ng the principles of Jacobinism in Holstein and the ... Germany, and generally in all the northern parts of ... Many emissaries, English, Scotch, and Irish, have ...atched from time to time from Hamburgh to Great Bri... ...Ireland, and to various parts of the continent, as cir... ...es required. There has recently been established at ...h. Altona, and the neighbourhood, a society called ...hilanthropic Society," for the purpose of correspondence with the republicans of all countries, upon the plan of the Corresponding Societies established in Great Britain and Ireland; and whose avowed object is the reform of all kingdoms and states. The leading members of this Society, who direct all the rest, compose a committee of about twenty persons, British, French, Dutch, and Germans. The members of the subordinate societies at Hamburgh and Altona are all under the control of the committee, or principal society before mentioned. This committee constantly corresponds with Great Britain and Ireland, and all parts of Germany. It has secretaries skilled in different languages, and corresponding agents in different towns, particularly in London. It may become a formidable engine in the hands of the French Directory, and it appears to be making considerable progress; but there is reason to hope that it has at length attracted the notice of the governments of those places.

Conclusion.

Upon a review of all the circumstances which have come under the consideration of your Committee, they are deeply impressed with the conviction—that the safety and tranquillity of these kingdoms have, at different periods from the year 1791 to the present time, been brought into imminent hazard, by the traitorous plans and practices of societies, acting upon the principles, and devoted to the views, of our inveterate foreign enemy:

That, although the Society of United Irishmen in Ireland has alone been enabled to attain its full strength and maturity; yet the societies instituted on similar principles in this country had all an undoubted tendency to produce similar effects, if they had not been checked by the general demonstrations of the zeal and spirit of his Majesty's faithful subjects, and by the timely and judicious use of those extraordinary powers, which Parliament has, in its wisdom, from time to time confided to his Majesty's government:

That, either directly or indirectly, a continual intercourse and connexion has been maintained between all these societies in Great Britain and Ireland, and that the real objects of the instigators of these proceedings, in both kingdoms, were no other than the entire overthrow of the British constitution, the general confiscation of property, and the erection of a democratic republic, founded on the ruins of all religion, and of all political and civil society, and framed after the model of France.

The vigorous resistance opposed to the rebellion in Ireland, the success of the measures which have been employed for detecting and defeating the designs of the conspirators here, and the general and ardent spirit of loyalty and attachment to the laws and constitution, have hitherto counteracted the progress mischief, and wented impending danger; but even these circumstances by no means appear to your Committee to justify that the mischief is eradicated, or the danger past. ... principles and views of the conspirators remain ... Their reliance on the assistance and co-operation of ..., by which they expect ultimately to effect their purpose, was undiminished; and the system of those secret societies are at once the instruments of seditious conspiracy at home, a channel of treasonable correspondence with France, though in parts broken and interrupted, is by no means destroyed. ... Committee have already referred to the positive ... laid before them, stating that hostile preparations are ... ing with extraordinary vigour and exertion, in ... of ... of France, for the invasion of this country, or of Ireland. ... activity of seditious and treasonable societies, in their correspondence with France, and in their endeavours to gain proselytes keeps pace with the preparations of the enemy; and the principle of secrecy, generally enforced by unlawful oaths, which is ... characteristic of these societies, peculiarly fits them for ... desperate enterprises, and, by holding out a prospect of ... ty, increases the means of seduction. It has, ... an obvious tendency to elude detection in the first instance, a defeat legal inquiry in the next. To this principle ... in the opinion of your Committee, such further measures as ... ment in its wisdom may think fit to adopt for the public ... should be more immediately and decisively pointed.

...ur Committee have seen, with satisfaction, the powers which, ...formity to the ancient practice and true principles of the ...lution, have from time to time, as the urgency required, been ...ted to his Majesty's Government; and they feel it their duty ...ularly to remark, that the power of arresting and detaining ...ted persons (a remedy so constantly resorted to by our an...s, in all cases of temporary and extraordinary danger) has, ... the present new and unprecedented circumstances, been found ...larly efficient. It has greatly interrupted and impeded the ...spondence with the enemy, and has checked, from time to ...the progress and communication of sedition and treason ... But from particular circumstances which have come under ...servation of your Committee in the course of their inquiry, ...feel it their duty to remark, that the good effects of this mea... would be rendered more complete, and the public tranquillity ... secured, if the leading persons who have been, or may be ...after, detained on suspicion of treasonable practices shall hereafter be kept in custody in places sufficiently distant from the me...

...whole of the secret information which has been laid before ...ommittee has strongly confirmed them in their opinion of ...cessity of confiding these extraordinary powers to his Ma-

jesty's

jesty's Government; and the very circumstances which cre
this necessity, and which continue at this time to operate r
powerfully than ever, have rendered it their peculiar duty to
tain from disclosing, in its full extent, the particular informa
of which they have stated to the House the general result, an
which their judgment is founded; but they trust that they
laid before the House sufficient grounds to justify their persua
that the multiplied and various attempts, by which the enemi
their country carry on their dangerous conspiracies, can onl
defeated by a corresponding vigilance on the part of Governm
and by the exercise of such additional powers, as may from tin
time be entrusted to it by Parliament, and may be best adapt
the peculiar exigency of the moment. And although your C
mittee do not think it any part of their province to suggest p
cular measures, the consideration of which must be left to the
dom of Parliament, they cannot forbear particularly and earn
pressing their unanimous opinion, that the system of secret soci
the establishment of which has, in other countries, uniformly
ceded the aggression of France, and, by facilitating the progre
her principles, has prepared the way for her arms, cannot be
fered to exist in these kingdoms compatibly with the safety of
government and constitution, and with their security again
reign force and domestic treason.

Your Committee have great satisfaction in adding, that i
growing and formidable evil can be effectually repressed, a
the same system of vigilance and precaution which has been
cessfully adopted for some years past, is adhered to, there is
reason to look forward with confidence to the ultimate disapp
ment and defeat of the projects which have been so long pu
by our foreign and domestic enemies. Impressed with a just
of the blessings enjoyed under our happy constitution, which
tinguish this country from every nation in Europe, all rank
conditions of society have shown their determination to pre
those blessings entire, and have stood forward with a becomin
dour and alacrity in their defence. While this laudable spirit
tinues to pervade every part of the kingdom, and while the wi

From the Committee of Secrecy, appointed by the British House of Lords, June 1799.

The Lords Committees who were appointed to inspect the ers delivered by his Majesty's command (sealed up) containing secret information received by his Majesty's Gov..., relative to the proceedings of different persons and so... Great Britain and Ireland, engaged in a treasonable con... and to the design carried on by our enemies, in concert ... h persons and societies, for effecting the separation of ... in this kingdom, have agreed to report ...
... the said papers, and the other informations which have been ... ore them, contain the most decisive evidence of a ... piracy carried on with unremitted industry, both in Great ... and in Ireland, for the destruction of the laws and govern... for the overthrow of every existing establishment both in ... and state; and for imposing, by force, ... the people of ... alms, under the influence and by the aid of France, ... subversive of public order, morality, and religion. ... e formation and progress of this conspiracy, your Com... ave seen a constant and systematic adherence to ... having opened the way to all the calamities and crimes of ... has since been uniformly pursued by all those who, in va... arts of Europe have engaged in similar designs; and your ttee are therefore decidedly of opinion, that the criminal ings which have been established in evidence before them, to be considered merely as the acts of unconnected and ... dividuals, but as branches and members of an extensive ... plicated system, which aims at nothing less than to sub... whole order of society as now established in Europe. The ... which are every where ultimately looked to for the accom... pt of this design, have been exhibited in France in their fullest ... n and extent; they have unhappily been (though in a less ... exemplified in Ireland; and it is the painful duty of your ttee to lay before this House a general view of the plan ... as been pursued by a part of their fellow-subjects in this ... in order to prepare the way here for similar scenes of ... ion, rebellion, and civil bloodshed. The necessity of en... g this Report into a detailed and historical enumeration of ... rent transactions which are included under this general de... is, however, superseded by the distinct and particular ... t of them, which is contained in the Report of the Secret ttee of the House of Commons, which has been communi... your Lordships, and referred to your Committee. ... whole of that most important document, your Committee ... earnestly to recommend to the particular attention of ... rdships.

They

They have found it supported throughout by the evidence which has been laid before the Committees of both Houses; and the truth of several of the facts there stated, as well as the authenticity of the sources of information from which they were drawn, have received additional confirmation from circumstances which have been disclosed even since the date of that Report.

In any attempt to trace the outlines and leading features of the system established and acted upon by the disaffected in this kingdom, the first point which claims attention is the indefatigable industry employed for deceiving and misleading the people at large, and particularly the lower classes of the community. To poison the minds of persons of this description with opinions destructive of their own happiness, and inconsistent with the very ends and nature of all government, has always, and in every country, been the principal endeavour of those who are engaged in these conspiracies for promoting the principles of the French revolution. Your Committee deem it almost unnecessary to recall to the recollection of this House, to what extent and with what success this measure was first adopted in France. They have seen abundant proof that, for many years past, and down to the present moment, the same means have been unremittedly pursued here by those who have unquestionably had the same objects in view. It would be an endless and most disgusting task to enumerate the almost infinite variety of impious, immoral, and seditious publications with which the press has of late years been loaded, both in Great Britain and in Ireland, and which appear to have in great part, if not wholly, proceeded from the persons engaged in this conspiracy. From this system of attack nothing has been held sacred. To revile our holy religion, to undermine the foundations of our faith, to subvert every established principle both of political and moral duty, to destroy all sense of allegiance to our Sovereign, all attachment to the forms and principles of our happy constitution, to eradicate every sentiment of national character, and to render the people of these realms indifferent both to the dangers and to the successes of their country, have been the invariable objects of these multiplied and continued endeavours.

The zeal with which these doctrines have been disseminated, the peculiar mode of their circulation, are, however, deserving of particular attention. They appear to be principally addressed to that class of society whose habits might enable them, in some degree, to judge of the tendency of such opinions, but to those whose station and occupations have in great measure debarred them even from that degree of knowledge. With this view, these writings have been printed in numerous editions, and in the cheapest forms; they have even been distributed gratis, and in large quantities, and their circulation among the labouring classes has been princip

...ncipal occupation of emissaries deputed to various parts of the ...ntry from the societies established in this metropolis.

The same object has been pursued by inflammatory language, ...ditious discourses, by lectures publicly delivered, by tumul... ...us assemblies convened in the neighbourhood of the capital, ...d of other populous places, and by every other means which ...peared best calculated to excite throughout the country, a spirit ... general hostility to its religion and government, and to delude ...he commission of the most atrocious crimes, those whose situa...ion most exposed them to this seduction.

In this close imitation of the beginnings of the French revolu...n, the advantage which in that country had been derived to ... supporters of these principles, from their success in corrupting ... soldiery, could not escape the observation of those who, in ...se kingdoms, were labouring in the same cause. Your Com...ee have accordingly found, by clear and multiplied proofs, ...t repeated endeavours have been employed to taint his Majesty's ... and armies, by the introduction of a spirit of insubordination ...d mutiny, inconsistent with the duty of subjects, and still more ...h that discipline which is the indispensable foundation of all ...litary service. Wherever in any part of those gallant and me...orious bodies of men any trace of such a spirit has appeared, ...this cause it is principally to be ascribed; and it is much more to ...r loyalty, fidelity, and steady sense of duty, than to any want ...industry employed to mislead them, that the ultimate failure of ...s part of the conspiracy is to be attributed.

Following the same example of the progress and success of the ...asures employed to promote the cause of the revolution in ...nce, the next object to which the conspirators in these king...ms appear to have turned their attention was the formation of ...ular societies, which, like those established in the earlier pe...ds of the French revolution, might supersede the authority of ...vernment, of whatever description, and enable their leaders to ...me, and exercise, at their discretion, the whole power of the ...try, civil and military.

The history of these successive attempts in England, in Scotland, ...d in Ireland, is so particularly and distinctly detailed in the ...ort of the Secret Committee of the House of Commons, that ... Committee deem it unnecessary to repeat it here.

...ey will only remark, that these attempts, followed up as they ... been with unremitting activity and perseverance, have suc...ely assumed every shape, and covered themselves under every ...nce, which might best elude the vigilance of the King's Go...ment, and promote the wicked and dangerous designs, which ... in the contemplation of the leaders of these societies.

... effects which this most powerful instrument of treason and ...ion is capable of producing, have been but too strongly

VOL. VIII.　　　　　3 G　　　　　shown

shown in Ireland, where, under the name of United Irishmen, a very large proportion of the lower class of the people throughout whole districts, counties, and provinces, have been combined into a systematic body leagued against the Government, and protected from detection and punishment by the nature of their establishment, by mutual oaths of secrecy, and still more, by the general terror which their menaces, crimes, and outrages, have naturally inspired, till at length the whole system burst forth into an open rebellion, which is even at this hour rather repressed than subdued.

It is under these circumstances that this establishment of United Irishmen, which has been so injurious to the peace and interest of Ireland, appears to have extended itself to this kingdom, and particularly to the metropolis, where there is always among the labouring classes a large number of Irish. It has also been closely imitated by the formation (precisely on the same model) of bodies of United Scotsmen and United Britons, which do not however as yet appear to have made such progress in this kingdom as was probably expected by their leaders.

The system of Corresponding Societies, which had preceded these, and prepared the way for them in this kingdom, is however scarcely, if at all, less dangerous, and appears to have been carried on to an extent well deserving the most serious attention of this House. Your Committee have annexed to this Report two lists, one extracted from the papers found at different periods in the possession of the secretary of the London Corresponding Society and at the General Committee Room of that Society; the other a copy of a paper found in the possession of a member of what is called the Executive Committee of that body.

They contain the names of different places in this kingdom with which that Society entertained correspondence. Your Committee have reason to believe that even these lists do not include the whole, but they appear to your Committee to furnish ample proof of the necessity of some new and more efficient provision to guard against the danger of such establishments, the extent of influence of which has already been manifested both in France and in Ireland, and can by no means be considered as an object of slight concern in the present state of this country.

To this imitation of the course of the proceedings which has led to such fatal consequences in France, your Committee find that the disaffected in these kingdoms have added the crime of treasonable communication and connexion with the enemy at various periods during the present war.

Intelligence of the state of both kingdoms, with a view to the facility and success of invasion, has been repeatedly transmitted to the French government, both from London and from Dublin. The invasion of Ireland was planned in personal intercourse between
two

(411)

...of the Irish rebels and the French general charged with... ...of that measure; a resident envoy continued for... time in France, regularly accredited by the body of... ... The communications were also maintained by... ...ies of persons who were addressed from the conspirators to the members of the societies in this kingdom, and ...nce passed over to the continent. One of these, being ... in the very act of procuring his passage for France, ...d executed here: and it appears that at the time of the ... person, and of Mr. Arthur O'Connor, who was along ... him, his Majesty's Government were in full ... e knowledge of the treasonable designs which the ... ...fessed.

...mmittee have, however, too much reason to apprehend ... the punishment of the offender already mentioned, and ...is accomplices who have suffered in Ireland, nor the ...nt of others, has yet stopped the course of this trea... ...recourse with the enemy. It indeed has appeared to ...ittee that, during the detention of the prisoners, who ...ed on this account in Dublin, they found the means of ... communications with some of their confederates ... ...rge; and recent evidence has been furnished to you ... of the continuance of a treasonable correspondence... ...United Irish and the enemy, with the object of ca... ...nd aiding an invasion of his Majesty's kingdom of...

...vhole result of their examination, your Committee ...e strongest grounds to be persuaded, that if the dan... ...ns of these conspirators have been so far checked and ... this kingdom, as to prevent an actual interruption of ...ranquillity, this could only have been effected by the ... his Majesty's Government, aided by the exercise of ...ordinary and occasional powers which Parliament has ... time judged it proper, after the example of their an... ...onfide to his Majesty; and supported by the extraor... ...nprecedented display of zeal, energy, and public spirit ... of the great body of his Majesty's faithful subjects. So ...e continue, and as the attention of Parliament is con... ...ied to supply any defects in the means which the pre... ...nay afford to meet the exigencies of this new and un... ...ous, they are confident that, under the Divine Provi... ...anger is to be apprehended to the laws and happy ... of this kingdom. But they are on the other hand ...inced, that this object requires a continued and active ...d they feel it their duty to add, that no form of go... ...e in their opinion, be considered as secure, under ...em of secret societies, such as it is described in the

Report of the Secret Committee of the House of C
as it has appeared in evidence before them, is permit

List of Places with which the London Corresponding
  corresponded, as appears by the Papers found in th
  their Secretary, and at the General Committee
  Queen of Bohemia's Head.

Bradley,	Nottingham,	Newcastle upon	Br
Norwich,	Derby,	Tyne,	Tr
Sheffield,	Banbury,	Chevening,	
Manchester,	Adderbury,	Oxford,	M
Chester,	Bromley,	Wolverhamp-	St
York,	Leeds,	ton	W
Liverpool,	Leicester,	Whitchurch,	Li
Halifax,	Exeter,	Cardiff,	Fi
St. Albans,	Deptford,	Gravesend,	Cr
Bradford,	Rochester,	Loughborough,	Cr
Coventry,	Ashton,	Stourbridge,	Ai
Maidstone,	Trowbridge,	Battle,	
Portsmouth,	Alton,	Wakefield,	Fr
Edinburgh,	Dudley,	Birmingham,	Ga
Glasgow,	Paisley,	Woodchurch,	Se
Perth,	Helstone,	Kent,	Cr
Dundee,	Berwick,	Bath,	Ro

A List of the United Corresponding Societies of Gr
  the year 1797, found in the possession of a person
  Member of the Executive Committee.

Portsmouth,	Hampshire.	Bath,	So
Newcastle un-		Bristol,	So
der Line,	Staffordshire.	Loughborough,	Le
Salford, near		Wolverhampton	St.
Manchester.		Stourbridge,	W
Manchester,	Lancashire.	Wakefield,	Yo
Sheffield,	Yorkshire.	Melbourne,	D
Norwich,	Norfolk.	Leicester,	Le
Bradford,	Yorkshire.	Edinburgh,	N
Nottingham,	Nottinghamsh.	Glasgow,	D
Birmingham,	Warwickshire.	Perth,	Di
Halifax,	Yorkshire.	Dundee,	Di
St. Alban's,	Hertfordshire.	Paisley,	N
Exeter,	Devonshire.	Helstone,	Co
Chester,	Cheshire.	Berwick,	Co
High Wycombe,	Bucks.	Newcastle upon	
Whitchurch,	Shropshire.	Tyne,	Co
Leominster,	Herefordshire.	Oxford,	O
York,	Yorkshire.	Chevening,	K

(413)

nd,	Kent.	Grantham,	Lincolnshire.
the,	Ditto.	Southampton,	Hampshire.
er,	Ditto.	Kendal,	Westmoreland.
d,	Ditto.	Wooton,	Hertfordshire.
r,	Ditto.	Bromley,	Yorkshire.
	South Wales.	Kegworth,	Leicestershire.
urch,	Kent.	Banbury,	Oxford
	Cornwall.	Adderbury,	Ditto.
	Derbyshire.	Tamworth,	Warwickshire.
ld,	Staffordshire.	Stockport,	
ge,	Hampshire.	Warrington,	
	Yorkshire.	Gosport,	Hampshire.
ter,	Hampshire.	Ipswich,	
ol,	Lancashire.	Philips Norton,	Somersetshire.
h,	North Britain.	Ashton under	
,	Middlesex.	Line,	Lancashire.
nock,	North Britain.	Coventry,	
er,	Ditto.	Tunbridge,	
,	Staffordshire.	Rochdale.	
	Yorkshire.		

PARLIA-

PARLIAMENTARY PAPERS.

BRITISH PARLIAMENT.

In the House of Commons, Thursday, November 22, 1798, M[r. Pitt] brought up the following Message from his Majesty.

HIS Majesty having taken into his consideration the [great] and meritorious services performed by Rear-admiral Nelson, in the memorable and decisive victory obtained [over the] superior French fleet off the mouth of the Nile, not only honourable to himself, but eminently beneficial to these [king]doms; and his Majesty being desirous to confer upon him [a] considerable and lasting mark of his royal favour in testim[ony of] his approbation of his great services, and therefore to gi[ve and] grant to the said Rear-admiral Lord Nelson, and the tw[o next] heirs male to whom the title of Baron Nelson of the Nile [and] Burnham Thorpe in the county of Norfolk, shall descend, fo[r their] lives the net sum of 2000l. *per annum*: but his Majesty not [having] it in his power to grant any annuity to that amount, or for a [term] beyond his own life, his Majesty recommends it to his f[aithful] Commons to consider of the means of enabling his Majesty [to ex]tend and secure an annuity of 2000l. *per annum* to Rear-a[dmiral] Lord Nelson, and the two next heirs male on whom the t[itle of] Baron Nelson of the Nile and Burnham Thorpe in the co[unty of] Norfolk shall descend, in such manner as shall be most advant[ageous] to their interests.

[The message being read, it was ordered, on the motion [of Mr.] Pitt, to be referred to a Committee of Supply for the next d[ay.]

On the 26th of November, in the House of Commons, Mr. S[heridan] gave Notice of a Motion to the following Effect, for the T[hursday] Se'nnight.

THAT it is the duty of his Majesty's ministers not to ent[er into] any engagements that may prevent or impede any nego[tiation] for peace, whenever there shall appear a disposition on the [part of] France to accede to terms of peace that may be consistent w[ith the] interests and honour of the British nation.

...sday, November the 27th, Mr. Pitt made the following Motion in the House of Commons.

THAT leave be given to bring in a bill for continuing, for a time to be limited, the act of the 38th of his Majesty, enabling his Majesty to avail himself of the voluntary offers of the English ... to serve out of the kingdom. [Leave granted.]

... 28th of November, Lord Grenville brought down a Message from his Majesty to the House of Lords similar to that presented to the Commons, relative to settling an Annuity on Lord Nelson ...

The message being read, Lord Grenville moved an address of thanks for his Majesty's gracious communication, which was ... to, nem. diss.

... the 3d of December, Mr. Tierney, in the House of Commons, ...

DEFERRED his motion relative to engagements with foreign powers, so far as they might interfere with a peace between Great Britain and France, until the Tuesday se'nnight following.

...onday the 10th of December, Sir Francis Burdett, in the House of Commons, made the following Motion.

THAT a list be laid on the table of this House of the names of the persons committed in virtue of an act entitled, "An Act to empower his Majesty to secure and detain such Persons as his Majesty shall suspect are conspiring against his Person and Government," and of the Prisons in which such Persons have been confined.—Agreed to.

...sday the 11th of December, Mr. Tierney, pursuant to Notice, made the following Motion in the House of Commons.

THAT it is the duty of his Majesty's ministers to advise his Majesty against entering into any engagements which may preclude or impede a negotiation for peace, whenever a disposition shall be shewn on the part of the French republic to treat on terms consistent with the security and interest of the British empire.

[The motion was negatived without a division.]

On

On the 19th of December, Mr. Secretary Dundas gave Notice, in the House of Commons,

THAT it was his intention to move to-morrow for leave to bring in a bill to renew and continue for a time to be limited, the bill for suspending the Habeas Corpus act.

On the 21st of December, Mr. Pitt, in the House of Commons,

MOVED the second reading of the bill for continuing the suspension of the Habeas Corpus act.
[After a long debate a division took place on this motion.—Ayes 96.—Noes 6.—Majority 90.]

MR. Dundas on the same day moved for leave to bring in a bill to exempt persons serving in volunteer corps from being balloted for to serve in the militia, under certain regulations.—Leave given.
[The bill was then brought up, read a first time, and ordered to be read a second time, next day.]

On the 31st of December, Mr. Pitt, in the House of Commons,

MOVED the order of the day for the third reading of the 10 *per cent.* or Income bill.
[A long debate ensued, and the House divided on the motion.—Ayes 93.—Noes 2.—Majority 91.]

On the 4th of January 1799, Lord Grenville, in the House of Lords,

MOVED the order of the day for the third reading of the bill for suspending the Habeas Corpus act.
[The order being read by the clerk, a debate ensued, after which the House divided.—For the third reading of the bill 26.—Against it 1.—Majority 25.]

On Tuesday, January the 8th, in the House of Lords,

THE Income bill was read a third time, and passed without a division.

On the 22d of January, Mr. Secretary Dundas, in the House of Commons, brought up the following Message from his Majesty.

G. R.

HIS Majesty is persuaded that the unremitting industry with which our enemies persevere in their avowed design of effecting the separation of Ireland from this kingdom, cannot fail to engage the particular attention of Parliament; and his Majesty recommends it to this House to consider of the most effectual means of counteracting, and finally defeating, this design; and he trusts that a review of all the circumstances which have recently occurred (joined to the sentiment of mutual affection and common interest) will dispose the Parliaments of both kingdoms to provide in the manner which they shall judge most expedient for settling such a complete and final adjustment as may best tend to improve and perpetuate a connexion essential for their common security, and to augment and consolidate the strength, power, and resources of the British empire.

[The message being read, it was ordered, on the motion of Mr. Secretary Dundas, to be taken into consideration the following day.]

Same Day, in the House of Lords,

LORD Grenville presented a similar message, which was ordered, on the motion of his Lordship, to be taken into consideration the next day.

On the 23d of January, in the House of Commons, the Order of the Day for taking his Majesty's Message relative to an Union with Ireland into Consideration, being read,

MR. Secretary Dundas moved an address of thanks, stating in substance, that the House would proceed with all due dispatch to the consideration of the several interests recommended to their serious attention in the message.

To this Mr. Sheridan moved an amendment, to the following effect:

"At the same time to express our surprise and deep regret, that the final adjustment which took place in 1782, and which the Parliaments of the two countries expected would add to the security and promote the happiness of Ireland, had not produced those effects; and farther to observe, that this House being led to fear that it is the intention of his Majesty's ministers to propose an union between the two kingdoms, they think it their duty to implore his Majesty not to listen to the counsels of those persons who

Vol. VIII.   3 H   advise

advise his Majesty to adopt such a measure at the present c
and under the present circumstances of the empire."

This amendment, after a long debate, was withdrawn;
original motion was then put and carried, and the address ord
to be presented to his Majesty the next day.

SAME day Mr. Dundas presented, by command of his Maj
several papers relative to the rebellion and conspiracy in Irela

---

SAME day, in the House of Lords, Lord Grenville moved
order of the day for taking his Majesty's most gracious messag
lative to an union with Ireland into consideration.

The order of the day being read, Lord Grenville moved ar
dress to the following effect:

"That this House beg leave to return his Majesty their hur
thanks, for his Majesty's most gracious communication in his
sage of last night; and to assure his Majesty, that this House
be ready to co-operate in, and to support and forward any r
sure, which, upon due and mature examination and deliberat
should be deemed necessary to strengthen, support, and consoli
the general interests of the British empire."

The question was then put on the address, which was v
nem. diff.

On January the 24th, on the Motion of Mr. Secretary Dundas, i
House of Commons,

A SECRET Committee was balloted for, to consider of
papers laid before the House relative to the rebellion and
spiracy in Ireland.

On January the 31st, Mr. Pitt moved, in the House of Commons,
the following Resolutions and Address be referred to a Committe

I. THAT, in order to promote and secure the essential intere
Great Britain and Ireland, and to consolidate the stren
power, and resources of the British empire, it will be advisab
concur in such measures as may best tend to unite the two k
doms of Great Britain and Ireland into one kingdom, in such n
ner, and on such terms and conditions, as may be established by
of the respective Parliaments of his Majesty's said kingdoms.

II. That it appears to this Committee that it would be f
propose, as the first article, to serve as a basis of the said un

That the said kingdoms of Great Britain and Ireland, shall, upon a day to be agreed upon, be united into one kingdom, by the name of The United Kingdom of Great Britain and Ireland.

III. That for the same purpose it appears also to this Committee that it would be fit to propose, That the succession to the monarchy and the imperial crown of the said united kingdoms shall continue limited and settled in the same manner as the imperial crown of the said kingdoms of Great Britain and Ireland now stands limited and settled according to the existing laws, and to the terms of the union between England and Scotland.

IV. That for the same purpose it appears also to this Committee that it would be fit to propose, That the said united kingdom be represented in one and the same Parliament, to be styled The Parliament of the United Kingdom of Great Britain and Ireland; and that such a number of Lords spiritual and temporal, and such a number of members in the House of Commons, as shall be hereafter agreed upon by acts of the respective Parliaments as aforesaid, shall sit and vote in the said Parliament on the part of Ireland, and shall be summoned, chosen, and returned in such manner as shall be fixed by an act of Parliament of Ireland previous to the said union; and that every member hereafter to sit and vote in the said Parliament of the united kingdom shall, until the said Parliament shall otherwise provide, take and subscribe the same oath, and make the same declarations as are by law required to be taken, subscribed, and made by the members of the Parliaments of Great Britain and Ireland.

V. That for the same purpose it appears also to this Committee that it would be fit to propose, That the churches of England and Ireland, and the doctrine, worship, discipline, and government thereof, shall be preserved as now by law established.

VI. That for the same purpose, it appears also to this Committee that it would be fit to propose, That his Majesty's subjects in Ireland shall at all times hereafter be entitled to the same privileges, and be on the same footing in respect of trade and navigation in all ports and places belonging to Great Britain, and in all cases with respect to which treaties shall be made by his Majesty, his heirs, or successors, with any foreign power, as his Majesty's subjects in Great Britain. That no duty shall be imposed on the import or export between Great Britain and Ireland of any articles now duty free, and that on other articles there shall be established, for a time to be limited, such a moderate rate of equal duties, as shall previous to the union be agreed upon, and approved by the respective Parliaments; subject, after the expiration of such limited time, to be diminished equally with respect to both kingdoms; but in no case to be increased:—That all articles which may at any time hereafter be imported into Great Britain from foreign parts, shall be importable through either kingdom into the other, be regulated from time to time by the united Parliaments.

VII. That for the like purpose it would be fit to propos[e] the charge arising from the payment of the interest, or sinki[ng] for the reduction of the principal of the debt incurred i[n each] kingdom before the union, shall continue to be separately [borne] by Great Britain and Ireland respectively; and for a nu[mber of] years to be limited, the future ordinary expenses of th[e united] kingdom in peace or war, shall be defrayed by Great Brit[ain and] Ireland, jointly, according to such proportions as shall [be esta]blished by the respective-Parliaments previous to the unio[n; and] that after the expiration of the time to be so limited, the [propor]tion shall not be liable to be varied, except according to su[ch rules] and principles as shall be in like manner agreed upon pre[vious to] the union.

VIII. That for the like purpose it would be fit to [propose] That all laws in force at the time of the union, and all th[e courts] of civil or ecclesiastical jurisdiction within the respectiv[e king]doms, shall remain as now by law established within th[em, but] subject only to such alterations or regulations from time [to time] as circumstances may appear to the Parliament of the unite[d king]dom to require.

That the foregoing resolutions be laid before his Majest[y in] an humble address, assuring his Majesty that we have p[roceeded] with the utmost attention to the consideration of the impor[tant sub]jects recommended to us in his Majesty's gracious message.

That we entertain a firm persuasion that a complete a[nd entire]

lated to form the basis of such a settlement, leaving it to his Majesty's wisdom, at such time and in such manner as his Majesty, in his parental solicitude for the happiness of his people, shall judge fit, to communicate these propositions to his Parliament of Ireland, with whom we shall be at all times ready to concur in all such measures as may be found most conducive to the accomplishment of this great and salutary work. And we trust that, after full and mature consideration, such a settlement may be framed and established by the deliberative consent of the Parliaments of both kingdoms, as may be conformable to the sentiments, wishes, and real interests of his Majesty's faithful subjects in Great Britain and Ireland, and may unite them inseparably in the full enjoyment of the blessings of our free and invaluable constitution, in the support of the honour and dignity of his Majesty's Crown, and in the preservation and advancement of the welfare and prosperity of the whole British empire.

On the question being put for the Speaker's leaving the chair, Mr. Sheridan objected to it, for the purpose of moving the two following resolutions:

"That no measures can have a tendency to improve and perpetuate the ties of amity and connexion now existing between Great Britain and Ireland, which have not for their basis the manifest, fair, and free consent and approbation of the Parliaments of the two countries.

"That whoever shall endeavour to obtain the appearance of such consent and approbation, in either country, by employing the influence of Government for the purposes of corruption or intimidation, is an enemy to his Majesty and to the constitution."

The House then divided on the question of the Speaker's leaving the chair.—Ayes 140.—Noes 15.—Majority 125.

On the 7th of February, in the House of Commons, Mr. Sheridan moved the following Resolution.

THAT it is the opinion of this House, that no measures can have a tendency to improve and perpetuate the ties of amity and connexion between Great Britain and Ireland that have not for their basis the unanimous, fair, and free consent of the Parliament of the two countries; and that whoever shall endeavour to obtain such consent by corruption and intimidation, shall be considered an enemy to his Majesty's government and the British constitution.

[The resolution was lost by the motion for the previous question, on which the House divided.—For the previous question—Ayes 141.—Against it 25.]

On February the 11th, Mr. Sheridan moved the following Resolution in the House of Commons.

THAT it be an instruction to the Committee, in the first instance to consider, how far it would be consistent with justice and policy, and conducive to the general interests, and especially to the consolidation of the British empire, were civil incapacities, on account of religious distinctions, to be done away throughout his Majesty's dominions.

[It was negatived without a division.]

On the 20th of February, Mr. Dundas moved to the following Effect in the House of Commons.

THAT leave be given to bring in a bill to enlarge the time of an Act for granting certain privileges to persons extending their service from local to whole districts, for reducing the Militia of England, &c.—Agreed to.

On the 1st of March, Mr. Pitt, in the House of Commons, brought down the following Message from his Majesty.

G. R.

HIS Majesty being desirous of making competent provision for the honourable support and maintenance of his dearly beloved sons, Prince Edward and Prince Ernest Augustus, which the monies applicable to the purposes of his Majesty's civil government would be insufficient to defray; and being also desirous of being enabled to extend to his beloved daughter, the Princess Amelia, the provision which he has been enabled to make out of the hereditary revenue for the other branches of his Royal family, desires the assistance of Parliament for this purpose: and his Majesty relies on the affection of his faithful Commons, that they will make such provision as the circumstances of the case may appear to require.

[The message was ordered to be referred to a Committee of Supply.]

On Monday, March the 18th, Lord Grenville, in the House of Lords, brought up

A PROCLAMATION, for prohibiting all persons, except those in his Majesty's service, from quitting Ireland without passports previously obtained from the Lord Lieutenant, &c. * [was ordered to be laid on the table.]

---

* This Proclamation will be found among the Gazettes at the end of the volume, p. 154.

of April, Mr. Secretary Dundas, in the House of Commons, presented the following Message from his Majesty.

"H[is] Majesty thinks proper to acquaint the House of Commons, [i]n consequence of representations received from his Lord [lieutenan]t of Ireland, his Majesty has thought it [necessary f]or [the peace] and security of that kingdom, to give directions, that [severa]l persons who were in custody in Dublin and Belfast, [on account o]f the active part taken in the rebellion, or for treasonable [practices] connected with the same, should be immediately re[move]d of that kingdom to a place of safe custody; and h[is Majesty h]as accordingly ordered them to be brought over to this [country a]nd they are now confined in Fort George.

[This m]essage was ordered to be taken into consideration on the [day following.]

[The same] day Lord Grenville, in the House of Lords, brought [up a si]milar message.

[On the 1]9[t]h of April, the following Protest was entered on the [Journals of the]House of Lords, against the Address in favour of [an Union with Ir]eland.

"[BEC]AUSE the measure of a legislative union between Great [Bri]tain and Ireland, the policy of which is highly question[able, t]he importance of which demands the most calm, dispas[sion]ed deliberate examination, is persisted in and urged for [the] compliment to his Majesty's ministers, under circum[stances w]hich ought imperiously to have deterred us from the [adoptio]n of it.

[At a m]oment of civil disturbance and division, when the ne[cessity of m]ilitary law is alleged by ministers, and acknowledged [by Parliam]ent, seems ill calculated for ensuring the full and un[biassed c]onsent of the Irish people, without which even the sup[porters of ']the measure must confess it to be illusory, and dangerous [as an ex]treme. And to commit the Parliament of Great Britain [to the a]dom of a project which the Commons of Ireland have [rejected,] and to which the inhabitants of that kingdom are disin[clined, ap]pears to us a whimsical expedient for securing the con[nection of ']the two countries, and consolidating the strength of the [empire.]

[Be]cause, as no jealousy or division has existed between the [legis]latures, the present dangers and discontents in Ireland [cannot be]attributed to the independence of Parliament, but must [be c]onsidered as the bitter fruits of a coercive system of
policy,

policy, suggested by his Majesty's advisers, and enforced under the sanction of the executive power with unconstitutional and wanton severity.

3dly, Because, though the possibility of a different will in the two separate legislatures cannot be controverted, yet possible inconveniences in remote and extreme cases from supposed legislative measures, or possible instances of additional embarrassment to the executive government, are no arguments for the subversion of a system in which no such inconveniences have been experienced, and no such difficulties encountered. For the consequences of such reasoning would lead us to consolidate into one the different branches of our own excellent constitution; to remove all the checks which the jealousy of our ancestors has imposed on the executive government; to condemn whatever theory might suppose difficult, though practice had shown it to be easy; and to substitute hypothesis and speculation for history, fact, and experience.

4thly, Because the notion that a legislative union will either conciliate the affections of the discontented in Ireland, or furnish more effectual means for defeating the design of the enemy in that country, seems unsupported by reasoning, and in direct contradiction to analogy and experience. Were we to admit the beneficial consequences of a union, yet the benefits which, according to such hypothesis, are likely to result to Ireland from the measures, are, at least, progressive and distant, and can furnish, therefore, no reasonable hope of allaying immediate discontent, suppressing actual rebellion, or defeating designs already on foot. If indeed, the enemies of the connexion endeavoured to effectuate a separation of the two kingdoms, by sowing jealousies and dissensions between the two Parliaments (as was the case in Scotland immediately previous to the union), the measure proposed would manifestly be an effectual, it might be represented as the only, remedy for the evil: but if it be true that their object is to disseminate jealousy, and foment discontent, not between the distant legislatures and governments of England and Ireland, but between the people and Parliament, between the governed and government of that country; and if, by representing their legislature as the corrupt agent of British ministers, and slavish engine of British tyranny, they have succeeded in alienating a large portion of his Majesty's subjects; and if it be farther true, as stated in the Report of the Committees of Secrecy of the Irish Parliament, that the misrepresentations of a few individuals have been found sufficient to seduce the allegiance of one whole province in Ireland; we are indeed at a loss to conceive how the danger of such designs is to be averted, or the force of such misrepresentations diminished, by a measure, which reduces the number of representatives of the Irish people, transfers the legal organ of their will out of the bosom of their own

country,

country, and annihilates all independent and executive authority in that kingdom.

An examination of the immediate consequences which the union formerly produced in Scotland, and a contemplation of the recent effects of its discussion in Ireland, suggest yet stronger reasons for doubting its efficacy either in healing discontents, or furnishing the means of resistance to any attempt of the enemy. We learn from the most authentic documents of those times, that in Scotland its agitation produced disorder and tumult; that, six years after it passed, nearly all the Scotch Peers voted for its dissolution, and founded that vote on the discontents it had occasioned; that it remained for a long period a subject of sullen discontent; that a promise of its dissolution was considered by the agents of the Pretender as advantageous to his cause in Scotland; and that two rebellions broke out in that kingdom, subsequent to its accomplishment.

Furthermore, from what information we have been able to procure, we observe, with the deepest concern and alarm, that its discussion in Ireland has already been attended with the most fearful symptoms. From the increased powers with which it has recently been deemed necessary to arm the executive power, we cannot but infer, that the prospect of an incorporating union has failed to conciliate the minds of the disaffected; and, from the ferment occasioned by its discussion, it is evident that all other parties in Ireland are alienated or divided, and the means of resistance in case of insurrection or foreign invasion thereby materially weakened.

We thought it therefore more prudent, in this moment of alarm, to desist from the prosecution of a measure, which might become a fresh subject of complaint, and a new source of discontent and division. And we were more disposed to seek for the re-establishment of mutual confidence, in the adoption of conciliatory laws, in the removal of odious disabilities, in the redress of grievances, and the operation of a milder system of policy on the affections of the Irish people, than in any experiment of theory and nominal union of governments.

Lastly, Because, at a time when the danger of innovation has been deemed a sufficient pretext for the continuation of abuses, the suspension of improvement, and the preservation of a defective representation of the people, we cannot regard without jealousy and alarm an innovation of direct contrary tendency, viz. the introduction of a number of members into the British Parliament, from a legislature, one branch of which has acknowledged the imperfection of its own constitution; and against the other branch of which the sale of peerages has been publicly alleged, and as publicly offered to be proved.

VOL. VIII.   3 I   And,

And, however invidious it might be to cite any example in [con]firmation of such opinion, we are not so blind to matters of [va]riety, or so deaf to the lessons of experience, as not to appre[hend] from a measure of this nature an enormous increase of the influ[ence] of the Crown; neither could we perceive, either in the pr[esent] temper of the Irish people, inflamed by civil animosity, and e[xas]perated by recent rebellion, or in the general moderation o[f his] Majesty's present advisers, any thing to allay our apprehen[sions] or remove our jealousies; and we were unwilling to give our [as]sent, at a period when new burdens are every day imposed, [and] new sacrifices every day required of the people, to a measure w[hich] must supply additional reasons for doubting the adequacy of [our] representation, and suspecting the independence of Parliament[.]

(Signed) HOLLAN[D.]
THANET
KING.

On the 19th of April, in the House of Commons, Mr. Pitt, [in a] Committee of the whole House upon a Report of the Secret C[om]mittee, proposed the two following Resolutions.

1st, THAT leave be given to bring a bill to continue the [act] of his present Majesty.

2dly, That leave be given to bring in a bill for the more effe[ctual] suppression of certain Societies, and for other purposes.

[After a long debate, both resolutions were agreed to witho[ut a] division.]

On the 5th of June, in the House of Commons, Mr. Pitt ma[de the] following Motion.

THAT leave be given to bring in a bill for the reducti[on of] the militia, for the purpose of enabling his Majesty to inc[rease] the regular forces, for the purpose of more vigorously carryin[g on] the war.—[Leave was granted.]

On the 6th of June, Mr. Secretary Dundas, in the House of Com[mons,] brought down the following Message from his Majesty.

G. R.

HIS Majesty thinks proper to acquaint this House, that h[e has] some time since concluded an eventual engagement wit[h his] good brother and ally, the Emperor of Russia, for employing f[orty-] five thousand men against the common enemy in such mann[er as] the state of affairs in Europe at that period appeared to render advantageous. The change of circumstances which has since arisen, having rendered a different application of that force more desirable, his Majesty has recently had the satisfaction to learn that the views of the Emperor of Russia in that respect are entirely conformable to his own. But his Majesty has not yet received any account that the formal engagements to that effect have been regularly concluded. He has, however, the satisfaction of knowing that the same promptitude and zeal in support of the common cause, which his ally has already manifested in a manner so honourable to himself, and so signally beneficial to Europe, have induced him already to put this army in motion towards the place of its destination, as now settled by mutual consent. His Majesty therefore thinks it right to acquaint the House of Commons, that the pecuniary conditions of this treaty will oblige his Majesty to pay the sum of two hundred and twenty-five thousand pounds in stipulated instalments, as preparation-money; and to pay a monthly subsidy of seventy-five thousand pounds, as well as to engage for a farther payment, at the rate of thirty-seven thousand five hundred pounds per month; which payment is not to take place till after the conclusion of a peace made by common consent.

His Majesty relies on the zeal and public spirit of his faithful Commons, to enable him to make good these engagements.

And his Majesty being desirous of continuing to afford the necessary succours to his ally the Queen of Portugal, as well as to give timely and effectual assistance at this important conjuncture to the Swiss Cantons for the recovery of their ancient liberty and independence, and to make every other exertion for improving to the utmost the signal advantages which, by the blessing of God, have attended the operations of the combined arms on the continent, since the commencement of the present campaign; recommends it also to the House of Commons to enable his Majesty to enter into such farther engagements, and to take such measures, as may be best adapted to the exigency of affairs, and most likely, by continued perseverance and vigour, to complete the general deliverance of Europe from the insupportable tyranny of the French republic.

[The message was referred to the Committee of Supply.]

The above message was taken into consideration on the 7th of June, in the House of Commons, in a Committee of Supply; when, on the motion of Mr. Pitt, the following resolutions were put and agreed to:

"That it is the opinion of this Committee that the sum of 225,000l. be granted to his Majesty to enable his Majesty to make good his engagement with Russia, in such manner as may be best adapted to the exigencies of the case.

"That it is the opinion of this Committee that a sum of 2,000,000l. be granted to his Majesty, to enable him to make good

good such further engagements as his Majesty may deem it exp[e]dient to enter into."

SAME day, in the House of Lords, Lord Grenville brou[ght] down a similar message to the above from his Majesty, which w[as] ordered to be taken into consideration on Tuesday the 11th.

On the 11th of June, in the House of Lords, Lord Grenville m[ade] an Address to his Majesty, which was an Echo of his Majes[ty's] Message relative to the Russian Subsidy.

EARL Fitzwilliam moved an amendment, the substance [of] which was, that in that part of the address which mentio[ns] the deliverance of Europe from the " insupportable tyranny [of] the French republic," the words " insupportable tyranny" shou[ld] be left out ; by which omission the sentence would then conclu[de] in the following words: " the deliverance of Europe from t[he] French republic."

An amendment was also moved by Lord Holland, the substan[ce] of which was, " that his Majesty, conformable to the language [he] had held on several previous occasions, would be ready to resu[me] the negotiation whenever a spirit of conciliation should appear [in] France, and a disposition to treat on fair, just, and honoura[ble] terms."

Both these amendments were negatived without a division, a[nd] the original address put and carried.

On the 25th of June, Mr. Abbot moved, in the House of Commons,

THE order of the day for the House to resolve itself into a Co[m]mittee upon the bill for repealing so much of the acts [of] Queen Anne and George the Second as limits the forfeiture [in] cases of high treason to the lives of the Pretender and his heirs[.]
[The House divided on the question for the Speaker's leavi[ng] the chair.—Ayes 57.—Noes 8.—Majority 49.]

On the 3d of July, in the House of Commons, Mr. Pitt made [the] following Motion.

THAT the House should resolve itself into a Committee of [the] whole House, to consider of a motion for leave to bring i[n a] bill to enable his Majesty, by an order in council, to permit su[ch] goods to be imported as should be specified in that order, in sh[ips] belonging to countries in amity with his Majesty.

[T

[The motion was agreed to, and the House having resolved itself into the said Committee, Mr. Pitt moved for leave to bring in such a bill.]

On the 4th of July, the following Protest was entered in the House of Lords against committing the Treason Forfeiture Bill.

Die Jovis, 4 Julii, 1799.

Dissentient,

FIRST, Because this statute, which it is by this bill proposed to make perpetual, appears to us to be unjust and impolitic, and contrary to the mild spirit of the laws of England—unjust, because it reduces to poverty and ruin children for the crimes of their ancestors; impolitic, because, instead of healing the divisions and animosity occasioned by civil war, it tends to make them continue.

It appears to us to be contrary to the express declaration of Magna Charta, which says, that no person shall be disinherited or deprived of his franchises unless he be heard in his defence; for in this case we disinherit persons who cannot be heard, and who have committed no crime.

Secondly, Because it does not appear that any urgent necessity calls for the immediate adoption of this law at this late period of the session, when it cannot receive the due consideration which a question of this sort deserves, and when the attendance is so thin in this House.

Thirdly, Because we have the satisfaction of thinking it is not necessary for the preservation of his Majesty, whose throne cannot be more secure by severe penal statutes. We therefore will not agree to destroy that hope which Sir William Blackstone exultingly says our posterity may entertain—that corruption of blood may one day be abolished and forgotten.

PONSONBY,
HOLLAND.

On the 8th of July, in the House of Lords, on the Motion for the third reading of the Treason Forfeiture Bill, the Duke of Norfolk moved the following Amendment.

THAT the act should continue in force for one year, and no more. This amendment he further amended, by moving that the word *suspended* should be substituted for "*repealed*."

[A division took place on this amendment so altered, when there appeared—Non-contents 11.—Contents 5.— Majority 6.—The bill was then read a third time.]

Same

Same Day, in the House of Lords, on the Motion for committing Seditious Societies Bill, the Duke of Norfolk made the follow Motion.

THAT the words " printed in this kingdom" be inserted in bill. His Grace stated, that otherwise the penalty en cted in bill might attach on persons vending foreign books.

The motion was withdrawn.

On the 12th of July, in the House of Lords, the following Protest entered against the third reading of the Militia Reduction Bill.

Dissentient,

BECAUSE the measures prescribed by the bill are destructiv the constitutional force of the country ; by making the mil ballot a fund for the supply, and its discipline a drill for the commodation of other corps, and by degrading its officers to humiliating situation of commanding the miserable remnant their regiments rejected by recruiting serjeants of the line.

Because the subversion of this constitutional force must be inevitable consequence, as it is probably the object, of these n sures ; for it cannot be imagined that gentlemen of property (l as are required by the still remaining wreck of the militia la should hereafter come forward in times of difficulty and dan with a zeal and patriotism so much applauded, and so bitterly sulted; that men of the highest consideration and fortune, such alone can form a constitutional force, should quit their dome comforts and family occupations without personal views, or p fessional allurements, to fill a station so degrading to them as of drill serjeants for the army. But exclusive of this great and superable objection, we consider this bill as framed under circu stances of gross inattention to the public interest, to private ri of various descriptions, and to the clearest and most impor principles of the constitution ; and we should esteem ourse neglectful of our own characters, as well as deficient in pu duty, if we did not record our marked and unreserved reproba of a measure of such dangerous tendency : First, because the promoters of this bill have, contrary to every principle of comm justice, established an arbitrary proportion, by which the resp tive counties are hereafter to be burdened with the expense raising their future militia, deviating from the established so approved and sanctioned by the acts of the twenty-sixth and thi seventh of the King, without any grounds laid before Parliam by which the justice of such deviation could be estimated ; the in a few days, and with no expense, the annual list for the cou ballots returned to the lieutenants of each county, and dire

5

(by the 26th of George the Third, chap. 107, clause 50) to be transmitted to the Secretary of State, would without error have produced a correct scale.

Secondly, Because all militia-men, not arriving (after the enrolment) at their respective regiments at the exact time contained in any order which may be given to them, are declared to be deserters, liable to be taken from service in the militia for five years within the kingdom, and condemned to serve in regiments of the line for life in any part of the world, by sentence of a regimental court martial, where neither the judge nor the witnesses are upon oath; and by an additional injustice the county which paid the service of the man is liable to the further charge of supplying his place

Thirdly, Because the difficulties and embarrassments which men enrolled to serve in the militia are exposed to by this bill are so obviously cruel and unjust, that it affords no slight ground of suspicion that they are intended to promote the recruiting the regular forces from the militia by the forced desertions of the unfortunate individuals who shall be engaged in the militia service; for the man, as soon as he is enrolled, perhaps many hundred miles from his regiment, is ordered to join it, but by this bill no pay is to commence nor allowance to be granted till he actually arrives at his regiment; he is deprived of all former sources of subsistence, and is not entitled to the means of present support; plunder or charity alone can maintain him on the road: and if under all these insurmountable difficulties he does not arrive within the time limited in his orders, he is liable to be treated as a deserter.

Fourthly, Because by this bill the regiments of militia are invited to a state of disorder and mutiny by anticipation, as the bill has publicly declared that desertion before the period of its passing into a law was to be made an offence not necessarily followed by punishment, but that every man may by such desertion take leave of absence till August, if by that time he shall enlist into the regular service. The bill encourages immediate desertion from a service to which the man had sworn fidelity, and the King is empowered to authorize the deserter's entrance into another service, discharged from any claim by the militia regiment to which he belongs.

Fifthly, Because by this bill the most important and incontrovertible principle of the constitution is flagrantly impeached. Whether it is legal or not, to appropriate public money by an order of the Commissioners of the Treasury, and levy money on the land-owners by a similar order, without consent of Parliament, is stated by this bill as a matter of doubt entertained by Parliament; and on the grounds of this pretended doubt, a clause of indemnity is introduced, of which the title of the bill gave no intimation, and to which the attention of the Legislature had not been directed.

In

In the general neglect, overthrow, and denial of private justi[ce]
public principles, and national rights, it is not to be wondered
that little attention should be paid to the feelings of individua[ls]
however called by their country to stations of considerable con[fi]
dence and trust; yet we cannot but express our disapprobati[on]
of the grating directions to commanding officers of militia reg[i]
ments, to crimp for another service their associates and fello[w]
soldiers, and become at once the instruments both of their o[wn]
disgrace, and of that of the militia establishment, to which th[ey]
are zealously attached.

      CARNARVON.
      RADNOR.
      WENTWORTH FITZWILLIAM.

Same Day, the Speaker of the House of Commons appeared at the B[ar]
of the House of Lords, and previous to his Majesty reading [his]
Speech, addressed him in the following Words.

Most gracious Sovereign,

IN the name of the Commons of Great Britain, in Parliame[nt]
assembled, it is my duty humbly to tender to your Majesty t[he]
bills by which their grants are completed for the public service [of]
the year.

The magnitude of the supply, and the cheerfulness with whi[ch]
it has been given, combined with the flourishing state of commer[ce]
and of the revenue, and with the manifestations of zeal and pu[b]
lic spirit which universally prevail, may justly be considered
indications, the most encouraging and decisive, of the unimpai[red]
resources of the British empire, and of the unshaken firmness [of]
your faithful people. To your Commons, it is a subject of pri[de]
and satisfaction to reflect, that in providing for the exigency [of]
the present conjuncture, they have been enabled to adopt a me[a]
sure which, though attended with sacrifices unprecedented in th[eir]
amount, is eminently calculated to administer effectual support [to]
public credit, upon the depreciation and expected failure of whi[ch]
the enemy have long been induced to found the vain hope of d[e]
stroying the liberties and independence of these kingdoms.

The conduct, however, of your Commons has not been inf[lu]
enced by a limited and partial view of the situation and circu[m]
stances of this country, and of the causes which operate upon [its]
welfare and security. They know that its interests are clos[ely]
connected with those of other states; and they have accordin[gly]
conformed to the principles of a sound and enlarged policy,
affording to your Majesty the most ample means of promoting a[nd]
assisting the exertions of those powers, who, justly estimating [the]
danger with which they are threatened, are convinced that a f[ar]
              aggravat[ion]

...tion...uld be the probable confequence of compro-
...e and fupin...is; and that to be fuccefsfully repelled, it muft
...ppofed by fuch efforts as will be fufficient to prove to the enemy
that their fyftem of ambition and conqueft is equally nefarious and
extravagant, and that its objects are unattainable.

Your Commons, Sire, are deeply fenfible of the importance of
the ftake for which your Majefty is ftill unavoidably contending,
and of the duties which they are bound to difcharge. It is, they
are perfuaded, upon the wifdom and fortitude of the Britifh Parliament, that, under the favour of Divine Providence, muft chiefly
depend the prefervation of whatever is truly valuable in civil
fociety, and of all that conftitutes the happinefs of private
life.

Actuated by thefe fentiments, and relying with perfect confidence upon the juftice and moderation of your Majefty's views,
your Commons have not hefitated to continue to your Majefty that
cordial and decided fupport in the profecution of the conteft,
which can alone juftify the hope of concluding it by a fafe and
durable peace.

---

*...e Day, his Majefty came with his ufual Attendance, and delivered
the following Speech in the Houfe of Lords.*

My Lords and Gentlemen,

THE favourable appearances which I announced to you at the
commencement of the prefent feffion, have fince been followed by fucceffes beyond my moft fanguine expectations.

By the progrefs of the Imperial arms, under the command of
the Archduke Charles of Auftria, a great part of Switzerland has
already recovered its ancient religion, laws, and liberties: and the
uninterrupted and brilliant victories of the combined armies under
the command of Field-marfhal Suwarroff, have, in the fhort period
which has elapfed fince the opening of the campaign, nearly accomplifhed the deliverance of Italy from the degrading yoke of
the French republic.

The decifion and energy which diftinguifh the councils of my
ally the Emperor of Ruffia, and the intimate union and concert
happily eftablifhed between us, will enable me to employ, to the
greateft advantage, the powerful means which you have entrufted
to me, for eftablifhing, on permanent grounds, the fecurity and
honour of this country, and the liberty and independence of
Europe.

I have the fatisfaction of feeing, that internal tranquillity is in
fome degree reftored in my kingdom of Ireland.

The removal of the only remaining naval force of the enemy to
a diftant quarter muft nearly extinguifh even the precarious hope
which

which the traitorous and difaffected have entertained of foreign affiftance.

But our great reliance for the immediate fafety of that country muft ftill reft on the experience, zeal, and bravery of my troops of all defcriptions, and on the unfhaken loyalty and voluntary exertions of my faithful fubjects in both kingdoms.

Its ultimate fecurity can alone be enfured by its intimate and entire union with Great Britain; and I am happy to obferve that the fentiments manifefted by numerous and refpectable defcriptions of my Irifh fubjects juftify the hope that the accomplifhment of this great and falutary work will be proved to be as much the joint wifh, as it unqueftionably is the common intereft, of both my kingdoms.

The provifions which you have made for fuppreffing thofe dangerous and feditious focieties which had been formed for the purpofe of diffeminating the deftructive principles of the French revolution, are peculiarly adapted to the circumftances of the times, and have furnifhed additional fecurity to the eftablifhed conftitution.

Gentlemen of the Houfe of Commons,

The unufual facrifices which you have made in the prefent moment, on behalf of my fubjects, are wifely calculated to meet effectually the exigencies of this great crifis. They have, at the fame time, given additional fecurity to public credit, by eftablifhing a fyftem of finance, beneficial alike to yourfelves and to pofterity; and the cheerfulnefs with which thefe heavy burdens are fupported evinces at once the good fenfe, the loyalty, and the public fpirit of my people.

My Lords and Gentlemen,

It is impoffible to compare the events of the prefent year with the ftate and profpects of Europe at the diftance of but a few months, without acknowledging, in humble thankfulnefs, the vifible interpofition of Divine Providence, in averting thofe dangers which fo long threatened the overthrow of all the eftablifhments of the civilized world.

It may be permitted to us to hope that the fame protecting Providence will continue to us its guidance through the remainder of this eventful conteft; and will conduct it finally to fuch an iffue as fhall tranfmit to future ages a memorable example of the inftability of all power founded on injuftice, ufurpation, and impiety; and fhall prove the impoffibility of ultimately diffolving the connexion between public profperity and public virtue.

Then the Lord Chancellor, by his Majefty's command, faid—

My Lords and Gentlemen,

It is his Majefty's royal will and pleafure, that this Parliament be prorogued to Tuefday, the 27th day of Auguft next, to be then here have holden; and this Parliament is accordingly prorogued to Tuesday, the 27th day of August next.

His Majesty's most gracious Speech to both Houses at the Meeting of Parliament on the 24th of September 1799.

My Lords and Gentlemen,

I HAVE called you together at this unusual season, in order to recommend it to you to consider of the propriety of enabling me, without delay, to avail myself, to a further extent, of the voluntary services of the militia, at a moment when the increase of our active force abroad may be productive of the most important and beneficial consequences.

We have seen the happy effects of the measure which you adopted on this subject in the last session; and the forces which I was thereby enabled to employ, have already displayed, in the face of the enemy, a courage, discipline, and steadiness, worthy of the character of British soldiers.

In the short interval since the close of the last session our situation and prospects have, under the blessing of Providence, improved beyond the most sanguine expectation. The abilities and valour of the commanders and troops of the combined Imperial armies have continued to be eminently displayed. The deliverance of Italy may now be considered as secured by the result of a campaign, equal in splendour and success to any of the most brilliant recorded in history; and I have had the heart-felt satisfaction of seeing the valour of my fleets and armies successfully employed to the assistance of my allies, to the support of our just cause, and to the advancement of the most important interests of the British empire.

The kingdom of Naples has been rescued from the French yoke, and restored to the dominion of its lawful sovereign, and my former connexions with that power have been renewed.

The French expedition to Egypt has continued to be productive of calamity and disgrace to our enemies, while its ultimate views against our Eastern possessions have been utterly confounded. The desperate attempt which they have lately made to extricate themselves from their difficulties has been defeated by the courage of the Turkish forces, directed by the skill, and animated by the heroism of a British officer, with a small portion of my naval force under his command; and the overthrow of that restless and perfidious power, who, instigated by the artifices, and deluded by the promises of the French, had entered into their ambitious and destructive projects in India, has placed the British interests in that quarter in a state of solid and permanent security.

The vigilance, decision, and wisdom of the Governor-general

abled them to obstruct our progress, I have the strongest g
expect that the skill of my generals, and the determined re
and intrepidity of my troops, and of those of my allies,
surmount every obstacle; and that the fleet which, u
usurped dominion of France, was destined to co-operate i
vasion of these islands, may speedily, I trust, under its
standard, partake in the glory of restoring the religion, lib
independence of those provinces so long in intimate u
alliance with this country.

While you rejoice with me in the events which add
lustre to the British character, you will, I am persuaded,
dially join in the sentiments so justly due to the condu
good and faithful ally the Emperor of Russia; to his mag
and wisdom directing to so many quarters of Europe the
his extensive and powerful empire, we are, in a great de
debted for the success of our own efforts, as well as for
and favourable change in the general situation of affairs.
directed copies to be laid before you of those engagement
have consolidated and cemented a connexion so consona
permanent interests of my empire, and so important at
sent moment to every part of the civilized world.

Gentlemen of the House of Commons,

The ample supplies which you have granted to me in t'
of the last session, will, I trust, so nearly provide for the e
of the public service, even on the extensive scale which
sent operations require, as to enable me, without furthe
continue those exertions to the close of the present year

benefit would be derived to both countries from that important measure; and I trust that the disposition of my Parliament, there will be found to correspond with that which you have manifested for the accomplishment of a work which would tend so much to add to the security and happiness of all my Irish subjects, and to consolidate the strength and prosperity of the empire.

[An address, which was, as usual, an echo to the Speech, was moved the same day, in the House of Lords, by the Marquis of Buckingham, seconded by Lord Amherst, and agreed to *nem. diff.*

A similar address was moved same day, in the House of Commons, by Mr. Shaw Le Fevre, seconded by Colonel Elford, and agreed to *nem. con.*]

On the 26th of September, in the House of Lords, Lord Grenville gave Notice,

THAT it was his intention to move the thanks of the House to Lord Mornington, and the officers and army under him, to whose important services this country was so much indebted for the glorious termination of the war in India.—Agreed to.

Same Day, in the House of Commons, Mr. Dundas moved,

THAT the thanks of the House be given to General Abercrombie, the officers and army under his command, for their gallant conduct at the Helder; to Admiral Mitchell, and the officers and seamen under his command, for safely conducting the armament to its destination, and the final capture of the Dutch fleet; and to Sir Sidney Smith, for his gallant defence of St. Jean D'Acre:—all which were agreed to, *nem. con.*

Same Day, in the House of Commons, Mr. Dundas made the following Motion.

THAT leave be given to bring in a bill to enable his Majesty to receive an additional aid for the prosecution of the war, by availing himself of the voluntary services of the militia.—Agreed to.

On the 4th of October, in the House of Lords,

ON the motion for the second reading of the Militia Service Extension bill, a debate took place; after which the House divided.—Contents 26.—Non-contents 3.—Majority 23.

The

The following Protest was entered on the Journals against it.

Dissentient,

1st, Because, by this bill, and by the recited act of the last session, whose powers are by this bill aggravated and extended, the constitutional purposes of the militia establishment are totally and finally subverted.

2dly, Because all the purposes of procuring men for the army might have been easily obtained, by disbanding the supplementary war militia (which by its extraordinary increase had confessedly occasioned a scarcity of men, without reducing the permanent militia establishment to a service, in which no gentleman could hereafter hope that his patriotic and disinterested industry would enable him to form his county regiment to a continued state of discipline, at the head of which he might, with credit and honour to himself, answer the purpose of his institution in the defence of his country against invasion.

3dly, Because, by this measure, all that system and arrangement which nourished the zeal of independent country gentlemen is irrecoverably done away in the existing pressure of a formidable and alarming war, and the peace establishment of the militia (if, mangled as it is by this bill, it can survive the war) will necessarily be reduced to a mere standing army of the worst sort: independent of an annual vote of Parliament—deprived of all its former constitutional advantages—connected with the people by nothing but the unequal and oppressive burdens it imposes on them, and commanded by such persons as may be procured to be regulating officers to a mere drill of army recruits.

4thly, Because the landed interest of England and Wales, already so heavily burdened, is most materially affected by this total revolution in the militia system; inasmuch as the peculiar expenses of a militia, originally formed for our unalienable domestic defence and insular garrison, are unjustly continued on the oppressed owners and occupiers of land in England and Wales, when they are by this measure deprived of the advantages which they had purchased, namely, those of security, resulting from a permanent domestic protection for their wives and children, which, under the faith of Parliament, was held out to them as the valuable consideration for heavy taxes imposed solely on them.

5thly, Because this bill operates with most unjustifiable partiality; it does not fairly and equally extend to Scotland: Scotland is still protected in the enjoyment of a constitutional militia; neither reduced to the disgraceful condition of a drill for the army, nor liable to be employed in the defence of England: from its services (confined and limited solely to the boundaries of Scotland), England and Wales can derive no protection, whilst the reduced

remnants

remnants of the militia of England and Wales may be removed from the defence of their own homes, to that of the most remote parts of Scotland.

     CARNARVON.
     WENTWORTH FITZWILLIAM.
All but the second reason.
     BUCKINGHAMSHIRE,

On the 5th of October, Mr. Pitt, in the House of Commons, made the following Motion.

THAT leave be given to bring in a bill to enable his Majesty to assemble Parliament at a short notice in case of its separation by a long adjournment.—Leave given.

On the 11th of October, in the House of Lords, Lord Holland moved the following Address to his Majesty.

THAT an humble address be presented to his Majesty, to return our most humble thanks for the gracious communication of the two treaties which his Majesty, by the advice of his ministers, has been pleased to enter into with his Majesty the Emperor of all the Russias; to express our sincere satisfaction at perceiving that his Majesty has entered into no engagement with the powers at war with France which can lead to an interference with the internal affairs of that country, or preclude the conclusion of peace upon just and equitable terms with the French republic.

That though, considering the unparalleled sacrifices which his Majesty's faithful subjects have already made, and that we are now engaged in the seventh year of an expensive and destructive war, from the calamities of which Russia has been hitherto exempt, we might have expected a more gratuitous exertion of the force of that powerful empire in the common cause; we shall, nevertheless, not fail to concur in such measures as the wisdom of Parliament may suggest for the purpose of meeting the additional and heavy expenses which his Majesty's engagements with the Emperor of all the Russias will necessarily occasion. To assure his Majesty that our anxious desire to maintain his Majesty's personal honour inviolate will induce us also to concur in a legislative provision to enable his Majesty to fulfil the 7th article of the treaty of 22d June 1799, which engages for the maintenance of a body of Russian troops within these kingdoms, upon certain contingencies. But at the same time humbly to represent to his Majesty that we have seen the stipu-
                   lation

lation, above alluded to with the most serious concern and anxi(ety?)
as, from the unprecedented manner in which it has been c(on)
cluded, and in which it has been communicated to this Ho(use?)
there is too much reason to fear that those persons who h(ave?)
advised his Majesty to this measure (and whose conduct in t(his?)
instance we cannot too severely condemn) entertain an opin(ion?)
that a power is vested in the Crown, of introducing and ma(in?)
taining within these kingdoms, a foreign force without the c(on?)
sent or sanction of Parliament; and that we therefore feel o(ur?)
selves particularly called upon to guard against the establishm(ent?)
of such a power, which is totally inconsistent with the anc(ient?)
laws of this realm, and with the security of those indubita(ble?)
rights which our ancestors asserted at the Revolution, and wh(ich?)
we are determined to maintain.

Further to express to his Majesty, that in cheerfully adopti(ng?)
such measures as may be necessary for a vigorous prosecution (of?)
the war, we entertain a confident expectation that his Maje(sty?)
will faithfully adhere to the pledge, which he has so solemn(ly?)
given to this country and to Europe, in his declaration (o)f (the?)
28th of October 1797, and humbly to suggest to his Maje(sty?)
that the present moment seems peculiarly favourable to the ado(p?)
tion of moderate and pacific counsels; when the improved sit(ua?)
tion of affairs, and the successes of his Majesty and his all(ies?)
will give an additional grace and dignity to measures of a c(on?)
ciliatory nature, and when the joint weight of the allies (sin?)
cerely exerted in a fair and honourable negotiation for pe(ace?)
may be expected to produce the happiest effects. That it is (far?)
from the wish or intention of this House to reflect upon any (of?)
his Majesty's allies, or to excite suspicions injurious to t(he?)
sincere and cordial co-operation which is no less essential t(o a?)
successful prosecution of the war than to an effective negotiat(ion?)
for peace. But we cannot conceal from ourselves, nor will (we?)
by an ill-timed flattery, dissemble from his Majesty the dang(er?)
which may result from not endeavouring in time to set on foot a j(oint?)
negotiation for peace, whilst the confederacy against France
remains unbroken. The former events of the present war (suf?)
ficiently prove that Great Britain may be left alone, to supp(ort?)
the whole burden of the contest against a formidable and irrita(ted?)
enemy, notwithstanding the sacrifices she had made for the co(m?)
mon interest, and in defiance of the most solemn engageme(nts?)
not to conclude a peace but by the common consent. We h(ave?)
not learnt that such treaties at present exist with all the pow(ers?)
now engaged in the war: nor have we seen such decisive (and?)
unequivocal symptoms of a perfect union and concert in t(he?)
views and objects as to silence the apprehensions which we (think?)
it our duty to state to his Majesty: that by new concessi(ons?)
which France has such abundant means of making without

diminut(ion?)

tinuation of her incorporated territory; some of the members of the confederacy may be separated from the common cause, and Great Britain again lose the inestimable advantage which now offers of opening a negotiation for peace, supported by the whole weight, authority, and power of her present allies.

That, whilst we are aware that it is neither practicable nor prudent to define the precise terms and conditions upon which peace must ultimately be concluded, which we are sensible must alter with the circumstances of the war, and the different degrees of security, which different situations and the various interests of the powers engaged may require; we conceive nevertheless that it is not only perfectly practicable and safe, but at this moment it would be attended with important advantages, to state what are now the principles which, with the consent and concurrence of his allies, his Majesty would be willing to adopt as the basis of immediate negotiation. At least, we cannot forbear most earnestly to entreat his Majesty to disclaim such views as must render peace with the republic of France utterly unattainable, and the suspicion of which cannot fail to unite the people of that country in a furious zeal and hatred against the British nation, as being engaged in the unjustifiable project of imposing upon them a government, by force, or of dismembering their ancient empire.

Recurring, therefore, to his Majesty's royal declaration of 1797, we humbly beseech his Majesty to reject all such counsels as would lead him to depart from the principles of moderation therein expressed; persuaded that some unequivocal proof of a sincere desire for the re-establishment of peace on just and reasonable grounds would afford the best hope of producing a corresponding disposition in the enemy; or if, contrary to that just expectation, from ambition, from pride, or from a spirit of revenge, such honourable overtures as his Majesty might be advised to make, should be rejected, that it would produce the double advantage of destroying the confidence of the people of France in their present rulers, and of increasing the zeal, energy, and spirit, of all descriptions of his Majesty's faithful subjects, in the necessary prosecution of just and unavoidable hostilities.

[On a division there appeared, for the address, Contents 2, Non-contents 15.]

IRISH PARLIAMENT.

Speech of his Excellency the Lord Lieutenant from the Throne on the 22d of January 1799, at the Meeting of Parliament.

My Lords and Gentlemen,

I HAVE received his Majesty's commands to meet you in Parliament.

I congratulate you on the happy effects which have followed the unparalleled achievement of the detachment of his Majesty's fleet under the command of Rear-admiral Lord Nelson; on the total defeat of the French squadron off the coasts of this kingdom, by that under the command of Sir J. B. Warren; and on the brilliant and important conquest of Minorca. Those events, while they afford to us, in common with every other description of his Majesty's subjects, matter of just pride and satisfaction, must, at the same time, give confidence to other powers, and show to all Europe the beneficial effects of a system of vigour and exertion, directed with manly perseverance against the destructive projects of the common enemy.

I feel much concern in being obliged to acquaint you, that a spirit of disaffection still prevails in several parts of this kingdom, and that the secret agents of the enemy are active in raising an expectation of fresh assistance from France.

In this situation, and under the evident necessity of continuing the war with vigour, his Majesty firmly relies upon that spirit and magnanimity which have hitherto marked all your exertions in support of the honour of his Crown, of the interest of this kingdom, and of the general cause of the empire.

Gentlemen of the House of Commons,

I have ordered the public accounts and estimates to be laid before you; and as I am confident your wisdom will raise the supplies which may be necessary in the manner least burdensome to the subject, so you may depend upon my attention to their prudent and economical application.

It is with great satisfaction I observe, that, notwithstanding our internal calamities, this kingdom, blended as its interests are in the general prosperity of the empire, has participated in the effects of the increasing wealth and commerce of Great Britain, and that our revenues and trade have increased.

My Lords and Gentlemen,

It is my duty to recommend to your attention the various objects of internal regulation which have so long enjoyed the benefit of your protection and support. Your agriculture, your manufactures, and particularly the linen manufacture, the Protestant

charter

charter schools, and other charitable institutions, will require, and will, I am sure, continue to receive that aid and encouragement which they have uniformly experienced from the liberality of Parliament. I am confident you will feel a particular anxiety to give further attention to the just and honourable claims of those who have suffered from their loyalty during the rebellion.

His Majesty depends upon your persevering energy to repress, by every wise effort, the spirit of disaffection, which still requires the exercise of extraordinary powers to check its malignant effects. In recurring, where the occasion has required it, to acts of indispensable severity, I have not been inattentive to the suggestions of mercy, and have endeavoured to mitigate the effects of penal justice, and the necessary exertions of the powers of the state, with as much forbearance and lenity as could be consistent with the public safety.

In the general cause which engages the empire, our prospect is highly encouraging; but in proportion as a successful termination of the war becomes probable, our efforts should be redoubled in order to secure it.

The zeal of his Majesty's regular and militia forces, the gallantry of the yeomanry, the honourable co-operation of the British fencibles and militia, and the activity, skill, and valour of his Majesty's fleets, will, I doubt not, defeat every future effort of the enemy. But the more I have reflected on the situation and circumstances of this kingdom, considering on the one hand the strength and stability of Great Britain, and, on the other, those divisions which have shaken Ireland to its foundations, the more anxious I am for some permanent adjustment which may extend the advantages enjoyed by our sister kingdom to every part of this island."

The unremitting industry with which our enemies persevere in their avowed design of endeavouring to effect a separation of this kingdom from Great Britain, must have engaged your particular attention; and his Majesty commands me to express his anxious hope, that this consideration, joined to the sentiment of mutual affection and common interest, may dispose the Parliaments in both kingdoms to provide the most effectual means of maintaining and improving a connexion, essential to their common security, and of consolidating, as far as possible, into one firm and lasting fabric, the strength, the power, and the resources of the British empire.

Same Day, in the House of Lords, an Address of Thanks, which was, as usual, an Echo to the Speech, was moved by the Earl of Glandore.

LORD Powerscourt proposed an amendment, expressing in substance,

That the House entertained a doubt of the competence ‹
liament to enact an incorporating legiflative union with
Britain; expreffing the ftrongeft attachment to Britifh conn
and promifing to ufe every effort confiftent with the freedc
independence of Parliament to ftrengthen that connexion.

The Earl of Ennifkillen feconded the amendment.

The Earl of Bellamont propofed an amendment to it, by 1
out that part which went to doubt the competence of Parlia
to which Lord Powerfcourt confented.

The Lord Chancellor oppofed the withdrawing of the o
amendment for the purpofe of introducing the propofed alter

On the queftion being put for leave to withdraw the a
ment, there appeared on a divifion—Contents 19.—No
tents 46.—Majority 25.

The amendment was then negatived without a divifion.

Lord Bellamont propofed an amendment to the addrefs, b;
ing out that part which approved of the confolidation of the
and refources of both kingdoms into one firm and lafting
and to infert in its place, " a determination of that H‹
ftrengthen the connexion happily fubfifting between Irelar
Great Britain, as far as it is confiftent with the dignity of
dent tutelary legiflature, eftablifhed and recognifed."

[The queftion being put on this amendment, the Ho1
vided—

  Contents - 16.——Proxy 1.———17
  Non-contents 49.——Proxies 3.———52
      Majority — — 35

The original addrefs was then put and carried, on a di
by a majority of 32.]

Same Day, in the Houfe of Commons,

LORD Tyrone moved a fimilar addrefs, which was fe‹
by Colonel Fitzgerald.

Mr. George Ponfonby propofed an amendment, by intro
the following words in the paffage of the addrefs expreffing :
ingnefs to enter into a confideration of meafures tending t‹
firm the common ftrength of the empire : " maintaining,
ever, the undoubted birthright of the people of Ireland, to
refident and independent legiflature, fuch as was recogni
the Britifh Parliament in 1782, and was finally fettled at t
juftment of all differences between the two countries."

Sir Laurence Parfons feconded the amendment.

The queftion was not put until half paft twelve on Wed:
the 23d, when there appeared for the amendment 105—;
it 106.—On the addrefs for it 107,—Againft it 105.

On the 22th of January, in the House of Commons, on reading the Report of the Address of Thanks for the Speech from the Throne,

SIR Laurence Parsons opposed the paragraph which stated the willingness of the Commons to devise such measures as would tend to consolidate the British empire.

On the question being put, that the paragraph do stand part of the address, the House divided—Ayes, for retaining the paragraph, 106.—Noes, for expunging, 111.—Majority 5.

The question on the address so amended was then put and carried without a division.

On the 28th of January, in the House of Commons, Sir Henry Cavendish moved three Resolutions to the following Effect:

THAT any insult or assault offered to any member of Parliament coming to or going from that House, in consequence of any thing said or done in Parliament, or any attempt to intimidate any member from any vote in that House, or any tumultuous assemblage of persons meeting in the passages to that House to awe or intimidate its members to or from any vote on any measure, is an high infringement on the privileges of that House.

[The resolutions were agreed to.]

On the 15th of February, in the House of Commons, Lord Corry moved,

THAT the House do forthwith resolve itself into a Committee of the whole House, to take into consideration the state of the nation.

[The question being put, there appeared on a division—Ayes 103.—Noes 123.—Majority 20.]

On the 18th of February, in the House of Commons, Mr. Toler, the Attorney General, moved for Leave

TO bring in a bill for the suppression of the rebellion in the kingdom.—[The motion passed *nem. con.*]

Same Day, in the House of Commons, Mr. Fitzgerald, late Prime Serjeant, moved

FOR leave to bring in a bill, to enact, that whenever Providence think fit to submit these kingdoms to the temporary government

ment of a Regent, that the Regent of England should be also Regent of Ireland.—[Leave was given.]

On the 22d of February, in the House of Commons, Mr. Barrington moved,

THAT the proper officer do lay before the House an account of the names of such persons, who having been mentioned in the bill for transporting certain persons therein named out of his Majesty's dominions, and for preventing their return, have been since discharged or otherwise liberated.

Also an account of the names of such persons, who having been convicted of treasonable practices, under the laws of war, since the commencement of the late rebellion, and whose sentences had been confirmed by an act of the last session, have never since been liberated.

[The two motions passed in the affirmative.]

On the 23d of February, in the House of Commons, Mr. Barrington moved

FOR leave to bring in a bill to amend an act passed in the 23d year of his present Majesty, entitled, "An Act for the better securing the Independence of the House of Commons."

The motion was lost by the order of the day, which was moved upon it and carried.

On the 1st of March, in the House of Commons, in the Committee on the Rebellion Bill, Mr. O'Donnel moved the following Amendment.

PROVIDED always, &c. that all general officers or others, to whom his Excellency the Lord Lieutenant shall issue his commission for executing martial law, shall, from time to time, institute courts martial for trial of all persons aiding and assisting to the said rebellion, or of attacking the persons or injuring the properties of his Majesty's loyal subjects for rebellious purposes, which courts martial shall be composed of five or more officers, to be on oath, the majority to decide on the guilt of the accused, and on the punishment to be inflicted. That no person shall be punished by virtue of this act, until previously so tried; and that no persons shall be subject to the penalties herein mentioned for any crime committed previous to the passing of this act.

[This amendment was negatived without a division.]

Same

Same Time and Place Mr. Edgeworth moved the following Amendment:

" THAT the duration of the bill should only be for two months," instead of until the next session of Parliament, and two months after the commencement of the said session.

This amendment was also negatived without a division.

Mr. Dobbs gave Notice of his Intention to propose the following Resolutions in a Committee of the House on the State of the Nation.

THAT all sinecure places be abolished, making compensation to their present possessors.

That no man should hold a seat in Parliament who had held any office created since 1782.

That the Catholics should be wholly emancipated, reserving a Protestant representation in Parliament, until such time as the good conduct of the Catholics should prove that no danger could result from admitting them into Parliament.

That an abolition of tithes should take place.

That a provision should be made for the Roman Catholic bishops and clergy.

On the 29th of March, in the House of Lords, in the Committee on the Rebellion Bill, the Lord Chancellor moved the following Amendment:

TO arrest and take into custody all who shall be engaged or suspected of being engaged in the said rebellion, or in any manner assisting thereto; and to hold trial on the same by court martial in a summary manner, whether taken in open arms, or in any other manner assisting to rebellion.

[The amendment was agreed to.]

His Lordship also moved two other amendments to the following effect, which were also agreed to.

Provided always, that no officer, non-commissioned officer or private, for any thing done in pursuance of this act, shall be subject to the courts of common law; and that they shall be responsible to such courts martial only as by the articles of war they would be liable to, had this bill not been enacted.

Provided always, that nothing herein contained shall militate against the acknowledged prerogatives of the Crown to resort to martial law for the purpose of opposing invasion or rebellion, with or without the advice of a privy council, or other person or persons; and to use that prerogative in same manner as if this act had not been made.

On

On the 2d of April, in the House of Commons, Lord Castlereagh brought down a Message from the Lord Lieutenant, the Substance of which was,

THAT he was commanded by his Majesty to acquaint the House, that his Majesty had received different voluntary offers of service in Great Britain, or any of his Majesty's dominions in Europe, from several Irish militia regiments ; that his Majesty was graciously pleased to express his satisfaction at their zeal and spirited conduct, and desired that the House would make a provision for enabling his Majesty to accept such voluntary offers.

[The message, on the motion of Lord Castlereagh, was ordered to be referred to a Committee.]

On the 18th of April, in the House of Commons, on the Question for receiving the Report of the Regency Bill,

LORD Castlereagh moved that the further consideration of the Report be deferred till the 1st of August, which was carried in the affirmative ; and of course the bill was lost.

His Excellency's Speech to both Houses on the 1st of June 1799, on proroguing the Parliament.

My Lords and Gentlemen,

I HAVE received his Majesty's commands to release you from your further attendance in Parliament, in order that the various parts of the kingdom, which are still agitated by the projects of the disaffected, may reap the advantage of your more immediate vigilance and protection.

I am at the same time to thank you in his Majesty's name, for the continued and undiminished zeal which you have manifested for counteracting the wicked plots of internal conspirators, and for the defeat of every hostile attempt which the desperation of the enemy may meditate.

The situation of affairs on the continent has been materially improved in the period which has elapsed since the commencement of the session. The signal advantages already obtained by the Austrian arms, and the vigorous and decisive exertions on the part of Russia, must be subjects of great joy and congratulation to all who can estimate the value of established order and legitimate government. I know the pleasure you must derive from the consoling prospect that Europe may be ultimately rescued from the ravaging arms and the desolating principles of France.

Gentlemen

Gentlemen of the House of Commons,

I thank you, in his Majesty's name, for the large and extraordinary supply which you have so honourably voted to meet every ⟨...⟩ of the Government, and every exigency of the state. You must reflect with the highest satisfaction on the liberal co-operation which in every moment of difficulty you have experienced from the British Parliament; and I have the fullest confidence that the public spirit of t⟨...⟩ ⟨...⟩ will not be found inferior to that of Great Britain, in su⟨...⟩ ⟨...⟩ such temporary burdens as the safety of the community may require.

I sincerely regret that so extensive a demand should be made on your liberality; but when no measure has been left untried by the malice of our enemies to sever this kingdom from the British empire, and to involve you in all the horrors of rebellion and massacre, you have displayed true wisdom in proportioning your exertions to the blessings you have to preserve, and the miseries you have to avert.

My Lords and Gentlemen,

I am to return you his Majesty's acknowledgments for the many important measures you have accomplished this session. Your liberality and justice to those who have suffered from their loyalty will confirm the exertions of the well-disposed; and your judicious provisions for the regulation of paper currency are calculated to preserve its credit from depreciation without diminishing the necessary circulation.

I am sensible of the confidence which you have reposed in me, by enabling me to exercise the powers of martial law in the manner best adapted to the present circumstances of the country. It will be my care to employ those powers for the purposes for which they were given, by taking the most effectual and summary measures for the suppression and punishment of rebellious proceedings, interfering as little as possible with the ordinary administration of justice among his Majesty's peaceable subjects.

I have his Majesty's particular commands to acquaint you, that a joint address of the two Houses of Parliament of Great Britain has been laid before his Majesty, accompanied by resolutions proposing and recommending a complete and entire union between Great Britain and Ireland, to be established by the mutual consent of the Parliaments, founded on equal and liberal principles, on the similarity of laws, constitution, and government, and on a sense of mutual interests and affections. His Majesty will receive the greatest satisfaction in witnessing the accomplishment of a system, which, by allaying the unhappy distractions too long prevalent in Ireland, and by promoting the security, wealth, and commerce of his respective kingdoms, must afford them at all times, and especially

especially in the present moment, the best means of jointly opposing an effectual resistance to the destructive projects of foreign and domestic enemies; and his Majesty, as the common father of his people, must look forward with earnest anxiety to the moment, when, in conformity to the sentiments, wishes, and real interests of his subjects in Great Britain and Ireland, they may all be inseparably united in the full enjoyment of the blessings of a free constitution, in the support of the honour and dignity of his Majesty's crown, and in the preservation and advancement of the welfare and prosperity of the whole British empire.

I feel most sensibly the arduous situation in which I am placed, and the weight of the trust which his Majesty has imposed upon me at this most important crisis; but if I should be so fortunate as to contribute in the smallest degree to the success of this great measure, I shall think the labours and anxieties of a life devoted to the service of my country amply repaid, and shall retire with the conscious satisfaction that I have had some share in averting from his Majesty's dominions those dangers and calamities which have overspread so large a portion of Europe.

APPENDIX.

APPENDIX.

HISTORY OF THE WAR.

From the LONDON GAZETTE, March 13, 1798.

Admiralty Office, March 13.

Extract of a Letter from Vice-admiral Kingsmill, Commander in Chief of his Majesty's Ships and Vessels on the Coast of Ireland, to Evan Nepean, Esq. dated at Cork the 4th instant.

THE Greyhound captured a Spanish ship, named La Porta de Buenos Ayres, laden with hides and tallow, from Monte Video to Bilboa, which stood into the convoy. She is brought in here by the Magnanime, along with the James of Liverpool, outward-bound Guineaman, which having beaten off one French privateer, had since stood an action of an hour and a half with another; but was captured after losing her master and boatswain, who were killed, and had two seamen wounded; one of whom is since dead. This ship was recaptured by the Magnanime on the 28th ultimo, in latitude 45 deg. 52 min. longitude 11 deg. 7 min.

From the LONDON GAZETTE, March 17, 1798.

Admiralty Office, March 17.

Copy of a Letter from Sir John Borlase Warren, K.B. to Evan Nepean, Esq. dated on board his Majesty's Ship Canada, Isle Dieu, March 8.

Sir,

I TAKE the liberty of acquainting you, that this morning a convoy of the enemy was discovered within Isle Dieu, to whom I immediately gave chase with his Majesty's ships under my orders; but the breeze dying away, I made the signal for the boats of my squadron to chase, and I have the satisfaction to inform you, that the vessels mentioned on the enclosed list were captured by them. A schooner gun-vessel and an armed lugger escaped into the Fromentine passage, near the island of Normentier.

Two of the prizes are numbered, and laden with naval stores for the armament equipping at Brest for the intended expedition against England; the rest have wine and brandy for their cargoes, and were bound from Rochefort to the above port.

I have the honour to remain, Sir,
Your most obedient humble servant,
JOHN WARREN.

A List of Vessels captured by the Squadron under the Orders of Sir Jo. Borlase Warren, Bart. K. B.

Two brigs, from Rochefort, bound to Brest, numbered, and lade with naval stores as transports. Five brigs, from ditto to ditto, laden with wine and brandy. Three chasse marées, from ditto to ditto, laden with wine and brandy. A chasse marée, from ditto to ditto, laden with ditto, burnt, being on shore.

(Signed)   JOHN WARREN.

From the LONDON GAZETTE, March 20, 1798.

Admiralty Office, March 20.

Extract of a Letter from Admiral Sir Peter Parker, Bart. Commander in Chief of his Majesty's Ships and Vessels at Portsmouth and Spithead, to Evan Nepean, Esq. dated the 17th instant.

THE Telemachus cutter arrived this morning from Dartmouth. In her way to Spithead she captured La Sophie, a French cutter privateer, of four guns, and twenty men, as reported in the enclosed letter from Lieutenant Newton.

Sir,   *Telemachus, at Spithead, March 17.*

I HAVE the pleasure of acquainting you, that yesterday, at three o'clock in the afternoon, three miles from the Berry Head, I fell in with and gave chase to a cutter. At nine o'clock, two or three leagues to the northward of the Caskets lights, I came up and captured her. She is called La Sophie, French cutter privateer, of four guns and twenty men belonging to St. Maloes; had been from that place two days, and has taken nothing. I am happy to say, that she was prevented from taking three English brigs that were very near her when I gave chase. At half past seven his Majesty's brig Sea Gull joined in the chase, and was in sight when I captured her.

I have the honour to be, &c. &c. &c.

Admiral Sir Peter Paker, Bart.   THO. NEWTON.

From the LONDON GAZETTE, March 31, 1798.

Admiralty Office, March 31.

Copy of a Letter from Admiral the Earl of St. Vincent, Commander in Chief of his Majesty's Ships and Vessels on the Coast of Portugal, to Evan Nepean, Esq. dated on board the Ville de Paris, at Sea, the 21 February.

Sir,

YOU will herewith receive letters from Captain Lord Henry Powle of his Majesty's ship the Thalia, and Captain Downman, of the Speedy sloop; the first giving an account of the capture of a French privateer, and the latter detailing an action between the Speedy and another of the enemy's privateers, which does great honour to her captain, officers, and company.   I am, &c.

ST. VINCENT.

Sir, *Thalia, at Sea, February 6.*

ON the 5th instant, at four A. M. Cape Finisterre bearing S. W. seventy leagues, I came up with and captured the Antoine French privateer brig, mounting sixteen guns and having seventy men. She was returning from a cruise to Rochelle, having captured five neutral vessels.

I remain, Sir, &c. &c. &c.

H. POWLETT.

My Lord, *Speedy, Tagus, Feb. 16.*

I HAVE the honour to acquaint you, that on the 3d instant, at daylight, being seventeen leagues west of Vigo, we discovered a brig bearing down on us with all sail set. At three P. M. being within half a mile of us, she hauled her wind, and opened her fire; on which we made all sail to close, engaging her until half past five, when she tacked, and made sail from us. I immediately tacked, continuing to engage till half past seven, when, from her advantage of sailing and little wind, she got out of gun-shot. Owing to the great swell, we received little damage, having only our fore-topmast shot through, with some of the running rigging cut. It falling calm, and the vessels separating against all our efforts with the sweeps, I had the mortification, about twelve o'clock, to see her fire several guns at our prize that we had taken the day before. Owing to the good conduct of the master, who, with twelve men, were on board the prize, battened down twenty-six Spaniards, and made their escape in a small boat. At daylight a breeze of wind sprung up, which enabled us to fetch her. At eight o'clock she, being within gun-shot, tacked, and made all sail from us, rowing with her sweeps at the same time. We chased her until noon, when they finding she had the heels of us, shortened sail, wore, and stood towards us, with a red flag flying at the main-topgallant-mast head. At half past twelve, being within pistol-shot, we began to engage her, with the wind upon the larboard quarter. At two, observing her fire to slacken, I thought it a good opportunity to lay her on board, but at that instant she wore, and came to the wind on the starboard tack; but finding us close upon her starboard quarter, and from our braces and bow-lines being shot away, our yard coming square, she took the opportunity to put before the wind, and made all sail from us. We immediately wore after her, firing musquetry at each other for twenty minutes, and so soon as the lower mast was secured, set our studding-sails, and continued the chase until seven P. M. when we lost sight of her, from her superior sailing. I then hauled our wind, and made short tacks all night to fall in with our prize; at daylight saw her to windward; at ten P. M. retook her, with ten Frenchmen on board. I learn from the prize-master, the brig is called the Pappilon, 360 tons burden, pierced for eighteen guns, mounting fourteen, four twelve and ten nine pounders, manned with 160 men. We had five men killed, and four badly wounded. I have to regret the loss of Lieutenant Dutton and Mr. Johnston, boatswain, amongst the killed. I beg leave to recommend to your Lordship's notice Mr. Marshall, master, for his good conduct during the action. Every praise is due to the ship's company for their good behaviour. All our lower masts, bowsprit, main boom, both topmasts, and most of the yards shot through, with all the standing and running rigging cut, I thought proper to put into Lisbon to repair our damage. I have, &c.

HUGH DOWNMAN.

Copy of another Letter from Admiral the Earl St. Vincent, K. B. to Evan Nepean, Esq. dated in the Tagus, March 3.

Sir,

I ENCLOSE a letter from Captain Waller, of his Majesty's ship the Emerald, acquainting me of his having captured Le Chasseur Barke privateer, of sixteen guns, on the 12th ultimo.

I am, &c. ST. VINCENT.

My Lord, *Emerald, at Sea, Feb. 13.*

I BEG leave to acquaint you, that last night, nearly in lat. 38 deg. 14 min. N. and long. 14 deg. 66 min. W. we captured a French privateer Le Chasseur Barque, belonging to Bayonne, a brig pierced for sixteen guns, but mounts only eight, and seventy-two men; she had been out a month, and had not taken any thing. I beg also to inform your Lordship, that on the 10th I chased another French brig privateer for thirty-six hours, without being able to come up with her, owing to light winds. I have, &c.

T. M. WALLER.

Extract of a Letter from Vice-admiral Sir Richard Onslow, Bart. to Evan Nepean, Esq. dated on board his Majesty's Ship Monarch, Yarmouth Roads, March 30.

BE pleased to acquaint my Lords Commissioners of the Admiralty, that his Majesty's sloop Echo arrived here yesterday afternoon, having, on the 23d instant, driven on shore to the northward of Camperdown, and destroyed, a French cutter privateer, mounting ten guns.

Sir, *His Majesty's Ship Apollo, off the Texel, March 27.*

ON the 23d instant his Majesty's sloop Echo, being on the look ahead, discovered a cutter, which she immediately chased, and soon caused to run on shore a few miles to the northward of Camperdown; the boats of the squadron were sent to endeavour to get her off, but owing to the surf, and the lateness of the evening, could not effect it; she was therefore destroyed. The crew quitted her at the approach of the boats. She mounted ten guns, and by papers found on board, she appears to have sailed from Dunkirk. I am, &c.

Vice-admiral Sir Richard Onslow, Bart. P. HALKETT.

Extract of a Letter from Captain Wallis, Commander of his Majesty's Ship Proserpine, to Vice-admiral Sir Richard Onslow, Bart. dated Yarmouth Roads, the 29th of March.

I HAVE the honour to inform you, that his Majesty's ship under my command anchored here this evening. On Monday morning last, St. Abb's Head bearing S. W. twelve or fourteen leagues, I fell in with a Dutch galliot, bound from Rotterdam to Altona; ten days out. Finding him close on wind, which was then at N. W. by W. I was well assured he could not be bound to Altona, and have an idea that he was bound north about to France; and having neither brief, register, or any paper to warrant his being on the coast of Scotland, I have thought proper to bring him in here: he now says he was bound to Montrose, and that he promised an Englishman at Rotterdam to carry the cargo there; he has no paper of any kind to show any such transaction. The vessel was built

in

in Holland laſt year, and the maſter of her ſays ſhe belongs to himſelf and a gentleman at Limbourg. He (the maſter) has been a priſoner in England eighteen months of this war, and was taken commanding a Dutch veſſel. He and his ſhip's company are all natives of Holland. Under theſe circumſtances I have no doubt but both the veſſel and cargo ought to be condemned.

Extract of a Letter from Captain Sir John Borlaſe Warren, K. B. Captain of his Majeſty's Ship Canada, to Evan Nepean, Eſq. dated Portius d'Antioche, the 14th of March.

I BEG leave to inform you, that on the night of the 13th inſtant I ſtood into the Portius d'Antioche, with his Majeſty's ſhips under my orders, and anchored near Baſque Road; and have the ſatisfaction of acquainting you that the boats of the ſquadron captured the veſſels mentioned in the liſt which accompanies this letter.

A Liſt of Veſſels belonging to the French Republic, captured by the Squadron under the Orders of Commodore Sir John Borlaſe Warren, K. B. in the Portius d'Antioche, on the 14th of March.

Brig L'Eſperance, from Bourdeaux, bound to Nantz, laden with brandy, wine, &c. &c.
Brig Heureux Succes, from Bourdeaux to Rochfort, laden with ditto.
Brig Martin Marie, from ditto to ditto, laden with ditto.
Brig St. Etienne, from ditto to ditto, laden with ditto.
Brig La Virginie, from ditto to ditto, laden with ditto.
Chaſſe marée St. Juliana, from ditto to ditto, laden with ditto.
Chaſſe marée, from ditto to ditto, laden with ditto.
Chaſſe marée, from ditto to ditto, laden with ditto.
Chaſſe marée, from ditto to ditto, laden with ditto.

(Signed)   JOHN WARREN.

From the LONDON GAZETTE, April 3, 1798.

Admiralty Office, April 2.

A Letter, of which the following is a Copy, from Captain Sir J. B. Warren, of his Majeſty's Ship Canada, to Admiral Lord Bridport, K. B. Commander in Chief, &c. &c. has been received at this Office.

My Lord,   *Canada, Plymouth Sound, March 30.*

I BEG leave to inform your Lordſhip, that on the 22d inſtant, at ſeven A. M. the Anſon having diſcovered a ſail in the eaſt quarter, which appeared a large frigate, I made the ſignal for a general chaſe, and continued the purſuit, with variable winds, until half paſt twelve at midnight, when Captain Stopford, in the Phaeton, brought her to action. The enemy endeavoured to eſcape into the river Garonne, but ſtruck upon the Olive Rocks, near the Cordovan light-houſe; ſhe was left by moſt of her crew, who had previouſly thrown her guns overboard. The ſhip being bilged, and having otherwiſe ſuffered much, it is probable, from the ſituation ſhe remained in, it will not be eaſy to get her off.

I have the honour to be, my Lord,
Your Lordſhip's moſt obedient humble ſervant,
JOHN WARREN.

Admiralty

Admiralty Office, April 3.

Copy of a Letter from Vice-admiral Sir Hyde Parker, Knt. Commander in Chief of his Majesty's Ships and Vessels at Jamaica, to Evan Nepean, Esq. dated on board the Queen, in Port Royal Harbour, the 6th January.

Sir,

HAVING yesterday received a letter from Captain Ricketts, of his Majesty's ship Magicienne, giving an account of his having, with the ships under his command, attacked and captured the vessels therein mentioned, in Guadilla Bay in the island of Porto Rico, and under the protection of the enemy's forts, I transmit herewith a copy of the said letter, for the information of the Right Honourable the Lords Commissioners of the Admiralty, who I am confident will, with me, highly approve of his gallant conduct, as well as that of the captains, officers, seamen, and marines, under his command.

I am, &c.

H. PARKER.

Sir, *La Magicienne, off the Isle of Zacha, December 28, 1797.*

HAVING received information that several brigs and schooners, belonging to the enemy, were in Guadilla Bay, in the island of Porto Rico, I proceeded there with the King's ships named in the margin *. On the 27th, at noon, we anchored close abreast of the forts; and after an hour and a half cannonading, captured every vessel under their protection. To Captain Carthew I am indebted, for the gallant and able support that I on this occasion met with (as well as upon many others since the Regulus has been under my orders). Captain Mends, who commanded the boats that took possession of the vessels, executed that service much to his own honour, and highly to my approbation. Indeed, every officer and man belonging to the squadron is fully entitled to my best thanks and praises. I have the honour to be, Sir,

Your most obedient humble servant,

W. H. RICKETTS.

La Magicienne, 5 wounded.
Regulus, none killed or wounded.
Diligence, 1 wounded.

Vessels captured in Guadilla Bay.

Le Brutus privateer of 9 guns.
One ship.
One schooner.

Vice-admiral Sir Hyde Parker,
Commander in Chief, &c. &c.

Extract of another Letter from Vice-admiral Sir Hyde Parker, Knt. to Evan Nepean, Esq. dated on board his Majesty's Ship Queen, in Port Royal Harbour, the 1st of January.

I AM to desire you will be pleased to acquaint the Right Honourable the Lords Commissioners of the Admiralty, that, since my letter of the

---

* La Magicienne, Regulus, Diligence.

29th October, the French corvette La Republique Triomphante, of 14 guns and 110 men, has been captured by his Majesty's ships Severn and Pelican.

From the LONDON GAZETTE, April 10, 1798.

Admiralty Office, April 10.

Extract of a Letter from Captain Gunter, of his Majesty's Sloop Nautilus, to Evan Nepean, Esq. dated at Sea, April 4.

I BEG you will be pleased to acquaint the Lords Commissioners of the Admiralty, that at noon this day, twelve leagues to the eastward of Scarborough, with the convoy and Narcissus cutter in company, I fell in with two French privateers, a brig and schooner; and after a chase of six hours, I came up with and captured the brig, which proves to be the Legere, three days from Dunkirk, with ten guns on board, pierced for sixteen, and sixty men. On my getting near them they parted; when I made the Narcissus' signal to chase the schooner, but without success, as she escaped by superior sailing.

Extract of a Letter from Sir Edward Pellew, Captain of his Majesty's Ship Indefatigable, to Evan Nepean, Esq. dated Falmouth, April 7.

I HAVE the honour to inform you, that his Majesty's ship Cleopatra arrived here this day. By the enclosed letter from Captain Pellew, their Lordships will be informed of his having captured L'Emilie, of 16 guns and 110 men.

Sir,   *Cleopatra, Falmouth, April 6.*

I HAVE to request you will inform the Right Honourable the Lords Commissioners of the Admiralty, that after separation from Sir Edward Pellew, agreeable to his orders, I had the good fortune, on the 26th ult. at half past two in the morning, to discover a ship standing to the northward, and immediately gave chase, and in an hour and a half came alongside, and after giving her all our larboard guns, she struck, and proved to be the Emilie, French ship privateer, en razée; a very fast sailer, from L'Orient, mounting 16 six-pounders and 2 brass twelves, manned with 110 men, out thirty-nine days.

I have the honour to be, &c.

To Sir Edward Pellew, Bart. &c. &c.   ISRAEL PELLEW.

Copy of a Letter from Captain Sir Edward Pellew, Bart. of his Majesty's Ship Indefatigable, to Evan Nepean, Esq. dated Falmouth, April 5.

I HAVE the honour to inform you that his Majesty's ship Cambrian anchored in this port to-day, blown in by the late gales.

I have the pleasure to enclose a letter from Captain Legge, giving an account of his having captured two privateers, and retaken an American ship.

Sir,   *Cambrian, at Sea, March 27.*

I HAVE the honour to inform you, that I have this day captured Le Cæsar, a French ship privateer of 16 guns and 80 men, belonging to St. Maloes, and fifty-five days from Brest.

On

On the 21ft, in company with his Majesty's ship Cleopatra, I recaptured the William Penn, of Philadelphia.
Sir Edward Pellew, Bart. I remain, &c.
&c. &c. &c. ARTHUR K. LEGGE.

Sir, *Cambrian, at Sea, March 30.*
I HAVE the honour to inform you that I have this day captured Le Pont de Lode, French ship privateer, of 16 guns and 102 men: she was five days from Bourdeaux, on her first cruise (being quite a new vessel), and had not taken any thing. I remain, Sir, &c.
Sir Edward Pellew, Bart. &c.&c.&c. ARTHUR K. LEGGE.

Prince of Wales, Carlisle Bay, Barbadoes, Dec. 15, 1797.
I HAVE to acquaint you, for the information of their Lordships, that Captain Weston, in his Majesty's ship Tamer, has captured the undermentioned privateers, belonging to Guadaloupe, and sent them into this Bay. The first was taken the 4th instant, the latter the 7th, a few leagues to windward of Barbadoes.

Le Dragon schooner, of 12 guns and 80 men.
Le Dix-huit de Fructidor sloop, of 10 guns and 73 men.

These vessels are fast sailers, and well equipped; the former had taken an American brig, which was recaptured by the Tamer: the latter had been out five days, and taken nothing.
I have the honour to be, &c.
Evan Nepean, Esq. HENRY HARVEY.

Sir, *Prince of Wales, Fort Royal Bay, Martinique, Jan. 4.*
I AM to acquaint you, for the information of their Lordships, that Captain Totty, in his Majesty's ship Alfred, captured the 16th ultimo, off Martinique, La Decidée French privateer schooner, belonging to Guadaloupe, of 10 guns and 89 men, which he sent to this bay. She had been out three days, but had not taken any thing.
I have the honour to be, &c.
Evan Nepean, Esq. HENRY HARVEY.

Sir, *Prince of Wales, Fort Royal Bay, Martinique, Feb. 9.*
I HEREWITH enclose, for the information of their Lordships, a letter addressed to me from Captain Mainwaring, of his Majesty's ship La Babet, relative to the capture of the French privateer schooner La Desirée, by the boats of that ship, under the direction of Lieutenant Samuel Pym, who performed the service with great gallantry and good conduct. I have the honour to be, &c.
Evan Nepean, Esq. HENRY HARVEY.

Sir, *His Majesty's Ship Babet, off Fort Royal Bay, Martinique, Jan. 17.*
IT is with great pleasure I acquaint you that Lieutenant Pym, of his Majesty's ship under my command, yesterday afternoon captured (in the pinnace, the launch following), after a most desperate resistance, the French republican schooner La Desirée, mounting six carriage guns, and having on board forty-six men. I discovered her in the morning, half way between Martinique and Dominique, standing towards me; soon after the wind died away, and she, having made us out distinctly, took

to her sweeps, rowed off, which Lieutenant Pym observing, in the handsomest manner volunteered attacking her in the boats. To this I alone consented from the knowledge I had of his resolution and good conduct on former occasions. I hope you will be of opinion that he merited the confidence placed in him, with every encomium I can bestow, when you know that the two boats contained but twenty-four men, that he was three leagues from the ship, and had been rowing four hours before he got within reach of their cannon, from which they kept up an incessant firing till he boarded. He reports that the officers and men under him behaved with the greatest coolness and intrepidity. I am sorry to add that we lost a very valuable seaman, and had five wounded; amongst the latter a Mr. Aslinhurst, a young gentleman of very promising expectations, and a volunteer on this occasion. The enemy had three killed and fifteen badly wounded. She had been out six days from Guadaloupe, had taken one American brig from St. Vincent bound to Boston. I have the honour to be, &c. &c. &c.
Henry Hervey, Esq. Rear-admiral   JEM. MAINWARING.
of the Red, &c. &c. &c.

   Sir,   *Prince of Wales, Fort Royal Bay, Martinique, Feb.* 19.
I AM to acquaint you, for the information of their Lordships, that his Majesty's ship Matilda, Captain Mitford, captured the 12th ult. off Antigua, La Ceres, a French ship privateer, pierced for 14 guns, mounting only two, bound to Guadaloupe from St. Bartholomew's, for her further equipment, with a cargo of pitch and tar, completely furnished, except in men and guns, having only 45 of the former on board when taken.
   You will also be pleased to acquaint their Lordships, that his Majesty's sloop Zephyr, Captain Champion, captured, the 8th instant, off Deseada, L'Espoire, French privateer sloop, belonging to Guadaloupe, of eight guns and 66 men: she had been out sixteen days, but had not made any captures.   I have the honour to be, &c.
                                      HENRY HARVEY.

   Sir,   *Prince of Wales, Fort Royal Bay, Martinique, Feb.* 19.
I HAVE the pleasure to acquaint you, for the information of their Lordships, that his Majesty's ship Alfred, Captain Totty, on the 16th instant, captured, off Guadaloupe, Le Scipion French national corvette of 20 guns and 160 men: she was taken near the Road of Basse Terre, within fire of the enemies' batteries, which they opened on the Alfred, both with shot and shells; but by the exertions and good conduct of Captain Totty she was brought off, and without any damage to the ships.
   This corvette has been for a considerable time about these islands, and a very active cruiser, to the great annoyance of our trade.
                     I have the honour to be, &c.
                                      HENRY HARVEY.

   Sir,   *Prince of Wales, Fort Royal Bay, Martinique, Feb.* 9.
I HAVE to acquaint you, for the information of their Lordships, that the undermentioned French privateers, belonging to Guadaloupe, have been captured and sent into different islands, at the periods, and by the ships and vessels of his Majesty's squadron under my command, as

against their several names expressed, and I have the pleasure to add without having made any captures.

By La Concorde, Captain Barton, January 3, 1798, off St. Bartholomew's, La Caye du Pont schooner, of 16 guns and 129 men; sailed from Guadaloupe the 1st, with troops, for St. Martin's and St. Eustatia.— January 8, 1798, off Montserrat, La Proserpine schooner, of eight guns and 82 men.

By the Lapwing, Captain Harvey, January 9, off Martinique, L'Intrique sloop, of six guns and 64 men.

By the Alfred, Captain Totty, January 20, 1798, to windward of Dominica, La Rencontre sloop, of six guns and 49 men.

By the Amphitrite, Captain Ekins, February 2, 1798, off St. Lucia, Le Battreu republican sloop, of four guns and 38 men.

Four small row-boats, armed with swivels, have likewise been captured under the island, by the several cruisers, and sent into port.

I have the honour, &c. &c.
(Signed)   HENRY HARVEY.

Evan Nepean, Esq.

Admiralty Office, April 10.

Copy of another Letter from Rear-admiral Harvey, to Evan Nepean, Esq. dated on board the Prince of Wales, Fort Royal Bay, Martinique, the 9th of February.

Sir,

ENCLOSED is an account of recaptured merchant-vessels by the ships of his Majesty's squadron under my command, as against their respective names expressed, between the 4th December last and the date hereof; also an account of vessels detained under neutral colours, and libelled in the Court of Admiralty for the causes stated in the said account during the said period.

I have the honour to be, &c.
HENRY HARVEY.

An Account of Merchant Ships and Vessels captured and recaptured, likewise such as have been detained under neutral Colours, by his Majesty's Ships and Vessels, respectively expressed against their Names, under the Command of Henry Harvey, Esq. Rear-admiral of the Red, Commander in Chief, &c. &c. Leeward Island Station, between the 6th December 1797, and the 9th February 1798.

Schooner Amazon, 90 tons, from Baltimore to Surinam, laden with provisions; detained by the Scourge, December 4th, 1797, to the windward of Dominica, and sent to St. Pierre, Martinique.—Taken by the Hannibal French privateer.

Brig Vulture, 170 tons, 8 men, S. Walton owner, from Boston to Grenada, laden with lumber; detained by the Tamer, December 2, 1797, off Barbadoes, and sent to Barbadoes—being in possession of a French privateer.

Ship Henry, 161 tons, 12 men, J. Treadwell owner, from Surinam to Rhode Island, laden with sugar and coffee; detained by the Lapwing, November 30, 1797, off St. Bartholomew's, and sent to St. Kitt's— being Dutch property.

Brig Blossom, 110 tons, 3 men, from Portsmouth, New Hampshire,

shire, for a market, laden with beef, pork, fish, &c. detained by the Vengeance, December 10, 1797, off Basse Terre, Guadaloupe; sent to Roseau, Dominica—having been taken by a French privateer.

Schooner La Prudence, 35 tons, 8 men, Courtney and Badie owners; bound to the windward ports in Martinique, laden with provisions, pottery, and timber; detained by the Alfred, December 18, 1797, off St. Pierre, Martinique; sent to Fort Royal, Martinique. Recaptured.

Sloop Stirling, 70 tons, 6 men; from Guadaloupe to St. Bartholomew; laden with bread: detained by the Invincible, November 29, 1797, off Guadaloupe, and sent to St. Pierre, Martinique. No register.

Ship Williamson, 229 tons, 12 men, 2 guns, Kelly and Leishman owners; from London to Martinique; laden with army provisions: detained by the Zephyr, January 1, 1798, windward of Mariegalante; sent to Fort Royal, Martinique. Recaptured, having been taken by a French privateer.

Ship Granville, 300 tons, 15 men, 6 guns, J. Maland owner; from London to Martinique; laden with horses, mules, asses, &c. detained by the Alfred, December 30, 1797, windward of Mariegalante; sent to Fort Royal, Martinique. Recaptured, having been taken by a French privateer.

Ship Brazillie, 289 tons, 18 men, 6 guns, J. Mills and G. Trattle owners; from Portsmouth to Martinique; laden with provisions: detained by the Alfred, January 8, 1798, windward of Mariegalante; sent to Fort Royal, Martinique. Recaptured, having been taken by a French privateer.

Ship Intrepid, 240 tons, 16 men, 4 guns, T. Critico owner; from Guadaloupe to Korigno, Italy; laden with sugar and coffee: detained by the Lapwing, December 25, 1797, off St. Bartholomew's; sent to St. Kitt's. English ship, condemned at Guadaloupe; cargo supposed to be French property.

Ship Sea Nymph, 303 tons, 19 men, 8 guns, R. M'Burny; from London to Martinique; laden with provisions for the army: detained by the Invincible, January 3, 1798, in lat. 14 deg. 6 min. N. long. 59 deg. 30 min. W.: sent to Martinique, having been captured by a French privateer.

Snow Neptune, 240 tons, 10 men, 4 guns, Fisher and Co. owners; from Dublin to Barbadoes and Martinique: detained by the Concord, January 14, 1798, off Deseada; sent to St. Kitt's, having been captured by a French privateer.

Schooner Union, 80 tons, 4 men; from Point Petre to St. Bartholomew, in ballast: detained by the Vengeance, January 16, 1798, off Point Vieux, Guadaloupe; sent to Roseau, Dominica, having no register, and being French property.

Schooner Columbus, 113 tons; from Point Petre to Baltimore; laden with cotton, &c. detained by the Zephyr, January 20, 1798, off Montserrat; sent to Roseau, Dominica; supposed to be French property.

HENRY HARVEY.

Admiralty Office, April 10.

Copy of a Letter from Admiral Earl St. Vincent to Evan Nepean, Esq. Secretary of the Admiralty, dated Ville de Paris, in the Tagus, March 9.

Sir,

I ENCLOSE a letter from Lord Henry Paulett, captain of his Majesty's ship Thalia, acquainting me with his having captured a brig and schooner, Spanish privateers: another from Captain Hood, of the Zealous, giving an account of his taking the Dragon (formerly a French frigate), from Buenos Ayres, with a valuable cargo; and I desire you will acquaint the Lords Commissioners of the Admiralty, that El Pid, a ship with a similar lading, which sailed in company with the last-mentioned, was captured, on the 20th ult. by Lieutenant Worth, of his Majesty's hired cutter the Stag.

I am, Sir,
Your most obedient humble servant,
ST. VINCENT.

My Lord, *Thalia, March* 6.

I HAVE the honour to inform you, that on the 27th of February, being forty leagues N. W. of Lisbon, after a chase of six hours, I captured the Spanish schooner San Joseph, mounting six guns and ten swivels, with 40 men on board: she sailed from Villa Nuova the 15th of February, and had taken nothing. And on the 4th of March, at sun-rise, being off the Rock of Lisbon, I discovered a brig in shore, which I gave chase to, and at nine o'clock arrived up with her, when she proved to be the Victoria Spanish brig, of 14 guns and ten swivels; she took an English brig in ballast the day before, off St. Ube's, and sent her into that port.

I am, &c.
H. PAULETT.

To the Right Hon. Earl St. Vincent,
&c. &c.

My Lord, *Zealous, off the Tagus, 5th of March.*

I LOST sight of the Culloden on the 27th ult. off Cape St. Vincent, by chasing a cutter to the N. W. The following day, standing to the southward, a sail was discovered west by south: on the 1st instant made her sail out to be suspicious; in the evening it became almost calm, and a possibility of her escape, if it came on bad weather or foggy. I sent the launch and barge, with the first and second lieutenants of the Zealous, towards her, she having, before dark, hoisted Spanish colours. By the judicious attack of the boats in the night, they obliged her to strike before the Zealous came within shot. She proved to be a Spanish merchant-ship, named the Dragon, of 600 tons, eight guns, and 45 men, four months from Monte Video, for Cadiz, with a valuable cargo. Her being a bad sailer, and the wind holding to the east, I thought it my duty to see her safe to the Bar of Lisbon.

SAM. HOOD.

Earl St. Vincent.

Admiralty Office, April 10.

Copy of a Letter from Admiral Earl St. Vincent, Commander in Chief of his Majesty's Ships and Vessels employed on the Coast of Portugal, to Evan Nepean, Esq. dated on board the Ville de Paris, in the Tagus, the 22d March.

Sir,

I ENCLOSE, for the information of the Lords Commissioners of the Admiralty, letters from the commanders of his Majesty's sloops Speedy and King's Fisher, acquainting me with their farther success, in capturing, separately, two of the enemy's privateers, Le Lynx, a French ship, pierced for 18 guns, by the latter; and San José Spanish lugger, by the former. I am, &c.

ST. VINCENT.

My Lord, *Speedy, River Tagus, March* 18.

I HAVE the honour to acquaint you, that his Majesty's sloop Speedy captured, on the 15th instant, twenty leagues west of Cape Mondego, the St. Jozé, alias El Gavelan, Spanish lugger privateer, of six carriage guns and 44 men, out from Vigo three days; not made any captures.

I have the honour to be, &c.

Right Hon. Admiral Earl St. Vincent, H. DOWNMAN.
K. B.

My Lord, *King's Fisher, in the Tagus, March* 18.

I HAVE the honour to inform your Lordship, that on the 15th instant, Oporto bearing S. E. by E. distant 40 leagues, I fell in with, and, after a chase of three hours, captured Le Lynx, copper-bottomed ship privateer, pierced for 18, but mounting only ten guns, four-pounders, and 70 men: she had been six days from Rochelle, but had not made any capture.

I have the honour to be, &c.

CHA. H. PIERREPONT.

Right Hon. Admiral Earl St. Vincent,
K. B.

From the LONDON GAZETTE, April 14, 1798.

Admiralty Office, April 14.

Copy of a Letter from Vice-admiral Kingsmill, Commander in Chief of his Majesty's Ships and Vessels on the Coast of Ireland, to Evan Nepean, Esq. dated Cove of Cork, the 6th instant.

Sir,

I HEREWITH transmit, for the information of my Lords Commissioners of the Admiralty, a letter to me from the Hon. Captain De Courcy, of his Majesty's ship Magnanime, containing particulars of the capture of two French privateers.

I have the honour to be, &c.

R. KINGSMILL.

Sir,

Sir, *Magnanime, Cork Harbour, April* 6.

I AVAIL myself of the earliest means of acquainting you, that when the service assigned to me by your order of the 6th of March had been nearly accomplished, chase was given by his Majesty's ship under my command to a French privateer brig, which, at the distance of about five miles, was, on the dawn of the 16th of the same month, observed to haul athwart the fore-foot of the little convoy submitted to my guidance.

The gale being fresh, and favourable to the Magnanime's best sailing, it was trusted she would very speedily arrive up with the object of pursuit; but that end was not attained till, at the expiration of twenty-four hours, a space had been run of 256 miles, although the privateer had, in her flight, given a very manifest advantage, by steering in a circuitous manner.

The satisfaction of capturing so fast-sailing a privateer has been much increased by a knowledge, subsequently obtained, of its having been the design of her commander, in a confidence of his vessel's unrivalled sailing, to hover round the convoy till a favourable moment should occur for attacking its least protected part. The privateer is named L'Eugenie, was captured in latitude 42 and longitude 12; was manned, when chased, with 107 men, and armed with 18 guns, eight of which appear to have been thrown overboard, whilst pressed in the pursuit.

Under similar circumstances of wind and weather, pursuit was again given, by the ship under my command, to a ship which reconnoitred us, early on the morning of the 1st of April.

The chase was continued with doubtful effect for some time, when at length, after a pursuit of 180 miles, in eighteen hours, she made a signal of surrendering. Her force consisted of 20 guns (but pierced for 22), and 137 men, and, like L'Eugenie, appears to be coppered and perfectly new. Her name L'Audacieux.

The ease with which she ran round us, within six hours after being taken possession of, manifested how much we were indebted for the capture of her to her very bad steering. Sixteen of her guns were thrown overboard in the chase.

I have the honour to be, &c.

Vice-admiral Kingsmill. M. DE COURCY.

Admiralty Office, April 14.

Copy of a Letter from Admiral Peyton, Commander in Chief of his Majesty's Ships and Vessels in the Downs, to Evan Nepean, Esq. dated on board the Overyssel, April 10.

Sir,

I HEREWITH enclose to you a letter I have received from Lieutenant Lowen, commanding his Majesty's hired armed brig Terrer, stating his having captured a French schooner privateer, armed with one 6-pounder and eight swivels, with 21 men; which letter you will please to lay before their Lordships.

I am, &c.

JOS. PEYTON.

Sir,

Sir, *His Majesty's armed Brig Terrier, April 8.*

I HAVE the honour to inform you, that this evening, Oftend bearing S. S. E. seven leagues, I fell in with and captured the Sans Pareil French schooner privateer, mounting one six-pounder and eight swivel guns, manned with 21 men, and commanded by Monf. Jacques François Dore, from Oftend this day; had not taken any thing.

I have the honour to be, &c.

THO. LOWEN.

Admiralty Office, April 14.

Copy of a Letter from Captain Thomas Campbell, Commander of his Majesty's armed Veffel the Wright, to Evan Nepean, Efq. dated at North Shields the 8th inftant.

Sir,

YOU will be pleafed to acquaint my Lords Commiffioners of the Admiralty, that I yefterday, about six leagues from Huntcliffe, recaptured the three brigs named in the margin *, laden with coals, who had been taken by a French privateer the same morning: about three o'clock, the veffels being all fecured, I gave chafe to the privateer, who was running to the N. E. and being highly favoured by the winds, had the pleafure to take her at half paft fix: she proved to be the Merveilleufe fchooner privateer, of Dunkirk, commanded by Pierre Lefevre, mounting fix guns (five of which were thrown overboard in the chafe), and 39 men. She had been eight days from Dunkirk, and had taken only one, a brig laden with coals, the day before we fell in with her.

I am, Sir, &c.

THO. CAMPBELL.

From the LONDON GAZETTE, April 17, 1798.

Admiralty Office, April 16.

Copy of a Letter from Captain Sir Henry Trollope, of his Majesty's Ship Ruffel, to Mr. Nepean, dated at Spithead, the 14th of April.

Sir,

I BEG leave to acquaint you, that on the 14th ult. his Majefty's ship Jafon, in company with the Ruffel, burnt a fmall French brig, in ballaft, bound from Breft to Nantz; and on the 20th ult. his Majefty's ships Ruffel and Jafon captured the Bon Citoyen, a French brig privateer, of 12 guns and 65 men, from Granville; had been out fourteen days, and taken nothing.

I have the honour to be, &c.

HENRY TROLLOPE.

---

* Spalding, of Bofton; Ranger, of Yarmouth; Elizabeth, of Wells.

From the LONDON GAZETTE, April 24, 1798.

Admiralty Office, April 24.

Extract of a Letter from Vice-admiral Sir Hyde Parker, Knight, Commander in Chief of his Majesty's Ships and Vessels at Jamaica, to Evan Nepean, Esq. dated on board the Queen, Cape Nicola Mole, March 12.

HEREWITH you will receive, for their Lordships' information, a list of such armed vessels, &c. as have been captured by the ships and vessels under my command, since my last return.

A List of armed Vessels captured and destroyed by his Majesty's Squadron under my Command, since the 29th October 1797.

A French schooner privateer, of 10 guns—destroyed by the Jamaica.

La Fortunée French schooner privateer, of two 4-pounders—captured by the Jamaica.

Le Petit Resource French privateer, of one 3-pounder and two swivels—captured by the Swallow.

La Creole French schooner privateer, of 6 guns and a cargo—captured by the Ceres.

Le Brutus French privateer, of 9 guns—captured by La Magicienne, Regulus, and Diligence.

A French schooner privateer—captured by the Gannett cutter.

A privateer—captured by the Recovery schooner.

La Magicienne French ship privateer, of 16 guns and 178 tons—captured by the Valiant and squadron.

Le Bien Venue French schooner privateer, of 14 guns, but only 8 mounted—captured by the Carnatic and squadron.

A large Spanish gun-boat—destroyed near the Havannah by the Ceres, Trent, and squadron.

A Spanish schooner packet, armed with swivels and with a cargo—captured, together with four Spanish brigs, loaded with hides, tallow, dying woods, and a great quantity of gunpowder, &c. by the squadron.

Together with several schooner-rigged row-boats—taken by the squadron at the Mole, under the orders of Rear-admiral Bligh.

(Signed)   H. PARKER.

War Office, Dublin Castle, February 26.

CAMDEN.

IT is his Excellency the Lord Lieutenant's order, that all officers belonging to regiments of the line, militia, and fencibles, in this kingdom, do join their respective corps on or before the 25th day of March next, notwithstanding any leave of absence, except those that shall be employed on the recruiting service.

By his Excellency the Lord Lieutenant's command.

T. PELHAM.

From the LONDON GAZETTE, April 28, 1798.

Admiralty Office, April 28.

Copy of a Letter from the Right Hon. Admiral Lord Bridport, K. B. to Evan Nepean, Esq. dated on board his Majesty's Ship Royal George, at Sea, the 22d inst.

Sir,

I HAVE the satisfaction to acquaint you, for their Lordships' information, that L'Hercule, of 74 guns, was taken by his Majesty's ship Mars last night.

The enclosed copy of a letter from Lieutenant Butterfield will best show to their Lordships the spirit and judgment manifested upon this occasion. No praise of mine can add one ray of brilliancy to the distinguished valour of Captain Alexander Hood, who carried his ship nobly into battle, and who died of the wounds he received in supporting the just cause of his country. It is impossible for me not to sincerely lament his loss, as he was an honour to the service, and universally beloved: he has fallen gloriously, as well as all those who are so handsomely spoken of by Lieutenant Butterfield. I have appointed him to the command of L'Hercule, to carry her into port, and I have given a temporary appointment to Captain James George Shirley to command the Mars, and Lieutenant George White, first of the Royal George, to command the Megæra. Lieutenant Henry Combe, the second, will deliver to you this dispatch.

I have the honour to be, Sir,
Your most obedient humble servant,
BRIDPORT.

My Lord, *Mars, at Sea, April 22.*

I BEG leave to acquaint your Lordship, that the ship chased by his Majesty's ship Mars yesterday, per signal, endeavoured to escape through the Passage du Raz, but the tide proving contrary, and the wind easterly, obliged her to anchor at the mouth of that passage, which afforded Captain Hood the opportunity of attacking her, by laying her so close alongside as to unhinge some of the lower-deck ports, continuing a very bloody action for an hour and a half, when she surrendered.

I lament being under the necessity of informing your Lordship, that his Majesty has, on this occasion, lost that truly brave man Captain Hood, who was wounded in the thigh late in the conflict, and expired just as the enemy's ship had struck her colours. This ship proves to be L'Hercule, of 74 guns, and 700 men, her first time at sea, from L'Orient, to join the Brest fleet.

I cannot sufficiently commend the bravery and good conduct of the surviving officers and men, who merit my warmest thanks. I must particularly recommend to your Lordship's notice Mr. Southey, the signal midshipman.

Lieutenants Argles and Tord are the only officers wounded. Captain Hood, and Captain White of the marines, are killed. Lieutenant Argles, though badly wounded, never quitted the deck.

From a number of the people being with Lieutenant Bowker in charge of the prize, I cannot at present inform your Lordship the exact

exact number of killed and wounded; but from the best information circumstances afford, I think about 30 killed, and as many wounded, most of them dangerously.

I have the honour to be, my Lord,
Your Lordship's most obedient humble servant,
W. BUTTERFIELD.

Admiral Lord Bridport, K. B. &c. &c.

From the LONDON GAZETTE, May 1, 1798.

Admiralty Office, May 1.

Copy of a Letter from Lieutenant Wollaston, commanding his Majesty's Cutter Cruiser, to Vice-admiral Sir Richard Onslow, Bart. dated at Sea, the 27th of last Month.

Sir,

AGREEABLE to your signal, I gave chase to the S. W. and, after a chase of three hours, came up with and captured the French lugger privateer Jupiter, mounting eight carriage-guns, and manned with 36 men; out fourteen days from Bologne.

Admiralty Office, May 1.

Extract of a Letter from the Right Hon. Admiral Lord Bridport to Evan Nepean, Esq. dated on board his Majesty's Ship the Royal George, at Sea, the 26th of April.

HEREWITH you will receive, for their Lordships' information, a copy of a list, transmitted to me by Captain Stirling, of the killed, wounded, and missing of the Mars, on the 21st instant.

List of killed and wounded, &c. on board his Majesty's Ship Mars, in Action with the French National Ship L'Hercule, the 21st of April.

Alexander Hood, captain, killed.
James Blythe, second midshipman, killed.
Seamen, 11 killed; 3 died of their wounds.
George Argles, third lieutenant, wounded.
George Arnaud Ford, fifth lieutenant, wounded.
Thomas Southey, midshipman, wounded.
Seamen, 36 wounded, 3 missing.
Boys, 2 wounded.

MARINES.

Joseph White, captain, killed.
One corporal killed.
Privates, 2 killed, 2 died of their wounds.
Serjeants, 2 wounded.
One drummer wounded.
Privates, 16 wounded, 5 missing.

Total—17 killed, 5 died of their wounds, 60 wounded, and 8 missing—in all 90.

From the LONDON GAZETTE, May 5, 1798.

Admiralty Office, May 5.

Copy of a Letter from Captain John Tremayne Rodd, Commander of his Majesty's Sloop Scorpion, to Evan Nepean, Esq. dated in the River Humber, April 30.

I HAVE the honour of acquainting you, for the information of my Lords Commissioners of the Admiralty, that his Majesty's sloop Scorpion, under my command, Flamborough Head S. W. between two and three miles, fell in with, on the night of the 26th instant, and captured the Batavian republican brig Le Courier, pierced for 12, and mounting six four-pounders, and a number of swivels, commanded by Lieutenant John Ysbrands, and manned with 30 men, sailed eight days before from Helvoetsluys, and taken the Lark brig, of Whitby, coal laden, which the Scorpion retook. I have the honour to be, &c.

J. T. RODD.

Copy of a Letter from Admiral Sir Peter Parker, Bart. Commander in Chief of his Majesty's Ships and Vessels at Portsmouth and Spithead, to Evan Nepean, Esq. dated the 3d instant.

ENCLOSED is a letter from Lieutenant Newton, commanding the Telemachus cutter, giving an account of the capture of La Sans Souci, a small French lugger privateer, which he discovered close in with the Bill of Portland, the 30th of last month.

P. PARKER.

Telemachus, Plymouth Sound, May 1.

YESTERDAY, in his Majesty's armed cutter under my command, close in with the Bill of Portland, I fell in with and captured, after a chase of twelve hours, La Sans Souci French privateer lugger, mounting one twelve-pounder carronade and two brass fours, and 27 men. She sailed from La Hogue the night before, and had not taken any thing.

THO. NEWTON.

From the LONDON GAZETTE, May 8, 1798.

Admiralty Office, May 8.

Extract of a Letter from Captain Halsted, of his Majesty's Ship Phœnix, to Mr. Nepean, dated Plymouth Sound, the 6th instant.

Sir,

BE pleased to inform their Lordships, that his Majesty's ship under my command arrived here this day, in company with Le Brave French privateer, pierced for 22 guns, and carrying 18, which are eighteens and twelves, with 160 men. She was captured on the night of the 24th ult. in latitude 49 deg. N. longitude 16 deg. W. after some resistance, by which she had a few men killed, and 14 wounded. The Phœnix received some trifling damage in her sails and rigging, but no person hurt.—She is a very fine ship, of 600 tons, coppered, and sails exceedingly fast. It is an additional pleasure to me to say there were about fifty English prisoners on board her at the time, none of whom received any injury from our shot. On the 25th we retook the Thetis, a valuable American ship, from Charlestown to London, which this privateer captured a few days before.

Admiralty Office, May 8.

Copy of a Letter from Rear-admiral Harvey, Commander in Chief of his Majesty's Ships and Vessels at the Leeward Islands, to Evan Nepean, Esq. dated on board the Prince of Wales, Fort Royal Bay, Martinique, the 13th of March.

Sir,

BE pleased to acquaint their Lordships, that Captain Barton, in his Majesty's ship Concorde, has captured the undermentioned French privateers, belonging to Guadaloupe.

Le Hardy schooner, of eight guns and 60 men.
Le Hazard schooner, of two guns and 27 men.

The first was taken the 11th ult. off Bermuda, and the latter the 15th, off Montserrat; and both were sent to St. Christopher's.

I have the honour to be, &c.

HENRY HARVEY.

Sir,   *Prince of Wales, Fort Royal Bay, Martinique, March 10.*

I AM to acquaint you, for the information of their Lordships, that his Majesty's ship Lapwing, Captain Thomas Harvey, captured, the 18th of last month, off Nevis, Le Mutine French privateer schooner, belonging to Guadaloupe, of eight guns and 61 men; and that his Majesty's ship Roebuck, Captain Burrowes, captured, on the 19th, off Martinique, La Parfaite French privateer schooner, belonging to Guadaloupe, of 10 guns and 60 men; both of them had been out some time, but had not made any captures.

You will also be pleased to acquaint their Lordships, that his Majesty's sloop Cyane, Captain Manning, captured a small schooner, off St. Vincent, the 26th ult. of four guns and 22 men. I am, &c.

Evan Nepean, Esq.   HENRY HARVEY.

From the LONDON GAZETTE, May 12, 1798.

Admiralty Office, May 12.

Copy of a Letter from Captain Hotham, of his Majesty's Ship Adamant, to Evan Nepean, Esq. dated at anchor off the Islands of St. Marçou, the 8th of May.

Sir,

I HAVE the satisfaction of enclosing for the information of my Lords Commissioners of the Admiralty, a letter I yesterday received from Lieutenant Price, commanding officer on the islands of Marçou, in which it will be found, that, by his firm and steady resistance against a very considerable force, those islands have been saved falling into the hands of the enemy.

The calm weather had for some days prevented his Majesty's ships under my orders from checking the progress which the flotilla from La Hogue might attempt to make; and, judging from the information I received from Lieutenant Price, on the morning of the 6th, that it was on its way to the islands, I necessarily approached them as near as the state of
the

the weather would permit me to do. On the same afternoon, however, I was obliged to anchor; but taking advantage of a light breeze in the evening, I again weighed and stood in. At ten o'clock that night, it again falling quite calm, and fearing the flood-tide would carry us too far to the eastward, the ship once more anchored, the islands bearing W. by S. six miles.

A little before the dawn of day, the enemy commenced the attack, and the boats were soon afterwards seen placed and keeping up a constant fire. A light breeze springing up at that time from the N. N. W. with an ebb tide, the signal was made to weigh, and Captains Talbot, of the Eurydice, and Hagget, of the Orestes, were directed by me to stand in as fast as possible, and attack the enemy in the manner they should judge most effectual towards destroying them, on arriving up. While going down, however, it was perceived the enemy was making his retreat in a very hasty and confused manner; and I am not altogether without hope, that the near approach of his Majesty's ships in some measure confirmed the enemy in his inclination of abandoning an enterprise, which, from the very able conduct and well-directed fire of Lieutenant Price, he would at all events have been ultimately obliged to do. It again falling calm, and the ships not having steerage-way, rendered pursuit on our side impossible, and enabled them to make their retreat to La Hogue.

It would be great injustice in not joining with him in his very well bestowed commendation on the conduct of the several officers and men under his command.

It may not be deemed improper to mention, that I this morning saw some pieces of paper taken from the vessel which has been towed in, and that amongst them there is a sort of return of the crew, by which it appears that it consisted of 144 men; the total force, therefore, may have been very considerable, and there is every reason to believe has suffered great loss.

I have the honour to be, &c.

W. HOTHAM.

Sir, *Badger, Isles St. Marçou, May 7.*

I BEG leave to represent to you, that in consequence of the information I received yesterday, and the movements of the enemy at La Hogue, I conjectured they would attack us in the night, about high water; I therefore dispatched a guard-boat, belonging to the Sandfly, with Mr. Moore, midshipman of the Eurydice, in her, to watch the motions of the enemy. About twelve o'clock he got amongst them, and made the signal of their being in motion, and about the same time we clearly heard the enemy talk, but it was so dark we could not discover them.

At daybreak I observed their line drawn abreast of the S. W. face of the western redoubt, and having all my guns I could bring to bear well pointed, I began a steady, well directed fire on them, until the flat boats came within musket-shot, when I observed six or seven of them go down, whilst the other took out the living part of the crews; one I am towing into the islands, and the remainder, consisting of forty-three, are returning into La Hogue. I am clear, from the crowded state of their deck, that they must have received great damage and slaughter; but I am sorry to add, we had one marine killed, and three severely wounded, and one seaman wounded.

Lieutenant Bourne took every method in his power to assist me; but from the situation of the attack, the East island was deprived for some time

time of doing much; but with the shells from the 68-pounders over the West island, latterly did them great damage, by flanking the N. W. side of the West island.

I beg leave to represent likewise to you, that Lieutenants Maughan and Enfor, with the marines, Serjeant Henderson and the party of artillery, and the seamen under my command, behaved as well as officers and men could do. I am, Sir, your humble servant,

Capt. Hotham, senior Officer, &c. CHA. P. PRICE.

Lieutenant Price, in a letter to Mr. Nepean, dated the 9th, repeats the intelligence contained in the above, and concludes thus:

I AM sorry to announce the death of Thomas Hall, private marine, killed; Richard Dunn and Peter Williamson, marines, wounded; and Thomas Banks, seaman, wounded. But considering our receiving the fire of near eighty heavy bow-guns, from 36 to 18 pounders, for upwards of two hours, I look upon our damage as not great. We had four guns dismounted, but I got them fit for service before night. Enclosed I send you Lieutenant Bourne's letter to me, the morning after the action.

I am, &c. CHA. P. PRICE.

Sir, *Sandfly, East Island, St. Marçou, 7th May.*
I HAVE the pleasure to inform you, that in the affair of this morning there were no killed or wounded in this island. I cannot speak in terms sufficiently strong, of the firm and manly conduct displayed on this occasion by the officers and men under my command; and I feel particularly indebted to Lieutenant Lawrence, of the marines, Ensign Carter, of the invalids, Messrs. Trotter and Moore, mates of the Adamant and Eurydice, and Mr. John Mather, commissary of ordnance stores, for their assistance, and ready execution of my orders during the action.

Lieut. Price, &c. &c. I have the honour to be, &c.
Senior Officer at the Islands of St. Marçou. RICH. BOURNE.

Admiralty Office, May 12.
Extract of a Letter from Captain Pakenham, of his Majesty's Ship Resistance, to Evan Nepean, Esq. dated off Fort Victoria, Amboyna, October 21, 1797.

Sir,
I HAVE the honour to inform you, that the islands of Amboyna and Banda are in a very respectable state of defence, and the seamen and troops in very good health and spirits, and, from the enemy's cruisers being all captured or destroyed, as per margin, are at present very well supplied.

Prizes taken by his Majesty's Ship Resistance.

Young Frank, sloop, 10 guns and 8 swivels, cut out from Ternate; Juno, sloop, loaded with rice, coming into Ternate; Young Lausin, sloop, 10 guns and 8 swivels; Limbi, ketch, 6 guns, off Celebes, and loaded with rice; a large corra-corra, 6 rantackers, carrying a pound ball, a paddawackan, with 6 swivels; Walker, sloop, 10 guns and 8 swivels, at Gonontalo, island of Celebes, by the boats of the Resistance. Resource, coppered brig, 6 guns, at Copang, island of St. Timor; a large paddawackan.

From

From the LONDON GAZETTE, May 22, 1798.

Admiralty Office, May 22.

Captain Winthrop, of his Majesty's Ship Circe, arrived here this Day with a Dispatch from Captain Home Riggs Popham, of his Majesty's Ship Expedition, to Evan Nepean, Esq. Secretary of the Admiralty, of which the following is a Copy.

Sir, His Majesty's Ship Expedition, Ostend Roads, May 20.

I BEG you will do me the honour to inform my Lords Commissioners of the Admiralty, that, in pursuance of their orders of the 8th instant, I proceeded to sea the 14th, with the ships and vessels named in the margin *, having on board the troops under the command of Major-general Coote, for the purpose of blowing up the basin gates and sluices of the Bruges canal, and destroying the internal navigation between Holland, Flanders, and France. On the 18th, P. M. I spoke the Fairy, when Captain Horton told me he had taken a cutter from Flushing to Ostend, and he understood from the people on board, that the transport schuyts fitting at Flushing were to go round immediately by the canals to Dunkirk and Ostend; and although it was impossible that any information could give additional spirit to the troops forming this enterprise, or increase the energy and exertions of the officers and seamen under my command, yet it convinced Major-general Coote and myself that it was of the greatest importance not to lose any time, but to attempt, even under an increased degree of risk, an object of such magnitude as the one in question; and as the weather appeared more favourable than it had been, I made the signal for Captain Bazely, in the Harpy, to go ahead, with the vessels appointed to lie as beacons N. W. of the town of Ostend, and for Captain Bradby, in the Ariadne, to keep between the Expedition and Harpy, that we might approach as near the coast as possible, without the chance of being discovered from the shore.

At one A. M. we anchored; and soon afterwards the wind shifted to west, and threatened so much to blow, that the General and myself were deliberating whether it would not be better to go to sea and wait a more favourable opportunity, when a boat from the Vigilant brought a vessel alongside, which she had cut out from under the light-house battery; and the information obtained from the persons who were on board her, under separate examinations, so convinced us of the small force at Ostend, Newport, and Bruges, that Major-general Coote begged he might be landed to accomplish the great object of destroying the canals, even if the surf should prevent his retreat being so successful as he could wish. I of course acceded to his spirited propositions, and ordered the troops to be landed as fast as possible, without waiting for the regular order of debarkation. Many of the troops were on shore before we were discovered, and it was not till a quarter past four that the batteries opened on the ships,

---

* To anchor to the eastward Hecla bomb, J. Oughton. Harpy, H. Bazely. Ariadne, J. Bradby. Expedition, H. Popham. Minerva. J. M'Kellar. Savage, N. Thompson. Biter, D Purvis. Dart, S Revel. Circe, R. Winthrop. Vestal, C. White. Hebe, W. Birchall. Dædalus, C. Apthorp. Tartar, T. Lowen. Vesuve, W. Elliott. Furnace, M. W. Suckling. To the westward, for the purpose of making a feint to land there. Champion, H. Kent. Dart, R. Rayner. Wolvereene, L. M. Mortlock. Crash, B. M. Praid. Blazer. J Cossert. Acute, J. Seaver.

which

[24]

which was instantly returned in a most spirited manner t
lock of the Wolvereene, Lieutenant Edmonds of the
nant Norman of the Biter. The Hecla and Tartarus
opened their mortars, and threw their shells with gr
precision. The town was on fire several times, and m
done to the ships in the basin. By five o'clock all the
land, except those from the Minerva, were on shore w
miners, wooden petards, tools, and gunpowder; and b
heard from General Coote, that he had no doubt of blow
I now became very anxious for the situation of the Ma
the state of the weather; and I ordered all the gun-boat
ed to the eastward of the town, to get as near the sh
cover and assist the troops in their embarkation. Th
town continued their fire on the Wolvereene, Asp, and
Wolvereene had received much damage, and the Asp h
four hours within 300 yards of the battery; I made the
and soon after directed the Dart, Harpy, and Kite, to
that the enemy might be prevented from turning th
troops; but it being low water, they could not get so
manders wished. At half past nine the Minerva came in
an additional number of troops would only add to t
General, from the little probability of being abl
I sent Captain Mackellar on shore to report his arriv
companies of the guards. In his absence, Colonel W
boats with his officers and men, and was proceeding
join the battalion of guards, without considering the dang
to in crossing the surf, when Captain Bradby fortuna
advised him to return immediately to his ship. At tw
tea I had the pleasure of seeing the explosion take pla
the troops assembled on the Sand Hills near the shore;
high, that it was impossible to embark a single man; ther
make every arrangement against the wind moderated; a
daylight I went on shore in the Kite, for the purpos
assistance, but I had the mortification to see our army
enemy's troops; and as I had no doubt the General had
ed all the ships to anchor farther out, and sent in a
Colonel Boone of the guards and Captain Brown of the
to the commandant, a copy of which I enclose for t
formation. At ten this morning, the General, aid
Williamson, came on board, and though it was ve
General Coote was wounded, after all his exertions, ye
factory to learn, that, under many disadvantageous c
after performing a service of such consequence to our
killed and wounded, was only between fifty and
privates; and that the General capitulated, in consequ
rounded by several thousands of the national troops.

I enclose, for their Lordships' information, a copy
were left me by Captain Wilson, from which their Lo
sluice-gates and works are completely destroyed, and
tended for transports, burnt.

I this morning learnt that the canal was quite dry,
destroyed yesterday had taken the sluice of Bruges five y

I hope their Lordships will be satisfied that the en

and every thing they wished was accomplished, although the loss of the troops far exceeded any calculation, except under the particular circumstances of the wind's coming to the northward and blowing very hard. If the weather had continued fine, the troops would have been embarked by twelve, at which time the return of killed and wounded did not exceed four rank and file.

I cannot help again noticing the particular good conduct of Captain Mortlock, Lieutenant Edmonds, and Lieutenant Norman, and beg to recommend them to their Lordships' protection.

General Coote sent to inform me that he was highly pleased with the uncommon exertions of Captains Winthrop and Bradby, and Lieutenant Bradby, who had acted on shore as his aid-de-camp: he also noticed the assistance he had derived from Captain Mackellar, after his landing.

I take the liberty of sending this dispatch by Captain Winthrop, of the Circe, who commanded the seamen landed from the different ships; and as he had the particular charge of getting the powder and mines up for the destruction of the works, in which he so ably succeeded, he will be enabled to inform their Lordships of every circumstance. Captain Mackellar, with the officers and men on shore, were included in the capitulation: but I have not yet been able to collect an exact return of the number of seamen taken.

I transmit you a list of killed and wounded on board his Majesty's ships; and I have the honour to be, Sir,

Your most obedient humble servant,
HOME POPHAM.

Sir, *His Majesty's Ship Expedition, Ostend Roads, May* 20.

I HAVE just heard with concern that the British troops and seamen under the command of Major-general Coote, and Captain Mackellar, of the royal navy, have capitulated to the troops of the republic, and I trust they will be treated with that attention which is due to officers and men executing the orders of their sovereign.

It has been the invariable rule of the British government to make the situation of prisoners as comfortable as possible; and I am sure, Sir, in this instance you will do the same to the troops, &c. who have fallen into your hands.

It will not be against any rule to exchange the prisoners immediately, but on the contrary add to your name by marking it with humanity and liberality: and I give you my word the same number of troops, or other prisoners, shall be instantly sent from England to France, with such officers as you shall name, or as shall be named by the National Convention, provided no public reason attaches against the release of any particular person.

I have sent the officers what things they left on board the ship, and I am confident you will order them to be delivered as soon as possible.

I beg you will allow the officers and men to write letters to England by this flag, as a satisfaction to their families, it being impossible for me to know who have fallen or received wounds, which I hope will be very inconsiderable, from the accounts I have received from the shore.

I beg your answer to this letter without loss of time; and confiding in your liberality towards the troops under capitulation to you, I have the honour to be, Sir, Your most obedient humble servant,

To *the Officer commanding the Troops of the* HOME POPHAM.
National Convention at Ostend.

Vol. VIII. D *Extract*

Extract from the Minutes left on board the Expedition by **Captain Williamson,** *Aid-de-camp to General Coote, dated 10 A. M. May 20, Ostend Roads.*

SLUICE-GATES destroyed in the most complete manner. Boats burnt, and every thing done, and the troops ready to embark by twelve o'clock. When we found it impossible to embark, took the strongest position on the Sand Hills, and about four in the morning were attacked by a column of 600 men to our left, an immense column in front, with cannon, and a very large column on the right.

The General and troops would have all been off, with the loss of not more than three or four men, if the wind had not come to the northward soon after we landed, and made so high a sea. We have not been able to ascertain the exact number of men killed and wounded, but it is supposed they amount to about fifty or sixty.

The officers killed and wounded are,

Major-general Coote, wounded.
Colonel Hely, 11th regiment, killed.
Colonel Campbell, wounded.
Captain Walker, royal artillery, wounded.

A List of Killed and Wounded in his Majesty's Ships and Vessels under the Command of Home Popham, Esq. 19th May, Ostend Roads.

Seamen, &c. of Wolvereene—1 killed, 10 wounded.
23d regiment, on board the Wolvereene—1 killed, 5 wounded.
Asp—1 seaman killed, Lieutenant Edmonds wounded.

HOME POPHAM.

Parliament Street, May 22.

A DISPATCH, of which the following is a copy, has been this day received by the Right Honourable Henry Dundas, one of his Majesty's principal Secretaries of State, from Lieutenant-colonel Warde, of the 1st regiment of guards, dated on board the Expedition frigate, eight o'clock, P. M. May 20.

Sir,

IN consequence of the Minerva frigate (on board which were the four light infantry companies of the 1st regiment of foot guards) having unfortunately lost her situation in the squadron under the command of Captain Popham, of the royal navy, during the night of the 18th instant, the command of the remainder of the troops, from that accident, has devolved upon me; and I have the honour to transmit to you the most correct account that I have been enabled to collect.

Early on the morning of the 19th instant, the following troops, under the command of Major-general Coote, viz.

Two companies, light infantry, Coldstream guards—two ditto, ditto, 3d guards—11th regiment of foot—23d and 49th, flank companies, with six pieces of ordnance, disembarked, and effected their landing, at three o'clock in the morning, to the eastward of Ostend, and completed the object of the expedition, by burning a number of boats destined for the invasion of England, and by so completely destroying the locks and basin gates of the Bruges canal, that it was this morning without a drop of water; and as I understand all the transports fitting out at Flushing were intended to be brought to Oftend and Dunkirk by the inland navigation, to avoid our cruifers, that arrangement will be defeated, and it will be a long time before the works can be repaired, as they were five years finifhing, and were efteemed the moft complete works of the kind in Europe. The troops had retreated, and were ready to re-embark by twelve o'clock the fame morning, with the lofs of only one rank and file killed, and one feaman wounded, but found it impoffible, from the wind having increafed, and the furf running to high, as entirely to prevent their regaining the boats; upon which they took up a pofition on the Sand Hills, above the Reach, where they lay the whole of that day and night upon their arms. The enemy taking advantage of the length of time and the night, collected in very great force, and foon after daybreak this morning attacked them on every fide, when, after a moft noble and gallant defence, I am grieved to add, they were under the neceffity of capitulating to a very great fuperiority of numbers.

I herewith enclofe a lift of the killed and wounded, and I have every reafon to believe it correct.

Lieutenant-colonel Hely, 11th foot, killed; Major-general Coote, wounded; Colonel Campbell, 3d guards, wounded; Major Donkin, 44th foot, wounded; Captain Walker, royal artillery, wounded; and near 60 rank and file killed and wounded.

I have the honour to be, &c.
HENRY WARDE,
Capt. and Lieut. Col. 1ft Guards.

Admiralty Office, May 22.

Copy of a Letter from Admiral Earl St. Vincent, Commander in Chief of his Majefty's Ships and Veffels employed on the Coaft of Portugal, to Evan Nepean, Efq. dated on board the Ville de Paris, off Cadiz, the 10th of May.

Sir,

I ENCLOSE a letter from Captain Caulfield, of his Majefty's floop the Petterel, giving an account of the capture of one of the enemy's privateers, on his paffage from St. Domingo to Lifbon.

I have the honour to be, &c.
ST. VINCENT.

Petterel, May 2, 1798, Latitude 38 deg. 46 min. N.
My Lord, Longitude 17 deg. 30 min. W.

I HAVE the honour to inform your Lordfhip, that, on the 30th ultimo, in latitude 37 deg. 52 min. N. longitude 22 deg. 1 min. W. I fell in with and captured Le Leopard, French letter of marque, mounting 12 fix-pounders and 14 fwivels, and carrying 100 men; had been out twenty days, and had not taken any thing.

I have the honour to be, &c.
(Signed) T. GORDON CAULFIELD.
To the Right Hon. Earl St. Vincent, K. B.
&c. &c. &c.

Admiralty Office, May 22.

Copy of a Letter from the Right Honourable Lord Viscount Duncan to Evan Nepean, Esq. dated the 19th instant.

THE enclosed letter I send for the information of the Lords Commissioners of the Admiralty, and am, Sir,

Your very humble servant,

DUNCAN.

My Lord, *Astrea, Elsineur, May 2.*

I BEG to acquaint your Lordship, that on the 22d of last month, on the Dogger Bank, I captured the Renommée French schooner privateer, of five guns and 54 men: Her guns are nine-pounders; fixed on slides a-midship, so as to fight all on either side. She is one of the most complete vessels I ever saw, and sails remarkably fast.

I have the honour to be, &c. &c. &c.

Admiral Lord Viscount Duncan, &c. &c. &c. R. DACRES.

Admiralty Office, May 22.

Copy of a Letter from Captain Wollaston, of his Majesty's Sloop Cruiser, to Evan Nepean, Esq. dated at Sheerness, May 20.

Sir,

I BEG you will inform their Lordships, that on the 19th inst. Lowestoff N. W. by W. six or seven leagues, we fell in with two French republican luggers, one of which carried away her main and foremast during the chase, when we continued in chase of the other until five P. M. at which time we could just see the mast-head to leeward; as the chase was then gaining on us, and the one that had struck was not secured, I left off chase and stood for her. Upon taking possession I found her to be La Chasseur, from Honfleur, out eight days, mounting four six-pounders, and manned with 48 men; had not taken any thing. Her consort was La Dragon, mounting four six-pounders, both new vessels, and sailed from Honfleur together, and were going to cruise on the Dogger Bank. During the chase La Dragon hove overboard her boat and several other things, but I could not perceive whether she threw her guns over or not. I am, &c. C. WOLLASTON.

From the LONDON GAZETTE, May 29, 1798.

Whitehall, May 29.

DISPATCHES, of which the following are copies, have been received from his Excellency the Lord Lieutenant of Ireland, by his Grace the Duke of Portland, his Majesty's principal Secretary of State for the home department.

My Lord, *Dublin Castle, May 24.*

THE intelligence contained in my last dispatches must have prepared your Grace to hear of some attempts being made by the rebels to carry their traitorous designs into execution, before every possibility of success was destroyed by the vigorous measures which have lately been pursued.

For some days, orders had been issued by the leaders of the United Irishmen, directing their partisans to be ready at a moment's notice, as the measures of Government made it necessary for them to act immediately. Yesterday information was received, that it was probable the city and the adjoining

adjoining districts would rise in the evening; subsequent information confirmed this intelligence. In consequence of which, notice was sent to the general officers in the neighbourhood, and Dublin was put in a state of preparation. The measures taken in the metropolis prevented any movement whatsoever; but I am concerned to acquaint your Grace, that acts of open rebellion were committed in the counties of Dublin, Meath, and Kildare. About half past two o'clock this morning, there was a regular attack made by a rebel force upon the towns of Naas, where Lord Gosford commanded, with part of the Armagh militia, and detachments of the 4th dragoon guards and Ancient British. The rebels consisted of about a thousand men, armed with muskets and pikes, and they made their attack with regularity, but were soon repulsed by the Armagh militia, and then charged and pursued by the 4th dragoon guards and Ancient British, and I understand their loss amounted to near two hundred. Two officers and a few privates have been lost of his Majesty's forces. It gives me pain to relate, that a small detachment at the town of Prosperous has been surprised, and a detachment at the village of Clare cut their way to Naas, with some loss. There was also an attack on a small party of the 9th dragoons, near Kilcullen, which suffered; but in the course of the day, General Dundas was enabled to come up with a considerable body of the rebels near the hills of Kilcullen, where they were entirely routed with the loss of two hundred men. There were also several bodies collected last night in different parts near Dublin, which were attacked by the Rathfarnham cavalry, and by a detachment of the 5th dragoons, and dispersed with some loss, and some prisoners and horses were taken. A rebel party however assembled at the borders of the county of Dublin, near Dunboyne, and overpowered some constables, and afterwards took the baggage of two companies, guarded by a small party of the Reay fencibles, coming to town, and have during the course of this day committed many outrages; several of them however have been killed, but the body remains undispersed. The city is tranquil, and I have no doubt will remain so this evening, and I trust that to-morrow we shall entirely disperse that body of the insurgents which has not been entirely routed to-day.

I must add, that the mail-coach going to the north was attacked, within a few miles of Dublin, by a select body, well armed; the passengers were taken and the coach burned. The Galway mail-coach was also attacked in the town of Lucan, but the rebel party was driven off before its destruction was effected.

In consequence of this desperate conduct of the rebellious, I issued the enclosed proclamation, with the advice of the Privy Council.

I shall in a future dispatch detail to your Grace the particular services which have been performed, but at present I am not furnished with regular reports, except from Lord Gosford, who appears to have acted with great firmness and decision.   I am, &c. &c.

His Grace the Duke of Portland, &c. &c. &c.   CAMDEN.

Extract of a Letter from Lord Viscount Gosford, Colonel of the Armagh Militia, and Major Wardle, of the Ancient British Light Dragoons, to Lieut. General Lake, dated Naas, Thursday Morning, Eight o'Clock, 24th of May.

THIS morning, about half past two o'clock, a dragoon from an outpost came in and informed Major Wardle, of the Ancient British, that a very considerable armed body were approaching rapidly upon the town.

The whole garrison were instantly under arms, and took up their positions according to a plan previously formed, in case of such an event happening. They made the attack upon our troops, posted near the gaol, with great violence, but were repulsed: they then made a general attack in almost every direction, as they had got possession of almost every avenue into the town. They continued to engage the troops for near three quarters of an hour, when they gave way, and fled on all sides. The cavalry immediately took advantage of their confusion, charged in almost every direction, and killed a great number of them. A great quantity of arms and pikes were taken, and within this half hour many hundreds more were brought in, found in pits near the town, together with three men with green cockades, all of whom were hanged in the public street. We took another prisoner, whom we have spared, in consequence of his having given us information that will enable us to pursue these rebels; and from this man we learnt that they were above one thousand strong: they were commanded, as this man informs us, by Michael Reynolds, who was well mounted, and dressed in yeoman uniform, but unfortunately made his escape; his horse we have got.

When we are able to collect further particulars, you shall be made acquainted with them. About thirty rebels were killed in the streets; in the fields, we imagine, above an hundred; their bodies have not yet been brought together.

It is impossible to say too much of the cavalry and infantry; their conduct was exemplary throughout.

Dublin Castle, May 25, Half past Three, P. M.

Extract of a Letter from Lieutenant-general Dundas to Lord Viscount Castlereagh, dated Naas, May 25.

IN addition to the account I had the honour of sending you yesterday, I have the satisfaction to inform your Lordship, that about two P. M. yesterday I marched out again to attack the rebels, who had assembled in great force on the north side of the Liffey, and were advancing toward Kilcullen bridge: they occupied the hills on the left of the road leading to Dublin, the road itself, and the fields highly enclosed on the right. The attack began between three and four; was made with gallantry; the infantry forcing the enemy on the road, and driving them from the hills on the left; the cavalry, with equal success, cutting off their retreat. The affair ended soon after four. The slaughter was considerable for such an action: one hundred and thirty lay dead—No prisoners.

I have the further satisfaction of stating to your Lordship, that his Majesty's troops did not suffer in either killed or wounded. The rebels left great quantities of all kinds of arms behind them, and fled in all directions.

This morning all is in perfect quietness. General Wilford, from Kildare, joined me last night, an officer with whom I serve with unspeakable satisfaction.

The troops of every description, both officers and men, showed a degree of gallantry which it was difficult to restrain within prudent bounds.

Captain La Touche's corps of yeomanry distinguished themselves in a high style.

My Lord, *Dublin Castle, May 24.*

I HAVE the honour to send to your Grace a copy of a message which I sent this day to both Houses of Parliament, in consequence of the proclamation

lamation referred to in my other difpatch of this day; and I requeft you will lay the fame before his Majefty.

Both Houfes of Parliament have unanimoufly voted addreffes in anfwer to the faid meffage, which I fhall have the honour to tranfmit to you tomorrow, with an account of what paffed in each Houfe upon the occafion. I have the honour to be,

With great truth and refpect, my Lord,
Your Grace's moft obedient humble fervant,

His Grace the Duke of Portland,   CAMDEN.
&c. &c. &c.

CAMDEN.

I HAVE thought it my indifpenfable duty, by and with the advice of the Privy Council, under the prefent circumftances of this kingdom, to iffue a proclamation *, a copy of which I have ordered to be laid before the Houfe of Commons.

Dublin Caftle, May 24.

From the LONDON GAZETTE EXTRAORDINARY, May 31, 1798.

Whitehall, May 30.

A DISPATCH, of which the following is a copy, has been received from his Excellency the Lord Lieutenant of Ireland, by his Grace the Duke of Portland, his Majefty's principal Secretary of State for the Home department.

My Lord,   *Dublin Caftle, May* 26, *Ten o'Clock A. M.*

I HAVE detained a packet, in order to tranfmit to your Grace the information received this morning.

I have ftated, in a private letter to your Grace, that a party of the rebels, to the amount of feveral hundreds, were attacked by a detachment of the Antrim militia, a fmall party of cavalry, and Captain Stratford's yeomanry, and that being driven into the town of Baltinglas, they loft about one hundred and fifty men.

This morning an account has been received from Major Hardy, that yefterday a body of between three and four thoufand had collected near Dunlavin, when they were entirely defeated, with the lofs of three hundred men, by Lieutenant Gardner, at the head of a detachment of the Antrim militia, and Captain Hardy's and Captain Hume's yeomanry.

The troops and yeomanry behaved with the utmoft gallantry in both actions.

Lieutenant-general Craig left Dublin yefterday morning, in hopes of meeting the body of the rebels which had collected near Dunboyne, and parties were fent in different directions to furround them. They however fled in the night, on hearing the approach of the troops. The General came up, however, with a party, confifting of about five hundred, fome of whom were put to the fword.

---

* For this proclamation the reader is referred to the fetenth volume of this work, p. 558.

By

By accounts received from the North, it appears that the province of Ulster is quiet. I have the honour to be, with great respect,

My Lord, your Grace's most faithful and obedient servant,

His Grace the Duke of Portland. CAMDEN.

P. S. The city of Dublin has been perfectly tranquil, owing to the precautions which have been taken; and it is impossible to describe, in terms sufficiently strong, the indefatigable zeal, patience, and spirit of the yeomanry corps. Too much praise cannot be given to his Majesty's regular and militia forces; and the latter have had opportunities of evincing their steadiness, discipline, and bravery, which must give the highest satisfaction to his Majesty, and inspire the best-grounded confidence in their exertions, should they have a more formidable enemy to contend with.

Extract of a Letter from Lieutenant Macaulay, of the Antrim Militia, to Major Hardy, commanding in the County of Wicklow, dated Baltinglass, the 24th May.

BETWEEN twelve and one o'clock to-day, the insurgents appeared in the neighbourhood, to the amount of at least four or five hundred. Thirty of the Antrim militia, under my command, and Cornet Love, with twenty of the 9th dragoons, were sent to attack them. At the instant that we were advancing upon them, in the town of Stratford upon Slaney, Captain Stratford appeared at the other end of the town with part of his corps. We attacked the rebels on both sides, and completely routed them, having between one and two hundred killed, besides many wounded, who made their escape.

There are several of our men wounded, and one of the 9th dragoons very severely. I have great pleasure in telling you, that every man behaved as well as possibly could be wished.

Dublin Castle, May 26.

Extract of a Letter from Hacketstown, May 25.

IN consequence of an information received this morning, that a large body of rebels were marching to attack the town, Lieutenant Gardner and Captain Hardy, with the men under their command, went out to meet them. Having reconnoitred their force, which amounted to between three and four thousand, they took their post on the hill under the church; and when the rebels came tolerably near, the officers and men made a feint, and retreated into the barracks, where they prepared to repel them, in case of an attack. On the rebels seeing the military retreat, they came on with a great shout, imagining the day to be their own. In a few minutes Captain Hume came up, with about thirty of his yeomanry troop, and instantly charged them, on which the rebels retreated, and a general pursuit took place; and I have the satisfaction to inform you, that above three hundred of the miscreants lie dead on the field of battle.

To say that the Antrim regiment behaved well, is nothing new to you; but the yeomen, under Captain Hume's command, behaved astonishingly.

Whitehall, May 30, Ten P. M.

A DISPATCH, of which the following is a copy, has been received this evening from his Excellency the Lord Lieutenant of Ireland by his Grace the Duke of Portland, his Majesty's principal Secretary of State for the home department.

My

My Lord, Dublin Castle, May 27.

I HAVE the satisfaction to inform your Grace, that the body of the rebels, who for some days had been in considerable force to the northward of Dublin, were yesterday defeated, with very great loss on their part, by a party of the Reay fencibles, and the neighbouring yeomanry corps, on the hill of Taragh.

Five companies of the Reay fencibles, under the command of Captain Scobie, had halted yesterday at Dunshaughlin, on their march to Dublin; and hearing that the rebels were in great force, and had taken a station on Taragh hill, Captain Scobie detached three of the companies, under the command of Captain M'Lean, with one field-piece, to the spot; who, being accompanied by Lord Fingal and his troop of yeomanry, Captain Preston's and the Lower Kells yeomanry cavalry, and Captain Molloy's company of yeomanry infantry, attacked the rebels, who, after some resistance, fled in all directions. Three hundred and fifty were found dead in the field this morning, among whom was their commanding officer, in his uniform; many more were killed and wounded. Some horses were taken, and great quantities of arms. The loss, on the part of the King's troops, was nine rank and file killed, and 5 wounded.

The town is perfectly quiet, and the only part of the country from whence any attack is threatened is from Wicklow. I shall have the honour of addressing your Grace again to-morrow night.

I have the honour to remain, with perfect truth,
Your Grace's most obedient humble servant,
His Grace the Duke of Portland. CAMDEN.

From the LONDON GAZETTE EXTRAORDINARY, June 1, 1798.

Whitehall, June 1.

A DISPATCH, of which the following is a copy, has been this day received from his Excellency the Lord Lieutenant of Ireland, by his Grace the Duke of Portland, his Majesty's principal Secretary of State for the home department.

Dublin Castle, May 28, Half past Four o'Clock, P. M.
My Lord,
INTELLIGENCE has been received that the insurrection is spreading southward, and it has broke out in great force in the county of Wexford; and I have to inform your Grace, with infinite concern, that the rebels in that quarter have assembled in such force, that they have cut off a party of one hundred men of the North Cork militia, who were sent to meet them. Colonel Foote, who has returned to Wexford, states the numbers of the rebels to be at least four thousand, and a great number of them mounted. Measures are taken to march against this body, and I hope they will be met and defeated.

I have received accounts from Colonel Campbell, at Athy, between whom and General Dundas the communication has been stopped, that he has had partial engagements with the rebels: that at Monasterevan and Carlow they have been defeated, and four hundred killed at the latter place, and fifty at the former. He also informs General Lake, that his

Vol. VIII. E

his men are in high spirits. I will not close this letter till the last mo
ment of the mail leaving Dublin, that I may give your Grace the la
information.   I have the honour to be, &c.
(Signed)   CAMDEN.

Nine o'Clock, P. M.
No farther accounts have been received from the country since th
middle of the day. General Lake went to Naas last night, and is no
yet returned.

___

From the LONDON GAZETTE, June 2, 1798.

Dublin Castle, May 29.
Official Report from Major-general Sir James Duff, dated Monasterevo
May 29.

I MARCHED from Limerick on Sunday morning, with sixty dr
goons, the Dublin militia, their field-pieces, with two curricle guns,
open the communication with Dublin, which I judged of the utmo
importance to Government. By means of cars for the infantry,
reached this place in forty-eight hours. I am now, at seven o'clock th
morning (Monday), marching to surround the town of Kildare, t
head-quarters of the rebels, with seven pieces of artillery, one hundr
and forty dragoons, and three hundred and fifty infantry. I have left t
whole country behind me perfectly quiet and well protected, by mea
of the troops and yeomanry corps. I hope to be able to forward th
to you by the mail-coach, which I will escort to Naas. I am sufficien
strong. You may depend on my prudence and success. My guns a
well manned, and the troops in high spirits. The cruelties that ha
been committed on some of the officers and men have exasperated th
to a great degree. Of my future operations I will endeavour to info
you.   I have the honour to be, &c.
J. DUFF.

Tuesday, Two o'Clock, P. M. Kildare.
P. S. We found the rebels retiring from the town, on our arriv
armed. We followed them with the dragoons. I sent on some of
yeomen, to tell them, on laying down their arms, they should not
hurt. Unfortunately, some of them fired on the troops: From t
moment they were attacked on all sides. Nothing could stop the r
of the troops. I believe from two to three hundred of the rebels w
killed. We have three men killed, and several wounded. I am
much fatigued to enlarge.
(Signed)   J. DUFF.

___

From the LONDON GAZETTE EXTRAORDINARY, June
1798.

Whitehall, June 2.
A DESPATCH, of which the following is a copy, has been this
r... ... ... by Lord Lieutenant of Ireland, by
G

Grace the Duke of Portland, his Majesty's principal Secretary of State for the home department.

My Lord,   *Dublin Castle, May* 29.

I HAVE only time to inform your Grace, that I learn from General Dundas, that the rebels in the Curragh of Kildare have laid down their arms, and delivered up a number of their leaders.

By a dispatch I have this instant received, I have the farther pleasure of acquainting your Grace, that Sir James Duff, who, with infinite alacrity and address, has opened the communication with Limerick (that with Cork being already open), had arrived at Kildare whilst the rebels had possession of it, completely routed them, and taken the place.   I have the honour to be, &c.

CAMDEN.

P. S. The South is entirely quiet, and the rebels in the neighbourhood of Dublin are submitting and delivering up their arms.

From the LONDON GAZETTE, June 5, 1798.

Admiralty Office, June 5.

Copy of a Letter from Rear-admiral Harvey, Commander in Chief of his Majesty's Ships and Vessels at the Leeward Islands, to Evan Nepean, Esq. dated on board the Prince of Wales, Fort Royal Bay, Martinique, the 8th of April.

Sir,

BE pleased to acquaint their Lordships, that his Majesty's sloop Hawke, Captain Rotherham, captured, the 15th ult. off Grenada, and sent into that island, Le Furet, French privateer schooner, belonging to Guadaloupe, of two guns and 27 men, and that his Majesty's ship Lapwing, Captain Harvey, captured, the 31st ultimo, off St. Bartholomew's, and sent into Martinique, Le Hardi, French privateer schooner, belonging to Guadaloupe, of four guns and 47 men. They had both been out some time, but had not made any captures.

You will also be pleased to acquaint their Lordships, that his Majesty's ship La Concorde, Captain Barton, captured, the 1st instant, to windward of Montserrat, La Rosiere, French privateer schooner, of two guns and 15 men, which he sent into St. Christopher's. She had been out but one day, and had not captured any thing.

I have the honour to be, &c.
(Signed)   HENRY HARVEY.

Dublin Castle, June 2.

ACCOUNTS have been received from Major-general Eustace, at New Ross, stating, that Major-general Fawcett having marched with a company of the Meath regiment from Duncannon Fort, this small force was surrounded by a very large body between Taghmon and Wexford, and defeated. General Fawcett effected his retreat to Duncannon Fort.

Accounts have also been received, that the rebels are in possession of Wexford; but that a large force was marching to dislodge them.

Whitehall, June 5.

A DISPATCH, of which the following is a copy, has been this day received from his Excellency the Lord Lieutenant of Ireland by his Grace the Duke of Portland, his Majesty's principal Secretary of State for the home department.

My Lord, *Dublin Castle, June 2.*

I HAVE the honour to acquaint your Grace, that a dispatch was this day received by Lieutenant-general Lake from Colonel L'Estrange, of the King's County militia, which states, that the town of Newtown Barry had been attacked yesterday morning by a considerable body of rebels from Vinegar Hill. They surrounded the town in such a manner, that Colonel L'Estrange at first retreated, in order to collect his force: he then attacked the rebels, drove them through the town with great slaughter, and pursued them several miles, until night obliged him to return. Above five hundred of the rebels were killed.

Colonel L'Estrange's detachment consisted of two hundred and thirty of the King's County militia, seventeen dragoons, and about one hundred yeomen. Colonel L'Estrange speaks in the highest terms of the conduct of the troops, and gives much praise to Major Marlay, who volunteered on the occasion.

I have accounts from Mr. Cornwall, that a picquet guard of his yeomen surprised, in the night, a party of rebels endeavouring to enter the county of Carlow, and completely defeated them.

I have the honour to be, &c.

CAMDEN.

From the LONDON GAZETTE, June 9, 1798.

Whitehall, June 9.

A DISPATCH, of which the following is a copy, has been received from his Excellency the Lord Lieutenant of Ireland by his Grace the Duke of Portland, his Majesty's principal Secretary of State for the home department.

My Lord, *Dublin Castle, June 4.*

YESTERDAY a dispatch was received from Major-general Loftus, conveying information from Lieutenant Elliott, of the Antrim militia, that the troops in Gorey, consisting of thirty of the Antrim militia, a subaltern detachment of the North Cork, the Gorey yeomen cavalry, Ballykeer, and part of the Camolin cavalry, attacked the rebels at Ballycanoe about three o'clock, on the 1st instant, defeated them, and killed above one hundred of them.

I have the satisfaction to inform your Grace that the city remains tranquil. The patience, the spirit, and continued exertions of the yeomanry are unequalled; and I cannot sufficiently applaud the indefatigable zeal of Major-general Myers, who has undertaken the arrangement of them with a promptitude and ability which has been of the most essential advantage.

I have the honour to be, &c.

CAMDEN.

His Grace the Duke of Portland, &c. &c. &c.

Dublin

Dublin Castle, June 5, Five o'Clock, P. M.

MAJOR Marlay is just arrived from Major-general Loftus, and brings an account that the Major-general, finding that Colonel Walpole's detachment had received a check, thought it prudent to move to Carrew, which he effected without the loss of a man.

It appears that Colonel Walpole had met with the main body of the rebels in a strong post near Slievebuy mountain, and having attacked them, he was unfortunately killed by a shot in the head in the beginning of the action, when his corps being in a situation where it could not act with advantage, was forced to retire to Arklow. The loss was 54 men killed and missing, and two six-pounders. Captain Stark, Captain Armstrong, Captain Duncan, were wounded, but not dangerously; and Sir Watkin Williams Wynne received a contusion in the hand.

From the LONDON GAZETTE EXTRAORDINARY, June 11, 1798.

Whitehall, June 10.

A DISPATCH, of which the following is a copy, has been received from his Excellency the Lord Lieutenant of Ireland by his Grace the Duke of Portland, his Majesty's principal Secretary of State for the home department.

My Lord, *Dublin Castle, June 8.*

I AM to acquaint your Grace that early this morning Lieutenant-general Lake received an express from Major-general Johnson, dated the 5th instant, at New Ross. The Major-general states, that the rebels had, on that morning, attacked his position at New Ross, with a very numerous force, and with great impetuosity; but that after a contest of several hours they were completely repulsed. The loss of the rebels was prodigiously great. An iron gun on a ship carriage was taken, and late in the evening they retreated entirely to Carrick Byrne, leaving several iron ship guns, not mounted.

General Johnson states, that too much praise cannot be given to the forces under his command; and that to Major-general Eustace, and indeed to every individual, he was in the highest degree indebted for their spirited exertions.

The Major-general severely regrets the loss of that brave officer Lord Mountjoy, who fell early in the contest. A return of killed and wounded of his Majesty's forces has not been received, but it appears not to have been considerable.

I have the honour to be, &c. &c.
(Signed) CAMDEN.

His Grace the Duke of Portland, &c. &c. &c.

From the LONDON GAZETTE, June 12, 1798.

Whitehall, June 12.

DISPATCHES, of which the following are copies, have been this day received from his Excellency the Lord Lieutenant of Ireland, by his
Grace

Grace the Duke of Portland, his Majesty's principal Secretary of State for the home department.

My Lord, *Dublin Castle, June* 9.

IT is with the utmost concern I acquaint your Grace an insurrection has broken out in the county of Antrim; and in order to give your Grace the fullest information in my power, I enclose to you an extract of a letter received this morning by Lord Castlereagh from Major-general Nugent. I am in great hope, from the numbers and spirit of the loyal in that part of the country, the insurgents may be quickly checked. I have the honour to be, &c.

His Grace the Duke of Portland. CAMDEN.

My Lord, *Belfast, June* 8.

I HAVE the honour to report to your Lordship, that in consequence of information, which I received early yesterday morning, of an intended insurrection in the county of Antrim, having, for its first object the seizure of the magistrates, who were to assemble that day in the town of Antrim. I apprehended several persons in Belfast. I did not receive the intelligence early enough to prevent the insurgents from taking possession of Antrim, and I am not therefore acquainted with their first proceedings there, but I prevented many magistrates from leaving Belfast; and many others, being officers of yeomanry, on permanent duty, did not attend the meeting. I ordered the 64th regiment and light battalion, and 100 of the 22d light dragoons, under Colonel Clavering and Lieutenant-colonel Lumley, with two five-inch and a half howitzers, and two curricle six-pounders, to proceed with the utmost dispatch through Lisburn to Antrim. I also ordered from the garrison 250 of the Monaghan militia, with Lieutenant-colonel Ker, and 50 of the 22d dragoons, together with the Belfast yeomanry cavalry, with Major Smith, to proceed under the command of Colonel Durham, with two curricle six-pounders, through Carmoney and Temple Patrick, to Antrim, to co-operate with the other detachment. The dragoons under Lieutenant-colonel Lumley having made the attack upon the town, without waiting for the light battalion, were fired upon from the windows of the houses, and were consequently obliged to retreat, with the loss of, I am sorry to add, three officers of that excellent regiment killed and wounded, and the two curricle six-pounders.

Colonel Clavering, on his arrival near Antrim, finding the rebels pouring into that town in great force, very judiciously took post on a hill on the Lisburn side, and reported his situation to M. General Goldie. In the mean time Colonel Durham, with his whole detachment, proceeded to within half a mile of Antrim, and after a cannonade of half an hour, drove the insurgents completely out of the town, and retook the two curricle guns, together with one brass six-pounder, very badly mounted, of which it seems the rebels had two, supposed to have been smuggled out of Belfast. The Colonel then proceeded without the loss of a man, through the town (which, for obvious reasons, suffered much), to Shane's Castle and Randelstown, in which direction the principal part of the rebels fled. He remains there still, for orders from me. Lord O'Neil, I am sorry to say, is dangerously wounded. Lieutenant-colonel Leslie, of the Tay fencibles, reports to me, from Carrickfergus, that Lieutenant Small, with a detachment of

twenty

twenty men of that corps, in the barrack at Larne, defended themselves most gallantly against the attack of a numerous body, and maintained their post with the lofs of two killed and three wounded, including the Lieutenant. I have ordered them into the head-quarters at Carrickfergus. The Glenarm yeomanry (sixty strong) being also threatened by an attack, in the courfe of the day took poffeffion of Glenarm Caftle, where they will maintain themfelves, if poffible. Brigadier-general Knox, having heard of a party of the Toome yeomanry being made prifoners by the infurgents, fent to me very early this morning, to offer to march, by Toome Bridge, into the county of Antrim; which I have defired him to do, in order to liberate Colonel Durham's detachment, and enable them to crofs the country on their return to Belfaft.

Although the infurrection has been pretty general in the country, I do not find they had much fuccefs; but I have not received as yet any reports from Ballycaftle, Ballymena, Ballymoney, Portglenore, and other places in the northern parts, in which yeomanry are ftationed. As my information led to a general rifing in the county of Down, I have been obliged to call in all the fmall detachments of the York fencibles to Newtown Ardes. Colonel Stapleton has every thing in readinefs to move at a moment's warning. The yeomanry are all on permanent duty throughout the counties of Down and Antrim; and I have diftributed arms to 140 loyal men in Belfaft, who will be attached to the Monaghan and Fifefhire regiments, and thereby become very ufeful. Offers of fervice are very numerous.

I cannot clofe this letter without expreffing to your Lordfhip my entire approbation of the conduct of the troops of all defcriptions in this part of the northern diftrict. Their zeal and attention to their duties cannot be furpaffed, and I truft that, when occafion offers, they will act in that concert which is fo much to be wifhed for in military fervice. Lieutenant-colonel Lumley, I am afraid, is badly wounded in the leg; Cornet Dunn is killed; and Lieutenant Murphy flightly wounded; all of the 22d dragoons. I underftand, but not officially, that fome yeomanry from Hertford's eftate (I believe the Derriaghy) were with the dragoons when they made the unfuccefsful attack on Antrim, and they retired to Antrim Caftle, where they were relieved by Colonel Durham. Colonel Durham deferves my warmeft praife for his judicious and fpirited conduct. He fpeaks in high terms of the detachment under him, and particularly of the Monaghan militia. The Rev. Steele Dickfon was taken up the night before laft, and fent prifoner here, where he will be confined in a place of fafety, as well as many others, whom it is now neceffary to apprehend. Your Lordfhip may depend upon my individual exertions in this unpleafant conteft; and as I am ably fupported, I make no doubt that we fhall prevent the rebels from gaining any advantages, and ultimately oblige them to return to their allegiance. I fhall write again to-morrow, fhould any material event occur.

I have the honour to be, &c.

G. NUGENT, Major-general.

Lord Vifcount Caftlereagh, &c.

My

My Lord,   *Dublin Castle, June 9.*

I HAVE the honour to enclose herewith to your Grace, further particulars respecting the action at New Ross, which have been received in a letter from Major-general Johnson to Lieutenant-general Lake, of which I transmit your Grace an extract, with two returns annexed.

                     I have the honour to be, &c.

His Grace the Duke of Portland.   CAMDEN.

Extract of a Letter from Major-general Johnson to Lieutenant-general Lake, dated at Ross, June 7.

I SEND you a return of the killed, wounded, and missing of the troops engaged on the 5th instant. Their numbers you will, I trust, find not great, when you take into consideration the numbers they were opposed to.

I likewise send a return of the ordnance, ammunition, and standards, taken from the rebels. The number killed cannot be ascertained. In my former letter I was prevented, by a pressure of business, doing justice to the merits of several officers to whom I am highly indebted for their extraordinary exertions.

General Eustace, Colonel Crawfurd, A. Q. M. G. Lieutenant-colonels, Stewart, 89th regiment, commanding light infantry; Maxwell, Donegal militia; Majors, Vandeleur, Clare militia; Vesey, county of Dublin militia; Mellifont, my aid de camp, and Major of Brigade Sandford, are entitled to my fullest praise. I should not omit Lieutenant Eustace, the General's aid de camp, who is a very promising young man. To Lieutenant-colonel James Foul., commanding the Mid-Lothian cavalry, and Captain Irvine, commanding the detachment of the 5th and 9th dragoons, I am no less indebted. I cannot say too much in favour of Captain Bloomfield, B. H. artillery, and Captain Thornhill, commanding the Royal Irish flying artillery, whose very great exertions contributed very essentially to our success. We had a great loss in Colonel Lord Mountjoy. Captain Tottenham, yeoman cavalry, and Captain Boyd, with the debus of his corps, have rendered me every possible assistance. In making mention of these particulars, I would not wish you to suppose I do not feel myself much indebted to every individual, a very few excepted.

Return of the killed, wounded, and missing of the Troops engaged at Ross on the 5th of June.

Killed—1 colonel, 1 cornet, 1 quarter-master, 4 serjeants, 3 drummers, and 0 rank and file. Also 54 horses.

Wounded—1 captain, 57 rank and file. Also 5 horses.

Missing—1 captain, 3 lieutenants, 1 ensign, 2 serjeants, 2 drummers, 72 rank and file, and 4 horses.

Names of Officers killed, wounded, and missing.

Colonel Lord Mountjoy, county of Dublin militia, killed.
Cornet Ladwell, 5th dragoons, killed.
Captain Sinclair, Donegal militia, wounded.
Captain Warburton and Lieutenant Flinter, Queen's County militia, missing.

                                           Lieutenant

Lieutenant Harford, Kilkenny militia, missing.
Lieutenant Blake and Lieutenant Buller, of the 89th, attached to the light battalion, missing.
Quarter-master Hay, of Mid-Lothian fencibles, killed.

HENRY JOHNSON.

Return of Ordnance Stores, &c. taken from the Rebels in the Action of the 5th of June 1798.

	Guns
5½ inch howitzer, on ship carriage	1
Iron four-pounder, on ship carriage	1
Swivels	14
Iron three pounder	1
Iron two-pounder	1
Total	18

Fourteen shots of different sizes.
An immensity of pikes, which were broken as soon as taken.
Also muskets, likewise destroyed.
A variety of standards and colours.

HENRY JOHNSON, Major-general.

From the LONDON GAZETTE EXTRAORDINARY, June 14, 1798.

Whitehall, June 14.

DISPATCHES, of which the following are copies, have been this day received from his Excellency the Lord Lieutenant of Ireland by his Grace the Duke of Portland, his Majesty's principal Secretary of State for the home department.

My Lord, *Dublin Castle, June 10, 1798.*

I HAVE the satisfaction to acquaint your Grace, that yesterday evening a very large body of the Wexford rebels was driven back with great loss from their attack upon Major-general Needham's post at Arklow.

The enclosed extract from the Major-general's letter to Lieutenant-general Lake, will furnish your Grace with the details of this important advantage. I have the honour to be, &c.

His Grace the Duke of Portland. CAMDEN.

Sir, *Arklow, June 10, Half past Five, A. M.*

ABOUT three o'clock, P. M. yesterday, the rebel army presented itself at my out-post in very great numbers.

They approached from Coolgrexny road, and along the sand-hills on the shore, in two columns, while the whole of the intermediate space embracing my entire front was crowded by a rabble, armed with pikes and fire-arms, and bearing down on me without any regular order. The position I had chosen was a very strong one in front of the barrack.

As soon as the enemy approached within a short distance, we opened a heavy fire of grape, which did as much execution as, from the nature of the ground and the strong fences of which they possessed themselves,

Vol. VIII. F could

could have been expected. This continued inceffantly from fix until half paft eight o'clock, when the enemy defifted from their attack, and fled in diforder on every fide. The numbers killed have not been afcertained. Our lofs is inconfiderable, and no officer is wounded. A principal leader is among the flain.

Colonel Sir W. W. Wynne, with fome of the 4th dragoon guards and 5th dragoons, and part of his own regiment, and the yeomanry, charged the rebels moft gallantly, and routed a ftrong column of them attempting to gain the town by the beach. Colonel Maxwell offered his fervices to burn fome houfes in his front, near the end of the action, and effected it moft handfomely, and without lofs. Colonel Skerrot, of the Durham fencibles, on whom the brunt of the action fell, acted in the moft fpirited and determined manner, as did alfo Colonel O'Hara, who commanded the Antrim, and covered the road on my right. The coolnefs and good conduct of Colonel Cope, of the Armagh, does him infinite credit; and it is with the moft real fatisfaction I add, that the zeal and fpirited conduct of the yeomanry corps were every thing I could wifh.

To Lieutenant-colonel Blackwood, of the late 33d, and Lieutenant-colonel Cleghorn, of the Meath, who did me the honour to ferve with me upon this occafion, I am indebted for the moft effential fervices, and I am happy thus to acknowledge my obligations to them both; and of the fpirited exertions of Mr. Whaley I cannot fpeak too highly.

I muft, in juftice to my aid-de-camp, Captain Moore, of the 4th dragoon guards, and major of brigade, Captain Needham, of the 9th dragoons, mention their great alertnefs. To the great activity and information of the former I am much indebted, and he will detail to you all other particulars.

    (Signed)   FRANCIS NEEDHAM.

Lieutenant-general Lake, &c. &c. &c.

  My Lord,   *Dublin Caftle, June* 17, 1798.

I HAVE the honour to acquaint your Grace, that a letter has been this day received by Lieutenant-general Lake from Major-general Nugent, at Belfaft, dated the 9th inftant, ftating, that the rebels in the county of Antrim were difperfed in all directions, except at Toome, whither Brigadier-general Knox and Lieutenant-colonel Clavering were proceeding; and that many of them had laid down their arms.

Major-general Nugent alfo ftates, that Mr. M'Cleverty had returned from Donegorr-hill, whither he had been carried prifoner by a body of 2000 rebels. Whilft they were in this ftation they difagreed, and quarrelled amongft themfelves, and from his influence and perfuafion, above 1500 left the camp, broke and deftroyed their arms, and declared that they would never again carry an offenfive weapon againft his Majefty or his loyal fubjects. Many more difperfed, and the commander of them was left with fifty men only.

      I have the honour to be, &c.

His Grace the Duke of Portland.   CAMDEN.

From the LONDON GAZETTE, June 16, 1798.

Whitehall, June 16.

DISPATCHES, of which the following are copies, have been received from his Excellency the Lord Lieutenant of Ireland by his Grace the Duke of Portland, his Majesty's principal Secretary of State for the Home department.

My Lord,   *Dublin Castle, June 11.*

I AM concerned to acquaint your Grace that the accounts received from Major-general Nugent this morning, are not so favourable as, from the details which were yesterday received, I had reason to hope. A body of rebels having assembled near Saintfield, they were attacked by a detachment under Colonel Stapleton, who at first suffered some loss; but he afterwards put the rebels to flight. Being ordered to proceed to Newtown Ardes, Colonel Stapleton found the rebels in possession of the town, upon which General Nugent ordered him to retire until his force could be augmented.

There is no official account as to the body of rebels which were to be attacked by Brigadier-general Knox, at Toome Bridge. Private accounts state that they have been dispersed.

I have the honour to be, &c.

His Grace the Duke of Portland.   CAMDEN.

My Lord,   *Dublin Castle, June 12.*

I HAVE the honour to acquaint your Grace, that accounts have been this day received from Major-general Nugent, who is at Belfast, which state, that the information he had received of a large body of rebels having entrenched themselves near Toome Bridge, was unfounded. One arch of the bridge had been broken down by an inconsiderable party, which had been dispersed; the bridge has been since rendered passable.

Colonel Clavering has reported from Antrim to Major-general Nugent, that the disaffected in the neighbourhood of that town had expressed a desire to submit, and to return to their duty. At Ballymena, 150 muskets and 800 pikes had been given up to the magistrates. Many arms, 500 pikes, and a brass field-piece, have been surrendered to Major Seddon.

Major-general Nugent expresses his warmest acknowledgments to the regulars, militia, and yeomanry forces under his command, for their alertness, zeal, and spirit.

Other advices state, that Lieutenant-colonel Stewart, having marched from Blaris, with a part of the Argyle fencibles, 30 cavalry, and some yeomanry, arrived at Ballynahinch as the rebels were beginning to collect. He relieved some yeomen who were in their possession, and the rebels fled into Lord Moira's wood, whither they were pursued, about 40 of them killed, and the remainder dispersed.

By a letter received this morning from Major-general Sir Charles Asgill, it appears, that he had attacked, with 300 men, a rebel camp, at the Roar, near Ross, which he completely dispersed; 50 men were killed, and their leader.   I have the honour to be, &c.

His Grace the Duke of Portland.   C

Admiralty Office, June 16.

Extract of a Letter from Captain Brifac, Commander of his Majefty's Ship Iris, to Evan Nepean, Efq. dated at Leith the 11th *inftant.*

I HAVE the pleafure to fay, that on the 1ft inftant, off the Scaw, after a chafe of fixteen hours, I captured the Leger French lugger privateer, carrying four four-pounders, who had the impudence to fire at his Majefty's fhip under my command, and by the papers I found on board had 35 men, commanded by a Monfieur Lallemand, who, with the crew, efcaped on fhore about three leagues to the eaftward of the Scaw, in fifhing-boats: fhe had taken three veffels, and fent them to Arundel in Norway.

From the LONDON GAZETTE EXTRAORDINARY, June 18, 1798.

Whitehall, June 18.

A DISPATCH, of which the following is a copy, has been this day received from his Excellency the Lord Lieutenant of Ireland, by his Grace the Duke of Portland, his Majefty's principal Secretary of State for the home department.

Dublin Caftle, June 14.

I HAVE the honour to acquaint your Grace, that intelligence arrived this day, from Major-general Nugent, ftating, that he had marched againft a large body of rebels, who were pofted at Saintfield. They retired, on his approach, to a ftrong pofition on the Saintfield fide of Ballynahinch, and there made a fhow of refiftance, and endeavoured to turn his left flank; but Lieutenant-colonel Stewart arriving from Down, with a pretty confiderable force of infantry, cavalry, and yeomanry, they foon defifted, and retired to a very ftrong pofition behind Ballynahinch.

General Nugent attacked them next morning at three o'clock, having occupied two hills on the left and right of the town, to prevent the rebels from having any other choice than the mountains in their rear for their retreat: he fent Lieutenant-colonel Stewart to poft himfelf with part of the Argyle fencibles, and fome yeomanry, as well as a detachment of the 22d light dragoons, in a fituation from which he could enfilade the rebel line; whilft Colonel Leflie, with part of the Monaghan militia, fome cavalry, and yeoman infantry, fhould make an attack upon their front. Having two howitzers and fix fix-pounders with the two detachments, the Major-general was enabled to annoy them very much, from different parts of his pofition.

The rebels attacked, impetuoufly, Colonel Leflie's detachment, and even jumped into the road, from the Earl of Moira's demefne, to endeavour to take one of his guns; but they were repulfed, with flaughter. Lieutenant-colonel Stewart's detachment was attacked by them with the fame activity, but he repulfed them alfo, and the fire from his howitzer and fix-pounder foon obliged them to fly in all directions. Their force was, on the evening of the 12th, near 5000; but as many perfons are preffed into their fervice, and almoft entirely unarmed, the General does not fuppofe that on the morning of the engagement their numbers were fo confiderable.

About

(45)

About 400 rebels were killed in the attack and retreat, and the remainder were difperfed all over the country. Parts of the town of Saintfield and Ballynahinch were burnt. Major-general Nugent ftates, that both officers and men deferve praife for their alacrity and zeal on this, as well as on all occafions; but he particularly expreffes his obligations to Lieutenant-colonel Stewart for his advice and affiftance throughout the bufinefs, and to Colonel Leflie for his readinefs to volunteer the duty at all times. The yeomanry behaved with extreme fteadinefs and bravery. Three or four green colours were taken, and one fix pounder, not mounted, but which the rebels fired very often, and a confiderable quantity of ammunition. Their chief was Muuro, a fhopkeeper of Lifburn.

Major-general Nugent regrets the lofs of Captain Evatt, of the Monaghan militia; Lieutenant Ellis, of the fame regiment, was wounded; the lofs of rank and file, five killed and 14 wounded. Several of the yeoman infantry were killed or wounded.

The Major general expreffes his acknowledgments to Lieutenant-colonel Peacock, and Major of Brigade Machinnon, who were of the greateft fervice.

The Portaferry yeomanry, on the 11th inftant, under the command of Captain Matthews, made a moft gallant defence againft a large body of the rebels, who attacked the town of Portaferry—the yeomanry having taken poffeffion of the market-houfe, from which poft they repulfed the rebels, who left behind them above 40 dead; many more were carried off. Captain Hopkins, of a revenue cruifer, brought his guns to bear on the town, and was of great fervice in defending it.

Advices from Major-general Sir Charles Afgill, dated from Kilkenny, the 13th inftant, ftate, that on the evening of the 12th, having heard that a large body of the rebels had marched from the county of Wexford againft Borris, under the command of Mr. Bagnal Harvey, and were burning the town, he proceeded to its relief with 400 men, but the rebels had fled before he could arrive. They had attacked Mr. Kavenagh's houfe, in which were 29 men of the Donegal militia, who, notwithftanding the inceffant fire kept up on them for fome hours, defended themfelves in the moft gallant manner, and killed feveral of the rebels. Nothing could furpafs the determined bravery of thofe few men. The rebels effected their efcape into the county of Wexford.

A letter, received by Lieutenant-general Lake, from Major-general Johnfon, dated the 13th inftant, at New Rofs, ftates, that having received information that the rebels had fitted out feveral boats and other craft, for the purpofe of effecting their efcape, he had fent Lieutenant Hill, with fuch armed veffels as could be fpared from Feathard, where they were collected, with orders to deftroy the whole; which Lieutenant Hill effected with his ufual fpirit, and without lofs. Thirteen large failing hookers and a great many boats were burnt.

I have the honour to be, &c.

His Grace the Duke of Portland, &c. CAMDEN.

From the LONDON GAZETTE, June 23, 1798.

Dublin Castle, June 16.

THIS morning advices were received from Major-general Nugent. By them it appears, that the rebels, who had been defeated at Ballynahinch, have petitioned for pardon, and offered to surrender up all their arms and ammunition. The Major-general, in reply, promised to accept their submission, on the condition of giving up their leader, Munroe, and the other principal traitors who had instigated them to their late wicked practices. They were to surrender by twelve o'clock on the 15th. Munroe was, however, taken by General Nugent early on that morning.

Major-general Nugent, alluding to the affair at Ballynahinch, states the loss of the rebels to have exceeded 500 men, and that many have been since made prisoners. The General particularly states his acknowledgments for the services of Major-general Barber.

He mentions also, with great satisfaction, the conduct of Mr. Boyd, of Ballycastle. Mr. M'Naghten had sent to warn him of his danger, which induced him to retreat on Friday last to Coleraine, where he collected the Dunseverich and Giant's Causeway corps, with which, together with his own, he returned to Ballycastle, and beat the rebels out of the place, and he is now proceeding to punish them between that town and Glenarm.

Captain Stewart, of the Glenarm yeomanry, and Captain Matthews, of the Portaferry yeomanry, have behaved uncommonly well in repulsing large bodies of rebels, who attacked them with great fury.

General Nugent speaks generally of the conduct of all the yeomanry in his district, in the warmest terms of approbation, and mentions that he has thanked them all.

My Lord, *Dublin Castle, June 17.*

I AM to acquaint your Grace, that, since the defeat of the rebels at Ballynahinch, advices have been received from Major-general Nugent, that they have not re-assembled in the county of Down, but are submitting, and delivering up their arms in various places.

I have the honour to be, &c.

His Grace the Duke of Portland, &c. &c. &c. CAMDEN.

My Lord, *Dublin Castle, June 19.*

I HAVE the honour to acquaint your Grace, that accounts were this day received from Brigadier-general Barnett, stating, that on the 17th instant a considerable body of rebels attacked Kinbeggan, but were repulsed by a detachment of 50 of the Northumberland fencibles, under the command of Captain Thatcher; 120 of the rebels were killed, and a great many wounded: the detachment behaved with the greatest gallantry.

Brigadier-general Grose reports, from Kilcock, that Colonel Irwine, with a detachment under his command, had this day engaged a body of above 2000 rebels at Ovidstown Hill, about a mile from Hortland. The loss of the rebels was upwards of 200 slain.

The number of killed and wounded of his Majesty's troops does not amount to more than 23. Ensign Sutter, of the Inverness fencibles, was killed;

killed; Colonel Irwine was himself wounded slightly in the cheek; Sir Richard Steele, of the 4th dragoon guards, was also wounded, but it is hoped not dangerously. Colonel Irwine reports to General Grose, that he is highly indebted to all the officers and men who served under him, and that he was much benefited by the assistance he received from Colonel Burrowes, who volunteerd on the occasion,

The accounts received from the north are favourable; and state, that the rebels are disperfed in all quarters. I have, &c. &c.

His Grace the Duke of Portland, &c. CAMDEN.

From the LONDON GAZETTE, June 26, 1798.

Parliament Street, June 26.

A DISPATCH, of which the following is a copy, has been received by the Right Honourable Henry Dundas, one of his Majesty's principal Secretaries of State, from Brigadier-general the Honourable Thomas Maitland, commanding his Majesty's forces in the island of St. Domingo; dated on board his Majesty's ship Thunderer, off Mole St. Nicholas, the 10th of May 1798.

Sir,

I EMBRACE the very first opportunity of informing you, that on the 22d of last month I came to the resolution of immediately evacuating the towns of Port-au-Prince and St. Marc's, with their dependencies, together with the parish of Arcahaye; and it is now with great pleasure I have the honour of acquainting you, that this measure has been carried into complete effect, without the smallest loss of any kind, and in a manner, I flatter myself, to give perfect satisfaction, as far as, under the circumstances, it was possible, to all the French inhabitants and planters, whether these choose to follow the fortune of his Majesty's arms, or to remain in the part of the colony about to be evacuated.

In confidering the modes of effecting this very difficult but important object, there seemed to me but two in any degree practicable; the one, to withdraw the small British force and such of the colonial troops as it was immediately posfible to induce to go with us, in a precipitate manner, after blowing up the forts; the other, to state fairly my determination, and, acting as events occurred, to endeavour, in a deliberate way, to withdraw the whole of our stores and force, and, at the same time, to attempt to obtain some terms for the numerous inhabitants, who, either from neceffity or choice, wished to remain.

The first of these measures seemed to me (however safe to the British nation) to be so perfectly contrary to the spirit of generosity and liberality which has ever actuated the British nation, and so certain of being attended with immediate and shocking scenes of bloodshed among the inhabitants, whose natural impetuosity of character would be increased by contending passions, deluded hopes, and different interests, that I determined at once to set it aside; and begun the 23d ultimo, in consequence of adopting the second, to embark the heavy stores of every description; stating my full determination to all the parties concerned, and sending, at the fame time, a flag of truce to General Touflaint l'Ouverture, of Gonaives, to acquaint him with my resolution, and leaving to his option either to obtain the poffeflions we evacuated in a state of ruin, or in a state of perfect order, provided he would guarantee, in a

solemn

solemn manner, the lives and properties of such persons as chose to remain.

General Toussaint immediately agreed to the last proposition, and sent to Port-au-Prince on the 28th instant a confidential officer, who, having met Lieutenant-colonel Nightingall, deputy adjutant-general, on my part, on the 30th of April, the accompanying agreement was mutually exchanged and ratified by both parties.

The stipulation in favour of the inhabitants and planters afforded them the only security in my power to obtain, and with which they were so entirely satisfied, that although at first they had universally resolved to follow the King's forces, yet, upon hearing of this agreement in their favour, many of them who had actually embarked relanded, and I think I may safely assure you, there are not ten rich proprietors who have, ultimately, upon this occasion, quitted their properties.

By the 6th instant the whole of the heavy British stores of every description being embarked, and all the French brass guns, mortars, with such of the inhabitants as voluntarily wished to go, and all the merchandise belonging to British merchants, I ordered the parish of L'Arcahaye to be evacuated, which was accordingly done the 7th at noon. The 8th, at two o'clock in the morning, I withdrew the whole of the force from Port-au-Prince, and embarked it at Fort Bizoton, and on the 9th, in the morning, the whole fleet sailed to its different destinations.

I have not heard from Colonel Grant, who commanded at St. Marc's, but I have every reason to believe he evacuated that place on the 6th or 7th of this month; and I entertain no doubt but that he is now at the Mole, where I ordered him to proceed with his garrison.

You will readily believe, that on such an occasion much military precaution, and much exertion in all the departments, must have been necessary, as well for the honour and security of his Majesty's arms, as to enable me to move off within a reasonable period.

Of the conduct of the officers and men of his Majesty's British and colonial forces, I have nothing to say, but what tends infinitely to their credit.

To the heads of departments I feel myself extremely indebted for the zeal and activity with which they seconded my wishes, most particularly to Lieutenants-colonel Nightingall and Littlehales, deputies adjutant and quarter-master generals, and to Captain Spicer, commanding the royal artillery; nor can I here omit doing myself the pleasure of signifying to you what very essential aid I have received from the zeal and intelligence of Mr. Wigglesworth, his Majesty's Commissary General.

To the royal navy I am under every obligation for their cordial assistance throughout the whole of this service; to Captains Cochet and Ogilvie, of his Majesty's ships Abergavenny and Thunderer, it is principally owing that I was enabled to carry my wishes into early effect.

Lieutenant Young, of the navy, chief agent of transports, conducted himself, in the execution of this arduous task, in such a manner, that I should neglect a very material, though pleasant part of my duty, were I not to seize this opportunity to recommend him in the strongest manner to your notice. He is a very old officer, but his length of services has neither impaired his zeal or diminished his activity. I have the honour to be, &c.

THOMAS MAITLAND,
Brigadier-general, commanding in St. Domingo.

Admiralty

y of a Letter from
s Majesty's Ships
dated on board his

Sir,

I ENCLOSE a letter from
...rora, acquainting me with
...patches from the Havannah.

Earl St. Vincent, &c. &c. &c.

py of a Letter from Rear-
Majesty's Ships and Vessels
dated on board the Prince
May 13.

Sir,

I HEREWITH enclose,

...ving his convoy.   I have

Sir,   *Victorieuse, St. Kitt's, May 12.*
I BEG leave to inform you, that on the 7th instant, passing to leeward of Guadaloupe, in his Majesty's sloop Victorieuse, under my command, with the trade of Trinidada for St. Kitt's, we saw two French

E. S. DICKINSON.

py of a Letter from Rear-admiral Harvey, Commander in Chief of his
Majesty's Ships and Vessels at the Leeward Islands, to Evan Nepean, Esq.
dated on board the Prince of Wales, St. Christopher's, May 13.

Sir,

I AM to acquaint you, for the information of their Lordships, that Captain Warren, in his Majesty's sloop Scourge, on the 1st instant chased

VOL. VIII.   G   on

on shore, on St. Martin's, a French privateer brig, of 14 guns. The crew, after setting fire to her, got on shore, and she blew up before the boats which were sent from the Scourge could get to her, and was consequently totally destroyed. I have the honour to be, &c.

HENRY HARVEY.

Sir, *Prince of Wales, Basseterre Road, St. Christopher's, May* 13.

I HAVE to acquaint you, for the information of their Lordships, that the undermentioned French privateers, which had been fitted out at Guadaloupe and Porto Rico, have been captured and sent into the different islands at the periods, and by the ships and vessels of his Majesty's squadron under my command, as against their names expressed:—By the Solebay, Captain Poyntz, 17th March, off Antigua, Augustus schooner, of two guns, and 23 men.—By the Maitland, Captain Mitford, 29th and 31st of March, to the northward of Antigua, La Vantour sloop, of 10 guns, and 64 men; and L'Aigle brig, of 12 guns, and 86 men.—By L'Aimable and Scourge, Captains Lobbe and Warren, 6th and 8th ult. off Porto Rico, La Triumphe brig, of 14 guns, and 88 men; also Chasseur schooner, of two guns, and 18 men; and on the 20th, by L'Aimable alone, L'Espiegle schooner, of two guns and 18 men.—By the Requin, commanded by Lieutenant Senhouse, the 1st instant, off St. Bartholomew, Mutine sloop, of six guns, and 44 men.—By the Tamer, Captain Webster, 2d instant, to windward of Barbadoes, Bran le Bas schooner, of eight guns, and 82 men. I have the honour to be, &c.

Evan Nepean, Esq. HENRY HARVEY.

THE Honourable Brigadier-general Maitland, commanding in chief his Britannic Majesty's forces in the island of St. Domingo, having intimated to General Toussaint l'Ouverture, commanding the French army in the said island, his intention to evacuate the towns of Port-au-Prince, St. Marc's, and their dependencies, with the parish of l'Arcahaye; and having proposed to General Toussaint l'Ouverture, to send a person to Port-au-Prince, charged with full powers, that this object might be effected in a manner most consonant to the interests of humanity and the views of each party; and General Toussaint l'Ouverture having consented to the above proposals, and having sent to Port au-Prince Monsieur Huin, Adjutant-general to the French army, did meet on board his Majesty's ship Abergavenny, the 30th of April 1798, when the following conditions were mutually agreed on, and have been since ratified on the one part by Brigadier-general Maitland, commanding in chief his Majesty's forces; and on the other by General Toussaint l'Ouverture, commanding the French army.

Conditions agreed upon between Lieutenant-colonel Nightingall, Deputy Adjutant-general to his Britannic Majesty's Forces, and Monsieur Huin, Adjutant-general to the Army of General Toussaint l'Ouverture, who are respectively invested with full Powers for that Purpose.

1st The towns of Port-au-Prince, St. Marc's, and their dependencies, with their present works, and the parish of L'Arcahaye, shall be left to General Toussaint l'Ouverture in the state agreed upon between us, viz. all the iron guns to be rendered unserviceable, except three or four, by verbal agreement between us, in a given time, which shall be fixed at the period when the British forces can conveniently be withdrawn.

2d.

2d. As an express condition, and in consequence of the first article, General Toussaint l'Ouverture engages, in the most solemn and positive manner, to guarantee the lives and properties of all the inhabitants who may choose to remain.

3d. In order to facilitate and accomplish these conditions, it is agreed, that there shall be a suspension of arms for a limited time, not exceeding five weeks from this day.

Done on board his Majesty's ship Abergavenny, in the road of Port-au-Prince, this 30th day of April 1798.

(Signed)

HUIN, Adjutant-general of the Army of the French Republic.
M. NIGHTINGALL, D. A. General to his Majesty's Forces.

Whitehall, June 26.

A DISPATCH, of which the following is a copy, has been received from his Excellency the Lord Lieutenant of Ireland by his Grace the Duke of Portland, his Majesty's principal Secretary of State for the home department.

My Lord, *Dublin Castle, June 21.*

I HAVE the honour to acquaint your Grace, that Brigadier-general Dunn has reported, from Monasterevan, that on the 19th instant he had sent a strong patrole, under the command of Captain Pack, of the 5th dragoon guards, towards Prosperous, from Rathangan; and that Captain Pack having fallen in with 100 of the rebels, well mounted and appointed, he instantly attacked and defeated them, taking eight horses, and killing from 20 to 30 men.

Lieutenant-colonel Stewart, of the 5th dragoons, having been detached to Prosperous on the evening of the 19th instant, found a body of rebels posted on a hill on the left of the town, which fled into the neighbouring bog on his approach. His advanced guard having been fired upon as he approached, from the town, he brought two curricle guns to bear upon it, and set fire to part of the town. Much cattle was left behind by the rebels, which they had pinned up near the mess-room of the barracks, together with many pikes and drums. Eight of the rebels were killed.

Yesterday morning a detachment from Mount Kennedy, under command of Lieutenant M'Lann, of the Reay fencibles, and Lieutenant Gore, of the Mount Kennedy cavalry, attacked a body of near 300 rebels, near Ballinarush. The fire commenced from the rebels, who were posted behind a hedge on the top of a commanding hill. After an engagement of about twenty minutes, they gave way in every quarter, leaving 20 dead behind them.

It appears, by letters from Cork, that an engagement has taken place between a detachment of the Caithness fencibles, assisted by a party of the Westmeath militia, and a considerable body of rebels. The latter were defeated, with the loss of above 100 men. His Majesty's troops appear to have suffered but little in the action.

The north remains quiet.

I have the honour to be, &c.

His Grace the Duke of Portland, CORNWALLIS.
&c. &c. &c.

From the LONDON GAZETTE EXTRAORDINARY, June 26, 1798.

Whitehall, June 26.

A DISPATCH, of which the following is a copy, has been this day received from his Excellency the Lord Lieutenant of Ireland, by his Grace the Duke of Portland, his Majesty's principal Secretary of State for the home department.

My Lord,   *Dublin Castle, June 24.*

I HAVE the honour to transmit to your Grace a dispatch received by Lord Viscount Castlereagh, this day, from Lieutenant-general Lake, dated Wexford, the 22d inst. together with a letter from Brigadier-general Moore, containing an account of his important successes.

I also enclose a copy of the proposals made by the rebels in the town of Wexford, to Lieutenant-general Lake, and his answer.

I have the honour to be, &c.
(Signed)   CORNWALLIS.

His Grace the Duke of Portland, &c. &c. &c.

My Lord,   *Wexford, June 22.*

YESTERDAY afternoon I had the honour to dispatch a letter to your Lordship, from Enniscorthy, with the transactions of the day, for his Excellency the Lord Lieutenant's information; and the enclosed copy of a letter from Brigadier-general Moore to Major-general Johnson, will account for my having entered this place without opposition. General Moore, with his usual enterprise and activity, pushed on to this town, and entered it so opportunely as to prevent it from being laid in ashes, and the massacre of the remaining prisoners, which the rebels declared their resolution of carrying into effect the next day; and there can be little doubt it would have taken place, for the day before they murdered above seventy prisoners, and threw their bodies over the bridge.

Enclosed is a copy of my answer to the proposal of the inhabitants of this town, transmitted in my letter of yesterday to your Lordship. The evacuation of the town by the rebels renders it unnecessary. I have the pleasure to acquaint your Lordship, that the subscriber of the insolent proposals, Mr. Keughe, and one of their principal leaders, Mr. Roach, with a few others, are in my hands, without negotiation. The rebels are reported to be in some force within five miles of this place; it is supposed for the purpose of submission, to which the event of yesterday may strengthen their inclination. I have reason to think that there are a number so disposed, and that I shall be able to secure some more of their leaders; but should I be disappointed in my expectations, and find they collect in any force, I shall lose no time in attacking them.

I have the honour to be, &c.
(Signed)   G. LAKE.

P. S. From inquiry, the numbers killed yesterday were very great indeed.

Lord Viscount Castlereagh.

Dear General,   *Camp above Wexford, June 22.*

AGREEABLE to your order I took post, on the evening of the 19th, near Fook's Mill, in the park of Mr. Sutton. Next day I sent a strong

strong detachment, under Lieutenant-colonel Wilkinson, to patrole towards Tintern and Clonmines, with a view to scour the country, and communicate with the troops you directed me to join from Duncannon. The Lieutenant-colonel found the country deserted, and got no tidings of the troops. I waited for them until three o'clock in the afternoon, when, despairing of their arrival, I began my march to Taghmon. We had not marched above half a mile when a considerable body of the rebels was perceived marching towards us. I sent my advanced guard, consisting of the two rifle companies of the sixtieth regiment, to skirmish with them, whilst a howitzer and a six-pounder were advanced to a cross road above Goff's Bridge, and some companies of light infantry formed on each side of them, under Lieut.-colonel Wilkinson. The rebels attempted to attack these, but were instantly repulsed and driven beyond the bridge. A large body were perceived at the same time moving towards my left. Major Aylmer, and afterwards Major Daniel, with five companies of light infantry and a six-pounder, were detached against them. The sixtieth regiment, finding no farther opposition in front, had of themselves inclined to their left, to engage the body which was attempting to turn us. The action here was for a short time pretty sharp. The rebels were in great numbers, and armed with both muskets and pikes; they were, however, forced to give way, and driven, though they repeatedly attempted to form, behind the ditches. They at last dispersed, flying towards Enniscorthy and Wexford.

Their killed could not be ascertained, as they lay scattered in the fields over a considerable extent, but they seemed to be numerous. I enclose a list * of ours. The troops behaved with great spirit; the artillery and Hompesch's cavalry were active, and seemed only to regret that the country did not admit of their rendering more effectual service. Major Daniel is the only officer whose wound is bad; it is through the knee, but not dangerous.

The business, which began between three and four, was not over till near eight. It was then too late to proceed to Taghmon. I took post for the night on the ground where the action had commenced. As the rebels gave way, I was informed of the approach of the second and twenty-ninth regiments, under Lord Dalhousie. In the morning of the 21st we were proceeding to Taghmon, where I was met by an officer of the North Cork from Wexford with the enclosed letters. I gave, of course, no answer to the proposal made by the inhabitants of Wexford, but I thought it my duty immediately to proceed here and to take post above the town, by which means I have perhaps saved the town itself from fire, as well as the lives of many loyal subjects who were prisoners in the hands of the rebels. The rebels fled, upon my approach, over the bridge of Wexford, and towards the barony of Forth. I shall wait here your farther orders. Lord Kingsborough has informed me of different engagements he had entered into with respect to the inhabitants. I have declined entering upon the subject, but have referred his Lordship to you or General Lake.

I received your pencilled note during the action of the 20th; it was impossible for me then to detach the troops you asked for, but I hear you have perfectly succeeded at Enniscorthy with those you had. Mr.

---

* This list was omitted.

Roche,

Roche, who commands the rebels, is encamped, I hear, about
miles off. He has sent to Lord Kingsborough to surrender upon ter
Your presence speedily is upon every account extremely necessary.

I am, &c.

Major-general Johnson.   JOHN MOORE

P. S. It is difficult to judge of the numbers of rebels, they appear such crowds and so little order. Information states those we beat to h been between five and six thousand.

Proposals of the Rebels.

June 21

THAT Capt. M'Manus shall proceed from Wexford towards Oul accompanied by Mr. E. Hay, appointed by the inhabitants of all religi persuasions, to inform the officer commanding the King's troops that t are ready to deliver up the town of Wexford without opposition, down their arms, and return to their allegiance, provided that their p sons and properties are guaranteed by the commanding officer; and t they will use every influence in their power to induce the people of country at large to return to their allegiance also. These terms we h Captain M'Manus will be able to procure.

Signed, by order of the inhabitants of the town of Wexford,

MATTHEW KEUGHE

Answer.

Enniscorthy, June 22

LIEUTENANT-General Lake cannot attend to any terms offe by rebels in arms against their sovereign. While they continue so, must use the force entrusted to him with the utmost energy for their struction.

To the deluded multitude he promises pardon, on their delivering his hands their leaders, surrendering their arms, and returning with cerity to their allegiance.

(Signed)   G. LAKE

To the Inhabitants of Wexford.

From the LONDON GAZETTE, June 30, 1798.

Whitehall, June 30.

A DISPATCH, of which the following is a copy, has been ceived from his Excellency the Lord Lieutenant of Ireland by his G the Duke of Portland, his Majesty's principal Secretary of State for home department.

My Lord,   *Dublin Castle, June* 2

I HAVE the honour of enclosing to your Grace the copy of a le received this day by Lord Castlereagh, from Major-general Sir Ch: Asgill, and a return of the killed, wounded, and missing, by the att on Vinegar Hill and the town of Enniscorthy.

I have the honour to be, &c.

His Grace the Duke of Portland.   CORNWALLIS

My Lord, Kilkenny, June 24, Nine o'clock, P. M.

I HAVE the honour to inform you, that early on the morning of the 23d instant I received information that the rebels, amounting to several thousands, had escaped from the county of Wexford, and formed a camp at Killymount, and were proceeding to Gores Bridge. I instantly assembled all the force I could collect, and marched towards them. I did not arrive in time to prevent their defeating a detachment at that place, and taking 24 men of the Wexford militia prisoners. They marched off rapidly towards Leighlin. The troops from thence, consisting of a small party of the 9th dragoons, commanded by Lieutenant Higgins, Lieutenant-colonel Rochfort's, and Captain Cornwall's yeomanry, killed 60 of them. Night coming on, I could not pursue them any further. By the position they took up near Sharkill, I conceived their intentions were to form a junction with the colliers at Castlecomer. As soon as the troops were able to move, I marched with 900 men to attack them, and was sorry to find they had burnt the whole town, and forced the soldiers who were in it, to retire before my arrival. Having cleared the town with the guns, I attacked them on all sides: about 400 were killed, the remainder fled. They were commanded by a priest called Murphy, and their numbers are said to amount to 5000. Our loss was inconsiderable. My force consisted of the Wexford and Wicklow militia, under the command of Lord Loftus and the Honourable Colonel Howard. The dragoons were commanded by Major Donaldson of the 9th dragoons, and Major Barnard, of the Romney fencibles, with several yeomanry corps from this county and Carlow, who, as well as the other troops, are entitled to my warmest praise for their bravery and alertness, on this and every occasion.

I have the honour to be, &c.

C. ASGIL, Major Gen.

Return of the killed, wounded, and missing, on the 21st of June, in the Attack of Vinegar Hill and the Town of Enniscorthy.

Lieutenant-general Dundas's corps.—Major-general Sir James Duff's brigade—89th regiment, 1 rank and file killed.

Needham's brigade.—7th dragoon guards, 1 captain wounded.

Wilford's brigade.—9th dragoons, 1 rank and file killed. Dunlavin yeoman cavalry, 1 rank and file wounded. 1st battalion of light infantry, 1 subaltern killed; 1 sergeant wounded; 2 rank and file killed; 18 ditto wounded; 3 ditto missing. Sligo militia, 1 field-officer wounded; 2 rank and file killed; 3 ditto wounded. Suffolk fencibles, 2 rank and file wounded.

Names of Officers killed and wounded.

Colonel King, of the Sligo corps, wounded. Captain Dunne, of the 7th dragoon guards, wounded. Lieutenant S. Sands, of the Longford corps, killed.

Major-general Johnson's corps.—Royal British artillery, 1 rank and file wounded. Mid-Lothian, 1 subaltern wounded; 1 rank and file wounded. Hompesch's hussars, 2 rank and file wounded. 5th battalion, 60th regiment, 1 captain wounded, 1 sergeant missing; 5 rank and file killed, 5 ditto wounded. 4th battalion, 1 subaltern killed, 1 ditto wounded; 1 sergeant killed; 3 rank and file killed, 22 ditto wounded, 1 ditto

ditto missing. Royal Meath regiment, 1 sergeant killed. Roscommon ditto, 1 rank and file wounded, 1 ditto missing. Dublin county ditto 1 field-officer wounded; 2 rank and file killed, 6 ditto wounded.

Names of Officers killed and wounded.

Lieutenant Baines, of the 13th foot, attached to 4th battalion, killed. Major Veley, of Dublin county regiment, wounded. Captain Schnuda, of 5th battalion, 60th regiment, wounded. Lieutenant Barker, of the Kildare, attached to the 4th battalion, wounded. Lieutenant Hill, of the Mid-Lothian, wounded.—Total, 2 field-officers wounded; 2 captains wounded; 2 subalterns killed, 2 ditto wounded 2 sergeants killed; 1 ditto wounded; 1 ditto missing; 16 rank and file killed, 62 ditto wounded, 5 ditto missing.

G. HEWETT, A.G.

Admiralty Office, June 29.

Copy of a Letter from Captain Sir Thomas Williams, Commander of h. Majesty's Ship Endymion, to Evan Nepean Esq. dated off Wexford, the 22d of June.

I BEG to acquaint you, for the information of my Lords Commissioners of the Admiralty, that, when cruising at the entrance of S. George's Channel with the squadron under my command, I received information, on the 19th, that the King's troops were to commence the attack on the rebels at Wexford on the 20th or 21st. I immediately proceeded off that harbour with the ships named in the margin*, and five cutters which I had collected. Lieutenant Carpenter, sen. lieutenant of the Endymion, was immediately dispatched in command of the cutters and ships' launches, manned and armed with carronades in their prows, to blockade the inward part of the entrance of the harbour, and to prevent the escape of the rebel armed vessels, and others, of which they were in possession, to the amount of forty or fifty sail. On the 21st was joined by the Chapman and Weazel sloops, which, being of light draught of water, anchored much nearer in than the frigates could venture, and thereby gave more effectual protection to the cutters and launches destined to attack the harbour and fort at the entrance of which fired on them. On the arrival of Captain Keen, of the Chapman, I directed him to conduct the operations of the cutters and launches, and endeavour to possess himself of the harbour and for the tides being so low, and the wind blowing out, that neither of the sloops could get in. The launches proceeded to attack the fort, which they soon possessed themselves, upwards of 200 of the rebels precipitately retreating from it, leaving behind them their colours flying and three six-pounders. The launches then immediately proceeded up the harbour; and, upon their arrival at the town, had the happiness to find the King's troops were just marching into it, they having entirely defeated the rebels in two separate attacks on the 20th and 21st, and who are now flying in all directions. Two of their generals, Hay and Roche, taken prisoners.

---

* Endymion, Phœnix, Glenmore, Melampus, Unicorn.

As the object of the squadron remaining at anchor here is now fully accomplished, it is my intention to get to sea to-morrow, if possible; and I am happy to be informed, since the reduction of Wexford, that the appearance of his Majesty's ships and vessels off the harbour, and the measures pursued by them, has been attended with the happiest consequences, and greatly contributed to check the farther progress of the horrible massacres that have been committed in the town of Wexford, disgraceful to humanity.

There being a number of boats and small vessels along the coast, belonging to the rebels, which I conceived would be employed in facilitating the escape of the fugitives, I have ordered the boats of the squadron in, and destroyed about 100 of them; in some, pikes were found concealed.

The public service has greatly benefited by the judicious arrangements of Captain Keen and Lieutenant Carpenter, and by the zeal and activity manifested by them and the officers and people employed in the different ships, boats, and launches under their command, and otherwise.

Admiralty Office, June 30.

Extract of a Letter from Captain Halsted, of his Majesty's Ship Phœnix, to Evan Nepean, Esq. dated at Plymouth, the 5th instant.

I HAVE the honour of acquainting you, for their Lordships' information, that his Majesty's ship under my command arrived here this morning, in company with the Caroline French privateer, and the Henry of Liverpool, her prize. The above ships were captured by the Phœnix on the 31st ult. in lat. 49 deg. 2 min. N. long. 15 deg. 38 min. W. The Caroline is a very handsome ship, coppered, only eight months old, and sails exceedingly fast. She is pierced for twenty guns, carrying twelves and sixes, most of which were thrown overboard in chase, and 105 men; had been ten days from Nantz, without making any other capture than the Henry and a Danish ship. The Henry is a valuable ship, bound to Jamaica, and was captured by the above privateer on the 3d ult. on which day we also sent in an American ship, which had been taken some days before.

This privateer is one of those I went in search of the 28th ult. agreeably to intelligence I received from the Success transport, and by which ship I had the honour of acquainting you, for their Lordships' information, by letter of that day's date.

From the LONDON GAZETTE, July 3, 1798.

Whitehall, July 3.

DISPATCHES, of which the following are copies, have been received from his Excellency the Lord Lieutenant of Ireland, by his Grace the Duke of Portland, his Majesty's principal Secretary of State for the home department.

My Lord, *Kilkenny, June 26.*

FEARING the consequences that must result from allowing the rebels who fled from Wexford to remain any length of time in this country, I preferred attacking them with a small number of men to waiting till a reinforcement arrived. My force amounted to eleven hundred men. The rebels consisted of about five thousand. I attacked them this morning, at six o'clock, in their position at Kilconnel Hill, near Gore's Bridge, and soon defeated them. Their chief, called Murphy, a priest, and upwards of one thousand men, were killed. Ten pieces of cannon and two swivels, the colours, and quantities of ammunition, arms, cattle, &c. were taken; and I have the pleasure to add, that some soldiers who were made prisoners the day before, and who were doomed to suffer death, were fortunately released by our troops.

Our loss consisted of seven men killed and wounded.—The remainder of the rebels were pursued into the county of Wexford, where they dispersed in different directions.

I feel particularly obliged to Major Mathews, of the Downshire militia, who, at a short notice, and with great alacrity, marched with 400 men of his regiment, and Captain Poole's and Captain Gore's yeomanry corps, from Maryboro, to co-operate with me. Lord Loftus, and Colonel Ram, of the Wexford militia; Lieutenant-colonel Howard, and Lieutenant colonel Radcliffe, of the Wicklow; Major Donaldson, of the 9th dragoons, who commanded the cavalry, as well as all the officers and privates, are entitled to my thanks for their spirited exertions. Nor can I withhold the praise justly due to all the yeomanry corps employed on this occasion.

I also beg leave to mention my aide-de-camp, Captain Ogle, and Lieutenant Higgins, of the 9th dragoons, who acted as my brigade-major.

I have the honour to be, &c.

Lord Viscount Castlereagh, &c. &c. &c.

CHA. ASGILL, Major-general.

My Lord,   *Dublin, June* 25.

I HAVE the honour to acquaint your Grace, that this day advices were received from Lieutenant Gardner, of the Antrim militia, dated from Baltinglass, the 26th instant, which state, that early on the morning of the 25th, a very large body of rebels attacked his post at Hacketstown. They were in number many thousands. Lieutenant Gardner's force consisted of 50 Upper Talbotstown, and 24 Shillelagh cavalry, 50 of the Antrim regiment, 46 Hacketstown, and 20 Coolattin yeoman infantry. He at first took an advantageous situation in front of the town; but after a few shots without effect, the rebels filed off in every direction to surround him. He then retreated into the town to defend the barracks. A contest took place in the midst of flames, for near nine hours, for the rebels set fire to the town. They were at last repulsed with considerable loss: many dead were found in the streets and ditches, and 30 cart-loads of killed and wounded were carried off in their retreat.

Lieutenant Gardner speaks in the highest terms of the gallantry of his whole detachment. He particularly praises Lieutenant Rowan of the Antrim, Captain Hume of the Upper Talbotstown cavalry, Captain and Lieutenant Charnley of the Coolattin, Lieutenants Saul and Thoms of the Hacketstown cavalry, and Lieutenants Braddell and Taylor of the Shebagh cavalry; and he strongly mentions the good conduct of Sergeant Nixon of the Antrim regiment.

He severely laments the loss of a good officer, Captain Hardy of the Hacketstown yeoman infantry, who fell early in the action. His other loss

.consists of 10 privates killed, and one sergeant, and 19 privates wounded.

I enclose to your Grace a further account of the action near Gore's bridge, and a return of killed and wounded, which has been received from Major-general Sir Charles Asgill.

I have the honour to be, &c.

To Grace the Duke of Portland,   CORNWALLIS.
&c. &c. &c.

My Lord,   *Kilkenny, June* 27.

I HAVE the honour to send you enclosed a return of the killed and wounded in the action with the rebels at Kilconnel Hill, on the 26th of June, and a return of the ordnance, ammunition, &c. &c. taken on that day. I have the pleasure to assure you, that every thing they possessed has fallen into our hands; and from subsequent accounts, the loss they sustained was much greater than I had the honour of stating to you in my former dispatch. I have no doubt but this victory will restore the counties of Kilkenny and Carlow to peace and tranquillity.

I have the honour to be,
CHA. ASGILL.
Right Hon. Viscount Castlereagh.   Major-general.

Return of Ordnance, Colours, and Ammunition taken.

One colours, five four-pounders, five one-pounders, four swivels, and 7 guns, and a number of pikes, which were destroyed as soon as taken. A number of shot of different sizes, with a quantity of lead and moulds.

Return of Stores taken.

Black cattle	—	—	—	170
Sheep	—	—	—	100
Horses	—	—	—	700
			Total	970

Also a vast quantity of bedding, blanketting, and wearing apparel.
J. LEWIS HIGGINS,
Lieut. 9th Dragoons, acting Brigade Major.

Return of the killed, wounded, and missing of the Troops engaged at Kilconnel Hill, on the 26th instant, June 1798, under the Command of Major-general Sir Charles Asgill.

Mount-Leinster yeoman infantry—1 lieutenant killed.
5th dragoons—1 horse missing.
9th dragoons—1 sergeant wounded, 1 horse killed.
Hompesch's hussars—1 rank and file wounded.
Maryborough yeoman cavalry—1 rank and file wounded, 4 horses killed.
Total—1 lieutenant, 1 corporal killed; 1 sergeant and 3 rank and file wounded; five horses killed, and one missing.

Officer killed.
Lieutenant Stones, of the Mount-Leinster yeoman infantry.

Admiralty Office, July 3.

Extract of a Letter from Captain *Wood*, of his Majesty's Sloop *Hound*, to Evan Nepean Esq. dated at Sea, the 15th June.

I HAVE to acquaint you, for the information of their Lordships, that at one A. M. on the 14th inftant, Skaw bearing E. S. E. 10 leagues, I captured the Dutch lugger Sea Hound, pierced for fourteen guns, but having only seven mounted, and four swivels, manned with thirty men, she has been six weeks from Holland.

Admiralty Office, July 3.

Copy of a Letter from *Vice-admiral Sir Hyde Parker*, Knight, Commander in Chief of his Majesty's Ships and Vessels at Jamaica, to *Evan Nepean*, Esq. dated Queen, Cape Nicola Mole, May 29.

Sir,

LIEUTENANT Rofs, commander of his Majesty's schooner Recovery, having captured the privateers mentioned in the letter to Captain Brooking, and which has been transmitted to me, I send you enclosed a copy of the said letter, which I desire you will be pleased to lay before my Lords Commissioners of the Admiralty, not doubting but they will highly approve of the conduct of that officer.

You will also receive on the other side a lift of armed vessels taken or destroyed by the cruisers under my command, since my laft.

I am, &c.
H. PARKER.

Acafta, L'Hirondelle, French privateer, 10 guns.—Ditto, 6 guns.—Ditto (pierced for 10), 6 guns, and 40 men.—Ditto and Ceres, St. Mary de Louvaine, 2 guns, and 25 men.

Sir, *Montego Bay, May* 1.

I BEG leave to inform you, that on the 17th ultimo, at ten A. M. the French privateer schooner La Revanche struck to his Majesty's schooner Recovery, under my command, after engaging from 45 to 50 minutes. La Revanche is pierced for 12 guns, and had 10 guns and 54 men on board when she engaged. She belonged to Cape François, captured 10 vessels laft cruise, and 19 the preceding one. She was commanded by Citizen Antoine Martin, who shortened sail and hove to, to engage me. I had the weather-gage of him, and went within piftol-fhot before we commenced firing. The enemy had three men killed, and nine wounded, four of them not expected to recover; the hull and rigging very much damaged with our fhot. In the latter part of the action, he endeavoured to effect his escape by the use of his sweeps, for he had not a sail to set except his ftanding jib.

I am happy to add, that his Majesty's schooner has not received any damage, excepting one gun difmounted, and some small fhot in her mafts, &c. nor are any of her small crew hurt. They are most of them young and inexperienced boys and lads; but it is with real fatisfaction I assure you, that all of them difplayed the greateft cheerfulness and firmness during the action, and that their conduct would do much honour to the moft experienced feamen.

On the 29th ultimo, at noon, a little to leeward of St. Ann's Bay, I fell in with the French privateer schooner L'Incredule, two long fix-pounders, four swivels, and 33 men: after two hours chafe to leeward, I captured her, and was obliged to come in here to land the prisoners. She is coppered, and sails very fast; had only captured a Danish vessel and a shallop with twenty hogsheads of sugar, which was afterwards retaken by a merchant-ship. I am, with much respect, &c.

WILLIAM ROSS.

Admiralty Office, July 3.

Extract of a Letter from Vice-admiral Kingsmill, Commander in Chief of his Majesty's Ships and Vessels at Cork, to Evan Nepean, Esq. dated June 27.

PLEASE to inform my Lords Commissioners of the Admiralty, that his Majesty's ship Shannon has captured and sent in here a fine French privateer out of Nantes, mounting 18 guns and 120 men; further particulars of which will be seen in the accompanying letter to me from Captain Fraser.

Sir, *Shannon, at Sea, June 26.*

I HAVE the honour to acquaint you, that on the 23d instant, at five P. M. being in latitude 50 degrees north, and longitude 21 degrees west, I fell in with, and after a chase of twelve hours captured La Julie, privateer, of Nantes, commanded by Citizen Gautreau, mounting 18 twelve and six pounders, and manned with 120 men. She had been from Corunna ten days; and it gives me much satisfaction to have taken this privateer, being quite new, copper bottomed; and, though not of large dimensions, is a remarkable fine vessel, and sails extremely well. Her length is 78 feet keel, 27 feet breadth of beam, 11 feet depth of hold, and is about 270 tons burden. I have the honour to be, &c.

Vice-admiral Kingsmill. ALEX. FRASER.

From the LONDON GAZETTE, July 7, 1798.

Admiralty Office, July 7.

Copy of a Letter from the Earl of St Vincent, Commander in Chief of his Majesty's Ships and Vessels in the Mediterranean, to Evan Nepean, Esq. dated on board the Ville de Paris, off Cadiz, June 8.

Sir,

HEREWITH I transmit Captain Luke's letter, of the 27th ult. acquainting me with the capture of La Zenodone, French Polacca privateer.

I am, Sir, &c.

ST. VINCENT.

My Lord, *Caroline, Roses Bay, May 24.*

I BEG leave to inform your Lordship, that on the 23d instant, Cape Palos bearing N. by E distance six leagues, I fell in with and captured La Zenodone, French Polacca privateer, mounting two sixes, six fours, and two three pounders, carrying 61 men, commanded by Captain Coffin, from Carthagena, out twenty-two days, but had not taken any thing.

I have the honour to be, &c.

The Earl of St. Vincent, K. B. &c. WILL. LUKE.

From

From the LONDON GAZETTE, July 10, 1798.

Admiralty Office, July 10.

Copy of a Letter from Rear-admiral Sir Hugh Cloberry Christian, K. B. Commander in Chief of his Majesty's Ships and Vessels at the Cape of Good Hope, to Evan Nepean, Esq. dated on board the Tremendous, in Simon's Bay, April 29.

Sir,

PLEASE to acquaint my Lords Commissioners of the Admiralty, that the Indispensable letter of marque, of 14 guns, and 32 men, arrived in Table Bay, on the 6th instant; the master of which informed me of his having captured, about 35 leagues S. W. of Cape Horn, a Spanish letter of marque, named Union, carrying 12 guns and 32 men, laden with tallow, hides, and herb-tea. The prize has since arrived in Table Bay, was bound from Monte Video to Lima, and is estimated at about 10,000*l*.

I have the honour to be, &c. &c.

HUGH C. CHRISTIAN.

From the LONDON GAZETTE, July 14, 1798.

Admiralty Office, July 14.

Extract of a Letter from Vice-admiral Vandeput, Commander in Chief of his Majesty's Ships and Vessels at Halifax, to Evan Nepean, Esq. dated on board the Asia, Halifax Harbour, June 23.

ON the 15th of April, I put to sea with the squadron, and proceeded to the S. E. as far as latitude 29 deg. 30 min. and longitude 76 deg. On the 22d we fell in with L'Amiable Juana, a Spanish privateer, of six guns and 46 men, which was captured by the Hind, and was sent to Halifax. On the 27th, we fell in with, and, after a chase of fifteen hours, the Resolution captured a schooner French privateer, from Curaçoa, of four guns and 35 men; this privateer had some time before taken an American vessel belonging to Baltimore. On the 15th of May, with the Topaze and Hind in company, having gotten intelligence that three privateers were cruising off Charlestown, I ordered Captain Larcam to go in search of them, and then, with the Topaze, I proceeded towards this port, where we arrived on the 28th ultimo. On the 7th instant arrived a French schooner privateer, called the Revenge, of 14 guns and 84 men, a prize to the Thetis, who took her in latitude 38, longitude 72; she had not taken any thing. On the day following came in the Thetis and Rover, the former from a cruise, in which she had taken a French privateer of six guns, which was sent to New Providence. The Rover, on her passage towards Bermuda, on the 17th of May, captured and sent in a French sloop privateer of 14 guns, with 57 men; she was last from Porto Rico, and had taken three American ships, as per margin *.

---

* Ship Thomas, from Liverpool to Philadelphia—Ship Merchant, from New York to Bristol.—Ship Diana, from New York to Demarara.

Admiralty

Admiralty Office, July 14.

a Letter from the Right Hon. Admiral Lord Bridport, K. B. to
Nepean, Esq. dated on board the Royal George, at Sea, July 11.

e enclosed copies of letters will inform their Lordships of the taking
eine, and the loss of his Majesty's ship La Pique. On both these
I can add nothing more than to express my satisfaction on this
nt capture, and real concern for the accidents that have attended
ptain Milne, with all his officers and people, are on board La

I am, &c.
BRIDPORT.

y Lord,   *Jason, Pointus Breton, July 2.*

Friday last, at seven A. M. his Majesty's squadron under my com-
consisting of the ships named in the margin †, gave chase to a
frigate off the Saintes; at eleven at night the Pique brought her
n, and continued a running fight, till the Jason passed between
. At this instant the land near the Point de la Trenche was seen
n our larboard bow, and before the ship could answer her helm,
k the ground close to the enemy, which we immediately perceived
ounded also: most unfortunately, as the tide rose, we hung only for-
and therefore swung with our stern close to the enemy's broadside,
lthough he was dismasted, did not fail to take advantage of his
position; but a well directed fire was kept up from a few guns
and at half past two she struck. Our opponent, called La Seine,
mmanded by Le Capitaine Brejot, her force 42 guns, eighteen and
ounders, with cannonades, and 610 men, including troops; she
rom L'Isle de France three months ago, bound to L'Orient.
he early part of the battle, I had the mortification to be wounded,
s obliged to leave the deck; but my misfortune is palliated by the
on that the service did not suffer by my absence, for no man could
lled my place with more credit to himself, and benefit to the state,
y first lieutenant, Mr. Charles Inglis; whom I beg leave to re-
nd in the strongest manner for his bravery, skill, and great ex-

me now, my Lord, to the painful part of my narrative, which I
esitated to make more prolix than I otherwise should, from the
r circumstances attending the engagement; and first I mention the
the Pique, whose officers and crew deserved a better fate. Captain
had led her to the fight in an officer-like manner; but it was his mis-
, that the main-topmast being carried away, he was obliged to drop
ardour urging him on to renew the combat, he did not hear me
n to anchor, and the ship therefore grounded on our off-side, near
to receive the enemy's shot over us, although very awkwardly
for the returning fire. In the morning every attempt was made
the ships off, but the Jason was alone successful: I therefore, on
the Pique was bilged, directed the captain to destroy her, and to
his abilities and activity to save the prize; which he, with great
ty, got afloat yesterday evening, after throwing her guns, &c.
ard.
carnage on board La Seine was very great; 170 men were killed,

---

† Jason, Pique, and Mermaid.

and about 100 wounded, many of them mortally. I enclose a list of the sufferers on board the Jason; and it is with great concern that among the killed I place the name of Mr. Anthony Richard Robotier, my second lieutenant, who died fighting gloriously, and by whose fall is lost a most amiable man and excellent officer. Lieutenant Riboleau commanded on the main deck afterwards, and behaved with great spirit; as did Mr Lockwood, the master, and Lieutenant Symes, of the marines; my other officers, of every description, behaved vastly well; and the bravery and excellent conduct of the crew deserve much praise.

The Pique was exceedingly shattered in her rigging, and the Jason ha not one mast or yard but what is much damaged, nor a shroud or rope but what is cut, with all the sails torn to pieces. If our ship could have remained in her first position, or our companion could have occupied th situation he wished, the business must have been sooner finished, withou so much injury being done aloft.

It is but justice to observe that every effort was made on board th Mermaid, during our long chase, to approach the enemy; and I too much indebted to Captain Newman for heaving this ship off, as that wa the only possible means to save her. So soon as we were afloat, the squa dron under Captain Stopford was seen in the offing, and being called in by signal, was of infinite service.

I have the honour to be, &c.
CHARLES STIRLING.

A List of killed and wounded on board his Majesty's Ship Jason, in th Action with La Seine.

Lieutenant Robotier, killed—One corporal of marines, killed—Fiv seamen, killed—Captain Stirling, wounded—Mess. Bedford and Luscom wounded—Nine seamen, wounded.—Total killed, 7; wounded, 12.
(Signed) CHARLES STIRLING.

My Lord, *On board La Seine, late French Frigate, July 3.*
IT is with real concern I have to inform your Lordship of the loss o his Majesty's ship Pique, under my command, on the night of the 30t ult. in action with the French frigate La Seine, by running on shore i the Passage Breton, where, at low water, she was entirely bulged. Fo the transactions of that day, I leave your Lordship to Captain Stirling dispatches; but must take the liberty of mentioning the entire satisfactio I had from the steady and cool behaviour of the officers and men I ha the honour to command; particularly Mr. Lee, first lieutenant; M Devonshire, second; and Mr. Watson, acting third; and Lieutenar M'Donald of the marines; as likewise Mr. Edween, the gunner, who conduct in his department deserves my warmest praise.

It is some small satisfaction to me, my Lord, for the loss of h Majesty's ship, that the prize was got off by the assistance given from the S Fiorenzo; and her being a very strong and nearly new ship, she does no appear to have received any material damage in her hull, except from sho as she makes very little water.

I have the honour to enclose a list of killed and wounded of his Majesty ship Pique. I have the honour to be, &c.
Right Hon. Lord Bridport, K. B. &c. DAVID MILNE.

Return of killed and wounded on board his Majesty's Ship La Pique in the Action with the French Frigate La Seine, on the 30th of June.

James Collins, sailmaker, killed—Mr. Robinson, boatswain, wounded—Thomas Andrews, boatswain's mate, wounded—Benjamin Lockwood, seaman, wounded—William Richards, seaman, missing—Benjamin Masland, Robert Sallass, and Joseph Furlman, marines, wounded.

From the LONDON GAZETTE, July 21, 1798.

Parliament Street, July 21.

THE dispatches, of which the following are copies, were received on the 17th instant by the Right Hon. Henry Dundas, one of his Majesty's principal Secretaries of State, from Major-generals Coote and Burrard; no opportunity to transmit them having occurred until the return of Mr. Jobernes, by whom they were forwarded.

Sir, *Ostend, June 23.*

NOT having had it in my power to send my dispatches by my aid-de-camp, Captain Williamson, I take the opportunity by Mr. Jobernes, the staff surgeon, who was ordered to Ostend by his Royal Highness the Commander in Chief. I have the honour to be, &c.

Right Hon. Henry Dundas,
&c.
EYRE COOTE,
Major-general.

On a Ridge of Sand Hills, three Miles to the
Sir, *East of Ostend, May 19.*

I HAVE the most sincere satisfaction to acquaint you of the complete and brilliant success attending the expedition entrusted by his Majesty to the care of Captain Popham, of the royal navy, and myself. The squadron reached Ostend about one o'clock this morning.

The able and judicious arrangements of Captain Popham, and great exertions of himself, the officers and seamen under his command, enabled us to disembark the troops at the place from which I have the honour of dating this dispatch; and from Captain Popham's local knowledge, I gained such information as very much removed the difficulties we had to encounter on shore, and contributed greatly to the success of the enterprise.

General Sir Charles Grey sent you, Sir, an outline of the disposition of the troops, and of the plans, previous to our sailing from Margate; these were carried into execution, with a little alteration, which I was obliged to make, in consequence of the whole of the troops not having landed.

Soon after we disembarked, I detached Major-general Burrard, with four companies of light infantry of the guards, the 23d and 49th grenadiers, and two six-pounders, to take possession of the different posts and passes that it was necessary to occupy, to enable us to carry our plan into execution. In effecting this, he met with strong opposition from a considerable body of sharp-shooters, who were gallantly repulsed with some loss, and, by a rapid march, cut off from the town of Ostend.

During the time Lieutenant Brownrigg, of the engineers, was employed in bringing up the powder and other materials to effect the destruction of the sluices of the Bruges canal, the troops were posted as follows: the grenadiers of the 11th and 23d regiments, with cannon, &c. at the lower ferry, to prevent the enemy crossing from Ostend. A detachment of Colonel Campbell's company of guards, under the command of Captain Duff, and the grenadiers of the 49th regiment, under the command of Captain Lord Aylmer, at the upper ferry, for the same purpose. The remainder of Colonel Campbell's, with three other companies of the guards, under the command of Colonel Calcraft, at the sluices and country around, to cover the operation.

The 11th regiment on the south-east front, to secure a safe retreat for the troops, if pressed.

The light infantry companies of the 11th and 23d regiments, under Major Donkin, to cover the village of Bredin, and extend to the Blankenburg road, near the sea, as well as to co-operate with the 11th regiment.

The greater part of the 23d regiment remained on board the ships of war, stationed to the westward of the town, as well to divert the enemy's attention to that point, as to land and spike the cannon, should an opportunity offer.

By the time the troops were properly posted, the necessary materials were brought up to the sluices, by the indefatigable exertions and extraordinary good conduct of Captains Winthrop, Bradby, and M'Kellar, and Lieutenant Bradby, of the royal navy, whose services on shore cannot be too highly praised. Lieutenant Brownrigg, of the royal engineers, in about four hours, made all his arrangements, and completely destroyed the sluices, his mines having, in every particular, the desired effect, and the object of the expedition thereby attained; and which, I have the satisfaction to add, was accomplished with the trifling loss of only five men killed and wounded. Several vessels of considerable burden were also destroyed in the canal near the sluices. No danger, even for an instant, abated the ardour of the seamen and soldiers. To their unanimity, his Majesty and the country are indebted for our success. No language of mine can do justice to the forces employed upon this occasion; and, as it is impossible to name each individual, I beg leave to state the great exertions of a few. To that excellent officer, Major-general Burrard, I shall feel everlasting obligation; to his counsel, exertions, and ability, I am in a great measure to attribute the success of the enterprise. His Majesty's guards, conspicuous upon all occasions, on this service have added to their former laurels. To Colonel Calcraft, who commanded them; Colonels Cunningham and Campbell, of the same corps; Major Skinner, of the 23d regiment, commanding the grenadiers; Major Donkin, of the 44th regiment, commanding the light infantry; and Captain Walker, commanding the royal artillery; I feel myself much indebted for their good conduct in the various services in which I employed them. In Lieutenant Brownrigg, of the royal engineers, I found infinite ability and resource. His zeal and attention were eminently conspicuous; and, in my opinion, this gentleman bids fair to be of great future service to his country. I should not do justice to the zeal and spirit of Lieutenant Gillem, of the Suffex militia, if I did not state to you that, anxious to be employed in the service of his country, and to learn his profession, he applied to his commanding officer at Dover, the night before we sailed, for permission to join our force. He left Dover in a violent gale of wind, and came on board the morning we got under weigh. I attached him to Colonel Campbell's company of the battalion of guards, where he acquitted

quitted himself much to his honour. Captain Viffcher, Sir Charles Grey's aid-de-camp, Captain Williamfon, my aid-de-camp, and Major of Brigade Thorley, I fent to attend the guards, light infantry, and grenadiers, in their different pofitions, as well to give their affiftance to the refpective commanding officers, as to apprife me of any circumftance that might occur, fo as to require my immediate information, they being thoroughly acquainted with the nature of the expedition. They conducted themfelves to my moft perfect fatisfaction, as did Lieutenant Clifton, of the royal artillery, who attended me, Captain Cumberland, of the 83d regiment, and Cornet Nixon, of the 7th light dragoons, who acted as aid-de-camp to Major-general Burrard.

In my letter of the 13th inftant, I had the honour to inform you of my having accepted the fervices of Mr. Jarvis, a furgeon of Margate. His great attention was unremitting, and his conduct upon this occafion is highly praifeworthy. To Colonel Twifs I fhall ever feel great obligation for the able affiftance he gave me at Dover, in preparing the neceffary inftruments for deftroying the fluice-gates, as well as for the inftructions he was fo kind to give Lieutenant Brownrigg for this fervice. As a feint to cover the operation of bringing up the materials, and of deftroying the fluices, Captain Popham and myfelf fent a fummons to the commandant of Oftend to furrender the town and its dependencies to his Majefty's forces under our command, which had the defired effect. I have the honour to enclofe you a copy of the fummons, with the commandant's anfwer. By an unavoidable accident, the four light companies of the 1ft guards, under command of Lieutenant-colonels Warde and Boone, were not landed in the morning; I think it however but juftice to declare, that every thing that brave men then could attempt, was done at the imminent rifk of their lives to accomplifh it; and I am confcious the zeal and courage they manifefted to partake in the dangers of their brother-foldiers, would have made them ample fharers in any honour to be acquired, or danger to be encountered on fhore, had they been able reach it. I have fent a difpatch to Sir Charles Grey by his aid-de-camp, Captain Viffcher; and Captain Williamfon, my aid-de-camp, will have the honour to deliver you this. Both thefe gentlemen are well qualified to give you any farther information, and I beg leave to recommend them to your notice and protection. I have the honour to be, &c.

EYRE COOTE,

Right Hon. Henry Dundas, &c. Major-general.

Copy of the Summons fent for the Town of Oftend to furrender, Dated Eaft of the Harbour of Oftend, May 19,

Sir,

WE the officers commanding the fea and land forces of his Majefty the King of Great Britain, think it neceffary to apprife you, that we fhall be obliged to bombard and cannonade the town of Oftend, unlefs you, as commandant, fhall immediately furrender the fame, with its dependencies, troops, and military ftores, belonging to the republic, to the arms of our fovereign. We leave to you to take into your ferious confideration the very formidable force now lying before the town and port of Oftend, as you cannot but be refponfible for the confequences of a vain and fruitlefs refiftance. We are willing to grant half an hour for your full confideration of the above terms, and are convinced that your humanity and good fenfe will point out the neceffary fteps to be taken to accede to our propofals,

posals, as, in default thereof, we shall be under the necessity of i
diately commencing hostilities. We have the honour to be, &c.
To his Excellency the Commandant   EYRE COOTE, Major-g
 of Ostend.   HOME POPHAM, Cap.

Translation of the Commandant of Ostend's Answer to the Summons
    Liberty—Equality.

Garrison of Ostend, 30th Floreal, 6th Year of the Rep
Muscar, Commandant of the Garrison of Ostend, to the Commander in
   of the Troops of his Britannic Majesty.

GENERAL, The council of war was sitting when I receive
honour of your letter; we have unanimously resolved not to surrende
place until we shall have been buried under its ruins.
    (Signed)   MUSCAR,
         Commandant of the Gar

 Sir,   *Ostend, May*
 MAJOR-GENERAL Coote, in his dispatch yesterday, had the h
to inform you of the brilliant success of the enterprise of which he ha
command, as far as related to the destruction of the gates and sluices 
canal of Bruges. The General having been severely wounded this mor
I have the painful task of detailing our unavoidable surrender soon
On our return yesterday to the beach, at eleven o'clock A. M. whe
had disembarked, we found that, from an increase of wind and surf
communication with the fleet was nearly cut off, and that it was impo
to re-embark the troops. The General, well aware of the risk we r
staying in an enemy's country, naturally-exasperated against us fo
damage we had recently done them, attempted to get off some compa
but the boat soon filled with water, and it was with extreme difficult
lives of the men were saved. It then became necessary to examine car
the ground we were likely to fight upon; and such a choice was ma
might have ensured us success, had any thing like an equal force pres
itself. Major-general Coote took every precaution the evening an
night afforded to make our post among the sand-hills upon the sh
tenable as possible, by directing Lieutenant Brownrigg, of the
engineers, to make small entrenchments where it was necessary, an
planting the few field-pieces and the howitzer we had on the most fa
able spots, to annoy the enemy in their approach to attack us. In
mentary expectation of them, we impatiently looked for a favou
opportunity to get into our boats, but unfortunately it never pres
itself. About four o'clock this morning (the wind and surf havir
creased during the night) we perceived plainly two strong columns 
enemy advancing on our front, and soon after we found several
columns upon our flanks.

 The action began by a cannonade from their horse artillery, which
answered from our field-pieces and howitzer with great animation.
artillery was served admirably; and had not the enemy soon after t
our flanks, which, from their very great numbers, could not be
vented, they would have paid dear indeed for any advantage their
riority of numbers gave them. The force they employed, we have
found, was assembled from Ghent, Bruges, and Dunkirk; and Ge
Coote and myself were very soon convinced that our case was despe

at we had no choice left but to defend our poſt, ſuch as it was, for nour of his Majeſty's arms, as long as we were able. We maintthis very ſevere and unequal conflict for nearly two hours, in extreme hot fire was interchanged, particularly on our left flank, , as well as our right, was now completely turned. Wiſhing how- o make one ſtrong effort, Major-general Coote ordered Major n, of the 44th regiment, on the left, with a company of light ry, to endeavour to turn that flank of the enemy which had made impreſſion upon us, and Colonel Campbell, with his own light iny of the guards, to effect the ſame purpoſe by a concealed and march round the ſand-hills. The uncommon exertions of theſe two able officers, when the ſignal was made for them to advance, are all praiſe; their companies in the attempt were much cut down, ol. Campbell and Major Donkin, with one ſubaltern (Capt. Duff), wounded. About this time Major-general Coote perceived that if the 11th regiment, towards our left, had given way, and was to diſtreſs the other parts of the front neareſt to it. At the moment s endeavouring to rally them, and had put himſelf at their head to the loſt and advantageous ground from which they had retreated, at oſt critical period, when moſt conſpicuous for gallantry and conduct, eived a very ſevere wound in his thigh; and being unable to go on, it for me from the right, where I was ſtationed.

both found that our front was broken, and our flanks completely l, the enemy pouring in upon us on all ſides, and ſeveral valuable s and many of our beſt men killed and wounded. It was evident uld not hold out for ten minutes longer; and therefore we thought e our duty to preſerve the lives of the brave men we commanded, to ſacrifice them to what, we conceived, was a miſtaken point of ir. Had we acted differently it is probable that in leſs time than I have juſt mentioned, their fate would have been decided by the et. Major-general Coote, by whoſe order I am writing, has enjoined repeat the praiſes (and I am wi he has juſtly beſtowed them) officers and men which he had the honour to mention in his diſ- of yeſterday. And we hope, that although we have not been ſucceſsful in re-embarking, our conduct and exertions, in having ed the object of the enterpriſe, will be deemed honourable by his ty and our country; and we rely upon his gracious acceptance of ideavours and zeal in the attempt to extricate the troops entruſted to harge from difficulties both unavoidable and inſurmountable.

ijor general Coote and myſelf would willingly beſtow praiſe where ue; but, among many competitors, it is difficult to ſelect without ring to overlook others well deſerving. We have, Sir, however, onour of mentioning to you Col. Campbell, of the 3d guards light ry, and Major Donkin, of the 44th, whoſe conduct, if any thing have protracted our fate, had been equal to the difficulty of effecting Captain Walker, commanding the royal artilery, Captains Wilſon Godfrey, and Lieutenants Simpſon, Hughes, and Holcroft, all of me diſtinguiſhed corps, after having done every thing which men do, ſpiked their guns, and threw them over the banks, at the mo- the enemy were poſſeſſing themſelves of them. The latter gentle- Lieutenant Holcroft, when all his men were wounded except one, ned at his gun doing duty with it to the beſt of his ability. Captain , of the 11th, and Captain Halkett, of the 23d light infantry,

eminently

eminently distinguished themselves by their cool, intrepid conduct during the whole time. All the gentlemen of the staff conducted themselves much to the satisfaction of Major general Coote and myself. To Captain Cumberland, of the 83d, and Cornet Nixon, of the 7th light dragoons, who flatteringly offered to accompany me, and who acted as my aid-de-camp, I am much indebted; their attention and activity I found of most material service. Mr. Lowen, volunteer, attached to the 23d light infantry, was twice wounded, and was particularly conspicuous, and remarked as a promising soldier. We think it but justice to the enemy to say, that our wounded are treated with humanity; many of them are in the hospital of this town, and are well attended by their surgeons. Our numbers on shore were about 1000 men, of which we are afraid there are from 100 to 150 killed and wounded. The enemy, by all accounts, have lost about the same number; but it is impossible to give any just return of the number we have lost till we hear from Bruges, where the prisoners were sent.

I have the honour to be, &c.
(Signed)   HARRY BURRARD, Major-gen.

The Right Hon. H. Dundas, &c.

P. S. A return of the killed and wounded is now more regularly transmitted by Major-general Coote.
(Signed)   EYRE COOTE, Major-gen.

Ostend, June 17.

Return of Officers, Non-commissioned Officers, Rank and File, and Seamen, killed, wounded, and missing, on the Sand Hills, near Ostend, 20th May.

Royal artillery, 6 rank and file killed; 1 captain, 5 rank and file wounded; 20 rank and file missing. Royal engineers, 2 rank and file killed; 5 rank and file wounded. 17th light dragoons, 1 rank and file wounded. 1st guards, 1 rank and file wounded. 2d guards, 4 rank and file killed; 2 drummers missing. 3d guards, 6 rank and file killed; 1 colonel, 1 captain, 1 lieutenant, 1 sergeant, 7 rank and file wounded; 25 rank and file missing. 11th regiment of foot, 1 lieutenant-colonel, 1 sergeant, 9 rank and file, killed; 2 sergeants, 28 rank and file wounded. 23d regiment of foot, 4 rank and file killed; 11 rank and file wounded. 44th regiment of foot, 1 major wounded. 49th regiment of foot, 1 rank and file wounded. Royal navy, 11 seamen killed, 3 seamen wounded.—Total, 1 lieutenant-colonel, 1 sergeant, 31 rank and file, 11 seamen killed; 1 colonel, 1 major, 2 captains, 1 lieutenant, 3 sergeants, 59 rank and file, 3 seamen, wounded; 2 drummers, 45 rank and file, missing.

Names and Rank of Officers killed and wounded.

Major-general Coote badly wounded; Colonel Campbell, 3d guards, badly wounded (since dead); Colonel Hely, 11th regiment of foot, killed; Major Donkin, commanding battalion of light infantry, wounded slightly; Captain Walker, commanding royal artillery, wounded (since dead); Captain Duff, 3d guards, slightly wounded; volunteer Lowen, attached to the 23d light infantry, wounded severely.—Royal navy,

navy, Mr. Wisdom, Mr. Belding, master's mates of his Majesty's ship Circe, killed.

From the best accounts.

Ostend, July 10.   M. THORLEY, Major of Brigade.

Return of Officers, Non-commissioned, and Rank and File, under the Command of Major-general Coote, surrendered Prisoners of War on the Sand Hills, near Ostend, May 20.

Royal artillery, 2 captains, 5 lieutenants, 8 serjeants, 2 drummers, 60 rank and file, at Lisle and Ostend. Royal engineers, 1 second lieutenant, at Lisle. 17th light dragoons, 1 serjeant, 8 rank and file, at Lisle. 4 companies of guards, 2 captains, 5 lieutenants, 1 quartermaster, 1 surgeon, 16 serjeants, 9 drummers, 260 rank and file, at Lisle. 11th regiment of foot, 1 major, 6 captains, 11 lieutenants, 4 ensigns, 1 adjutant, 1 surgeon, 40 serjeants, 16 drummers, 400 rank and file, at Douay, Fort L'Escarpe. 23d regiment grenadiers and light infantry, 1 lieutenant-colonel, 1 major, 3 captains, 6 lieutenants, 8 serjeants, 4 drummers, 160 rank and file, at Lisle. 44th regiment, 1 major, at Lisle. 49th grenadiers, 1 captain, 3 lieutenants, 1 surgeon, 4 serjeants, 2 drummers, 78 rank and file, at Lisle.—Total, 1 lieutenant-colonel, 3 majors, 14 captains, 30 lieutenants, 1 second lieutenant, 4 ensigns, 1 adjutant, 1 quarter-master, 3 surgeons, 77 serjeants, 33 drummers, 966 rank and file. Royal artillery, Captains Wilson and Godfrey; Lieutenants Simpson, Clifton, Hughes, Holcroft, and Hibbert; second lieutenant Brownrigg, royal engineers. Four companies of guards, Colonels Calcraft and Cunningham. Captains and Lieutenants, Wheatley, acting adjutant; Armstrong, Bean, Duff, and Stephens; Surgeon Fullelove. 11th regiment, Major Armstrong; Captains Sirce, Martin, and Evans; Aylmer, captain-lieutenant. Lieutenants Blair, adjutant; Collyer, M'Lean, Newnan, Ogilvie, and Armstrong; Ensigns Simpson, Miller, Cromie, and M'Kenzie. 11th flank companies, Captains, Knight, grenadiers; Gibbs, light infantry. Lieutenants Hely, Grant, and Campbell, grenadiers; Fenwick, Maxwell, and Elton, light infantry. Surgeon Harlet. 23d regiment, Lieutenant-colonel Talbot; Major Skinner. Captains Bradford and Bury, grenadiers; Halket, light infantry. Lieutenants Hanson, Vischer, and Lloyd, grenadiers; Craton, Cochland, and Roberts, light infantry. 44th regiment, Major Donkin. 49th regiment, Captain Lord Aylmer, grenadiers; Lieutenant Martin, Purson, and Williams, ditto; Surgeon Cobb. General officers and staff, Major-general Coote; Aide-de-camp, Captains Williamson and Vischer, and Lieutenant Gilborn; Captain Thorley, major of brigade; Major-general Burrard; Aide-de-camp, Captain Cumberland and Cornet Nixon.

From the best accounts.

M. THORLEY, Major of Brigade.

Sir,   *Ostend, May* 27.

IT is with inexpressible concern that I am to acquaint you that Colonel Campbell, of the 3d guards, died this morning of the wounds he received in the action of the 20th instant. The loss of this invaluable officer to the service is irreparable, and by his country ever to be lamented. Major-general Burrard, with all the officers (three or four excepted,

cepted, that were left with me) and soldiers, are removed to Lisle, where I expect to be sent as soon as I am sufficiently recovered of my wounds.
I have the honour to be, &c.

To the Right Hon. Henry Dundas, &c.   EYRE COOTE, M. G.

My Lord,   *Drogheda, July* 15.

HAVING received information from different quarters on Friday afternoon, that a large body of rebels had assembled about Garristown, and were marching towards this, I went out with what force I thought it prudent to take from the garrison here, to Duleek, where I arrived at ten o'clock at night the 13th, and got information that the rebels were strongly posted upon a hill three miles off to the right. Not knowing the country, I remained in Duleek till one o'clock. When I marched to the hill, I found the rebels left it on our coming into Duleek the evening before, and halted at a village near it. I followed them to the village. They had left it about five hours before towards Slane. I thought it probable, from a note I had received from General Meyrick, that he was to march from Taragh Hill to attack the rebels at Garristown, that I should hear of him at the Black Lion, and went on about half a mile, when I saw General Meyrick's division coming into the Black Lion. We, immediately, proceeded by two roads towards Slane, as we were informed they were posted above Lord Boyne's house. When we came there, they had left it about three hours, and had passed the Boyne above Slane. Finding that we did not come up with them, General Meyrick sent on Lieutenant-colonel Ord, with the Durham cavalry, to overtake them, and keep them in check, which he did, about four or five miles from us on the north side of the Boyne road to Ardee, and sent back for a reinforcement of cavalry. I ordered Colonel Maxwell with the Dumfries, with General Meyrick, to move on, and they found the rebels very strongly posted behind a defile between two bogs, the pass only allowing them to pass by fours. The cavalry drove in their advanced post, and charged with great spirit; but from the position of the enemy, Colonel Maxwell thought it better to wait till the infantry came up, which I did, with the Sutherland highlanders, in a very short time, and advanced with my battalion guns. Whenever the rebels perceived us, I saw them get into confusion, and they immediately broke in all directions.

I then ordered the cavalry and yeomanry to attack, and I followed with the infantry, to support them. The rebels got into the bogs, and the cavalry advanced, killed all they met with, and surrounded the bog to the right on the opposite side. The highlanders got into the bog and killed all that were in it. Those who got out on the opposite side were met by the cavalry. From the manner in which they dispersed, I cannot give an exact account of the killed. We took a great quantity of pikes, pistols, swords, muskets, &c. and two standards. General Meyrick got one prisoner, who gave him some information, and promised him more. He took him with him to Navan, so that I cannot report any thing with accuracy about him.

The troops behaved with great spirit, and bore a great deal of fatigue; particularly General Meyrick's division, with a reinforcement from this of the Dumfries, and my light company, have been out three nights. I am particularly indebted to the gentlemen yeomanry and to Mr. Trentu Lublin, who served me as a guide. Any body of the rebels

...left went on towards Ardee. A great many got round the hill on
r right, and came back to Slane, where they assembled near it, crossed
e Boyne, and went back towards Garristown, where I hope General
... will fall in with them. I reported this to General Campbell last
... being under his command, and just now received a note from
... to inform you of it.

    (Signed)   W. WEMYSS, M. G.
Marquis Cornwallis.

From the LONDON GAZETTE, July 24, 1798.

Admiralty Office, July 24.

*...act of a Letter from the Earl of St. Vincent, K. B. Commander in
Chief of his Majesty's Ships and Vessels in the Mediterranean, to Evan
Nepean, Esq. dated on board the Ville de Paris, off Cadiz, June 30.*

I ENCLOSE a letter from Captain Pierrepont, of his Majesty's sloop
King's Fisher, relating the capture of a small Spanish privateer.

 My Lord,   *King's Fisher, Oporto Roads, May 31.*

I HAVE the honour to inform your Lordship, that on the 26th inst. being off Vigo, I fell in with and captured L'Avantvis Ferro-
l, Spanish lugger privateer, mounting one carriage gun and four swi-
..., and manned with 26 men.

    I have the honour to be, &c.
      CHARLES H. PIERREPONT.
Right Hon. Earl St. Vincent.

*...act of another Letter from the Earl of St. Vincent, K. B. to Evan
Nepean, Esq. dated on board the Ville de Paris, the 3d of July.*

I ENCLOSE, for the information of the Lords Commissioners of
Admiralty, the report Captain Digby, of his Majesty's ship the Au-
ra, has made of his last cruise. The active service of this young
... cannot be too highly commended.

          June 16.

I GAINED my station, and sent Lieutenant Lloyd, during a fog, to
... with two boats armed, a vessel that had been seen, report-
... on his return, having followed her into Curmes, where two Spa-
... vessels were at anchor. I stood into the bay, to cover him in the
... taking or destroying them, which he effected by burning a brigan-
... loaded with hemp and iron, scuttling a schooner with various mer-
...andise, and brought the boats off with three men wounded, two of
... slightly, by the musketry from the town, and a wall-piece from an
... mount.

...ding on the 19th for Cape Prior, in thick hazy weather, a ship,
... five merchant brigs, was seen steering along the land to the east-
..., the wind westerly. By two P. M. I could distinctly see the ship
... enemy, carrying 18 or 20 guns, making, with the brigs, for the
... of Cedeira, which he entered about four; every preparation
... made, if possible, to destroy them in that port, which I stood in
... at half past four opened a fort on the N. E. side of the town, which,
... the ship under French colours, commenced a fire on the Aurora,

Vol. VIII.   K.   which

which was returned, in hopes still of driving all the vessels on shore; b soon losing the wind, and being nearly land-locked, I was obliged avail myself of the way the ship had not yet lost, to tack and stand o leaving with certainty only two brigs on shore, the corvette or privat ship at the extremity of the harbour, which the charts describe as sho. the fort damaged, and silent probably from the bursting of a gun, wh: a seaman on the look-out aloft supposes to have happened: about six Aurora, by sweeps and towing, was out of the harbour, without mage.

Chasing a cutter on the 20th, and a lugger on the 21st (belonging Guernsey), carried me far into the bay. On the 22d I chased a ship Cape Machichicao, scudding with a N. W. wind, in a direction betwe me and the land. It soon proved to be a corvette, or large French p vateer ship, carrying, to appearance, 20 guns; for on distinguishing frigate, she hauled in for the land, and anchored in an opening unde fort between three and four P. M. At four I brought the ship to wind, within half a gun-shot of the enemy, her colours flying, on a b sho e, with three anchors a-head. After giving her three or four bro sides, her cables and masts shot away, she went on shore, the sea maki a fair passage over her; on which I made sail to clear the eastern la carrying out from thirteen to nineteen fathoms water; the fort fir without effect.

By the reports of a Spanish fishing-boat on the 24th, off Bilboa, understand the place where she was lost to be Baquio, or near it; th account of her loss of men killed and wounded appears exaggerate her name they did not know; but I believe she last sailed from St. A dero, where she had lately carried in a valuable English vessel.

The wind being easterly, I sent this evening Lieutenant Lloyd to e mine, and, if necessary, destroy a coasting vessel in an inlet called nis: he returned in an hour, having scuttled and set fire to her, loa with wrought iron, bringing two Spaniards on board.

H. DIGBY.

From the LONDON GAZETTE, July 28, 1798.

Admiralty Office, July 26.

A LETTER, of which the following is a copy, has been transm ted by Admiral Lord St. Vincent, commander in chief of his Ma ty's ships and vessels off Cadiz, to Evan Nepean, Esq. secretary of Admiralty.

Sea Horse, June 27, Isle of Pantellaria
My Lord,   *W.N.W. 12 Leagues.*

AFTER a chase of twelve hours, and a close action of eight nutes, his Majesty's ship under my command, this morning, at f o'clock, captured the Sensible, a French 36-gun frigate, 12 pound and 300 men, commanded by M. Bourde, Capitaine de Vaisseau; new coppered, copper-fastened, and had a thorough repair at Tou two months ago. A general of division, Baraguey D'Hilliers, with suite, was on board, going to Toulon with an account of the capt of Malta. The Sea Horse's officers and men conducted themselves in to my satisfaction; and I received that assistance from Mr. Wilm the first lieutenant, which I might naturally expect from an officer had been in nine actions, and received eight wounds. Two master's mates and nine men belonging to the Culloden evinced the same steady courage as the crew of that ship have done on every occasion.

The enclosed is a list of the killed and wounded.
I have the honour to be, &c.
(Signed)   EDWARD JAMES FOOTE.
The Right Hon. Earl St. Vincent, Admiral
of the Blue, &c. &c.

Sea Horse—1 seaman, 1 drummer, killed; Mr. Wilmott, first lieutenant, slightly, 13 seamen, 1 corporal of marines, 1 private marine, wounded.

Sensible—18 killed; Monsieur Bourde, capitaine et capitaine de vaisseau, second capitaine, 35 men, wounded.

From the LONDON GAZETTE, July 31, 1798.

Admiralty Office, July 31.

Copy *of a Letter from Rear-admiral Harvey, Commander in Chief of his Majesty's Ships and Vessels at the Leeward Islands, to Evan Nepean, Esq. dated on board the Prince of Wales, Fort-Royal Bay, Martinique, June 12.*

Sir,

I HAVE to acquaint you, for the information of their Lordships, that since my letter to you of the 13th ultimo, the undermentioned French privateers, belonging to Guadaloupe, have been captured at the periods and by the ships and vessels of his Majesty's squadron under my command, as against their names expressed.

By the Matilda, Captain Mitford, 29th ult. to windward of Antigua, L'Annibal brig, of 14 guns and 97 men.

By the Lapwing, Captain Harvey, 29th ult. off St. Bartholomew's, L'Intrepid sloop, of 10 guns and 58 men.

By the Charlotte armed sloop, commanded by Lieutenant John Williams, 29th ult. off Dominica, La Mort schooner, of 4 guns and 36 men.

Neither of the above privateers had made any captures since their leaving Guadaloupe. I have the honour to be, &c.

HENRY HARVEY.

From the LONDON GAZETTE, August 11, 1798.

Admiralty Office, August 11.

Copy *of a Letter from Captain Robert Hall, Commander of his Majesty's Sloop Lynx, to Evan Nepean, Esq. dated at Sea, the 11th of July.*

Sir,

BE pleased to acquaint the Lords Commissioners of the Admiralty, that on the 13th of last month, in lat. 28 deg. N. long. 72 deg. W. I captured a small French schooner privateer, called L'Isabelle, of two guns and 30 men; and on the 27th of the same month, in lat. 30¼ deg. N. long. 71 deg. W. a French brig privateer, called Le Mentor, of 14 fix-pounders, fix of which she threw overboard in the chafe, and 79 men: they were both from Porto Rico, bound to the coaft of America, on a cruife. I yefterday alfo recaptured the American fhip Liberty, from Philadelphia, bound to Liverpool, which had been taken fix days before, a few hours after her getting out of the Delaware.

Copy of a Letter from Admiral Lord Bridport to Evan Nepean, Efq. dated the 9th Auguft.

I TRANSMIT a copy of a letter from Sir Charles Hamilton, captain of his Majefty's fhip Melpomene, on the taking of L'Aventurier corvette brig, for their Lordfhips information, and which appears to do fo much credit to the officers and men employed in the execution of this fervice.

My Lord, *Melpomene, Auguft 4, off Aberack.*

HAVING determined to make an attack with the boats on the port of Corigiou, where a national brig and feveral veffels under her protection were at anchor, on the evening of the 3d inft. I ordered the boats of his Majefty's fhip Melpomene and Childers floop to be manned and armed, and at 10 P. M. difpatched them under command of Lieutenant Shortland, who proceeded, in the moft judicious manner, to the attack, which took place about three A. M. The badnefs of the night from heavy rain, vivid lightning, and frequent fqualls, very much favoured the execution of the defign. They boarded the brig in different places, nearly at the fame moment, and carried her, though not without more refiftance than fuch a furprife gave reafon to expect. The forts which command this inlet being now alarmed, and the wind having unfortunately veered round to the N. N. W. and blowing frefh directly into the paffage, the merchant veffels no longer became an object of acquifition, and the intricacy of the channel made it doubtful whether the corvette even could be got out: the attempt, however, was made; and, after working to windward, under a heavy fire from the batteries, for upwards of two hours, it was at length, with great perfeverance, effected. The brig appears to be the Aventurier, carrying 14 four-pounders and 79 men, commanded by Citizen Raffy, Lieutenant de Vaiffeau. As no merit can redound to me from this enterprife, I do not hefitate to announce it to your Lordfhip as one of the moft gallant nature, and on which no encomiums of mine can do fufficient juftice to the conduct of Lieutenant Shortland, the officers, and the men who performed it. Lieutenant Rofs, of the marines, Mr. Boomley purfer of the Childers, and Meffrs. Morgan, Palmer, and Erfkine particularly diftinguifhed themfelves.

Captain O'Bryen, whom I had appointed to cover the boats, gave all the affiftance that the circumftances could poffibly admit of, and not without great rifk, from the badnefs of the night, and the dangers on the coaft.

Our lofs is one man killed, one miffing; Mr. Froft, midfhipman, and three feamen, wounded.

The enemy have 16 wounded, and feveral mortally.

I have the honour to be, &c.
(Signed) CHARLES HAMILTON.

Admiral Lord Bridport, K. B. &c.

Fron

From the LONDON GAZETTE, August 14, 1798.

Admiralty Office, August 14.

Copy of a Letter from Vice-admiral Sir Alan Gardner, Bart. to Evan Nepean, Esq. dated on board his Majesty's Ship Royal Sovereign, at Sea, the 10th of August.

Sir,

ENCLOSED I transmit, for the information of the Lords Commissioners of the Admiralty, a copy of a letter I received yesterday afternoon from Sir Edward Pellew, Bart. captain of his Majesty's ship Indefatigable, dated at sea the 5th instant, giving an account of the capture of the French ship privateer L'Heureux, of 16 guns and 112 men, after a chase of thirty-two hours.

I am, Sir, &c.

A. GARDNER.

Sir, *Indefatigable, at Sea, Aug. 5.*

I HAVE much pleasure in communicating to you the capture of the French ship privateer L'Heureux, mounting 16 guns, and manned with 112 men; a very handsome ship, coppered, and perfectly new, and in every respect fit for his Majesty's service.

I fell in with this ship at daylight on the 4th instant, on her return from a cruise, in company with a merchant-ship, her prize, called the Canada, John Sewell master, from Jamaica to London (last from Charlestown), laden with sugar, rum, and coffee.

These vessels separated upon different courses, the latter steering direct for Bayonne; the former, after a circular chase of thirty-two hours, led us in sight of Bayonne, and the Canada, which ship, after exchanging the prisoners, we drove on shore under that town, where at least her cargo must be destroyed, as the sea ran very high, and the wind dead on the shore.

I have also the honour to enclose a list of the captures made by the privateer, and remain, Sir, &c. &c.

Sir Alan Gardner, Bart. &c. &c. EDWARD PELLEW.

A List of Captures made by L'Heureux French Ship Privateer, on her last Cruise of eight Weeks from Bourdeaux.

Zephyr brig, from Jersey, 8 guns, 30 men, privateer.
Dartmouth lugger, from Guernsey, 6 guns, 26 men, privateer.
Alliance, American ship, from New York to Liverpool, tobacco.
Canada, English ship, from Jamaica to London, with rum, sugar, and coffee, drove on shore, near Bayonne, by his Majesty's ship Indefatigable.

EDWARD PELLEW.

From the LONDON GAZETTE, August 21, 1798.

Admiralty Office, August 21.

Copy of a Letter from the Right Honourable Lord Bridport, K. B. to Nepean, Esq. dated on board his Majesty's Ship Royal George, at Se 15th instant.

Sir,

HEREWITH you will receive a copy of a letter from Sir E(Pellew, of his Majesty's ship Indefatigable, addressed to Vice-ad Sir Alan Gardner, stating the capture of the French national co La Vaillante. I am, &c. &c.

BRIDPOR

Sir, *Indefatigable, at Sea, Augus*

I HAVE great pleasure in communicating to you the capture c French national corvette La Vaillante, commanded by the Lieutena Vaisseau La Porte, mounting 20 guns, nine pounders, pierced fo and manned with 175 men.

This ship sailed from Rochefort the 1st, and from L'Isle de Rl 4th instant, with 25 banished priests, 27 convicts, and Madame R and family, for Cayenne. We fell in with her at daybreak on the between Bourdeaux and the Isle of Rhe, and the chase continued tw four hours, when she struck, after firing a few guns. She is of dimensions, only eighteen months old, coppered, and copper fast sails fast, and will, I trust, be found fit for his Majesty's service.

I have the honour to be, &c.
Sir Alan Gardner, Bart. EDWARD PELLE'

From the LONDON GAZETTE, September 1, 1798.

Whitehall, September 1.

A DISPATCH, of which the following is a copy, has beer ceived here this day from Dublin.

Sir, *Dublin Castle, Aug.*

IN the absence of my Lord Lieutenant, I beg leave to acquaint for the information of his Grace the Duke of Portland, that early o 27th instant the French attacked Lieutenant-general Lake in a positic had taken at Castlebar, before his forces were collected, and comp him to retire. The Lieutenant-general reports that his loss of m not considerable, but that he was obliged to leave behind him six p of cannon. It appears by a letter I have received this day from Lord Lieutenant, that the French have advanced upon Tuam. Excellency was assembling forces at Athlone.

I have the honour to be, &c.
William Wickham, Esq. CASTLEREAG

Copy of a Letter from Captain Butterfield, of his Majesty's Sloop Ha dated Cork Harbour, 26th August, to Vice-admiral Kingsmill, &c. &

ON the morning of the 7th instant, I fell in with and captur American snow, which had been taken by a French privateer or

4th; and, in consequence of the information given me by the American master, went in pursuit of the enemy. On the 12th I fell in with a French privateer, mounting 24 guns, which I chased during two days. When we got nearly within gun-shot of her, I had the mortification to see her guns thrown overboard, by which means she started from us, and gained so considerably, that, finding it impossible to come up with her, and seeing another suspicious ship to windward, being then in lat. 46 deg. 12 min. longitude 18 deg. 23 min. I altered my course and gave chase, and at four P. M. being within gun-shot, she hauled up her courses, hoisted French colours, and fired a shot.

An action immediately commenced between us, which lasted an hour and fifty minutes, when she struck, and proved to be Le Neptune national armed ship, manned with 50 seamen, and 270 troops on board, from the Isle of France, bound to Bourdeaux, pierced for 20 guns, mounting 10, all of which she fought on the same side. During the action, she attempted several times to board us; the soldiers in her kept up a very heavy fire of musketry, and a privateer, with French colours flying, was in sight to leeward the whole time. The enemy had between 20 and 30 men killed and wounded, and fortunately wounded only six on board of us. I beg to recommend to your notice my first lieutenant, Mr. J. Fairweather, whose able assistance and good conduct on this, and all other occasions, merit my warmest encomiums. I have also great reason to be satisfied with Mr. Dathan, my second lieutenant, and Mr. Lancaster, the master, and likewise Mr. Edward Davis, the purser, who volunteered his services, and commanded the marines on the quarter-deck, their proper officers being dangerously ill. In short, all my officers and ship's company behaved themselves in a manner which does them infinite credit. The Hazard is not materially injured, having only a few shot in her hull and rigging.

From the LONDON GAZETTE, September 4, 1798.

Admiralty Office, September 4.

Extract of a Letter from the Right Hon. Lord Bridport, K. B. Admiral of the White, &c. to Evan Nepean, Esq. dated on board his Majesty's Ship Royal George, at Sea, the 30th of August.

YOU will receive herewith copies of letters from Captain Pierrepont, of the Naiad, stating the capture of the French settee privateer, La Tigre.

My Lord, *His Majesty's Ship Naiad, at Sea, 18th Aug.*

BY La Tigre French privateer, captured by his Majesty's ship under my command, on the 11th instant, I have the honour to transmit your Lordship a copy of a letter written by me to Captain De Courcy, on that occasion; but not having been able to communicate with the Magnanime since, I have thought it right to make known unto you myself, by the opportunity which offers, the capture of the privateer.

I have the honour to be, &c. &c.

W. PIERREPONT.

Right Hon. Lord Bridport, K. B. &c. &c.

Sir,

Sir, *His Majesty's Ship Naiad, at Sea, Aug. 12.*

I BEG to make known to you, for the information of the Admiral Lord Bridport, that yesterday, at five P. M. Cape Finisterre bearing E. S. E. 42 leagues distant, I captured, in his Majesty's ship under my command, after a chase of four hours, the French settee privateer La Tigre, mounting eight carriage guns, four pounders, and eight swivels, bearing a complement of 53 men; 22 of that number had been sent into different vessels, captured by Stephen Bonaventure Aggaret, the commander of La Tigre, since his sailing from Groire ten days ago.

I have the honour to be, &c.

W. PIERREPONT.

Hon. M. De Courcy, Captain of his Majesty's Ship Magnanime.

From the LONDON GAZETTE, September 8, 1798.

Admiralty Office, September 8.

Extract of a Letter from the Right Hon. Lord Bridport, K. B. Admiral of the White, &c. to Evan Nepean, Esq. dated on board his Majesty's Ship Royal George, at Sea, the 1st of September.

Sir,

HEREWITH you will receive, for their Lordships' information the copy of a letter of the 31st ult. from Captain Stopford, of his Majesty's ship Phaeton, stating the capture of the French privateer ship Le Mercure. I am, Sir, &c.

BRIDPORT.

My Lord, *Phaeton, at Sea, Aug. 31.*

I HAVE the honour to inform your Lordship, that this day his Majesty's ship under my command, in company with the Anson, captured a French ship privateer of 18 guns (pierced for 20), and 135 men, called Le Mercure: she sailed from Bourdeaux yesterday, bound on a cruise; is quite a new vessel, copper bottomed and fastened.

I am, my Lord, &c.

ROBERT STOPFORD.

Right Hon. Lord Bridport, K. B. &c.

Admiralty Office, September 8.

BY letters received at this office, from the Hon. Captain De Courcy, of his Majesty's ship Magnanime, dated the 21st and 25th ult. addressed to Evan Nepean, Esq. it appears, that on the 16th of that month he had fallen in with and captured La Colombe French privateer, of 12 guns and 64 men, quite a new vessel, coppered, copper fastened, and a very fast sailer: had been only four days from Bayonne, bound to the West Indies. That on the 24th following, at two P. M. two ships of war were observed steering to the S. E. under a crowd of sail, which proved to be his Majesty's ship Naiad, Captain Pierrepont, in chase of a French frigate. At five P. M. the two British ships neared the enemy, who, after a well-directed fire for the space of one hour from her stern-chase guns, at the Naiad, struck, and was immediately taken possession of. She proves to be La Decade, commanded by Le

Citoyen

Citoyen Villeneau, manned with 336 men, and pierced for 44 guns, 10 of which however had been landed at Cayenne, from whence she had just returned. Captain Pierrepont makes the strongest acknowledgments of the ardour by which his officers and men were animated during an anxious chase of thirty-two hours, in constant expectation of battle, and most particularly of the services which he experienced from his first lieutenant, Mr. Marshall.

Both his Majesty's ships, with the prizes, have arrived at Plymouth.

Admiralty Office, September 8.

Copy of a Letter from Sir Thomas Williams, Captain of his Majesty's Ship Endymion, to Evan Nepean, Esq. dated at Spithead the 5th instant.

Sir,

YOU will be pleased to inform my Lords Commissioners of the Admiralty, that his Majesty's ship Endymion, under my command, is arrived at Spithead, having taken from the enemy the three ships herein described; the Britannia English extra India ship, from Bengal to London, valuably laden, taken by the Huron French privateer. La Sophie French ship privateer, of 20 guns and 130 men, eighty-two days out; had taken nothing. La Sophie is a very fine ship, quite new, and well adapted for his Majesty's service, being an extraordinary fast sailer; she having been chased eight different times, during her last cruise, by our ships of war, and each time escaped by superior sailing. The May Flower, of New York, from Lisbon to London, taken by Le Telemaque French cutter privateer.

I have the honour to be, &c.
THO. WILLIAMS.

Admiralty Office, September 8.

Copy of a Letter from Rear-admiral Harvey, Commander in Chief of his Majesty's Ships at the Leeward Islands, to Evan Nepean, Esq. dated Prince of Wales, Fort Royal Bay, Martinique, July 14.

I HAVE to acquaint you, for the information of their Lordships, that since my letter to you of the 12th ult. the undermentioned French privateers, belonging to Guadaloupe, have been captured at the periods, and by the ships and vessels of his Majesty's squadron under my command, as against their several names expressed. By the Solebay, Captain Poyntz, 13th ult. off Martinique, Le Destin schooner, of four guns and 46 men. By the Matilda, Captain Mitford, 23d ult. to the northward of Antigua, L'Etoile sloop, of six guns and 53 men. By the Hawke, Captain Rotheram, 8th instant, off St. Lucia, Le Mahomet schooner, of four guns and 34 men.

From the LONDON GAZETTE EXTRAORDINARY,
September 14, 1798.

Whitehall, September 14.

A DISPATCH, of which the following is a copy, has been received this morning from his Excellency the Lord Lieutenant of Ireland, by his Grace the Duke of Portland, one of his Majesty's principal Secretaries of State.

My Lord, Camp, near St. John's Town, Sept. 8.

WHEN I wrote to your Grace on the 5th, I had every reason believe, from the enemy's movement to Drumahain, that it was the intention to march to the north; and it was natural to suppose that th[ey] might hope that a French force would get into some of the bays in th[at] part of the country; without a succour of which kind every point direction for their march seemed equally desperate.

I received, however, very early in the morning of the 7th, accoun[t] from Lieutenant-general Lake, that they had turned to their right Drumkeirn, and that he had reason to believe that it was their inte[n]tion to go to Boyle, or Carrick on Shannon; in consequence of whi[ch] I hastened the march of the troops under my immediate command, order to arrive before the enemy at Carrick, and directed Major gen[e]ral Moore, who was at Tubercurry, to be prepared, in the event of t[he] enemy's movement to Boyle.

On my arrival at Carrick, I found that the enemy had passed t[he] Shannon at Balintra, where they attempted to destroy the bridge; b[ut] Lieutenant-general Lake followed them so closely, that they were n[ot] able to effect it.

Under these circumstances, I felt pretty confident that one mo[re] march would bring this disagreeable warfare to a conclusion; and ha[v]ing obtained satisfactory information that the enemy had halted for t[he] night at Cloone, I moved with the troops at Carrick, at ten o'clock [on] the night of the 7th, to Mohill, and directed Lieutenant-general Lake proceed at the same time to Cloone, which is about three miles from M[o]hill; by which movement I should be able either to join with Lieut[e]nant-general Lake in the attack of the enemy, if they should remain [at] Cloone, or to intercept their retreat, if they should (as it was mo[st] probable) retire on the approach of our army.

On my arrival at Mohill, soon after daybreak, I found that t[he] enemy had begun to move towards Granard; I therefore proceeded wi[th] all possible expedition to this place, through which I was assured, on a[c]count of a broken bridge, that the enemy must pass in their way [to] Granard, and directed Lieutenant-general Lake to attack the enem[y's] rear, and impede their march as much as possible, without bringing t[he] whole of his corps into action. Lieutenant-general Lake performed th[is] service with his usual attention and ability; and the enclosed lett[er] which I have just received from him, will explain the circumstances whi[ch] produced the immediate surrender of the enemy's army.

The copy of my orders, which I enclose, will show how much reas[on] I have to be satisfied with the exertions of the troops; and I request th[at] your Grace will be pleased to inform his Majesty, that I have receiv[ed] the greatest assistance from the general and staff officers who have serv[ed] with the army. I have the honour to be, &c.

CORNWALLIS.

P. S. I am sorry to find that the wounds of Lieutenant Stephens, the carabineers, are more dangerous than they had been reported.

His Grace the Duke of Portland, &c. &c. &c.

Letter from Lieutenant-general Lake to Captain Taylor, private Secretary to his Excellency the Lord Lieutenant, dated Camp, near Ballinamuck, September 8.

Sir,

I HAVE the honour to acquaint you, for the information of his Excellency the Lord Lieutenant, that finding, upon my arrival at Ballaghy, that the French army had passed that place from Castlebar, I immediately followed them, to watch their motions. Lieutenant-colonel Crawfurd, who commanded my advanced corps, composed of detachments of Hompesch's and the first fencible cavalry, by great vigilance and activity hung so close upon their rear, that they could not escape from me, although they drove the country, and carried with them all the horses.

After four days and nights most severe marching, my column, consisting of the carabineers, detachments of the 23d light dragoons, the first fencible light dragoons, and the Roxburgh fencible dragoons, under the command of Colonel Sir Thomas Chapman, Lieutenant-colonel Maxwell, Earl of Roden, and Captain Kerr, the third battalion of light infantry, the Armagh, and part of the Kerry militia, the Reay, Northampton, and Prince of Wales's fencible regiments of infantry, under the command of Lieutenant-colonel Innes, of the 64th regiment, Lord Viscount Gosford, Earl of Glandore, Major Ross, Lieutenant-colonel Bulkeley, and Lieutenant-colonel Macartney, arrived at Cloone about seven o'clock this morning, where, having received directions to follow the enemy on the same line, whilst his Excellency moved by the lower road, to intercept them, I advanced, having previously detached the Monaghan light company, mounted behind dragoons, to harass their rear.

Lieutenant-colonel Crawfurd, on coming up with the French rear guard, summoned them to surrender; but as they did not attend to his summons, he attacked them, upon which upwards of 200 French infantry threw down their arms: under the idea that the rest of the corps would do the same thing, Captain Packenham, Lieutenant-general of ordnance, and Major-general Craddock, rode up to them. The enemy, however, instantly commenced a fire of cannon and musketry, which wounded General Craddock; upon which I ordered up the third battalion of light infantry, under the command of Lieutenant-colonel Innes, and commenced the attack upon the enemy's position. The action lasted upwards of half an hour, when the remainder of the column making its appearance, the French surrendered at discretion. The rebels, who fled in all directions, suffered severely.

The conduct of the cavalry was highly conspicuous. The third light battalion, and part of the Armagh militia (the only infantry that were engaged), behaved most gallantly, and deserve my warmest praise. Lieutenant-colonel Innes's spirit and judgment contributed much to our success.

To Brigadier-general Taylor I have to return my most sincere thanks, for his great exertions and assistance, particularly on this day; also to Lord Roden, Sir Thomas Chapman, Major Kerr, and Captain Ferguson, whose example contributed much to animate the troops. I ought not to omit mentioning Lieutenant-colonel Maxwell, Major Packenham, and Captain Kerr, whose conduct was equally meritorious;

and I feel infinitely thankful to all the commanding officers of corps, who, during so fatiguing a march, encouraged their men to bear it with unremitting perseverance.

To Captain Packenham, Lieutenant-colonel Clinton (who came to me with orders from Lord Cornwallis), and Major-general Craddock (who joined me in the morning), I am highly indebted for their spirited support; the latter, though early wounded, would not retire from the field during the action.

I acknowledge, with gratitude, the zeal and activity displayed, on all occasions, by Lieutenant-colonel Meade, Major Hardy (assistant quarter-master-general), Captains Taylor and Eustace, of the engineers, Captain Nicholson, and my other aides-de-camp.

I cannot conclude my letter without expressing how much our success is to be attributed to the spirit and activity of Lieutenant-colonel Crawfurd; and I beg leave to recommend him as a most deserving officer.

I have the honour to be, &c.

G. LAKE.

General Orders.

Head-quarters, near St. John's Town, September 9.

LORD Cornwallis cannot too much applaud the zeal and spirit which have been manifested by the army from the commencement of the operations against the invading enemy, until the surrender of the French forces.

The perseverance with which the soldiers supported the extraordinary marches which were necessary to stop the progress of the very active enemy, does them the greatest credit; and Lord Cornwallis heartily congratulates them on the happy issue of their meritorious exertions.

The corps of yeomanry, in the whole country through which the army has passed, have rendered the greatest services, and are peculiarly entitled to the acknowledgments of the Lord Lieutenant, from their not having tarnished that courage and loyalty which they displayed in the cause of their king and country, by any acts of wanton cruelty towards their deluded fellow-subjects.

Return of the killed, wounded, and missing, of the King's Forces at Battle of Ballinamuck, September 8.

Officers—1 wounded.
Privates—3 killed, 12 wounded, 3 missing.
Horses—11 killed, 1 wounded, 8 missing.

Ordnance, Arms, and Ammunition taken.

3 light French 4-pounders.
5 ditto ammunition waggons, nearly full of made-up ammunition.
1 ditto tumbril, 700 stand of arms, with belts and pouches, and a great number of pikes.

Officer wounded—Lieutenant Stephens, of the carabineers.

Return of the French Army taken Prisoners at the Battle of Ballinamuck, September 8.

General and other officers	96
Non-commissioned officers and soldiers	746
Troops, about	100

N: B. Ninety-six rebels taken, three of
y the names of Roach, Blake, and Te   g.

*** The enemy, in their   l   t tr   com-
nnd, were compelled to aband   ne   s c   on   I they
ad taken in the former actions with   nty's
                                       G. I   LE, Lieut.-Gen.

*ames of the principal Officers of the French Force taken at the Battle of
Ballinamuck, September 8.*

Humbert—General en chef.
Sarazin—General de division.
Fontaine—General de brigade.
Laserure—Chef de brigade attaché à l'etat major.
Dufour—Ditto.
Aulty—Chef de battalion.
Demanche—Ditto.
Touffaint—Ditto.
Babin—Ditto.
Silbermon—Ditto.
Menou—Commiffaire ordonnateur.
Brillier—Commiffaire de guerre.
Thibault—Payeur.
Puton—Aid-de-camp.
Framair—Ditto.
Moreau—Capitaine waguemeftre-general.
Ardouin—Chef de brigade.
Serve—Chef de battalion.
Hais—Ditto.
Mauchaud—Ditto.
Brand,   } Officiers de fanté.
Maffonnet,   }

Recapitulation.

Sous officiers	96
Grenadiers	78
Fufiliers	440
Carabiniers	33
Chaffeurs	60
Cannoniers	41
Total	748
Officiers	96
	844

Certifié par le Chef de Brigade,
                             P. ARDOUIN.

From the LONDON GAZETTE, September 18, 1798.

Admiralty Office, September 17.

Extract of a Letter from Vice-admiral Sir Richard Onslow, Bart. to Evan Nepean, Esq. dated on board his Majesty's Ship Monarch, Yarmouth Road, September 16.

BE pleased to inform my Lords Commissioners of the Admiralty, that his Majesty's ship America has sent into this port a French privateer lugger, called the Hussar, mounting 14 guns, and had on board 34 men: she belongs to Harfleur, which place she left the 6th of April last, and put into Norway, to refit.

Copy of a Letter from the Right Hon. Admiral Lord Bridport, K. B Commander in Chief of the Channel Fleet, to Mr. Nepean, dated Royal George, Torbay, September 14.

Sir,
HEREWITH you will receive, for their Lordships' information, a copy of a letter from the Hon. Captain Stopford, of his Majesty's ship Phaeton, stating the capture of the French frigate La Flore, together with a copy of one from Captain Fraser, of his Majesty's ship Nymphe, stating the capture of the Spanish ship L'Edad de Oro, also the recapture of the English sloop Charlotte. I am, &c.

BRIDPORT.

Copy of a Letter from the Honourable Captain Stopford, of his Majesty's Ship Phaeton, to Admiral Lord Bridport, dated at Sea, 8th September.

My Lord,
I HAVE the honour to inform your Lordship, that, having received intelligence of a French frigate being about to sail from Bourdeaux, I stood to the southward, in company with the Anson, to try to intercept her; and after a search of seven days, and a chase of twenty hours from yesterday noon, I have the pleasure to inform your Lordship, that La Flore French frigate, of 36 guns and 255 men, was captured by the Anson and Phaeton.

She has been eight days from Bourdeaux, bound on a cruise.
I have the honour to be, &c. &c.
ROB. STOPFORD.

My Lord, *La Nymphe, Cawsand Bay, September.*
I HAVE the honour to acquaint your Lordship, that on the 6th instant, and about six miles distant from Corunna light-house, I fell in with and captured the Spanish ship L'Edad de Oro, from the Havannah and La Guaira, bound to Corunna, laden with cocoa; his Majesty's ship Aurora, and the Lord Hawke privateer, now in company; and the latter, availing herself of her sweep, came up first and brought her to.

I have also to acquaint your Lordship, that on the 7th instant I recap-

aptured the Charlotte sloop from London
have thought proper to see the Spanish p
                                I am, &c.
Right Hon. Lord Bridport, K. B.   PERCY FRASER.
     &c. &c. &c.

               Admiralty Office, September 18.

py of a Letter from Admiral Earl St. Vincent, Commander in Chief of his Majesty's Ships and Vessels in the Mediterranean, to Evan Nepean, Esq. dated on board the Ville de Paris, off Cadiz, August 20.

Sir,
I ENCLOSE a letter from Captain Dixon, of his Majesty's ship the on, acquainting me with his success in capturing his Catholic Majesty's frigate El Dorothea.
Captain Dixon seems to have displayed great judgment and cool urage on this occasion.   I am, &c.
                                    ST. VINCENT.

py of a Letter from Captain Dixon, of his Majesty's Ship the Lion, to Admiral the Earl of St. Vincent, dated at Sea, the 10th *July.*

My Lord,
IT is with the greatest pleasure I have the honour to inform your rdship, that yesterday morning at nine o'clock, Carthagena bearing 79 W. distant 29 leagues, I had the good fortune to fall in with a adron of Spanish frigates, as per margin*, and that, after having ought them to close action, about a quarter past eleven o'clock, ich lasted with great warmth till ten minutes past one P. M. the my was totally defeated and put to flight, leaving the Dorothea to her e, having hoisted an English ensign with the union downwards; and I considered her in the greatest distress, I lost not a moment in taking session, which was done in the face of the three remaining frigates, tant about two miles on my weather-bow.
In detailing the particulars of the above affair, I have to inform your rdship, that at the hour the frigates were descried in the S. E. quar-, the Lion was steering E. with a crowd of sail, the wind moderate W. S. W.; and as I soon discovered, by the uvres, they were enemies, I immediately ich being effected in the shortest time I ever quainted the officers and ship's company with tely bringing the frigates to the closest action e cheerfulness with which it was received, I ment to profit thereby; and accordingly to ft reefs of the topsails, in order to secure t ttery, and hauled up towards the frigates, wh

---
* Pomona, of 42 guns and 350 men, Felix O'Neil commodore, Don Francis lamil captain
Dorothea, of 42 guns and 370 men, Don Manuel Gerraro captain.
Cafilda, of 42 guns and 350 men, Don Deam. Eriara captain.
Proferpine, of 42 guns and 350 men, Quaj Bial captain
They all sailed from Carthagena the 8th instant, on a cruise

Lion.

Lion. Having secured the weather-gage, I bore down on the enemy, who was forming in a close order of battle on the larboard line of bearing: the third frigate from the van had lost her fore-topmast. It immediately occurred to me that the crippled ship was my object, in order to secure a general action; supposing that a Spaniard (from the nobleness of his character) would never, with so superior a force, forsake a friend in distress. In this I fortunately succeeded; and steering for and closing with the crippled ship, which was now become the sternmost in the line of battle, the other three frigates tacked in succession, and passed the Lion very gallantly within musket-shot; but as their line after tacking was by no means a close one, they each received a well-directed broadside from the Lion; the good effect of which was very visible by their standing a considerable time on that tack. I still continued to steer for the crippled ship, who, nearly failing as well as the Lion, galled her very considerably in the rigging by her stern-chafes.

The three frigates made a second close attempt, but not so close as the former, to support her, and were each fully repaid by an exchange of broadsides. At length we closed with the crippled ship, and poured in a destructive fire, the yard-arms being just clear of each other; he nevertheless did not strike for some time after. At this period I found the Lion totally ungovernable, having all her braces, bowlines, clue-garnets, &c. shot away, the foresail nearly rendered useless, and the other sails much torn.

The three frigates a third time made a distant and feeble effort to protect and cover the distressed frigate, but in vain; they did not dare to approach within the entrance to do so; and by great exertions being enabled to wear round on the same tack with the frigate that had now struck her colours, and substituted the English ensign in its place, I closed with and took possession of her as before related.

During the remainder of the day we were lying to, fully employed in repairing the rigging, bending new canvas, and securing the prize, in order to enable me, if possible, to go in pursuit of the three frigates, which were making off close by the wind to the N. W.

Now, my Lord, it is with the greatest and most heartfelt pleasure to me that this service has been effected with the probable loss of only one poor man, who has had his thigh amputated; as likewise Mr. Patey, midshipman, slightly wounded in the shoulder: this youth did not quit his quarters in consequence of the wound, and was, from first to last, particularly active: but, my Lord, there have been several miraculous recoveries in the Lion, owing to the great ability and humane attention of the surgeon, Mr. Young, I therefore never despair of a man while there is life.

I have now the satisfaction of declaring to your Lordship, that nothing could exceed the cool and collected bravery and determined resolution of every individual in the Lion. I have taken the Dorothea in tow, as she has her mizen-mast and fore-topmast carried away, and sails and rigging cut to pieces, her rudder and mainmast much damaged, as well as on account of the necessary attendance of the surgeon to the relief of the wounded men on board, the surgeon of the Dorothea being an inexperienced man, and without the necessary instruments.

I can get, my Lord, but an imperfect account of the killed on board the Dorothea: their complement at the commencement of the

action

action was called 350, and now there are victualled on board the Lion, 351: many volunteers embarked on board at Carthagena; the captain and officers suppose there might be from 20 to 40 killed in the action, and the wounded now on board the Lion are 32.

I am, &c. &c.
MANLEY DIXON.

Extract of a Letter from Vice-admiral Vandeput, Commander in Chief of his Majesty's Ships and Vessels at Halifax, to Evan Nepean, Esq. dated on Board the Asia, Halifax Harbour, 12th August.

BY a letter which I have received from Captain Hall, of the Lynx, dated the 13th July, he informs me, that the ship he writes by (an American), called the Liberty, from Philadelphia, bound to Liverpool, laden with tobacco and rice, having been captured by a French privateer on the edge of soundings off the coast, had been retaken by him six days afterwards in latitude 35 deg. and in the longitude of Bermuda; and that he had likewise taken two French privateers, one only of two guns and 30 men, which he carried to Providence; the other, called the Mentor, he took on the 27th of June, in latitude 30 deg. 30 min. longitude 71 deg. and sent to Bermuda: he says, she is a fine brig, of 14 six-pounders and 79 men.

From the LONDON GAZETTE, September 22, 1798.

Admiralty Office, September 22.

Copy of a Letter from the Right Hon. Admiral Earl of St. Vincent, K.B. to Evan Nepean, Esq. dated Ville de Paris, before Cadiz, 20th Aug.

I ENCLOSE the representation of a very gallant and obstinate action, fought by his Majesty's sloop L'Espoir, of 14 six-pounders, against a Ligurian pirate of very superior force, which reflects such lustre upon his Majesty's arms, that too much cannot be said in praise of it.

The loss of Mr. Sollby, the Master, is greatly to be lamented, as he was a very promising young man.

My Lord,   *His Majesty's Sloop L'Espoir, Gibraltar, 10th Aug.*

I HAVE the honour to acquaint your Lordship, that having under my charge part of the Oran convoy, on the 7th instant, at about five P. M. I discovered a large ship seemingly steering to cut off the convoy, or for Malaga, Cape Windmill bearing N. E. by N. four or five leagues. If she proved an enemy, I saw the preservation of the convoy depended upon my opposing her; I therefore hauled out from them, and made all sail to meet her. A little before seven P. M. perceiving her to be a man of war, and hove to to receive me, I hoisted our colours, that we might know each other, being then within musket-shot; she did not think proper to display hers; but when we came upon her weather-quarter, hailed, which I answered. He then ordered me, in a very imperious manner, and in good English, to go to leeward of him, and strike, or he would sink me, firing one shot into us, and instantly after his whole broadside, which we returned, and continued a very heavy fire of great guns and small arms on both sides, till about three quarters past ten P. M. when we had the satisfaction to hear him call

call out for quarter, begging us not to fire any more; he was a Genoese. I told him again we were a British man of war, and ordered him to lower all his sails, and come on board of me; but he paid no further attention, and kept shooting up, to gain a situation to rake us. We brought our broadside to bear, and thinking his force too great to be trifled with, gave it to him with its full effect, and he returned it; but on our shooting ahead, and tacking, to give him the other, he again cried out, begging us not to fire again; that he was badly wounded, but would obey my orders immediately; and on his lowering his sails, all firing ceased about eleven P. M. The vessel is called the Liguria, Don Franc. de Orso commander, a Dutch frigate, sold to the Genoese, and mounting 12 eighteen-pounders, four twelve-pounders, 10 six-pounders, 12 long wall-pieces, and four swivels, with 120 men on board, of all nations.

It would give me infinite pleasure if I could close this without having to inform your Lordship, that in the first hour of the action I lost my master, Mr. Solsby; a loss I felt more severely, for he was brave with the greatest coolness, and knew his duty well. I had six men wounded, two badly; the Liguria had seven killed, and 14 wounded; among them the boatswain was killed, and the first captain very dangerously wounded.

No panegyric of mine can do justice to either warrant-officers or men; for the great disparity between the vessels shows that, had it not been for their spirited exertions, we must have fallen a sacrifice to these pirates, or whatever else they may be. The service is much indebted to the spirited conduct of Captain Brown, of the 28th regiment, who happened to be on board, by his animation inspiring all around, and by his attention to the guns; nor should I do justice, if I did not beg leave, in the strongest terms, to recommend to your Lordship's notice Mr. Hemphill, the purser, who, vith my leave, came up from below, where he was stationed; and by his assiduity in attending the guns, saved me much; as, after the loss of the master, my attention was more particularly required in manœuvring the helm and sails.

I have the honour to be, &c.

LOFTUS OTWAY BLAND.

Admiral the Earl of St. Vincent, K. B. &c.

From the LONDON GAZETTE EXTRAORDINARY, October 2, 1798.

Admiralty Office, October 2.

THE Honourable Captain Capel, of his Majesty's sloop Mutine, arrived this morning with dispatches from Rear-admiral Sir Horatio Nelson, K. B. to Evan Nepean, Esq. Secretary of the Admiralty, of which the following are copies.

Sir, *Vanguard, Mouth of the Nile, August 7.*

HEREWITH I have the honour to transmit you a copy of my letter to the Earl of St. Vincent, together with a line of battle of the English and French squadrons, also a list of killed and wounded. I have the pleasure to inform you, that eight of our ships have already top-gallant yards across, and ready for any service; the others, with the prizes, will

soon

be ready for sea. In an event of this importance, I have thought it right to send Captain Capel with a copy of my letter (to the commander in chief) over land, which I hope their Lordships will approve; and beg leave to refer them to Captain Capel, who is a most excellent officer, and fully able to give every information; and I beg leave to recommend him to their Lordships' notice.

I have the honour to be, &c.

HORATIO NELSON.

P. S. The island I have taken possession of, and brought off the two thirteen-inch mortars, all the brass guns, and destroyed the iron ones.

Evan Nepean, Esq.

My Lord,   *Vanguard, off the Mouth of the Nile, Aug.* 3.

ALMIGHTY God has blessed his Majesty's arms in the late battle, by a great victory over the fleet of the enemy, whom I attacked at sunset on the 1st of August off the mouth of the Nile. The enemy were moored in a strong line of battle for defending the entrance of the Bay (of Shoals), flanked by numerous gunboats, four frigates, and a battery of guns and mortars, on an island in their van; but nothing could withstand the squadron your Lordship did me the honour to place under my command. Their high state of discipline is well known to you; and with the judgment of the captains, together with their valour and that of the officers and men of every description, it was absolutely irresistible.

Could any thing from my pen add to the characters of the captains, I would write it with pleasure; but that is impossible.

I have to regret the loss of Captain Westcott, of the Majestic, who was killed early in the action; but the ship was continued to be so well fought by her first lieutenant, Mr. Cuthbert, that I have given him an order to command her till your Lordship's pleasure is known.

The ships of the enemy, all but their two rear ships, are nearly dismasted; and those two, with two frigates, I am sorry to say, made their escape; nor was it, I assure you, in my power to prevent them. Captain Hood most handsomely endeavoured to do it; but I had no ship in a condition to support the Zealous, and I was obliged to call her in.

The support and assistance I have received from Captain Berry cannot be sufficiently expressed. I was wounded in the head, and obliged to be carried off the deck, but the service suffered no loss by that event. Captain Berry was fully equal to the important service then going on, and to him I must beg leave to refer you for every information relative to this victory. He will present you with the flag of the second in command, that of the commander in chief being burnt in the L'Orient.

Herewith I transmit you lists of the killed and wounded, and the lines of battle of ourselves and the French.

I have the honour to be, &c.

Admiral the Earl of St. Vincent.   HORATIO NELSON.

Line of Battle.

1. Culloden, T. Troubridge captain, 74 guns, 590 men.
2. Theseus, R W. Miller captain, 74 guns, 590 men.
3. Alexander, Alexander J. Ball captain, 74 guns, 590 men.

4. Van-

4. Vanguard, Rear-admiral Sir Horatio Nelson, K. B. Edward Berry captain, 74 guns, 595 men.
5. Minotaur, Thomas Louis captain, 74 guns, 640 men.
6. Leander, T. B. Thompson captain, 50 guns, 343 men.
7. Swiftsure, B. Hallowell captain, 74 guns, 590 men.
8. Audacious, Davidge Gould captain, 74 guns, 590 men.
9. Defence, John Peyton captain, 74 guns, 590 men.
10. Zealous, Samuel Hood captain, 74 guns, 590 men.
11. Orion, Sir James Saumarez captain, 74 guns, 590 men.
12. Goliath, Thomas Foley captain, 74 guns, 590 men.
13. Majestic, George B. Westcott captain, 74 guns, 590 men.
14. Bellerophon, Henry D. E. Darby captain, 74 guns, 590 men.
La Mutine brig.

HORATIO NELSON.

Vanguard, off the Mouth of the Nile, Aug. 3.

French Line of Battle.

1. Le Guerrier, 74 guns, 700 men.—Taken.
2. Le Conquerant, 74 guns, 700 men.—Taken.
3. Le Spartiate, 74 guns, 700 men.—Taken.
4. L'Aquilon, 74 guns, 700 men.—Taken.
5. Le Souverain Peuple, 74 guns, 700 men.—Taken.
6. Le Franklin, Blanquet first contre amiral, 80 guns, 800 men.—Taken.
7. L'Orient, Brueys admiral and commander in chief, 120 guns, 1010 men.—Burnt.
8. Le Tonant, 80 guns, 800 men.—Taken.
9. L'Heureux, 74 guns, 700 men.—Taken.
10. Le Timoleon, 74 guns, 700 men.—Burnt.
11. Le Mercure, 74 guns, 700 men.—Taken.
12. Le Guillaume Tell, Villeneuve second contre amiral, 80 guns, 800 men.—Escaped.
13. Le Genereux, 74 guns, 700 men.—Escaped.

Frigates.

14. La Diane, 48 guns, 300 men.—Escaped.
15. La Justice, 44 guns, 300 men.—Escaped.
16. L'Artemise, 36 guns, 250 men.—Burnt.
17. La Serieuse, 36 guns, 250 men.—Dismasted, and sunk.

HORATIO NELSON.

Vanguard, off the Mouth of the Nile, August 3.

A Return of the killed and wounded in his Majesty's Ships under the Command of Sir Horatio Nelson, K. B. Rear-admiral of the Blue, in Action with the French, at Anchor, on the 1st of August 1798, off the Mouth of the Nile.

Theseus—5 seamen killed; 1 officer, 24 seamen, 5 marines, wounded.—Total 35.

Alexander—1 officer, 13 seamen, killed; 5 officers, 48 seamen, 5 marines, wounded.—Total 72.

Vanguard—3 officers, 20 seamen, 7 marines, killed; 7 officers, 60 seamen, 8 marines, wounded.—Total 105.

Minotaur—

Minotaur—2 officers, 18 seamen, 3 marines, killed; 4 officers, 54 seamen, 6 marines, wounded.—Total 87.
Swiftsure—7 seamen, killed; 1 officer, 19 seamen, 2 marines, wounded.—Total 29.
Audacious—1 seaman killed; 2 officers, 31 seamen, 2 marines, wounded.—Total 36.
Defence—3 seamen, 1 marine, killed; 9 seamen, 2 marines, wounded.—Total 15.
Zealous—1 seaman killed; 7 seamen wounded.—Total 8.
Orion—1 officer, 11 seamen, 1 marine, killed; 5 officers, 18 seamen, 6 marines, wounded.—Total 42.
Goliath—2 officers, 12 seamen, 7 marines, killed; 4 officers, 28 seamen, 9 marines, wounded.—Total 62.
Majestic—3 officers, 33 seamen, 14 marines, killed; 3 officers, 124 seamen, 16 marines, wounded.—Total 193.
Bellerophon—4 officers, 32 seamen, 13 marines, killed; 5 officers, 126 seamen, 17 marines, wounded.—Total 197.
Leander—14 seamen wounded.
Total. 16 officers, 156 seamen, 46 marines, killed; 37 officers, 562 seamen, 78 marines, wounded.—Total 895.

Officers killed.

Vanguard—Captain Taddy, marines; Mr. Thomas Seymour, Mr. John G. Taylor, midshipmen.
Alexander—Mr. John Collins, lieutenant.
Orion—Mr. Baird, captain's clerk.
Goliath—Mr. William Davies, master's mate; Mr. Andrew Brown, midshipman.
Majestic—George B. Westcott, captain; Mr. Zebedee Ford, midshipman; Mr. Andrew Gilmore, boatswain.
Bellerophon—Mr. R. Savage Daniel, Mr. Ph. W. Launder, Mr. George Joliffe, lieutenants, Mr. Thomas Ellison, master's mate.
Minotaur—Lieutenant J. S. Kirchner, master; Mr. Peter Walters, master's mate.

Officers wounded.

Vanguard—Mr N. Vassal, Mr. J Adye, lieutenants; Mr. J. Campbell, admiral's secretary; Mr. M. Austin, boatswain; Mr. J. Weatherston, Mr. George Antrim, midshipmen.
Theseus—Lieutenant Hawkins.
Alexander—Alexander J. Ball, Esq captain; Captain J. Creswell, marines, Mr. W. Lawson, master; Mr. G. Bully, Mr. Luke Anderson, midshipmen.
Audacious—Mr. John Jeans, lieutenant; Mr. Christopher Font, gunner.
Orion—Sir James Saumarez, captain; Mr. Peter Sadler, boatswain; Mr. Phil. Richardson, Mr. Ch. Miell, Mr. Lanfesty, midshipmen.
Goliath—Mr. William Wilkinson, lieutenant, Mr. Law. Graves, midshipman; Mr. P. Strachan, schoolmaster; Mr. James Payne, midshipman.
Majestic—Mr. Charles Seward, Mr. Charles Royle, midshipmen; Mr. Robert Overton, captain's clerk.

Bellero-

Bellerophon—H. D. Darby, Efq. captain; Mr. Ed. Kirby, mafter; Captain John Hopkins, marines; Mr. Chapman, boatfwain; Mr. Nicholas Bettfon, midfhipman.

Minotaur—Mr. Thomas Irwin, lieutenant; Lieutenant John Jewell, marines; Mr. Thomas Foxten, fecond mafter; Mr. Martin Wills, midfhipman.

Swiftfure—Mr. William Smith, midfhipman.

HORATIO NELSON.

Sir, *Vanguard, off the Mouth of the Nile, Aug. 11.*
HEREWITH I fend you a copy of my letter to the Earl of St. Vincent, of this date. I have the honour to be, &c.
Evan Nepean, Efq. HORATIO NELSON.

My Lord, *Vanguard, off the Mouth of the Nile, Aug. 11.*
THE Swiftfure brought in this morning La Fortune French corvette, of 18 guns and 70 men. I have the honour to be, &c.
Earl St. Vincent. HORATIO NELSON.

From the LONDON GAZETTE, October 9, 1798.

Downing Street, October 9.

BY letters from Switzerland, of the 18th September, it appears, that on the 8th and 9th of that month the troops of the canton of Underwalden were, after a moft obftinate refiftance, totally defeated by the French army.

The moft horrible carnage enfued. Stanz, the principal town of the canton, has been reduced to afhes, and old men, women, and children, put to the fword, without mercy. The French had to contend with 1600 of the inhabitants of Underwalden, who were joined by a few hundred volunteers from the neighbouring cantons. A fmall body of peafants from Schweitz performed prodigies of valour, and was the means of faving the colours of the canton. The wretched remains of this unfortunate army have taken refuge in the mountains.

Admiralty Office, October 9.

Extract of a Letter from the Hon. Robert Stopford, Captain of his Majefty's Ship Phaeton, to the Right Hon. Lord Bridport, dated at Sea, the 1ft of October.

I TRANSMIT to your Lordfhip a letter which I this day received from Captain Gore, informing me of his having, on the 28th ultimo, captured a French fchooner privateer.

Sir, *Triton, at Sea, 1ft Oct.*
I HAVE the fatisfaction to inform you, that on the 28th of September laft, in a heavy gale of wind, his Majefty's fhip under my command fell in with and captured L'Araignée French fchooner privateer, mounting four four-pounders and one nine-pounder carronade, but pierced for 10 guns, carrying 38 men: fhe had been four days from Cape Machichaco, with an intention to cruife three months in the Gulf
of

of St. Lawrence: she is coppered, built at Liverpool, and appears to sail well. I am, Sir, &c. &c.
The Hon. Rob. Stopford, &c.

JOHN GORE.

Admiralty Office, October 9.

Copy of a Letter from Rear-admiral Harvey, Commander in Chief of his Majesty's Ships and Vessels at the Leeward Islands, to Evan Nepean, Esq. dated at Fort Royal Bay, Martinique, *August* 8.

Sir,

I AM to acquaint you, for the information of their Lordships, that his Majesty's armed sloop Charlotte, commanded by Lieutenant John Williams, captured, the 9th ultimo, off Demerara river, de Este Oudenenung Dutch privateer schooner, belonging to Surinam, of eight guns and 38 men, which he sent to Demerara; she was upon a three months cruise, had been out nineteen days, but made no captures.

I have the honour to be, &c. &c.

HENRY HARVEY.

Admiralty Office, October 9.

Copy of a Letter from Vice-admiral Sir Hyde Parker, Knight, Commander in Chief of his Majesty's Ships and Vessels at Jamaica, to Evan Nepean, Esq. dated in Port Royal Harbour, the 27th *July*.

Sir,

HAVING received a letter from Captain Lane, of the Acasta, giving an account of the proceedings and success of that ship, and the Ceres, Captain Otway; and having also received a letter from Captain Eyre, of his Majesty's ship Regulus, acquainting me with the capture of the vessels therein mentioned (copies of which you will receive herewith), I am to desire you will be pleased to lay the same before the Right Hon. the Lords Commissioners of the Admiralty, for their information.

I have the honour to be, &c.

H. PARKER.

Acasta, at Sea, Zacheo S. W. distant seven Leagues, 13th July.

Sir,

I HAVE the pleasure to inform you, that since my letter of the 9th May, the Acasta and Ceres have taken, burnt, and destroyed, the following vessels, viz.

By the Acasta.

May 1—The St. Mary, of four guns and 28 men; pierced for four guns.

May 12—St. Antonio; pierced for 14 guns.

May 20—La Vengeance, six guns, 71 men; pierced for 10 guns.

June 30—La Trump, two guns, 10 men; pierced for 10 guns.

July 2—St. Josef de Victorio, eight guns, 50 men; pierced for 16 guns. Burnt.

July 13—St. Michael Acandea, six guns, 28 men; pierced for six guns.

By the Ceres.

May 12—Sally, seven men.

May 18—Goulette, 11 men.
May 30—L'Avanture, 14 men.
June 1—La Mutinie, 18 guns, 150 men; pierced for 18 guns.
June 8—Cargo, two guns, five men; pierced for four guns.
June 20—Two small schooners. Scuttled.
June 20—Two small sloops. Scuttled.

The Ceres chased on the 1st of June La Mutinie, French privateer brig, of 18 guns and 150 men, to windward of St. Juan; but, from the state of the weather and shoal water, was unable, for some days, to take possession of her; the crew, in the interim, had warped her close in shore, for the purpose of defending her from the beach; Captain Otway however sent his boats the first moment the weather permitted (covering them with the Ceres), under the command of Lieutenant Wooldridge. The enemy having set fire to her, quitted, and formed in great numbers on the beach, keeping up a very heavy fire on the boats: while taking possession of her, and striking the colours, some of the Ceres' shot having taken place below her water-line, she filled, which making it impracticable to bring her off, the fire was permitted to take effect. The St. Josef de Victorioso, of eight guns (but pierced for 16), and 50 men, from Europe, was chased on shore by the Acasta, six leagues to windward of St. Juan; the boats of which ship being sent to take possession, and finding it impossible to bring her off, set fire to and completely destroyed her. The Ceres chased to windward, on the morning of the 6th of May, a sail to the eastward into the Mona Passage. Intelligence was received, upon which was placed great dependence, that the French privateers were doing incredible mischief off the N. E. end of Porto Rico, and of two Spanish frigates being daily expected at St. Juan: we immediately proceeded thither, and made all the above captures off that port; but both ships being extremely short of provisions and water, the Ceres not having more than two days of all species on board, I thought it most advisable, under the existing circumstances, to recruit at St. Thomas's; to which island we made the best of our way, and returned in four days from the time we left our former station, to it again. I am sorry to add, that the day previous to our arrival at St. Thomas's, one of the enemy's frigates (the Venus) got into St. Juan, the other we are anxiously looking for, and you may rely upon our remaining out until the last moment, in hopes of falling in with her: having this instant captured a polacre ship from St. Juan, bound to Vera Cruz, under Creek colours, affords me the opportunity of sending this letter, which ought to have gone by the last prize, but by some accident was left behind.

Lieutenant Denman will be able to give you every information respecting both ships you may wish for. The Ceres is now in chase, and has made the signal for an enemy, which we take to be a privateer brig. I have the honour to be, &c. &c.

Vice-admiral Sir Hyde Parker, Knt. RICHARD LANE.

Sir, *Regulus, Cape Nichola Mole, July* 17.

I HAVE the honour to inform you, that on the 11th instant, having discovered five vessels at anchor in Aguada Bay, at the north-west end of the island of Porto Rico, I manned La Pouline, a French schooner, of four guns and 32 men, which I had captured a few days before, and sent her, together with the boats of the Regulus, under the
command

command of Lieutenant Good, to endeavour to cut them out, proceeding in with the ship for their protection and support; the wind unfortunately failing, neither the Regulus nor schooner could get in near enough to be of any material service; the whole effort consequently fell upon the boats; and it is with great satisfaction I have to add, that through the judicious arrangement and very spirited conduct of Lieutenant Good, well supported by Lieutenant Holman and the junior officers and men under their command, three of the largest vessels, consisting of a ship, a brig, and an armed schooner, were brought away, and had there been the smallest breath of wind, the same would have been the case with the other two, both which were also boarded, and in our possession for a considerable time; but it falling a dead calm at the moment the cables were cut, and not having boats sufficient to tow so many vessels, it became necessary to quit some, in order to secure those which appeared of the most importance.

I have great pleasure in representing to you the very good conduct and determined bravery which was conspicuously shown by every officer and man in the boarding and towing out those vessels under a very heavy and incessant fire from the batteries, close to which they had previously been brought as a security from such an attempt.

I am sorry, in concluding, to be obliged to acquaint you with the loss which we have sustained in Mr. Thomas Finch, master's mate, a very promising young man, who was killed by a grape-shot from one of the batteries, and was the only person hurt upon this occasion.

I have the honour to be, &c.
GEORGE EYRE.

Vice-admiral Sir Hyde Parker, Knt.

From the LONDON GAZETTE, October 16, 1798.

Admiralty Office, October 16.

Copy of a Letter from the Earl of St. Vincent, K. B. Admiral of the Blue, and Commander in Chief of his Majesty's Ships and Vessels in the Mediterranean, to Evan Nepean, Esq. dated off Cadiz the 8th of September.

Sir,

I ENCLOSE a letter from Captain Bartholomew James, commander of his Majesty's sloop El Corso, acquainting me with the capture of Le François French privateer.

I am, &c. &c. &c.
ST. VINCENT.

My Lord, *El Corso, Gibraltar, Aug. 27.*

I HAVE the honour to acquaint your Lordship, that on the 24th inst. (Alboran, east, seven leagues) I captured Le François French privateer, Clement Roux commander, mounting two carriage-guns and six swivels, and manned with 23 men, from Malaga five days, and taken nothing.

I have the honour to be, &c. &c.
BARTH. JAMES.

Admiral the Earl of St. Vincent, K. B. &c.

Admiralty Office, October 26.

Copy of a Letter from the Right Honourable Lord Bridport, K. B. Admiral of the White, to Evan Nepean, Esq. dated at Sea the 10th instant.

Sir,

HEREWITH you will receive, for their Lordships' information, a copy of a letter from the Hon. Captain Stopford, commander of his Majesty's ship Phaeton, stating his having captured, on the 8th inst. a French brig privateer, called the Levrier, pierced for 16 guns, and carrying 70 men. I am, Sir, &c. &c.

BRIDPORT.

My Lord, *Phaeton, at Sea, Oct. 9.*

I HAVE the honour to inform your Lordship, that on the 8th inst. his Majesty's ship under my command captured a French brig privateer, called Le Levrier, pierced for 16 guns, and carrying 70 men: she sailed from Rochelle on the 5th instant, and was bound on a cruise.

I have the honour to be, &c.

ROBERT STOPFORD.

Right Hon. Lord Bridport, K. B. &c. &c.

From the LONDON GAZETTE EXTRAORDINARY,
October 21, 1798.

Admiralty Office, October 21.

LIEUTENANT Waterhouse arrived here late last night with the duplicate of a dispatch from Sir John Borlase Warren, Bart. and K. B. Captain of his Majesty's ship Canada, to Vice-admiral Kingsmill, of which the following is a copy:

Sir, *Canada, Lough Swilly, Ireland, 16th October.*

IN pursuance of the orders and instructions I received by the Kangaroo, I proceeded with the ships named in the margin*, off Achill Head, and on the 10th inst. I was joined by his Majesty's ships Melampus and Doris, the latter of whom I directed to look out for the enemy off Tory Island and the Rosses: in the evening of the same day the Amelia appeared in the offing, when Captain Herbert informed me he had parted with the Ethalion, Anson, and Sylph, who, with great attention, had continued to observe the French squadron since their sailing on the 17th ult. In the morning of the 11th, however, these two ships also fell in with us, and at noon the enemy were discovered in the N. W. quarter, consisting of one ship of 80 guns, eight frigates, a schooner, and a brig. I immediately made the signal for a general chase, and to form in succession as each ship arrived up with the enemy, who, from their great distance to windward, and a hollow sea, it was impossible to come up with before the 12th.

The chase was continued in very bad and boisterous weather all day of the 11th and the following night, when, at half past five A. M. they

---

* Canada, Robust, Foudroyant, and Magnanime.

were

were seen at a little distance to windward, the line-of-battle ship having lost her main-topmast.

The enemy bore down, and formed their line in close order upon the starboard tack; and from the length of the chase, and our ships being spread, it was impossible to close with them before seven A. M. when I made the Robust's signal to lead, which was obeyed with much alacrity, and the rest of the ships to form in succession in the rear of the van.

The action commenced at 20 minutes past seven o'clock, A. M. the Rosses bearing S. S. W. five leagues, and at eleven the Hoche, after a gallant defence, struck; and the frigates made sail from us: the signal to pursue the enemy was made immediately, and in five hours afterwards three of the frigates hauled down their colours also; but they, as well as the Hoche, were obstinately defended, all of them being heavy frigates, and, as well as the ship of the line, entirely new, full of troops and stores, with every necessary for the establishment of their views and plans in Ireland.

I am happy to say, that the efforts and conduct of every officer and man in the squadron seemed to have been actuated by the same spirit, zeal, and unanimity, in their king and country's cause; and I feel myself under great obligations to them, as well as the officers and men of this ship, for their exertions upon this occasion; which will, I hope, recommend them to their Lordships' favour.

I left Captain Thornborough after the action, with the Magnanime, Ethalion, and Amelia, with the prizes; and am sorry to find he is not arrived; but trust they will soon make their appearance.

I have the honour to remain, Sir,
Your most obedient humble servant,
JOHN WARREN.

P. S. The ships with us in the action were, the Canada, Robust, Foudroyant, Magnanime, Ethalion, Melampus, and Amelia.

The Anson joined us in the latter part of the action, having lost her mizen-mast in chase the day before.

I have sent my first lieutenant, Turguand, to take the command of the Hoche.

BY a letter from Lord Viscount Castlereagh to Mr. Wickham, Under-secretary of State for the home department, dated Dublin Castle, the 18th instant, it appears that the Melampus had arrived off Lough Swilly with another French frigate in tow, in pursuit of which she had been sent.

THE following is the copy of an official bulletin published in Dublin:

Dublin Castle, October 18.

Extract of a Letter received this Morning from Sir John Borlase Warren, to Lord Viscount Castlereagh, dated from his Majesty's Ship the Canada in Lough Swilly, the 16th inst.

My Lord,
I TAKE the liberty of communicating to you, for the information of his Excellency the Lord Lieutenant, that I fell in with the enemy's squadron

squadron on the 12th inftant, the Roffes bearing S. S. W. five leagues; and after an action, which continued moft of the day, four of their fhips ftruck their colours.

I believe a brig, with Napper Tandy on board, was in company, as fhe left the French at the commencement of the bufinefs. The enemy's fhips had numbers of troops on board, arms, ftores, and ammunition; and large quantities of papers were torn and thrown overboard after they had ftruck.

I am of opinion that few of the frigates which efcaped will arrive in France, as they had received much damage in their mafts and rigging; and, from the violent gales that followed the next day, they muft be in a crippled ftate, and may, in all probability, be picked up by fome of the fquadrons on the coaft of France, or by Admiral Kingfmill's cruifers. They had thrown every thing overboard, boats, fpars, arm-chefts, &c.

I left the prizes with the Robuft, Magnanime, Ethalion, and Amelia. The Hoche, of 84 guns, was one of the fhips taken.

I am, &c.
J. B. WARREN.

It appears, by a letter from Major-general the Earl of Cavan, of a later date, that the Melampus had arrived off Lough Swilly, with another frigate in tow, which fhe had been fent in purfuit of; fo that the number of prizes amount to five.

From the LONDON GAZETTE, October 23. 1798.

Admiralty Office, October 23.

Copy of a Letter from Captain Graham Moore, Commander of his Majefty's Ship Melampus, to Sir John Borlafe Warren, dated at Sea, off Lough Swilly, the 16th inftant.

Sir,

I HAVE the honour to inform you, that on the 13th inftant, at midnight, being well up towards St. John's Point, we difcovered two large fhips clofe to us on our weather-beam; on feeing us, they hauled up on the oppofite tack: as I had not the leaft doubt of their being two of the enemy's frigates, we tacked and clofed with the neareft in an hour, going ten knots. After hailing, and ordering her to bring to, without effect, fhe trying to get away athwart our ftern, we opened fuch a fire upon her, as completely unrigged her in about twenty-five minutes, and forced her to bring to, and furrender: fhe proved to be La Refolue French frigate, commanded by Jean Pierre Barqueau, mounting 40 guns, and 500 feamen and troops on board; the other frigate was L'Immortalité, of 44 guns, 24 pounders, on the main deck, and 600 feamen and foldiers: fhe made feveral fignals whilft we were occupied with her confort, but gave us no difturbance.

Both on this occafion, and during the action of the 12th, the officers, feamen, and marines of his Majefty's fhip under my command difplayed the utmoft degree of zeal, alacrity, and gallant fpirit; Mr. Martin (the firft lieutenant, an old and good officer), with Lieutenants Price, Ellifon, and Hole of the marines, conducted themfelves much to my satisfaction; and I experienced very great assistance from the steady good conduct of Mr. Emory, the master.

As a very heavy gale of wind came on immediately after our boarding La Resolue, the second lieutenant, Mr. John Price, with 21 men, were all that could be thrown on board of her, with the loss of our two cutters. That officer deserves very great credit for his active exertion in clearing her of the wreck of her masts and rigging, and in keeping company in so violent a storm; as our object was to disable our antagonist before her consort could assist her. La Resolue had only 10 men killed, and a great number wounded; but I am inexpressibly happy to add, that in the action of the 12th we had only one man wounded; and the affair of the 13th did not deprive their country of the services of a single man of the brave crew of the Melampus.

I have the honour to be, &c.

GRAHAM MOORE.

Admiralty Office, October 23.

Copy of a Letter from the Earl of St. Vincent, K. B. Admiral of the Blue, &c. to Evan Nepean, Esq. dated off Cadiz the 30th of September.

Sir,

I ENCLOSE two letters, representing eminent services performed by officers and part of the crew of his Majesty's ships the Goliath and Alcmene. I am, &c.

ST. VINCENT.

Sir, *Goliath, off the Mouth of the Nile, the 25th August.*

I HAVE great pleasure in informing you, that at half after one this morning the boats of his Majesty's ship Goliath, under the direction of Lieutenant William Debusk, attacked and carried, after an obstinate action of fifteen minutes, the French national armed ketch Torride, of 70 men, commanded by Mr. Martin Bedat, lieutenant de vaisseaux, mounting three long eighteen pounders, four swivels, and well appointed in small arms: the Castle of Bequier, under the guns of which the Torride was moored, also fired for her support; but the skill and courage of Lieutenant Debusk, and those under his command, were such as to baffle every attempt to save her. The French captain is badly wounded; I have therefore sent him on shore with a flag of truce. Lieutenant Debusk is slightly wounded, and one of his people likely to suffer amputation of his left arm: the prize had three killed and 10 wounded; several of the prisoners escaped to the shore by swimming.

I have, &c.

To Captain Hood, Zealous. THO. FOLEY.

Sir, *Alcmene, off Alexandria, Aug. 22.*

I BEG leave to inform you that La Legere French gunboat, mounting two 6-pounders, some swivels, and 61 men, was captured this day by his Majesty's ship under my command.

Though every preparation was made for running alongside and boarding her, to save any dispatches she might have for Buonaparte, we could

not

not prevent their being thrown overboard, which was however perceived by John Taylor and James Harding, belonging to the Alcmene, who, at the risk of their lives (the ship then going between five and six knots), dashed overboard, and saved the whole of them.

Both men were most fortunately picked up by the boat that was sent after them; and I conceive it my duty to make known the very spirited conduct they showed on this occasion, for the good of the service.

I am, &c.

To *Samuel Hood, Esq.*   GEORGE HOPE.
Captain of his Majesty's Ship Zealous.

La Legere is forty days from Toulon, bound to Alexandria, with dispatches for General Buonaparte.

Extract of another Letter from the Earl of St. Vincent, K. B. to Evan Nepean, Esq. dated off Cadiz the 28th September.

HEREWITH I enclose copies of two letters from Captain Digby, of his Majesty's ship the Aurora, relating to captures lately made by that ship.

My Lord,   *His Majesty's Ship Aurora, Lisbon,* 19*th Sept.*

I HAVE the honour to acquaint you of my arrival in the Tagus with La Velos Aragonesa, Spanish-built frigate (lettre de marque), of 30 guns and 90 men, Jase Eloy Sanchez commander, with a cargo from La Guayra: she sails very fast. A defect in her rudder, and fore-topsail being reefed, prevented her escape. Many of her guns were thrown overboard during the chase on the 16th instant, twenty leagues to the westward of the Bayones.   I have, &c.

H. DIGBY.

My Lord,   *His Majesty's Ship Aurora, River Tagus.*

I HAVE enclosed a list of vessels taken during my last cruise [*].

La Velos Aragonesa is a very complete ship, as large as our four and twenties: left Old Spain the 10th of April last, in company with a ship of the line and two frigates, that went to Cuba. Her cargo, by register, consists of 3702 fanegas, 87lb. cocoa, 98,466lb. coffee, 3381lb. indigo — Though very deep, she sails well. The Petterel in sight at the commencement of the chase.

I have the honour to be, &c. &c.

Earl St. Vincent, K. B. &c.   H. DIGBY.

Philadelphia, June 25.

MR. Marshall, one of the three commissioners at Paris, who lately arrived here from France by way of New York, has been received with much distinction. He was met at some miles distance from Philadelphia by the secretary of state, and some members of the senate, escorted into town by a party of the new-raised volunteer corps; and a public dinner has been since given to him by the principal members of the two Houses of Congress.

* Omitted to be sent.

Philadelphia,

Philadelphia, July 16.

THE measures adopted with a view to place this country in a state of preparation for a war with France, continue to be carried on with considerable spirit. The defenceless situation of the different seaport towns is particularly felt; and the erection or repair of the fortifications necessary for the protection of the most exposed places is begun all along the coast of the Atlantic with a great degree of energy. In some parts of the country, particularly at New York, individuals have offered their personal service, gratis, for the construction of batteries. The sum appropriated to this object, by Congress, is four hundred and thirty thousand dollars: and an act has been passed, that when any individual state, that happens to be indebted to the general union, shall, with the approbation of the President, complete any fortification already begun, or erect any additional works, the money thus applied shall be placed to the credit of that state.

The three frigates ordered by Congress to be completed and equipped, the United States of 44 guns, the Constitution of 44, and the Constellation of 36 guns, have found no difficulty in procuring their full complement of men, although the monthly pay, seventeen dollars to able-bodied seamen, and ten dollars to ordinary seamen, is much inferior to the wages given at present by the captains of merchant-vessels.

A considerable addition to the number of these large frigates is likely to be made by voluntary subscription; the merchants of Philadelphia have undertaken to construct one of 44 guns: at Boston upwards of one hundred thousand dollars have been subscribed for a similar purpose: at Baltimore, one hundred thousand: at New York, Alexandria, Norfolk, Richmond, Charlestown, and almost all the considerable towns of the Union, proportionate sums have been generously contributed.

The Congress have authorized the President to build a considerable number of vessels of inferior size:—six of 32 guns, 12 of from 20 to 22 guns, six of 18 guns, and 10 gallies. The number of revenue cutters, which carry from eight to 14 guns each, are also to be multiplied along the coasts, and the President is empowered to increase their complement of men to the number of 70. These vessels have been authorized by act of Congress to take all French armed vessels, and to retake such American vessels as may have been captured. The exertions of the officers and crews have been encouraged by a law, securing to them a certain share in the value of the prizes they may make. The French privateer lately brought in by the American sloop of war the Delaware, has been regularly libelled, and condemned in the court of admiralty here. The crews have been considered as prisoners of war, and are to be confined in Lancaster jail.

Congress has further ordered the formation of a corps of marines, to consist of five hundred men, under the directions of a major and a proper number of subaltern officers; and it appears that it is likely to be raised without difficulty.

Much time has been spen
and disciplining the militia.
chase thirty thousand stand of small
militia that are most in want of them,
nient situations, and to be either lent
at prime cost.

The regular army of the United States is also to receive some increase;
Congress

(104)

Congress has authorized the raising of twelve new regiments of infantry, and six troops of light dragoons (which, with the two troops already existing, will form a regiment), in addition to the provisional army of ten thousand men, which the President has it in his power to levy in case of a threatened invasion. By this means the regular army will amount upon the whole to between twelve and thirteen thousand men, exclusive of the provisional one just mentioned.

The volunteer corps proceed with very great success. The spirit of enlistment has been in some degree increased by a plan, adopted by Congress, empowering the volunteers to form themselves into legions; that is to say, as it is understood here, into corps composed of infantry, cavalry, and artillery.

A body of this kind has very suddenly acquired numbers and respectability, and is likely soon to have the full complement of two thousand men. It is expected that those volunteers who may offer their service, in the whole extent of the United States, may in the end amount to from ninety to a hundred thousand men.

Vienna, October 4.

THE last accounts from Malta, which were dated the 26th of August, brought intelligence that the French troops, to the number of about two thousand five hundred men, and in consequence of the discontents of the inhabitants, which had broken out into acts of violence, retired within the forts, whither they had transported the powder, and as much flower as they could lay up in the magazine; and that, in order to avoid the diminution of this store, they compelled the inhabitants and the town, by the firing of a cannon laden with ball, over their houses, to bring them, from time to time, sufficient provisions for their present consumption.

Constantinople, September 8.

IMMEDIATELY upon receiving the news of the victory off the mouth of the Nile, the Grand Signior directed a superb diamond aigrette (called a *chelengh*, or plume of triumph), taken from one of the Imperial turbans, to be sent to Admiral Sir Horatio Nelson, together with a pelice of sable fur, of the first quality.

He directed also a purse of two thousand zequins to be distributed among the British seamen wounded at the battle of the Nile.

These presents are to be conveyed to Sir Horatio Nelson in a Turkish frigate.

The following is a translation of the note delivered to Mr. Smith, his Majesty's minister plenipotentiary upon the occasion:

TRANSLATION.

' It is but lately, that by a written communication it has been made known, how much the Sublime Porte rejoiced at the first advice received of the English squadron in the White Sea having defeated the French squadron off Alexandria in Egypt.

By recent accounts, comprehending a specific detail of the action, it appears now more positive, that his Britannic Majesty's fleet has actually destroyed, by that action, the best ships the French had in their possession.

This joyful event, therefore, laying this empire under an obligation, and the service rendered by our much esteemed friend, Admiral Nelson, on this occasion, being of a nature to call for public acknowledgment, his
· · Imperial

perial Majesty, the powerful, formidable, and most magnificent Grand
nior, has destined, as a present in his Imperial name to the said Admi-
, a diamond aigrette *(chelengk)*, and a sable fur with broad sleeves; be-
s two thousand zequins to be distributed among the wounded of his
w. And as the English minister is constantly zealous to contribute by his
eavours to the increase of friendship between the two courts, it is
ped he will not fail to make known this circumstance to his court, and
solicit the permission of the powerful and most august King of England,
the said Admiral to put on and wear the said aigrette and pelice.

September 8, 1798.

Constantinople, September 19.

VICE-ADMIRAL Ouschakoff's squadron is now actually under
igh for the Dardanelles, &c.

By letters just received from Smyrna, it appears that the general mea-
es of police adopted against the French have been pursued there with
ore exemplary rigour than elsewhere. The individuals of the French
tion have been thrown into the common prisons, and the whole French
sion, including Jean Bon St. André, and his papers, laden on half a
sen mules, are upon their way hither under an escort.

Three French vessels have been captured in the harbour, and the whole
ench property on shore confiscated.

Admiralty Office, October 23.

*py of a Letter from Rear-admiral Harvey, Commander in Chief of his
Majesty's Ships and Vessels at the Leeward Islands, dated on board the
Prince of Wales, Fort Royal Bay, Martinique, the 8th August.*

Sir,

I AM to acquaint you, for the information of their Lordships, that
s Majesty's armed sloop Charlotte, commanded by Lieutenant John
illiams, captured the 9th ult. off Demarara river, De Este Andeneming
utch privateer schooner, belonging to Surinam, of eight guns and 38
en, which he sent to Demarara. She was upon a three months cruise,
d been out nineteen days, but made no captures.

I have, &c.

HENRY HARVEY.

Sir, *Prince of Wales, Fort Royal Bay, Martinique, 8th Sept.*

I HAVE to acquaint you, for the information of their Lordships, that
ce my letter to you of the 10th February last, the ships and vessels of his
ajesty's squadron under my command have recaptured six British and
teen American vessels, of different denominations, bound to and from
se islands. I have, &c.

Evan Nepean, Esq. HENRY HARVEY.

Admiralty Office, October 23.

*py of another Letter from Rear-admiral Harvey, Commander in Chief of
his Majesty's Ships and Vessels at the Leeward Islands, to Evan Nepean,
q. dated on board the Prince of Wales, Fort Royal Bay, Martinique,
th September.*

Sir,

I AM to acquaint you, for the information of their Lordships, that
ce my letter to you of the 8th ultimo, his Majesty's ships Concorde

and Lapwing have captured the undermentioned French privateers (schooners) belonging to Guadaloupe:

Le Buonaparte, of eight guns and 72 men.
L'Amazone, of 10 guns and 80 men.
Le Sauveur, of four guns and 20 men, and
La Fortune, of two guns and 20 men.

And the Lapwing captured, on the 11th ult. the Invariable schooner letter of marque, of four guns and 20 men, laden with dry goods, from St. Bartholomew's, bound to Guadaloupe.

I have the honour to be, &c.

HENRY HARVEY.

From the LONDON GAZETTE, October 27, 1798.

Admiralty Office, October 27.

Copy of a Letter from the Right Honourable Lord Bridport, K. B. Admiral of the White, &c. to Evan Nepean, Esq. dated at Spithead, the 24th instant.

Sir,

THE enclosed copy of a letter, which I received this morning, will manifest to their Lordships the courage, skill, and intrepidity of Captain Martin, his officers, and ship's company, in the capture of the French frigate L'Immortalité, after a persevering and brilliant action against a ship of such superior force. I am, Sir, &c.

BRIDPORT.

My Lord, *Fishguard, Plymouth Sound, Oct. 22.*

IN compliance with your order of the 17th instant, I proceeded with all possible dispatch to the southward; and on the 20th instant, having arrived in latitude 48 deg. 23 min. north, longitude 7 deg. west, I had the satisfaction to fall in with a free French frigate, and, after an hour's running fight, came to close act. n with her, which lasted for twenty-five minutes, when the Fishguard became perfectly ungovernable; the bowlines, braces, topsail-ties, backstays, and the whole of the running rigging being cut to pieces. At this critical moment she endeavoured to make off; but the activity of the officers and ship's company in repairing the damages and making sail, soon enabled us to close with her again, and the fight was renewed, and continued with great spirit and resolution for an hour and fifty minutes, when she surrendered to his Majesty's ship, and proved to be L'Immortalité, a new frigate, mounting 42 guns, twenty-four pounders on the main-deck, and nine-pounders, with forty-two pound carronades, on the quarter-deck and forecastle, commanded by Citizen Le Grand, who was killed in the action. She was one of the squadron that composed the expedition to Ireland; and at the commencement of the action had on board 580 men, including General Menage, second in command of the troops (who was also killed in the action), Adjutant General Crazey, and some soldiers. I should wish to recommend the steady good conduct of Mr. Corden, first lieutenant of the Fishguard, on this occasion, but not to the prejudice of any other person, as every officer and man on board behaved with that courage and intrepidity which at all times distinguish his Majesty's subjects in the presence of the enemy.

Annexed

...exed is a list of the killed and wounded. I am sorry to say, thirteen
...ur wounded men have suffered so much as to preclude all hope of their
...very.   I have the honour to be, &c.
T. B. MARTIN.

List of killed and wounded on board his Majesty's Ship Fisgard.

Killed.—William Bennet, Richard Wallis, John Caird, Edward Paine, ...mas Sketton, George Snalum, George Morton, Solomon M'Cormick, ...n Maxworthy, John Williams.

Wounded.—Lieutenant Gerrard, marines; seamen 23; marines 2.

Total killed and wounded 36.

Killed and wounded on board L'Immortalité.

Killed.—Officers 10; men 44.
Wounded.—Sixty-one.
Total killed and wounded 115.

T. B. MARTIN.

From the LONDON GAZETTE, October 30, 1798.

Admiralty Office, October 30.

...of a Letter from Captain Durham, Commander of his Majesty's Ship Anson, to Evan Nepean, Esq. dated in Plymouth Sound.

...BEG leave to enclose you a copy of a letter, sent by this post, to the ...t Hon. Admiral Lord Bridport.

My Lord,   *Anson, in Plymouth Sound, Oct. 27.*

...ROM the disabled state of his Majesty's ship under my command, in ...ction of the 13th instant, and the wind remaining to the S. W. I was ...voidably separated from the squadron under the command of Sir John ...ase Warren, Bart. K. B. and drove considerably to the N. W. of ...nd.

...have great satisfaction in informing your Lordship, that on the 18th, ...aylight in the morning, I discovered a large ship to leeward, for-...tely for me, with the loss of her fore and main topmasts (the Anson ...g by no means in a situation to chase), her mizen-mast gone, main-... and main-crosstrees; the bowsprit and foreyard shot through in ...ral places.

...immediately bore up, and got alongside of her: after an action of ... hour and a quarter, most gallantly disputed, which does the greatest ...our to Citizen Joseph Andrien Segune, her commander, she struck; ...ed to be La Loire, one of the largest and finest frigates belonging to ...epublic, presented by the city of Nantz, quite new, and never before ..., pierced for 50 guns, mounting 46 (eighteen-pounders), having on ...d 664 men (troops included), among whom are a number of artillery, ...major for three regiments. La Loire had 48 men killed and 75 ...nded, was one of the four frigates which the Anson engaged the ..., and was making her escape from the coast.

...beg leave particularly to acknowledge the steady and good behaviour of ...fficers and petty officers; cannot avoid recommending to your Lord-...'s notice my first lieutenant, Mr. John Hinton, whose conduct, not only

O 2   upon

upon this occasion but many others, has met with my fullest approbation; not derogating from the behaviour of Lieutenants Meager, Manderson, and Mr. William Chrishop, the master.

I have also to acknowledge the services of Lieutenants Bell and Derring, of the marines, who commanded the carronades: as to my ship's company, they have been my faithful companions during four years in pretty active service, and whose conduct upon all occasions merits my warm approbation.

Having fallen in, the night before the action, with his Majesty's brig Kangaroo, I ordered Captain Brace, from the Anson's disabled state, to continue in company, and am much indebted to him for the services he has rendered me in taking possession of La Loire.

Herewith I send a list of the killed and wounded.

Killed.—Alexander Duncan, quarter-master; Matthew Birch, seaman.

Wounded.—Mr. W. Abell, first lieutenant of marines; Mr. William Robilliard, Mr. Francis R. Payler, midshipmen; Henry Wilson, James Davis, John Adams, John Houston, William Shaw, Peter Willman, William Thomas (second), Patrick Kelly, seamen; James Cummings, Robert Dillon, marines.

Enclosed is a list of the stores, &c. found on board La Loire republican frigate:

Clothing complete for 3000 men.—1020 musket in cases.—200 sabres.—360 pouches.—25 cases of musket ball cartridges.—1 brass field-piece, with a great quantity of ammunition of different kinds, intrenching tools, &c. &c. I have the honour, &c. &c.

(Signed) H. DURHAM.

Admiralty Office, October 30.

Copy of a Letter from Admiral Peyton, Commander in Chief of his Majesty's Ships and Vessels in the Downs, to Evan Nepean, Esq. dated 29th October.

Sir,

I HEREWITH enclose, for their Lordships' information, a letter I have received from Captain Cheshire, of his Majesty's ship Plover, stating his having captured a French schooner privateer, of 10 carriage-guns and eight swivels, that left Calais on Saturday last in the forenoon, but had not taken any thing. I am, &c. &c.

JOS. PEYTON.

Plover, at Sea, Oct. 28.

Sir,

I BEG leave to acquaint you, for the information of my Lords Commissioners of the Admiralty, that on Sunday morning the 28th inst. I observed a suspicious schooner between three and four leagues S. W. of Farleigh, to which I gave chase; at ten, after firing five or six chase guns, she struck; on boarding found her to be Le Corsair L'Eringobrah, of 10 carriage guns and eight swivels, viz. eight three-pounders, and two four-pounders, part of which she threw overboard: she had between 40 and 50 men; she sailed from Calais on Saturday forenoon, had taken nothing.

I have the honour to be, &c.

Joseph Peyton, Esq. JOHN CHESHIRE.

Copy of a Letter from Admiral Peyton, Commander in Chief of his Majesty's Ships in the Downs, to Evan Nepean, Esq. dated 29th of October.

HIS Majesty's sloop Racoon is just arrived in the Downs, and I herewith enclose a letter I have received from her commander, stating his having chased three French lugger privateers and captured one of them, Le Vigilant, of 12 four-pounders, and two long sixes (55 men), which soon after sunk.

Sir, *His Majesty's Ship Racoon, Downs, Oct. 20.*

I BEG leave to acquaint you, that at six A. M. on this morning, Blackness bearing S. E. by E. distance three leagues, I discovered three large luggers ahead; immediately made all sail and gave chase; after a running fire of two hours, had the pleasure to come up with and capture one of them, Le Vigilant lugger, mounting 12 four-pounders and two long sixes, carrying 55 men (six or seven of which were left on shore at Boulogne), commanded by Citizen Muirbasse. On sending my boats on board, I found that, in consequence of her being hulled in several places, she was sinking very fast, which detained me a considerable time (in endeavouring to stop the leak), otherwise I must inevitably have taken another before they could possibly have reached the coast of France. I have the pleasure to say that all the prisoners got safe on board, except those killed by firing, and every exertion was used to save the vessel, but to no effect; at nine A. M. she sunk: she was entirely new, had been out two cruises only, and taken nothing. One of the luggers in company had captured a brig, which I observed his Majesty's sloop the Plover to take possession of, off Folkstone, at eleven A. M.

I have the honour to be, &c.

To Joseph Peyton, Esq. Admiral of the   ROB. LLOYD.
Blue, &c. &c. &c. Downs.

From the LONDON GAZETTE, November 3, 1798.

Admiralty Office, November 3.

Copy of a Letter from Captain Thomas Woolley, Commander of his Majesty's Ship Arethusa, to Evan Nepean, Esq. dated off Havre, the 24th ultimo.

Sir,

I HAVE to acquaint you, for the information of their Lordships, that on the 21st of this month, his Majesty's ship Arethusa, under my command, drove on shore a lugger privateer on the rocks of Cape La Hogue (where she bilged and upset), mounting, as we suppose, about six guns, carrying 40 men, and retook a sloop her prize. We had one man wounded by musketry from the shore. The Eurydice had chased her from Guernsey, where she had taken the sloop, and joined us in the evening. I have the honour to be, &c. &c. &c.

J. WOOLLEY.

From the LONDON GAZETTE, November 6, 1798.

Admiralty Office, November 6.

Copy of a Letter from Admiral Lord Viscount Duncan to Evan Nepean, Esq. dated on board the Kent, Yarmouth Roads, Nov. 5.

I HAVE the satisfaction to enclose you, for the information of the Lords Commissioners of the Admiralty, a letter I received last night from Captain King, of his Majesty's ship Sirius, acquainting me of his having captured two Dutch frigates, in which he has displayed equal spirit and address. I am, Sir, &c.

DUNCAN.

My Lord, *Sirius, Grimsby Roads, Nov. 1.*

I HAVE the honour to inform your Lordship, that in pursuance of orders I received from Vice-admiral Sir Richard Onslow, Bart. I parted company with the fleet on the evening of the 23d ultimo, to reconnoitre the force of the enemy in the Texel. At eight A. M. on the following morning, the Texel bearing S. by E. ten leagues, I fell in with the two Dutch frigates named in the margin *, at about two miles distance from each other.

Passing within gun-shot of the leewardmost of them, I stood on until I could (upon tacking) nearly fetch the weathermost (the Waakzaamheid), my object being to prevent their junction, and by this means, that being accomplished, I had the satisfaction to cut off the latter, and bring her to about nine o'clock, when she hauled down her colours and fired a gun to leeward; as soon as the prisoners were exchanged, I made sail after the other, and although nearly out of sight, I had the good fortune, before five P. M. to bring her to a kind of running action, which continued about half an hour, within musket shot at times, during which she kept up a smart but ill-directed discharge of cannon and musketry, when she struck to his Majesty's ship. She is called the Furie, and under the orders of the Captain of the Waakzaamheid, and had the commandant of the troops and a number of officers on board. I am happy to add there was only one man wounded by a musket ball, and that his Majesty's ship suffered but little; one shot through her bowsprit; her rigging, &c. &c. but little cut. The loss on board the Furie was eight killed and 14 wounded: her hull, masts, &c. have suffered much. I should be wanting in gratitude were I not to express my acknowledgments of the spirited conduct manifested by all my officers and ship's company on this occasion; particularly to on account of the reduction of numbers, by manning the other prize (on which I sent Mr. Gossett, my senior lieutenant), and securing the officers, troops, &c. taken out of her.

This expedition has been waiting an opportunity of sailing since the 2 of July last. They left the Texel at eleven o'clock the preceding night.

I have the honour to be, &c.

RICHARD KING.

---

* Waakzaamheid, Captain Neurop, ten captain, mounting 26 guns, 24 nine pounders on the main-deck, two 6 pounders on the forecastle, having 100 Dutch seamen and 122 French troops, total 222, on board, also 2000 stand of arms, besides other ordnance stores.

Furie, Captain Petz, of 36 guns, 26 twelve pounders on the main-deck, and six pounders on her quarter-deck and forecastle, with 153 Dutch seamen and 165 French troops (total 318) on board, also 4000 stand of arms, besides other ordnance stores.

From the LONDON GAZETTE, November 10, 1798.

Admiralty Office, November 10.

Extract of a Letter from Captain George Countess, Commander of his Majesty's Ship Ethalion, to Evan Nepean, Esq. dated in Plymouth Sound, Nov. 8.

I HAVE to request you will be pleased to inform my Lords Commissioners of the Admiralty, that since my letter of the 22d of September, by Captain White, of the Sylph, I continued to watch the motions of the French squadron, in his Majesty's ship under my command (having with me the Anson and Amelia), until the 4th October at noon, when a hard gale of wind coming on, we lost sight of them in lat. 53 deg. 13 min. north, and long. 16 deg. 15 min. west, Sligo Bay bearing north 77 east, distance 91 leagues. The wind being off shore, we carried sail to get in with the land, to give the necessary information.—The Amelia separated in the night of the 8th. I had previously desired, in case of separation, each ship to make the best of her way to give the alarm. On the 11th we fell in with the squadron under Sir J. B. Warren; but it blowing strong, could not get on board to communicate any intelligence; but seeing the Amelia with him, I was satisfied he had all the information I could give. Soon after our joining the above squadron, the Anson made the signal for the enemy, whom we discovered coming down; but they had hauled to the wind on observing us. We chased, and kept close to them during the night, and next morning the attack commenced, which no doubt you have been fully informed of by Sir John Borlase Warren. After the Hoche struck, we pursued the weathermost frigate, who was making off, and sailed very fast. After a considerable chase, we came up with and engaged her: she made an obstinate resistance for an hour and fifty minutes, after we got abreast of her, when she struck her colours, most of her sails having come down, and five feet water in her hold. She proved to be the Bellone, of 36 guns, 12 pounders, having 300 soldiers on board, besides her crew. The squadron chased to leeward, and of course was separated, being obliged to remain by the prize, and have been under the necessity of keeping the sea ever since.

I cannot speak too highly of the bravery and conduct of all my officers during the action, as well as of their extreme vigilance in watching them for seventeen days. Mr. Sayers, first lieutenant, is in the prize; and I can with pleasure say his Majesty has not a more zealous or a better officer. We had one man killed and three wounded: the enemy appears to have had 20 killed.

From the LONDON GAZETTE, November 13, 1798.

Naples, September 25.

HIS Majesty's ships the Culloden, Captain Troubridge, the Alexander, Captain Ball, and the frigate Bonne Citoyen, came into this port on the 18th instant, in the evening. His Sicilian Majesty went out in his boat into the bay, to meet them, as did numerous English and Neapolitan boats. The ships gave the royal salute to his Majesty. Admiral Sir Horatio

ratio Nelson, in the Vanguard, accompanied by the Thalia frigate, did not make his appearance in this bay until Saturday laſt, the 22d inſtant, having been becalmed off Sicily.

The King of Naples not only went off to meet the Admiral, but inſtantly went on board the Vanguard, and ſtaid on board until that veſſel was at anchor in the port. The royal ſalute was given by all the king's ſhips, both on his Sicilian Majeſty's arrival on board the Vanguard and on his leaving the ſhip. The day being remarkably fine, numerous boats, with colours and muſic, attended the Vanguard, and all the ſhores and wharfs of Naples were crowded with a multitude of rejoicing people; and when the Admiral came on ſhore, the reception the Neapolitans gave him was expreſſive of the utmoſt kindneſs and gratitude.

Naples, September 28.

EVERY aſſiſtance has been given to the Vanguard, the Culloden, and Alexander; ſo that theſe ſhips will be fit to go again to ſea in a few days. Yeſterday his Majeſty's ſhip Coloſſus, Captain Murray, with four victuallers, from Gibraltar, came to an anchor in this port. This morning Sir Horatio Nelſon has received a letter from Sir James Saumarez, dated from the port of Auguſta in Sicily, the 17th inſtant, reporting all well in the ſquadron under his command; and that he hoped, having got water and freſh proviſions, to ſail from thence for Gibraltar the Wedneſday following.

Naples, September 29.

CAPTAIN Gage, in the Terpſichore, arrived here this morning: he left Malta the 26th inſtant, when Sir James Saumarez, with his ſquadron, in conjunction with the Portugueſe ſquadron under the command of Marquis Nizza, had ſummoned the French to ſurrender and evacuate Malta, which was refuſed by M. Vaubois, the commander in chief of the Valetta; and that Sir J. Saumarez was proceeding with his ſquadron and French prizes to Gibraltar, having left the Portugueſe to block Malta, and having, at the requeſt of the Malteſe inſurgents, ſupplied them with a large quantity of ammunition, and 1200 ſtand of arms from his French prizes. The Malteſe ſay, that the French are in the greateſt want at Valetta.

Vienna, October 27.

INTELLIGENCE was received on Thurſday afternoon from General Bellegarde, of the Auſtrians having, at the formal requeſt of the Griſons government taken poſſeſſion of Coire and the important poſt of Richenau, and of detachments being on their march to occupy the reſt of the country.

From the LONDON GAZETTE, November 17, 1798.

Admiralty Office, Nov. 16.

Copy of a Letter from Captain Columbine to Evan Nepean, Eſq. dated Haſtings, November 15.

I AM to acquaint you, that this morning a French privateer having appeared off this place, and Mr. Wenham having offered himſelf and cutter, after, the Lion, to go after her, I put on board her as many of the sea encibles as I thought necessary, chased, and after a little firing, in which one Frenchman was killed, we took and brought her into this road. She is the Success, of Cherbourg, Nicholas Dubois master, with four guns and 24 men; had been out four days without making any capture. I beg leave to add, that the Hastings men came forward on the occasion with the greatest zeal and readiness.

I have the Honour to be, &c.

E. H. COLUMBINE.

From the LONDON GAZETTE, November 20, 1798.

Downing Street, November 20.

A DECREE having been published by the French Directory, declaring, that all persons, natives of, or originally belonging to neutral countries, or countries in alliance with France, who may form a part of the crews of any of the King's ships of war, or any other British vessel, shall be considered and treated as pirates; his Majesty has directed it to be signified to the commissary for the French prisoners in Great Britain, that if this decree shall, in any instance, be carried into effect against any such persons taken in any vessels the property of his Majesty, or of his Majesty's subjects, and navigated under the British flag, it is his Majesty's determination to exercise the most vigorous retaliation against the subjects of the French republic, whom the chance of war has now placed, or may hereafter place, at the King's disposal.

Admiralty Office, November 20.

Copy of a Letter from Commodore Sir John Borlase Warren, K. B. &c. to Evan Nepean, Esq. dated on board the Canada, Plymouth Dock, 18th November.

Sir,

I HAVE been waiting with great anxiety the arrival of the Robust and La Hoche at this port, to enable me to make a return of the killed and wounded in the different ships under my orders upon the 12th October last; but as I understand those ships may be still further detained by repairs at Lough Swilly, I send the enclosed, which it was impossible for me to obtain before the present moment, as the whole squadron was separated in chase of the flying enemy, and have successively arrived at this port; it was impracticable, therefore, to communicate the particulars to their Lordships sooner, or to state the very gallant conduct of Captains Thornborough and De Courcy, in the Robust and Magnanime, who, in the van on that day, were enabled to close with the enemy early in the action, and were zealously and bravely seconded by every other ship of the squadron, as well as by the intrepidity displayed by the Anson in the evening, in obeying my signal to harass the enemy, and in bearing off their frigates. For further particulars I refer their Lordships to the letters they may have received from Captains Countess and Moore of the Ethalion and Melampus.

I am happy in reflecting that so many advantages to his Majesty's arms have

Vol. VIII. P

have been purchased with so inconsiderable a loss in the ships of the squadron. I have the honour to remain, Sir,
Your most obedient humble servant,
JOHN WARREN.

A Return of the killed and wounded on board the Squadron of his Majesty's Ships under the Orders of Sir John Borlase Warren, Bart. K. B. in the Action with a Squadron of French Ships, on the 12th October.

Canada—1 seaman wounded (since dead).
Foudroyant—9 seamen wounded.
Robust—no return. But I understand the first lieutenant, Mr. M'Colby, lost his arm, and one marine officer was killed.
Magnanime—7 seamen wounded.
Ethalion—1 seaman killed, 4 seamen wounded.
Melampus—1 seaman wounded.
Amelia—no return.
Anson—2 seamen killed; 2 petty officers, 8 seamen, 3 marines, wounded.
Total—3 seamen killed; 2 petty officers, 30 seamen, 3 marines, wounded.

(Signed) JOHN WARREN.

A List of a Squadron of the French Republic in the Engagement on the 12th October, on the Coast of Ireland, with a Squadron of his Majesty's Ships under the Orders of Captain Sir John Borlase Warren, Bart. K. B.

La Hoche, 84 guns (no return), Commodore Bompard, Monsieur Hardi, commander in chief of the army, Monsieur Simon, adjutant-general—taken by Sir John Borlase Warren's squadron.
La Coquille, 40 guns, 580 men, Captain Deperon—taken by ditto.
L'Ambuscade, 36 guns, 559 men, Captain Clement La Konsieur—taken by ditto.
La Resolue, 36 guns, 510 men, Captain Berjeat—taken by ditto.
La Bellone, 40 guns, 240 seamen, 340 troops, Captain Jacob—taken by ditto.
L'Immortalité, 40 guns, 580 men, Captain Le Grand; General of brigade, Monsieur Menage—taken by the Fishguard.
La Romaine, 40 guns, Captain Berquiere—escaped.
La Loire, 44 guns (no return), Captain Second—taken by the Anson.
La Semillante, 36 guns, Captain La Costune—escaped.
La Biche, 8 guns (schooner)—escaped.

Killed and wounded on board the French Ships.

La Coquille—18 killed, 31 wounded.
L'Ambuscade—15 killed, 26 wounded.
La Resolue, 15 killed, 16 wounded.
La Bellone, 20 killed, 45 wounded.
Total—68 killed, 118 wounded.
Evan Nepean, Esq. &c. JOHN WARREN.

From the LONDON GAZETTE, November 24, 1798.

Admiralty Office, November 24.

Copy of a Letter from the Right Hon. Lord Bridport, K. B. Admiral of the White, &c. to Evan Nepean, Esq. dated London, the 22d instant.

Sir,

HEREWITH you will receive, for their Lordships' information, a copy of a letter from Captain White, of his Majesty's sloop Sylph, stating the capture of a French armed lugger, on the 17th instant.

I am, Sir, &c. &c. &c.

BRIDPORT.

My Lord,   *Sylph, at Sea, November 18.*

I BEG leave to acquaint your Lordship, that we last night fell in with two armed luggers, the escort of a small convoy from Nantz to Brest; one of the former, La Fouine, of eight guns and 26 men, we took, and run the other on shore. The convoy escaped in Hodierne.

I have the honour to be, &c.

J. C. WHITE.

Right Hon. Admiral Lord Bridport, K. B. &c.

Copy of a Letter from Lieutenant Charles Patey, commanding his Majesty's hired Cutter the George, to Evan Nepean, Esq. dated at Plymouth the 20th Nov.

Sir,

I BEG leave to acquaint you, for the information of my Lords Commissioners of the Admiralty, of my having fallen in with, yesterday afternoon, off Alderney, and captured, after a short chase of four hours, L'Enterprise French privateer lugger, mounting two swivels, with muskets, pistols, swords, half-pikes, &c. Jaques Adam master, with 16 men; only two days from Granville; quite new, and had not taken any thing.   I have the honour to be, &c.

CHARLES PATEY.

Admiralty Office, November 24.

Copy of a Letter from Captain Thomas Thompson, of his Majesty's late Ship the Leander, to Evan Nepean, Esq. dated on board the Lazaretto, at Trieste, the 14th of October.

Sir,

UPON my arrival at this place, I immediately acquainted Sir Horatio Nelson with the capture of his Majesty's ship Leander under my command, and beg leave to enclose you a copy of my letter to the Rear-admiral, for the quicker information of my Lords Commissioners of the Admiralty.

I have the honour to be, &c.

THOMAS THOMPSON.

Admiralty Office, November 24.

Copy of a Letter from Captain Thompson, late Commander of his Majesty's Ship Leander, to Rear-admiral Sir Horatio Nelson, K. B. dated Trieste, the 13th of October.

IT is with extreme pain I have to relate to you the capture of his Majesty's ship Leander, late under my command, by a French seventy-four gun ship, after a close action of six hours and a half. On the 18th of August last, being within five or six miles of the west end of Goza, near the island of Candia, we discovered at daybreak a large sail on the S. E. quarter, standing directly for the Leander; we were then becalmed, but the stranger bringing up a fine breeze from the southward, we soon made him to be a large ship of the line. As the Leander was in officers and men upwards of eighty short of her complement, and had on board a number which were wounded on the 1st, I did not consider myself justified in seeking an action with a ship that appeared of such considerable superiority in point of size; I therefore took every means in my power to avoid it: I however soon found that our inferiority of sailing made it inevitable, and I therefore, with all sails set, steered the Leander a course which I judged would receive our adversary to the best advantage, should he bring us to battle. At eight o'clock the strange ship (still continuing to have the good fortune of the wind) had approached us within a long random shot, and had Neapolitan colours hoisted, which he now changed to Turkish; but this deception was of no avail, as I plainly made him to be French. At nine he had ranged up within a half gun-shot of our weather quarter; I therefore hauled the Leander up sufficiently to bring the broadside to bear, and immediately commenced a vigorous cannonade on him, which he instantly returned. The ships continued nearing each other until half past ten, keeping up a constant and heavy firing. At this time I perceived the enemy intending to run us on board, and the Leander being very much cut up in rigging, sails, and yards, I was unable, with the light air that blew, to prevent it. He ran us on board on the larboard bow, and continued alongside us for some time: a most spirited and well-directed fire, however, from our small party of marines (commanded by the sergeant), on the poop and from the quarter-deck, prevented the enemy from taking advantage of his good fortune, and he was repulsed in all his efforts to make an impression on us. The firing from the great guns was all this time kept up with the same vigour, and a light breeze giving the ships way, I was enabled to steer clear of the enemy, and soon afterwards had the satisfaction to luff under his stern, and passing him within ten yards, distinctly discharged every gun from the Leander into him. As from henceforward was nothing but a continued series of heavy firing within pistol shot, without any wind, and the sea as smooth as glass, I feel it unnecessary to give you the detail of the effects of every shot, which must be obvious from our situation. I shall therefore content myself with assuring you, that a most vigorous cannonade was kept up from the Leander, without the smallest intermission, until half past three in the afternoon. At this time, the enemy having passed our bows with a light breeze, and brought himself on our starboard side, we found that our guns on that side were nearly all disabled by the wreck of our own spars, that had all fallen on this side. This produced a cessation of our fire, and the enemy took this time to ask us if we had surrendered. The Leander was now totally ungovernable,

not

not having a thing standing but the shattered remains of the fore and main masts and the bowsprit, her hull cut to pieces, and the decks full of killed and wounded; and perceiving the enemy, who had only lost his mizen-topmast, approaching to place himself athwart our stern; in this defenceless situation, I asked Captain Berry if he thought we could do more? He coinciding with me, that further resistance was vain and impracticable, and, indeed, all hope of success having for some time vanished, I therefore now directed an answer to be given in the affirmative, and the enemy soon after took possession of his Majesty's ship.

I cannot conclude this account without assuring you how much advantage his Majesty's service derived during this action from the gallantry and activity of Captain Berry of the Vanguard; I should also be wanting in justice, if I did not bear testimony to the steady bravery of the officers and seamen of the Leander in this hard contest, which, though unsuccessful in its termination, will still, I trust, entitle them to the approbation of their country. The enemy proved to be the Genereux, of 74 guns, commanded by M. Lejoillie, chef de division, who had escaped from the action of the 1st of August, and, being the rearmost of the French line, had received little or no share of it, having on board 900 men, about 100 of whom we found had been killed in the present contest, and 188 wounded. I enclose a list of the loss in killed and wounded in the Leander, and have the honour to be, &c.

THOMAS THOMPSON.

A Return of Officers and Men killed and wounded on board his Majesty's Ship Leander, on the 18th August.

Officers killed—Mr. Peter Downs, midshipman; Mr. Gibson, midshipman of the Caroline; Mr. Edward Haddon, midshipman.
Twenty-four seamen killed.
Marines killed—Sergeant Dair and 7 privates.
Total—3 officers, 24 seamen, 1 sergeant, 7 marines, killed.
Officers wounded—Captain Thompson, badly; Lieutenant Taylor; Lieutenant Swiney; Mr. Lee, master; Mr. Mathias, boatswain, badly; Mr. Lacky, master's mate; Mr. Nailor, midshipman.
Forty-one seamen.
Nine marines.
Total.—7 officers, 41 seamen, 9 marines, wounded.

THOMAS THOMPSON.

Admiralty Office, November 24.

LETTERS, of which the following are extract and copy, have been received at this office.

Extract of a Letter from Captain Samuel Hood, of his Majesty's Ship Zealous, to Rear-admiral Lord Nelson, K. B. dated off Alexandria, Sept. 19.

I SHOULD have dispatched the Emerald to you on the 2d instant, agreeably to your orders, but knowing the French had possession of Damietta, also having information they had some vessels likely to sail from thence, I directed Captain Hope, in the Alcmene, to proceed off the place with the Fortune polacre, and endeavour to destroy any vessels he might fall in with, that were belonging to, or assisting the enemy.

On the 2d instant his Majesty's ships Seahorse and Emerald chased in shore, where she anchored near the town of the Arabs, the French gunboat

boat (aviso) L'Anemone, commanded by Enſigne de Vaiſſeau Garbon, of four guns and 62 men, having on board General Camin and Citoyen Valette, aid-de-camp to General Buonaparte, with diſpatches from Toulon, which place they left the 27th of July, and Malta the 26th of Auguſt. On the approach of the boats of our ſhip, ſhe fired on them, cut her cable, and ran on ſhore into the breakers. General Camin and Aid-de-Camp Valette, having landed with the diſpatches, and the whole of the crew, were immediately attacked by the Arabs. The two former, and ſome others, making reſiſtance, were killed, and all the reſt ſtripped of their clothes. Her commander and a few of the men, about ſeven, made their eſcape naked to the beach, where our boats had by this time arrived, and begged on their knees to be ſaved. I am happy in ſaying the humanity of our people extended ſo far as to ſwim on ſhore with lines and ſmall caſks to ſave them, which they fortunately effected. Amongſt theſe was particularly diſtinguiſhed a young gentleman, midſhipman of the Emerald, who brought off the commander Garbon, at the hazard of his own life, through the ſurf.

Sir, *Alcmene, off Damietta, Sept. 21.*
I HAVE the honour of informing you that I arrived yeſterday off Damietta, and, purſuant to your orders, cut out all the veſſels that were anchored in that road, being eight in number, loaded with wine and other neceſſaries for the French army. I am, &c.

To Samuel Hood, Eſq. Captain of   GEORGE HOPE.
his Majeſty's Ship Zealous, &c.

From the LONDON GAZETTE, December 4, 1798.

Admiralty Office, December 4.
Copy of a Letter from the Right Honourable Admiral Lord Bridport, K. B. to Evan Nepean, Eſq. dated the 2d inſtant.

Sir,
ENCLOSED is the copy of a letter I have received from the Hon. Captain Stopford, of his Majeſty's ſhip Phaeton, which I tranſmit to you for their Lordſhips' information.
I have the honour to be, &c.
BRIDPORT.

My Lord, *Phaeton, at Sea, Nov. 24.*
I HAVE the honour to inform your Lordſhip, that his Majeſty's ſhip under my command has this day captured a French brig privateer, called La Reſolue, mounting 18 guns, and carrying 70 men.

She was returning from a cruiſe, in which ſhe had captured one Engliſh merchant-ſhip, called the General Wolfe, from Poole, bound to Newfoundland; and an American ſloop, from Boſton to Hamburgh, which latter was recaptured by the Stag laſt night. The Phaeton having continued the chaſe after the privateer, the two ſhips ſeparated, but I am in hopes that we ſhall ſoon again join. I have the honour to be, &c.

The Right Hon. Lord Bridport, K. B.   ROBERT STOPFORD.

From the LONDON GAZETTE, December 8, 1798.

Admiralty Office, December 8.

Copy of a Letter from the Earl of St. Vincent, K. B. Admiral of the Blue, and Commander in Chief of his Majesty's Ships and Vessels in the Mediterranean, to Evan Nepean, Esq. dated at Gibraltar, October 31.

I ENCLOSE a letter from Captain Bland, of L'Espoir, acquainting me with the capture of a small French cutter (La Fulminante). This vessel is so admirably adapted for an advice-boat, of which we are in extreme want, and so well found, that I immediately ordered Commissioner Inglefield to cause her to be surveyed and estimated, and she proceeded to sea the day after she was taken.

I am, Sir, &c. &c.
ST. VINCENT.

My Lord, *L'Espoir, October 29.*
I HAVE the pleasure to inform your Lordship, that his Majesty's ship under my command has captured a French national cutter that was cruising between Tarifa and Tangiers, who had the impudence to attack us.
I am, &c. &c.
LOFTUS BLAND.

Extract of another Letter from the Earl of St. Vincent, K. B. to Evan Nepean, Esq. dated at Gibraltar, November 15.

YOU will perceive by the enclosed copy of a letter and list of captures and recaptures from Captain Middleton, of his Majesty's ship the Flora, that the position I placed her and the Caroline in, furnished a considerable degree of protection to the outward-bound African and West India trade.

My Lord, *His Majesty's Ship Flora, off the Salvages, Oct. 4.*
I HAVE the honour to inform your Lordship, that the Salvages bearing N. by W. six or seven leagues distant, I fell in with his Majesty's ship the Caroline in chase of a cutter; after passing the private signal, I joined in the chase until nine A. M. when she struck. She proves to be the President Parker, of L'Orient, Citizen Ferry commander; a new vessel, sails well, and belongs to the republic, but has a letter of marque for six months. In the chase she hove all her guns overboard, also the shot and a quantity of provisions. She had captured the Bird, of Liverpool, Robert Tyne master, bound to Africa, which Captain Bowen, of the Caroline, had recaptured this morning at four o'clock. Annexed I send your Lordship a list of guns thrown overboard; and have the honour to be, my Lord, &c. R. G. MIDDLETON.

A List of Guns, &c. thrown overboard by the Cutter, during the Chase.

Eight carronades, 36 pounders, 1 long gun, 9 pounder; six months' provisions, of all species (nearly), and all her boats.

A List of Ships and Vessels captured, recaptured, and destroyed, by his Majesty's Ships Flora and Caroline, between the 19th of July and the 5th of November.

Captured, the Spanish packet Grimaldi, of 2 guns and 28 men; the Spanish ship La Carlota, of 19 men; the French cutter privateer, President

dent Parker, of 12 guns and 50 men, belonging to Dunkirk, bound from L'Orient on a cruife; and the French fhip polacre privateer Le Baret, 12 guns and 77 men, belonging to Malaga, bound from Grand Canary on a cruife.

Recaptured, the Portuguefe brig Noftra Senora de Monte, of 12 men, belonging to Madeira; and the Englifh fhip Bird, of 10 guns and 30 men, belonging to Dunkirk, bound to the Coaft of Guinea.

Deftroyed, the French lugger privateer L'Efperance, 1 gun, with mufkets, and 38 men, belonging to Santa Cruz.

R. G. MIDDLETON.

Philadelphia, Nov. 4.

THE contagion, which has for the laft three months raged fo violently in this city, has as heretofore yielded at length to a fucceffion of froft which has prevailed during the laft week, and the committee of health has invited the inhabitants to return to their homes, under an affurance of perfect fafety, under proper precautions, as to cleanfing and airing their houfes, bedding, and clothing. The coldnefs of the feafon has worked the fame happy change in New York, Bofton, New London, and Wilmington, where the fame fpecies of difeafe raged at the fame time, and proved infinitely more malignant than the former difeafes with which thofe places have been vifited.

From the LONDON GAZETTE, December 15, 1798.

Admiralty Office, December 15.

Copy of a Letter, dated at Ramfgate the 6th inftant, from Mr. Thomas Robert Ridge, Commander of the Badger Excife Cutter, to the Honourable the Commiffioners of Excife, and tranfmitted to this Office.

Honourable Sirs,

I BEG leave to inform your Honours, that being cruifing with the Badger cutter, on the morning of the 5th inftant, I fell in with and captured, between Folkftone and Dungennefs, a French lugger privateer, of four carriage guns and manned with 18 men, called the Calaifen, Citoyen Jaques Guillaume Lamey commander, of and from Calais, out eighteen hours and had captured nothing, quite new, being her firft cruife. I have put in here with the prize, owing to its blowing very ftrong from the fouthward, and as foon as it moderates I fhall proceed to Dover with her.

I am, your Honours, &c.

THOS. R. RIDGE.

From the LONDON GAZETTE, December 22, 1798.

Admiralty Office, December 22.

My Lord, *Ambufcade, at Sea, Dec. 13.*

I BEG to acquaint your Lordfhip, I this day captured the letter of mart Faucon, from Guadaloupe, bound to Bourdeaux, loaded with fugar, coffee, &c. She is near two hundred tons, has been for forty-fix days on her paffage, and had not taken any thing.

I have the honour to be, my Lord, &c.

Right Hon. Lord Bridport, K. B. HENRY JENKINS.

Earl

Earl of St. Vincent to Evan Nepean, Esq. dated Le Souverain, Gibraltar,
November 23.

I ENCLOSE a letter from Lieutenant Coryndon Boger, of the Majestic, who commands his Majesty's sloop El Corso, in the absence of Lord William Stuart, her captain, giving an account of the capture of one of the most mischievous of the enemy's privateers which infest the entrance of the Straits; and his activity on the occasion does him great credit. I am, &c.

ST. VINCENT.

My Lord, *Tangier Bay, Nov. 21.*

I HAVE the honour to acquaint your Lordship, that after seeing the convoy into the Bay of Gibraltar, I chased two French privateers, one of which, L'Adolphe, mounting six carriage guns and 42 men, I captured yesterday evening; the other I drove on shore, about two miles to the westward of Tariff; but from the day being far advanced, and very hazy weather, I found it impossible with safety to attempt destroying her.
I am your Lordship's, &c.
CORYNDON BOGER.

From the LONDON GAZETTE EXTRAORDINARY,
December 24, 1798.

Downing Street, December 23.

CAPTAIN Gifford, first aid-de-camp to General the Hon. Charles Stuart, arrived this afternoon at the office of the Right Hon. Henry Dundas, one of his Majesty's Principal Secretaries of State, with a dispatch from the General, of which the following is a copy.

Sir, *Ciudadella, November 18.*

I HAVE the honour to acquaint you, that his Majesty's forces are in possession of the island of Minorca, without having sustained the loss of a single man.

As neither Commodore Duckworth or myself could procure any useful information relative to the object of the expedition at Gibraltar, it was judged advisable to dispatch the Peterell sloop of war to cruise off the harbour of Mahon for intelligence; where, after remaining a few days, she joined the fleet near the Colombrites, without having made any essential discovery. So circumstanced, it was agreed to attempt a descent in the Bay of Addaya; and the wind proving favourable on the 7th instant, a feint was made by the line of battle ships at Fornelles, and boats were assembled for that purpose under the direction of Captain Bowen, Captain Polden, and Captain Pressland. Previous to the landing of the troops, a small battery at the entrance of the bay was evacuated, the magazine blown up, the guns spiked, and shortly after the first division, consisting of 800 men, was on shore. A considerable explosion to the westward indicated that the Spaniards had also abandoned the works at Fornelles. Nearly the same moment 2000 of the enemy's troops approached in several different directions, and threatened to surround this inconsiderable force, but were repulsed with some loss on the left, while the guns of the Argo checked a similar attempt on the right flank; and the post was maintained until the debarkation of the different divisions afforded the means of establishing a position, from whence the enemy's troops would have been attacked with considerable advantage, had they not retired in the beginning of the night.

The strength of the ground, the passes, and the badness of the roads in Minorca, are scarcely to be equalled in the most mountainous parts of Europe; and what increased the difficulty of advancing upon this occasion was the dearth of intelligence; for although near 100 deserters had come in from the Swiss regiments, and affirmed that the remaining force upon the island exceeded 4000 men, no particular account of the enemy's movements was obtained. Under this uncertainty it was for a few minutes doubtful what measures to pursue, but as quickly determined to proceed by a forced march to Mercadal, and thereby separate the enemy's force by possessing that essential pass, in the first instance, and from thence advancing upon his principal communications to either extremity of the island, justly depending upon Commodore Duckworth's zeal and exertions to forward from Addaya and Fornelles such supplies of provisions and ordnance stores as might favour subsequent operations.

To effect this object, Colonel Graham was sent with 600 men, and by great exertion arrived at Mercadal, a very few hours after the main force of the enemy had marched towards Ciudadella, making several officers and soldiers prisoners, seizing various small magazines, and establishing his corps in front of the village.

The persevering labour of 250 seamen, under the direction of Lieutenant Buchannan, during the night, having greatly assisted the artillery in forwarding the battalion guns, the army arrived at Mercadal on the 9th, where, learning that Mahon was nearly evacuated, a disposition was instantly made to operate with the whole force in that direction, and Colonel Paget detached under this movement with 300 men, to take possession of the town; upon his arrival, he summoned Fort Charles to surrender, and made the Lieutenant-governor of the island, a colonel of artillery, and 160 men, prisoners of war, removed the boom obstructing the entrance of the harbour, and gave free passage to the Cormorant and Aurora frigates, which were previously sent by Commodore Duckworth to make a diversion off that port. But these were not the only advantages immediately resulting from this movement; it favoured desertion, intercepted all stragglers, and enabled the departments of the army to procure beasts of burden for the further progress of his Majesty's arms.

Having ascertained that the enemy's troops were throwing up works and intrenching themselves in front of Ciudadella, it was resolved to force their position on the night of the 13th instant; and preparatory to this attempt, Colonel Paget, with 200 men, was withdrawn from Mahon; Colonel Moncrief sent forward with a detachment to Ferarias; three light twelve pounders, and five and a half inch howitzers, and 90 marines landed from the fleet; when, in consequence of its having been communicated to Commordore Duckworth, that four ships, supposed of the line, were seen between Majorca and Minorca, steering towards the last-mentioned island; he decided to pursue them, requested that the seamen and marines might re-embark, and signified his determination of proceeding with all the armed transports to sea; but weighing the serious consequences which would result to the army from the smallest delay on the one hand, and the advantages to be reasonably expected from a spirited attack on the other, it was thought advisable to retain them with the army; and, on the 12th instant, the whole force marched to Alpius, and

from

ce proceeded, on the 13th, to Jupet, Colonel Moncrief's detaching in a parallel line on the Ferarias road to Mala Garaba, :cautions, and the appearance of two columns approaching the luced the enemy to retire from their half-conftructed defences e walls of Ciudadella; and in the evening of the fame day, a chment, under Captain Muter, was fent to take poffeffion of. den Quart, whereby the army was enabled to advance on the ,arently in three columns, upon Kane's, the Ferarias, and Ford, to the inveftment of the town at daybreak, occupying ground y the pofition the enemy had relinquifhed: thus ftationed, in heavy artillery, and every article neceffary for a fiege, it was ;pedient to fummon the Governor of Minorca to furrender; preliminary articles were immediately confidered; but doubts the part of the enemy, whether the invefting force was fuperior r to the garrifon, two batteries of three twelve pounders, and three half inch howitzers, were erected in the courfe of the following hin eight hundred yards of the place, and at daybreak, the main he troops formed in order of battle, confiderably to the right of ,ad, leaving the picquets to communicate between them and Moncrief's poft. This line, partly real and partly imaginary, four miles in front of the enemy's batteries, from whence two ,ound fhot were immediately fired at the troops; but a timely id the diftant appearance of the fquadron, occafioned a ceffation ies, and renewed a negotiation, which, through the addrefs of neral Sir James St. Clair Erfkine, terminated in the annexed)n.

'eeks falt provifions for the garrifon, befides the enclofed lift of ftores, were found in the town of Ciudadella.

fiftance received from Commodore Duckworth, in forwarding artillery and provifions, greatly facilitated the rapid movements ny; and I am happy in the opportunity of declaring my obliga- ,ord Mark Kerr and Captain Caulfield for the fupplies they fent, hon, and their exertions to land two mortars, which, in the 'urther refiftance, might have proved of the utmoft importance g the army, or compelling the enemy to furrender.

ipport I have experienced from Major-general Sir James St. fkine, Brigadiers-general Stuart and Oakes, the exertion of it-colonel Stewart, my adjutant-general, the zeal, fpirit, and nce of both the officers and men of the different regiments under ,and, have eminently contributed to the fuccefs of the expedition; orize me to reprefent their fervices as highly deferving his moft gracious approbation.

a Gifford, my firft aid de-camp, who is perfectly acquainted y circumftance concerning the capitulation of Ciudadella, and tion of the ifland of Minorca, will have the honour to deliver, tch. I have the honour to be, &c. &c.
ht Hon. *Henry Dundas.* (Signed) CHARLES STUART.

Capitulation demanded for the Surrender of the Fortrefs of Ciudadella to the Arms of his Britannic Majefty.

: garrifon fhall not be confidered as prifoners of war, but fhall it free, with their arms, drums beating, colours flying, with unds of cartridge per man.

Anfwer.

Answer.—The town and fortress of Ciudadella, and the fort of St. Nicholas, together with all artillery, ammunition, stores, provisions, or effects, the property of his Most Catholic Majesty, shall be surrendered to his Britannic Majesty's arms; and the gate of Mahon, and the fort of St. Nicholas, shall be delivered up to the British army to-morrow at noon.

II. They shall be preceded by four brass four pounders, and two two-inch howitzers, with lighted matches, and twelve rounds for each.

Answer.—The garrison shall march out as proposed in the first and second articles, but the guns must be left with the artillery.

III. The said garrison shall be sent with all due convenience to Spain, at the expense of his Britannic Majesty, to one of the nearest ports of the Peninsula, excepting the first battalion of the Swiss regiment of Yan, and the detachment of the dragoons of Numancia, with their horses and furniture, who shall be sent to Majorca, as belonging to corps which garrison that island.

Answer.—The garrison shall be conveyed to the nearest port of his Most Catholic Majesty.

IV. The officers in this island and fortress shall keep their arms, horses, and equipage, with the funds of their regiments, and shall be permitted to go to Mahon, for the purpose of bringing away their families, and removing or disposing of their property there.

Answer.—Admitted, they paying their just debts; and the officers who have occasion to go to Mahon to bring away their families, or dispose of their property, will have passports, on applying to the British commander in chief.

V. The officers of the war department, the revenue, and marine, together with the persons employed in every branch thereof, shall be permitted to follow the garrison, and are to be included in the articles III. IV. and V.

Answer.—Admitted.

VI. Whatever officers and troops have been made prisoners in Mahon, or other parts of the island, since the 7th instant, are comprehended in the above five articles.

Answer.—People who have already surrendered cannot be included in the above capitulation.

VII. The deserters from this army, who have given themselves up to the protection of his Britannic Majesty since the said 7th instant, shall be restored to our army.

Answer.—Refused.

VIII. Beasts of burden, both great and small, shall be granted at the ordinary prices, for those who may be desirous of going to Mahon.

Answer.—Admitted.

IX. During the time the garrison may remain in this island, their necessary wants shall be supplied at the expense of Spain.

Answer.—There will be no obstacle to the garrison's being supplied with provisions by its own officers while it remains, which will be as short a time as possible, and be regulated by the commander in chief.

X. The sick and wounded shall remain in the hospitals, and their treatment be at the expense of their regiments.

Answer.—Admitted.

XI. The inhabitants of this island shall be allowed to continue in the free exercise of their religion, enjoying peaceably the revenues, property, and privileges which they possess and enjoy at present.

XII. The

XII. The episcopal see of the island shall remain established in it, according to the bull for its new creation, enjoying the honours, authority, and rents, belonging to the bishopric, and subsisting with its ecclesiastical chapter and as suffragan of the Archbishop of Valencia.

XIII. The universities (or corporations) of the island shall be maintained in the enjoyment of the particular privileges and franchises which have been granted to them by the ancient King of Spain, as they now possess them, and as they have been allowed to them in the treaties which have taken place as often as this island has passed from one dominion to another.

Answer.—XI. XII. and XIII. are articles which do not properly belong to this capitulation; but of course due care will be taken to secure the peaceable inhabitants in the enjoyment of their religion and property.

XIV. The merchant-ship named Experiencia, which is in Mahon, coming from Smyrna, and belonging to the consulate of Cadiz, and its cargo, shall remain free, and a passport be granted for its safe conduct to Spain.

Answer.—Refused.

XV. Commissioners will be appointed on both sides to settle the detail of the execution of this treaty, and to deliver and receive all stores, &c. the property of his Most Catholic Majesty.

(Signed)   CHARLES STUART,
General and Commander in Chief.
J. T. DUCKWORTH,
Commodore and Naval Commander in Chief.
JUAN NEPOMUSENO DE QUESADA.

Ciudadella, 15th Nov.

Return of Ordnance taken in the Island of Minorca.

Camp, opposite Ciudadella, Nov. 18.

Ciudadella and Fort St. Nichola—5 brass 3¼ inch howitzers; brass ordnance, four 4-pounders, mounted; iron ordnance, six 18, ten 12, eight 9, and two 6-pounders, mounted.

Mahon—One 13-inch, 3 brass 10¼ inch, mortars; 3 brass 6¼ inch howitzers; iron ordnance, fifteen 32, twelve 18, seventeen 12, and three 6-pounders, mounted; 3 brass 8¼ inch howitzers; brass ordnance, three 24, four 12-pounders; iron ordnance, two 24, one 18, and five 12-pounders, dismounted.

Lower Musquito—iron ordnance, one 6-pounder, mounted.
Upper Musquito—iron ordnance, three 9, two 6-pounders, mounted.
Calaucolim—iron ordnance, four 12-pounders, mounted.
St. Teresa—brass ordnance, four 12-pounders, mounted.
Fornelles—iron ordnance, fourteen 18-pounders, mounted.
Pointa Prima—iron ordnance, four 12-pounders, mounted.
Calacoufa—iron ordnance, four 12-pounders, mounted.

Total—one 13, three 10¼ inch mortars; three 8¼, three 6¼, five 3¼ inch howitzers; fifteen 32, five 24, thirty-three 18, fifty-two 12, eleven 9, eight 6, four 4-pounders.

Return of the Ammunition and Stores taken on the Island of Minorca.

Fifty 13, one hundred 10½, one hundred and eighty 8½, seventy-eight 6½ inch shells.

One thousand nine hundred and eighty 32, three thousand one hundred and thirty-one 18, four thousand four hundred and sixty 12, one thousand four hundred and forty 9, one thousand four hundred and thirty-three 6, seven hundred and sixty-four 4-pound round shot.

Sixty-eight 32, three hundred and twenty 12-pound grape shot.

Forty-seven 32, sixty 18, one hundred and sixty-eight 12, six 9, forty-eight 6-pound double-headed shot.

Ninety-nine 4-pound round shot, fixed ammunition.

One hundred and forty-four hand granades.

Two hundred and seventy thousand musket-ball cartridges.

Two thousand flints.

Six hundred and ninety-eight 18, one thousand and ten 12, one hundred and sixty 9, two hundred and thirteen 6-pound cartridges, filled.

Eight hundred and twenty-one whole, and three half barrels of gunpowder.

HAYLORD FLAMINGHAM,
Captain, commanding the Royal Artillery.

His Excellency General the Honourable Charles Stuart, Commander in Chief.

Copy of an Embarkation Return delivered by his Excellency Don Juan Nepomuseno de Quesada, to his Excellency General the Honourable Charles Stuart, Commander in Chief of the British Forces in the Island of Minorca.

Fortress of Ciudadella, in the Island of Minorca.

General State of the Spanish Troops who are to embark for the Evacuation of this Island.

153 officers.
3528 sergeants, drummers, and rank and file.
56 horses.

General staff 16, including 1 governor, 1 lieutenant-governor, 1 major-general, &c.

(Signed)   PEDRO QUADRADO,
Ciudadella, Nov. 17.   Major-general.

I certify the above to be a true copy; and that since the landing of the British forces, and previous to the surrender of Ciudadella, on the 16th instant, nearly 300 deserters have come over to the British army.

RD. STEWART, Adjt.-general.

N. B. The corps composing the Spanish force in this island are as follows---viz. regiment of Valencia, 3 battalions; Swifs regiment of Ruttiman, 2 battalions; Swifs regiment of Yann, 1 battalion; a detachment of the dragoons of Numancia; and a detachment of artillery.

Admiralty

Admiralty Office, Dec. 23.

LIEUTENANT Jones, of his Majesty's ship Leviathan, arrived here this afternoon, with a dispatch from Admiral the Earl of St. Vincent to Mr. Nepean, of which the following is a copy:

Sir, *Le Souverain, Gibraltar, Dec.* 6.

I ENCLOSE the copy of a letter from Commodore Duckworth, with other documents relating to the conquest of the island of Minorca; upon which important event I request you will congratulate the Lords Commissioners of the Admiralty.

Lieutenant Jones, first of the Leviathan, is the bearer of this dispatch, who, from the report of Commodore Duckworth, and my own observation, while my flag was on board that ship, is highly deserving their Lordships' favour and protection.

I am, Sir, &c.
ST. VINCENT.

Leviathan, off Fournelles, Minorca,
My Lord, 19*th Nov.*

IN pursuance of your Lordship's instructions to me of the 18th and 20th of October, I proceeded with the ships under my orders, and the troops under the command of the Honourable General Charles Stuart, to the rendezvous off the Colombrettes; and after having been joined by his Majesty's sloop Peterell, and the arrangements for landing had been completed, on the 5th in the afternoon I stood for Minorca; but in consequence of light winds, I did not make that island till daybreak on the 7th, then within five miles of the port of Fournelles, where finding the wind directly out of that harbour, and the enemy prepared for our reception I (having previously consulted the General) made the signal for Captain Bowen, of the Argo, accompaniend by the Cormorant and Aurora, to assist in covering the landing, to lead into the Creek of Addaya, there not being water or space enough for the line-of-battle ships, which he executed in a most officer-like and judicious manner; and in hauling round the northern point, a battery of four 12-pounders fired one gun, but on seeing the broadside, the enemy left it, blowing up their magazines, and spiking the guns, when the transports were got in without damage, though there was scarcely room for stowing them in tiers During this service, which was rapidly executed, the Leviathan and Centaur plied on and off Fournelles, to divert the attention of the enemy; but knowing an expeditious landing to be our greatest object, as soon as I observed the transports were nearly in the creek, I bore away, and anchored with the Leviathan and Centaur off its entrance, to see that service performed. One battalion was put on shore by eleven o'clock, and directly took the height, which proved fortunate, as the enemy very quickly appeared in two divisions, one of which was marching down towards the battery before mentioned, when I ordered the covering ships to commence a cannonade, which effectually checked their progress, and the General kept them at bay with the troops he had; and by six o'clock in the afternoon the whole were on shore, with eight 6-pounders, field-pieces, and eight days provisions, as also two howitzers. On the same evening, after ordering the Cormorant and Aurora to proceed off Port Mahon, with seven transports, to form a diversion, I
got

got under weigh with the Leviathan and Centaur, and turned up to Fournelles, with an intent to force the harbour; but on my entering the passage, I found the enemy had evacuated the forts, and the wind throwing out caused me to anchor, when I made the Centaur's signal (which was following me) to haul off, landed the marines of the Leviathan, took possession of two forts of four guns each, and one of six; but soon after the General requesting I would not enter this port, I ordered Captain Digby to embark the marines, and to put to sea, and cruise under the command of Captain Markham, who was employed in covering the port of Fournelles and Addaya, and preventing succour being thrown in, whilst my pennant was hoisted on board the Argo, where I continued two days, aiding and directing the necessary supplies for the army. In this I was ably assisted by Captain Bowen. During these two days, I visited head-quarters, to consult with the General, when it was decided, as the anchorage at Addaya was extremely hazardous, and the transports in hourly risk of being lost, to remove them to Fournelles, which was executed under cover of the Leviathan and Centaur. On the 11th I ordered the Centaur off Ciudadella to prevent reinforcements being thrown in, and anchored the Leviathan at Fournelles, landed some 12-pounder field-pieces and howitzers, the sailors drawing them up to the army, shifted my pennant to the Leviathan, and left the Argo at Addaya, ordering Captain Bowen to continue there till all the depots were re-embarked and removed, which was effected that day. Late that evening I received information from the General, that four ships, supposed to be of the line, were seen between Minorca and Majorca. In the middle of the night the General sent me another corroborating report from the look out man, of the four ships seen being of the line. I instantly put to sea (though one-fifth of the crews were on shore) with two ships of the line, a forty-four, and three armed transports, and stood towards Ciudadella; when, at daylight the next morning, that place bearing S. E. by S. eight or nine miles, five ships were seen from the mast-head standing directly down for Ciudadella. I instantly made the signal for a general chase, when I soon observed the enemy haul their wind for Majorca; but I continued the pursuit, to prevent the possibility of their throwing in succour to Minorca; and at noon I discovered the enemy, from the fore-yard, to be four large frigates and a sloop of war; this latter keeping her wind, I made the Argo's signal to haul after her; and Captain Bowen, by his letter of the 15th, informs me he took her at half past three that afternoon, and proved to be his Majesty's sloop Peterell, which had been captured the preceding forenoon by the squadron of frigates I was in chase of. For further particulars on that head, I shall refer you to Captain Bowen's letter, where I am convinced you will observe, with great concern, the very harsh treatment the officers and crew of the Peterell met with when captured; and he has since added, that one man, who resisted the Spaniards plundering him of forty guineas, was murdered, and thrown overboard.

I continued the chase till eleven o'clock that night, when I was within three miles of the sternmost frigate; but finding the wind become light, I feared it would draw me too far from the island of Minorca; I therefore hailed the Centaur, and directed Captain Markham to pursue the enemy, steered directly for Ciudadella, which I made the subsequent afternoon (the 14th) with the Calcutta and Ulysses. The next morning (the 15th), at daybreak, the Argo joined us off Ciudadella. Having had no communication

munication from the General, I sent the first lieutenant, Mr. Jones, though a very hazardous night, in the ship's cutter, with a letter to the General, propoling to cannonade Ciudadella, if it would facilitate his operations. In the morning of the 16th Lieutenant Jones returned with duplicates of two letters I had previously received by Captain Gifford, the General's aid-de-camp, acquainting me that he had summoned the town on the 14th, and that terms of capitulation were agreed upon on the 15th to surrender to his Majesty's arms. When I went on shore, I signed the capitulation the General had made, on which fortunate event I most truly congratulate your Lordship. The Centaur joined, not having been so fortunate as to capture either of the Spanish frigates, though within four miles of the sternmost, Captain Markham being apprehensive the continuance of the chase would carry him to a great distance from more essential service.

From the 10th in the morning, when Fort Charles was put into our possession, and Lord Mark Kerr in the Cormorant, with the Aurora, Captain Caulfield, entered the port, those ships have been employed for the defence of the harbour, guarding the prisoners; and I have the pleasure to assure your Lordship, in the performance of the various services incident to the movements I have stated, I cannot pass too high encomiums on the captains, officers, and seamen, under my command. From Captains Poulden and Pressland, agents of transports, I received every possible assistance in their departments; and when it was necessary I should proceed to sea, to bring to action a reputed superior force, they showed great spirit, and used every exertion to accompany me in their armed transports, as did Lieutenant Simmonds, the other agent, in his. I must now beg leave to mention my first lieutenant, Mr. George Jones, who, in the various and hazardous services he had to undergo, during the attack of the island, has proved highly deserving my praise; I have therefore put him to act as commander of the Peterell, which ship I have presumed to recommission, to convey the present dispatches. There is also high merit due to my second lieutenant, Mr. William Buchannan, whom I landed as second in command under Captain Bowen, with more than 250 seamen: there were likewise the Leviathan's and Centaur's marines with the army, to the number of 100; but other essential service calling Captain Bowen on board his ship, the command of the seamen devolved on Lieutenant Buchannan; and, as will appear by the strongest accompanying testimony given him from the commander in chief of the army, he performed the services with the army with the greatest ability and exertion.

I should feel myself remiss was I to close this without noticing to your Lordship the particular exertions, activity, and correctness of Lieutenant Whitton, of the Constitution cutter, in the various services and messages he had to execute.

The General having signified his wish that his dispatches should be sent without delay, I have not yet been able to visit the port of Mahon, to obtain a return of the state of the dock-yard, or vessels captured in that place, but I understand from Captain Lord Robert Mark Kerr, that there are no ships of war, and only one merchant ship of value; the particulars of which I will transmit by the earliest opportunity.

I have the honour to be, &c.

Earl St. Vincent.   J. T. DUCKWORTH.

Sir, *Argo, at Sea,* 15*th Nov.*

I HAVE the honour to acquaint you, that at half paſt three P. M. on the 13th inſtant, I had the good fortune to come up with the ſhip that I hauled the wind after round Cape Rouge, conformable to your ſignal: ſhe proved to be his Majeſty's ſhip Peterell, in poſſeſſion of Don Antonio Franco Gandrada, ſecond captain of the Spaniſh frigate Flora, who, in company with the three others named in the margin *, captured her the day before.

Theſe frigates had come from Carthagena, had touched at Barcelona, ſailed from thence on Saturday laſt bound to Mahon, with eight millions of rials, to pay the troops.

Deeming it abſolutely neceſſary to make the Peterell uſeful until your return, I took all the Spaniards out (72 in number), and gave her in charge of my firſt lieutenant, Mr. Lynne, with a mate, two midſhipmen, 30 ſeamen, and 12 marines, directing them to land an officer and guide at Fornells, with a letter for General Stuart, and to return here immediately.

I am ſorry to inform you the Spaniards behaved very ill to the officers and ſeamen of the Peterell, having robbed and plundered them of every thing. Great part of the captain's and officers' clothes I have recovered. I returned off this place yeſterday, but being calm I could not get near the ſhore. I have, &c.

Commodore Duckworth. J. BOWEN.

Sir, *Before Ciudadella, Nov.* 18.

I HAVE the honour to return you and the gentlemen employed on ſhore under your command, my ſincere thanks for your activity, zeal, and aſſiſtance, in forwarding the light artillery of the army; neither can too much praiſe be given to the ſeamen for their friendly and cheerful exertions under very hard labour; exertions which were accompanied with a propriety of behaviour which I greatly attribute to your management, and which will ever merit my acknowledgmeuts, and affords me the ſatisfaction of aſſuring you that I am, with ſincere regard, Yours, &c.

Lieutenant Buchannan. CHARLES STUART.

A Liſt of Stores found in the Arſenal at Port Mahon.

The keel and ſtern frame for a man-of-war brig, on the ſtocks, with all the timbers, and part of the clothing, all the rigging, &c.

14 gun-boats, hauled up, with all their rigging in good order, but the boats very old.

13 boats from 36 to 20 feet in length, all their rigging in good order, and fit for ſervice.

2 cables of 17 inch.
2 cables of 0 inch.
2 cables of 5½ inch.
Rope of 5 inch, 400 fathoms.
Rope of 3 inch, 400 fathoms.
Rope of 2½ inch, 600 fathoms.

---

* Caſilda, of 40 guns; Pomona, of 40; and Proſerpine, of 40.

Rope of 1¼ inch, 400 fathoms.
Rope of 1 inch, 300 fathoms.
Rope of ¾ inch, 400 fathoms.
Old junk, 6000 pounds.
6 anchors, from 14 to 17 hundred weight.
7 grapnels, of seven hundred weight.
A large quantity of all sorts of iron-work.
A brass mortar, of 13 inch.
3 ditto, of 12 ditto.
Some shells, of 13 inch and of 8 inch.
2 topmasts for 74-gun ships.
3 lesser ones.
Several caps and spars.
1000 fir planks.
Several knees, and some oak plank.
20 tons of nails, of all sorts.
30 bolts of new, and about 400 yards of old canvas.
14 Spanish pennants.
Blocks for the sheers and heaving ships down of all descriptions, with various other small articles.

    (Signed)   J. WOOLDRIDGE,
Nov. 18.   Lieutenant of the Cormorant.

List of Ships and Vessels found at Port Mahon, and taken Possession of.

1 ship of 540 tons, partly laden with cotton, gum, and drugs.
1 ship of 200 tons, in ballast.
A zebec of 60 tons, laden with horn.
And 4 small tartans.

    (Signed)   J. WOOLDRIDGE,
Nov. 18.   Lieutenant of the Cormorant.

From the LONDON GAZETTE, December 25, 1798.

Admiralty Office, December 25.

Copy of a Letter from Admiral Earl of St. Vincent, K. B. Commander in Chief of his Majesty's Ships and Vessels in the Mediterranean, to Evan Nepean, Esq. dated on board Le Souverain, Gibraltar, November 27.

HEREWITH you will receive the copy of a letter from Rear-admiral Lord Nelson, enclosing one from Captain Ball, of his Majesty's ship Alexander, with the capitulation of the island of Goza.

 My Lord,   *Vanguard, at Sea, Nov.* 1.
I HAVE the honour to transmit you a letter received from Captain Ball, dated October 30, together with the capitulation of the castle of Goza, and a list of ordnance, &c. found in it; the prisoners are now embarked in the Vanguard and Minotaur, till I can get a vessel to send them to France. Captain Ball, with three sail of the line, a frigate, and fireship, is entrusted with the blockade of Malta, in which are two sail of the line and three frigates ready for sea; and from the experience I have had of Captain Ball's zeal, activity, and ability, I have no doubt
but

but that in due time I shall have the honour of sending you a good account of the French in the town of Valetti.

I am, with the greatest respect,
Your Lordship's most obedient servant,

Admiral Earl of St. Vincent. HORATIO NELSON.

Sir, *Alexander, off Malta, Oct. 30.*

I HAVE the honour to acquaint you, that the commandant of the French troops in the castle of Goza signed the capitulation the 28th inst. which you had approved I ordered Captain Creswell, of the marines, to take possession of it in the name of his Britannic Majesty, and his Majesty's colours were hoisted. The next day the place was delivered up in form to the deputies of the island, his Sicilian Majesty's colours hoisted, and he acknowledged their lawful sovereign.

I embarked yesterday all the French officers and men who were on the island of Goza, amounting to 217.

I enclose the articles of capitulation, and an inventory of the arms and ammunition found in the castle, part of which I directed to be sent to the assistance of the Maltese, who are in arms against the French. There were 3200 sacks of corn in the castle, which will be a great relief to the inhabitants, who are much in want of that article.

I have the honour to be, &c.

(Signed)   ALEX. JOHN BALL.

Rear-admiral Sir Horatio Nelson.

Articles of Capitulation between Alexander John Ball, Esq. Captain of his Britannic Majesty's Ship Alexander, appointed to conduct the Blockade of Malta, under Rear admiral Sir Horatio Nelson, K. B. on the Part of Great Britain, and Lieutenant-colonel Lochey, Auj. de Batt. Commander of the French Troops in the Castle of Goza.

I. THE French troops shall march out of the castle of Goza with the honours of war, and shall lay down their arms as they get out of the gate.

II. The castle of Goza, with all the military implements and stores, shall be delivered up to the British officer appointed to take charge of them.

III. The French officers and troops shall be protected in their persons and effects, and the officers allowed to retain their side-arms; they shall be embarked immediately on board his Britannic Majesty's ships, and sent to France in transports, at the expense of the French government. They are not to serve against his Britannic Majesty, or his allies, during the war, until regularly exchanged.

Rear-admiral Sir Horatio Nelson, K. B. has entered into articles with the inhabitants of Goza, that if the French surrender to the British, they shall be considered as under their protection, and they will not offer them the smallest insult or molestation.

Signed the 28th of October 1798,

ALEX. JOHN BALL,
Captain of his Britannic Majesty's Ship Alexander.
LOCHEY, Auj. de Battalion.

Approved.—HORATIO NELSON.

Extract

Extract of Articles found in the Castle of Goza, the 28th October.

50 barrels of powder.
9000 ball cartridges.
1000 musket cartridges, without ball.
1700 flints.
38 eighteen-pound cartridges, filled.
140 twelve-pound ditto.
450 six-pound ditto.
268 four-pound ditto.
25 three-pound ditto.
88 two-pound ditto.
18 eighteen-pounder guns, good, and 200 shot.
2 twelve-pounder guns, good, and 900 shot.
4 six-pounder guns, good, and 2985 shot.
400 hand-granades, filled.
90 pikes, and 90 halberts.
3200 sacks of corn

N. B. No small-arms, except those laid down by the French troops.

Admiralty Office, December 25.

Copy of a Letter from the Right Honourable Lord Bridport, K. B. Admiral of the White, &c. to Evan Nepean, Esq. dated the 22d inst.

ENCLOSED is a copy of a letter from Captain Keats, of his Majesty's ship the Boadicea, to Vice-admiral Sir Alan Gardner, Bart. which is transmitted to you for their Lordships' information.

I have the honour to be, &c. &c.

BRIDPORT.

Sir, *Boadicea, at Sea, Dec. 9.*

I HAVE the honour to inform you, that a ship privateer, named the Invincible Buonaparte, mounting 20 guns (12 and 18-pounders), with a crew of 170 men, of various nations, quite new, sixteen days from Bourdeaux, and never having made any capture, was this day taken by his Majesty's ship Boadicea

I have the honour to be, &c.

Vice-admiral Sir Alan Gardner, Bart. R. G. KEATS.

Copy of another Letter from the Right Hon. Lord Bridport, K. B. to Evan Nepean, Esq. dated the 21st instant.

Sir,

ENCLOSED is a copy of a letter from the Hon. Arthur Kay Legge, captain of his Majesty's ship Cambrian, to me, together with another copy of a letter to Sir Harry Neale, Bart. captain of his Majesty's ship St. Fiorenzo, which are transmitted to you for their Lordships' information. I have the honour to be, &c.

BRIDPORT.

My

My Lord,   *Cambrian, at Sea, Dec.* 8.

ENCLOSED I have transmitted to your Lordship a copy of my letter, of this day's date, to Sir Harry Neale, Bart. captain of his Majesty's ship St. Fiorenzo.   I am, Sir, &c. &c. &c

A. K. LEGGE.

Sir,   *Cambrian, at Sea, Dec.* 8.

I HAVE to inform you, that I have this morning captured Le Cantacre, a French brig privateer, of 14 guns and 60 men. She is three days from Bayonne, quite new, on her first cruise, and a very fine vessel.   I am, Sir, &c. &c.

A. K. LEGGE.

Copy of a Letter from the Right Hon. Lord Bridport, K. B. Admiral of the White, &c. to Evan Nepean, Esq. dated Dec. 23.

Sir,

ENCLOSED are copies of two letters from the Hon. Captain Stopford, of his Majesty's ship Phaeton, and the Hon. Captain Legge, of his Majesty's ship Cambrian, which are transmitted to you for their Lordships' information.   I have the honour to be, &c.

BRIDPORT.

My Lord,   *Phaeton, at Sea, Dec.* 6.

I HAVE the honour to inform your Lordship, that this day his Majesty's ship under my command, in company with the Stag, captured a French brig privateer, called Le Resource, carrying 10 guns and 66 men; two days out from Rochelle, bound on a cruise upon the coast of Africa.   I have the honour to be, &c. &c.

Right Hon. Lord Bridport, K. B. &c.   R. STOPFORD.

My Lord,   *Cambrian, at Sea, Dec.* 12.

I HAVE the honour to inform you, that this morning at one o'clock we recaptured the Dorothea, a Danish brig from Amsterdam, bound to Tangiers, laden with bale-goods. She had been taken on the 9th instant by the Rusée, a French brig privateer from Bayonne, in lat. 42 deg. 30 min. N.   I have the honour to be, &c.

Right Hon. Lord Bridport, K. B.   ARTHUR K. LEGGE.

Copy of a Letter from Rear-admiral Harvey, Commander in Chief of his Majesty's Ships at the Leeward Islands, to Evan Nepean, Esq. dated on board the Prince of Wales, Fort Royal Bay, Martinique, 8th September.

Sir,

I HAVE to acquaint you, for the information of their Lordships, that since my letter to you of the 10th February last, the ships and vessels of his Majesty's squadron under my command have recaptured six British and sixteen American vessels of different denominations, bound to and from these islands, and have also detained twenty vessels under neutral colours, on suspicion of having enemy's property on board.   I have the honour to be, &c.

HENRY HARVEY.

Copy of another Letter from Rear-admiral Harvey to Evan Nepean, Esq. dated on board the Prince of Wales, Fort Royal Bay, Martinique, September 8.

Sir,

I AM to acquaint you, for the information of their Lordships, that since my letter to you of the 8th ultimo, his Majesty's ships Concorde and Lapwing have captured the undermentioned French privateers (schooners), belonging to Guadaloupe.

Le Buonaparte, of 8 guns and 72 men.
L'Amazone, of 10 guns and 80 men.
Le Sauveur, of 4 guns and 21 men.
La Fortune, of 2 guns and 22 men.

And the Lapwing captured, on the 12th ultimo, the Invariable schooner letter of marque, of four guns and 20 men, laden with dry goods, from St. Bartholomew's, bound to Guadaloupe.

I have the honour to be, &c.

HENRY HARVEY.

Copy of another Letter from Rear-admiral Harvey to Mr. Nepean, dated Oct. 22.

Sir,

YOU will be pleased to acquaint their Lordships, that since my letter to you of the 8th ultimo three French privateers, belonging to Guadaloupe, have been captured and sent to this island by his Majesty's ships under my command, as under mentioned.

By the Bittern, September 8th, off Marigalante, Le 10 Aout brig, of 12 guns and 50 men: she had been cruising on the American coast, where she had taken three American vessels and one Dane, and was returning to Guadaloupe.

By the Matilda, the 5th instant, off the north-east end of Antigua, L'Intrepid brig, of 14 guns and 74 men: had been out three days from Guadaloupe, without making any captures.

By the Pearl, the 14th instant, off the east end of Antigua, the Scevola sloop, of 10 guns and 73 men: had been out two days, and taken nothing.

And the Pearl, a few days previous to the last capture, likewise destroyed a small French privateer row-boat, under Dominica.

I have the honour to be, &c.

HENRY HARVEY.

From the LONDON GAZETTE, December 29, 1798.

Admiralty Office, December 29.

Copy of a Letter from the Right Hon. Lord Bridport, K.B. Admiral of the White, &c. to Evan Nepean, Esq. dated the 24th instant.

Sir,

ENCLOSED is a copy of a letter from Sir Harry Neale, Bart. captain of his Majesty's ship St. Fiorenzo, which I transmit to you for their Lordships' information.

I have the honour to be, &c. &c.

BRIDPORT.

My

My Lord, *St. Fiorenzo, at Sea, Dec.* 13.

I HAVE the honour to inform your Lordship, that the St. Fiorenzo and Triton captured, on the 11th and 12th inst. the vessels named in the margin *, which are sent to Plymouth.

I have the honour to be, &c. &c.
H. NEALE.

Copy of a Letter from the Earl of St. Vincent, K. B. Commander in Chief of his Majesty's Ships and Vessels in the Mediterranean, to Evan Nepean, Esq. dated at Gibraltar, Dec. 3.

Sir,

LIEUTENANT Boger, during his temporary command of his Majesty's sloop El Corso, has given good earnest of what may be expected of him when promoted. My letter of the 23d last, gave an account of his capturing the Adolphe, French privateer, which had done much mischief in the Gut, and the enclosed relates his having taken another small one, name unknown. I am, Sir, &c. &c.
ST. VINCENT.

My Lord, *El Corso, Rosia Bay, Dec.* 2.

I HAVE the honour to acquaint your Lordship, that I yesterday afternoon chased a French privateer on shore, about three leagues to the eastward of Cape Malabar, and, with the assistance of the Espoire's boats, was enabled to bring her off. On boarding, we found that the crew had deserted her. She mounts two carriage-guns, two swivels, and several small arms.

I have the honour to be, &c.

Admiral the Earl of St. Vincent, K. B. &c. C. BOGER.

From the LONDON GAZETTE, January 1, 1799.

Dublin Castle, December 24, 1798.

IT is his Excellency the Lord Lieutenant's pleasure, that the yeomanry brigade majors proceed to their respective counties forthwith, and report their arrival at their stations to the War Office. Those who shall fail to comply with this order previous to the 4th of next month, will be considered as absent without leave, and consequently will be superseded.

---

* St. Joseph, Spanish privateer, mounting 14 long brass six-pounders, complement 64 men.

La Revue French brig, coppered, just off the stocks, and in every respect fit for his Majesty's service, mounting 14 four-pounders, complement 60 men.

Recaptured the George brig, of London, from Bristol, bound to Lisbon, loaded with coals, copper, and bottles.

From

From the LONDON GAZETTE,

Admiralty Office, January 8.
Copy of a Letter from Sir Edward Pellew, Bart.

Sir,   *Indefatigable, at Sea, Jan.* 1.
I HAVE the pleasure to inform you, that at dawn of day, yesterday morning, Ushant bearing N. E. five leagues, we captured the French ship privateer La Minerve, carrying 16 guns and 140 men, twenty-eight days from St. Malo. She was lying-to, waiting to proceed into Brest, and took this ship for her prize, the Asphalon, of Newcastle, from Halifax, bound to London, laden with sugar, coffee, and tobacco; which ship we chased all day, and this morning had the satisfaction to retake off the rocks of Albrevrak.

I have the honour to enclose a list of vessels captured by the privateer during her cruise.   I am, &c.
                                                EDWARD PELLEW.
Vice-admiral Sir Alan Gardner, Bart.

List of Vessels captured by La Minerve French Ship Privateer, of St. Malo, between the 11th and 31st of December 1798.

Martinus, a Bremen brig, from Lisbon, bound to Bremen, with sugar, coffee, and hides.

Tagus, Portuguese brig, from Lisbon, bound to Bristol, with lemons and oranges.

Minerva, English snow, from Providence to London, with sugar, coffee, and cotton.

Ann and Dorothea, Danish schooner (captured under the name of Beata Maria), from St. Thomas, bound to Hamburgh, with cocoa and cotton—retaken by his Majesty's ship Indefatigable.

Asphalon, ship of Newcastle, John Edgar master, from Halifax, bound to London, with sugar, coffee, and tobacco, &c. &c.—retaken by his Majesty's ship Indefatigable.

From the LONDON GAZETTE, January 12, 1799.

Admiralty Office, January 12.
Copy of a Letter from the Right Honourable Lord Bridport, K. B. Admiral of the White, &c. to Evan Nepean, Esq. dated the 7th inst.

Sir,
ENCLOSED is a copy of a letter from Captain Griffith, of his Majesty's ship Triton, which I transmit for their Lordships' information.   I have the honour to be, Sir, &c.
                                                BRIDPORT.

My Lord,
AGREEABLE to the orders which I received from Sir Harry Neale, I have returned to Cawsand Bay in the Triton. A few days ago, after I parted company with the St. Fiorenzo, I captured a French privateer brig of 14 guns and 64 men, just come out of Corunna, and was bound on a cruise off the Western Islands: she is new off the stocks

stocks, coppered, and sails well. This, with the two brigs I captured in company with Sir Harry Neale, is the amount of our success.
I have the honour to be, &c.
EDWARD GRIFFITH.

Right Hon. Admiral Lord Bridport, K. B. &c.

Admiralty Office, January 12.

Extract of a Letter from Admiral Sir Peter Parker, Bart. Commander in Chief of his Majesty's Ships and Vessels at Portsmouth, to Evan Nepean, Esq. dated the 11*th instant.*

ENCLOSED is a letter which I have received from Lieutenant Shepheard, commander of his Majesty's cutter the Pigmy, giving an account of his having captured, on the 8th instant, La Rancune French cutter privateer, and retaken two brigs, laden with bar-iron, which had been taken by the said privateer.

Sir, *Pigmy Cutter, Portland Road, Jan.* 9.

I HAVE the honour to acquaint you, that yesterday noon, Durlstone Head bearing N. W. two miles, I observed a cutter and two brigs off St. Alban's, standing to the southward, and immediately gave chase. At forty minutes past one came up, and retook the brig Lark, Francis Artis master, from Cardiff to London, laden with bar-iron; and the brig Dion, Esdras Best master, from Cardiff to London, laden with the same. Continued the chase, and at four captured the French cutter privateer La Rancune, commanded by Ant. Fran. Vic. Jos. Panpeville; manned with 21 men, and carrying two swivel guns, small-arms, &c. from Cherbourg twenty-six hours: had made no other capture than the two brigs before mentioned, which she had taken that morning. I have the honour to be, &c.
W. SHEPHEARD.

Sir Peter Parker, Bart. Admiral of the White,
Commander in Chief, &c.

Copy of a Letter from Captain Edward Buller, commanding the Sea Fencibles along the Coast of Devon, dated Dartmouth, Jan. 10.

Sir,

I BEG leave to acquaint you, for the information of the Lords Commissioners of the Admiralty, that the brig Susannah left this port yesterday morning, seven o'clock, for Torbay, and was captured while at anchor off West Down Head, five miles from this place, at half past one P. M. by the French privateer L'Heureux Speculateur, mounting 14 guns. The Brixham sea fencibles, perceiving an armed vessel, concluded her to be an enemy; and, from her boarding the above brig, supposed she had captured her; in consequence of which went off in a boat armed with pikes and muskets, succeeded in recapturing the brig, which, on their appearance, was deserted by the Frenchmen, whom they also pursued, and took.

Lieutenant Nicholas, with his usual zeal, with Collector Brooking's assistance of small-arms and boat, went also from this port with part of the sea fencibles, accompanied by a boat from his Majesty's cutter Nimble, in hopes of capturing the privateer, but was not fortunate enough

nough to succeed in the attempt. The recaptured brig he towed into his harbour. I am, Sir, &c.
ED. BULLER.

From the LONDON GAZETTE, January 19, 1799.
Admiralty Office, January 19.

Copy of a Letter from Admiral Lord Bridport, K. B. Commander in Chief of his Majesty's Ships and Vessels employed in the Channel, to Evan Nepean, Esq. dated Bath, January 18.

Sir,
ENCLOSED is the copy of a letter from Captain Cunningham, of his Majesty's ship Clyde, which I transmit to you for their Lordships' information. I have the honour to be, &c. &c.
BRIDPORT.

My Lord, *Clyde, Carusand Bay, Jan. 15.*
I HAVE the honour to inform you, that on the 10th instant, his Majesty's ship Clyde, under my command, captured L'Air schooner letter of marque, from Brest to St. Domingo; and on the 13th, a brig privateer, called Le Bon Ordre, carrying 16 guns and 65 men. She sailed from Granville on the 20th December, and had captured one brig from Newfoundland, on the 6th instant.
I have the honour to be, my Lord, &c.
(Signed) CHA. CUNNINGHAM.
The Right Hon. Lord Bridport, K. B. &c.

From the LONDON GAZETTE, January 22, 1799.
Whitehall, January 22.

LETTERS, of which the following are copies, were yesterday received from the Earl of Balcarras, by his Grace the Duke of Portland, one of his Majesty's Principal Secretaries of State.

My Lord, *Jamaica, Nov. 7, 1798.*
ON the 31st of October I received a dispatch from the Bay of Honduras.
Lieutenant-colonel Barrow informs me, that the settlers had been attacked by a flotilla, consisting of thirty-one vessels, having on board 2000 and troops and 500 seamen. Arthur O'Neil, governor-general of Yucatan, and a field marshal in the service of Spain, commanded in person. I have great satisfaction in transmitting the letter of the Lieutenant-colonel, by which your Grace will be informed, that this armament has been repulsed, and the expedition entirely frustrated.
The Lieutenant-colonel speaks in the handsomest manner of the conduct of Captain Moss, of his Majesty's ship Merlin, and of the wonderful exertions of the settlers and their negro slaves, who manned the gunboats.
The conduct of Lieutenant-colonel Barrow, and of the settlers, in putting the port of Honduras Bay into a respectable state of defence, as well as the gallant manner in which it was maintained, give me entire satisfaction, and it is with pleasure that I report their services to your Grace. I have the honour to be, &c. &c. &c.
To his Grace the Duke of Portland. BALCARRAS.

My Lord, *Honduras, September 23, 1798.*

AFTER the date of my laſt diſpatch of the 11th, 14th, and 21ſt Auguſt, by the expreſs-boat Swift, I continued to ſtrengthen our flotilla, which now conſiſts of,

No. 1. Towſer, 1 gun, eighteen pounder.
No. 2. Tickler, 1 gun, eighteen pounder.
No. 3. Mermaid, 1 gun, nine pounder.
No. 4. Swinger, 4 guns, ſix pounders, and 2 guns, four pounders.
No. 5. Teazer, 6 guns, four pounders.

Beſides eight flat gunboats, carrying each a nine pounder in the prow.

No. 1 and 2 are commanded by Mr. Gelſton and Mr. Hoſmer, maſters of merchant-veſſels, who, with ſome of their crews, volunteered the buſineſs in a very handſome manner: to thoſe gentlemen I am much indebted for their able and active ſervices. The maſters and crews of all the other veſſels conſiſt entirely of volunteers from the colonial troops, and together amount to 354 men now on float. The enemy was ſo well watched by the ſcout-boats and canoes, that not a ſingle movement could be made by him without our knowledge; and finding that he aimed at the poſſeſſion of St. George's Key, the armed veſſels, No. 1, 4, and 5, were ſent to that place to guard the narrow channels leading to that commodious harbour.

On the 3d of September the enemy endeavoured to force a paſſage over Montego Key Shoal with five veſſels, two of which carried heavy metal, but was repulſed: he renewed his attempt on the following day; but our little ſquadron, being now reinforced by ſix gunboats, beat them off with great eaſe, and the five veſſels returned to the main body of the fleet, then at anchor about two leagues to the northward. This movement gave our people an opportunity of drawing and deſtroying all the beacons and ſtakes which the enemy had placed in this narrow and crooked channel, and without the uſe of which nothing but veſſels of a very eaſy draught of water can paſs. On the 5th, the ſame veſſels, accompanied by two others, and a number of launches, endeavoured to get over this ſhoal by another paſſage, but were repulſed, apparently with loſs. On this, as well as on the two preceding days, the Spaniards expended an immenſe quantity of ammunition to no manner of purpoſe; while our people fired comparatively little, but with a ſteadineſs which ſurpaſſed my moſt ſanguine hopes.

Captain Moſs, in his Majeſty's ſhip Merlin, left his anchorage at Belize on the evening of the 5th, and arrived at St. George's Key about noon on the 6th of September. The Spaniards having found a paſſage through the leeward channels impracticable, had got under weigh on the morning of that day, with the whole of their fleet, ſeemingly with a view of forcing a paſſage through the windward, a ſand-bore paſſage, to the eaſtward of Long Key; but on ſeeing the Merlin beating into the harbour of St. George's Key, and that our fleet was reinforced by the armed veſſels No. 2 and 3, and a large gunboat, they returned to their former anchorage between Long Key and Key Chappel.

I was now of opinion that the enemy would alter his mode of attack, and endeavour to make a landing on the main land to the northward of our poſts, at the Haul-over. Under this idea I began to prepare ſmall veſſels and gunboats, in which I meant to embark with 200 men, including detachments of his Majeſty's 63d and 6th Weſt India regiments, and of the royal artillery, with one howitzer and two field-pieces, ſix

pounders;

pounders: with this force it was my intention to block up the channel between the main and the western point of Hicks's Keys, and to obstruct as much as possible a landing in that quarter; or, if foiled in both these objects, to throw the whole strength into the works at the Haul-over, and to defend that post to the last extremity; while a body of experienced bush-men, all good shots, and under orders for that purpose, should hang on the flanks and rear of the enemy.

On the morning of Monday the 10th of September, fourteen of the largest vessels of the Spanish fleet weighed anchor, and at nine o'clock brought to about a mile and a half distant from our fleet. Captain Moss was then of opinion, that they meant to delay their attack till the following day; but nine of them got under weigh about noon: these carried each two twenty-four pounders in the bow, and two eighteen pounders in the stern; one schooner carried twenty-two, and all the rest from eight to 14 guns in their waist; and every one of them, besides being crowded with men, towed a large launch full of soldiers. The other five vessels, with several large launches all full of men, remained at this last anchorage, at the distance of a mile and a half.

Our fleet was drawn up with his Majesty's ship Merlin in the centre, and directly abreast of the channel: the sloops with heavy guns and the gunboats in some advance to the northward, were on her eastern and western flanks.

The enemy came down in a very handsome manner, and with a good countenance, in a line abreast, using both sails and oars. About half after two o'clock, Captain Moss made the signal to engage, which was obeyed with a cool and determined firmness, that, to use his own expression to me on the occasion, would have done credit to veterans. The action lasted about two hours and a half, when the Spaniards began to fall into confusion, and soon afterwards cut their cables, and sailed and rowed off, assisted by a great number of launches which took them in tow.

Captain Moss, on seeing them retreat, made a signal for our vessels to chase; but night coming on, and rendering a pursuit too dangerous in a narrow channel and difficult navigation, they were soon after recalled.

At half past three in the afternoon I received a letter from Captain Moss, stating that the enemy was preparing to attack him, and requiring all the assistance which I could give. I immediately ordered as many men to embark and proceed to his assistance, as small craft to carry them could be procured. The alacrity shown on this occasion was great indeed; but as a requisition of this nature was by no means expected, the necessary arrangements had not been made for so speedily embarking the troops, and of consequence some irregularity ensued; for the cannonade being distinctly heard, and a certainty of an engagement having taken place, it became impossible to restrain the eagerness of the colonial troops, who, possessing canoes, dories, and pit-pans, without thought or respect to those left behind, hastened with impetuosity to join their companions, and share their danger: hence arose difficulty and disappointment to the regular troops, who being under arms, anxious to proceed with all expedition, suffered delay from want of the necessary boats and craft to embark in.

As soon as I saw seventeen craft of different descriptions, having on board 200 men, set off with orders to rally round the Merlin, I immediately joined them, in hopes of assisting Captain Moss and harassing the enemy;

enemy; but although we were only two hours in getting on board the Merlin, a diftance of three leagues and a half, in the wind's eye, we were too late to have any fhare in the action. But I am of opinion, that the fight of fo many craft full of men, coming up with velocity, haftened the return of the enemy; and that their appearance on the following day, as well as the junction of two armed fhips, the Juba and Columbia, which I had ordered round to St. George's Key on the 9th, induced the fleet to prepare for returning to their refpective pofts. The Spaniards remained under Key Chappel until the 15th; on the morning of which they made various movements, and in the courfe of the day fome of them anchored under Key Caulker. On the morning of the 16th, it was difcovered that they had ftolen off; eight of their largeft veffels got out to fea, and ftood to the northward; the remainder, being twenty-three in number, fhaped their courfe for Baccalar.

We have every reafon to believe that the enemy fuffered much in the action of the 10th, as well in killed and wounded as in the hulls and rigging of the veffels engaged; and I am happy to inform your Lordfhip that we had not a fingle man hurt, and that no injury was done to any of our veffels deferving of notice.

It would be unjuft, my Lord, to mention the names of any officers, either of the military or militia, on account of any particular fervice performed by them; for the conduct of all being fuch as to merit my beft thanks, no particular diftinction can be made.

It is alfo unneceffary for me to fay any thing refpecting Captain Mofs: his penetration in difcovering, and activity in defeating, the views of the enemy; his coolnefs and fteady conduct in action, point him out as an officer of very great merit. He firft fuggefted to me the very great ufe which might be made of gunboats againft the enemy, and gave me much affiftance by the artificers belonging to his fhip in fitting them out. I am happy to fay, that the moft cordial co-operation has always exifted between us. On the 13th inftant I fent out two fcout-canoes well manned, with orders to pafs the Spanifh fleet in the night; and, proceeding to the northward, to board the firft fmall veffel they could fall in with. On the 16th they captured a fmall packet-boat with five hands, when taking out the prifoners, letters, &c. and deftroying the boat, they returned here on the 17th. At daylight of that day the canoes were entangled with the retreating Spanifh fleet near Savanna Quay, and efcaped with difficulty.

The expedition was commanded by Arthur O'Neil, a field-marfhal in the armies of Spain, and captain-general of the province of Yucatan. The Campeachy fleet was commanded by Captain Bocca Negra: 2000 foldiers were embarked and diftributed in proportion to the dimenfions of the veffels on board of the fleet, which confifted of

The veffels which made the attack, in number — —	9
Referve of equal force — — — — —	5
A very large floop of equal force, and fix fchooners not fo large, but armed in the fame manner as thofe which came down to the attack, and drawing too much water, remained with the tranfports and victuallers	7
Tranfports, victuallers, &c. all carrying bow and fide guns of different calibres — — — — —	11
Total	32

And

And navigated by 500 seamen, principally from the Havannah and Campeachy. I am, &c.

THO. BARROW,
Lieutenant-colonel Commandant.
BALCARRAS.

To the Earl of Balcarras.
(True copy.)

Admiralty Office, January 22.

Extract of a Letter from Vice-admiral Sir Hyde Parker, Knt. Commander of his Majesty's Ships and Vessels at Jamaica, to Evan Nepean, Esq. dated on board his Majesty's Ship Abergavenny, in Port Royal Harbour, the 6th November 1798.

Sir,

YOU will be pleased to acquaint the Right Hon. the Lords Commissioners of the Admiralty, that I have received dispatches from Captain Mots, of his Majesty's sloop Merlin, dated Honduras, 27th September; copy of which, describing the defeat of the Spanish flotilla, is herewith inclosed.

Sir, *Merlin, St. George's Key, September 27, 1798.*

MY letters by the Swift schooner, which sailed from Honduras express on the 21st of August, have informed you of the enemy's force, intended for the reduction of this settlement, and their situation at that time; since which our look-out canoes have watched them so closely, that all their movements were known to me as they happened. On the 4th of this month they were visible from our mast-heads at Belize, and the look-outs reported to me thirty-one sail of all descriptions, but their exact force by no means certain. The next day six of their heaviest vessels attempted to force their passage over Montego Key shoals, by putting their provisions and stores into other vessels: had they effected this, it would have secured them all a passage to Belize, over shoal water, where I could by no means act. I ordered three of our armed vessels to annoy them in their endeavours, which succeeded so far as to occasion their removal at dark; and a small channel they had marked by driving down stakes was also taken up by our canoes. I now clearly saw that their next effort would be to get possession of St. George's Key, from which place (only nine miles from Belize) they might go down through the different channels leading to it, and continue to harass the inhabitants and destroy the town at their leisure, and drive me from my anchorage there: this determined me to gain the Key before them, if possible; I therefore left Belize on the evening of the 5th, and secured this place, at the instant twelve of their heaviest vessels were attempting the same; they hauled their wind and returned to Long Key, on my hauling my wind towards them. They continued working and anchoring among the shoals until the 11th, at the distance of three or four miles, when having made their arrangements, at one P.M. nine sail of sloops and schooners, carrying from 12 to 20 guns, including two twenty-four and two eighteen pounders each had in prow and stern, with a large launch astern of each, full of men, bore down through the channel leading to us in a very handsome, cool manner; five smaller vessels lay to windward, out of gun-shot, full of troops, and the remainder of their squadron at Long Key Spit to wait the event, each of which carried small prow-guns, with swivels fore and aft. At half past one P.M. seeing their intention to board the two sloops, and that they meant to come no nearer, but had anchored, I made the signal to engage,

which

which began and continued near two hours; they then cut their cables, and rowed and towed off by signal, in great confusion over the shoals. I had placed the Merlin as near the edge of them as possible, and nothing that I had was equal to follow them unsupported by the Merlin. At dark they regained their other vessels, and continued in sight till the 15th at night, when they moved off with a light southerly wind: some are gone to Bacalar, and, some prisoners taken report, others to Campeche. I am happy to add, that the service was performed without a man killed on our side. The enemy, I think, must have suffered much from the great number of men on board, and the precipitate manner they made their retreat. This armament was commanded by General O'Neil, governor of the province; troops and sailors included, about 2500 men: and so certain were the Spaniards of success, that the letters found in a canoe taken were actually directed to Belize and St. George's Key.

The behaviour of the officers and crew of his Majesty's ship gave me great pleasure, and had we had deep water to follow them in, I think many of them would have fallen into our hands. The spirit of the negro slaves that manned our small crafts was wonderful, and the good management of the different commanders does them great credit.

Our force, besides the Merlin, as follows:
Two sloops, with 1 eighteen pounder and 25 men.
One sloop, with 1 short nine pounder and 25 men.
Two schooners, with 6 four pounders and 25 men each.
Seven gun-flats, with 1 nine pounder and 16 men each.

I have the honour to be, Sir, &c. &c.

JNO. R. MOSS.

Admiralty Office, January 22.

Extract of a Letter from Sir Thomas Williams, Knt. Captain of his Majesty's Ship Endymion, to Evan Nepean, Esq. dated in the Downs, the 20th instant.

YOU will be pleased to inform their Lordships, that the Endymion has captured two Spanish privateers:
La Prudencia schooner, of 1 six pounder, 8 swivels, and 34 men.
La Casualidad, of 6 six pounders, 8 swivels, and 40 men.

From the LONDON GAZETTE, January 26, 1799.

Admiralty Office, January 26.

Copy of a Letter from Vice-admiral Kingsmill, Commander in Chief of his Majesty's Ships and Vessels on the Coast of Ireland, to Evan Nepean, Esq. dated Cork, January 17.

Sir,

PLEASE to lay before my Lords Commissioners of the Admiralty the accompanying letter I have just received from Captain Frafer, of his Majesty's ship Shannon, who has brought in a French privateer, out of Granville, mounting 18 carronades and 2 long twelve pounders, and 125 men, which he captured on the 25th instant.

I have the honour to be, &c. &c.

R. KINGSMILL.

Sir,

Sir, Shannon, Cove of Cork, January 17.

I BEG leave to acquaint you, that being, on the morning of the 5th inſtant, in lat. 49 deg. 40 min. and long. 9 deg. 30 min. W. with his Majeſty's ſhip under my command, proceeding to the rendezvous preſcribed by Captain Faulknor, I ſaw, and after a chaſe of ſeven hours captured Le Grand Indien, a ſhip privateer, from Granville, commanded by Gand Olivier Vabois, carrying 18 braſs carronades, eighteen pounders, and two long twelve pounders, manned with 125 men.

She was only five days from Granville, had taken nothing, is quite new, with proviſions and ſtores for three months cruiſe.

From the circumſtance of the prize having carried her main-maſt by the board while chaſed (and as the Shannon alſo ſprung a main-topmaſt, and tore to pieces two boats while ſhifting priſoners), the wind blowing ſtrong with a heavy ſea, I hope you will approve of my having accompanied her into port. I have the honour to be, Sir, &c. &c.
Robert Kingſmill, Eſq. ALEX. FRASER.

From the LONDON GAZETTE, February 9, 1799.
Admiralty Office, February 8.
Copy of a Letter from the Right Hon. Admiral Lord Bridport, to Evan Nepean, Eſq. dated February 1.

Sir,
HEREWITH you will receive a copy of a letter from Captain Gore, of his Majeſty's ſhip Triton, which I tranſmit you for their Lordſhips' information. I have the honour to be, &c.
BRIDPORT.

My Lord, *His Majeſty's Ship the Triton, at Sea, Jan. 29.*
I HAVE the ſatisfaction to inform your Lordſhip, that after a chaſe of eight hours and a half, his Majeſty's ſhip Triton captured the French brig L'Aimable Victoire, mounting 16 braſs eight pounders, two iron ſix pounders, and 86 men; ſailed from Cherbourg yeſterday evening, has not taken any thing.

I have reaſon to feel ſatisfied at this capture, as ſhe ſails very faſt, is of large dimenſions, and being her firſt cruiſe, might have injured the trade of this country. She is quite new, and I think fit for his Majeſty's ſervice. I have the honour to be, &c.
JOHN GORE.
The Right Hon. Lord Bridport, Admiral of the White, &c.

From the LONDON GAZETTE, February 12, 1799.
Admiralty Office, February 12.
Copy of a Letter from the Earl of St. Vincent, K. B. Commander in Chief of his Majeſty's Ships and Veſſels in the Mediterranean, to Evan Nepean, Eſq. dated at Gibraltar, the 7th of January.

Sir,
HEREWITH I encloſe a liſt of veſſels captured by his Majeſty's ſhips under the orders of Commodore Duckworth, at and near Minorca.
I am, &c.
ST. VINCENT.

Vol. VIII. T Liſt

List of Vessels captured by the Squadron under the Orders of Commodore Duckworth.

Spanish ship Francisco Xavier, alias Esperanfa, laden with drugs and bale-goods, bound to Cadiz, taken possession of by the Cormorant, in the harbour, November 10, 1798.

French privateer Le Tartar, on a cruise, taken possession of by the Cormorant, at sea, October 27, 1798.

Spanish ship Misericordia, of Minorca, laden with paper, bound for a market, taken possession of by the Coromandel, Nov. 15, 1798.

Spanish ship Virgin Dolorosa, of Minorca, laden with merchandise, bound to Minorca, taken possession of by the Ulysses, Nov. 18, 1798.

Spanish ship Virgin del Rosario, of Minorca, laden with merchandise, bound to Minorca, taken possession of by ditto, same day.

Spanish ship San Antonio, laden with beans, bound to Barcelona, taken possession of by the Centaur, at sea, Nov. 19, 1798.

French ship Marie Rose, laden with wine and merchandise, bound to La Cala, taken possession of by the Leviathan, in the harbour, Nov. 22, 1798.

Spanish ship Virgin Solidad, laden with rags, bound to Barcelona, taken possession of by the Argo, at sea, same day.

Spanish ship San Antonio di Cadua, laden with rags, bound to Barcelona, taken possession of by the Dolphin's boats in the harbour, Dec. 8, 1798.

Spanish ship St. Vincent Fiza, laden with merchandise, bound to Yarca, taken possession of by the Leviathan, at sea, Dec. 8, 1798; part of a cargo lying in store, belonging to the Genoese and Spaniards, value about 2000*l*.
(Signed) J. DUCKWORTH.

Copy of a Letter from Captain Horton, of his Majesty's Sloop Fairy, to Evan Nepean, Esq. dated at Sea, January 11.

Sir,

I HAVE the satisfaction to advise you, for the information of my Lords Commissioners of the Admiralty, that at half past six, A. M. I gave chase to a brig in the S. W. and at half past eleven came up with and captured her: she proves to be the Nostra Senora del Pont St. Buonaventa, mounting six carriage guns, two carronades, and carrying 55 men, fifteen of whom, it appears, are on board two prizes she had taken from Newfoundland, which, from the information I have obtained, I am in hopes of retaking.

I have further to advise you, for their Lordships' information, that I this day retook the John M'Donald, from Newfoundland to Lisbon, with fish, having been captured on the 6th instant by Il Volario privateer, out of Vigo. I have sent the John M'Donald for Lisbon; but for the present I detain the Buonaventa, as it blows too fresh at present to make the necessary arrangements.

I am, &c. &c.
JOSHUA SYDNEY HORTON.

From the LONDON GAZETTE, February 16, 1799.

Admiralty Office, February 16.

Copy of a Letter to the Earl of St. Vincent, K. B.

My Lord, Santa Dorothea, off Alberan, Dec. 1.

I HAVE the honour to acquaint you with the capture of a Spanish man of war brig, on the evening of the 28th ult. mounting 16 six pound-

ers and 88 men, in company with the Strombolo, Perseus, and Bull Dog.
H. DOWNMAN.

Extract of a Letter from the Earl of St. Vincent, K. B. to Evan Nepean, Esq. dated at Gibraltar, December 23, 1798.

Sir,

I ENCLOSE a list of prizes taken by his Majesty's ships Flora and Caroline. I am, &c.
ST. VINCENT.

List of Vessels captured by his Majesty's Ships Flora and Caroline, between the 5th of November and 4th of December 1798.

Spanish ship El Bolante, four guns and 19 men, laden with dry goods, bound from Corunna to Montevedio, taken Nov. 21, 1798, twenty-seven leagues W. of Madeira.

French ship La Garonne, 10 guns and 47 men, laden with dry goods, bound from Bourdeaux to Guadaloupe, taken Nov. 23, 1798, fifteen leagues W. N. W. of Madeira.

Admiralty Office, February 16.

Extract of another Letter from the Earl of St. Vincent, dated at Gibraltar, December 23, 1798.

Sir,

BY some accident Captain Middleton's relation of the gallant action performed by the boats of his Majesty's ship Flora, commanded by the first lieutenant (Russel) of that ship, in cutting out the Mondovi French corvette, from Cerigo, was not transmitted to you: it is now enclosed.
I am, &c.
ST. VINCENT.

His Majesty's Ship Flora, off Cerigo, Archipelago, May 14, 1798.

My Lord,

HAVING chased a French national brig into Cerigo, and finding it impracticable to follow in the ship, from the narrow entrance of the harbour, and the commanding situation of the forts; on the evening I sent the boats of his Majesty's ship, under the command of Lieutenant Russel, with officers as per margin *, who volunteered their services in a very handsome manner, with such of the ship's company as chose to go, to cut her out, which they did in a very gallant manner, under a severe fire from the forts, the brig, and several vessels in the harbour. She proves to be Le Mondovi brig corvette, of 16 guns, 12 brass six pounders, and four iron twelve pounders, manned with 68 men, commanded by Citizen Bonnevie, Lieutenant de Vaisseau, a new Venetian-built brig, sails well, though not coppered, is well found, and in my opinion fit for his Majesty's service. I cannot express to your Lordship the high sense I have of the gallant behaviour of Lieutenant Russel, and of the officers and men sent on this service, which they effected with little loss, notwithstanding the enemy were prepared to receive them. I have sent Lieutenant Brown to command them for the time being: as I think it

---

* Lieutenant Russel (1st), Lieutenant Hepenstall (2d); Lieutenant Parry (marines); Mr. Morton (mate), Mr. Iancock (gunner); Mr. Petley (midshipman); Mr. Hawkins (midshipman).

probable,

probable, during the cruife, we may meet a fhip of equal force, it will be proper to give Lieutenant Ruffel that opportunity of promotion, in cafe of fuccefs he fo highly merits on this occafion, as well as many others, fince under my command. I fend a lift of killed and wounded.
Have the honour to remain, &c.
ROBERT G. MIDDLETON.

I beg leave to acquaint your Lordfhip, that I anchored, on the 11th inftant, at St. Nicholas, on the ifland of Cerigo, and cut out a French polacre fhip from under that fort. She being in ballaft, I found it neceffary to fcuttle her, and have landed her prifoners with Le Mondovi, on getting a proper receipt for them from the governor at Cerigo.

A Lift of the killed and wounded belonging to his Majefty's Ship Flora, Robert G. Middleton, Efq. Captain, at the Capture of the French national Brig Le Mondovi, on the Night of May 13, 1798.

Killed—One private marine.
Wounded—Three officers and 5 feamen.
Name of the killed—John Perks.
Names of the officers wounded—Lieutenant Parry, of the marines, flightly in the hand; Mr. Morton, mafter's mate, dangeroufly in the back; Mr. Tancock, gunner, flightly in the head.

Lift of the Enemy killed and wounded.

One feaman killed, 1 officer and 4 feamen jumped overboard, and fuppofed to be drowned.
Eight feamen and foldiers dangeroufly wounded.

Copy of a Letter to the Earl of St. Vincent.

My Lord,   *Caroline, Lifbon, Dec.* 15, 1798.
THIS ferves to advife your Lordfhip, on the 4th inftant, P. M. lat. 38 deg. 45 min. long. 12 deg. I obferved a ftrange fail to windward; but the weather being hazy, and fhe at a great diftance, I could not form a perfect idea of her being a cruifer; and having at that time the charge of two prizes, with which I was on my way to Lifbon, I, by way of a decoy, made a fignal for the fame to form a line, taking care to keep the Caroline's ftern towards the ftranger; I had the fatisfaction, in a fhort time, to find the ftratagem fucceed; for the cruifer (as fhe turned out), feeing I took no notice of her, chafed me, and as before obferved, the weather being hazy, fhe got within the fuperior failing of the Caroline before fhe difcovered her miftake; fhe, however, led me a chafe of four hours, in the conclufion of which I had the fatisfaction of fecuring her; fhe proves to be a French brig privateer, her name Le Serailleur, commanded by Capt. Malbernac, out of Bourdeaux fifty-fix days: fhe mounts 10 brafs four pounders and two brafs fix pounders; her complement was 82 men, but when captured had only 58 on board, the reft being difperfed in two Americans fhe had captured.
I am, my Lord, &c.
THOS. BOWEN.

Copy of a Letter to Lord Bridport.

My Lord, *Anson, at Sea, Feb. 2.*

I HAVE the honour to inform your Lordship, that his Majesty's ship under my command has this day captured (in company with the Ethalion) Le Boulonnois French cutter privateer, of 14 guns and 70 men, belonging to Dunkirk: the capture of her gives me great satisfaction, as she has greatly annoyed the trade in the North Seas.

P. C. DURHAM.

Extract of a Letter from Admiral Sir Peter Parker, Bart. Commander in Chief of his Majesty's Ships and Vessels at Portsmouth and Spithead, to Evan Nepean, Esq. dated the 12th instant.

PLEASE to acquaint their Lordships that his Majesty's sloop the Fly arrived this morning from a cruise, in the course of which she captured Le Gleneur, a French privateer cutter, of six guns and 32 men, as described in the enclosed letter from Captain Mudge.

Sir, *Fly, at St. Helen's, Feb. 12.*

I BEG leave to acquaint you with the arrival of his Majesty's sloop under my command at this roadsted, having, on the 6th instant, captured a French cutter privateer, called Le Gleneur, off Portland, mounting six four-pounders and 32 men, Emanuel Tone commander: had sailed from Cherbourg the night before, where she had been chased in two days prior to her capture.

I have the honour to be, &c. &c.

ZACHARY MUDGE.

Copy of a Letter to Vice-admiral Kingsmill.

Sir, *Phœnix, at Sea, Jan. 23.*

I HAVE the pleasure to inform you that his Majesty's ship Phœnix, under my command, captured this day, at noon, in lat. 48 deg. 19 min. N. long. 17 deg. 28 min. W. the Foudroyant French privateer ship, pierced for 24 guns, and mounting 20 twelves and sixes; the former brass, with 160 men. Eight of the guns were thrown overboard during the chase, which lasted from twelve last night, in which we ran upwards of one hundred and twenty miles. She was launched at Bourdeaux about three months ago, and sailed from thence on this cruise nine weeks since. She had made three captures, two of them English and one American. She is coppered, and appears to be a most complete vessel. I am, &c.

L. W. HALSTED.

Names of the Vessels the above Ship captured.

English brig Malbridge, from Martinico to London.
Ditto brig Duncan, from Halifax to London.
American ship Argo, from Sweden to Charlestown.

Admiralty Office, Feb. 16.

Copy of a Letter from Rear-admiral Harvey, Commander in Chief of his Majesty's Ships and Vessels at the Leeward Islands, to Evan Nepean, Esq. dated on board his Majesty's Ship Prince of Wales, Fort Royal Bay, Martinique, Dec. 10, 1798.

Sir,

I HAVE the pleasure to acquaint you, for the information of their Lordships, that since my letter to you of the 7th ultimo, the undermentioned French privateers, belonging to Guadaloupe, have been captured, and sent to the different islands by the ships and vessels of his Majesty's squadron under my command, as against their several names expressed.

By the Amphitrite, Captain Ekins—La Guadaloupienne schooner, of 10 guns and 80 men; La Prise de Malthe schooner, of eight guns and 65 men; La Bordelais sloop, of six guns and 38 men.

By the Solebay, Captain Poyntz—La Prosperité schooner, of eight guns and 61 men.

By the Pearl, Captain Ballard—L'Independence brig, of 12 guns and 65 men.

By the Santa Margarita, Captain Parker—Le Quatorze Juillet, coppered brig, 14 guns and 65 men.

By the Cyane, Captain Matson—La Iombie cutter, of eight guns and 72 men.

And I have further to acquaint you, that his Majesty's sloop Victorieuse, Captain Dickson, destroyed on the 10th ultimo a French privateer schooner of 12 guns, which he found at anchor at Rio Caribbe, on the island of La Margaritta. The conduct of Captain Dickson in performing this service was highly spirited; as the privateer lay under the protection of two batteries, one of four and the other of two guns, which kept up a fire on the Victorieuse, who received but little damage in her masts and rigging, but had two men killed and two wounded.—The crew of the privateer escaped on shore.

I have the honour to be, &c. &c.
HENRY HARVEY.

From the LONDON GAZETTE, February 19, 1799.

Admiralty Office, February 19.
Copy of a Letter to Lord Bridport.

My Lord,   *Sylph, in Cawsand Bay, Feb.* 14.

I HAVE the honour to inform your Lordship, that on the 7th and 8th instant we captured, off Cape Ortegal, two fast-sailing Spanish letter of marque brigs (coppered), one the St. Antonio, from Porto Rico, bound to Bilboa, laden with cocoa; the other the Primavera, from the Havannah, bound to St. Andero, laden with sugar, cocoa, indigo, and logwood.—These vessels being valuable, I thought proper to convoy them home, and with the former arrived here this evening: the latter parted company from us on Monday night, in a gale of wind, twelve leagues S. E. of the Lizard; but being an excellent vessel, and in good hands, I expect her here every hour.

I beg

I beg leave further to add, that on the 20th January we retook the sloop Three Sisters, laden with butter, from Cork to Lisbon. This vessel has arrived at this port.

I have the honour, &c.

JOHN C. WHITE.

From the LONDON GAZETTE, February 26, 1799.

Admiralty Office, February 26.

Extract of a Letter from Vice-admiral Sir Charles Thompson, Bart. to Evan Nepean, Esq. dated on board the Queen Charlotte, in Torbay, the 22d of February.

Sir,

ENCLOSED is a letter from Captain Keates, of his Majesty's ship Boadicea.   I am, &c.

CHARLES THOMPSON.

Sir,   *Boadicea, at Sea, Feb. 20.*

I HAVE the honour to inform you, that a French cutter privateer, of 14 guns and 44 men, named Le Milan, was this day taken by the Boadicea and Atalante.

I have ordered Captain Griffith to see the prize into port, and having landed the prisoners, to return, and rejoin me upon my station.

I have the honour to be, &c.

R. G. KEATES.

Vice-admiral Sir Charles Thompson, Bart. &c.

From the LONDON GAZETTE, March 5, 1799.

Admiralty Office, March 5.

Copy of a Letter from Rear-admiral Harvey, Commander in Chief of his Majesty's Ships at the Leeward Islands, to Evan Nepean, Esq. dated Prince of Wales, Fort Royal Bay, Martinique, Jan. 22.

Sir,

I ENCLOSE you, for their Lordships' information, copies of two letters, one of which I received from Captain Fahie, of his Majesty's ship Perdrix, and the other from Captain Dickson, of La Victorieuse. The spirited conduct of the captains, officers, and men, on both occasions, will manifest to their Lordships their zeal and exertion for the King's service.

I have the honour to be, &c.

HENRY HARVEY.

Sir,   *His Majesty's Ship La Perdrix, Tortola, Dec. 13.*

I HAVE the honour to acquaint you, that on the 7th instant I spoke, to leeward of St. Thomas's, an American, who informed me, that he had been boarded the preceding evening by a French ship of war, seven leagues to the eastward of Virgin Gorda.

I used

I used every exertion to get to windward of that island; but from the strong gales which prevailed, accompanied by frequent and heavy squalls, I did not effect it until the 10th. On the 11th, at daylight, a sail was discovered from the mast-head in the S. E. which, by our glasses, was soon distinguished to be a ship, and evidently a cruiser.

Not a moment was lost in pursuing her; and, after a chase of sixteen hours, I brought her to close action, which lasted forty-two minutes, when she ceased firing, and lay an unmanageable wreck on the water.—She proved to be L'Armée d'Italie, a French private ship of war, mounting 14 nine and 4 twelve-pounder long guns, with 117 men, commanded by Citizen Colachy, eleven days from Guadaloupe, and had captured the Bittern brig and Concorde schooner, of Martinique; part of the crews of which vessels were on board.

It is impossible for me, Sir, sufficiently to express the high sense I have of the steady and spirited conduct of Lieutenants Edward Ottley and James Smith, and of Mr. Moses Crawford, the master: Mr. Samuel Piguenet, the purser, is also entitled to my warmest thanks, having volunteered the danger of the deck. In short, Sir, I cannot more forcibly acknowledge the merit of the officers and crew of his Majesty's ship at large, than by saying their conduct was such as, even at the present day, to render them worthy of the name of British seamen; and I have the pleasure to add that but one man was wounded.—The enemy's loss, as far as I can obtain information, is six killed and five wounded.

Our sails and rigging are much cut; but in other respects we have not sustained any material injury.

I am, Sir, &c. &c.

Rear-admiral Harvey, &c. &c.   W. CHARLES FAHIE.

Sir,   *Victorieuse, off the Islands Testigos, Dec.* 6.

ON the 29th of last month I received intelligence of three privateers to leeward. I proposed to Colonel Picton, as the only sure method of keeping the trade open, to attack Rio Caribe and Gurupano, destroy their forts, and bring off their guns, as the privateers would then have no shelter, if chased by us. He perfectly agreed with me, and ordered Major Laureil, with forty of the royal rangers, to embark, and proceed with me.

On the 2d I pushed down, in company with the Zephyr; and having reached Cape Three Points, we destroyed the schooner Proserpine, a Dutch privateer, of two guns and 13 men, from Caraçao, on a cruise—On the 3d, having reached within eight miles of Rio Caribe, at two in the morning I landed the troops, with a party of seamen, to attack the forts in the rear, while the brigs attacked in front. At daylight the commandant sent to beg we would not fire, as he would give us possession without resisting. We immediately re-embarked the troops, took off the guns, and made sail for Gurupano, where we arrived at four in the evening. Observing a French privateer in the harbour, I sent a flag of truce to the commandant, to say I was determined to take her out; and on his peril to fire on me. He answered, he would protect her; and that I should give him up the guns I had taken at Rio Caribe.

I found there was no time to be lost, and ordered Major Laureil, with
the

e troops, Lieutenants Cafe and M'Renfey, with 30 feamen from the Victorieufe and Zephyr, to land, and carry the forts by ftorm, while the brigs attacked in front.

At five we anchored, and opened a fmart fire on both forts; in ten minutes the troops and feamen carried the lower fort, and I obferved the Spanifh flag ftruck at the upper one, but inftantly replaced by French colours; in five minutes the upper fort was carried.

I have taken the guns and ammunition off, deftroyed the forts, and fent the privateer to Trinidad: fhe had fix guns and 80 men.

I cannot conclude my letter without informing you, I never faw more real courage difplayed than by Major Laureil, Lieutenants Cafe and M'Renfey, of the Victorieufe, and the foldiers and feamen under their command, by attacking two forts with 70 men, defended by at leaft 200. Great zeal was alfo fhown by the officers and feamen of the Victorieufe and Zephyr; and I am much indebted to Captain Champain, to whom I beg to refer you for further information.

I have the honour to be, Sir, &c. &c. &c.
E. S. DICKSON.

Rear-admiral Harvey, Commander in Chief, &c. &c.

Admiralty Office, March 5.

Extract of a Letter from Vice-admiral Dickfon, commanding Officer for the Time being, of his Majefty's Ships and Veffels at Yarmouth, to Evan Nepean, Efq. dated the 4th inftant.

HEREWITH I tranfmit, for their Lordfhips' information, the copy of a letter from Captain Temple, of his Majefty's floop Jaloufe.

Sir, *His Majefty's Sloop Jaloufe, off the Texel, Feb. 24.*

I HAVE the pleafure to inform you, that yefterday I captured Le --fon French privateer, that morning out of the Texel: fhe is a brig, of 14 guns and 52 men, belonging to Dunkirk.

I have the honour to be, &c.
J. TEMPLE.

Archibald Dickfon, Efq. Vice-admiral of the Red, &c.

From the LONDON GAZETTE, March 12, 1799.

My Lord, *Melpomene, 3d March, off Breft.*

I HAVE the honour to inform you, that on the 28th ult. about nine leagues from the Saints, I captured a fhip privateer named Le ---lé, mounting 16 guns and 69 men. As foon as I had fhifted the prifoners, I went in purfuit of her prize (the Betfey, a valuable Englifh brig, from Santa Cruz, bound to Liverpool), and was within a mile of her when fhe run on fhore among the rocks of the Penmarks.

I have the honour to be, &c. &c.
(Signed) C. HAMILTON.

The Right Hon. Lord Bridport, K. B. &c. &c.

Vol. VIII. U Extract

Admiralty Office, March 12.
Extract of a Letter from Captain Thomas Hamilton, commanding the Sea Fencibles at Margate, to Evan Nepean, Esq. dated the 9th inst.

I HAVE the honour to acquaint you, that yesterday morning, about ten o'clock, a small cutter was observed boarding two brigs eight or nine miles from the North Foreland. The wind being to the eastward, with a flood tide, prevented the Camperdown cutter, lying in Westgate Bay, from chasing. I sent an orderly dragoon to the Admiral at Deal, not knowing the force of the privateer.

The moment the capture was perceived, forty or fifty of the sea fencibles pushed off in three boats, and near three o'clock recaptured the two brigs, the privateer having made off.

From the LONDON GAZETTE, March 16, 1799.

By the King.—A Proclamation.

GEORGE R.

WHEREAS we have reason to apprehend that divers persons engaged in the treasonable conspiracy against us in our kingdom of Ireland, which lately manifested itself in open acts of rebellion and war against us in our said kingdom, have not abandoned their treasonable designs against us; and, acting in concert with our foreign enemies, are preparing to assist our said enemies in an invasion of our kingdoms, and for that purpose are endeavouring to incite and stir up rebellion and war against us in this kingdom: we have therefore thought it necessary, for the safety of our kingdoms, to prevent all persons engaged in such treasonable designs from passing from our said kingdom of Ireland into this kingdom; and we do, for that purpose, by and with the advice of our Privy Council, order, and do hereby strictly charge and command, that, from and after the 20th day of March instant, no person whatsoever be permitted to pass from our said kingdom of Ireland into this kingdom, except such persons as shall be in our service, and actually so employed; and such persons as shall obtain a passport for that purpose from our Lord Lieutenant of our said kingdom of Ireland, his chief or under secretaries, the mayor, or other chief magistrate of some city or town in Ireland, or one of our general officers commanding our forces within the several districts in our said kingdom: and by and with the advice aforesaid, we do further order, and hereby strictly charge and command, that no person whatsoever (except as aforesaid), coming from our said kingdom of Ireland, be permitted to land in this kingdom without our licence for that purpose first obtained; and that all such persons (except as aforesaid) who shall land, or attempt to land, in this kingdom, without such licence as aforesaid, shall be forthwith taken into custody, and detained in custody until our pleasure shall be further known. And we do further order and require, that all persons having such passports as aforesaid, shall produce the same to some officer of our customs, at the port or place to which such person shall come, before such persons shall be permitted to land at such port or place: and we do hereby, by and with the advice aforesaid, strictly enjoin, require, and command, all and singular justices of the peace, mayors,

mayors, sheriffs, bailiffs, constables, and all other our officers and subjects, to use their utmost endeavours for the due execution of these our commands.

 Given at our Court at St. James's, the 15th day of March one thousand seven hundred and ninety-nine, in the thirty-ninth year of our reign.

    God save the King.

From the LONDON GAZETTE, March 23, 1799.

Admiralty Office, March 23.

Copy of a Letter from Admiral Kingsmill, Commander in Chief of his Majesty's Ships and Vessels on the Coast of Ireland, to Evan Nepean, Esq. dated the 2d instant.

Sir,

PLEASE to inform my Lords Commissioners of the Admiralty, that his Majesty's ship Melampus arrived here yesterday evening, and has brought in with her a French ship privateer, named Le Mercure, of 16 guns and 103 men, from St. Maloes, which was returning into port from a successful cruise in the Channel.

 I have the honour to be, &c.

    R. KINGSMILL.

A Copy of a Letter from Admiral Sir Richard King, Bart. Commander in Chief of his Majesty's Ships and Vessels at Plymouth, to Evan Nepean, Esq. dated the 20th instant.

Sir,

I HAVE the pleasure to transmit, for their Lordships' information, a letter I received from Lieutenant Worth, commanding his Majesty's hired armed brig Telegraph, giving an account of his having captured, off the Isle of Bas, L'Hirondelle, a French corvette, carrying 16 guns, nine and six pounders, and 89 men.

 I am, &c.

    R. KING.

Sir,   *Telegraph armed Brig, Torbay, March 19.*

I HAVE the honour to inform you, I arrived here at seven o'clock this evening with L'Hirondelle brig corvette, mounting 16 guns, long nine and six pounders, and 89 men, when she sailed from St. Maloes three days since; but having captured an American schooner and an English sloop, reduced her complement to 72. I discovered L'Hirondelle on Monday morning at daylight, two miles on the lee-bow, the Isle de Bas S. E. nine leagues. She immediately tacked, and stood towards me: at half past seven, being close alongside, an action commenced, which continued for three hours and a half; and after several attempts to board on both sides, she being totally unrigged, she struck, and proved to be the vessel above described: five of her crew were killed, and 14 wounded; the Telegraph had five wounded. I am proud to say the company of the Telegraph behaved as English sailors always do on such occasions; and to acknowledge the very able assistance I received

from

from Mr. George Gibbs, the master. I shall return to Plymouth the moment the wind will allow me.

I have the honour to be, &c.

Sir Richard King, Bart.   J. A. WORTH.

Extract of a Letter from the Right Hon. Lord Bridport, K. B. Admiral of the White, &c. to Evan Nepean, Esq. dated the 20th instant.

ENCLOSED are two copies of letters from Captain Pierrepont, of his Majesty's ship Naiad, which are transmitted to you for their Lordships' information.

His Majesty's Ship Naiad, Plymouth Sound, March 19.

My Lord,

I HAVE the honour to inform your Lordship of my arrival at this anchorage with the ship I command, in order to land 103 French prisoners, being the crew of a French privateer taken on the 5th instant, off the Loine, by the Naiad and St. Fiorenzo. The Naiad has likewise sent into Falmouth a smuggling cutter, laden with tobacco and spirits.   I have the honour to be, &c.

The Right Hon. Lord Bridport, &c.   W. PIERREPONT.

Sir,   *His Majesty's Ship Naiad, at Sea, March 5.*

THE ship L'Heureux Hazard, French privateer, mounting 16 sixes and nine-pounders, but pierced for 20 guns, and having on board 94 men, was this day taken by his Majesty's ship under my command. This ship sails very fast, left Nantz only yesterday; and was completely found and equipped for a cruise of three months.

I have the honour to be, &c.

W. PIERREPONT.

Sir Harry Neale, Bart. Captain of his Majesty's Ship Saint Fiorenzo, at Sea.

From the LONDON GAZETTE, March 26, 1799.

Downing Street, March 21.

THE King has been pleased to cause it to be signified by the Right Hon. Lord Grenville, his Majesty's principal Secretary of State for foreign affairs, to the ministers of neutral powers residing at this Court, that the necessary measures having been taken by his Majesty's command, for the blockade of the ports of the United Provinces, the said ports are declared to be in a state of blockade, and that all vessels which may attempt to enter any of them after this notice, will be dealt with according to the principles of the law of nations, and to the stipulations of such treaties subsisting between his Majesty and foreign powers, as may contain provisions applicable to the cases of towns, places, or ports, in a state of blockade.

From the LONDON GAZETTE, March 30, 1799.

Corfu, March 3.

THIS day the French garrison surrendered by capitulation to the united forces of the Russians and Turks. The Leander and the Bruno frigate were taken in the port.

Admiralty Office, March 30.
Copy of a Letter from the Right Hon. Lord Bridport, K. B. Admiral of the White, to Evan Nepean, Esq. dated the 25th inst.

Sir,

ENCLOSED is a copy of a letter from Captain Countess, of his Majesty's ship Ethalion, which is transmitted to you for their Lordships' information. I have the honour to be, &c. &c.
BRIDPORT.

My Lord, *Ethalion, at Sea, March 6.*

I HAVE the pleasure to inform your Lordship, that this day his Majesty's ship under my command captured the Indefatigable privateer ship of Nantz, of 18 guns and 120 men, after a chase of ten hours: she is quite new, coppered, victualled for four months, and had been out but one day. I purpose seeing her safe in, and taking that opportunity of getting rid of the prisoners. Yesterday evening we fell in with the Naiad, when she captured another privateer of Nantz, of 18 guns, which is the only success we have had since the Anson parted company; but we have had very severe weather.

I have the honour to be, &c. &c. &c.
GEORGE COUNTESS.

The Right Hon. Lord Bridport, K. B. &c.

Extract of a Letter from Admiral Sir Hyde Parker, Knt. Commander in Chief of his Majesty's Ships and Vessels at Jamaica, to Evan Nepean, Esq. dated the 10th Feb.

I ENCLOSE a list of the armed vessels taken or destroyed, with the number of merchant vessels taken or destroyed, by his Majesty's ships and vessels under my command, since the last report; and I have the pleasure to state, for their Lordships' information, that, from the activity of the cruisers, few privateers are at sea.

A List of Ships and Vessels captured or destroyed by the Squadron under my Command, between the 4th of June 1798, and 10th of February 1799.

By the Queen—the Spanish armed schooner L'Aimable Marseilles, of four guns and 40 men—taken.

By the Queen and Lark—a French schooner privateer, name unknown, of four guns and 30 men—cut out of Port Nieu.

By the Acasta—the French brig privateer Active, of eight guns and 36 men; the Spanish armed schooner Cincinnatus, of two guns and 33 men—taken. A French schooner privateer, name unknown, of six guns and 60 men—burnt.

Ey

By the Trent and Acasta—the Spanish armed ship Penada, of 14 guns and 40 men—taken

By the Renommée—the French sloop privateer Le Triomphant, of six guns and 56 men—taken.

By the Renommée and Squirrel—the Spanish armed brig Neptune, of four guns and 23 men—taken.

By the Magicienne—the Spanish armed schooner Julie, of four guns and 12 men—taken.

By the Surprise—the French schooner privateer Laurette, of six guns and 46 men—taken.

By the Swallow—the French schooner privateer Buonaparte, of six guns and 50 men—taken.

By the Pelican—the French schooner privateer La Belle en Cuisse, of four guns and 57 men—taken.

By the Amaranthe and Surprise—the French schooner privateer Petite Française, of four guns and 35 men—taken.

Total.—Thirteen privateers and armed vessels, carrying 72 guns, with 518 men.

Merchant Vessels.

Taken.—By the Queen and Lark 4—Brunswick 1—Thunderer 1—York 2—Acasta 3—Trent 4—Trent and Hannibal 4—Trent and Acasta 4—Regulus 10—Regulus and Swallow 2—Renommée and Squirrel 7—Magicienne 7—La Prompte 1—Jamaica 6—Jamaica and Lark 2—Serpent 2—La Legere 2—Lark 7—Diligence 13—Rattler 1—Pelican and Brunswick 1—Drake and Serpent 2—Amaranthe 2—Stork 1—Total 89.

Destroyed.—By the Acasta 3—Trent and Acasta 7—Regulus 4—Regulus and Swallow 1—Magicienne 1—Jamaica 2—Jamaica and Lark 1—La Legere 1—Lark 1.—Total 21.

HYDE PARKER.

Copy of a Letter from Vice-admiral Harvey, Commander in Chief of his Majesty's Ships and Vessels at the Leeward Islands, to Evan Nepean, Esq. dated at Martinique the 6th February.

Sir,

I HAVE to acquaint you, for the information of their Lordships, that Captain Westbeech, in his Majesty's sloop Favourite, on the 8th December last captured a Genoese ship from Rio de Plate, bound to the Havannah, laden with jerked beef, tallow, and hides, and carried her into Tobago; and that on the 20th ult. Captain Warren, of the Scourge, captured a Spanish brig from Cadiz, bound to Laguira, laden with wine, brandy, and merchandise, which he carried into Trinidad.

I have the honour to be, &c. &c.

HENRY HARVEY.

Extract of a Letter from the Earl of St. Vincent, K. B. Commander in Chief of his Majesty's Ships and Vessels in the Mediterranean, to Evan Nepean, Esq. dated at Gibraltar, the 26th of Feb.

I ENCLOSE letters from Captain Bowen, of his Majesty's ship Argo, and Captain Sanders, of his Majesty's sloop L'Espoir, giving an account

account of the capture of the Santa Teresa Spanish frigate and Africa xebeque; also a letter from Captain Markham, of his Majesty's ship Centaur, relating the events of his cruise on the coast of Catalonia.

Sir, *Argo, off Port Mahon, Feb. 8.*

I HAVE great pleasure in acquainting you, that in carrying your orders into execution, in company with the Leviathan, on the 6th instant, at four P. M. drawing round the east end of Majorca under storm staysails, with a violent gale westerly, I discovered two large Spanish frigates at anchor, near a fortified tower on the south point of the Bahia de Alcudé, who, immediately on seeing us, cut their cables, and made sail to the N. N. E. We instantly gave chase with all the canvas the ships could bear; unfortunately, the Leviathan's main-topsail gave way, which caused her to drop astern; the enemy seeing this, took the advantage of it, and after the close of day spoke each other and separated; one hauling her wind to the northward, and the other set top-gallant sails and kept away before it; which latter I followed. The darkness of the night precluded the Leviathan from seeing their manœuvre, as also my signal to her to alter her course to port; however, the Leviathan kept sight of the Argo, and was near up with us at midnight, when I got alongside of the enemy, who still persevered in his endeavours to get off (although his small sails were either shot or carried away in the chase), and did not surrender until he had received our whole broadside, which wounded two men, and did much mischief to his rigging. She proved to be the Santa Teresa, commanded by Don Pable Perez, mounting in all 42 guns besides swivels and cohorns, and manned with 280 seamen and marines, besides 250 soldiers; in all 530 persons on board.

My first lieutenant, Mr Thomas Lyne, has much merit in keeping sight and observing the different shifts of the enemy, by which great advantage was gained by the Argo during the chase; much commendation is due to his professional skill and great exertions, after taking possession of the prize, in saving her tottering mast from tumbling overboard, which he could not have done, had not Captain Buchanan sent him speedy assistance of officers and men from the Leviathan, to whom I feel myself much indebted.

Great praise is due to all my officers and seamen, for their vigilance and exertions in shortening and making sail in squalls during the chase; and had the enemy given them an opportunity of showing further proofs of their zeal and loyalty, I am convinced they would have behaved as British seamen always do upon these occasions.

I have the honour to be, &c. &c. &c.
JAMES BOWEN.

P. S. The Santa Teresa is just out of dock, rebuilt, new coppered, and is in every respect almost as good as a new ship; she was completely stored and victualled for four months, and is esteemed one of the fastest-sailing frigates out of Spain, of large dimensions, upwards of 950 tons, and fit for immediate service. Her consort, the Proserpine, that made her escape, is of the same force, but not so large.

Extract of a Letter from Captain Cuthbert, of his Majesty's Ship Majestic, to the Earl of St. Vincent, dated at Sea the 23d Feb.

I HAVE the honour of enclosing a letter to your Lordship, received from Captain Sanders, commander of his Majesty's brig L'Espoir, giving an account of his having engaged and captured the Africa, a Spanish xebec, mounting 14 guns, long four-pounders, and four brass four-pound swivels, in the service of the King of Spain, and commanded by Josepho Subjado.

Having been an eye witness to the action, it's not in the power of my pen sufficiently to extol the meritorious conduct of Captain Sanders and his ship's company on the occasion.

Sir,   *L'Espoir, at Sea, Feb. 22.*

AT a quarter past noon, town of Marbello bearing N. N. W. three leagues, a brig and two xebecs in the S. E. quarter, appearing suspicious, I hoisted my colours to them, when the brig and one of the xebecs hoisted Spanish; upon which a Moorish brig in tow was cast off, and L'Espoir hauled to the wind in chase: it was soon perceived they were armed vessels; but not being so fortunate as to weather them, we exchanged broadsides with both in passing. L'Espoir being tacked, soon brought the xebec to close action, which continued for an hour and a half, when a favourable opportunity of boarding her was embraced, and after a sharp contest of about twenty minutes she surrendered, and proved to be the Africa, commanded by Josepho Subjado, in the service of the King of Spain, mounting 14 long four-pounders and four brass four-pound swivels, having on board 75 seamen and 38 soldiers, from Algofamus, bound to Malaga. Lieutenant Richardson (in whom I have much confidence), and all the officers and seamen of his Majesty's sloop I have the honour to command, behaved with the same courage they have done on former occasions.

During the action the brig (which, I have since learned, mounted 18 guns) stood in shore, and anchored.

I enclose a list of the killed and wounded, and am, with respect, Sir, &c. &c.

                                      JAMES SANDERS.

List of the killed and wounded.

L'Espoir—2 seamen killed; 2 ditto wounded.

Africa—1 officer, 8 seamen killed; 1 captain, 2 officers, and 25 seamen wounded.

Captain Cuthbert, Majestic.

Sir,   *Centaur, at Sea, 16th Feb.*

I HAVE the honour to inform you, that in obedience to your orders I proceeded to Sallo Bay in his Majesty' ship under my command, after the Spanish frigates: and having been joined by the Cormorant alone, of the squadron under Captain Bowen, I at length, after beating against heavy gales of wind from the 28th January till the 9th February, reached Sallo Bay, in which I found twenty-one Swedish and Danish merchantmen, but no men of war had been in sight of Sallo since

since the 2d of February. Having looked into Fangel Bay, and Tarragona also, where Lord M. Kerr, in the Cormorant, took a tartan, and drove another on shore, I proceeded towards Majorca, and at daylight the Cormorant took a settee laden with oil, and I chased two large xebecs and a settee, all privateers in the royal Spanish service; one of which, La Vierga de Rosario, I captured at two o'clock, mounting 14 brass twelve-pounders, and 90 men; the other two escaped, by the wind shifting at dark, when within shot. The same night the Aurora joined and proceeded for Tarragona, in consequence of intelligence I received of two Spanish frigates being bound there with Swiss troops from Palma. On the 15th I fell in with the Argo and Leviathan, and the next morning stood in for Sallo Bay. Finding the frigates were not in the neighbourhood, I attacked the town of Cambrelles, and the Spaniards having quitted their guns on a tower, sent the boats in under Lieutenant Grossett, of the Centaur, who, after dismounting the guns, burnt and captured as per margin*; La Velon Maria was taken in the offing, from Auguilas, bound to Barcelona. The Proserpine frigate, consort to the Santa Teresa, taken by the Argo, after having escaped to Palamor, has since, I am informed by Captain Bowen, hauled close into the bar of Barcelona.

I have, &c. &c. &c.
JOHN MARKHAM.

From the LONDON GAZETTE, April 2, 1799.

Downing Street, April 2.

A LETTER, of which the following is a copy, has been received from Mr. Consul Foresti, by the Right Hon. Lord Grenville, his Majesty's principal Secretary of State for the foreign department.

Port of Corfu, March 3, 1799, on board of the Russian Ship of War the St. Paul, commanded by Vice-admiral Uchakoff.

My Lord,

I HAVE the honour to inform your Lordship, that on the 1st instant an attack was made by the united Turkish and Russian forces on the island situated in this port, called Lo Scoglio di Vido, and by the French, L'Isle de la Paix. After a very brisk fire of about two hours and a half from the ships of war, the troops were landed, and the said island was captured. An attack was made at the same time on the outworks of the town, and Fort St. Salvador was taken by the Russian and Turkish troops, and the French themselves evacuated another outwork, called Il Monte di Abram.

On the morning of the 2d, a flag of truce was sent off by the French commander of the garrison of the town of Corfu to the Russian Viceadmiral, for the purpose of informing him of the wish of the garrison

---

* Five settees—burnt.
Tartan, name unknown, laden with wine—taken.
Settee, name unknown, laden with hoops and staves—taken.
Settee, name unknown, laden with wine—taken.
Settee, name unknown, lading unknown—taken.
La Velon Maria, tartan, armed as a letter of marque, with one brass and two iron 12-pounders, and two 3 ditto, 14 men, laden with wheat—taken.

to capitulate; a Russian officer was therefore sent to the town, with the propositions of the Russian and Turkish commanders, and they were accepted of, with little variation.

The capitulation of the garrison, of which I have the honour to enclose a copy, was signed this afternoon, on board of the Russian Vice-admiral's ship. I have the honour to be, &c.

SPEREDION FORESTI.

The Citizens Dufour, chief of brigade, Vareze, naval agent, Briche, commissary of the executive power, and Grouvelle, aide-de-camp and commodore, appointed by the council of war in the town of Corfu, to stipulate in the name of the French republic the articles of capitulation for the surrender of the town and forts of Corfu, conjointly with Vice-admiral Uchakoff, the Capitan Bey Cadir Bey, commanding the combined Russian and Turkish squadrons, met on board the Russian Admiral's ship, where they respectively agreed upon the following articles, subject to the ratification of Citizen Dubois, commissary-general of the government, and of Citizen Chabot, general of division, commanding in the Levant islands.

Art. I. The French shall give up to the Turkish and Russian commissaries the town and the forts of Corfu, together with the artillery, ammunition, provisions, stores, and all other public effects, as they actually exist in the arsenals and magazines. The Turkish and Russian commissaries shall give receipts for every thing that may be delivered to them upon inventories.

II. The garrison shall march, with all military honours, out of all the forts and posts which they may occupy, one day after the signature of the present capitulation. They shall be drawn up in line of battle, upon the esplanade, where they shall lay down their arms and standards, with the exception of the officers, as well civil as military, who shall retain their arms; after which the allied troops shall take possession of the posts. The French shall enter immediately after into the citadel, where they shall continue to be lodged until the time of their embarkation, which shall take place at the port of Mandaccio. The commissary-general and the staff shall have a Russian guard of honour until their embarkation.

III. The garrison shall be conveyed to Toulon in vessels furnished by the combined squadron, and at the charge of the said squadron, and shall be convoyed by ships of war, after having given their word of honour not to bear arms for eighteen months against his Majesty the Grand Signior, his Majesty the Emperor of all the Russias, or against their allies, the King of England, the King of the Two Sicilies, and the present allies of the two empires.

IV. All the other Frenchmen employed in the island of Corfu, as well civil as military, are comprehended in the preceding article: as also the civil and military officers and crews of the ship the Leander, the corvette La Brune, and of every vessel belonging to the republic: they are permitted to carry away with them (as are also all the individuals composing the garrison of Corfu) all their effects and moveables which are their own private property.

V. All Frenchmen, who have been made prisoners during the blockade and siege, are in like manner admitted and entitled to the advantages specified in articles III. and IV. They shall only be bound by the parole of honour not to carry arms against the contracting powers during the present

sent war, unless an exchange be made with the Turkish and Russian empires.

VI. A ship of war, of not less than 20 guns, shall be granted, in order to transport the commissary-general, the general, and staff.

VII. The general of division, Chabot, and his staff, a secretary selected by the commissary-general, the two chiefs of administration of land and sea, with their families, and two secretaries for each, shall be permitted to go either to Toulon or to Ancona, at their pleasure, and at the expense of the contracting powers; but if they prefer to go to Ancona, their passage shall take place within one month from the present day.

VIII. All public property, whether belonging to the town or to the garrison (the ship the Leander, the corvette La Brune, and all other vessels belonging to the French republic included), shall be given up entirely to the commissaries of the Turkish and Russian powers.

IX. The commanders of the allied squadron declare, that every individual, of what religion or nation soever, as well as all the inhabitants of the town and island of Corfu, shall be respected in their persons and property. They shall not be prosecuted, molested, or pursued, on account of the political opinions which they may have held, or for their actions, or for the employments which they may have filled under the French government up to the date of the capitulation. The space of two months is granted to all those of the said inhabitants who may be desirous of removing themselves and property elsewhere.

X. The sick, who cannot accompany the garrison, shall be treated in the same manner as the Turks and Russians, and at the expense of the said powers; and shall also, when cured, be sent to Toulon. The French general shall be permitted to leave at Corfu an officer with a sum of 6000 livres, and also the necessary number of officers of health, to dress and take care of the sick.

XI. The garrison, the officers, and those employed in a civil or military capacity, shall receive, as well on shore as on board the vessels, the same number of rations which are allowed to them, according to their rank, in conformity to the French laws, until their debarkation at Toulon or at Ancona.

XII. The ships of war and transports which shall be employed in conveying the French either to Toulon or Ancona, shall not make any prizes either in going or returning, and the commissary-general engages, in the name of the French government, to cause the said vessels to be respected by the French ships and vessels, and to guarantee their return to Corfu, in like manner as the Turkish and Russian admirals respectively promise in the name of their courts to cause all the French comprised in the present capitulation to be conveyed to the destination agreed upon.

Done on board the Russian admiral's ship St. Paul, the 20th February 1799, Russian old style; 13th Ventose, 7th year of the republic.

(Signed)   T. BRICHE,
DUFOUR,   VAREZE,
J. GROUVELLE, Aide-de-Camp.

(L.S.) TURKISH ADMIRAL.
(L.S.) RUSSIAN VICE-ADMIRAL.

The above capitulation is ratified and accepted in the name of the French government by the undersigned.

 (L. S.) DUBOIS, Commiffary-general of the Executive Directory of the French Republic.
 (L. S.) CHABOT, General of Divifion.

Admiralty Office, April 2.

Copy of a Letter from the Right Hon. Lord Bridport, K. B. Admiral of the White, &c. to Evan Nepean, Efq. dated at Spithead, the 1ft inftant.

Sir,

HEREWITH you will receive a copy of a letter from Captain Keats, of his Majefty's fhip Boadicea, which is tranfmitted for their Lordfhips' information; and I am very much concerned for the misfortune which happened to the prize brig La Requin, by which fo many valuable lives have been loft to the fervice of their king and country.

I have the honour to be, &c. &c. &c.

BRIDPORT.

My Lord, *Boadicea, at Sea, 20th March.*

I HAVE the honour to inform your Lordfhip, that on the 7th inft. I retook an American from Charleftown, bound to Hamburgh: on the 8th, fell in with and liberated a neutral fhip from Charleftown, bound to Embden, and took the privateer La Requin, a brig, pierced for 18, mounting 14 guns, with 70 men, which, when I firft difcovered her, was in the act of taking poffeffion of the neutral. It is with extreme concern I add, that on the day following, in a violent gale of wind, the Requin overfet, although at the time fhe had no canvas fpread; by which misfortune, Mr. W. Clay, mafter's mate of the Boadicea, a young man of much merit, nine valuable feamen, and one prifoner, loft their lives.

I have the honour to be, &c. &c. &c.

Right Hon. Admiral Lord Bridport, R. C. KEATS.
K. B. &c. &c. &c.

From the LONDON GAZETTE, April 6, 1799.

Admiralty Office, April 6.

Copy of a Letter from the Right Honourable Lord Bridport, K. B. Admiral of the White, &c. to Evan Nepean, Efq. dated at Spithead the 30th ultimo.

Sir,

HEREWITH you will receive the copy of a letter from Captain Newman, of his Majefty's fhip Mermaid, dated the 24th inftant; alfo one from Captain White, of his Majefty's floop Sylph, dated the 21ft, which I tranfmit for their Lordfhips' information.

I have the honour to be, &c. &c.

BRIDPORT.

My Lord, *Mermaid, at Sea, March 24.*

I HAVE the honour to inform your Lordfhip, I this day, after a chafe of fifteen hours (Sylph in company), captured the Spanifh packet
        Golondrina,

Golondrina, Don Juan El Busto captain, from the Havannah, bound to Corunna, out thirty-nine days, pierced for 20 guns, but has only four on board, coppered, 200 tons burden, and a remarkable fast sailer: she has a cargo of sugar, cocoa, and indigo.

I have the honour to be, &c. &c.

Right Hon. Lord Bridport.   J. N. NEWMAN.

My Lord,   *Sylph, at Sea, March 21.*
I HAVE the honour to inform your Lordship, that La Debut French brig (letter of marque), of eight guns, pierced for 16, from Bourdeaux to Cayenne, laden with different sorts of merchandise, was this day captured by the sloop under my command, fifteen leagues N.W. of Cape Ortegal.   I am, &c.

Right Hon. Lord Bridport, K. B. &c.   J. C. WHITE.

From the LONDON GAZETTE, April 9, 1799.

Admiralty Office, April 9.

Copy of a Letter from Admiral Sir Richard King, Bart. Commander in Chief of his Majesty's Ships and Vessels at Plymouth.

Sir,   *His Majesty's Sloop Spitfire, Plymouth Sound, April 7.*
I HAVE the honour to acquaint you, that the Spitfire captured in the violent gale of the 31st ultimo, Scilly bearing N. N. W. fourteen leagues, the French brig privateer Resolu, of 14 six and eight pounder guns, and 65 men, perfectly new, being her first cruise, out two days from St. Maloes; had not made any capture.

I am, Sir, &c. &c. &c

Sir Richard King, Admiral of the   MICHAEL SEYMOUR.
White, &c. &c. &c.

Admiralty Office, April 9.

Copy of a Letter from Captain D'Auvergne, Prince of Bouillon, Commander of his Majesty's Ship Bravo, to Evan Nepean, Esq. dated at Jersey, the 6th instant.

Sir,
ENCLOSED, I have the honour to transmit you, for the information of my Lords Commissioners, Captain Lord Proby's report to me of the capture, in his Majesty's ship Danae, commanded by him, of a French national armed vessel that had only left St. Maloes a few hours before he fell in with her yesterday.

I have the honour to be, &c. &c.

D'AUVERGNE, Prince of Bouillon.

Sir,   *St. Helier, Danae, April 4.*
I HAVE the honour to acquaint you, that his Majesty's ship under my command captured the French national lugger Le Sans Quartier, this morning, off Les Isles de Chosey. The prize is pierced for 14 guns, but all she had on board were thrown overboard in the chase; she has 56 men.   I have the honour to be, &c. &c.

Captain D'Auvergne, Prince of Bouillon, &c.   PROBY.

From

From the LONDON GAZETTE, April 13, 1799.

Admiralty Office, April 13.

Copy of a Letter from the Right Hon. Lord Bridport, K. B. Admiral of the White, &c. to Evan Nepean, Esq. dated on board his Majesty's Ship Royal George, at St. Helen's, the 10th instant.

Sir,

HEREWITH you will receive a copy of a letter from Captain Keats, of his Majesty's ship Boadicea, stating the capture of the French brig privateer L'Utile, which is transmitted for their Lordships' information.

I have the honour to be, Sir, &c.

BRIDPORT.

My Lord, *Boadicea, at Sea, April 1.*

I HAVE the honour to inform your Lordship of the capture of a third privateer this cruise, by the Boadicea, viz. L'Utile, a very fine brig of 16 guns, eight pounders, 10 of which are brass, and 120 men, quite new, and three weeks from Bourdeaux.

I have the honour to be, &c.

The Right Hon. Lord Bridport, K. B. &c. R. G. KEATS.

Hamburgh, April 5.

ACCORDING to the most recent accounts from the Austrian army, it appears, that after the action of the 21st ultimo, General Jourdan retreated, in the night between the 21st and 22d, to Stockach and Engen. He then occupied the line from Schaffousen through Engen to Dutlingen: in the neighbourhood of which last place he assembled the principal part of his army. The Archduke advanced towards him on the 25th, when General Jourdan attacked the Austrians. His left wing was at first successful; but his centre and right having been defeated, he was obliged to retreat with his whole army in great disorder; his right wing towards Swisserland, and he himself, with the remainder of his army, towards Fribourg and Offenbourg by the Black Forest.

Whilst this was passing in Suabia, General Massena in person attacked, on the 23d, the position of Feldkirk, where General Jellachich commanded in the absence of General Hotze. The French were repulsed with very great loss, and driven over the Rhine. General Hotze is since returned to Feldkirk from Buckhorn, with the corps of 12,000 men, which he had marched to that place, the French having retreated from thence in consequence of the Archduke's victory on the 21st.

The loss on both sides, in these different actions, which appear to have been hard fought, has been very considerable, but much greater on the part of the French than on that of the Austrians, who have, however, lost several officers of distinction. On the 21st, the French are stated to have lost 4000 men—on the 23d, 3000—and on the 25th, their loss is stated to have been much more considerable than on either of the preceding days.

On the 26th, the Archduke marched in pursuit of the enemy.

From the LONDON GAZETTE, April 16, 1799.

Admiralty Office, April 16.

Copy of a Letter from Vice-admiral Harvey, Commander in Chief of his Majesty's Ships at the Leeward Islands, to Evan Nepean, Esq. dated Prince of Wales, Fort Royal Bay, Martinique, March 4.

Sir,

YOU will be pleased to acquaint their Lordships, that Captain Barton, of his Majesty's ship Concorde, captured on the 14th ultimo, to windward of Antigua, La Prudent French ship privateer, copper-bottomed, of 18 guns and 100 men. She had been cruising to windward of Barbadoes for six weeks, without making any other captures than two schooners, one from Halifax, and the other an American, and was on her return to the Spanish port of Saint Domingo, where she belonged, and from whence she had sailed early in December last.

I have the honour to be, &c.
HENRY HARVEY.

Copy of a Letter from Vice-admiral Dickson, commanding Officer of his Majesty's Ships and Vessels at Yarmouth, to Evan Nepean, Esq. dated Veteran, at Yarmouth, 15th April.

Sir,

HEREWITH I transmit, for their Lordships' information, a letter from Captain Dacres, of his Majesty's ship Astrea, addressed to Captain Sotheron, of the Latona, acquainting him with the capture of Le Marsouin French lugger privateer. I am, Sir, &c. &c.
ARCH. DICKSON.

Astrea, at Sea, April 13.
Sir,

I BEG leave to acquaint you, that on the 10th instant, the Texel bearing E. nine or ten leagues, I fell in with, and captured after a chase of three hours, Le Marsouin French lugger privateer, of 14 guns and 58 men. She left Dunkirk the day before; had taken nothing.

I have the honour to be, &c.
R. DACRES.

From the LONDON GAZETTE, April 20, 1799.

Admiralty Office, April 20.

Extract of a Letter from Captain Reynolds, of his Majesty's Ship La Pomone, to Evan Nepean, Esq. dated Falmouth, April 17.

Sir,

I BEG leave to acquaint you, for the information of the Lords Commissioners of the Admiralty, of my arrival in this port.

I have also to inform you, that on the 31st ult. in lat. 42 deg. 25 minutes N. long. 9 deg. 16 min. W. we retook the Minerva, a valuable Liverpool West India ship, that had been captured sixteen days before, by the Argus French privateer, belonging to Bourdeaux; and I have the pleasure to add that, on the 3d instant, we fortunately fell in with the Argus, and, after a long chase of one hundred and eight miles, running twelve knots

knots an hour, took her close under Cape **Finisterre**. She is a beautiful new ship, not six months off the stocks, carrying 18 brass nine pounders, pierced for 22, and 130 men; is copper-bottomed, and a remarkable swift sailer. Besides the Minerva, the Argus had captured this cruise, two brigs belonging to Teignmouth; the masters and crews of both I found on board her. And, on the 9th of this month, we retook an American schooner from the Carracas, bound to Corunna, laden with cocoa and indigo, that had been taken eight days before by the Gironde privateer, from Bourdeaux. Previous to the above, his Majesty's ship Pomone had captured, off Carthagena, the Mutius Scævola French privateer, belonging to Genoa, and a Spanish coaster: particulars of which I transmitted in a letter on service to the Earl of St. Vincent.

I have the honour to be, Sir, &c.
R. C. REYNOLDS.

Venice, March 29.

EARLY on the morning of the 26th instant, the French made an attack on the ultra advanced posts at Santa Lucia and Buffolengo, before the expiration of the truce, but were repulsed with considerable loss at both places. A thousand French prisoners, with two pieces of cannon, have been sent to Verona. The Austrians had many officers and men killed and wounded.

General Kray repulsed the enemy at Legnago, killed 3000, made 2000 prisoners, took 17 pieces of cannon, and pursued the remainder towards Mantua. The Piedmontese insurgents are become so formidable against their new lords, as to threaten the capital. Continual reinforcements of Austrian cavalry and infantry pass every day by forced marches; and his Imperial Majesty never had, during the war, such a numerous and fine army, as we see at present in Italy.

[This gazette likewise contains the proclamation of his Royal Highness Archduke Charles to the Swiss, which will be found under the head Proclamations.]

From the LONDON GAZETTE, April 23, 1799.

Admiralty Office, April 23.

Extract of a Letter from Sir Harry Burrard Neale, Bart. Captain of his Majesty's Ship St. Fiorenzo, to Evan Nepean, Esq. dated Plymouth, the 17th April.

Sir,

I BEG you will acquaint their Lordships that I arrived with the St. Fiorenzo in Plymouth Sound this morning, with a French brig, prize, from St. Domingo, bound to L'Orient, with sugar and coffee. I also captured a French brig, in ballast, on the same day, not yet arrived.

I enclose, for their Lordships' information, a copy of my letter to Lord Bridport, of the 16th instant.

H. NEALE.

My Lord, *St. Fiorenzo, at Sea, April 16.*

I HAVE the honour to inform your Lordship, that on the 9th instant, after reconnoitring two French frigates at anchor in the port of L'Orient, I stood towards Belle Isle. On our approach I saw some ships at anchor in the Great Road, but as the weather was hazy, and the ships under

under the land, I could not sufficiently ascertain their strength until we had run the full length of the island, when I clearly distinguished them to be three French frigates, and a large sailing gun-vessel, with their topsail-yards ready hoisted to come out to us. At this instant a heavy and sudden squall of wind from the N. W. carried away the Amelia's main-topmast and her fore and mizen-topgallant-masts; the fall of the former tearing a great part of the mainsail from the yard.

The enemy, who were apparently waiting our near approach, got under weigh immediately, and made sail towards us in a line ahead. Circumstanced as we now were, I felt we had but one duty to perform, and that we could do nothing more than testify our readiness to meet them; I therefore made the signal to prepare for battle; and when they had advanced a little to leeward of us, I shortened sail, so as for the Amelia to keep under command, with her fore and mizen topsails only, and made the signal to bear up, preserving the weather-gage and keeping close order. The enemy tacked to meet us, and we instantly commenced an action, receiving the fire from one of the batteries on the island at the same time. The enemy were so little disposed to close quarters, we were under the necessity of bearing down upon them three times, until they were close upon the islands of Houatt and Hedic. After engaging them one hour and fifty-five minutes, they wore ship and stood from us. I am extremely sorry we had it not in our power to do any thing more with the enemy (who had a port close on each side of them) than compel them to relinquish an action which, from their superiority, and the crippled state of the Amelia previous to the action, had inspired them with the hope of success.

Soon after the action ceased they bore up for the Loire, two of them apparently much shattered; and the gun-vessel returned to Belle Isle.

It is with peculiar satisfaction I acquaint your Lordship, that the active and spirited conduct of Captain Herbert is deserving of the highest applause; and I feel that no encomiums of mine can do justice to his merit.

The officers and ships' companies of both ships conducted themselves with the greatest order and most determined courage:—they are entitled to every commendation I can bestow.

I take the liberty of naming in particular Lieutenants Farnall and Holmes, the first lieutenants of each ship, as very deserving officers.

The damage sustained by his Majesty's ships is principally confined to the masts, sails, and rigging.

By a vessel captured since the action, I learn the frigates we engaged were La Cornelie, La Vengeance, and La Semillante:—they have been lately stationed at Belle Isle to guard the coast.

Enclosed is a list of killed and wounded in each ship.

I have the honour to be, &c.

Right Hon. Lord Bridport, K. B. H. NEALE.

Return of killed and wounded on board his Majesty's Ships St. Fiorenza and Amelia, on the 9th Day of April.

St. Fiorenza.—One seaman killed; 18 seamen wounded, two of them dangerously.

Amelia.—Mr. Bayley, midshipman, and one seaman, killed; 17 seamen wounded, one of them dangerously.

Total—Three killed and 35 wounded.

Admiralty Office, April 23.
Copy of a Letter from Mr. Daniel Hamon to Evan Nepean, Esq. dated at Jersey the 16th instant.

Sir,

I HAVE the honour to acquaint you, for the information of the Lords Commissioners of the Admiralty, that the Phoenix lugger private ship of war under my command, on the 5th instant, St. Sebastian bearing S. E. four leagues, I fell in with and captured the French lugger privateer Le Coureur, commanded by Gabriel de la Garats, mounting four guns, four pounders, and six swivels, having on board 46 men; she belonged to St. Jean de Luz, sailed last from St. Sebastian, had captured nothing.

I have the honour to be, &c. &c. &c.

DANIEL HAMON.

Vienna, April 10.

THE enemy has been entirely expelled from the Tyrol, and dislodged from the posts of Funster-Munster and St. Maria, in the Engadine. They have also been driven from the Adige, beyond the Mincio.

Hamburgh, April 16.

ON the 30th ultimo the French attacked the Austrians on the Upper Adige, between Verona and Roveredo. At first they obtained some success; but they were on the same day repulsed with very considerable loss.

Accounts have been received from the Tyrol, that the French force which had penetrated into that country had been obliged to evacuate it completely; and that General Jourdan's army, as well as a great part of Bernadotte's, had repassed the Rhine, having left a garrison in Manheim, and in the works of Kehl, but had abandoned the blockade of Philipsburg. The Austrians have advanced to Friburg and Offenburg, and have summoned Kehl to surrender.

Advices from Rastadt of the 8th April mention that General Staray had gained a very considerable advantage over the French General St. Cyr, as the latter was retreating from Freudenstadt to Offenburg, on his way to Kehl; and that the French had lost a considerable park of artillery.

From the LONDON GAZETTE, April 27, 1799.

Admiralty Office, April 27.

Copy of a Letter from Captain Graham Moore, of the Melampus, to Admiral Kingsmill, and by him transmitted to Evan Nepean, Esq.

Sir,   *Melampus, at Sea, April 15.*

I HAVE the honour to inform you, that we have this morning captured the French privateer brig Le Papillon, of Nantz, mounting 10 nine pounders, and four brass thirty-six pounder carronades, and 123 men, after a chase of twenty-five hours; she is a remarkable fine new vessel, and sails admirably.   I am, Sir, &c. &c.

GRAHAM MOORE.

Vienna, April 10.

HIS Royal Highness the Archduke Charles and Lieutenant-general Kray have transmitted the following detailed accounts of the actions which

have

have taken place near Stockach in Germany, and in the neighbourhood of Legnago and Verona in Italy.

Account of the Battle near Stockach, on the 25th and 26th March.

AFTER the action at Osterach, the enemy retreated by Pfulendorff and Stockach; the greatest part of their forces took a position near Engen. General Ferino's division and the brigade of Rubi were posted near Singen, and in the country behind Radolpzell; that of St. Cyr halted at Liptingen.

The main body of the advanced guard of his Royal Highness, under the command of the Count de Nauendorff, pursued the enemy as far as Ach; General Prince de Schwartzenberg, with his brigade, drove them from Stirflingen; General Count de Meerfeld forced them from Swandorff, and took post there on the 23d of March. This general attacked, on the 24th, the advanced guard of St. Cyr, which had taken a position in front of Neuhausen, and drove them back with a considerable loss in killed and wounded, as far as Liptingen, and took 200 men prisoners, and three pieces of cannon.

On the same day the army put itself in motion, in two columns, and encamped near Stockach. The right wing occupied the heights of Malfpieren, and extended itself towards Nellenberg; the left wing took a position below Nellenberg, near the custom-house, and stretched as far as the neighbourhood of Walwis. In order to cover this position on the side of the great road from Radolpzell, two battalions of Lascey and the regiments of cuirassiers of Anspach were posted on the heights of Erperingen. This wing had the advantage of an open country, which was for the most part covered by marshy grounds and steep hills.

On the 24th the Archduke received intelligence from M. de Nauendorff, that the enemy had concentred the main body of their army near Engen; his Royal Highness immediately sent some battalions of infantry to the Count de Meerfeld, who had no other infantry with him than the free corps of Wurmser; with orders to attack, on the following day (the 25th), the division of St. Cyr, which was posted near Liptingen, and to endeavour to compel him to repass the Danube. His Royal Highness resolved to reconnoitre in person, on the same day, the main body of the enemy's army near Engen. But the enemy on his side had resolved on that day not only to attack the right wing of the Archduke's army with the principal part of their forces, but also to take his army in the rear, in order to cut off its communication with Pfulendorff. For this purpose, and with a view to conceal their motions, the enemy sent two divisions from Engen to Liptingen; and in order to draw the attention of his Royal Highness to their left wing, caused an attack to be made on the 25th, at five o'clock in the morning, on the village of Ach, with five or six battalions, and endeavoured to gain the defile which is there. Prince Schwartzenberg was attacked at the same time at Steiflingen by the division of Ferino and the brigade of Rubi. His Royal Highness received intelligence of this attack at the moment when he was passing through Ach; and he had hardly arrived near Count Nauendorff, before he also received from the General in Chief Wallis, at the right wing, an account that the Count de Meerfeld was totally incapable of making any further resistance to the superior forces of the enemy, and that he was retreating from Liptingen to the wood about three miles in the rear of that place.

His Royal Highnefs immediately gave orders to M. de Nauendorff and to Prince Schwartzenberg, to retire, by degrees, to their pofitions; that is to fay, M. de Nauendorff to the heights of Nellenberg, and Prince Schwartzenberg to the left wing. Both of thefe movements were executed in the moft fkilful manner, and with the greateft regularity, infomuch that the enemy, notwithftanding their great fuperiority, was compelled to pay dear for every inch of ground. General Jourdan in perfon commanded at this attack, and fent at the fame time General Van Damme to harafs his Royal Highnefs's communication with Pfulendorff. It was not till one o'clock in the afternoon that the enemy were able to reach the pofition of our left wing on the fide of Shiflingen, and it was near evening before they reached it on the fide of Ach. His Royal Highnefs returned to this wing, gave the command of it to Lieutenant-general Stader, and haftened in perfon to the right wing. General Stader immediately detached two battalions of infantry and three of grenadiers to the heights of Nellenberg, in order to defend thofe heights, as the centre of the pofition which his Royal Highnefs had chofen, jointly with the advanced guard under M. de Nauendorff, or, if it fhould become neceffary to reinforce the right wing, to draw them by this means nearer to each other. As there was more cavalry in the left wing than could be employed, General Prince de Furftenberg was detached towards Dentwang with the regiment of cuiraffiers of the Archduke Francis; Lieutenant-general Petrafch had at this time, in confequence of orders from General Wallis, pofted two battalions of infantry to the right of Malfpieren, on the heights of Zizenhangen, in order to cover his right flank; this general had orders to attack the enemy, who had already penetrated through the wood, with thofe troops, and the regiments of Kirpen and Gemmingen, on the right of the high road to Stutlingen, whilft Lieutenant-general Prince de Furftenberg, with the regiments Emperor and Benjoffsky, notwithftanding a heavy fire of grape and mufketry from the enemy, advanced along the high road, and on the left of it, for the purpofe of giving fupport to the heights: the Prince was killed by a grape fhot in the courfe of this attack, which he conducted with fo much intrepidity. Colonel Prince of Anhalt Bernberg was alfo dangeroufly wounded, and died foon after on the field of battle; his body was found amongft the dead. The lofs of thefe two brave officers is feverely felt by the army. The Archduke immediately gave the command of part of the Prince of Furftenberg's divifion to General Major Stipfitz, who executed his orders with no lefs fkill than courage, and with the greateft fuccefs. He himfelf received a contufion on the arm by a mufket ball, but this did not prevent him from remaining at the head of his troops. All the officers and foldiers diftinguifhed themfelves by their courage. The Prince of Anhalt Cothen, who perceived that his cavalry could not get up to the enemy, and that the infantry were in want of generals, difmounted his horfe, and made an offer to the Archduke to lead the other part of the Prince of Furftenberg's divifion to the enemy. The Archduke granted him his permiffion, and he performed, at the head of this corps, all that could be expected from the moft tried conduct and courage. The enemy, who oppofed us on this point with their choiceft troops, made not only a moft obftinate refiftance, but fucceeded, in fpite of the intrepidity of our troops, fometimes in repulfing them, and at others in keeping them at check; fo much fo, that this action remained, during many hours, undecided, which gave them hopes that they fhould finally carry the point

he

be aimed at. At this crisis, with a view to secure the fortune of the day, the Archduke ordered two battalions, under the skilful conduct of Colonel Ulm and Major Richter, to advance on the left of the high road. Captain Bibra particularly distinguished himself on this occasion. The grenadiers which his Royal Highness had sent from the left wing, and from the Hellenberz, arrived at the same time. They advanced in one column along the high road, under the command of Lieutenant-general Count de Kollowrath. The battalions of Thegethof and Bajokowsky were at the head of it. In this order they reached the point of the wood, before which they extended themselves in front towards the left, forming a flank, whilst the battalions of Teschner and Lippe, which followed them, extended themselves towards the right, and, advancing in order of battle, took the enemy in the rear, and forced a half brigade to surrender themselves prisoners. During these manœuvres, and this success of our brave grenadiers near Neuhaus, on the high road to Duttingen, the enemy hazarded an attack, with four regiments of cavalry, on the flank of our grenadiers. They were received with great steadiness; and, by a well-directed fire, followed by a charge on the part of the cuirassiers of Nassau and Mack, who had formed themselves with the greatest expedition in a hollow ground, under the orders of Lieutenant-general Riesen, the enemy was completely overthrown, and forced to fly. We pursued them as far as Liptingen, and took one piece of cannon. Night coming on, prevented us from pursuing them farther on this wing. Whilst this was going on, the enemy had detached a division under General Van Damme towards Moskirch, for the purpose of turning our right wing. The Prince of Wirtemberg, who had formed near to Dentwangen with the cuirassiers of the Archduke Francis, took, of his own accord, the resolution to attack the enemy, who was already in possession of the villages of Millingen and Dentwangen, and who, we learnt by the reports of a prisoner, intended to carry off our artillery of reserve. He executed this attack, with the assistance of a small body of light infantry, who were on their march to rejoin the army, retook the two villages, and pursued the enemy as far as the little wood near Birkel, to which place General Van Damme had already sent considerable reinforcements to the support of his troops. This well-combined enterprise perfectly succeeded. The enemy was also repulsed on this point, with a great loss in killed and wounded, and the Prince of Wirtemberg rejoined our right wing.

On the left wing, under Lieutenant-general Studer, the enemy pushed their attacks with vigour. Our light infantry was withdrawn from the village of Lenzingen, of which the enemy took possession. The Nellenberg still remained occupied by our troops. The enemy made every effort, by repeated attacks, to dislodge them from thence. They were foiled by a well-directed fire from our field-batteries, as also from that on the Nellenberg. After these unsuccessful attempts, the enemy endeavoured to establish batteries against us, in which attempt, however, they were equally unsuccessful; for no sooner did one battery begin to play than it was dismounted, and the attack repulsed. The enemy directed all their force towards the village of Walwis, and made repeated efforts to carry it; but the excellent dispositions made by Lieutentant-general Prince Reuss, who had this village in his front, and who had entrusted the defence of it to two battalions of infantry, added to the well-directed fire of our batteries, caused this enterprise equally to fail. The repeated attacks on the village of Walwis were continued till the night was far advanced; and thus ended this important day.

On the 26th, at half past four in the morning, the enemy renewed their attack on Walwis, and made the greatest efforts to take that village. Some time after they seemed also inclined to attack our left wing on the road to Radolpfell. This attack was again repulsed, and the enemy was obliged to retreat. During the continuance of this day they still maintained themselves behind Liptingen. Our advanced guard followed them close in the rear. His Royal Highness cannot exactly state our loss; however, it is supposed that it amounts to 3000 men in killed, wounded, and missing. The enemy must have lost 5000, among whom 2000 were made prisoners. His Royal Highness gives here an exact account of all the officers who have distinguished themselves, of whom the principal are already mentioned in the report of the different actions in which they commanded.

His Royal Highness, since the date of this report, has communicated to government that the enemy, after having been defeated at Stockach, had retired as far as Neustadt, Hornberg, and Freudenstadt. His Royal Highness had pushed his advanced guards to positions abandoned by the enemy; and on the 3d of April he was encamped on the heights of Villengen.

An Account of the Battle which took place near Legnago, on the 26th of March.

On the 26th, at daybreak, we heard at a great distance a severe cannonade in the neighbourhood of Verona and Pastrengo. About eight o'clock the advanced posts near Legnago were also attacked; upon which Lieutenant-general Kray removed, as soon as possible, the camp at Bevilaqua to Legnago. The garrison of the town occupied the ramparts, and the road, which was not yet quite repaired. A battalion of the regiment de Giulay, and another of Latterman, were posted in front of the town, near the canal of Busco, in order to defend the bridges. The enemy attempted, in every direction, to advance towards the town, but were repulsed in all quarters. They had stationed their principal forces upon the Adige, and near Anquiari, where they were sheltered. After two very furious attacks, they were obliged to retreat to that place. Another formidable attack was made since that of St. Pierre de Legnago, from whence the high road leads to Manterre. After the garrison of Legnago alone had thus checked the progress of the enemy for three hours and a half, the advanced guard of the corps of Bevilaqua arrived, of which the first division, under the command of General Frolich, was employed to attack the enemy in their turn. This attack was directed in every road leading from Legnago, inasmuch as the country, intersected by the lands, would permit. The principal attack was made upon St. Pierre. Major Reinwald, of the regiment of Wartenfleben, commanded the advanced guard. Colonel Abfaltern, with the regiment of Nadasty, followed him with the main body of the column. Major Count Paar conducted the advanced guard on the road towards St. Pierre, to attack the rear of the enemy. Colonel Rudt, with a part of the regiment of Latterman, followed him with the remainder of the column. Colonel Somariva, of the regiment of Lobkowitz, commanded the attack upon Anquiari. Besides these principal attacks, several partial ones, on different points, had been made, and all the troops conducted themselves with the greatest bravery, every one having amply discharged his duty. The artillery, as well that within the town, as that which was in the plain near it, resisted all the different

their prefence of mind, and their good example, infpired
courage and confidence. The commander in chief beftowed the fame praifes
mafter-general, Marquis Chat
poft, did not fail to give, on
his ability, activity, and zeal
fuftain the moft fevere attack,

the morning,
had hitherto a
great credit i
made; by the
meafures which
Lieutenant-colo₁
general in chief, his entire a
every where put to flight.
taro; but it was impoffible
terfect the land, to purfue
would have been infinitely
amounts to 2000 men; am

ers, of whom 22 are officers, nine f
Our lofs amounts to one fuperior officer, three officers, 103 from the fergeant to the common foldier. In wounded, 24 officers, 863 rank and file, including non-commiffioned officers; 82 miffing or taken prifoners.

Battle of Verona, of the 26th of March.

According to a more recent report of Lieutenant-general Kray, Lieutenant-general Keim had received advice that the enemy were concentrating their forces near Villa Franca and Caftelnuovo. This general was thus upon his guard ever fince the 24th, when he received the information, he communicated it alfo to General Count de Hohenzollern, who immediately quitted Vicence, and arrived at Verona on the 25th, with two battalions of Giulay, one battalion of Stenz grenadiers, three battalions of Mitrowfky, two fquadrons of Lovenehr, five fquadrons of Karaczay. General Liptay likewife arrived at Verona in the night between the 24th and 25th, with a battalion of Klebeck and two battalions of Furftenberg. General Keim was thus enabled to ftrengthen the pofition of Paftienge with three battalions of Schroder, and one battery of artillery. In the intrenched lines of this pofition, where Generals Elnitz and Goddfheim commanded, were feven battalions of infantry and three fquadrons of the new regiment of huffars, No. 5. The advanced chain commenced from the Lake of Garda, and extended along the frontier as far as the environs of Beirlaque; it was defended by a battalion of Ogulins, a battalion of Warafdins, four companies of the
chaffeurs

chaſſeurs of Aſpre, and one ſquadron of huſſars. In order to facilitate their retreat, and alſo to preſerve a communication with the left bank of the Adige, two bridges of boats were fixed near Pol, upon that river,¹ ſtrengthened by a double *tête de pont*, defended by artillery. As this poſition could not keep up a communication with Verona upon the right bank of the Adige, by reaſon of their diſtance from each other, they contented themſelves with ſending a diviſion of huſſars from Verona to Caſa Cam, to keep up the communication as well as they could: but the advanced chain of Verona, through Tombetta, Tomba, St. Lucia, St. Maſſimo, Croce Biancha, which extended from one bank of the Adige to the other, was defended by three battalions of infantry, and was ſupported on the glacis of Verona at the new gate. Two battalions, Mitrowſky, one battalion of Hungarians, No. 48, and ſix ſquadrons of cavalry, were poſted near the Porta Nuova; four battalions of infantry and five ſquadrons of cavalry were poſted as a reſerve behind the Porto Zeno. In this ſituation, the enemy attacked our chain of advanced poſts very early in the morning of the 26th. Lieutenant-general Keim immediately marched thither, and finding that the enemy's attack was principally directed againſt St. Lucia, he took meaſures to reinforce thoſe points. He ſent thither an additional battalion. General Liptay, who was with his troops at St. Lucia, had been already wounded at half paſt four o'clock. General Keim then entruſted the command of that place to General Morſkwitz, and marched to Croce Biancha, to endeavour to fall upon the flank of the enemy, which was attacking St. Lucia. This diverſion was intended to be made between Lugugna and Maſſimo, towards Doſſobon. By the firſt priſoners that were taken, it was learnt that the enemy conſiſted of two complete diviſions under Generals Victor and Grenier; that one part of the diviſion of Serrurier had been added to them, together with 6000 Piedmonteſe, Swiſs, and Poliſh emigrants; that the enemy was, therefore, forming an attack upon Verona, with a force amounting to between 25 and 30,000 men, in the firm expectation of taking that city by ſurpriſe. The enemy had, therefore, put in the general orders of the army, that as they had already ſubſiſted fifteen days without pay, they ſhould be indemnified with two hours pillage of the city of Verona. General Keim immediately ordered the corps of reſerve to advance, ſent General Hohenzollern to the left wing, with orders to ſupport General Minkwitz; and he went himſelf to St. Maſſimo. At ſix o'clock the enemy muſtered all their forces, and directed their principal attacks upon St. Lucia and St. Maſſimo. The firſt poſt was ſoon carried by the enemy; and notwithſtanding that General Hohenzollern learnt that General Minkwitz had been wounded, he ſucceeded twice in retaking it; it could not, however, be preſerved, and the enemy remained in poſſeſſion of it during the whole day. They did not ſucceed equally well at St. Maſſimo. They made ſeven ſucceſſive attacks upon it, and carried the poſt ſeven times with freſh forces, and ſeven times they were repulſed from it by our brave troops. This place occaſioned an immenſe loſs to the enemy; we not only remained maſters of it during the whole day, but our chain of advance poſts was likewiſe maintained with the exception of the poſt of St. Lucia. Our loſs is conſiderable; that of the enemy twice as great. General Keim ſays, that all the troops under his command performed prodigies of valour; and that there is no example of ſo deadly a fire of muſket ſhots having been ſuſtained during eighteen hours, without the

ſmalleſt

smallest interval, by reason of the superiority of the enemy, who continually advanced with fresh troops. This heroic effort of courage and perseverance is so much the more wonderful, as the troops were not able to procure, during the whole attack, any refreshment or comfort. Towards twelve o'clock, General Kehn was wounded. He did not quit his post, without recommending to all the generals not to abandon the post of St. Massimo, and to continue the diversions in the flank and rear of the enemy, which would necessarily make them repent of the audacity of their enterprise. It was owing to the want of troops, and the exhausted state of those who had been so long fighting, that hindered us from profiting of the advantages which we had gained by attacking Busfolengo and Villa Franca. We took one cannon, one ammunition-waggon, 316 prisoners, amongst whom were two chiefs of battalions, and 35 officers. The General says, that it is impossible for him to make a list of those who distinguished themselves; each had shown the most invincible courage, and every individual reflected by his conduct the greatest honour upon the army of his Majesty, of which he was a part. Our losses consist of 11 officers and 90 men killed, 42 officers and 2675 men wounded. At the attack of St. Lucia 1000 prisoners fell into the hands of the enemy. The loss of the enemy cannot be estimated at less than from 8 to 10,000 men.

Second Battle of Verona, of the 30th March.

Immediately after the battle of Legnago, as it has been said in the preceding report, General Kray lost no time in marching with the greater part of the army to Verona.

On the 29th General Victor sent an officer to the commander in chief, to propose to him a truce for twenty-four hours, in order to carry off the slain which still remained in the field of battle, and occasioned a dangerous infection. To this proposal General Kray consented, but fixed its duration to the following day at twelve o'clock; but at ten o'clock the enemy began to attack our advanced posts upon the left bank of the Adige, posted opposite to their front at Pola. The advanced posts were insensibly repulsed; and at the same time the enemy filed off across the mountains near St. Ambroso, in order to turn Verona. The retreat of the advanced posts, as well as of the battalions of Schrieder, of Sordy, and of Tellachech, was already effectuated as far as Parona, when the regiment of Nadasti, the battalions of Weber, Fequelmont, Mercantin et Korher, together with the regiments of cavalry of Lobkowitz Karaczay, and the 7th regiment of hussars, who had been kept in readiness, put themselves in motion, attacked and overcame the enemy in a moment. The attack was made in three columns, of which one was conducted along the Adige; the other upon the Chauffee of the Tyrol; the third along the mountains. The attacks were performed with such promptness, that the enemy could not maintain themselves on any side, and we thus reached their bridge, where they had planted, on the opposite bank, a battery of twelve cannon, which obliged us for a moment to suspend our fire: but after a short pause the assault of the bridge was ordered. The grenadiers of Korber, Fequelmont, and Weber, immediately carried and destroyed it. The enemy, who had marched over the mountains to turn Verona, found themselves cut off, and were obliged to surrender themselves pri-

Vol. VIII.　　　　　　　　　L　　　　　　　　　soners.

soners. A great number are wandering in the mountains, who will be brought in by degrees. It is remarkable that the enemy in this expedition had but one piece of cannon. They must have entertained the hope of surprising and taking Verona by storm. Our loss does not exceed 46 in killed, and 166 in wounded. The enemy has lost 1000 men, and 1112 prisoners. The enemy made this attack with the whole division of Serrurier, and with the half of that of Victor, amounting in the whole to 15,000 men. According to a still more recent account from General Kray, the enemy had, on the 1st April, made a retrograde movement, which induced him to direct the advanced guard, commanded by Count Hohenzollern, and consisting of two regiments of cavalry, and five battalions of infantry, to proceed forward as far as Castel Nuovo. This advanced guard was supported by a division of General Zopff, which had passed the Adige, and encamped under Verona. On the 2d of April, detachments were sent to Peschiera and Villa Franca; and Major-general Fulda, of the 5th regiment of hussars, with two squadrons, made 29 officers and 800 privates prisoners at Villa Franca, and took two pieces of cannon, nine ammunition-waggons, and 300 small arms. Several shells from two howitzers were thrown into Peschiera to alarm the enemy; and on the same day (2d April) the General crossed the Adige with his whole army, and took possession of a camp in front of Verona, supported on the left by Tomba, and on the right by St. Lucia.

The enemy still occupies the ground between the Adige and the Tartaro, towards Legnago; but has so entirely evacuated the whole space near the Lago de Garda, that the communication with the Tyrol, by the valley of the Adige, is open; and the Count de St. Julien has already advanced from the Tyrol as far as Rivoli, and has sent patroles as far as Peschiera. At present the enemy appear inclined to cross the Adige, having with them 40 pontoons.

This passage may be expected to be attempted near Ronco and Roverschiano; but the Commander in Chief is prepared against every design which the enemy may endeavour to effect, in consequence of our movements forward, and will attack them in front, or with still greater advantage in the rear. General Klenau has patrolled along the river Po as far as Ostiglia, and has alarmed the whole country. The enemy, who occupied that space with a few troops only, have retreated in every direction; and the General, as well as his patroles, were received with acclamations of joy on both sides of the Po. General Klenau has sunk, in the Lago Oscuro, a small armed vessel, and another has been dragged on shore; since which the enemy have sunk all their vessels armed with cannons, and have sent the crews to Ferraro. The French General has proposed to General Kray to exchange the officers who had been made prisoners on the 26th and 30th. He was answered, that he must first send his Majesty's officers, and then an equal number of French officers, of those whom we had made prisoners, would be returned.

Vienna, April 10.

FIELD-MARSHAL-LIEUTENANT Count de Bellegarde has sent as courier the first lieutenant Baron Sterndahl with the following account:

Schluderns, April 5.

The enemy having penetrated into the Tyrol, and the general of division Deroles having quitted, in the night of the 30th to the 31st, his position at Mals and Aurent, advanced towards Tauffers and St. Marie. The

The Field-marshal-lieutenant Count de Bellegarde judged it highly necessary to drive them from a post where they manifested an intention of establishing themselves, having already begun to throw up intrenchments, in order to act with the greater effect whenever circumstances would permit. Field-marshal-lieutenant Count Bellegarde accordingly assembled his troops on the 4th instant, at two o'clock in the morning, and having made the necessary dispositions, marched against the enemy at break of day.

The attack commenced at half past four o'clock: our left wing soon gained possession of a hill which commanded the enemy's flank, but they maintained their principal position, from whence they annoyed us by a very brisk fire of artillery and musketry. Our right wing experienced a still greater resistance, from the enemy's being, as it were, intrenched behind two old castles, of which they had taken possession. The Field-marshal-lieutenant then ordered the whole of the artillery and the corps de reserve to advance, from which time the attack became general. The manœuvres and good countenance of the Imperial troops enabled them to gain ground considerably on the top of the mountain that commanded the right flank of the enemy, who now began to give way, abandoning their position and retreating towards the village of Tauffers; but being pursued with great spirit, they retreated with precipitation, and with great loss, to the heights behind Tauffers, from whence, however, they were soon dislodged by General Bellegarde. The enemy then fell back upon Munster, where they made a vigorous stand, but they were also driven from thence with great loss in prisoners, and closely pursued by our troops.

The enemy retreated to Czernez, near which place Petrioni, chief of the staff, risked an attack with all his forces. He succeeded in driving back some battalions; but the enemy were again routed with the loss of three pieces of cannon, and from that time they continued to retreat without halting. Several of the enemy's staff officers have been wounded, and a great number of subalterns. We have made 300 prisoners, besides three pieces of cannon, 11 gun-carriages, 14 ammunition-waggons, and 1000 muskets. An hospital, with a number of officers, and above 150 non-commissioned officers and men, have fallen into our hands.

On our side the loss has been by no means inconsiderable, as the enemy made an obstinate resistance. Many officers of merit have been either killed or wounded.

From the report of Field-marshal-lieutenant Kray, of the 4th instant, it appears that the advanced guard of General Count Hohenzollern had taken more than 500 prisoners; and General Count Klenau states, that being desirous of attacking, with one company, two gunboats, which were in the Po d'Ariano, and having passed the river for that purpose, the inhabitants of the island of Ariano had shown great satisfaction, had taken up arms, had seized upon the boats, and made 60 Frenchmen prisoners.

On the 2d, the enemy attempting to reconnoitre from Ostiglia to Merlava, were stopped by the armed peasantry, and forced to retire.

Vienna, April 12.

THE Field marshal-lieutenant Kray has sent the following account:

The enemy, after the check sustained on the 30th ult. near Verona, had descended the Adige, and taken post between that river and the Tartaro, from whence they threatened to repass the Adige. But Field-marshal-lieutenant

lieutenant Kray, underſtanding that they had been unable to rally all their forces, took the reſolution of attacking them immediately. The enemy's head-quarters were at Iſola della Scala; one camp near Magnan, oppoſite to our army under Verona, and a ſecond near Lecca, on the rivulet Menego, oppoſite to Legnano. Field-marſhal-lieutenant Kray's plan was, firſt to attack the enemy's camp near Magnan, and to penetrate, if poſſible, as far as Iſola della Scala. He accordingly drew near the enemy on the 5th inſtant, and at ten in the morning attacked them with three columns, ſupported by a fourth. The action ſoon became general; the enemy made a moſt obſtinate reſiſtance. The ground was a long time diſputed, but the firmneſs and bravery of the Imperial troops obtained the victory. The enemy were routed on all ſides, and driven from their camp at Magnan. Night coming on put an end to the combat. During the night, the Imperial troops formed a line by Leccedre Caſtel d'Azano, Hutta Freda, and Valeſe, to watch the motions of the enemy, after this ſecond defeat.

At the departure of the courier we had already taken 11 pieces of cannon, 30 ammunition-waggons, ſeven ſtandards, and above 2000 priſoners. Our loſs in killed and wounded is eſtimated by Field-marſhal-lieutenant Kray at 2000 men; that of the enemy muſt be far more conſiderable, as his Majeſty's troops performed prodigies of valour.

Vienna, April 13.

ACCORDING to two accounts of the 5th and 7th inſtant, from his Royal Highneſs the Archduke Charles, it appears that the enemy, who were poſted at Freudenſtadt, Homberg, and Neuſtadt, moved and attacked a part of his Royal Highneſs's army with great force at Alpierſbach, Frieberg, and Turwangen, and at the ſame time ordered their advanced poſts to march towards Sultz on the Necker, where there was a ſmall Auſtrian corps. His Royal Highneſs immediately ſent General Nauendorff forward with a reinforcement of ſeveral battalions, and ordered him to attack the enemy on every point, and to endeavour to drive them back to the mountains. General Gorger at the ſame time marched towards Alpierſbach, whilſt Generals Meerfeld and Guiley moved to Frieberg and St. George, where they attacked the enemy, diſperſed them, took many priſoners, and one ammunition-waggon. At the ſame time, General Klingling moved towards Neuſtadt, which poſt the enemy left on his approach. General Kienmeyer, who had been to the neighbourhood of Shaffhauſen and Stain, repulſed a ſtrong detachment of the enemy, and purſued them as far as Shaffhauſen, where his (General Kienmeyer's) advanced poſts now are. The enemy having ſome apprehenſions for Stain and Diſſenhoſen, burnt the bridges at both places.

On the 5th, it was reported at all the advanced poſts, that the enemy had retreated from every quarter, as far as Freudenſtadt, where the rear of the French General St. Cyr's diviſion was ſtill poſted. Lieutenant-colonel Steinhofer, of the Blankenſtein regiment of huſſars, purſued the enemy with great ſpirit near Homberg, fell in with them, killed ſome, and took ſeveral priſoners. On the 7th, the enemy retreated alſo from Freudenſtadt, and abandoned ſeveral poſts on the Kniebiſs, from whence they marched by Oberkirch towards Kehl, to which place ſeveral other columns, who were directing their march to Laar through Offenburgh, had retreated. The column from Freyburg took the road to Old Breyſach, where they paſſed the Rhine and broke down the bridge behind them. His Royal Highneſs ordered his light troops to purſue the enemy in every direction,

direction, and took poffeffion of all the principal pofitions which the enemy had abandoned, the army being now pofted in the neighbourhood of Villengen, Donauefchingen, and Engen.

From the LONDON GAZETTE, April 30, 1799.

Admiralty Office, April 29.

Extract of a Letter from Admiral Kingsmill, Commander in Chief of his Majefty's Ships and Veffels on the Coaft of Ireland, to Evan Nepean, Efq. dated at Cork, the 22d April.

Sir,

PLEASE to lay before my Lords Commiffioners of the Admiralty the enclofed letter received from Captain Moore, of his Majefty's fhip Melampus, juft returned from her cruife, giving account of a French privateer of 20 guns, faid to be Le Nantois, which he was in chafe of, having overfet, and that unfortunately none of her crew could be faved.

I am, &c. &c. &c.
R. KINGSMILL.

Sir, *Melampus, at Sea, April 19.*

I HAVE the honour to inform you, that yefterday morning, in latitude 50 deg. 23 min. north, longitude 15 deg. 20 min. weft, we chafed a fhip, which, on our firing at her, hoifted French colours. The wind blowing exceedingly hard at N. W. with a very high fea, fhe got before the wind when within half gunfhot of her, and, fetting all poffible fail, obftinately perfifted in attempting to efcape: after carrying away our ftudding-fail-booms, we continued firing our chafe guns, when fhe fuddenly gave a broad yaw to windward, inftantly overfet, and in the fpace of two minutes fhe went down, and not an atom of the wreck could be feen. The greateft exertion and the utmoft expedition were ufed in bringing the Melampus to the wind as near the fpot as poffible, with the view of faving thefe unfortunate people, but nothing remained on the furface.

I find, by the information of the captain and officers of Le Papillon, which failed from Nantes about the fame time with this fhip, and who knew her both from her appearance and the fignals fhe made to us, that fhe was Le Nantois, of 14 twelve and fix pounders, and 150 men; and I am very forry to add, that from other circumftances there is no room for doubt, that the mafter and part of the crew of the Echo, of Poole, which fhe had taken, were amongft the fufferers on this melancholy occafion.

I am, &c.
Admiral Kingsmill, Cork. G. MOORE.

Vienna, April 15.

FROM the lateft reports received from Field-marfhal-lieutenant Kray, it appears, that after the battle of the 5th, near Magnan, the enemy had abandoned, on the 6th inftant, Ifola della Scala and Villa Franca; had pofted their rear guard at Roverbella; had retired upon the 7th beyond the Mincio near Goito, and having left a ftrong garrifon in that place, the reft of the rear guard had directed their march towards La Volta, probably in the defign either of reinforcing the garrifon of Pefchiera, or of throwing provifions into it.

This

This induced Field-marshal-lieutenant Kray to push forward his advanced guard as far as Villa Franca, to cause three battalions and some chasseurs to advance as far as Vallegio upon the Mincio, to defend the bridge of that place, and four divisions to support them.

We found at Isola della Scala 200 wounded, the greater part of whom were French; but some of them our own people. Amongst the former was General Pigeon, who died on the 7th of his wounds.

On the departure of the courier we had already made 2500 prisoners, of whom 130 were officers; we also took 16 pieces of cannon, and 40 ammunition-waggons. The loss of the enemy is estimated at 8000 men. The disorder was so great among them, that the generals were plundered by their own soldiers.

Vienna, April 16.

FIELD-MARSHAL-LIEUTENANT Kray, exclusive of the circumstantial details which he gives of the movements in the last battle near Magnan, and of the consequences which resulted from them, adds, that Major-general Klenau had penetrated as far as Governello with his light troops; that he had taken from the enemy 18,000 muskets, 60 oxen, a great quantity of brandy, and made 150 men and two officers prisoners.

At the same time Colonel Dretkovich, supported by the inhabitants of the Po di Goro, near Ariano, seized three gun-boats, with 13 cannon, 17,032 sacks of salt, 24 merchant-vessels with their cargoes, and 20 others unladen.

Vienna, April 17.

LETTERS have been received from General Bellegarde, from Schludern, dated the 9th instant, but nothing of moment had passed in that quarter since the defeat of the French at Munster and Santa Maria.

Vienna, April 18.

HIS Royal Highness the Archduke Charles has sent an account here, dated the 14th instant, of General Count Nauendorff having taken possession of Schaffhausen, on the 13th in the evening, after having made several attacks upon the town with part of his advanced guard.

The said general punctually obeyed the orders of his Royal Highness in sparing the town as much as possible, and wished also to enter into an engagement with the enemy not to destroy the beautiful bridge, which is considered a masterpiece of workmanship; the enemy, however, rejected this proposition, and placed themselves in a posture of defence, but were driven back with precipitation. They then set fire to the bridge, which soon became a prey to the flames, and also two houses that were situated close to it. In all other respects the town remained uninjured. His Royal Highness will soon transmit the particulars of this affair.

By a further account received from General Kray, dated the 8th inst. it appears that General Count Klenau had taken possession of the post of Governolo, the only one which the enemy was still able to retain on the Lower Mincio; and in that, as well as in the fortress near Ponte Molino, 100 men and several officers were made prisoners; by which circumstance we are entire masters of the Tartaro and Tions.

From

From the LONDON GAZETTE, May 4, 1799.

Vienna, April 19.

Particulars of the Battle of Osterach, which took place on the 21st March, between the Imperial Troops, under the Orders of the Archduke Charles, and the French Forces commanded by General Jourdan.

INFORMATION having been repeatedly received that the enemy continued to make further progress in Suabia, and that they had driven back our advanced posts and detached corps, his Royal Highness determined to march against them.

On the 20th March, his Royal Highness was informed that the enemy had attacked the whole line of our out-posts along the Osterach; that they had succeeded in driving them in on one side; but that, notwithstanding the inferiority of numbers, our troops had not only stopped their progress, but had even repulsed them as far as Polstern. On the side of Attchaufan the enemy could penetrate no further than Hofzirchen, from whence they were shortly after dislodged.

The enemy had concentrated the greatest part of their forces behind Osterach, and placed their advanced guard on the right bank of the river of that name.

His Royal Highness took the necessary measures for attacking them on the following day; during the night, he divided his troops into three columns, the first was to march from Sulgau to Pfokenstadt; the second, under the command of the Archduke, pushed forward upon Kussen; and the third from Atschaufen to Ratzenreite; each column had its advanced guard.

Early on the 21st, all our advanced guards attacked the enemy, and were soon followed by the columns, who charged the enemy on all sides. By the good disposition and bravery of our troops, the enemy, in spite of their obstinate resistance, were defeated and driven back every where. They retreated during the night with great precipitation to Stochbach, where our advanced guard pursued them. The French General Ferino, who, with his division and that of General Aubi, had driven back one of our brigades, finding himself, by the defeat of General Jourdan's army, obliged to make a retreat, owed his safety only to the extreme expedition with which he effected it. We, however, made a great number of prisoners, and took three pieces of cannon. The loss of the enemy amounts to 5000 men. We have lost 2160 killed and wounded.

Supplement to the Battle of Tauffers and St. Marie, on the 4th of April.

We found at St. Marie a very considerable magazine of ammunition, containing more than ninety casks filled with cartridges and powder.

Account of the Events of the 8th of April.

Field-marshal lieutenant Bellegarde ordered General Count Alvini to harass the enemy by different movements, in order to facilitate the operations of the army of Italy. He beat and drove back the enemy wherever he met with them.—Having halted with his corps before Rocca d'Anfo, he pushed forward his advanced guard, and took possession of Bagalino.

Our loss in these different actions is very inconsiderable compared to that of the enemy. We took from them one cannon, one standard, and made many prisoners.

Accounts

Accounts are this moment received that we are in poſſeſſion of Rocca d'Anſo, and that the enemy are retreating upon Veſtone and Breſcia.

SUPPLEMENT.

General Melas, who is arrived at the army of Italy, has ſent intelligence of the enemy having retreated by Azola, behind Chieſa; that our advanced guards extend beyond the Mincio: that they are before Goito, and upon the heights before La Volta and Monzanbano.—Peſchiera is already ſurrounded at a certain diſtance, on the ſide of Suave and Mazinirola. Our patroles have advanced as far as the citadel, without meeting with any of the enemy's picquets.

General Kiainau has alſo inveſted Mantua, on the ſide of Molinella. That general has made himſelf maſter of the enemy's poſts at Lago Sacro, and of four pieces of cannon.

General Melas informs us, that the people are every where very favourably diſpoſed, particularly in the neighbourhood of Mantua; that our troops are received in all places with ſhouts of joy; that the populace in general give evident marks of their attachment to the old conſtitution, as well as of their hatred to the French, and a democratical government.

Admiralty Office, May 4.

A Liſt of Ships and Veſſels taken and deſtroyed by the Squadron under the Command of Sir Hugh Cloberry Chriſtian, K.B. Rear-admiral of the White, and Commander in Chief of his Majeſty's Ships and Veſſels at the Cape of Good Hope, between the 13th of March 1798, and the 23d of November following; tranſmitted to Evan Nepean, Eſq. Secretary of the Admiralty.

BY the Jupiter, Raiſonable, Imperieuſe, Braave, Rattleſnake, and Star—The 13th March, the Daniſh ſhip Matilde Marie, from Copenhagen, bound to the Mauritius, laden with naval ſtores and ſundries: naval ſtores condemned. The 20th March, the Daniſh ſloop Fanny, from Roderiga, bound to the Mauritius, laden with paddy and Indian corn: veſſel ſunk, cargo condemned. The 20th March, the French brig Le Dragon, from Madagaſcar, bound to the Mauritius, laden with ſlaves: veſſel ſunk, cargo condemned. The 22d March, the Daniſh ſloop Forſoget, from Serampore, bound to the Mauritius, laden with piece-goods: under trial. The 27th of March, the French ſloop Francis Auguſtus, in ballaſt: condemned. The 31ſt March, the French brig L'Abondance, from Madagaſcar, bound to the Mauritius, in ballaſt: condemned.

By the Jupiter, Raiſonable, Imperieuſe, Braave, Rattleſnake, Star, Tremendous, Sceptre, Stately, and Garland—The 29th May, the Daniſh ſhip Chriſtianus Septimus, from Batavia, bound to Copenhagen, laden with coffee and ſugar: under trial.

By L. Oiſeau—The 8th July, the Daniſh ſhip Angelique, from Madras and Tranquebar, bound to Manilla, laden with piece-goods; cargo belonging to American reſidents at Madras: under trial. The 30th Auguſt, the Daniſh ſhip Goede Henſigt, from Copenhagen, bound to the Mauritius, laden with naval ſtores and ſundries: under trial. The 31ſt Auguſt, a French brig; cut out by the boats from the river Noire, Iſle of France: condemned. A French brig; cut out by the boats from the river Noire, Iſle of France, and afterwards ſent in with priſoners. A French ſloop: ſunk. The 1ſt September, the French brig Henrietta, from Bourbon, bound to the Mauritius, laden with rice: condemned. The French brig Reunion,

Reunion, from the Mauritius: corvette, six guns, and 27 men: condemned.

By the Stately, Braave, Garland, and Star—The 26th July, the French ship Necessarie, from the Mauritius, in ballast, run on shore by the Garland, on the rocks at St. Luce, Madagascar, and lost. A French sloop, from the Mauritius, in ballast: run on shore by the Braave. The 16th August, the French ship Bonne Intention, from the Mauritius, taken at Foul-point, and sent to assist the Garland; since arrived at the Cape. The 16th August, the French sloop Ca Ira, from the Mauritius, in ballast: taken at Foul-point, and afterwards destroyed. The 17th August, the French brig L'Elizabeth, from the Mauritius, in ballast: taken at Tamatave, Madagascar, and sent to assist the Garland; since arrived at the Cape. The 18th August, the French sloop L'Esperance, from the Mauritius, in ballast: taken at Foul-point, and sent to assist the Garland; since arrived at the Cape. The French brig L'Ursilie, from Madagascar, bound to the Isle of France, laden with rice: condemned.

By the L'Oiseau and Rattlesnake—The 21st November, the Spanish schooner Santa Rosa, from Buenos Ayres, bound to the Mauritius, laden with 12,300 dollars, beef, pork, and flour; arrived at the Cape 23d December 1798.

(Signed) LAUGHLAN M'LEAN,
Late Secretary to Sir H. C. Christian deceased.

From the LONDON GAZETTE, May 7, 1799.

Admiralty Office, May 7.

Extract of a Letter from Captain Charles Cobb, Commander of his Majesty's Ship Glatton, to Evan Nepean, Esq. dated in Yarmouth Roads, the 4th instant.

AT six A. M. arrived Le Vengeur French cutter privateer, mounting 12 guns and 98 men, taken by his Majesty's sloop Martin, off the Scaw. The master of the Martin has just brought me Captain St. Clair's letter to Vice-admiral Dickson, which I enclose for their Lordships' information.

Sir, *His Majesty's Sloop Martin, at Sea, April 29.*

I BEG leave to inform you, I arrived safe at Elsineur with the convoy; I found the Roads full of ice, and no trade come down from the eastward; and in consequence of which, and information of several privateers off the coast of Norway, I left the place, and on the 28th instant, at ten A. M. the Scaw bearing S. W. by W. five leagues, descried one lugger and two cutter privateers; I immediately gave chase, came up with, and captured one cutter at seven in the evening; she proved to be Le Vengeur, commanded by Citizen Charles Tack, a very fine vessel, 14 guns, and 105 men, from Christiansand, taken nothing since out: I used all expedition in getting out the prisoners, and made sail after the others; but it coming on dark, I was not so fortunate as to come up with them; had the daylight continued two hours longer, I must inevitably have taken them.

I have the honour to be, &c. &c.

Vice-admiral Dickson, &c. &c. M. ST. CLAIR.

Vienna, April 24.

A LETTER from Marshal Suwarrow, dated Veliggio, April 18, states, that the French had repassed the Adda, after throwing 15,000 men into Mantua, and 5,000 into Peschiera; and that the Marshal was preparing to follow them, after leaving General Kray with a corps of about 20,000 men to invest those two places. Marshal Suwarrow's patroles had been pushed as far as Cremona, and General Klenau's to the neighbourhood of Bologna, without meeting any considerable body of the enemy.

By accounts received in the evening of the same day, it appears that the enemy were employed in throwing up intrenchments at Lodi and Cassano. Marshal Suwarrow, with a body of between 45 and 50,000 men, was to have marched on the 19th to Monta Chiaro on the Chiesa, in order to occupy Brescia, and then to advance on the Oglio and Adda.

Vienna, April 24.

HIS Royal Highness the Archduke Charles has reported the following particulars relative to the taking of Schaffhausen:

As the enemy still retained possession of the town of Schaffhausen and the suburb of Constance, called Petershausen, both situated on the right bank of the Rhine, with an apparent view to assemble there, and particularly in Schaffhausen, a number of troops, and to make an advantageous attack from both points upon the corps of Lieutenant-general Count Nauendorff, which was posted in the neighbourhood, his Royal Highness directed that the enemy should be driven from those two points, and that their stations should be occupied by our troops.

In consequence of this arrangement, Lieutenant-general Count Nauendorff was charged to order Lieutenant-general Count Baillet to advance against Schaffhausen with a considerable body of light infantry and cavalry, supported by four battalions of the line and some reserve artillery. He obeyed these orders, and summoned the enemy to abandon the town in the course of half an hour, and to retire to the left bank of the river. The officer who commanded in Schaffhausen sought to gain time by negotiation, with a view to draw unto himself a reinforcement; but Lieutenant-general Count Baillet, aware of the enemy's object, ordered his artillery, which he had posted to great advantage, to fire upon the bridge and the gate of the town, and without further delay he attacked the enemy in the town; and notwithstanding a very obstinate resistance, he drove them across the Rhine, the bridge over which they burnt in their retreat.

The enemy lost upon this occasion several hundred men killed and wounded, and 100 taken prisoners; 17 pieces of cannon, and arms of various descriptions, were taken. Our loss does not exceed 20 men.

Lieutenant-general Count Baillet particularizes the spirited conduct of a private of the regiment of Lacy, who voluntarily swam across the Rhine, and, under the protection of our fire, loosened two vessels which were on the left bank, and got back with them as far as the middle of the river, where, however, the current drove him against the burning bridge, which set fire to the two vessels. This circumstance obliged the man to dive, and to swim back to the right bank. His example encouraged another: both plunged into the Rhine, and brought over some vessels; the consequence of which was, that 17 or 18 more men, of the regiment of Lacy, followed the others, and got possession of many more vessels. His
Royal

Royal Highness, as a reward for so meritorious a zeal, and as an encouragement to others, gave the first man the golden medal, and the second the silver medal.

On the 14th, at daybreak, Major-general Piaczeck made an attack upon Petershausen with great spirit and decision, drove the enemy from it, and sunk the ships which were on the opposite bank.

The detachment which was sent through Pforzheim and Bruckfal, towards Philipsburg, on the same day that it had re-established the communication with that fortress, had pushed on patroles towards Manheim.

At the same time Lieutenant-general the Rhinegrave of Salm, commandant of Philipsburg, reported that a patrole of the inconsiderable detachment of the dragoons of Bamberg, which formed a part of the garrison, had pushed forward through Waghausel, and had taken four French chasseurs with their horses. The Rhinegrave took this opportunity of commending the conduct of the above detachment, as well as the remainder of the garrison during its blockade.

From the LONDON GAZETTE, May 18, 1799.

Admiralty Office, May 18.

Extract of a Letter from Vice-admiral Dickson, to Evan Nepean, Esq. dated on board his Majesty's Ship Monarch, off the Texel, the 14th instant.

HEREWITH I transmit, for their Lordships' information, a letter from Lieutenant Searle, commanding the Courier hired cutter, acquainting me of his having captured the Ribotteur French schooner privateer, on the 13th instant.

Sir, *Courier, off the Texel, May 14.*

HAVING received orders from Captain Cobbe, of his Majesty's ship Glatton, to proceed from Yarmouth Roads, and put myself under the command of Captain Sotheron, of the Latona, I left Yarmouth the 11th instant; and on the morning of the 12th I observed a brig in the act of capturing a merchant sloop, about eight or nine leagues off Winterton: I immediately made all sail, and at half past one brought her to close action, proving to be a French privateer of 16 guns, of six and nine pounders: we continued in close action an hour and forty minutes, when, after every exertion being used, her superiority of sailing, together with having the advantage of the wind, she accomplished her escape, though, I flatter myself, in that shattered state as to render her incapable of continuing her cruise. We continued in chase of her till midnight, when it came on thick and foggy weather, we lost sight of her. At daylight in the morning, we perceived a vessel in the north-east; supposing it to be the brig we had previously engaged, again made sail: at eight came up with and captured the Ribotteur French schooner, of six three pounders, two of which were thrown overboard in chase, and 26 men, which we found to be in concert with the brig above mentioned. I have to observe, that, at the time of my engaging the brig, a lugger privateer was then lying at some distance to leeward, but showed no inclination to assist the vessel we were then engaging.

I have the pleasure and satisfaction to inform you, that no men could have acted with a greater spirit of gallantry than all on board the Courier; and have particularly to mention Lieutenant Campbell, of the Latona, and Lieutenant Glanvill, of the Ranger, for their great assistance during the whole of the engagement, as well as Messrs. Trescott and Campbell, mates of the Latona, and Mr. Willis, mate of the Ranger.

I am sorry to add we had five men wounded; but have every reason to believe the enemy suffered considerably more.

I have the honour to be, Sir, &c.

Archibald Dickson, Esq. Vice-admiral   T. SEARLE.
of the Red, &c.

Vienna, April 26.

HIS Royal Highness the Archduke writes from Stockach, the 20th instant, that, as the enemy, after having been driven from Schafhausen and Petershausen, still occupied an advantageous position in the small town of Eglisau, on the right bank of the Rhine, he had directed Prince Schwartzenberg to dislodge them from that post; that, in pursuance of these directions, he approached the place, and summoned the enemy to surrender; that, upon an answer in the negative being returned, he had attacked them with such impetuosity that they were soon compelled to abandon their station, and retreat. Our loss, in this affair, consists of only 14 men killed and wounded.

His Royal Highness also states, that, from the report of Field-marshal-lieutenant Kospoth, it appears, that a detachment had been sent from Fribourg to Vieux Brisac, in order to demolish the intrenchments that the enemy had raised there, but immediately had abandoned. The following day a detachment of the enemy, consisting of 300 cavalry and 700 infantry, made their appearance on the right bank of the Rhine. In the mean time, in another quarter, we fell in with an enemy's picquet of 10 horsemen, who were made prisoners.

General Melas sends the following account of the proceedings of the army in Italy, dated the 15th instant.

ON the 14th the whole army passed the Mincio, and encamped near Campagnola and Monte Olivetano, pushing the advanced posts as far as Marcaria on the Ogno, and Monte Chiaria on the Chiese.

The enemy retreated on the right beyond the Oglio, and on the left beyond the Chiese.

General Vukassovich instantly occupied Salo, by which he established his communication with the army.

On the 18th the army encamped between Capriano and Caffello. Mantua is left to its own means of defence: it is blockaded at a certain distance; and our patroles advance to its very gates.

We took from the enemy, at Cassel Maggiore, a convoy of 36 pontoons, dispersed the escort, and made five officers and 180 men prisoners.

One of our detachments even entered Cremona, where they learnt that there were only 400 Frenchmen at Pizzighetoni; that the enemy's army had retreated beyond the Adda, and their head-quarters were at Lodi.

A detachment from our Venetian flotilla had cast anchor at the mouth of the Premuna, where it had made several prizes, and released several of our boats.

In the Lago Sacro we took 128 prisoners (of whom six were officers), with 15 brass cannon in a vessel, and 200 pieces of iron ordnance, without carriages, on the shore.

The

The armed peasants, supported by one single detachment of General Klenau, attacked a detachment of Cisalpines near Mirandola, who had two pieces of cannon, and made 234 prisoners.

General Suwarrow has already taken the command of the combined Italian army. When these accounts came away, the first column of Russian troops were at Villa Franca; the remainder were following by forced marches.

In addition to the above, Major-general Hohenzollern mentions the capture of two large merchantmen, several chests filled with uniforms, great quantities of ammunition, one cannon, and several gun-carriages, with some prisoners at Cremona.

At Castel Nuovo a park of 14 pieces of artillery, four mortars, a prodigious quantity of ammunition, 20 horses, and several prisoners, fell into our hands.

Major-general Vukassovich, on taking possession of Salo, seized a large vessel fully equipped, having on board three chests full of muskets and other military stores.

Two lieutenants, with 50 men, attacked a post near Brescia at two o'clock in the morning, consisting of three officers and 100 men, of whom 25 were killed, 20 made prisoners, and the remainder, many of them wounded, fled.

Vienna, April 29.

LIEUTENANT Gugenos, of the regiment of Nadasty, arrived here this day, with the news that the town and fortress of Brescia were taken on the 20th instant, in the following manner: Field-marshal-lieutenant Kray, charged with this enterprise, detached for this purpose Field marshal-lieutenant Otto, with his division, who had already marched on the 17th from his position at Monte Chiaro, by Castel Edolo, to reconnoitre the town.

The 20th, at midnight, Field-marshal Otto quitted his camp with his division in two columns. The battalion of Nadasty, posted in Rezato, advanced upon the high road by Euphemia, as far as the entrance of the suburbs of Brescia.

Colonel Biteskuti advanced on the high road leading from Castel Edolo to Brescia, with a battalion of Anthony Esterhazy, which he commanded, and two battalions of Nadasty, commanded by Colonel Absaltern, with the necessary artillery. The battalion of Esterhazy was posted on the left of the high road near the town, to cover the bomb batteries, and the battalion of Nadasty was posted on the right to keep up the communication with the battalion stationed at St. Euphemia. The third battalion of Nadasty remained in reserve near St. Polo.

These battalions directed their attack against the gate of Torre Longa. One battalion of Esterhazy, commanded by Major-general Kraus, which was at Chedi, marched on the high road of Cremona by St. Zeno, against the gate of St. Alexander. This column was augmented by a corps of horse artillery; and all the rest of the cavalry, commanded by Colonel Sommariva, pushed forward as far as the high road to Cremona, to cover the left wing.

This enterprise was supported by 500 Cossacks, 1000 foot chasseurs, and 500 grenadiers, under the orders of the two Russian generals, the Princes Gortbecop and Bagration. The division of Field-marshal-lieutenant Zoph was kept in reserve in case of necessity.

After

After these dispositions Field-marshal-lieutenant Otto sent a second summons to the French commander; and a refusal having been returned, the town began to be bombarded at six o'clock in the morning, and in the space of an hour and a half several cannon were dismounted. This circumstance, together with the approach of the battalion of Nadasty to the gate of Peschiera, caused the enemy to give way, and to retire with precipitation into the citadel.

Our pioneers immediately forced the gate, and, by the exhortations of Field-marshal-lieutenant Kray, the inhabitants assembled upon the ramparts lowered the drawbridge. The battalion of Nadasty then entered the town, drums beating and colours flying.

One wing of the dragoons of Lobkovitz, which was posted in the rear, under the orders of Major Count Harach, and a battalion of the regiment of Esterhazy, took possession of the avenues and streets of the town, of all the roads leading to the citadel, and thus secured this important place.

The enemy kept up a continual fire from the citadel, but without doing any mischief. This induced Field-marshal-lieutenant Kray to summon the commander of the citadel, who first demanded permission to withdraw his troops unconditionally; but perceiving the preparations of the Imperial and Russian troops to take the citadel by assault, he resolved to capitulate. By this capitulation, the garrison, consisting of 1000 men, was made prisoners of war. Forty pieces of cannon, 18 mortars, 480 hundred weight of powder, a great number of muskets and gun-carriages, with ammunition and provision of every kind, and a great quantity of stores, have fallen into our hands. This important conquest cost us only one artillery-man.

The articles of capitulation, and further particulars, will be given hereafter.

Vienna, May 4.

FIELD-marshal-lieutenant Count Bellegarde has written, on the 24th of April, from Nauders, that he (in order to strengthen the operations of the Italian army, on their advancing over the Chiesa towards the Oglio) has given orders to Major-general Vickaslovich to co-operate with his troops to the utmost. At the same time, the General received an order from Field-marshal Suwarrow to advance across Fetzone, towards Isco, to support the movement of the army.

Before Count Bellegarde knew of the movements of the army of Italy, he gave orders to Colonel Strauch, of the regiment of M. Wallis, to enter into the Val Camonica, and to advance from Tonal over Ponte di Legno, towards Edolo.

After a most fatiguing march over mountains covered with snow more than two feet deep, the Colonel arrived at Vione. The first posts of the enemy retired without much resistance; but the enemy defended themselves with obstinacy behind the intrenchments at Vione, but were driven from them by the bayonet.

Colonel Strauch marched then to Vezza, and took possession of Anounzino, and the passes which lie between Ponte di Legno and Edolo, towards Camonica.

Our loss was but trifling; and Colonel Strauch says, that his troops in this very fatiguing enterprise, and with such unfavourable weather, have shown a praiseworthy and indefatigable perseverance, and in their battles an uncommon bravery.

Field-

Field-marshal Count Bellegarde gave orders on the 2ad to reconoitre in different directions on the borders of the Engadein and the rettigau, to examine the mountains, which were not paſſable, according to reports.

Theſe different detachments were ſo directed, that they might join, and act offenſively: but the reports from all quarters were alike, ſtating, that the great quantity of ſnow, and the continued fall of it, made their progreſs impoſſible.

Theſe circumſtances determined Field-marſhal Count Bellegarde to delay reconnoitring; but Major Smid, of Naugebauer, who was ordered to make a diverſion towards Fimba-joch with a battalion of his regiment, had not received the counter order.

This active and ſkilful officer commenced therefore his march, in the evening of the 21ſt, over Blockig Alpe, towards Fimba-joch, marched with his troops over this very difficult point, and met the firſt picquets of the enemy near Jarnſenboden, who gave way without reſiſtance, and retreated towards Manas. The advanced guard purſued the enemy warmly into the village, where an obſtinate battle enſued. To diſengage the advanced guard, and put an end to the battle, Major Smid ordered more troops to advance to take the village, by which the engagement became general.

The enemy, in the mean time, ſucceeded in bringing up their reſerve to haraſs the retreat of our troops, fatigued by ſo difficult a march. Major Smid had, on this occaſion, the misfortune to fall into the hands of the enemy, with a part of his troops and ſome officers. The reſt of the battalion returned to Yſgal.

From the LONDON GAZETTE EXTRAORDINARY, May 22, 1799.

Downing Street, May 22.

A DISPATCH, of which the following is an extract, has been this day received from the Right Hon. Sir Morton Eden, K. B., by the Right Hon Lord Grenville, his Majeſty's principal Secretary of State for the foreign department, dated Vienna, May 7, 1799.

AN officer arrived here yeſterday from Milan, with an account of Marſhal Suwarrow having forced the paſſage of the Adda on the 27th paſt, completely beaten the enemy, and eſtabliſhed his head-quarters on the 30th at Milan. By this victory, all the Milaneſe, except the caſtle of Milan, is wreſted from the French, and it muſt alſo ſoon fall, as the garriſon does not exceed 1200 men, of which only 400 are French. The diſorder of the enemy in their flight was extreme; and it is ſuppoſed that they went towards the Po. Another body of the enemy, it is ſaid, are throwing up works at Reggio and Parma, in order to cover Mantua. I encloſe the Extraordinary Gazette publiſhed late laſt night on the occaſion, and moſt ſincerely congratulate your Lordſhip on theſe brilliant and important events.

It is with great ſatisfaction that I add, that by accounts juſt received from General Bellegarde, it appears that that general has driven the enemy from nearly the whole of the Lower Engadine. On the 3d inſtant inftant he himfelf was at Suz, and General Haddick was at Zernetz; Schuls was alfo occupied by the Auftrians.

This government is greatly hurt at the unfortunate event that has taken place near Raftadt, with regard to the French plenipotentiaries. Bonnier and Roberjot are faid to be dead, and Jean de Brie badly wounded. A fevere inquiry has been fet on foot, the refult of which will be made public, and the guilty exemplarily punifhed.

Tranflation of the Vienna Extraordinary Gazette of Monday, May 6.

COUNT Bokarme, who arrived here this morning as courier from Field-marfhal Count Suwarrow Rimnifkoy, has brought the following details of the movements of the united Imperial armies, from the time of their paffing the Oglio, until their entrance into Milan.

On the 24th of April the enemy abandoned the Oglio, on the approach of Colonel Strauch, of Michael Wallis's regiment, who with feven battalions forced his way from the Tyrol through the Val Camonica towards Lovere on the north point of the Lago d'Ifio.

The Imperial army paffed the Oglio in two columns, the right commanded by General Rofemberg, by the way of Palazuolo to Bergamo, the left under the command of General Melas by Ponte Oglio, Martinengo, Sola, as far as the River Serio.

The next day the army marched in three columns to the Adda. The right, confifting of General Vukaffowich's brigade, and fome of the Ruffian troops, advanced by Ponte St. Pietro and Pontilla, towards Lecco; the fecond, confifting of the divifions of Field-marfhal Lieutenant Ott and Zoph, marched againft Baprio, and encamped oppofite the village; the third, commanded by the General of cavalry Melas, marched by the great road through Garavazio, Trevillo, and encamped oppofite Caffano.

In the mean time the enemy had ftrongly fortified Caffano. This place and the right bank of the Adda were defended by formidable batteries, and a tête-de-pont on this fide the river.

The head-quarters of General Moreau were at Inzago, and two divifions of his army were pofted there in order to prevent our paffing the Adda.

Near Lecco the enemy was alfo ftrongly fortified, and had a tête-depont on the left bank. A divifion of the enemy, under General Serrurier, defended the Upper Adda, one half of which was pofted behind Lecco, a part near Porto Imberzago, and another near Trezzo.

On the Lower Adda, towards Lodi, the enemy had a detachment under General Delmas, and a ftrong garrifon in Pizzighetone.

On the 26th of April the Ruffian troops attacked the enemy before Lecco, and Prince Pangrazian, commander of the chaffeurs, fupported by two grenadier battalions, drove the enemy back to the bridge, in fpite of their advantageous pofition.

The fame day General Seckendorf marched out of the camp near Trevillo, with two battalions and two fquadrons, as far as Crema, where the enemy had fhown themfelves 1500 ftrong, and fent his patroles towards Lodi.

General Count Hohenzollern, who had already advanced to Cremona, fent out fome ftrong parties to Pizzighetone, and as far as Parma over the Po.

The enemy intrenched himself on the Adda upon every side, determined to defend himself to the very last. Field-marshal Suwarrow resolved on the 27th to force the passage of this river.

With this intention, General Vukassowich crossed the river in the night near Brivio, by the means of a flying bridge, which had been early destroyed by the enemy, but was afterwards quickly repaired, and took, with four battalions, two squadrons, and four pieces of canon, a good position on the right bank near Brivio, sending his patroles towards Ogliate and Garlate, where they met with the enemy.

An Austrian column arrived at nine o'clock in the evening behind the village Gervasto, opposite to Trezzo, consisting of the division of Field-marshal-lieutenant Ott, as advanced guard; and that of Field-marshal-lieutenant Zoph, to support it. The captain of the pontooners, who had been previously sent forward, reported, that it was impossible to throw a bridge, owing to the declivity of the mountains and the sharp turnings of the river.

On receiving this report, the quarter-master-general, Marquis Chasseler, went to the place himself, and finding the execution of this design difficult, though not quite impossible, resolved, with the assistance of the fourth Bannat battalion, and that of the chasseurs (whose colonel volunteered the service), to have the pontoons carried down by men, and to attempt to re-establish the bridge.

Between twelve at night and five in the morning all the pontoons and beams were fortunately brought down, and at half past five the bridge was completed. Thirty chasseurs of the corps of Asper, and fifty volunteers of Nadasty, were carried over in a boat to the opposite side, and remained at the foot of the rugged mountain on which the castle of Trezzo is built, without making the least noise.

The bridges being finished, Major Retzer, with six companies of the above-mentioned chasseurs, and one regiment of Russian Cossacks, crossed the Adda: one battalion of Nadasty, two of Esterhazy, and the fourth Bannat battalion, then passed the river, under the command of Colonel Bideskuti, and fell upon the enemy in and behind Trezzo.

The French, who considered the building of this bridge impossible, had not the least notice thereof. The above brigade was followed by the seventh hussars and two Cossack regiments. The enemy was driven back as far as Pozzo, where Field-marshal-lieutenant Ott, whose whole division crossed the river, fell upon that of the enemy, commanded by General Grenier, which was on the point of advancing against General Vukassowich at Brivio.

The battle was very obstinate; the enemy took post between Pozzo and Brivio, where it was most vigorously attacked. On this occasion, the brave Colonel Bideskuti was wounded in the head.

The enemy, who in the mean time had drawn reinforcements from Victor's division, was on the point of turning our right wing, and the first battalion had already begun to give way, when General Chasseler led up the two grenadier battalions Pers and Stentoch, which formed the head of Field-marshal-lieutenant Zoph's division, just then coming up against the enemy.

The battalion Pers, having attacked in front, suffered considerably; and the Stentoch battalion, with two squadrons of hussars, of Archduke Joseph's regiment, under the command of Captain Kirchner, led

VOL. VIII. B 6 on

on by Lieutenant Bokarme of the engineers (to the found of military mufic), fell on the enemy's left flank, which was totally routed; and the huffars, having broken through the French, made 300 prifoners, and cut 200 to pieces.

The village Pozzo was carried fword in hand. The enemy in the mean time had received reinforcements, and marched his troops up in order in the road that leads from Baprio to Milan, but was again attacked, and Major Retzer, with the Nadafty battalion, took Baprio, and made 200 prifoners.

The enemy was purfued; and near Gergonzollo the French General Beker and 30 wounded officers were taken prifoners.

At the fame time General Melas marched againft Caffano, and battered the intrenchments acrofs the Ritorto canal with twelve-pounders and howitzers; and, as the French fell back, caufed a flying brid'ge to be thrown over the canal di Ritorto. Firft lieutenant of the pioneers, Count Kinfki, completed it in fpite of the heavy fire of the enemy. General Melas immediately ordered the Reifky's regiment againft the intrenchments which covered the bridge, which, with three cannons, was carried with fo much rapidity, that the bridge, which had been fet on fire by the French, was faved by our troops.

General Melas croffed, with his whole column, the Adda; and the fame evening marched to Gergonzollo, and the next day early (28th) to Milan.

The two divifions Frolich and Ott advanced to Milan on the 28th; the right, under General Rozemberg, paffed the Adda at Brivio on the 27th; but General Vukaffowich, who had already paffed the river, formed the advanced guard, met with a divifion of French under General Serrurier at Bertero, which, after a moft obftinate engagement, was beaten, and forced to capitulate. The whole corps laid down its arms, the officers were permitted to return to France on their parole, and the privates remained prifoners of war.

After this affair, General Vukaffowich marched to Corno, and the Ruffians to the right of Milan.

In Milan confiderable magazines of clothing, arms, and provifions were found, of which an inventory is now making. A general with 500 men were alfo taken prifoners here.

The lofs of the enemy, as far as could be afcertained when the meifenger left the army, amounted to four generals and upwards of 5000 men taken prifoners, and 6000 killed. Eighty pieces of cannon were taken, of which 46 are heavy befieging artillery; feveral ftandards were alfo taken.

Field-marfhal Suwarrow, after having given due praife to the Auftrian and Ruffian troops who fignalized themfelves on this important occafion, paffes the higheft enconiums on the following officers:

General of cavalry Melas, Field-marfhal-lieutenant Ott, Major-general Vukaffowich, Colonel Knefevich of Archduke Jofeph's huffars, Colonel d'Afpre of the chaffeurs, Colonel Bidefkuti, Captain Count Reipperg, and efpecially Captain Kirchner, who, though his battalion was but weak, forced his way with the bayonet through the enemy; Captains Meffieri, Rothfchuz, the laft of whom received two wounds; Lieutenants Count Bokarme, of the engineers, and Habinay, of Nadafty; as alfo the fecond lieutenant Rittko, of the fame regiment.

But

Field-marshal Suwarrow principally praises the discernment and [servi]ce of Quarter-master-general Marquis Chasteller; as also Lieutenant-[C]olonel Thelen, his aid-de-camp.

[Wit]h regard to the Russian troops, the Field-marshal Suwarrow part[icular]ly commends General Prince Kozakow, Colonel Laborow, Ma[j]or [R]omanzow and Rosan, and Captain Stalerakow.

[The] articles of capitulation granted to General Serrurier and his divi[sion w]ill be added in our next.

[Fiel]d-marshal Suwarrow has left Field-marshal Kray, with a sufficient [force] in the environs of Mantua and Peschiera. Mantua is block[ed a]nd Peschiera besieged.

From the LONDON GAZETTE, May 25, 1799.

Admiralty Office, May 25.

[Copy of] a Letter from Sir Hyde Parker, Knt. Commander in Chief of his [Maj]esty's Ships and Vessels at Jamaica, to Evan Nepean, Esq. dated [on b]oard the Queen, Port Royal Harbour, the 15th of April.

S[ir,]

[CA]PTAIN Otway, of his Majesty's ship Trent, having acquainted [me b]y his letter of the 30th of last month, with his having succeeded [in cutt]ing out a ship and schooner then lying in a small bay to the north[ward] of Cape Roxo, under the protection of a five-gun battery, I have [the ho]nour to enclose herewith a copy of the said letter, for the inform[ation] of the Right Honourable the Lords Commissioners of the Ad[miralt]y; and am to desire you will be pleased to communicate the [same] to their Lordships; and further acquaint them, that, since my [last of] the 10th of February, the squadron under my command have [taken] or destroyed eight armed vessels, and 67 merchant vessels of every [descrip]tion, as per enclosed list. I likewise enclose a copy of a letter [from] Captain Vesey, of the Amaranthe, for their Lordships' information.

I am, Sir, &c.
H. PARKER.

Trent, at Anchor off the west End of Porto Rico, March 30.

S[ir,]

[I H]AVE the honour to inform you, that having discovered a Spa[nish sh]ip and three schooners in a small bay about seven leagues to the [lee]ward of Cape Roxo, I sent the boats under the command of [Lieute]nants Belchier and Balderston, and covered them with the Spar[row c]utter; the vessels being in shoal water, close in shore, and under [the pro]tection of a five-gun battery.

[Lieu]tenant M'Gee, with his party of marines, were landed, and [the] seamen, under the orders of Lieutenant Belchier, who imme[diately] stormed the battery, bayonetted five, and wounded several, and [fin]ally destroyed the guns, &c.

[The] ship and schooner were, in the mean time, boarded, and brought [off by] the boats; the other two schooners were scuttled by the enemy. [Great] praise is due to Lieutenant Wylie, for his spirited conduct in the [Sparr]ow, as likewise the officers and men of his Majesty's ship em[ployed] on this service.

I am

I am happy to add, only two seamen and one corporal were wounded on the occasion.

R. W. OTWAY.

A Lift of armed Veffels captured and deftroyed by his Majefty's Squadron under my Command, fince the 12th February.

By the Maidftone—A French fchooner privateer, of 10 guns and 79 men. Taken.

By the Aquilon—A French fchooner, pierced for 16 guns, eight mounted, coppered, with a cargo of coffee for Europe. Taken.

By the Surprife—A French fchooner privateer, of five guns (pierced for 10), and 60 men; named La Lione. Taken.

By La Prompte—The Urea Caraodora, a Spanifh fhip, of 1300 tons burden; commanded by a lieutenant, pierced for 26 guns, mounting 12 fix-pounders, copper fheathed, quite new: loaded with fhip timber for the navy yard at Havannah. Set fire to, and burnt near the Matanzas.

By the Rattler—A French fhip, pierced for 16 guns, 10 mounted, and 42 men. Taken.

By the Lark—A French fchooner privateer, captured. A Spanifh latine veffel, of one fix-pounder and two fwivels. Taken.

By L'Amaranthe—Le Vengeur French fchooner privateer, of fix guns and 50 men. Taken.

H. PARKER.

A Lift of Merchant Veffels captured and deftroyed by the Squadron under my Command, fince the 12th of February.

By the Queen—1 taken.
By the Hannibal—2 taken.
By the Thunderer—2 taken.
By the Renommée—1 taken.
By the Trent and Sparrow—4 taken, 2 deftroyed.
By the Maidftone—2 taken.
By the Aquilon—5 taken.
By the Alarm—1 taken.
By the Surprife—6 taken.
By the Squirrel—5 taken, 1 deftroyed.
By the Jamaica—2 taken.
By the Carnatic, Maidftone, and Greyhound—4 taken.
By the Regulus and Swallow—1 taken.
By the Swallow—1 taken.
By the Diligence—7 taken.
By the Lark—7 taken.
By the Rattler—3 taken.
By the Pelican—4 taken.
By La Legere and Pelican—1 taken.
By the Albicore—1 taken.
By the Serpent—1 taken.
By the Merlin—1 taken.
By L'Amaranthe—2 taken.
Total—64 taken, 3 deftroyed.

H. PARKER.

Sir,

L'Amaranthe, at Sea, east End of Jamaica bearing
Sir, *S. S. W. 25 Leagues, six P. M. April 13.*

I HAVE the pleasure to inform you, that I this day captured Le Vengeur French schooner letter of marque, mounting six four-pounders, after a long chase S. W. and a brave resistance of an hour and eight minutes, nearly within pistol-shot; in which his Majesty's sloop under my command had one quarter-master killed and three seamen slightly wounded. By the best account I can get, she had 36 men on board, including passengers; of whom 14 were killed outright, and five wounded, one of whom is just dead, and another not likely to live.— She was from St. Jago de Cuba, bound to Jeremie, with a cargo of flour; is a very fine copper-bottomed schooner, capable of mounting 10 carriage-guns, nearly new, and sails uncommonly fast; and was a privateer last cruise.

F. VESEY.

Samuel Miles, quarter-master, killed.
Joseph White, Piers Johns, George Montgomery, wounded.
Sir Hyde Parker, &c. &c. &c.

Admiralty Office, May 25.

Copy of a Letter from Captain Charles Wollaston, Commander of his Majesty's Sloop Cruiser, to Evan Nepean, Esq. dated at Yarmouth the 23d instant.

I BEG leave to acquaint you, for the information of my Lords Commissioners of the Admiralty, that, St. Abb's Head bearing north, on the 21st instant, at eleven A. M. I discovered two luggers to the southward, to which I gave chase, but the weather being very unsettled and hazy, I could only discern them at times, they being well to windward, and finding in the intervals of clear, that we headed them fast, I took the advantage of tacking, and had the satisfaction of seeing them nearly abreast when the weather cleared up; and about half past four P. M. were nearly within gunshot of them, when a sudden gust of wind from off the shore carried away our fore-topmast, and with it the main topgallant-mast: this obliged me to bring to for some time, to clear the wreck, which being accomplished, I made what sail I could, and was thereby enabled to keep sight of them until nine P. M. when finding they steered a course directly along the shore, I continued standing to the southward all night, having during the night got up another topmast, and refitted the ship.—At daylight in the morning, Scarborough Castle bearing W. half N. three leagues, I discovered one of them about eight miles to leeward, to which I gave chase, and after a chase of six hours captured her. She proved to be the Deux Freres, Captain Jacques Bellet, of 14 guns (twelve of which she threw overboard during the chase), and 50 men, belonging to Calais; sailed from thence on the 16th of April last, and has been cruising ever since. The lugger (the captain informs me) in company with him the day before, was the Tippoo Saib, of 12 guns, and having thrown all her guns, boat, &c. overboard, during the chase, has gone either to France or Norway. Having 26 men away in prizes, and 50 prisoners on board, I judged proper to come into this port, the
wind

wind being northerly, to land the prisoners, and shall as soon as possible repair to my station.

CHARLES WOLLASTON.

From the LONDON GAZETTE EXTRAORDINARY, May 25, 1799.

Downing Street, May 25.

DISPATCHES, of which the following are extracts, have been received from the Right Hon. Sir Morton Eden, K. B. and from Lieutenant-colonel Robert Craufurd, by the Right Hon. Lord Grenville, his Majesty's principal Secretary of State for the foreign department.

Vienna, May 8.

I HAVE the honour of enclosing to your Lordship the Gazette of this place of this evening, containing the capitulation of General Serrurier.

Terms of Capitulation proposed by Serrurier, General of Division, commanding a Corps in the Service of the French Republic, to General Vukassowich, of his Imperial Majesty's Service.

Proposals.

ALL the French and Piedmontese troops stationed at Verderio give themselves up as prisoners of war, on the following conditions.

Answ. Agreed.

Art. I. All generals, staff-officers, and field-officers, shall keep their swords, horses, and baggage. The French and Piedmontese soldiers, both cavalry and infantry, to retain their baggage also.

Answ. Agreed.

Art. II. On both sides, in the usual order, an exchange shall first take place at the army.

Answ. Agreed.

Art. III. Until a general exchange of prisoners takes place, an immediate exchange of those on the spot, in possession of each army, shall be made.

Answer. Disallowed.

Art. IV. The remaining French, subject to this capitulation, shall continue prisoners of war. The generals, staff and field-officers, both French and Piedmontese, shall be allowed to return to France and Piedmont, on their parole, not to serve against his Majesty the Emperor and King, or his allies, until regularly exchanged.

Answ. Agreed.

Art. V. The same indulgence as contained in the foregoing article shall be granted to the non-commissioned officers and soldiers of cavalry who remain prisoners.

Answ. Disallowed.

(Signed) SERRURIER.

Verderio, the 9th Floreal, 7th year of the Republic, 28th April 1799.

Observation

Observation.

General Vukassovich promises, that the soldiers, prisoners of war, shall not be sent back further than the ex-Venetian states, until such time as General Serrurier shall have arranged with his government the means of exchanging the same numbers, rank for rank, and man for man.

Vienna, May 11.

A MESSENGER arrived this morning, with letters from Marshal Suwarrow, of the 4th instant, from an obscure village near Cremona, and with the colours taken at Peschiera*.

The Marshal states, that the enemy is flying on all sides, without daring to make head against him; that the Austrians are in possession of Novara on one side, and of Pavia, whither the head-quarters were to be transferred that evening, and the castle of Placentia on the other; that Vercelli is abandoned; that on the 7th he proposed to batter Pizighetone; that a detachment had been at Modena, which they found evacuated by the enemy; that 400 Croats and a numerous body of peasants closely blockaded Ferrara; that preparations were making for forming and pushing with vigour the siege of Mantua; that great quantities of cannon, ammunition, and other stores, had been taken at different places, particularly at Peschiera, where the booty far exceeded all expectation; that the inhabitants of the different countries showed the utmost gratitude for their deliverance; that the Piedmontese officers who have been taken, are, under the auspices of the Marshal, drawing up a proclamation, inviting their brother officers and soldiers to rise and join them, for the purpose of assisting in the re-establishment of their sovereign on the throne.

Extract of a Dispatch from Lieutenant-colonel Craufurd to Lord Grenville, dated Lindau, the 10th instant.

PART of General Bellegarde's army has advanced from the Upper Engadine, in the direction towards Coire, and has passed the Albula. The French, who were in the Upper Engadine, have retired towards the Splugen. It is reported that there has been a considerable insurrection of the inhabitants of the Upper Valais and Uri; but the particulars are not known.

From the LONDON GAZETTE, May 28, 1799.

Admiralty Office, May 28.

Copy of a Letter from Vice-admiral Lutwidge, Commander in Chief of his Majesty's Ships and Vessels in the Downs, to Evan Nepean, Esq. dated the 26th instant.

Sir,

ENCLOSED herewith is a letter I have received from Lieutenant Richard Young, commanding his Majesty's hired armed cutter Ann, stating his having captured L'Aimable Therese, a small French lugger

---

* A dispatch of a preceding date, supposed to contain the details of the taking of Peschiera, is not yet arrived.

privateer,

privateer, carrying four carriage-guns and 27 men, which letter you will be pleased to lay before their Lordships.
I am, Sir, &c. &c.
SKEFF. LUTWIDGE.

Sir, *Downs, May 26.*
IN obedience to your orders of the 23d inſtant, I proceeded with his Majeſty's hired armed cutter Ann, under my command, for the protection of the fiſhery off Folkeſtone. I laſt night weighed with five boats; at eight P. M. ſaw a lugger, and gave chaſe: after a running fight of two hours, I came up with and captured her. She proves to be L'Aimable Thereſe, of four carriage-guns and 27 men.
I am, Sir, &c. &c.
R. YOUNG.

Extract of a Letter from Admiral the Earl of St. Vincent, Commander in Chief of his Majeſty's Ships and Veſſels in the Mediterranean, to Evan Nepean, Eſq. dated Gibraltar, March 8.

HEREWITH I tranſmit you a letter from Lieutenant George Miller, late acting commander of his Majeſty's ſloop Transfer, giving an account of the capture of a ſmall French privateer.
I am, &c. &c.
ST. VINCENT.

My Lord, *Transfer, at Sea, Feb. 13.*
I HAVE the ſatisfaction to inform your Lordſhip, that on the 11th inſtant I captured, off Avamonte, the French privateer L'Eſcamotaur, carrying three ſix-pounders and 34 men.
I have the honour to be, &c. &c.
(Signed) GEORGE MILLER.
Right Hon. Lord Keith, &c.

From the LONDON GAZETTE EXTRAORDINARY, May 30, 1799.

Downing Street, May 30.
DISPATCHES, of which the following are copies and extracts, have been received from the Right Honourable Sir Morton Eden, K. B. and Lieutenant-colonel Robert Craufurd, by the Right Honourable Lord Grenville, his Majeſty's principal Secretary of State for the foreign department.

Extract of a Letter from Sir Morton Eden, K B. dated Vienna, May 11.

IT is with the greateſt ſatisfaction that I inform your Lordſhip of the ſurrender of the fortreſs of Peſchiera, by capitulation, on the 6th inſtant, to General Kray, an event which will greatly facilitate the further operations in Italy.
I have the honour of encloſing the Extraordinary Gazette publiſhed on the occaſion, and an Extraordinary Gazette of Wedneſday laſt, containing

containing an account of the operations of the army under General Bellegarde, of the loss sustained by the army of Italy in the different engagements on the Adda, and of the great joy with which the army was received at Milan.

Accounts from Brindisi state, that on the 15th the French troops, in consequence of orders brought to them over-land, evacuated the place, and with such precipitation, as to leave both their magazines and booty.

Supplement to the Vienna Court Gazette, May 11.

THE first lieutenant of artillery, Wopaterny, sent as courier from General Baron Kray, who was left behind by Field-marshal Count Suwarrow, brought the agreeable intelligence, that, on the 5th instant, when every thing was ready to open the trenches, and to bombard Peschiera, he offered at the same time a capitulation to the garrison, which, according to the enemy's reports, consisted of 1500 men, by which they are permitted to march out, on promising not to serve against us for six months.

The serious preparations of siege, and the artillery already produced to bombard the place, dismayed the enemy, and induced them to accept of the capitulation offered, and to surrender the fortress immediately to our troops, with all the artillery, military stores, and provisions.

As far as General Kray now mentions, the artillery of the fortress consists of 90 pieces of cannon and mortars; at the same time 18 gunboats, with every thing belonging to them, a large quantity of military stores, and considerable quantities of provisions, fell into our hands.

On the 6th, early in the morning, General Kray ordered a company to occupy one gate of the fortress, and made the Imperial officers take a list and inventory of all the magazines, which will be reported hereafter.

General Kray praises the restless activity with which General Count St. Julien conducted all the operations of siege, as well as the zealous co-operation of the lieutenant-colonel of engineers, Danno, and the major of artillery, Gillet, with all the officers belonging to the besieging army.

General Kray thought it a very happy circumstance that, at the moment when he summoned the garrison, and forced them to capitulate, his Imperial Highness the Grand Duke Constantine arrived there, to remain till the garrison shall march out, when he intends to continue his journey to the head-quarters of Field-marshal Count Suwarrow.

Capitulation of Peschiera, concluded between the Imperial General Count St. Julien and the French Adjutant-general Coutheaux, May 6.

Art. I. The garrison, and all belonging to the French army, shall march out with all the honours of war.

Answ. Granted; but such of the troops as are not Frenchmen shall freely return home.

Art. II. The garrison will evacuate the place as soon as possible, after signing the capitulation; it will march out with arms and baggage, music playing, matches lighted, colours flying, and four pieces of cannon, to go under proper escort to the next post of the French army.

Answ.

Anfw. Granted: the garrifon fhall march out at eight o'clock to-morrow morning by the Brefcia gate, lay down arms, and take the fhorteft road to the firft pofts of the French army; it fhall oblige itfelf not to ferve againft his Majefty the Emperor or King, nor his allies, for fix months after the prefent capitulation. The gate of Verona is immediately to be opened to the Imperial troops, and at two o'clock in the afternoon the garrifon of Pefchiera is to quit that part of the place fituated on the left bank of the Mincio.

Art. III. The fick who cannot be conveniently removed fhall remain in the hofpital till their entire recovery; they fhall afterwards experience the treatment ftipulated in the preceding article, and the neceffary number of carriages is to be granted for the conveyance of thofe that are unable to reach their deftination.

Anfw. Granted.

Art. IV. All the officers and other perfons employed in the French army are to take with them their baggage, carriages, horfes, and other effects belonging to them.

Anfw. Granted, according to the general tenour of the capitulation.

Art. V. All thofe effects are not to be fearched, and waggons are to be provided for the removal of fuch as want them.

Anfw. Granted, under the reftriction in the foregoing article.

Art. VI. The inhabitants are never and no wife to be called to an account either for ferving in the French army, or owing to their political and religious opinions and principles.

Anfw. This article, being not of a military nature, muft be referred to the government.

Art. VII. Should any objections be made hereafter refpecting the prefent articles between his Imperial Majefty and the French republic, they are to be decided according to the rules of juftice.

Anfw. One may depend, in this refpect, upon the well-known honour, integrity, and love of juftice of the Auftrian army.

Art. VIII. The Auftrian government fhall alone guarantee the ftrict execution of thefe articles of capitulation.

Anfw. Well underftood.

Additional article. All the plans, military ftores, artillery, naval ftores, and all the provifions of every kind, belonging to the French nation, fhall be faithfully delivered up.

Concluded on the walls of Pefchiera, 17th Floreal (May 6th), 1799.

(Signed) COUNT ST. JULIEN,   COUTHEAUX,
Imperial Maj. Gen.   Adjut. Gen.

Accepted.   BARON KRAY,
General of Artillery.

Firft Supplement Extraordinary to the Vienna Court Gazette, May 8.

Vienna, May 8.

FIELD-Marfhal Count Bellegarde has forwarded, by Lieutenant Dietrich, the preliminary details of the offenfive operations of the army under his orders, from the 30th of April till the 3d of May.

The weather having become a little more favourable towards the laft
days

days of April, and the passes more practicable, Field-marshal Count Bellegarde determined to execute, without delay, the plan of attack which he had prepared. It was made on the 30th of April, in two columns, and several detachments. The first, being the principal one, was commanded by the Field-marshal Count Bellegarde, and the second by the Field-marshal Haddick. Each of those columns was supported in its operations by detachments, which sometimes attacked and at other times only made demonstrations.

The first column penetrated from Nauders into the Engadine. It was necessary to pass the Inn at several fords, which the troops, notwithstanding the extreme cold, performed with the greatest willingness: several were lost by the rapidity of the current.

As soon as the signal for attack was given, all the advanced posts of the enemy were attacked at the same time by the first column, and by the detachments which had taken the roads leading to the Lower and Upper Lovellen: the greatest part of them were killed, and the rest put to flight. The reserved posts of the enemy, however, availing themselves of the advantage of the ground, disputed every inch.

From Strada to Ramiss, the first column and the detachments were obliged to climb the most impracticable mountains, fighting at the same time, in order to drive the enemy from several advantageous positions.

Towards twelve o'clock this column arrived before Ramiss; the enemy was driven from the heights which command the valley of Ramiss, from the village itself, as far as the intrenched position behind Ramiss.

This position, naturally very advantageous, was rendered still more so by the works which the enemy had raised on the front and right flank.

The most decisive attack against this intrenched position was made upon its left wing on the side of Manas.

Field-marshal-lieutenant Bellegarde had ordered a particular column to penetrate from Isyi and Spils by the mountains as far as Schleims and Manas, and afterwards to pass the rivulet of Ramiss above Manas. This column had, from the place at which it was formed, already made some extremely painful marches over the steepest mountains; so that, in advancing from Manas by the valley, full of ravines, the soldiers had almost exhausted their strength.

On that side the enemy had secured themselves by three intrenchments, placed one before the other, which could only be reached by a very narrow path. That column, however, in spite of the exhausted state of the soldiers, carried two of those intrenchments; but by the obstinate resistance of the enemy, and their own extreme fatigue, they could not reach the third.

It was the intention of Field-marshal Bellegarde, that an attack should be made upon the intrenchments on the enemy's right flank, as soon as this column had reached his left.

The troops destined for this assault advanced to the intrenchment thick set with palisadoes, and in spite of a very brisk fire of artillery and musketry, climbed up the steep height upon which the intrenchment was made. They forced the palisadoes; but their fatigue did not suffer them to penetrate as far as the intrenchment. In the constant hope of being able to drive the enemy out of this intrenchment, who had already several times given way, but who, with forces repeatedly renewed,

renewed, defended themselves behind their parapet with obstinacy, the attacking division sustained itself for a long time at a few paces from the ditch, without either side losing an inch of ground.

Night came on, and Field-marshal Bellegarde was obliged to defer till next day the assault of the camp.

During that time, Field-marshal Haddick had succeeded in penetrating with his column over the top of the Scharl, and into the valley as far as the bridge near Schius. Count Bellegarde had relied upon his success. The enemy could no longer maintain themselves in their position behind the rivulet of Ramiss, and the less so, as the column of Field-marshal Bellegarde had got behind their right wing.

The column of Count Haddick, from its point of formation until that of the attack, had to make a very difficult stage of ten hours over the steepest mountains covered with snow; he made his troops take some hours repose upon the summit of one of them; but only being able to allow a few fires, they necessarily suffered from the extreme cold.

About four o'clock in the morning, the advanced guard, commanded by Colonel Rousseau, attacked the advanced posts of the enemy. They were immediately driven away. The troop of reserve of the enemy maintained themselves in their post near the village Scharl; they did not yield till after an obstinate battle of an hour, during which we took several prisoners.

The column pushed before them the defeated divisions of the enemy, under a continual fire, till half past one o'clock: but the advanced guard found themselves unexpectedly before a position which was strongly fortified both by nature and art, the front of which could only be reached by a narrow path, and all the attempts of Colonel Rousseau to penetrate to it were rendered fruitless by the vigorous resistance of the enemy.

At length, the Colonel detached some companies, under the command of the first Lieutenant Giwchak, which, by taking a very long by-road through an abatis, got beyond the intrenchments of the left flank of the enemy, and as they could from the top of a hill distress the right flank, more energy could be employed in attacking the front: in this manner, the enemy was soon forced to abandon this position with a considerable loss. The column pushed forward, but met with an almost insurmountable obstacle. The only way by which it could pass was a narrow hollow path, on the declivity of a rock, which was entirely exposed to the fire from the enemy's intrenchments.

Field-marshal-lieutenant Haddick, finding it impossible to approach the enemy in front, determined to attack their intrenchments in the rear, from a height which appeared almost inaccessible, and to dislodge them from their position by an attempt which they by no means expected. The chief Chasseur Mathieu, of the corps of Le Loup, with some other Chasseurs, and Captain Enyeter, with a company and an half of the regiment of Antoine Esterhazi, were charged with this enterprise, who, by means of cramp-irons, scaled the highest summit of the mountain undiscovered by the enemy; and while their attention was engaged by our cannonade from the mountains in their front, the whole detachment, headed by Captain Enyeter, gained their intrenchments, by descending a frozen ravine in their rear.

This

This bold attempt totally disconcerted the enemy, and gave our advanced guard time and opportunity to penetrate by the narrow path in their front. The intrenchments being carried by assault, the enemy took a new position further back; but they were attacked, and dislodged from it with great loss. To cover their retreat, they destroyed a wooden bridge, which could not be repaired in less than an hour and a half.

The Field-marshal-lieutenant Haddick pushed on, by a forced march, as far as Schlus; but he was forced to halt upon the heights of the right bank of the Inn near Schlus, as his troops, exhausted by a twenty-four hours march, were unable to make another attack, the bridge over the Inn near Schlus being destroyed, and the only fordable passage being commanded by the enemy's batteries.

The remaining detachments on the left, commanded by Lieutenant-colonel Count Veissenwolf, of the regiment of Michael Wallis, was destined to alarm the enemy in the valley of Tschiffer, and to keep them at Czernitz. This division was also compelled to make a very long and difficult march to arrive at the point of attack. His advanced guard soon drove in all the enemy's outposts to their reserve, which was posted behind an abatis, and for some time there was only a partial discharge of musketry. The enemy, however, being reinforced, attacked our advanced guard, but were repulsed. About noon, the enemy made a sortie from their abatis in greater force, and renewed the attack: our advanced guard was driven back upon the reserve, and were obliged to retire by the narrow path already described, as they could not advance against the enemy on account of the snow being no longer strong enough to bear them. Part of the rear-guard fell into the enemy's hands.

The first column has made several officers (among whom are a chef de brigade) and some soldiers prisoners; one cannon and several waggons loaded with powder fell into our hands.

The column of Field-marshal-lieutenant Haddick has also made some prisoners.

On the 1st of May, at daybreak, the vanguard advanced as far as Fottan, and the first column joined the second between Schlus and Fottan.

The posts of the enemy were between Garda and Lavin. On account of the great fatigues of the preceding days, the troops were not able to proceed farther than to the lofty and steep heights of Fottan.

On the 2d of May the reunited columns marched from Fottan towards Lavin, and took post on the high road. A small column, under the orders of Colonel Zeegradt, of the regiment of Beaulieu, marched towards the right bank of the Inn in the same direction as the first column.

The enemy having destroyed the bridge near the Lower Garda, and it being indispensably necessary to have a bridge of communication, a small bridge was constructed there, which could not be completed in less than four hours. In the mean while the position of the enemy was reconnoitred, and the disposition for attack made. While they were doing this, Field-marshal lieutenant Bellegarde placed the vanguard before Garda and the main body behind the village. The vanguard, as well as the column where Field-marshal-lieutenant Bellegarde was in person, advanced under the orders of Field-marshal-lieutenant Haddick,

dick, upon the high road which leads to Cus. The division of Colonel Zeegradt, reinforced by two battalions, made a column apart under the orders of General Count Robilt, who was to march upon the right bank of the Inn in the same direction as the principal columns.

The two columns marched directly to Lavin, and forced the enemy's advanced guards to retire as fast as possible. The village of Lavin was carried by the advanced guard; but the enemy having reassembled behind the village, another obstinate engagement took place, which however ended to our advantage, by means of the divisions sent to the mountains to take the enemy in flank.

As the ground behind Lavin was proper for cavalry manoeuvres, a detachment of hussars, of the regiment of Erdsby, was sent forward, to follow the enemy's infantry, which was flying into the plain. On this occasion Demont, a brigadier-general of the enemy, was taken prisoner.

Our army was obliged to open a way among impracticable mountains, and obstructed by continual attacks, finding every where the most obstinate resistance; but as the enemy, whatever position they took, found themselves threatened on both their flanks, they did not stay either in the village of Cus, or in the valley of Floda.

The village was taken by the advanced guard of Field-marshal-lieutenant Haddick, and at the same time the heights which command it were taken possession of, where the enemy had rallied with its corps-de-reserve. A very brisk fire was kept up on both sides, and on a sudden the enemy fell rapidly on the village, but was repulsed by the Gorchen regiment of grenadiers and the third regiment of Antoine Esterhazi.

Field-marshal Bellegarde, at the moment that the grenadiers made their attack with the bayonet, advanced his columns to the two banks of the Inn, where they fell upon the enemy with so much bravery as to oblige them to fly in the utmost disorder to Czernetz.

The general of division of the enemy La Courbe was wounded in the arm, in his retreat. The rear-guard of the French did not immediately abandon Czernetz, but retreated during the night; and their last posts retreated in the morning of the 3d of May towards the Upper Engadine. They set fire to the bridges near Czernetz, but only the lower bridge was destroyed.

Our loss in the two engagements of the 20th of April and 3d of May is considerable, of which Lieutenant-general Bellegarde intends soon to transmit an exact account.

Second Supplement Extraordinary to the Vienna Court Gazette, May 8. The Account of Field-marshal Suwarrow, relative to the forcing of the Passage of the Adda, and the taking of Milan.

THE general of cavalry Melas, in a particular account, describes the general satisfaction expressed at the arrival of our troops in that city. The Archbishop and his suite, with all the nobility, met the army at Cresenzago, and delivered the keys of the city, but could not find language expressive of their respect and affection for his Majesty, and of their joy at the recovery of their religion and their ancient constitution.

From that place as far as the town, which is at three miles distance, the e army was accompanied by the people. The continued cries of "Long live our religion and Francis the Second!" were so power-l, that even Turkish music, which is heard in the midst of battle, uld not be distinguished. In the evening a general illumination took ace. It was almost impossible to pass through the streets; yet, not-ithstanding the general confusion, the military force was not employed, r was there a single excess committed; so pure and so sincere was the y of the people.

Our loss in the different engagements in which we were concerned the Adda amounts to 240 men and 105 horses killed; 368 men and 50 horses wounded; 307 men and 28 horses missing: in the whole, 21 men and 283 horses.

I HAVE the honour of enclosing to your Lordship the Extraordinary azette published on Monday last.

Vienna, May 13.

THE first lieutenant Eck brought yesterday to his Majesty, from eld-marshal Suwarrow, the intelligence of 14 standards having been ken from the enemy in the late engagements. The Field-marshal had oved with his army from Milan to Pavia, leaving 4000 men under e command of General Latterman to blockade the citadel of Milan, d to support other operations. On the departure of the courier, he d advanced beyond Pavia.

The enemy had left in Pavia 12 pieces of cannon, of different sizes, cases full of muskets for infantry, and a great many barrels of wder, with ammunition for the infantry and cavalry.

General Bukassowich found at Novara 16 pieces of cannon, four ortars, 250 casks of cartridges, 15 barrels of case-shot, and several her military effects.

The enemy had also been repulsed as far as the little town of Li-vrno.

Field-marshal-lieutenant Kaim being employed to take possession of zzighetone, had regulated his dispositions in such manner as to en-re an attack upon that place at seven o'clock in the morning. In nsequence of which, three sixteen-pounders taken from the enemy, twelve-pounders, 10 howitzers, and a part of the Russian artillery, ere sent to him.

Field-marshal Kray, availing himself of the passage of the courier, rwarded the farther particulars of the surrender of Peschiera, by hich he informs us, that, owing to the capitulation, the garrison, of 500 men, had quitted the town in the morning on the 6th; that e number of cannons and mortars, according to the inventory, ounted to 100; that, instead of only 16 sloops of war, there were nnd 19 completely equipped.

General Kray, of the artillery, advanced, on the 6th, towards Man-a, in order to besiege that town, and to possess himself of the Po, that the provisions destined for our army, which moves on but wly, should not in any way be intercepted.

General-major Klenau makes very considerable incursions beyond the and in the neighbourhood of Regio, Modena, and Cento; besides ich, Captain Buday, who is in front of Modena, announces, that the 4th, in the afternoon, he had sent a detachment forward, in er to disarm those people whom the enemy had armed in order to defend

defend the town; that having entered the town, he immediately detached thirty huffars from Fort Orbano, as far as the river Panaro, within three miles of Modena. The fame day, at eight o'clock in the morning, 150 Cifalpines were gone from thence; and their retreat was fo hafty, that they left behind them a confiderable quantity of provifions; 50 barrels of powder were left in the citadel. The above-mentioned captain, having learnt that there were at Svilambetto (which is about nine miles from Modena) 90 quintals of powder, a quantity of faltpetre, and other articles of ammunition, had them all conveyed to a place of fafety, during the night, by a patrole that he had difpatched thither. A Cifalpine captain, who could not efcape the day before, was made prifoner at five o'clock in the morning by Captain Buday, who has fent him to Sachetta.

Our troops were received by the inhabitants with the moft lively joy, and their eagerneſs to fee us was fo great, that the army could fcarcely advance; the enthufiafm of fome carried them fo far as even to kifs our horfes. Captain Buday alfo fays, that from the reports of feveral of the peafants that came there, he learnt that the Tufcan territories had been moſt ſhamefully pillaged; that the contributions which had been exacted from them were infupportable; and that even deputies from Florence had arrived at Modena, to implore affiſtance againſt the exactions of the enemy.

His Royal Highneſs the Archduke Charles informs us, that fince the late events nothing of confequence had happened, but that the enemy moſt probably was endeavouring to engage our attention by manœuvres and continual changes in the line of his advanced pofts. In return, the patroles fent forward by Generals Gorger, Merveld, and Guilay, to make incurfions, harafs the enemy continually, do him great injury, and are perpetually making prifoners. There have alfo been two battles at Odenwald, in which the peafants have taken a part. It was near the village of Birkenau, and above and below Stainau, with the aid of the divifion commanded by the Firſt Lieutenant Goringer and the huffars of Szeekler, that the enemy was repulſed with confiderable loſs.

The huffars took 20 horfes from the enemy.

Upon the Bergſtraſſe, another party of the fame huffars took upon the Rhine, in the neighbourhood of Raſtadt, a tranfport, with 180 barrels of flour, which they conveyed to Gerfbach.

Vienna, May 16.

AN officer arrived in the night from Italy, with the news of the furrender of Pizzighetone, on the 10th, by capitulation, to General Kaim.

The intelligence brought by this officer further ftates, that a part of the Ruffian troops was already in poffeffion of the town of Tortona.

Head-quarters of Lieutenant-general Hotze, Mayenfeld, May 14.

My Lord,

I HAVE the honour to inform your Lordfhip, that this day General Hotze made a general and completely fuccefsful attack on the French corps in the Grifons country, diflodged them from all their pofitions, from Saint Lucius Steig (which is on the northern boundary) to Coire, inclufive, and took 16 pieces of cannon and 2000 prifoners. I have the honour to be, &c.

(Signed) ROB. CRAUFURD.

P. S.

S. The immediate departure of a courier from General Hotze
ents my giving, at present, any further detail.
ight Hon. Lord Grenville, &c.

Palermo, May 1.

Y accounts from the continent it appears that Salerno has been
n by Captain Hood, of his Majesty's ship Zealous, who had placed
e a garrison, composed of a detachment of marines and of loyal
bitants. The King's colours were also flying at Castel del Mare.
n the 25th of April General Macdonald left Naples for Capua,
all his troops, except 500, which were left in the Castle of St.
o.

From the LONDON GAZETTE, June 1, 1799.

Admiralty Office, June 1.

' *of a Letter from Captain John Clements to Evan Nepean, Esq.
dated Leith,* 29th May.

Sir,

OU will be pleased to inform my Lords Commissioners of the
hiralty, that La Ruse French lugger, mounting 14 guns, and car-
g 60 men, arrived here this day: she was taken on the 20th inst.
the Schaw, by his Majesty's sloop of war Kite, on her return with
bonvoy from Elsineur. I am, &c.

JOHN CLEMENTS.

From the LONDON GAZETTE, June 4, 1799.

*tract of a Letter from Sir Morton Eden to Lord Grenville, dated
May* 18.

My Lord,

HAVE the honour of enclosing an Extraordinary Gazette, publish-
n Thursday last, containing intelligence from the army of Italy.

Vienna, May 16.

IELD-marshal-lieutenant Kaim, charged by Field-marshal Suwar-
with the siege of Pizzighetone, has sent his first lieutenant, Runcle,
the particulars of the capture of that place on the 10th.
eneral Baron Sekendorff and Count Hohenzollern had previously
ounded the fortress with a small body of troops, and with the as-
nce of the inhabitants of the environs had begun to construct
ries.
n the 5th, Field-marshal-lieutenant Kaim received orders to attack
place with his division, and to push forward the siege vigorously.
he night of the 5th, and during the whole day of the 6th, they
ked with such dispatch to construct batteries, that in the night of the
some cannon were mounted.
n the 7th, before daybreak, they began to attack the fortress, and
hrow in some howitzers, the fourth of which set fire to a consi-
ble magazine of hay, straw, and wood, which continued burning all
lay.
wo hours afterwards, Field-marshal-lieutenant Kaim summoned the
els to surrender. The Governor replied, that he had orders from
oL. VIII.   D d   his

his government to defend himself, and that he could not enter into negotiation. The fire was therefore continued by our brave cannoneers with such success, that in the evening a small powder magazine blew up, several batteries dismounted, and even the embrasures demolished. In the night of the 7th, and in the morning till nine o'clock, we continued our works in such a manner that our batteries were not farther than musket-shot from the fortress.

The fire in the town, the apprehension that a quantity of powder in the casemates might catch fire, and the proximity of our batteries connected by trenches, induced the enemy's commandant to send proposals of negotiation in writing to Field-marshal-lieutenant Kaim, by one of his artillery officers.

The Field-marshal-lieutenant sent the Quarter-master-general's first lieutenant into the fortress with the following capitulation: adding, that no change whatever could be made in it. The enemy's commandant, after holding a council of war, required liberty to return with his garrison to France, and persisted in this point till ten at night: but Field-marshal-lieutenant Kaim having then informed him that he could wait no longer, the capitulation was agreed upon, and was ratified and exchanged on the morning of the 10th. The garrison, although consisting of 600 men and 30 officers, of whom two were on the staff, was commanded by a captain.

Ninety-five pieces of cannon, ammunition sufficient for a siege of six months, provisions to supply a garrison of 5000 men for fourteen months, and a great quantity of powder, were found in the place.

This siege cost us only one man killed and two wounded.

Articles of Capitulation concluded between Field-marshal-lieutenant Kaim and Captain Francis Jaquey, Commandant of the Fortress of Pizzighetone.

Art. I. The garrison shall evacuate the fortress, and shall leave the cannon, ammunition, and every thing that belongs to the civil and military administration.

II. The garrison shall march out on the 11th of May with all the honours of war, shall lay down their arms on the glacis, and be made prisoners of war. The French officers and their allies shall keep their arms, baggage, horses, and military ornaments. Every facility of transport shall be furnished them, and a proper escort through the countries occupied by the Imperial and Royal troops.

III. The garrison shall retain their effects and knapsacks. Hostages shall be mutually given. Those of the French shall remain in the fortress until every thing shall have been faithfully delivered up to the Imperial troops.

IV. Immediately on the signature of the capitulation, the gate of Cremona shall be delivered up to the Imperial and Royal troops, and the gate opposite to Geza shall be occupied by General Sekendorff, who commands at Geza.

V. The inhabitants shall not be molested for any sentiments they may have manifested during the stay of the French.

VI. The sick and wounded shall be attended by a French surgeon, and shall remain at the hospital under the protection of Austrian probity. On their recovery, they shall be sent under escort to France.

VII.

VII. The French commissaries of war, and those employed by the Cisalpine governments, shall remain in the place until all the magazine shall have been delivered over to the persons named by Field-marshal-lieutenant Kaim.

All persons not having borne arms shall be set at liberty, and conducted to the French outposts.

Concluded and signed at Regano, the 9th of May 1799.

KAIM, Field-marshal-lieutenant.
JAQUEY, Captain and Commandant.

Field-marshal-lieutenant Kaim had orders to follow the army immediately after the surrender of Pizzighetone. On the 11th he marched towards Toghera, where our army was posted when the courier departed, and from whence General Gottescheim, who commanded the advanced guard, sent out patroles to the environs of Turin.

The Russian troops, with Karaczay's regiment of dragoons, under the orders of General Dollen, have entered Tortona. The enemy, after having been driven from the town by the Russians, threw themselves into the castle, which is at some distance; but it is blockaded, as well as that of Milan.

The General of artillery Kray writes, on the 9th instant, that the garrison of Mantua, reported to be 12,000 strong, having learnt that the greater part of the force that blockaded it had marched towards Peschiera, made a general sortie; but that on the 7th he had recalled eight battalions, in consequence of the complete evacuation of that fortress. This corps was advantageously employed at Roverbella, under General Elsnitz, who defeated the enemy on every side with considerable loss, and took prisoners a captain, aid-de-camp to General Monet, a lieutenant, and 40 men.

General Kray, of the artillery, not being able to give an exact statement of his loss, on account of the extent of his posts, has deferred making any return for the present.

Our army distinguished itself very much in resisting this sally, particularly in the commencement, when the enemy, infinitely superior in strength, had considerably advanced, and discharged a brisk fire of artillery.

A secretary of General Monet, and a trumpeter, were taken prisoners. The Field-marshal-lieutenant Kray sent them both to Mantua, after delivering to them a copy of the capitulation of Peschiera. At the same time he signified to the garrison, that the cannonade which they had conceived to be a signal from the French army, and which had induced them to make this sally, was in reality the bombardment of Pizzighetone, of which the garrison might convince themselves by sending one of their officers to the very spot.

According to a report from the Archduke Charles, the enemy had attacked on the 9th current the advanced posts of General Merveli, between Biberach and Gegenbach, and had taken some hostages from the latter place, on his retreat.

On the following day the enemy renewed his attack with more energy, and made our front posts rather give way, but retired to his former position.

All the rest of the enemy's line remained perfectly quiet.

Extract of a Letter from Sir Morton Eden to Lord Grenville, dated Vienna, Saturday, May 18.

A COURIER arrived this morning from Marſhal Suwarrow with accounts of the further progreſs of the army under his command. The head-quarters were, on the 13th inſtant, at Tortona, the citadel of which had only an inconſiderable garriſon.

General Moreau had collected all the French troops which had been ſcattered through Piedmont, and was encamped near to Alexandria with about 17,000 men. The Imperial troops occupied Verçelli on the ſide of Arona on the ſouthern extremity of the Lago Maggiore, and Jurea on the Dora Baltea. The advanced poſts were at Chivaſſo, near Turin; and the inhabitants of that part of the country had taken arms for the purpoſe of aiding the Auſtrians. The Canton of Uri had riſen, and driven out the French; the Valais were alſo in arms, and General Kaim had been ſent with a conſiderable detachment to ſupport them, and furniſh them with arms, ammunition, &c.

The greateſt part of the Valteline was likewiſe in poſſeſſion of the Auſtrians.

Admiralty Office, June 3.

BY advices which have been received it appears that the Childers brig and Succeſs frigate had joined the Britiſh ſquadron under the orders of Vice-admiral Lord Keith, in the bay of Cadiz, on Friday the 3d of May, with information of the ſailing of the French fleet from Breſt, and the Spaniſh ſquadron from Ferrol; that the morning of the following day the Breſt fleet, conſiſting of 33 ſhips of war, had appeared off Cadiz; and that his Lordſhip, wiſhing rather to meet the enemy under ſail than receive him at anchor with the Spaniſh fleet of 22 ſhips of the line in view, at anchor to leeward, and at no greater diſtance than ſeven or eight miles, had got under ſail with his ſquadron, conſiſting of fifteen ſail of the line, to give battle to the enemy, and ſtood off and on from the port of Cadiz; that during the courſe of that day the French fleet, though ſhips ſent to reconnoitre had nearly approached the Britiſh ſquadron, had made no attempt to attack it, or to form a junction with the Spaniſh fleet; and that on the morning of the 5th the wind, which had blown freſh all the afternoon of the preceding day, with cloudy weather, increaſing to a perfect ſtorm, and blowing right on the ſhore, he had loſt ſight of the enemy, excepting four ſhips of the line which had ſeparated, and which he had endeavoured ineffectually to cut off.

That his Lordſhip had continued on his ſtation until the 9th, when he proceeded with his ſquadron off Cape Spartel, and having reaſon to believe that the enemy had paſſed the Straits, proceeded on the 10th into Gibraltar Bay, where he is ſuppoſed to have anchored on the ſame day.

It alſo appears, by advices from Gibraltar of the 9th of May, that the Childers brig had joined Lord St. Vincent on the 4th; that his Lordſhip had in conſequence taken the neceſſary means for apprizing the commanders of his Majeſty's ſhips of the enemy's approach, and had made his arrangements with a view to collecting his force and purſuing the enemy, which had paſſed the Straits and proceeded up the Mediterranean in the afternoon of the 5th.

An account has alſo been received, that the ſquadron under Rear-admiral

admiral Whitshed, consisting of five ships of the line, was off the Tagus on the 16th, and, from the state of the winds, would be likely to reach the Bay of Gibraltar on the 18th.

From the LONDON GAZETTE EXTRAORDINARY, June 6, 1799.

Downing Street, June 5.

"DISPATCHES, of which the following are extracts, have been received from Sir Morton Eden, K. B. and Lieutenant-colonel Robert Craufurd, by the Right Hon. Lord Grenville, his Majesty's principal Secretary of State for the foreign department.

Extract of a Letter from Sir Morton Eden, K. B. dated Vienna, May 23.

I HAVE the honour of enclosing three Extraordinary Gazettes of this place, with the translations, together with the translation of an article in the Ordinary Gazette of yesterday, and sincerely congratulate your Lordship on the happy turn of affairs in the Grisons and the Little Cantons, which must contribute so essentially to the further success of the campaign in Italy, and so greatly facilitate the operations of the Russian army, which entered this country on the 15th instant, and of that under the command of the Archduke Charles.

Vienna, May 18.

"CAPTAIN Vimmer, of the regiment of Lobkowitz cavalry, arrived here yesterday from Field-marshal Suwarrow, with the following account of his further operations. As every account agreed that the enemy had only a small garrison in Tortona, Field-marshal Suwarrow ordered Prince Pangrazrion, who was at Pavia, to cross the Po without delay with the advanced guard, consisting of a regiment of chasseurs, two battalions of grenadiers, two battalions of infantry, and two regiments of Cossacks, under the command of Colonel Grekow. They passed the river near Corvesino, in barges and flat-bottomed boats, and pushed forward to Voghera. On reconnoitring, it was discovered that the enemy had strengthened the garrison of Tortona. In consequence of which, General Karaiczay received orders to join the Prince, who crossed the river with two battalions of the regiment of Frolich, two squadrons of Lobkowitz's dragoons, and two of Karaiczay's, which passed the Scrivia near Castel Nuovo, and formed near Torre di Garrofole, between Tortona and Alexandria. But the following day, having learnt that Moreau was posted near Alexandria, on the banks of the river, with the two divisions of Victor and Grenier, and whatever force he had been able to collect from Turin and other places, the Field-marshal resolved to march with his whole army against Tortona. The two divisions Zopfi and Frolich, under the orders of the General of cavalry Melas, marched from their camp at Casal Pusterlengo to Plaisance, where they passed the Po, after having previously carried the important post of Bovis (leaving there General Morzin, with three battalions and two squadrons), and encamped near Castel St. Giovanni. The following day they passed through Voghera, and on the 9th arrived by Ponte Coronne at Tortona. At dusk the same day Major-general Marquis Chatelet attacked the gate of Voghera with two battalions of the regiment of Alvinczy, a reserve of grenadiers,

and

and a squadron of Lobkowitz, under the orders of Colonel Spanochl, and with the affiftance of the inhabitants, who at heart are faithful to their king, the gate was forced notwithftanding the fire from the citadel. Thus fell the fortrefs of Tortona, the key of Piedmont. The Ruffian General Prince Gortzakow witneffed their operation. The troops were received with fhouts of joy by the inhabitants. The town was illuminated the whole night, and the next day (the 10th) high mafs and *Te Deum* were fung at the churches. There were but few cannon in the town. The enemy, 700 men ftrong, have retired to the citadel, which is blockaded by four battalions, and the works are already begun. The enemy left behind them 250 wounded or fick, of whom 12 are officers. The army paffed the Scrivia on the 10th, which was fo fwoln and fo rapid as to render it impoffible to conftruct a bridge. The men paffed through the water up to their middle, and joined the Ruffian advanced guard near Torre di Garrofole. General Vukaffovich advanced with his brigade beyond Novara to Vercelli; and his advanced guard, under Colonel Prince Charles of Rohan, took the important fortrefs of Ivrea, which fecures to us the Valley of Aoft. Thirty pieces of cannon and a great quantity of ammunition were found in the place. A detachment of the fame corps has alfo taken feventeen guns on the Lago Maggiore. Colonel Prince Victor of Rohan pufhed forward with a corps of about 2000 men as far as the lake of Como, where he took one gun-boat, and obliged the enemy to burn two others. Being fupported by the peafants, who take up arms every where, he has marched againft a body of French who have retreated to the environs of Chiavenna. The canton of Uri, and the diftricts of Bellinzone, are alfo in infurrection againft the French. Major Luzioni, who entered Piedmont with thirty huffars, has armed all the peafants who join our troops, and has already advanced by Dorra Paldea as far as Chivas, two pofts from Turin. Colonel Strauch, detached from the Tyrol with 5000 men, has penetrated into the Valley of Brembona, and has driven the enemy from Morbegno. Major Fredigoni, of the Tyrolefe chaffeurs, with 800 men, is on his march from Ecola to Terano, in the Valteline, againft the enemy. The Field-marfhal hopes, that by means of thefe different operations, combined with thofe of Field-marfhal-lieutenant Bellegarde, the enemy will be fpeedily driven from the Valteline. Field-marfhal Suwarrow has detached Field-marfhal-lieutenant Otto, with 5000 infantry and 1500 horfe, againft General Montrichard, who is pofted at Bologna. This corps has already advanced as far as Modena, and the enemy has retired towards Ponte Tremoli. By this means our army will draw fupplies from the fertile provinces of Ferrara, Bologna, and Modena, and at the fame time the territory of Parma is wrefted from the hands of the French. Field-marfhal-lieutenant Kaim, with fix battalions and four fquadrons, joined the grand army before Tortona after the reduction of Pizzighetone. General Hohenzollern was fent with four battalions to Milan, where are already fix battalions, commanded by General Latermann, with orders to prefs the fiege of the caftle of that city. The four fquadrons of cavalry being unneceffary for the fiege, have received orders to reinforce the army in Piedmont.

Vienna, May 19.

THE Archduke Charles has fent by his firft lieutenant, Lefbrich de Spleny, an account that Lieutenant-general Hotze had, agreeably to the inftructions he had received, attacked the paffes of Lucien's Steig on the

morning

morning of the 14th inftant, and had fucceeded in taking poffeffion of them, and made prifoners almoft the whole of the 14th demi-brigade, and took eight pieces of cannon. Lieutenant-general Hotze entertained great hopes that he fhould be able to take a great number of prifoners as he advanced, the enemy being ftill in the Pratigau, and our troops having already reached the bridge of Zollbrucke, which leads from the Valley of Pratigau to Coire, where his Royal Highnefs prefumes our troops had arrived on the 14th. His Royal Highnefs will give as foon as poffible the details of this important operation.

Vienna, May 21.

CAPTAIN Comte Caramelli, of the Emperor's regiment of cuiraffiers, arrived here this day, as courier from his Royal Highnefs the Archduke Charles, with the particulars refpecting the fubfequent operations of Field-marfhal-lieutenant Hotze in the Grifons. The enemy's divifions, which had been driven to the mountains by Colonel Plunket, and the column of General Heller, retreated to Furna, in the defign of efcaping either by Zizers or by Coire. But finding that the Field-marfhal-lieutenant Hotze occupied thefe two points, and that he had already pofted two battalions in the latter, they furrendered themfelves prifoners of war. The total of the prifoners amounts to 1000 privates, 80 officers; a pair of colours has alfo been taken. Befides this, in the purfuit after the affair of Lucien's Steig, on the 14th, we took four pieces of cannon, and made two companies of grenadiers prifoners, without counting the eight pieces of cannon and the demi-brigade already mentioned. Field-marfhal-lieutenant Hotze reconnoitred the enemy on the 15th, near Reichenau; at the fame time he appeared in great force againft Ragatz, where the enemy had 2000 men. This demonftration produced an engagement, and the enemy being obliged to retreat, burnt the bridge over the rivulet Pfefferer. We, however, purfued them beyond Fettes: part of them were driven into the Valley of Sargans, where an officer and 30 men were made prifoners. We had a few men wounded. We took three more cannon from the enemy near Ragatz, which with thofe already mentioned make 15 guns. After this laft attack, the enemy withdrew in the night between the 15th and 16th with fuch precipitation, and had loft fo much ground, that when the account came away, Field-marfhal Hotze was already at Sargans; at the fame time the Field-marfhal-lieutenant received intelligence that Colonel Count St. Julien was at Lenz, and Field-marfhal lieutenant Count Haddick at Felifur. The enemy is retiring on the fide of Fufis, probably in order to join the camp at Reichenau, and to attempt to continue their retreat towards St. Gothard by the only road now left them, viz. Ilianz and the Devil's Bridge. But as the Upper League of the Grifons was preparing to rife, Colonel Strauch clofed the paffage of Splugen, and Field-marfhal-lieutenant Hotze that of the Gunkels. It is alfo probable that Field-marfhal-lieutenant Count de Bellegarde will advance towards Coire and Fufis. From all which it may be concluded, that this corps of the enemy, confifting of 7000 men, is in a moft critical fituation, from which it will be extremely difficult to difengage itfelf. In order to affift as much as poffible Field-marfhal-lieutenant Hotze in the attack of Lucien's Steig, his Royal Highnefs the Archduke Charles made at the fame time a demonftration towards the Rhine with fuch fuccefs, that a corps of the enemy, of 17,000 men, affembled near Schaffhaufen, were prevented from fending any detachment againft Field-marfhal-lieutenant

Hotze.

Hotze. It appears, by accounts sent by Field-marshal-Lieutenant Colpoth to his Royal Highness, that on the night of the 14th, General Merfeldt surprised the enemy's post at Dundenheim, and killed three officers and 60 grenadiers who resisted. One officer and four soldiers were made prisoners. We took also 14 horses.

Vienna, May 22.

WHAT Lieutenant-general Bellegarde had announced previous to the bulletins of the 22d and 23d inst. which his Royal Highness the Archduke Charles had ordered to be published relative to the operations of Lieutenant-general Hotze, is connected with what follows, although the intelligence from Lieutenant-general Bellegarde arrived later. According to this account, Colonel and Brigadier Strauch, after very fatiguing marches, reached Chiavenna with his brigade on the 9th instant, at which place Colonel Le Loup, of the van-guard of General Vukassovich, had arrived on the preceding day. From the 7th the enemy had commenced their retreat from Chiavenna, by the Valley of Giacomo, leaving at the first place 32 pieces of cannon, of which we have taken possession. Colonel Strauch, being reinforced by three battalions of light troops, and the remainder of the third battalion of Michael Wallis, commanded by Colonel Carneville, pursued the enemy to the heights; and Colonel Prince Victor de Rohan went with his force to Beilinzone, to dispute the passage of the Bernadin. The brigade of Colonel Strauch had many difficulties to surmount at Morpegon, in the Valley of Camonica. He was obliged to wait two days at Piacca, in order to dig a road through the snow near Casa St. Marco, as it was impossible for the soldiers to march, the snow being fifteen feet deep, and not hard enough to bear. By this means, the communication is re-established with the principal corps of Lieutenant-general Bellegarde, by Silva, Plana, Malagio, and Caffatsch. Demonstrations were made for the purpose of alarming the enemy on the hills of Julie and Albula, in order to facilitate the operations of General-lieutenant Hotze, whom General Bellegarde was prepared to support on the side of Javos and the hill of Albula. Colonel Du Marseille, of the regiment Clairfayt, had brought from Albula two pieces of cannon belonging to the enemy. At Malagio, and at several other places on the road to Chiavenna, were found a great quantity of ammunition, muskets, and waggons. The enemy had destroyed a part of them in retreating. The first intention of the enemy was to proceed to Chiavenna, by the mountain of Septume, in order to join General La Courbe, near Lenz; but the detachment of the van-guard of General Bellegarde, which had advanced from Pernada as far as Malagio and Caffatsch, prevented this, and obliged them to retreat by the Splugen.

Extract of a Letter from Colonel A. Crawfurd, dated Head-quarters of General Hotze, Mayenfeldt, May 22.

ON the 14th inst. I had the honour to write your Lordship a few lines, containing the account of the successful attack made by General Hotze on the enemy's post at St. Lucien's Steig, and his other positions in the Grison country. In the course of the evening of the 14th, above 1600 more prisoners were brought in, so that the number taken in this affair amounted in the whole to between 3 and 4000 men. The difficulties attending this operation were extremely great, and its success reflects the highest honour on the General and the troops. The fortified post of St. Lucien's Steig completely closes and defends the direct passage from

kirch into the Grifon country; its natural and artificial ftrength is fuch
render a direct attack upon it in front extremely difficult and impru-
and its flanks are fo well fupported as to render it impoffible to turn
thout marching over fuch mountains as might almoft have been
ed impracticable for troops. The firft or right-hand column marched
Veldkirch, on the great road, ftraight to the Steig. The deftination
is column was to form in front of the poft, to make fuch demonftra-
as to threaten an attack, and endeavour to draw off the enemy's
tion from his right flank, and to be in readinefs to purfue the enemy
the cavalry and flying artillery as foon as the other columns fhould
obliged him to abandon the Steig. The fecond column, commanded
[ajor-general Yellachitz, confifting entirely of infantry, made a con-
ible detour to the left, effected this march by extraordinary exertions
the chain of mountains by which the right flank of the pofition of the
is covered, and defcended about daybreak in the rear of that flank,
place where, from the extreme difficulty of the ground, the enemy
l not expect an attack. This column diflodged the enemy from the
, and made prifoners great part of the infantry that defended it. The
and fourth columns, commanded by General Hiller and Colonel
ket, marched from Veldkirch up the Montafune valley, from
ice they with great difficulty croffed at different points the chain of
atains which feparates it from the valley called Brettigaw, and driving
:nemy from the different pofitions he occupied on this fide, they
nded into the valley of the Rhine by Marchlines and Zizers; the
aced guard of the firft column purfuing the enemy from the Steig,
ed at Zizers time enough to cut off the retreat of the enemy from the
igaw. Of the remains of the enemy's corps in the Grifons, one
nn retired through Coire to Reichenau, where they took poft behind
thine, and another paffed that river at the Zollbrueke, and marched
igh Ragatz towards Sargans, leaving a rear-guard at Ragatz. On
15th, General Hotze reconnoitred the enemy at Reichenau; but
ng them very ftrongly pofted, and not having any infantry at hand,
uld not attack them. The fame day, however, he ordered Colonel
icini to attack them at Ragatz, from whence they were driven with
derable lofs. About 52 prifoners and two pieces of cannon were
1. The advanced pofts were pufhed forward to Sargans. On the
, the enemy retired from Reichenau towards Difentis, where they were
ked on the 18th, and obliged to retreat with the lofs of two cannon
feveral men. On the fame day they were driven from Wallenftadt
Werdenberg, on which occafion they loft three pieces of cannon.
he 19th, the enemy with a very fuperior force made a fevere attack
he corps commanded by Colonel Cavacini at Wallenftadt, but was
pletely repulfed on this occafion. The battalion of Swifs emigrants,
nanded by Colonel Rovorco (which formed a part of Colonel Cava-
i corps), were engaged for the firft time; it fuffered a good deal, and
ved with great bravery. The enemy is now in full retreat from the
enbourg and canton of Appenzell. The Auftrian patroles entered
fall the night before laft, and found between Rheineck and that place
en pieces of ordnance, befides a confiderable quantity of ammunition,
h the French had abandoned in their retreat. On the whole, the
y's lofs in this quarter, from the 14th to this day, exclufive of killed
wounded, may be eftimated at 4000 prifoners, and 36 pieces of
on. General Bellegarde is at Chiavenna.

o1. VIII.   E *   From

From the LONDON GAZETTE, June 11, 1799.

Downing Street, June 11.

DISPATCHES have been this day received from the Right Hon. Sir Morton Eden, K. B. dated Vienna, May 30th, with the intelligence that the caftle of Milan had furrendered by capitulation on the 24th ultimo; that the Imperial troops had alfo occupied the towns of Ferrara, Cafale, and Ceva; which latter place was feized by the peafants of the country, and at their defire garrifoned by the Auftrians.

From the LONDON GAZETTE EXTRAORDINARY, June 13, 1799.

Downing Street, June 12.

DISPATCHES, of which the following are copy and extracts, have been received from the Right Honourable Sir Morton Eden, K. B. and Lieutenant-colonel Robert Craufurd, by the Right Honourable Lord Grenville, his Majefty's principal Secretary of State for the foreign department.

Extract of a Letter from Sir Morton Eden, K. B. dated Vienna, May 30.

I HAVE the honour of tranfmitting to your Lordfhip an Extraordinary Gazette of this day, containing an account of the progrefs of the army under the command of the Archduke Charles in Switzerland, and of General Bellegarde's determination (the object of refcuing the Grifons from the French being now attained) to proceed with the troops under his command to fupport the operations of the army in Italy, and a detailed relation of the attack of Lucien's Steig and the neighbouring pofts by General Hotze.

Vienna, May 24.

FROM two reports received from his Royal Highnefs the Archduke Charles, dated at Stockach the 20th inft. and at Singen the 21ft inft. it appears, that General Bay, whom Lieutenant-general Hotze had detached to attack the enemy near Afmos, had driven him from that poft, carried a fleche, and taken one piece of cannon and a tumbril. General Bay proceeded to ftorm the enemy's intrenchments, and purfued him in his retreat to Werdenberg; in the courfe of which he took one more piece of cannon. Notwithftanding a very obftinate attempt of the enemy to make a ftand at Werdenberg, our brave troops fucceeded in repulfing him upon this occafion, and one of the enemy's companies was, with the exception of 30 men, cut to pieces. While General Bay was executing the above operation, Colonel Gavafini, of the regiment of Kerpen, who was ordered by Lieutenant-general Hotze to advance to Wallenftadt, reached Wallenftadt on the 19th, and pofted his troops about half a league on the fide of the Lake. He was foon after attacked by a very fuperior number of the enemy, who continued fending frefh troops through Flums againft his flank, but could not gain a foot of ground. On the contrary, Colonel Gavafini, in the end, fucceeded in bringing a fmall column to act upon the enemy's right flank, and in repulfing him towards funfet, with confiderable flaughter, as far as Murk. His Royal Highnefs here obferves, that Colonel Gavafini upon this occafion gave frefh proofs of his fpirit

and

and intelligence, having prevented the enemy, notwithstanding his superiority, from gaining the least advantage. Our loss was, however, not inconsiderable, as it amounted to 300 men killed and wounded, among whom were eight officers, three killed and five wounded. A legion formed of Swiss emigrants, which were engaged for the first time, distinguished itself very much, and the country people have every where risen in mass with enthusiasm. The rapid progress of Lieutenant-general Hotze obliged the enemy to abandon the neighbourhood of St. Gall, as well as the banks of the Rhine, near Constance and Schaffhausen, and to retreat beyond Winterthur. Lieutenant-general Nauendorff, who observed this, immediately crossed the Rhine with a part of his advanced guard, and pushed forward the light cavalry to observe the enemy's further movements. He was informed that the enemy had abandoned the Toar and the Thor, and had fallen back towards Zurich. Lieutenant-general Nauendorff sent patroles of light troops towards St. Gall, to establish a communication with those of the corps which was advancing from that quarter, under Lieutenant-general Hotze. His Royal Highness on the 21st moved his camp from Stockach to Singen, at which latter he also established his head-quarters on that day. As soon as Lieutenant-colonel Williams learnt that the enemy had evacuated Rheineck, he directed the cruise of the whole of his flotilla towards Arbon, with a view to impede their retreat. He further sent to Roschach, Count Tuscoms, one of the officers acting under him, who seized there eight pieces of cannon, of different calibres, three mortars, a quantity of shells, ships' stores, and ammunition, and six gun-boats which were not quite built, all which were brought to Bregentz. A further report from his Royal Highness, dated on the 22d, at Singen, states, that Lieutenant-colonel Williams had reported from Roschach, that he had advanced with a division of the regiment of Waldeck dragoons, which had reached that place under Lieutenant Burschied, as far as St. Gall, from which town the enemy had retreated a short time before. He occupied it, and took three pieces of cannon and two tumbrils. Lieutenant-general Hotze also reported, that Captain Count Leiningan, of the regiment of Bender, had, with the assistance of some armed peasants, taken in Altstetten two cannon, five tumbrils, and a considerable proportion of arms and ammunition; and that General Bay had, in the prosecution of his attack upon Werdenberg, taken two more cannon and 400 firelocks. Lieutenant-general Nauendorff already occupies Frauenfeld and Winterthur, and his patroles are in the direction of Zurich and Balach. In Diffenhofen, where he established a bridge of pontoons, he found nine pieces of cannon, 100 firelocks, and a supply of ammunition. Major Morbert, who belonged to his advanced guard, fell in with a detachment of the enemy at Munsterlingen, on the borders of the Lake of Constance, which being attacked at the same time by the crew of one of the vessels forming part of the flotilla who had landed, was dispersed, and the greater part were taken. This detachment formed the escort of a transport of their artillery, which fell into our hands, and which consisted of four cannon, one howitzer, and one tumbril. Lieutenant-general Kospoth reported to his Royal Highness, that Captain Luck, of the 13th regiment of dragoons, had, at the desire of Colonel Frenelle, fallen upon and surprised the 3d regiment of French hussars, which was encamped near Leimen, not far from Heidelberg, had cut to pieces about 100 men, and dispersed the remainder, taking several prisoners and 60 horses. On his side, one officer

officer and two men only were flightly wounded. His Royal Highnefs fpeaks in the ftrongeft terms of the meritorious conduct, upon feveral occafions, of the above-named two officers.

General Melas reports, that Lieutenant-general Ott had ordered the light battalion of Mihanovich to attack the enemy in Pontremoli, from which poft he was diflodged. Major Mihanovich particularly diftinguifhed himfelf upon the occafion, having, befides driving the enemy, who occupied fo advantageous a poft with no lefs a force than 800 men, taken two cannons, 17 mules laden with ammunition, and 30 prifoners, and having purfued the remainder of the enemy into the mountains.

With a view to give effectual fupport to the operations of Colonel Strauch and Prince Victor of Rohan, after the enemy had affembled near Bellinzone a confiderable number of troops, General Count Hohenzollern was fent with five battalions againft Chiavenna, and directed alfo to take the command of the whole corps there, while General Latterman carries on the blockade of the citadel of Milan, with the troops that remained there.

General Vukaffovich reports, that at Cofignano, in Piedmont, the armed peafants had rifen upon and difarmed 100 French foldiers; that they had done the fame in Carmagnola, and had wounded two French generals, one of whom had died of his wounds.

Lieutenant-general Bellegarde reports, that, in order to fupport moft effectually the operations of Lieutenant-general Hotze in the Grifons, he had marched his corps forward in four columns; that the firft, under General Count Nobili, advanced from Sus over Mount Flolo againft Davos; the fecond, under Lieutenant-general Haddick, from Pont acrofs the Albula; the third, under Colonel La Marfeille, over Mount Julies, into the Upper Stein Valley, while he himfelf, with the remainder of the troops, moved upon Lenz. The enemy did not any where make much oppofition, and the column of Count Nobili alone was obliged to force an abattis near Dorfli; after which however the enemy retreated with the utmoft expedition, but not without the lofs of one captain, two lieutenants, and 150 men, who were taken prifoners.

Lieutenant-general Bellegarde adds, that fince the object in view, namely the conqueft of the Grifons, is now accomplifhed, he fhould, without delay, proceed to co-operate with the army of Italy, leaving, however, Colonel Count St. Julien with his brigade to cover the Engadin, to keep up the communication with Lieutenant-general Hotze, and, if neceffary, to co-operate further with him.

THE following is the detailed report promifed in the Extraordinary Gazette of the 2ad, which has now been received from his Royal Highnefs, of the attempt made by Lieutenant-general Hotze upon the Grifons:

Relation of the Circumftances which attended the Attack made on the 14th, 15th, and 16th May, by Order of his Royal Highnefs the Commander in Chief, upon the Grifons, by the Corps ftationed in the Voralburg.

HIS Royal Highnefs the Archduke Charles had directed Lieutenant-general Hotze to fupport the advance of Lieutenant-general Count Bellegarde into the Engadin, by combining with him his attacks upon the Grifons, and by advancing with the utmoft celerity to Coire. In obedience to fuch directions, Lieutenant-general Hotze, after communicating with Lieutenant-general Count Bellegarde, fixed the 14th of May for the attack,

nd was promised by the latter that a'd
nen, stationed in Montafuner under Maj
iment of Neugebauer, should be at his
column should, on the 14th, also adva
s Davos. Lieutenant-general Hotze was
ucien's Steig could not be attacked in
ion that the troops which occupied that
at the enemy's commandes in chief, Mas
een there, in order to render the pass
e: he therefore determined to leave a co
ence between Feldkirch and Bregentz, i
the infantry and cavalry destined for t
commanded by Lieutenant-general Ho
the night of the 13th at Baduz and Ba
es which the enemy had established on
denberg, and which rendered the narrow
. On the same night Lieutenant-gener
twelve pounders, near Balzers, with a
leads along the Rhine from Werdenber
n, under General Zellachich, assembled,
Mount Mavenfeld in the Alps. The thi
was assembled by him between the 13
in the Alps. The fourth column, unde
ded on the evening of the 13th, at the
llen. The first column was destined to
emy's front and flanks, while the second
and to penetrate to the rear of the en
and thereby enable the first to advance t
o take post. The third battalion was to
ched position near Sevis, to hasten to
ld gain possession, and if necessary to rei
ne battalion, and with the remainder to
oll bridge on the Langwart, and the l
. Finally, the fourth column was ord
n at Kloster and Keeblis, immediately to
rg to Davos, and with the remainder to
reinforce General Hiller. It was furtl
s and Conters, in order to block up the
ger Valley. The second, third, and fou
the highest and steepest mountains, and
es; to make their way through snow f
for twelve hours before they could n
the attack was to be made. The extre
mmits of the Alps of Mayenfeld, Sevis
ible to fix upon any other point for the
d firmness and courage with which the
le set them by their officers, braved all t
antly admired.
e excellent inhabitants of the Valley of
to the utmost in facilitating the march, a
sporting the ammunition and provisions
ldest and most experienced of the inha

prise at the security with which the passage of the artillery and cavalry of the fourth column was effected across the summit of Mount Slapin.

Companies formed of the inhabitants of Vorarlberg and Montafuner were distributed to each column, who not only served as guides, but were upon all occasions most useful in action.

On the 14th, at daybreak, each column reached the enemy's advanced picquets. The first column remained prepared in front of Balzers, waiting the attack to be made by the second upon the enemy's rear.

General Zellachich had directed the march of his column in such manner as might enable Major Elvos, commanding the fourth Peterwardein battalion, with two companies of riflemen under Lieutenant Raiacfich, to pass over the Klek, and attack the Steig from the rear.

The General took post on the heights betwixt Mayenfeld and Zenins, took possession of these places, and attacked Mattans, while another detachment advanced to the Lower Zoll bridge on the Rhine. The enemy retreated into the wood, leaving behind one cannon, one ammunition-waggon, and three artillerymen.

As soon as Major Elvos heard the fire of General Zellachich's column, he ordered Lieutenant Raiacfich with his riflemen, supported by three companies of Peterwardeiners, to attack the right flank of the Steig; Captain Mirich, of the fourth Peterwardein battalion, to advance direct against the enemy's camp, while Lieutenant Rovich made an attack along a very narrow road on the left.

Although the enemy directed the fire of his whole artillery against these divisions, still such was the vigour and impetuosity of their attack, that the garrison was obliged to lay down their arms. Six pieces of cannon, two howitzers, and nine ammunition-waggons, were found on the Steig: the commandant, a number of officers, and 700 men, were made prisoners. The remainder of the garrison, consisting of 300 men, fell into the hands of the division of the regiment of Kaunitz, which General Hotze had stationed on the left flank, to make a diversion.

As soon as the gate of the Steig was open, General Hotze and General Bay advanced with the cavalry, in order to reach the Langwart, and secure that position. The enemy had burnt the upper bridge on that river; but Captain Brudtschneider, with a detachment of Hulans, forded the stream, in spite of its extreme rapidity, and forced two companies of the rear guard to lay down their arms. Captain Kiselevski pursued the enemy, with his squadron of Hulans, as far as the lower bridge, but could not prevent its being set on fire at both ends. As soon as Captain Garneka, of the dragoons of Modena, observed this, he put himself at the head of some detachments of the regiment of Kerpen, and of the third Peterwardein battalion, and, in spite of a heavy fire of musketry, passed the burning bridge, dispersed the enemy, and took one cannon. Lieutenant Serpes, of the dragoons of Waldeck, assisted by the armed peasants of the Vorarlberg, drove the enemy over the Rhine near Flasch: he then sent Corporal Platz, of the dragoons of Waldeck, across the river, who, with the aid of the peasants, carried off three guns, although fired on with grape-shot by the enemy.

General Hiler having assembled the third column about midnight, near Geneier Bade, sent a battalion of Bender, under Captain Bach, supported by another battalion of the same regiment, under Major Rhineck, to attack the enemy's abattis and strong redoubts near Sevis: he followed

with

with the rest of the column at the same time. In order to facilitate this attack, he detached Lieutenant Bilhaker, with a company of Bender, over a very high mountain in the enemy's rear. The whole operation was conducted with such spirit that the redoubts were almost immediately carried. Ensign Kreff, of Bender, who commanded the volunteers, and contributed much to the success, was wounded. Captain Bach pursued the enemy to the Schlofs bridge, and as he there attempted some resistance, Lieutenant Foulon, with the volunteers of Bender, carried the bridge by storm, and made several prisoners: Captain Bach was unfortunately killed. General Hiller, in order to cut off the enemy from the roads still open to him, sent at the same time several detachments into the mountains, advanced with his column to Zitzers, and ordered Lieutenant Metzmacher to push on with the volunteers of Bender, who entered Chur the same evening. The enemy, thus surrounded on every side, was obliged to surrender, to the amount of 26 officers and 1110 privates: considerable magazines of arms, ammunition, and clothing, were found in Zitzers and Chur.

The fourth column advanced from Slapin at break of day, through a narrow path, which they were obliged to pass in single files, against the enemy's outposts. Colonel Plunket also detached 200 men of the regiment of Neugebauer, in order to drive in the picquet which guarded the mouth of the defile. This detachment was observed: the enemy took the alarm, and, in spite of every exertion, made good his retreat across the Langwart to Schrins, in order to join the rest of the corps. Colonel Plunket also detached Major Colloredo over the mountain of Gavia towards Keeblis and Conters, in order, if possible, to cut off the enemy's retreat; but he too was discovered, and found it impossible to effect his purpose. Colonel Plunket immediately sent a battalion of Gemingen along with his cavalry and the armed peasants, to join General Hiller at the Schlofs bridge; and as soon as he was assured that General St. Julien had reached Dorfli, he ordered Major Stahremberg to join him, and advanced himself to the Schlofs bridge.

On the 15th Lieutenant-general Hotze occupied Chur with two battalions of Bender and two squadrons of Modena, and reconnoitred the enemy's position near Reichenau. A heavy cannonade ensued, and the enemy burnt the bridge of Reichenau. Major Jacobi, of Waldeck, also advanced with a strong escort towards Ragatz, in order to reconnoitre it: this produced an attack, which ended in the retreat of the enemy, after burning the village of Ragatz. Major Jacobi pursued the enemy through Pfeffers to Veris, occupied that debouché of the pass of Kunkels, and pushed his advanced posts near to Sargans. These advantages were the more important, as there now remained no retreat open to the enemy, excepting the foot road to Illentz and Difentis, which the rising of the peasants of the Upper League must have rendered very insecure. Two dismounted guns were found in Ragatz. The enemy retired in the greatest confusion towards the Lake of Wallenstadt and Difentis. Many of his detachments, dispersed in the mountains, have since surrendered.

On the 16th the enemy abandoned Reichenau and Sargans, which were immediately occupied by our troops. The precaution which the enemy took of burning or destroying all the bridges on his route, made it difficult to follow him quickly. All the troops distinguished themselves by their perseverance and steadiness, and those who were particularly engaged

gaged gave signal proofs of their courage. Lieutenant-general Hotze commends in a particular manner the conduct of the regiment of Bender, the Major's division of the second Uhlan regiment, the third battalion of the Peterwardeiners, and the division of Brooder (riflemen). In the opinion of Lieutenant-general Hotze, General Hiller gave fresh proofs of his extensive military knowledge, great resolution, and exemplary steadiness, which he had manifested on so many previous occasions. To the good conduct and unwearied activity of Generals Zellachich and Count Bay, as well as of Colonel Plunket, and to the precision with which they executed the orders entrusted to them, is in a great measure to be imputed the fortunate result of the undertaking. Major Wachtenburg, of the artillery, gave great satisfaction in the measures he took, and in the judicious manner in which he posted his guns. Captain Romberg, of the Quarter-master-general's department, distinguished himself on the 1st instant by his personal bravery, and by the great judgment he evinced in the attack at Flasch; and in the action of the 14th, his conduct was so meritorious that Lieutenant-general Hotze thought himself in justice obliged to send him from the field of battle to his Royal Highness the Archduke, with the first account of the victory. Lieutenant-general Hotze, in a very particular manner, praises Captain Meyer, of the Quarter-master-general's department, whose accurate knowledge of the ground decided him in his disposition for the attack, and who contributed, by this means, very much towards the defeat of the enemy. Captain Gratze, of the first Wallachian regiment, who, ever since the opening of the campaign, had been most usefully and actively employed by Lieutenant-general Hotze, is mentioned by that General in high terms of commendation. The commanding officers of the several columns have praised the conduct of the following officers for their particular good conduct: in the first column—of the Major's division of the second Uhlan regiment, Major Count Trautmannsdorf, Captains Kisselveski and Bredschneider, Lieutenants Koniasch and Cserna—of the Modena dragoons, Major Petz and Captain Garnika—of the dragoons of Waldeck, Major Jacobi, First-lieutenant Baron Serpes, and Corporal Platz—of the regiment of infantry of Kerpen, Colonel Count Gavasini, Captain Niederman, and Ensign Count Kinburgh—of the horse artillery, First-lieutenant Karnof—of the militia, Captain Wochener and his whole company. In the second column, Major Elves, of the fourth battalion of Peterwardein, to whom Lieutenant-general Hotze gives the credit of the taking possession of the post, Captain Mixich, Second-lieutenant Wassich, and Sergeant Kovacs of the third battalion; First-lieutenant Novich, and Second-lieutenant Geigen, of the fourth battalion of Peterwardein; First-lieutenant Raiacsich, and Ensign Illich, of the first Brooder battalion. Captain Gerbeth, of the grenadiers of Breschainville, who commanded the militia of Oberland, distinguished himself very much by his good conduct and bravery—of the regiment of Bender infantry, Major Rhineck, Captain Bach, First-lieutenants Lagoutte, Metzmacher, Sodan, Billharts, and Maldini, Second-lieutenant Foulon, and Ensign Krafft. General Hiller speaks of Captain Baumgarten, of the Quarter-master-general's department, in the highest terms. Of the militia of Montafuner, Captain Patlock and his company. In the fourth column, Major Richter, of the Quarter-master-general's staff, and Count Stahremberg of the third regiment of Neugebauer—of the militia, Captains Fournier and Kosler,

Our

"Our loss in all does not amount to more than 700 killed and wounded; that of the enemy may be reckoned at 1000 killed, wounded, and drowned. The prisoners brought in amount to nearly 3000 men, among whom are 100 officers. No precise account can yet be sent, as numbers are daily brought in. Thirteen pieces of cannon, two howitzers, and 28 ammunition-waggons, have fallen into our hands. The enemy, in their retreat, set fire to and blew up a number of the latter. Lieutenant-general Hotze finally praises the good conduct and active services of his aid-de-camp, Captain Nestor.

Vienna, May 31.

"GENERAL Count Hohenzollern, who was entrusted with the siege of the citadel of Milan, has sent Captain Ottol, of the engineers, with a report, that in consequence of the orders he had received on the night of the 14th, to blockade the citadel of Milan, and to support Colonel Prince Rohan, against whom the enemy was advancing with very superior numbers, he, on the 15th, left General Lattermann at Milan, with five battalions and one squadron, and hastened with the remaining five battalions to join the Prince, whose advanced posts were opposite to those of the enemy at Ponte Ceresa, in Anio. Notwithstanding the great distance, General Count Hohenzollern on the 17th had advanced beyond Ponte Ceresa, and formed a junction with the Prince. The enemy's position was immediately reconnoitred, and the attack to be made upon them, in three columns, near Caverna, was fixed for the 18th. It was accordingly made, and with such vivacity, that the enemy was driven back for the space of five leagues, and spread over the rivulet Ancre. A detailed report of this operation will follow. From the extent of the position to be occupied by Colonel Prince Rohan, Count Hohenzollern reinforced him with one battalion, and left his corps posted near Luciono, Ponte Ceresa, and Lugano, with his advanced posts in Caverna. His march back to Milan with the remaining four battalions was so expeditious that he reached it early on the morning of the 20th.

In the night between the 20th and 21st, the trenches were opened before the citadel of Milan. On the 23d, notwithstanding the very heavy fire from the besieged, the batteries were in a sufficient state of forwardness to begin playing upon the works. Upon a second summons being sent, the enemy agreed to capitulate; and the garrison, consisting in the whole of 2230 men, of which nine chiefs of battalions, 158 officers, are not to serve against their Imperial Majesties for the space of one twelvemonth: 110 pieces of cannon, and a quantity of ammunition and military stores of every description, were found in the citadel. The total number of killed on our side does not exceed 146 men.

"Major-general Count Hohenzollern praises, in the strongest terms, the conduct of all the officers and men employed in the siege. The inhabitants of Milan expressed the greatest joy upon this occasion, and were very liberal in their presents of money, &c. to the troops.

"General Melas, in a report of the 19th, from Cafa Flima, states, that the enemy had abandoned the position near Valenza, which the Austro-Russian troops had occupied.

"General Vukassovich reported on the 17th, that the movements he had made had obliged the enemy to abandon Cumle and its citadel. His corps marched out of the camp at Tofe di Garafolo, and early on the 19th encamped behind the rivulet of Capa, whence he will proceed to

Vol. VIII.   F f   Mor-

Mortanu. In the night between the 18th and 19th, two deputies arrived in the camp from Montoni, with an account that the armed peasants, to the number of 10,000, had, after a blockade of nine days, taken the Piedmontese fortress of Ceva, the French garrison of which, consisting of 325 men, they had made prisoners of war, and conveyed to Mondovi, there to be confined in the citadel. At the request of these deputies, an adequate detachment was immediately marched to occupy the above important fortress. One of the deputies proceeded with it as a guide, while the other offered to remain as an hostage with our troops. Indeed the inhabitants of every district in Italy have given proofs of the most favourable disposition towards the great just cause in which we are engaged.

General Kray, in a report of the 22d, states, that General Count Klenau had taken Ferrara by capitulation, and was proceeding to attack its citadel. The particulars of the capitulation will appear shortly.

My Lord, *Head-quarters, near Winterthur, 31st May.*
I HAVE the honour to inform your Lordship, that on the 21st inst. the advanced guard of the Archduke's army (commanded by General Nauendorff) passed the Rhine without opposition between Diffenbofen and Schaffhausen, and moved forward to Andelfingen on the Thur.— The army passed in the following days, and encamped near Paradies. On the 22d, the main body of General Hotze's corps also crossed the Rhine at different points between Balzers and the Lake of Constance, and on the 23d the General took his head-quarters at St. Gallen. Lieutenant-general Petrarsch, who during the operations against the Grison country had been posted with the right wing of General Hotze's corps for the defence of the Rhine from Feldkirch to the Lake, marched in the night from the 24th to the 25th with six battalions of infantry and the regiment of Kinsky Chevaux Leger, from St. Gallen towards Frauenfeld, in order to form a junction with the Archduke's army, the advanced posts of which were already pushed forward to Nefelbach. The rest of Lieutenant-general Hotze's corps marched in the forenoon of the 25th to Schwartzenbach, where it encamped behind the Thur, and its advanced guard took post two leagues in front of that river, on the road towards Elgg. In the course of this day (25th) the enemy attacked all the corps that had passed the Thur.— He drove back Lieutenant-general Nauendorff's advanced posts from Nefelbach, and obliged them to repass the river at Andelfingen. Lieutenant-general Petrarsch's corps was attacked just as. it arrived on the heights behind Frauenfeld; the affair lasted the whole day, and in the evening the enemy succeeded in obliging Lieutenant-general Petrarsch to retreat, and to take a position about half way between Frauenfeld and Wyll. During this affair, the enemy had pushed forward a column to the bridge of Pfin, with a view of covering the left flank of the corps that was engaged with General Petrarsch. The advanced guard of General Hotze's left was also attacked, but it repulsed the enemy and drove him as far as Elgg: in consequence however of the retreat of General Petrarsch's corps, it was also ordered to fall back.— Early in the morning of the 26th, a column of the Archduke's army, under Lieutenant-general Prince Reuss, arrived at Pfin, and in the course of the day encamped near Frauenfeld, where it was joined in the evening by Lieutenant-general Petrarsch's corps. In the night from the

26th to the 27th, General Hotze's and Prince Reuss's columns advanced in connexion with each other, to attack the enemy's position near Winterthur. The manœuvre was executed with the greatest precision, and the attack was made soon after daylight of the 27th, with much regularity, and in a very military manner. The enemy was driven from his position, but the ground being extremely favourable and much intersected with wood, he effected his retreat in tolerable order, and took post behind the Tress, where he remained till the evening: the bridge over the Thur, at Andelfingen, had been destroyed on the 25th, and an unfortunate delay in the construction of the pontoon bridge, in the night from the 26th to the 27th, prevented the Archduke's right wing (under Lieutenant-general Nauendorff) arriving in time to take part in the affair of this day, which otherwise might have been more decisive. The banks of the Tress are so steep that it affords an excellent position; but Massena did not think proper to make any farther attempt to defend it: he therefore retreated, and took post behind the Glat; to which he was induced not only by the affair of Winterthur, but perhaps also by the march of General Nauendorff's column towards his left flank. The advanced posts of the two armies are now separated by the Glat, and the enemy has an intrenched camp, said to be advantageous, about a league on this side of Zurich; but I have no doubt of his soon being obliged to abandon it. He has retired from Raperfweil, and destroyed the bridge. Colonel Roverea, with the Swifs corps, is at Notre Dame d'Einsidlen, in the canton of Schweitz; he has been joined by some of the inhabitants, and is supported by an Austrian corps under Colonel Cavafini. Official accounts have been this day received of part of General Bellegarde's corps having passed the St. Gothard.

I have the honour to be, &c.
ROBERT CRAUFURD.

From the LONDON GAZETTE, June 15, 1799.

Admiralty Office, June 15.

Extract of a Letter from Admiral the Earl of St. Vincent, K. B. Commander in Chief of his Majesty's Ships and Vessels in the Mediterranean, to Evan Nepean, Esq. dated Gibraltar, 27th April.

Sir,

HEREWITH I transmit you, for the information of my Lords Commissioners of the Admiralty, the copy of a letter from the Right Hon. Lord Mark Robert Kerr, captain of his Majesty's ship Cormorant, to Rear-admiral Duckworth, giving an account of the capture of a Spanish corvette.

ST. VINCENT.

Sir, *Thursday, 19th March, Colombrettes W.N.W. 7 Leagues.*

I HAVE the honour to acquaint you, that having parted company with his Majesty's ship Centaur on the 16th instant, in chase of a Spanish frigate, I proceeded to the rendezvous; and on the 19th, perceiving a brig to leeward, I gave chase, and after four hours brought her to.

She proved to be a Spanish brig of war, named El Vincelo, mounting 18 six-pounders on her gun-deck, and six brass four-pounders on her quarter-deck, and two on her forecastle, and having 144 men on board. During her chase, she threw six of her six-pounders overboard. I have the honour to be, &c. &c.

M. R. KERR.

J. T. Duckworth, Commodore, &c. &c. &c.

Admiralty Office, June 15.

Copy of a Letter from Admiral Kingsmill, Commander in Chief of his Majesty's Ships and Vessels at Cork, to Evan Nepean, Esq. dated on board the Polyphemeus, Cork Harbour, the 8th of June.

PLEASE to lay before my Lords Commissioners of the Admiralty the enclosed letter which I have received from Captain Twysden, of his Majesty's ship La Revolutionnaire, informing me of his having captured Le Victoire French brig privateer, from Bayonne. This prize arrived here yesterday: was captured in lat. 48 deg. 30 min. and 19 deg. long. W. and left La Revolutionnaire going in quest of a large ship privateer, which she had gained information of.

Sir, *His Majesty's Ship Revolutionnaire, at Sea, 30th May.*

I HAVE the honour to inform you, that this evening, after a chase of eight hours, his Majesty's ship under my command captured Le Victoire French brig privateer, mounting 16 nine-pounders, and 160 men; out nine days from Bayonne, fitted for a three months cruise, but had not taken any thing. Le Victoire is a very fine new vessel, and sails remarkably fast. I have the honour to be, &c. &c.

THO. TWYSDEN.

Admiralty Office, June 15.

Copy of a Letter from the Honourable Henry Curzon, Captain of his Majesty's Ship Indefatigable, to Evan Nepean, Esq. dated at Sea, the 31st ult.

Sir,

I BEG you will inform their Lordships, that I have fallen in with and captured the French privateer brig La Venus, mounting 12 four and two nine-pounders, and manned with 101 men; out nine weeks from Rochefort. She had captured the schooner Clarence, from Lisbon, bound to London; and a ship from Lisbon, bound to Hamburgh, laden with salt. I have the honour to be, Sir, &c. &c. &c.

H. CURZON.

From the LONDON GAZETTE EXTRAORDINARY, June 22, 1799.

Downing Street, June 21.

A DISPATCH, of which the following is a copy, has been received from Lieutenant-colonel Robert Craufurd, by the Right Honourable Lord Grenville, his Majesty's principal Secretary of State for the foreign department.

My

My Lord, Zurich, June 7.

I HAVE the honour to inform your Lordship that, in consequence of a very severe action which took place on the 4th inst. Massena has been obliged to abandon his intrenched camp before this place, and that the Austrians took possession of the town yesterday afternoon.

In my dispatch of the 31st ult. I had the honour to acquaint your Lordship that after the affair of Winterthur the enemy retreated behind the Glat. In the subsequent days the right wing of the Archduke's army, under General Nauendorff, advanced towards Buclach, the centre of Prince Reuss's column, towards Kloten, and General Hotze's to Bassersdorf.

In order to threaten the enemy's right flank, and in hopes of thereby inducing him to quit the position of Zurich (the real strength of which was not known), General Zellachich was sent with a column round the Greifensee, and afterwards advanced towards Zurich, in connexion with another part of General Hotze's corps, which crossed the Glat below Greifensee, but considerably to the enemy's right. As these demonstrations, however, were without effect, an attack was determined upon.

Between the Glat and Limmat is a considerable chain of hills, running nearly parallel to these rivers, and covered in most parts with thick woods. On this ridge, just in the front of Zurich, Massena had chosen a most excellent and not very extensive position, which for several weeks past he had caused to be strengthened by numerous intrenchments, and in which, after the affair of Winterthur, he collected a considerable part of the army. The right wing was posted on the hill called the Zurich-Berg, which is greatly elevated above every other part of the ridge within its reach, and is covered with very thick woods, in which the enemy had made considerable abbatis, entirely surrounding the hill, and defended by redoubts; and this being the most interesting and decisive point of the position, it was occupied by a large body of infantry; the right flank of which was thrown back *en potence* towards the town. The left wing of the army was placed on the continuance of the above-mentioned chain of hills; likewise protected by extensive woods, abbatis, and intrenchments: in the centre the ground was much lower, quite free from wood, and of easy access. Through this open space (which is not quite a cannon-shot in extent from wood to wood) pass the roads leading from Kloten and Winterthur to Zurich. This is the only part of the position in which cavalry could have acted; but it was completely covered by a chain of closed redoubts, considerably retired, and serving as a curtain to connect the two wings, by which it was so flanked and defended as to render the attack of this line extremely difficult so long as the wings of the army maintained the heights on each side of it. The left flank was further covered by a corps posted between Regensberg and the Glat, having its retreat towards Baden. The only defect of the position in front of Zurich was, that in case of defeat the whole would have been obliged to defile through the town, situated close behind the right of the position, and in which there is but one bridge over the Limmat; for (whether owing to the rapidity of the river, or what other cause I know not) the enemy had not, as it was supposed he would have done, constructed any pontoon bridges in the rear of his centre or left.

From the above-mentioned circumstances of the enemy's situation, it was evident that, if the Zurich-Berg was forced, it must have brought on the total defeat of their army; whose retreat through the town, just at the foot of this hill, would have been attended with the greatest difficulty.

Early in the morning of the 4th instant, the army marched to attack the enemy. General Hotze's corps marched off to the left, crossed the Glat, formed on the enemy's right flank, and began the attack of Zurich-Berg. The enemy defended this post with the greatest obstinacy, and although a considerable part of Prince Reuss's column was sent to assist in the attack, it was found impossible to force it: the enemy was driven indeed from some of the abbatis and intrenchments, but maintained his principal position on the Zurich-Berg, till night put an end to the action.

During the night, and the whole of the next day, both parties remained exactly where they had stood at the end of the affair, the Austrian infantry of the left wing being in many places almost within musket-shot of the enemy's abbatis and works. The great fatigue which the troops had undergone on the 4th determined the Archduke to defer till the 6th the renewal of the attack: but the enemy, whose loss in the affair of the 4th had been very great, and who foresaw the total ruin of his army if the Zurich-Berg should be forced, retired in the night from the 5th to the 6th, leaving in his intrenchments 35 pieces of cannon, three howitzers, and a great number of ammunition-waggons. In the afternoon of the 6th the Austrians occupied the town.

In the attack of the 4th instant the Austrian infantry suffered a considerable loss in killed and wounded; among the latter were General Wallis, Lieutenant-general Hotze, and Major-general Hidler. General Hotze received a musket-shot in the arm early in the affair, but it did not hurt the bone, and fortunately does not prevent his continuing to command his corps. His absence at this moment would have been sensibly felt and sincerely regretted.

Cherin (general of division and chief of the staff), together with two other French generals, were severely wounded, and two adjutants-general are among the prisoners, of which there are a considerable number.

I am, &c.
(Signed)   ROB. CRAUFURD

From the LONDON GAZETTE, June 22, 1799.

Admiralty Office, June 22.

Extract of a Letter from Captain Sir William Sidney Smith, to Mr. Nepean, dated Tigre, off Tripoly, in Syria, the 2d of April.

I BEG leave to transmit, for the information of my Lords Commissioners of the Admiralty, a copy of my report to the Right Hon. Earl St. Vincent, of the late events in this quarter.

My Lord,   *Tigre, off St. John d'Acre, 23d March.*

I HAVE the honour to inform you that, in consequence of information from Gezar Pacha, governor of Syria, of the incursion of General Buonaparte's army into that province, and approach to its capital, Acre, I hastened, with a portion of the naval force under my orders,

ders, to its relief, and had the satisfaction to arrive there two days before the enemy made his appearance.

Much was done in this interval under the direction of Captain Miller, of the Theseus, and Colonel Phelypeaux, towards putting the place in a better state of defence, to resist the attack of an European army; and the presence of a British naval force appeared to encourage and decide the Pacha and his troops to make a vigorous resistance.

The enemy's advanced guard was discovered at the foot of Mount Carmel, in the night of the 17th, by the Tigre's guard-boats: these troops, not expecting to find a naval force of any description in Syria, took up their ground close to the water-side, and were consequently exposed to the fire of grape-shot from the boats, which put them to the rout the instant it opened upon them, and obliged them to retire precipitately up the side of the Mount. The main body of the army finding the road between the sea and Mount Carmel thus exposed, came in by that of Nazareth, and invested the town of Acre to the east, but not without being much harassed by the Samaritan Arabs, who are even more inimical to the French than the Egyptians, and better armed.

As the enemy returned our fire by musketry only, it was evident they had not brought cannon with them, which were therefore to be expected by sea, and measures were taken accordingly for intercepting them; the Theseus was already detached off Jaffa (Joppa). The enemy's flotilla, which came in from sea, fell in with and captured the Torride, and was coming round Mount Carmel, when it was discovered from the Tigre, consisting of a corvette and nine sail of gun-vessels: on seeing us, they hauled off. The alacrity of the ship's company in making sail after them was highly praiseworthy: our guns soon reached them, and seven, as per enclosed list, struck; the corvette, containing Buonaparte's private property, and two small vessels, escaped, since it became an object to secure the prizes without chasing further; their cargoes, consisting of the battering train of artillery, ammunition, platforms, &c. destined for the siege of Acre, being much wanted for its defence. The prizes were accordingly anchored off the town, manned from the ships, and immediately employed in harassing the enemy's posts, impeding his approaches, and covering the ship's boats sent further in shore to cut off his supplies and provisions conveyed coastwise. They have been constantly occupied in these services for these five days and nights past; and such has been the zeal of their crews, that they requested not to be relieved, after many hours excessive labour at their guns and oars.

I am sorry to say we have met with some loss, as per enclosed list, which, however, is balanced by greater on the part of the enemy, by the encouragement given by the Turkish troops from our example, and by the time that is gained for the arrival of a sufficient force to render Buonaparte's whole project abortive. I have had reason to be perfectly satisfied with the gallantry and perseverance of Lieutenants Bushby, Inglefield, Knight, Stokes, and Lieutenant Burton of the marines, and of the petty officers and men under their orders.

I have the honour to be, &c. &c.

(Signed) W. SIDNEY SMITH.

Right Hon. Earl St. Vincent, Commander in Chief.

(232)

List of the Gun-vessels composing the French Flotilla bound from Alexandria and Damietta to St. John d'Acre, taken off Cape Carmel by his Majesty's Ship Tigre, Commodore Sir Sidney Smith, K. S. the 18th March, eight o'Clock P. M. after a Chase of three Hours.

La Negresse, of six guns and 53 men.—La Foudre, of eight guns and 52 men.—La Dangereuse, of six guns and 23 men.—La Maria Rose, of four guns and 22 men.—La Dame de Grace, four guns and 35 men. —Les Deux Freres, of four guns and 23 men.—La Torride, taken in the morning of that day, and retaken, of two guns and 30 men.

Total—7 gun-boats, 34 guns, and 238 men.

These gun-boats were loaded, besides their own complements, with battering cannon, ammunition, and every kind of siege equipage, for Buonaparte's army before Acre.

(Signed)   W. S. SMITH.
On board the Tigre, off Acre, March 23.

N. B. The Marianne gun-boat was taken previously, and the transport No. 1, subsequently, by the Tigre.

Return of the killed and wounded in the Boats of his Majesty's Ships Tigre and Theseus, and in the Gun-vessels employed against the French Army before Acre, from the 17th to the 25th March.

Tigre—Mr. Arthur Lambert, Mr. John Goodman, and Mr. John Gell, midshipmen, and eight seamen, killed; 20 seamen wounded, of which eight are among the 20 prisoners.

Theseus—Mr. John Carra, midshipman, killed; Mr. John Waters, midshipman, and six seamen, wounded.

Total—4 midshipmen and eight seamen killed; one midshipman and 26 seamen wounded.

On board the Tigre, March 23.   W. S. SMITH.

N. B. The officers, petty officers, and seamen, employed on this service were volunteers. The dead bodies of Mr. Gell, and Peter M'Kircher, seaman, which fell into the hands of the enemy, were buried by them with the honours of war.

Admiralty Office, June 22.

Copy of a Letter from the Right Hon. Lord Keith, Vice-admiral of the Red, to Evan Nepean, Esq. dated on board the Barfleur, off Cadiz, the 27th April.

Sir,

I HAVE the honour to enclose a copy of a letter received from Captain Hope, of his Majesty's ship Majestic, announcing his having destroyed a French ship privateer, mounting 16 long guns and carronades, which I have also communicated to the Commander in Chief.   I have the honour to be, &c. &c. &c.

KEITH.

Majestic,

My Lord, Majestic, 6th April.

I HAVE the honour of informing your Lordship, that a French ship privateer, coppered, and mounting 16 long guns and carronades, was yesterday drove on shore by his Majesty's ship Majestic and Transfer brig, under cover of a fort a few leagues to the eastward of Velez Malaga, where, finding it impossible to get her off, she was destroyed by the boats of the Majestic, under the command of Lieutenant Roger.

I have the honour to be, &c. &c. &c.

(Signed) GEO. HOPE.

Right Hon. Lord Keith, K. B. *&c. &c. &c.*

Downing Street, June 22.

DISPATCHES, of which the following are extracts, have been received from the Right Hon. Sir Morton Eden, by the Right Hon. Lord Grenville, his Majesty's principal Secretary of State for the foreign department.

Extract of a Letter from Sir Morton Eden to Lord Grenville, dated June 1.

I HAVE the honour of transmitting to your Lordship the Extraordinary Gazette of this place, containing the official relation of the surrender of the castle of Milan.

Capitulation between Major-general I. and R. C. Hohenzollern and the French Commander of the Citadel of Milan, Bechaud, concluded May 24.

Art. I. All the garrison shall march on the 25th May, drums beating, and with all the honours of war: all that make part of the garrison shall be conducted to the French advanced posts, and given up to the general who commands the French army in Italy.

Answ. The garrison shall not serve, during a year and a day, against the troops of his Imperial Majesty, unless the whole or part of them shall be exchanged in the interval. The officers shall keep their arms; the garrison shall march out to-morrow morning at nine o'clock, with the usual military honours and drums beating, and shall lay down their arms upon the glacis.

II. All those in general who have not carried arms, as well as the women and children, shall be conducted to the French advanced posts.—Granted.

III. Ten small carts, which are, with their equipages, in the citadel, shall depart with the officers, without being searched.—Granted.

IV. The necessary waggons shall be furnished to transport the sick, the women, and children, if the small carts are not sufficient.—Granted.

V. Those officers who have horses shall be allowed to take them with them freely, and the troops shall keep what belongs to them.—Granted.

VI. Every attention that humanity demands shall be shewn to the sick of the garrison, and proper attendants shall remain with them till their perfect re-establishment.—Granted.

VII. The garrison, during their march to the French advanced posts, shall be under the protection of the Austrian troops, and the officer who shall command them shall be responsible for all the bad treatment and all the injuries that the garrison may suffer on the part of the inhabitants.—Granted.

Vol. VIII. G g VIII.

VIII. The troops of the allies, of whatever nation, belonging to the garrison, shall be treated with the same attention as the French troops.—Granted.

Additional article. Lieutenant Jankovich shall be immediately exchanged for an officer of the garrison; both of them may serve forthwith.

Second additional art. A commissary at war shall remain in the fortress, to deliver up all the magazines, and, in a word, every thing which belongs to the French republic.

Done at the citadel of Milan, the 12th May.
LATTERMAN,
Major-general, L. and R.
BECHAUD,
Chief of Battalion and Commandant.
COUNT HOHENZOLLERN,
Major-general, I. and R. Commandant of the Siege.

Extract of a Letter from Sir Morton Eden, dated Vienna, June 3.

I HAVE the honour of enclosing to your Lordship two Extraordinary Gazettes of this place, the one with a supplement, published yesterday evening, the other this day.

Vienna, June 3.

GENERAL Baron Kray has sent Lieutenant Diforifki, of the regiment of Nauendorff, with the intelligence of the capture of the citadel of Ferrara, on the 2 d of May.

Major-general Count Klenau states, in his report, that, not having succeeded in his endeavours, when he took possession of the town, to make the enemy evacuate the citadel, a regular pentagon, in perfect repair, abundantly supplied with artillery, ammunition, and provisions, he was induced to direct Colonel Orefkovich to order Captain Victora of the artillery to erect two batteries; which work was carried on with so much activity and spirit that they were finished in the evening of the 22d.

On the 23d, at three o'clock in the morning, the enemy had already evacuated the town, which General Klenau garrisoned with the light battalion of Bach. At eight o'clock Count Klenau summoned the commandant of the fortress to surrender, but a negative answer was returned.

The batteries being ready, and the artillery and ammunition having been conveyed into them at daybreak, General Klenau ordered shells to be thrown both from mortars and howitzers into the citadel. Two magazines in the fortress having caught fire, the commandant was summoned a second time, and after some delay, a flag of truce was sent about nine o'clock in the evening with proposals of capitulation, which were concluded at one o'clock in the morning. The enemy's fire killed two privates of the artillery and wounded an artificer.

On the 24th, in the morning, the copies of capitulation were exchanged, hostages mutually delivered up, and the gate of Soccorso was occupied an hour after.

Seventy-two new brass cannon, with their ammunition, and six months provisions, were found in the fortress. The hospital stores alone are estimated at one million five hundred thousand French livres.

General

General Klenau gives praise to Colonel Oreſkovich, Captain Victora, and Lieutenant Cantori, the two latter of whom not only erected their batteries one hundred feet from the covered way, but by their ſkill and bravery alſo ſet fire to the enemy's magazines, which obliged them ſoon to ſurrender.

Count Alberti, Lieutenant Diſerſki, and others, diſtinguiſhed themſelves upon this occaſion, but particularly Colonel Skall, who joined General Klenau as a volunteer, and who proved both an able engineer and an experienced negotiator.

Capitulation concluded on the 23d May, between the Auſtrian General Count Klenau and the French Commandant La Poniſe, for the Surrender of the Citadel of Ferrara.

Art. I. The citadel of Ferrara ſhall be ſurrendered to General Klenau.

Anſw. The citadel ſhall be occupied by the Auſtrian troops within thirty hours after the ſignature of the preſent capitulation.

II. The troops of which the garriſon conſiſts ſhall march out with all the honours of war; namely, with their arms, baggage, and one field-piece and its tumbril, for each battalion.

Anſw. The garriſon ſhall march through the gate of Soccorſo, with the honours of war; namely, with arms, baggage, and a field-piece, as far as the glacis, but ſhall there lay down their arms, and the cavalry give up their horſes. Officers will be permitted to keep their ſwords.

III. The garriſon ſhall be forwarded to the head-quarters of the French army, under ſuch eſcort as the Auſtrian general ſhall order, with whom it will alſo reſt to decide upon the route upon which they are to march, obſerving, however, that it ſhould be by the ſhorteſt way.

Anſw. The garriſon engage not to ſerve againſt the troops of his Imperial Majeſty, or of his allies, during ſix months.

IV. The troops ſhall be provided with the neceſſary means for the conveyance of their effects, either by land or water, whether theſe effects are the property of the whole corps or of individuals; alſo for the removal of the horſes belonging to officers and ſuch other perſons as are entitled to have any.—Granted.

V. The garriſon ſhall be ſupplied, from ſtation to ſtation, with the neceſſary proviſions, at the rates and according to the rules obſerved in the French ſervice.—Granted.

VI. The ſick and wounded whoſe immediate removal is impracticable, will remain in the hoſpital at Ferrara until their entire recovery, when they ſhall, together with the medical officers who are left to attend them, be eſcorted to the French advanced poſts.

Anſw. Granted. Theſe ſick and wounded, however, when they recover, to be ſubject to what is ſpecified in anſwer to the third article.

VII. Engineer and artillery officers ſhall be reciprocally appointed to take inventories of the writings and plans in the fortreſs, and of the artillery and other articles which they exchange.

Anſw. Theſe individuals will meet in the citadel immediately after the exchange of the preſent articles.

VIII. Commiſſaries ſhall be named on both ſides, to take inventories of the magazines of every deſcription, and to receive or deliver them up.

Anſw.

Anſw. Granted, on the ſame condition as above.

IX. All perſons not being military, who are ſhut up in the fortreſs, and may wiſh to accompany the garriſon, will either be permitted to do it, or to repair to wherever they pleaſe.—Granted.

X. The Ciſalpine and Piedmonteſe troops ſhall be treated in every reſpect as the French.—Granted.

XI. The officers or other perſons belonging to the army departments, whom their affairs may detain for a ſhort time in Ferrara, ſhall be permitted to remain there as long as the Auſtrian general ſhall deem it proper.—Granted.

XII. No ſoldier, or other individual belonging to the garriſon, ſhall, upon any account, be moleſted or detained.—Granted.

XIII. The Auſtrian troops will, immediately after the ſignature of the preſent capitulation, occupy the town ſide of the half-moon at the entrance of the citadel.

Anſw. The Auſtrian troops will take poſſeſſion of the gate of Soccorto.

XIV. Hoſtages will be exchanged as ſecurities for the execution of the above articles.

Anſw. Of courſe.

ALBERTY, Captain of the Auſtrian Engineers.
DESAU, Chief of Battalion Triqueurt.
SEALL, Colonel of the Quarter-maſter-general's Staff.

Confirmed by the Commandant of the Citadel of Ferrara,
Ferrara, May 23.   LA PONITE.

As it is a principle in the Auſtrian ſervice to diſtinguiſh brave ſoldiers, I conſent to the requeſt of the commandant La Ponite, that non-commiſſioned officers may keep their ſide-arms; and I approve in general of the above articles of capitulation.

COUNT KLENAU, Major-gen.

The French garriſon conſiſted of 1525 men. Ammunition of every ſort, and in great abundance, was found in the place.

Whilſt this operation was carried on againſt Ferrara, Lieutenant Grill was ordered upon another expedition againſt Ravenna.

According to his report of the 26th to General Kray, he embarked on the 24th, with four companies of the regiment of Stuart, and entered Porto di Goro on the 25th.

On the 26th he landed his troops at Porto Primaro with two three-pounders, having previouſly concerted upon the mode of attack with Major Pooz, the commander of the flotilla, and Jacobi, the chief of the inſurgents at Commachio.

Major Pooz entered the canal of Ravenna with his flotilla, and landed his ſailors. Lieutenant Grill marched to Ravenna through Pozzuolo, with three companies and two pieces of cannon; and 300 of the inſurgents marched at the ſame time from St. Alberto.

On his approach, the enemy ſhut their gates and defended themſelves, but the gates were ſoon forced open, and, after a ſhort reſiſtance, they retreated by the way of Lugo. They loſt, in their retreat, one piece of cannon, a lieutenant-colonel, an officer, and about 100 priſoners. Major Pooz was very active in the landing, and ſoon after the forcing of the

the gates, he came to the affistance of Lieutenant Grill with 60 armed failors.

cures the coast, Ferrara, in the province of Ferrara.

An account from General Melas, of the 21ft of May, from Candia, ftates, that, after fome very fatiguing marches, the three divifions of Kaim, Frolich, and Zoph, with the Ruffian troops under the command of General Forfter, had entered the camp between Langafco and Candia, on the Sefia, where the Ruffian general Rofenberg was already ftationed with the reft of his troops, who, together with General Vukaffovich, occupied, the ftrong points of Valenza and Cafale.

SUPPLEMENT.

Conformable to a Report from his Royal Highnefs, dated Head-quarters, Winterthur, 28th of May.

GENERAL Maffena, commander in chief in Switzerland, made a general attack on our troops on the 25th, and occupied Frauenfeld at the moment when Field-marfhal-lieutenant Petrafh, who had been detached by Field-marfhal-lieutenant Hotze with the dragoons of Kinfky and the brigade of General Prince Rofenberg, arrived there to occupy that poft. The engagement lafted the whole day with the greateft obftinacy. Our infantry, who had marched the whole of the preceding night, diftinguifhed themfelves by their intrepid conduct, notwithftanding their fatigue: they were fupported with energy by the dragoons of Kinfky's regiment, under the command of General Prince Rofenberg, who, on account of the ground being unfavourable for cavalry, ferved on foot in the hotteft fire, with diftinguifhed bravery. The Prince received a contufion, which, however, did not prevent him from continuing the command.

The lofs was confiderable on both fides. Night coming on put an end to the engagement; but the poft was abandoned by the enemy, who had attacked it with three divifions.

Field-marfhal-lieutenant Petrafh highly commends the fteadinefs of the regiments of Kaunitz and Gemmingen: he extols particularly the bravery of General Prince Rofenberg, and the fkill difplayed by him in availing himfelf of every advantage that the ground afforded. He praifes in the higheft terms, the co-operation and the efforts of the officers of the ftaff, and more efpecially the courage difplayed by the whole regiments during the action.

The number of prifoners taken on this occafion, at firft ftated to be only 300 men, amounts to more than 500.

The Archduke Charles having determined to quit Fyn and Vyll, in order to attack the enemy with the left wing of the army, ordered Fieldmarfhal-lieutenant Prince Reufs to march on the 26th with his divifion by Fyn, and form a junction with Field-marfhal-lieutenant Hotze, for the purpofe of acting in concert.

The attack took place on the 27th, under the orders of Field-marfhallieutenant

Lieutenant Hotze and Prince Reuss, whilst the right wing of the army remained upon the Fyn.

This attack had the wished-for success. The enemy was driven back every where with considerable loss. All our troops acting in Switzerland formed a junction on the 27th near Winterthur at eleven o'clock in the morning. This obliged the enemy to retreat to their position near Zurich. We took on that day 300 prisoners and four pieces of cannon.

This first success of our troops determined General Massena to recall General Lorch with his division, who was already on his march for Italy.

Vienna, June 1.

BY accounts received from General Melas, of the 26th, it appears that the two divisions of Kaim and Frolich had pass'd the Stura and advanced against Turin, the capital of Piedmont, the left wing being placed upon the Reggio and Dora, and the right behind Madonna della Campagna.

The suburb was occupied by two battalions of Guilay. The Russian troops, with the division of General Karaiczy, also passed the Stura and the Dora, and placed themselves in front of La Certosa, so that their right wing extended to Cruliasko.

General Vukassovich, being reinforced with one battalion, advanced on the right bank of the Po, and occupied the heights; and at nine o'clock at night every thing was prepared for the bombardment of the town.

Lieutenant-colonel and Adjutant-general Thelen arrived here yesterday morning, with a farther account from Field-marshal Suwarrow, that on the 27th General Vukassovich, who commanded the advanced guard, summoned the town of Turin to surrender. Being refused, General Vukassovich ordered some shells to be thrown into the town, which set fire to one of the houses near the gate of the Po, when the well-disposed citizens, notwithstanding the opposition of the French, opened the said gate to General Vukassovich.

Two squadrons of the seventh regiment of hussars immediately forced their way into the town, and pursued the enemy as far as the gate of the citadel, and made 40 prisoners. In the mean time General Vukassovich occupied the town with his infantry, and opened the rest of the gates. Captain Veczay took this opportunity to pursue the enemy with a detachment of cavalry and the piquet of Guilay, in the suburb of Palino, and took several prisoners.

The enemy having thrown themselves into the citadel, General Kaim's division was ordered to blockade it from within the town, and the Russian general, Prince Pankrazion, with five battalions, four companies of rangers, and four squadrons of Lewenohr, from without.

The division of General Frolich has been stationed on the road of Pignerelo, near Orbassano, to which place Zoph's division and the rest of the Russian troops have also been ordered.

Upwards of 360 pieces of cannon, a considerable quantity of ammunition and stores of every kind, were found on the ramparts and in the arsenal. The enemy left 215 sick in the hospital. General Melas entertains no doubt that he will be able to discover an additional quantity of stores.

Immediately

Immediately upon our entering Turin, the enemy cannonaded the town from the citadel for upwards of an hour, and commenced the cannonade again at daybreak, which lasted till five o'clock. A convention was afterwards agreed upon, by which the enemy engaged to do no farther injury to the town.

General Seckendorff, who advanced with his troops against Alessandria, between the Orba and Bormida, whilst the Russian Lieutenant-general Schweihowsky invested the citadel on the left bank of the Tanaro, is now blockading it from the side of the town, and his advanced posts extend from the Serivia through Novi Casine and Carantino to Masso upon the Tanaro; the Russian Cossacks being also stationed between Masso and Casale.

It is reported that the enemy are collecting their main force near Cuneo.

Downing Street, June 22.

THE Emperor of Russia having, as a mark of friendship towards his Majesty, and of esteem and regard towards his Majesty's naval service, and particularly towards the officers and crews of the ships who served on the 1st of August 1798, under the command of Rear-admiral Lord Nelson, signified to his Majesty's minister at Petersburgh his desire, that the Leander, of 50 guns, which having been engaged in that action, was, after a most gallant and distinguishable resistance, captured by a French ship of the line of 74 guns, and has since been recaptured from the enemy, by his Imperial Majesty's arms, at the surrender of Corfu, should be presented to his Majesty in his Imperial Majesty's name, with a view to its being restored to his naval service.

The King has been pleased to accept, with the highest satisfaction, this distinguished mark of attention and friendship on the part of his ally, and has directed that the Leander should be received accordingly from such officer as the Emperor of Russia may direct to deliver the same, and should again be placed among the ships composing his Majesty's fleet employed in the Mediterranean.

From the LONDON GAZETTE EXTRAORDINARY, June 26, 1799.

Downing Street, June 26.

A DISPATCH, of which the following is an extract, has been received from the Right Honourable Sir Morton Eden, K. B. by the Right Honourable Lord Grenville, his Majesty's principal Secretary of State for the foreign department.

Vienna, June 12.

I HAVE the honour of enclosing to your Lordship two Extraordinary Gazettes of this place, one published yesterday evening, the other this day.

Vienna, June 11.

BEFORE communicating to the public the statement of his Royal Highness, which was brought yesterday by the First-lieutenant Leibinger

ger of the regiment of Spleny, we will give, in their order, the preceding reports, hitherto delayed from the irregularity of the post.

On the 25th May the enemy, probably with the intention of preventing us from forming a junction with Field-marshal-lieutenant Hotze, attacked the whole line of our outposts with so superior a force as to oblige them to fall back as far as Thur, and enabled the enemy to occupy the bridge of Andelfingen.

Our artillery, which was p'anted on the banks of the river, checked their progress; they were at length dislodged from the bridge and driven back with considerable loss.

General Kienmayer and Colonel Merfery greatly distinguished themselves by the almost total destruction of a regiment of the enemy's hussars, which endeavoured to surround them in the beginning of the affair.

General Piatfchek was wounded in the very outset.

Nevertheless, the enemy attacked Field-marshal-lieutenant Hotze's advanced guard with great impetuosity and alternate success five different times: the regiments of Kounitz and Gemmingen particularly distinguished themselves on this occasion; but towards evening we were obliged to yield to the superior numbers of the enemy, and to fall back upon Field-marshal lieutenant Hotze. The enemy then took the direction of Pfyn, and occupied the bridge.

General Simfchon was sent with a battalion of Callenberg and a detachment of cavalry, to dislodge the enemy. He could not arrive before night-fall. The attack was made after dark by General Pfecher, and with such success, that the enemy were not only dislodged from the bridge, but also driven back with great loss.

The enemy, finding that their attempts had failed, retired the 26th on all sides. They were followed by our advanced guard. The enemy, notwithstanding, attacked the advanced guard of Field marshal-lieutenant Nauendorff on the 27th at Embrach, with the design of forcing the passage of the Thofs, and penetrating, by that means, to the rear of our communication. This attack was repulsed; the enemy were driven from Embrach, and we took post at this large village.

In the night of the 28th the enemy withdrew entirely behind the Klatt; in consequence of which the advanced guard of our left wing took post before Baffefdorff, and that of our right wing before Bulach. These checks, and the appearance we shewed, induced the enemy to detain the columns which were already in motion to join the army of Moreau in Italy.

The above-mentioned Lieutenant Leibinger was sent, on the 6th inst. by his Royal Highness from Kiatten, with accounts that the enemy had abandoned all the right bank of the Klatt, and, after destroying all the bridges in the rear, had taken post on the left bank of that river.

In order to approach the strong intrenchments which the enemy had raised near Zurich, and to drive them from the right bank of the Klatt, for the purpose of forming a considerable advanced guard there, his Royal Highness ordered Field-marshal-lieutenant Hotze and General Prince Rotenberg to pass the Klatt near Tubendorff at four in the morning, and to drive the enemy from the bridge of Klatt, which was executed, notwithstanding a most obstinate resistance: at the same time, Field-marshal-lieutenant Prince Joseph of Lorrain advanced from Villikon, and General Jellachich from Zullikon, with such vigour against the flank of the intrenchments, that General Jellachich penetrated into the upper suburbs of Zurich, and the Prince of Lorrain as far as the abbatis upon the Zurich-Berg, which was defended by redoubts and fleches.

It being of the utmost importance to the enemy to keep us as far distant as possible from their intrenched camp, they sent such powerful reinforcements to their troops posted on the Klatt, and brought such a number of batteries to bear upon us, that they not only checked the progress of the division under Field-marshal-lieutenant Hotze, before Schwammendingen, but also repulsed the troops which had advanced to the abbatis, and even threatened the right flank of Prince Rosemberg's corps, near Seebach: this induced his Royal Highness to reinforce the advanced guard near Seebach with a brigade of infantry under Prince Reuss and part of Prince Anhalt Cotheu's division of cavalry; at the same time Field-marshal lieutenant Count Wallis was ordered to march with two battalions of grenadiers and the Archduke Ferdinand's regiment of infantry, by Schwammendingen to the Zurich-Berg, and to carry the enemy's intrenchments and abbatis by the bayonet. The grenadiers speedily gained possession of the first fleche, and penetrated into the abbatis, where General Hiller was wounded, as well as Field-marshal-lieutenant Count Wallis.

The enemy being posted behind the abbatis in superior force, it was impossible to advance; but they were however prevented from attacking the Prince of Lorrain: this gave an opportunity for Field-marshal-lieutenant Petrasch (who commanded in the place of General Hotze, who was wounded in the first attack) to push forward the advanced guard under Prince Rosemberg to within musket-shot of the intrenchments, and to form there at dusk.

His Royal Highness reconnoitred the enemy's intrenchments on the 5th, and notwithstanding their strength and their advantageous situation, he resolved to attack them at two o'clock in the morning, and to take them by storm: his Royal Highness, in consequence, ordered his troops to be refreshed, and to take rest in sight of the enemy. This unexpected and menacing aspect disconcerted them; and to avoid the risk of this fresh attempt they retired on the 5th with the main body of their army, in the greatest precipitation, towards Baden, leaving in their intrenchments 25 cannon, three howitzers, and 18 ammunition-waggons.

The following day his Royal Highness took possession of the intrenchments with a strong advanced guard, and soon after the town of Zurich. He gave orders to the commanders of the outposts to send out numerous patroles to watch the motions of the enemy.

All the generals and the officers of the staff who commanded the troops deserve the highest praise. The success of this day is to be attributed to their courage and skill.

One chief of brigade and two adjutant-generals are among the prisoners.

The enemy estimates their loss at 4000 men. Ours will be made known immediately.

Vienna, June 12.

AS already mentioned, the corps under the command of the Field-marshal-lieutenant Count Bellegarde has, in consequence of the fortunate change of affairs in the Tyrol and the Grison country, received orders

orders to advance into Italy to support the operations of the army there. The arrival of Count Bellegarde in Chiavenna is already known.

In conformity to particular orders since received from the commander in chief of the Italian army, a part of the Count's corps was to operate in the right flank of the army of Italy, and to take a post near Migiasidone and Domo d'Asola; by this means to secure a communication between the Italian army and that under the command of his Royal Highness the Archduke Charles; and he himself to proceed expeditiously with the remainder of his corps to Como, and thence through Milan and Pavia against Tortona.

The Field-marshal-lieutenant Count Hadik having already placed himself at the head of the troops collected at Bellinzone, the greatest part of which consisted of the brigades of the Colonels Prince de Rohan, Strauch, and Count St. Julien, Count Bellegarde has destined this corps to the above-mentioned operations on the right wing of the army, and he himself has embarked with the rest of the troops on the Lake Como, to proceed to his farther destination.

By three reports from the Count, dated Como, May 30, 31, and June 3, we learn, that Field-marshal lieutenant Count Hadik had received advice of the intention of the French General Loison to get reinforcements, and to maintain his position near Airolo and on the Mount St. Gotthard, and he thought it expedient to counteract this design.

With this view, on the 28th of May, in the evening, at six o'clock, he attacked the enemy on this side at the foot of the Mount St. Gotthard: the obstinate defence of the enemy fully demonstrated how important this post was to them. The centre had the most difficult part of the battle, on account of the perpendicular rocks, and the left column could not immediately give any support, because the enemy had broke down the bridge over the Ticino. Finally, the perseverance of the light-infantry, under the command of its chief Lieutenant-colonel Le Loup, supported by a division of Bannalis's, surmounted all those obstacles which opposed the centre. Now the battle became general; the enemy using every means that could result from number, local advantage, and courage, and it remained for some time doubtful: but when the Colonel Prince Victor de Rohan had crossed the Ticino with the left column, and ascended the steepest rock on the right flank of the enemy, and the Major Siegenfeld with his column posted himself upon that mountain which commands the left of the Mount St. Gotthard, it was impossible for the enemy to maintain their position in this important pass.

In this critical situation the enemy was attacked on the following morning, the 29th, by Colonel Count St. Julien, on the other side of Mount St. Gotthard, who set off in the morning at half past one o'clock from Selva in Upper Rhinethal, ascended Mount Ursula, drove down the picquets of the enemy, and leaving behind him a battalion, in case of a retreat on his part, he descended with impetuosity to attack the enemy's position at the Devil's Bridge, and to Urseren, compelled the enemy, by the briskness of the attack, to abandon this advantageous and important post with such precipitancy, that even the battalion destined to cover their retreat, by a well-directed fire in its flank from a division of De Vins, commanded by the Lieutenant Kall of the general quarter-master staff, fell in disorder, and the commander of it,

with

with some officers and many privates, by a quick pursuit, were made prisoners.

In the heat of the pursuit our troops, animated by victory, forgot all the fatigues of the preceding nocturnal march over Mount Ursula and the exertions of the battle, and followed the enemy over Gestum and Waassen, a space of five leagues, to the Stile, and prevented the enemy from taking a position; took prisoners several divisions of its rear, and would have driven the enemy to Altdorf at the Lake of Lucerne, if the battalion placed at the Stile had not collected the fugitives, and prevented our further pursuit by breaking down the bridge, which was prepared and preconcerted in case of a flight. In that they could the better succeed, as the column who had orders to pass the Mount Kritzly to the Stile found the road impassable, and could not arrive in time, even by the acknowledgment of the people of the country.

The principal view of the attack (the junction with Field-marshal-lieutenant Count Hadik, and the possession of Mount St. Gotthard, with all the passes leading from the Russthal) having completely succeeded, the Colonel Count St. Julien contented himself with taking a position near Waassen and Gertina, and supporting it by all necessary means.

In these continued and obstinate battles our loss is not inconsiderable, but that of the enemy much greater. A more minute account will in time be given. When the report was sent off, 531 prisoners were brought in, among whom are a commander of a battalion and 12 officers.

The enemy left behind in Airolo 450 sacks of rice, 100 casks of wine, some casks of brandy, and other provisions, together with one four-pounder and a considerable quantity of ammunition ready for the infantry.

The Field-marshal-lieutenant Count Hadik and the Colonel Count St. Julien universally extol the courage and perseverance of the troops. Count Hadik particularly praises the Lieutenant-colonel Le Loup, the Major Siegenfeld, and the Captain Sokolovich of the staff of the general-quarter-master, who commanded the columns which chiefly contributed to the decision of the battle, by their accurate judgment of the local, by leading them to the most essential points, and by their personal examples of bravery. Further the Field-marshal-lieutenant Hadik praises the intrepidity of Captain Lossberg, of the regiment of Michael Wallis, who, with the fore-mentioned Captain Sokolovich, leaped the first into the Ticino, by which they inspired the troops with a resolution to follow.

The Colonel Count St. Julien particularly acknowledges the judicious and spirited conduct of Captain Wesselich, of Mungatsi, Captain Sudna, of De Vins, and Captain Lehn, of Neugebauer, commanders of battalions; and that of Lieutenant Kall, of the general-quarter-master staff, who facilitated not only the victory, but much contributed to secure the prisoners, of which two companies were compelled by Captain St. Ivany, of De Vins, to surrender their arms in the wood.

The Colonel also applauds the conduct of Corporal Zerini, of the third battalion of artillery, who not only invented frames of ordnance for the eight one-pounders belonging to the brigade, to apply them in all places, but personally attended them on all occasions, and particularly in these latter actions, with as much ability as effect.

Finally,

Finally, a confiderable quantity of filk and other merchandife, which the enemy had confifcated, was found in Alrolq, but which our troops have left untouched, although the place was taken by affault. The Field-marfhal-lieutenant Hadik took upon him to reftore the goods to the former proprietors.

In confequence of the reports to the 3d of June from the General of the cavalry De Melas, the pofition of the army of Turin, and furrounding it, has not been confiderably altered.

The divifion of Field-marfhal-lieutenant Frolich has extended itfelf over Pignerol, Boncaliere, and Carignan; and the General Vukaffovich has befet with his van, Carmagnol, Alba, and Cherafco.

In Cherafco he has taken fix metal eight and fixteen pounders, five of iron heavy artillery, one howitzer, three metal and 10 iron guns, two bombs, and a quantity of ammunition and ftores.

According to a farther report of the General of cavalry Melas, the preparations for befieging the caftle of Turin are urged on with vigour. To this purpofe, fome of the guns found in this town and ammunition are applied.

The two companies of the regiment of Anton Efterhazy, fent to the fortrefs Ceva (taken from the enemy by the country people of Piedmont), have happily arrived there by the judicious guidance of the inhabitants, notwithftanding the enemy patrolled that whole country, and the fortrefs was fupplied with provifions for thirty days.

Since that time the enemy has collected troops round this place, blockaded it, and thrown fhells in it fince the 28th of May. But the General Vukaffovich has advanced with his van towards Ceva, and forced the enemy to raife the blockade and to quit Mondovi.

The Field-marfhal-lieutenant Frolich has occupied Foffano with his divifion. He ftaid near Savigliano, and fent his patroles towards Cuneo.

The General Lufignan has orders to repulfe the enemy, which is at Feneftrell; and the General Alcaini has already commenced the bombardment of the citadel of Tortona.

The General of artillery Kray reports from Caftlelucio, dated the 4th of June, that the Field-marfhal-lieutenant Ott, who had received reinforcements from him, is pofted very advantageoufly near Fornovio, which pofition covers Parma and Piazenza, and that he himfelf is inceffantly urging forward the moft ferious preparations for the fiege of Mantua.

From the LONDON GAZETTE, July 2, 1799.

Admiralty Office, July 2.

Extract of a Letter from Mr. William Le Lacheur, Commander of the Cutter private Ship of War the Refolution, to Evan Nepean, Efq. dated at Guernfey the 20th ult.

"ON the 25th May, in lat. 43 N. long. 16 W. I fell in with and captured the French fchooner privateer La Vigie, of 14 long fourpounders and 71 men, belonging to Bourdeaux.

"W. LE LACHEUR."

Extract

Extract of a Letter to Lord Duncan, dated his Majesty's Ship Champion, Yarmouth Roads, June 30.

"My Lord,

"ON the morning of the 26th instant I observed a brig off the Dudgeon, and, after a chase of three days and two nights, I had the satisfaction to capture the Anacreon French privateer, commanded by Citizen Blanckeman, belonging to Dunkirk, of 16 guns and 125 men.

Admiral Lord Duncan. "G. E. HAMOND."

From the LONDON GAZETTE, July 6, 1799.

Admiralty Office, July 6.

Extract of a Letter from Vice-admiral Harvey, Commander in Chief of his Majesty's Ships and Vessels at the Leeward Islands, to Evan Nepean, Esq. dated at Fort Royal Bay, Martinique, May 17.

"Sir,

"THE following merchant vessels belonging to the enemy have been captured by the ships and vessels of his Majesty's squadron under my command."

By the Bittern—The Spanish ship Amistad, letter of marque.
By the Lapwing—Two French schooners, La Revanche and L'Asmable.
By the Concorde—The French schooner La Recherche.
By the Southampton—The French schooner Caroline.
By the Pearl—The Dutch schooner Maria.
By the Victorieuse—A small Spanish schooner.

"Since my letter to you of the 8th of September last, three British and 12 American vessels, of different denominations, have been recaptured, and 14 vessels under neutral colours detained on suspicion of having enemy's property on board, by the squadron under my command.

HENRY HARVEY."

From the LONDON GAZETTE, July 9, 1799.

Downing Street, July 9.

DISPATCHES, of which the following are extracts, have been received from the Honourable Lord Henley and Lieutenant-colonel Craufurd, by the Right Honourable Lord Grenville, his Majesty's principal Secretary of State for the foreign department.

Zurich, June 24.

"I HAVE the honour to inform your Lordship, that a courier arrived this afternoon from Turin, with official dispatches from General Kray to the Archduke Charles, informing his Royal Highness, that Marshal Suwarrow had marched with a part of his army against General Macdonald, who was attempting to effect a junction with Moreau, and had defeated him in an action which took place at Gionni, near Bobbio.

General Haddick has received orders from Marshal Suwarrow to return

turn by the Simplon into the Valais, which will, no doubt, occasion a material alteration in the position of the armies.

Vienna, June 23.

I THINK it right to lose no time in informing your Lordship, that, by accounts just arrived from Marshal Suwarrow, dated the 13th, from Asti, the intelligence of the enemy's fleet having effected a disembarkation at Genoa appears to have been unfounded, as well as that of the exaggerated amount of the force of General Moreau's army.

Letters were at the same time received from General Kray, of the 19th, which agree with those of the Marshal in stating, that the enemy were moving with a force, which the most authentic accounts made to amount to about 25,000 men, through the Modenese, in the direction of Mantua, probably with the view of raising the siege of that fortress. General Kray, who had already marched with a few of his cavalry, in obedience to Marshal Suwarrow's orders, had, in consequence, determined to return to his station before Mantua: the Marshal had detached to him reinforcements, and intended immediately to march himself to Valentia; and the Austrian troops, which occupied Reggio, Parma, and Modena, &c. had retired, and were concentrating themselves towards Mantua.

Admiralty Office, July 9.

Extract of a Letter from Lord Viscount Duncan, Admiral of the White, &c. &c. to Evan Nepean, Esq. dated on board the Kent, off the Texel, the 4th July.

I ENCLOSE, for their Lordships' information, a letter I received yesterday from Captain Winthrop, of his Majesty's ship Circe.

My Lord, *Circe, at Sea, June 29.*

HAVING received information that several Dutch gun-vessels were lying at the back of the Island of Ameland, and Captains Temple and Boorder of his Majesty's sloops Jalouse and L'Espeigle, having very handsomely volunteered their services to cut them out, I ordered the boats of his Majesty's ships named in the margin * to proceed under their command on the night of the 27th instant for that purpose, and anchored with the ships as near the shore as possible, in readiness to afford every assistance in my power.

I am sorry to say it now appears that the gun-vessels had previously shifted their berth with the ebb tide, and were lying aground when the boats got in, at a place where it was impossible to get near them: the officers and men were therefore ordered to cut out as many vessels from the Wadde as it might be practicable to bring away; and I have the satisfaction to add they succeeded in getting out twelve without a man being killed or wounded, though the enemy annoyed them as much as possible from their batteries. Six of the vessels have valuable cargoes, and were bound to Amsterdam; the others are in ballast.

I have the honour to remain, &c. &c.

R. WINTHROP.

Admiral Lord Viscount Duncan, &c. &c. &c.

* Circe, Jalouse, Pylades, L'Espeigle, Typhoon.

From

From the LONDON GAZETTE EXTRAORDINARY, July 10, 1799.

Downing Street, July 10.

DISPATCHES, of which the following are copies, have been this day received from the Right Honourable Lord William Bentinck, by the Right Honourable Lord Grenville, his Majesty's Secretary of State for the foreign department.

My Lord, *Placenza, June 22.*

BEFORE I begin to relate the different actions which have taken place, and which I am happy to say have terminated in the most complete success, it will be necessary previously to state to your Lordship the situation of the allied army, by which you will be better able to understand the views of the enemy, and the movements by which they have been defeated. The great and extensive plan of operations undertaken by Field-marshal Suwarrow have necessarily very much divided his force. Besides the siege of Turin, Mantua, Alexandria, and Tortona, were blockaded. The passes of Susa, Pignerol, and the Col d'Assiette, have been occupied. Major-general Hohenzollern was posted at Modena with a considerable corps. Lieutenant-general Ott, with 10,000 men, at Reggio, observed the movements of the enemy on that side, while Field-marshal Suwarrow remained at Turin with the rest of the army. This divided state of the army appears to have presented to General Moreau the most favourable opportunity of retrieving the French affairs in Italy. He hoped, by strongly reinforcing the army of Naples, that General Macdonald would be able to defeat the separate corps of Generals Ott and Hohenzollern, and afterwards to effect a junction with the army under his own command; and he probably conceived that the Field-marshal was too distant to afford assistance. With this view, the army of Macdonald, which had advanced very far to the north of Italy, was joined by the division of Victor, and, from the report of the French officers taken, must have amounted to near 30,000 men, composed entirely of French, with the exception of one Polish legion. Field-marshal Suwarrow having received information of the intentions of the enemy, immediately collected all the force at Alexandria, whence he marched on the 15th with 17 battalions of Russians, 12 battalions of Austrian dragoons, and three regiments of Cossacks. In the mean time General Macdonald had fallen upon Major-general Hohenzollern, and had obliged him to cross the Po with considerable loss. Lieutenant-general Ott had also been obliged to retire from Reggio to Placenza.

On the 17th, the French attacked General Ott, and compelled him to fall back upon Castel S. Gioanni, when the arrival of the army under the command of Field-marshal Suwarrow enabled Lieutenant-general Ott to repulse the French behind the Tidone river, with the loss of one piece of cannon and several prisoners.

On the 18th, the army marched in three columns, to attack the enemy. The Russian General Rosenberg commanded the right column, the Russian General Foerster the centre, and General Melas the left. The Russian Major-general Prince Prokration commanded the advanced guard, Prince Lickstenstein the reserve. The columns moved at twelve o'clock. The country is perfectly flat, and very much intersected with ditches

ditches and rows of vines. It does not appear that the enemy occupied any particular position. An advanced corps of two battalions and two guns at Caſſaleggio was attacked by the Ruſſian grenadiers, and the whole made priſoners. The French line retired behind the Trebbia. It was too late, and the troops were too much fatigued, to make a general attack, which was ordered for the next morning. The Trebbia is the moſt rapid torrent in Italy: the diſtance from one bank to the other is near a mile. The intermediate ſpace is an open ſand, divided by ſeveral ſtreams, which at this ſeaſon are fordable any where. The French occupied the right bank, the allies the left.

On the 19th, while the allies were preparing to make the attack, the French began a very heavy fire upon the whole line. For a moment they ſucceeded in turning the right of the Ruſſians at Caſſaleggio, and obliged them to fall back; but at this inſtant Prince Prokration, who had been detached with the ſame intent on the enemy's left, fell upon their rear and flank, and took one piece of cannon and many priſoners: the French did not however give up their object. They renewed the attack repeatedly upon the village of Caſſaleggio, but they were always defeated by the obſtinate valour of the Ruſſians. The attack upon the centre and left was equally violent: for ſome time the ſucceſs was doubtful, but at night the whole French line was repulſed behind the Trebbia. It was the intention of the Field-marſhal Suwarrow to have followed up the ſucceſs the next morning, but the French army retired in the night.

On the 20th, in the morning, the army purſued the enemy in two columns. The Ruſſians on the right marched by Settima, Monturuno, and Zena, where the rear-guard of the French, after an obſtinate reſiſtance, laid down their arms: the left column, compoſed of Auſtrians, marched on the great road from Placenza to Parma, as far as Ponte Nura.

On the 21ſt the army moved on to Fiorenzola. Lieutenant-general Ott was detached with a corps of Auſtrians in purſuit of the enemy. Several priſoners have already been ſent in. General Ott has reported that the French are retiring in two columns, one upon Parma, the other upon Forte Novo. Prince Hohenzollern has again advanced to Parma. Seven pieces of cannon, four French generals, and above 10,000 priſoners, have fallen into the hands of the allies. General Moreau has advanced to Tortona, where he gained a ſlight advantage over the advanced poſts of General Pellegarde. General F——'s army, from all reports, does not exceed 12,000 men, among whom are a vaſt number of Genoeſe. Not having ſeen any return of the killed and wounded of the Auſtrians, it is impoſſible for me to ſay what their loſs has been; it muſt have been conſiderable.

(Signed) WILLIAM BENTINCK.

My Lord, Placenzia, June 23.

SINCE I had the honour of writing to your Lordſhip yeſterday, the very important news of the ſurrender of the citadel of Turin has arrived. The garriſon is to return to France immediately, to be exchanged for an equal number of Auſtrian priſoners. General Fiorella, the commandant of the citadel, and all the French officers taken with him, are detained as hoſtages till the articles of the capitulation are executed. Field-marſhal Suwarrow arrived here this morning with the main army; he will march to-morrow towards ——————— in order to cover the sieges of that town and of Tortona. General Ott has formed a junction with Major-generals Klenau and Hohenzollern. In Piedmont General Macdonald has retreated, with his whole corps, by Pietra Bonia, towards Genoa.

(Signed)   WILLIAM BENTINCK.

From the LONDON GAZETTE, July 18, 1799.

Admiralty Office, July 16.

Extract of a Letter from Captain Griffiths, Commander of his Majesty's Ship Diamond, to Evan Nepean, Esq. dated at Spithead the 14th inst.

"ON the 29th ult. the Révolutionaire captured L'Hipolite French letter of marque; and in lat. 46 deg. N. and long. 24 deg. W. we recaptured the brig Margaret, from Greenock, bound to Savannah, taken but a few hours before by the Determiné French ship privateer, then in sight; and which, after a chase of fourteen hours, was captured by the Révolutionaire. I have brought her to Spithead: she is pierced for 24 guns, mounts 18 brass twelve and nine pounders."

From the LONDON GAZETTE, July 20, 1799.

Admiralty Office, July 20.

Extract of a Letter from the Honourable Henry Curzon, Captain of his Majesty's Ship Indefatigable, to Lord Bridport.

His Majesty's Ship Indefatigable, at Sea, May 31.

"IN lat. 43 deg. 7 min. N. and long. 11 deg. W. I fell in with and captured the French privateer brig La Venus, of 12 four and two nine pounders, and manned with 101 men, from Rochfort.

Right Hon. Lord Bridport, K. B. &c.   "H. CURZON."

Extract of a Letter from Captain Henry Digby, Commander of his Majesty's Ship Alcmene, to Earl St. Vincent.

My Lord,   *His Majesty's Ship Alcmene, July 6.*
RECEIVING information of several large privateers that had been hovering on the coast of Portugal having gone to the westward, I thought it expedient to exceed the limits of my station, and on the 22d of June, in lat. 38 deg. 50 min. N. long. 31 deg. W. a ship boarding an American was seen, which I chased; the parting, the American made to, and told me she was French, then distant two leagues; the weather being clear, I saw his manœuvres, and acted accordingly throughout the night; and by using every possible exertion, I got round the island of Corvo, in calms and light winds, on the 23d; the enemy, equally active, in his endeavours to avoid, preserved his distance, by towing and sweeping to the westward.

On the 24th and 25th I passed two English brigs, and upwards of 40 sail of merchant vessels, steering for Lisbon.

A breeze from the northward, on the 26th, brought me, by six in the morning, within gunshot of the enemy: a running fight commencing

Vol. VIII.   I   mencing

mencing, she struck after seven, in lat. 39 deg. 29 min. N. long. 33 deg. W. having suffered in her hull, sails, and rigging; is named the Courageux, of Bourdeaux, pierced for 32, but carrying only 28 twelves and nine-pounders (of which some were thrown overboard during the chase), with 253 men, commanded by Jean Bernard; 23 days last from Passage, expressly to intercept a Brazil convoy.

I have the honour to be, &c.

H. DIGBY.

Earl of St. Vincent, K. B. Admiral of the White, &c.

Extract of a Letter from Vice-admiral Harvey, Commander in Chief of his Majesty's Ships and Vessels in the Leeward Islands, dated June 8, to Evan Nepean, Esq.

"CAPTAIN Ekins, of his Majesty's ship Amphitrite, captured on the 22d ult. to windward of Antigua, Le Duquesne French privateer coppered brig, 16 guns, nine-pounders, and 129 men, belonging to Guadaloupe, which he sent to Barbadoes."

Extract of a Letter from Captain Winthrop, of his Majesty's Ship Circe to Lord Viscount Duncan.

My Lord, *Circe, off Ameland, July 11.*
I FEEL great pleasure in acquainting your Lordship, that the boats of our little squadron* made another dash into the Watt, at the back of Ameland, last night, and brought out three valuable vessels, deeply laden with sugar, wine, and brandy; they also burnt a large galliot, laden with brass ordnance and stores, which could not be brought off, notwithstanding the perseverance of Captain Mackenzie, to whom I am very much indebted for his coolness and judgment in the management of this affair; and also to Captain Boorder, whose local knowledge has been of great use to me.

"I have the honour, &c.

Admiral Lord Viscount Duncan, &c. "R. WINTHROP."

Extract of a Letter from Captain Wood, of his Majesty's Sloop Hound, to Vice-admiral Dickson.

"Sir, *H. M. Sloop Hound, off East Rice, June 23.*
"ON the 20th instant, the Scaw bearing S. S. W. distance 8 leagues, at two A. M. I fell in with and captured the French lugger privateer L'Hirondelle, mounting five guns, two swivels, and 26 men, from Dunkirk.

Arch. Dickson, Esq. Vice-admiral, &c. "J. WOOD."

Extract of a Letter from Captain Wollaston, of his Majesty's Sloop Cruiser, to Evan Nepean, Esq. dated Leith Roads, July 15.

"Sir,
"ON the 13th instant, in lat. 56 deg. N. I fell in with and captured, after a chase of three hours, the French lugger privateer Le

---

* Circe, Pylades, L'Espeigle, Courier cutter, and Nancy cutter.

Courageux,

Courageux, of 14 guns and 47 men, belonging to Dunkirk; she had taken four prizes, one of which I captured on the 12th.

"C. WOLLASTON."

Downing Street, July 20.

DISPATCHES, of which the following are copy and extract, have been received from Lieutenant-colonel Robert Craufurd, by the Right Hon. Lord Grenville, his Majesty's principal Secretary of State for the foreign department.

My Lord,   *Zurich, July 6.*

I HAVE the honour to inform your Lordship, that on the 3d inst, a considerable corps of the right wing of General Massena's army, under the command of the General of Division Le Courbe, attacked General Yellachitz's position in the canton of Schweitz, on the whole extent of his front, from the Sill to Schweitz and Brunnen.

The affair lasted the greater part of the day; and although the French at first gained some ground, they were afterwards completely repulsed; and General Yellachitz's corps reoccupied all its former posts, except Brunnen, of which the enemy retained possession on the evening of the 3d, but from whence he was also repulsed on the next morning.

Major-general Yellachitz bestows great praise on the conduct of the contingent troops of the cantons of Glaris and Schweitz.

I have the honour to be, &c.

ROB. CRAUFURD.

Extract of a Letter from Lieutenant-colonel Craufurd, to Lord Grenville, dated Zurich, 7th July.

I HAVE much satisfaction in being able to inform your Lordship, that, in consequence of the total defeat of General Macdonald's army, and the retreat of Moreau, General Haddick's corps, the destination of which has been so frequently changed, is now decidedly on the point of entering the Valais.

From the LONDON GAZETTE, July 23, 1799.

Downing Street, July 23.

DISPATCHES, of which the following are extracts, were this day received from the Right Honourable Lord Henley, by the Right Honourable Lord Grenville, his Majesty's principal Secretary of State for the foreign department.

Extract of a Letter from Lord Henley, to Lord Grenville, dated Vienna, July 6.

THE letters from Constantinople, of the 18th past, state, that official intelligence had been received by the Turkish government from Acre, that the garrison of that place had made, on the 21st of May, a general sally against the army of General Buonaparte, had completely defeated it, and put a great part of it to the sword; that General Buonaparte had, in consequence, found himself obliged to set fire to his camp and baggage, and to avail himself of the darkness of the night to retire towards Joppa; that Gezzar Pacha had immediately not only sent his cavalry in pursuit of him,

him, but had dispatched orders to the proper places, in order, as far as might be possible, to straiten or cut off his retreat; and that the heads of 13 French generals and 300 French officers, sent by different Tartars, had arrived at Constantinople, and had been exposed, according to custom, on the gate of the palace, with a suitable inscription.

A second messenger from Marshal Suwarroff, dispatched from Alessandria, on the 1st instant, is just arrived. I am informed that besides a detailed relation of the brilliant successes of the Imperial army on the 17th, 18th, and 19th past, and by which it appears that the loss of the French amounts in all to 20,000 men killed and taken prisoners, he brings an account of the Austrians having reoccupied the town of Tortona.

Extract of a Letter from Lord Henley to Lord Grenville, dated July 9.

AN express arrived yesterday with dispatches from General Kray of the 1st instant, mentioning the surrender of Bologna, by capitulation, to General Klenau, on the preceding day.

In addition to the intelligence, which I lately conveyed to your Lordship, of the defeat of General Buonaparte, and his flight towards Joppa, I have now to state, that this government has received official accounts from Constantinople, dated the 22d past, that Joppa had been taken by the allied force (meaning, it is supposed, that under Sir Sidney Smith and a body of Turks); that Buonaparte had reached El Arish, on the frontier of Syria, in his flight; and that it was scarcely to be believed, that in his present circumstances of distress he would be able to gain in safety the Egyptian side of the desert.

Extract of a Letter from Lord Henley to Lord Grenville, dated Vienna, July 11.

IT is with great and unfeigned pleasure that I inform your Lordship, that a messenger arrived here about an hour ago from Florence, with letters, dated the evening of the 6th instant, stating, that on the preceding day the people having assembled in great force, and cut down what is styled the tree of liberty; the French centinels and corps de garde had retired into the forts, and that the following day all the French troops had left that town and Pistola, and marched towards Leghorn; the old magistrates had immediately resumed their functions, and had replaced the arms of the Grand Duke in the places from which they had been taken down. No disorder whatever had taken place, and the greatest demonstrations of joy had been exhibited by all ranks of people.

General Klenau writes, on the 7th, from Bologna, that in consequence of the instances of the magistrates of Florence, he had sent thither a detachment of troops under the command of Colonel D'Aspre; these troops were attacked by the French garrison that marched out of Bologna, but succeeded in repelling them.

Admiralty Office, July 23.

Extract of a Letter from Captain Ball to Captain Losack.

His Majesty's Ship Dædalus, Table Bay, Cape of Good Hope,
" Sir,   February 16.
" ON the 9th instant, in latitude 31 deg. 30 min. south, lon. 33 deg. 30 min. east, a little past daylight in the morning, we saw two sail on the starboard

starboard bow; gave chase to a large ship at six. At half past twelve P.M. came up alongside of the chase, and brought her to action; in fifty-seven minutes after which she struck. She proved to be La Prudente French national frigate, from the Isle of France, manned with 297 men, and mounts 26 twelve-pounders on the main-deck, two long six-pounders and two brass howitzers on the quarter-deck; she is pierced for 42 guns, 14 on a side, beside the bridle-port on the main-deck, was built at Brest. The ship in her company, when we first saw her, was an American, which they had sent to the Isle of France as a prize.

" Enclosed I transmit a list of the killed and wounded on board the two ships. I am, Sir, &c.

To George Losack, Esq. &c. Cape of Good Hope. "H. L. BALL."

Return of the killed and wounded on board his Majesty's Ship Dædalus, and the French National Frigate La Prudente.

Dædalus.—One seaman and one marine killed.—Eleven seamen and one marine wounded.

La Prudente.—Twenty-seven men killed.—Twenty-two wounded.

H. L. BALL.

From the LONDON GAZETTE, July 27, 1799.

Admiralty Office, July 27.

Extract of a Letter from the Earl of St. Vincent, K. B. Commander in Chief of his Majesty's Ships and Vessels in the Mediterranean, to Evan Nepean, Esq. dated at Port Mahon, June 14.

" Sir,

" I ENCLOSE a letter from Captain Peard, of his Majesty's ship the Success, recounting a very gallant exploit, which appears to me equal to any enterprise recorded in the naval history of Great Britain.

"ST. VINCENT."

" My Lord, *Success, Port Mahon, June 13.*

" THE 9th instant, standing towards Cape Creaux, in pursuance of Instructions I had received from Lord Keith, I discovered a polacca in the N. W. to whom I gave chase, but in consequence of her being near the land, I could not prevent her getting into the harbour of La Selva, a small port two leagues to the northward of the Cape; however, as she had shown Spanish colours, and there being no appearance of batteries to protect her, and the weather very favourable, I was induced to send the ship's boats to try to bring her out, with instructions to Lieutenant Facey, who commanded, to return, should he find any opposition of consequence: at four in the afternoon, Lieutenant Facey in the barge, Lieutenant Stupart in the launch, and Lieutenant Davison of the marines in the cutter, all volunteers on this occasion, put off from the ship; and at eight, after a good deal of firing, I had the satisfaction of seeing the polacca coming out round the point, which had kept them from our sight for more than an hour. During the time the boats were engaged, several of the enemy's gun-boats endeavoured to get in, but were prevented by our shot. The captured vessel proved to be the Bella Aurora, from Genoa, bound to Barcelona, laden with cotton, silk, rice, &c. mounting 10 carriage guns, nine and six pounders, and having on board, when attacked, 113 men:

the

she was surrounded by a netting, and supported by a small battery, and a large body of musketry from the shore.

"I am sorry to inform your Lordship that our loss has been great, three of those gallant fellows having been killed on the spot; and Lieutenant Stupart, an officer inferior to none in his Majesty's service for zeal, courage, and ability, with nine others, badly wounded; one of whom died this morning. The conduct of Lieutenant Facey, my Lord, who commanded, does him, in my opinion, great honour: he appears to have been the first on board, and to have shown, throughout the whole, great firmness and good example.

"The attack, my Lord, was made in the face of day by 42 men, in three boats, against a ship armed with 113 men, secured with a boarding netting, and supported by a battery, and a large body of men at small arms on the shore. I trust, my Lord, this fair statement of facts will be a sufficient recommendation of Lieutenants Facey and Stupart, and Lieutenant Davison of the marines, together with the petty officers and men who acted with them. I have the honour to be, &c. &c. &c.

Admiral the Earl of St. Vincent, K.B. &c. &c. &c. "S. PEARD."

List of killed and wounded on board the Boats of his Majesty's Ship Success, on the 9th of June.

Barge.—John Grey, killed.— John Londres, ditto.—James Shaw (2d), wounded.—Thomas Edwards, ditto.—John Hughes, ditto.—William Robinson, ditto.

Launch.—William Orr, killed.—Lieutenant G. Stupart, wounded.— Richard Hornsby, ditto.— William Madden, ditto.—James Shaw (2d), ditto.

Cutter.—Thomas Needham, wounded.—William Lamb, ditto.

Admiralty Office, July 27.
Extract of another Letter from Admiral the Earl of St. Vincent, K.B. to Evan Nepean, Esq. dated at Port Mahon, June 17.

"HEREWITH I enclose the copy of a letter from Captain Young, of his Majesty's ship Ethalion, who has been cruising off the Bay of Palma, the west end of the island of Majorca, where he captured and sent into this port, seven vessels, laden with wheat, sheep, and other articles of provisions; and three others this day.

"Likewise the copy of letter from Captain Cockburn, of La Minerve, giving an account of his having captured, in company with the Emerald, off the S.E. end of Sardinia, La Caroline French privateer ship, of 16 guns and 90 men, which he has sent into this port."

"My Lord, *His Majesty's Ship Ethalion, off Palma Bay, June 11.*

"I PROCEEDED off Palma Bay with the Ethalion under my command. On the morning of the 10th instant we discovered a number of vessels standing into the Bay, with a light air at east. The Ethalion being becalmed, I hoisted the boats out, and sent them under the direction of Lieutenants Pym and Jauncey, to endeavour to cut them off from Palma Bay. After a long and fatiguing row they took possession of two brigs and five tartans, from Barcelona, laden with wheat and sheep, for Majorca.

"I have the honour to be, &c. &c. &c.
To the Right Hon. the Earl of St. Vincent, "JAMES YOUNG."
Commander in Chief, &c. &c. &c.

My Lord, *La Minerve, at Sea, June 2.*

I HAVE the honour to inform your Lordship that the Emerald and Minerve captured this morning, off the S. E. end of Sardinia, La Caroline French privateer ship, of 16 guns and 90 men.

GEORGE COCKBURN.

Extract of another Letter from Earl St. Vincent, K. B. to Evan Nepean, Esq. dated at Port Mahon, the 22d June.

"YOU will herewith receive a letter from Vice-admiral Lord Keith, enclosing one from Captain Markham, of his Majesty's ship Centaur, giving an account of the capture of a squadron of French frigates, which had made their escape from Alexandria."

"My Lord, *Queen Charlotte, at Sea, June 19.*

"I HAVE the honour to inform your Lordship of the capture of five French vessels by the squadron under my command, and to enclose your Lordship Captain Markham's letter. KEITH."

My Lord, *Centaur, June 19.*

I HAVE the honour to inform you, that, pursuant to your signal of yesterday for a general chase to the N. E. I came up with and captured three frigates on the evening of this day.

The Bellona and Santa Teresa frigate being nearest when the two stern-most struck, I made their signals to take possession of them, whilst I pursued the third, which struck also in an hour afterwards. The Emerald in the mean time took the Salamine brig, and the Captain, the Alerte.

This squadron was commanded by Rear-admiral Perré, thirty-three days from Jaffa, bound to Toulon; for their names and force I refer you to the list. J. MARKHAM.

Vice-admiral Lord Keith, &c. &c. &c.

La Junon, Rear-admiral Perré, Porquerer captain, 40 guns, eighteen pounders, 500 men.
La Courageux, Buille captain, 22 guns, twelve-pounders, 300 men.
L'Alceste, Barée captain, 36 guns, twelve-pounders, 300 men.
La Salamine brig, Sandry lieutenant, 18 guns, six-pounders, 120 men.
L'Alerte brig, Dumay lieutenant, 14 guns, six-pounders, 120 men.

Admiralty Office, July 26.

Copy of another Letter from Admiral the Earl of St. Vincent, K. B. Commander in Chief of his Majesty's Ships and Vessels in the Mediterranean, to Evan Nepean, Esq. dated on board his Majesty's Ship Argo, Gibraltar Bay, July 6.

"I ENCLOSE a letter I have received from Captain Gage, of his Majesty's ship the Terpsichore."

"My Lord, *Terpsichore, at Sea, June 23.*

"I CHASED this morning, at daybreak, a Spanish xebec and an armed brig; the latter (St. Antonio) I captured, having carried away her main-top mast in the chase; she has 14 brass guns, twelve and six pounders, with 70 men; from Malaga, in company with the xebec.

"I have the honour to be, &c.

The Right Hon. the Earl St. Vincent, "W. G. GAGE."
K. B. &c. &c. &c.

Admiralty Office, July 27.

Copy of a Letter from Sir Hyde Parker, Knt. Commander in Chief of his Majesty's Ships and Vessels at Jamaica, to Evan Nepean, Esq. dated Port Royal Harbour, Jamaica, June 1.

"HEREWITH you will receive an account of privateers and merchant-vessels taken and destroyed by the squadron under my command, since my last returns by his Majesty's ship La Renommée, dated the 6th ultimo. H. PARKER."

An Account of Privateers, armed Vessels, and Merchant Vessels, captured and destroyed by the Squadron under my Command, since my last Returns, dated the 6*th May, by his Majesty's Ship La Renommée.*

Privateers and armed Vessels.

By the Magicienne—The French armed schooner L'Esperance, pierced for 14 guns, only four on board, and plenty of small arms, with a cargo of flour, hams, and butter; was chased on shore, but got off with the loss of her false keel, the crew escaped: taken.—A French schooner, pierced for 10 guns: chased on shore and burnt.

By the Acasta, in company with the Aquilon and Squirrel—A Danish schooner, from Jacquemel to St. Thomas, with a cargo of coffee and dollars: taken.

By the Acasta—A Spanish polacre of two guns and 130 tons, with a cargo of brandy, wine, and dry goods: taken by the boats.—The French schooner L'Aimable Eustatie, of one gun, and a cargo of 268 bags of coffee: taken.—The Spanish ship La Juno, of eight guns, pierced for 16, laden with cocoa and indigo: taken.—Two French row-boats, schooner-rigged: destroyed.—Two Spanish droggers, sloop-rigged: destroyed.

By the Surprise—The French armed schooner Les Amis, of one gun, and a cargo of coffee: taken.

By the Albicore—A settee Spanish privateer, armed with small arms, &c. cut out of a small bay to the eastward of St. Jago de Cuba, by the boats.

By the La Legere—The national brig L'Eclair letter of marque, with a cargo of dry goods and provisions from St. Thomas, pierced for 16 guns, had eight mounted: taken.

By the Sprightly—The French schooner L'Esperance, of six guns and 22 men, with a cargo of sugar and coffee: taken.

Merchant Vessels taken and destroyed.

By the Magicienne—The Spanish brig Nostra Senora del Carmen, with salt taken.—A Spanish schooner (same name as the brig), laden with flour, indigo, cinnamon, &c.: taken.—A French schooner, from Aux Cayes to St. Thomas, laden with coffee: taken.—The French schooner Speculator, from Curraçoa to Jacquemel, laden with provisions and dry goods: taken.

By the Squirrel and Musquito—A Spanish schooner from Port au Plat, with dollars: taken.

By the Acasta—A Spanish sloop, with plantains, taken by the boats, and broke up.—The Spanish sloop Nostra Senora del Carmen, with plantains, taken by the boats, and cut adrift.—The French schooner La Capricieuse, from Jeremie bound to St. Thomas, with a cargo of 115 bags of coffee, taken off Ocoa Point, by the boats.—A Spanish sloop, taken

off

off Ocoa Point, with a cargo of sugar.—A Danish ship from St. Juan, Porto Rico, bound to St. Thomas, with a cargo of 30 tons of fustick, cut out of a small bay, ten leagues to leeward of St. Juan, by the boats.—The Spanish schooner Polly: burnt by the boats.—The Spanish sloop La Magicienne, with plantain, corn, and stock: taken by the boats, and cut adrift.—The schooner Lucas, under Danish colours, from Mayoguave, bound to St. Thomas, with a cargo of 78 bags of coffee: taken by the boats.

By the Surprise—The American brig Juno, from Barracoa to Baltimore, laden with sugar and coffee; taken by a French privateer: retaken.

By the Pelican—A ship under American colours, from Jeremie, laden with coffee: taken.

H. PARKER.

Admiralty Office, July 27.

Extract of a Letter from Admiral Lord Viscount Duncan, Commander in Chief of his Majesty's Ships and Vessels in the North Sea, to Evan Nepean, Esq. dated off the Texel, the 22d instant.

"I TRANSMIT a letter I have just received from Captain Wood, of his Majesty's sloop the Hound, giving an account of his having destroyed a lugger privateer on the coast of Norway."

My Lord, *His Majesty's Sloop Hound, June 28.*

SINCE my last letter to you of the 20th instant, acquainting you of the capture of L'Hirondelle French privateer, being off this harbour, I received information from the consul of a large lugger of 16 guns, which was cruising in the Bight, or off the Scaw. On the 25th, at two A.M. I fell in with her, and after a chase of fourteen hours, having shot away her main-mast, I drove her ashore on the coast of Jutland, between Robinout and Hartshall; blowing very hard, with a heavy sea on the beach, she was soon dashed to pieces; and, I fear, many of the lives of the crew were lost. It gives me pleasure in having destroyed her, as she was following the rear of the Baltic convoy when I fell in with her.

I have, &c.

Lord Viscount Duncan, &c. &c. &c. J. WOOD.

Admiralty Office, July 27.

Extract of a Letter from Lieutenant Bond, commanding his Majesty's Gun-vessel Netley, to Evan Nepean, Esq. dated at Sea, July 9.

"I ENCLOSE copies of two letters, written by me to the Earl of St. Vincent."

My Lord, *Netley, Oporto, May 10.*

ON the 1st instant, after a long chase, we took L'Egyptienne French schooner privateer, pierced for 14, but carrying only eight guns, four of which she hove overboard during our pursuit. She had been eight days from Vigo, had made four neutral prizes, and had on board when taken only 35 men. I have the honour likewise to acquaint your Lordship, that on the same evening we recaptured an English brig, from Cork, bound to Oporto, laden with provisions, which had been taken the day before by a lugger privateer, off Vianna; also a galliot, laden with wine, from Oporto, one of the captures of the schooner before mentioned.

I have the honour to be, &c. &c.

The Earl of St. Vincent, K. B. &c. &c. &c. F. G. BOND.

My

My Lord,   Netley, Oporto, June 28.

ON the 10th ultimo I had the honour to communicate to your Lordship the proceedings of his Majesty's schooner under my command. She sailed from Oporto on the 20th of the same month, and, on the 14th inst. recaptured a brig from Lisbon to that port; the following day we took possession of a schooner laden with corn, &c. and, on the subsequent day, retook another schooner, also with corn. These vessels were part of a Portuguese convoy from Lisbon, that had been taken by a French privateer.

During the Netley's last cruise, we burnt a coasting vessel in Vigo Bay, and run on shore a brig, a little to the northward.

I have the honour to be, my Lord, &c. &c.

The Earl of St. Vincent, K. B. &c. &c. &c.   F. G. BOND.

Vienna, July 8.

Farther Particulars of the Battles which were fought on the 17th, 18th, and 19th of June, between the Rivulet of Tidone and the River Trebia, and of the Pursuit of the Enemy on the 20th, over the River Nura.

WHILE the royal Imperial and Russian troops were in the neighbourhood of Turin, and making preparations to besiege the citadel, advices were received that General Macdonald, with a reinforcement from Florence, and the division of General Victor, which had been sent to join him by the way of Lucca, was advancing toward the Lower Po.

Field-marshal Count Suwarrow committed the siege of the citadel of Turin to the care of Field-marshal-lieutenant Kaim, with nine battalions, six squadrons, and two regiments of Cossacks, to watch the passages from Savoy and the Riviera towards Piedmont; and led the army, by forced marches, to Alessandria. News arrived here that Macdonald had already appeared on the 12th before Modena, had forced General Hohenzollern to retreat with his small corps, with some loss, over the Po, and General Klenau to remain inactive; that he had afterwards advanced through Reggio and Parma; in which last place he had been joined by a battalion of the Duke's troops, and had threatened to attack Field-marshal-lieutenant Ott, who was posted at For-Novo, and between Parma and Piacenza.

Field-marshal Ott had, however, received orders not to weaken his force by a hazardous battle, but to yield to a superior force, and to retreat towards the army which was advancing to his support.

The Field-marshal marched with the army from Alessandria, leaving Field-marshal-lieutenant Count Bellegarde for the blockade of the citadel and that of Tortona, and hastened to the support of Field-marshal-lieutenant Ott: he arrived on the 17th, at four o'clock P. M. with the van-guard above St. Giovanni, at the moment when General Ott had, with great judgment, given way. Two regiments of Cossacks, Gocgow and Basdeyew, and the van-guard of Prince Pangrazion, reinforced the right wing of Field-marshal-lieutenant Ott; the first threw themselves, with a velocity peculiar to them, into the left wing of the enemy, during which time the said right wing of the infantry, in spite of the hedges and ditches, attacked the left wing of the enemy with fixed bayonets. The right wing and flank of the enemy were attacked by the Russian general Prince Gorzakow with two regiments of Cossacks, Semernikow and Moltsanow, two battalions of Russian grenadiers, ten companies of the regiment of Froelich and of the Imperial Russian grenadier battalion of Wouvermann; while Field-marshal-first-lieutenant Ott advanced upon the centre with his troops on the high road: every obstacle was furmounted; the moft impaffable ground did not prevent the companies of General Froelich from marching againft the enemy with fixed bayonets, and the huffars of the Archduke Joseph were every where ready to support the attack of our infantry, and make the retreat of the enemy as deftructive as poffible. The regiments of Karaczay, Loevenehr, and Lobkowitz, contributed in the moft effectual manner to the victory, and purfued the enemy as far as over the ftream of the Tidone, with great lofs.

The infantry arrived on the left bank of the Tidone about the clofe of the evening, but were prevented from rallying on the other fide by a brifk fire of artillery and fmall arms. The battle did not ceafe till late at night. The fruits of this victory, gained over the enemy on the 17th, are 1000 men killed, a proportionable number wounded, and 400 made prifoners.

The army broke up from the left bank of the Tidone at ten o'clock in the morning of the 18th, forded the river in three columns, and found the whole force of the enemy (which, according to their own report, confifted of fix divifions and more than 30,000 men) drawn up in a line of battle along the river Trebia.

The country being croffed with hedges and ditches, made our attack infinitely difficult. The van-guard, under the command of Prince Pangrazion, with four fquadrons of Karaczay, and four regiments of Coffacks, could not reach the left wing of the enemy till one o'clock P. M. It was immediately attacked by the infantry with fixed bayonets, turned, and overtaken by the cavalry: 500 remained dead in the field of battle; the adjutant-general, two colonels, and 600 privates, of the Polifh divifion of Dembrowfky, were made prifoners, and two pieces of cannon and one pair of colours taken.

In the mean time the enemy received new reinforcements, and put himfelf again into a pofture of defence, with a body of 15,000 men. General de Rofenberg, attentive to the defigns of the enemy, added the whole divifion of Sweykowfky to the van-guard of Prince Pangrazion. The attack was renewed, and the enemy driven over the river Trebia. The lofs of the enemy in this affair confifted of 1000 men killed, and 300 taken prifoners: the centre column, under the command of General-lieutenant Foerfter, with its light van-guard, confifting of one regiment of Coffacks and one fquadron of Loevenehr, fell in with the van-guard of the enemy, which confifted of 1000 horfe, fupported by fome hundreds of infantry, pofted half way between Tidone and the river Trebia: it was attacked, and, by the affiftance of fome companies under the command of Colonel Lawarrow, was forced to give way. The centre of the enemy was then attacked with fixed bayonets, and driven to the other fide of the river.

The enemy being determined to hazard the utmoft, and having received frefh reinforcements, with a ftrong divifion of cavalry, broke through the ranks of our infantry, and croffed the river with a body of 10,000 men. The Imperial Ruffian column waited its arrival with courage, threw themfelves with impetuofity upon the advancing enemy, and forced them once more, with the lofs of 600 killed and 60 taken prifoners, on the other fide of the river, where they were forced to remain, being kept in check by the fire of our cannon and mufketry, which continued till eleven o'clock at night.

The

General Hohenzollern had already arrived from Mantua, and found 200 of the enemy's wounded: Field-marſhal-lieutenant Ott took 110 priſoners on his march there.

The 22d the army reſted at Fiorenzolo; but as the news of General Moreau advancing with 18,000 men from Genoa by Bochetta into the plains between Tortona and Aleſſandria, had reached them, the army broke up on the 23d from Fiorenzolo, and got by forced marches already as far as the river Scrivia by the 25th, but Moreau did not find it prudent to wait their arrival. General Csubarrow, in conſequence of this, took poſſeſſion of the town of Tortona with four battalions, and blockaded the citadel as before.

Moreau had been engaged on the 20th with Field-marſhal-lieutenant Count Bellegarde, who had but an inconſiderable body of men to oppoſe to the ſuperior force of the enemy, being obliged to keep Aleſſandria blockaded: he, however, ſucceeded, though with the ſevere loſs of 203 killed, 578 wounded, and 1229 priſoners, in ſuch a manner that the enemy remained full four days inactive, and on the fifth commenced their retreat through Novi, and on the 26th were continuing their retreat over Bochetta.

Thus was the army of the enemy in the ſpace of ten days almoſt entirely annihilated, the ſiege of the citadel of Mantua once more ſecured, the whole of the river Po liberated, Tortona again blockaded, and Moreau driven back to his former poſition.

The advantages gained during the whole of this conteſt conſiſt in a loſs, on the part of the enemy, of 6000 killed, 5085 taken priſoners on the field of battle, 7183 wounded, made priſoners in Piacenza, amongſt whom are four generals, eight colonels, 502 officers of the ſtaff and commiſſioned officers; in the whole, 18,268 men: laſtly, ſeven cannons and eight ſtandards.

The loſs on our ſide conſiſts, in killed, 10 ſtaff and commiſſioned officers, and 244 non commiſſioned officers and privates; in wounded, 87 officers of the ſtaff and commiſſioned officers, and 1816 non-commiſſioned officers and privates.

The Imperial Ruſſian army loſt, in killed, one lieutenant-colonel, four officers, and 675 privates; in wounded, three generals, three colonels, one lieutenant-colonel, five majors, 35 commiſſioned officers, and 2041 privates.

Vienna, July 10.

ACCORDING to the information ſent here the 1ſt inſtant by the General of artillery Kray, the van-guard of Field-marſhal-lieutenant Ott, commanded by General Count Klenau, came up with the rear of General Macdonald at Bologna, on the 30th June, and compelled General Hulin, commander of it, to evacuate immediately, and ſurrender that place on the fo'lowing terms of capitulation:

Article I. I demand two hours to march out of the town with the garriſon and the ſick.

Anſw. I ſhall occupy immediately all the gates except that of Florence.

II. The inhabitants ſhall not be interrogated or perſecuted for their opinions and principles.

Anſw. This article is of a political nature, with which the military are not to interfere.

III.

III. The French, who have been made prisoners of war in the attack of the bridge and the other post, shall be immediately returned on their parole not to serve.—Granted.

IV. The baggage of the officers and of the staff, as well as the chest of the garrison, shall march out at the head of the troops, and be accompanied by an Austrian officer.

Answ. Granted; as far as the entrance of the mountains Pietro Mali.

HULIN,
General Commander of the Rear of the third Division of the Army of Naples.

COUNT DE KLENAU,
Imperial Royal Major-general.

Farther particulars concerning the ammunition and provisions found in Bologna, and other circumstances of this undertaking, are expected.

HIS Royal Highness the Archduke Charles has sent accounts, dated the 28th and 29th ult. that General Count Meerveld has advanced over Haslach, by the orders of Field-marshal-lieutenant Count Sztarray, on a reconnoitring party, by which the enemy have been driven from the environs of Offenburg, which General Count Meerveld had occupied the 26th.

The enemy retired to Kehl; and the Generals Meerveld and Goerger posted themselves, the first at Gengenbach, the latter at Oppenau.

By this expedition one colonel, six officers, and 240 privates have been brought in prisoners; the 10th and 23d French regiments of cavalry have been nearly cut to pieces. Our loss was not considerable.

The Field-marshal-lieutenant Count Sztarray purposes to send in the names of those who have signally distinguished themselves on this occasion.

We communicate here the detailed relation of the battle near Zurich, on the 4th of June, sent in by his Royal Highness.

THE French army, after their losses near Winterthur, on the 27th of May, having been compelled to retire over the Klatt, and having unsuccessfully attacked our right wing on the Thoes by Rohrbast and Under Embrach on the 1st of June, with a body of 10 or 12,000, and having been forced to withdraw their rear-guard from the right bank of the Klatt, his Royal Highness determined to dislodge them, and to drive them, if not beyond the Limat, at least into their intrenched position of Zurich, in order to put himself in a condition to ascertain exactly that position, of which his Royal Highness had received such various accounts, and to be enabled to arrange and order an attack upon it.

Immediately after taking Winterthur, his Royal Highness ordered General Jellachich to march to Pfeffikon, to cover the left flank of the army; and as soon as the enemy had passed the Klatt, the General Count Bey was ordered to march to Greiffensee, and General Jellachich to Grimmengen, to proceed from thence to the lake of Zurich, and along the lake to Kussnach.

On the 2d of June the army advanced to the Klatt, and took the bridge of Tubendorff. The General Count Bey dispersed the enemy, and

and passed the Klatt in the environs of Schwerzenbach, whence he proceeded to Wittikon, at the same time that General Jellachich drove the enemy from Zollikon with great loss, and took post there.

The Field-marshal-lieutenant Hotze had placed the Field-marshal Prince Joseph of Lorrain, near Tubendorff, with orders to render himself master of the heights of Wittikon in conjunction with Count Bey; he himself, with his column, was at Wallisellen, upon the chauffee from Winterthur to Zurich; his Royal Highness had conferred on him the command of all the troops on his left, and conduct of the attack.

The Field-marshal Prince of Reuss was placed on the right, before daybreak, with his division, upon the heights on the right bank of the Klatt at the chauffee leading from Klotten to Zurich; the General Prince Rosenberg, who commanded the van-guard, having already possessed himself of the Klatt bridge. Early in the morning of the 4th, the enemy succeeded in setting fire to the bridge over the Klatt at Wallisellen, and it was neither possible to extinguish the flames, nor form another bridge across, because the enemy, with his numerous artillery upon the declivity of the mountains called the Zurichberg, commanded the whole space from Stettbach to Schwammerdingen, so that all attempts to form a bridge would have been vain: the Field-marshal-lieutenant Hotze, in consequence of this, left behind the 60th Hungarian regiment, with a division of cavalry and a battery of horse artillery, under the direction of the Colonel Count Monquet, with orders to make continual feints, as if it was seriously intended to pass there; in the mean while the Field-marshal marched with the column to Tubendorff, to attack from that side the right flank of the enemy posted from Stettbach to Schwammerdingen.

The left wing was already engaged with the enemy; General Jellachich took several forts from them, and drove them over the Riebach, as far as the ramparts of Zurich; the General Count Bey, drove them from Wittikon, and dislodged them from the village of Kirchland; the General Count Oreilly, who commanded the van-guard of the Prince Joseph of Lorrain, compelled them to abandon Aldersbergen, and Dobelhof, and maintained himself there, while the Field-marshal-lieutenant Prince of Lorrain took his position at Wittikon, and by that means formed his junction with the Count Bey.

This movement of the column of the Field-marshal-lieutenant had the completest effect; the attack was made with as much judgment as valour and order, and the enemy retired on all sides; but, much to the regret of his Royal Highness, Field-marshal-lieutenant Hotze, was slightly wounded in the arm by a musket-ball at Stettbach, notwithstanding which he remained for some time with the column, and led them to Schwammerdingen, where he was obliged to resign his command to Field-marshal-lieutenant Petrasch.

His Royal Highness, in order to approach the left wing of the position of the enemy, and by that means favour the advance of Field-marshal-lieutenant Petrasch, placed the division of the Prince Reuss in a column, and the Prince of Rosenberg received orders to cross the Klatt with his van-guard, to drive back the enemy from Seebach and its environs.

The corps de reserve took place of the division of Reuss; the Prince of Rosenberg drove the enemy from Seebach, and advanced towards Orlisen

Orliken and Affoltern: in the meanwhile Prince Reufs followed with his division, and formed a line upon the heights of Seebach.

When the column of the Field-marshal-lieutenant Petrasch had advanced to Schwammerdingen, the Colonel Count Plouquet croffed the Klatt with his regiment, and rejoined the column.

From our continual advance, the enemy began to entertain apprehenfion for the security of their position: they advanced the grenadiers which had been placed as a reserve behind them, principally to strengthen the right wing, where General Maffena was; but all their exertions were ineffectual against the ardour of our troops.

Field-marshal-lieutenant Petrasch advanced from Schwammerdingen so far, that his van-guard came nearly in the midst of the enemy's abbatis, which ascends from the chauffée of Schwammerdingen to the Zurcherberg. The Prince of Rosenberg at the same time obliged the enemy to quit the village of Orliken, in spite of their advantageous position on the rising ground, protected by the artillery of all the surrounding batteries. He occupied the village, the rising ground, and the little forest before Orliken; by which means a complete junction was effected between the Prince of Rosenberg and the Field-marshal-lieutenant Petrasch: immediately after which four divisions of cavalry were placed along a gentle acclivity between Orliken and the chauffée leading from Schwammerdingen to Zurich. This eminence protected them from the fire of the enemy, and they were in a situation to fall on the flank of the enemy, in case of their attempting any thing from the centre of their position: they did not, however, make any attempt of the kind, but from their left wing attacked the division of Prince Reufs on the heights of Seebach, in order to force the Prince of Rosenberg to retire, by taking the heights.

They repeated this attack several times, but were always repulsed with a great lofs.

In the interim his Royal Highness observed that the fire on the principal eminence toward the Zurich-Berg, where the right wing of the position of the enemy and their abbatis were, remained always at the same place by the Aldersberger Hof: he therefore ordered the battalions of grenadiers Tegetthof and Tuch under the command of the General Hiller, and the two battalions of Archduke Ferdinand under the command of the General Sebottendorf, to march to Schwammerdingen and to proceed to the abbatis, and if poffible to break through, in order to enable General Oreilly to advance on his side.

His Royal Highness conferred the command of this column, and of the whole left wing, on the General of artillery Count Wallis, who advanced at the head of the grenadiers, fallied out of the forest by the Zurichberger Hof, formed his troops, and marched with the greatest bravery towards the enemy: but he soon received a contusion in the leg by a cartridge-ball, and shortly after General Hiller was wounded in the same manner by a musket-shot.

Both were obliged to quit the field of battle, because the difficulties of the ground were such that they could not lead on their troops except on foot. The attack however was continued under the command of the General Baron Sebottendorf. The grenadiers, with a battalion of Archduke Ferdinand's, attacked with the bayonet, broke through the abbatis, and took a fort; but they were obliged to relinquish these advantages, because the enemy, with their corps de reserve, made at the

Vol. VIII.   L l   same

same time an attack on the head of the columns which had partly entered the abbatis, and on the reft who were endeavouring to follow them.

The approach of the night rendered every farther attempt impoffible, for which reafon General Sebottendorf retired with the column, lined the wood towards the Zurichberger Hof with a battalion of Archduke Ferdinand's, and pofted the reft of the troops near Schwammerdingen: the battle lafted till nine o'clock in the evening.

We obtained the advantage of driving the enemy back to their pofition, and approached fo near as to enable his Royal Highnefs to examine it, and to form a plan of attack.

On this day all the troops moft eminently fignalized themfelves.

The generals, particularly the General of artillery Count Wallis, the Field-marfhal-lieutenants Baron Hotze, Prince Reufs, and de Petrafch; the Major-generals de Jellachich, Count Bey, Count Oreilly, and Prince of Rofenberg, moft contributed to the happy iffue of the battle by their military knowledge and their own example of diftinguifhed bravery.

The Field-marfhal-lieutenants Hotze and Petrafch praife particularly the activity and zeal of the Colonel Count Plonquet of the 60th regiment of infantry; of the Lieutenant-colonel de Wiederberg, and the Captain Froelich, of the Sclavonian huffars; of the Lieutenant-colonel Altftaetten, of Bender; of the Major Etvoes, of the 4th battalion of Peterwardein; of the Captains Romberg and Baumgarten; of the general-quarter-mafter ftaff; of the Captain Gratze, of the 1ft regiment of Wallachians; and of the Major Wachenburgh, of the artillery, who performed all that could be expected from the greateft zeal and knowledge.

The Field-marfhal-lieutenant Prince of Lorrain, who diftinguifhed himfelf by the greateft activity, recommends particularly the Captain Sarette, of the general-quarter-mafter ftaff, who was conftantly along with the General Count Oreilly at the head of the van-guard, and animated the troops by his own example; the Firft Lieutenant de Dalquen, of the regiment of dragoons of Cobourg, adjutant of the Count Oreilly; of the Lieutenant Prince of Bernburgh Witkenftein, of the fame regiment; and of his adjutant the Firft Lieutenant Baron of Thuillen.

The General Jellachich recommends the Colonel Jonfon and the Lieutenant-colonel Lamarine, of Emperor infantry; the Captains Brettfchneider and Harnifcher, of the fecond regiment of Uhlans; the Major Baron Jacobi, and the Captain Steigert, of Waldeck; the Lieutenant-colonel de Schoenthal, the Captains Zuraba and Bermanns, and the Lieutenant Munzhaufen, of Stein infantry; the Captain Count Bartolozzi, of Modena dragoons, and the Engineer Kutten, of the artillery; the Firft Lieutenant Petrichevich, his adjutant, and the Captain Meyer, of the quarter-mafter ftaff.

The General Sebottendorf praifes in general the bravery of the grenadiers, and the regiments of Archduke Ferdinand, and particularly the Colonel Candiani and the Major Mellitz, of Archduke Ferdinand; the Lieutenant-colonel Tegetthoof, the Captains Hanmer and Helmoes, of the grenadiers, the Captain Czolich, and the Firft Lieutenant Fier, of the general-quarter-mafter ftaff, and his adjutant the Firft Lieutenant Kuherr de Vins.

The lofs of the enemy in killed and wounded amounts to 4000 men;

ongst the latter, as it is said, are the Generals Cheraw, Oud...
Humbert, the General of the engineers de Ville, and the Ad...
eral de Billy. We made 500 prisoners, amongst whom are
...ant-generals.
...s, in killed, wounded, and prisoners, may amount to 1600

...ay after the battle, namely, the 5th, the position of the enemy
...noitred: it had every thing that nature and art could afford to
...a military position. The extremity of the right wing ex...
...the lake, and was covered by the batteries of the ramparts
...wn of Zurich: from thence, up the ascents as far as the right
...e abbatis, upon the Zurcherberg, before the villages Hottingen
...ern, towards Hirschland, the ground is so broken by deep
...ays, ditches, and ravines, that in most places it would have
...ossible to reach the enemy's position on foot.
...the steep declivities of the Zurcherberg, as far as the Chur...
...hwammerdingen, was formed an abbatis, well defended by re...
...d artillery: before the right side there was an open small plain,
...the enemy could make their cavalry operate with much more
..., because all the avenues leading from Adleiberger Hof and
...to this plain, were entirely exposed to the fire of the batteries,
...impossible to make an attack on that side, because our artillery
...ry could not be brought to oppose theirs, and the infantry could
...rmed to the attack under the cartridge fire of the enemy.
...ntre of the position of the enemy was placed upon a deep and
...in of mountains, whose surface, declining towards Oniken en...
...ormed a gentle curve, defended by the fire of the artillery
...lve redoubts and fléches. The left wing of the enemy was
...ody elevation equally advantageous, and was strengthened in
...nanner with a good abbatis and with redoubts. The left wing
...d in the rear of Hong with three batteries, commanding the
...ong the Limat. To all these advantages was added, that of
...e position strongly concentrated, and that from every point of
...ole country around could be seen for three miles distance.
... of these obstacles, which appeared insurmountable, his Royal
...had made all the dispositions for the attack, and had fixed
...6th of June with the more confidence, as our troops were
...sembled so near the position on all sides, and had rendered
...s masters of the ground, that in all probability, without much
...ne, they might have approached the forts, and stormed them
...usual courage.
...nemy, however, did not wait for this attack, but retreated
...e night with such precipitancy, that at break of day they had
...bandoned their position, and left behind in their intrenchments
...n, three howitzers, and 18 powder-carts.
...p the Prince of Rosenberg entered Zurich with the van-guard,
...e the cavalry of his right wing advance towards Wittikon,
..., and Altstietten. In the town were found 140 pieces of ar...
...different sizes and calibres, which made in all 177 pieces of

...my of the enemy retreated over the mountain Albis towards
...along the Limat.

I l 2   From

From the LONDON GAZETTE, July 30, 1799.

Vienna, July 10.

IT is already known how the armed peasantry in Piedmont took possession of the fortress of Ceva, and by their deputies requested the commander in chief of the army to send Austrian troops into the fortress.

The following is the journal of the march of Captain Schmelzer, of Anton Esterhazi, as well as of the attack of the enemy on the fortress, and its defence.

Journal from the 19th of May to the 2d of June, of the taking Possession of the Piedmontese Fortress of Ceva by the Imperial Royal Troops; of their Preparations of Defence; of the Circumstances attending the Blockade and Bombardment of the Fortress, and its Deliverance.

ON the 19th of May orders were issued by the Major-general Baron Sekendorf to the regiment Esterhazi, to send a division of 250 men by forced marches, with the necessary ammunition, a corporal of the artillery, eight gunners, and 14 assistants, to Ceva, to garrison this fortress.

At ten o'clock in the morning on the same day, Captain Schmelzer set off with the division to which he was appointed, and marched over Tresonaro, Rivolta, to Acqui; the Imperial royal troop, however, were not permitted to pass here, because they were mistaken by the people for French dressed in Imperial uniform.

Although Captain Schmelzer adduced every possible testimony of veracity, yet he could not succeed in removing this error from the minds of the people: he therefore took a position upon an eminence before the town, placed his picquets, sent out patroles from the peasantry in the adjacent country, and, on account of the proximity of the enemy, ordered his troops to be partly under arms. He himself went to Acqui; and, by the active mediation of the Archbishop of that town, he succeeded in obtaining the passage for the following day.

On the 20th he continued his march with all necessary circumspection: but, because the report had spread itself over the whole country to Ceva, that his troops were French disguised, he always sent half an hour before him, several peasants, who had been previously fully convinced that they were Imperial soldiers, in order to pacify the armed peasantry, who had threatened to assail them. This was the more necessary, as Captain Schmelzer received information that the French soldiers, of the division of General Grouchy, who were plundering in the mountains of Cassano, had been acquainted with his march, and collected themselves to pursue him.

In order that Captain Schmelzer might have timely information of the motions of the enemy, he sent about 50 peasants to the mountains, with directions to impede their march as much as possible, and to inform him of their approach by signal shots. In the mean while he proceeded with forced marches along the left bank of the Bormida, after he had sent before him some peasants across the river, to observe General Victor, who, with his division, was posted between Acqui and Spigna.

In this manner he fortunately passed with his detachment through two columns of the enemy to the environs of Monastero and Cesule, where
he

he rested his troops, till the repeated fire from the peasants in the mountains gave the signal to break up. He now went forward to Corte Maglia, where he again halted: but an hour after, some peasants arrived with the intelligence that the enemy were approaching; he therefore, during the night, passed the mountains to Cara Vanzana, where his troops rested till the break of day.

On the 21st of May he passed over Niela and Belbo, and arrived at Ceva, where they made some scruples of receiving him, occasioned by the above-mentioned report: he therefore went into the fortress, and convinced the commandant Francolino, and several other chiefs of the armed peasantry, of their mistake; that his detachment was sent to them from the commander in chief of the Austrian army in Italy. He then, conformable to his orders, entered the fortress, drums beating, &c.

Captain Schmelzer observing great disorder in the fortress, reproached the commander Francolini, who apologized, by saying, that he was unable to keep the people in order and subordination; and that a serious exertion to restrain them had frequently endangered his life.

In order to make every necessary arrangement for defence with the greatest energy, Captain Schmelzer took on himself the command of the fortress, but retained the late commandant, to avail himself of his local knowledge. This officer, who, as chief of the peasants, by taking the fortress, showed his attachment to the good cause, fulfilled every expectation of the Captain Schmelzer, by his willingness to undertake every service during the blockade.

On the 22d of May he made application to the magistrates of the town to supply the fortress with provisions, having found there only sufficiency for three days. The magistrates complied very willingly, and requested a memorial of the necessaries, which he sent.

Then he went to the magazines of ammunition, where he found much neglect, the floor being covered with powder. Although the peasants had taken a vast quantity of ammunition, and more than 210,000 cartridges, yet there still remained a copious supply. To establish order in the magazines, he permitted no ammunition to be taken without his knowledge; for which purpose he placed sentinels before them. He ordered the scattered powder to be collected, and the magazines to be cleaned: this was performed by the Corporal Stowasser and eight gunners in the most expeditious manner.

In the fortification he every where found traces of the destruction committed by the peasants; palisadoes, great and small gates of the outworks, were burnt, the iron works demolished, even the fascines torn up in such a manner that whole traverses had fallen.

To remedy this, in some degree, he sent for three cartwrights, one joiner, two smiths, two locksmiths, and one gunsmith of the town, whom he kept in the fortress: he succeeded in replacing the palisadoes and the most essential gates, being supplied with every thing he wanted by the town.

The greatest part of the gun-carriages upon the ramparts and in the magazines being unserviceable, the Captain Schmelzer placed them on those places where an attack was least probable, and disposed the rest in the most eligible manner.

From the LONDON GAZETTE, August 3, 1799.

Admiralty Office, August 3.

Copy of a Letter from Sir William Sidney Smith, Knight, Captain of his Majesty's Ship Tigre, to Evan Nepean, Esq. dated at Acre, the 3d of May.

Sir,

I HAVE the honour to enclose you copies of my letters to Earl St. Vincent, of the 7th of April and 2d instant, for the information of my Lords Commissioners of the Admiralty; as also a sketch of the position of the forces. The enemy have made two attempts since yesterday morning to force the two English ravelines, but were repulsed with loss. The works have now cannon mounted on them, and are nearly completed. We have thus the satisfaction of finding ourselves, on the 46th day of the siege, in a better state of defence than we were the first day the enemy opened their trenches, notwithstanding the increase of the breach, which they continue to batter with effect; and the garrison, having occasionally closed with the enemy, in several sorties, feel greater confidence that they shall be able to resist an assault, for which they are prepared. I have the honour to be, &c. &c.

W. SIDNEY SMITH.

My Lord, *Tigre, St. Jean d'Acre Bay, April 7.*

I HAVE the honour to inform your Lordship, that as soon as the return of fine weather, after the equinoctial gale, allowed me to approach this unsheltered anchorage, I resumed my station in the bay with the squadron under my orders. I found the enemy had profited, by our forced absence, to push their approaches to the counterscarp, and even in the ditch of the N. E. angle of the town-wall, where they were employed in mining the tower, to increase a breach they had already made in it, and which had been found impracticable when they attempted to storm on the 1st inst. The Alliance and prize gunboats, which had been caught in the gale, had fortunately rode it out except one; and Captain Wilmot had been so indefatigable in mounting the prize-guns, under the direction of an able officer of engineers, Colonel Phelipeaux, that the fire therefrom had already slackened that of the enemy; still, however, much was to be apprehended from the effect of the mine, and a sortie was determined on, in which the British marines and seamen were to force their way into it, while the Turkish troops attacked the enemy's trenches on the right and left. The sally took place this morning, just before daylight; the impetuosity and noise of the Turks rendered the attempt to surprise the enemy abortive, though in other respects they did their part well. Lieutenant Wright, who commanded the seamen pioneers, notwithstanding he received two shot in his right arm, as he advanced, entered the mine with the pikemen, and proceeded to the bottom of it, where he verified its direction, and destroyed all that could be destroyed in its then state, by pulling down the supporters.

Colonel Douglas, to whom I had given the necessary step of rank to enable him to command the Turkish colonels, supported the seamen in this desperate service with his usual gallantry, under the increased fire of the enemy, bringing off Lieutenant Wright, who had scarcely strength left to get out of the enemy's trench, from which they were not dislodged, as also Mr. Janverin, midshipman of the Tigre, and the rest of the wounded. The action, all together, speaks for itself, and says more than could be said by me in praise of all concerned. I feel doubly indebted to Colonel Douglas for having preserved my gallant friend Lieutenant Wright, whose life, I am happy to say, is not despaired of by the surgeon. We have, however, to lament the loss of a brave and tried officer, Major Oldfield, who commanded the Theseus's marines, and fell gloriously on this occasion, with two of the men under his command.

Our loss in wounded is 23, among which is Lieutenant Beatty, of the marines, slightly. The Turks brought in above 60 heads, a greater number of muskets, and some intrenching tools, much wanted in the garrison. A farther attack on the enemy's second parallel was not to be attempted without a greater number of regular troops. The return of the detachment was well covered by the Theseus's fire, Captain Miller having taken an excellent position to that effect.

The result of our day's work is, that we have taught the besiegers to respect the enemy they have to deal with, so as to keep at a greater distance. The apprehensions of the garrison are quieted as to the effect of the mine, which we have besides learnt how to countermine with advantage, and more time is gained for the arrival of the reinforcements daily expected. I have the honour to be, &c.

W. SIDNEY SMITH.

Right Hon. Earl St. Vincent, Commander in Chief, &c.

My Lord, *Tigre, moored under the Walls of Acre, May 2.*

THE enemy continue to make the most vigorous efforts to overcome our resistance in the defence of this place. The garrison has made occasional sorties, protected by our small boats, on their flank, with field-pieces, in which the most essential service has been performed by Lieutenant Brodie and Mr. Atkinson, of the Theseus, and Mr. Joes, master of the Tigre, who commanded them.

Yesterday the enemy, after many hours heavy cannonade from 30 pieces of artillery brought from Jaffa, made a fourth attempt to mount the breach, now much widened, but were repulsed, with loss. The Tigre moored on one side, and the Theseus on the other, flank the town walls, the gun-boats, launches, and other rowing-boats, continue to flank the enemy's trenches, to their great annoyance. Nothing but desperation can induce them to make the sort of attempts they do to mount a breach practicable only by the means of scaling-ladders, under such a fire as we pour in upon them; and it is impossible to see the lives, even of our enemies thus sacrificed, and so much bravery misapplied, without regret.

Our loss is as per list enclosed; and we have therein to lament some of the bravest and best among us. Captain Wilmot was shot on the 8th ult. by a rifleman, as he was mounting a howitzer on the breach; his loss is severely felt.

We have run out a ravelin on each side of the enemy's nearest approach, in which the marines of the Tigre and Theseus have worked
under

under a heavy and inceſſant fire from the enemy, in a way that commands the admiration and gratitude of the Turks, as it is evident the flanking fire produced from them contributed much to ſave the place yeſterday. Colonel Phelipeaux, of the engineers, who projected and ſuperintended the execution, has fallen a ſacrifice to his zeal for this ſervice; want of reſt and expoſure to the ſun having given him a fever, of which he died this morning: our grief for this loſs is exceſſive on every account. Colonel Douglas ſupplies his place, having hitherto carried on the work under his direction, and is indefatigable in completing it for the reception of cannon. I muſt not omit to mention, to the credit of the Turks, that they fetch the gabions, faſcines, and thoſe materials which the garriſon does not afford, from the face of the enemy's works, ſetting fire to what they cannot bring away. The enemy repair in one night all the miſchief we do them in the day, and continue within half piſtol-ſhot of the walls, in ſpite of the conſtant fire kept up from the ramparts under the direction of Lieutenant Knight.

I hope I need not aſſure your Lordſhip that we ſhall continue to do our duty to the utmoſt of our power, in ſpite of all obſtacles; among which, climate, as it affects health, and the expoſed nature of our rocky anchorage, are the moſt formidable, ſince they are not to be overcome, which I truſt the enemy are by our exertions.

I am, &c.
W. SIDNEY SMITH.

The Right Hon. Earl St. Vincent, Commander in Chief, &c. &c.

Return of the killed and wounded belonging to his Majeſty's Ships Tigre, Theſeus, and Alliance, at the Sortie from the Town of Acre, againſt the French beſieging that Town, on the 7th Day of April.

Tigre—Lieutenant Wright, Mr. Janverin, midſhipman, and 11 men, wounded.

Theſeus—Major Oldfield, of marines, and two private marines, killed; Lieutenant Beatty, of marines, Mr. James M. B. Forbes, midſhipman (ſlightly), Sergeant Cavanagh, and four private marines, wounded.

Alliance—One ſeaman and two marines, wounded.

Total—One major and two private marines killed; one lieutenant, one lieutenant of marines, two midſhipmen, one ſergeant, ſix private marines, and 12 ſeamen, wounded.

On board his Majeſty's Ship Tigre, off Acre, April 8.
W. SIDNEY SMITH.

Return of the Caſualties, killed, and wounded, belonging to his Majeſty's Ships Tigre, Theſeus, and Alliance, between the 8th of April and the 2d of May following, employed in the Defence of Acre.

Tigre—Mr. Edward Morris, midſhipman, and James Maugham, Andrew Wall, and Robert Bennet, ſeamen, killed; Lieutenant Knight, a contuſion on his breaſt; John Bolton, boatſwain's mate, William Hutchinſon, William Pickard, James Bailey, Joſeph Hudſon, Joſeph Viaſquez, and William Price, ſeamen, wounded.

Theſeus—John Rich, ſeaman, killed; John Chidlow, marine, wounded.

Alliance—

Alliance.—Captain Wilmot, killed by the enemy, as he was mounting a howitzer on the breach.

Total—One captain, one midshipman, and four seamen, killed; one lieutenant, one Boatswain's mate, six seamen, and one marine, wounded.

W. SIDNEY SMITH.

On board his Majesty's Ship Tigre, St. Jean d'Acre Bay, the 2d Day of May.

Admiralty Office, August 3.

Extract of a Letter from Mr. Christopher Anderson, Commander of the Bull-dog Privateer, to Evan Nepean, Esq. dated in the River of [illegible], Portugal, the 11th July.

I TAKE the liberty to acquaint you, that on the 7th instant, being in Vigo Bay, I took and destroyed four small coasters, having on board empty pipes from Ferrol to Vigo, and sent the crews on shore in a fishing-boat.

On the 9th, coming out of Marim Bay, I fell in with the El Diego Spanish schooner privateer, commanded by Remo Rodrigues Trelles, of 10 muskets, 10 pistols, and 10 [illegible], manned with 16 [illegible], of the burden of about 10 tons, quite new, and coppered, had sailed from Ferrol two days before, and had not taken any thing, which vessel I brought to this place.

From the LONDON GAZETTE, August 10, 1799.

Admiralty Office, August 10.

Copy of a Letter from Vice-admiral Rainier, Commander in Chief of his Majesty's Ships and Vessels in the East Indies, to Evan Nepean, Esq. dated in Bombay Harbour, April 1.

Sir,

I HAVE much pleasure in acquainting you, for their Lordships' information, that Captain Cooke, of his Majesty's ship La Sybille, captured the French national frigate La Forte, of much superior force, on the 28th of February last, off the Sand-heads of Bengal river, after a well-fought night-action, wherein Captain Cooke appears to have displayed the greatest degree of courage, presence of mind, and professional abilities, and to have been nobly supported by the intrepid conduct of the officers and crew, part of which consisted of a company of his Majesty's Scotch brigade, embarked by order of his Excellency the Governor-general, on La Sybille's ship's company having been so much reduced by deaths, and debilitated by the severe illness contracted last year at Calcutta, during the repair of that ship, on which account many of them were left ashore at the hospital, and most of the remainder of her old and valuable crew in a weak state of convalescency.

I feel the most sensible concern in acquainting you, that the universal joy and satisfaction, diffused over every countenance on hearing the news of this gallant capture, of so much importance to the trading part of the community, and also to the public service, was considerably damped, on being informed that Captain Cooke's wounds were of so dangerous a nature as almost to preclude every hope of his recovery.

I transmit

I transmit a copy of Lieutenant Hardyman's letter on the occasion, containing a brief account of the action, addressed to General Sir Alured Clarke, K. B. Vice-president of the government of Fort William, as it was communicated to me by his Excellency the Earl of Mornington, then at Fort Saint George, who has been pleased to testify the most sincere regret for Captain Cooke's melancholy situation.

It may be proper to inform you, that my not having received Lieutenant Hardyman's account of the action is owing to the uncertainty where to address me, but which I shall enclose, if it arrives in time.

I am informed, by an officer in the marine of this port, who was on board La Forte last September at the Mauritius, that she mounted thirty four pounders on the main-deck, 14 nine-pounders, and eight thirty-six-pounders, carronades, with a line of brass swivels on a flush deck, continued from the quarter-deck to the forecastle.

It appears she passed Achin Head nearly about the same time his Majesty's ship Sceptre did with the convoy from the Cape of Good Hope, and did not reach the Sand-heads till the usual time was expired for expecting any of the enemy's cruisers thereabouts.

You will please to inform their Lordships, that I shall order La Forte to be purchased and commissioned for his Majesty's service, and appoint Lieutenant Hardyman to the command, till their Lordships' pleasure is known.

I have the honour to be, &c. &c. &c.

PETER RAINIER.

His Majesty's Ship La Sybille, Balysore Roads,
March 2.

Sir,

I BEG leave to inform you, that in consequence of a report that the French frigate La Forte was in the bay, his Majesty's frigate La Sybille sailed from Madras on the 19th February to cruise for her, had the good fortune to fall in with her in these roads on the 28th, when, after an action of one hour and forty minutes, during which she was totally dismasted, with very little comparative damage to his Majesty's ship, I have the satisfaction to acquaint you that she struck.

I much lament that to this intelligence I must add that of the death of Captain Davis, of Lord Mornington's staff, who came a volunteer on this occasion, and who unfortunately fell early in the action; and with great regret I must also acquaint you, that Captain Cooke is (it is feared mortally) wounded.

The number of killed and wounded on board La Forte is not yet correctly known, but is stated to be very considerable: on board La Sybille, three killed, wounded 19.

I have to request that you will order as speedy a conveyance as possible for Captain Cooke, who, if he survives, will proceed to Calcutta; and that you will please to give the necessary orders that conveyances to Calcutta may be provided for the prisoners and the wounded.

I have the honour to be, &c. &c. &c.

L. HARDYMAN, First Lieutenant.

General Sir Alured Clarke, &c. &c. &c.

From the LONDON GAZETTE EXTRAORDINARY, August 17, 1799.

Downing Street, August 16.

DISPATCHES from the Right Honourable Lord Henley and the Right Honourable Lord William Bentinck, of which the following are copies and extract, have been this day received by the Right Honourable Lord Grenville, his Majesty's principal Secretary of State for the foreign department.

Copy of a Letter from Lord Henley, to Lord Grenville, dated Vienna, July 31.

My Lord,

I HAVE the honour of enclosing to your Lordship two Extraordinary Gazettes of this place, the one published yesterday evening with the important intelligence of the surrender of the citadel of Alexandria on the 21st past, and the other published this afternoon with the articles of capitulation of that fortress.

The batteries against Mantua were finished on the 23d; and on the following day a most formidable and tremendous fire was opened upon that place, from 111 pieces of artillery.

M. Fiorella, late commandant of the citadel of Turin, having endeavoured to inculcate into the minds of the inhabitants of a small place near to Verona, where he resided on his parole, his own seditious principles, has been sent to the castle of Ruffstein; and it has been notified to some of the principal Cisalpine prisoners, for the information of the French Directory, that if any cruelty be exercised on any of the French emigrants in the service of this country, made prisoners by the French, severe reprisals will be made on them (the Cisalpines), and such other prisoners as are not natives of France.

It is with great pleasure that I mention, that the report of M. de Chastelet's death, which was confidently reported, is not true.

I have the honour to be, &c.

HENLEY.

Vienna, July 30.

'GENERAL Melas has sent, from the head-quarters at Alessandria, the agreeable news of the surrender of that citadel. An approach was made from the second parallel against the glacis, on the night between the 19th and 20th, and by this means thirty paces were gained from the glacis towards the covered way. As the batteries of the second parallel were now finished and the artillery placed in them, the firing was recommenced with the utmost energy. The enemy then abandoned the covered way, and retired within the works, as the assault projected against the covered way was now no longer necessary. Field-marshal-lieutenant Bellegarde determined on the following day to attack the counter-guard, to maintain himself there, and in the mean time to crown the salient angles of the covered way, and to re-establish the necessary communications. On the 21st, this work was completed upon the salient angles, and especially upon that of the counter-guard of the ravelin between the bastions Amadeo and St. Carno. A demi-sappe was also pushed forward in the centre, to within twenty paces of the angle of the bastion Amadeo, and by means of three boyaux on the left wing, to within thirty paces of the palisadoes. In the mean time our batteries continued firing in the two parallels, and the enemy answered

answered them briskly. General Gardanne, commander of the citadel, seeing the approaching danger, and probably unwilling to sustain an assault, sent, at three in the afternoon, of the 21st, his Adjutant-general Louis, with a letter to Field-marshal-lieutenant Bellegarde, to the following effect:—"That the answer which he had given him to his first summons to surrender was such as his duty required of him, and such as the Field-marshal-lieutenant would have made had he been in his situation; but that now, being enabled to listen to the voice of humanity, without acting against his conscience or fear of reproach, he was disposed to enter into negotiation for a capitulation, upon conditions which Frenchmen could accept, who knew how to sacrifice every thing for their honour."—As the bearer had no full power, he was immediately sent back with injunctions to procure instructions and full powers within two hours, and to inform the Commandant that he should be responsible for any loss occasioned by this delay.—At eight in the evening the firing on both sides ceased; the capitulation was concluded; the garrison in consequence was made prisoners of war; they marched out on the 22d, at four in the afternoon, laid down their arms on the glacis, and were sent by Paris into the Hereditary States. General Melas means hereafter to transmit the articles of capitulation, together with a list of the effects found in the citadel, and an account of our loss during this obstinate siege. By an unfortunate accident, General Chastelet was severely wounded by a ball in quitting the trenches. Field-marshal-lieutenant Kray writes under date of the 22d, that eleven batteries had been constructed before Mantua, and that the artillery would be placed in them the following night, in order to batter the body of the fortress.

There were found in the citadel 105 guns, of different calibres; the other stores were not particularized at the departure of the express. The number of prisoners of war of the garrison was 2400, except the sick that were left behind.—According to the reports of General Klenau to General Melas, dated the 20th, from Florence, the people of Tuscany, encouraged by the victories of the Imperial armies, and by the love of their country and of their prince, and a hatred of the enemy, have invested Leghorn, Pisa, Lucca, and Pescia. According to this report, the insurgents of Florence have invested the fortresses of Antignano and Piombino, made 200 Frenchmen prisoners of war, took eight guns, and a French privateer with three guns and 21 men. Volterra, and the whole country about Rome are free; and only Perugia and Civita Vecchia are occupied by the enemy, of whom, however, a great number are fled to Ancona.

Vienna, July 31.

GENERAL Melas dispatched Baron Ertel with six pair of colours, taken from the garrison at Alexandria, and with the following articles of capitulation:

Capitulation of the Citadel of Alexandria, between Field-marshal Count de Bellegarde, in the Service of his Majesty the Emperor and King, and the French General Gardanne, Commander of the Citadel.

Art. I. The garrison of the citadel of Alexandria shall march out of the gate of Asti, with all military honours, drums beating, colours flying, and matches lighted, carrying with them two four-pounders, with the necessary carts, horses, ammunition, and artillery.

The garrison shall take post upon the glacis, from the gate of Asti to the

the gate of Alexandria, without laying down their arms. They shall return to France, but not to serve against the armies of his Majesty the Emperor and of his allies until their exchange, which is to take place before any other, and with a preference of Auftrian and Ruffian prisoners of war, except such persons as are diftinguifhed in the second article as not in the number of prisoners of war.

Anf.—The garrison shall march out with all military honours, drums beating, colours flying, matches lighted, and two guns, through the gate of Afti; but upon the glacis they are to lay down their arms, and surrender as prisoners of war, to be sent to the dominions of his Majesty the Emperor.

II. The following persons shall not be considered as prisoners of war; the General of Brigade Gardanne, commander of the division of Tonaro; General-adjutant Lewis, the other adjutants, the officers belonging to the staff, together with 300 military persons whom General Gardanne is to select from the garrison.

Anf.—The Commander, the Adjutant-general Lewis, the other adjutants, and the whole general staff, must share the fate of the garrison.

III. The officers shall keep their arms, horses, military equipage, and in general all their property; the men shall keep their knapsacks, and the other officers and persons following the army their horses and other effects. Care shall be taken that the officers recovering from illness, and the other military persons that have no horses, shall be provided with them from one ftage to another. The garrison of the Piedmontese, Cifalpines, and Swifs, making a part of the French army, shall enjoy the advantages of this article equally with the French troops.

Anf.—The officers of the higher ranks, as General Gardanne, General-adjutant Lewis, the chiefs of artillery and of the other corps, shall keep their arms; the officers in general will retain their horses and military accoutrements; the men their knapsacks, and the officers and other persons their horses and effects. Care shall be taken to supply them with horses upon their march. The Piedmontese, Cifalpines, and Swifs, are prisoners of war equally with the French.

IV. There shall be granted ten covered waggons to contain the effects of the staff, and of the different corps, and the military cheft; in case some corps shall not be provided with ammunition-waggons or horses, the Auftrian army will provide them with these articles from one ftage to another, to the borders of Genoa.

Anf.—The poffession of the personal effects is granted; but as for the reft, it is underftood that all military chefts or magazines, plans, archives, and military ftores whatever, whether they belong to the French or Piedmontese government, muft be moft faithfully delivered.

V. The fick shall be treated with humanity in the hofpitals of Alexandria; the neceffary furgeons and attendants shall be left, and after their recovery, they are to enjoy the benefit of this capitulation equally with thofe who remain at Alexandria on account of their business.—The fick are not to be confidered as prisoners of war.

Anf.—The fick and wounded are prisoners of war, and shall be treated with our ufual humanity. The garrifon are to leave behind the neceffary furgeons and attendants.

VI. Three hours after the figning of this capitulation, the outer guards of the gate of the Vineyard, and of the gates of St. Michael and of St. Antonio, shall be given up to the Auftrian troops; but the entrance into
the

the citadel is only to be granted to the Auſtrian commiſſaries, and to thoſe who are ſent by the commander of the ſiege. The Auſtrian army are not to enter into the citadel till it is evacuated by the French garriſon.

Anſ.—Three hours after the ſigning of this capitulation the forces of his Majeſty ſhall garriſon the inner gate of Aſti, as well as the outer guard-poſts of the gate.

VII. In caſe that the French army ſhould not return to the neighbourhood of Genoa, leave will be granted to ſend an officer to the head-quarters of the commanding general with a copy of this capitulation.—Granted.

VIII. If there ſhould be found in the capitulation any dubious article, it is to be explained in favour of the garriſon.

Anſ.—On this head a fair explanation and agreement ſhall take place.

IX. The garriſon are to be allowed a ſufficient eſcort to the borders of Genoa.

Anſ.—The garriſon, in conformity to the capitulation, will be furniſhed with a ſufficient eſcort.

ADDITIONAL ARTICLES.

Directly after ſigning the capitulation, the hoſtages of Piedmont, ſecured in the citadel, together with their effects, are to be delivered. Two hoſtages, an officer of the general ſtaff and a captain, are to be exchanged, until the complete fulfilling of this capitulation. An officer of the artillery corps and a commiſſary ſhall be ſent into the citadel, to whom are to be given up, without the leaſt reſerve, all plans, magazines, and all other military effects belonging to government. The horſes of the cavalry, and all others belonging the French government, ſhall be reſtored.

The garriſon are to march out to-morrow, the 2d of July 1799, at four o'clock in the afternoon, through the gate of Aſti: thoſe that remain on account of the ſurrender of the military effects, may ſtay in the citadel till the complete execution of their buſineſs.

All horſes or other effects belonging to the Emperor, to the Auſtrian officers, or to any body that ſerves in the armies, ſhall be reſtored.

In witneſs of this, two copies have been made, ſigned, and ratified and exchanged.

In the camp before the citadel of Alexandria, July the 24th, ten o'clock at night, 1799.

COUNT de BELLEGARDE, Field-marſhal.
GARDANNE,
A. LEWIS, } Generals of Brigade.

Extract of a Letter from Lord Henley to Lord Grenville, dated Vienna, Auguſt 3.

IT gives me the greateſt ſatisfaction to be enabled to cloſe my official correſpondence from this place, with the important intelligence of the ſurrender of Mantua to the Imperial arms. A courier is juſt arrived from General Kray, with diſpatches of the 30th paſt, ſtating, that on the 27th the horn-work was taken; on the 28th the town was ſummoned; on the 29th the capitulation was ſigned; and on the 30th the place was occupied by the Imperial troops. The garriſon are priſoners of war; the privates have liberty to return to France, on the condition of not ſerving againſt the Emperor and his allies till they are exchanged againſt an equal number of Auſtrians. The exchange, it is ſtipulated, ſhall take place immediately

ly; and the officers are to be kept for three months in this country, as hostages for the exact fulfilment of this stipulation.

Permit me, my Lord, to convey to you my most sincere congratulations on this most fortunate and important event, which will furnish such facilities to the further progress of the allied arms; and to add my most cordial wishes, that the successes of the allies may be continued with the same brilliancy and rapidity which have distinguished all the operations of this remarkable campaign.

My Lord,   *Head-quarters, Bosco, July 30.*

I HAVE the satisfaction to enclose the capitulation of Mantua. The trenches had been opened only fourteen days. The garrison, I am informed, amounts to near 13,000 men; the sick, including the non-combatants, are about 500. The loss of the Austrians does not exceed 200 men.   I have the honour to be,

Right Honourable Lord Grenville.   W. BENTINCK.

Capitulation made between his Excellency Baron Kray, General of Artillery, and Commander in Chief of the Troops of his Imperial Majesty at the Siege of Mantua, and the General of Division Foissac la Tour, Commandant of the Town and Citadel of Mantua.

Art. I. THE garrison of Mantua will march out the 30th of July 1799, at twelve o'clock, with the honours of war, six pieces of cannon in front. The garrison shall be prisoners of war; and, in order to prevent the disgrace and misery of confinement, the General commanding in chief, the other generals under his orders, the officers of the staff, and all the officers of the garrison, consent to remain prisoners in the nearest part of the Hereditary States in Germany, in order to serve as hostages for the non-commissioned officers and soldiers, who shall be sent back into France by the shortest road, and shall not serve against the troops of the Emperor or his allies till after their exchange.

Ans.—Granted in its fullest extent; and in consideration of the open, brave, and honourable conduct of the garrison of Mantua, the commandant, the officers of the staff, and the other military officers of the garrison, after having remained three months in the Hereditary States, shall be at liberty to return to their respective countries upon their word of honour not to serve against his Imperial Majesty or his allies until they are reciprocally exchanged. The period of three months shall begin from the day on which the capitulation is signed.

The garrison will lay down their arms upon the glacis of the citadel. The officers will keep their swords, baggage, and the number of horses allowed by their own military regulations. The non-combatants shall be sent back to France. The generals shall keep their secretaries, and all the officers their servants. A pair of colours shall be granted to the General of Division Foissac la Tour, in consideration of the energy of his defence.

II. The Cisalpines, Swiss, Poles, and Piedmontese, shall be considered and treated in every respect as troops of the French republic.—Granted.

III. Three covered waggons shall be allowed the commander for the carriage of his papers, baggage, and personal property. These waggons shall not be examined, and shall be subject to his orders only.—Granted.

IV. The chief of the staff, and the other chiefs of departments, shall have the power of taking with them all papers relating to their own concerns, and shall have the sole charge of the waggons destined for this purpose, and

for

for the carriage of their own personal effects. The commissaries shall be responsible that nothing belonging to the place is taken away.—Granted.

V. An appeal is made to the justice and generosity of the Austrian government, in favour of those citizens who have been employed in the Cisalpine republic (which was formerly acknowledged by the Emperor at the treaty of peace concluded at Campo Formio), as well as of all those who have manifested republican opinions, the Imperial commissaries, and the citizens who acted as artillery-men, having been treated in the same manner, according to the terms of the noble capitulation made by Buonaparte with General Wurmser.—Granted.

VI. Engineer and artillery officers shall be appointed to receive all articles relating to their departments.—Granted.

VII. Commissaries shall also be named to take charge of the magazines of provisions.—Granted.

VIII. The sick and wounded who cannot be removed shall continue to receive the necessary care; for which purpose the French surgeons and physicians who now attend them shall remain. The General in chief shall name an officer who shall have the particular charge of the sick; and as soon as they may be sufficiently recovered to travel, they shall be furnished with the means of following the army if it is exchanged, or of going into France or Germany, according to the same conditions with all the rest, every one complying with what is decided for his rank.—Granted.

IX. There shall be furnished by the Austrian troops escorts sufficient to protect all individuals whatever comprised in the present capitulation, against insult or popular commotion, for which the commander of the escort shall be made particularly responsible.—Granted.

X. All doubts that may arise out of the present capitulation, shall be explained in favour of the garrison, consistently with the laws of equity.—Granted.

XI. After the signature of the present capitulation, hostages shall be mutually exchanged. On the part of the French, a brigadier and a captain; on that of the Austrians, a colonel and a captain.—Granted.

XII. During the management of the capitulation, there shall be a cessation of hostilities on both sides.—Granted.

XIII. Mignarello shall be occupied by a battalion of Austrians, from which 50 men shall be detached to occupy the outer part of the gate of Ceres. The two armies shall have no communication with each other, commanding officers, and those who have leave from their respective generals, excepted.—Granted.

XIV. The commissary of the executive power, and the inspector general of the police of the Cisalpine republic at Mantua, shall have leave to go wherever they please.—Granted.

XV. A sufficient number of carriages shall be allowed for the carriage of the effects, not only of the officers composing the garrison, but of all such as, not being present, may have left their baggage.—Granted.

XVI. Two carriages shall be granted for the suite of the general, and for such others as shall have been ordered by him to follow the lot of the garrison.—Granted.

XVII. The generals and other officers may send any part of their baggage to France with the troops:—unless indeed General Kray, who always acts like a man of the highest honour and liberality, consents that the officers should share the same fortune with the men, and be permitted to return to France prisoners on their parole.

Ans.—Regulated by article I.

ADDITIONAL ARTICLES.

All deserters shall be given up to their respective Battalions.—General Kray promises them their life.

(Signed) FOISSAC LA TOUR, le General de Division.
(Signed) BARON KRAY, General d'Artillerie.
(Signed) MONBERT, Chef de brigade, Commandant en Chef de Genie.

Le Chef de Brigade Boitron, Commandant d'Artillerie, n'a pas signé des Motifs qui lui font personels.

(Signed) FOISSAC LA TOUR.

Head quarters, Castelleccio, July 28.

From the LONDON GAZETTE, August 17, 1799.

Admiralty Office, August 13.

Extract of a Letter from Rear-admiral Lord Nelson, K. B. to Evan Nepean, Esq. dated Bay of Naples, 27th of June.

I AM happy in being able to congratulate their Lordships on the possession of the city of Naples. St. Elmo is yet in the hands of the French; but the castles of Ovo and Nuovo I took possession of last evening, and his Sicilian Majesty's colours are now flying on them.

Extract of another Letter from Rear-admiral Lord Nelson, K. B. to Evan Nepean, Esq. dated Bay of Naples, 14th of July.

HEREWITH I have the honour of sending you copies of my letters to the commander in chief, and the capitulation granted to the French in St. Elmo. All the chief rebels are now on board his Majesty's fleet. Capua and Gaieta will very soon be in our possession, when the kingdom will be liberated from anarchy and misery.

My Lord, *Foudroyant, Bay of Naples, 13th July.*

I HAVE the pleasure to inform you of the surrender of Fort St. Elmo (on the terms of the enclosed capitulation), after open batteries of eight days, during which time our heavy batteries were advanced within 160 yards of the ditch. The very great strength of St. Elmo, and its more formidable position, will mark with what fortitude, perseverance, and activity, the combined forces must have acted. Captain Troubridge was the officer selected for the command of all the forces landed from the squadron. Captain Ball assisted him for seven days till his services were wanted at Malta, when his place was ably supplied by Captain Hallowell, an officer of the most distinguished merit, and to whom Captain Troubridge expresses the highest obligation. Captain Hood, with a garrison for the castle of Nuovo, and to keep good order in the capital, an arduous task at that time, was also landed from the squadron: and I have the pleasure to tell you, that no capital is more quiet than Naples. I transmit you Captain Troubridge's letter to me, with returns of killed and wounded. I have also to state to your Lordship, that although the abilities and resources of my brave friend Troubridge are well known to all the world, yet even he had difficulties to struggle with in every way, which the state of the capital will easily bring to your idea, that has raised his great character even higher than it was before. I am, &c.

Right Hon. Lord Keith, Commander in Chief, &c. &c. &c. NELSON.

My Lord, *Antignano, near St. Elmo, July* 13.

AGREEABLE to your Lordſhip's orders I landed with the Engliſh and Portugueſe marines of the fleet on the 27th of June; and after embarking the garriſons of the caſtles Ovo and Nuovo, compoſed of French and rebels, I put a garriſon in each, and on the 29th took poſt againſt Fort St. Elmo, which I ſummoned to ſurrender; but the commandant being determined to ſtand a ſiege, we opened a battery of three thirty-ſix pounders and four mortars, on the 3d inſtant, within 700 yards of the fort, and on the 5th, another of two thirty-ſix pounders. The Ruſſians, under Captain Baillie, opened another battery of four thirty-ſix pounders and four mortars againſt the oppoſite angle, intending to ſtorm it in different places as ſoon as we could make two practicable breaches in the work. On the 6th I added four more mortars; and on the 11th, by inceſſant labour, we opened another battery of ſix thirty-ſix pounders within 180 yards of the wall of the garriſon, and had another of one eighteen pounder and two howitzers, at the ſame diſtance, nearly completed. After a few hours cannonading from the laſt battery, the enemy diſplayed a flag of truce, when our firing ceaſed, and their guns being moſtly diſmounted, and their works nearly deſtroyed, the encloſed terms of capitulation were agreed to and ſigned.

In performing this ſervice I feel much ſatisfaction in informing your Lordſhip, that I received every poſſible aſſiſtance from Captain Ball for the firſt ſeven days, when your Lordſhip ordered him on other ſervice, and did me the honour to place Captain Hallowell under my orders in his room, whoſe exertions and abilities your Lordſhip is well acquainted with, and merit every attention.

Lieutenant-colonel Strickland, Major Creſwell, and all the officers of marines and men, merit every praiſe I can beſtow; as does Antonio Saldineo de Gama, and the officers and men belonging to her Moſt Faithful Majeſty the Queen of Portugal; their readineſs on all occaſions does them great honour. The very commanding ſituation of St. Elmo rendered our approaches difficult, or I truſt it would have been reduced much ſooner; the ready acquieſcence to all our demands, and the aſſiſtance received from the Duke de Solandie, I beg may be made known by your Lordſhip to his Sicilian Majeſty.

I feel myſelf alſo much indebted to Colonel Tſchudy for his great zeal and exertions on all occaſions.

I have the honour to be, &c.

The Right Hon. Lord Nelſon, K. B.   J. TROUBRIDGE.

Articles of Capitulation agreed upon between the Garriſon of Fort St. Elmo and the Troops of his Sicilian Majeſty and his Allies.

Art. I. The French garriſon of Fort St. Elmo ſhall ſurrender themſelves priſoners of war to his Neapolitan Majeſty and his allies, and ſhall not ſerve againſt any of the powers actually at war with the French republic until regularly exchanged.

II. The Engliſh grenadiers ſhall take poſſeſſion of the gate of the fort in the courſe of the day.

III. The French garriſon ſhall march out of the fort to-morrow, with their arms, and drums beating. The troops ſhall lay down their arms on the outſide of the gate of the fort; and a detachment of Engliſh, Ruſſian, Portugueſe, and Neapolitan troops ſhall take poſſeſſion of the caſtle.

IV. The officers ſhall keep their arms.

V. The

V. The garrison shall be embarked on board the English squadron, until the necessary shipping are provided to convey them to France.

VI. When the English grenadiers take possession of the gate, all the subjects of his Sicilian Majesty shall be delivered up to the allies.

VII. A guard of French soldiers shall be placed round the French colours, to prevent their being destroyed: that guard shall remain until all the garrison has marched out, and it is relieved by an English officer and guard, to whom orders shall be given to strike the French flag, and hoist that of his Sicilian Majesty.

VIII. All private property shall be reserved for those to whom the same appertains; and all public property shall be given up with the fort, as well as the effects pillaged.

IX. The sick, not in a state to be removed, shall remain at Naples, with French surgeons, and shall be taken care of at the expense of the republic. They shall be sent back to France as soon as possible after their recovery.

Done at Fort St. Elmo, the 22d Messidor, in the seventh year of the French republic, or 12th July 1799.

(Signed) The DUKE DELLA SALANDRA, Captain-general of the Forces of his Majesty the King of the Two Sicilies.

THOMAS TROUBRIDGE, of his Majesty's Ship Culloden, and Commander of the British and Portuguese Troops at the Attack of St. Elmo.

CHEVALIER BELLE, Captain-lieutenant, commanding the Troops of his Imperial Russian Majesty at the Attack of St. Elmo.

JH. MEJAU, commanding Fort St. Elmo.

Return of killed and wounded at the Siege of the Castle St. Elmo, which surrendered July 12.

Five officers, 32 rank and file, killed.
Five officers, 79 rank and file, wounded.

Foudroyant, Naples Bay, July 13.

Copy of a Letter from Rear-admiral Lord Nelson, K. B. to Vice-admiral Lord Keith, K. B. dated Foudroyant, Naples Bay, July 13.

My Lord,

HIS Sicilian Majesty arrived in this Bay on the 10th, and immediately hoisted his standard on board the Foudroyant, where his Majesty still remains with all his ministers.

I have the honour to be, &c.

NELSON.

Downing Street, August 17.

DISPATCHES, of which the following are extracts, have been received by Lord Grenville, his Majesty's principal Secretary of State for foreign affairs.

Extract of a Letter from the Honourable William Windham to Lord Grenville, dated Florence, July 15.

DEPUTIES from all the principal towns and from the armies have been sent to Vienna, to entreat his Royal Highness to return to Tuscany; or at least to send a regent to act with full powers in his name: I profit of the occasion of a deputation from Arezzo going this day to Vienna to send this to your Lordship.

The Aretin army has really performed wonders; in every action it has beat the French, killing numbers of them, making many prisoners, and driving the enemy from their strong posts. The army consists of about 40,000 Tuscans, chiefly mountaineers, who encounter every danger, and march forward with the firm determination to conquer or die.

I can venture to assure your Lordship, that in a few days the French will be entirely expelled from Tuscany; and this country will be happy in the repossession of its beloved sovereign, the re-establishment of its laws, and the return of industry and commerce.

Extract of a Letter from Mr. Windham, dated Florence, July 18.

THE departure of a deputation of the senate of this city for Vienna this evening does not allow me time to write so fully as I could desire.

The victories of the Tuscan army, which, by degrees, was grown formidable, has enabled them to take a position within a few miles of Leghorn: in the mean time the Austrians likewise increased their force in the Modenese, and threatened a considerable invasion of Tuscany.

General Moreau's army having been again completely beaten in the Riviera of Genoa, an express arrived on the 15th inst. to the French general commanding the forces at Leghorn, to withdraw all the French troops from Tuscany, and to march immediately towards Sarzana; in consequence of which he entered into a capitulation with the Tuscan General Lavilette, a copy of which I have the honour to enclose for your Lordship.

I make no doubt but in the present situation of French distress, a capitulation more honourable and more advantageous might have been made; but, however, it is a great consolation to know that all Tuscany is completely evacuated by the French without bloodshed or any inconvenience.

This night a column of Austrians and Aretins united marched towards Lucca, to dislodge the French, who are in small numbers in that country, and who it appears are disposed to evacuate it without opposition.

In Tuscany there is no farther cause of fear of the French, who are in every part of Italy too weak to be able to return; besides, the people armed in mass, already accustomed to the use of arms, and provided with plenty of artillery and ammunition, are determined to support their religion and sovereign against any force that could be sent against them.

I have sent off an express to Lord Nelson at Naples, with this intelligence. The presence of a squadron off this coast, and that of Genoa, would prevent the French from carrying off immense treasures robbed from the various states of Italy.

Head-

Head quarters, Leghorn, the 28th Messidor (July 16), 7th Year of the French Republic.

DARCOUBET, General of Brigade, commandant of Leghorn, Pisa, and Lucca, proposes to General De Lavilette, Governor of Leghorn, and to the Chamber of Commerce, to evacuate that city on the following conditions:

Art. I. The Chamber of Commerce and General De Lavilette shall promise succour and protection to all the French sick, and to those who shall remain in the hospitals of the city of Leghorn; after their recovery, they shall be conducted to the French army.

II. General De Lavilette and the Chamber of Commerce shall bind themselves moreover to receive the garrison of Porto Ferrajo; and the day after their arrival to permit them to evacuate the town, and to afford them security and protection till they join the French army.

III. They shall moreover cause the trading companies to afford a just indemnity and compensation to the several individuals who have been ruined by the requisitions of lead and salt-petre furnished to the French army; to which purpose all the magazines belonging to the French at Leghorn, and all other effects belonging to them, in right of conquest, shall be applied.

General De Lavilette, the Auditor Alliata, conjointly with the deputies of the Chamber of Commerce, have subscribed the articles of the above-mentioned treaty, and will guarantee the execution of it to the French General Darcoubet, commandant of Leghorn, Pisa and Lucca, in faith of which they have hereunto set their hands.

  DE LAVILETTE, General.
  GIOV. ALLIATA, Auditor, President of the Comm.
  GIOV. GIACOMO BILLIET, President of the Department of Commerce.
  DARCOUBET, French General.

(A true Copy.) GIOV. ALLIATA, Auditor.

From the LONDON GAZETTE, August 20.

Admiralty Office, August 20.

Copy of a Letter from Vice-admiral Harvey, Commander in Chief of his Majesty's Ships and Vessels at the Leeward Islands, to Evan Nepean, Esq.

Martinique, June 21.

Sir,

YOU will be pleased to acquaint their Lordships that Captain Ekins, in his Majesty's ship Amphitrite, captured, on the 31st ult. off Martinique, after a very long chase, the Democrat French schooner privateer, belonging to Guadaloupe, of 12 guns and 80 men, and carried her to Barbadoes. She is a fast sailer, and had, for some time past, eluded the vigilance of our cruisers.

I have the honour to be, &c.
  HENRY HARVEY.

From

From the LONDON GAZETTE, August 24, 1799.

Admiralty Office, August 24.
Copy of a Letter from Vice-admiral Dickson to Evan Nepean, Esq. dated at Yarmouth the 20th instant.

Sir,

HEREWITH I transmit, for their Lordships' information, a letter from Captain Boorder, of his Majesty's sloop L'Espiegle, stating his success, in company with the Pylades, in having cut out, burnt, and took possession of the vessels therein mentioned; and beg to recommend Captain Boorder to their Lordships' particular notice, for his activity and zeal for the service, not only exemplified in this but other preceding instances.

I am, Sir, &c. &c. &c.
ARCH. DICKSON.

His Majesty's Sloop L'Espiegle, Yarmouth Roads, August 20.

Sir,

I HAVE to acquaint you of my arrival at this anchorage with his Majesty's sloop under my command, and of my having, in company with the Pylades sloop and Courier cutter, cut out and took possession of, on the 11th instant, from Shiermannikoog, the Crash gun-brig (formerly in our service), mounting 12 guns, eighteen, twenty-four, and thirty-two pounders; as also having burnt a schooner of 70 men; likewise took possession of a row-boat, of 30 men: we then landed on the island (having previously drove the men from the battery), spiked four pieces of cannon, and brought off two brass field-pieces, four pounders.

The Crash made an obstinate resistance from forty to fifty minutes, and then struck.

I am happy to add, not more than two men were killed on our side, and three wounded, and recommend the Crash as an excellent vessel, well calculated for his Majesty's service, being of a small draught of water.

I cannot but express my satisfaction in our keeping the ships afloat, as in many places our soundings proved there to be not more than fourteen feet, the Espiegle drawing twelve.

I am, Sir, &c. &c. &c.
JAMES BOORDER.

Vice-admiral Dickson.

INDEX.

A.

ABERCROMBIE, Sir Ralph—His letter to the officer commanding the Dutch troops, 320—His Proclamation to the Dutch, 336

Adams, Mr.—His speech upon opening the Congress, 1—Answer of the Senate thereto, 6—His reply, 7—Answer of the House of Representatives to his speech, 8—His reply thereto, 10—His address on presenting the correspondence of the French minister and Mr. Gerry, 129—His message to Congress, on laying before it a report of the Secretary of State on the above correspondence, 229—His message to Congress, 228—His message relative to a new negociation with France, 261—He nominates new ministers to negotiate with France, 263—His proclamation, discontinuing an act for the suspension of the commercial intercourse between France and the United States, 290

Address of Gen. Jourdan to the French army, declaring his intention to advance into the territory of the German Empire, 69—Of the Executive Directory of the Helvetic republic to the general of the French army in Helvetia, approving his conduct, 101—Of Citizen Cole, aid-de-camp of the General in Chief of St. Domingo, to the merchants of France, refuting the report of a plan of independence or criminal connivance of that general, Toussaint, and the English, 152—Of the Archduke Charles to all the generals of the Imperial armies at the opening of the campaign, 158—Of the President of the United States, on presenting the correspondence of the French minister and Mr. Gerry, 129—Of the Emperor of Germany to the people of Lombardy, 167

Agency of St. Domingo. Its arrêté in favour of the American trade with that island, 186

Alquier—His letter to the Bavarian minister, demanding payment of certain sums stipulated by the treaty of Pfaffenhoien, 109—He complains that the English minister at Munich had charged him with labouring to excite troubles in Bavaria, 149

Amsterdam—Letter from General Brune to that municipality on the landing of the English troops in Holland, 333

Answer of the Senate of the United States to the speech of the President, 6—Of the House of Representatives to the same, 8—Of General Mack to General Championnet, 108—Of the Count de Viceroy to the minister Alquier, during that the sums demanded by the latter, forpass the pretensions refuting from the treaty of Pfaffenhoien, 112—Of the Commandant of Philipsburg to the summons of General Bernadotte, 156—Of the Duc of Razilbon respecting Citizen Bacher, 179—Of General Macdonald to Commodore Troubridge, 181—Of General Maffena to the Helvetic Directory, relative to the union of the Grison league, 184—Of the Insurgents of Arezzo to the French proclamation addressed to the President of the government of Florence, 209—Of the President of the Batavian Directory to the minister of the French republic, on presenting his credentials, 311—Of Gilquin, the officer commanding the Dutch troops, to Sir Ralph Abercrombie, 321—Of Admiral Story to the summons of Lord Duncan, 333—Answer ordered to be given to the summons of Lord Duncan by the Batavian Directory, 334—Of the Commandant of Philipsburg to the summons of General Laroche, 338—Of the King of Spain to the manifesto of the Emperor of Russia, 342

Armistice, concluded between General Championnet and Captain-general Pignatelli, Viceroy of the kingdom of Naples, xviii

Articles of engagement proposed by Tippoo Sultaun to the French Directory, 366—Separate article to the treaty between Great Britain and Russia, xiv

Aulic, Imperial, decree relative to the assassination of the French ministers at Rastadt, 285—Decree on the renewal of the war between France and Austria, 297

Austria—Note published by Austria in the College of Princes, 73

Bacher,

B

Barker, French chargé d'affaires at the Diet of Ratisbon, is ordered abruptly away by the Archduke Charles, 71—Answer of the Diet of Ratisbon respecting him, 179

Barthélemy—His letter to Baron d'Albini respecting the insecurity of Rastadt, 74—His letter to the ministers of the French republic on the same subject, 75—His letter to the deputies at Ratisbon to answer to their note communicating to him the assassination of the French ministers, ibid.

Batavian republic—Answer of the President of the Batavian Directory to the French minister on presenting his credentials, 311—Letter of the Batavian Directory to the first Chamber, on transmitting the speech of the French minister Fouché, and the answer of the President Director, 313—Message of the Batavian Directory, relative to the answer to be given to Admiral Lord Duncan's summons, 331—Their decree, directing the answer to be given to the above summons, 334—Their proclamation, inviting the people to rise in a mass, 343.

Bernadotte—He summonses the fortress of Philipsburg to surrender, 155—His proclamation, inviting the Germans to declare war against the House of Austria, 174

Bissengen, Count—His proclamation to the inhabitants of Infpruck, 177

Bouchard, Neapolitan general, summonses the French troops in the castle of St. Angelo in Rome to surrender, 110

Bruix, French admiral—His proclamation previous to his leaving Carthagena, 289

Bruix, minister of marine—His letter relative to American vessels, 214—His letter, ordering the discharge of American sailors, ibid.

Buonaparte—His proclamation to the inhabitants of Cairo, 150—He orders that all the vessels that navigate the Nile shall carry the tri-coloured flag, 153—His letter to Gherrif Pacha, stating his only object in Egypt, 161

C

Campo Formio, Treaty of, iii.
Cafe, Citizen, vindicates General Toussaint against the charge of a criminal connivance with the English, in St. Domingo, 252
Championnet—Treaty between him and Prince Pignatelli, xvii.—His letter to General Mack, 107—His proclamation to his army, containing general orders, 117—He invites the Neapolitans to place themselves under his protection, 118—His letter to the Roman consuls, ibid.—His re-

INDEX.

e Executive Directory, raising the
go laid on American vessels, 815—
ve to the re-establishment of com-
al connexions between St. Domingo
he United States of America, 274—
nal Aulic decree to the German Diet
tisbon, respecting the assassination of
ench ministers at Rastadt, 285—
ial Aulic, to the Diet of Ratisbon,
re to the war, 297—Of the Prince
zil, declaring himself Regent of Por-
300

a, Charles—His observations on Tal-
d's vindication, 302
eaux, Secretary of the French Di-
y at Guadaloupe—His declaration of
ainst the United States, 265
—His letter to the Rajah of Tra-
e's minister at Aleppo, 367—To
o Sultaun, 368

Lord—His summons to the Com-
r of the Dutch fleet, 333

E.

the Emperor of Russia, laying an
go on Hamburg, 175
Order of Buonaparte concerning the
tion of the Nile, 153—Buonaparte's
l motive for the expedition to Egypt,

stein—Notes respecting the supply-
with provisions, 48, 50, 54, 57,
3, 73, 75
of Cologne—The declaration of his
er relative to the war, 179
on Swedish vessels in France, 294
of Germany—Proclamation issued
uncer, assigning his motives for or-
g his armies to advance, 160—Mes-
om the Directory to the Councils,
ing to declare war against him, 152
—Its opinion on the renewal of the
ith the Emperor, and the future of its
er on the chusing, ensuing war, 343
m nah—Decree of the Exe-
ire t ry, respecting ship laden there-
h 6

ron of witness relative to the assas-
in of the French ministers at Ras-
260
e Directors of the French republic
er proclamation, fixing the religious
ketting their entrance, 65—
proclamation of the French on the
t of the assassination of the plenipo-
ries at Rastadt, 69—Their notice
to all persons in vessels suspected
of the French plenipotentiaries at
dt, 9—Their decree relative to
laden with English merchandize, 105
eir decree respecting the French in
111—Their message to the Council
b. VIII.

of Five Hundred, proposing to declare war
against the Kings of Naples and Sardinia,
114—Their address to the French armies
on the same subject, 115—Their message
to the Council of Five Hundred, stating
all their grounds of complaint against the
Kings of Naples and Sardinia, in justifi-
cation of their hostile proceedings, 119—
Their message to the Council of Five
Hundred, relative to privateering, 135—
Their message to the Councils, informing
them of the adoption of measures of reprisal against Turkey, 150—Their message to the Council of Five Hundred, announcing that the Neapolitan government
was proclaimed, 155—Their message to
the Councils, proposing to declare war
against the Emperor of Germany and the
Grand Duke of Tuscany, 162—Their
letter to General Jourdan, with instructions
for his conduct, particularly in Suabia,
169—Their decree relative to neutral vessels, 172—Extract from the Registry of
the deliberations of their agency at St.
Domingo in favour of the United States of
America with respect to their trade with
that island, and securing it from French
privateers, 186—Their decree, restraining
abuses committed on the American trade
in the West Indies by French privateers,
197—Their decree, raising the embargo
laid on American vessels, 215—Their
decree, signed by their agent at St. Domingo, for the re-establishment of commercial connexions between that island and
the United States, 274—Their letter to
the Batavian Directory, relative to the invasion of Holland by the English, 324—
Their letter to the Batavian Directory,
promising aid, 334
Executive Directory of the Batavian republic—Answer of its President to the French
minister, on presenting his credentials, 311
—Their letter, on sending to the First
Chamber of the Legislative Body, the
speech of the French minister Touche, and
the answer of the President, 312—Their
message to the First Chamber, relative to
the answer to be given to Admiral Duncan's summons, 332—They decree the
answer to be given to the summons of Lord
Duncan, 334—Their proclamation, inviting the people to rise in a mass, 345
Executive Directory of the Helvetic republic, declare their attachment to the French
army in Helvetia, 101—Their message to
the Grand Council, on the disposition and
conduct of foreign powers to the Helvetic
republic, 172—Their proposal to the two
Councils, to declare war against the Emperor, 179—Their letter to General Massena, on the subject of the union of the
Grison league, 183.

Fir-

INDEX.

F.

Fitzgerald, Lord Robert—His letter to Lord Grenville, complaining of an illicit commerce carried on in the East Indies, under the sanction of the Royal College at Copenhagen, 178

French republic—Its treaty of commerce with the Helvetic republic, xx—Its treaty with Tippoo Saib, xxiii

G.

Gauthier—His proclamation to the people of Florence, 284

Gerry, Mr.—His letter from Paris to the American Secretary of State, after the departure of his colleagues from France, 11—From the same to the same, announcing his intended departure, 13—His letter to the French minister, proposing to present to his Government any amicable propositions, 15—From the same to the same, requesting that certain captured dispatches should be given up to him, 16—From the same to the same, including the names denoted by certain initials, 17—From the same to the same, advising an amicable arrangement, ibid.—He receives a letter from the French minister, complaining of the President's speech, 18—His letter to the French minister, vindicating the President, and further recommending accommodation, 19—A letter from the French minister to him, containing propositions as the basis of a negotiation, 21—His letter to the French minister, with observations on the propositions offered, and stating the impossibility of applying to his Government for the necessary powers to conduct the negotiation, 26—He solicits the necessary passports for his return, 27—He is further solicited by the French minister to resume the negotiation, 28—His letter to the French minister, containing a further vindication of the President's speech, avowing his inability to treat separately, and soliciting the necessary documents for his return, 31—A letter to him from the French minister, containing two notes, stated to be necessary in the progress of the negotiation, and urging the inconvenience of abandoning the discussion, 39—His letter to the French minister, further defending the President and Senate of the United States, and renewing his demand for passports, 42—His letter to the French minister, containing a general review of his conduct and that of his colleagues, 190—His letter to the French minister, acknowledging the receipt of the arrêté of the Directory, 196—He charges Mr. Haute-val with a misstatement in a public post, 198—His letter to the minister of the United States at London, 200—His letter to Doctor Tazewell, 201—His conference with the Dutch minister, 201—His letter to the President, on his return from France, accompanying the correspondence transmitted, 216

Gilquin, officer commanding the Dutch troops—His answer to Sir Ralph Abercrombie, 321

Grisons—Treaty with the Helvetic republic, xx—Proclamation of Massena to them, 72

Grouchy, General—His proclamation, enjoining certain regulations in the city of Turin, 145

Guillemardet, the French ambassador in Spain—His letter, enclosing two notes from the Spanish Secretary of State, relative to French insurgents who had escaped to that kingdom, 340

H.

Hamburg—Embargo laid on it by the Emperor of Russia, 175—Notice published by its Senate, concerning libels on political affairs, 278

Hauteval is charged by Mr. Gerry with a misstatement, 198—His answer to the charge, 199—His letter to the French minister for foreign affairs, 209.

Hedouville, General—His proclamation to the inhabitants of St Domingo, 131

Helvetia—Massena's proclamation to the inhabitants of Helvetia, 268

Helvetic republic—Its treaty with the Grisons, xx—Its treaty with the French republic, ibid.—Its minister at Paris complains of its grievances, and proposes certain modes of redress, 100—Its Directory present to the general of the French army in Helvetia a decree of the Legislative body, approving his conduct, 101

Hewitt, Adjutant-general—His circular letter, apprizing the commanders in the several districts of Ireland of an intended invasion by the French, 151

I.

Impeachment of the French Ex-directors, 294

India—Papers relative to the war with Tippoo Sultaun, 346

Instructions to the commanders of armed vessels in the service of the United States, 262

Ireland—Letter from the Adjutant-general's office to the commanders, in the several districts, announcing an intended invasion from France, 151—Proclamation of his Majesty,

INDEX

Majesty, prohibiting any person to land in England from Ireland without a passport, 154
Jean Debry—His letter to the French minister for foreign affairs, on the subject of the assassination of the French ministers at Rastadt, 92
Joubert—His general orders, complaining of the King of Sardinia, 113—He announces to the Executive Directory the installation of a provisional government at Turin, 129
Jourdan—His address to the French army under his command, 69—His orders to the military, in favour of the reigning Prince of Hohenzollern Heckingen, 161—His letter to the commander in chief of the Austrian troops in Suabia, declaring the orders of the French Government, to penetrate into Suabia in spite of resistance, 170

K.

King of Great Britain—His treaty with the Emperor of Russia, vi—Convention between the same powers, x
Klenau—His proclamation to the inhabitants of Outre-Po, 266
King, Rufus, minister of the United States at London—His letter to the American Secretary of State, 250

L.

Laroche, French general—His summons to Count Salm, commandant of Philipsburg, 337
Lavilletre, Major-general in the service of the Grand Duke of Tuscany—His notification respecting the landing of forces from an English and Portuguese squadron at Leghorn, 154
Law of the 23d Thermidor, respecting privateers, 180
Leghorn is summoned by the commander of an English and Portuguese squadron to allow troops to be disembarked there, 254

L.

Letter of Mr Gerry, after the departure of his colleagues from Paris, to the American Secretary of State, 11—His letter, announcing his intended departure, 13—Of the same to the French minister, proposing to be the bearer of any amicable propositions to his Government, 15—Of the same, requesting the restoration of certain intercepted dispatches, 16—Of M. Talleyrand, requesting a communication of the names of the persons designated by certain initials, ibid.—Of Mr. Gerry, including the names, 17—Of the same, recommending an amicable arrangement, 18—Of the French minister, complaining of the President's speech, 19—Of Mr. Gerry, defending the President's conduct, 19—Of the French minister, offering certain propositions as the basis of negotiation, 21—Of Mr. Gerry, with observations on the propositions of the French minister, but pleading his want of powers to resume the negotiation, 26—Of the same, soliciting passports for his return, 27—Of the French minister, pressing Mr. Gerry to resume the negotiation, 28—Of Mr. Gerry, containing a further vindication of the President, and repeating his demand for passports, 31—Of the French minister, still pressing the resumption of the negotiation, 33—Of Mr. Gerry, demanding passports, 40—Of the French minister, enclosing the passports required, ibid.—Postscript to the above, complaining of an order issued by the United States against French vessels, 45—Of the French minister to Bernadotte, in favour of the Elector Palatine, 160—Of Buonaparte to Ghezzar Pacha, 162—Of the Executive Directory to General Jourdan, 169—Of Jourdan to the commander of the Austrian troops in Suabia, 170—Of Massena, to the Helvetic Directory, 171—From Barthélemy to Baron D'Albini, respecting the integrity of Rastadt, 78—To the French minister, on the same subject, 77—To the deputies of Rastadt, on the subject of the assassination of the French ministers, ibid.—From Jean Debry's secretary Bellu to Citizen Noblet, on the same subject, 80—From Jean Debry, concerning the assassination of the French ministers at Rastadt, 92—From the Archduke Charles to General Massena, on the same subject, 93—From the French minister of war to the Executive Directory, stating the reasons for the adoption of hostile measures in Helvetia, 102—Of General Championnet to General Mack, 107—Of Citizen Alquier to the Bavarian minister, 109—Of General Macdonald to General Mack, in answer to the summons to the commander of St. Angelo, 111—Of General Championnet to the Roman consuls, 112—Of the King of Naples to his subjects, after his return to his capital, 128—From Joubert to the Executive Directory, announcing the installation of a provisional government at Turin, 129—Of General Mack to Championnet, proposing an armistice, 134—Of General Championnet to General Mack, rejecting the proposal of an armistice, ibid.—Of the King of Naples to General Pignatelli, reproaching him for having concluded the armi-

INDEX.

armistice with General Championnet, 143—Of the French prisoners at Constantinople to Mr. Spencer Smith, returning thanks for his exertions in procuring their liberation, 144—Of Toussaint Louverture to his secretary at Paris, vindicating his conduct, particularly with respect to the English, 148—Of the French minister Alquier, complaining that he was wrongfully charged by the English minister at the court of his Electoral Highness, with labouring to excite troubles in Bavaria, 149—From the Adjutant-general's office to the generals, &c. commanding the several districts in Ireland, apprizing them of an intended expedition by the French against that country, 151—Of the Governor in council at Fort St. George to the Directors of the East India Company, complaining of improper conduct in the government of Tranquebar, respecting its refusal to surrender certain French prisoners, and other particulars, ibid.—Of Toussaint Louverture, complaining of the conduct of General Hedouville in St. Domingo, 153—Of the minister for foreign affairs to Bernadotte, desiring him to take off the sequestration laid upon the revenue at Manheim, and recommending the Elector Palatine to his protection, 160—Of Buonaparte to Ghezzar Pacha, declaring that his only intention in Egypt was to expel the Mamelukes, 161—Of the Executive Directory to General Jourdan, with instructions for his conduct, particularly in Suabia, 169—Of Jourdan to the commander of the Austrian troops in Suabia, stating the orders of his Government to penetrate by force, if necessary, into that country, 170—Of Lord Robert Fitzgerald, complaining of an illicit traffic carried on in the East Indies, under the sanction of the Royal College of Commerce of Copenhagen, 178—Of Commodore Troubridge to General Macdonald, respecting the property of Sir William Hamilton at Naples, &c. 181—Of General Macdonald, complaining of cruelty exercised by the King of Naples on the person of the French vice-consul at Messina, 182—Of the Helvetic Directory to General Massena, relative to the union of the Grison league, 183—Of Mr. Gerry to the French minister, containing a general review and defence of the conduct of himself and his colleagues, 190—Of the French minister to Mr. Gerry, declaring the intention of the Directory to prevent any violence to the commerce of the United States in the West Indies, 194—Of the same to the same, enclosing a decree of the Executive Directory in favour of the commerce of the United States in the West Indies, 196—Of Mr Gerry, acknowledging the receipt of the above decree, ibid.—Letter containing the decree of the French Directory, restraining the abuses committed by privateers against the American commerce in the West Indies, 197—Of Mr. Gerry to Mr. Hauteval, charging him with a misstatement in a public print, 198—Of Mr. Hauteval in answer, 199—Of Mr. Gerry to the minister of the United States at London, 200—Of Mr. Gerry to Mr. Tazewell, 201—Of Hauteval to the French minister for foreign affairs, 209—Of Mr. Skipwith to the Secretary of State for the United States, enclosing an arrêté of the French Directory concerning French privateers in the West Indies, 211—From the same to the same, enclosing a letter on the same subject, ibid.—Of Talleyrand to Citizen Skipwith, on the same subject, 212—Of Mr. Skipwith to the American Secretary of State, relative to maritime affairs, and announcing an arrêté of the Directory for raising the embargo laid on American vessels in the ports of France, ibid.—Of Talleyrand to Mr. Skipwith, enclosing letters of the French minister of marine, on maritime affairs, 213—Of the minister of marine, relative to American vessels, 214—Of the same, ordering the discharge of American prisoners, ibid.—Of Mr. Gerry, on his return from France, accompanying the correspondence transmitted to the President, 216—Of Mr. Pickering, the American Secretary of State, to Mr. Gerry, 228—Of Rufus King, minister of the United States at London, 250—Of the Consul of the United States at the Havannah, relative to the capture of American vessels by a British squadron, 258—Of Benjamin Stoddert to the commanders of armed vessels in the service of the United States, 261—Of Talleyrand to Citizen Pichon, relative to a new negociation between France and the United States, 262—Of the Batavian minister Schimmelpenninck to the French minister, 303—Of the Batavian Executive Directory, on sending to the First Chamber the speech of the French minister, and the answer of the President Director, 312—Of Archduke Charles to all the princes of the Empire, relative to the furnishing of their contingents, 318—Of Sir Ralph Abercromby to the officer commanding the Dutch troops, 320—Of the French Directory to the Batavian Directory, relative to the invasion of Holland by the English, 324—Of the French ambassador, on the same subject, ibid.—Of Lord Duncan to the commander of the Dutch fleet, 333—Of the French Directory to the Batavian Directory, promising assistance against invasion, 334—Of General Brune to the municipality of Amsterdam, 335—Of the Archduke Charles to the commandant of Philipsburg, on the raising of the siege

5

INDEX.

of what fortress,' 338—Of the French ambassador in Spain, enclosing two notes from the Spanish Secretary of State, respecting French insurgents who had taken refuge in Spain, 340—Of Tippoo Sultaun to the French Executive Directory, 364—Of Dubuc to the Rajah of Travancore's minister at Aleppo, 367—Of the same, to Tippoo Sultaun, 368
Ligurian people—Proclamation addressed to them by Moreau, 288
Liston, Robert—His official correspondence respecting the United States, 282, 283
Lombardy—Proclamation of Count Cocastelli to its inhabitants, 285
Lucerne—Proclamation of Suwarrow to its inhabitants, 278

M.

Macdonald, General—His letter to General Mack, 111—His answer to the letter of Commodore Trowbridge, 182—His letter to the Neapolitan minister, complaining of cruelty exercised on the person of the French vice-consul at Messina, ibid.
Mack, General—His answer to the letter of General Championnet, 108—He proposes an armistice to General Championnet, 134
Manifesto of the Executive Directory to all governments, on the subject of the assassination of the plenipotentiaries at Rastadt, 99—Of the Roman consuls against the King of the Two Sicilies, 103—Of the King of Naples, published previous to the commencement of hostilities, 106—Of George Count Zouccato to the Roman nation, on the approach of the Austro-Russian armies, 291—Of Count Suzarray to the Beh tant, 294—Austro-Russian, on entering the territory of Genoa, 315
Masseredo, Spanish admiral—His proclamation previous to leaving Carthagena, 290
Massena—His proclamation to the Grisons, 72—His proclamation to the French army, 170—His letter to the Helvetic Directory, 171—His proclamation to the Helvetians, 180—He receives a letter from the Helvetic Directors, relative to the union of the Grison league, 183—His answer to the letter of the Helvetic Directory, 184—His proclamation to the inhabitants of Helvetia, 268
Merlin, Ex-director—His vindication, 325
Message from the Directory to the Council of Five Hundred, proposing a formal declaration of war against the Kings of Naples and Sardinia, 114—Of the Executive Directory to the Council of Five Hundred, detailing all the grounds of complaint against the King of Naples and Sardinia,

119—Of the Executive Directory to the Council of Five Hundred, containing general views relative to privateering, and its consequences, 135—Of the Directory to the Councils, stating that the French Government had adopted measures of reprisal against Turkey, 155—Of the Executive Directory, announcing that the Neapolitan government was proclaimed, 154—Of the Executive Directory of the French republic to the Councils, proposing to declare war against the Emperor of Germany and the Grand Duke of Tuscany, 162—Of the Helvetic Directory to the Grand Council, on the conduct and disposition of foreign powers, 171—Of the President of the United States to Congress, 119—Of the Secretary of State to the President of the United States, ibid.—Of the President of the United States to Congress, 228—Of the President, relative to a new negotiation between the United States and France, 261—Of the Batavian Directory to the First Chamber, announcing the reply to be given to the letter and summons of Admiral Duncan, 333
Milloradowitz, Austrian general—His proclamation to the inhabitants of the Val Vallais, 271
Minister of the Elector of Cologne—Declaration annexed to his vote relative to the war, 179
Miollis—He orders the Consul of the French republic at Leghorn to put seals on all the property belonging to English or English merchants, &c. 176
Moreau—His proclamation to the Ligurian people, 288—His proclamation to the Piedmontese, 292
Mornington, Earl of—His letter to the Court of Directors of the East India Company, detailing the grounds and circumstances of the war in India with Tippoo Sultaun, 346
Morocco—Its treaty with Spain, 242
Morton, G. C. Esq. acting Consul of the United States at the Havannah—His letter relative to the capture of part of the American fleet by a British squadron, 258—His letter to L. Trezevant and W. Timmons, requesting a correct statement of the capture, 259
Muffet—His proclamation to the Piedmontese, 267
Musquiz, the Spanish ambassador—His speech on presenting his credentials to the Directory at Paris, 344

N.

Naples—Treaty concluded between its Viceroy and General Championnet, 111—Manifesto

INDEX.

Manifesto of the Roman Consuls against its King, 103 — Manifesto of its King, published before the commencement of hostilities, 106 — His letter to his subjects after his return to his capital, 128 — He reproaches Pignarelli for having concluded the armistice with the French, 143 — City of, is entered by the French, 146 — The whole kingdom declared free, ibid. — Its inhabitants are ordered to be disarmed, 148

Neapolitans — They are invited by Championet to place themselves under his protection, 114

Negotiation at Seltz, 1

Note — Upon the twelfth article of the Convention between France and the United States, 36 — Upon the fifteenth article of the same, 38 — From the Helvetic minister at Paris to the minister for foreign affairs, recommending a redress of the grievances of the Helvetic republic, 100 — Note, an answer by the Sublime Porte to the ambassador of the republic of Poland, ordering him to quit Constantinople, 144 — Note, diplomatic, distributed in Germany by order of the Court of Vienna, 175 — Of the French ambassador, Bertolio, to the Roman conclave, 177 — Of the Spanish Secretary of State, promising that French insurgents who had fought refuge in Spain should be delivered up, 340 — A second note from the same, to the same effect, 341

Notice of the Senate of Hamburg against libellous remarks on political affairs, 278

Notification of the commander of the garrison of Leghorn, relative to the landing of some troops belonging to his Sicilian Majesty in that port, from a squadron of English and Portuguese ships of war, 154

O.

Observations, by Charles Delacroix, on the Reflections published by Talleyrand, 302

Opinion of the Empire, on the renewal of the war of the Empire, 343

Orange, Prince of — His proclamation to the Dutch, 313 — His proclamation to the people of the Netherlands, 331

Orders, general, of Joubert, complaining of the conduct of the Court of Turin, 113 — Of Buonaparte in Egypt, 153 — Of Jourdan, in favour of the reigning Prince of HohenzollernHeckingen, 161 — General, of the Archduke Charles to all the generals of his army, 174 — Russian, prohibiting the entrance of Danish ships into any of the ports of the Russian dominions, 317

Orders, Emperor of — His treaty with Russia, xv

Osope — General R...., p. ...tion to its inhabitants, 200

P.

Parliamentary papers, 414 — British Parliament, ibid. — Message from his Majesty, brought up by Mr. Pitt, ibid. — Mr. Tierney's notice of a motion against any engagements that might impede a negotiation for peace, ibid. — Mr. Pitt's mission relative to the voluntary offers of the English militia to serve out of the Kingdom, 415 — Address to his Majesty for his Majesty's message relative to settling an annuity on Lord Nelson, ibid. — Motion of Sir Francis Burdett relative to persons committed under the Bill for suspending the Habeas Corpus Act, ibid. — Motion in the House of Commons, by Mr. Tierney, against any engagements that might interfere with a negotiation for peace, ibid. — Mr. Dundas's notice, relative to the suspension of the Habeas Corpus Act, 416 — His motion, for leave to bring in a bill to exempt volunteers from the service of the militia, ibid. — The bill for the suspension of the Habeas Corpus Act, read a third time, ibid. — The income bill, to enable his Majesty to carry on the war, was passed in the House of Lords, ibid. — Message from his Majesty to both Houses of Parliament, relative to an Union with Ireland, 417 — Address of thanks in consequence of the message, in the House of Commons, ibid. — Amendment to the address, moved by Mr. Sheridan, ibid. — Address in consequence of the message, in the House of Lords, 418 — A Secret Committee appointed in the House of Commons to consider certain papers, relative to the rebellion in Ireland, presented by the command of his Majesty, ibid. — Resolutions and address relative to the Union with Ireland, moved by Mr. Pitt in the House of Commons, ibid. — Resolutions on the same subject, by Mr. Sheridan, 421 — Mr. Sheridan's resolutions, relative to an Union with Ireland, ibid. — Mr. Sheridan's motion in the House of Commons, relative to the abolition of civil incapacities arising out of religious distinctions, 422 — Mr. Dundas's notice, relative to the reduction of the militia, ibid. — Message from his Majesty, relative to a support for Prince Edward, and Ernest Augustus, ibid. — Lord Grenville, in the House of Lords, brought up his Majesty's proclamation prohibiting persons from leaving Ireland without passports, ibid. — Message from his Majesty to both Houses, relative to the removal of the Irish state prisoners to Fort George, 423 — Protest in the House of Lords against the address in favour of an Union with Ireland, ibid. — Mr. Pitt's resolutions in the House of Commons, relative to the ...

INDEX

pression of seditious societies, 426—Bill ordered to be brought in for the reduction of the militia, ibid.—His Majesty's message to both Houses, relative to the Russian treaty, ibid.—Address in consequence of the message in the House of Lords, 428—Amendment to the address, moved by Lord Holland, ibid.—Mr. Pitt's motion in the House of Commons, relative to the importation of goods in neutral vessels, ibid.—Mr. Abbot's bill for extending forfeiture in cases of treason, ibid.—Protest in the House of Lords against committing the treason forfeiture bill, 429—Amendment, moved by the Duke of Norfolk, to the treason forfeiture bill, ibid.—Amendment, moved by the Duke of Norfolk, to the seditious societies bill, 430—Protest in the House of Lords against the militia reduction bill, ibid.—Address of the Speaker of the House of Commons at the bar of the House of Lords, previous to his Majesty reading his speech, 431—His Majesty's speech on proroguing the Parliament, 433—His Majesty's speech to both Houses at the meeting of Parliament on the 24th September 1799, 435—Thanks of the House of Commons given to General Abercrombie, Admiral Mitchell, Sir Sydney Smith, &c. 437—The bill ordered to enable his Majesty to avail himself of the voluntary services of the militia, ibid.—Protest in the House of Lords against the militia service extension bill, 438—Bill, ordered in the Commons, to enable his Majesty to assemble Parliament at a short notice, in case of adjournment, 439—Lord Holland's address to his Majesty, ibid.

Irish Parliament, 442—Speech of the Lord Lieutenant on the opening of Parliament on the 22d of January 1799, ibid.—Address, in consequence, in the House of Lords, 443—Lord Powerscourt's amendment thereto, doubting the competence of Parliament to pass a legislative Union with Great Britain, 444—Lord Ballamont's amendment, by leaving out the word "relative to competence," ibid.—Lord Bellamont's amendment, proposing concessions in preference to the words importing an Union, ibid.—Amendment to the address in the House of Commons, moved by George Ponsonby, objecting to the Union with Great Britain, ibid.—Sir H. Cavendish's motion, relative to tumultuous assemblies near the House, 445—Lord Cole's motion in the House of Commons, for a Committee to inquire into the state of the nation, ibid.—On the motion of Mr Tighe, bill ordered for the suppression of the rebellion, ibid.—Mr. Fitzgerald's motion, for leave to bring in a Regency bill, ibid.—Motion of Mr. Barrington, relative to persons convicted of treasonable practices, or ordered to be transported, 446—His motion for leave to bring in a bill to secure the independence of Parliament, ibid.—Amendment, moved by Mr. O'Donnel, to the rebellion bill, ibid.—Mr. Edgeworth's amendment to the same, 447—Resolutions proposed to be moved by Mr. Dobbs, for tranquillizing the country, ibid.—Amendment, moved by the Lord Chancellor, in the House of Lords, to the rebellion bill, ibid.—Message of the Lord Lieutenant to the House of Commons, relative to the proffered service of the English militia, in Ireland, 448—His Excellency's speech on proroguing the Parliament, ibid.

Pascal Vallouge—His letter to Mr. Speaker Smith, on the subject of the liberation of himself and fellow-prisoners, 144

Philipsburg is summoned to surrender to the French, 155

Pickering, Timothy, the American Secretary of State—His letter to Mr. Gerry, 228—His Report on the transactions relating to the United States and France, 229

Piedmontese—Muffet's proclamation to them, 267—Proclamation of Suwarrow to the same, 330.

Pignatelli—His treaty with Championet, xviii

Pomerania, Duke of—His Declaration to the Diet of the Empire, 279

Portugal—Prince of Brazil declares himself Regent, 300

President of the French Directory—His reply to the speech of M. Musquiz, the Spanish ambassador at Paris, 344

Prince of Brazil declares himself Regent of Portugal, 300

Proclamation of the French Directory, ordering the French armies, in consequence of the silence of the Emperor of Germany respecting the march of the Russian troops, to take such positions as circumstances may require, 63—Of Masséna to the Grisons announcing his entry into their country, 72—Of the Executive Directory on the assassination of the French plenipotentiaries at Rastadt, 96—Proclamation of the Executive Directory to the French armies, stating the reason for going to war with Naples and Sardinia, 111—Of Championet in his entry, restraining general orders, 107—Of the same to the Neapolitan, inviting them to put themselves under his protection, 113—Of General Serrurier to the French troops, on their entering the territories of the Grand Duke of Tuscany, and the republic of Lucca, 114—Of Bonaparte to the inhabitants of Cairo, ibid.—Of General Hedouville to the inhabitants of St. Domingo, 111—Of the Governor to the several provinces of

INDEX.

Naples, declaring the armistice concluded by Pignatelli null, and recommending active measures, 142—Of General Grouchy, enjoining certain regulations in the city of Turin, 145—Of Championnet to the Neapolitans, inviting them to return to order, and to surrender their arms, 146—Of the same to all the inhabitants of the kingdom of Naples, declaring them free, and pointing out the conduct they are expected to pursue, ibid.—Of the same to the inhabitants of Naples, ordering a disarming, 148—Of the Sublime Porte to the French army in Egypt, offering a safe conduct to such of them as would wish to leave that country, 150—Of General Ernouf, 157—Of the Duke of Wurtemberg, enjoining his subjects to behave friendly to the French in their passage through part of his territories, ibid.—Proclamation issued by order of the Emperor of Germany, assigning the reasons for ordering his troops to advance, 160—Of General Massena to the French army, 170—Of the King of Prussia, protesting against any alienation of property by the inhabitants in the provinces of Cleves, Gueldres, and Meurs, before the conclusion of peace, 171—Of Bernadotte to the people of Germany, calling upon them to declare war against the House of Austria, 174—Of the King of Great Britain, declaring the ports of the United Provinces in a state of blockade, 176—Of the Duke of Tuscany, in consequence of the determination of the French to occupy Florence, ibid.—Of the Governor of Inspruck, 177—Of the Archduke Charles to the Swiss, stating his motives in entering their country, ibid.—Of Massena to the Helvetians, complaining of violence exercised against the French troops, 180—Of the King of Great Britain, regulating the commercial intercourse between the islands of Jamaica and St. Domingo, 184—Turco-Russian to the people of Corfou, after its capitulation, 264—Of General Klenau to the inhabitants of Outre-Po, 266—Of Musset to the Piedmontese, 267 —Of Massena to the Helvetians, 268—Of Suwarrow to the inhabitants of Lucerne and St. Martin, 271—Of Suwarrow to the Italians, 272—Of Millerndowitz to the inhabitants of the Bas-Vallais, ibid. —Of Suwarrow to the nations of Italy, 273—Second proclamation of the Archduke Charles to the Swiss, 281—Third proclamation of the same to the Swiss, 282—Of Gauthier to the people of Florence, 284—Of Count Cocastelli, the Imperial commissioner, to the people of Lombardy, 285—Of Moreau to the Ligurian people, 288—Of the provisionary government of Zurich, 280—Proclamations of the French and Spanish animal previous to their leaving Carthagena, ibid. 290—Of the President of the United States, discontinuing an act for suspending the commercial intercourse between the United States and France, ibid.—Of Moreau to the Piedmontese, 292—Of the Prince of Orange, 313—Of General Muller, 321—Of the Batavian Directory to the Batavian people, on the subject of the English expedition, 322—Of Suwarrow to the Piedmontese, 330—Of the Prince of Orange to the people of the United Netherlands, 331—Of Sir Ralph Abercrombie to the Dutch, 336—In the name of his Sicilian Majesty to the inhabitants of Rome, 339 —Of the Batavian Directory, inviting the country to rise in a mass, 345

Protest of the King of Sardinia against the conduct of the French, in driving him from his dominions, 157

Provisionary government of Zurich—Its proclamation, 289

Prussia, King of—He protests against any alienation of property by the inhabitants in his provinces of Cleves, Meurs, and Gueldres, 171—Secret convention between the King of Prussia and the French republic, 315

Rastadt—Conclusum of the deputation of the Empire, in which they object to charging the right bank of the Rhine with the communal debts of the left, and other conditions, 46—Second conclusum of the deputation of the Empire, in reply to the second note of the French legation concerning the supplying of Ehrenbreitstein with provisions, 48—Memorial of the Prussian ministers to the same, on the same subject, 50—First note from the French minister, in which they insist upon the conditions objected to in the first conclusum of the deputation of the Empire respecting the transfer of the communal debts from the left to the right bank of the Rhine, and other conditions respecting the inhabitants of the latter side, 51—Second note from the same to the same, in which they insist that the question respecting the supplying of Ehrenbreitstein with provisions belongs to the military department, and is unconnected with the negotiations for peace, 54 —Note of the Imperial minister assenting to the cession of the isles on the left of the Thalweg to France, but requesting in return, on the part of the French government, the cession of that isle of Rudeshein, and objecting to the abolition of the toll of Elsbeth, 55—Note of the French minister, consenting that the communal debts on the left bank of the Rhine shall remain to the charge of the French, and that the property of the isles on the left bank of the Thalweg belonging to private persons, shall be possessed by them, on certain conditions,

INDEX

—Second note from the same to the same, declining the question concerning Ehrenbreitstein, 57—Address of the deputation of the Empire to the Imperial plenipotentiary, acceding to all the articles of the ultimatum of the French legation generally, leaving such as require precise determinations for future discussion, 58—Answer of the French plenipotentiaries, containing their acceptance of the last ultimatum of the deputation of the Empire, and proposing now to treat on the principle of indemnity by way of secularization, 60—Decree of the Imperial commission, communicating the ultimatum of the deputation of the Empire to the French ministers, ibid.—Note from the French ministers to Chateauneuf Randon, acquainting him with the acceptance of their ultimatum by the deputation of the Empire, 61—Note from the French ministers to the deputation of the Empire, protesting against the entry of the Russian troops on the territory of the Empire as a violation of its neutrality, ibid. —Note from Count Metternich to the French ministers, in answer to their complaint respecting the march of the Russian troops, 62—Note from the French ministers to the Emperor, as King of Hungary and Bohemia, stating the grant of a free passage through his states to the Russian troops would be considered as a ground of rupture, ibid.—Resolutions adopted at the Diet of Ratisbon, stating that no requisition had been made to the Empire, concerning the entry of the Russian troops, 63—Note from the Imperial minister to the deputation of the Empire, complaining that the conditions on which he had acceded to the French ultimatum were not observed, but, on the contrary, that Ehrenbreitstein was still more severely pressed, ibid —Memorial from Count D'Erbach to the deputation of the Empire, relative to the contributions imposed by the French in the circle of Westphalia, 64—The Emperor's answer, relative to the march of the Russian troops, 65—Resolution of the deputation of the Empire, on the same subject, ibid.—Decree of the Imperial commission, approving the resolution of the deputation of the Empire, 66—Note of the French ministers, declining to pursue the negotiation until they had first received a categorical answer on the subject of the march of the Russian troops, ibid.—Note of the French minister to the Austrian, pressing for an explicit declaration and assurance respecting the march of the Russian troops, ibid.—Vote of Mentz, 67—Note from the French ministers to the deputation of the Empire, transmitting a proclamation of the French Directory, and the copy of an address of General

Vol. VIII.

Jourdan to his army, 68—Proclamation transmitted with the foregoing note, ordering the French armies to take the necessary positions, ibid.—Address of General Jourdan to his army, declaring his intention to advance into Germany, transmitted with the above, 69—Conclusum of the deputation of the Empire, on the subject of the proclamation of the Directory, the address of General Jourdan, and the note with which these documents were accompanied, 71—Note from the French ministers, respecting the announced movement of the French army, and containing a proclamation of General Massena, ibid.—Proclamation of General Massena to the Grisons, announcing his intention to defend their country against the German troops, 72—Note of the French ministers to the deputation of the Empire, complaining that the Archduke Charles had ordered Citizen Bacher, the French chargé d'affaires, to withdraw abruptly from Ratisbon, ibid.—Note published by Austria in the College of Princes, objecting to the interference of France respecting the march of the Russian troops, and alleging the necessity of precaution in consequence of the obviously hostile measures of the French government, 73—Verbal declaration of the motives which induced the Imperial committee to refuse its sanction to the conclusum of the deputation of the Empire, 74—Note of the French ministers to Count Metternich, urging the pacific intentions of the French government, 76—The French ministers declare their intention to leave Rastadt, 78—Letter from Barbacfy to the French ministers, stating the insecurity of Rastadt, 79—He declares his horror of the assassination of the French ministers, ibid.—Letter from Jean Debry's secretary, on the same subject, 80—, Report of the ministers plenipotentiary on the circumstances of the assassination of the French ministers, ibid.

Ratisbon, Diet of—Its resolutions respecting the march of the Russian troops, 63—Its answer to the note of the deputation of the Empire, respecting Citizen Bacher, 179

Reflections on the communications made by the President of the United States to the American Congress, 202

Reinhart—His resolution respecting the persons attached to the Grand Duke of Tuscany and his family, 174

Renunciation—Act of renunciation of the King of Sardinia, 116

Report of the Secretary of State, on the transactions relating to the United States and France, 220—Of the Secret Committee of the British House of Commons, on certain treasonable papers referred to them

P p

INDEX.

...en by his Majesty's command, 371—Containing a view ...the nature and system of the Soc... of United Irishmen, as established in Ireland, 373—Their institution in 1791, and rise of different societies in Great Britain, 375—Their first open attempt in Scotland, 377—Attempts to assemble a convention of the people in England, 380—Further proceedings subsequent to the arrests in 1794, 383—Progress of the Society of United Irishmen in Ireland till the rebellion, its intercourse with France, and leading members of societies in Great Britain, 388—Further intercourse between the United Irishmen, the French government, and the British societies; formation of new societies, and their proceedings, 392—Societies at Hamburgh, 403—Conclusion, 404—Report of the Secret Committee of the British House of Lords, on the same subject, 407—List of places with which the London Corresponding Society corresponded, 412

Resolution of Citizen Reinhart, relative to the persons attached to the service of the Grand Duke of Tuscany, 171

Roman Consuls—Their manifesto against the King of the Two Sicilies, 103

Russia—Treaty between the Emperor of, and King of Great Britain, vi—Convention between the same powers, x—Treaty between it and Turkey, xv—The Emperor's edict, laying an embargo on Hamburgh, 175—The Emperor declares war against Spain, 313

Russian troops—Their entry on the territory of the Empire objected to by the French ministers at Rastadt, 61—Same subject continued, 62, 63, 65, 66, 68

S.

Salm—The Rhinegrave Salm is summoned to surrender Philipsburg to the French, 155—His answer, 156

Sardinia, King of—His act of renunciation, 116—He protests against the conduct of the French in driving him from his dominions, 157

Schimmelpenninck, the Batavian minister—His letter to the French minister, 304

Seltz—Secret negotiation at it, 1

Serrurier, General—His proclamation to the French troops on entering the territories of the Grand Duke of Tuscany, and the republic of Lucca, 120

Skipwith, Fulwar—His letter to the Secretary of State of the United States of America, enclosing an arrêté of the Executive Directory, concerning French privateers in the West Indies, 211—His letter to the same, enclosing a letter on the same subject, ib.—His letter to the American Secretary of State, enclosing an arrêté of the French Directory for raising the embargo imposed on American vessels in the ports of the Republic, 212

Spain—Treaty between it and Morocco, xxiv—Answer of the King of Spain to the manifesto of the Emperor of Russia, 342

Speech—Of the President of the Batavian Directory, on the surrender of the fleet, 335—Of the President of the Directory to the Spanish ambassador at Paris, on his taking leave, 344—Of the new Spanish ambassador on presenting his credentials, ib.1

Storey, Dutch admiral—His answer to the summons of Lord Duncan, 333

Stoddert, Benjamin—His letter to the commander of armed vessels in the service of the United States, 261

Summons—Of the Neapolitan general to the commander of the French troops in the castle of St. Angelo in Rome, 110—Of General Bernadotte to the Rhinegrave Salm, commander of Philipsburg, requiring him to surrender that fortress, 155—Of Lord Duncan to the commander of the Dutch fleet, 333—Of the French general Laroche to Count Saint, commandant of Philipsburg, 337

Suwarrow—His proclamation to the inhabitants of Lucerne and St. Martin, 271—His proclamation to the Italians, 272—His proclamation to the nations of Italy, 273—His proclamation to the Piedmontese, 330

Swiss—First proclamation of the Archduke Charles to them, 177—Second ditto, 281—Third ditto, 282

Szatmary—His manifesto to the Belgians, 294

T.

Talleyrand, Ch. Mau—His letter to Mr Gerry, proposing to resume the negotiation, 13—He requests a communication of the persons denoted by certain initial, and complain. of the interference of intriguers, 16—He complains of the President's speech, 18—His letter to Mr. Gerry, in which he resumes the negotiation by proposing certain propositions, 21—His letter to Mr. Gerry, containing further solicitations to resume the negotiation, 28—His letter to Mr. Gerry, transmitting fresh notes as necessary in the progress of the negotiation, and urging the inconvenience of adjourning the discussion, 33—His letter to Mr. Gerry, enclosing the passport for his return to America, 40—Postscript to the same, complaining of an order issued by the United States, for attacking and stopping French vessels, 45—His letter to Bernadotte, in favour of Manheim and the Elector Palatine, 160—His letter to M. Gerry, declaring that measures are adopted to prevent any violence to the American trade in the West Indies, 194—His letter

INDEX.

to Mr. Gerry, enclosing a decree of the Executive Directory for protecting the American trade in the West Indies, 196—His letter to Citizen Skipwith on the same subject, 212—From the same to the same, enclosing letter of the French minister of marine on the same subject, 213—His letter to Citizen Pichon, relative to a new negotiation with the United States, 262—His vindication, 301

Tippoo Saib—His treaty with the French Republic, xxiii—Articles of engagement proposed by him to the French Directory, 366

Toussaint Louverture—His letter to his secretary at Paris, vindicating his conduct, particularly with respect to the English, 148—He complains of General Hedouville's conduct in St. Domingo, 153

Treaties—Of Campo Formio, iii—Provisional, between the King of Great Britain and the Emperor of Russia, vi—Of defensive alliance between the Emperor of the Ottomans and the Emperor of Russia, xv—Between Championnet and Prince Pignatelli, viceroy of Naples, xviii—Conditions of a treaty of union between the Grisons and the Helvetic republic, xx—Of commerce between the French and Helvetic republic, *ibid*—Between Tippoo Saib and the French republic, xxiii—Between Spain and Morocco, xxix

Trezevant—His account of the capture of part of an American fleet by a British squadron, 259

Troubridge, Commodore—He complains of the detention of the English ambassador's property at Naples, 181

Turco-Russian proclamation to the people of Corfou, after its capitulation, 264

Turkey—Note of the Porte transmitted to the embassador of the Batavian republic, enjoining him to quit Constantinople, 144—The Sublime Porte offers a safe conduct to the to the French army in Egypt as they wish to return from that country, 155

Tuscany, Grand Duke of—Reasons assigned by the Executive Directory of the French republic for declaring war against him, 162—His proclamation in consequence of the determination of the French to occupy Florence, 176

U.

United States of America—Speech of the President on the opening of Congress, 1—Mr Gerry's letter to the American secretary of state, after the departure of his colleagues from France, 11—From the same to the same, on his own departure, 13—Correspondence between Mr Gerry and the French minister, 15—Same continued, 16—Same continued, 17, 18, 19, 21, 26, 27, 28, 31, 33, 40, 190, 196—Mr. Gerry charges Mr. Hauteval with a misstatement in the public prints, 198—Mr. Gerry's letter to the minister of the United States resident at London, 200—Mr. Gerry's letter to the President of the United States, accompanying the correspondence transmitted on his return from France, 216—The President's address on presenting the correspondence of the French minister and Mr. Gerry, 219—Message of the President to Congress on laying before it a Report of the Secretary of State on the documents transmitted by Mr. Gerry after his return, *ibid*—Message of the President relative to a new negotiation with France, 261—He nominates new ministers for that purpose, 263—The agent of the French Directory at Guadaloupe declares hostilities against the United States, 265—The commercial connexions between the colony of St. Domingo and the United States are re-established, 274—The government of the United States complain of the interference of Colonel M'Kee, respecting a proposed modification of the Grenville treaty, with regard to the Shawanese Indians, 282—The President discontinues the act for suspending the commercial intercourse between the United States and France, 297.

United Irishmen, society thereof, and all its proceedings. *See* Report.

Urquijo, Spanish secretary of state—His notes, promising that French insurgents, who had fled to Spain, should be delivered up, 340, 341

W.

Wirtemberg, Duke of—His proclamation to the inhabitants of his communes, enjoining them to behave friendly to the French troops in their passage, 159

V.

Viderts, Bavarian minister—His answer to Citizen Alquier's letter demanding the payment of certain sums of money, 111

Vindication of Talleyrand, 301—Of the Ex-director Merlin, 325

Von Steiger, Mayor of Berne—Declaration of the United Swiss, published by him, 271

Z.

Zeltner, the Helvetic minister at Paris—His note to the minister for foreign affairs, proposing regulations for the advantage of his country, 160

Zoinoesto, George Count—His manifesto to the Russian nation, on the approach of the Austro-Russian army, 292

Zurich, provisionary government of—Its proclamation, 289

END OF THE EIGHTH VOLUME.

Printed for J. DEBRETT.

AN
ASIATIC ANNUAL REGISTER;
Comprehending a View of the HISTORY, POLITICS, COMMERCE, and LITERATURE of HINDUSTAN;

Together with a connected Detail of the principal Occurrences, Civil, Military, and Commercial, of BRITISH INDIA.

For 1799.

Dedicated, by Permission,
To the Right Honourable HENRY DUNDAS,
One of his Majesty's Principal Secretaries of State, and President of the Board of Commissioners for the Affairs of India;

And also, by Permission,
To the Honourable the COURT of DIRECTORS of the EAST INDIA COMPANY.

The First Volume will be published January 1800, Price 10s. 6d.

⁂ The Plan submitted to the Public for its patronage, is so general and extensive, and the execution of it requires so much information, assiduity, and attention, that those who may be the most inclined to encourage the undertaking, will very naturally ask, Whether men, who thus boldly promise, be sufficiently qualified to perform? and whether such boldness does not rather belong to the rashness of ignorance, than to the confidence of knowledge? To this the Editors can only answer, that they have resided in India, and have long made the subjects of the proposed Work their peculiar study. Without, therefore, arrogating any superiority of talents, they think it would be unworthy of that kindness expected of a generous Public, as well as deficient in duty to themselves and to their Country, were they to permit a timid supposition of incapacity to deter them from doing what they deem may be beneficial to Society, and what, with the promised assistance of their Friends, they trust they shall satisfactorily perform.

The Editors of the ASIATIC ANNUAL REGISTER respectfully entreat Orders for the Work to be transmitted to Mr. DEBRETT, opposite Burlington House, Piccadilly, to whom all Communications intended for the Asiatic Register are to be addressed.

Printed by S. GOSNELL, Little Queen Street, Holborn.